Psychological Testing and Assessment

An Introduction to Tests and Measurement

FIFTH EDITION

Ronald Jay Cohen
ST. JOHN'S UNIVERSITY

Mark E. Swerdlik
ILLINOIS STATE UNIVERSITY

ONLINE LEARNING CENTER
www.mhhe.com/psychtesting5

Boston   Burr Ridge, IL   Dubuque, IA   Madison, WI   New York
San Francisco   St. Louis   Bangkok   Bogotá   Caracas   Kuala Lumpur
Lisbon   London   Madrid   Mexico City   Milan   Montreal   New Delhi
Santiago   Seoul   Singapore   Sydney   Taipei   Toronto

McGraw-Hill Higher Education

A Division of The McGraw-Hill Companies

1 2 3 4 5 6 7 8 9 0 VON/VON 0 9 8 7 6 5 4 3 2 1

Library of Congress Cataloging-in-Publication Data

Cohen, Ronald Jay.
    Psychological testing and assessment : an introduction to tests and measurement / Ronald Jay Cohen, Mark E. Swerlik. — 5th ed.
        p. cm.
    Includes bibliographical references and index.
    ISBN 0-7674-2157-4
    1. Psychological tests.   I. Swerdlik, Mark E.   II. Title.

BF176.C63   2001
150'.28'7—dc21   2001041015

Sponsoring editor, Kenneth King; *production editor,* April Wells-Hayes; *manuscript editor,* Sheryl Rose; *design manager and cover designer,* Violeta Diaz; *text designers,* Cloyce J. Wall and Michael Remener; *illustrators,* Judith Ogus and Robin Mouat; *manufacturing managers,* Randy Hurst and Pam Augspurger. The text was set in 10/12 Palatino by G&S Typesetters, Inc., and printed on acid-free, 45# New Era Matte (not recycled) by Von Hoffmann Press in black and PMS 3015.

Cover image: Naomi Shea

INTERNATIONAL EDITION ISBN 0-07-113134-5

www.mhhe.com

*This book is dedicated to the victims of America's September 11th tragedy.
It is our hope that progress in the field of psychological assessment may
better aid civilized society in profiling and identifying misguided individuals
intent upon perpetrating senseless violence against innocent people.*

—Ronald Jay Cohen

BRIEF Contents

Contents

PART 1 *An Overview*

PART 3 *The Assessment of Intelligence*

PART 4 *The Assessment of Personality*

PART **5** *Testing and Assessment in Action*

17   Computer-Assisted Psychological Assessment   545

Preface

I remember walking with some of my fellow clinical psychology interns at Bellevue Hospital, entering a building in the NYU-Bellevue Medical Center complex, and hearing someone pointing to a man in the distance say, "There's David Wechsler!" Indeed, there stood one of the living legends in the field of psychology. As a graduate student I had learned to administer each of the Wechsler intelligence tests and had even been privileged enough to serve as an examiner in the restandardization of one of them. Seeing this psychologist in person for the first time as a fellow employee at Bellevue inspired a sense of awe.

It was during my internship year at Bellevue that I first began to think about writing a textbook on testing, assessment, and measurement in psychology. I was gaining a great deal of clinical experience in the area of assessment, was completing a doctoral dissertation that involved projective testing, and I had access to some of the most renowned human resources in the field of clinical psychology. In settings as diverse as the Bellevue child, adolescent, and adult in-patient services, the Bellevue psychiatric emergency room, the Bellevue prison service, the Bellevue adult outpatient clinic, and the Bellevue in-hospital court room, academic instruction was complemented by supervised experience with a wide variety of assessment-related dilemmas and solutions. This growing body of knowledge and experience reinforced my developing views about the need for an alternative to measurement texts of the day.

My education and experience in the area of testing and assessment continued after my internship year with my appointment as Senior Psychologist on the NYU-Bellevue staff. I handled a regular stream of assessment cases, instructed clinical psychology interns on assessment and supervised their work, and routinely made numerous assessment-related case presentations to colleagues. One day while chatting informally with David Wechsler—the luminary I had come to know as a colleague—he related a story about the time that Dan Rather and a CBS camera crew set up shop in his Upper East Side apartment. They had come to conduct an in-depth interview with him on the subject of intelligence for use on *CBS Reports*. Dr. Wechsler quipped that it wasn't until that day that the people in his building got an inkling that he must be kind of an important person—he had to be, if Dan Rather was coming to interview him! Even as Dr. Wechsler spoke, I envisioned a time when I, too, would request a formal interview with him, the better to provide some "insider" insights for this book. But the interview was not to be; Dr. Wechsler's death preceded that request.

Although we did not have the benefit of Dr. Wechsler's personal input for the first edition of this textbook, we have been, through the quarter-century or so in which the present edition of this textbook has evolved, fortunate enough to obtain the input of dozens of other authorities in areas such as intelligence, personality, statistics, and culture. In the course of that time period, the authors collectively gained not only greater knowledge about how to effectively convey measurement principles in a textbook, but greater personal experience using tests in clinical, school, business, and organizational settings. This vast bank of expertise was complemented by countless hours of library and online research, and by formal and informal reviews of alternative versions of manuscripts by faculty and students. Assimilating all such sources of information, draft after draft of this manuscript was created. Each draft was designed to succeed even more than its predecessor in terms of making the material accessible to students and stimulating independent thought on the subject matter.

The first proposal for this book was sent to a publisher in the mid-1970s. In that document, we envisioned a measurement text that was different in key ways from any existing book. The text would be comprehensive yet readable. It would be scholarly and academic in its presentation, yet include ample real-life examples illustrating the authors' hands-on experience with the subject matter. Illustrations would be used to stimulate thinking and imagination, not simply to break up long stretches of text. The organization of the book would be logical. Chapters were designed to flow in discussion from what a construct like intelligence or personality is, to why it is measured, to how it is measured. Designed to build a core knowledge in psychometrics early on, many of the subsequent chapters allowed for flexibility in order of assignment at the discretion of the instructor. The proposed book contained content areas never visited in any existing text. Coverage of neuropsychological and forensic assessment was included, as were culture-related issues and coverage of assessment in business and organizations. None of this may seem very revolutionary now. But it was then.

After initial writing had begun under contract, we received advice—some solicited and some unsolicited—from many colleagues who taught measurement courses. We were encouraged by some to fashion "a professor's book" rather than a "student's book." In this context, one colleague advised us half-jokingly, "If you're going to write a measurement text, make sure it's not very clear." Asked why, he responded, "Because if the writing's clear, few measurement experts and statisticians will think it's very good." Call us naive, but our vision of this book was quite the opposite. It was an era in which many psychology and education majors dreaded taking a required course in assessment, and many universities were dropping the course as a requirement. We believed a "student's book" was sorely needed to help reverse that trend.

The first edition of this book was finally published in 1988 by Mayfield Publishing Company, a relatively small, privately owned publishing house. At that time, in contrast to much larger, corporately owned publishers, Mayfield had only a handful of salespeople to promote the text. Despite this fact, and promotion efforts that were modest by any standard, word-of-mouth propelled our text to become one of the most frequently used books in measurement courses. We have been very proud of the reception the professional community gave us. We attribute it to the fact that we stayed true to our objectives and really delivered on our promises.

Revisions of tests, changes in the law, innovation in methods of assessment, new insights on the role of culture in assessment, and other factors have necessitated the publication of new editions of this text from time to time. Accordingly, the organization, content, and other variables related to each new edition have been tweaked—for the better, we trust—in each new edition. What has remained unchanged through the years is our commitment to keeping the presentation of material fresh, current, and forward-looking. The specific objectives we outlined in the first edition of this book have remained much the same in succeeding editions. They are:

1. To provide a thorough, state-of-the-art, and readable description of basic measurement concepts at a level of technical complexity sufficient to equip students to understand technical terms in professional journals, test manuals, and test reports and to be able to develop an educated opinion about the psychometric soundness of any psychological test

2. To present up-to-date, reasonably detailed, and well-balanced discussion of various issues in measurement ranging from the issue of heritability in intelligence, to general legal/ethical issues, to administration, scoring, and interpretation concerns with respect to computer-assisted psychological assessment

3. To blend theoretical and applied material in such a way as to provide the student with both a rationale for and a hands-on feel of the assessment process

4. To provide ample case illustrations of the wide range of real-world contexts in which psychological testing and assessment occur, including clinical, counseling, neuropsychological, educational, and business-related contexts

5. To provide a person-oriented perspective on measurement by including biographical material on many past and present contributors to the field

6. To excite genuine interest in the field of testing and assessment by writing with warmth, even occasional humor, and liberally illustrating with relevant material

7. To impart a sense of the authors' belief in and respect for the psychological assessment enterprise balanced by a healthy and realistic degree of self-criticism and an eye toward the challenges that lie ahead

"What else is new in this edition?" you may ask. The answer: "Way too much to detail here." In addition to coverage of new or updated tests, some new or updated material has to do with test development, such as the new material in Chapter 4 on the practice of concurrent validation by test developers and publishers. Some of the material has to do with specific constructs, such as the new material on the Cattell-Horn theory of intelligence, John Carroll's three-stratum theory, and the Cattell-Horn-Carroll theory. There is a wealth of new material having to do with sundry aspects of assessment such as the process of test revision, techniques of self-monitoring, substance abuse assessment, and pre-retirement assessment, and a fresh look at clinical versus actuarial prediction. Interwoven throughout, you will find a great deal of new content related to issues of culture and assessment.

In the past, whenever anyone asked me a question about the possibility of color in this text, my stock response would be, "The color is in the writing." With this fifth edition, I am now pleased to be able to add, "and in the blue ink on the pages, too!" In keeping with the objective of making this book as student-friendly as possible, we have also created a glossary; explanations of key words printed in bold throughout the text may be found there. In the companion workbook and student study guide (Cohen, 2002), each chapter now opens with a crossword puzzle keyed to the corresponding chapter in this text.

Our thanks to the many people who gave their time, knowledge, and talents to assist in the development of this fifth edition, especially the many measurement professionals who provided either solicited or unsolicited input. I thank the following individuals for their constructive review of the fifth edition manuscript: Nancy S. Breland, The College of New Jersey; Amy Herstein Gervasio, University of Wisconsin, Stevens Point; Janet L. Kottke, California State University, San Bernardino; and Terry G. Newell, California State University, Fresno. Special thanks to the people at Mayfield Publishing Company, the former publisher of this book, especially Frank Graham and Boyce Nute, who believed in this book from the outset. They, as well as many other staff people, supported us in our efforts to continually make it as good as it could be. Sincere thanks to my wife, Susan, for her assistance in various stages of this work, and for her above-and-beyond help in creating the crossword puzzles for the *Exercises* workbook; all those years of watching and playing *Wheel of Fortune* may not have been for naught. Thanks to all of the editorial staff who have worked behind the scenes to make certain this book is all that it can be. A partial listing of this editorial staff includes April Wells-Hayes, Sheryl Rose, and Ken King. Thanks also to Thalia Dorwick at our new publisher for the warm welcome to the McGraw-Hill family.

To the student taking this course: Welcome! We, your textbook authors, have done our best to convey a great deal of technical information in a way that you can understand, and with a style that you may (we hope) find appealing. To the instructor who has assigned this textbook, we sincerely thank you for the privilege of allowing us into your classroom, and we accept with a great sense of responsibility and humility the trust you have placed in us. We will continue to do our best to keep pace with the pulse of the field of testing and assessment and to provide readable, innovative, and thought-provoking coverage of that field to your students.

Ronald Jay Cohen, Ph.D.
Diplomate, American Board of Assessment Psychology

1

Psychological Testing and Assessment

All fields of human endeavor use measurement in some form, and each field has its own set of measuring tools and measuring units. If you're recently engaged or thinking about becoming engaged, you may have obtained an education on a unit of measure called the "carat." If you've been shopping for a computer, you may have learned something about a unit of measurement called a "byte." And if you're in need of an air conditioner, you'll no doubt want to know about the Btu (British thermal unit). Other units of measurement you may or may not be familiar with include a mile (land), a mile (nautical), a ton (long), a ton (short), a hertz, a henry, miles per hour, cycles per second, and candela per square meter. Professionals in the fields that employ these units know the potential uses, benefits, and limitations of such units in the measurements they make. So, too, users and potential users of psychological measurements need a working familiarity with the commonly used units of measurement, the theoretical underpinnings of the enterprise, and the tools employed.

Testing and Assessment

Detailed and intriguing accounts of efforts to assess people psychologically as early as the eleventh century B.C.E. in China (Yan, 1999) provide compelling testimony to the historic need for the assessment enterprise. However, the roots of contemporary psychological testing and assessment can be found in early-twentieth-century France. In 1905, Alfred Binet and a colleague published a test that was designed to help place Paris schoolchildren in appropriate classes. As history records, however, Binet's test would have consequences well beyond the Paris school district. Binet's test would serve as a catalyst to the field of psychological measurement as no test had before it. Within a decade, an English-language version of Binet's test was prepared for use in schools in the United States. In 1917, the United States declared war on Germany and entered World War I. The military needed a way to quickly screen large numbers of recruits for intellectual as well as emotional problems, and psychological testing provided the methodology. During World War II, the military would depend even more on psychological tests to screen recruits for service. The government's large-scale reliance on psychological tests served as a great impetus to the psychological testing enterprise. Following the war, an expanding number of tests purporting to measure a wide array of psychological variables burst onto the American scene.

The heyday of psychological testing was the 1950s and early 1960s. At many mental health facilities, both public and private, clients were administered groups of tests that typically included an intelligence test, a personality test, and a test to screen for neurological impairment. In the schools, the role of various psychological and educational tests in making placement and other decisions broadened. Corporate America, as well as many government agencies, also embraced psychological testing. A wide assortment of tests was being used to make critical decisions about the hiring, firing, and general utilization of personnel.

Paralleling greater reliance on data derived from psychological tests was greater public concern about such data. From the perspective of the public, psychological tests were suspect because they were so shrouded in mystery. Individuals compelled by an employer or a prospective employer to sit for a psychological test were understandably apprehensive. On the basis of data derived from the test, and for reasons not at all clear to the examinee, the testing might result in the denial of a desirable transfer or promotion, even the denial of employment. Examinees were not guaranteed any information about how well they did on the test, and they were seldom informed about the criteria on which their performance was being judged. Before long, the courts, even the Congress, would be grappling with a number of thorny questions and issues. Do psychological tests violate one's constitutional right of privacy? Do the tests really measure what they purport to measure? What kinds of decisions can and cannot be made on the basis of test data, and how should those decisions be made? What credentials, if any, are necessary to administer and interpret psychological tests? What rights do examinees undergoing psychological evaluation have?

Public scrutiny of psychological testing reached its zenith in 1965 with a series of probing and unprecedented congressional hearings (see Amrine, 1965). Against a backdrop of mounting public concern about—as well as legal challenges to—psychological testing, many psychologists in the 1960s began to look anew at the testing enterprise. Beyond being a mere instrument of measurement, a psychological test was conceptualized by many as a tool of a highly trained examiner. The value of a particular test was intimately and irrevocably linked to the expertise of the test user.

Testing and Assessment Defined

The world's receptivity to Binet's test in the early twentieth century spawned not only more tests, but more test developers, more test publishers, more test users, and the emergence of what, logically enough, has become known as a "testing" industry. "Testing" was the term used to refer to everything from the administration of a test (as in "Testing in progress") to the interpretation of a test score ("The testing indicated that . . ."). During World War I, the process of testing aptly described the group screening of thousands of military recruits. We suspect it was at that time that "testing" gained a powerful foothold in both the lay and professional vernaculars. We can find references to testing in the context of test administration and test interpretation, as well as everything in between, not only in postwar (World War I) textbooks (such as Anastasi, 1937; Bingham, 1937; Chapman, 1921; Hull, 1922; Spearman, 1927) but in varied test-related writings for decades thereafter. However, by the time of World War II, a semantic distinction between "testing" and another, more inclusive term, "assessment," began to emerge.

During World War II, the United States Office of Strategic Services (OSS) employed a variety of procedures and measurement tools—psychological tests among them—for the purpose of selecting military personnel for highly specialized positions involving spying, espionage, intelligence gathering, and the like. As summarized in *Assessment of Men* (OSS, 1948) and elsewhere (Murray & MacKinnon, 1946), the assessment data generated were subjected to thoughtful integration and evaluation by the highly trained assessment center staff. The OSS model of using an innovative variety of evaluative tools, with the data derived from the evaluations analyzed by highly trained assessors, would later inspire what is now referred to as the "assessment center" approach to personnel evaluation (Bray, 1982).

Personnel evaluations, clinical evaluations, and educational evaluations are but a few of the many contexts that entail behavioral observation and active integration by an assessor of test scores and other data from various sources. In such situations, as well as other evaluations involving more than a simple test-scoring process, the term "assessment" may be preferable to "testing." Such a preference for the term "assessment" acknowledges that tests represent only one type of tool used by professional assessors. It also reflects an appreciation for the value of a test being most intimately linked with the knowledge, skill, and experience of the assessor. As Sundberg and Tyler (1962) observed, *"Tests are tools.* In the hands of a fool or an unscrupulous person they become pseudoscientific perversion" (p. 131, emphasis in the original). In many, perhaps most, evaluation contexts it is the process of assessment that breathes life and meaning into test scores; test scores are what result from testing.

Psychological Assessment, a measurement textbook by Maloney and Ward (1976), echoed the uneasiness of psychologists with the anachronistic use of "psychological testing" to describe their many varied assessment-related activities. By articulating several differences between testing and assessment, Maloney and Ward clarified the rich texture of the thoughtful, problem-solving processes of psychological assessment, which had been mistakenly clumped under the same rubric as the more technician-like tasks of psychological testing.

Maloney and Ward conceived of this problem-solving process as ever variable in nature and the result of many different factors, beginning with the reason the assessment is being undertaken. Different tools of evaluation—psychological tests among them—might be marshaled in the process of assessment depending on the particular objectives, people, and circumstances involved, as well as other variables unique to the particular situation. By contrast, psychological testing was seen as much narrower in scope, referring only to "the process of administering, scoring, and interpreting psychological tests" (Maloney & Ward, 1976, p. 9). Testing was also seen as differing from assessment because the process is "test-controlled"; decisions, predictions, or both are made solely or largely on the basis of test scores. The examiner is more key to the process of assessment, in which decisions, predictions, or both are made on the basis of many possible sources of data (including tests). Maloney and Ward also distinguished "testing" from "assessment" in regard to their respective objectives. In testing, a typical objective is to measure the magnitude of some psychological trait. For example, one might speak of "intelligence testing" if the purpose of administering a test was confined to obtaining a numerical gauge of the examinee's intelligence. In assessment, by contrast, the objective more typically extends beyond obtaining a number; rather, the aim would be to reflect the strength or absence of some psychological trait. According to this view, "assessment" would be preferable to "testing" if an evaluation of a student's intelligence was undertaken, for example, to answer a referral question about the student's ability to function in a regular classroom. Such an evaluation might explore the student's intellectual strengths and weaknesses. Further, the assessment would likely integrate the clinician's findings during the course of the intellectual evaluation that pertained to the student's social skills and judgment. Maloney and Ward (1976) further distinguished testing from assessment by noting that testing

> could take place without being directed at answering a specific referral question and even without the tester actually seeing the client or testee. For example, tests could be (and often are) administered in groups and then scored and interpreted for a variety of purposes. (p. 9)

. . . while psychometric tests usually just add up the number of correct answers or the number of certain types of responses or performances with little if any regard for the how or mechanics of such content, clinical assessment is often far more interested in *how* the individual processes rather than the results of what he processes. The two operations, in fact, serve very different goals and purposes. (p. 39)

Regarding the collection of psychological assessment data, Maloney and Ward (1976) urged that far beyond the use of psychological tests alone, "literally, any method the examiner can use to make relevant observations is appropriate" (p. 7). Years later, Roberts and Magrab (1991) argued that assessment was not an activity to be confined to the consulting room. In presenting their community-based, interdisciplinary model for the assessment of children, they envisioned a place for traditional testing but viewed more global assessment as key to meaningful evaluation:

Assessment in this model does not emphasize stable traits but attempts to understand a problem in the larger ecological framework in which it occurs. For assessment to be ecologically valid, a broad range of information must be collected and new methods may be required to obtain the necessary information. These methods could include routine visits to the home and the community or naturalistic observations. (p. 145)

The semantic distinction between "psychological testing" and "psychological assessment" is of more than academic interest. Society at large is best served by clear definition and differentiation between terms such as "psychological testing" and "psychological assessment," as well as related terms such as "psychological test user" and "psychological assessor." In the section "Test-User Qualifications" in Chapter 2, we argue that clear distinctions between such terms will not only serve the public good but might also help avoid the turf wars now brewing between psychology and various users of psychological tests. Admittedly, the line between what constitutes testing and what constitutes assessment is not always as straightforward as we might like it to be. However, by acknowledging that such ambiguity exists, we can work toward sharpening our definition and use of these terms; denying or ignoring their distinctiveness provides no hope of a satisfactory remedy. For our purposes, we will define **psychological assessment** as the gathering and integration of psychology-related data for the purpose of making a psychological evaluation, accomplished through the use of tools such as tests, interviews, case studies, behavioral observation, and specially designed apparatuses and measurement procedures. We will define **psychological testing** as the process of measuring psychology-related variables by means of devices or procedures designed to obtain a sample of behavior.

We elaborate on these definitions in the sections below as we discuss tests and other tools of assessment. However, having defined *assessment,* it would be useful at this juncture to define *alternate assessment.* Why? Read on.

Alternate assessment   The **Individuals with Disabilities Education Act Amendments,** PL 105-17, became law in 1997. This law reauthorized and amended the Individuals with Disabilities Education Act (widely referred to as the **IDEA**), originally passed in 1975. According to Pitasky (1998), the amended IDEA "performed radical surgery on a law for which major repairs were recommended" (p. 1) and "is responsible for the most wide-sweeping and rampant changes in the history of the 27-year-old law" (p. 12). Indeed, the revisions, most of which became effective as of June 4, 1997, contained dramatic changes concerning the way that students in special education programs are educated and evaluated. Many of the provisions of the IDEA amendments are discussed elsewhere in this book. Here, let's simply point out that among other things, the new law seeks to include students with disabilities in assessments carried out at a statewide level, as well as at the level of the individual school district. Specifically, section 612 (a) (17) of the law reads, in part, as follows:

> Children with disabilities are included in general State and district-wide assessment programs, with appropriate accommodations, where necessary. As appropriate, the State or local educational agency—(i) develops guidelines for the participation of children with disabilities in alternate assessments for those children who cannot participate in State and district-wide assessment programs; and (ii) develops and, beginning not later than July 1, 2000 conducts those alternate assessments.

The law does not expressly define "alternate assessments." However, past practice by assessors involved in evaluating students with special needs informs us what would probably pass muster with a court, should the utility of any alternate assessments be challenged. In essence, the critical question confronting assessors in special education settings may be phrased as, "What alternative assessment procedure, or adaptation of an existing procedure, shall be employed in order to assess this special education student?"

The question posed above is a familiar one to professional assessors who work in educational settings with special education students. Its answer will vary with the unique needs of each individual student. So, for example, the student who has difficulty reading the small print of a particular test may be accommodated with a large-print version of the same test or a test environment with special lighting. A student with a hearing impairment may be administered the test by means of sign language. A child with attention deficit disorder might have an extended evaluation time, with frequent breaks during periods of evaluation. So far, the process of alternate assessment may seem fairly simple and straightforward; in practice, however, it may be anything but.

Consider, for example, the case of a student with a vision impairment scheduled to be tested on a written, multiple-choice test by an alternate procedure. There are several options for the exact form of this alternate procedure. For instance, the test could be translated into Braille and administered in that form, or it could be administered by means of audiotape. Whether the test is administered by Braille or audiotape may affect the test scores—with some students doing better with a Braille administration and some doing better with an audiotaped administration. Students with superior short-term attention and memory skills for auditory stimuli would seem to have an advantage with regard to the audiotaped administration. Students with superior haptic (sense of touch) and perceptual-motor skills might have an advantage with regard to the Braille administration. We could raise a number of questions regarding the equivalence of various alternate assessments, as well as the equivalence of each of the alternate assessments to the traditional measurement method. Perhaps the key question is, "To what extent is each method really measuring the same thing?" Related questions include, "How equivalent is the alternate test to the original test?" and "How does modifying the format of a test, the time limits of a test, or any other aspect of the way a test was originally designed to be administered affect test scores?"

With this brief introduction to alternate assessment as background, we propose this definition of this somewhat elusive process: **Alternate assessment** is an evaluative or diagnostic procedure or process that varies from the usual, customary, or standardized way a measurement is derived, either by virtue of some special accommodation made to the assessee or by means of alternative methods designed to measure the same variable(s). In this definition, we have steered clear of the thorny issue of equivalence of methods; unless the alternate procedures have been thoroughly researched, there is no reason to expect that they would be equivalent—and in most cases, because the alternate procedures have been so individually tailored, there is seldom compelling research to support equivalence. State guidelines for alternate assessment will no doubt include ways of translating measurement procedures from one format to another. Other guidelines may suggest substituting one tool of assessment, such as a test, with another tool of assessment. You might ask, "What are those other tools of assessment?"

The Tools of Psychological Assessment

The test   A **test** may be defined simply as a measuring device or procedure. When the word *test* is prefaced with a modifier, what is being referred to is a measuring device or procedure designed to measure a variable related to that modifier. Consider, for example, the term *medical test,* which refers to a measuring device or procedure designed to measure some variable related to the practice of medicine (including a wide range of tools and procedures such as X rays, blood tests, and testing of reflexes). In a like manner, the term **psychological test** refers to a measuring device or procedure designed to measure variables related to psychology (for example, intelligence, personality, aptitude, interests, attitudes, and values). And whereas a medical test might involve the analysis of a sample of blood, tissue, or the like, a psychological test almost always involves the analysis of a sample of behavior. The behavior sample could range from responses to a pencil-and-paper questionnaire to oral responses to questions to performance of some task (Figure 1–1). The behavior sample could be elicited by the stimulus of the test itself or could be naturally occurring behavior (under observation).

Psychological tests may differ on a number of variables such as content, format, administration procedures, scoring and interpretation procedures, and psychometric or technical quality. The content (subject matter) of the test will, of course, vary with the focus of the particular test. But even two psychological tests purporting to measure the same construct—for example, "personality"—may differ widely in item content because of factors such as the test developer's definition of personality and the theoretical orientation of the test. For example, items on a psychoanalytically oriented personality test may have little resemblance to those on an existentially oriented personality test, yet both are "personality tests." The term **format** pertains to the form, plan, structure, arrangement, and layout of test items as well as to related considerations such as time limits. "Format" is also used to refer to the form in which a test is administered—computerized, pencil and paper, or some other form. When making specific reference to a computerized test, "format" also refers to the form of the software—IBM- or Apple-compatible. Additionally, "format" may be used with reference to the form or structure of other evaluative tools and processes, such as the conduct of interviews, the performance of tasks, and the nature of work samples and portfolios.

For sports enthusiasts, "score" typically refers to the number of points accumulated by competitors. For music aficionados, "score" refers to the written form of a musical composition. For students of psychometrics, **score** refers to a code or summary statement, usually but not necessarily numerical in nature, that reflects an evaluation with regard to performance on a test, task, interview, or some other sample of behavior. Accordingly, **scoring** is the process of assigning such evaluative codes or statements to performance on tests, tasks, interviews, or other behavior samples. As you pursue the study of the measurement of psychological and educational variables, you will learn about many different types of scores and scoring methods. You will also discover that tests differ widely in terms of their guidelines for scoring and interpretation. Some tests are designed to be scored by testtakers themselves, others are designed to be scored by trained examiners, and still others may be scored by computers. Some tests, such as most tests of intelligence, come with test manuals that are very explicit not only about scoring criteria but also about the nature of the interpretations that can be made from the

Figure 1–1
Price (and Judgment) Check in Aisle 5

Hamera and Brown (2000) described the development of a context-based Test of Grocery Shopping Skills. Designed primarily for use with persons with psychiatric disorders, this assessment tool may be useful in evaluating a skill necessary for independent living.

calculated score. Other tests, such as the Rorschach Inkblot Test (discussed in Chapter 12), are sold with no manual; the (qualified) purchaser buys the stimulus materials and then selects and uses one of many available guides for administration, scoring, and interpretation.

Tests differ with respect to their technical or psychometric quality. At this point, suffice it to say that a good test measures what it purports to measure in a consistent way and that if two tests purport to measure the exact same (identically defined) construct, the test that measures the construct better is the better (that is, the technically superior or more psychometrically sound) instrument. We have more to say about what constitutes a good test later in this chapter, and all of Part 2 is concerned with issues related to the psychometric quality of a test. Let's also note here that it is easier to identify a good test than to identify a good assessment process. A developing body of knowledge and a proving ground of experience have yielded methodologies with which tests can be evaluated for psychometric soundness. However, it is generally more difficult to evaluate the soundness of an assessment procedure because there are typically many more variables involved. Unlike a test, which may be designed to measure a particular trait, psychological assessment is undertaken in an effort to provide more information relevant to specific questions, issues, or previous conclusions, and the nature of the tools used and the procedures followed will vary accordingly. Because of the diversity of assessors' backgrounds, it is conceivable that two assessors might use entirely different sets of tools and procedures to answer any given assessment question. Can one approach to assessment be more valid than another? Yes. But determining the answer to that question with a fair amount of certainty is sometimes an ambitious undertaking. As Maloney and Ward (1976, p. 4) put it: "We do have ways of assessing test-as-tools efficiently. On the other hand, it is much more difficult to determine the efficiency of the process of psychological assessment, primarily because there is much less agreement on what this process is or what it entails."

Consistent with common practice, we sometimes use the word "test" (as well as related terms such as "test score") in a generic sense when discussing general principles applicable to various measurement procedures. These measurement procedures range from those widely labeled as "tests" (such as paper-and-pencil examinations), to procedures that measurement experts might label with more specific terms (such as situational performance measures).

The interview   Another widely used tool in the process of psychological assessment is the interview—a word that may conjure images of face-to-face talk. But an interview as a tool of psychological assessment involves more than talk. If the interview is being conducted face to face, the interviewer will probably be noting nonverbal as well as verbal behavior. For example, the interviewer may make notations regarding the interviewee's dress, manner, and eye contact. A face-to-face interview need not involve any speech if the interviewee suffers from a hearing impairment; the entire interview might be conducted in sign language. An interview may be conducted over the telephone, in which case the interviewer might make inferences regarding the content of what is said as a function of changes in the interviewee's voice quality. An interview of sorts may also be conducted by means of other electronic media, such as e-mail. In its broadest sense, then, we can define an **interview** as a method of gathering information through direct, reciprocal communication.

Interviews differ with regard to many variables, such as the purpose for which they are initiated, the time or other restrictions under which they are conducted, and the willingness of the interviewee to candidly provide information. An interview may be used by psychologists and others in clinical, counseling, forensic, or neuropsychological settings as a tool to help make diagnostic or treatment decisions. School psychologists and others in an educational setting may use interviews to help make decisions related to the appropriateness of various educational interventions or class placements. An interview may be used as a tool to help psychologists in the field of human resources to make more informed recommendations regarding the hiring, firing, and advancement of personnel. Interviews are used by psychologists who study consumer behavior to answer the questions of corporate America regarding the market for various products and services, as well as questions related to how best to advertise and promote such products and services. Researchers in psychology and related fields use interviews to explore varied psychological variables ranging from the quality of life of homeless persons (Sullivan et al., 2000), to psychological differences between Gulf War veterans with and without unexplained symptoms (Storzbach et al., 2000).

The popularity of the interview as a method for gathering information extends far beyond psychology. Just try to think of one day when you were *not* exposed to an interview on television, radio, or on the Net! However, regardless of the forum, the quality, if not the quantity of useful information produced by an interview depends to some degree on the skill of the interviewer. Interviewers differ with respect to variables such as the pacing of interviews, the extent to which they develop a rapport with interviewees, and the extent to which they convey genuineness, empathy, and a sense of humor. As you look at Figure 1–2, think about other dimensions on which you might characterize interviewers you see on television (such as juvenile versus adult, and eager-to-speak versus eager-to-listen). What types of interviewing skills do you think are necessary for

Figure 1–2
On Interviewing and Being Interviewed

Different interviewers have different styles of interviewing. How would you characterize the interview style of Howard Stern versus that of Jay Leno?

the host of a talk show? Do these skills differ from those that are necessary for a professional in the field of psychological assessment?

The portfolio In recent years, the popularity of **portfolio** (work sample) assessment in many fields, including education, has been rising. Some have argued, for example, that the best evaluation of a student's writing skills can be accomplished not by the administration of a test but by asking the student to compile a selection of writing samples. From the perspective of education administrators, portfolio assessment would seem to also have distinct advantages in assessing the effectiveness of teachers. By examining teachers' portfolios and seeing how teachers approach their coverage of various topics, educational evaluators have another tool that can help anchor judgments to work samples.

Case history data In a general sense, **case history data** refers to records, transcripts, and other accounts made in written, pictorial, or other form, in any media, that preserve archival information, official and informal accounts, as well as other data and items relevant to an assessee. Case history data may include files or excerpts from files maintained at diverse institutions and agencies such as schools, hospitals, employers, religious institutions, and criminal justice agencies. Other possible examples of case history data include letters and written correspondence, photos, family albums, newspaper or magazine clippings, and home videos, movies, and audiotapes. Work samples, artwork, doodlings, and accounts and pictures pertaining to interests and hobbies are yet other examples of case history data.

As we will see, case history data can be a very useful tool in a wide variety of assessment contexts. In a clinical evaluation, for example, case history data can be useful in shedding light relevant to an individual's past and current adjustment, as well as the events and circumstances that may have contributed to any changes in adjustment. Case history data can be of critical value in neuropsychological evaluations, where it often provides information relevant to neuropsychological functioning prior to the occurrence of a trauma or other event that results in a deficit. School psychologists rely on case history data to, among other things, answer questions about the course of a student's developmental history.

Another use of the term "case history," one synonymous with "case study," has to do with the assembly of case history data into an illustrative account. For example, a case study might detail how a number of aspects of an individual's personality combined with environmental conditions to produce a successful world leader. A case study of an individual who attempted to assassinate a high-ranking political figure might shed light on what types of individuals and conditions might lead to similar attempts in the future. In fact, as we will see in Chapter 13, The U.S. Secret Service relies heavily on behavioral case study data in its assessments of dangerousness.

Behavioral observation   "To the extent that it is practically feasible, direct observation of behavior frequently proves the most clinically useful of all assessment procedures" (Goldfried & Davison, 1976, p. 44). **Behavioral observation** as a tool of assessment may be defined as monitoring the actions of others or oneself by visual or electronic means, while recording quantitative and/or qualitative information regarding the actions, typically for diagnostic or related purposes and either the design of an intervention or the measurement of the outcome of an intervention. Behavioral observation has proved to be a very useful assessment procedure, particularly in institutional settings such as schools, hospitals, prisons, and group homes. Using published or self-constructed lists of targeted behaviors, staff can observe firsthand the behavior of the person under observation and design interventions accordingly. In a school situation, for example, behavioral observation in the playground of a culturally different child suspected of having linguistic problems might reveal that the child does have English language skills but is unwilling—for reasons of shyness, cultural upbringing, or whatever—to demonstrate those abilities to an adult.

Despite the potential usefulness of behavioral observation in settings ranging from the private practitioner's consulting room to the interior of a space shuttle, it tends to be used infrequently outside institutional settings. For private practitioners, it is typically not economically feasible to spend hours out of the consulting room engaged in behavioral observation.

Role play tests   Some assessment tools require assessees to role play or play themselves in some hypothetical situation and then respond accordingly. An individual being evaluated in a corporate, industrial, organizational, or military context for managerial or leadership ability, for example, might be asked to mediate a hypothetical dispute between personnel at a work site. The context of the role play may be created by various techniques ranging from live actors to computer-generated simulation. Outcome measures for such an assessment might include ratings related to various aspects of the individual's ability to resolve the conflict, such as effectiveness of approach, quality of resolution, and number of minutes to resolution.

Beyond corporate, industrial, organizational, and military settings, role play as a tool of assessment may be used in clinical settings, particularly in work with substance abusers. Clinicians may attempt to obtain a baseline measure of abuse, cravings, or coping skills by administering a **role play test** prior to therapeutic intervention, and then again at the completion of a course of treatment.

Computers as tools   Traditionally, the key advantage of automated techniques has been saving assessors time in test administration, scoring, and interpretation. In interpreting test data, the ability of computers to analyze voluminous amounts of data while simultaneously comparing such data with other data in memory is especially advantageous. Related advantages of using computers in assessment include:

- *Automatic tailoring of a test's content and length for each testtaker.* Depending on their response to initial items, the content of the items testtakers are presented with may vary for each testtaker. In addition, the actual length of the test for different testtakers may also vary. The objective of this computer-adaptive testing is to tailor tests to the ability (or to the strength of some other trait) that the testtaker is presumed to possess.

- *Measurement of traits or abilities by techniques that could not be measured by more traditional methods.* For example, Mirka et al. (2000) described an assessment methodology that employs video, computer, and other components to obtain continuous assessment of back stress (Figure 1–3).

- *Quick and efficient comparisons to other testtakers.* Computers can be programmed and periodically updated with test findings for large numbers of other current or

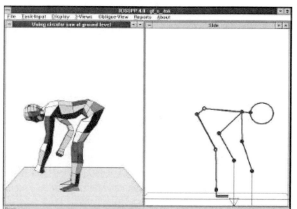

Figure 1–3
A Method to Quantify Back Stress

A new assessment methodology designed to quantify back stress involves capturing an image with a video camera (in this illustration, the act of sawing at ground level), computerized representation of the action, and laboratory simulation (Mirka et al., 2000).

previous testtakers, thus facilitating speedy comparison of results with other individuals and groups.

- *Financial savings.* In cost-conscious times, computer-assisted psychological assessment's (CAPA) promise of significant savings over time has enticed many large corporations to invest in it.

Because of the great proliferation of computerized testing, discussion of CAPA will be integrated throughout this book. In Chapter 17, we explore in detail the benefits as well as the issues that remain unresolved with regard to computer-assisted assessment.

Other tools   Varied instruments of measurement can be used in psychological assessment. Video monitors wired to simple videocassette players have become more widespread as a tool of assessment. Specially created videos are used not only in job training, for example, but also in evaluating the learning and competencies of personnel. Although many math- or language-related skills can be reasonably assessed by paper-and-pencil tests, assessment by means of video adds a component of realism and attention to detail (Outtz, 1994) that is desirable in many personnel-assessment situations. Corporate managers may be asked to respond to a variety of hypothetical incidents of sexual harassment in the workplace. Police personnel may be asked about how they would respond to various types of emergencies either reenacted for the assessment video or actually recorded on tape as they happened. Psychotherapists may be asked to respond with a diagnosis and a treatment plan for each of several clients presented to them on videotape. The list of potential applications for video assessment is endless.

Psychologists and others who devise tools to assess people with disabilities and members of other special populations have been most innovative. For example, Wilson et al. (1982) described a dental plate activated by the tongue as a mechanism for test response to be used by testtakers who lack the capacity for speech or control of their hands or limbs. The device permits five kinds of response, depending on the area of the plate depressed by the tongue.

As researchers learn more about various psychology-related matters, new tools will be pressed into service to measure relevant variables. For example, a new tool in diagnosing dyslexia may be a multimedia computer device that assesses one's ability to process rapid sounds (Katz et al., 1992). Old tools may also be put to new uses based on new information. For example, ordinary blood pressure or body temperature readings may become tools of assessment in a psychological study, especially if analyzed with measures of stress or other psychological variables (see, for example, McCubbin et al., 1991; Ussher & Wilding, 1991). Biofeedback equipment is useful in obtaining measures of bodily reactions (such as muscular tension or galvanic skin response) to various sorts of stimuli. An instrument called a penile plethysmograph, which gauges male sexual arousal, has found application in sexual therapy programs with normal males experiencing sexual difficulties as well as in the treatment of sexual offenders. Impaired ability to identify odors is not uncommon in disorders such as Alzheimer's disease and Down's syndrome, in which the central nervous system (CNS) may be affected. Tests such as the University of Pennsylvania Smell Identification Test (UPSIT) have been helpful in assessing the extent of olfactory deficit in these and other diseases where there is suspected CNS involvement, such as acquired immunodeficiency syndrome (AIDS) (Brody et al., 1991). The UPSIT testtaker is sequentially exposed to 40 scratch-and-sniff odors and asked to identify each odor from a four-item word list.

There has been no shortage of innovation on the part of psychologists in devising measurement tools, or adapting existing tools, for use in psychological measurement. Yet all such tools tend to be based on a dozen or so assumptions that we now review.

Twelve Assumptions in Psychological Testing and Assessment

What follows is a listing of basic assumptions in psychological testing and assessment. Be forewarned that these assumptions are deceptively simple. One can state, for example, that psychologists who use tests to measure psychological traits assume that such traits (1) exist, (2) can be quantified, and (3) can be measured. Yet it is also true that psychologists who use tests to measure psychological traits have engaged in intense debate about the nature of the existence of psychological traits, as well as how—even if—psychological traits can be meaningfully quantified and measured. Indeed, controversy surrounds some of the most fundamental assumptions about psychological testing and assessment. As you read on, and with every successive chapter in this book, your appreciation for the complexity of the issues involved will deepen.

Assumption 1: Psychological traits and states exist. A **trait** has been defined as "any distinguishable, relatively enduring way in which one individual varies from another" (Guilford, 1959, p. 6). **States** also distinguish one person from another but are relatively less enduring (Chaplin et al., 1988).

The word *distinguishable* conveys the idea that behavior labeled with one trait term can be differentiated from behavior that is labeled with another trait term. Thus, for example, behavior within a certain context that might be viewed as religious should ideally be distinguishable from behavior within the same or another context that might be viewed as deviant. Note here that it is important to be aware of the *context* or situation in which a particular behavior is displayed when distinguishing between trait terms that may be applicable: A person who is kneeling and talking to God inside a church may be described as religious, whereas another person engaged in the exact same behavior in a public restroom might more readily be viewed as deviant. The trait term that an observer applies, as well as the strength or magnitude of the trait presumed to be present, is based on an observation of a sample of behavior. The observed sample of behavior may be obtained in a number of ways, ranging from direct observation of the assessee (such as by actually watching the individual going to church regularly and praying) to the analysis of the assessee's statements on a self-report, pencil-and-paper personality test (on which, for example, the individual may have provided an indication of great frequency in church attendance).

The phrase "relatively enduring way" in the definition serves as a reminder that a trait cannot be expected to be manifest in an individual 100% of the time. Whether a trait manifests itself, and to what degree, is presumed to depend not only on the strength of the trait in the individual but also on the nature of the situation. Stated another way, exactly how a particular trait manifests itself is, at least to some extent, situation-dependent. For example, a violent parolee may generally be prone to behave in a rather subdued way with her parole officer and much more violently in the presence of her family and friends. John may be viewed as dull and cheap by his wife but as charming and extravagant by his secretary, business associates, and others he keenly wants to impress.

The definitions of "trait" and "state" we are using also refer to a *way in which one individual varies from another.* This phrase should serve to emphasize that the attribution of a trait or state term is always a relative phenomenon. For example, in describing one person as "shy," or even in using terms such as "very shy" or "not shy," most people are typically making an unstated comparison with the degree of shyness that could reasonably be expected to be emitted by the average person under the same or similar circumstances. In psychological testing and assessment, assessors may also make such comparisons with respect to the hypothetical average person. Alternatively, assessors may make comparisons among people who, because of their membership in some group or for any number of other reasons, are decidedly not average. As you might expect, the reference group with which comparisons are made can greatly influence one's conclusions or judgments. For example, suppose a psychologist administers a test of shyness to a 22-year-old male who earns his living as an erotic dancer. The interpretation of the test data will almost surely differ as a function of whether the reference group with which the testtaker is compared is other males in his age group or other male erotic dancers in his age group.

The term **psychological trait,** much like the term *trait* itself, covers a very wide range of possible characteristics. Thousands of psychological trait terms can be found in the English language (Allport & Odbert, 1936). Among them are psychological traits that relate to intelligence, specific intellectual abilities, cognitive style, adjustment, interests, attitudes, sexual orientation and preferences, psychopathology, personality in general, and specific personality traits. New concepts or discoveries in research may bring new trait terms to the fore. For example, a trait term seen with increasing frequency in the professional literature on human sexuality is *androgynous* (referring to a lack of primacy of male or female characteristics). Cultural evolution may bring new trait terms into common usage as it did in the 1960s when people began speaking of the degree to which women were *liberated* (or freed from the constraints of gender-dependent social expectations). A more recent example is the trait term *new age,* used in the popular culture to refer to a spiritual, almost mystical orientation.

Few people deny that psychological traits exist. Yet there has been a fair amount of controversy regarding just *how* they exist. For example, do traits have a physical existence, perhaps as a circuit in the brain? Although some have argued in favor of such a conception of psychological traits (Allport, 1937; Holt, 1971), compelling evidence to support such a view has been difficult to obtain. For our purposes, a psychological trait exists only as a **construct**—an informed, scientific idea developed or constructed to describe or explain behavior. We can't see, hear, or touch constructs, but we can infer their existence from overt behavior. In this context, "overt behavior" refers to an observable action or the product of an observable action, including test- or assessment-related responses. A challenge facing test developers is to construct tests that are at least as telling as observable behavior like that illustrated in Figure 1–4.

Assumption 2: Psychological traits and states can be quantified and measured.   Amy scored 36 on a test of marital adjustment, and her husband Zeke scored 41 on the same test. *Question:* What does this information tell us about Amy, Zeke, and their adjustment to married life? *Answer:* Virtually nothing. To respond professionally to this question, we would need to know much more about (1) Amy; (2) Zeke; (3) how the construct "marital adjustment" was defined on the marital adjustment test they took; (4) the meaning of the test scores according to the test's author; and (5) research relevant to substantiating the test's guidelines for scoring and interpretation.

Test authors, much like people in general, have many different ways of looking at and defining the same phenomenon. Just think, for example, of the wide range of ways a term such as "aggressive" is used. We speak of an "aggressive salesperson," an "aggressive killer," and an "aggressive dancer," and in each of those different contexts "aggressive" carries with it a different meaning. If a personality test yields a score purporting to provide information about how aggressive a testtaker is, a first step in understanding the meaning of that score is understanding how "aggressive" was defined by the test developer. More specifically, what types of behaviors are presumed to be indicative of someone who is aggressive as defined by the test?

From a world of behaviors presumed to be indicative of the targeted trait, a test developer has a world of possible items that can be written to gauge the strength of that

Figure 1–4
Measuring Sensation Seeking

The psychological trait of sensation seeking *has been defined as "the need for varied, novel, and complex sensations and experiences and the willingness to take physical and social risks for the sake of such experiences" (Zuckerman, 1979, p. 10). A 22-item Sensation-Seeking Scale (SSS) seeks to identify people who are high or low on this trait. Assuming the SSS actually measures what it purports to measure, how would you expect a random sample of people lining up to bungee jump to score on the test, as compared with another age-matched sample of people shopping at the local mall? What are the comparative advantages of using paper-and-pencil measures, such as the SSS, and using more performance-based measures, such as the one pictured here?*

trait in testtakers.[1] For example, if the test developer deems knowledge of American history to be one component of adult intelligence, then an item that asks "Who was the second president of the United States?" may appear on the test. Similarly, if social judgment is deemed to be indicative of adult intelligence, then it would be legitimate to include an item that asks "Why should guns in the home always be inaccessible to children?" Such items having been included on an adult test of intelligence, one of the many complex issues the test developer will have to deal with is the comparative weight such items are given. Perhaps correct responses to the social judgment questions should earn more credit than correct responses to the American history questions. Perhaps, for example, a correct response to a social judgment question should be assigned a numerical value of 2 or 3 points toward the overall point total, and each correct response to the American history questions should be assigned a numerical value of 1 point. Weighting the comparative value of a test's items comes about as the result of a complex interplay among many factors, including technical considerations, the way a construct has been defined for the purposes of the test, and the value society attaches to the behaviors being evaluated.

Measurement is the assignment of numbers or symbols to characteristics of people or objects according to rules. An example of a measurement rule, this one for scoring

---

1. In the language of psychological testing and assessment, the word *domain* is substituted for *world* in this context. As we will see subsequently, assessment professionals speak, for example, of **domain sampling,** which may refer to either (1) a sample of behaviors from all possible behaviors that could conceivably be indicative of a particular construct, or (2) a sample of test items from all possible items that could conceivably be used to measure a particular construct.

each item on a spelling test, is "Assign the number 1 for each correct answer according to the answer key, and 0 for each incorrect answer." Another example of a measurement rule, this one for each item on a test designed to measure depression, is "Using the test's answer key as a guide, assign the number 1 for each response that indicates that the assessee is depressed, 0 for all other responses." For many varieties of psychological tests, some number representing the score on the test is derived from the examinee's responses. The test score, presumed to represent the strength of the targeted ability or trait or state, is frequently based on a cumulative model of scoring.[2] Inherent in cumulative scoring models is the assumption that the more the testtaker responds in a particular direction as keyed by the test manual as correct or consistent with a particular trait, the higher that testtaker is presumed to be on the targeted ability or trait. The rules for assigning all numbers have typically been published in the test's manual. Ideally, scientifically acceptable evidence to support the test's measurement rules, as well as all other related claims of the test author, are also included in the test's manual.

A **scale** is a set of numbers (or other symbols) whose properties model empirical properties of the objects or traits to which numbers are assigned. As we will see in Chapter 3 and again in Chapter 7, different types of scales exist, each with its own assumptions and limitations. **Scaling** may be defined as assigning numbers in accordance with empirical properties of objects or traits. Entire volumes have been written on scaling, and many different strategies of scaling can be applied in the development of a new test. An underlying assumption in all scaling efforts is that traits and abilities can be meaningfully quantified and measured. The body of professional literature on scaling provides theoretical rationales and mathematical techniques helpful in deciding how such quantification and measurement can best proceed.

Assumption 3: Various methods of measuring aspects of the same thing can be useful. A number of different tests and measurement techniques may exist to measure the same trait, state, interest, ability, attitude, or other construct, or some aspect of same. Some tests are better than others in various ways, such as the extent to which meaningful predictions can be made on the basis of the scores derived. In fact, tests can differ in a great many ways.

Tests vary in the extent to which they are linked to a theory. For example, the items for a personality test called the MMPI-2 were not developed with reference to any one theory of personality. By contrast, the items for another test, the Myers-Briggs Type Indicator, were developed on the basis of Carl Jung's theory of personality types.

Tests may also differ according to whether the items were selected on a rational or an empirical basis. As its name implies, a rational basis for a particular test item exists when the item logically taps what is known about the targeted trait. Logically, for example, we would expect people in a state of severe depression to report that they feel sad much of the time. On a rational basis, then, a test for severe depression might include a true-false item such as "I feel sad much of the time." However, test items can also be developed empirically—that is, on the basis of experience. For example, suppose researchers discovered that severely depressed people tend to agree with the following statement: "The best part of waking up is coffee in my cup." If that were the case—it is not—such a statement could be included on a strictly empirical, not rational, basis as a test item. When tests are developed empirically, the items may or may not seem to belong on the test from the standpoint of reason or logic.

There is a wide array of ways in which test items can be presented. Most familiar to you, perhaps, are items structured in a true-false, a multiple-choice, or an essay form.

---

2. Other, less widely used models of scoring are discussed in Chapter 7.

However, test items may be structured in other ways, so that, for example, the examinee's task is to manipulate stimulus materials by reordering or rearranging them, substituting or correcting them, or presenting them in some new form or way. A test of creative musical ability, for example, might explore the examinee's facility in manipulating a given series of musical notes.

Tests differ in their administration, scoring, and interpretation procedures. Some tests are individually administered; others are designed for group administration. Some tests have strict time limits; others are not timed. Some tests can be scored and interpreted by machines or computers; other tests are designed for submission to a committee of experts who must apply their expertise in the process of scoring and interpreting the test data.

Tests differ in the extent to which their stimulus materials are verbal or nonverbal. Tests differ in the way that they compel examinees to think and reason; success on various tests may require anything from factual recall to social judgment to great creativity—or some combination of those or other skills. Tests differ with respect to their application. One test of depression might be developed for use in an acute-care setting to identify severely depressed individuals. Another test of depression might have been developed to evaluate the effectiveness of a new drug in treating depression. In general, the utility of tests must be proved for the settings in which they were originally designed to be used, and then proved again for any additional settings in which their use is contemplated.

Assumption 4: Assessment can provide answers to some of life's most momentous questions.

Every day, throughout the world, momentous questions are addressed on the basis of some type of assessment process. Is this person competent to stand trial? Who should be hired, transferred, promoted, or fired? Who should gain entry to this special program or be awarded a scholarship? Which parent shall have custody of the children? The answers to these kinds of questions are likely to have a significant impact on many lives. If they are to sleep comfortably at night, users of tests and other assessment techniques must believe that the process of assessment employed to answer such questions is fully up to the task.

Assumption 5: Assessment can pinpoint phenomena that require further attention or study.

In addition to their function in evaluation for the purpose of making sometimes momentous judgments, an assumption in measurement is that tools of assessment can be used for diagnostic purposes. **Diagnosis** may be defined broadly as a description or conclusion reached on the basis of evidence and opinion through a process of distinguishing the nature of something and ruling out alternative conclusions. A **diagnostic test** may be defined as a tool used to make a diagnosis, usually for the purpose of identifying areas of deficit to be targeted for intervention.

In the field of medicine, a diagnosis is perhaps best associated with a name of some illness. A medical diagnosis may be arrived at on the basis of a physical examination, medical test data, and knowledge of the patient's medical history. In the field of education, similar tools may contribute to a comprehensive assessment. For example, a child with a reading problem may be given a thorough optometric examination and a diagnostic reading test. The resulting data will be interpreted in the context of the child's educational history. A precise statement regarding the specifics of the child's reading problem—a diagnosis—will be made.

In psychology, as in medicine, diagnosis is perhaps best associated in the public mind with the names of various illnesses, albeit mental illnesses. For example, one speaks of a diagnosis of depression or schizophrenia. In reality, however, *diagnosis* is used in a much broader sense, one that in general has to do with pinpointing psychological or behavioral phenomena, usually for further study. For example, a psychologist specializing in measurement might use diagnostic techniques to analyze how behavior and thinking involved in taking a test administered by computer differs from behavior and thinking involved in taking that same test administered in a paper-and-pencil format. A psychologist specializing in jury research might use diagnostic techniques to analyze what is and is not compelling to a jury about various arguments. A psychologist specializing in engineering psychology might use diagnostic techniques to analyze the pros and cons of different positionings of a new control on an automobile's dashboard.

Assumption 6: Many sources of data are part of the assessment process.   To understand a student, a convict, an employee, a therapy client, or any person in any role or capacity, data from a test can be helpful. However, testing and assessment professionals understand that decisions that are likely to significantly influence the course of an examinee's life are ideally made not on the basis of a single test score but, rather, from data from many different sources. Exactly what type of additional information is needed will, of course, vary with the questions the assessment procedure was initiated to answer. A partial listing of some other types of data that may be relevant to the decision-making process would include information about the examinee's current as well as past physical and mental health and academic and occupational status. Relevant family history and current family status may also make important contributions to the decision-making process, as may knowledge of the examinee's values, aspirations, and motivation.

Assumption 7: Various sources of error are part of the assessment process.   In everyday conversation, we use the word *error* to refer to mistakes, miscalculations, and the like. In the context of the assessment enterprise, "error" need not refer to a deviation, an oversight, or something that otherwise violates what might have been expected. To the contrary, "error" in the context of psychological testing and assessment traditionally refers to something that is not only expected but actually considered a component of the measurement process. In this context, **error** refers to a long-standing assumption that factors other than what a test attempts to measure will influence performance on the test. Because error is a variable in any psychological assessment process, we often speak of **error variance.** Test scores earned by examinees are typically subject to questions concerning the degree to which the measurement process includes error. For example, a score on an intelligence test could be subject to debate concerning the degree to which the obtained score truly reflects the examinee's IQ, and the degree to which it was due to factors other than intelligence.

Potential sources of error are legion. An examinee's having the flu or not having the flu when taking a test is one source of error variance. In a more general sense, then, examinees are sources of error variance. Examiners, too, are sources of error variance. For example, some examiners are more professional than others in the extent to which they follow the instructions governing how and under what conditions a test should be administered. Tests themselves are another source of error variance; some tests are simply better than others in measuring what they purport to measure. There are other sources of error variance, and we will discuss them in greater detail in Chapter 5.

Instructors who teach the undergraduate measurement course will, on occasion, hear a student refer to error as "creeping into" or "contaminating" the measurement process. Yet measurement professionals tend to view error as simply an element in the process of measurement, one for which any theory of measurement must surely account. In what is referred to as "classical" or "true score" theory, an assumption is made that each testtaker has a "true" score on a test that would be obtained but for the random action of measurement error. This point is elaborated on elsewhere in this book, as well as in this chapter's *Close-up.*

Error of Measurement and the True Score Model

Kathy applies for a job as a word processor at The Rochester Wrenchworks (TRW). To be hired, Kathy must be able to word-process accurately at the rate of 50 words per minute. The personnel office administers a total of seven brief word processing tests to Kathy over the course of seven business days. In words per minute, Kathy's scores on each of the seven tests are as follows:

52   55   39   56   35   50   54

If you were in charge of hiring at TRW and you looked at these seven scores, you might logically ask, "Which of these scores is the best measure of Kathy's 'true' word processing ability?" or, stated more succinctly, "Which is her 'true' score?"

The "true" answer to the question posed above is that we cannot say with absolute certainty from the data we have exactly what Kathy's true word processing ability is—*but* we can make an educated guess. Our educated guess would be that her true word processing ability is equal to the mean of the distribution of her word processing scores plus or minus a number of points accounted for by error in the measurement process. Error in the measurement process can be thought of as any factor entering into the process that is not directly relevant to whatever it is that is being measured. If Kathy had the misfortune on one occasion of drawing a word processor that had not been properly serviced and was of lesser quality than the other word processors she

had been tested on, that is an example of error entering into the testing process. If there was excessive noise in the room on a testing occasion, if Kathy wasn't feeling well, if light bulbs blew . . . the list could go on, but the point is that any number of factors other than an individual's ability can enter into the process of measuring that ability. We can try to reduce error in a testing situation such as Kathy's by making certain, to the extent that it is possible, that all word processing equipment is functioning equally well, that the test room is free of excessive noise and has adequate lighting, and so forth. However, we can never entirely eliminate error. The best we can do is estimate how much error entered into a particular test score and then intelligently interpret the score with that information.

The tool used to estimate or infer the extent to which an observed score deviates from a true score is a statistic called the **standard error of measurement,** also known as the **standard error of a score.** In practice, few developers of tests designed for use on a widespread basis would investigate the magnitude of error with respect to a single testtaker. Typically, an average standard error of measurement is calculated for a sample of the population on which the test is designed for use. More detailed information on the nature and computation of the standard error of measurement will be presented in Chapter 5. As we will see, measures of reliability assist us in making inferences about the proportion of the total variance of test scores attributable to error variance.

Assumption 8: Tests and other measurement techniques have strengths and weaknesses. Competent test users understand a great deal about the tests they use. They understand, among other things, how a test they use was developed, the circumstances under which it is appropriate to administer the test, how the test should be administered and to whom, how the test results should be interpreted and to whom, and what the meaning of the test score is. Competent test users understand and appreciate the limitations of the tests they use, as well as how those limitations might be compensated for by data from other sources. All of this may sound quite commonsensical. It probably is. Yet this deceptively simple assumption—that test users know the tests they use and are aware of the tests' limitations—is emphasized repeatedly in the codes of ethics of associations of assessment professionals.

Assumption 9: Test-related behavior predicts non-test-related behavior. Many tests involve tasks such as blackening little grids with a number 2 pencil or simply pressing keys on a computer keyboard. The objective of such tests typically has little to do with predicting future grid-blackening or key-pressing behavior. Rather, the objective of the test is more typically to provide some indication of other aspects of the examinee's behavior. For example, patterns of answers to true-false questions on the MMPI are used as indicators of the presence of mental disorders. The tasks in some tests mimic the actual behaviors that the test user is attempting to understand. By their nature, however, such tests yield only a sample of the behavior that can be expected to be emitted under nontest conditions. And in general, testing and assessment are conducted with the presumption that meaningful generalizations can be made from test data to behavior outside the testing situation.

Assumption 10: Present-day behavior sampling predicts future behavior.   Tests sample what a person does on the day the test is administered. The obtained sample of behavior is typically used to make predictions about future behavior, such as predicted work performance of a job applicant. A rare exception to this assumption occurs in some forensic (legal) matters, where psychological tests may be used not to predict behavior but to postdict it—that is, to aid understanding of behavior that has already taken place. For example, there may be a need to understand a criminal defendant's state of mind at the time of the commission of a crime. Although it is beyond the capability of any known testing or assessment procedure to reconstruct one's state of mind, behavior samples taken at one point may be useful under certain circumstances in shedding light on the nature of one's state of mind at some point in the past. Additionally, other tools of assessment, such as case history data or the defendant's personal diary during the period in question, might all be of great value in such an evaluation.

Assumption 11: Testing and assessment can be conducted in a fair and unbiased manner.   If we had to pick the one of these 12 assumptions that is more controversial than the remaining 11, this one is it. Decades of court challenges to various tests and testing programs have sensitized test developers and users to the societal demand that tests be developed so as to be fair and that tests be used in a fair manner. Today, all major test publishers strive to develop instruments that, when used in strict accordance with guidelines in the test manual, are fair. One source of fairness-related problems is the test user who attempts to use a particular test with people whose background and experience are different from the background and experience of people for whom the test was intended. In such instances, it is useful to emphasize that tests are tools that, like other, more familiar tools (hammers, ice picks, shovels, and so on), can be used properly or abused.

Some potential problems related to test fairness are more political than psychometric in nature, such as the use of tests in various social programs. For example, heated debate often surrounds affirmative action programs in selection, hiring, and access or denial of access to various opportunities. In many cases, the real question to be debated is, "What do we as a society wish to accomplish?" not "Is this test fair?"

Assumption 12: Testing and assessment benefit society.   At first glance, the prospect of a world devoid of testing and assessment might seem very appealing, especially from the perspective of a harried student preparing for a week of midterm examinations. Yet a world without tests would most likely turn out to be more of a nightmare than a dream. In such a world, people could hold themselves out to the public as surgeons, bridge builders, or airline pilots regardless of their background, ability, or professional credentials. In a world without tests, teachers and school administrators could arbitrarily place children in different types of special classes simply because that is where they believed the children belonged. Considering the many critical decisions that are based on testing and assessment procedures, as well as the possible alternatives (including decision making on the basis of human judgment, nepotism, and the like), we can readily appreciate the need for the assessment enterprise and be thankful for its existence.

Who, What, and Why?

Who are the parties in the assessment enterprise? What types of settings are assessments conducted in? Why is assessment conducted? Think about the answer to each of these important questions before reading on. Then, check your own ideas against those that follow.

Who Are the Parties?

The primary parties to the assessment enterprise are developers and publishers of tests or other methods of assessment, users of tests and other methods of assessment, and people who are evaluated by means of tests and other methods of assessment. A fourth and frequently overlooked party is society at large. Referring to these parties, respectively, as (1) the test developer, (2) the test user, (3) the testtaker, and (4) society at large, let's take a closer look at each in the context of the assessment enterprise.

The test developer　Test developers create tests or other types of methods of assessment. The **American Psychological Association (APA)** estimates that upward of 20,000 new psychological tests are developed each year (APA, 1993). Among these new tests are some that were created for a specific research study, some that were created in the hope that they would be published, and some that represent refinements or modifications of existing tests.

The people who create tests bring a wide array of backgrounds, skills, and interests to the test development process. To learn more about them and the test development process, we sent letters requesting biographical information to a number of developers of some famous and not so famous tests. We inquired about major influences on these people, noteworthy aspects of the test development process, and the pros and cons of being a test developer. Many of these profiles provide not only a fascinating biographical sketch but an intriguing inside look at the test development process. Space limitations precluded us from presenting the profiles here. However, *Test Developer Profiles* can be accessed at our Internet Web site: *www.mhhe.com/psychtesting.*

Recognizing that tests and the decisions made as a result of their administration can have a significant impact on testtakers' lives, a number of professional organizations have published standards of ethical behavior that specifically address aspects of responsible test development and use. Perhaps the most detailed document addressing such issues is one jointly written by the American Educational Research Association, the American Psychological Association, and the National Council on Measurement in Education (NCME). Referred to by many psychologists simply as "the *Standards*," *Standards for Educational and Psychological Testing* covers issues related to test construction and evaluation, test administration and use, and special applications of tests, such as special considerations when testing linguistic minorities. The *Standards* is an indispensable reference work for professional users and developers of psychological and educational tests. Initially published in 1954, revisions of the *Standards* were published in 1966, 1974, 1985, and 1999.

The test user Tests are used by a wide range of professionals, including clinicians, counselors, human resources personnel, and teachers and other school personnel. The *Standards,* as well as the official guidelines of various other professional organizations, have much to impart to test users about how, why, and the conditions under which tests should be used. For example, the principles of professional ethics promulgated by the National Association of School Psychologists (Jacob-Timm & Hartshorne, 1998) stress that school psychologists should select and use the test or tests that are most appropriate for each individual student. NASP (2000) further emphasizes that any questions that serve to prompt the psychological assessment of students be answered in as comprehensive a manner as possible—that is, with as much background information and other data as possible, including data from behavioral observation.

The test user has ethical obligations that must be fulfilled even before any testtaker is exposed to a test. For example, the test must be stored in a way that reasonably ensures that its specific contents will not be made known in advance—leaving open the possibilities of irregularities later. Note that we used the term *specific contents* in describing what must be secured from testtakers in advance of the test. In the case of some specific types of tests, mostly tests of achievement, acquainting the testtaker with the general type of questions the test will contain helps to lift the veil of mystery that may surround a test and minimize the associated test anxiety (see, for example, the booklets prepared for prospective Scholastic Aptitude Test or Graduate Record Examination examinees). With some types of tests, such as intelligence tests and projective tests of personality, such pretest descriptions of the test materials would not be advisable because they might compromise the resulting data. Another obligation of the test user before the test's administration is to ensure that a prepared and suitably trained person administers the test properly. The test administrator (or examiner) must be familiar with the test materials and procedures and have at the test site all the materials needed to properly administer the test—a sufficient supply of test protocols and other supplies, a stopwatch, if necessary, and so forth.[3] The test examiner must also ensure that the room in which the test will be conducted is suitable and conducive to the testing (Figure 1–5). To the extent that it is possible, distracting conditions such as excessive noise, heat, cold, interruptions, glaring sunlight, crowding, inadequate ventilation, and so forth should be avoided. Even a badly scratched or graffiti-grooved writing surface on a desk can act as a contaminating influence on the test administration; if the writing surface is not reasonably smooth, the written productions made on it may in some instances lead a test scorer to suspect that the examinee had a tremor or some type of perceptual-motor deficit. In short, if the test is a standardized one, it is the obligation of the test administrator to see that reasonable testing conditions prevail during the test administration; if for any reason those conditions did not prevail during an administration of the test (for instance, there was a fire drill or a real fire), an accounting of such unusual conditions should be enclosed with the test record.

Especially in one-on-one or small-group testing, rapport between the examiner and examinee is important. In the context of the testing situation, **rapport** may be defined as a working relationship between the examiner and the examinee. Such a working relationship can sometimes be achieved with a few words of small talk when examiner and examinee are introduced. If appropriate, some words regarding the nature of the test as well as why it is important for examinees to do their best may also be helpful. In other

---

3. **Protocol** in everyday usage refers to diplomatic etiquette. A less common usage of the word is as a synonym for the first copy or rough draft of a treaty or other official document before its ratification. This second meaning comes closer to the way the word is used with reference to psychological tests, as a noun referring to the form or sheet on which the testtaker's responses have been entered.

Figure 1–5
Less-Than-Optimal Testing Conditions

In 1917, new Army recruits sat on the floor as they were administered the first group tests of intelligence—not ideal testing conditions by current standards.

instances, as with the case of a frightened child, the achievement of rapport might involve more elaborate techniques such as engaging the child in play or some other activity until the child is deemed to have acclimated to the examiner and the surroundings. It is important that attempts to establish rapport with the testtaker not compromise any rules of the test's standardized administration instructions.

Evidence exists to support the view that, depending on the test, examiners themselves may have an effect on test results. Whether the examiner is familiar or a stranger (Sacks, 1952; Tsudzuki et al., 1957), whether the examiner is present or absent (Bernstein, 1956), and the general manner of the examiner (Exner, 1966; Masling, 1959; Wickes, 1956) are some factors that may influence performance on ability as well as personality tests (see also Cohen, 1965; Kirchner, 1966; Masling, 1960). In assessing children's abilities, the effect of examiner sex, race, and experience has been studied with a mixed pattern of results (Lutey & Copeland, 1982). Whereas some studies have indicated that students receive higher scores from female than from male examiners (for example, Back & Dana, 1977; Gillingham, 1970; Samuel, 1977), others have found that the key variable is whether the examiner and student are of the same or opposite sex. For example, Smith, May, and Lebovitz (1966) and Cieutat (1965) found that students perform better with examiners of the opposite sex, but Pedersen, Shinedling, and Johnson (1968) found that students perform better with examiners of the same sex. Examiner race and experience have been examined in a number of studies, and reviews of these studies have concluded that these variables have little effect on student performance (Sattler, 1988; Sattler & Gwynne, 1982).

No matter how psychometrically sound a test is, the purpose of the test will be defeated if the test user fails to competently manage all phases of the testing or assessment process. For that reason alone, it is undeniably necessary for all test users, as well as all potential users of tests, to have a working familiarity with principles of measurement.

The testtaker   Testtakers approach an assessment situation in different ways, and test users must be sensitive to the diversity of possible responses to a testing situation. On the day of test administration, testtakers may vary on a continuum with respect to numerous variables, including:

- The amount of test anxiety they are experiencing and the degree to which that test anxiety might significantly affect the test results.

- Their capacity and willingness to cooperate with the examiner or to comprehend written test instructions.

- The amount of physical pain or emotional distress being experienced.

- The amount of physical discomfort brought on by not having had enough to eat, having had too much to eat, or other physical conditions.

- The extent to which they are alert and wide awake as opposed to nodding off.

- The extent to which they are predisposed to agreeing or disagreeing when presented with stimulus statements.

- The extent to which they have received prior coaching.

- The importance they may attribute to portraying themselves in a good—or bad— light.

- The extent to which they are, for lack of a better term, "lucky" and can "beat the odds" on a multiple-choice achievement test (even though they may not have learned the subject matter).

As we will see, testtakers have a number of rights in assessment situations. For example, testtakers have the right to informed consent to testing, the right to have the results of the testing held confidential, and the right to be informed of the findings.

Before leaving the subject of "testtaker" as a party in the assessment process, let us make brief mention of the very rare and exceptional case where the person being assessed is deceased. Such is the case in what has been referred to as a **psychological autopsy,** or a reconstruction of a deceased individual's psychological profile on the basis of archival records, artifacts, and interviews previously conducted with the assessee or people who knew the assessee. For interested readers, a fascinating case study that employed the technique of psychological autopsy is presented by Neagoe (2000).

Society at large

> The uniqueness of individuals is one of the most fundamental characteristic facts of life.... At all periods of human history men have observed and described differences between individuals.... But educators, politicians, and administrators have felt a need for some way of organizing or systematizing the many-faceted complexity of individual differences. (Tyler, 1965, p. 3)

The societal need for "organizing" and "systematizing" has historically manifested itself in such varied questions as "Who is a witch?" "Who is schizophrenic?" and "Who is qualified?" The nature of the specific questions asked has shifted with societal concerns. The methods used to determine the answers have varied throughout history as a function of factors such as intellectual sophistication and religious preoccupation. Palmistry, podoscopy, astrology, and phrenology, among other pursuits, have had proponents who argued that the best means of understanding and predicting human behavior was through the study of the palms, the feet, the stars, bumps on the head, tea leaves, and so on. Unlike such pursuits, the assessment enterprise has roots in science. Through systematic and replicable means that can produce compelling evidence, the assessment enterprise responds to what Tyler (1965, p. 3) referred to as the societal "need for some way of organizing or systematizing the many-faceted complexity of individual differences."

Other parties   Beyond the four primary parties we have focused on here, let's briefly make note of others who may participate in varied ways in the testing and assessment enterprise. Organizations, companies, and governmental agencies sponsor the development of tests for various reasons, such as to certify personnel. Companies and services offer test scoring or interpretation services. In some cases, these companies and services are simply extensions of test publishers, and in other cases they are independent. There are people whose sole responsibility has to do with the marketing and sales of tests. Sometimes these people are employed by the test publisher, sometimes they are not. There are academicians who review tests and make evaluations as to their psychometric soundness. All of these people may also be considered parties to the enterprise.

In What Types of Settings Are Assessments Conducted and Why?

Educational settings   From your own experience, you are probably no stranger to the many types of tests administered in the classroom. You have taken achievement tests—some constructed by teachers, others constructed by measurement professionals. You may have taken tests designed to assess your ability, aptitude, or interest with respect to a particular occupation or course of study. You may have also taken a group-administered test of intelligence, now also termed a **school ability test.** Such tests are frequently administered, in part to help identify children who may not be achieving at a level commensurate with their capability. Where appropriate, further evaluation with more specialized instruments may follow to assess the need for special education intervention. *Public Law 94-142* mandated that appropriate educational programs be made available to individuals with disabilities between the ages of 3 and 21 who require special education. *Public Law 99-457* specified that services be delivered to preschoolers with disabilities (birth to age 2) and encouraged services to at-risk infants, toddlers, and their families.

Tests are often used in educational settings to diagnose learning or behavior problems or both and to establish eligibility for special education programs. Individually administered intelligence and achievement measures are most often used for diagnostic purposes and are generally administered by school psychologists, psychoeducational diagnosticians, or similarly trained professionals. Interviews, behavioral observation, self-report scales, and behavior checklists are also widely used in educational settings.

Another variety of assessment that takes place daily throughout the country, in every classroom, and at every educational level is informal assessment. Evidence of such assessment comes not in test scores but in a variety of ways ranging from a sincere, enthusiastic "Good!" verbalized by instructors to nonverbal expressions of disappointment. As complex and interesting as the study of informal assessment may be, this text will limit its scope to testing and assessment of the more formal variety.

In recent years, we have witnessed the birth of a new type of achievement test: a certification of education. Particularly at the high school level, students in some areas of the country are being evaluated at the end of their course of study to determine if they indeed have acquired the minimal knowledge and skills expected of a high school graduate. Students unable to pass this certification test receive a certificate of attendance as opposed to a high school diploma. Needless to say, the cutting score (in this case, the dividing line between passing and failing) on such a test is one with momentous consequences, and its determination must be made only by persons with a very sound technical knowledge of tests and measurement.

Another type of test administered in educational settings is that used for educational selection. Many colleges and universities require scores on standardized tests such as the Scholastic Aptitude Test (SAT) or the Graduate Record Examination (GRE) as part of the undergraduate or graduate school admission process. Foreign applicants to North American universities may be required to take a standardized test of English proficiency as part of their admission application. Few, if any, universities rely solely on standardized test scores in making admissions decisions. Typically, such decisions are based on an assessment of a number of factors ranging from grade-point average to letters of recommendation to written statements by the applicant to extracurricular interests and activities. To fulfill affirmative action requirements, variables such as ethnic background and gender may sometimes enter into the admission decision as well. Chapter 10 covers in detail psychological testing and assessment in educational settings.

Counseling settings   The use of assessment in a counseling context may occur in environments as diverse as schools, prisons, or government or privately owned institutions. Regardless of where it is done, assessment is typically undertaken to identify various strengths or weaknesses, with the ultimate objective being an improvement in the assessee's adjustment, productivity, and general quality of life. Measures of social and academic skills or abilities and measures of personality, interest, attitudes, and values are among the many types of tests that a counselor might administer to a client. Objectives in testing for counseling purposes vary with stage of life and particular situation; questions to be answered range from "How can this child work and play better with other children?" to "What career is the client best suited for?" to "What activities are recommended for retirement?" Because the testtaker is in many instances the primary recipient and user of the data from a test administered by a counselor, it is imperative that a well-trained counselor fully explain the test results. Alternatively, the results of the test should be readily interpretable by testtakers themselves through easy-to-follow instructions.

Clinical settings   Tests and other methods of assessment (such as interviews, case studies, and behavioral observation) are widely used in clinical settings such as inpatient and outpatient clinics; public, private, and military hospitals; private-practice consulting rooms; schools; and other institutions to screen for or diagnose behavior problems. Situations that might call for tests and other tools of clinical assessment include the following:

- A private psychotherapy client wishes to be evaluated to see if the assessment can provide any nonobvious clues regarding his maladjustment.

- A school psychologist clinically evaluates a child experiencing learning difficulties to determine if her problem lies in a deficit of ability, a problem of adjustment, a discrepancy between teaching techniques being employed and the child's favored receptive and expressive modalities, or some combination of such factors.

- A psychotherapy researcher uses assessment procedures to determine if a particular method of psychotherapy is effective in treating a particular problem.

- A psychologist-consultant retained by an insurance company is called on to give an opinion as to the reality of a client's psychological problems; is the client really experiencing such problems or malingering?

- A court-appointed psychologist is asked to give an opinion as to a defendant's competency to stand trial.
- A prison psychologist is called on to give an opinion regarding the extent of a convicted violent prisoner's rehabilitation.

The tests employed in clinical settings may be intelligence tests, personality tests, neuropsychological tests, or other specialized instruments, depending on the presenting or suspected problem area. The hallmark of testing in clinical settings is that the test or measurement technique is employed with only one individual at a time; group testing can be used only for screening at best—identifying those individuals who require further diagnostic evaluation. In Chapter 13 and elsewhere, we will look at the nature, uses, and benefits of clinical assessment.

Business settings   In the business world, tests are used in many areas, particularly human resource management. As we will see in Chapter 16, personnel psychologists use tests and measurement procedures to assess whatever knowledge or skills an employer needs to have assessed—be it the ability of a prospective air traffic controller to sustain attention to detail for hours on end or the ability of a prospective military officer to lead others. A wide range of achievement, aptitude, interest, motivational, and other tests may be employed in the decision to hire as well as in related decisions regarding promotions, transfer, performance or job satisfaction, and eligibility for further training. Engineering psychologists also employ a variety of existing and specially devised tests to help people at home and in the workplace, in part by designing ergonomically efficient consumer and industrial products—products ranging from office furniture to spaceship cockpit layout.[4]

Another example of a business-related application of testing and assessment is in the area of consumer psychology. Consumer psychologists help corporate America in the development, marketing, and sale of products. Using tests as well as other techniques, psychologists who specialize in this area may be involved in taking the pulse of consumers—helping to predict the public's receptivity to a new product, a new brand, or a new advertising or marketing campaign. "What type of advertising will appeal to which type of individual?" Tests of attitudes and values have proved to be one valuable source of information to consumer psychologists and marketing professionals who endeavor to answer such questions.

Other settings   Testing and assessment procedures are used in many other areas. Credentialing professionals is one such area. Before they are legally entitled to practice medicine, physicians must pass an examination. Law school graduates cannot hold themselves out to the public as attorneys until they pass their state's bar examination. Psychologists, too, must pass an examination entitling them to present themselves to the public as psychologists. And just as physicians can take further training and a test indicating that they are "Board certified" in a particular area, so can psychologists specializing in

---

4. "Ergonomically efficient"? An **erg** is a unit of work and **ergonomics** is the study of work; more specifically in the present context, it is the relationship between people and tools of work. Among other endeavors, engineering psychologists are involved in designing things so that we can see, hear, reach, or generally use them better. For example, it was through extensive research by engineering psychologists that the division of letters and numbers that appears on a telephone was derived. Interested in obtaining a firsthand look at the kind of work engineering psychologists do? Take a moment to look through journals like *Ergonomics, Applied Ergonomics,* and *Man-Environment Systems* next time you're in your university library.

certain areas be evaluated for a diploma from the American Board of Professional Psychology (**ABPP**) to recognize excellence in the practice of psychology. Another organization, the American Board of Assessment Psychology (**ABAP**), awards its diplomate to test users, test developers, and others who have distinguished themselves in the field of testing and assessment.

Measurement may play an important part in program evaluation—be it a large-scale government program or a small-scale privately funded one. Is the program working? How can the program be improved? Are funds being spent in the areas where they ought to be spent? These are the types of general questions that tests and measurement procedures used in program evaluation are designed to answer.

Psychological assessment plays a valuable role in the process of psychological theory building; tests and measures may be employed in basic research to confirm or disprove hypotheses derived from behavioral theories. Tests, interviews, and other tools of assessment may be used to learn more about the organization of psychological traits and serve as vehicles by which new traits can be identified.

The courts rely on psychological test data and related expert testimony as one source of information to help answer important questions such as "Is this convict competent to be executed?" "Is this parent competent to take custody of the child?" and "Did this defendant know right from wrong at the time the criminal act was committed?" Issues such as these are covered in the forensic psychology section of Chapter 13.

Issues about testing people with disabling conditions have become increasingly prominent in recent years, and our survey of these issues as well as a glimpse at specialized measurement procedures used in this area appears in Chapter 15. In Chapter 14 we detail some of the methods used by neuropsychologists to help in the diagnosis and treatment of neuropsychological deficits.

In addition to bringing you a firsthand look at the test development process, we also want to provide a glimpse of test use "in the trenches." We sent out letters to colleagues who use tests, requesting a paragraph or two about how and why they use them. Interested readers will find these responses at our *Test User Forum* on the Internet at *www.mhhe. com/psychtesting.* And by the way, if you are a user of psychological or educational tests and would like your essay posted on that site, please write to us care of our publisher.

Evaluating the Quality of Tests

We know which psychological tests are most frequently used (Archer et al., 1991; Hutton et al., 1992; Lees-Haley et al., 1996; Lubin et al., 1985; Piotrowski & Keller, 1989, 1992; Piotrowski & Lubin, 1990; Sweeney et al., 1987), but we need to know which tests are good. This of course raises a question.

What Is a Good Test?

Purely from a logical standpoint, the criteria for a good test would include clear instructions for administration, scoring, and interpretation. It would also seem to be a plus if a test offered economy in the time it takes to administer, score, and interpret it. Most of all, a good test would seem to be one that measures what it purports to measure. Ideally, the results of the assessment procedure lead to an improved quality of life for the testtaker and others.

Beyond simple logic, there are technical criteria that assessment professionals use to evaluate the quality of tests and other measurement procedures. These technical considerations have to do with psychometrics. Synonymous with *psychometry,* **psychometrics** may be defined as the science of psychological measurement.[5] Test users often speak of the "psychometric soundness" of tests, two key aspects of which are reliability and validity.

Reliability   A good test or, more generally, a good measuring tool or instrument is *reliable.* As we will explain in Chapter 5, the criterion of reliability has to do with the *consistency* of the measuring tool, the precision with which the test measures, and the extent to which error is present in measurements. In theory, the perfectly reliable measuring tool consistently measures in the same way. For example, to determine if a digital scale was a reliable measuring tool, we might take repeated measures of the same standard weight, such as a 1-pound gold bar. If the scale repeatedly indicated that the gold bar weighed 1 pound, we would say that the scale was a reliable measuring instrument. If another scale repeatedly indicated that the gold bar weighed exactly 1.3 pounds, we would still say that the scale was reliable (although inaccurate and invalid), because the scale provided a consistent result. But suppose we weighed the bar ten times and six of those times the scale registered 1 pound, on two occasions the bar weighed in at a fraction of an ounce less than a pound, and on two other occasions it weighed in at a fraction of an ounce more than a pound . . . would the scale still be considered a reliable instrument?

Whether we are measuring gold bars, behavior, or anything else, unreliable measurement is a problem to avoid. We want to be reasonably certain that the measuring tool or test we are using will yield the same numerical measurement every time we observe the same thing under the same conditions. Psychological tests, like other tests and instruments, are reliable to varying degrees. Specific procedures for making determinations as to the reliability of an instrument will be introduced in Chapter 5, as will the various types of reliability.

Validity   A good test is a *valid* test, and a test is considered to be valid for a particular purpose if it in fact measures what it purports to measure. In the gold bar example cited earlier, the scale that consistently indicated that the 1-pound gold bar did, in fact, weigh 1 pound is a valid scale. Likewise, a test of reaction time is a valid test if it truly measures reaction time. A test of intelligence is a valid test if it truly measures intelligence. A potential problem, however, is that although there is relatively little controversy about the definition of a term such as reaction time, a great deal of controversy exists about the definition of intelligence. The validity of a particular test might be questioned with regard to the definition of whatever that test purports to measure. A test creator's conception of what constitutes intelligence might be different from someone else's, and therein lies the basis for a claim that the test is invalid.

Questions regarding a test's validity may focus on the items that collectively make up the test. Do the items adequately sample the range of areas that must be sampled to adequately measure the construct? Individual items will also come under scrutiny in an investigation of a test's validity; how do individual items contribute to or take away from the test's validity? The validity of a test may also be questioned in regard to the scores derived from an administration of the test; what do the scores really tell us about the targeted construct? How are high and low scores on the test related to testtakers' behavior? In general, how do scores on this test relate to scores on other tests purporting

---

5. Variants of these words include the adjective *psychometric* and the nouns *psychometrist* and *psychometrician.* Traditionally, a **psychometrist** holds a master's degree and is qualified to administer specific tests. A **psychometrician** holds a doctoral degree in psychology or some related field (such as education) and specializes in areas such as individual differences, quantitative psychology, or theory of assessment.

to measure the same construct? How do scores on this test relate to scores on other tests purporting to measure opposite types of constructs? For example, we might expect one person's score on a valid test of introversion to be inversely related to that same person's score on a valid test of extraversion. That is, the higher the introversion test score, the lower the extraversion test score, and vice versa.

As we will see when we discuss validity in greater detail in Chapter 6, questions concerning the validity of a particular test or assessment procedure extend beyond the specific test or procedure per se. Critical validity-related questions concern the way in which data from a particular test or assessment procedure are used.

Other considerations   If the purpose of a test is to compare the performance of the test-taker with the performance of other testtakers, a good test is one that contains adequate **norms.** Also referred to as *normative data,* norms provide a standard with which the results of measurement can be compared. These types of tests are referred to as **norm-referenced,** and a common goal of such tests is to yield information on the testtaker's standing or ranking relative to some comparison group of testtakers. The SAT and the GRE are two examples of norm-referenced tests; scores reflect the testtaker's standing relative to other testtakers. As an aid to a prospective test user in judging the appropriateness of administering, scoring, and interpreting a norm-referenced test, a complete description of the **norm group** or **normative sample** (the people who were tested with the instrument and with whom current testtakers' performance is being compared) is required. Unfortunately, manuals for norm-referenced tests differ widely in the specificity they employ in describing the norm group. Because of its greater specificity, a description such as "200 male, Hispanic, freshman community college students between the ages of 18 and 20 at New York City Community College" is preferable to one such as "many minority college students from a large community college in the East." In general, the closer the match between the norm group and the examinee(s), the more appropriate the test may be for a given purpose. Some norm-referenced tests are better than others because of the size of the normative sample; all other things being equal, the larger the normative sample, the better.

In contrast to norm-referenced tests, some tests, particularly in the fields of educational and industrial or organizational assessment, are **criterion-referenced.**[6] Whereas norm-referenced tests yield information about a testtaker's relative standing, criterion-referenced tests yield information about an individual's mastery of a particular skill. Has this applicant mastered the skills necessary to be a pilot for this airline? Has this student mastered the ability to spell "sand"? Has this group home member mastered the skills necessary for independent living? These are the types of questions criterion-referenced tests may seek to answer. When evaluating a criterion-referenced test, key issues concern the definition of the criterion used by the test developer, the relevance of the test's criterion to the objectives of the current assessment, and the evidence in hand that supports the use of the test for the contemplated purpose (see *Everyday Psychometrics.*)

---

6. As we will point out in Chapter 4, the criterion-referenced approach has been referred to of late with various terminology such as "domain-referenced," "content-referenced" and "objective-referenced." Our view is that this plethora of alternate terminology, although offered in the spirit of precision, tends to muddle rather than clarify distinctions between norm-referenced and criterion-referenced approaches. Assessment with reference to a criterion has traditionally been associated with the assessment of learning outcomes as opposed to mere content (or domain). Terms such as "content-referenced" and "domain-referenced" speak more to learning content (or domain) than to a learning outcome. Further, and what can be so confusing, is that a norm-referenced test may be content- or domain-referenced in the sense that it is linked or referenced to a particular content area; still, only the term "criterion-referenced" is used as if synonymous with "content-" or "domain-referenced."

Putting Tests to the Test

For experts in the field of testing and assessment, a number of questions occur almost reflexively when evaluating a test or measurement technique. You may not be an assessment expert yet, but your consideration of questions such as the following will represent a significant first step in that direction. Try to think of these questions when you come across mention of various tests in this book, in other books and journal articles, and in life. These questions will help you evaluate the psychometric soundness of tests and other measurement methods.

Why Use This Particular Instrument or Method?

A choice of measuring instruments typically exists when it comes to measuring a particular psychological or educational variable, and the test user must therefore choose from many available tools. Published information, such as test catalogues, test manuals, and published test reviews, can be of great value in coming to a decision regarding the use of a particular test. Unpublished sources of information, such as information obtained by writing directly to the test developer or test publisher, may also be a possibility. Some of the questions the prospective test user will raise relate to the objectives of the test and the goodness of fit between those objectives and the objectives of the testing or assessment. What type of information will result from an administration of this test? Do alternate forms of this test exist and, if so, how might they be used? How long does it take to administer this test? What is the recommended age range for test-takers and what reading level is required? How will this resulting information be applied to answer the test referral question? What types of decisions can or cannot be made on the basis of information from the use of this test? What other information will be required in order to adequately answer the test referral question?

Are There Any Published Guidelines Relevant to the Use of This Test?

Measurement professionals make it their business to be aware of published guidelines from professional associations and related organizations relevant to the use of tests and measurement techniques. So, for example, suppose you are a psychologist called upon to provide input to a court in the matter of a child custody decision. More specifically, the court has asked you for your professional opinion regarding the parenting capacity of one parent. How would you proceed? Many psychologists who perform such evaluations

use a psychological test as part of the evaluation process. However, the psychologist performing such an evaluation is—or should be—aware of the guidelines promulgated by the American Psychological Association's Committee on Professional Practice and Standards (1994). These guidelines describe three types of assessments relevant to a child custody decision: (1) the assessment of parenting capacity, (2) the assessment of psychological and developmental needs of the child, and (3) the assessment of the goodness of fit between the parent's capacity and the child's needs. Clearly, an evaluation of a parent, or even two parents, does not provide the evaluator with sufficient information to express an opinion as to custody. Rather, only an evaluation of the parents (or others seeking custody), the child, and the goodness of fit between the needs and capacity of each of the parties can provide information relevant to an educated opinion about child custody.

There are many psychological tests and measurement procedures used to obtain information about parenting capacity (Holden & Edwards, 1989; Lovejoy et al., 1999; Touliatos et al., 1991). According to Heinze and Grisso (1996), some of the most commonly used instruments are the Ackerman-Schoendorf Scales for Parent Evaluation of Custody, the Bricklin Perceptual Scales, the Bricklin Perception of Relationships Test, the Child Abuse Potential Inventory (CAP), the Parent-Child Relationship Inventory, and the Parenting Stress Index (PSI). Regardless of the particular test(s) employed, the psychologist will use other sources of data, such as interviews, behavioral observation, and document analysis, in the evaluation of parenting capacity. This is consistent both with accepted professional practice as well as the published guideline that encourages psychologists to "use multiple methods of data gathering" (APA, 1994a, p. 679). Data from multiple sources of data can have the effect of providing varied sources of support for a professional opinion, conclusion, or recommendation.

The area of child custody evaluation provides a useful illustration of why mere knowledge of assessment or of a test may not adequately equip an assessor to assess. Assessors who undertake child custody evaluations must have working familiarity not only with the specific tools they use and the current literature in psychological assessment in general, but with the ever-changing laws and professional guidelines applicable to such evaluations, as well as the current literature in areas such as child development, family dynamics, and divorce. Executing a competent child custody

(continued)

Putting Tests to the Test (continued)

evaluation is no simple matter, and there are many published resources designed to assist professionals who wish to become involved in this type of work (for example, Ackerman, 1995; Bushard & Howard, 1994; Schultz et al., 1989; Stahl, 1995).

Is This Instrument Reliable?

Earlier, we introduced you to the psychometric concept of reliability and noted that it had to do with the consistency of measurement. Here, we hope to pique your interest in learning more about this concept by pointing out that measuring reliability is not always a straightforward matter. As an example, consider one of the tests that might be used in the evaluation of parenting capacity, the Bricklin Perceptual Scales (BPS; Bricklin, 1984). The BPS was designed to explore a child's perception of father and mother. A measure of one type of reliability, referred to as test-retest reliability, would indicate how consistent a child's perception of father and mother is over time. However, the BPS test manual contains no reliability data because as Bricklin (1984, p. 42) put it, "there are no reasons to expect the measurements reported here to exhibit any particular degree of stability, since they should vary in accordance with changes in the child's perceptions." Such an assertion has not stopped others (such as Speth, 1992) from exploring the test-retest reliability of the BPS. But whether or not one accepts Bricklin's assertion regarding the need for reliability data, such opinions illustrate the complexity of reliability questions—as well as the need for multiple sources of data to strengthen arguments regarding the confirmation or rejection of a hypothesis.

Is This Instrument Valid?

Validity, as you have learned, refers to the extent that a test measures what it purports to measure. Like reliability, questions related to the validity of a test can be complex and colored more in shades of gray than black or white. So, for example, even if data from a test such as the BPS were valid for the purpose of gauging children's perceptions of their parents, the data would not necessarily be valid as the sole source on which to base an opinion regarding child custody (Brodzinsky, 1993). In this context, Heinze and Grisso (1996) bemoaned what they saw as a trend by experts to rely on data concerning perceptions of the desirability of parents:

> Questions of parental desirability cannot be answered without reference to the characteristics, needs, and demands of the specific child who is in need of parenting. We suspect that no instrument that only assesses parents (e.g., whether through children's perceptions or direct observations of parents themselves) can ever meet basic scientific standards for making judgments about "preferred parents," or for making comparisons between parents that would justify suggesting that one parent's abilities are more desirable than the other's. (p. 310)

Instruments designed to measure variables such as stressful reactions to parenting (such as the PSI) and the potential for child abuse (such as the CAP) have yielded valuable data that could be very useful to courts as they evaluate all of the elements necessary for an informed judgment in child custody matters (Heinze & Grisso, 1996). However, in the courtroom and beyond, questions concern-

Must you be an assessment expert in order to be able to know a good test when you see one? Not necessarily. In some cases, all you need is to be good at retrieving relevant information about a particular test. In many instances, such information is as close as your university library and as available as cyberspace.

Reference Sources for Test Information

Many reference sources exist for learning more about published tests. These sources vary with respect to detail; some merely provide descriptions of tests, whereas others provide very technical information regarding reliability, validity, norms, and other such matters.

ing which test or combination of tests is valid for what purpose under what conditions sometimes stimulate heated debate and controversy.

What Inferences May Reasonably Be Made from This Test Score and How Generalizable Are the Findings?

The *raison d'être* (or *reason for being*) of many psychological tests and other tools of psychological assessment is to make inferences about behavior. In evaluating a test, it is therefore critical to consider the inferences that may reasonably be made as a result of administering that test. Will we learn something about a child's readiness to begin first grade? How prepared a student is for the first year of college at a particular institution? Whether the odds favor success for an independent life outside an institution for a person with a disability? Whether one is harmful to oneself or others to the extent that involuntary institutionalization is required? These represent but a small sampling of critical questions for which answers must be inferred on the basis of test scores and other data derived from various tools of assessment.

Intimately related to considerations regarding the inferences that can be made are considerations regarding the generalizability of the findings. Even from our brief introduction of the subject of norms, you are probably aware that normative data provide a context in which to interpret and generalize from test results. And following the discussion above regarding the complexity of measuring reliability and validity, you may have (correctly) anticipated comments about the complexity of gauging the generalizability of test findings. Consider, for example, that the normative sample for the Parenting Stress Index (PSI) consisted of 2,633 parents, drawn primarily from the state of Virginia. The majority of the children in the sample were under 5 years of age and Caucasian. How generalizable would you say the findings from an administration of the PSI are to non-Caucasian parents? If this is a question that occurred to you, you are in good company (see, for example, Krauss, 1993; McBride, 1989; Teplin et al., 1991; Younger, 1991). In fact, adaptations of the PSI have been made to include parents from different cultures (Abidin, 1990; Beebe et al., 1993; Black et al., 1993).

In addition to issues regarding the applicability of the norms, a number of other factors may give rise to questions regarding the generalizability of a test or a particular administration of a test. The wording of test items, for example, may have the effect of biasing scores in some way. So, for example, it may be that all other things being equal, the BPS is biased toward more favorable perceptions of mothers. Mothers and fathers may score similarly on all of the subtests except the Supportiveness subscale on which mothers tend to score higher (Heinze & Grisso, 1996).

The question of generalizability of findings may also be raised with regard to issues concerning a particular administration of a test. Most published tests have very explicit directions that test administrators—or a computer, if the test is computer-administered—must follow to the letter. If test administration is compromised in any way—whether by design, negligence, or any other reason—the generalizability of the data derived from the testing has also been compromised.

And so, although you may not yet be an expert in measurement, you are now armed with a working knowledge of the types of questions such experts ask when evaluating any test or measurement technique.

Test manuals   Detailed information concerning the development of a particular test, the normative sample, the test's reliability and validity, and other such information should be found in the manual for the test itself. The chances are good that somewhere within your university (be it the library or the counseling center), a collection of popular psychological test manuals is maintained. If not, most test publishers are willing to sell a test manual by itself, sometimes within some sort of sampler kit.

Test catalogues   Perhaps one of the most readily accessible sources of information about a test is a catalogue distributed by the publisher of the test. Because most test publishers make available catalogues of their offerings, this source of test information can be tapped

Figure 1–6
Oscar Krisen Buros (1906–1978)

Buros is best remembered for being the creator of the Mental Measurements Yearbook *(MMY), a kind of* Consumer Reports *for tests and a much needed source of "psychometric policing" (Peterson, 1997, p. 718). His work lives on at the Buros Institute of Mental Measurements at the University of Nebraska, Lincoln. In addition to the MMY, which is updated periodically, the institute publishes a variety of other test-related publications.*

by a simple telephone call, e-mail, or note. As you might expect, however, publishers' catalogues usually contain only a brief description of the test and seldom contain the kind of detailed technical information that a prospective user of the test might require. Further, the objective of the catalogue is to sell the test. Expect any quotations from reviews critical of the test to be excluded from the description.

Reference volumes   The Buros Institute of Mental Measurements provides "one-stop shopping" for a great deal of test-related information including lists of test publishers and recently published or newly revised tests, as well as test reviews. The initial version of what would evolve into the *Mental Measurements Yearbook* (MMY) was compiled by Oscar Buros (Figure 1–6) as early as 1933. At this writing, the latest edition of this authoritative compilation of test reviews is the *13th Mental Measurements Yearbook* (Impara & Plake, 1998), although the *14th* cannot be far behind. The Buros Institute also publishes *Tests in Print* as well as a number of other test-related reference works. For a list of its latest offerings, as well as links to a number of other useful test-related test databases, visit the Institute's Web site at *http://www.unl.edu/buros/*.

Journal articles   Articles relevant to the development and use of sundry tests and measurement methods can be found in the pages of a wide array of behavioral science journals (such as *Psychological Bulletin, Psychological Review, Professional Psychology: Research and Practice,* and *Journal of Personality and Social Psychology*), as well as journals that focus more specifically on matters related to testing and assessment (such as *Psychological Assessment, Educational and Psychological Measurement, Applied Measurement in Education,* and the *Journal of Personality Assessment*). Journals such as *Psychology, Public Policy, and Law* and *Law and Human Behavior* frequently contain highly informative articles on legal and ethical issues and controversies as they relate to psychological testing and assessment.

In addition to articles relevant to specific tests, journals are a rich source of information regarding important trends in testing and assessment. For example, with reference to clinical psychological assessment, the negative impact of managed health care and the reluctance or refusal of insurers to pay for assessment services has spurred a great deal of self-evaluation on the part of those in the business of evaluation (Acklin, 1996; Backlar, 1996; Camara et al., 2000; Eisman et al., 1998; Miller, 1996; Piotrowski et al., 1998). While

Table 1–1
Some Internet Web Site Addresses for Test Publishers

Academic Therapy www.academictherapy.com	James Stanfield Company www.stanfield.com	Pro-Ed www.proedinc.com
American Guidance Service www.agsnet.com	Lafayette Instruments www.licmef.com	Riverside Publishing www.riverpub.com
Consulting Psychologists Press www.cpp-db.com	Meritech, Inc. www.meritech.com	Scholastic Testing Service www.ststesting.com
CTB McGraw-Hill www.ctb.com	Multi-Health Systems www.mhs.com	Slosson Educational Publications www.slosson.com
Educator's Publishing Service www.epsbooks.com	National Computer Assessments www.ncs.com	Sopris West www.sopriswest.com
Harcourt Brace Educational Measurement www.hbem.com	Psychological Assessment Resources www.parinc.com	Stoelting www.stoeltingco.com
Institute for Personality and Ability Testing www.ipat.com	The Psychological Corporation www.psychcorp.com	Vort www.vort.com

critics of clinical assessment argue that testing and assessment is too expensive, too time consuming, and of too little value (Griffith, 1997), more informed reviews of the issues find abundant empirical support for the value of the enterprise (Kubiszyn et al., 2000).

Online databases   The American Psychological Association (APA) maintains a number of databases useful in locating psychology-related information in journal articles, book chapters, and doctoral dissertations. PsycINFO is a database of abstracts dating back to 1887. ClinPSYC is a database derived from **PsycINFO** that focuses on abstracts of a clinical nature. PsycSCAN: Psychopharmacology contains abstracts of articles having to do with psychopharmacology. PsycARTICLES is a database of full-length articles dating back to 1988. **PsycLAW** is a free database available to everyone that contains discussions of selected topics having to do with psychology and law. It can be accessed at *http://www.psychlaw.org.* For more information on any of these databases, visit APA's Web site at *http://www.apa.org.*

Educational Testing Service (ETS), "the world's largest and most influential testing organization" (Frantz & Nordheimer, 1997), maintains its own Web site at *http://www.ets.org.* The site contains a wealth of information about college and graduate school admission and placement tests, as well as many related resources. If you wanted to try your hand at some practice questions for a test such as the Graduate Record Examination (GRE), for example, this is the place to go. For more information, ETS can be contacted by e-mail at *etsinfo@ets.org.* A list of Web sites for publishers of other educational and psychological tests is presented in Table 1–1.

Other sources   Your school library contains a number of other sources that may be used to acquire information about tests and test-related topics. For example, two sources for exploring the world of unpublished tests and measures are the *Directory of Unpublished Experimental Measures* (Goldman & Mitchell, 1995) and *Tests in Microfiche* available from Test Collections. APA makes available *Finding Information About Psychological Tests* (1995), its own guide to locating test-related information.

Armed with a wealth of background information about tests and other tools of assessment, let's explore various historical, cultural, and legal/ethical aspects of the assessment enterprise.

Self-Assessment

Test your understanding of elements of this chapter by seeing if you can explain each of the following terms, expressions, and abbreviations:

ABAP	psychological testing
ABPP	psychometrics
alternate assessment	psychometry
assessment	Public Law 94-142
behavioral observation	Public Law 99-457
case history data	rapport
construct	reliability
diagnosis	role play test
diagnostic test	scale
erg	scaling
ergonomics	score
error	scoring
error variance	standard error of measurement
format	state
interview	test
measurement	test catalogue
MMY	test developer
norms	testing
portfolio	test manual
protocol	testtaker
PsycINFO	test user
psychological assessment	trait
psychological autopsy	validity
psychological test	

The same words or terms may appear at the end of different chapters. So, for example, you will see words such as "norms," "reliability," and "validity" at the end of some succeeding chapters—at which point you may be able to provide a more detailed explanation of what these words mean.

Another aid to self-assessment and learning is the crossword puzzles presented in the companion study guide and workbook to this textbook, *Exercises in Psychological Testing and Assessment* (Cohen, 2002). Each chapter begins with a puzzle that contains "clues" to key concepts, terms, and/ or names presented in the chapter.

2

Historical, Cultural, and Legal/Ethical Considerations

Our broad overview of the field of psychological testing and assessment continues. We begin this chapter with a look backward so we can better appreciate the historical context of the enterprise. Also in this chapter, we present food for thought regarding cultural and legal/ethical matters. Consider this "food" only as an appetizer; material on historical, cultural, and legal/ethical considerations is interwoven where appropriate throughout this book.

A Historical Perspective

Antiquity to the Nineteenth Century

A primitive form of proficiency testing existed in China as early as 2200 B.C.E. (DuBois, 1966, 1970) where some form of examination of public officials by the Chinese emperor was conducted every third year. Civil service examinations began in China during the Chan dynasty in 1115 B.C.E. and ended in 1905 when a reform measure abolished the system. For three thousand years, the open and competitive system of examinations in China provided for evaluation of proficiency in areas such as music, archery, horsemanship, writing, and arithmetic. Proficiency was also examined with respect to skill in the rites and ceremonies of public and social life, civil law, military affairs, agriculture, revenue, and geography (Figure 2–1).

The historical significance of the testing program in ancient China is that thousands of years ago there existed a civilization concerned with some of the same basic principles of psychometrics that we are concerned with today. Modern readers might note with fascination that activities such as archery and horsemanship were included among the tests, but keep in mind that the test users of the day felt that civil servants should be proficient in those skills; stated another way, the tests were content-valid. In a period of history when nepotism was no doubt rampant, it is admirable that employment was based on open competitive examinations.

Fascinating from a historical perspective are Greco-Roman writings that proposed various physiological bases for personality and temperament. Also intriguing are accounts of attempts during the Middle Ages to answer diagnostic questions of critical importance to society at the time—such as, "Who is in league with the Devil?" However, it was not until the Renaissance that measurement in behavioral science as we recognize

Figure 2–1
Testing Booths in China

Unlike exams for a position with the U.S. Postal Service, testing in China went on for days, and examinees occasionally died of the strain in these hundreds of civil service examination cubicles in Nanking. This photograph was taken about twenty years after the cessation of such testing in 1905.

it today began to emerge. By the eighteenth century, Christian von Wolff (1732, 1734) had anticipated psychology as a science and psychological measurement as a specialty area within that science.

The Nineteenth Century

In 1859, a book entitled *On the Origin of Species by Means of Natural Selection* by Charles Darwin (1809–1882) was published. In this important, far-reaching work, Darwin argued that chance variation in species would be selected or rejected for survival by nature according to adaptivity and survival value, and that humans had descended from the ape as a result of such chance genetic variations. This revolutionary notion aroused interest, admiration, and a good deal of enmity—the enmity primarily from members of the religious community who interpreted Darwin's ideas as an affront to the biblical account of creation in Genesis. Of primary importance to the field of psychology is the fact that the notion of an evolutionary link between human beings and animals conferred a new scientific respectability on experimentation with animals. It also raised questions about how animals and humans compare with respect to states of consciousness—questions that would beg for answers in laboratories of future behavioral scientists.[1]

History records that it was Darwin who spurred scientific interest in individual differences. Darwin (1859) wrote:

---

1. The influence of Darwin's thinking is also apparent in the theory of personality formulated by Sigmund Freud. From a Darwinian perspective, it would be the strongest persons with the most efficient sex drives that would have been most responsible for contributing to the human gene pool. In this context, Freud's notion of the primary importance of instinctual sexual and aggressive urges can be better understood.

> The many slight differences which appear in the offspring from the same parents . . . may be called individual differences. . . . These individual differences are of the highest importance. . . . [for they] afford materials for natural selection to act on. (p. 125)

Indeed, Darwin's writing on individual differences kindled interest in research on heredity in his half cousin, Francis Galton. In the course of his efforts to explore and quantify individual differences between people, Galton became an extremely influential contributor to the field of measurement (Forrest, 1974). Galton (1869) aspired to classify people "according to their natural gifts" (p. 1) and to ascertain their "deviation from an average" (p. 11). Along the way, Galton would be credited with devising or contributing to the development of many contemporary tools of psychological assessment including questionnaires, rating scales, and self-report inventories.

Galton's initial work on inheritance was done with sweet peas, in part because there tended to be fewer variations among the peas in a single pod. In this work, Galton pioneered the use of a statistical concept central to psychological experimentation and testing: the coefficient of correlation. Although Karl Pearson (1857–1936) developed the product-moment correlation technique, the roots of this technique can be traced directly to the work of Galton (Magnello & Spies, 1984). From heredity in peas, Galton's interest turned to heredity in humans and various ways of measuring aspects of people and their abilities. At an exhibition in London in 1884, Galton displayed his Anthropometric Laboratory where, for three or four pence, depending on whether you were already registered or not, you could be measured on variables such as height (standing), height (sitting), arm span, weight, breathing capacity, strength of pull, strength of squeeze, swiftness of blow, keenness of sight, memory of form, discrimination of color, and steadiness of hand. Through his own efforts and his urging of educational institutions to keep anthropometric records on their students, Galton excited widespread interest in the measurement of psychology-related variables.

Assessment was also an important activity at the first experimental psychology laboratory, founded at the University of Leipzig in Germany by Wilhelm Max Wundt (1832–1920), a medical doctor whose title at the university was professor of philosophy. Wundt and his students tried to formulate a general description of human abilities with respect to variables such as reaction time, perception, and attention span. The focus at Leipzig was not how individuals differed but how individuals were the same. In fact, individual differences were viewed by Wundt as a frustrating source of error in experimentation. Wundt attempted to control all extraneous variables in an effort to reduce error to a minimum. As we will see, attempting to control extraneous variables for the purpose of minimizing error is a routine component of contemporary assessment. Standardized conditions are used to help ensure that differences in scores are the result of true differences among individuals.

In spite of the prevailing research orientation that focused on how people tended to be the same, one of Wundt's students at Leipzig, an American named James McKeen Cattell (Figure 2–2), completed a doctoral dissertation that dealt with individual differences, specifically, individual differences in reaction time. After receiving his doctoral degree from Leipzig, Cattell returned to the United States and taught at Bryn Mawr and then at the University of Pennsylvania before leaving for Europe to teach at Cambridge. At Cambridge, Cattell came in contact with Galton, whom Cattell later described as "the greatest man I have known" (Roback, 1961, p. 96).

Inspired by his contact with Galton, Cattell returned to the University of Pennsylvania in 1888 and coined the term "mental test" in an 1890 publication. Boring (1950, p. 283) has noted that "Cattell more than any other person was in this fashion responsible for getting mental testing underway in America, and it is plain that his motivation was similar to Galton's and that he was influenced, or at least reinforced by Galton." Cattell went

Figure 2–2
The Cattells, James McKeen and Psyche

The psychologist who coined the term mental test, *James McKeen Cattell (1860–1944), has often been mistakenly credited (along with another psychologist, Raymond B. Cattell—no relation) with the authorship of a measure of infant intelligence called the Cattell Infant Intelligence Scale (CIIS). Actually, it was Psyche (1893–1989), the third of seven children of Cattell and his wife, Josephine Owen, who created the CIIS. From 1919 through 1921, Psyche assisted her famous father in statistical analyses for the third edition of* American Men of Science. *In 1927, she earned a doctor of education degree at Harvard. In 1931, she adopted a son, becoming one of the first unmarried women to do so (Sokal, 1991). Later in the decade she adopted a daughter. Her book* The Measurement of Intelligence in Infants and Young Children *was published in 1940, and it was in that book that the CIIS was introduced. Later in her career, she would write a popular book,* Raising Children with Love and Limits, *which refuted the permissiveness being advocated by child-rearing authorities such as Benjamin Spock.*

on to become professor and chairman of the psychology department at Columbia University, and for the 26 years he was there not only trained many psychologists but also founded a number of publications (such as *Psychological Review, Science,* and *American Men of Science*). In 1921, Cattell was instrumental in founding the Psychological Corporation, which named 20 of the country's leading psychologists as its directors. The goal of the corporation was the "advancement of psychology and the promotion of the useful applications of psychology." Originally, the corporation's stock was held by 170 psychologists. Today the Psychological Corporation is still very active in providing services related to psychological testing and assessment to the profession and the public.

Other students of Wundt at Leipzig included Charles Spearman, Victor Henri, Emil Kraepelin, E. B. Titchener, G. Stanley Hall, and Lightner Witmer. Spearman is credited with being the originator of the psychometric concept of test reliability. Victor Henri is the Frenchman who would collaborate with Alfred Binet on papers suggesting how mental tests could be used to measure higher mental processes (for example, Binet & Henri, 1895a, 1895b, 1895c). Psychiatrist Emil Kraepelin was an early experimenter with the word association technique as a formal test (Kraepelin, 1892, 1895). Lightner Witmer received his Ph.D. from Leipzig and went on to succeed Cattell as director of the psychology laboratory at the University of Pennsylvania. In March 1896, Witmer was challenged by a public school teacher to provide a solution in the case of a "chronic bad speller" (see Brotemarkle, 1947). Later that year, Witmer founded the first psychological clinic in the United States at the University of Pennsylvania. In 1907, Witmer founded the journal *Psychological Clinic* with the first article entitled "Clinical Psychology" (Witmer, 1907). Witmer has been cited as the "little known founder of clinical psychology" (McReynolds, 1987).

The Twentieth Century

The early 1900s witnessed the birth of the first formal tests of intelligence. As such tests were welcomed into various cultures throughout the world, the testing movement began to gain momentum. As we will see in the rest of this section, there was initially great receptivity to instruments that could purportedly measure mental characteristics—at first, intelligence and later other characteristics such as those related to personality, interests, attitudes, and values.

The measurement of intelligence   Much of the nineteenth-century testing that could be described as psychological in nature involved the measurement of sensory abilities, reaction time, and the like. One person who had a vision of broadening testing to include the measurement of cognitive abilities was Alfred Binet (1857–1911). As early as 1895, Binet and his colleague Victor Henri published several articles in which they argued for the measurement of abilities such as memory and social comprehension. Ten years later, Binet and collaborator Theodosius Simon published a 30-item "measuring scale of intelligence" designed to help identify mentally retarded Paris schoolchildren (Binet & Simon, 1905). The Binet test would go through many revisions and translations—and in the process launch both the intelligence testing movement and the clinical testing movement. Before long, psychological tests were used in settings as diverse as juvenile courts, reformatories, prisons, children's homes, and schools (Pintner, 1931).

In 1939, David Wechsler, a clinical psychologist at Bellevue Hospital in New York City, introduced a test designed to measure adult intelligence—defined as "the aggregate or global capacity of the individual to act purposefully, to think rationally, and to deal effectively with his environment" (p. 3). The test, originally called the Wechsler-Bellevue Intelligence Scale, was revised and renamed the Wechsler Adult Intelligence Scale (WAIS). The WAIS has since been periodically revised. Later, we will examine Wechsler's definition of intelligence as it was reflected in the series of adults', children's, and young children's intelligence tests that bear his name.

A natural outgrowth of the individually administered intelligence test devised by Binet was the *group* intelligence test. Group intelligence tests came into being in the United States in response to the military's need for an efficient method of screening the intellectual ability of World War I recruits. Because of military manpower needs during World War II, psychologists were enlisted into government service to develop, administer, and interpret group psychological test data. Psychologists returning from military service brought back a wealth of applied testing skills that would be useful not only in government service but also in settings as diverse as private industry, hospitals, and schools.

The measurement of personality   The general receptivity to tests of intellectual ability spurred the development of a number of other types of tests (Garrett & Schneck, 1933; Pintner, 1931), including tests of personality. Only eight years after the publication of Binet's scale, the field of psychology was being criticized for being too test oriented (Sylvester, 1913). By the late 1930s, approximately four thousand different psychological tests were in print (Buros, 1938), and "clinical psychology" was synonymous with "mental testing" (Institute for Juvenile Research, 1937; Tulchin, 1939).

World War I brought not only the need to screen the intellectual functioning of recruits but also the need to screen for personality problems. A government Committee on Emotional Fitness chaired by psychologist Robert S. Woodworth was assigned the task of developing a measure of adjustment and emotional stability that could be administered quickly and efficiently to groups of recruits. The committee developed several experimental versions of what in essence were paper-and-pencil psychiatric interviews. To disguise the true purpose of the test, the questionnaire was labeled and referred to as a Personal Data Sheet. Draftees and volunteers were asked to indicate "yes" or "no" to a series of questions that probed the existence of various kinds of psychopathology. For example, one of the questions on the test was, "Are you troubled with the idea that people are watching you on the street?"

The Personal Data Sheet developed by Woodworth and his colleagues never went beyond the experimental stages, for the armistice ending the war preceded the final form of the test. After the war, Woodworth developed a personality test for civilian use that was based on the Personal Data Sheet and called it the Woodworth Psychoneurotic Inventory. This inventory was the first widely used self-report test of personality—a method of assessment that would soon be employed in a long line of succeeding personality tests. Personality tests that employ self-report methodologies have both advantages and disadvantages. On the one hand, the person answering the question is—assuming sound judgment and insight—arguably the best qualified person to provide answers. On the other hand, the person may possess neither good judgment nor good insight. And regardless of judgment or insight, respondents might be unwilling to reveal anything that could place them in a negative light. Given these shortcomings of personality assessment by self-report, a need existed for alternative types of personality tests.

One type of test that provided a means of drawing inferences about personality without relying on self-report was the projective test. As we will see in Chapter 12, the projective test is one in which an individual is assumed to "project" onto some ambiguous stimulus his or her own unique needs, fears, hopes, and motivation. The ambiguous stimulus might be an inkblot, a drawing, a photograph, or something else. Perhaps the best known of all projective tests is the Rorschach Inkblot developed by the Swiss psychiatrist Hermann Rorschach. The use of pictures as projective stimuli was popularized in the late 1930s by Henry A. Murray, Christiana D. Morgan, and their colleagues at the Harvard Psychological Clinic. In addition to projective tests, other alternatives to self-report for personality assessment have been and continue to be developed. A sampling of these instruments and a general discussion of personality assessment will be presented in Chapters 11 and 12.

Measurement in various settings   Like the development of the parent field of psychology, the development of psychological measurement can be traced along two distinct threads: the academic and the applied. In the tradition of Galton, Wundt, and other scholars, psychological testing and assessment are practiced today in university psychology laboratories as a means of furthering knowledge about the nature of the human experience. There is also a very strong applied tradition—one that dates back in modern times to the work of people like Binet and in ancient times to China and the administration of competitive civil service examinations. Which child should be placed in which class? Who of these military recruits should be rejected on the basis of intellectual or personality problems? Which person is best suited for the job? Society requires answers to questions such as these, and tests and measures used in a competent manner can help provide answers. However, because we live in a multicultural society, tests must be developed and used with cultural sensitivity. In the section that follows we overview some of the major issues that such sensitivity entails. We elaborate on these and related issues throughout this book.

Culture and Assessment

Culture may be defined as "the socially transmitted behavior patterns, beliefs, and products of work of a particular population, community, or group of people" (Cohen, 1994, p. 5). As taught to us by parents, peers, and societal institutions such as schools, culture prescribes many behaviors and ways of thinking. Spoken language, attitudes toward elders, and techniques of child rearing are but a few critical manifestations of culture. Culture teaches specific rituals to be performed at birth, marriage, death, and other momentous occasions. Culture imparts much about what is to be valued or prized, as well as what is to be rejected or despised. Culture teaches a point of view about what it means to be born of one or another gender, race, or ethnic background. Culture teaches us something about what we can expect from other people and what we can expect from ourselves. Indeed, the influence of culture on an individual's thoughts and behavior may be a great deal stronger than most of us would acknowledge at first blush.

Professionals involved in the assessment enterprise have shown increasing sensitivity to the role of culture in many different aspects of measurement. This sensitivity is manifested in greater consideration of cultural issues with respect to every aspect of test development and use, including decision making on the basis of test data. Unfortunately, it was not always that way.

Evolving Interest in Culture-Related Issues

Soon after Alfred Binet introduced intelligence testing in France, the United States Public Health Service began using such tests to measure the intelligence of people seeking to immigrate to the United States (Figure 2–3). Henry Goddard (1913), the chief researcher assigned to the project and a specialist in the field of mental retardation, early raised (and studied) questions about how meaningful such tests are when used with people from various cultural and language backgrounds. Goddard used interpreters in test administration, employed a bilingual psychologist, and administered mental tests to selected immigrants who appeared mentally retarded to trained observers (Goddard, 1917). This last point is the basis of the false (though widely circulated) claim that Goddard estimated over 80% of all immigrants to be mentally retarded. Goddard states accurately that his research could not make such an estimate about immigrants in general because his subjects were selected for low mental ability.

Thus, the impact of language and culture on the results of scores on mental ability tests was recognized by psychologists even in the early 1900s. One way for the early test developers to deal with this psychometric fact of life was to develop culture-specific tests. That is, the test would be designed for use with people from one culture but not from another. Representative of this approach to test development were early versions of some of the best-known tests of intelligence. For example, the 1937 revision of the Stanford-Binet Intelligence Scale, which enjoyed widespread use until it was revised in 1960, included no minority children in its standardization sample. Similarly, the Wechsler-Bellevue Intelligence Scale, a forerunner of a widely used measure of adult intelligence, contained no minority members in its published standardization sample data. The test's author, David Wechsler (1944), noted that "a large number" of Blacks were tested during the standardization trials but that those data were omitted from the final test manual "because we did not feel that norms derived by mixing the populations could be interpreted without special provisos and reservations." Hence, Wechsler (1944) stated at the outset that the Wechsler-Bellevue norms could not be used for "the colored populations of the United States." Similarly, the inaugural edition of the Wechsler Intelligence Scale for Children (WISC), first published in 1949 and not revised until 1974, contained no minority children in its standardization sample.

Figure 2–3
Psychological Testing at Ellis Island

Immigrants coming to America via Ellis Island were greeted not only by the Statue of Liberty but also by immigration officials ready to evaluate them with respect to physical, mental, and other variables. Here, a block design test, one measure of intelligence, is administered to a would-be American. Immigrants who failed physical, mental, or other tests were returned to their country of origin at the expense of the shipping company that had brought them. Critics would later charge that at least some of the immigrants who had fared poorly on mental tests were sent away from our shores not because they were indeed mentally deficient but simply because they did not understand English well enough to execute instructions. Additionally, the criterion against which these immigrants from many lands were being evaluated was questioned: Who served as the standardization sample, and how appropriate was that sample for this application?

Even though many published tests were, in essence, culture-specific, it soon became apparent that the tests were being administered—improperly—to people from different cultures. Perhaps not surprisingly, testtakers from minority cultures tended to score lower as a group than people from the group for whom the test was developed and standardized. As a specific example, consider this item from the 1949 WISC: "If your mother sends you to the store for a loaf of bread and there is none, what do you do?" Whether or not you perceive any problem with this item may depend on your own cultural background. In fact, the item could be problematic for children from Hispanic homes, many of whom had routinely been sent to the store for tortillas; whether they would even know the meaning of "a loaf of bread" was open to question.

Translation of test materials for people who speak a language different from the one in which the test was initially written typically poses several problems. Some items may be easier or more difficult than originally intended when translated directly into another language. For example, the old Stanford-Binet vocabulary item *skunk* would have to be changed for administration in Puerto Rico, where skunks are nonexistent. Some vocabulary items may change meanings or have dual meanings when translated. For example, a WISC item such as "Why should most government positions be filled through examinations?" might have to be modified to refer to "civil service examinations" in languages or cultures where *examinations* most typically refers to medical examinations. Indeed, many items require some change or modification to be both meaningful to the testtaker from another culture and psychometrically equivalent to the original item with respect to its overall contribution to the test score.

Today, test developers typically take many steps to ensure that a major test developed for national use is indeed suitable for use nationally. Those steps might involve trying out a preliminary version of the test on a tryout sample of testtakers. The data from the tryout sample are typically analyzed in many ways. Test items deemed to be biased with regard to race, gender, or other factors will be eliminated. Further, a panel of independent reviewers may be asked to go through the test items and review them for possible bias. Examiners who administer the test may be asked to relate their impressions regarding various aspects of the test administration. For example, subjective impressions such as the examiner's impressions of the testtaker's reaction to the test materials may be noted, as might opinions regarding the clarity of instructions and the design of the materials. A national standardization of the test may be executed with the sample of participants mirroring the latest U.S. Census data on age groups by sex, geographical region of the United States, race or ethnic group, and socioeconomic status (as gauged by the highest educational attainment of the head-of-household). Again, the data from the standardization sample will typically be rigorously analyzed to root out any possible sources of bias. More details regarding the contemporary process of test development will be presented in Chapter 7.

Some Issues Regarding Culture and Assessment

There are many fertile areas for further exploration of the subject of culture and assessment, among them, some basic considerations relevant to culture and verbal and nonverbal communication.

Verbal communication   Language, the means by which information is communicated, is a key, yet sometimes overlooked, variable in the assessment process. Most obviously, the examiner and the examinee must speak the same language for an assessment to proceed. If a test is in written form complete with written instructions, the testtaker must be able to read and comprehend what is written. When the language in which the assessment is conducted is not the assessee's primary language, questions may arise as to the extent to which the examinee comprehends all that the examiner verbally communicates. Perhaps to a lesser degree, questions about comprehension also remain when an assessment is conducted with the aid of a translator; subtle nuances of meaning and unusual idioms may become lost in the translation and affect the test user's conclusions.

In interviews or other situations in which an evaluation is made on the basis of an oral exchange between two parties, a trained examiner may detect through verbal or nonverbal means that the examinee's grasp of the language is deficient. Such is not the case with written tests. If anything, there well may be an assumption that everyone being administered a written test is capable of understanding it and responding appropriately. In the case of written tests, then, it is clearly essential that the testtaker be able to read and comprehend what is written lest the exercise be more reflective of language competency than whatever it is the test purports to measure.

When assessing an individual whose proficiency in the English language is limited or nonexistent, a number of questions arise: How proficient is the assessee in his or her primary language? What level of proficiency in English is required on the part of the testtaker? Can a meaningful assessment take place through a trained interpreter? Can an alternative and more appropriate assessment procedure be devised to meet the objectives of the assessment? Some of these questions must be considered on a case-by-case basis.

If a test developed and standardized on English-speaking people is to be translated into another language, precautions must be taken to ensure that the translation is indeed an equivalent form. Focusing on problems related to test translation and recognizing the increasing interest in cross-cultural assessment around the world, Van de Vijver and Hambleton (1996) described three types of bias for which the translator must remain vigilant. Construct bias refers to the nonequivalence of constructs across cultural groups. Method bias is the result of problems related to the administration of the instrument. Item bias may result from an incorrect word choice in the translation, which renders the item useless. Hambleton (1994) emphasized the need for demonstrated similarity in meaning across cultural groups for everything from the test administration instructions, to the individual items, to the guidelines for scoring. Ultimately, verifying that foreign language translations of standardized tests are indeed equivalent psychometrically to the original may require a standardization study in its own right. The reliability and validity of a translated test should be established for the specific group for whom the test is to be used. Thus, for example, if an English-language test designed for use in this country is translated into Spanish, its reliability and validity should be established separately with each of the various Spanish-speaking groups of testtakers with whom it might be used (such as Mexicans, Puerto Ricans, and Guatemalans).

Obvious exceptions to these cautions are tests that have been designed expressly to assess proficiency in the English language. However, an orally administered test of English proficiency should not be construed as representative of written proficiency (and vice versa).

Examiners must ideally be knowledgeable about relevant aspects of the culture from which the testtakers come. For example, a child may present as noncommunicative and having only minimal language skills when verbally examined. This finding may be due to the fact that the child is from a culture where elders are revered, where children speak to adults only when they are spoken to and then only in as short a phrase as possible.

In addition to linguistic barriers, the contents of tests from a particular culture are typically laden with items and material—some obvious, some very subtle—that draw heavily from that culture. Test performance may, at least in part, reflect not only whatever variables the test purports to measure but also one additional variable—the degree to which the testtaker has assimilated the culture. One way of attempting to ensure that all bases are covered in translating and adapting a test for use with a specific population of testtakers is to use what Ana Felicia Muñoz-Sandoval refers to as "consensus translation." Read about this translation process in Muñoz-Sandoval's *Test Developer Profile* on our Internet site, *www.mhhe.com.psychtesting*.

Less obvious language-related issues may arise when the examiner and the examinee are native to the same country and speak the same language. Even then, language can sometimes play a subtle role in test outcomes. This is especially true when regional differences in familiarity with particular terms contribute to regional differences in test scores. Consider the word *lavaliere* in the context of a vocabulary test. The chances that you know the meaning of the word vary depending on the part of the United States in which you live. In some areas of the country, particularly the Midwest, a lavaliere, or pendant, is given by the male to the female in a dating relationship as a sign of commitment. In the East, a parallel custom involves pinning on a pin or giving a ring. Owing primarily to cultural practices and not necessarily to major differences in vocabulary ability, people from the East would be far less likely to answer this vocabulary item correctly. As you might imagine, if a vocabulary test had a number of items that were more familiar to students from the Midwest than to students from the East, testtakers from the

Midwest would tend to score higher on the test than those from the East. Would it be fair to conclude on the basis of such test results that the vocabulary of students in the Midwest exceeds that of students in the East? Probably not. At best, such a test might have value in highlighting the vocabulary differences between people raised in different areas of the United States.

The spoken dialect of a language may also influence test results. Although Standard American English is the established language in the United States, many variants and dialects of Standard American English are routinely spoken in various communities throughout the country (Wolfram, 1971). Assessors must be sensitive to the differences, if any, between the language familiar to the assessee and the language in which the assessment is conducted. The assessor must also be sensitive to the degree to which the testtaker has been exposed to the dominant culture or has made a conscious choice not to become assimilated into the dominant culture. Stephens (1992) observed that in some cases, language may be used by the assessee as a defensive tool to maintain distance from the evaluative relationship.

Nonverbal communication and behavior   Humans communicate not only through verbal means but also through nonverbal means. Facial expressions, finger and hand signs, and shifts in one's position in space may all convey messages. Of course, the messages conveyed by such body language may be different from culture to culture. For example, in American culture, one who fails to look another person in the eye when speaking may be viewed as being deceitful or having something to hide. However, in other cultures, such failure to make eye contact when speaking may be a sign of respect.

Having gone on or conducted a job interview, you may have developed a firsthand appreciation for the value of nonverbal communication in an evaluative setting. Interviewees who show enthusiasm and interest have the edge over interviewees who appear to be drowsy or bored. In clinical settings, an experienced evaluator may develop hypotheses to be tested in the interview from the nonverbal behavior of the interviewee. For example, a person who is slouching, moving slowly, and exhibiting a sad facial expression may be depressed. Then again, such an individual may be experiencing physical discomfort as a result of a muscle spasm or an arthritis attack. It will remain for the assessor to determine which of those hypotheses, if any, best accounts for the observed behavior.

Certain theories and systems in the mental health field go beyond more traditional interpretations of body language. For example, in psychoanalysis, a theory of personality and psychological treatment developed by Sigmund Freud, symbolic significance is assigned to many nonverbal acts. From a psychoanalytic perspective, an interviewee's fidgeting with a wedding band during an interview may be interpreted as a message regarding an unstable marriage. As evidenced by his thoughts on "the first chance actions" of a patient during a therapy session, Sigmund Freud (1913) believed he could tell much about motivation from nonverbal behavior:

> The first . . . chance actions of the patient . . . will betray one of the governing complexes of the neurosis. . . . A young girl . . . hurriedly pulls the hem of her skirt over her exposed ankle; she has betrayed the kernel of what analysis will discover later; her narcissistic pride in her bodily beauty and her tendencies to exhibitionism. (p. 359)

By the way, this quote from Freud is also useful in illustrating the influence of culture on diagnostic and therapeutic views. Freud lived in Victorian Vienna. In that time and in that place, sex was not a subject for public discussion. In many ways, Freud's views regarding a sexual basis for various thoughts and behaviors were a product of the sexually repressed culture in which he lived.

An example of a nonverbal behavior on which people differ is the speed at which they characteristically move to complete tasks. The overall pace of life in New York City, for example, is stereotypically faster than it is in the South. In a similar vein, there are differences in pace of life across cultures, and these differences may enhance or detract from test scores on tests involving timed items (Knapp, 1960). In a more general sense, Hoffman (1962) raised questions about the value of timed tests of ability containing multiple-choice items in education settings. Hoffman argued that such tests tapped the variable of quickness or facility and might therefore discriminate against the "deep, brooding" thinker. Indeed, one might wonder how well deep, brooding thinkers would fare on tests such as the SAT or the GRE. In some circumstances, a test user might extend the time limit of a test in order to explore the capabilities of the testtaker. However, the test user must be aware that such exceptions—changing time limits for tests normed with those time limits—makes interpretation of the resulting test scores tenuous at best.

Standards of evaluation Suppose that master chefs from over a hundred nations entered a contest designed to discover the best chicken soup in the world. Who do you think would win? The answer to that question hinges on the evaluative standard to be employed. If the sole judge of the contest was the owner of a kosher delicatessen on the Lower East Side of Manhattan, the entry that came closest to the "Jewish mother home-made" variety might well be declared the winner. However, other judges might have other standards and preferences. For example, soup connoisseurs from Arabic cultures might prefer a variety of chicken soup that includes fresh lemon juice in the recipe. Judges from India might be inclined to give their vote to a chicken soup flavored with curry and other exotic spices. For other Asian judges, soy sauce might be viewed as an indispensable ingredient, and any chicken soup prepared without it might lose by default. Ultimately, it probably is not the case that one soup is truly better than all the rest; judging which soup is best will be very much a matter of personal preference and the standard of evaluation employed.

Similarly, judgments related to certain psychological traits can also be culturally relative. For example, whether specific patterns of behavior are considered to be male- or female-appropriate will depend on the prevailing societal standards regarding masculinity and femininity. In some societies, for example, it is role-appropriate for women to fight wars and put food on the table while the men are occupied in more domestic activities. Whether specific patterns of behavior are considered to be psychopathological also depends on the prevailing societal standards. In Sudan, for example, there are tribes that live among cattle because they regard the animals as sacred. Judgments as to who might be the best employee, manager, or leader may differ as a function of culture, as might judgments regarding intelligence, wisdom, courage, and other psychological variables.

A challenge inherent in the assessment enterprise has to do with tempering test- and assessment-related outcomes with good judgment regarding the cultural relativity of those outcomes. In practice, this means raising questions about the applicability of assessment-related findings to specific individuals. Thus, in addition to attempting to answer questions such as "How intelligent is this person?" or "How assertive is this individual?" by means of evaluative methods, some additional questions must also be raised. How appropriate are the norms or other standards that will be used to make the evaluation? To what extent has the individual been assimilated into the culture from which the test is drawn, and what influence might such assimilation (or lack of it) have on the test results? What research has been done on the test that bears on its applicability for use in evaluating this particular individual? Increasingly, these questions are being raised not only by careful test users but by the courts as well.

Tests and Group Membership

Tests and other evaluative measures administered in the context of vocational, education, counseling, and other settings leave little doubt that people differ—not only from one another on an individual basis but from group to group on a collective basis. The mandate of the assessment enterprise, perhaps since the first evaluative measures were ever administered, has been to identify individual differences and take effective action with respect to them. "Effective action" in this sense might mean a number of things such as targeting areas of intervention, gauging the progress of interventions, facilitating optimal selection and hiring practices, learning about the human development process, learning about human temperament and personality, making predictions regarding behavior under specific conditions, and so on.

In the area of vocational assessment, test users are sensitive to legal and ethical mandates requiring that test scores, as well as any other criteria used to evaluate candidates, be related to one's ability to do the job. Indeed, logic alone dictates that if a test is designed to measure ability to perform a particular job, scores should reflect that. Scores on such ability tests should be influenced only by job-related variables and not by other variables such as hair length, group membership, or any other factor extraneous to the ability to perform the job. It is in the interest of society as a whole for the results of vocational assessments not to discriminate against members of any racial, ethnic, religious, or other group, if membership in the group in no way affects ability to perform the job in question. Few would argue against contemporary public policy that strives to promote equal opportunity for all. Ethical guidelines promulgated by professional organizations, as well as legislation, case law, and administrative regulations, are safeguards designed to protect individuals from test-related discrimination as a result of group membership. Major test developers and publishers, in their public statements and by their actions, seem dedicated to the principle of equal opportunity. Still, claims of test-related discrimination against reputable test developers and publishers abound, as do claims of unfairness regarding evaluative criteria used by employers, schools, and others who rely on test data. Why?

Claims of test-related discrimination against major test publishers may be best understood as evidence of the great complexity of the assessment enterprise rather than any conspiracy to systematically use tests to discriminate. This complexity leaves ample room for confusion in distinguishing between practices that are psychometrically sound and practices that may be construed as discriminatory. In the area of vocational assessment, for example, conflicts may arise from disagreements concerning the criteria deemed necessary to perform a particular job. The potential for controversy looms over almost all selection criteria an employer sets, regardless of whether the criteria are physical, educational, psychological, or experiential in nature. At its core, the critical question with regard to hiring, promotion, and other selection decisions in almost any work setting can be phrased as, "What criteria must be met to do this job?" A state police department may have a requirement that all applicants for the position of police officer must meet certain physical requirements, including a minimum height of 5 feet, 4 inches. A person who is 5 feet 2 inches and from a cultural background where the average height of adults is less than 5 feet 4 inches is effectively barred from applying. The result may be a class action lawsuit charging discrimination against this cultural group by the police force; the police force evaluation policies have the effect of systematically excluding specific group members. Whether the police department's height requirement is reasonable and job related, and whether discrimination in fact occurred, are very complex questions that will have to be considered by a court. Compelling arguments may be presented on both sides, as benevolent, fair-minded, knowledgeable, and well-intentioned people may have honest differences about the necessity of the prevailing height requirement for the job of police officer in this state.

In some instances, applicants may be eliminated from consideration for a job for reasons directly or indirectly related to their membership in some group. As an example, consider an opening for a quality control supervisor at a busy catering company. The position requires, among other things, managerial experience and superior taste discrimination ability as measured by a taste discrimination test. As most of the company's clients retain the company's services for weekend parties, candidates are required to work on weekends as well as provide their own transportation to party sites. One applicant who has excellent managerial experience happens to obtain an exceptionally high score on the company's taste discrimination test. The company arranges a personal interview, excited about the prospect of hiring such a promising candidate. However, the outcome of the interview is not a hire but rather a reopening of the candidate search. Why? The candidate was an observant Jew whose appearance was markedly different from any of the other personnel in the company. The candidate had a full beard and always wore a hat of one sort or another (in accordance with religious custom). The company evaluator's immediate concern was that the candidate's appearance and dress might contribute to him being socially isolated from fellow workers, even clients. The evaluator also sensed that even if this candidate were hired, his chances of making it to the executive suite would be slim—in reality, an unfortunate fact of corporate life for observant Jews (Korman, 1988; Mael, 1991; Zweigenhaft, 1984). The candidate would have been unable to work on weekends, for the Jewish Sabbath begins at sundown on Friday and lasts through sundown on Saturday. During the Sabbath, custom would forbid him from riding in motorized vehicles. Yet, even if all concerns about the candidate's appearance could be allayed and even if the work schedule could be adjusted so that he would not have to report on the Sabbath or any holy day on the Jewish calendar, there would still be the matter of his diet. The candidate would eat only kosher food, and then not in combination with other types of food. Given the established selection criteria, then, candidates who are members of the group known as observant Jews are effectively excluded from working at any field job for this company.

In discussing individual and group differences with respect to evaluative criteria, most of us can readily appreciate that such differences exist regarding variables such as height or religious preference. However, suggesting that these differences exist with respect to abilities and psychological attributes, such as intelligence, easily arouses skepticism, if not charges of discrimination, bias, or worse. If systematic differences were found to exist on psychological or ability test scores, as a function of group membership, the playing field could be leveled by revising the test-scoring procedures so as to differentially weight the scores of people in the affected groups (McNemar, 1975). But does this best serve the interests of society? Wouldn't these same differences in test scores by group also tend to predict differential real-world performance? In fact, there is evidence to suggest that group differences in scores on professionally developed tests do reflect differences in real-world performance (Gottfredson, 2000; Halpern, 2000; Hartigan & Wigdor, 1989; Kubiszyn et al., 2000; Neisser et al., 1996; Schmidt, 1988; Schmidt & Hunter, 1992). Given this state of affairs, attempting to equalize group differences by means of differential manipulation of test scores might be tantamount to introducing "inequity in equity" (Benbow & Stanley, 1996).

As sincerely committed as they may be to principles of egalitarianism and fair play, test developers and test users must ultimately look to society at large—and, more specifically, to laws, administrative regulations, and other rules and professional codes of conduct—for guidance regarding test scores. Here we cross interdisciplinary boundaries into a vast middle ground between psychometric theory and real-world applications, an area that lies conceptually between technical and philosophical aspects of measurement. This middle ground is the area of public policy and social values.

Psychology, tests, and public policy   Psychologists, as well as other professional groups, are pledged to use their knowledge for the welfare of the individual and the public good. To that end, psychologists have used their research know-how and applied skills to help address a wide range of urgent social problems, such as those related to AIDS, drunk driving, and urban violence and gangs. Psychologists have also used their skills to champion not so publicized but equally life-threatening problems. So, for example, as long as there are significant numbers of people who fail to buckle up behind the wheel although it is in their best interest to do so, there will always be psychologists exploring ways to increase the frequency of seatbelt-buckling behavior. As long as there are people who must cut down on their food intake, increase their exercise, or make other positive changes in their lifestyles, there will be psychologists researching ways to best effect such changes. And as long as the quality of the world's environment continues to deteriorate, there will be psychologists researching ways to motivate "green" behavior.

Psychological tests and assessment procedures are used to accomplish many things in the service of such objectives. For example, they are used to measure outcomes, pinpoint problem areas, and help make policy decisions. Few members of the general public would object to using psychological tests in the service of such noble causes. Then again, few such people would be aware of these uses of tests. However, many people are aware of the use of tests in high profile contexts, such as when an individual or a group has a great deal to gain or to lose as a result of a test score or an assessor's report. In these more visible situations, where a test score or an assessment may have a momentous and immediate impact on one's life, tests and assessment can be easily perceived as tools used to *deny*. Denial of educational advancement, job opportunities, parole, custody—these are some of the more threatening consequences and images that members of the public may associate with psychological tests and assessment procedures. To guard against such denials, legislators pass laws, administrative agencies make regulations, judges hand down rulings, and citizens call for referendums either to reflect and enforce prevailing public policy or to modify it. So, in 1997, for example, legislation was enacted to, among other things, help prevent the misdiagnosis and mislabeling of children who are culturally different from the majority. That legislation, along with various other legal and ethical issues, is discussed in the section that follows.

Legal and Ethical Considerations

A society's **laws** are rules that individuals must obey for the good of the society as a whole—or rules thought to be for the good of society as a whole. Some laws are and have been relatively uncontroversial. For example, the law that mandates driving on the right side of the road has been neither a subject of debate, nor a source of emotional soul-searching, nor a stimulus to civil disobedience. For safety and the common good, most people are willing to relinquish their freedom to drive anywhere on the road they might please. But what about laws pertaining to abortion? to busing? to capital punishment? to euthanasia? to deprogramming of religious cult members? to affirmative action in employment? Exactly how laws regulating matters such as these should be written and interpreted are issues of heated controversy—as are some of the laws that pertain to psychological measurement.

Whereas a body of laws is a body of rules, a body of **ethics** is a body of principles of right, proper, or good conduct. Thus, for example, an ethic of the Old West was "Never shoot 'em in the back." Two well-known principles subscribed to by the seafaring set are "Women and children leave first in an emergency" and "A captain goes down with his ship."[2] The ethics of journalism dictate that reporters present all sides of a controversial issue. A research principle is that the scientist should never fudge data; all data must be reported accurately. What kinds of ethical guidelines do you think should govern the professional behavior of psychologists involved in psychological testing and assessment? The answer to this question is important; to the extent that a code of ethics is recognized and accepted by members of a profession, it defines the standard of care expected by members of that profession.

Members of the public and members of the profession have at times in recent history been on different sides of the fence with respect to issues of ethics and law. We now trace some concerns of the public and the profession.

The Concerns of the Public

The assessment enterprise has never been very well understood by the public. Even today, it is unfortunate that we may hear statements symptomatic of misunderstanding with regard to tests (for example, "The only thing tests measure is the ability to take tests"). Possible consequences of public misunderstanding include fear, anger, legislation, litigation, and administrative regulations.

Perhaps the first time the American public evidenced widespread concern about psychological testing came in the aftermath of World War I. At that time, various professionals (as well as nonprofessionals) sought to adapt group tests developed by the military (such as the Army Alpha and Beta tests) for civilian use in schools and industry. As noted by Haney (1981), many articles in the periodical literature of the early 1920s reflected discomfort with the growing testing industry. Representative of this discomfort were articles by Walter Lippmann in the popular *New Republic* magazine, such as "The Abuse of Tests" in November 1922 and "The Mental Age of Americans" in October 1922. In the latter article, Lippmann asserted, among other things, that an intelligence test amounted to a "vain effort to discount training and knowledge." The renowned Stanford psychologist Lewis Terman attempted to respond to Lippmann's sensational and misleading remarks in the same magazine. However, because the issues were complex and the forum of the debate was a lay magazine, Terman was the loser in the eyes of the readership. As Cronbach (1975, p. 12) observed, Terman had "tried to play the same game and was hopelessly overmatched."

Constructive criticism regarding the psychometric soundness of tests of the day was evident in the writings of Ruch (1925), a measurement specialist who proposed standards for tests that in many ways anticipated the criteria that are currently in place. Ruch (1933) also anticipated the creation of a Buros-like institute when he wrote of "the urgent need for a fact-finding organization which will undertake impartial, experimental, and statistical evaluations of tests." Earlier, Kelley along with six other measurement experts took on the (overly) ambitious task of attempting to rank all published tests designed for use in educational settings. The results were published in a pioneering book (Kelley, 1927) that provided test users with information needed to compare the merits of

---

2. We leave the question of what to do when the captain of the ship is a woman to a volume dedicated to an in-depth exploration of seafaring ethics.

published standardized tests. However, given the pace at which test instruments were being published, this type of resource would be quickly outdated if not periodically updated. Thus, although Oscar Buros may not have been the first measurement professional to undertake a comprehensive testing of the tests, he was certainly the most tenacious in terms of updating and revising the information.

The widespread military testing that took place during the 1940s as a result of World War II did not appear to arouse as much popular interest as did the testing that had been undertaken during World War I. The periodical literature was relatively free of articles dealing with psychological testing until the 1960s, when considerable media attention was focused on gifted children. Perhaps the greatest stimulus to that attention was an event that occurred in the Soviet Union on October 4, 1957. On that day, the Russians launched into space a satellite they called *Sputnik*—and the race to space was on. About a year after the Russian launch, Congress passed the National Defense Education Act, which provided federal money to local schools for the purpose of ability and aptitude testing, in an effort to identify gifted and academically talented students.

The subsequent proliferation of large-scale testing programs in the schools combined with the increasing use of ability as well as personality tests in government, military, and business employment selection led to renewed widespread public concern about the efficacy of psychological tests. This concern was reflected in magazine articles such as "Testing: Can Everyone Be Pigeonholed?" (*Newsweek,* July 20, 1959) and "What the Tests Do Not Test" (*New York Times Magazine,* October 2, 1960), and in books (for example, Gross, 1962) that seemed by their nature to be designed more to incite than to inform. The upshot of the heightened public concern was congressional hearings on the subject of testing (Amrine, 1965).

In 1969, widespread media attention was accorded the publication of an article in the prestigious *Harvard Educational Review,* and once again public concerns with respect to testing were aroused. The article was entitled "How Much Can We Boost IQ and Scholastic Achievement?" and its author, Arthur Jensen, argued that "genetic factors are strongly implicated in the average Negro-white intelligence difference" (1969, p. 82). An outpouring of public and professional attention to nature versus nurture issues regarding intelligence focused attention on the instruments used to gauge intellectual differences—instruments we commonly refer to as intelligence tests. The United States Select Committee on Equal Education Opportunity, in preparation for hearings on the matter of the relationships between intelligence, genetics, and environment, compiled a document of over six hundred pages called *Environment, Intelligence and Scholastic Achievement* (1972). However, according to Haney (1981), the hearings "were canceled because they promised to be too controversial" (p. 1026). More recently, public concern about testing was reinvigorated by heavy media attention given *The Bell Curve* (Herrnstein & Murray, 1994), a book that is essentially an updated and more politicized version of Jensen's work.

The extent of public concern about psychological assessment is reflected in the extensive involvement of the government in many aspects of the assessment process in recent decades. Assessment has been affected in numerous and important ways by activities of the legislative, executive, and judicial branches of federal and state governments, as the following examples illustrate.

In recent years, the U.S. Congress has passed or amended several laws that impact psychological assessment. For example, the *Americans with Disabilities Act of 1990* bans discrimination in employment, transportation, public accommodations, and telecommunications on the basis of physical or mental disability. The law defines a disability as a condition that "substantially limits a major life activity." Facilities must be accessible to individuals with disabilities, and employers must make "reasonable accommodation" for disabled workers to perform their duties. Implications of this act for psychological assessment include designing employment testing materials and procedures to measure the skills essential to the particular job. For example, using paper-and-pencil tests in selecting employees is not appropriate if such skills are not job related and if the applicant's performance on these measures would reflect his or her handicap. Tests with time limits are considered inappropriate when speed is not essential to the skill being assessed.

The *Civil Rights Act of 1964* was amended in 1991 by the federal legislature. Also known as the *Equal Opportunity Employment Act*, this law provides for nondiscrimination in employment. The 1991 amendment makes explicit the implications for testing: Section 106 states, "It shall be unlawful employment practice . . . to adjust the scores of, use different cutoff scores for, or otherwise alter the results of, employment related tests on the basis of race, religion, sex, or national origin."

The *Education for All Handicapped Children Act (Public Law 94-142)* was first enacted in 1975 and then amended in 1984, twice in 1988, and again in 1990. In Section 612, the law mandates that all children with suspected mental or physical handicaps be identified through the use of screening instruments, "regardless of the severity of their handicap." Section 101 of the 1990 amendment specifies the broad range of conditions covered by the law: "mental retardation, hearing impairments including deafness, speech or language impairments, visual impairments including blindness, serious emotional disturbance, orthopedic impairments, autism, traumatic brain injury, other health impairments, or specific learning disabilities." Once identified, each individual child must be evaluated by a professional team qualified to determine that child's special educational needs, and then periodically reevaluated during the course of an individualized educational program. Psychological assessment is used extensively in the wide range of evaluations associated with this law.

Records generated as a result of testing have also been subject to federal legislation. For example, the *Family Education Rights and Privacy Act* (1974) mandated that parents and eligible students be given access to school records. Additionally, the act formally granted parents and students the right to challenge findings in those records in a hearing.

In 1997, sweeping amendments to the *Individuals with Disabilities Education Act (IDEA)* of 1975 were embodied in *PL 105-17*, a law that changed the way that candidates for special education were evaluated and educated. Among the many provisions of this law was an extension of existing disability-related protections to infants and toddlers from birth to age 3. Professionals who assess candidates for special education were mandated to include extratest information, such as information about a preschooler's involvement in activities or a student's involvement and progress in the general curriculum. The law contained provisions designed to deter inappropriate placement in special education programs due to cultural differences and limited proficiency in the English language. As was noted in Chapter 1, PL 105-17 encouraged accommodation of existing test instruments and other alternate means of assessment for the purpose of gauging the progress of special education students as measured by state- and district-wide assessments. These provisions sought to generate greater accountability in the schools for the educational progress of special education students.

The making of laws to govern the assessment process has not been limited to the federal legislature. In the 1970s, numerous states enacted **minimum competency testing programs**—formal testing programs designed to be used in decisions regarding various aspects of students' education (such as award of diplomas, grade promotions, and identification of areas in which the student needs remedial instruction). These laws grew out of grassroots support for the idea that high school graduates should have, at the very least, "minimal competencies" in areas such as reading, writing, and arithmetic.

In some jurisdictions, laws provide that a student may be denied a high school diploma if such minimal competencies cannot be demonstrated on a test.

Truth-in-testing legislation was also passed at the state level, beginning in the 1980s. The primary objective of these laws is to provide testtakers with a means of learning the criteria by which they are being judged. In reaching that objective, some laws mandate the disclosure of questions and answers of postsecondary and professional school admissions tests within 30 days of the publication of test scores. Some require that information relevant to a test's development and psychometric soundness be kept on file. Some truth-in-testing laws require providing descriptions of (1) the test's purpose and its subject matter, (2) the knowledge and skills the test purports to measure, (3) procedures for ensuring accuracy in scoring as well as procedures for notifying testtakers of errors in scoring, and (4) procedures for ensuring the testtaker's confidentiality. Truth-in-testing laws create special difficulties for test developers and publishers, who argue that it is essential for them to keep the test items secret. They note that there may be a limited item pool for some tests and that the cost of developing an entirely new set of items for each succeeding administration of a test is prohibitive.

To the extent that state and federal legislators respond to the concerns of the people they represent, the legislative acts described above suggest that Americans are concerned about the way in which psychological testing may affect their lives. The laws that grow out of these concerns often mandate the involvement of the executive branch of government in their application. For example, Title VII of the Civil Rights Act of 1964 created the Equal Employment Opportunity Commission (EEOC) to enforce the act. EEOC has published sets of guidelines concerning standards to be met in constructing and using employment tests. In 1978, the EEOC, the Civil Service Commission, the Department of Labor, and the Justice Department jointly published the *Uniform Guidelines on Employee Selection Procedures.* One sample guideline is as follows:

> The use of any test which adversely affects hiring, promotion, transfer or any other employment or membership opportunity of classes protected by Title VII constitutes discrimination unless (a) the test has been validated and evidences a high degree of utility as hereinafter described, and (b) the person giving or acting upon the results of the particular test can demonstrate that alternative suitable hiring, transfer or promotion procedures are unavailable for . . . use.

Note in this excerpted guideline that a definition of discrimination as exclusionary coexists with the proviso that a valid test that evidences "a high degree of utility" (among other criteria) will not be considered discriminatory. Generally, however, the public has been quick to label a test as unfair and discriminatory regardless of its utility. As a consequence, a great public demand for proportionality by group membership in hiring and college admissions now coexists with a great lack of proportionality by group membership in skills (Gottfredson, 2000). Gottfredson (2000) noted that while selection standards can often be improved, the opportunistic manipulation of such standards "will produce only lasting frustration, not enduring solutions." She recommended that enduring solutions be sought by addressing the problem related to gaps in skills between groups, and not by lowering hiring and admission standards or forcing hiring and admissions proportionality through legislation. Yet it is in the latter direction that the tide seems to be turning, at least in some recent legislation.

In Texas, state law now mandates that the top 10% of graduating seniors from all Texas high schools be admitted to a state university regardless of SAT scores. This means that regardless of the quality of education in any particular Texas high school, a senior in the top 10% of the graduating class is guaranteed college admission regardless of how he or she might score on a nationally standardized measure. There have been reports that in some Texas high schools, as many as 25% of the students are in the top 10% of their class (Kronholz, 1998). In California, there has been a decreasing use of skills tests in the public sector as a result of the passage of Proposition 209, which banned racial preferences (Rosen, 1998). One consequence has been the deemphasis of the Law School Admissions Test (LSAT) as an admission criterion to the University of California, Berkeley, law school. Additionally, the law school has stopped weighing grade point averages from undergraduate schools in their admission criteria, so that "A 4.0 from California State is now worth as much as a 4.0 from Harvard" (Rosen, 1998, p. 62). Gottfredson (2000) argued that organizations advocating such reversals of achievement standards obtain "nothing of lasting value by eliminating valid tests" and that such action actually hinders progress "while providing only the illusion of progress." She opined that society is best served by activities that focus on skills training and the reversal of unfortunate social trends in family structure. Society is ill served by unfounded criticism of tests in the wanton pursuit of proportionality in groups in employment and university settings, despite large skills gaps between groups.

Beyond activity in state and federal legislative bodies, it is instructive to look at activity in the courts relevant to testing and assessment. Through the years, a number of cases have focused on ability and intelligence testing in the schools. *Hobson v. Hansen* (1967) raised these issues relative to an ability tracking system in a desegregated school. Children at this school were tracked on the basis of their scores on an ability test, and the result was that the school had effectively become resegregated: Black students were grouped together in lower-track classes. The Supreme Court found that ability tests developed on Whites could not lawfully be used to track Black students within the school system.

Similar concerns were raised in a California case, *Diana v. State Board of Education* (1970). Although children with Spanish surnames constituted only about 18% of the student body, fully 33% of the students in classes for the educable mentally retarded (EMR) had Spanish surnames. All testing had been done in English using intelligence tests developed primarily on White children. When nine Spanish-speaking children were retested in Spanish, eight scored in the nonretarded range. This case resulted in several changes in the California Education Code. Placement in EMR classes must involve a comprehensive developmental and educational assessment of the child, not just the results of an intelligence test.

Another California case, *Larry P. v. Riles* (1979), involved the placement of Black students in EMR classes using intelligence tests. Six such children were retested using the same intelligence test, with some items reworded to reflect the children's cultural background. Intelligence test scores on retesting increased by 17 to 38 points, and all six children scored in the nonretarded range. Also, as with *Diana,* a higher proportion of Black children were in the EMR classes than in the student body. The judge in this case found that the use of intelligence tests to place Black children in EMR classes was unconstitutional, because such tests are "racially and culturally biased" and have a "discriminatory impact on Black children." This decision was appealed but upheld in 1984. The California judge who made the 1979 ruling affirmed it in 1986 by stating "in no uncertain terms . . . that schools in that state may not use IQ tests to assess Black children for placement in special education classes" (Landers, 1986, p. 18).

The minimum competency legislation discussed above has also created some activity in the judicial system. For example, in *Debra P. v. Turlington* (1981), suit was brought against Florida's Commissioner of Education (Turlington) by ten Black students after they had been denied high school diplomas. The students had failed a statewide test of minimum competency, which was essentially a literacy test. The plaintiffs argued that if the minimum competency test were to be sanctioned as a requirement for the reward of a diploma, 20% of the Black high school seniors in Florida would be denied high school diplomas, as compared with only 2% of the White high school seniors. In 1979, a federal judge ruled that the minimum competency testing program in Florida was unconstitutional because it perpetuated the effects of past discrimination. A moratorium on such testing was ordered. In 1981, the United States Court of Appeals affirmed the lower court's ruling, holding that such a program violated the equal protection clause of the Constitution, because it punished Black students for prior discrimination in schooling.

Not all court cases surrounding psychological testing involve education. The use of tests to select or promote employees, and the potential for such practices to result in racial discrimination, has been examined in a series of cases brought under the Civil Rights Act. Through these cases, we see the courts struggling with how to apply the act when different groups score differently on employment tests.

In *Griggs v. Duke Power Company* (1971), Black employees brought suit against a private paper company for discriminatory hiring practices. The company used measures of general ability, such as a high school diploma and the Wonderlic Personnel Test, resulting in the hiring of a relatively small number of Blacks. The Supreme Court agreed with the plaintiffs, finding problems with "broad and general testing devices." Instead, the Court stated that tests must "fairly measure the knowledge or skills required by a particular job." The Court ruled that employment tests must "measure the person for the job and not the person in the abstract."

A similar issue was explored in *Albemarle Paper Company v. Moody* (1976). The paper mill's industrial psychologist had found that scores on a general ability test predicted measures of job performance, such as supervisors' ratings of competence, and so had been using the general ability test to select employees. The complaint was that, as a group, Whites scored better than Blacks on the general ability test and therefore were given preference in hiring decisions. The U.S. District Court found this use of the test to be sufficiently job related to be valid, but the decision was reversed on appeal with the argument that discrimination had occurred despite the paper mill's "absence of discriminatory intent."

Allen v. District of Columbia (1993), involved a test that had been developed to assist with promotion decisions in the city's fire department. The promotional test was not one of general ability but drew questions from specific aspects of the job of firefighter. Blacks scored lower on the test than Whites, with the result that a smaller proportion of Blacks were promoted than there were in the pool of candidates for promotion. As in *Albemarle*, validity information had been collected showing that the test accurately predicted future job success and was related to others' evaluations of the candidate's abilities. However, in this case, the use of the test was supported by the court: "Because the promotional examination . . . was a valid measure of the abilities and probable future success of those individuals taking the test, the exam serves the legitimate employment goals of the department."

Drawing a consistent lesson from the results of court cases in this area is difficult. Courts at various levels have worked toward a description of what constitutes discriminatory use of tests in the employment setting, but a consistent understanding has not yet been reached. Courts disagree about whether validated tests on which there are racial differences can be used to assist with employment-related decisions. Perhaps the fact that courts have been somewhat inconsistent should not surprise, given the great diversity of opinions expressed by the experts who testify in them (see *Everyday Psychometrics*).

State and federal legislatures, executive bodies, and courts have been involved in many aspects of the psychological assessment process. This involvement demonstrates both the extent and the nature of public concern about testing. Such concerns are not limited to people outside psychology but often come from professionals as well.

Expert Testimony

Unfortunately the validity and reliability of many psychological tests are currently being decided by the courts; it should not be that way but it is." So said Ralph Reitan (1994), a neuropsychologist and developer of the Halstead-Reitan Neuropsychological Test Battery. Reitan should know. He served as an expert witness in *Chapple v. Ganger* (1994), a case involving alleged neuropsychological injury. As we will discuss in Chapter 14 ("Neuropsychological Assessment"), Reitan's testimony concerned his administration of what is referred to as a "fixed" test battery. Other experts provided testimony regarding their administration of a "flexible" test battery. The court's ruling in *Chapple* may well have implications for the administration of fixed versus flexible text batteries, as well as other aspects of psychological assessment.

Data from psychological assessments are ideally used to benefit individual people as well as society at large. However, in legal matters where the parties have conflicting interests, professionals often disagree on assessment-related matters. The appropriateness of administering a particular test under a particular set of circumstances and the appropriateness of the conclusions drawn are two likely areas of dispute. When facts related to the administration or interpretation of psychological tests are contested in the courtroom, experts for each side may express diametrically opposite opinions.

The dynamics of legal battles regarding psychology-related issues is itself a fascinating topic. Each side in such contests may retain their own experts to support their views. One attorney even boasted, "[I]n virtually any case, I can find a psychiatric witness to make whatever recommendation I want" (Shell, 1980, p. 8). One solution to this problem of expert shopping by attorneys entails court-appointed experts who are presumably neutral. Yet, the neutrality of these court-appointed experts has also been a matter of contention, as observed by Howard (1991, p. 101): "It is slightly mysterious that it should be thought that experts are venal mountebanks when engaged by the parties but transformed into paragons of objectivity when employed by the courts."

When an assessor is also the assessee's therapist, the assessor-assessee relationship coexists with a therapist-client relationship. There is typically no ambivalence in either relationship, and the client (assessee) can be reasonably confident that the therapist (assessor) is acting in a way that is consistent with the client's own objectives. Conceivably, however, there are many instances when the assessor does not share the objectives of the assessee. An assessor may be the agent of a court, of some administrative agency, or

even of a legal adversary. In the latter situations, it would seem that there would be greater ambiguity surrounding the motivation and loyalties of the assessor, at least in the eyes of the assessee. We can only speculate how this would affect the findings in individual cases. Suppose, for example, an individual demands insurance compensation on the basis of a psychiatric disability. The insurer obtains authorization to administer a battery of psychological tests to rule out malingering. Depending on the ways the parties to such an assessment approach the process, the objectives, nature, tone, and results obtained from that assessment could differ to a very large degree from the same assessment conducted by the insured's own therapist.

Scenarios such as that have grown increasingly common as psychologists and other professionals involved in assessment have been called upon to serve as experts in diverse types of legal actions. Assessors may serve as experts in cases involving competency to stand trial, insanity as a defense, charges of malingering or fraud, petitions to die with dignity, and petitions to be held at or released from a mental institution. Experts may be called on to testify as to the mental state of an individual at some time in the past or present or even offer predictions regarding future behavior.

One area in which the interpretations made and the conclusions reached are most likely to be legally contested is assessment for the purpose of determining child custody. As Acklin (1997) put it, "The very nature of the task, occurring in the midst of divorce conflict and posing a threat to the most intimate family bonds, exposes the evaluator to intense suspicion or ambivalence, and in some cases, potential ethical or malpractice complaints. In few areas of practice is the capacity to do harm more pronounced" (p. 448). If the matter of custody is not decided by means of an out-of-court settlement and goes to trial, the value of the tests and procedures employed by assessors, as well as the competence of the assessors, quickly becomes the focal point of contention and judicial scrutiny. During the proceedings, parents may hear themselves referred to by assessors in terms they find extremely unflattering, if not libelous. This may result in retaliation against the expert, which may take the form of an ethics complaint or a lawsuit alleging malpractice. To prevail in malpractice litigation, the plaintiff must prove by the preponderance of the evidence that the care provided by the professional was substandard and that some loss resulted (Cohen, 1979). In a bygone era, if the expert had been appointed by the court to conduct the evaluation, the expert would be

(continued)

Expert Testimony *(continued)*

immune from liability. However, if a recent decision made by a federal circuit court is a harbinger of things to come, mental health professionals in private practice contracted by a court to conduct an evaluation no longer qualify for immunity (Hafemeister, 2001). The decision in this case may have a number of implications for mental health professionals involved in assessment. It may, for example, deter professionals from accepting evaluation referrals from courts.

Perhaps the most significant recent court case with regard to issues related to expert testimony was *Daubert v. Merrell Dow Pharmaceuticals,* heard in the United States Supreme Court in June, 1993. The origins of this case can be traced to the use of the prescription drug Bendectin in order to relieve nausea during pregnancy. The plaintiffs sued Merrell Dow Pharmaceuticals, the manufacturer of Bendectin, when their children were born with birth defects. Their claim was that Bendectin had caused the defects.

Attorneys for the plaintiffs were armed with research that they claimed would prove that Bendectin causes birth defects. However, the trial judge refused to admit their reseach into evidence, ruling that the research failed to meet the criteria necessary to be admissible. In the end, the judge ruled against the plaintiffs.

The plaintiffs appealed to the next highest court, which also ruled against them. Once again, the plaintiffs appealed, this time to the Supreme Court of the United States. A question before the Supreme Court was whether the judge in the original trial acted properly by not allowing the plaintiffs' research to be admitted into evidence.

A major precedent regarding the admissibility of research into evidence was the 1923 case of *Frye v. the United States.* In *Frye,* the Court held that scientific research will be admissible into evidence when the research study or method enjoys general acceptance. A less rigorous standard for admissibility of research had been set forth by Congress in the *Federal Rules of Evidence* (FRE 1975). Rule 702 of the FRE opened the door to expert witnesses testifying as to the admissibility of research and research methods. An expert might offer an opinion to a jury concerning the acceptability of a research study or method, regardless of whether the opinion represented the opinion of other experts. Rule 702 was designed to assist juries in their fact-finding by helping them to understand the issues involved.

In *Daubert,* the plaintiffs argued that Rule 702 was ignored by the trial judge. The defendant, Merrell Dow Pharmaceuticals, countered that the trial judge ruled appropriately, as high standards of evidence admissibility were necessary to protect juries from "scientific shamans who, in the guise of their purported expertise, are willing to testify to virtually any conclusion to suit the needs of the litigant with resources sufficient to pay their retainer."

Ultimately, the Supreme Court ruled that the *Daubert* case be retried with the trial judge being given wide discretion in terms of deciding what does and does not qualify as scientific evidence. In effect, federal judges were charged with a gatekeeping function. The ruling superseded the long-standing policy as set forth in *Frye,* one of admitting into evidence scientific testimony that had won general acceptance in the scientific community. In *Daubert,* factors such as general acceptance in the scientific community or publication in a peer-reviewed journal were simply relevant factors for judges to consider. Other factors judges might consider included the extent to which a theory or technique had been tested and the extent to which the theory or technique might be subject to error. Under *Frye,* a variety of controversial theories and methods had been admitted into evidence, essentially as the result of expert testimony to the effect that the theory or method was "generally accepted" in the field. In essence, *Daubert* let the trial judge decide what the jury could consider.

The Concerns of the Profession

As early as 1895, the infant American Psychological Association (APA) formed its first committee on mental measurement, a committee charged with investigating various aspects of the new practice of standardized testing. Another APA committee on measurements was formed in 1906 to further study the issues and problems attendant upon test standardization. In 1916 and again in 1921, symposia dealing with various issues surrounding the expanding uses of tests were sponsored (*Mentality Tests,* 1916; *Intelli-*

... the Ancients measured facial beauty by the millihelen, *a unit equal to that necessary to launch one ship...*

The *Daubert* standard for admission to evidence was modified by the Supreme Court decision in the case of *General Electric v. Joiner* (1997). In that case, the Court emphasized that the trial court had a duty to exclude unreliable expert testimony evidence. Subsequently, in the case of *Kumho Tire Company v. Carmichael* (1999), the Supreme Court expanded the principles expounded in *Daubert* to the testimony of all experts, whether or not they claim a basis for their testimony in scientific research. Thus, for example, a psychologist's testimony based on personal experience in practice rather than scientific evidence may be admitted into evidence if the trial judge chooses to admit it (Mark, 1999).

Taken together, *Daubert, Joiner,* and *Kumho* will probably raise the level of scrutiny by the court to expert testimony by clinicians, and raise questions regarding how the available research supports clinicians' opinions (Shuman & Sales, 1999). Various commentators have speculated on just how *Daubert* and related cases might affect the admissibility of expert testimony in cases involving mental capacity (Frolik, 1999), child custody (Krauss & Sales, 1999), criminal prosecution (Slobogin, 1999), civil litigation (Lipton, 1999), and related matters (Grove & Barden, 1999; Saxe & Ben-Shakhar, 1999; Tenopyr, 1999).

gence and Its Measurement, 1921) and in 1923 an APA committee recommended that nonpsychologists' use of tests be monitored. However, that recommendation was voted down by the APA membership. In 1954, the association published its *Technical Recommendations for Psychological Tests and Diagnostic Tests,* a document that set forth testing standards and technical recommendations. The following year, another professional organization, the National Educational Association (working in collaboration with the National Council on Measurements Used in Education—now known as the National Council on Measurement) published its *Technical Recommendations for Achievement Tests.*

Collaboration between these professional organizations led to the development of testing standards.

Paralleling APA's ongoing concerns regarding the ethics of psychological testing were concerns about general ethics in the field of psychology. In 1953, APA published its *Ethical Standards of Psychologists,* a culmination of the work of many APA committees that had been established over the years to study ethical standards and practices for various types of professional and scientific activities. That publication has been updated periodically over the years. At this writing, a draft version of the latest proposed ethical guidelines was presented to the APA membership for review and discussion (Jones, 2001). APA and other professional organizations in the United States have made available numerous reference works and publications, all designed to delineate ethical and sound practice in the field of psychological testing and assessment.[3] Along the way, these professional organizations have grappled with some thorny questions such as: Who should be privy to test data? Who should be able to purchase psychological test materials? Who is qualified to administer, score, and interpret psychological tests? What level of expertise in psychometrics is required to be qualified to administer which type of test? A consideration of these important questions follows.

Test-user qualifications   Should anyone be allowed to purchase and use psychological test materials? If not, who should be permitted to use psychological tests? As early as 1950, an APA Committee on Ethical Standards for Psychology published a report called *Ethical Standards for the Distribution of Psychological Tests and Diagnostic Aids.* This report defined three levels of tests in terms of the degree to which the test's use required knowledge of testing and the subject matter of psychology:

- *Level A:* Tests or aids that can adequately be administered, scored, and interpreted with the aid of the manual and a general orientation to the kind of institution or organization in which one is working (for instance, achievement or proficiency tests).

- *Level B:* Tests or aids that require some technical knowledge of test construction and use, and of supporting psychological and educational fields such as statistics, individual differences, psychology of adjustment, personnel psychology, and guidance (for example, aptitude tests, adjustment inventories applicable to normal populations).

- *Level C:* Tests and aids that require substantial understanding of testing and supporting psychological fields, together with supervised experience in the use of these devices (for instance, projective tests, individual mental tests).

The report included descriptions of the general levels of training corresponding to each of the three levels of tests. Although many test publishers continue to use this three-level classification, some do not. In general, professional standards promulgated by APA (AERA, 1999), NASP (2000; Jacob-Timm & Hartshorne, 1998), and other professional organizations are clear that test use should only be assumed by or delegated to persons qualified to use them by virtue of their education, training, and experience. Further, there is an ethical mandate to take reasonable steps to prevent the misuse of the tests and the information they provide. The obligations of professionals who use tests to testtakers are set forth in a document called the *Code of Fair Testing Practices in Education.* Jointly authored and/or sponsored by the Joint Committee of Testing Practices (a coalition of APA, AERA, NCME, the American Association for Measurement and Evaluation

---

3. Unfortunately, while organizations in many other countries have verbalized concern about ethics and standards in testing and assessment, relatively few of these organizations beyond North America have actually taken meaningful and effective action (Gregoire, 1999).

in Counseling and Development, and the American Speech-Language-Hearing Association), this document presents standards for educational test developers in four areas (1) developing/selecting tests, (2) interpreting scores, (3) striving for fairness, and (4) informing testtakers. Readers so inclined may read this document in its entirety on the companion Web site to this textbook at *www.mhhe.com/psychtesting.*

Beyond efforts to promote high standards in testing and assessment among professionals, APA has initiated or assisted in litigation to limit the use of psychological tests to qualified personnel. Skeptics label such measurement-related legal action by APA and state licensing boards as symptomatic of jockeying for turf, with the financial spoils of a measurement monopoly hanging in the balance. A more charitable—and in our view, more realistic—reading of APA's proclamations and actions would be that for the benefit of society at large, it is absolutely critical to have adequately trained measurement professionals, regardless of formal professional affiliations.

Today, psychological tests are used not only by psychologists but by educators, counselors, social workers, physicians, nurses, and other professionals. In reaction to perceived efforts by APA and state psychology boards to restrict the use of psychological tests, the Association of Test Publishers, as well as members of more than 30 professional associations, with a combined membership of more than 520,000 members, have allied to form Fair Access Coalition on Testing (FACT). Incorporated in North Carolina, the mission of this organization is to monitor attempts to restrict access to psychological tests on the national or state level. Beyond monitoring, FACT may also take an active role in legal conflicts, as it did in one California case involving the use of a test called the Myers-Briggs Type Indicator (MBTI). The California Board of Psychology had ruled that the MBTI was a psychological test, and as such could only be administered in California by a California-licensed psychologist. However, that ruling was reversed, in part as the result of the efforts of FACT. FACT argued that:

> (a) the MBTI is widely used by those in many professions and is not just a diagnostic tool but has business, group, religious, educational, and career applications; (b) the MBTI was not developed by a psychologist; (c) because MBTI type assessments are readily available in bookstores and on the Internet, enforcement of "psychologist only" laws against nonpsychologist professionals is not only impossible but also cannot be viewed as public protection. (Clawson, 1997, p. 91)

A psychologist licensing law designed to serve as a model for state legislatures has been available from APA since 1987. The law contains no definition of psychological testing. In the interest of the public, the profession of psychology, and other professions that employ psychological tests, it may now be time for that model legislation to be rewritten, with terms such as "psychological testing" and "psychological assessment" clearly defined and differentiated. In complementary fashion, it would be helpful if terms such as "test-user qualifications" and "psychological assessor qualifications" were clearly defined and differentiated. Part of the problem surrounding legal conflicts regarding psychological test usage stems from confusion of the terms "psychological testing" and "psychological assessment." People who are not considered by society to be professionals may be qualified to be users of psychological tests (psychological testers); however, these same people may not be qualified to engage in psychological assessment. As we argued in the previous chapter, psychological assessment requires certain skills, talents, expertise, and training in psychology and measurement over and above that required to engage in psychological testing. In the past, psychologists have been lax in differentiating the two terms. However, continued laxity may prove to be a costly indulgence given current legislative and judicial trends.

Amid the legal battles, turf wars, and other potential conflicts regarding testing and assessment, there is at least one development that many measurement experts in the field of psychology have found gratifying. In 1993 the American Board of Assessment Psychology (ABAP) was founded with a mandate to identify highly competent assessment psychologists. Applicants for ABAP's Diplomate in Assessment Psychology must meet ABAP's standards in terms of general qualifications (including academic excellence, moral character, scientific integrity, and relevant training and experience) and applied knowledge, as evidenced by a formal oral or written examination and by the work product such as a published test or a report of an assessment. Assessment professionals who are awarded the ABAP Diplomate become members of the American Academy of Assessment Psychology, the education and training arm of ABAP. For more information on ABAP, write to this organization at 1000 Brickell Avenue, Suite 910, Miami, Florida 33131.

Testing people with disabilities   Difficulties analogous to those concerning testtakers from linguistic and cultural minorities are present when testing people with disabling conditions. Specifically, these difficulties may include (1) transforming the test into a form that can be taken by the testtaker, (2) transforming the responses of the testtaker so that they are scorable, and (3) meaningfully interpreting the test data.

The nature of the transformation of the test into a form ready for administration to the individual with disabling conditions will, of course, depend on the nature of the disability. Then, too, some test stimuli do not translate easily. For example, if a critical aspect of a test item contains artwork to be analyzed, there may not be any meaningful way to translate this item for use with testtakers who are blind. With respect to any test converted for use with members of a population for which the test was not originally intended, a number of choices must inevitably be made regarding exactly how the test materials will be modified, what standards of evaluation will be applied, and how the results will be interpreted. As you might expect, professional assessors do not always agree on the answers to such questions.

Another issue on which there is little consensus among professional assessors has to do with the most exceptional case in which the assessee is terminally ill and has requested aid in dying. Because such a request may only be granted contingent on the findings of a psychological evaluation, life or death literally hangs in the balance of such assessments. Some ethical and related issues surrounding this relatively new and rare phenomenon are discussed in this chapter's *Close-up*.

Computerized test administration, scoring, and interpretation   The widespread availability of relatively inexpensive computers has had a great impact on the field of psychological testing. An ever-growing number of psychological tests can be purchased on disk, and their administration, scoring, and interpretation are as simple as pressing keys on a keyboard. In many respects, the relative simplicity, convenience, and range of potential testing activities that computer technology brings to the testing industry have been a great boon. Test users have under one roof the means by which they can quickly administer, score, and interpret a wide range of tests. However, if the growing computer-assisted testing industry looks rosy at first, a more careful look reveals a welter of thorns.

The availability of psychological tests that can be administered, scored, and interpreted by computer may be a temptation to the public. Employers who currently use personnel psychologists to screen prospective employees, for example, might believe it to be more efficient and economical to have evaluations done by computer and supervised by a clerical worker. This raises the question of access to psychological tests—on disk or otherwise. Who should have access? Why?

Another question—this one a step backward from the access question—involves the issue of the soundness of the test software itself. If the test is a computer version of a paper-and-pencil test, how does one know whether the two versions of the test are indeed equivalent? If the test contains a program for providing a narrative interpretation

Life or Death Psychological Assessment

The state of Oregon has the distinction—dubious to some people, depending on one's values—of having enacted the nation's first aid-in-dying law. Oregon's *Death with Dignity Act* (ODDA) provides that a patient with a medical condition thought to give that patient six months or less to live may end his or her own life by voluntarily requesting a lethal dose of medication. The law requires that two physicians corroborate the terminal diagnosis, and that either may request a psychological evaluation of the patient by a state-licensed psychologist or psychiatrist to ensure that the patient is competent to make the life-ending decision, and to rule out impaired judgment due to psychiatric disorder as a reason for the request. Aid-in-dying will be denied to persons "suffering from a psychiatric or psychological disorder, or depression causing impaired judgement" (ODDA, 1997).

The ODDA was hotly debated prior to its passage by referendum, and it remains controversial today. Critics of the law question whether suicide is ever a rational choice under any circumstances, and they fear that such aid-in-dying condoned by the state will serve to destigmatize suicide in general (Callahan, 1994; see also Richman, 1988). It is argued that the first duty of health and mental health professionals is to do no harm (Jennings, 1991). Some fear that professionals willing to testify to almost anything (so-called "hired guns") will corrupt the process and accommodate those who can pay their fees with any professional opinion desired. Critics also point with concern to the experience of the Dutch death-with-dignity legislation. In the Netherlands, relatively few individuals requesting physician-assisted suicide are referred for psychological assessment. Further, the highest court of that land ruled that "in rare cases, physician-assisted suicide is possible even for individuals suffering only from mental problems rather than from physical illnesses" (Abeles & Barleve, 1999, p. 233). On moral and religious grounds, it has been argued that death should be viewed as the sole province of divine and not human intervention.

Supporters of death-with-dignity legislation argue that life-sustaining equipment and methods can extend life beyond a time when it is meaningful, and that the first obligation of health and mental health professionals is to relieve suffering (Latimer, 1991; Quill et al., 1992; Weir, 1992). Additionally, they may point to the dogged determination of people intent on dying and to stories of how many terminally ill people have struggled to end their lives using all kinds of less than sure methods—enduring even greater suffering in the process. In marked contrast to such horror stories, the first patient to die under the ODDA is said to have described

Sigmund Freud
(1856–1939)
It has been said that Sigmund Freud made a "rational decision" to end his life. Suffering from terminal throat cancer, having great difficulty in speaking, and experiencing increasing difficulty in breathing, the founder of psychoanalysis asked his physician for a lethal dose of morphine. For years it has been debated whether a decision to die, even on the part of a terminally ill patient, can ever truly be "rational." Today, in accordance with death-with-dignity legislation, the responsibility for evaluating just how rational such a choice is falls on mental health professionals.

how the family "could relax and say what a wonderful life we had. We could look back at all the lovely things because we knew we finally had an answer" (cited in Farrenkopf & Bryan, 1999, p. 246).

Professional associations such as the American Psychological Association and the American Psychiatric Association have long promulgated codes of ethics requiring the prevention of suicide. The enactment of the law in Oregon has placed clinicians in that state in a unique, if not awkward, position. For years, many of these same clinicians have devoted their

(continued)

Life or Death Psychological Assessment
(continued)

efforts to suicide prevention; now, they have been thrust into the position of being a potential party to, if not a facilitator of, physician-assisted suicide—regardless of how the aid-in-dying process is referred to in the legislation. Note that the Oregon law scrupulously denies that its objective is the legalization of physician-assisted suicide. In fact, the language of the act mandates that action taken under it "shall not, for any purpose, constitute suicide, assisted suicide, mercy killing or homicide, under the law." The framers of the legislation perceived it as a means by which a terminally ill individual could exercise some control over the dying process. Couched in these terms, the sober duty of the clinician drawn into the process may be made more palatable, if not ennobled.

Psychologists and psychiatrists called upon to make death-with-dignity competency evaluations may accept or decline the responsibility (Haley & Lee, 1998). Judging from a recent survey of 423 psychologists in clinical practice in Oregon (Fenn & Ganzini, 1999), many of the psychologists who could be asked to make such a life-or-death assessment might decline to do so. About one-third of the sample responded that an ODDA assessment would be outside the scope of their practice. Another 53% of the sample said they would either refuse to perform the assessment and take no further action, or refuse to perform the assessment themselves and refer the patient to a colleague.

Although firm guidelines as to what an ODDA assessment should entail have yet to be established, Farrenkopf and Bryan (1999) offered several useful suggestions (summarized in the accompanying table).

Clearly, professionals in the field of psychological assessment have much more to do in working through their relatively new role vis-à-vis death-with-dignity legislation. Toward that end, the American Psychological Association established a working group on assisted suicide and end-of-life decisions, charged with making recommendations about this new and ethically perilous challenge.

The ODDA Assessment Process

1. Review of Records and Case History

   With the patient's consent, the assessor will gather records from all relevant sources, including medical and mental health records. A goal is to understand the patient's current functioning in the context of many varied factors ranging from the current medical condition and prognosis to the effects of medication and substance use.

2. Consultation with Treating Professionals

   With the patient's consent, the assessor may consult with the patient's physician and other professionals involved in the case to better understand the patient's current functioning and current situation.

3. Patient Interviews

   Sensitive but thorough interviews with the patient will explore the reasons for the aid-in-dying request, including the pressures and values motivating the request. Other areas to explore include: (a) the patient's understanding of his or her medical condition, the prognosis, and the treatment alternatives; (b) the patient's experience of physical pain, limitations of functioning, and changes over time in cognitive, emotional, and perceptual functioning; (c) the patient's characterization of his or her quality of life, including exploration of related factors including personal identity, role functioning, and self-esteem; and (d) external pressures on the patient, such as personal or familial financial inability to pay for continued treatment.

4. Interviews with Family Members and Significant Others

   With the permission of the patient, separate interviews should be conducted with the patient's family and significant others. One objective is to explore from their perspective how the patient has adjusted in the past to adversity, and how the patient has changed and adjusted to his or her current situation.

5. Assessment of Competence

   Like the other elements of this overview, this aspect of the assessment is complicated and only the barest of guidelines can be presented here. In general, the assessor seeks to understand the patient's reasoning and decision-making process, including all information relevant to the decision and its consequences. Some formal tests of competency are available (Appelbaum & Grisso, 1995a, 1995b; Lavin, 1992), but the clinical and legal applicability of such tests to an ODDA assessment has yet to be established.

6. Assessment of Psychopathology

   To what extent is the decision to end one's life a function of pathological depression, anxiety, dementia, delirium, psychosis, or some other pathological condition? This is a question the assessor addresses using not only interviews but formal tests. Examples of the many possible instruments the assessor might employ include intelligence tests, personality tests, neuropsychological tests, symptom checklists, and depression and anxiety scales; refer to the Appendix in Farrenkopf and Bryan (1999) for a complete list of these tests.

7. Reporting Findings and Recommendations

   Findings, including those related to the patient's mental status and competence, family support and pressures, and anything else relevant to the patient's aid-in-dying request, should be reported. If treatable conditions were found, treatment recommendations relevant to those conditions may be made. Nontreatment types of recommendations may include recommendations for legal advice, estate planning, or other resources. In Oregon, a Psychiatric/Psychological Consultant's Compliance Form with the consultant's recommendations should be completed and sent to the Oregon Health Division.

Adapted from Farrenkopf and Bryan, 1999.

of the test results, how does one know that the interpretation is valid? In Chapter 17, we will explore these and related issues in greater detail.

The Rights of Testtakers

As prescribed by the *Standards,* some of the rights test users accord to testtakers are as follows: the right to **informed consent,** the right to be informed of test findings, the right not to have privacy invaded, the right to the least stigmatizing label, the right to obtain feedback, and the right to have findings held confidential.

The right to informed consent Testtakers have a right to know why they are being evaluated, how the test data will be used, and what, if any, information will be released to whom. The disclosure of such information must, of course, be in language the testtaker can understand. Thus, for a testtaker as young as 2 or 3 years of age or an individual who is mentally retarded with limited language ability, a disclosure before testing might be worded as follows: "I'm going to ask you to try to do some things so that I can see what you know how to do and what things you could use some more help with" (APA, 1985, p. 85). If a testtaker is incapable of providing an informed consent to testing, such consent may be obtained from a parent or a legal representative. Ideally, the consent should be written rather than oral, and the written form should specify (1) the general purpose of the testing, (2) the specific reason it is being undertaken in the present case, and (3) the general type of instruments to be administered. Many school districts now routinely send home such forms before testing children. Such forms typically include the option to have the child assessed privately if the parent so desires. In instances where testing is legally mandated (as in a court-ordered situation), obtaining informed consent to test may be considered more of a courtesy (undertaken in part for reasons of establishing good rapport) than a necessity.

One gray area with respect to the testtaker's right of fully informed consent before testing involves research and experimental situations wherein the examiner's complete disclosure of all facts pertinent to the testing (including the experimenter's hypothesis and so forth) might irrevocably contaminate the test data. In such instances, professional discretion is in order; testtakers might be given a minimum amount of information before the testing (for example, "This testing is being undertaken as part of an experiment on obedience to authority. . . .") with a full and complete disclosure and debriefing made after the testing. As Rupert et al. (1999) observed, due attention must be given to informed consent and related issues regarding the protection of the rights and well-being of people who contribute to training in assessment. One such related issue is the right to feedback.

The right to be informed of test findings In a bygone era, the inclination of many psychological assessors, particularly many clinicians, was to tell testtakers as little as possible about the nature of their performance on a particular test or test battery and in no case to disclose diagnostic conclusions that could arouse anxiety or precipitate a crisis. This orientation was reflected in at least one authoritative text where testers were advised to keep information about test results superficial and focus only on "positive" findings so that the examinee would leave the test session feeling "pleased and satisfied" (Klopfer et al., 1954, p. 15). But all of that has changed, and giving realistic information about test performance to examinees is not only ethically and legally mandated, but may be useful from a therapeutic perspective as well (see Berg, 1985).

Testtakers have a right to be informed, in language they can understand, of the nature of the findings with respect to a test that they took. They are also entitled to know what recommendations are being made as a consequence of the test data. If the test results, findings, or recommendations made on the basis of test data are being voided for any reason (such as irregularities in the test administration), testtakers have a right to know that, as well.

Because of the possibility of untoward consequences as a result of providing individuals with information about themselves—their ability, their lack of ability, their personality, their values—the communication of results of a psychological test is a most important part of the evaluation process. With sensitivity to the situation, the test user will inform the testtaker (and the parent or the legal representative or both) of the purpose of the test, the meaning of the score relative to those of other testtakers, and the possible limitations and margins of error of the test. And regardless of whether such reporting is done in person or in writing, a qualified psychologist should ideally be available to answer any further questions testtakers (or their parents) have about the test scores. Further, the resource of counseling should ideally be available for testtakers who become distraught at learning how they scored on a particular test.

The right not to have privacy invaded   The concept of **privacy** "recognizes the freedom of the individual to pick and choose for himself the time, circumstances, and particularly the extent to which he wishes to share or withhold from others his attitudes, beliefs, behavior, and opinions" (Shah, 1969, p. 57). When people in court proceedings "take the Fifth" and refuse to answer a question put to them on the grounds that the answer might be self-incriminating, they are asserting a right of privacy provided by the Fifth Amendment to the Constitution. The information withheld in such a manner is termed *privileged;* it is information that is protected by law from disclosure in a legal proceeding. State statutes have extended the concept of **privileged information** to parties who communicate with each other in the context of certain relationships, including the lawyer-client relationship, the doctor-patient relationship, the priest-penitent relationship, and the husband-wife relationship. In most states, privilege is also accorded to the psychologist-client relationship. Privilege is extended to parties in these relationships because it has been deemed that the parties' right to privacy serves a greater public interest than would be served by having their communications vulnerable to revelation during legal proceedings. Stated another way, it is for society's good if people feel confident that they can talk freely to their attorneys, clergy, physicians, psychologists, and spouses. Professionals such as psychologists who are parties to such special relationships have a legal and ethical duty to keep their clients' communications confidential. Distinguishing **confidentiality** from *privilege,* Jagim, Wittman, and Noll (1978, p. 459) pointed out that whereas "confidentiality concerns matters of communication outside the courtroom, privilege protects clients from disclosure in judicial proceedings."

Privilege is not absolute; there are occasions when a court can deem the disclosure of certain information necessary and can order the disclosure of that information. Should the psychologist or other professional so ordered refuse to make the ordered disclosure, he or she does so under the threat of going to jail, being fined, or both. Note also that the privilege in the psychologist-client relationship belongs to the client; the competent client can direct the psychologist to disclose information to some third party (such as an attorney or an insurance carrier), and the psychologist is obligated to make the disclosure. In some rare instances, the psychologist may be ethically (if not legally) compelled to disclose information if that information will prevent harm to either the client or some endangered third party. An illustrative case would be the situation where a client details a plan to commit suicide or homicide. In such an instance, the psychologist would be legally and ethically compelled to take reasonable action to prevent such an occurrence—the preservation of life being deemed an objective more important than the nonrevelation of privileged and confidential communications. The guiding principle here was set forth in the 1981 revision of APA's *Ethical Principles of Psychologists:*

Psychologists have a primary obligation to respect the confidentiality of information obtained from persons in the course of their work as psychologists. They reveal such information to others only with the consent of the person or the person's legal representative, except in those unusual circumstances in which not to do so would result in clear danger to the person or to others.

Of course, determining when there exists one of "those unusual circumstances . . . which . . . would result in clear danger to the person or to others" is no easy matter. Further, a wrong judgment on the part of the clinician might lead to premature disclosure of confidential information and untoward consequences for not only the examinee and the examiner but the profession as well. A landmark court case that set forth the principle that "protective privilege ends where the public peril begins" was the 1974 case *Tarasoff v. Regents of University of California.* In that case, a therapy patient had made known to his psychologist his intention to kill an unnamed but readily identifiable girl two months before the murder. The court in *Tarasoff* held that the therapist had a duty to warn the endangered girl of her peril. The *Tarasoff* precedent was expanded upon by the Vermont Supreme Court in *Peck v. the Counseling Service of Addison County, Inc.* (Stone, 1986). A 1983 United States Court of Appeals (9th Circuit) decision in *Jablonski v. United States* placed a burden upon mental health professionals of being able to predict violent behavior even if no threat of violence had been made; key here was matching the profile of the intended victim with the profile of prior victims. Buckner and Firestone (2000) reviewed the effects that the landmark *Tarasoff* case and the "duty to warn" has had on clinical practice.

In recent years, there has been a great deal of debate about a psychologist's duty to warn in cases involving HIV-positive clients and assessees (Buckner & Firestone, 2000; Melchert & Patterson, 1999; Melton, 1988; Perry, 1989). Most states have enacted legislation that specifies limits to confidentiality regarding an HIV-positive diagnosis. However, at this writing, only one state has enacted legislation designed to protect mental health professionals from liability in the event of a good-faith disclosure to a third party who may be at risk of HIV infection (Montana Health and Safety Code, 1997). Basic issues regarding the concepts of confidentiality, privilege, and the duty to warn have been discussed in detail elsewhere by Cohen (1979; Cohen & Mariano, 1982).

The right to the least stigmatizing label   The *Standards* advise that the least stigmatizing labels should always be assigned when reporting test results. To better appreciate the need for this standard, consider the case of Jo Ann Iverson.[4] Jo Ann was 9 years old and suffering from claustrophobia when her mother brought her to a state hospital in Blackfoot, Idaho, for a psychological evaluation. Arden Frandsen, a psychologist employed part-time at the hospital, conducted an evaluation of Jo Ann, during the course of which he administered a Stanford-Binet Intelligence test. In his report, Frandsen classified Jo Ann as "feeble-minded, at the high-grade moron level of general mental ability." Following a request from Jo Ann's school guidance counselor, a copy of the psychological report was forwarded to the school—and embarrassing rumors concerning Jo Ann's mental condition began to circulate.

Jo Ann's mother, Carmel Iverson, brought a libel (defamation) suit against Frandsen on behalf of her daughter.[5] Mrs. Iverson lost the lawsuit, the court ruling in part that the

---

4. See *Iverson v. Frandsen,* 237 F. 2d 898 (Idaho, 1956) or Cohen (1979, pp. 149–150).

5. An interesting though tangential aspect of this case was the argument advanced by Iverson that she had brought her child in for claustrophobia and, given that fact, the administration of an intelligence test was unauthorized and beyond the scope of the consultation. However, the defendant proved to the satisfaction of the court that the administration of the Stanford-Binet was necessary to determine if Jo Ann had the mental capacity to respond to psychotherapy.

psychological evaluation "was a professional report made by a public servant in good faith, representing his best judgment." But although Mrs. Iverson did not prevail in her lawsuit, we can certainly sympathize with her anguish at the thought of her daughter going through life with a label such as "high-grade moron"—this despite the fact that the psychologist had probably merely copied that designation from the test manual. We would also add that, in retrospect, it might have been possible to prevail in a suit against the guidance counselor for breach of confidentiality, because there appeared to be uncontested testimony that it was from the guidance counselor's office that rumors concerning Jo Ann first emanated.

The right to have findings held confidential   Testtakers have a right to have their test results held confidential and be released only to third parties who have a legitimate need for access to those records—and such release must also be contingent on the informed consent of the testtaker. Whereas the word *confidentiality* was once thought of solely as a matter of professional ethics, it is now true that "case law, statutes, and licensing regulations in many states have given this standard of conduct legal status as well. For example, a practitioner is legally liable for breach of confidentiality" (Swoboda et al., 1978, p. 449).

Test users must take reasonable precautions to safeguard test records. If these data are stored in a filing cabinet, the cabinet should be locked and preferably made of steel. If these data are stored in a computer, electronic safeguards must be taken to ensure only authorized access. We might also mention here that it is not a good idea for individuals and institutions to store records *in perpetuity*. Rather, the individual or institution should have a reasonable policy covering (1) the storage of test data—when, if at any time, these records will be deemed to be outdated, invalid, or useful only from an academic perspective, and (2) the conditions under which requests for release of records to a third party would be entertained.

While on the subject of the rights of testtakers, let's not forget about the rights—of sorts—of students of testing and assessment, including the right to learn more about technical aspects of measurement. Exercise that right in the succeeding chapters.

Self-Assessment

Test your understanding of elements of this chapter by seeing if you can explain each of the following terms, expressions, abbreviations, events, or names in terms of their significance in the context of psychological testing and assessment:

Albemarle Paper Company v. Moody

Binet

Cattell

Code of Fair Testing Practices in Education

confidentiality

culture

Darwin

Daubert v. Merrell Dow Pharmaceuticals

Debra P. v. Turlington

Diana v. State Board of Education

duty to warn

ethics

Frye v. the United States

Galton

General Electric v. Joiner

Griggs v. Duke Power Company

Hobson v. Hansen

informed consent

Jensen

Kumho Tire Company v. Carmichael

Larry P. v. Riles

laws

Morgan

Murray

ODDA

Personal Data Sheet

privilege

Public Law 105-17

Rorschach

Sputnik

*Standards for Educational and
    Psychological Testing*

Tarasoff

Wechsler

Witmer

Woodworth

World War I

World War II

Wundt

3

A Statistics Refresher

From the red-pencil number circled at the top of your first spelling test to the computer printout of your college entrance examination scores, tests and test scores touch your life. They seem to reach out from the paper and shake your hand when you do well and punch you in the face when you do poorly. They can point you toward or away from a particular school or curriculum. They can help you to identify strengths and weaknesses in your physical and mental abilities. They can accompany you on job interviews and influence a job or career choice. Test scores are indeed a very important part of your life. But what makes those numbers meaningful?

In your role as a student, you have probably found that the nature of your relationship to tests has been primarily that of a testtaker. But as a psychologist, teacher, researcher, or employer, you may find that the primary nature of your relationship with tests is that of a test user—the person who breathes life and meaning into test scores by applying the knowledge and skill needed to interpret them appropriately. You may one day create a test, whether in an academic or a business setting, and then have the responsibility for reasonably scoring and interpreting the data derived. An understanding of the theory underlying test use and principles of test score interpretation is essential to the prospective test user.

Test scores are frequently expressed as numbers, and statistical tools are used to describe, make inferences from, and draw conclusions about numbers.[1] In this statistics refresher, we cover scales of measurement, tabular and graphic presentations of data, measures of central tendency, measures of variability, and standard scores. If these statistics-related terms look painfully familiar to you, we ask your indulgence and remind you that overlearning is the key to retention. However, if these terms are unfamiliar, we urge you to get—and spend ample time reviewing—a good elementary statistics text. The brief review of statistical concepts that follows is designed only to supplement an introductory course in statistics.

---

1. Of course, a test score may be expressed in other forms, such as a letter grade or a pass/fail designation. Unless stated otherwise, words such as *test score, test data, test results,* and *test scores* will be used throughout this book in reference to numeric descriptions of test performance.

Scales of Measurement

Measurement is the act of assigning numbers or symbols to characteristics of objects (people, events—whatever) according to rules. The rules used in assigning numbers are guidelines for representing the magnitude (or some other characteristic) of the object being measured. An example of a measurement rule is "Assign the number 12 to all lengths that are exactly the same length as a 12-inch ruler." A **scale** is a set of numbers (or other symbols) whose properties model empirical properties of the objects to which the numbers are assigned. Various types of scales exist. One way of labeling a scale is to label it with reference to the type of variable being measured. Thus a scale used to measure a continuous variable might be referred to as a "continuous scale," whereas a scale used to measure a discrete variable might be referred to as a "discrete scale." If, for example, research subjects were to be categorized as being either female or male, the categorization scale would be said to be discrete in nature because it would not be meaningful to categorize a subject as anything other than a female or a male.[2] By contrast, a continuous scale exists when it is possible theoretically to divide any of the values of the scale. A distinction must be made, however, between what is theoretically possible and what is practically desirable; the units into which a continuous scale will actually be divided may depend on the purpose of the measurement. Thus, although it may be theoretically possible to divide measurements of length into millimeters or even micrometers, it may be impractical to do so if the purpose of the measurement is to install venetian blinds.

Measurement using continuous scales always involves some error. For example, the length of the window you measured to be 35.5 inches could, in reality, be 35.7 inches; it's just that your measuring scale is conveniently marked off in more gross gradations of measurement. Most scales used in psychological testing are continuous in nature and therefore can be expected to contain error. A consideration of sources of error in testing was presented in Chapter 1. Error will arise from the mere use of a continuous scale; the number or score used to characterize the trait being measured on a continuous scale should be thought of as an approximation of the "real" number. Thus, for example, a score of 25 on some test of anxiety should not be thought of as a precise measure of anxiety but rather as an approximation of the real anxiety score had the measuring instrument been calibrated to yield such a score. In such a case, perhaps the score of 25 is an approximation of a real score of 24.7 or 25.44. In contrast to numbers or scores used to characterize traits in continuous scales, the numbers or scores used in discrete scales are presumed to be exact.

Measurement can be further categorized with respect to the amount of quantitative information the assigned numbers possess. It is generally agreed that there are four different levels or scales of measurement. Numbers at different levels or scales of measurement convey different kinds of information. In testing and in research in general, it is important to know which scales of measurement are being employed, for the kind of scale will be one factor in determining which statistical manipulations of the data would or would not be appropriate.[3]

---

2. We acknowledge that if all females were labeled "1" and all males were labeled "2," some people, most visibly individuals born with a gender-related genetic abnormality, might seem to qualify as a 1.5. Such exceptions aside, however, all cases on a discrete scale must lie on a point on the scale, and it is theoretically impossible for a case to lie between two points on the scale.

3. For the purposes of our statistics refresher, we present what Nunnally (1978) called the "fundamentalist" view of measurement scales—a view that "holds that 1. there are distinct types of measurement scales into which all possible measures of attributes can be classified, 2. each measure has some 'real' characteristics that permit its proper classification, and 3. once a measure is classified, the classification specifies the types of mathematical analyses that can be employed with the measure" (p. 24). Nunnally and others have acknowledged that alternatives to the "fundamentalist" view may also be viable.

The French word for black is *noir* (pronounced "n'wăre"). We bring this up here only to call attention to the fact that this French word is a useful acronym for remembering the four levels or scales of measurement; each letter in *noir* is the first letter of each of the succeedingly more rigorous levels. *N* stands for "nominal," *o* for "ordinal," *i* for "interval," and *r* for "ratio" scales.

Nominal Scales

Nominal scales are the simplest form of measurement. These scales involve classification or categorization based on one or more distinguishing characteristics where all things measured must be placed into mutually exclusive and exhaustive categories. For example, people may be characterized by gender in a study designed to compare performance of men and women on some test. In such a study, all males might be labeled "men," "1," "B," or some other symbol, and all females might be labeled "women," "2," or "A." In the specialty area of clinical psychology, one often-used nominal scale is the American Psychiatric Association's *Diagnostic and Statistical Manual of Mental Disorders IV (DSM-IV)*. Each disorder listed in the manual is assigned its own number. Thus, for example, the number 303.00 identifies alcohol intoxication and the number 307.00 identifies stuttering. But these numbers are used exclusively for classification purposes and cannot be meaningfully added, subtracted, ranked, or averaged (the number 305 does *not* equal an intoxicated stutterer).

Individual items may also employ nominal scaling. Items found on an employment application are common examples:

Instructions: Answer either "yes" or "no."

Are you actively contemplating suicide?

Are you currently under professional care for a psychiatric disorder?

Have you ever been convicted of a felony crime?

In each case, a "yes" or "no" response results in the placement into one of a set of mutually exclusive groups: suicidal or not, under care for psychiatric disorder or not, and felon or not. Arithmetic operations that can legitimately be performed with nominal data include counting for the purpose of determining how many cases fall into each category and some consequential determination of proportion or percentages.[4]

Ordinal Scales

Like nominal scales, **ordinal scales** permit classification. However, in addition to classification, rank-ordering on some characteristic is also permissible with ordinal scales. In business and organizational settings, job applicants may be rank-ordered according to their desirability for a position. In the clinical setting, people on a waiting list for psychotherapy may be rank-ordered according to their need for treatment. In these examples, individuals are compared with others and assigned a rank (perhaps "1" to the best applicant or the most needy wait-listed client, "2" to the next, and so forth).

---

4. Nominal data may also be analyzed by means of nonparametric statistical techniques, log linear modeling, and other techniques (see Gokhale & Kullback, 1978).

Although he may have never used the term "ordinal scale," Alfred Binet, the developer of the intelligence test that today bears his name, believed strongly that the data derived from an intelligence test are ordinal in nature. He emphasized that what he tried to do in the test was not *measure* people as one might measure a person's height, but merely *classify* (and rank) people on the basis of their performance on the tasks. Binet made this point clear:

> I have not sought . . . to sketch a method of measuring, in the physical sense of the word, but only a method of classification of individuals. The procedures which I have indicated will, if perfected, come to classify a person before or after such another person, or such another series of persons; but I do not believe that one may measure one of the intellectual aptitudes in the sense that one measures a length or a capacity. Thus, when a person studied can retain seven figures after a single audition, one can class him, from the point of his memory for figures, after the individual who retains eight figures under the same conditions, and before those who retain six. It is a classification, not a measurement . . . we do not measure, we classify. (Binet, cited in Varon, 1936, p. 41)

Assessment instruments applied to the individual subject may also use an ordinal form of measurement. The Rokeach Value Survey uses such an approach, with a list of personal values (like freedom, happiness, and wisdom) to be put in order according to their perceived importance to the testtaker (Rokeach, 1973). If a set of ten values is rank-ordered, the testtaker may assign a value of "1" to the most important and "10" to the least important.

Ordinal scales imply nothing about how much greater one ranking is than another. Even though ordinal scales typically employ numbers to represent the rank ordering, the numbers do not indicate units of measurement: The difference between the best and the second-best job applicants may be very small, but there may be a large difference between them and the third-best applicant. Likewise, a person completing the Rokeach Value Survey may be able to identify easily the characteristic ranked "1" as the most important value but might struggle with the ordering of the next three items, suggesting that the strength of these values is similar. Furthermore, ordinal scales have no absolute zero point; without units, zero is without meaning. In the case of values, for example, each item on the test is assumed to be of some value to the testtaker.

Because unequal units of measurement may exist in ordinal scales, and because there is no zero point, the ways in which data from such scales can be treated statistically are limited. One cannot average the qualifications of the first- and third-ranked job applicants, for example, and expect to come out with the qualifications of the second-ranked applicant.

Interval Scales

In addition to the features of nominal and ordinal scales, **interval scales** contain equal intervals between numbers; each unit on the scale is exactly equal to any other unit on the scale. But, like ordinal scales, interval scales contain no absolute zero point. With interval scales, we have reached a level of measurement at which it *is* possible to take the average of a set of measurements and get a meaningful result.

Intelligence scale scores are often taken to be at an interval level of measurement. The difference in intellectual ability represented by IQs of 80 and 100, for example, is thought to be similar to that existing between IQs of 100 and 120. However, if an individual were to achieve an IQ of 0 (something that is not even possible on many intelligence scales), that would not mean an absence of intelligence.

Ratio Scales

In addition to having all the properties of nominal, ordinal, and interval measurement, a **ratio scale** has a true zero point. All mathematical operations can meaningfully be performed because there exist equal intervals between the numbers on the scale as well as a true or absolute zero point.[5]

In psychology, ratio-level measurement is used on some items assessing the functioning of the nervous system. An example would be the amount of pressure one can exert with one's grip: Someone who can exert 20 pounds of pressure is exerting twice as much as one who can exert 10. Here, a meaningful zero point exists, representing individuals incapable of squeezing at all, perhaps because of paralysis in the hand. Some intelligence test items use ratio-level measurement. The time taken to complete a puzzle is an example, with 30 seconds being half the time taken to complete the puzzle in 60 seconds. Here, one can meaningfully talk about a zero point in theory, though in reality no subject will complete the puzzle that quickly.

Measurement Scales in Psychology

The ordinal level of measurement is most frequently used in psychology. As Kerlinger (1973, p. 439) put it, "Intelligence, aptitude, and personality test scores are, *basically and strictly speaking*, ordinal. They indicate with more or less accuracy not the amount of intelligence, aptitude, and personality traits of individuals, but rather the rank-order positions of the individuals." Kerlinger allowed that "most psychological and educational scales approximate interval equality fairly well," though he cautioned that if ordinal measurements were treated as if they were interval measurements, the test user must "be constantly alert to the possibility of *gross* inequality of intervals" (pp. 440–441).

Why would psychologists want to treat their assessment data as interval when those data would be better described as ordinal? Why not just say that they are ordinal? The attraction of interval measurement for users of psychological tests is in the flexibility with which such data can be manipulated statistically, a flexibility that is not available with ordinal data. What kinds of manipulation are we talking about? The remainder of this statistics refresher discusses ways in which test data can be described in a manageable, interpretable form, using computations like the mean, or average, and employing tables and graphs. Some of these techniques can be used if data are interval but not if they are ordinal. We continue with a review of the various ways test data can be described—as well as some ways it should not (see *Everyday Psychometrics*).

Describing Data

Suppose you have magically changed places with the professor teaching this course, and you have just administered an examination that consists of 100 multiple-choice items (where one point is awarded for each correct answer). The distribution of scores for the

---

5. Note that the distinction between ordinal scales and interval scales is the result of the empirical observations on which numerical assignments are based. The difference between interval and ratio scales seems more closely related to theoretical considerations related to the attribute being measured. It has been suggested that another useful scale of measurement lies between the interval and ratio level of measurement (Narens & Luce, 1986).

Consumer (of Graphed Data), Beware!

One picture is worth a thousand words," and one purpose of representing data in graphic form is to convey information at a glance. However, although two graphs may be accurate with respect to the data they represent, their pictures—and the impression drawn from a glance at them—may be vastly different. As an example, consider the following hypothetical scenario involving a hamburger restaurant chain we'll call "The Charred House."

The Charred House chain serves very charbroiled, microscopically thin hamburgers formed in the shape of little, triangular houses. In the ten-year period since its founding in 1993, the company has sold, on average, 100 million burgers per year. On the chain's tenth anniversary, The Charred House distributes a press release proudly announcing "Over a Billion Served."

Reporters from two business-type publications set out to research and write a feature article on this hamburger restaurant chain. Working solely from sales figures as compiled from annual reports to the shareholders, Reporter 1 focuses her story on the differences in yearly sales. Her article is titled "A Billion Served—But Charred House Sales Fluctuate From Year to Year," and its graphic illustration is reprinted here.

Quite a different picture of the company emerges from Reporter 2's story, titled "A Billion Served—And Charred House Sales Are as Steady as Ever," and its accompanying graph. The latter story is based on a diligent analysis of comparable data for the same number of hamburger chains in the same areas of the country over the same time period. While researching the story, Reporter 2 learned that yearly fluctuations in sales is common to the entire industry and that the annual fluctuations observed in the Charred House figures were—relative to other chains—insignificant.

Compare the graphs that accompanied each story. Although both are accurate insofar as they are based on the correct numbers, the impression they are likely to leave is quite different.

Incidentally, custom dictates that the intersection of the two axes of a graph be at 0, and that all of the points on the vertical axis (also known as the *ordinate* or the *Y*-axis) be in equal and proportional intervals from 0. This custom is followed in Reporter 2's story, where the first point on the ordinate is 10 units more than 0, and each succeeding point is also 10 more units away from 0. However, the custom is vio-

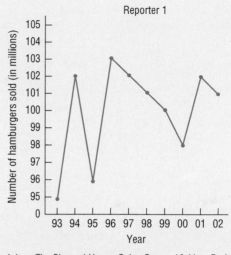

(a)   The Charred House Sales Over a 10-Year Period

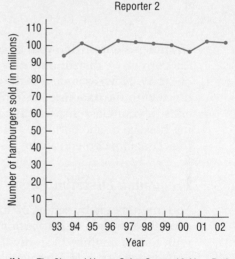

(b)   The Charred House Sales Over a 10-Year Period

lated in Reporter 1's story, where the first point on the ordinate is 95 units more than 0, and each succeeding point increases only by 1. The fact that the custom is violated in Reporter 1's story should serve as a warning to evaluate pictorial representations of data all the more critically.

Table 3–1	Student	Score (number correct)
Data from Your Measurement Course Test	Judy	78
	Joe	67
	Lee-Wu	69
	Miriam	63
	Valerie	85
	Diane	72
	Henry	92
	Esperanza	67
	Paula	94
	Martha	62
	Bill	61
	Homer	44
	Robert	66
	Michael	87
	Jorge	76
	Mary	83
	"Mousey"	42
	Barbara	82
	John	84
	Donna	51
	Uriah	69
	Leroy	61
	Ronald	96
	Vinnie	73
	Bianca	79

25 students enrolled in your class could theoretically range from 0 (none correct) to 100 (all correct). A **distribution** may be defined as a set of test scores arrayed for recording or study. Now, assume it is the day after the examination and you are sitting in your office with the data listed in Table 3–1. One task at hand is to communicate the test results to your class in a way that will best assist each individual student in understanding how he or she performed on the test in comparison with all the other testtakers in the class. How do you accomplish this objective?

Frequency Distributions

You might begin by setting up a distribution of the raw scores; rather than just a listing of all the raw data, a distribution will help you compare the performance of one student with that of another. One way the scores could be distributed is by the frequency with which they occur. In a **frequency distribution,** all scores are listed alongside the number of times each score occurred. The scores might be listed in tabular or graphic form. Table 3–2 lists the frequency of occurrence of each score in one column and the score itself in the other column.

Before we see how these data would look in graphic form, we should note that there exists another kind of frequency distribution, a **grouped frequency distribution,** which further summarizes the data. In a grouped frequency distribution, test-score intervals, also called *class intervals*, replace the actual test scores. The number of class intervals used and the size or "width" of each class interval (that is, the range of test scores contained in each class interval) will be a matter left for you to decide as regards the data in need of summarizing; the width that most conveniently summarizes the data will be best. But how do you decide?

Table 3–2	Score	f (frequency)
Frequency Distribution of Scores from Your Test	96	1
	94	1
	92	1
	87	1
	85	1
	84	1
	83	1
	82	1
	79	1
	78	1
	76	1
	73	1
	72	1
	69	2
	67	2
	66	1
	63	1
	62	1
	61	2
	51	1
	44	1
	42	1

Table 3–3	Class Interval	f (frequency)
A Grouped Frequency Distribution	95–99	1
	90–94	2
	85–89	2
	80–84	3
	75–79	3
	70–74	2
	65–69	5
	60–64	4
	55–59	0
	50–54	1
	45–49	0
	40–44	2

In most instances, a decision as to the size of a class interval in a grouped frequency distribution is made on the basis of convenience and with the knowledge that virtually any decision will represent a trade-off; a convenient, easy-to-read summary of the data is the trade-off for the loss of detail. To what extent must the data be summarized? How important is detail? These types of questions must be reckoned with. In the grouped frequency distribution in Table 3–3, the test scores have been grouped—simply on the basis of the need for convenience in reading the data as opposed to the need for detail—into 12 class intervals with each class interval being equal to 5 points.[6] The highest class

6. Technically, each number on such a scale would be viewed as ranging from as much as 0.5 below it to as much as 0.5 above it. For example, the "real" but hypothetical width of the class interval ranging from 95 to 99 would be the difference between 99.5 and 94.5, or 5. The true upper and lower limits of the class intervals presented in the table would be respectively 99.5 and 39.5.

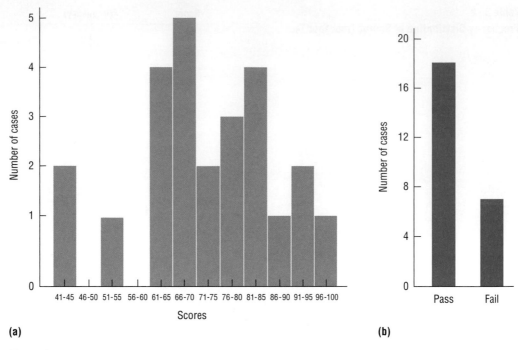

(a)   (b)

Figure 3–1
Graphic Illustrations of Data from Table 3–3

A histogram (a), a bar graph (b), and a frequency polygon (c) all may be used to graphically convey information about test performance. Of course, the labeling of the bar graph and the specific nature of the data conveyed by it depend on the variables of interest; in (b) the variable of interest is the number of students who passed the test (assuming for the purpose of this illustration that a raw score of 65 or higher had been arbitrarily designated in advance to be a passing grade).

interval (95 to 99) and the lowest class interval (40 to 44) are referred to respectively as the upper and lower limits of the distribution.

Frequency distributions of test scores can also be illustrated graphically. A **graph** is a diagram or chart composed of lines, points, bars, or other symbols that describe and illustrate data. With a good graph, the place of a single score in relation to a distribution of test scores can be grasped easily by a casual inspection of the data. Three kinds of graphs used to illustrate frequency distributions are the histogram, the bar graph, and the frequency polygon (Figure 3–1). A **histogram** is a graph with vertical lines drawn at the true limits of each test score (or class interval) forming a series of contiguous rectangles. It is customary for the test scores (either the single scores or the midpoints of the class intervals) to be placed along the graph's horizontal axis (also referred to as the abscissa or X-axis), and numbers indicative of the frequency of occurrence are placed along the graph's vertical axis (also referred to as the ordinate or Y-axis). In a **bar graph,** numbers indicative of frequency also appear on the Y-axis, and reference to some categorization (such as yes/no/maybe, male/female, and so forth) appears on the X-axis; here the rectangular bars typically are not contiguous. Data illustrated in a **frequency polygon** are expressed by a continuous line connecting the points where test scores or class intervals (as indicated on the X-axis) meet frequencies (as indicated on the Y-axis). As illustrated in *Everyday Psychometrics,* graphs may obscure or distort information as well as convey it.

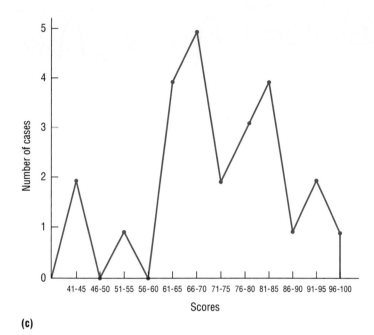

(c)

Returning to the question posed earlier—the one in which you are playing the role of instructor and must communicate the test results to your students—which type of graph would best serve your purpose? Why?

As we continue our review of descriptive statistics, you may wish to return to your role of professor and formulate your response to challenging related questions such as "Which measure(s) of central tendency shall I use to convey this information?" and "Which measure(s) of variability would convey the information best?"

Frequency distributions of test scores may assume any of a number of different shapes (Figure 3–2)—this is because of a variety of factors, including the variable(s) being researched, the measurement technique(s), and the sampling procedures. The "normal" or bell-shaped curve is of particular interest to us, and it is discussed in greater detail later in this chapter. Distributions are also described according to characteristics such as their central tendency, variability, skewness, and kurtosis.

Measures of Central Tendency

A **measure of central tendency** is a statistic that indicates the average or middle-most score between the extreme scores in a distribution. The center of a distribution can be defined in different ways. Perhaps the most commonly used measure of central tendency is the *arithmetic mean* (or simply, **mean**), referred to in everyday language as the "average." The mean takes into account the actual numerical value of every score. In special instances, such as when there are only a few scores and one or two of the scores are extreme in relation to the remaining ones, a measure of central tendency other than the mean may be desirable. Other measures of central tendency we review include the *median* and the *mode.* Note that in the formulas that follow, the standard statistical

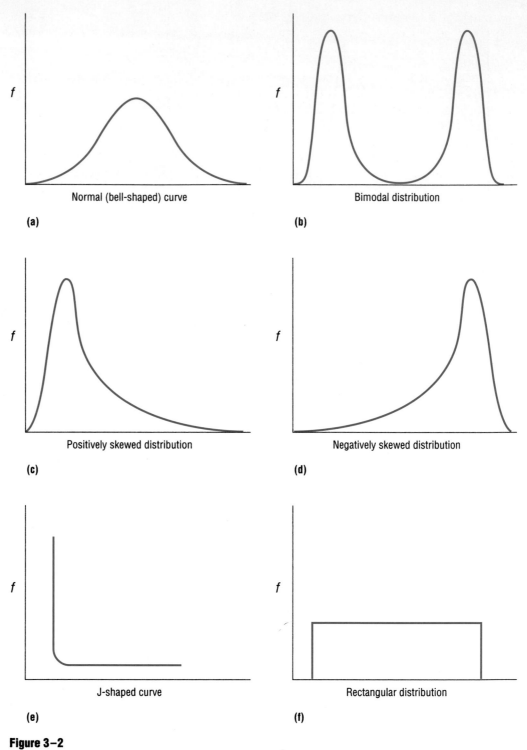

Figure 3–2
Shapes Frequency Distributions Can Take

shorthand called "summation notation" (*summation* meaning "the sum of") is used. The Greek uppercase letter sigma, Σ, is the symbol used to signify "sum"; if X represents a test score, then the symbol ΣX means "add all the test scores."

The arithmetic mean   The **arithmetic mean,** denoted by the symbol $\overline{X}$ (pronounced "X bar") is equal to the sum of the observations (or test scores in this case) divided by the number of observations. Symbolically written, the formula for the arithmetic mean is $\overline{X} = \Sigma X/n$, where n equals the number of observations or test scores. The arithmetic mean is typically the most appropriate measure of central tendency for interval or ratio data when the distributions are believed to be approximately normal. An arithmetic mean can also be computed from a frequency distribution. The formula for doing this is

$$\overline{X} = \frac{\Sigma fX}{n}$$

where ΣfX means "multiply the frequency of each score by its corresponding score and sum."

As we explain certain concepts, we will urge you to get involved with the subject matter by doing more than merely reading. Your learning may be facilitated if you take an extra step and become a participant-observer. Begin by using the two arithmetic mean formulas we've just discussed to compute the arithmetic mean for your examination data (contained in Table 3–1 and Table 3–2). As a check on your understanding of how to apply the formulas, note that you should get the same answer using either one.

The median   The **median,** defined as the middle score in a distribution, is another commonly used measure of central tendency. Determine the median of a distribution of scores by ordering the scores in a list by magnitude—in either ascending or descending order. When the total number of scores ordered is an odd number, the median will be the score that is exactly in the middle, with one-half of the remaining scores lying above it and the other half of the remaining scores lying below it. When the total number of scores ordered is an even number, the median can be calculated by determining the arithmetic mean of the two middle scores. For example, suppose that ten people took a preemployment word processing test at The Rochester Wrenchworks (TRW) Corporation and obtained the following scores, presented here in descending order:

66

65

61

59

53

52

41

36

35

32

The median in these data would be computed by obtaining the average (that is, the arithmetic mean) of the two middle scores, 53 and 52 (which would be equal to 52.5). The median is an appropriate measure of central tendency for ordinal, interval, and ratio data, especially if data are highly skewed.

Remember Kathy from the Chapter 1 *Close-up?* You may recall that she applied for a job at TRW and was administered seven word processing tests over the course of seven business days. TRW's policy is not to hire word processors unless they can accurately word-process 50 words per minute. Kathy's word processing scores in words per minute are reprinted below. Should she be hired?

52   55   39   56   35   50   54

If you were to obtain the arithmetic mean for this distribution of scores, the resulting figure would be below 50. Thus, if the company's policy were to routinely take an average of word processing test scores and reject people whose average score did not meet the minimum of 50 words per minute, Kathy would have to be dismissed from further consideration. However, if you as the personnel officer had some discretion, you might have used the median and not the mean as the preferred measure of central tendency in this situation. You would have grouped these scores from highest to lowest and located the middle score in the distribution:[7]

56

55

54

52   (the middle score)

50

39

35

If Kathy's résumé looked good in all respects, if the company needed to hire clerks immediately, or for any other good reason, a decision to hire Kathy could be justified by the use of the median as the measure of central tendency—in this case, as a measure of Kathy's word processing ability. The median may well be the most appropriate measure to use with such a distribution of scores. On the days when Kathy's score was in the thirties, she might not have been feeling well, the word processor used for the test might not have been operating properly, or other factors could have influenced the score. Whereas the mean is the preferred measure of central tendency for symmetrical distributions, the median is the preferred measure for skewed distributions like this.

The mode   The most frequently occurring score in a distribution of scores is the **mode**.[8] As an example, determine the mode for the following scores obtained on the TRW test by another applicant for a word processing position, Bruce:

43   46   45   51   42   44   51

The most frequently occurring score in this distribution of scores is 51. Again, place yourself in the role of the corporate personnel officer. Would you hire Bruce? If your hiring guideline dictated that you use the arithmetic mean, you would not hire him, be-

---

7. Consult an appropriate statistics text for specialized formulas used to calculate the median of (a) a large, unwieldy group of scores (that is, a group of scores so large it would be impractical merely to order them in ascending order and locate the middle score), (b) a grouped frequency distribution, or (c) a distribution where various scores are identical.

8. If adjacent scores occur equally often and more often than other scores, custom dictates that the mode be referred to as the "average."

cause his mean performance falls below 50 words per minute. But even if you had the leeway to use another measure of central tendency, you still might not hire him; even a casual look at these data indicates that Bruce's typical performance would fall below the level required by the company.

Distributions that contain a tie for the designation as "most frequently occurring score" can have more than one mode. Consider the following scores—arranged in no particular order—obtained by 20 students on the final exam of a new trade school called the Home Study School of Elvis Presley Impersonators:

| 51 | 49 | 51 | 50 | 66 | 52 | 53 | 38 | 17 | 66 |
| 33 | 44 | 73 | 13 | 21 | 91 | 87 | 92 | 47 | 3 |

The distribution of these scores is said to be **bimodal** because it contains two scores (51 and 66) that occur with the highest frequency (a frequency of two). Except for use with nominal data, the mode tends not to be a very commonly used measure of central tendency. Unlike the arithmetic mean, which has to be calculated, the value of the modal score is not calculated—one simply counts and determines which score occurs most frequently. Because the mode is arrived at in this manner, the modal score may be a totally atypical score—one at an extreme end of the distribution—but nonetheless one that occurs with the greatest frequency. In fact, it is theoretically possible for a bimodal distribution to have two modes that each fall at the high or the low end of the distribution—thus violating our expectation that a measure of central tendency should indicate a point at the middle of the distribution.

Even though the mode is not calculated and even though the mode is not necessarily a unique point in a distribution (a distribution can have two, three, or even more modes), the mode can be useful in conveying certain types of information. For example, suppose you wanted an estimate of the number of journal articles published by clinical psychologists in the United States in the past year. To arrive at this figure, you might total the number of journal articles accepted for publication by each clinical psychologist in the United States, divide by the number of psychologists, and arrive at the arithmetic mean—an indication of the average number of journal articles published. Whatever that number would be, we can say with certainty that it would be more than the mode. It is well known that most clinical psychologists do not write journal articles; therefore, the mode for publications by clinical psychologists in any given year is zero. The mode in this instance provides useful information in addition to the mean because it tells us that no matter what the figure is for the average number of publications, most clinicians do not publish.

Because the mode is not calculated in a true sense, it is a nominal statistic and cannot legitimately be used in further calculations. The median is a statistic that takes into account the order of scores and is, itself, ordinal in nature. The mean is the most stable and generally the most useful measure of central tendency, and it is an interval statistic.

Measures of Variability

Variability is an indication of how scores in a distribution are scattered or dispersed. As Figure 3–3 illustrates, two or more distributions of test scores can have the same mean, though differences in the scatter or dispersion of scores around the mean can be wide. In both distributions A and B, test scores could range from 0 to 100. In distribution A, we see that the mean score was 50 and the remaining scores were widely distributed around the mean. In distribution B, the mean was also 50, though few if any people scored higher than 60 or lower than 40.

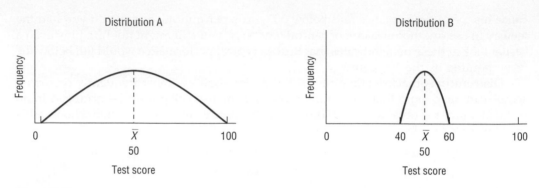

Figure 3–3
Two Distributions with Differences in Variability

Measures of variability—statistics that describe the amount of variation in a distribution—include the range, the interquartile range, the semi-interquartile range, the average deviation, the standard deviation, and the variance.

The range   The **range** of a distribution is equal to the difference between the highest and the lowest scores. We could describe distribution B of Figure 3–3, for example, as having a range of 20 if we knew that the highest score in this distribution was 60 and the lowest score was 40 (60 − 40 = 20). With respect to distribution A, if we knew that the lowest score was 0 and the highest score was 100, the range would be equal to 100 − 0, or 100. The range is the simplest measure of variability to compute, but it is also of limited use; one extreme score can radically alter the value of the range, because the range is based entirely on the value of the two extreme scores. Suppose, for example, that there was one score in distribution B equal to 90. The range of this distribution would now be equal to 90 − 40, or 50. Yet in looking at the data in the graph for distribution B, it is clear that the vast majority of scores tend to be between 40 and 60.

As a descriptive statistic of variation, the range provides a quick but gross description of the spread of scores. Better measures include the interquartile range and the semi-interquartile range.

The interquartile and the semi-interquartile ranges   A distribution of test scores (or any other data for that matter) can be divided into four parts such that 25 percent of the test scores occur in each quarter. As illustrated in Figure 3–4, the dividing points between the four quarters in the distribution are the **quartiles;** there are three of them and they are respectively labeled "Q_1," "Q_2," and "Q_3." Note that "quartile" refers to a specific point, whereas "quarter" refers to an interval; an individual score may, for example, fall *at* the third quartile or *in* the third quarter (but *not* "in" the third quartile or "at" the third quarter). It should not come as a surprise to you that Q_2 and the median are exactly the same. And just as the median is the midpoint in a distribution of scores, so quartiles Q_1 and Q_3 are "quarter-points" in a distribution of scores. Formulas may be employed to determine the exact value of these points. The **interquartile range** is equal to the difference between Q_3 and Q_1 and, like the median, it is an ordinal statistic. A related measure of variability is the **semi-interquartile range,** which is equal to the interquartile range divided by two. Knowledge of the relative distances of Q_1 and Q_3 from Q_2 (the median) provides the seasoned test interpreter with immediate information as to the shape of the distribution of scores. In a perfectly symmetrical distribution, Q_1 and Q_3 will be exactly the same distance from the median. If these distances are unequal, there will be a lack of symmetry, referred to as "skewness" and discussed later in this chapter.

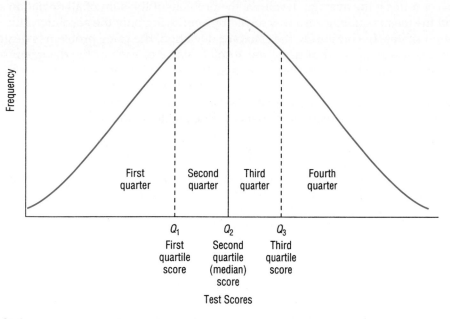

First quarter | Second quarter | Third quarter | Fourth quarter

Q_1
First quartile score

Q_2
Second quartile (median) score

Q_3
Third quartile score

Test Scores

Figure 3–4
A Quartered Distribution

The average deviation Another tool that could be used to describe the amount of variability in a distribution is the **average deviation,** or *AD* for short. Its formula is

$$AD = \frac{\Sigma \, |x|}{n}$$

The lowercase, italicized "x" in the formula signifies a score's deviation from the mean; it is obtained by subtracting the mean from the score $(X - \text{mean}) = x$. The bars on each side of x indicate that you must use the absolute value of the deviation score (ignoring the positive or negative sign and treating all deviation scores as positive). All the deviation scores are then summed and divided by the total number of scores (n) to arrive at the average deviation. As an exercise, compute the average deviation for the following distribution of test scores:

85   100   90   95   80

Begin by calculating the arithmetic mean. Next obtain the absolute value of each of the five deviation scores and sum them (and note what would happen if you did not ignore algebraic signs—all the deviation scores would sum to 0). Divide the sum of the deviation scores by the number of measurements (5). Did you obtain an *AD* of 6? The *AD* tells us that the five scores in this distribution varied, on average, 6 points from the mean.

The *AD* is a very rarely used statistic, because the deletion of algebraic signs renders it a useless measure with respect to any further operations. An understanding of how the *AD* is arrived at, however, is useful in understanding another much more widely used statistic, the standard deviation.

The standard deviation and variance The **standard deviation** is a measure of variability that is equal to the square root of the average squared deviations about the mean. We could define a standard deviation more succinctly by saying simply that it is equal to the square root of the variance. The **variance** is equal to the arithmetic mean of the squares of the differences between the scores in a distribution and their mean.

In computing the average deviation, the problem of the sum of all deviation scores around the mean equaling zero was solved by employing only the absolute value of the deviation scores. In computing the standard deviation, the same problem is dealt with in a different way; instead of using the absolute value of each of the deviation scores, each score is squared; thus, the sign of the negative deviations becomes positive. Because all the deviation scores are squared, we know that before we are finished with our calculations, we must go back and obtain the square root of whatever number we reach. The formula used to calculate the variance (s^2) using deviation scores is

$$s^2 = \frac{\Sigma x^2}{n}$$

Simply stated, the variance is calculated by squaring and summing all the deviation scores and dividing by the total number of scores. The variance can also be calculated in other ways. For example, from raw scores, first calculate the summation of the raw scores squared, divide by the number of scores, and then subtract the mean squared:

$$s^2 = \frac{\Sigma X^2}{n} - \overline{X}^2$$

The variance is a widely used measure in psychological research. To make meaningful interpretations, the test-score distribution should be approximately normal, which means that the greatest frequency of scores occurs near the arithmetic mean and correspondingly fewer and fewer scores relative to the mean occur on both sides of it as scores differ from the mean.

For some hands-on experience with—as well as a sense of mastery of—the concepts of variance and standard deviation, why not allot the next 10 or 15 minutes or so to computing the standard deviation for the test scores originally contained in Table 3–1? Use both formulas to verify that they produce the same results.

Using deviation scores, your calculations should look similar to these:

$$s^2 = \frac{\Sigma x^2}{n}$$

$$s^2 = \frac{\Sigma (X - \text{mean})^2}{n}$$

$$s^2 = \frac{[(78 - 72.12)^2 + (67 - 72.12)^2 + \cdots (79 - 72.12)^2]}{25}$$

$$s^2 = \frac{4972.64}{25}$$

$$s^2 = 198.91$$

Using the raw-scores formula, your calculations should look similar to these:

$$s^2 = \frac{\Sigma X^2}{n} - \overline{X}^2$$

$$s^2 = \frac{[(78)^2 + (67)^2 + \cdots (79)^2]}{25} - 5201.29$$

$$s^2 = \frac{135005}{25} - 5201.29$$

$$s^2 = 5400.20 - 5201.29$$

$$s^2 = 198.91$$

In both cases, the standard deviation is the square root of the variance (s^2). According to our calculations, the standard deviation of the test scores is 14.10. If $s = 14.10$, 1 standard deviation unit is approximately equal to 14 units of measurement, or with reference to our example and rounded to a whole number, 14 test-score points. The test data did not provide a good normal curve approximation; rather, they were positively "skewed," a concept we will review shortly. Some things you need to know about test-score interpretation when the scores are *not* skewed—that is, when the test scores are approximately normal in distribution—are presented later in the section "Area Under the Normal Curve."

The symbol for standard deviation has variously been represented as *s, S*, SD, and the lowercase Greek letter sigma (σ). One custom—the one we adhere to—has it that *s* refers to the sample standard deviation and σ refers to the population standard deviation. The number of observations in the sample is *n* and the denominator $n - 1$ is sometimes used to calculate what is referred to as an "unbiased estimate" of the population value—it's actually only *less* biased (see Hopkins & Glass, 1978). Unless *n* is 10 or less, the use of *n* or $n - 1$ tends not to make a meaningful difference.

But whether the denominator is more properly *n* or $n - 1$ has been something of a matter of debate. Lindgren (1983) has argued for the use of $n - 1$, in part because this denominator tends to make correlation formulas simpler. By contrast, most texts recommend the use of $n - 1$ only when the data constitute a sample; *n* is preferable when the data constitute a population. For Lindgren (1983), it matters not whether the data are from a sample or a population. Perhaps the most reasonable convention—and the one we will follow—is to use *n* when either the population has been assessed (as we might legitimately assume it has when dealing with the examination scores of one class of students—including all the people about whom we're going to make inferences) or no inferences to the population are intended. $\overline{X}$ represents a sample mean, *M* (mu) a population mean. The formula for the population standard deviation is

$$\sigma = \sqrt{\frac{\Sigma (X - M)^2}{n}}$$

The standard deviation is a very useful measure of variation, since each individual score's distance from the mean of the distribution is employed in its computation. You will come across it frequently in the study of measurement.

Skewness

Distributions can be characterized by their **skewness,** or the nature and extent to which symmetry is absent. Skewness is an indication of how the measurements in a distribution are distributed. A distribution is said to be skewed positively when relatively few of the scores fall at the high end of the distribution. Results from an examination that are positively skewed may indicate that the test was too difficult; more items that were easier would have been desirable to discriminate better at the lower end of the distribution of test scores. A distribution is said to be skewed negatively when relatively few of the scores fall at the low end of the distribution. Results from an examination that are negatively skewed may indicate that the test was too easy; in such an instance, more items of a higher level of difficulty would have been desirable so that better discrimination between scores could have been made with respect to the upper end of the distribution of scores. (See Figure 3–2 for examples of skewed distributions.)

Experience in teaching measurement courses has indicated to the authors that the term *skewed* carries with it negative implications for many students, perhaps because of an association with abnormality—given that a skewed distribution deviates from a normal distribution. However, the presence or absence of symmetry in a distribution (skewness) is simply one characteristic by which a distribution can be described, and skewness is not in and of itself bad (or good). We might expect a distribution of household income

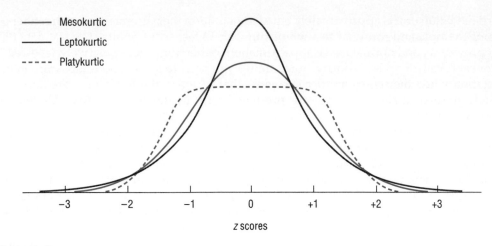

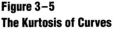

Figure 3–5
The Kurtosis of Curves

in dollars to be skewed negatively if samples such as Beverly Hills residents or Harvard Law School graduates were employed—because of the clustering that could be expected at the higher end of possible household incomes. A hypothetical Marine Corps Endurance Test used to screen male applicants might consistently yield positively skewed distributions; its built-in difficulty level would be designed to guarantee that only a few would pass—consistent with the advertised objective that the Corps isn't seeking a lot of good men but rather only "a few good men." A test purporting to measure abilities that are assumed to be normally distributed in the population would be expected to yield distributions that are also approximately normal in distribution. If testing with such an instrument using samples from the general population repeatedly yielded skewed distributions, the assumptions made by such a test would have to be reconsidered.

Various formulas exist for measuring skewness. One way of gauging the skewness of a distribution is through examination of the relative distances of quartiles from the median. In a positively skewed distribution, $Q_3 - Q_2$ will be greater than the distance of $Q_2 - Q_1$. In a negatively skewed distribution, $Q_3 - Q_2$ will be less than the distance of $Q_2 - Q_1$. In a distribution that is symmetrical, the distances from Q_1 and Q_3 to the median are the same.

Kurtosis

The term testing professionals use to refer to the steepness of a distribution in its center is **kurtosis,** and the descriptive suffix *kurtic* is added to either *platy, lepto,* or *meso* to describe the peakedness/flatness of three general types of curves (Figure 3–5). Distributions are generally described as being either **platykurtic** (relatively flat), **leptokurtic** (relatively peaked), or—somewhere in the middle—**mesokurtic.** Many methods exist for measuring kurtosis. Some computer programs feature an index of skewness that ranges from −3.00 to +3.00. In many ways, however, technical matters related to the measurement and interpretation of kurtosis are controversial among measurement specialists.

The Normal Curve

Development of the concept of a normal curve began in the middle of the eighteenth century with the work of Abraham DeMoivre and, later, Pierre Simon de Laplace. At the beginning of the nineteenth century, Karl Friedrich Gauss made some substantial contributions to the normal curve concept with work on his "theory of errors" (work that resulted in a statistical technique known as the method of least squares). In the early nineteenth century, the normal curve was referred to as the "Laplace-Gaussian curve." It was Karl Pearson who first referred to this curve as the "normal curve," perhaps in an effort to be diplomatic. Diplomacy aside, referring to the curve as "normal" instead of assigning someone's name to it created some confusion at the time, especially because many wondered aloud whether all other curves should be thought of as abnormal. Somehow, the name "normal curve" stuck—but don't be surprised if you're sitting at some scientific meeting one day and you hear this distribution or curve referred to as "Gaussian" in nature.

Theoretically, the **normal curve** is a bell-shaped, smooth, mathematically defined curve highest at the center and then gradually tapered on both sides approaching the X-axis *asymptotically* (meaning that it approaches, but never touches, the axis). In theory, the distribution of the normal curve ranges from negative infinity to positive infinity. The curve is perfectly symmetrical, with no skewness, so if you folded it in half at the mean, one side would lie exactly on top of the other. Because it is symmetrical, the mean, the median, and the mode all have the same exact value.

Why is the normal curve important in understanding the characteristics of psychological tests? See this chapter's *Close-up.*

Area Under the Normal Curve

The normal curve can be conveniently divided into areas defined in standard deviation units. A hypothetical distribution of "National Spelling Test" scores with a mean of 50 and a standard deviation of 15 is illustrated in Figure 3–6. In this example, a score equal to 1 standard deviation above the mean would be equal to 65 ($\overline{X} + 1s = 50 + 15 = 65$).

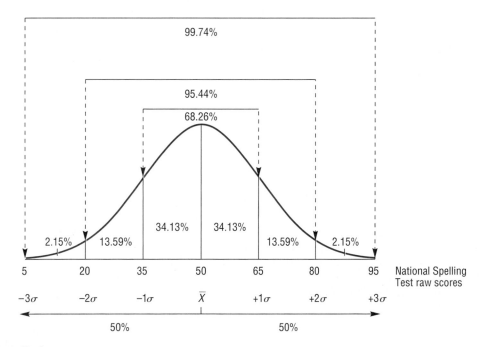

Figure 3–6
Area Under the Normal Curve

The Normal Curve and Psychological Tests

Scores on many psychological tests are often approximately normally distributed, particularly when the tests are administered to large numbers of subjects. Few, if any, psychological tests yield precisely normal distributions of test scores (Micceri, 1989). As a general rule, with ample exceptions, the larger the sample size and the wider the range of abilities measured by a particular test, the more the graph of the test scores will approximate the normal curve. A classic illustration of this was provided by E. L. Thorndike and his colleagues (1927). Thorndike et al. compiled intelligence test scores from several large samples of students. As you can see in Figure 1, the distribution of scores closely approximated the normal curve.

The following sample gives more varied examples of the wide range of characteristics that psychologists have found to be approximately normal in distribution:

■ The strength of handedness in right-handed individuals, as measured by the Waterloo Handedness Questionnaire (Tan, 1993).

■ Scores on the Women's Health Questionnaire, a scale measuring a variety of health problems in women across a wide age range (Hunter, 1992).

■ Responses of both college students and working adults to a measure of intrinsic and extrinsic work motivation (Amabile et al., 1994).

■ The intelligence scale scores of girls and women with eating disorders as measured by the Wechsler Adult Intelligence Scale-Revised and the Wechsler Intelligence Scale for Children-Revised (Ranseen & Humphries, 1992).

■ The intellectual functioning of children and adolescents with cystic fibrosis (Thompson et al., 1992).

■ Decline in cognitive abilities over a one-year period in people with Alzheimer's disease (Burns et al., 1991).

■ The rate of motor-skill development in developmentally delayed preschoolers, as measured by the Vineland Adaptive Behavior Scale (Davies & Gavin, 1994).

■ Scores on the Swedish translation of the Positive and Negative Syndrome Scale, which assesses the presence of positive and negative symptoms in people with schizophrenia (von Knorring & Lindstrom, 1992).

■ The scores of psychiatrists on the Scale for Treatment Integration of the Dually Diagnosed (people with both a drug problem and another mental disorder). The scale examines opinions about drug treatment for this group of patients (Adelman et al., 1991).

■ Responses to the Tridimensional Personality Questionnaire, a measure of three distinct personality features (Cloninger et al., 1991).

■ Scores on a self-esteem measure among undergraduates (Addeo et al., 1994).

In each case, the researchers made a special point of stating that the scale under investigation yielded something close to a normal distribution of scores. Why?

One benefit of a normal distribution of scores is that it simplifies the interpretation of individual scores on the test. In a normal distribution, the mean, the median, and the mode take on the same value. For example, if we know that the average score for intellectual ability of children with cystic fibrosis is a particular value, and that the scores are normally distributed, we know quite a bit more. We know that the average is the most common score and the score

Before reading on, take a minute or two to calculate what a score exactly at 3 standard deviations below the mean would be equal to. How about a score exactly at 3 standard deviations above the mean? Were your answers 5 and 95, respectively? The graph tells us that 99.74% of all scores in these normally distributed spelling test data lie between ±3 standard deviations. Stated another way, 99.74% of all spelling test scores lie between 5 and 95. This graph also illustrates other characteristics true of all normal distributions:

■ 50% of the scores occur above the mean, and 50% of the scores occur below the mean.

■ Approximately 34% of all scores occur between the mean and 1 standard deviation above the mean.

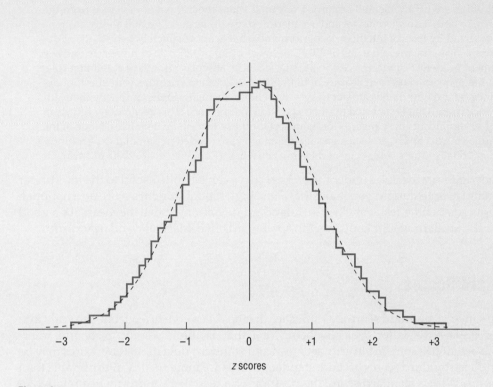

Figure 1
Graphic Representation of Thorndike et al. Data

The solid line outlines the distribution of intelligence test scores of sixth-grade students (N = 15,138). The dotted line is the theoretical normal curve (Thorndike et al., 1927).

below and above which half of all the scores fall. Knowing the mean and the standard deviation of a scale, and knowing that it is approximately normally distributed, tells us that approximately two-thirds of all testtakers' scores are within a standard deviation of the mean. Approximately 95% of the scores fall within 2 standard deviations of the mean.

The characteristics of the normal curve provide a ready model for score interpretation that can be applied to a wide range of test results.

- Approximately 34% of all scores occur between the mean and 1 standard deviation below the mean.
- Approximately 68% of all scores occur between the mean and ±1 standard deviation.
- Approximately 95% of all scores occur between the mean and ±2 standard deviations.

A normal curve has two "tails." The area on the normal curve between 2 and 3 standard deviations above the mean is referred to as a **tail;** so is the area between −2 and −3 standard deviations below the mean. As observed in a thought-provoking article entitled "Two Tails of the Normal Curve," an intelligence test score that falls within the limits of either tail can have momentous consequences in terms of the tale of one's life:

> Individuals who are mentally retarded or gifted share the burden of deviance from the norm, in both a developmental and a statistical sense. In terms of mental ability as operationalized by tests of intelligence, performance that is approximately two standard deviations from the mean (i.e., IQ of 70–75 or lower or IQ of 125–130 or higher) is one key element in identification. Success at life's tasks, or its absence, also plays a defining role, but the primary classifying feature of both gifted and retarded groups is intellectual deviance. These individuals are out of sync with more average people, simply by their difference from what is expected for their age and circumstance. This asynchrony results in highly significant consequences for them and for those who share their lives. None of the familiar norms apply, and substantial adjustments are needed in parental expectations, educational settings, and social and leisure activities. (Robinson et al., 2000, p. 1413)

Knowledge of the areas under the normal curve can be quite useful to the interpreter of test data. If, for example, you know that some high school student's score on a national, well-reputed spelling test was close to 3 standard deviations above the mean, it's a good bet that the student would know how to spell words like *asymptotic* and *leptokurtic*.

Standard Scores

Simply stated, a **standard score** is a raw score that has been converted from one scale into another scale—the latter typically being one that is more widely used and interpretable—that has some arbitrarily set mean and standard deviation. Raw scores may be converted to standard scores because standard scores are more readily interpretable than raw scores. With a standard score, the position of a testtaker's performance relative to other testtakers is readily apparent. Different types of systems for standard scores exist, each unique as regards its respective mean and standard deviations. One type of standard score scale has been referred to as the "zero plus or minus one" scale because it has a mean set at zero and a standard deviation set at one. Raw scores converted into standard scores on the "zero plus or minus one scale" are more popularly referred to as "z scores."

z *Scores*

A **z score** is equal to the difference between a particular raw score and the mean divided by the standard deviation. In essence, a z score expresses a score in terms of the number of standard deviation units the raw score is below or above the mean of the distribution. Using an example from the normally distributed "National Spelling Test" data in Figure 3–6, we can convert a raw score of 65 to a z score using the following formula:

$$z = \frac{X - \bar{X}}{s} = \frac{65 - 50}{15} = \frac{15}{15} = 1$$

In this test a raw score of 65 is equal to a z score of +1. Knowing simply that someone obtained a raw score of 65 on a spelling test conveys virtually no usable information because information about the context of this score is lacking. However, knowing that someone obtained a z score of 1 on a spelling test provides context and meaning to the score; drawing on our knowledge of areas under the normal curve, for example, we would know that only about 16% of the other testtakers obtained higher scores.

Standard scores provide a convenient way to compare raw scores within and between tests. It helps us little to know, for example, that Crystal's raw score on the "Main

Street Reading Test" was 24 and that her raw score on the "Main Street Arithmetic Test" was 42. Knowing Crystal's z scores on the two tests would be more informative. If we were to compute z scores based on the performance of other students in Crystal's class, we might find that her z score on the reading test was 1.32 and her z score on the arithmetic test was −0.75. Thus, although her raw score in arithmetic was higher than in reading, the z scores tell us that Crystal performed above average on the reading test and below average on the arithmetic test, relative to the other students in her class (provided, of course, that the scores on the tests are normally distributed). An interpretation of exactly how much better she performed could be obtained by reference to tables detailing distances under the normal curve (and the resulting percentage of cases that could be expected to fall above or below a particular standard deviation point, or z score).

Of course, to make meaningful comparison of z scores on different tests, the groups on which the z score calculations are based should be similar. For example, it would be pointless to compute Crystal's z score on the reading test relative to non-English-speaking children and then compare that with her z score on the arithmetic test computed relative to college mathematics majors; at best, such a comparison might allow us to conclude that Crystal's reading skills are better relative to non-English speakers than her arithmetic skills are relative to college math majors. If the previous statement seemed like nonsense to you, that's because it described the nonsensical situation of comparing z scores using different comparison groups. Meaningful comparison of any standard scores requires similarity between the comparison groups on which the standard scores are computed.

T *Scores*

If the scale used in the computation of z scores is called a "zero plus or minus one" scale, then the scale used in the computation of **T scores** is called a "fifty plus or minus ten" scale: a scale that has a mean set at 50 and a standard deviation set at 10. Devised by W. A. McCall (1922, 1939) and named a T score in honor of his professor E. L. Thorndike, this standard score system is composed of a scale that ranges from 5 standard deviations below the mean to 5 standard deviations above the mean. Thus, for example, a raw score that fell exactly at 5 standard deviations below the mean would be equal to a T score of 0, a raw score that fell at the mean would be equal to a T of 50, and a raw score that fell at a point that was 5 standard deviations above the mean would be equal to a T of 100. An advantage in using T scores is that none of the scores is negative. By contrast, in a z score distribution, scores can be positive and negative, making further computation cumbersome in some instances.

T scores were the measure of choice for the developers of the Minnesota Multiphasic Personality Inventory (MMPI), a widely used personality test that will be discussed in Chapter 11. Through the years, however, a technical problem with the use of T scores in that test emerged. It was observed that many more respondents exhibited elevated T scores than would be expected in a normal distribution. Also associated with this phenomenon was a lack of percentile equivalence of T scores.

These problems were recognized by Colligan and his associates (1980, 1983, 1984a, 1984b; Colligan & Offord, 1989), who suggested that normalized standard scores be used in place of the linear T scores. To accomplish this normalization, Colligan and his colleagues used what is called the "Box-Cox power transformation method" (Box & Cox, 1964). In the late 1980s, with the restandardization of the MMPI under way, the MMPI-2 Restandardization Committee also believed that percentile comparability was a desirable end. They differed, however, from Colligan and his associates on how that end could best be achieved. Ultimately, the MMPI-2 Restandardization Committee concluded that **normalized T scores** represented an extreme departure from the linear T scores.

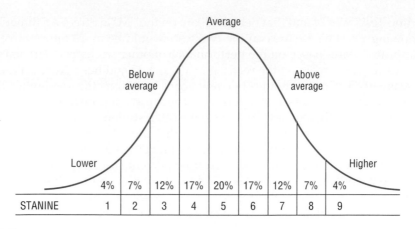

Figure 3–7
Stanines and the Normal Curve

Switching "from linear T scores to normalized scores would have meant substantial changes in the frequencies and clinical implications of elevated T scores and T score profiles" (Tellegen & Ben-Porath, 1992, p. 147); this not only would have "required marked departures from familiar MMPI interpretations based on previous research," but would have "accentuated discontinuities between the original MMPI and the MMPI-2" (p. 147). The committee sought out a "less disruptive method" of achieving percentile comparability. The end result was the development of what they called a **uniform T (UT) score** in place of a normalized T score (see Tellegen & Ben-Porath, 1992).

Other Standard Scores

Numerous other standard scoring systems exist. Researchers during World War II developed a standard score with a mean of 5 and a standard deviation of approximately 2. Divided into nine units, the scale was christened a **stanine,** deriving from a contraction of the words *sta*ndard and *nine*. This scale was subsequently refined statistically (see Kaiser, 1958).

Stanine scoring may be familiar to many students from achievement tests administered in elementary and secondary school, where test scores are often represented as stanines. Stanines are different from other standard scores in that they take on whole values from 1 to 9, which represent a range of performance that is ½ a standard deviation in width (Figure 3–7.) The 5th stanine indicates performance in the average range, from ¼ standard deviation below the mean to ¼ standard deviation above the mean, capturing the middle 20% of the scores in a normal distribution. The 4th and 6th stanines are also ½ standard deviation wide, and capture the 17% of cases below and above the 5th stanine, respectively. When "computer" was synonymous with the use of IBM punch cards, one attraction of the stanine scale was that its whole-number, single-digit values could be readily manipulated computationally.

Raw scores on tests such as the Scholastic Aptitude Test (SAT) and the Graduate Record Examination (GRE) are converted to standard scores such that the resulting distribution has a mean of 500 and a standard deviation of 100. If the letter A is used to represent a standard score from a college or graduate school admissions test whose distribution has a mean of 500 and a standard deviation of 100, then the following is true:

$$(A = 600) = (z = 1) = (T = 60)$$

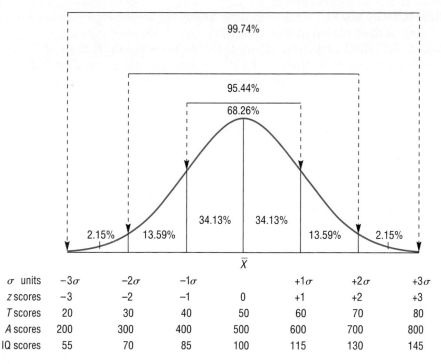

σ units	−3σ	−2σ	−1σ		+1σ	+2σ	+3σ
z scores	−3	−2	−1	0	+1	+2	+3
T scores	20	30	40	50	60	70	80
A scores	200	300	400	500	600	700	800
IQ scores	55	70	85	100	115	130	145

Figure 3–8
Some Standard Score Equivalents

The relationship of z, T, and A scores to each other in a normal distribution is illustrated in Figure 3–8.

Another kind of standard score that you may be familiar with is the "deviation intelligence quotient," or **deviation IQ,** or simply "IQ" for short. If you are not familiar with this type of score, rest assured that after studying Part 3 of this textbook you will be. For most IQ tests, the distribution of raw scores is converted to IQ scores, whose distribution typically has a mean set at 100 and a standard deviation set at 15 (note that we say "typically" because there is some variation in standard scoring systems depending on the test used). The typical mean and standard deviation for IQ tests results in approximately 95% of deviation IQs ranging from 70 to 130—that is, 2 standard deviations below and above the mean, respectively (see Figure 3–8). We will have much more to say about deviation IQs in Part 3. We will also see that each of the individual subtests of the Wechsler set of intelligence tests is a standard score itself, with a mean set at 10 and a standard deviation set at 3.

Standard scores converted from raw scores may involve either linear or nonlinear transformations. A standard score obtained by a **linear transformation** is one that retains a direct numerical relationship to the original raw score, and the magnitude of differences between such standard scores exactly parallels the differences between corresponding raw scores. Sometimes scores may undergo more than one transformation; for example, the creators of the SAT did a second linear transformation on their data to convert z scores into a new scale that has a mean of 500 and a standard deviation of 100. A **nonlinear transformation** may be required when the data under consideration are not normally distributed and comparisons with normal distributions need to be made. When such a nonlinear transformation is done, the original distribution is said to have been "normalized."

Normalized standard scores   A test developer interested in developing an instrument that yields a normal distribution of scores may find that, even after very large samples have been tested with the instrument, skewed distributions result. If the test developer is intent on having scores on this test be distributed normally, the distribution can be normalized. Conceptually, **normalizing a distribution** involves "stretching" the skewed curve into a shape of a normal curve and creating a corresponding scale of standard scores—a scale that is technically referred to as a **normalized standard score scale.**

Normalization of a skewed distribution of scores may also be desirable for purposes of comparability. One of the primary advantages of a standard score on one test is that it can readily be compared with a standard score on another test. However, comparison of standard scores is appropriate only when the distributions from which they derived are the same—and in most instances they are the same because the two distributions are approximately normal. But if, for example, distribution A was normal and distribution B was highly skewed, z scores in these respective distributions would represent different amounts of area subsumed under the curve. A z score of -1 with respect to normally distributed data tells us, among other things, that about 84% of the scores in this distribution were higher than this score. A z score of -1 with respect to data that were very positively skewed might mean, for example, that only 62% of the scores were higher.

For test developers intent on creating tests that yield normally distributed measurements, it is generally preferable to fine-tune the test according to difficulty and/or other relevant variables so that the resulting distribution will approximate the normal curve—as opposed to trying to normalize skewed distributions. This is so because there are technical cautions to be observed before attempting normalization. Transformations should be made only when there is good reason to believe that the test sample was large and representative enough and the failure to obtain normally distributed scores was due to the measuring instrument. In situations where the distribution is not perfectly normal but closely approximates normal, normalization is not typically conducted because the normalized standard score (derived from a nonlinear transformation) will closely approximate the standard score (derived from a linear transformation). Further, the score derived from a nonlinear transformation will be limited with respect to additional computations that can legitimately be performed with it, whereas the score derived from the linear transformation will not.

And speaking of transformations, it's about time to make one to Chapter 4. It may be helpful at this time to review this statistics refresher to make certain that you indeed feel refreshed. Apply what you have learned about frequency distributions, graphing frequency distributions, measures of central tendency, measures of variability, and the normal curve and standard scores to the question of the data listed in Table 3–1. How would you communicate the data from Table 3–1 to the class? Which type of frequency distribution might you use? Which type of graph? Which measure of central tendency? Which measure of variability? Might reference to a normal curve or to standard scores be helpful? Why or why not?[9]

Come to the next class session prepared with your thoughts on the answers to these questions, as well as your own questions regarding any of the material that could stand a bit more explanation. We will be building on your knowledge of basic statistical principles in the chapters to come, and it is important that such building be on a rock-solid foundation.

---

9. A detailed, step-by-step illustration of the computation of each of various statistics for these data is presented in Cohen (2002).

Self-Assessment

Test your understanding of elements of this chapter by seeing if you can explain each of the following terms, expressions, and abbreviations:

average deviation (AD)

bar graph

bimodal

distribution

frequency distribution

frequency polygon

graph

grouped frequency distribution

histogram

interquartile range

interval scale

kurtosis

leptokurtic

mean

measurement

measure of central tendency

median

mesokurtic

mode

nominal scale

normal curve

normalized standard score

ordinal scale

platykurtic

quartile

range

ratio scale

scale

semi-interquartile range

skewness

standard deviation

standard scores

stanine

T score

variability

variance

z score

Norms, Correlation, and Inference

Each year, thousands of college-bound students, with number 2 pencil firmly in hand, blacken thousands of little grids on college entrance examination answer forms. After months of anticipation, the mail brings a computer-generated statement with the test scores. Typically enclosed with the scores is a booklet or leaflet explaining how the scores should be interpreted. Students are advised to judge their own individual performance in comparison with the performance of some other group of students that took the test—a *normative sample* (also variously known as a *norm group* or a *standardization sample*). Let's take a closer look at these terms.

Norms

Norm in the singular is used in the scholarly literature to refer to behavior that is usual, average, normal, standard, expected, or typical. In social psychology, for example, we may read about the norm of reciprocity (Burger et al., 1997). Reference to a particular variety of norm may be specified by means of modifiers such as age (as in "age norm") or gender (as in "gender norm"), and each specific type of norm may convey different information depending on the context in which it is used. For example, in an educational context, an age norm might refer to the level of academic work one is capable of doing relative to one's age. In the context of marriage, an age norm might refer to the age at which most people in a given culture get married. In an organizational context, an age norm might refer to "the ages viewed as typical for a given role or status by the modal group of members of a social system" (Lawrence, 1996, p. 209).

"Norms" is the plural form of norm. In a psychometric context, **norms** are the test performance data of a particular group of testtakers that are designed for use as a reference for evaluating or interpreting individual test scores. The technical manuals of all major standardized tests contain norms for the test. The "particular group of testtakers" may be defined broadly (for example, "a sample representative of the adult population of the United States") or narrowly (for example, "inpatients at Community Hospital with a primary diagnosis of depression"). Whether broad or narrow in scope, members of the group will all be typical with respect to some characteristic(s) of the people for whom the particular test was designed. A test administration to this representative sample of testtakers yields a distribution (or distributions) of scores. These data constitute the norms for the test and typically are used as a reference source for evaluating and placing into context test scores obtained by individual testtakers. The data may be in the form of raw scores or converted scores. We will learn more about various types of converted scores shortly. Here, let's focus briefly on the meaning of raw score.

As its name implies, a **raw score** is a straightforward, unmodified accounting of performance, usually numerical and typically used for evaluative or diagnostic purposes. A raw score may reflect a simple tally as in "number of items responded to correctly" on an achievement test, or "number of items responded to indicative of faking" on a personality test. On each subtest of an intelligence test, for example, a raw score is obtained and then converted into another type of score. Clinical experience has taught the authors that when administering such tests, a raw score of zero on any one subtest or group of subtests can be very telling: A raw score of zero should serve as a red flag alerting the examiner to possibilities that the testtaker did not understand the instructions, was not physically capable of hearing the instructions, or was not physically capable of following the instructions.

The verb *to norm* and its derivatives, such as **norming**—psychometric terms that you probably will not find in a standard dictionary—refer to the process of deriving norms. Grant and Nash (1995), for example, described the standardization and norming of the Computer-Assisted Hypnosis Scale, a computer-administered measure of hypnotic susceptibility. "Norming" may be modified to describe a particular type of norming, as in *age norming*. **Race norming** is the controversial practice of norming on the basis of race or ethnic background. Race norming was once engaged in by some government agencies and private organizations, and the practice resulted in the establishment of different *cut scores* (discussed below) for hiring by cultural group; members of one cultural group would have to attain one score to be hired, whereas members of another cultural group would have to attain a different score. Although initially instituted in the service of affirmative action objectives (Greenlaw & Jensen, 1996), the practice was outlawed in the Civil Rights Act of 1991. The law left unclear a number of issues, however, including "whether, or under what circumstances in the development of an assessment procedure it is lawful to adjust item content to minimize group differences" (Kehoe & Tenopyr, 1994, p. 291).

A **cut score** (also referred to as a *cutoff score* or simply a *cutoff*) may be defined as a reference point, usually numerical, derived as a result of judgment and used to divide a set of data into two or more classifications. Some action will be taken or some inference will be made on the basis of these classifications. Cut scores on tests, usually in combination with other data, are used in schools in many contexts, such as grading and making decisions about the class or program to which a particular child will be assigned. Cut scores are used by employers as aids to decision making about personnel hiring and advancement. Consumer psychologists use cut scores in testing the receptivity of the marketplace to new products and new marketing campaigns. State agencies use cut scores for assistance in determining who shall be licensed as a professional in a given field. There are probably upwards of 20 different methods that can be used to formally derive cut scores (Dwyer, 1996), and some are more legally defensible than others. Sometimes, no formal method is used, as when a teacher proclaims, "You will pass with a score of 65 or more on this test, and you will fail with a score of under 65." And whether formally or informally derived, cut scores always involve human judgment, subjectivity, and to some extent, the values of the person or group of people responsible for setting them. As you might expect, cut scores also have effects on the people who are "cut." Some of these effects have been explored in innovative experimentation (Figure 4–1).

As an adjective, *normative* modifies a noun with reference to a norm or an acknowledged standard. Some examples of this term's use in the literature include references to

According to research by Victoria Husted Medvec and her colleagues (Medvec et al., 1995; Medvec & Savitsky, 1997), people who just make some categorical cutoff may feel better about their accomplishment than those who make the cutoff by a substantial margin. But those who just miss the cutoff may feel worse than those who miss it by a substantial margin. Evidence consistent with this view was presented in research with Olympic athletes. Bronze medalists were—somewhat paradoxically—happier with the outcome than silver medalists. Bronze medalists might say to themselves, "At least I won a medal" and be happy about it. By contrast, silver medalists might feel frustrated about having gone for the gold and missed winning it.

normative beliefs (Crick et al., 1996; Huesmann & Guerra, 1997), normative forms of aggression (Crick, 1997), normative mechanisms of influence (Amada, 1996; Green, 1998; Groeger & Chapman, 1997; Perez et al., 1997), and normative thresholds for heat-induced pain (Yarnitsky et al., 1995). In psychometrics, reference is often made to a **normative sample;** that is, a group of people whose performance data on a particular test may be used as a reference source for evaluating individual test scores. When the people in the normative sample are the same people on whom the test was standardized, the phrases "normative sample" and "standardization sample" are often used interchangeably. Increasingly, however, new norms for standardized tests for specific groups of test-takers—typically groups that may have been underrepresented or not represented in the original norms—are developed after a test has been published. In such instances, the normative sample for the new norms would not be identical to the standardization sample, and it would be inaccurate to use the terms interchangeably. Norming a test, especially with the participation of a nationally representative normative sample, can be a very expensive proposition. For this reason, some test manuals provide what are variously known as **user norms** or **program norms** (APA, 1985), which "consist of descriptive statistics based on a group of test takers in a given period of time rather than norms obtained by formal sampling methods" (Nelson, 1994, p. 283).

Standardization and Norming

The process of administering a test to a representative sample of testtakers for the purpose of establishing norms is referred to as "standardizing a test." A test is said to be **standardized** when it has clearly specified procedures for administration and scoring—including normative data. But how are norms obtained? In the process of developing a test, a test developer has targeted some defined group as the population for which the test is designed for use. This population is the complete universe or set of individuals with at least one common, observable characteristic. The common observable characteristic(s) might range from "high school seniors who aspire to go to college" to "the 16 boys and girls in Mrs. Smith's day care center," to "all housewives with primary responsibility for household shopping who have purchased over-the-counter headache remedies within the last two months." To obtain a distribution of scores, the test developer could have the test administered to every person in the targeted population; and if the total targeted population consists of something like "the 16 boys and girls in Mrs. Smith's day care center," there would be no problem. However, with tests developed for use with large or wide-ranging populations, it is usually impossible, impractical, or simply too expensive to administer the test to everyone, nor is it necessary.

The test developer can obtain a distribution of test responses by administering the test to a **sample** of the population—a portion of the universe of people deemed to be representative of the whole population. The size of the sample could be as small as one person, though as the size of the sample approaches the size of the population, possible sources of error as a result of insufficient sample size diminish.

Subgroups within a defined population may differ with respect to some characteristics, and it is sometimes essential to have these differences proportionately represented in the sample. Thus, for example, if you devised a "Public Opinion Test," and you wanted to sample the opinions of Manhattan residents with this instrument, it would be desirable to include in your sample people representing different subgroups (or strata) of the population, such as Blacks, Whites, Asians, other non-Whites, males, females, the poor, the middle class, the rich, professional people, business people, office workers, skilled and unskilled laborers, the unemployed, homemakers, Catholics, Jews, members of other religions, and so forth—all in proportion to the occurrence of these strata in the population of people who reside on the island of Manhattan. Such sampling, termed **stratified sampling,** would help prevent sampling bias and ultimately aid in the interpretation of the findings. If such sampling were *random* in nature (that is, if every member of the population had the same chance of being included in the sample), then the procedure would be termed **stratified-random sampling.**

Two other types of sampling procedures are *purposive sampling* and *incidental sampling*. If we arbitrarily select some sample because we believe it to be representative of the population, the sample we have selected is referred to as **purposive.** Manufacturers of products frequently use purposive sampling when they test the appeal of a new product in one city or market and then make assumptions about how that product would sell nationally. For example, the manufacturer might test a product in a market such as Cleveland because, on the basis of experience with this particular product, "how goes Cleveland goes the nation." The danger in using such a purposive sample is that the sample, in this case Cleveland residents, may no longer be representative of the nation or simply may not be representative of national preferences with regard to the particular product being test-marketed.

Another type of sample, and an all-too-frequently used type, is called an "incidental sample." When the authors think of this type of sample, we think of the old joke about the drunk searching for some money he lost under the lamppost; he may not have lost it there, but that's where the light is. Like the drunk searching for money under the lamppost, a researcher may sometimes employ a sample that is not necessarily the most appropriate but, rather, the most convenient. Unlike the drunk, the researcher employing this type of sample is not doing it as a result of poor judgment but because of budgetary limitations or other situational constraints. An **incidental sample** (also termed a **convenience sample**) is one that is convenient or available for use. You may have been a party to incidental sampling if you have ever been placed in a subject pool for experimentation with introductory psychology students. It's not that the students in such subject pools are necessarily the most appropriate subjects for the experiments—it's just that they are the most available. Generalization of findings made with respect to incidental samples must be made with caution.

Having obtained a sample, the test developer administers the test according to the standard set of instructions that will be used with the test. The test developer also provides a setting for the testtakers that will be the recommended setting for giving the test. This may be as simple as making sure that the room is quiet and well lit, or as complex as providing a specific set of toys to test an infant's cognitive skills. Establishing a standard set of instructions and conditions under which the test is given makes the test scores of the standardization (normative) sample more comparable with the scores of future testtakers. For example, if a test of concentration ability is given to a normative sample in the summer with the windows open and people mowing the grass and arguing about whether the hedges need trimming, the normative sample probably won't concentrate well. If a testtaker then completes the concentration test under quiet, comfortable conditions, that person may well do much better than the normative group, resulting in a high standard score. That high score would not be very helpful in understanding the testtaker's concentration abilities because it would reflect the differing conditions under which the test was taken. This example illustrates how important it is that the normative group take the test under a standard set of conditions, which are then repeated as closely as possible each time the test is given.

After all of the test data have been collected and analyzed, the test developer will describe the data using descriptive statistics including measures of central tendency and variability. In addition, it is incumbent on the test developer to provide a precise description of the standardization sample itself. Good practice dictates that the norms be developed with respect to data derived from a group of people who are presumed to be representative of the people who will take the test in the future. In order to best assist future users of the test, test developers are encouraged to "describe the population(s) represented by any norms or comparison group(s), the dates the data were gathered, and the process used to select the samples of testtakers" (*Code of Fair Testing Practices in Education,* 1988, p. 3).

In practice, descriptions of standardization samples vary widely in precision. Not surprisingly, test authors wish to present their tests in the most favorable light possible, and shortcomings in the standardization procedure (or elsewhere in the process of the test's development) may be given short shrift or be totally overlooked in a test's manual. Sometimes the sample may be scrupulously defined, but the generalizability of the norms to a particular group or individual is questionable. For example, a test carefully normed on school-age children who reside within the Los Angeles school district may be relevant only to some lesser degree to school-age children who reside within the Dubuque, Iowa, school district. How many children in the standardization sample were English speaking? How many were of Hispanic origin? How does the elementary school curriculum in Los Angeles differ from the curriculum in Dubuque? These are the types of questions that must be raised before the Los Angeles norms are judged to be generalizable to the children of Dubuque. Test manuals sometimes supply prospective test users with guidelines for establishing local norms—one of many different ways norms can be categorized.

Types of Norms

Some of the many different ways we can classify norms are as follows: age norms, grade norms, national norms, national anchor norms, local norms, norms from a fixed reference group, subgroup norms, and percentile norms. We begin with a detailed explanation of the term *percentile* because the norms for many tests are expressed as percentile norms. *Percentile norms* are the raw data from a test's standardization sample converted to percentile form.

Percentiles   In our discussion of the median, we saw that a distribution could be divided into quartiles where the median was the second quartile (Q_2), the point at which 50% of the scores fell at or below and the remaining 50% fell above. Instead of dividing a distribution of scores into quartiles, we might wish to divide the distribution into *deciles,* or ten equal parts. Alternatively, we could divide a distribution into 100 equal parts—100 *percentiles.* In such a distribution, the xth percentile is equal to the score at or below which x% of scores fall. Thus, the 15th percentile is the score at or below which 15% of the scores in the distribution fall; the 99th percentile is the score at or below which 99% of the scores in the distribution fall. If 99% of a particular standardization sample answered fewer than 47 questions on a test correctly, then we could say that a raw score of 47 corresponds to the 99th percentile on this test. It can be seen that a percentile is a ranking that conveys information about the relative position of a score within a distribution of scores.

A **percentile** is an expression of the percentage of people whose score on a test or measure falls below a particular raw score. A more familiar description of test performance, the concept of **percentage correct,** must be distinguished from the concept of a percentile. A percentile is a converted score that refers to a percentage of testtakers. "Percentage correct" refers to the distribution of raw scores—specifically, the number of items that were answered correctly multiplied by 100 and divided by the total number of items.

Because percentiles are easily calculated, they are a popular way of organizing test data—be they data from the standardization sample or otherwise. Additionally, percentiles are very adaptable for use with a wide range of tests. A problem with using percentiles with normally distributed scores is that real differences between raw scores may be minimized near the ends of the distribution and exaggerated in the middle of the distribution. This distortion problem may even be worse with highly skewed data. In the normal distribution, the highest frequency of raw scores occurs in the middle. That being the case, the differences between all those scores that cluster in the middle might be quite small, yet even the smallest difference will appear as differences in percentiles. The reverse is true at the extremes of the distributions, where differences between raw scores may be great, though we would have no way of knowing that from the relatively small differences in percentiles.

Age norms   Also known as *age-equivalent scores,* **age norms** indicate the average performance of different samples of testtakers who were at various ages at the time the test was administered. If the measurement under consideration is height in inches, for example, we know that children's "scores" (that is, heights) will gradually increase at various rates as a function of age up to their middle to late teens.

Carefully constructed age norm tables for physical characteristics such as height enjoy widespread acceptance and are virtually noncontroversial. This is not the case, however, with respect to age norm tables for psychological characteristics such as intelligence. Suppose you created the "National Intelligence Test" (NIT) and designed it for use with children between the ages of 5 and 14. And let's say that you obtained NIT norms using large, nationally representative, random samples of 5-year-olds, 6-year-olds—all the way through to 14-year-olds. Your standardization sample data tell you the average 6-year-old obtains a raw score of, say, 30 on your test, and the average 12-year-old obtains a raw score of 60. In the course of examining your data, you note that one 12-year-old, Adolf, scored 30 on your test. You also find that one 6-year-old, Anna, obtained a raw score of 60. Is it legitimate for you to make statements like "Adolf has a mental age of 6 and Anna has a mental age of 12"?

For many years psychologists have made statements like those referring to "mental ages" of testtakers. The child of any chronological age whose performance on a valid test of intellectual ability indicated that he or she had intellectual ability similar to that of the average child of some other age was said to have the mental age of the norm group in which his or her test score fell. The reasoning here was that irrespective of chronological age, children with the same mental age could be expected to read the same level of material, solve the same kinds of math problems, reason with a similar level of judgment, and so forth. But some have complained that the concept of mental age is too broad and that although a 6-year-old might, for example, perform intellectually like a 12-year-old, the 6-year-old might not be very similar at all to the average 12-year-old socially, psychologically, and otherwise. In addition to such intuitive considerations, the mental age concept has also been criticized on technical grounds.[1]

Grade norms   Designed to indicate the average test performance of testtakers in a given grade, **grade norms** are developed by administering the test to representative samples of children over a range of consecutive grade levels (such as first through sixth grade). Next, the mean or median score for children at each grade level is computed. Because the school year typically runs from September to June—ten months—fractions in the mean or median are easily expressed as decimals. Thus, for example, a sixth-grader performing exactly at the average on a grade-normed test administered during the fourth month of the school year (December) would achieve a grade-equivalent score of 6.4. Like age norms, grade norms have widespread application with children of elementary school age, the thought here being that children learn and develop at varying rates but in ways that are in some aspects predictable.

Suppose Raoul is in grade 12 but his score on a grade-normed spelling test is 6. Does this mean that Raoul has the same spelling abilities as the average sixth-grader? The answer is no: Accurately interpreted, all this finding means is that Raoul and a hypothetically average sixth-grader answered the same fraction of items correctly on that test. Grade norms do not provide information as to the content or type of items that a student could or could not answer correctly. Perhaps the primary use of grade norms is as a convenient, readily understandable gauge of how one student's performance compares with that of fellow students in the same grade.

Some experts in testing have called for a moratorium on the use of grade-equivalent as well as age-equivalent scores because such scores may so easily be misinterpreted. One drawback to using grade norms is that they are useful only with respect to years and months of schooling completed. They have little or no applicability to children who are not yet in school or who are out of school. Age norms are also limited in this regard, since, for many tests, the value of such norms is limited with an adult population.[2]

National norms   As the name implies, **national norms** are derived from a standardization sample that was nationally representative of the population. In the fields of psy-

---

1. For many years, IQ (intelligence quotient) scores on tests such as the Stanford-Binet were calculated by dividing mental age (as indicated by the test) by chronological age. The quotient would then be multiplied by 100 to eliminate the fraction. The distribution of IQ scores had a mean set at 100 and a standard deviation of approximately 16. A child of 12 with a mental age of 12 had an IQ of 100 ($12/12 \times 100 = 100$). The technical problem here is that IQ standard deviations were not constant with age; at one age, an IQ of 116 might be indicative of performance at 1 standard deviation above the mean, whereas at another age an IQ of 121 might be indicative of performance at 1 standard deviation above the mean.

2. But use of age norms in tests standardized with adult populations can be expected to rise in future years. With the graying of America, there is increased interest in performance on various types of psychological tests as a function of advancing age. Already, we are beginning to see more and more age-specific norms in the adult age range in the area of neuropsychological assessment.

chology and education, for example, national norms may be obtained through the testing of large numbers of students representative of different variables of interest such as socioeconomic strata, geographical location (such as North, East, South, West, Midwest), and different types of communities within the various parts of the country (such as rural, urban, suburban). Norms would typically be obtained for every grade to which the test sought to be applicable, and other factors related to the representativeness of the school itself might be criteria for inclusion in or exclusion from the standardization sample. For example, is the school the student attends publicly funded, privately funded, religiously oriented, military oriented, or something else? How representative are the pupil-teacher ratios in the schools under consideration? Does the school have a library and, if so, how many books are in it? These are only a sample of the types of questions that could be raised in assembling a standardization sample to be used in the establishment of national norms. The precise nature of the questions asked will depend on whom the test is designed for and what it is designed to do. Because norms from different tests all represented as national in nature may have nationally representative standardization samples that differ in many important respects, it is always a good idea to check the manual of the tests under consideration to see exactly how comparable the tests are. The greater the differences in standardization sample among such tests, the less the comparability of students' scores.

National anchor norms   Even the most casual survey of catalogues from various test publishers will reveal that, with respect to almost any human characteristic or ability, there exist many different tests purporting to measure the characteristic or ability. Dozens of tests, for example, purport to measure reading. Suppose we select a reading test designed for use in grades 3 to 6, which—for the purposes of this hypothetical example— we call the "Best Reading Test" (BRT). Suppose further that we now want to be able to compare findings obtained on another national reading test designed for use with grades 3 to 6, the "XYZ Reading Test," with the BRT. An equivalency table for scores on the two tests or **national anchor norms** could provide the tool for such a comparison. Just as an anchor provides some stability to a vessel, so national anchor norms provide some stability to test scores by anchoring them to other test scores.

The method by which such equivalency tables or national anchor norms are established typically begins with the computation of percentile norms for each of the tests to be compared. Using the **equipercentile method,** the equivalency of scores on different tests is calculated with reference to corresponding percentile scores. Thus, if the 96th percentile corresponds to a score of 69 on the BRT, and if the 96th percentile corresponds to a score of 14 on the XYZ, we can say that a BRT score of 69 is equivalent to an XYZ score of 14. We should note that the national anchor norms for our hypothetical BRT and XYZ tests must have been obtained on the same sample—each member of the sample took both tests and the equivalency tables were then calculated on the basis of these data.[3] Although national anchor norms provide an indication of the equivalency of scores on various tests, it would be a mistake, because of technical considerations, to treat these equivalencies as precise equalities (Angoff, 1964, 1966, 1971).

Subgroup norms   A standardization sample can be segmented by any of the criteria initially used in selecting subjects for the sample, and **subgroup norms** for any of these more narrowly defined groups can be developed. Thus, for example, suppose criteria used in selecting children for inclusion in the "XYZ Reading Test" standardization sample were age, educational level, socioeconomic level, geographic region, community type, and

---

3. When two tests are normed from the same sample, the norming process is referred to as *co-norming.* Co-norming is discussed later in this chapter.

handedness (whether the child was right-handed or left-handed). The test manual or a supplement to it might report normative information by each of these subgroups. A community school board member might find the regional norms to be most useful, whereas a psychologist doing exploratory research in the area of brain lateralization and reading scores might find the handedness norms most useful.

Local norms Typically developed by test users themselves, **local norms** provide normative information with respect to the local population's performance on some test. A local company personnel director might find some nationally standardized test useful in making selection decisions but might deem the norms published in the test manual to be far afield from local job applicants' score distributions. Individual high schools may wish to develop their own school norms (local norms) for student scores on some examination that is administered statewide. A school guidance center may find that locally derived norms for a particular test—say, a survey of personal values—are more useful in counseling students than the national norms printed in the manual.

Fixed Reference Group Scoring Systems

Norms provide a context for interpreting the meaning of a test score. Another type of aid in providing a context for interpretation is termed a **fixed reference group scoring system.** Here, the distribution of scores obtained on the test from one group of testtakers—referred to as the "fixed reference group"—is used as the basis for the calculation of test scores for future administrations of the test. Perhaps the test most familiar to college students that exemplifies the use of a fixed reference group scoring system is the SAT. This test was first administered in 1926. Its norms were then based on the mean and standard deviation of the people who took the test at the time. With passing years, more colleges—as well as a variety of different kinds of colleges—became members of the College Board, the sponsoring organization for the test. It soon became evident that SAT scores tended to vary somewhat as a function of the time of year the test was administered. In an effort to ensure perpetual comparability and continuity of scores, the custom of norming the SAT with respect to the group of testtakers who had taken a given administration of the test was abandoned in 1941.

The distribution of scores from the 11,000 people who took the SAT in 1941 was immortalized as a standard to be used in the conversion of raw scores on future administrations of the test. The scores obtained by this fixed reference group of 1941 paralleled successive administrations of the test. A new fixed reference group, the more than 2 million testtakers who completed the SAT in 1990, began to be used in 1995. A score of 500 on the SAT corresponds to the mean obtained by the 1990 sample, a score of 400 corresponds to a score that is 1 standard deviation below the 1990 mean, and so forth. As an example, suppose John took the SAT in 1995 and answered 50 items correctly on a particular scale. And let's say Mary took the test in 1996 and, just like John, answered 50 items correctly. Although John and Mary may have achieved the same raw score, they would not necessarily achieve the same scaled score. If, for example, the 1996 version of the test under discussion was judged to be somewhat easier than the 1995 version, scaled scores for the 1996 testtakers would be calibrated downward so that scores achieved in 1996 would be comparable to scores earned in 1995. The statistical procedures used to equate scores from one administration to the next are technically sophisticated.

Test items common to each new version of the SAT and each previous version of it are employed in a procedure (termed *anchoring*) that permits the conversion of raw scores on the new version of the test into what are technically referred to as "fixed reference group scores." Like other fixed reference group scores, including Graduate Record Examination scores (see *Everyday Psychometrics*), SAT scores are most typically interpreted with respect to local norms. Thus, for example, admissions offices of colleges usually rely on their own independently collected norms to make selection decisions. Judgments may, in part, be based on SAT scores for those who successfully completed their program as opposed to scores for dropouts. Conceptually, the idea of a "fixed reference group" seems analogous to the idea of a "fixed reference foot"—the foot of the English king that also became immortalized as a measurement standard (Angoff, 1962).

Norm-Referenced Versus Criterion-Referenced Interpretation

As we have seen, one way to derive meaning from test scores is to evaluate the test score in relation to other scores on the same test. This approach to testing and assessment is termed **norm-referenced;** test scores are understood relative to other test scores on the same test. Terms such as *norm group* and *normative group* may be used to describe the body of scores with which an individual testtaker's performance is being compared.

Unlike norm-referenced approaches to testing and assessment, a **criterion-referenced** approach does not describe test performance in terms of the testtaker's relative standing among others; rather, test scores are interpreted with regard to some standard or criterion. Examples of the criterion-referenced approach to measurement abound. A community might legislate as a standard that students must demonstrate at least a sixth-grade reading level as one requirement for the award of a high school diploma. An airline might require that all its pilots meet a certain set level of proficiency on a battery of tests. The professional community may decide that a particular level of performance on a licensing examination is necessary to demonstrate competence to practice as a psychologist.

The criterion in criterion-referenced assessments typically derives from the values or standards of an individual or organization. An airline, for example, may have little interest in how a particular pilot performs on a flight simulator relative to other pilots taking the same test on the same day. Rather, the airline requires assurance that the pilot demonstrates a reasonable level of proficiency—regardless of how well or how poorly all the other pilots performed.

What we are referring to as criterion-referenced tests have been variously called **domain-** or **content-referenced tests** because the focus of interest is not on individual scores in relation to other people's scores but on scores in relation to a particular content area or domain.[4] Generally speaking, it can be said that criterion-referenced interpretations provide information about what people can do, whereas norm-referenced interpretations provide information about how people have done in relation to other people. Criterion-referenced tests are frequently used to gauge achievement or mastery (and are sometimes referred to as "mastery tests" in this context). "Has this flight trainee mastered the material she needs to be an airline pilot?" This is the type of question that an airline personnel office might have to address with a test of mastery (that is, a criterion-referenced test). If a standard, or criterion, for passing on a hypothetical "Airline Pilot

---

4. Although acknowledging that "content-referenced" interpretations can be referred to as "criterion-referenced" interpretations, the 1974 edition of *Standards* also noted a technical distinction between interpretations referred to as "criterion-" and "content- referenced": "*Content referenced* interpretations are those where the score is directly interpreted in terms of performance at each point on the achievement continuum being measured. *Criterion-referenced* interpretations are those where the score is directly interpreted in terms of performance at any given point on the continuum of an *external* variable. An external criterion variable might be grade averages or levels of job performance" (p. 19; footnote in original omitted).

Good Ol' Norms and the GRE

Some time before or after you graduate from college, the Graduate Record Exam (GRE) may be on your "to do" list. Knowing that the GRE test scores may influence the choices you have in graduate schools and, by extension, your graduate career and your life in general, you are likely to read the test results eagerly but a bit fearfully as well. Assuming you have taken the GRE General Test, you will have three scores, one each for verbal ability, quantitative ability, and analytical ability. How do you understand those scores?

Knowing what you do about norms, and knowing that the GRE has a mean of 500 and a standard deviation of 100, you might feel confident about making certain interpretations about a given set of scores. However, what you also need to know is that the mean of 500 and the standard deviation of 100 apply to scores obtained by people who took the GRE in 1952; their scores were immortalized as a normative or fixed reference group. To know the meaning of a score earned today requires current normative tables supplied by the Educational Testing Service (ETS).

By way of explanation, consider the case of Dexter, an English literature major. In 2002, Dexter received the following GRE scores: 640 on verbal ability, 700 on quantitative ability, and 520 on analytical ability. Knowing that the GRE has a mean of 500 and a standard deviation of 100, and not taking the time to learn much more about the actual meaning of the scores, Dexter made some immediate conclusions about his abilities.

Dexter concluded that quantitative ability was his strong suit. After all, his quantitative score was 2 standard deviations above the mean—a score that exceeded the scores of over 97% of his fellow testtakers. "Perhaps English literature was the wrong major," he thought aloud. He then went on to analyze his analytic ability score. "Average to slightly above average compared with those I will be competing with for entrance to graduate school." So far, is Dexter's analysis accurate?

In a word, no. Dexter is wrongly assuming that the GRE among current testtakers has a mean of 500 and a standard deviation of 100. But the GRE uses a fixed reference group scoring system. The reference group for the verbal and quantitative portions of the test comprised people who took the GRE in 1952. On that occasion, the mean score of the people who took the test was set at 500, with a standard deviation at 100. In the 50-plus years since the fixed reference group was tested, there have been significant changes in the population taking the GRE. These changes in the population

of testtakers have necessitated changes in the way a contemporary GRE score report is interpreted.

ETS makes available the current norms of the GRE to individual students and institutions. The information is presented in terms of percentiles, with the percentage of examinees scoring below a particular score reported across the distribution of GRE scores. The report of scores sent to testtakers includes such percentile information for the scores earned by that testtaker. Had Dexter taken the time to read this information, he could have more accurately interpreted his scores relative to the college seniors and college graduates who took the test in the same period of time as he. In this hypothetical example, we will refer to this time period simply as "Now."

Suppose, for the sake of this example, that verbal ability scores of 640 are at the 87th percentile, quantitative ability scores of 700 are at the 79th percentile, and analytical ability scores of 520 are at the 35th percentile. With that information, a different picture of Dexter and his abilities emerges.

Relative to testtakers "Now," Dexter does best in the verbal ability area, scoring better than 87% of other testtakers. His quantitative ability performance, better than 79% of others, is clearly above the median but not as outstanding as his verbal performance. Dexter's analytical performance is actually below the median, with only 35% of testtakers scoring lower than he did. After reviewing his score report with a staff member in his school's counseling center, Dexter is reassured that English literature was a good choice of major after all.

Learning about the derivation and interpretation of GRE scores, you may wonder about the benefits of perpetuating what may seem to be a needlessly complicated and outdated system. Why retain decades-old data as a fixed reference norm group? Why the necessity for changing percentile values corresponding to specific GRE scores? Why hasn't ETS reset the GRE mean at 500 and its standard deviation at 100 for each new year, if not for each administration of the test? Certainly such a resetting would simplify interpretation of individual scores.

Frequent renorming of the GRE would make meaningful comparisons between people who sat for the examination at different times extremely difficult, if not impossible. By contrast, the system that is in place guarantees that meaningful comparisons between people and across time can be made. Indeed, the GRE exists for the purpose of assisting institutions in making decisions about matters such as graduate school admission and the awarding of scholarships. The test's ability to make meaningful comparisons is retained under the current system. A GRE score of 500 on the quantitative (or verbal) test means that the testtaker has performed at the average level of people who took the GRE in 1952. For this or any other specific score, the score represents a set level of performance regardless of when the test was taken.

When members of the fixed reference group took the test in 1952, the GRE scores were set with a mean of 500 and a standard deviation of 100. Assuming a normal distribution of scores, percentile values for a sampling of specific scores would be as follows:

GRE Score	Percentile Value in 1952
700	98
600	84
500	50
400	16
300	2

In our hypothetical example for the period of time we are referring to as "Now," the patterns of test scores have changed somewhat:

GRE Score	Percentile Value in 1952	Percentile Value "Now"	
		Verbal	Quantitative
700	98	95	79
600	84	79	56
500	50	51	31
400	16	19	11
300	2	3	2

As compared with 1952, the distribution of scores on the verbal ability test is not vastly different. Although the scores seem to have spread out a bit more in recent years, the median is essentially the same. A slightly larger proportion of people score both at the lower and at the higher ends of the scale. For example, 16% of students scored over 600 in 1952, and 21% of students scored over 600 in 1989 to 1992.

The distribution of scores on the quantitative ability test is considerably different for the two time periods. In this case, a greater proportion of people are getting higher scores than was the case in 1952. In 1952, students scoring

over 700 constituted only about 2% of the population of testtakers. In the "Now" sample, such students constituted fully 21% of the group.

A factor contributing to the change in the distribution of quantitative scores is that more international students now take the GRE than in 1952. Many of these students have better math ability than do U.S. students, causing a rise in the median ability level among all testtakers.

Returning to the issue of renorming the GRE more frequently, can you imagine how things would be different if that were the case? If the level of ability being tested in the population were to change, as it seems to have done for quantitative ability, then the meaning of specific scores would also change. This can be illustrated by the case of two students taking the GRE five years apart. The two students are applying for admission to the same competitive graduate program. During the five-year period separating the testings, an increasing proportion of people with good quantitative ability entered the population and took the GRE. The first student took the GRE with relatively few highly quantitatively skilled people and got a score of 660 on the quantitative test. The second student took the GRE with many highly quantitatively skilled people and also got a score of 660 on the quantitative test.

Under the current system, in which the test is not renormed annually, we would conclude that two students with similar scores have similar levels of quantitative performance; a direct comparison would be valid. However, if the test were renormed annually, the second student's score described above would actually represent better quantitative skill because that student was compared with more quantitatively skilled people. Clearly, renorming would diminish comparability of scores across different testings.

In this discussion, we have touched on issues related to the GRE verbal and quantitative test scores. As you might suspect, there are additional issues related to norms concerning the analytical ability scores and Subject Test scores. A consideration of these more complex norm-related issues awaits you after you have taken the GRE and earned a place in a graduate psychometrics program. Alternatively, you can write to Educational Testing Service, P.O. Box 6000, Princeton, NJ 08541-6000, for more information about the GRE or any of its other tests. Interested students may also wish to write to obtain current percentile values that correspond to GRE scores, as the "Now" data presented here were only hypothetical.

Test" (APT) has been set at 85% correct, then trainees who score 84% correct or less will not pass; it matters not whether they scored 84% or 42%. Conversely, trainees who score 85% or better on the test will pass whether or not they scored 85% or 100%; all who score 85% or better are said to have mastered the skills and knowledge necessary to be an airline pilot. Taking this example one step further, another airline might find it useful to set up three categories of findings based on criterion-referenced interpretation of test scores:

85% or better correct = pass

75% to 84% correct = retest after two-month refresher course

74% or less = fail

How should cut scores in mastery testing be determined? How many test items and what kinds of test items are needed to demonstrate mastery in a given field? The answers to these and related questions could be the subject of a text in itself; they have been tackled in such diverse ways as empirical analyses (for example, Panell & Laabs, 1979) and applications of decision theory (Glaser & Nitko, 1971) and other prediction techniques (Ferguson & Novick, 1973).

The criterion-referenced approach has enjoyed widespread acceptance in the field of computer-assisted education programs where mastery of segments of materials is assessed before the program user can proceed to the next level of material. This approach is also utilized in educational assessment to determine if students have mastered basic academic skills, including reading and arithmetic. The criterion-referenced approach is the basis for curriculum-based assessment. Critics of the criterion-referenced approach argue that if it is strictly followed, potentially important information about an individual's performance relative to other testtakers is lost. Another criticism is that although this approach may have value with respect to the assessment of mastery of basic knowledge, skills, or both, it has little or no meaningful application at the upper end of the knowledge/skill continuum. Although it might be meaningful to use criterion-oriented tests to see if pupils have mastered basic reading, writing, and arithmetic, the value of such tests would be at best questionable in gauging the progress of an advanced doctoral-level student in his or her area of specialization; stand-alone originality and brilliant analytic ability are not the stuff of which criterion-oriented tests are made. By contrast, brilliance and superior abilities are recognizable in tests that employ norm-referenced interpretations; they're the scores you see all the way to the right on the normal curve, past the third standard deviation.

Before leaving our comparison of norm- and criterion-referenced testing, let's note that all testing is in reality normative—even if the scores are as seemingly criterion-referenced as pass/fail in nature. Even in a pass/fail score, there is an inherent acknowledgment that a continuum of abilities exists—it's just that some dichotomizing cutoff point has been applied.

We now proceed to a discussion of another one of those words that—along with *impeach* and *percentile*—would easily make a national list of Frequently Used but Little Understood Terminology. The word is *correlation*—a word that enjoys widespread confusion with the concept of causation. Let's state at the outset that correlation is *not* synonymous with causation. But what does *correlation* mean? And what is meant by *regression?* Read on.

Correlation and Regression

Central to psychological testing and assessment is finding out how some things (such as traits, abilities, or interests) are related to other things (such as behavior). A **coefficient**

of correlation is the number that provides us with an index of the strength of the relationship between two things. An understanding of the concept of correlation and an ability to compute a coefficient of correlation is therefore central to the study of tests and measurement.

The Concept of Correlation

Simply stated, **correlation** is an expression of the degree and direction of correspondence between two things; a coefficient of correlation (r) expresses a linear relationship between two (and only two) variables, usually continuous in nature. It reflects the degree of concomitant variation between variable X and variable Y. The *coefficient of correlation* is the numerical index that expresses this relationship; it tells us the extent to which X and Y are "co-related."

The meaning of a correlation coefficient is interpreted by its sign (positive or negative—indicative of a positive or a negative correlation) and by its magnitude (the greater its absolute value, the greater the degree of relatedness). A correlation coefficient can range in value from $+1$ to -1. If a correlation coefficient is $+1$ or -1, this means that the relationship between the two variables is perfect—without error in the statistical sense. Here, "error" refers to variability or imprecision of measurement and not to a mistake. Perfect correlations in psychological work—or other work for that matter—are difficult to find (just as perfection in almost anything tends to be difficult if not impossible to find). If a correlation is zero, then no relationship exists between the two variables. If two variables simultaneously increase or simultaneously decrease, then those two variables are said to be *positively* (or directly) correlated. The height and weight of normal, healthy children ranging in age from birth to 10 years tends to be positively or directly correlated; as children get older, their height and their weight generally increase simultaneously. A positive correlation also exists when two variables simultaneously decrease (for example, the less preparation a student does for an examination, the lower the score on the examination). A *negative* (or inverse) correlation occurs when one variable increases while the other variable decreases. For example, there tends to be an inverse relationship between the number of miles on your car's odometer (mileage indicator) and the number of dollars a car dealer is willing to give you on a trade-in allowance; all other things being equal, as the mileage increases, the number of dollars offered as a trade-in decreases.

As we stated in our introduction to this topic, correlation is often confused with causation. It must be emphasized that a correlation coefficient is merely an index of the relationship between two variables, *not* an index of the causal relationship between two variables. If you were told, for example, that from birth to age 5 there is a high positive correlation between hat size and spelling ability, would it be appropriate to conclude that hat size causes spelling ability? Of course not; this is a time of maturation in *all* areas, including development in cognitive and motor abilities as well as growth in physical size. Thus, although intellectual development parallels physical development in these years and although it is true that a relationship clearly exists between physical and mental growth, it is not necessarily a causal relationship.

Although correlation does not imply causation, there *is* an implication of prediction. Stated another way, if we know that there is a high correlation between X and Y, we should be able to predict—with various degrees of accuracy, depending on other factors—the value of one of these variables if we know the value of the other.

The Pearson r

The *Pearson product-moment correlation*, also known as the *Pearson correlation coefficient* and simply as the **Pearson r,** is the most widely used of several alternative measures of

Almost Everything You May Want to Know About the Development of the Pearson *r*

If Galton is credited with developing correlation, why has the most widely used correlation coefficient become known as a "Pearson *r*"? What does that italicized *r* stand for? And why is it sometimes referred to as "product-moment" correlation? For the answers to these questions, we go back to the laboratory of Sir Francis Galton.

Investigating the role of genetics with respect to physical characteristics, Galton developed several statistical techniques. His interest in being able to describe the rank of each subject in contrast to the rank of every other subject led him to the development of the concept of a median—the point at which 50% of the sample falls above and below. Because physical measurements from generation to generation in humans had not been made, much of Galton's initial experimentation involved work with plants. Galton examined the diameter and weight of mother and daughter sweet pea seeds and through tables and graphs constructed ways of examining their relationship. Karl Pearson later recollected that these tables and graphs were the early precursors to more familiar correlation tables and scatterplots.

In an 1877 paper, "Typical Laws of Heredity," Galton presented his findings with formulas for a phenomenon he labeled "reversion"—and abbreviated by reference to the first initial *r*. The *r* used today to denote "correlation" is a statistical descendant of the *r* Sir Francis Galton used to describe what he called "reversion" (which has subsequently come to be referred to as "regression"). Galton had observed that the mother pea's magnitude of deviation from the population mean differed from the daughter pea's magnitude of deviation from the population mean. Although it was generally true that the larger the mother sweet pea, the larger the daughter, there was also some "reversion" in size toward the average ancestral type.

In 1884 Galton fulfilled a dream by setting up his Anthropometric Laboratory at the International Health Exhibition in

Karl Pearson and his daughter

South Kensington, England. One of the traits Galton was interested in measuring was "stature" (that is, height), specifically the stature of fathers and sons. During the course of the one-year Exhibition, approximately nine thousand people went through the doors of Galton's Laboratory. Even at that time, Galton was aware that the father did not contribute solely to that characteristic in his son; Galton described the

correlation (see *Close-up*). It can be the statistical tool of choice when the relationship between the variables is linear and when the two variables being correlated are continuous (that is, they can theoretically take any value). Other correlational techniques can be employed with data that are discontinuous and where the relationship is nonlinear. The formula for the Pearson *r* takes into account the relativity of each test score's position (or,

YOU STANDARD SCORES ARE A BUNCH OF
DEVIATES ABOUT A MEAN OF ZERO!

cal index of the strength of the reversion or regression is the "coefficient of regression" (symbolized by the letter r). But as a result of the work of Galton's contemporary, Karl Pearson, we have now come to view what Galton labeled r to be a measure of the slope (b) of a regression line. Pearson developed an alternative formula for Galton's r, and it is the latter r (the Pearson r) that has become the most-used measure of correlation. But why is the Pearson r referred to as a "product-moment" coefficient of correlation?

A *moment* is a relatively brief, indefinite time interval—according to one usage of that word. In psychometric parlance, the word *moment* is used to describe a deviation about a mean of a distribution.

Now consider the word *deviate*. Individual deviations about the mean of a distribution are referred to as *deviates*. In psychometric parlance, deviates are referred to as the "first moments" of the distribution. The "second moments" of the distribution are the moments squared. The "third moments" of the distribution are the moments cubed, and so forth.

The computation of the Pearson r in one of its many formulas entails multiplying corresponding standard scores on two measures. One way of conceptualizing standard scores is as "the first moments of a distribution"—this is because standard scores are deviates about a mean of zero. A formula that entails the multiplication of two corresponding standard scores can therefore be conceptualized as one that entails the computation of the *product* of corresponding *moments.* Because r is the average product of the first moments of two distributions, it may well have been referred to in terms such as "product-of-moments correlation," "average-product-of-first-moments correlation," or "average-product-of-corresponding-moments correlation." The simpler *product-moment correlation* is the term commonly used to refer to r.

contribution of the father to the son's height as a "partial" contribution—other ancestral or genetic factors were operative as well. In a paper read by Galton at a scientific meeting on December 5, 1888, he discussed his findings and promised that "it will be shown how the closeness of co-relation in any particular case admits of being expressed by a single number" (cited in Magnello & Spies, 1984).

Galton felt that a numerical index of the strength of the reversion or regression phenomenon could be obtained by calculating the slope for the *regression line*—the line of best fit through all the points in the scatterplot. The numeri-

stated more broadly, each measurement's position) with respect to the mean of its distribution of scores.

A number of formulas can be used to calculate a Pearson r. One formula necessitates converting each raw score to a standard score and then multiplying each pair of standard scores. A mean for the sum of the products is calculated, and that mean is the value of the Pearson *r*. Even from this simple verbal conceptualization of what a Pearson *r* is, it can be seen that the sign of the resulting *r* would be a function of the sign and the magnitude of the standard scores being used; if, for example, negative standard score values for measurements of *X* always corresponded with negative standard score values for *Y* scores, the resulting *r* would be positive (because the product of two negative values is positive). Similarly, if positive standard score values on *X* always corresponded with positive standard score values on *Y*, the resulting correlation would also be positive. However, if positive standard score values for *X* corresponded with negative standard score values for *Y* and vice versa, an inverse relationship would exist and a negative correlation would result. A zero or near-zero correlation could result when some products are positive and some are negative.

The formula used to calculate a Pearson *r* from raw scores is as follows:

$$r = \frac{\Sigma\, (X - \bar{X})\,(Y - \bar{Y})}{\sqrt{[\Sigma\, (X - \bar{X})^2]\,[\Sigma\,(Y - \bar{Y})^2]}}$$

This formula can and has been simplified for shortcut purposes. One such shortcut formula is a deviation formula employing "little *x*," or *x* in place of $X - \bar{X}$ and "little *y*," or *y* in place of $Y - \bar{Y}$:

$$r = \frac{\Sigma\, xy}{\sqrt{(\Sigma\, x^2)\,(\Sigma\, y^2)}}$$

Another formula for calculating a Pearson *r* is as follows:

$$r = \frac{N\,\Sigma\, XY - (\Sigma\, X)\,(\Sigma\, Y)}{\sqrt{N\,\Sigma\, X^2 - (\Sigma\, X)^2}\,\sqrt{N\,\Sigma\, Y^2 - (\Sigma\, Y)^2}}$$

Although this formula looks more complicated than the previous deviation formula, it is easier to use. *N* represents the number of paired scores; $\Sigma\, XY$ is the sum of the product of the paired *X* and *Y* scores; $\Sigma\, X$ is the sum of the *X* scores; $\Sigma\, Y$ is the sum of the *Y* scores; $\Sigma\, X^2$ is the sum of the squared *X* scores and $\Sigma\, Y^2$ is the sum of the squared *Y* scores. Similar results are obtained with the use of each formula.

The next logical question concerns what to do with the number obtained for the value of *r*. The answer is that you ask even more questions, such as "Is this number statistically significant given the size and nature of the sample?" or "Could this result have occurred by chance?" At this point, you will need to consult tables of significance for Pearson *r*—tables that are probably in the back of your old statistics textbook. In those tables you will find, for example, that a Pearson *r* of .899 with an *N* = 10 is significant at the .01 level (using a two-tailed test). You will recall from your statistics course that significance at the .01 level tells you, with reference to these data, that a correlation such as this could have been expected to occur by chance alone one time or less in a hundred if *X* and *Y* are not correlated in the population. You will also recall that significance at either the .01 level or the (somewhat less rigorous) .05 level—meaning that result could have been expected to occur by chance alone five times or less in a hundred—provides a basis to conclude with confidence that a correlation does indeed exist.

The value obtained for the coefficient of correlation can be further interpreted by deriving from it what is called a **coefficient of determination** or r^2. The coefficient of determination is an indication of how much variance is shared by the *X* and the *Y* variables. The calculation of r^2 is quite easy; simply square the correlation coefficient, multiply by 100, and express the result equal to the percentage of the variance accounted for. If, for example, you calculated an *r* to be .9, then r^2 would be equal to .81; the remaining variance, equal to $100\,(1 - r^2)$, or 19%, could presumably be accounted for by chance, error, or otherwise unmeasured or unexplainable factors. In an interesting but somewhat technical article, Ozer (1985) cautioned that the actual estimation of a coefficient of de-

Figure 4–2
Charles Spearman (1863–1945)

Charles Spearman is best known as the developer of the Spearman rho statistic and the Spearman-Brown prophecy formula, which is used to "prophesy" the accuracy of tests of different sizes. He has also been credited with being the father of factor analysis. He was fairly moderate in his views regarding statistical versus more intuitive approaches to the study of psychology. He wrote, "At one extreme, statistical zealots have accumulated masses of figures that remain psychologically senseless. At the other extreme, no less ardent typologists have been evolving an abundance of psychological ideas with little or no genuine evidence as to their truth" (Spearman, 1930–1936, Vol. 2).

termination must be made with scrupulous regard to the assumptions operative in the particular case; evaluating a coefficient of determination solely in terms of variance accounted for may lead to interpretations that underestimate the magnitude of a relation.

The Spearman Rho

The Pearson *r* enjoys such widespread use and acceptance as an index of correlation that if, for some reason, it is not used to compute a correlation coefficient, mention is made of the statistic that was used. One commonly used alternative statistic is variously called a **rank-order correlation coefficient,** a **rank-difference correlation coefficient,** or simply **Spearman's rho.** Developed by Charles Spearman, a British psychologist (Figure 4–2), this coefficient of correlation is frequently used when the sample size is small (fewer than 30 pairs of measurements) and especially when both sets of measurements are in ordinal (or rank-order) form. Special tables are used to determine if an obtained rho coefficient is or is not significant.[5]

Graphic Representations of Correlation

One type of graphic description of correlation is the **scatterplot** or **scatter diagram.** A scatterplot is a simple graphing of the coordinate points for values of the *X* variable (placed along the graph's horizontal axis) and the *Y* variable (placed along the graph's vertical axis). Scatterplots are useful because they provide a quick indication of the direction and magnitude of the relationship, if any, between the two variables. Figures 4–3 and 4–4

---

5. Another ranking method of correlation is embodied in a correlation coefficient with another Greek letter name: the tau (τ). It is also referred to as "Kendall's tau" and use of this coefficient rests on no special assumptions. Interested readers are invited to consult Kendall (1948) for a detailed discussion of its development and applications.

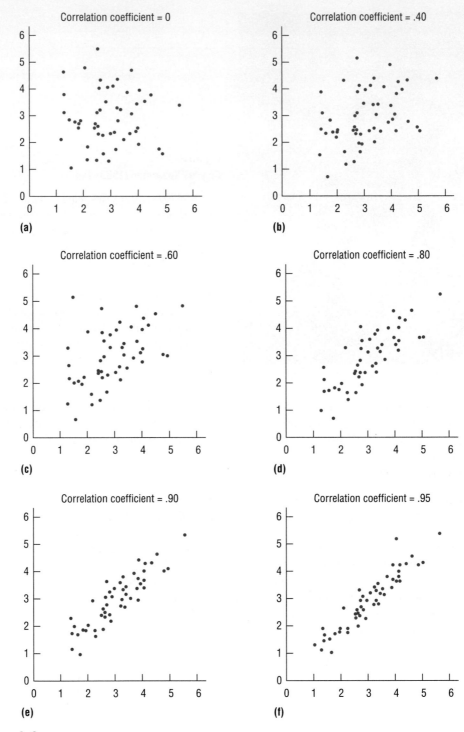

Figure 4–3
Scatterplots and Correlations for Positive Values of *r*

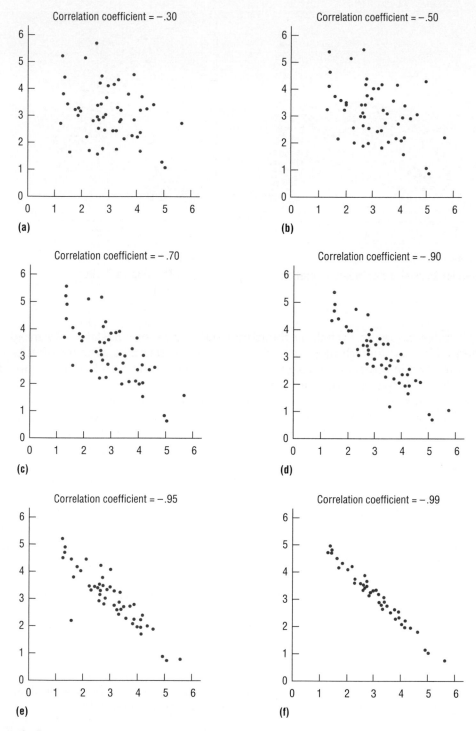

Figure 4–4
Scatterplots and Correlations for Negative Values of r

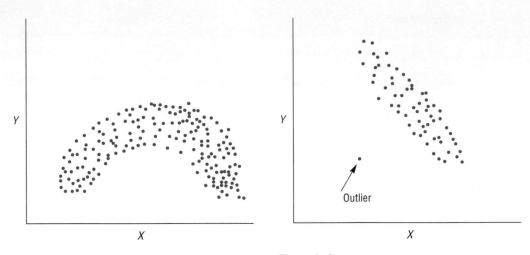

Figure 4–5
Scatterplot Showing a Nonlinear Correlation

Figure 4–6
Scatterplot Showing an Outlier

offer a quick course in eyeballing the nature and degree of correlation by means of scatterplots. In distinguishing positive from negative correlations, note the direction of the curve. And in estimating the strength of magnitude of the correlation, note the degree to which the points form a straight line.

Scatterplots are useful in revealing the presence of curvilinearity in a relationship. Remember that a Pearson *r* should be used only if the relationship between the variables is linear; if the graph does not appear to take the form of a straight line, the chances are good that the relationship is not linear (Figure 4–5). When the relationship is nonlinear, other statistical tools and techniques may be employed.[6]

A graph also makes the spotting of outliers relatively easy. An **outlier** is an extremely atypical point located at a relatively long distance—an outlying distance—from the rest of the coordinate points in a scatterplot (Figure 4–6). Outliers stimulate interpreters of test data to speculate about the reason for the atypical score. For example, the professor interpreting midterm examination data correlated with study time might wonder about Curly's performance on the test; Curly studied for ten hours and achieved a score of only 57. Was this outlier due to some situational emotional strain? Poor learning skills or study habits? Or was it simply reflective of using a very small sample? If the sample size were larger, perhaps more low-scorers who put in large amounts of study time would have been identified. Sometimes an outlier can provide a hint regarding some deficiency in the testing or scoring procedures.

Before leaving the subject of graphic representations of correlation, we should point out that the interpreter of such data needs to know, among other things, if the range of scores has been restricted in any way. To understand why this is the case, look at Figure 4–7. Let's say that graph A describes the relationship between Public University en-

---

6. The specific statistic to be employed will depend at least in part on the suspected reason for the nonlinearity. For example, if it is believed that the nonlinearity is due to one distribution being highly skewed because of a poor measuring instrument, the skewed distribution may be statistically normalized and the result may be a correction of the curvilinearity. If even after graphing the data a question remains concerning the linearity of the correlation, a statistic called "eta squared" (η^2) can be used to compute the exact degree of curvilinearity.

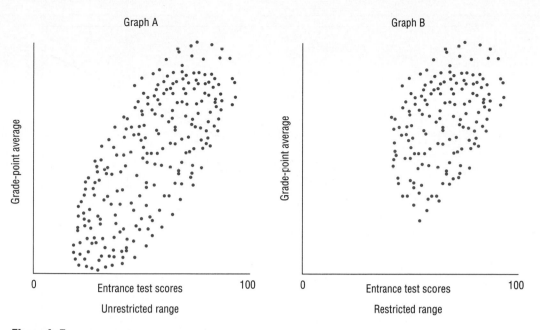

Graph A

Graph B

Grade-point average

Grade-point average

0 Entrance test scores 100

0 Entrance test scores 100

Unrestricted range

Restricted range

Figure 4–7
Two Scatterplots Illustrating Unrestricted and Restricted Ranges

trance test scores for 600 applicants (all of whom were later admitted) and their grade-point averages at the end of the first semester. The scatterplot indicates that the relationship between entrance test scores and grade-point average is both linear and positive. But what if the admissions officer had accepted only the applications of the students who scored within the top half or so on the entrance exam? To a trained eye, this scatterplot (graph B) appears to indicate a weaker correlation than that indicated in graph A—an effect attributable exclusively to the restriction of range. Graph B is less of a straight line than graph A, and its direction is not as obvious.

Regression

In everyday language, the word *regression* is synonymous with "reversion to some previous state." In the language of statistics, *regression* also describes a kind of reversion—a reversion to the mean over time or generations (or at least that is what was meant by it originally).

Regression may be defined broadly as the analysis of relationships among variables for the purpose of understanding how one variable may predict another. **Simple regression** involves one independent variable (X), typically referred to as the predictor variable, and one dependent variable (Y), typically referred to as the outcome variable. Simple regression analysis results in an equation for a regression line. The **regression line** is the "line of best fit," the straight line that, in one sense, comes closest to the greatest number of points on the scatterplot of X and Y.

Does the following equation look familiar?

$$Y = a + bX$$

In high school algebra, you were probably taught that this is the equation for a straight line. It's also the equation for a regression line. In the formula, a and b are **regression**

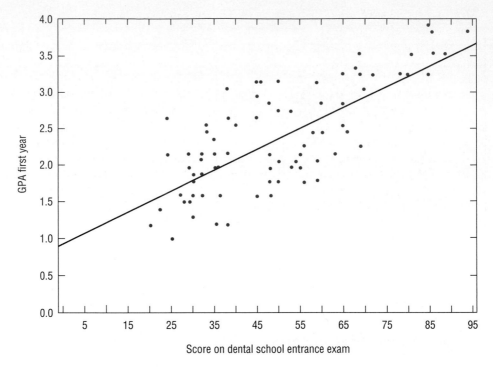

Figure 4–8
Graphic Representation of Regression Line

The correlation between X and Y is 0.76. The equation for this regression line is Y = 0.82 + 0.03(X); for each unit increase on X (the dental school entrance examination score), the predicted value of Y (the first-year grade-point average) is expected to increase by .03 unit. The standard error of the estimate for this prediction is 0.49.

coefficients; *b* is equal to the slope of the line, and *a* is the **intercept,** a constant indicating where the line crosses the *Y*-axis. The regression line represented by specific values of *a* and *b* is fitted precisely to the points on the scatterplot, such that the sum of the squared vertical distances from the points to the line will be smaller than for any other line that could be drawn through the same scatterplot. Although finding the equation for the regression line might seem difficult, the values of *a* and *b* can be determined through simple algebraic calculations.

The primary use of a regression equation in testing is to predict one score or variable from another. For example, suppose a dean at the "De Sade School of Dentistry" wishes to predict what grade-point average (GPA) an applicant might have after the first year at De Sade. The dean would accumulate data about current students' scores on the dental college entrance examination and end-of-the-first-year GPA. These data would then be used to help predict the GPA (*Y*) from the score on the dental college admissions test (*X*). Individual dental students are represented by points in the scatterplot in Figure 4–8. The equation for the regression line is computed from these data. This means that the values of *a* and *b* are calculated. In this hypothetical case:

$$GPA = 0.82 + 0.03 \text{ (entrance exam)}$$

This line has been drawn onto the scatterplot in Figure 4–8.

Using the regression line, the likely value of Y (the GPA) can be predicted based on specific values of X (the entrance exam) by plugging the X-value into the equation. A student with an entrance exam score of 50 would be expected to have a GPA of 2.3. A student with an entrance exam score of 85 would be expected to earn a GPA of 3.7. This prediction could also be done graphically by tracing a particular value on the X-axis (the entrance exam score) up to the regression line, then straight across to the Y-axis, reading off the predicted GPA.

Of course, all students who get an entrance exam score of 50 do not earn the same GPA. This can be seen in Figure 4–8 by tracing from any specific entrance exam score on the X-axis up to the cloud of points surrounding the regression line. This is what is meant by error in prediction: Each of these students would be predicted to get the same GPA based on the entrance exam, but in fact they earned different GPAs. This error in the prediction of Y from X is represented by the **standard error of the estimate.** As you might expect, the higher the correlation between X and Y, the greater the accuracy of the prediction, and the smaller the standard error of the estimate.

Multiple regression   Suppose that the dean suspects that the prediction of GPA will be enhanced if another test score—say, a score on a test of fine motor skills—is also used as a predictor. The use of more than one score to predict Y requires the use of a *multiple regression* equation.

The **multiple regression** equation takes into account the intercorrelations among all the variables involved. The correlation between each of the predictor scores and what is being predicted (in this case, the correlation of the entrance exam and the fine motor skills test with the GPA in the first year of dental school) is reflected in the weight given to each predictor. Predictors that correlate highly with the predicted variable are generally given more weight, meaning that their regression coefficients (referred to as b-values) are larger. This is logical, because one would want to pay the most attention to predictors that predict Y best.

The multiple regression equation also takes into account the correlations among the predictor scores. In this case, it takes into account the correlation between the dental college admissions test scores and scores on the fine motor skills test. If many predictors are used, and one is not correlated with any of the other predictors but is correlated with the predicted score, then that predictor may be given relatively more weight because it is providing unique information. In contrast, if two predictor scores are highly correlated with each other, they could be providing redundant information. If both were kept in the regression equation, each might get less weight, so that they would "share" the prediction of Y.

More predictors are not necessarily better. If two predictors are providing the same information, the person using the regression equation may decide to use only one of them for the sake of efficiency. If the De Sade dean observed that dental school admission test scores and scores on the test of fine motor skills were highly correlated with each other and that each of these scores correlated about the same with GPA, the dean might decide to use only one predictor because nothing was gained by the addition of the second predictor.

Inference from Measurement

Correlation, regression, and multiple regression are all statistical tools used to help ensure that predictions or inferences drawn from test data are reasonable and—to the extent that it is technically possible—accurate. Another statistical tool that can be helpful in achieving such objectives is meta-analysis.

Meta-Analysis

No single research study can precisely determine the correlation between two variables or the exact coefficients for a regression equation.[7] For example, in a study of height and weight, we would not expect the correlation to be exactly the same each time the study is repeated. The relationship between height and weight will probably be at least slightly different for each group of people studied. To most accurately estimate the correlation between height and weight, we might want to include data from all available studies. However, using information from several studies creates a problem, because the correlation (or the mean, or the regression coefficients) will differ from study to study. How is this diverse information understood? One option is to present the range of statistical values that appear in various studies: "The correlation between variable X and variable Y ranges from .73 to .91." Another option is to combine statistically the information across the various studies. This statistical combination of information across studies is termed **meta-analysis.** Meta-analysis produces a single estimate of the statistic being studied. For example, "Meta-analysis estimates the correlation between variable X and variable Y at .81." Meta-analysis gives more weight to studies that have larger numbers of subjects, information that is not readily available when ranges are used to describe the data. This weighting process results in more accurate estimates (Hunter & Schmidt, 1990). Meta-analysis may be used to combine results across studies in order to obtain an estimate of effect and to compare effects between studies in order to better understand moderating factors (Hall & Rosenthal, 1995). Multiple regression and subgroup analysis are two of the most common techniques used to search for moderators.

Meta-analysis is a research tool that has been growing in popularity in recent years. It has been used to revisit conclusions made from a wide variety of quantitative studies. For example, a meta-analysis of 23 studies focusing on the consequences of subliminal advertising on consumer choice yielded very little effect. Contrary to the belief and fear of many consumers, subliminal advertising does not appear to be particularly compelling (Trappey, 1996). Blumenthal (1998) meta-analyzed research on what has been called the "reasonable woman standard" (RWS) in sexual harassment litigation. The RWS criterion was proposed to reflect what was thought to be a wide divergence between men and women regarding perceptions of harassing behavior. The meta-analysis of the available research failed to identify any such major divergence as a function of gender. Other examples of meta-analysis in the scholarly literature include meta-analysis of studies related to screening and diagnostic tests (Hasselblad & Hedges, 1995), the stigma associated with AIDS (Crawford, 1996), the effectiveness of school-based drug prevention programs (Tobler & Stratton, 1997), the effect of number of hours worked on health (Sparks et al., 1997), and how predictive the GRE combined with undergraduate grade-point average is of performance in graduate school (Kuncel et al., 2001).

In many ways, a meta-analysis is the quantitative analogue to a qualitative literature review. And just as there are many ways to write a literature review on a particular topic, so there are many different ways to conduct a meta-analysis (Cook et al., 1992; Rosenthal, 1991). The methodological issues and potential problems that attend meta-analytic

---

7. This is true unless all members of the population of interest are included in the study, something that almost never occurs.

research are legion (Ioannidis, et al., 1998; Lepper, 1995; Shadish, 1996; Sharpe, 1997). In general, although it is appropriate to use meta-analysis to increase the precision of quantitative estimates with regard to general populations, caution is the rule when applying the same data to make any sort of inference or conclusion about an individual case. As Charlton (1996) warned, because of the diversity of variables that are so often present in the studies being meta-analyzed, many complex, assumption-laden adjustments might be necessary if these data are to be applied to an individual case. Ultimately, the value of any meta-analytic investigation is very much a matter of the skill and ability of the meta-analyst (Kavale, 1995).

Culture and Inference

In a series of experiments on conformity, Solomon Asch (1951, 1955, 1957a, 1957b) demonstrated the profound influence of the opinions of group members on an individual. In one version of the experiment, subjects were seated around a table and told that their task would be to verbally select one of three lines that was the same length as a stimulus line. Actually, only one of the group members was a bona fide subject; all of the other group members were confederates of the experimenter who would, on cue, unanimously name the same, wrong line. Interestingly, Asch found that under such circumstances 76% of the subjects conformed to the obviously wrong choice of the group at least once. Since the mid-1950s, 133 studies in 17 countries have employed the Asch line judgment paradigm to study conformity. A meta-analysis of such studies brought to light differences in the results as a function of whether the culture in which the study was conducted was collectivistic or individualistic. Bond and Smith (1996) concluded that collectivistic countries evidenced higher levels of conformity than countries identified as more individualistic in nature.

Bond and Smith's (1996) meta-analysis of international research employing Asch-type line judgment tasks provides a useful point of departure for emphasizing the role of culture in evaluation, measurement, and the process of making inferences. In describing people with the use of trait terms such as, for example, "conformist" versus "nonconformist," we need to be clear about standards of comparison; in this case, conforming or nonconforming with reference to whom? Consider in this context an individual who hails from a collectivistic country such as China, who relocates to a strongly individualistic country such as the United States. In China, the person may have been viewed as a nonconformist given the norm of conformity in China. However, in the United States, this person's behavior might be viewed as conformist. In all likelihood, the conformity-related trait of this individual's personality did not reverse itself as a result of boarding a jet for the United States. What changed was the background or context that framed the behavior under scrutiny. In the figure-ground relationship, we know that changing the ground can markedly affect one's perception of the figure.

In the everyday practice of testing and assessment, a test's norms typically provide the background and context to frame the behavior under scrutiny. In most instances, as in the case of the vast majority of standardized tests, the test norms come in the form of tables published in the test manual.[8] Test users and assessment professionals have an obligation to use the appropriate norms when attempting to derive meaning and make

---

8. Less frequently, as in the case of a projective test used by a clinician in idiosyncratic fashion, the "norms" are more subjective and intuitive—the product not of formal normative research but of the test user's own education, training, clinical experience, and personal predilections.

inferences from data derived from tests, interviews, and other tools of psychological assessment. In recognition of this professional mandate, it is increasingly common to read of published evaluations of existing norms for use with particular populations, as well as norming projects conducted after the publication of a particular test, typically with groups that were either not included in the original normative sample or were believed to be underrepresented in that sample.[9] Also, in recent years increasing attention has been given to the technical and multifaceted issues regarding the adaptation of a test standardized and normed with members of one culture, for use with members of another culture (Ben-Porath, 1990; Bracken & Barona, 1991).

Further discussion of culture as it relates to test development, administration, and interpretation, as well as the process of making inferences from assessment, will be found in subsequent chapters. Now, let's continue to build a sound foundation in testing and assessment with a discussion of the psychometric concept of reliability.

---

9. Other situations may prompt an evaluation of the adequacy of existing norms or stimulate the development of new norms. These situations include substituting one subtest for another subtest, abbreviating a test in some way, or making any deviation from the test administration instructions in the test's manual (see, for example, Lyons & Scotti, 1994; McCusker, 1994; Reynolds et al., 1996).

Self-Assessment

Test your understanding of elements of this chapter by seeing if you can explain each of the following terms, expressions, and abbreviations:

age-equivalent scores

age norming

coefficient of correlation

coefficient of determination

convenience sample

correlation

criterion-referenced testing and assessment

cut score

fixed reference group scoring

grade norming

incidental sampling

local norms

meta-analysis

multiple regression

national anchor norms

national norms

normative sample

norming

norm-referenced testing and assessment

outlier

Pearson *r*

percentile

percentile norms

program norms

purposive sampling

race norming

raw score

regression

sample

scatterplot

simple regression

Spearman rho

standard error of the estimate

standardization sample

stratified-random sampling

stratified sampling

subgroup norms

user norms

$Y = a + bX$

5

Reliability

In everyday conversation, *reliability* is a synonym for dependability or consistency—as in "the train is so reliable that you can set your watch by it" or "the reliable friend who is always there if you are in need." In the language of psychometrics, reliability refers, broadly speaking, to the attribute of consistency in measurement. And whereas in everyday conversation reliability always connotes something that is positively valued, reliability in the psychometric sense merely connotes something that is consistent—not necessarily consistently good or bad, but simply consistent.

It is important for us as users of tests and consumers of information about tests to know how reliable tests and other measurement procedures are. But reliability is seldom an all-or-none matter; there are different types and degrees of reliability. A **reliability coefficient** is an index of reliability. More technically, it is a proportion that indicates the ratio between the true score variance on a test and the total variance. In this chapter, we explore different kinds of reliability coefficients, including those for measuring test-retest reliability, alternate-forms reliability, split-half reliability, and inter-scorer reliability.

The Concept of Reliability

Recall from our discussion of classical test theory in Chapter 1 that a score on an ability test is presumed to reflect both the testtaker's true score on the ability being measured, as well as error.[1] In its broadest sense, "error" refers to the component of the observed score on an ability test that does not have to do with the testtaker's ability. If we use X to represent an observed score, T to represent a true score, and E to represent error, then the fact that an observed score equals the true score plus error may be expressed as follows:

$$X = T + E$$

---

1. For illustration purposes, ability as a trait being measured is frequently used. However, unless stated otherwise, the principles to which we refer with respect to ability tests also hold true with respect to other types of tests, such as tests for personality. Thus, according to the true score model, it is also true that the magnitude of the presence of a certain psychological trait (such as extraversion) as measured by testing with a test of extraversion will be due to (1) the "true" amount of extraversion and (2) other factors.

A statistic useful in describing sources of test score variability is the **variance** (σ^2) — the standard deviation squared. This statistic is useful because it can be broken into components. Variance from true differences is **true variance,** and variance from irrelevant, random sources is **error variance.** If (σ^2) represents the total variance, (σ_{tr}^2) represents the true variance, and (σ_e^2) represents error variance, then the relationship of the variances can be expressed as

$$\sigma^2 = \sigma_{tr}^2 + \sigma_e^2$$

In this equation, the total variance in an observed distribution of test scores (σ^2) equals the sum of the true variance (σ_{tr}^2) plus the error variance (σ_e^2). The term **reliability** refers to the proportion of the total variance attributed to true variance. The greater the proportion of the total variance attributed to true variance, the more reliable the test. Because true differences are assumed to be stable, they are presumed to yield consistent scores on repeated administrations of the same test as well as on equivalent forms of tests. Because error variance may increase or decrease a test score by varying amounts, consistency of the test score—and thus the reliability—would be affected. Note that a systematic source of error would *not* affect score consistency. If a measuring instrument, such as a weight scale, consistently underweighed everyone who stepped on it by 5 pounds, then the relative standings of the people would remain unchanged (even though the weights themselves would consistently vary from the true weight by 5 pounds). A scale underweighing all comers by 5 pounds is analogous to a constant being subtracted from (or added to) every test score. A systematic error source does not change the variability of the distribution or affect reliability.

Sources of Error Variance

Sources of error variance include test construction, administration, scoring, and/or interpretation.

Test construction One source of variance during test construction is **item sampling** or **content sampling,** a term that refers to variation among items within a test, as well as to variation among items between tests. Consider two or more tests designed to measure a specific skill, personality attribute, or body of knowledge. Differences in the way the items are worded and differences in the exact content sampled are sure to be found. Each of us has probably walked into an achievement test setting, thinking "I hope they ask this question" or "I hope they don't ask that question." With luck, only the questions we wanted to be asked appeared on the examination. In such situations, some testtakers achieve higher scores on one test than they would on another test purporting to measure the same thing, simply because of the specific content sampled on the first test, the way the items were worded, and so on. The extent to which a testtaker's score is affected solely by the content sampled on the test as well as the way the content is sampled (that is, the way in which the item is constructed) is a source of error variance. From the perspective of a test author, a challenge in test development is to maximize the proportion of the total variance that is true variance and minimize the proportion of the total variance that is error variance.

Test administration Sources of error variance that occur during test administration may influence the testtaker's attention or motivation; thus, the testtaker's reactions to those influences are the source of one kind of error variance. Examples of untoward influences during administration of a test include factors related to the test environment: the room temperature, the level of lighting, and the amount of ventilation and noise, for instance.

A relentless fly may develop a tenacious attraction to an examinee's face. A wad of gum on the seat of the chair makes itself known only after the testtaker sits down on it. Other environment-related variables include the instrument used to enter responses (such as a pencil with a broken point or a pen that has dried up) and the writing surface (which may be riddled with heart carvings—the legacy of past years' students who felt compelled to express their eternal devotion to someone whom by now they have long forgotten).

Other potential sources of error variance during test administration include test-taker variables such as degree of physical discomfort, amount of sleep the night before, degree of test anxiety, pressing emotional problems, or the effects of drugs. A testtaker may, for whatever reason, make a mistake in entering a test response. For example, the examinee might blacken a "b" grid when he or she meant to blacken the "d" grid. An examinee might look at a test question such as "Which is not a factor that prevents measurements from being exactly replicable?" and mistakenly read, "Which is a factor that prevents measurements from being exactly replicable?" One carelessly skipped question on a long list of multiple-choice grid-type questions could result in subsequent test responses being out of sync; thus, for example, the testtaker might respond to the eighteenth item but blacken the grid for the seventeenth item, because the twelfth item was inadvertently skipped. Formal learning experiences, casual life experiences, therapy, illness, and other such events that may have occurred in the period between administrations of parallel forms of a test will also be sources of examinee-related error variance.

Examiner-related variables that are potential sources of error variance include the presence or absence of an examiner, the examiner's physical appearance and demeanor, and the professionalism the examiner brings to the test situation. Some examiners in some testing situations might knowingly or unwittingly depart from the procedure prescribed for a particular test. On an oral examination, some examiners might unwittingly provide clues by posing questions that emphasize various words or convey information about the correctness of a response through head nodding, eye movements, or other nonverbal gestures.

Test scoring and interpretation   The advent of computer scoring and a growing reliance on objective, computer-scorable items have virtually eliminated error variance caused by scorer differences in many tests. However, not all tests can be scored from grids blackened by number 2 pencils. Individually administered intelligence tests, some tests of personality, tests of creativity, various behavioral measures, and countless other tests still require hand scoring by trained personnel. Manuals for individual intelligence tests tend to be very explicit about scoring criteria lest examinees' measured intelligence vary as a function of who is doing the testing and scoring. In some tests of personality, examinees are asked to supply open-ended responses to stimuli such as pictures, words, sentences, and inkblots, and it is the examiner who must then score (or perhaps more appropriately, assess) the responses. In one test of creativity, examinees might be given the task of creating as many things as they can out of a set of blocks. For a behavioral measure of social skills in an inpatient psychiatric service, the scorers or raters might be asked to rate patients with respect to the variable of "social relatedness." Such a behavioral measure might require the rater to check "yes" or "no" to items like "Patient says 'Good morning' to at least two staff members."

You can appreciate that as soon as a psychological measure uses anything but objective-type items amenable to reliable computer scoring, the scorer or the scoring system becomes a source of error variance. If subjectivity is involved in scoring, the scorer (or rater) can be a source of error variance. Indeed, despite very rigorous scoring criteria set forth in many of the better-known tests of intelligence, examiner/scorers occasionally are still confronted by situations where an examinee's response lies in a gray area. The element of subjectivity in scoring may be much greater in the administration of certain non-objective-type personality tests and certain academic tests (such as essay examinations) and even in behavioral observation. Consider the case of two observers given the task of rating one psychiatric inpatient on the variable of "social relatedness." On an item that asks simply whether two staff members were greeted in the morning, one rater might judge the patient's eye contact and mumbling of something to two staff members to qualify as a "yes" response, whereas another observer might feel strongly that a "no" response to the item is appropriate. Such problems in scoring agreement can be addressed through rigorous training designed to make the consistency—or reliability—of various scorers as near perfect as can be.

Other sources of error Certain types of assessment situations lend themselves to particular varieties of systematic and nonsystematic error. For example, consider assessing the degree of agreement between partners regarding the quality and quantity of physical and psychological abuse in their relationship. As Moffitt et al. (1997) observed, "Because partner abuse usually occurs in private, there are only two persons who 'really' know what goes on behind closed doors: the two members of the couple" (p. 47). Potential sources of nonsystematic error in such an assessment situation include forgetting, failing to notice abusive behavior, and misunderstanding instructions regarding reporting. A number of studies (O'Leary & Arias, 1988; Riggs et al., 1989; Straus, 1979) have suggested that there are also factors that may contribute to systematic error in the form of underreporting or overreporting of perpetration of abuse. Females, for example, may underreport abuse due to fear, shame, or social desirability factors and overreport abuse if they are seeking help. Males may underreport abuse due to embarrassment and social desirability factors and overreport abuse if they are attempting to justify the report.

Just as the amount of abuse one partner suffers at the hands of the other may never be known, so the amount of test variance that is true relative to error may never be known. A so-called true score, as Stanley (1971, p. 361) put it, is "not the ultimate fact in the book of the recording angel." Further, the utility of current methods for estimating true versus error variance is a hotly debated matter (see, for example, Collins, 1996; Humphreys, 1996; Williams & Zimmerman, 1996a, 1996b). Let's take a closer look at such estimates and the process of deriving them.

Reliability Estimates

Test-Retest Reliability Estimates

A ruler made from the highest-quality steel can be a very reliable instrument of measurement; every time you measure something that is exactly 12 inches in length, for example, your ruler will tell you that what you are measuring is exactly 12 inches in length. The reliability of this instrument of measurement may also be said to be stable over time; whether you measure the 12 inches today, tomorrow, or next year, the ruler is still going to measure 12 inches as 12 inches. By contrast, a ruler constructed of putty might be a very unreliable instrument of measurement. One minute it could measure some known 12-inch standard as 12 inches, the next minute it could measure it as 14 inches, and a week later it could measure it as 18 inches. One way of estimating the reliability of a measuring instrument is by using the same instrument to measure the same thing at two points in time. In psychometric parlance, this approach to reliability evaluation is called the "test-retest method," and the result of such an evaluation is an estimate of "test-retest reliability."

Test-retest reliability is an estimate of reliability obtained by correlating pairs of scores from the same people on two different administrations of the same test. The test-retest measure is appropriate when evaluating the reliability of a test that purports to measure something that is relatively stable over time, such as a personality trait. If the characteristic being measured is assumed to fluctuate over time, there would be little sense in assessing the reliability of the test using the test-retest method; insignificant correlations between scores obtained on the two administrations of the test would be found. Such insignificant correlations would be due to real changes in whatever is being measured rather than to factors inherent in the measuring instrument.

As time passes, people change; they may, for example, learn new things, forget some things, and acquire new skills. It is generally the case—though there are exceptions—that as the time interval between administrations of the same test increases, the correlation between the scores obtained on each testing decreases. The passage of time can be a source of error variance. The longer the time that passes, the more likely the reliability coefficient will be lower. When the interval between testing is greater than six months, the estimate of test-retest reliability is often referred to as the **coefficient of stability.** An estimate of test-retest reliability from a math test might be low if the testtakers took a math tutorial before the second test was administered. An estimate of test-retest reliability from a personality profile might be low if the testtaker either suffered some emotional trauma or received counseling during the intervening period. A low estimate of test-retest reliability might be found even when the interval between testings is relatively brief, if the testings occur during a time of great developmental change with respect to the variables they are designed to assess. An evaluation of a test-retest reliability coefficient must therefore extend beyond the magnitude of the obtained coefficient; it must extend to a consideration of possible intervening factors between test administrations if we are to come to proper conclusions about the reliability of the measuring instrument.

An estimate of test-retest reliability may be most appropriate in gauging the reliability of tests that employ outcome measures such as reaction time or perceptual judgments (including discriminations of brightness, loudness, or taste). However, even in measuring variables such as these and even when the time period between the two administrations of the test is relatively small, note that various factors (such as experience, practice, memory, fatigue, and motivation) may intervene and confound an obtained measure of reliability.[2]

Parallel-Forms and Alternate-Forms Reliability Estimates

If you have ever taken a makeup exam in which the questions on the makeup were not all the same as on the test initially given, you have had experience with different forms of a test. And if you have ever wondered whether the two forms of the test were really equivalent, you have wondered about the **alternate-forms,** or **parallel-forms,** reliability of the test. The degree of the relationship between various forms of a test can be evaluated by means of an alternate-forms or parallel-forms coefficient of reliability, which is often termed the **coefficient of equivalence.**

Alternate forms and *parallel forms* are terms sometimes used interchangeably, although there is a technical difference between them. **Parallel forms** of a test exist when for each

---

2. Although we may refer to a number as the summary statement of the reliability of individual tools of measurement, any such index of reliability can only be meaningfully interpreted in the context of the process of measurement—the unique circumstances surrounding the use of the ruler, the test, or some other measuring instrument in a particular application or situation.

form of the test, the means and the variances of observed test scores are equal. In theory, the means of scores obtained on parallel forms correlate equally with the true score. More practically, scores obtained on parallel tests correlate equally with other measures. **Alternate forms** are simply different versions of a test that have been constructed so as to be parallel. Although they do not meet the requirements for the legitimate designation of "parallel," alternate forms of a test are typically designed to be equivalent with respect to variables such as content and level of difficulty.

Estimates of alternate- and parallel-forms reliability are similar to an estimate of test-retest reliability in two ways: (1) Two test administrations with the same group are required, and (2) test scores may be affected by factors such as motivation, fatigue, or intervening events such as practice, learning, or therapy (although not as much as when the same test is administered twice). However, an additional source of error variance—item sampling—is inherent in the computation of an alternate- or parallel-forms reliability coefficient; testtakers may do better or worse on a specific form of the test, not as a function of their true ability, but simply because of the particular items that were selected for inclusion in the test.[3] Another potential disadvantage of an alternate test form is financial in nature; it is typically time-consuming and expensive to develop alternate or parallel test forms—just think of all that might be involved in getting the same people to sit for repeated administrations of an experimental test! A primary advantage of using an alternate or parallel form of a test is that the effect of memory for the content of a previously administered form of the test is minimized.

Certain traits are presumed to be relatively stable in people over time, and we would expect tests measuring those traits—alternate forms, parallel forms, or otherwise—to reflect that stability. As an example, we expect that there will be—and in fact there is—a reasonable degree of stability in scores on intelligence tests. Conversely, we might expect there to be relatively little stability in scores obtained on a measure of state anxiety (anxiety felt at the moment); the level of anxiety experienced by the testtaker could be expected to vary from hour to hour—let alone day to day, week to week, or month to month.

An estimate of the reliability of a test can be obtained without developing an alternate form of the test and without having to administer the test twice to the same people. Such an assessment entails scrutinizing the individual items that make up the test and their relation to one another. Because this type of reliability estimate is obtained not through comparison with data from an alternate form and not through a test-retest procedure but, rather, through an examination of the items of the test, it is referred to as an **"internal-consistency"** estimate of **reliability** or as an estimate of "inter-item consistency." Our focus now shifts to such types of reliability estimates, beginning with the "split-half" estimate.

Split-Half Reliability Estimates

An estimate of **split-half reliability** is obtained by correlating two pairs of scores obtained from equivalent halves of a single test administered once. It is a useful measure of reliability when it is impractical or undesirable to assess reliability with two tests or to have two test administrations (because of factors such as time or expense). The computation of a coefficient of split-half reliability generally entails three steps:

---

3. According to the classical true score model, the effect of such factors on test scores is indeed presumed to be measurement error. There are alternative models in which the effect of such factors on fluctuating test scores would not be considered error (Atkinson, 1981).

Step 1. Divide the test into equivalent halves.

Step 2. Compute a Pearson r between scores on the two halves of the test.

Step 3. Adjust the half-test reliability using the Spearman-Brown formula.

When it comes to calculating split-half reliability coefficients, there's more than one way to split a test—but there are some ways you should never split a test. Simply dividing the test in the middle is not recommended, because this procedure would probably spuriously raise or lower the reliability coefficient (because of factors such as different amounts of fatigue for the first as opposed to the second part of the test, different amounts of test anxiety, and differences in item difficulty as a function of placement in the test). One acceptable way to split a test is to randomly assign items to one or the other half of the test. A second acceptable way is to assign odd-numbered items to one-half of the test and even-numbered items to the other half (yielding an estimate that is also referred to as **odd-even reliability**).[4] A third way is to divide the test by content so that each half of the test contains items equivalent with respect to content and difficulty. In general, a primary objective in splitting a test in half for the purpose of obtaining a split-half reliability estimate is to create what might be called "mini-parallel-forms," with each half equal to the other—or as nearly equal as humanly possible—in format, stylistic, statistical, and related aspects.

Step 2 in the procedure entails the computation of a Pearson r, which requires little explanation at this point. However, the third step requires the use of the Spearman-Brown formula.

The Spearman-Brown formula   The **Spearman-Brown formula** allows a test developer or user to estimate internal consistency reliability from a correlation of two halves of a test; it is a specific application of a more general formula to estimate the reliability of a test that is lengthened or shortened by any number of items. Because the reliability of a test is affected by its length, a formula is necessary for estimating the reliability of a test that has been shortened or lengthened. The general Spearman-Brown (r_{SB}) formula is

$$r_{SB} = \frac{nr_{xy}}{1 + (n - 1)r_{xy}}$$

where r_{SB} is equal to the reliability adjusted by the Spearman-Brown formula, r_{xy} is equal to the Pearson r in the original-length test, and n is equal to the number of items in the revised version divided by the number of items in the original version.

By determining the reliability of one-half of a test, a test developer can then use the Spearman-Brown formula to estimate the reliability of a whole test. Because a whole test is two times longer than half a test, n becomes 2 in the Spearman-Brown formula for the adjustment of split-half reliability. The symbol r_{hh} stands for the Pearson r of scores in the two half tests:

$$r_{SB} = \frac{2r_{hh}}{1 + r_{hh}}$$

It is generally—though not always—true that reliability increases as test length increases, providing that the additional items are equivalent with respect to the content and the range of difficulty of the original items. Estimates of reliability based on consid-

---

4. One precaution here: With respect to a group of items on an achievement test that deals with a single problem, it is usually desirable to assign the whole group of items to one-half of the test. Otherwise—if part of the group were in one half and another part in the other half—the similarity of the half scores would be spuriously inflated; a single error in understanding, for example, might affect items in both halves of the test.

Table 5–1

Odd-Even Reliability Coefficients Before and After the Spearman-Brown Adjustment*

Grade	Half-Test Correlation (unadjusted r)	Whole-Test Estimate (r_{SB})
K	.718	.836
1	.807	.893
2	.777	.875

*For scores on a test of mental ability.

eration of the entire test therefore tend to be higher than those based on half of a test. Table 5–1 shows half-test correlations presented alongside adjusted reliability estimates for the whole test. You can see that all the adjusted correlations are higher than the unadjusted correlations—this because Spearman-Brown estimates are based on a test that is twice as long as the original half test. For the data from the kindergarten pupils, for example, a half-test reliability of .718 can be estimated to be equivalent to a whole-test reliability of .836.

If test developers or users wish to shorten a test, the Spearman-Brown formula may be used to estimate the effect of the shortening on the test's reliability. Reduction in test size for the purpose of reducing test administration time is a common practice in situations where the test administrator may have only limited time with the testtaker or in situations where boredom or fatigue could produce responses of questionable meaningfulness.

A Spearman-Brown formula could also be used to determine the number of items needed to attain a desired level of reliability. In adding items to increase test reliability to a desired level, the rule is that the new items must be equivalent in content and difficulty so that the longer test still measures what the original test measured. If the reliability of the original test is relatively low, it may be impractical to increase the number of items to reach an acceptable level of reliability. Another alternative would be to abandon this relatively unreliable instrument and locate—or develop—a suitable alternative. The reliability of the instrument could also be raised in some way—for example, by creating new items, clarifying the test's instructions, or simplifying the scoring rules.

Internal consistency estimates of reliability, such as that obtained by use of the Spearman-Brown formula, are inappropriate for measuring the reliability of heterogeneous tests and speed tests. The impact of test characteristics on reliability is discussed in detail later in this chapter.

Other Methods of Estimating Internal Consistency

In addition to the Spearman-Brown formula, other methods in wide use to estimate **internal consistency reliability** include formulas developed by Kuder and Richardson (1937) and Cronbach (1951). **Inter-item consistency** is a term that refers to the degree of correlation among all the items on a scale. A measure of inter-item consistency is calculated from a single administration of a single form of a test. An index of inter-item consistency is, in turn, useful in assessing the **homogeneity** of the test. Tests are said to be "homogeneous" if they contain items that measure a single trait. As an adjective used to describe test items, *homogeneity* (derived from the Greek words *homos,* meaning "same," and *genous,* meaning "kind") is the degree to which a test measures a single factor, the extent to which items in a scale are unifactorial.

In contrast to test homogeneity, **heterogeneity** describes the degree to which a test measures different factors. A *heterogeneous* (or *nonhomogeneous*) test is composed of items that measure more than one trait. A test that assesses knowledge only of color television repair skills could be expected to be more homogeneous in content than a test of electronic repair. The former test assesses only one area and the latter assesses several, such as knowledge not only of televisions but also of radios, video recorders, compact disc players, and so forth. The more homogeneous a test is, the more inter-item consistency it can be expected to have. Because the test would be sampling a relatively narrow content area, it would contain more inter-item consistency. A person who is skilled in color television repair might be somewhat familiar with the repair of other electronic devices such as radios and stereo systems but may know little about video recorders or compact disc players. Thus, there would be less inter-item consistency in this test of general repair ability than in a test designed to assess only color television repair knowledge and skills.

Test homogeneity is desirable because it allows relatively straightforward test-score interpretation. Testtakers with the same score on a homogeneous test probably have similar abilities in the area tested. Testtakers with the same score on a more heterogeneous test may have quite different abilities. But although a homogeneous test is desirable because it so readily lends itself to clear interpretation, it is often an insufficient tool for measuring multifaceted psychological variables such as intelligence or personality. One way to circumvent this potential source of difficulty has been to administer a series of homogeneous tests, each designed to measure some component of a heterogeneous variable.[5] In addition to some of the random influences that can affect reliability measures, error variance in a measure of inter-item consistency comes from two sources: (1) item sampling and (2) the heterogeneity of the content area. The more heterogeneous the content area sampled, the lower the inter-item consistency will be.

The Kuder-Richardson formulas   Dissatisfaction with existing split-half methods of estimating reliability compelled G. Frederic Kuder and M. W. Richardson (1937; Richardson & Kuder, 1939) to develop their own measures for estimating reliability. The most widely known of the many formulas they collaborated on is their **Kuder-Richardson formula 20** or *KR-20* (so named because it was the twentieth formula developed in a series). Where test items are highly homogeneous, KR-20 and split-half reliability estimates will be similar. However, KR-20 is the statistic of choice for determining the inter-item consistency of dichotomous items, primarily those items that can be scored right or wrong (such as multiple-choice items). If test items are more heterogeneous, KR-20 will yield lower reliability estimates than the split-half method. Table 5–2 summarizes items on a sample heterogeneous test. Assuming the difficulty level of all the items on the test to be about the same, would you expect a split-half (odd-even) estimate of reliability to be fairly high or low? How would the KR-20 reliability estimate compare with the odd-even estimate of reliability—would it be higher or lower?

We might guess that because the content areas sampled for the 18 items from this "Hypothetical Electronics Repair Test" are ordered in a manner whereby odd and even items tap the same content area, the odd-even reliability estimate will probably be quite high. With respect to a reasonable guess concerning the KR-20 reliability estimate, because of the great heterogeneity of content areas when taken as a whole, it could reasonably be predicted that the KR-20 estimate of reliability will be lower than the odd-even one. How can KR-20 be computed? The following formula may be used:

$$r_{\text{KR20}} = \left(\frac{k}{k-1} \right) \left(1 - \frac{\Sigma\, pq}{\sigma^2} \right)$$

---

5. As we will see elsewhere throughout this textbook, important decisions are seldom made on the basis of one test only. Psychologists frequently rely on a **test battery**—a selected assortment of tests and assessment procedures in the process of evaluation. A test battery is typically composed of tests designed to measure different variables.

Table 5–2	Item Number	Content Area
Content Areas Sampled for 18 Items of the Hypothetical Electronics Repair Test (HERT)	1	Color television
	2	Color television
	3	Black-and-white television
	4	Black-and-white television
	5	Radio
	6	Radio
	7	Video recorder
	8	Video recorder
	9	Computer
	10	Computer
	11	Compact disc player
	12	Compact disc player
	13	Stereo receiver
	14	Stereo receiver
	15	Video camera
	16	Video camera
	17	DVD player
	18	DVD player

where r_{KR20} stands for the Kuder-Richardson formula 20 reliability coefficient, k is the number of test items, σ^2 is the variance of total test scores, p is the proportion of test-takers who pass the item, q is the proportion of people who fail the item, and Σpq is the sum of the pq products over all items. For this particular example, k equals 18. Based on the data in Table 5–3, Σpq can be computed to be 3.975. The variance of total test scores is 5.26. Thus, $r_{KR20} = .259$.

An approximation of KR-20 can be obtained by the use of the twenty-first formula in the series developed by Kuder and Richardson, a formula known—you guessed it—as *KR-21*. KR-21 may be used if there is reason to believe that all the test items have approximately the same degree of difficulty—an assumption, we should add, that is seldom justified. Formula KR-21 tends to be outdated in an era of calculators and computers, because it was used as an approximation of KR-20 that required less computation. Another formula once used in the measurement of internal consistency reliability and now for the most part outdated was a statistic referred to as the **Rulon formula** (Rulon, 1939).

Though numerous modifications of Kuder-Richardson formulas have been proposed through the years (for example, Cliff, 1984; Horst, 1953), perhaps the one variant of the KR-20 formula that has received the most acceptance to date is a statistic called "coefficient alpha," sometimes referred to as "coefficient α-20" (α being the Greek letter alpha and 20 referring to KR-20).

Coefficient alpha   Developed by Cronbach (1951) and subsequently elaborated on by others (such as Kaiser & Michael, 1975; Novick & Lewis, 1967), **coefficient alpha** may be thought of as the mean of all possible—the good along with the bad—split-half correlations, corrected by the Spearman-Brown formula. As we have noted above, KR-20 is appropriately used on tests with dichotomous items. Additionally, coefficient alpha is appropriate for use on tests containing nondichotomous items: items that can individually be scored along a range of values. Examples of such tests include opinion and attitude polls, where a range of possible alternatives are presented; essay tests; and short-answer tests, where partial credit can be given. The formula for coefficient alpha is

$$r_\alpha = \left(\frac{k}{k-1} \right) \left(1 - \frac{\Sigma \sigma_i^2}{\sigma^2} \right)$$

Table 5–3
HERT Performance by Item for 20 Testtakers

Item Number	Number of Testtakers Correct
1	14
2	12
3	9
4	18
5	8
6	5
7	6
8	9
9	10
10	10
11	8
12	6
13	15
14	9
15	12
16	12
17	14
18	7

where r_a is coefficient alpha, k is the number of items, σ_i^2 is the variance of one item, $\Sigma\,\sigma_i^2$ is the sum of variances of each item, and σ^2 is the variance of the total test scores. In the age of computers and programmable calculators, few people who would have occasion to calculate this statistic would undertake the rather laborious calculations by hand—and the number of people who would prefer the old-fashioned way could reasonably be presumed to dwindle as the number of items on the test rises. Today, perhaps because of the ready availability of computers, coefficient alpha is the preferred statistic for obtaining an estimate of internal consistency reliability.

Measures of Inter-Scorer Reliability

When we are being evaluated, we usually would like to believe that no matter who is doing the evaluating, we would be evaluated in the same way.[6] For example, if the instructor of this course were to evaluate your knowledge of the subject matter by means of an essay test, you would like to think that the grade you receive on the essay test would be the same whether it was graded by your professor or any other professor who teaches this course. If you take a road test for a driver's license, you would like to believe that whether you pass or fail is solely a matter of your performance behind the wheel and not a function of who is sitting in the passenger's seat. Unfortunately, in some types of tests under some conditions, the score may be more a function of the scorer than anything else. This was demonstrated back in 1912 when researchers presented one pupil's English composition to a convention of teachers, and volunteers graded the papers—with grades that ranged from a low of 50% to a high of 98% (Starch & Elliott, 1912).

---

6. We say "usually" because exceptions do exist. Thus, for example, if you go on a job interview and the employer/interviewer is a parent or other loving relative, you might reasonably expect that the nature of the evaluation you receive would *not* be the same were the evaluator to be someone else. On the other hand, if the employer/interviewer is someone with whom you have had a run-in, it may be time to revisit the want ads.

Variously referred to as **"scorer reliability," "judge reliability," "observer reliability,"** and **"inter-rater reliability," inter-scorer reliability** is the degree of agreement or consistency that exists between two or more scorers (or judges or raters). Reference to levels of inter-scorer reliability for a particular test may be published (either in the test's manual or elsewhere), and if the reliability coefficient is very high, the prospective test user knows that test scores can be derived in a systematic, consistent way by various scorers with sufficient training. A responsible test developer who is unable to create a test that can be scored with a reasonable degree of consistency by trained scorers will go back to the drawing board to discover the reason for this problem. If, for example, the problem is a lack of clarity in scoring criteria, then the remedy might be to rewrite the scoring criteria section of the manual to include clearly written scoring rules. Lectures to raters on scoring rules are not as effective in promoting inter-rater consistency as is providing raters with the opportunity for group discussion along with practice exercises and information on rater accuracy (Smith, 1986).

Perhaps the simplest way of determining the degree of consistency that exists among scorers in the scoring of a test is to calculate a coefficient of correlation, a coefficient of inter-scorer reliability. Assuming, for example, that a 30-item test of reaction time was administered to one subject and scored by two scorers, the inter-scorer reliability would be equal to the value of the Spearman-Brown corrected correlation coefficient obtained with respect to 30 pairs of scores. If the reliability coefficient were found to be, say, .90, this would mean that 90% of the variance in the scores assigned by the raters stemmed from true differences in the subject's reaction time, whereas 10% could be attributed to factors other than the subject's reaction time (that is, error). In many cases, more than two scorers are used in such reliability studies. In such instances, scores obtained by the two scorers would be correlated, using Pearson r or Spearman rho, depending on the scale of measurement of the test score.

The kappa statistic   The **kappa statistic** was initially designed for use in the case where scorers make ratings using nominal scales of measurement (Cohen, 1960). The kappa statistic was subsequently modified by Fliess (1971) for use with multiple scorers. There are special instances where it may be appropriate to use kappa in a modified form (Conger, 1985) or to use another measure, such as Yule's Y (Spitznagel & Helzer, 1985).

Using and Interpreting a Coefficient of Reliability

We have seen that with respect to the test itself, there are basically three approaches to the estimation of reliability: (1) test-retest, (2) alternate or parallel forms, and (3) internal or inter-item consistency. The method or methods employed will depend on a number of factors—primary among them the purpose of obtaining a measure of reliability and the way that measure will be used.

The Purpose of the Reliability Coefficient

How repeatable are repeated measurements—with the same or alternate forms of a test—over short intervals of time? over long intervals? These are some of the questions we seek to answer with reference to a coefficient of reliability. If a specific test of employee performance is designed for use at various times over the course of the employment period, it would be reasonable to expect the test to demonstrate reliability across time—in which case knowledge of the instrument's test-retest reliability would be essential. For a

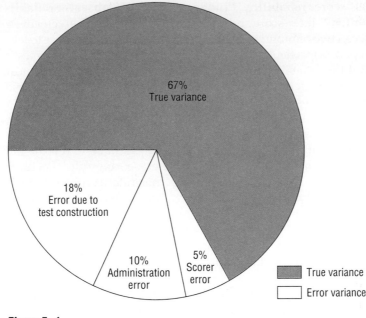

Figure 5–1
Sources of Variance in a Hypothetical Test

test designed for a single administration only, an estimate of internal consistency would be the coefficient computed. If the purpose of determining reliability is to analyze the error variance into its parts, as has been done for the illustration in Figure 5–1, then a number of reliability coefficients would have to be computed.

Note that the various reliability coefficients do not all reflect the same sources of error variance. Thus, an individual reliability coefficient may provide an index of error from test construction, test administration, or test scoring and interpretation. A coefficient of inter-rater reliability, for example, provides information about error as a result of test scoring. Specifically, it can be used to answer questions about how consistently two scorers score the same test items. For response to questions such as "How did illness affect this testtaker's score?" a different reliability coefficient would have to be calculated. Table 5–4 summarizes the different kinds of error variance that are reflected in different reliability coefficients.

The Nature of the Test

Closely related to considerations concerning the purpose and use of a reliability coefficient are considerations concerning the nature of the test itself. Included here are considerations such as whether (1) the test items are homogeneous or heterogeneous in nature; (2) the characteristic, ability, or trait being measured is presumed to be dynamic or static; (3) the range of test scores is or is not restricted; (4) the test is a speed or a power test; and (5) the test is or is not criterion-referenced. Some tests present special problems regarding the measurement of their reliability (see this chapter's *Close-up*).

Homogeneity versus heterogeneity of test items If the test is homogeneous in items (that is, if it is functionally uniform throughout because it is designed to measure one factor, such as one ability or one trait), it would be reasonable to expect a high degree of inter-

Table 5-4
Summary of Reliability Types

Type of Reliability	Number of Testing Sessions	Number of Test Forms	Source(s) of Error Variance	Statistical Procedures
Test-retest	2	1	Administration	Pearson r or Spearman rho
Alternate forms	1 or 2	2	Test construction Administration	Pearson r or Spearman rho
Internal consistency	1	1	Test construction	Pearson r between equivalent test halves with Spearman-Brown correction, or Kuder-Richardson for dichotomous items, or Coefficient alpha for multipoint items
Inter-scorer	1	1	Scoring and interpretation	Pearson r, or Spearman rho, or kappa coefficient

nal consistency. If the test is heterogeneous in items, an estimate of internal consistency might be low relative to a more appropriate estimate of test-retest reliability.

Dynamic versus static characteristics   Whether what is being measured by the test is dynamic or static is also a consideration in obtaining an estimate of reliability. Dynamic characteristics are presumed to be ever-changing as a function of situational and cognitive experiences. If, for example, one were to take hourly measurements of the dynamic characteristic of anxiety as manifested in a stockbroker throughout a business day, one might find the measured level of this characteristic to change from hour to hour. Such changes might even be related to the magnitude of the Dow-Jones index. Because the true amount of anxiety presumed to exist would vary with each assessment, a test-retest measure would be of little help in gauging the reliability of the measuring instrument. The best estimate of reliability could be obtained from an internal-consistency measure. Contrast this situation to one in which hourly assessments of this same stockbroker are made on a characteristic that is not dynamic in nature but presumed to be relatively unchanging or static (such as intelligence). In this instance, obtained measurement would not be expected to vary significantly as a function of time, and either the test-retest or the alternate-forms method would be appropriate.

Restriction or inflation of range   In using and interpreting a coefficient of reliability, the issue variously referred to as **restriction of range** or **restriction of variance** (or, conversely, **inflation of range** or **inflation of variance**) is important. If the variance of either variable in a correlational analysis is restricted by the sampling procedure used, then the resulting correlation coefficient tends to be lower. If the variance of either variable in a correlational analysis is inflated by the sampling procedure, then the resulting correlation coefficient tends to be higher. Also of critical importance is whether the range of variances employed is appropriate to the objective of the correlational analysis. Consider in the latter context, for example, a published educational test designed for use with children in grades 1 through 6. Ideally, the manual for this test should contain not one reliability value covering all the testtakers in grades 1 through 6, but reliability values for testtakers at each grade level. A corporate personnel officer who employs a certain screening test in the hiring process must maintain reliability data with respect to scores achieved by job applicants—as opposed to hired employees—if the range of measurements is not to be restricted (this because the people that were hired typically scored higher on the test than any comparable group of applicants).

The Reliability of the Bayley Scales of Infant Development

The Bayley Scales of Infant Development, second edition (BSID-II; Bayley, 1993) is a test designed to assess the developmental level of children between 1 month and 3½ years old. It is used primarily to help identify children who are developing slowly and might benefit from cognitive intervention (Bayley, 1993). The BSID-II includes three scales. Items on the Motor Scale focus on the control and skill employed in bodily movements. Items on the Mental Scale focus on cognitive abilities. The Behavior Rating Scale assesses behavior problems, such as lack of attention.

Is the BSID-II a reliable measure? The way in which reliability of the BSID-II is assessed depends in part on the nature of the test itself. For example, because the Mental, Motor, and Behavior Rating Scales are each expected to measure a homogeneous set of abilities, internal consistency reliability is an appropriate measure of reliability for the scales. Note that internal consistency reliability is not calculated across all three BSID-II scales at once, because the test as a whole is not assumed to be homogeneous. Rather, each of these three scales is expected to measure a somewhat different set of skills from those measured by the others. Other characteristics of the BSID-II also justify the evaluation of internal consistency reliability. The abilities measured are not expected to change during the course of the testing session (about 30 to 60 minutes). Further, the BSID-II is norm-referenced and is a power test. As noted later in this section, all of these characteristics are consistent with examining the test's internal consistency reliability.

Bayley (1993) reported coefficient alphas ranging from .78 to .93 for the Mental Scale (variations exist across the age groups), .75 to .91 for the Motor Scale, and .64 to .92 for the Behavior Rating Scale. From these reliability studies, Bayley (1993) concluded that the BSID-II is internally consistent.

Examining the test-retest reliability of the BSID-II poses a problem unique to instruments that undertake the assessment of infants. We know that cognitive development during the first months and years of life is uneven and fast. Children often grow in spurts, changing dramatically over a few days (Hetherington & Parke, 1993). The child tested just before and again just after a developmental advance may perform very differently on the BSID-II at the two testings. In such cases, a change in test score would not be the result of error in the test itself or in test administration. Instead, such changes in the test score could reflect an actual change in the child's skills. Still, of course, not all differences between the child's test performance at two test administrations need to result from changes in skills. The challenge in gauging the test-retest reliability of the BSID-II is to do it in such a way that it is not spuriously lowered by the testtaker's actual developmental changes between testings.

Bayley's solution to this dilemma entailed examining test-retest reliability over short periods of time. The median interval between testings was just four days. Correlations between the results of the two testing sessions were strong for both the Mental (.83 to .91) and the Motor (.77 to .79) Scales. The Behavior Rating Scale demonstrated lower test-retest reliability: .48 to .70 at 1 month of age, .57 to .90 at 12 months of age, and .60 to .71 at 24 to 36 months of age (Bayley, 1993).

Inter-scorer reliability is an important concern for the BSID-II, because many items require judgment on the part of the examiner. The test manual provides clear criteria for scoring the infant's performance, but by their nature many tasks involve some subjectivity in scoring. For example, one of the Motor Scale items is "Keeps hands open . . . Scoring: Give credit if the child holds his hands open most of the time when he is free to follow his own interests" (Bayley, 1993, p. 147). Sources of examiner error on this item can arise from a variety of sources: Different examiners may note the position of the child's hands at different times. Examiners may define differently when the child is "free to follow his

Speed versus power tests When a time limit is long enough to allow testtakers to attempt all items and if some items are so difficult that no testtaker is able to obtain a perfect score, then the test is a **power test.** By contrast, a **speed test** generally contains items of uniform level of difficulty (typically uniformly low) so that when given generous time limits, all testtakers should be able to complete all the test items correctly. In practice, own interests." And examiners may disagree about what constitutes "most of the time." As a second example, one of the Mental Scale items is "Attends to story . . . Scoring: Give credit if the child attends to the entire story. Attending includes decreasing motor activity and looking at the pictures, listening to the words, or talking to you about the pictures as you read" (Bayley, 1993, p. 114). Examiners may differ in noticing lapses of attention or in their strictness about attention to the whole story. Is a single distraction enough for the child to lose credit on this item?

Correlations between the scores assigned by the examiner and an observer sitting unobtrusively nearby during the same testing session were as follows: .96 for the Mental Scale, .75 for the Motor Scale, .57 to .82 for the different factors of the Behavior Rating Scale, and .88 for the total Behavior Rating Scale (Bayley, 1993).

An alternate or parallel form of the BSID-II does not exist, so alternate-forms reliability cannot be assessed. An alternate form of the test would be useful to have, especially in cases in which the examiner makes a mistake in administering the first version of it. Still, the creation of an alternate form of this test would almost surely entail a great investment of time, money, and effort. If you were the test's publisher, would you make that investment? In considering the answer to that question, don't forget that the ability level of the testtaker is changing rapidly.

Nellis and Gridley (1994) noted that a primary goal in the revision was to strengthen the test psychometrically. Based on the data provided in the test manual, Nellis and Gridley concluded that this goal was accomplished: The BSID-II does seem to be more reliable than the original Bayley Scales. However, there are still some important weaknesses. For example, the manual focuses on the psychometric quality of the BSID-II as administered to children without significant developmental problems; whether the same levels

Nancy Bayley, Ph.D.

of reliability would be obtained with children who are developmentally delayed is unknown.

For a glimpse of how the Bayley test has been used by practitioners and researchers, interested readers may review Alessandri et al. (1998), Drotar et al. (1999), Levy-Shiff et al. (1998), Nelson et al. (2000), and Raz et al. (1998).

however, the time limit on a speed test is established so that few if any of the testtakers will be able to complete the entire test. Score differences on a speed test are therefore based on performance speed, because items attempted tend to be correct. A reliability estimate of a speed test should be based on performance from two independent testing periods using one of the following: (1) test-retest reliability, (2) alternate-forms reliability, or (3) split-half reliability from two separately timed half tests. If a split-half procedure is used, the obtained reliability coefficient is for a half test and should be adjusted using the Spearman-Brown formula.

Because a measure of the reliability of a speed test should reflect the consistency of response speed, the reliability of a speed test should not be computed from a single administration of the test with a single time limit. If a speed test is administered once and some measure of internal consistency is computed, like the Kuder-Richardson or a split-half correlation, the result will be a spuriously high reliability coefficient. A couple of examples illustrate how this occurs. When a group of testtakers completes a speed test, almost all the items completed will be correct. If reliability is examined using an odd-even split, and if the testtakers completed the items in order, testtakers will get close to the same number of odd as even items correct. A testtaker completing 82 items can be expected to get approximately 41 odd and 41 even items correct. A testtaker completing 61 items may get 31 odd and 30 even items correct. When the number of odd and even items correct are correlated across a group of testtakers, the correlation will be close to 1.00—an impressive-looking value that tells us nothing about response consistency. A Kuder-Richardson reliability coefficient would yield a similar coefficient. Recall that KR-20 reliability is based on the proportion of testtakers correct (p) and the proportion of testtakers incorrect (q) on each item. In the case of a speed test, it is conceivable that p would equal 1.0 and q would equal 0 for many of the items. Toward the end of the test—when many items would not even be attempted because of the time limit being imposed—p might equal 0 and q might equal 1.0. For many, if not a majority, of the items, then, the product of pq would equal or approximate 0. When 0 is substituted in the KR-20 formula for Σpq, the reliability coefficient is 1.0 (a meaningless coefficient in this instance).

Criterion-referenced tests A **criterion-referenced** test is designed to provide an indication of where a testtaker stands with respect to some criterion such as an educational or a vocational objective. Unlike norm-referenced tests, criterion-referenced tests tend to contain material that has been mastered in hierarchical fashion; for example, the would-be pilot masters on-ground skills before attempting to master in-flight skills. Scores on criterion-referenced tests tend to be interpreted in pass/fail (or, perhaps more accurately, master/failed-to-master) terms, and any scrutiny of performance on individual items tends to be for diagnostic (and remedial) purposes. Traditional techniques of estimating reliability employ measures based on total test scores. In test-retest reliability, a reliability estimate is based on the correlation between the total scores on two administrations of the same test. In alternate-forms reliability, a reliability estimate is based on the correlation between the two total scores on the two forms. In split-half reliability, a reliability estimate is based on the correlation between scores on two halves of the test and then adjusted using the Spearman-Brown formula to obtain a reliability estimate of the whole test. These traditional procedures of estimating reliability are inappropriate for use with criterion-referenced tests. To understand why, recall that reliability is defined as the proportion of total variance (σ^2) attributable to true variance (σ_{tr}^2). Total variance in a test score distribution equals the sum of the true variance plus the error variance (σ_e^2):

$$\sigma^2 = \sigma_{tr}^2 + \sigma_e^2$$

A measure of reliability, therefore, depends on the variability of the test scores: how different the scores are from one another. In criterion-referenced testing and particularly in mastery testing, individual differences between examinees on total test scores may be minimal; the key issue is not the test scores in comparison with the other test scores but simply if a certain criterion score has been obtained. As individual differences (and the variability) decrease, a traditional measure of reliability would also decrease, regardless of the stability of individual performance. Traditional ways of estimating reliability are therefore not always appropriate for criterion-referenced tests, though there may be instances in which traditional estimates can be adopted (such as where the same test is used at different stages in some program—training, therapy, or the like—and variability in scores could reasonably be expected). Statistical techniques applicable to the assessment of the reliability of criterion-referenced tests are discussed in detail elsewhere (for example, Hambleton & Jurgensen, 1990).

Before proceeding to the discussion of alternatives to the true score model, read about a real-life application of the types of reliability coefficients we have discussed to this point in this chapter's *Everyday Psychometrics*.

Alternatives to the True Score Model

Thus far, and throughout this book unless specifically stated otherwise, the model we have assumed to be operative is the true score or classical model—the most widely used and accepted model in the psychometric literature today. Historically, the true score model of the reliability of measurement enjoyed a virtually unchallenged reign of acceptance from the early 1900s through the 1940s. The 1950s saw the development of an alternative theoretical model, one referred to as the "domain sampling theory" originally and as "generalizability theory" in one of its many modified forms. As set forth by Tryon (1957), the theory of domain sampling rebels against the concept of a true score existing with respect to the measurement of psychological constructs (in the same way that a true score might exist with respect to measurement in the physical sciences). Whereas those who subscribe to **true score theory** seek to estimate the portion of a test score that is attributable to error, proponents of domain sampling theory seek to estimate the extent to which specific sources of variation under defined conditions are contributing to the test score. In the latter model, a test's reliability is conceived of as an objective measure of how precisely the test score assesses the domain from which the test draws a sample (Thorndike, 1985). A *domain* of behavior—or the universe of items that could conceivably measure that behavior—can be thought of as a hypothetical construct: one that shares certain characteristics with (and is measured by) the sample of items that make up the test. In theory, the items in the domain are thought to have the same means and variances of those in the test that samples from the domain. Of the three types of estimates of reliability, measures of internal consistency are perhaps the most compatible with domain sampling theory.

Generalizability theory may be viewed as an extension of true score theory wherein the concept of a universe score replaces that of a true score (Shavelson et al., 1989). Developed by Lee J. Cronbach (1970) and his colleagues (Cronbach et al., 1972), this theory is based on the idea that a person's test scores vary from testing to testing because of variables in the testing situation. Instead of conceiving of all variability in a person's scores as error, Cronbach encourages test developers and researchers to describe the details of the particular test situation or **universe** leading to a specific test score. This universe is described in terms of its **facets,** which include things like the number of items in the test, the amount of training the test scorers have had, and the purpose of the test administration. According to generalizability theory, given the exact same conditions of all the facets in the universe, the exact same test score should be obtained. This test score is the **universe score,** and it is, as Cronbach noted, analogous to a true score in the true score model.

> "What is Mary's typing ability?" This must be interpreted as, "What would Mary's score be if a large number of measurements were collected and averaged?" The particular test score Mary earned is just one out of a *universe* of possible observations, any of which the investigator would be willing to base his conclusion or decision on. If one of these scores

The Reliability Defense
and the Breathalyzer Test

Breathalyzer" is the generic name for a number of different types of instruments used by law enforcement agencies to determine if a suspect, most typically the operator of a motor vehicle, is legally drunk. The driver is required to blow into a tube that is attached to the breathalyzer. The breath sample then mixes with a chemical that is added to the machine for each new test. The resulting mixture is automatically analyzed for alcohol content in the breath. The value for the alcohol content in the breath is then converted to a value for blood alcohol level. Whether the testtaker is deemed to be legally drunk will vary from state to state as a function of the specific legislation on the books regarding the blood alcohol level necessary to be declared intoxicated.

In the state of New Jersey, the blood alcohol level required to be declared legally drunk is one-tenth of 1 percent (.10%). Drivers in New Jersey found guilty of a first drunk-driving offense face fines and surcharges amounting to about $3,500, mandatory detainment in an Intoxicated Driver Resource Center, suspension of driving privileges for a minimum of six months, and a maximum of 30 days' imprisonment. Two models of a breathalyzer (model 900 and 900A made by National Draeger Inc.) have been used in New Jersey since the 1950s. Well-documented test-retest reliability regarding the 900 and 900A breathalyzers indicate that the instruments have a margin of error of about one-100th of a percentage point. This means that an administration of the test to a testtaker who in reality has a blood alcohol level of .10% (a "true score," if you will) might yield a test score of anywhere from a low of .09% to a high of .11%.

A driver in the state of New Jersey who was convicted of driving drunk appealed the decision on grounds relating to the test-retest reliability of the breathalyzer. The breathalyzer had indicated that the driver's blood alcohol level was .10%. The driver argued that the law did not take into account the margin of error inherent in the measuring instrument. However, the state supreme court ruled against the driver, finding that the legislature must have taken into consideration such error when it wrote the law.

Another issue related to the use of breathalyzers has to do with where and when they are administered. In some states, the test is most typically administered at police headquarters, not at the scene of the arrest. Expert witnesses were once retained on behalf of defendants to calculate what the defendant's blood alcohol was at the actual time of the

A suspect being administered a breathalyzer test

arrest. Working backward from the time the test was administered, and figuring in values for variables such as what the defendant had to drink and when, as well as the defendant's weight, they could calculate a blood alcohol level at the time of arrest. If that level was lower than the level required to be declared legally drunk, the case might be dismissed. However, in some states, such as New Jersey, such a defense would not be entertained. In such states, higher courts have ruled that because it was aware that breathalyzer tests would not be administered at the arrest scene, the legislature had intended the measured blood alcohol level to apply at the time of its administration at police headquarters.

One final reliability-related issue relevant to the use of breathalyzers has to do with inter-scorer reliability. When using the 900 and 900A models, the police officer who conducted the arrest also records the measured blood alcohol level. Although the vast majority of police officers are honest when it comes to such recording, there is potential for abuse. A police officer who wished to save face on a drunk-driving arrest, or even a police officer who simply wanted to add to a record of drunk-driving arrests, could record an incorrect breathalyzer value to ensure a conviction. In 1993, one police officer in Camden County, New Jersey, was convicted of and sent to prison for recording incorrect breathalyzer readings (Romano, 1994). Such an incident is representative of extremely atypical "error" entering into the assessment process.

is as acceptable as the next, then the mean, called the *universe score* and symbolized here by M_p (mean for person p), would be the most appropriate statement of Mary's performance in the type of situation the test represents.

The universe is a collection of possible measures "of the same kind," but the limits of the collection are determined by the investigator's purpose. If he needs to know Mary's typing ability on May 5 (for example, so that he can plot a learning curve that includes one point for that day), the universe would include observations on that day and on that day only. He probably does want to generalize over passages, testers, and scorers—that is to say, he would like to know Mary's ability on May 5 without reference to any particular passage, tester, or scorer. . . .

The person will ordinarily have a different universe score for each universe. Mary's universe score covering tests on May 5 will not agree perfectly with her universe score for the whole month of May. . . . Some testers call the average over a large number of comparable observations a "true score"; e.g., "Mary's true typing rate on 3-minute tests." Instead, we speak of a "universe score" to emphasize that what score is desired depends on the universe being considered. For any measure there are many "true scores," each corresponding to a different universe.

When we use a single observation as if it represented the universe, we are generalizing. We generalize over scorers, over selections typed, perhaps over days. If the observed scores from a procedure agree closely with the universe score, we can say that the observation is "accurate," or "reliable," or "generalizable." And since the observations then also agree with each other, we say that they are "consistent" and "have little error variance." To have so many terms is confusing, but not seriously so. The term most often used in the literature is "reliability." The author prefers "generalizability" because that term immediately implies "generalization to what?" . . . There is a different degree of generalizability for each universe. The older methods of analysis do not separate the sources of variation. They deal with a single source of variance, or leave two or more sources entangled. (Cronbach, 1970, pp. 153–154)

How can these ideas be applied? Cronbach and his colleagues suggested that tests be developed with the aid of a **generalizability study** followed by a **decision study.** A generalizability study examines how generalizable scores from a particular test are if the test is administered in different situations. Stated in the language of generalizability theory, a generalizability study examines how much of an impact different facets of the universe have on the test score. Is the test score affected by group as opposed to individual administration? Is the test score affected by the time of day in which the test is administered? The influence of particular facets on the test score is represented by **coefficients of generalizability.** These coefficients are similar to reliability coefficients under the true score model.

After the generalizability study is done, Cronbach et al. recommended that test developers do a decision study, which involves the application of information from the generalizability study. In the decision study, developers examine the usefulness of test scores in helping the test user make decisions. In practice, test scores are used to guide a variety of decisions, from placing a child in special education to hiring new employees and discharging mental patients from the hospital. The decision study is designed to tell the test user how test scores should be used and how dependable those scores are as a basis for decisions, depending on the context of their use. Why is this so important? Cronbach (1970) explained:

The decision that a student has completed a course or that a patient is ready for termination of therapy must not be seriously influenced by chance errors, temporary variations in performance, or the tester's choice of questions. An erroneous favorable decision may be irreversible and may harm the person or the community. Even when reversible, an erroneous unfavorable decision is unjust, disrupts the person's morale, and perhaps retards his development. Research, too, requires dependable measurement. An experiment is not very informative if an observed difference could be accounted for by chance variation. Large error variance is likely to mask a scientifically important outcome. Taking a better measure improves the sensitivity of an experiment in the same way that increasing the number of subjects does. (p. 152)

Generalizability has not replaced the true score model. Still, it has great appeal owing to its message that a test's reliability does not reside within the test itself. Rather, a test's reliability is very much a function of the circumstances under which the test is developed, administered, and interpreted.

Another alternative to the true score model (discussed in greater detail in Chapter 7) is **item response theory** (Lord, 1980), also referred to by the acronym "IRT" or the term "latent trait theory." This theory focuses on the extent to which individual test items are useful in evaluating individuals presumed to possess various amounts of a particular trait or ability.

Reliability and Individual Scores

The reliability coefficient helps the test developer build an adequate measuring instrument, and it helps the test user select a suitable test. However, the usefulness of the reliability coefficient does not end with test construction and selection. By employing the reliability coefficient in the formula for the standard error of measurement, the test user now has another descriptive statistic relevant to test interpretation, this one useful in describing the amount of error in a test or a measure.

The Standard Error of Measurement

The standard deviation of a theoretically normal distribution of test scores obtained by one person on equivalent tests is the **standard error of measurement,** abbreviated SEM or SEm. Also known as the **standard error of a score** and denoted by the symbol σ_{meas}, the standard error of measurement is an index of the extent to which one individual's scores vary over tests presumed to be parallel. In accordance with the true score model, an obtained test score represents one point in the theoretical distribution of scores the testtaker could have obtained. Further, the test user has no way of knowing the testtaker's true score. However, if the standard deviation for the distribution of test scores is known (or can be calculated) and if an estimate of the reliability of the test is known (or can be calculated), an estimate of the standard error of a particular score (that is, the standard error of measurement) can be determined with the following formula:

$$\sigma_{\text{meas}} = \sigma\sqrt{1 - r}$$

where σ_{meas} is equal to the standard error of measurement, σ is equal to the standard deviation of test scores by the group of testtakers, and r is equal to the reliability coefficient of the test. The standard error of measurement allows us to estimate the range in which the true score is likely to exist, with a specific level of confidence.

If, for example, a spelling test has a reliability coefficient of .84 and a standard deviation of 10, then:

$$\sigma_{\text{meas}} = 10\sqrt{1 - .84} = 4$$

To use the standard error of measurement to estimate the range of the true score, we make an assumption: If the individual were to take a large number of equivalent tests, scores on those tests would tend to be normally distributed with the individual's true score as the mean. Because the standard error of measurement functions like a standard deviation in this context, we can use it to predict what would happen if an individual took additional equivalent tests:

- Approximately 68% (actually, 68.26%) of the scores would be expected to occur within $\pm 1\sigma_{meas}$ of the true score.
- Approximately 95% (actually, 95.44%) of the scores would be expected to occur within $\pm 2\sigma_{meas}$ of the true score.
- Approximately 99% (actually, 99.74%) of the scores would be expected to occur within $\pm 3\sigma_{meas}$ of the true score.

Of course, we don't know the true score for any individual testtaker, and so we must estimate it. The best estimate available about the individual's true score on the test is the test score already obtained. Thus, if a student achieved a score of 50 on one spelling test, and if the test had a standard error of measurement of 4, then using 50 as the point estimate, we can be

- 68% (actually, 68.26%) confident that the true score falls within $50 \pm 1\sigma_{meas}$ (or between 46 and 54, including 46 and 54).
- 95% (actually, 95.44%) confident that the true score falls within $50 \pm 2\sigma_{meas}$ (or between 42 and 58, including 42 and 58).
- 99% (actually, 99.74%) confident that the true score falls within $50 \pm 3\sigma_{meas}$ (or between 38 and 62, including 38 and 62).

The standard error of measurement, like the reliability coefficient, is one way of expressing test reliability. If the standard deviation of a test is held constant, the smaller the σ_{meas} the more reliable the test will be; as r increases, the σ_{meas} decreases. For example, when a reliability coefficient equals .64 and σ equals 15, the standard error of measurement equals 9:

$$\sigma_{meas} = 15\sqrt{1 - .64} = 9$$

With a reliability coefficient equal to .96 and σ still equal to 15, the standard error of measurement decreases to 3:

$$\sigma_{meas} = 15\sqrt{1 - .96} = 3$$

In practice, the standard error of measurement is most frequently used in the interpretation of individual test scores. For example, intelligence tests are given as part of the assessment of individuals for mental retardation. One of the criteria for mental retardation is an IQ score of 70 or below (when the mean is 100 and the standard deviation is 15) on an individually administered intelligence test (American Psychiatric Association, 1994). One question that could be asked about these tests is how scores that are close to the cutoff value of 70 should be treated. Specifically, how high above 70 must a score be to conclude confidently that the individual is unlikely to be retarded? Is 72 clearly above the retarded range, so that if the person were to take a parallel form of the test, we could be confident that the second score would be above 70? What about a score of 75? a score of 79?

Useful in answering such questions is an estimate of the amount of error in an observed test score. The standard error of measurement provides such an estimate. Further, the standard error of measurement is useful in establishing what is called a **confidence interval;** that is, a range or band of test scores that is likely to contain the true score. Consider in this context the Wechsler Adult Intelligence Scale-III (WAIS-III), a test designed to measure adult intelligence. The technical manual for this test provides a great deal of information relevant to the reliability of the test as a whole, as well as more specific reliability-related information for each of its subtests. As reported in the manual, the standard deviation is 3 for the subtest scaled scores and 15 for the IQ and Index scores. Across all of the age groups in the normative sample, the average reliability coefficient for the Full Scale IQ (FSIQ) is .98, and the average standard error of measurement for the FSIQ is 2.3. The manual also provides much more specific information, including standard error of measurement data by individual subtest and age group. Knowing an individual testtaker's FSIQ score and the testtaker's age we can calculate a confidence interval. For example, suppose a 22-year-old testtaker obtained a WAIS-III FSIQ of 75. The test user can be 95% confident that this testtaker's true FSIQ falls in the range of 70 to 80. This is so because the 95% confidence interval is set by taking the observed score of 75, plus or minus 1.96 multiplied by the standard error of measurement. As reported on page 54 of the WAIS-III manual, the standard error of measurement of the FSIQ for a 22-year-old testtaker is 2.37. With this information in hand, the 95% confidence interval is calculated as follows:

$$75 \pm 1.96\sigma_{\text{meas}} = 75 \pm 1.96(2.37) = 75 \pm 4.645$$

The calculated interval of 4.645 is rounded to the nearest whole number, 5. We can therefore be 95% confident that this testtaker's true FSIQ on the WAIS-III lies somewhere in the range of the observed score of 75 plus or minus 5, or somewhere in the range of 70 to 80.

The standard error of measurement can be used to set the confidence interval for a particular score or to determine whether a score is significantly different from a criterion (such as the cutoff score of 70 described above). The standard error of measurement cannot be used to compare scores. To accomplish those kinds of comparisons, read on.

The Standard Error of the Difference Between Two Scores

Error related to any of the number of possible variables operative in a testing situation (such as item sampling, testtaker's physical or mental state, and the test environment) can contribute to a change in a score achieved on the same test, or a parallel test, from one administration of the test to the next. The amount of error in a specific test score is embodied in the standard error of measurement. But scores can change from one testing to the next for reasons other than error.

True differences in the characteristic being measured can also affect test scores. These differences may be of great interest, as in the case of a personnel officer who must decide which of many applicants to hire. Indeed, such differences may be hoped for, as in the case of a psychotherapy researcher who hopes to prove the effectiveness of a particular approach to therapy. Comparisons between scores are made using the **standard error of the difference,** a statistical measure that can aid a test user in determining how large a difference should be before it is considered statistically significant. As you are probably aware from your course in statistics, custom in the field of psychology dictates that if the probability is more than 5% that the difference occurred by chance, then for all intents and purposes it is presumed that there was no difference. A more rigorous standard is the 1% standard; by this criterion, no statistically significant difference would be deemed to exist unless the observed difference could have occurred by chance alone less than one time in a hundred.

The standard error of the difference between two scores can be the appropriate statistical tool to address three types of questions:

1. How did this individual's performance on test 1 compare with his or her performance on test 2?
2. How did this individual's performance on test 1 compare with someone else's performance on test 1?
3. How did this individual's performance on test 1 compare with someone else's performance on test 2?

As you might have expected, when comparing scores achieved on the different tests, it is essential that the scores be converted to the same scale. The formula for the standard error of the difference between two scores is

$$\sigma_{\text{diff}} = \sqrt{\sigma^2_{\text{meas 1}} + \sigma^2_{\text{meas 2}}}$$

where σ_{diff} is the standard error of the difference between two scores, $\sigma^2_{\text{meas 1}}$ is the squared standard error of measurement for test 1, and $\sigma^2_{\text{meas 2}}$ is the squared standard error of measurement for test 2. If we substitute reliability coefficients for the standard errors of measurement of the separate scores, the formula becomes

$$\sigma_{\text{diff}} = \sigma\sqrt{2 - r_1 - r_2}$$

where r_1 is the reliability coefficient of test 1, r_2 is the reliability coefficient of test 2, and σ is the standard deviation—both tests having the same standard deviation, because they would have had to have been on the same scale (or converted to the same scale) before a comparison could be made.

The standard error of the difference between two scores will be larger than the standard error of measurement for either score alone because the former is affected by measurement error in both scores. This also makes good sense: If two scores *each* contain error, such that in each case the true score could be higher or lower, we would want the two scores to be further apart before we conclude that there is a significant difference between them.

The value obtained when the standard error of the difference is calculated is used in much the same way as the standard error of the mean. If we wish to be 95% confident that the two scores are different, we would want them to be separated by two standard errors of the difference. A separation of only one standard error of the difference would give us 68% confidence that the two true scores are different.

As an illustration of the use of the standard error of the difference between two scores, consider the situation of a corporate personnel manager who is seeking a highly responsible person for the position of vice president of safety. The personnel officer in this hypothetical situation decides to use a new published test called the "Safety-Mindedness Test" (S-MT) to screen applicants for the position. After placing an ad in the employment section of the local newspaper, the personnel officer tests 100 applicants for the position, using the S-MT. The personnel officer narrows the search for the vice president to the two highest scorers on the S-MT: Moe, who scored 125, and Larry, who scored 134. Assuming the measured reliability of this test to be .92 and its standard deviation to be 14, should the personnel officer conclude that Larry performed significantly better than Moe? To answer this question, first compute the standard error of the difference:

$$\sigma_{\text{diff}} = 14\sqrt{2 - .92 - .92} = 14\sqrt{.16} = 5.6$$

Note that in this application of the formula, the two test reliability coefficients are the same because the two scores being compared are derived from the same test.

What does this standard error of the difference mean? For any standard error of the difference, we can be

- 68% confident that two scores differing by 1 σ_{diff} represent true score differences.

- 95% confident that two scores differing by 2 σ_{diff} represent true score differences.

- 99.7% confident that two scores differing by 3 σ_{diff} represent true score differences.

Applying this information to the standard error of the difference just computed for the "Safety-Mindedness Test," we see that the personnel officer can be

- 68% confident that two scores differing by 5.6 represent true score differences.

- 95% confident that two scores differing by 11.2 represent true score differences.

- 99.7% confident that two scores differing by 16.8 represent true score differences.

The difference between Larry's and Moe's scores is only 9 points, not a large enough difference for the personnel officer to conclude with 95% confidence that the two individuals actually have true scores that differ on this test. Stated another way, if Larry and Moe were to take a parallel form of the "Safety-Mindedness Test," the personnel officer could not be 95% confident that, at the next testing, Larry would again outperform Moe. The personnel officer in this example would have to resort to other means to decide whether Moe, Larry, or someone else would be the best candidate for the position.

As a postscript to the preceding example, suppose Larry got the job primarily on the basis of data from our hypothetical S-MT. And let's further suppose that it soon became all too clear that Larry turned out to be the hands-down, absolute worst vice president of safety that the company had ever seen. Larry spent much of his time playing practical jokes on fellow corporate officers, and he spent many of his off-hours engaged in his favorite pastime: flagpole sitting. The personnel officer might then have very good reason to question how well the instrument called the "Safety-Mindedness Test" truly measured safety-mindedness. Or, to put it another way, the personnel officer might question the *validity* of the test. Not coincidentally, the subject of test validity is taken up in the next chapter.

Self-Assessment

Test your understanding of elements of this chapter by seeing if you can explain each of the following terms, expressions, and abbreviations:

alternate forms	generalizability theory
coefficient alpha	heterogeneity
coefficient of equivalence	homogeneity
coefficient of generalizability	inflation of range
coefficient of stability	inter-item consistency
confidence interval	internal consistency
content sampling	inter-scorer reliability
criterion-referenced test	IRT
error variance	item sampling

kappa statistic

Kuder-Richardson formula

odd-even reliability

parallel forms

power test

reliability

reliability coefficient

restriction of range

Rulon formula

Spearman-Brown formula

speed test

split-half reliability

standard error of a score

standard error of measurement

standard error of the difference

test-retest reliability

true variance

variance

6

Validity

In everyday language, we say that something is valid if it is sound, meaningful, or well grounded on principles or evidence. For example, we speak of a valid theory, a valid argument, or a valid reason. In legal terminology, lawyers say that something is valid if it is "executed with the proper formalities" (Black, 1979), such as a valid contract and a valid will. In each of these instances, people make judgments based on evidence of the meaningfulness or the veracity of something. Similarly, in the language of psychological assessment, *validity* is a term used in conjunction with the meaningfulness of a test score—what the test score truly means.

The Concept of Validity

Stated succinctly, the word **validity** as applied to a test refers to a judgment concerning how well a test does in fact measure what it purports to measure. More specifically, it is a judgment based on evidence about the appropriateness of inferences drawn from test scores.[1] An **inference** is a logical result or deduction in a reasoning process. Characterizations of the validity of tests and test scores are frequently phrased in terms such as "acceptable" or "weak"—reflecting a judgment about how adequately the attribute the test was designed to measure is actually measured. Inherent in a judgment of validity is a judgment of usefulness. One respected psychometrician even defined validity as how "useful scientifically" an instrument of measurement is (Nunnally, 1978, p. 86).

    Validation is the process of gathering and evaluating validity evidence. Both the test developer and the test user may play a role in the validation of a test for a specific purpose. It is the test developer's responsibility to supply validity evidence in the test manual. It may sometimes be appropriate for test users to conduct their own **validation studies** with their own groups of testtakers. Such "local" validation studies are necessary when the test user plans to alter in some way the format, instructions, language, or content of the test (such as changing the test from written to Braille form). **Local validation studies** would also be appropriate when the test will be used with a population of testtakers that differs in some significant way from the population on which the test was standardized.

---

1. Recall from Chapter 1 that the word *test* is used in the broadest possible sense; it may therefore also apply to measurement procedures and processes that would not, strictly speaking, colloquially be referred to as "tests."

How does one go about evaluating the validity of a test? A prerequisite is the development of a more precise conceptualization of validity. One way of conceptualizing validity has been with respect to the following three-category taxonomy:

- content validity
- criterion-related validity
- construct validity

This view of validity—referred to by Guion (1980) as the "trinitarian" view—is clearly the prevailing one in the field of psychology today and has been at least since the 1950s. Accordingly, answers to questions about methods for determining the validity of a test tend to be couched in terms such as "content validation strategies," "criterion-related validation strategies," and "construct validation strategies." There are also references to other categories, such as "predictive validity" and "concurrent validity," but these two terms tend to be collapsed under the more general category of "criterion-related validity."

Within the context of the three-category taxonomy, the validity of a test may be evaluated by (1) scrutinizing its content, (2) relating scores obtained on the test to other test scores or other measures, and (3) executing a comprehensive analysis of not only how scores on the test relate to other test scores and measures but also how they can be understood within some theoretical framework for understanding the construct the test was designed to measure. These three approaches to validity assessment are not mutually exclusive; each should be thought of as one type of evidence that, with others, contributes to a judgment concerning the validity of the test. All three types of validity evidence contribute to a unified picture of a test's validity, though a test user may not need to know about all three types of validity evidence. Depending on the use to which a test is being put, one or another of these three types of validity evidence may not be as relevant as the next.

Some have expressed concerns about the traditional trinitarian conceptualization of validity (Landy, 1986; Messick, 1995). Messick, for example, condemned this approach as fragmented and incomplete. He called for a unitary view of validity, one that takes into account everything from the implications of test scores in terms of societal values to the consequences of test use. Messick described validity as a "social salient value" that "assumes both a scientific and a political role that can by no means be fulfilled by a simple correlation coefficient between test scores and a purported criterion (i.e., classical criterion-related validity) or by expert judgments that test content is relevant to the proposed test use (i.e., traditional content validity)" (1995, p. 742). As you learn more about "classical criterion-related validity," "traditional content validity," and other traditional conceptualizations of validity, you will be in a better position to evaluate their overall utility, as well as the extent to which such conceptualizations embody social values and judgments. And speaking of social values and judgments, let's begin with a look at one variety of validity that has "received little attention—and even less respect—from researchers examining the construct validity of psychological tests and measures" (Bornstein et al., 1994, p. 363). As Bornstein et al. (1994) aptly characterize, it is the "Rodney Dangerfield of psychometric variables" (p. 363). It is face validity.

Face Validity

Face validity relates more to what a test appears to measure to the person being tested than to what the test actually measures. Face validity is a judgment concerning how relevant the test items appear to be. Stated another way, if a test definitely appears to measure what it purports to measure "on the face of it," it could be said to be high in face validity. A paper-and-pencil personality test labeled "The Introversion/Extraversion Test" with items that ask respondents whether they have acted in an introverted or an extraverted way in particular situations will be perceived as a highly face-valid test by the respondents. On the other hand, a personality test in which respondents are asked about a variety of inkblots may generally be perceived as a test with low face validity; no doubt many respondents would wonder how on earth what they said they saw in the inkblots really had anything at all to do with personality.

In contrast to judgments concerning the reliability of a test and in contrast to judgments concerning the content, construct, or criterion-related validity of a test, judgments concerning the face validity of a test are frequently thought of from the perspective of the testtaker as opposed to that of the test user. It is conceivable that the lack of face validity could contribute to a lack of confidence with respect to the perceived effectiveness of the test—with a consequential decrease in the testtaker's cooperation or motivation to do his or her best. Also, parents may object to having their children tested with such an instrument. Their concern might stem from a belief that such testing will result in invalid conclusions. A test may in reality be very relevant and useful in a particular context, but if it is not perceived as such by examinees, negative consequences (ranging all the way from a negative testtaking attitude to a lawsuit) may result. From the perspective of the test user, face validity may also be important as it contributes (or fails to contribute) to users' confidence in the test. We can therefore conclude that face validity may have public relations value for both testtakers and test users. However, the face validity of a test—the mere appearance of validity—is not an acceptable basis for interpretive inferences from test scores.

Content Validity

Content validity describes a judgment concerning how adequately a test samples behavior representative of the universe of behavior the test was designed to sample. For example, the universe of behavior referred to as "assertive" is very wide-ranging. A content-valid paper-and-pencil test of assertiveness would be one that is adequately representative of these wide-ranging situations. We might expect that such a test would contain items sampling from hypothetical situations at home (such as whether the respondent has difficulty in making her or his views known to fellow family members), on the job (such as whether the respondent has difficulty in asking subordinates to do what is required of them), and in social situations (such as whether the respondent would send back a steak not done to order in a fancy restaurant).

With respect to educational achievement tests, it is customary to consider a test a content-valid measure when the proportion of material covered by the test approximates the proportion of material covered in the course. A cumulative final exam in introductory statistics would be considered content-valid if the proportion and type of introductory statistics problems on the test approximates the proportion and type of introductory statistics problems presented in the course.

The early stages of a test being developed for use in the classroom—be it one classroom or those throughout the state or the nation—typically entails research exploring the universe of possible instructional objectives for the course. Included among the many possible sources of information on such objectives are course syllabi, course textbooks, teachers who teach the course, specialists who develop curricula, and professors and supervisors who train teachers in the particular subject area. From the pooled information (along with the judgment of the test developer), a blueprint for the structure of the test will emerge—a blueprint representing the culmination of efforts designed to adequately sample the universe of content areas that could conceivably be sampled in such a test.[2]

For an employment test to be content-valid, the content of the test must be a representative sample of the job-related skills required for employment. One technique frequently used in blueprinting the content areas to be covered in certain types of employment tests is observation. The test developer will observe successful veterans on that job, note the behaviors necessary for success on the job, and design the test to include a representative sample of those behaviors. Those same workers (as well as their supervisors and others) may subsequently be called on to act as experts or judges in rating the degree to which the content of the test is a representative sample of the required job-related skills. Here is one method for quantifying the degree of agreement between such raters.

The Quantification of Content Validity

The measurement of content validity is important in employment settings, where tests used to hire and promote people are carefully scrutinized for their relevance to the job. Recall from Chapter 2 that courts often require evidence that employment tests are work related. Probably partly in response to this legal pressure, and doubtless also out of a concern for the quality of employment tests, methods for quantifying content validity have been created (for example, James et al., 1984; Lindell et al., 1999; Tinsley & Weiss, 1975). One widely used method of measuring content validity was developed by C. H. Lawshe. It is essentially a method for gauging agreement among raters or judges regarding how essential a particular item is. Lawshe (1975) proposed that each rater on the judging panel respond to the following question for each item: "Is the skill or knowledge measured by this item

- essential
- useful but not essential
- not necessary

to the performance of the job?" (p. 567). For each item, the number of panelists stating that the item is essential is noted. According to Lawshe, if more than half the panelists indicate that an item is essential, that item has at least some content validity. Greater levels of content validity exist as larger numbers of panelists agree that a particular item is essential. Using these assumptions, Lawshe developed a formula termed the **content validity ratio:**

$$CVR = \frac{n_e - N/2}{N/2}$$

where CVR = content validity ratio, n_e = number of panelists indicating "essential," and N = total number of panelists. Assuming a panel consists of ten experts, the following three examples illustrate the meaning of the CVR when it is negative, zero, and positive.

---

2. The application of the concept of blueprint and of blueprinting is, of course, not limited to achievement tests. Blueprinting may be used in the design of a personality test, an attitude measure, or any other test, sometimes employing the judgments of experts in the field.

Table 6–1	Number of Panelists	Minimum Value
Minimum Values of the Content Validity Ratio to Ensure That Agreement Is Unlikely to Be Due to Chance	5	.99
	6	.99
	7	.99
	8	.75
	9	.78
	10	.62
	11	.59
	12	.56
	13	.54
	14	.51
	15	.49
	20	.42
	25	.37
	30	.33
	35	.31
	40	.29

Source: Lawshe (1975)

1. *Negative CVR:* When fewer than half the panelists indicate "essential," the *CVR* is negative. Assume four of ten panelists indicated "essential":

$$CVR = \frac{4 - (10/2)}{10/2} = -0.2$$

2. *Zero CVR:* When exactly half the panelists indicate "essential," the *CVR* is zero:

$$CVR = \frac{5 - (10/2)}{10/2} = .00$$

3. *Positive CVR:* When more than half but not all the panelists indicate "essential," the *CVR* ranges between .00 and .99. Assume nine of ten indicated "essential":

$$CVR = \frac{9 - (10/2)}{10/2} = .80$$

In validating a test, the content validity ratio is calculated for each item. Lawshe (1975) recommended that if the amount of agreement observed has more than a 5% chance of occurring by chance, the item should be eliminated. The minimal *CVR* values corresponding to this 5% level are presented in Table 6–1. In the case where there are ten panelists, an item would need a minimum *CVR* of .62. In our third example (the one in which nine of ten panelists agreed), the *CVR* of .80 is significant; the item could therefore be retained. Subsequently, in our discussion of criterion-related validity, our attention shifts from an index of validity not based on test content, but on test scores. First, some perspective on culture as it relates to a test's validity.

Culture and the Relativity of Test Validity

Tests are often thought of as being either valid or not valid. A history test, for example, either does or does not accurately measure historical fact. However, it is also true that what constitutes historical fact depends in some cases on who is writing the history. Consider, for example, a momentous event in the history of the world, one that served as a catalyst for World War I. Archduke Franz Ferdinand was assassinated on June 28,

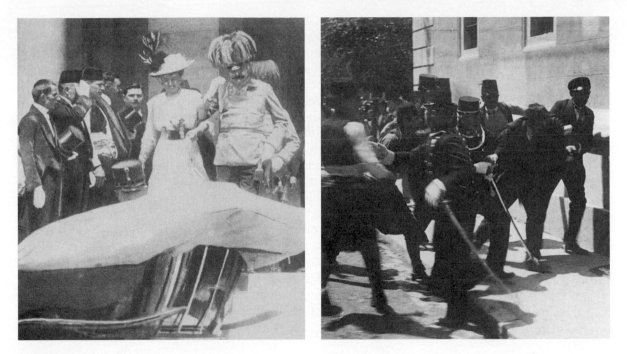

Figure 6–1
Cultural Relativity, History, and Test Validity

Austro-Hungarian Archduke Franz Ferdinand and his wife Sophia are pictured (left) as they left Sarajevo's City Hall on June 28, 1914. Moments later, Ferdinand would be assassinated by Gavrilo Princip, shown in custody at right. The killing served as a catalyst for World War I and is discussed and analyzed in history textbooks in every language around the world. Yet descriptions of the assassin Princip in those textbooks—and ability test items based on those descriptions—vary as a function of culture.

1914, by a Serb named Gavrilo Princip (Figure 6–1). Now think about how you would answer the following multiple-choice item on a history test:

Gavrilo Princip was

    a. a poet.

    b. a hero.

    c. a terrorist.

    d. a nationalist.

    e. all of the above.

For various textbooks in the Bosnian region of the world, choice "e"—that's right, all of the above—is the "correct" answer. According to Hedges (1997), textbooks in areas of Bosnia and Herzegovina that are controlled by different ethnic groups impart widely varying characterizations of the assassin. In the Serb-controlled region of the country, history textbooks, and presumably the tests constructed to measure students' learning, regard Princip as a "hero and poet." By contrast, Croatian students read that Princip was an assassin trained to commit a terrorist act. Muslims in the region are taught that Princip was a nationalist whose deed sparked anti-Serbian rioting.

As incredible as it may sound to Westerners, students in Bosnia and Herzegovina today are taught different versions of history, art, and language depending upon their ethnic background. Such a situation illustrates in stark relief the influence of culture on what is taught to students, as well as aspects of test construction, scoring, interpretation, and validation. The influence of culture thus extends to judgments concerning validity of tests and test items. Differences in judgments concerning the validity of tests and test items may be observed from country to country throughout the world, and in some cases, even from classroom to classroom. What is considered a valid history test in one classroom will not be considered so in another classroom. Moreover, interpretations made on the basis of testtaker responses will vary as a function of culture. So, for example, Croatian students in Bosnia who select choice "b" (hero) for the test item above may do more than depress their scores on the history test; they may draw unwanted scrutiny, if not a formal investigation, regarding their political loyalties. Such scenarios bring new meaning to the term "politically correct" as it applies to tests, test items, and testtaker responses.

The Bosnian region is hardly unique in this regard. Consider in this context a *60 Minutes* segment entitled "Brother Against Brother," first aired December 7, 1997. Correspondent Ed Bradley reported on the case of a Palestinian professor who included questions regarding governmental corruption on an examination. The Palestinian Authority responded by interrogating, confining, and torturing the professor—all in the interest of maintaining governmentally approved "content validity" of university examinations.

Criterion-Related Validity

Criterion-related validity is a judgment regarding how adequately a test score can be used to infer an individual's most probable standing on some measure of interest—the measure of interest being the criterion. Two types of validity evidence are subsumed under the heading "criterion-related validity." **Concurrent validity** is the form of criterion-related validity that is an index of the degree to which a test score is related to some criterion measure obtained at the same time (concurrently). **Predictive validity** is the form of criterion-related validity that is an index of the degree to which a test score predicts some criterion measure. Before we discuss each of these types of validity evidence in detail, it seems appropriate to raise (and answer) an important question.

What Is a Criterion?

A *criterion* may be broadly defined as the standard against which a test or a test score is evaluated. Operationally, a criterion can be most anything: "pilot performance in flying a Boeing 767," "grade on examination in Advanced Hairweaving," "number of days spent in psychiatric hospitalization." In short, there are no hard-and-fast rules for what constitutes a criterion; it can be a specific behavior or group of behaviors, a test score, an amount of time, a rating, a psychiatric diagnosis, a training cost, an index of absenteeism, an index of alcohol intoxication, and so on. But although a criterion can be almost anything, it should be reliable, relevant, valid, and uncontaminated.

Characteristics of a criterion   Like test scores, the criterion scores should be reliable. The reliability of the criterion and the reliability of the test each limit the magnitude of the validity coefficient according to the following theoretical relationship:

$$r_{xy} \leq \sqrt{(r_{xx})(r_{yy})}$$

Here, r_{xy} is the validity coefficient (the correlation between the test and the criterion), r_{xx} is the test reliability, and r_{yy} is the criterion reliability. The formula is read as follows: The validity coefficient is less than or equal to the square root of the test's reliability coefficient multiplied by the criterion's reliability coefficient.

An adequate criterion is also relevant. We would expect, for example, that a test purporting to tell us something about an individual's aptitude for a career in psychology had been validated using some sort of criterion involving data obtained from psychologists.

An adequate criterion measure must also be valid for the purpose for which it is being used. If one test (X) is being used as the criterion to validate a second test (Y), then evidence should exist that test X is valid. If the criterion used is a rating made by a judge or a panel, then evidence should exist that the rating is valid. If, for example, a test manual for a diagnostic test of personality reported that the test had been validated using a criterion of "diagnoses made by a blue ribbon panel of psychodiagnosticians," the test user might wish to probe further—either by reading on in the manual or by writing the test publisher—regarding variables such as (1) the specific definitions of diagnostic terms and categories, (2) the precise nature of the background, training, and experience of the "blue ribbon panel," and (3) the nature and extent of panel members' extra-test contact with the diagnosed subjects.

Ideally, a criterion is also uncontaminated. **Criterion contamination** is the term applied to a situation where the criterion measure itself has been based, at least in part, on predictor measures. Suppose that we just completed a study of how accurately a test called the MMPI predicted psychiatric diagnosis in the psychiatric population of the Minnesota state hospital system. In this study, the predictor is the MMPI, and the criterion is the psychiatric diagnosis that exists in the patient's record. Let's suppose further that, while we are in the process of analyzing our data, someone informs us that the diagnosis for every patient in the Minnesota state hospital system was determined, at least in part, by an MMPI test score. Should we still proceed with our analysis? The answer, of course, is no; because the predictor measure has contaminated the criterion measure, it would be of little value to find, in essence, that the predictor can indeed predict itself.

Concurrent Validity

If test scores are obtained at about the same time that the criterion measures are obtained, measures of the relationship between the test scores and the criterion provide evidence of *concurrent validity*. Statements of concurrent validity indicate the extent to which test scores may be used to estimate an individual's present standing on a criterion. If, for example, scores (or classifications) made on the basis of a psychodiagnostic test were to be validated against a criterion of already diagnosed psychiatric patients, the process would be one of concurrent validation. In general, once the validity of the inference from the test scores is established, the test may provide a faster, less expensive way to offer a diagnosis or a classification decision. A test with satisfactorily demonstrated concurrent validity may therefore be very appealing to prospective users because it holds out the potential of savings of money and professional time; what administrator, for example, wouldn't prefer to use an inexpensive paper-and-pencil test if he or she could obtain the same results with this test as through the use of highly trained mental health personnel (who might more efficiently and valuably be spending their time doing other things, such as conducting research or therapy)?

Sometimes the concurrent validity of a particular test (we'll call it Test A for the purposes of this example) is explored with respect to how it compares with another test (one we'll call Test B). In such studies, prior research has satisfactorily demonstrated the validity of Test B, and the question becomes, "How well does Test A compare with Test B?"

Here, Test B is used as what is referred to as the "validating criterion." In some studies, Test A is either a brand-new test or a test being used for some new purpose, perhaps with a new population. In the example of a concurrent validity study that follows, a group of researchers explored whether a test that had been validated for use with adults could be used with adolescents.

The Beck Depression Inventory (BDI, Beck et al., 1961, 1979; Beck & Steer, 1993) and its revision, the Beck Depression Inventory-II (BDI-II, Beck et al., 1996) are self-report measures used to identify symptoms of depression and quantify their severity. Although the BDI had been widely used with adults, questions were raised regarding its appropriateness for use with adolescents. Ambrosini et al. (1991) conducted a concurrent validity study to explore the utility of the BDI with adolescents. They also sought to determine if the test could successfully differentiate patients with depression from those without depression in a population of adolescent outpatients. Diagnoses generated from the concurrent administration of an instrument previously validated for use with adolescents (the Kiddie-Schedule for Affective Disorders and Schizophrenia) were used as the criterion validators. The findings suggested that the BDI is valid for use with adolescents.

We now turn our attention to another form of criterion validity, one in which the criterion measure is obtained not concurrently but at some future time.

Predictive Validity

Test scores may be obtained at one time and the criterion measures obtained at a future time—after some intervening event has taken place (such as training, experience, therapy, medication, or simply the passage of time). Measures of the relationship between the test scores and a criterion measure obtained at a future time provide an indication of the **predictive validity** of the test; that is, how accurately scores on the test predict some criterion measure. Measures of the relationship between college admissions tests and freshman grade-point averages, for example, provide evidence of the predictive validity of the admissions tests.

In settings where tests might be employed, such as a personnel agency, a college admissions office, or a warden's office, a test's high predictive validity can be a very useful aid to decision makers who must select successful students, productive workers, or convicts who are good parole risks. Whether a test result is valuable in making a decision depends on how well the test results improve selection decisions over those decisions made without knowledge of test results. In an industrial setting where volume turnout is important, if the use of a personnel selection test can have the effect of enhancing productivity to even a small degree, the enhanced productivity will pay off year after year and may translate into millions of dollars of increased revenue. And in a clinical context, no price could be placed on a test that has the effect of saving more lives from suicide or homicide if the test could provide predictive accuracy over and above existing tests with respect to such acts. Unfortunately, the difficulties inherent in developing such tests are numerous and multifaceted (see Mulvey & Lidz, 1984; Murphy, 1984; Petrie & Chamberlain, 1985).

Judgments of criterion-related validity, whether concurrent or predictive, are based on two types of statistical evidence: the validity coefficient and expectancy data.

The validity coefficient The **validity coefficient** is a correlation coefficient that provides a measure of the relationship between test scores and scores on the criterion measure. The correlation coefficient computed from a score (or classification) on a psychodiagnostic test and the criterion score (or classification) assigned by psychodiagnosticians is one example of a validity coefficient. Typically, the Pearson correlation coefficient is used to determine the validity between the two measures. However, depending on variables such as the type of data, the sample size, and the shape of the distribution, other correlation coefficients could be used. For example, in examining self-rankings of performance on some job with rankings made by job supervisors, the formula for the Spearman rho rank-order correlation would be employed.

Like the reliability coefficient and other correlational measures, the validity coefficient is affected by restriction or inflation of range. And as in other correlational studies, a key issue is whether the range of scores employed is appropriate to the objective of the correlational analysis. In situations where, for example, attrition in the number of subjects has occurred over the course of the study, the validity coefficient may be adversely affected. To illustrate, suppose that a clinical psychologist working in the psychiatric emergency room of a municipal hospital has developed a new test called the "Very Brief Psychodiagnostic Classification Inventory" (VBPCI). The psychologist hypothesizes that a patient's score or classification on this test will be predictive of the diagnosis on the patient's chart seven days from the day it was administered. Because the test takes only a minute or two to administer—it is indeed *very* brief—all people who present themselves at (or who are brought to) the psychiatric emergency room are administered the test as part of a validation study. The study runs for one month, at the end of which time a statistically significant validity coefficient describing the relationship between VBPCI score and the criterion diagnosis is computed. Should the psychologist immediately proceed to a test publisher's office, VBPCI in hand?

Not necessarily—at least not until the effects of attrition, if any, in the sample have been analyzed. The impressive VBPCI findings might well be an artifact of such attrition, and the findings might more accurately be interpreted as reflecting the fact that the VBPCI is an accurate predictor of psychiatric diagnosis for conditions in the middle range of psychopathology only; one may not be able to tell from the design of this study how well a predictor the VBPCI is at extreme ranges. Here's why: If the municipal hospital psychiatric emergency room in which the study was conducted is typical of others, the least disordered patients will have been discharged after a day or two—and therefore they will be eliminated from the sample. Attrition of the sample can be expected to occur not only with respect to the least disordered patients but at the other extreme as well; many of the severely disordered patients will have been transferred to a state hospital before seven days from the time of their initial admission. Because the data for the remaining subjects represent only the middle range of the wide range of psychodiagnostic types that could be encountered in a psychiatric emergency room, the reported measure of the VBPCI's validity would likely be deflated.[3]

The problem of restricted range can occur through a self-selection process in the sample employed for the validation study. Thus, for example, if the test purports to measure something as technical or dangerous as oil barge fire-fighting aptitude, it may well be that the only people who reply to an ad for the position of oil barge firefighter are people who actually are highly qualified for the position; hence, you would expect the range of the distribution of scores on some test of oil barge fire-fighting aptitude to be restricted. For less technical or dangerous positions, a self-selection factor might be operative if the test developer selects a group of newly hired employees to test (with the expectation that criterion measures will be available for this group at some subsequent

---

3. A more detailed discussion of the influence on correlation coefficients of (1) restriction of range and (2) combining data from different groups can be found in Allen and Yen (1979, pp. 34–36).

date). However, because the newly hired employees have probably already passed some formal or informal evaluation in the process of being hired, there is a good chance that ability to do the job among this group will be higher than ability to do the job among a random sample of ordinary job applicants. Consequently, scores on the criterion measure that is later administered will tend to be higher than scores on the criterion measure obtained from a random sample of ordinary job applicants; stated another way, the scores will be restricted in range.

Whereas it is the responsibility of the test developer to report validation data in the test manual, it is the responsibility of test users to carefully read the description of the validation study and evaluate the suitability of the test for their specific purposes. What were the characteristics of the sample used in the validation study? How matched are those characteristics to the people for whom an administration of the test is being contemplated? Are some subtests of a test more appropriate for a specific test purpose than is the entire test?

How high should a validity coefficient be for a user or a test developer to infer that the test is valid? There are no rules for determining the minimum acceptable size of a validity coefficient. In fact, Cronbach and Gleser (1965) cautioned against the establishment of such rules. They argued that validity coefficients need to be large enough to enable the test user to make accurate decisions within the unique context in which a test is being used. Essentially, the validity coefficient should be high enough to result in the identification and differentiation of testtakers with respect to target attribute(s), such as employees who are likely to be more productive, police officers who are less likely to misuse their weapons, and students who are more likely to be successful in a particular course of study.

Incremental validity   Test users involved in predicting some criterion from test scores are often interested in the utility of multiple predictors. The value of including more than one predictor depends on a couple of factors. First, of course, each measure being used as a predictor should have criterion-related predictive validity. Second, additional predictors should possess **incremental validity,** defined as the degree to which an additional predictor explains something about the criterion measure not explained by predictors already in use.

Incremental validity may be used when predicting something like academic success in college. Grade-point average (GPA) at the end of the first year may be used as a measure of academic success. A study of potential predictors of GPA may reveal that time spent in the library and time spent studying are highly correlated with GPA, and how much sleep one's roommate allows one to have during exam periods correlates with GPA to a smaller extent. What is the most accurate but most efficient way to predict GPA? One approach, employing the principles of incremental validity, is to start with the best predictor, the predictor that is most highly correlated with GPA. This may be time spent studying. Then, using multiple regression techniques, one would examine the usefulness of the other predictors. Even though time in the library is highly correlated with GPA, it may not possess incremental validity if it overlaps too much with the first predictor, time spent studying. Said another way, if time spent studying and time in the library are so highly correlated with each other that they reflect essentially the same thing, then only one of them needs to be included as a predictor; including both will provide little new information. In contrast, one may find that the amount of sleep one's roommate permits one to have during exams has good incremental validity because it reflects a different aspect of preparing for exams (resting) from the first predictor (studying). Incremental validity has been used to improve the prediction of job performance for Marine Corps mechanics (Carey, 1994) and the prediction of child abuse (Murphy-Berman, 1994). In both instances, predictor measures were included only if they demonstrated that they could explain something about the criterion measure that was not already known from the other predictors.

Expectancy data   **Expectancy data** provide a source of information that can be used in evaluating the criterion-related validity of a test. Using a score obtained on some test(s) or measure(s), expectancy tables illustrate the likelihood that the testtaker will score within some interval of scores on a criterion measure—an interval that may be seen as "passing," "acceptable," and so on. An **expectancy table** shows the percentage of people within specified test-score intervals who subsequently were placed in various categories of the criterion (for example, placed in "passed" category or "failed" category). An expectancy table may be created from a scatterplot according to the steps listed in Figure 6–2. An expectancy table showing the relationship between scores on a subtest of the Differential Aptitude Test (DAT) and course grades in American history for eleventh-grade boys is presented in Table 6–2. You can see that of the students who scored between 40 and 60, 83% scored 80 or above in their American history course.

To illustrate how an expectancy table might be used by a corporate personnel office, suppose that on the basis of various test scores and personal interviews, personnel experts rated all applicants for a manual labor position that entailed piecework as "excellent," "very good," "average," "below average," and "poor." In this example, then, the test score is actually a rating made by personnel experts on the basis of a number of test scores and a personal interview. Let's further suppose that because of a severe labor scarcity at the time, all the applicants were hired (a dream come true for a researcher interested in conducting a validation study with respect to the validity of the assessment procedure). Floor supervisors who were blind with respect to the composite score obtained by the newly hired workers provided the criterion measure in this validation study; specifically, they provided ratings of each employee's performance—"satisfactory" or "unsatisfactory." Figure 6–3 is the resulting **expectancy chart,** or graphic representation of an expectancy table. It can be seen that of all applicants originally rated "excellent," 94% were rated "satisfactory" on the job. By contrast, among applicants originally rated "poor," only 17% were rated "satisfactory" on the job. In general, this expectancy chart tells us that the higher the initial rating, the greater the probability of job success. Stated another way, it tells us that the lower the initial rating, the greater the probability of job failure. The company experimenting with such a rating system could reasonably expect to improve its productivity by using this rating system. Specifically, job applicants who obtained ratings of "average" or higher would be the only applicants hired.

Tables that could be used as an aid for personnel directors in their decision-making chores were published by H. C. Taylor and J. T. Russell in the *Journal of Applied Psychology* in 1939. Referred to by the names of their authors, the Taylor-Russell tables provide an estimate of the extent to which inclusion of a particular test in the selection system will actually improve selection. More specifically, the tables provide an estimate of the percentage of employees hired by the use of a particular test who will be successful at their jobs, given different combinations of three variables: the test's validity, the selection ratio used, and the base rate, or the proportion of people currently employed in positions similar to the vacant position who are considered successful. The value assigned for the test's validity is the computed validity coefficient. The selection ratio is a numerical value that reflects the relationship between the number of people to be hired and the number of people available to be hired. For instance, if there are 50 positions and 100 applicants, the selection ratio is 50/100, or .50. The base rate is an indication of the personnel office's

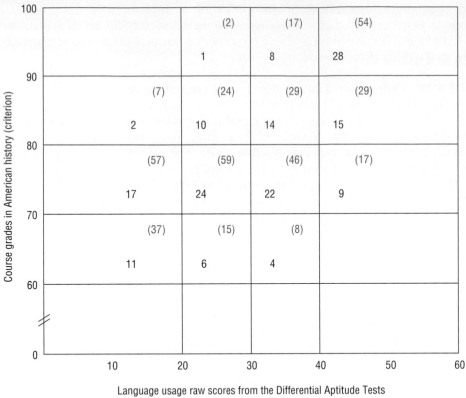

Language usage raw scores from the Differential Aptitude Tests
( ) percentage of points per cell

Figure 6–2
Seven Steps to an Expectancy Table

1. *Draw a scatterplot such that each point in the plot represents a particular test score–criterion score combination. The criterion should be on the Y-axis.*
2. *Draw grid lines in such a way as to summarize the number of people who scored within a particular interval.*
3. *Count the number of points in each cell (n_i) as shown in the figure.*
4. *Count the total number of points within each vertical interval (N_v). This number represents the number of people scoring within a particular test score interval.*
5. *Convert each cell frequency to a percentage (n_i/N_v). This represents the percentage of people obtaining a particular test score–criterion score combination. Write the percentages in the cells. Enclose the percentages in parentheses to distinguish them from the frequencies.*
6. *On a separate sheet, create table headings and subheadings and copy the percentages into the appropriate cell tables as shown in Table 6–2. Be careful to put the percentages in the correct cell tables. (Note that it's easy to make a mistake at this stage because the percentages of people within particular score intervals are written horizontally in the table and vertically in the scatterplot.)*
7. *If desired, write the number and percentage of cases per test-score interval. If the number of cases in any one cell is very small, it is more likely to fluctuate in subsequent charts. If cell sizes are small, the user could create fewer cells or accumulate data over several years.*

Table 6-2

DAT Language Usage Subtest Scores and American History Grade for 171 Eleventh-Grade Boys (Showing Percentage of Students Obtaining Course Grades in the Interval Shown)

Test Score	Course Grade Interval				Cases per Test-Score Interval	
	0–69	70–79	80–89	90–100	N_v	%
40 and above		17	29	54	52	100
30–39	8	46	29	17	48	100
20–29	15	59	24	2	41	100
below 20	37	57	7		30	101*

*Total sums to more than 100% because of rounding.

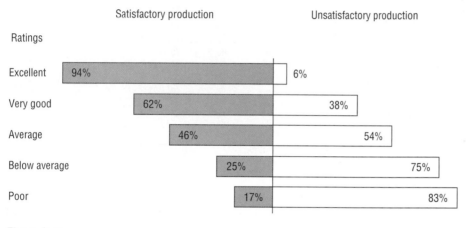

Figure 6-3
Expectancy Chart for Test Ratings and Job Performance

current "batting average" using whatever techniques it is currently using. If, for example, a firm employs 25 computer programmers and 20 are considered successful, the base rate would be .80. With knowledge of the validity coefficient of a particular test along with the selection ratio, reference to the Taylor-Russell tables would provide the personnel officer with an estimate of how much using the test would improve selection over existing methods.

A Taylor-Russell table is presented in Table 6-3. This table is for the base rate of .60, meaning that 60% of those hired under the existing system are successful in their work. Down the left-hand side are validity coefficients for a test that could be used to help select employees. Across the top are the various selection ratios. They reflect the proportion of the people applying for the jobs who will be hired. If a new test is introduced to help select employees in a situation with a selection ratio of .20, and if the new test has a predictive validity coefficient of .55, the table shows the base rate will increase to .88. This means that, rather than 60% of the hired employees being expected to perform successfully, a full 88% can be expected to do so. When selection ratios are low, as when only 5% of the applicants will be hired, even tests with low validity coefficients, such as .15, can result in improved base rates.

Table 6–3
Taylor-Russell Table for a Base Rate of .60

Validity (ρ_{xy})	Selection Ratio										
	.05	.10	.20	.30	.40	.50	.60	.70	.80	.90	.95
.00	.60	.60	.60	.60	.60	.60	.60	.60	.60	.60	.60
.05	.64	.63	.63	.62	.62	.62	.61	.61	.61	.60	.60
.10	.68	.67	.65	.64	.64	.63	.63	.62	.61	.61	.60
.15	.71	.70	.68	.67	.66	.65	.64	.63	.62	.61	.61
.20	.75	.73	.71	.69	.67	.66	.65	.64	.63	.62	.61
.25	.78	.76	.73	.71	.69	.68	.66	.65	.63	.62	.61
.30	.82	.79	.76	.73	.71	.69	.68	.66	.64	.62	.61
.35	.85	.82	.78	.75	.73	.71	.69	.67	.65	.63	.62
.40	.88	.85	.81	.78	.75	.73	.70	.68	.66	.63	.62
.45	.90	.87	.83	.80	.77	.74	.72	.69	.66	.64	.62
.50	.93	.90	.86	.82	.79	.76	.73	.70	.67	.64	.62
.55	.95	.92	.88	.84	.81	.78	.75	.71	.68	.64	.62
.60	.96	.94	.90	.87	.83	.80	.76	.73	.69	.65	.63
.65	.98	.96	.92	.89	.85	.82	.78	.74	.70	.65	.63
.70	.99	.97	.94	.91	.87	.84	.80	.75	.71	.66	.63
.75	.99	.99	.96	.93	.90	.86	.81	.77	.71	.66	.63
.80	1.00	.99	.98	.95	.92	.88	.83	.78	.72	.66	.63
.85	1.00	1.00	.99	.97	.95	.91	.86	.80	.73	.66	.63
.90	1.00	1.00	1.00	.99	.97	.94	.88	.82	.74	.67	.63
.95	1.00	1.00	1.00	1.00	.99	.97	.92	.84	.75	.67	.63
1.00	1.00	1.00	1.00	1.00	1.00	1.00	1.00	.86	.75	.67	.63

Source: Taylor and Russell (1939)

One limitation inherent in the use of the Taylor-Russell tables is that the relationship between the predictor (the test) and the criterion (rating of performance on the job) must be linear. If, for example, there is some point at which job performance levels off, no matter how high the score on the test gets, use of the Taylor-Russell tables would be inappropriate. Another limitation inherent in the use of the Taylor-Russell tables is the potential problem of having to identify a criterion score that separates "successful" from "unsuccessful" employees. This problem was avoided in an alternative set of tables (Naylor & Shine, 1965) that provide an indication of the difference in average criterion scores for the selected as compared with the original group. Use of the Naylor-Shine tables entails obtaining the difference between the means of the selected and unselected groups to obtain an index of what the test (or some other tool of assessment) is adding to already established procedures. Both the Taylor-Russell and the Naylor-Shine tables can assist in judging the utility of a particular test, the former by determining the increase over current procedures and the latter by determining the increase in average score on some criterion measure. With both tables, the validity coefficient used must be one obtained by concurrent validation procedures—a fact that should not be surprising because it is obtained with respect to current employees hired by the selection process in effect at the time of the study.

If hiring decisions were made solely on the basis of variables such as the validity of an employment test and the prevailing selection ratio, then tables such as those offered by Taylor and Russell and Naylor and Shine would be in wide use today. The fact is that many other kinds of variables might enter into hiring decisions (for example, minority status, general physical or mental health of applicant, or drug use by applicant). Given that many variables may affect a hiring—or some other—decision, of what use is a given test in the decision process? After publication of the Taylor-Russell tables, a number of articles probing ways to determine how appropriate the use of a given test is with respect to different types of assessment procedures began to appear (Brogden, 1946, 1949; Smith, 1948), and a literature dealing with test utility theory began to grow. Also during this period, statisticians such as Wald (1947, 1950) were involved in identifying statistical rules for developing a sequential analysis of a problem that would lead to an optimal decision; decision theory had been born, and it would be applied to answering questions about the utility of psychological tests.

Decision theory and test utility   Perhaps the most oft-cited application of statistical decision theory to the field of psychological testing is Cronbach and Gleser's *Psychological Tests and Personnel Decisions.* The idea of applying statistical decision theory to questions of test utility was conceptually appealing and promising, and an authoritative textbook of the day reflects the great enthusiasm with which this marriage of enterprises was greeted:

> The basic decision-theory approach to selection and placement . . . has a number of advantages over the more classical approach based upon the correlation model. . . . There is no question but that it is a more general and better model for handling this kind of decision task, and we predict that in the future problems of selection and placement will be treated in this context more frequently—perhaps to eventual exclusion of the more stereotyped correlational model. (Blum & Naylor, 1968, p. 58)

Stated generally, Cronbach and Gleser (1965) presented (1) a classification of decision problems, (2) various selection strategies ranging from single-stage processes to sequential analyses, (3) a quantitative analysis of the relationship between test utility, the selection ratio, cost of the testing program, and expected value of the outcome, and (4) a recommendation that in some instances job requirements be tailored to the applicant's ability instead of the other way around (a concept they refer to as "adaptive treatment").

Before we illustrate decision theory in action, let us briefly—and somewhat loosely—define five terms frequently encountered in discussions of decision theory as applied to psychological testing and measurement: base rate, hit rate, miss rate, false positive, and false negative.

A **base rate** may be defined as the extent to which a particular trait, behavior, characteristic, or attribute exists in the population (expressed as a proportion). As illustrated in this chapter's *Close-up*, due consideration must be given to the base rate of a targeted attribute in the sample of people being studied in predictive validity research, versus the base rate of that same attribute in the population at large. In psychometric parlance, a **hit rate** may be defined as the proportion of people a test accurately identifies as possessing or exhibiting a particular trait, behavior, characteristic, or attribute. For example, "hit rate" could refer to the proportion of people accurately predicted to be able to perform graduate school–level work, or the proportion of neurological patients accurately identified as having a brain tumor. In like fashion, a **miss rate** may be defined as the proportion of people the test fails to identify as having—or not having—a particular characteristic or attribute; a *miss* amounts to an inaccurate prediction. The category of "misses" may be further subdivided. A **false positive** is a miss wherein the test predicted that the testtaker did possess the particular characteristic or attribute being measured when the testtaker did not. A **false negative** is a miss wherein the test predicted that the testtaker did not possess the particular characteristic or attribute being measured when the testtaker did.

Suppose you developed a measurement procedure you called the "Vapor Test" (VT), which was designed to determine if alive-and-well subjects are indeed breathing. The procedure for the VT entails having the examiner hold a mirror under the subject's nose and mouth for a minute or so and observing if the subject's breath fogs the mirror.

Base Rates and Predictive Validity

For evaluating the predictive validity of a test, a test targeting a particular attribute may be administered to a sample of research subjects in which approximately half of the subjects possess or exhibit the targeted attribute and the other half do not. Questions may subsequently arise about the appropriateness of the use of such a test in which the base rate of the occurrence of the targeted attribute in the population being tested is substantially less than 50%. Such questions arose, for example, with regard to the use of a test called the Child Abuse Potential Inventory (CAP; Milner, 1986).

The CAP was designed to be a screening aid in the identification of adults at high risk for physically abusing children. A high score on the CAP, especially in combination with confirmatory evidence from other sources, might prompt the test user to probe further with regard to the testtaker's history of, or present intentions regarding, child abuse. Another use of the CAP is as an outcome measure in programs designed to prevent physical abuse of children (Milner, 1989). Participants would be administered the CAP upon entry to the program, and again upon exit.

Predictive validity research conducted with the CAP has "demonstrated an uncanny hit rate (about 90%) in discriminating abusers from nonabusers" (Melton & Limber, 1989, p. 1231). Yet as the author of the CAP has pointed out, "the reported 90% hit rate was determined in studies using groups that consisted of equal numbers of abusers and nonabusers that by design contain base rates of 50% which are optimal for classification purposes" (Milner, 1991, p. 80). Thus, as the base rate for child abuse decreases, the number of false positives in the group indicated as abusive will increase, while the number of false negatives in the group indicated as nonabusive will decrease. If these facts related to base rates and predictive validity are not known and appreciated by the test user, a potential for misuse of tests such as the CAP exists.

The base rate for child abuse in the general population is about 2–3% annually (Finkelhor & Dziuba-Leatherman,

Table 1
Application of the CAP in a Population with a High Base Rate of Child Abuse

	Actual Status		
	Abuser	Nonabuser	Row Totals
CAP results indicate:			
Abuser	91	13	104
Nonabuser	19	97	116
Column totals	*110*	*110*	*220*

1994). This base rate is low relative to the 50% base rate that prevailed in the predictive validity studies with the CAP. This fact must therefore be considered in any use of the CAP with members of the general population.

With this background, consider a study conducted by Milner et al. (1986) with 220 adults, including 110 known abusers and 110 nonabusers. All subjects completed the CAP and the test was scored. Fully 82.7% of the abusers and 88.2% of the nonabusers were correctly classified using the CAP (Table 1). Working down the columns of Table 1, note that of the 110 known abusers, 19 were incorrectly classified as nonabusers. Of the 110 known nonabusers, 13 were incorrectly identified as abusers. Of course, in most applications of the CAP, one would not know whether the person being tested was an actual child abuser; that would probably be the reason for administering the test. To gain an understanding of the errors that would be made, look at Table 1 again, but this time work across the rows. When the CAP indicates that a person is an abuser, the finding is correct 87.5% of the time (91 of 104 instances). When the CAP indicates that a person is not an abuser, it is correct 83.6% of the time (97 of 116 instances).

Let's say that 100 introductory psychology students are administered the VT, and it is concluded that 89 were, in fact, breathing (whereas 11 are deemed, on the basis of the VT, not to be breathing). Is the VT a good test? Obviously not. Because the base rate is 100% of the (alive-and-well) population, we really don't even need a test to measure the characteristic "breathing"—and if for some reason we did need a measurement procedure, we probably wouldn't use one that was inaccurate in approximately 11% of the cases. A test is obviously of no value if the hit rate is higher *without* using it; one measure

Table 2
Application of the CAP in a Population with a Low Base Rate of Child Abuse

	Actual Status		
	Abuser	Nonabuser	Row Totals
CAP results indicate:			
Abuser	41	112	153
Nonabuser	9	838	847
Column totals	*50*	*950*	*1000*

The picture changes dramatically, however, in a low base rate environment. For the purposes of this example, let's say that physical child abuse occurs in 5% of the population. In a hypothetical study, we test 1,000 people using the CAP. Because physical child abuse occurs in 5% of the population, we would expect 50 or so of our testtakers to be abusers. And let's say further that just as in the Milner et al. (1986) study, 82.7% of the abusers and 88.2% of the nonabusers are correctly identified in our study (Table 2). Working down the columns in Table 2, if 82.7% of the abusers are correctly identified, 41 will be identified as abusers, and the remaining 9 will be identified as nonabusers. If the test has an 88.2% accuracy rate for nonabusers, 838 of the nonabusers will be correctly identified, and the remaining 112 will be identified as abusers.

Now look at Table 2 again, this time working across the rows. If the CAP score indicates that the individual is an abuser, it is probably *in*correct. Most of the people (73.2% of them, in this example) with CAP scores indicating that they are abusers are, in reality, not abusers. This inaccuracy is entirely the product of working with a low base rate sample. Even if the CAP were more accurate, because abuse is a low

base rate phenomenon, using test results to identify abusers will still result in many identified abusers being wrongly classified. Stated another way, when the nonabusing population is much larger than the abusing population, the chances are that most of the mistakes will be made in classifying the nonabusing population.

Place yourself in the seat of the judge or the jury hearing a physical child abuse case. A psychologist testifies that the CAP, which has an accuracy rate of 85–90%, indicates that the defendant is a physical abuser. The psychologist attempts an explanation about population base rates and the possibility of error. Still, what might stick in your mind about the psychologist's testimony? Many people would reason that, if the CAP is right more than 85% of the time, and if the defendant is *identified* as a child abuser, there must be at least an 85% chance that the defendant *is* a child abuser. This conclusion, as you know now, would be incorrect and could result in justice not being served (Melton & Limber, 1989).

This example illustrates that the test developer's intended use of the test must be respected. Lacking any compelling psychometric evidence to deviate from the test developer's intended use of the test, such deviations may result in harm to the testtaker. The example further serves as a reminder that when data about the accuracy and consistency of a test are collected, the data are collected using a sampling of people from a particular population. Conclusions drawn from those psychometric data are applicable only to groups of people from a similar population.

Joel Milner, the author of the CAP, has urged test users to keep in mind that it is inappropriate to use any single psychological test as a diagnostic criterion. Milner (1991) went on to remind readers that "data from multiple sources, such as several tests, client interviews, collateral interviews, direct observations, and case histories should be used in making decisions regarding child abuse and treatment" (p. 81).

of the value of a test lies in the extent to which its use improves on the hit rate that exists without its use.

As a simple illustration of decision theory applied to testing, suppose a test is administered to a group of 100 job applicants, and some cutoff score is applied to distinguish applicants who will be hired (applicants judged to have passed the test) from applicants whose employment application will be rejected (applicants judged to have failed the test). And let's further suppose that some criterion measure will be applied some time later to ascertain whether the newly hired person worked out—whether the newly hired person was considered a success or a failure at the job. In such a situation, if the test is a perfect predictor (if its validity coefficient is equal to 1), two distinct types of outcomes can be identified: (1) Some applicants will score at or above the cutoff score on the test and be successful at the job, and (2) some applicants will score below the cutoff score and would not have been successful at the job. But because few, if any, employment tests are perfect predictors, two other types of outcomes are also possible: (3) Some applicants will score at or above the cutoff score, be hired, and fail at the job (the criterion), and (4) some applicants who scored below the cutoff score and were not hired could have been successful at the job. People who fall into group 3 could be categorized as "false positives," and those who fall into group 4 could be categorized as "false negatives."

In this illustration, logic alone tells us that if the selection ratio is, say, 90% (nine out of ten applicants will be hired), the cutoff score will probably be set lower than if the selection ratio is 5% (only five of the 100 applicants will be hired). Further, if the selection ratio is 90%, it is a good bet that the number of false positives (people hired who will fail on the criterion measure) will be greater than in a case where the selection ratio is 5%. Conversely, if the selection ratio is only 5%, it is a good bet that the number of false negatives (people not hired who could have succeeded on the criterion measure) will be greater than in a case where the selection ratio is 90%. Decision theory provides guidelines for setting optimal cutoff scores. In setting such scores, the relative seriousness of making false-positive or false-negative selection decisions is frequently taken into account. Thus, for example, it is a prudent policy for an airline personnel office to set cutoff scores on tests for pilots that might result in a false negative (a pilot who is truly qualified being rejected) as opposed to a cutoff score that would allow a false positive (hiring a pilot who is, in reality, unqualified).

In the hands of highly skilled researchers, principles of decision theory applied to problems of test utility have led to some enlightening and impressive findings. For example, Schmidt, Hunter, McKenzie, and Muldrow (1979) demonstrated in dollars and cents how the utility of a company's selection program (and the validity coefficient of the tests used in that program) can play a critical role in the profitability of the company. Focusing on one employer's population of computer programmers, these researchers asked supervisors to rate, in dollars, the value of good, average, and poor programmers. This information was used in conjunction with other information, including these facts: (1) Each year the employer hired 600 new programmers, (2) the average programmer remained on the job for about ten years, (3) the Programmer Aptitude Test currently in use as part of the hiring process had a validity coefficient of .76, (4) it cost about $10 per applicant to administer the test, and (5) the employer currently had in excess of 4,000 programmers in its employ.

Schmidt et al. (1979) made a number of calculations using different values for some of the variables. For example, knowing that some of the tests previously used in the hiring process had validity coefficients ranging from .00 to .50, they varied the value of the test's validity coefficient (along with other factors such as different selection ratios that had been in effect) and examined the relative efficiency of the various conditions. Among their findings was the fact that the existing selection ratio and selection process provided a great gain in efficiency over a previous situation (when the selection ratio was 5% and the validity coefficient of the test used in hiring was equal to .50)—a gain equal to almost $6 million per year. Multiplied over, say, ten years, that's $60 million. The existing selection ratio and selection process provided an even greater gain in efficiency over a previously existing situation in which the test had no validity at all and the selection ratio was .80; here, in one year, the gain in efficiency was estimated to be equal to over $97 million.

By the way, the employer in the study above was the United States government. Hunter and Schmidt (1981) applied the same type of analysis to the national workforce and made a compelling argument with respect to the critical relationship between valid tests and measurement procedures and our national productivity. In a subsequent study, Schmidt, Hunter, and their colleagues found that substantial increases in work output or reductions in payroll costs would result from using valid measures of cognitive ability as opposed to nontest procedures (Schmidt et al., 1986).

Employers are reluctant to use decision theory–based strategies in their hiring practices because of the complexity of their application and the threat of legal challenges Thus, although decision theory approaches to assessment hold great promise, their promise has yet to be fulfilled.

Construct Validity

Construct validity is a judgment about the appropriateness of inferences drawn from test scores regarding individual standings on a variable called a "construct." A **construct** is an informed, scientific idea developed or hypothesized to describe or explain behavior. "Intelligence" is a construct that may be invoked to describe why a student performs well in school. "Anxiety" is a construct that may be invoked to describe why a psychiatric patient paces the floor. Other examples of constructs are "job satisfaction," "personality," "bigotry," "clerical aptitude," "depression," "motivation," "self-esteem," "emotional adjustment," "potential dangerousness," "creativity," and "mechanical comprehension." Constructs are unobservable, presupposed (underlying) traits that a test developer may invoke to describe test behavior or criterion performance. The researcher investigating a test's construct validity must formulate hypotheses about the expected behavior of high scorers and low scorers on the test. From these hypotheses arises a tentative theory about the nature of the construct the test was designed to measure. If the test is a valid measure of the construct, the high scorers and the low scorers will behave as predicted by the theory. If high scorers and low scorers on the test do not behave as predicted, the investigator will need to reexamine hypotheses made about the construct (or reexamine the nature of the construct itself). One possible reason for obtaining results contrary to those that would have been predicted by the theory is that the test simply is not a valid measure of the construct. An alternative explanation could lie in the theory that generated hypotheses about the construct—perhaps that theory needs to be reexamined. Perhaps the reason for the contrary finding can be traced to the incorrect inclusion in the experimental design of a particular statistical procedure or the incorrect execution of the procedure. Thus, although confirming evidence contributes to a judgment that the test is indeed a valid measure of some construct, contrary evidence—on the bright side—provides a stimulus for the discovery of new facets of the construct or alternative ways to measure it.

Increasingly, construct validity has been viewed as the unifying concept for all validity evidence; all types of validity evidence, including the content and criterion-related varieties, are forms of construct validity. A group of validity coefficients for a given test when considered individually can be interpreted with respect to the test's criterion-related validity; collectively, however, these coefficients have bearing on the construct validity of the test (Guion, 1980).

Evidence of Construct Validity

A number of procedures may be used to provide different kinds of evidence that a test has construct validity. The various techniques of construct validation may provide evidence, for example, that

- The test is homogeneous, measuring a single construct.

- Test scores correlate with scores on other tests in accordance with what would be predicted from a theory that covers the manifestation of the construct in question.

- Test scores increase or decrease as a function of age, the passage of time, or an experimental manipulation as theoretically predicted.

- Test scores obtained subsequent to some event or to the mere passage of time (that is, posttest scores) differ from pretest scores as theoretically predicted.

- Test scores obtained by people from distinct groups vary as predicted by theory.

A brief discussion of each type of construct validity evidence and the procedures used to obtain it follows.

Evidence of homogeneity   **Homogeneity** refers to how well a test measures a single concept. A test developer can increase the homogeneity of an instrument in several ways. Consider, for example, a test of academic achievement that contains subtests in areas such as mathematics, spelling, and reading comprehension. The Pearson r could be used to correlate average subtest scores with average total test score. Subtests that in the test developer's judgment do not correlate very well with the test as a whole might have to be reconstructed (or eliminated) lest the test not measure the construct "academic achievement." Correlations between subtest scores and total test score are generally reported in the test manual as evidence of homogeneity.

One way a test developer can improve the homogeneity of a test containing items that are scored dichotomously (for example, right or wrong) is by eliminating those items that do not show significant correlation coefficients with total test scores. If all test items show significant, positive correlations with total test scores, and high scorers on the test tend to pass each item more than low scorers, then each item is probably measuring the same construct as the total test, thereby contributing to test homogeneity.

The homogeneity of a test in which items are scored on a multipoint scale can also be improved. For example, some attitude and opinion questionnaires require respondents to indicate level of agreement with specific statements by responding, for example, "strongly agree," "agree," "disagree," or "strongly disagree." Each response is assigned a numerical score, and items that do not show significant Spearman rank-order correlation coefficients are eliminated. If all test items show significant, positive correlations with total test scores, then each item is most likely measuring the same construct that the test as a whole is measuring (and thereby contributing to the test's homogeneity). Coefficient alpha may also be used in estimating the homogeneity of a test composed of multiple-choice items (Novick & Lewis, 1967).

As a case study illustrating how a test's homogeneity can be improved, consider the Marital Satisfaction Scale (MSS; Roach et al., 1981). Designed to assess various aspects of married people's attitudes toward their marital relationship, the MSS contains an approximately equal number of items expressing positive and negative sentiments with respect to marriage. For example, "My life would seem empty without my marriage" and "My marriage has 'smothered' my personality." In one stage of the development of this test, subjects indicated how much they agreed or disagreed with the various sentiments in each of 73 items by marking a 5-point scale that ranged from "strongly agree" to "strongly disagree." Based on the correlations between item scores and total score, the test developers elected to retain 48 items with correlation coefficients greater than .50, thus creating a more homogeneous instrument.

In addition to correlational measures of test homogeneity, let us also mention an item-analysis procedure that entails focusing on the relationship between testtakers' scores on individual items and their score on the entire test. Each item is examined with respect to how high scorers as opposed to low scorers on the test responded to it. If it is an academic test and high scorers on the entire test for some reason tended to get that particular item wrong and low scorers on the test as a whole tended to get the item right, the item is obviously not a good one. In fact, such an item should be eliminated in the interest of test homogeneity, among other considerations. If the test is one of, say, marital satisfaction and individuals who score high on the test as a whole respond to a particular item in a way that would indicate that they are not satisfied, whereas people who tend not to be satisfied respond to the item in a way that would indicate that they are satisfied, then again the item should probably be eliminated or at least reexamined for clarity.

Although test homogeneity is desirable because it assures us that all the items on the test tend to be measuring the same thing, it is not the "be-all and end-all" with respect to construct validity. Knowing that a test is homogeneous contributes no information about how the construct being measured relates to other constructs. It is therefore important to report evidence of a test's homogeneity along with other evidence of construct validity.

Evidence of changes with age   The nature of some constructs is such that changes in them would be expected to occur over time. "Reading rate," for example, tends to increase dramatically year by year from age 6 to the early teens. If a test score purports to be a measure of a construct that could be expected to change over time, it too should show the same progressive changes with age if the test score is to be considered a valid measure of the construct. We would expect, for example, that if children in grades 6, 7, 8, and 9 sat for a test of eighth-grade vocabulary, the total number of items scored as correct from all the test protocols would increase as a function of the higher grade level of the testtakers.

Some constructs lend themselves more readily to predictions concerning changes over time than other constructs do. Thus, although we may be able to predict, for example, that a gifted child's scores on a test of reading skills will increase over the course of the testtaker's years of elementary and secondary education, we may not be able to predict with such confidence how a newlywed couple will score through the years on a test of marital satisfaction. This fact does not relegate a construct such as "marital satisfaction" to any less stature than "reading ability"; rather, it simply means that measures of "marital satisfaction" may be less stable over time or more vulnerable to situational events (such as in-laws coming to visit and refusing to leave for three months) than is "reading ability" in specific instances. Evidence of change over time, like evidence of test homogeneity, does not in itself provide information about how the construct relates to other constructs.

Evidence of pretest/posttest changes   Evidence showing that test scores change as a result of some experience between a pretest and a posttest can be evidence of construct validity. Some of the more typical intervening experiences responsible for changes in test scores are formal education, a course of therapy or medication, and on-the-job experience. Of course, depending on the construct being measured, almost any intervening life experience could be predicted to yield changes in score from pretest to posttest. Reading an inspirational book, watching a TV talk show, undergoing surgery, serving a prison sentence, or the mere passage of time may each prove to be a potent intervening variable.

Returning to our example regarding the use of the Marital Satisfaction Scale, one investigator cited in Roach et al. (1981) compared scores on that instrument before and after a sex therapy treatment program. Scores showed a significant change between pretest and posttest. A second posttest given eight weeks later showed that scores remained stable (suggesting the instrument was reliable) whereas the pretest/posttest measures were still significantly different. Such changes in scores in the predicted direction after the treatment program contribute to evidence of the construct validity for this test. Conversely, we would expect a decline in marital satisfaction scores if a pretest were administered to a sample of couples shortly after they took their nuptial vows and a posttest was administered shortly after members of the couples first consulted their respective divorce attorneys (employing for the purposes of the experimental group in this study only couples who consulted divorce attorneys). The design of such pretest/posttest research ideally should include a control group as a way of ruling out alternative explanations of the findings. Thus, with reference to the two examples above, simultaneous testing of a matched group of couples who did not undergo sex therapy and simultaneous testing of a matched group of couples who did not consult divorce attorneys would be advisable. In both instances, there would presumably be no reason to expect any significant changes in the test scores of these two control groups.

Evidence from distinct groups   Also referred to as the **method of contrasted groups,** one way of providing evidence for the validity of a test is to demonstrate that scores on the test vary in a predictable way as a function of membership in some group. The rationale here is that if a test is a valid measure of a particular construct, then test scores from groups of people who would be presumed to differ with respect to that construct should have correspondingly different test scores. It would be reasonable to expect that on a test designed to measure depression (wherein the higher the test score, the more depressed the testtaker is presumed to be), individuals psychiatrically hospitalized for depression should score higher than a random sample of fans at the local baseball stadium. Suppose it was your intention to provide construct validity evidence for the Marital Satisfaction Scale by means of showing differences in scores between distinct groups; how might you go about doing that?

Roach and colleagues (1981) proceeded by identifying two groups of married couples, one relatively satisfied in their marriage, the other not so satisfied. The groups were identified by means of ratings by peers and by professional marriage counselors. A t test on the difference between mean score on the test was significant ($p < .01$)—evidence to support the notion that the Marital Satisfaction Scale is indeed a valid measure of the construct "marital satisfaction."

In a bygone era, the method many test developers used to create distinct groups was deception. For example, if it had been predicted that more of the construct would be exhibited on the test in question if the subject was made to feel highly anxious, an experimental situation might be designed to make the subject feel highly anxious. Virtually any feeling state (such as low self-esteem or impotence) the theory called for could be induced by an experimental scenario that typically involved giving the research subject some misinformation. However, given the ethical constraints of contemporary psychologists combined with the fact that academic institutions and other sponsors of research tend not to condone deception in human research, the method of obtaining distinct groups by creating them through the dissemination of deceptive information is seldom allowed today.

Convergent evidence   Evidence for the construct validity of a particular test may converge from a number of sources, such as other tests or measures designed to assess the same (or a similar) construct. Thus, if scores on the test undergoing construct validation tend to correlate highly in the predicted direction with scores on older, more established, and already validated tests designed to measure the same (or a similar) construct, this would be an example of **convergent evidence.**[4]

Convergent evidence for validity may come not only from correlations with tests purporting to measure an identical construct but also from correlations with measures purporting to measure related constructs. Consider, for example, a new test designed to measure the construct "test anxiety." Generally speaking, we might expect high positive correlations between this new test and older, more established measures of test anxiety. However, we might also expect more moderate correlations between this new test and measures of general anxiety.

Roach et al. (1981) provided convergent evidence of the construct validity of the Marital Satisfaction Scale by computing a validity coefficient between scores on it and scores on the Marital Adjustment Test (Locke & Wallace, 1959). The validity coefficient of .79 provided additional evidence of the construct validity of the instrument.

Discriminant evidence   A validity coefficient showing little (that is, a statistically insignificant) relationship between test scores and/or other variables with which scores on the test being construct-validated should *not* theoretically be correlated provides **discriminant evidence** of construct validity (also known as *discriminant validity*). In the course of developing the Marital Satisfaction Scale (MSS), its authors correlated scores on that instrument with scores on the Marlowe-Crowne Social Desirability Scale (Crowne & Marlowe, 1964). Roach et al. (1981) hypothesized that high correlations between these two instruments would suggest that respondents were probably not answering entirely honestly to items on the MSS but were instead responding in socially desirable ways. But the correlation between the MSS and the social desirability measure did not prove to be significant, and the test developers concluded that social desirability could be ruled out as a primary factor in explaining the meaning of MSS test scores.

In 1959, an experimental technique useful for examining both convergent and discriminant validity evidence was presented in the pages of *Psychological Bulletin*. This rather technical technique, called the **multitrait-multimethod matrix,** is presented in Cohen (2002), the companion study guide to this textbook. Here, let's simply point out that *multitrait* means "two or more traits" and *multimethod* means "two or more methods." The multitrait-multimethod matrix (Campbell & Fiske, 1959) is the matrix or table that results from correlating variables (traits) within and between methods. Values for any number of traits (such as aggressiveness or extraversion) as obtained by various methods (such as behavioral observation or a projective test) are inserted into the table, and the resulting matrix of correlations provides insight with respect to both the convergent and the discriminant validity of the methods used.[5]

Factor analysis   Both convergent and discriminant evidence of construct validity can be obtained by the use of factor analysis. **Factor analysis** is a singular, shorthand term used

---

4. Data indicating that a test measures the same construct as other tests purporting to measure the same construct are also referred to as **convergent validity.** One question that may be raised here concerns the necessity for the new test if it simply duplicates existing tests that measure the same construct. The answer, generally speaking, is a claim that the new test has some advantage over the more established test. For example, the new test may be shorter and capable of administration in less time without significant loss in reliability or validity. On a practical level, the new test may be less costly.

5. For an interesting, real-life application of the multitrait-multimethod technique, see Meier's (1984) examination of the validity of the construct "burnout." In a subsequent construct validity study, Meier (1991) used an alternative to the multitrait-multimethod matrix to examine another construct: "occupational stress."

to describe a class of mathematical procedures that are designed to identify *factors* or specific variables that are typically attributes, characteristics, or dimensions on which people may differ. In psychometric research, factor analysis is frequently employed as a data reduction method in which several sets of scores and the correlations between them are analyzed. In such studies, the purpose of the factor analysis may be to identify the factor or factors in common between test scores on subscales within a particular test, or the factors in common between scores on a series of tests. In general, factor analysis is conducted either on an exploratory or a confirmatory basis. **Exploratory factor analysis** typically entails "estimating, or extracting factors; deciding how many factors to retain; and rotating factors to an interpretable orientation" (Floyd & Widaman, 1995, p. 287). By contrast, in **confirmatory factor analysis,** "a factor structure is explicitly hypothesized and is tested for its fit with the observed covariance structure of the measured variables" (Floyd & Widaman, 1995, p. 287).

A term commonly employed in factor analysis is **factor loading,** which is "a sort of metaphor. Each test is thought of as a vehicle carrying a certain amount of one or more abilities" (Tyler, 1965, p. 44). Loading a factor in a test conveys information about the extent to which the factor determines the test score or scores. A new test purporting to measure bulimia, for example, can be factor-analyzed with other known measures of bulimia, as well as with other kinds of measures (such as measures of intelligence, self-esteem, general anxiety, anorexia, or perfectionism). High factor loadings by the new test on a "bulimia factor" would provide convergent evidence of construct validity. Moderate to low factor loadings by the new test with respect to measures of other eating disorders such as anorexia would provide discriminant evidence of construct validity.

Factor analysis frequently involves technical procedures so complex that few contemporary researchers would attempt to routinely conduct one without the aid of a prepackaged computer program. But although the actual data analysis has become work for computers, humans still tend to be very much involved in the *naming* of factors once the computer has identified them. Thus, for example, if a factor analysis identified a common factor being measured by two hypothetical instruments, a "Bulimia Test" and an "Anorexia Test," we would have to name this factor. One factor analyst looking at the data and the items of each test might christen the common factor an "Eating Disorder Factor." Another factor analyst examining exactly the same materials might label the common factor a "Body Weight Preoccupation Factor." A third analyst might name the factor a "Self-Perception Disorder Factor," and so forth. The point is that naming factors that emerge from a factor analysis has more to do with knowledge, judgment, and verbal abstraction ability than mathematical expertise. There is no rule book for naming factors; factor analysts exercise their own judgment concerning what factor name best communicates the meaning of the factor. Further, even the criteria used to identify a common factor, as well as related technical matters, can be a matter of debate, if not heated controversy (see, for example, Bartholomew, 1996a, 1996b; Maraun, 1996a, 1996b, 1996c; McDonald, 1996a, 1996b; Mulaik, 1996a, 1996b; Rozeboom, 1996a, 1996b; Schonemann, 1996a, 1996b; Steiger, 1996a, 1996b).

Factor analysis is a subject rich in technical complexity. Its uses and applications can vary as a function of the research objectives, as well as the nature of the tests and the constructs under study. It is a research technique that has the advantage of flexibility; but with that advantage come many potential pitfalls. If you are interested in learning more about the advantages (and pitfalls) of factor analysis, see Cohen (2002) and the companion Web site to this textbook, as well as instructive articles (such as Floyd & Widaman, 1995; Gorsuch, 1997; Panter et al., 1997) and books (such as Comrey, 1992).

Validity, Bias, and Fairness

In the eyes of many laypeople, questions concerning the validity of a test are intimately tied to questions concerning the fair use of a test and the issues of bias and fairness. Let us hasten to point out that validity, fairness in the use of a test, and test bias are three separate issues. It is possible for a valid test to be used fairly or unfairly. It is even possible for a biased test to be used fairly or unfairly. Furthermore, people can disagree about whether a test is biased, depending on the definition of bias being used.

Test Bias

For the general public, the term "bias" as applied to psychological and educational tests may conjure up many meanings having to do with prejudice and preferential treatment (Brown et al., 1999). For federal judges, the term "bias" as it relates to items on children's intelligence tests is synonymous with "too difficult" for one group as compared to another (Sattler, 1991). For psychometricians, **bias** is a factor inherent within a test that systematically prevents accurate, impartial measurement.

Psychometricians have developed the technical means to identify and remedy bias, at least in the mathematical sense. As a simple illustration, consider a test we will call the "flip-coin test" (FCT). The "equipment" needed to conduct this test is a two-sided coin. One side has the image of a profile (the "heads" side), and the other side does not (the "tails" side). The FCT would be considered to be biased if the instrument (the coin) were weighted so that either heads or tails would appear more frequently than it would by chance alone. If the test in question were an intelligence test, the test would be considered to be biased if it were constructed so that people who had brown eyes consistently and systematically obtained higher scores than people with green eyes—assuming, of course, that in reality people with brown eyes are not generally more intelligent than people with green eyes. *Systematic* is a key word in our definition of test bias. We have previously looked at sources of *random* or chance variation in test scores. *Bias* implies *systematic* variation.

To illustrate, let's suppose we need to hire 50 secretaries, and so we place an ad in the newspaper. In response to the ad, 200 people reply, including 100 people who happen to have brown eyes and 100 people who happen to have green eyes. Each of the 200 applicants is individually administered a hypothetical test we will call the "Test of Secretarial Skills" (TSS). Logic tells us that eye color is probably not a relevant variable with respect to performing the duties of a secretary; we would therefore have no reason to believe that green-eyed people are better secretaries than brown-eyed people or vice versa. We might reasonably expect that after the tests have been scored and the selection process has been completed, an approximately equivalent amount of brown-eyed and green-eyed people would have been hired (that is, approximately 25 brown-eyed people and 25 green-eyed people). But what if it turned out that 48 green-eyed people were hired and only 2 brown-eyed people were hired? Is this evidence that the TSS is a biased test?

Although the answer to this question seems simple on the face of it—"Yes the test is biased because they should have hired 25 and 25!"—a truly responsible answer to this question would entail statistically troubleshooting the test and the entire selection procedure (see Berk, 1982). To begin with, the following three characteristics of the regression lines (Figure 6–4) used to predict success on the criterion would have to be scrutinized: (1) the slope, (2) the intercept, (3) the error of estimate. And because these three factors of regression are functions of two other statistics (the validity coefficient and the reliability coefficient for both the test and the criterion) that could vary with respect to the two groups in question, a total of five characteristics must be statistically

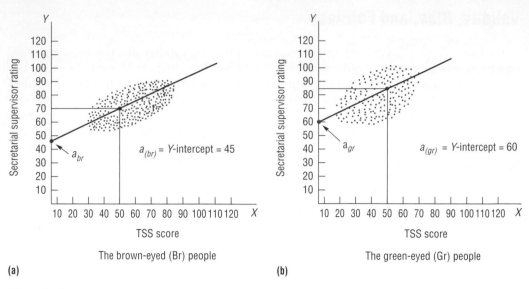

Figure 6–4
TSS Scores and Supervisor Ratings for Two Groups

Note the different points of the Y-intercept corresponding to a TSS score of 50 for the green-eyed and brown-eyed testtakers. If the TSS were an unbiased test, any given score on it would correspond to exactly the same criterion score for the two groups.

examined. A test of significance could indicate that our brown-eyed and green-eyed groups are the same or different with respect to any of these five characteristics. This binary choice (that is, same or different) taken to the fifth power (meaning that there are five ways that the two groups could conceivably differ) means that a comprehensive troubleshooting would entail examination of a total of 32 ($2^5 = 32$) possible ways the test could be found to be biased.

If, for example, a test systematically underpredicts or overpredicts the performance of members of a particular group (such as people with green eyes) with respect to a criterion (such as supervisory rating), it exhibits what is known as **intercept bias**—a term taken from the point where the regression line intersects the Y-axis. If a test systematically yields significantly different validity coefficients for members of different groups, it has what is known as **slope bias**—so named because the slope of one group's regression line is different in a statistically significant way from the regression line of another group.

Stone (1992) identified slope and intercept bias on the Differential Abilities Scale (DAS; Elliot, 1990a, 1990b). The DAS is designed to measure school-related ability and achievement in children and adolescents. The test yields a General Conceptual Ability score, which is a measure of general ability, and achievement scores in a variety of areas, including Basic Number Skills and Word Reading. Stone (1992) computed regression lines for two racial groups: Whites and Asian Americans. When Word Reading scores were predicted from General Conceptual Ability, the regression lines for the two races had different slopes, indicating slope bias. When Basic Number Skills were predicted from General Conceptual Ability, the regression lines for the two races crossed the Y-axis at different places, indicating intercept bias.

The presence of slope and intercept bias on the DAS has important practical implications for testtakers. We will look specifically at the slope bias that Stone found in relation to the Word Reading achievement test. To understand the impact of that bias, draw a graph, using Figure 6–4 as a guide. Place General Conceptual Ability on the X-axis and Word Reading on the Y-axis. Then draw two regression lines with different slopes. Both lines should have a positive slope and should cross the Y-axis in the same place. The line with the steeper slope represents the Asian American children, and the other line represents the White children.

On your drawing, examine the relative position of the regression lines on each graph for X-axis values that are in the intermediate range, representing realistic test scores. You should find that the regression line for the Asian American children is higher than the regression line for the White children. This means that Asian American children at a particular level of achievement generally have lower ability scores than White students achieving at the same level. To see how this is so, pick a point relatively high on the Y-axis, representing a high level of achievement. Then draw a horizontal line across to the two regression lines, and drop a vertical line down to the X-axis from where you cross each regression line (as was done in Figure 6–4). The resulting points on the X-axis represent the average ability levels for the level of reading achievement selected on the Y-axis. You should cross the line for the Asian American students first, meaning that those students have a lower X-value, corresponding to a lower ability level than the White students at the same level of performance.

Now let's assume that teachers nominate students to a program for gifted individuals based on classroom achievement. However, entry to the gifted program is based on ability. This is the approach that is taken in many programs for gifted students. Nominated students are given an ability test, and those above a specific score are admitted. The exercise you just completed indicates that a smaller percentage of nominated Asian American students would be accepted into the gifted program. The Asian American students may well feel discriminated against—they were doing as well in the classroom as their White counterparts but were denied a place in a special program in which they might receive extra attention and more challenging work. Note further that, because of the nonparallel nature of the lines, this will become a greater problem at higher levels of achievement. This is just one of several results of slope and intercept bias explored by Stone (1992). We refer interested students to the original article for a more detailed discussion.

One reason some tests have been found to be biased has more to do with the design of the research study than the design of the test; if there are too few testtakers in one of the groups (such as the minority group—literally), this methodological problem will make it appear as if the test is biased when in fact it may not be. A situation in which a test may justifiably be deemed biased is one in which some portion of its variance stems from some factor(s) irrelevant to performance on the criterion measure; as a consequence, one group of testtakers will systematically perform differently from another. Prevention during test development is the best cure for test bias, though a procedure called "estimated true score transformations" represents one of many available *post hoc* remedies (Mueller, 1949; see also Reynolds & Brown, 1984).[6]

Rating error A **rating** is a numerical or verbal judgment (or both) that places a person or an attribute along a continuum identified by a scale of numerical or word descriptors known as a **rating scale.** Simply stated, a **rating error** is a judgment resulting from the intentional or unintentional misuse of a rating scale. Thus, for example, a **leniency error** (also known as a **generosity error**) is, as its name implies, an error in rating that arises from the tendency on the part of the rater to be lenient in marking. From your own experience during course registration, you might be aware that a section of a particular

---

6. Lest you think that there is something not quite right about transforming data under such circumstances, we add that even though "transformation" is synonymous with "change," the change referred to here is merely a change in form—not meaning. Data may be transformed to place them in a more useful form, not to change their meaning.

course will fill very quickly if the section is being taught by a professor who has a reputation for committing leniency errors when it comes to end-of-term grading. At the other extreme from a leniency error in rating is a **severity error.** Movie critics who pan just about everything they review may be guilty of severity errors (assuming that these critics review a wide range of movies that might consensually be viewed as good and bad). Another type of error might be termed a **central tendency error.** Here the rater, for whatever reason, exhibits a general and systematic reluctance to giving ratings at either the positive or the negative extreme, and so all ratings tend to cluster in the middle of the rating continuum. One way to overcome what might be called "restriction of range rating errors" (central tendency, leniency, severity errors) is to use **rankings,** a procedure that requires the rater to measure individuals against one another instead of against an absolute scale. Now the rater is forced to select first, second, third choices and so forth.

Halo effect describes the fact that, for some raters, some ratees can do no wrong. More specifically, a halo effect may also be defined as a tendency to give a particular ratee a higher rating than he or she objectively deserves because of the rater's failure to discriminate among conceptually distinct and potentially independent aspects of a ratee's behavior. For example, suppose Mel Gibson consented to write and deliver a speech on multivariate analysis. His speech would probably earn much higher all-round ratings if given before the founding chapter of the Mel Gibson Fan Club than if delivered before and rated by the membership of, say, the Royal Statistical Society (even in the unlikely event that the members of each group were equally savvy with respect to multivariate analysis).

Criterion data may also be influenced by the rater's knowledge of the ratee's race or sex (Landy & Farr, 1980). Males have been shown to receive more favorable evaluations than females in traditionally masculine occupations. Except in highly integrated situations, ratees tend to receive higher ratings from raters of the same race (Landy & Farr, 1980). Returning to our TSS situation, a particular rater may have had particularly great—or particularly distressing—prior experiences with green-eyed (or brown-eyed) people and be making extraordinarily high (or low) ratings on that irrational basis.

Training programs to familiarize raters with common rating errors and sources of rater bias have shown promise in reducing rating errors and increasing measures of reliability and validity. Lecture, role playing, discussion, watching oneself on videotape, and computer simulation of different situations are some of the many techniques that could be brought to bear in such training programs. We revisit the subject of rating and rating error in our discussion of personality assessment in Chapter 11. Now, we take up issues related to test fairness.

Test Fairness

In contrast to questions of test bias, which may be thought of as technically complex statistical problems, issues of test fairness tend to be rooted more in thorny issues involving values (Halpern, 2000). Thus while questions of test bias can sometimes be answered with mathematical precision and finality, questions of fairness can be grappled with endlessly by well-meaning people who hold opposing points of view. With that caveat in mind, and with exceptions most certainly in the offing, we will define **fairness** in a psychometric context as the extent to which a test is used in an impartial, just, and equitable way.[7] Keep in mind, however, that apart from the most obvious unfair use of tests—sit-

---

7. On a somewhat more technical note, Ghiselli et al. (1981, p. 320) observed that "fairness refers to whether a difference in mean predictor scores between two groups represents a useful distinction for society, relative to a decision that must be made, or whether the difference represents a bias that is irrelevant to the objectives at hand." For more practical guidelines regarding fairness, at least as construed by legislative bodies and the courts, see Russell (1984).

uations that any reasonable person would consider unfair (for instance, the misuse of psychological tests in some countries to detain, even imprison)—what constitutes a fair and an unfair use of tests is a matter left to parties such as the test developer (in the test manual's usage guidelines), the test user (in the way the test is actually used in practice), and society (in the form of legislation, judicial decisions, and administrative regulations).

Although fairness as applied to tests is at best difficult to address, it is possible to discuss some rather common misunderstandings regarding what are sometimes perceived as unfair or even biased tests. Some tests, for example, have been labeled "unfair" because they discriminate among groups of people;[8] the reasoning is that although differences may exist among individuals, all people are created equal and any differences found among groups of people on any psychological trait must be an artifact of the unfair or biased test. Because this position is so rooted in faith as opposed to scientific evidence—in fact it flies in the face of scientific evidence—it is virtually impossible to refute; one either believes it or doesn't. We would all like to believe that people are equal in every way and are capable of rising to the same heights given equal opportunity, but a more realistic view would appear to be that each person is capable of fulfilling a personal potential. Because people differ so obviously with respect to physical traits, one would be hard put to believe that psychological differences found to exist between individuals—and groups of individuals—are purely a function of inadequate tests. Again, although a test is not inherently unfair or biased simply because it is a tool by which group differences are found, the *use* of the test data can, like the use of any data, be unfair.

Another misunderstanding of what constitutes an unfair or biased test is that it is unfair to administer to a particular population a standardized test that did not include members of that population in the standardization sample. In fact, it may well be biased, but that must be determined by statistical or other means; the sheer fact that no members of a particular group were included in the standardization sample does *not*, in and of itself, invalidate the test for use with that group. Consider in this context a test we will call the "7-Year Itch Test" (7-YIT). Initially designed to explore whether husbands really do become itchy (read "restless") after seven years of marriage, this hypothetical test of marital restlessness was originally standardized in the 2000s on a large sample of men who had been married for seven years. But in the 1990s, the test is being used to assess how itchy not only men but also women get after seven years of marriage. Suppose that a couple married seven years, Bob and Carole, take the 7-YIT and are informed that they each scored at the 95th percentile in marital itchiness. We can conclude that their 7-YIT scores are higher than 95% of the men who take the test. We would have no basis on these data alone, however, to draw any comparisons between Bob and Carole and other couples with respect to 7-YIT performance, nor any basis for conclusions about Carole's itchiness relative to other women who have also been married seven years.

A final source of misunderstanding is the complex problem of remedying situations where bias or unfair test usage has been found to occur. In the area of selection for jobs, positions in universities and professional schools, and the like, a number of different preventive measures and remedies have been attempted. As you read about the tools used in these attempts in this chapter's *Everyday Psychometrics,* form your own opinions regarding what constitutes a fair use of employment and other tests in a selection process.

---

8. The verb *discriminate* here is used in the psychometric sense, meaning, "to show a statistically significant difference between individuals or groups with respect to measurement." The great difference between this statistical, scientific definition and other colloquial definitions (such as "to treat differently and/or unfairly because of group membership") must be kept firmly in mind in discussions of bias and fairness.

Adjustment of Test Scores
by Group Membership:
Fairness in Testing or Foul Play?

Any test, regardless of its psychometric soundness, may be knowingly or unwittingly used in a way that has an adverse impact on one or another group. If such adverse impact is found to exist, and if social policy demands some remedy or an affirmative action program, then psychometricians have a number of techniques at their disposal to create change. The accompanying table lists some of these techniques.

Although psychometricians have the tools at their disposal to institute special policies through manipulations in test development, scoring, and interpretation, there are few clear guidelines in this controversial area (Brown, 1994; Gottfredson, 1994, 2000; Sackett & Wilk, 1994). The waters are further muddied by the fact that some of the guidelines seem to have contradictory implications. For example, although racial imbalance in employee selection (disparate impact) is unlawful, the use of valid and unbiased selection procedures virtually guarantees disparate impact. This state of affairs will change only when racial disparities in job-related skills and abilities are minimized (Gottfredson, 1994).

In 1991, Congress enacted legislation that would effectively bar employers from adjusting testtakers' test scores for the purpose of making hiring or promotion decisions. Section 106 of the Civil Rights Act of 1991 made it illegal for employers "in connection with the selection or referral of applicants or candidates for employment or promotion to adjust the scores of, use different cutoffs for, or otherwise alter the results of employment related tests on the basis of race, color, religion, sex, or national origin."

The law prompted concern on the part of many psychologists who believed it would adversely affect various societal groups and might reverse social gains made. Brown (1994, p. 927) forecasted that "the ramifications of the Act are more far-reaching than Congress envisioned when it considered the amendment and could mean that many personality tests and physical ability tests that rely on separate scoring for men and women are outlawed in employment selection." Arguments in favor of group-related test-score adjustment have been made on philosophical as well as technical grounds. From a philosophical perspective, increased minority representation is socially valued to the point that minority preference in test scoring is warranted. In the same vein, minority preference is viewed both as a remedy to past societal

wrongs and as a contemporary guarantee of proportional workplace representation among various groups. From a more technical perspective, it is argued that some tests require adjustment in scores because (1) the tests are biased and a given score on them does not necessarily carry the same meaning for all testtakers, and/or (2) "a particular way of using a test is at odds with an espoused position as to what constitutes fair use" (Sackett & Wilk, 1994, p. 931).

In contrast to advocates of test-score adjustment are those who view such adjustments in the context of a social agenda for preferential treatment of certain groups. These opponents of test-score adjustment reject the subservience of individual effort and ability to group membership as criteria in the assignment of test scores (Gottfredson, 1988, 2000). Hunter and Schmidt (1976, p. 1069) described the unfortunate consequences to all parties involved in a college selection situation wherein poor-risk applicants were accepted on the basis of score adjustments or quotas. With reference to the employment setting, Hunter and Schmidt (1976) described one case in which entrance standards were reduced so as to hire more members of a particular group. However, many of these new hires did not pass promotion tests—with the result that the company was sued for discriminatory promotion practice. Yet another consideration has to do with the feelings of "minority applicants who are selected under a quota system but who also would have been selected under unqualified individualism and must therefore pay the price, in lowered prestige and self-esteem" (Jensen, 1980, p. 398).

A number of psychometric models of fairness in testing have been presented and debated in the scholarly literature (Hunter & Schmidt, 1976; Petersen & Novick, 1976; Schmidt & Hunter, 1974; Thorndike, 1971). Despite a wealth of research and debate, a long-standing question in the field of personnel psychology remains: "How can group differences on cognitive ability tests be reduced while existing high levels of reliability and criterion-related validity can be retained?" According to Gottfredson (1994), the answer probably will not come from measurement-related research because differences in scores on many of the tests in question arise principally from differences in job-related abilities. For Gottfredson (1994, p. 963), "the biggest contribution personnel psychologists can make in the long run may be to insist collectively

Psychometric Techniques for Preventing or Remedying Adverse Impact and/or Instituting an Affirmative Action Program

Some of these techniques may be preventive if employed in the test development process, and others may be employed with already established tests. Some of these techniques entail direct score manipulation; others, such as banding, do not. Preparation of this table benefited from Sackett and Wilk (1994), and their work should be consulted for more detailed consideration of the complex issues involved.

Technique	Description
Addition of Points	A constant number of points is added to the test score of members of a particular group. The purpose of the point addition is to reduce or eliminate observed differences between groups.
Differential Scoring of Items	This technique incorporates group membership information, not in adjusting a raw score on a test, but in deriving the score in the first place. The application of the technique may involve the scoring of some test items for members of one group but not scoring the same test items for members of another group. This technique is also known as *empirical keying by group*.
Elimination of Items Based on Differential Item Functioning	This procedure entails removing from a test any items found to inappropriately favor one group's test performance over another's. Ideally, the intent of the elimination of certain test items is not to make the test easier for any group but simply to make the test fairer. Sackett and Wilk (1994) put it this way: "Conceptually, rather than asking 'Is this item harder for members of Group X than it is for Group Y?' these approaches ask 'Is this item harder for members of Group X with true score Z than it is for members of Group Y with true score Z?'"
Differential Cutoffs	Different cutoffs are set for members of different groups. For example, a passing score for members of one group is 65, whereas a passing score for members of another group is 70. As with the addition of points, the purpose of differential cutoffs is to reduce or eliminate observed differences between groups.
Separate Lists	Different lists of testtaker scores are established by group membership. For each list, test performance of testtakers is ranked in top-down fashion. Users of the test scores for selection purposes may alternate selections from the different lists. Depending on factors such as the allocation rules in effect and the equivalency of the standard deviation within the groups, the separate-lists technique may yield effects similar to those of other techniques, such as the addition of points and differential cutoffs. In practice, the separate list is popular in affirmative action programs where the intent is to overselect from previously excluded groups.
Within-Group Norming	Used as a remedy for adverse impact if members of different groups tend to perform differentially on a particular test, within-group norming entails the conversion of all raw scores into percentile scores or standard scores based on the test performance of one's own group. In essence, an individual testtaker is being compared only with other members of his or her own group. When race is the primary criterion of group membership and separate norms are established by race, this technique is known as *race-norming*.
Banding	The effect of banding of test scores is to make equivalent all scores that fall within a particular range or band. For example, thousands of raw scores on a test may be transformed to a stanine having a value of 1 to 9. All scores that fall within each of the stanine boundaries will be treated by the test user as either equivalent or subject to some additional selection criteria. A *sliding band* (Cascio et al., 1991) is a modified banding procedure wherein a band is adjusted ("slided") to permit the selection of more members of some group than would otherwise be selected.
Preference Policies	In the interest of affirmative action, reverse discrimination, or some other policy deemed to be in the interest of society at large, a test user might establish a policy of preference based on group membership. For example, if a municipal fire department sought to increase the representation of female personnel in its ranks, it might institute a test-related policy designed to do just that. A key provision in this policy might be that when a male and a female earn equal scores on the test used for hiring, the female will be hired.

and candidly that their measurement tools are neither the cause of nor the cure for racial differences in job skills and consequent inequalities in employment." Do you agree?

What is your opinion about the use of procedures to adjust test scores on the basis of group membership? Do you agree with Section 106 of the Civil Rights Act of 1991? Why?

If performance differences between identified groups of people on a valid and reliable test used for selection purposes are found, some hard questions may have to be dealt with if the test is to continue to be used. Is the problem due to some technical deficiency in the test, or is the test, in reality, too good at identifying people of different levels of ability? Regardless, is the test being used fairly? If so, what might society at large do about remedying the skill disparity between different groups as reflected on the test?

Our discussion of issues of test fairness and test bias may seem to have brought us far afield of the seemingly cut-and-dried, relatively nonemotional subject of test validity. However, the complex issues accompanying discussions of test validity, including issues of fairness and bias, must be wrestled with by us all. For further consideration of the philosophical issues involved, we refer you to the solitude of your own thoughts and the reading of your own conscience.

Self-Assessment

Test your understanding of elements of this chapter by seeing if you can explain each of the following terms, expressions, and abbreviations:

base rate	false negative
bias	false positive
central tendency error	generosity error
concurrent validity	halo effect
confirmatory factor analysis	hit rate
construct	homogeneity
construct validity	incremental validity
content validity	inference
covergent evidence	intercept bias
criterion	leniency error
criterion-related validity	local validation study
CVR	method of contrasted groups
discriminant evidence	miss rate
expectancy chart	multitrait-multimethod matrix
exploratory factor analysis	predictive validity
face validity	ranking
factor analysis	rating
factor loading	rating error
fairness	severity error

slope bias

Taylor-Russell tables

validation

validity

validity coefficient

7

Test Development

All tests are not created equal. The creation of a good test is not a matter of chance; it is the product of the thoughtful and sound application of established principles of test construction. In this chapter, we explore the basics of test development and examine in detail the processes by which tests are constructed. Although we focus on tests of the published, standardized variety, much of what we have to say also applies to custom-made tests such as those created by teachers, researchers, and employers.

The process of developing a test occurs in five stages:

1. test conceptualization
2. test construction
3. test tryout
4. item analysis
5. test revision

Briefly, once the idea for a test is conceived (test conceptualization), items for the test are drafted (test construction). This first draft of the test is then tried out on a group of sample testtakers (test tryout). Once the data from the tryout are collected, testtakers' performance on the test as a whole and on each of the test's items is analyzed. Statistical procedures, referred to as item analysis, are employed to assist in making judgments about which items are good as they are, which items need to be revised, and which items should be discarded. The analysis of the test's items may include analyses of item reliability, item validity, item discrimination, and—depending on the type of test it is—item-difficulty level. On the basis of the item analysis and related considerations, a revision or second draft of the test is created. This revised version of the test is tried out on a new sample of testtakers, the results are analyzed, the test further revised if necessary—and so it goes (Figure 7–1).

Test Conceptualization

The beginnings of any published test can probably be traced to thoughts—self-talk, in behavioral terms. The test developer says to himself or herself something like: "There

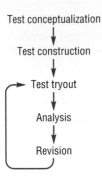

Figure 7–1
The Test Development Process

ought to be a test designed to measure [fill in the blank] in [such and such] way." The stimulus for such a thought could be almost anything. A review of the available literature on existing tests designed to measure a particular construct might indicate that such tests leave much to be desired in psychometric soundness—and the would-be test developer thinks he or she can do better. An emerging social phenomenon or pattern of behavior might serve as the stimulus for the development of a new test. If, for example, celibacy were to become a widely practiced lifestyle, we might witness the development of celibacy tests; tests that might measure variables like reasons for adopting a celibate lifestyle, commitment to a celibate lifestyle, and degree of celibacy by specific behaviors. The analogy in medicine is straightforward. Once a new disease comes to the attention of medical researchers, they attempt to develop diagnostic tests to assess its presence or absence as well as the severity of its manifestations in the body.

The development of a new test may be in response to a need to assess mastery in an emerging occupation or profession. For example, new tests may be developed to assess mastery in fields such as environmental engineering, wireless communications, and computer networking.

Some Preliminary Questions

Regardless of the stimulus for developing the new test, a number of questions immediately confront the prospective test developer. Here are some of those questions:

- *What is the test designed to measure?* This is a deceptively simple question; its answer is very closely linked to how the test developer defines the construct being measured and how that definition is the same or different from other tests purporting to measure the same construct.

- *What is the objective of the test?* In the service of what goal will the test be employed? In what way or ways is the objective of this test the same or different from other tests with similar goals?

- *Is there a need for this test?* Are there any other tests purporting to measure the same thing? In what ways will the new test be better than or different from existing ones? Will there be more compelling evidence for its reliability or validity? Will it be more comprehensive in its scope? Will it take less time to administer? In what ways would this test not be better than existing tests?

- *Who will use this test?* Clinicians? educators? others? For what purpose or purposes would this test be used?

- *Who will take this test?* Who is this test for? Who needs to take it? Who would find it desirable to take it? For what age range of testtakers is the test designed? What reading level is required of a testtaker? What cultural factors might affect testtaker response?

- *What content will the test cover?* Why should it cover this content? Is this coverage different from the content coverage of existing tests with the same or similar objectives? How and why is the content area different? To what extent is this content culture-specific?

- *How will the test be administered?* Individually or by groups? Is it amenable to both group and individual administration? What differences will exist between the test as administered to individuals and groups? Will the test be designed for or amenable to computer administration? How might differences between versions of the test be reflected in test scores?

- *What is the ideal format of the test?* Should it be true-false, Likert-scaled, or scaled in some other fashion? Why?

- *Should more than one form of the test be developed?* What does a cost/benefit analysis conclude regarding the creation of alternate forms?

- *What special training will be required of test users for administering or interpreting the test?* What background and qualifications will a prospective user of data derived from an administration of this test need to have? What restrictions, if any, should be placed on distributors of the test and on the test's usage?

- *What types of responses will be required by testtakers?* What variety of disability might preclude someone from being able to take this test? What real-world behaviors would be anticipated to correlate with testtaker responses?

- *Who benefits from an administration of this test?* What would the testtaker learn, or how might the testtaker benefit from an administration of this test? What would the test user learn, or how might the test user benefit? What social benefit, if any, derives from an administration of this test?

- *Is there any potential for harm as the result of an administration of this test?* What safeguards are built into the recommended testing procedure to prevent any sort of harm to any of the parties involved in the use of this test?

- *How will meaning be attributed to scores on this test?* Will a testtaker's score be compared to others taking the test at the same time? To others in a criterion group? Will the test evaluate mastery of a particular content area?

This last question provides a point of departure to elaborate on issues related to test development with regard to norm- versus criterion-referenced tests.

Norm-referenced versus criterion-referenced tests: Item development issues In this chapter, we explore some of the intricacies of test development, including a number of techniques designed to construct and select good items and tests. While reading about the test development process, keep in mind that different approaches to test development and individual item analyses are necessary depending upon whether the finished test is designed to be norm referenced or criterion referenced. Generally speaking, for example, a good item on a norm-referenced achievement test is an item for which high scorers on the test respond correctly; low scorers on the test tend to respond to that same item incorrectly. On a criterion-oriented test, it may be the case that the same pattern of test results occurs for an item: High scorers on the test get a particular item right, whereas low scorers on the test get that same item wrong. However, that is not what makes an item good or acceptable from a criterion-oriented perspective. Ideally, each item on a criterion-oriented test addresses the issue of whether the testtaker—a would-be physician, airline pilot, piano student, or whoever—has met certain criteria. In short, when it comes to criterion-oriented assessment, being "first in the class" does not count and very often is irrelevant. Although we can envision exceptions to this general rule, norm-referenced comparisons are typically insufficient and inappropriate when knowledge of mastery is what the test user requires.

Criterion-referenced testing and assessment is commonly employed in licensing contexts, be it a license to practice medicine or a license to drive a car. Criterion-referenced approaches are also employed in educational contexts in which mastery of particular material must be demonstrated before the student moves on to advanced material that conceptually builds on the existing base of knowledge, skills, or both.

In contrast to techniques and principles applicable to the development of norm-referenced tests (many of which are discussed in this chapter), the development of criterion-referenced instruments derives from a conceptualization of the knowledge or skills to be mastered. The required cognitive or motor skills may be analyzed into component parts for assessment. The test developer may attempt to sample criterion-related knowledge with regard to general principles relevant to the criterion being assessed. Pilot work with different items, tests, formats, or measurement procedures will help the test developer discover the best measure of mastery for the targeted skills or knowledge. In general, the development of a criterion-oriented test or technique entails pilot work with at least two groups of testtakers: one group known to have mastered the knowledge or skill being measured and another group known to have not mastered such knowledge or skill. For example, in developing a criterion-referenced written test for a driver's license, a pilot version of the test may be administered to one group of people who have been driving about 15,000 miles per year for ten years and have a perfect safety record (no accidents and no moving violations). The second group of testtakers might be a group of adults matched in demographic and related respects to the first group but who have never had any instruction in driving or driving experience. The items that best discriminate between these two groups would be considered "good" items.

Pilot Work

In the context of test development, terms such as **pilot work,** *pilot study,* and *pilot research* refer, in general, to the preliminary research surrounding the creation of a prototype of the test. Test items may be pilot studied to evaluate whether they should be included in the final form of the instrument. In developing a structured interview to measure introversion/extraversion, for example, pilot research may entail open-ended interviews with people believed for some reason (perhaps on the basis of an existing test) to be introverted or extraverted. Additionally, interviews with parents, teachers, friends, and others who know the subject might also be arranged. Another type of pilot study might entail physiological monitoring of the subjects (such as monitoring of heart rate) as a function of exposure to different types of stimuli.

In pilot work, the test developer typically attempts to determine how to best measure the targeted construct. The process may entail the creation, revision, and deletion of many test items, as well as literature reviews, experimentation, even soul-searching. Once pilot work has been completed, the process of test construction begins. Keep in mind, however, that depending on the nature of the test, and in particular its need for updates and revisions, the need for additional pilot research is always a possibility.

Psychometrics in the Classroom

Many concerns that professors and students have about testing are psychometric in nature. Professors want to give, and students want to take, reliable and valid measures of student knowledge. Even students who have not taken a course in psychological testing and assessment seem to understand psychometric issues regarding the tests they are administered in the classroom. As an illustration, consider each of the following pairs of statements. The first is a criticism of a classroom test you may have heard (or said yourself). The second statement is that criticism translated into the language of psychometrics.

"I spent all last night studying Chapter 3, and there wasn't one item on that test from that chapter!"
Translation: "I question the examination's content validity!"

"The instructions on that essay test weren't clear, and I think it affected my grade."
Translation: "There was excessive error variance related to the test administration procedures."

"I wrote the same thing for this short-answer question as my friend did—how come she got full credit and the professor took three points off my answer?"
Translation: "I have grave concerns about rater error affecting reliability."

"I didn't have enough time to finish; this test didn't measure what I know—only how fast I could write!"
Translation: "I wish the person who wrote this test had paid more attention to issues related to criterion-related validity and the comparative efficacy of speed as opposed to power tests!"

Like their students, professors have concerns about the tests they administer. They want their examination questions to be clear, relevant, and representative of the material covered. They sometimes wonder about the length of their examinations. Their concern is to cover voluminous amounts of material while still providing enough time for students to give thoughtful consideration to their answers.

For most published psychological tests, these types of psychometric concerns would be addressed in a formal way during the test development process. In the classroom, however, rigorous psychometric evaluation of the dozen or so tests that any one instructor may administer during the course of a semester is impractical. Classroom tests are typically created for the purpose of testing just one group of students during one semester. Tests change to reflect changes in lectures and readings as courses evolve. Also, if tests are reused, they are in danger of becoming measures of who has seen or heard about the examination previously, rather than measures of how well the students know the course material. Of course, although formal psychometric evaluation of classroom tests may be impractical, informal methods are frequently used.

Concerns about content validity are routinely addressed, usually informally, by professors in the test development process. For example, suppose an examination containing 50 multiple-choice questions and five short essays is to cover the reading and lecture material on four broad topics. The professor might systematically include 12 or 13 multiple-choice questions, and at least one short essay from each topic area. The professor might also draw a certain percentage of the questions from the readings and a certain percentage from the lectures. Such a deliberate approach to content coverage may well boost the test's content validity—although no formal evaluation of the test's content

Test Construction

Pilot work, as well as many of the other elements of test conceptualization and construction that we discuss in this chapter, is a necessity when constructing tests or other measuring instruments to be published and made widely available. Of course, pilot work and many of these other elements are not part of the process in the development of teacher-made tests for classroom use (see *Everyday Psychometrics*). As you read about more formal aspects of professional test construction, think about whether such technical procedures could be modified for everyday classroom use by teachers, and if so, what modifications would have to be made.

validity will be made. The professor may also make an effort to inform the students that all textbook boxes and appendices and all instructional media presented in class (such as videotapes) are fair game for evaluation (if that is indeed the case).

Criterion-related validity is difficult to establish on many classroom tests because no obvious criterion reflects the level of the students' knowledge of the material. Exceptions may exist for students in a technical or applied program who take an examination for licensure or certification. Informal assessment of something akin to criterion validity may occur on an individual basis in a student-professor chat; a student who obtained the lowest score in the class may demonstrate to the professor an unambiguous lack of understanding of the material. It is also true that by the same method, the criterion validity of the test may be called into question. For example, a chat with the student who scored the highest might also reveal that the student has not a clue about the material the test was designed to tap. Such a finding would give the professor pause.

The construct validity of classroom tests is often assessed informally as well, as when an anomaly in test performance may call attention to construct validity–related issues. For example, consider a group of students who have a history of performing at an above-average level on exams. Now suppose that on one exam, all students in this group perform poorly. If all these students report not having studied for the test or just not having understood the text material, then there is an adequate explanation for their low scores. However, if the students report that they studied and understood the material, as usual, then one might question the construct validity of the test as an explanation of the outcome.

Aspects of a classroom test's reliability can also be informally assessed. For example, a discussion with students can shed light on the internal consistency of the test. Then again, if the test was designed to be heterogeneous in nature, low internal consistency ratings might be desirable. On essay tests, inter-rater reliability can be explored by providing a group of volunteers with the criteria used in grading the essays and letting them grade some. Such an exercise might shed light on the clarity of the scoring criteria. In the rare instance when the same classroom test, for some reason, is given twice or in an alternate form, a discussion of the test-retest or alternate-forms reliability can be conducted. In practice, however, it is rare that classroom tests are administered twice or in alternate forms.

Have you ever taken an exam in which one student quietly asks for clarification about a specific question, and the professor then announces to the entire class the response to the student's question? This professor is attempting to reduce administration error (and increase reliability) by providing the same experience for all testtakers. When grading short-answer or essay questions, professors may try to reduce rater error by several techniques. For example, they may ask a colleague to decipher a student's poor handwriting or regrade a set of essays (blind to the original grades). Professors also try to reduce administration error and increase reliability when they eliminate items that many students misunderstand.

Tests developed for classroom use may not be perfect; few if any tests for any purpose are. Still, most professors are always on the lookout for ways—formal and informal—to make the tests they administer as psychometrically sound as possible.

Scaling

We have previously defined *measurement* as the assignment of numbers according to rules. **Scaling** may be defined as the process of setting rules for assigning numbers in measurement. Stated another way, scaling is the process by which a measuring device is designed and calibrated, and the way numbers (or other indices)—scale values—are assigned to different amounts of the trait, attribute, or characteristic being measured.

The prolific L. L. Thurstone is historically credited for being at the forefront of efforts to develop methodologically sound scaling methods. He adapted psychophysical scaling methods to the study of psychological variables such as attitudes and values

(Thurstone, 1959; Thurstone & Chave, 1929). Thurstone's (1925) article "A Method of Scaling Psychological and Educational Tests" introduced, among other things, the notion of **absolute scaling**—a procedure for obtaining a measure of item difficulty across samples of testtakers who vary in ability. Two years later came his influential paper on the "law of comparative judgment" (Thurstone, 1927). Thurstone once told his students that this law was his proudest achievement (Nunnally, 1978, pp. 60–61).

Types of scales   In common parlance, scales are instruments used to measure something, such as weight. In psychometrics, scales may also be conceived of as instruments used to measure something—that "something" typically being a psychological trait, characteristic, or attribute. Further, it is meaningful to speak of different types of scales as a function of various characteristics. We have seen, for example, that scales can be meaningfully categorized along a continuum of level of measurement and referred to as nominal, ordinal, interval, or ratio in nature. But we might also characterize scales in other ways. If the testtaker's performance on a test as a function of age is of critical interest, then the test might be referred to as an "age-based scale." If the testtaker's performance on a test as a function of grade is of critical interest, then the test might be referred to as a "grade-based scale." If all raw scores on the test are to be transformed into scores that can range from 1 to 9, then the test might be referred to as a "stanine scale." A scale might be described in other ways, such as unidimensional as opposed to multidimensional, and comparative as opposed to categorical.

Many books, articles, and monographs devoted exclusively to the subject of scaling can be found in the scholarly literature. Our treatment of the subject here is only a brief overview of some general principles. There is no one method of scaling. There is no one best type of scale. Test developers scale a test in the manner they believe is optimally suited to the way they have conceptualized measurement of the target trait(s).

Scaling methods   Speaking generally, a testtaker is presumed to have more or less of the characteristic measured by a (valid) test as a function of the test score; the higher or lower the score, the more or less of the characteristic he or she presumably possesses. But how are numbers assigned to responses so that a test score can be calculated? This is done through scaling the test items, using any one of several available methods.

For example, consider a moral issues opinion measure called the Morally Debatable Behaviors Scale-Revised (MDBS-R; Katz et al., 1994). Developed to be "a practical means of assessing what people believe, the strength of their convictions, as well as individual differences in moral tolerance" (p. 15), the MDBS-R contains 30 items. Each item contains a brief description of a moral issue or behavior on which testtakers express their opinion by means of a 10-point scale that ranges from "never justified" to "always justified." Here is a sample:

Cheating on taxes if you have a chance is:

1	2	3	4	5	6	7	8	9	10
never									always
justified									justified

This is an example of a **rating scale,** which can be defined as a grouping of words, statements, or symbols on which judgments concerning the strength of a particular trait, attitude, or emotion are indicated by the testtaker. Rating scales can be used to record judgments of oneself, others, experiences, or objects, and may take several forms (Figure 7–2).

On the MDBS-R, the ratings that the testtaker makes for each of the 30 test items are added together to obtain a final score. Scores range from a low of 30 (if the testtaker in-

Rating Scale Item A
I believe I would like the work of a lighthouse keeper.
True   False   (circle one)

Rating Scale Item B
Please rate the employee on ability to cooperate and get along with fellow employees:
Excellent _____ / _____ / _____ / _____ / _____ / _____ / _____ / Unsatisfactory

Rating Scale Item C
How did you feel about what you saw on television?

Figure 7–2
The Many Faces of Rating Scales

Rating scales can take many forms. "Smiley" faces, such as those illustrated here as Item C, have been used in social-psychological research with young children and adults with limited language skills. The faces are used in lieu of words such as positive, neutral, *and* negative.

dicates that all 30 behaviors are never justified) to a high of 300 (if the testtaker indicates that all 30 situations are always justified). Because the final test score is obtained by summing the ratings across all the items, it is termed a **summative scale.**

One type of summative rating scale, the **Likert scale** (Likert, 1932), is used extensively in psychology, usually to scale attitudes. Likert scales are relatively easy to construct. Each item presents the testtaker with five alternative responses (sometimes seven), usually on an agree/disagree or approve/disapprove type of continuum. If Katz et al. had used a Likert scale, an item on their test might have looked like this:

"Cheating on taxes if you have a chance"
        This is (check one):

| _____ | _____ | _____ | _____ | _____ |
| never justified | rarely justified | sometimes justified | usually justified | always justified |

Likert scales are usually reliable, which may account for their widespread popularity. Likert (1932) experimented with different weightings of the five categories but concluded that assigning weights of 1 (for endorsement of items at one extreme) through 5 (for endorsement of items at the other extreme) generally worked best.

The use of rating scales of any type results in ordinal-level data. With reference to the Likert scale item, for example, if the response "never justified" is assigned the value 1, "rarely justified" the value of 2, and so on, the higher the score, the more the response is indicative of permissiveness with regard to cheating on taxes. Respondents could even be ranked with regard to such permissiveness. However, the difference in permissiveness between the opinions of a pair of people who scored 2 and 3 on this scale is not necessarily the same as the difference between the opinions of a pair of people who scored 3 and 4.

Rating scales differ in the number of dimensions underlying the ratings being made. Some rating scales are unidimensional, meaning that only one dimension is presumed to underlie the ratings. Other rating scales are multidimensional, meaning that more than one dimension is thought to guide the testtaker's responses. Consider in this context an item from the MDBS-R regarding marijuana use. Responses to this item, particularly responses in the low to middle range, may be interpreted in many different ways. Such responses may reflect the view that people should not engage in illegal activities, or that people should not take risks with their health, or that people should avoid activities that could lead to contact with a bad crowd. Responses to this item may reflect other attitudes and beliefs, such as those related to the beneficial use of marijuana as an adjunct to chemotherapy for cancer patients. When more than one dimension is being tapped by an item, multidimensional scaling techniques are used to identify the dimensions.

Another scaling method that produces ordinal data is the method of paired comparisons. Testtakers are presented with pairs of stimuli (two photographs, two objects, two statements), which they are asked to compare. They must select one of the stimuli as per some rule (they agree more with one statement, they find one stimulus more appealing than the other, and so on). Had Katz et al. used the method of paired comparisons, an item on their scale might have looked like this:

Select the behavior that you think would be more justified:
a. cheating on taxes if you have a chance
b. someone accepting a bribe in the course of his or her duties

For each pair of options, testtakers would receive a higher score if they selected the option that was deemed more justifiable by the majority of a group of judges. The judges would have been asked to rate the pairs of options before the distribution of the test, and a list of the options selected by the judges would be provided along with the scoring instructions as an answer key. The test score would reflect the number of times the choices of a testtaker agreed with those of the judges. If we use Katz et al.'s (1994) standardization sample as the judges, the more justifiable option is cheating on taxes. A testtaker who selected that option might receive a point toward the total score if option "a" was selected, but no points if option "b" was selected. An advantage of the method of paired comparisons is that it forces testtakers to choose between items.

Another way of deriving ordinal information through a scaling system entails sorting tasks. In these approaches, printed cards, drawings, photographs, objects, or other such stimuli are typically presented to testtakers for evaluation. One method of sorting, **comparative scaling,** entails judgments of a stimulus in comparison with every other stimulus on the scale. A version of the MDBS-R that employs comparative scaling might feature each of the 30 items printed on a separate index card. Testtakers would be asked to sort the cards from most to least justifiable. Comparative scaling could also be accomplished by providing testtakers with a list of 30 items on a sheet of paper and asking them to rank the justifiability of the items from 1 to 30.

Another scaling system that relies on sorting is **categorical scaling.** Stimuli are placed into one of two or more alternative categories that differ quantitatively with respect to some continuum. In our running MDBS-R example, testtakers might be given 30 index cards on which are printed the 30 items. They would be asked to sort the cards into three piles: one pile of those behaviors that are never justified, one pile that are sometimes justified, and one pile that are always justified.

A **Guttman scale** (1944, 1947) is yet another scaling method that yields ordinal-level measures. Items on it range sequentially from weaker to stronger expressions of the attitude, belief, or feeling being measured. A feature of Guttman scales is that they are designed so that all respondents who agree with the stronger statements of the attitude will also agree with milder statements. Using the MDBS-R scale as an example, consider the following statements that reflect attitudes toward suicide.

Do you agree or disagree with each of the following:
a. All people should have the right to decide whether they wish to end their lives.
b. People who are terminally ill and in pain should have the option of having a doctor assist them in ending their lives.
c. People should have the option of signing away the use of artificial life-support equipment before they become seriously ill.
d. People have the right to a comfortable life.

If this were a perfect Guttman scale, all respondents who agree with "a" (the most extreme position) should also agree with "b," "c," and "d." All respondents who disagree with "a" but agree with "b" should also agree with "c" and "d," and so forth. Guttman scales are developed through the administration of a number of items to a target group. The resulting data are then analyzed by means of scalogram analysis. The objective is to obtain an arrangement of items wherein endorsement of one item automatically connotes endorsement of less extreme positions.

All the foregoing methods yield ordinal data. The method of equal-appearing intervals, first described by Thurstone (1929), is one scaling method used to obtain data that are presumed to be interval. Again using the example of attitudes about the justifiability of suicide, let's outline the steps that would be involved in creating a scale using Thurstone's equal-appearing intervals method.

1. A reasonably large number of statements reflecting positive and negative attitudes toward suicide are collected, such as "Life is sacred, so people should never take their own lives," and "A person in a great deal of physical or emotional pain may rationally decide that suicide is the best option available to him or her."

2. Judges (or experts in some cases) judge each statement as to how much it indicates that suicide is justified. Each judge is instructed to rate each statement on a scale *as if* the scale were interval in nature. For example, the scale might range from 1 (the statement indicates that suicide is never justified) to 9 (the statement indicates that suicide is always justified). Judges are instructed that the 1-to-9 scale is being used *as if* there is equal distance between each of the values; that is, as if it were an interval scale. Judges are cautioned to focus their ratings on the statements, and not their own views on the matter.

3. A mean and a standard deviation of the judges' ratings are calculated for each statement. For example, if 15 judges rated 100 statements on a scale from 1 to 9, then for each of these 100 statements, the 15 judges' ratings would be averaged together. Suppose five of the judges rated a particular item as a 1. Five other judges rated it as a 2, and the remaining five judges rated it as a 3. The average rating would be 2 (with a standard deviation of 0.816).

4. Items are selected for inclusion in the final scale based on several criteria, including the degree to which the item contributes to a comprehensive measurement of the variable in question and the test developer's degree of confidence that the items have indeed been sorted into equal intervals. Item means and standard deviations are also considered. Items should represent a wide range of attitudes reflected in a variety of means. A low standard deviation is indicative of a good item; the judges agreed about the meaning of the item with respect to how it reflected attitudes toward suicide.

5. The scale is now ready for administration. The way the scale is used depends on the objectives of the test situation. Typically, respondents are asked to select those statements that most accurately reflect their own attitudes. The values of the items that the respondent selects (based on the judges' ratings) are averaged together, producing a score on the test.

The method of equal-appearing intervals is an example of a scaling method of the direct estimation variety. In contrast to other methods that involve indirect estimation, there is no need to transform the testtaker's responses into some other scale.

The particular scaling method employed in the development of a new test will depend on many factors, including the variables being measured, the group for whom the test is intended (children may require a less complicated scaling method than adults, for example), and the preferences of the test developer.

Writing Items

In the grand scheme of test construction, considerations related to the actual writing of the test's items go hand in hand with scaling considerations. Three questions that the prospective test developer/item writer faces immediately are:

- What range of content should the items cover?
- Which of the many different types of item formats should be employed?
- How many items should be written?

When devising a standardized test using a multiple-choice format, it is usually advisable that the number of items for the first draft contain approximately twice the number of items that the final version of the test will contain.[1] If, for example, a test called "American History: 1940 to 1990" was to have 30 questions in its final version, it would be useful to have as many as 60 items—items that comprehensively sample the domain of the test—in the item pool. An **item pool** is the reservoir or well from which items on the final version of the test will be drawn or discarded. A comprehensive sampling provides a basis for content validity of the final version of the test. Because approximately half of these items will be eliminated in the test's final version, the test developer needs to ensure that the final version of the test also contains items that adequately sample the domain. Thus, if all the questions on the Persian Gulf War from the original 60 items were determined to be poorly written items, the test developer should either rewrite items sampling this period or create new items—and then subject the rewritten or new items to tryout as well. If this were not done, the content validity of the test would be jeopardized because some aspects of the test domain would not be represented in the final version of the test. Of course, the number of planned forms of the test is another consideration here; multiply the number of items required in the pool for one form of the test by the number of forms planned.

How does one develop items to place into the item pool? The test developer may write a large number of items from personal experience or academic acquaintance with the subject matter. Help may also be sought from others, including experts. For psychological tests designed for use in clinical settings, clinicians, patients, patients' family members, clinical staff, and others may be interviewed for insights that could assist in

---

1. Common sense and the practical demands of the situation may dictate that fewer items be written for the first draft of a test. If, for example, the final draft were to contain 1,000 items, it could be an undue burden to attempt to create an item pool of 2,000 items. Further, if the test developer was a very knowledgeable and capable item writer, it might be necessary to create only about 1,200 items for the item pool.

the item writing. For psychological tests designed for use by personnel psychologists, interviews with members of a targeted industry or organization will likely be of great value. For psychological tests designed for use by school psychologists, interviews with teachers, administrative staff, educational psychologists, and others may be invaluable. Searches through the research literature may be fruitful sources of inquiry, as might searches through nonresearch literature.

Considerations related to variables such as the purpose of the test and the number of examinees to be tested at one time enter into decisions regarding the format of the test. Thus, for example, if the purpose of a test is to screen large numbers of military recruits for minimal intellectual ability, a constructed-response format, such as one including essay items, would be impractical. Preferable would be a test format wherein an examinee must select one of many alternative answers—a selected-response format. Selected-response formats facilitate automated scoring and can readily accommodate a large number of examinees. Both selected- and constructed-response formats are described in the following section.

Item formats   **Item format** refers to the form, plan, structure, arrangement, or layout of individual test items, including whether the items require testtakers to select a response from existing alternative responses (**selected-response format**) or to construct a response (**constructed-response format**). If the test is designed to measure achievement, and the items are written in a selected-response format, then examinees must select the response that is keyed as correct. If the test is designed to measure the strength of a particular trait, and the items are written in a selected-response format, then examinees must select the alternative that best answers the question with respect to themselves. For the sake of simplicity, we'll confine our examples to achievement tests. The reader may wish to mentally substitute other appropriate terms for words such as *correct* because such substitutions might apply to personality or other types of tests that are not achievement tests.

Three types of selected-response item formats are multiple-choice, matching, and true-false items. As illustrated by Item A in the following example, a multiple-choice item has three elements: (1) a stem, (2) a correct alternative or option, and (3) several incorrect alternatives or options variously referred to as "distractors" or "foils":

Item A

Stem $\longrightarrow$ A psychological test, an interview, and a case study are:

Correct alt. $\longrightarrow$ a. psychological assessment tools

Distractors $\longrightarrow$ b. standardized behavioral samples
c. reliable assessment instruments
d. theory-linked measures

Now consider Item B:

Item B

A good multiple-choice item in an achievement test:

a.   has one correct alternative
b.   has alternatives that are grammatically parallel
c.   has alternatives of similar length
d.   has alternatives that fit grammatically with the stem
e.   includes as much as possible of the item in the stem to avoid unnecessary repetition
f.   avoids ridiculous distractors
g.   is not excessively long
h.   all of the above
i.   none of the above

If you answered "h" to Item B, you are correct. In the process of going through the list of alternatives, it may have occurred to you that Item B violated many of the rules it set forth!

A matching item is a variant of a multiple-choice item. The examinee is presented with two columns of responses, and the task is to determine which response from one column goes with which response from the other. An example follows:

Match the actors' names (*a* through *k*) with their roles (1 through 12) by writing the appropriate number next to the letter.

_____ a.	Anthony Hopkins	1. Ace Ventura
_____ b.	Jim Carrey	2. Ellen Ripley
_____ c.	Johnny Depp	3. Maximus
_____ d.	Mike Myers	4. Hannibal
_____ e.	Dustin Hoffman	5. Austin Powers
_____ f.	Antonio Banderas	6. Donnie Brasco
_____ g.	Barbra Streisand	7. Yu Shu
_____ h.	Robin Williams	8. Zorro
_____ i.	Sigourney Weaver	9. Professor Brainard
_____ j.	Michelle Yeoh	10. Tootsie
_____ k.	Russell Crowe	11. Yentl
		12. The Jackal

You may have noticed that there are different numbers of items in the two columns. If the number of items in the two columns were the same, then a person unsure about one of the actor's roles could deduce it by matching all the other options first. A perfect score would then result even though the testtaker did not actually know all of the material. Providing more options than are needed is designed to minimize such a possibility.[2]

A true-false item is another of the selected-response variety, this one in the form of a sentence that requires the examinee to indicate whether the statement is or is not a fact. A good true-false item contains a single idea, is not excessively long, and is not subject to debate; that is, it is indeed either true or false.

Like multiple-choice items, true-false items have the advantage of being readily applicable to a wide range of subject areas. Also like the multiple-choice items, acceptable levels of item reliability can be achieved with true-false items. True-false items need not contain a list of distractor alternatives. Therefore, true-false items tend to be easier to write than multiple-choice items. A disadvantage of true-false items is that the probability of obtaining a correct response purely on the basis of chance (guessing) on any one item is .5, or 50%.[3] By contrast, the probability of obtaining a correct response by guessing on a four-alternative multiple-choice question is .25, or 25%.

---

2. For the record, the answers to this matching question are as follows: a-4, b-1, c-6, d-5, e-10, f-8, g-11, h-9, i-2, j-7, and k-3.

3. We note in passing, however, that although the probability of guessing correctly on an individual true-false item on the basis of chance alone may be .5, the probability of guessing correctly on a *sequence* of true-false items decreases as the number of items increases. The probability of guessing correctly on two such items is equal to $.5^2$, or 25%. The probability of guessing correctly on ten such items is equal to $.5^{10}$, or .001; there is therefore a one-in-a-thousand chance that a testtaker would guess correctly on ten true-false items on the basis of chance alone.

Constructed-response format   An alternative to a selected-response format is a *constructed-response format*—one that requires the examinee to supply or to create the correct answer, as opposed to merely selecting it. Three types of constructed-response items are the completion item, the short answer, and the essay. A completion item requires the examinee to provide a word or phrase that completes a sentence, as in the following example.

The standard deviation is generally considered the most useful measure of _____.

A good completion item should be worded so that the correct answer is specific. Completion items that can be correctly answered in many ways can lead to scoring problems. The correct completion for the item above is *variability*. An alternative way of writing this item would be as a short-answer item:

What descriptive statistic is generally considered the most useful measure of variability? _____

A good short-answer item is written clearly enough that the testtaker can indeed respond succinctly—with a short answer. There are no hard-and-fast rules specifying how short an answer must be to be considered a short answer; a word, a term, a sentence, or a paragraph may suffice. Beyond a paragraph or two, the item might more properly be referred to as an "essay item." Here is an example of an essay item:

Compare and contrast definitions and techniques of classical and operant conditioning. Include examples of how principles of each have been applied in clinical as well as educational settings.

An essay is a useful type of item when the test developer wants the examinee to demonstrate a depth of knowledge about a single topic. In contrast to selected-response items and constructed-response items such as the short answer and the completion items, the essay question not only permits the restating of learned material but also allows for the creative integration and expression of the material in the testtaker's own words. It can also be appreciated that the skills tapped by essay-type items are different from those tapped by items of the true-false and matching genres. Whereas an essay requires recall, organization, planning, and writing ability, the other types of items require only recognition. Drawbacks to essay items as compared with short-answer items may include a more limited area of coverage relative to the amount of testing time and a degree of subjectivity in the scoring.

Scoring Items

Many different test-scoring models have been devised. In psychological testing, the **cumulative** model is the most common, perhaps because of its sheer simplicity and logic. Typically, the rule in a cumulatively scored test is that the higher the score on the test, the higher the testtaker is on the ability, the trait, or some other characteristic the test purports to measure. For each testtaker response to targeted items made in a particular way, the testtaker earns cumulative credit with regard to a particular construct.

In tests that employ a **class** or category approach to **scoring,** testtaker responses earn credit toward placement in a particular class or category with other testtakers whose pattern of responses is presumably similar in some way. This approach is used in some diagnostic systems, wherein individuals must exhibit a certain number of symptoms to qualify for a specific diagnosis. A third scoring model, **ipsative scoring,** departs radically in rationale from either cumulative or class models. A typical objective in ipsative scoring is the comparison of a testtaker's score on one scale within a test with another scale within that same test. Consider, for example, a personality test called the Edwards Personal Preference Schedule (EPPS), which is designed to measure the relative strength of different psychological needs. The EPPS ipsative scoring system yields information on the strength of various needs in relation to the strength of other of the testtaker's needs. The test does not yield information on the strength of a testtaker's need relative to the presumed strength of that need in the general population.

Once all of the groundwork for a test has been laid and a draft of the test is ready for administration, the next step is, logically enough, test tryout.

Test Tryout

Having created a pool of items from which the final version of the test will be developed, the test developer will try out the test. The test should be tried out on people similar in critical respects to the people for whom the test was designed. Thus, for example, if a test is designed to aid in decisions regarding the selection of corporate employees with management potential at a certain level, it would be appropriate to try out the test on corporate employees at the targeted level—and inappropriate to try out the test on introductory psychology students.

Equally important as questions concerning whom the test should be tried out on are questions regarding how many people the test should be tried out on. There are no hard-and-fast rules here, but some have recommended that there be no fewer than five subjects, and preferably as many as ten subjects, for every one item on the test. In general, the more subjects in the tryout the better; all other things being equal, ten subjects per test item is better than five because of less role of chance in subsequent analyses of the data, particularly in factor analysis. A definite risk in using too few subjects during test tryout comes during factor analysis of the findings, when what we might call "phantom factors"—nonexistent factors that are actually artifacts of the small sample size—may emerge.

The test tryout should be executed under conditions that are as identical as possible to the conditions under which the standardized test will be administered. This means that all instructions, and everything from the time limits allotted for completing the test to the atmosphere at the test site, should be as similar as possible. As Nunnally (1978, p. 279) so aptly phrased it, "If items for a personality inventory are being administered in an atmosphere that encourages frankness and the eventual test is to be administered in an atmosphere where subjects will be reluctant to say bad things about themselves, the item analysis will tell a faulty story." In general, the test developer endeavors to ensure that differences in response to the test's items are due in fact to the items, not to extraneous factors.

What Is a Good Item?

Before reading on, pick up a piece of paper and just jot down—using logic and common sense—what you believe are the criteria of a good test item. After you've done that, compare what you've written with the following discussion.

In the same sense that we can speak of a good test as being reliable and valid, we can speak of a good test item as being reliable and valid. Further, a good test item helps to discriminate testtakers; a good test item is one that high scorers on the test as a whole get right. An item that high scorers on the test as a whole do not get right is probably not a good item. We may also describe a good test item as one that low scorers on the test as a whole get wrong; an item that low scorers on the test as a whole get right may not be a good item.

How does a test developer identify good items? After the first draft of the test has been administered to a representative group of examinees, the test developer analyzes test scores and responses to individual items. The different types of statistical scrutiny that the test data can potentially undergo at this point are referred to collectively as **item analysis.** Note that although item analysis tends to be regarded as a quantitative endeavor, it may be, as we shall see, qualitative as well.

Item Analysis

Statistical procedures used to analyze items may become quite complex, and our treatment of this subject should be thought of only as introductory. We briefly survey some procedures typically used by test developers in their efforts to select the best items from a pool of tryout items. The criteria for the best items may differ as a function of the test developer's objectives. Thus, for example, one test developer might deem the best items to be those that optimally contribute to the internal reliability of the test. Another test developer might wish to design a test with the highest possible criterion-related validity—and select items accordingly. Among the tools test developers might employ to analyze and select items will be an index of an item's difficulty, an item-validity index, an item-reliability index, and an index of the item's discrimination. Brief coverage of each of these statistics appears in this section.

In the interest of simplifying our discussion and clearly illustrating the concepts presented, assume that you are the author of 100 items for a ninth-grade-level "American History Test" (AHT) and that this 100-item (draft) test has been administered to 100 ninth-graders. Hoping in the long run to standardize the test and have it distributed by a commercial test publisher, you have a more immediate, short-term goal: to select the 50 best of the 100 items you originally created. How might that short-term goal be achieved? As we will see, the answer lies in item-analysis procedures. Before elaborating on those procedures, however, we once again invite you to apply the following material—making translations in phraseology when appropriate—to tests other than achievement tests, such as tests of personality or tests designed to measure consumer preferences.

Item-Difficulty Index

Suppose every examinee got item 1 of the test correct. Can we say that item 1 is a good item? What if no one got item 1 correct? In either case, item 1 is not a good item. If everyone gets the item right, the item is too easy. If everyone gets the item wrong, the item is too difficult. Just as the test as a whole is designed to provide an index of degree of knowledge about American history, so each individual item on the test should be passed (scored as correct) or failed (scored as incorrect) on the basis of testtakers' differential knowledge of American history.[4]

---

4. An exception here may be a giveaway item. Such an item might be inserted near the beginning of a test to spur motivation and a positive testtaking attitude and lessen testtakers' test-related anxiety. In general, however, if an item analysis suggests that a particular item is too easy or too difficult, the item must be either rewritten or discarded.

An index of an item's difficulty is obtained by calculating the proportion of the total number of testtakers who got the item right. A lowercase, italicized p (p) is used to denote item difficulty, and a subscript refers to the item number (p_1 is read "item-difficulty index for item 1"). The value of an item-difficulty index can theoretically range from 0 (if no one got the item right) to 1 (if everyone got the item right). If 50 of the 100 examinees got item 2 right, then the item-difficulty index for this item would be equal to 50 divided by 100, or .5 ($p_2 = .5$). If 75 of the examinees got item 3 right, p_3 would be equal to .75, and we could say that item 3 was easier than item 2. Note that the larger the item-difficulty index, the easier the item. Because p refers to the percent of people passing an item, the higher the p for an item, the easier the item. The statistic referred to as an **item-difficulty index** in the context of achievement testing may be an **item-endorsement index** in other contexts, such as personality testing. Here, the statistic provides not a measure of the percent of people passing the item but a measure of the percent of people who said "yes" to, agreed with, or otherwise endorsed the item.

An index of the difficulty of the average test item for a particular test can be calculated by averaging the item-difficulty indices for all the test's items. This is accomplished by summing the item-difficulty indices for all test items and dividing by the total number of items on the test. For maximum discrimination among the abilities of the testtakers, the optimal average item difficulty is approximately .5, with individual items on the test ranging in difficulty from about .3 to .8. Note, however, that the possible effect of guessing must be taken into account when considering items of the selected-response variety. With this type of item, the optimal average item difficulty is usually the midpoint between 1.00 and the chance success proportion, defined as the probability of answering correctly by random guessing. In a true-false item, the probability of guessing correctly on the basis of chance alone is 1/2, or .50. Therefore, the optimal item difficulty is halfway between .50 and 1.00, or .75. In general, the midpoint representing the optimal item difficulty is obtained by summing the chance success proportion and 1.00 and then dividing the sum by 2, or:

$$.50 + 1.00 = 1.5$$
$$\frac{1.5}{2} = .75$$

For a five-option multiple-choice item, the probability of guessing correctly on any one item on the basis of chance alone is equal to 1/5, or .20. The optimal item difficulty is therefore .60:

$$.20 + 1.00 = 1.20$$
$$\frac{1.20}{2} = .60$$

Item-Validity Index

The **item-validity index** is a statistic designed to provide an indication of the degree to which a test is measuring what it purports to measure; the higher the item-validity index, the greater the test's criterion-related validity. The item-validity index can be calculated once the following two statistics are known:

- the item-score standard deviation
- the correlation between the item score and the criterion score

The item-score standard deviation of item 1 (denoted by the symbol s_1) can be calculated using the index of the item's difficulty (p_1) in the following formula:

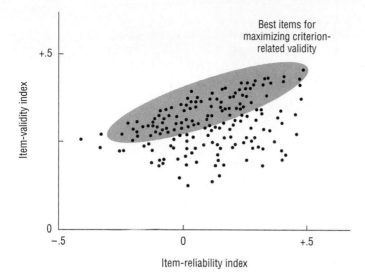

Figure 7–3
Maximizing Criterion-Related Validity

(Source: Allen & Yen, 1979)

$$s_1 = \sqrt{p_1(1 - p_1)}$$

The correlation between the score on item 1 and a score on the criterion measure (denoted by the symbol r_{1C}) is multiplied by item 1's item-score standard deviation (s_1), and the product is equal to an index of an item's validity ($s_1 r_{1C}$). The calculation of the item-validity index will be important when the test developer's goal is to maximize the criterion-related validity of the test. A visual representation of the best items on a test (if the objective is to maximize criterion-related validity) can be achieved by plotting each item's item-validity index and item-reliability index (Figure 7–3).

Item-Reliability Index

The **item-reliability index** provides an indication of the **internal consistency** of a test (Figure 7–4); the higher this index, the greater the test's internal consistency. This index is equal to the product of the item-score standard deviation (s) and the correlation (r) between the item score and the total test score.

Factor analysis and inter-item consistency   A statistical tool useful in determining whether items on a test appear to be measuring the same thing(s) is the technique of factor analysis. Through the judicious use of factor analysis, items that do not "load on" the factor that they were written to tap (that is, items that do not appear to be measuring what they were designed to measure) can be revised or eliminated. If too many items appear to be tapping a particular area, the weakest of such items can be eliminated. Additionally, factor analysis can be useful in the test interpretation process, especially when comparing the constellation of responses to the items from two or more groups. Thus, for example, if a particular personality test is administered to two groups of hospitalized psychiatric patients, each group with a different diagnosis, the same items may be found to load on different factors in the two groups. Such information will compel the responsible test developer to revise or eliminate certain items from the test or to describe the differential findings in the test manual.

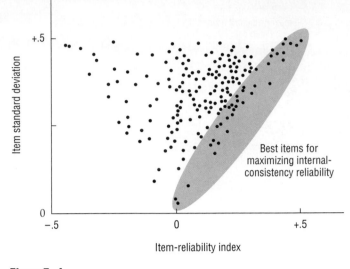

Figure 7–4
Maximizing Internal-Consistency Reliability

(Source: Allen & Yen, 1979)

Item-Discrimination Index

Measures of item discrimination indicate how adequately an item separates or discriminates between high scorers and low scorers on an entire test. In this context, a multiple-choice item on an achievement test is a good item if most of the high scorers answer correctly and most of the low scorers answer incorrectly. If most of the high scorers fail a particular item, these testtakers may be making an alternative interpretation of a response intended to serve as a distractor. In such a case, the test developer should interview the examinees to understand better the basis for the choice and then appropriately revise (or eliminate) the item. Common sense dictates that an item on an achievement test is not doing its job if it is answered correctly by respondents who understand the subject matter least. Similarly, an item on a test purporting to measure a particular personality trait is not doing its job if responses to it indicate that people who, for example, score very low on the test as a whole (indicating the absence or low level of the trait in question) tend to score very high on the item (indicating that they are very high on the trait in question—contrary to what the test as a whole indicates).

The **item-discrimination index** is a measure of item discrimination symbolized by a lowercase, italicized letter d (d). This estimate of item discrimination, in essence, compares performance on a particular item with performance in the upper and lower regions of a distribution of continuous test scores. The optimal boundary lines to demarcate what we are referring to as the "upper" and "lower" areas of a distribution of scores are scores within the upper and lower 27% of the distribution of scores—provided the distribution is normal (Kelley, 1939). As the distribution of test scores becomes more platykurtic (flat), the optimal boundary line for defining upper and lower gets larger and approaches 33% (Cureton, 1957). Allen and Yen (1979, p. 122) assure us that "for most applications, any percentage between 25 and 33 will yield similar estimates."

The item-discrimination index is a measure of the difference between the proportion of high scorers answering an item correctly and the proportion of low scorers answering the item correctly; the higher the value of d, the greater the number of high scorers answering the item correctly. A negative d value on a particular item is a red flag because

Table 7–1
Item-Discrimination Indices for Five Hypothetical Items

Item	U	L	U – L	n	d [(U – L)/n]
1	20	16	4	32	.13
2	30	10	20	32	.63
3	32	0	32	32	1.00
4	20	20	0	32	0.00
5	0	32	– 32	32	– 1.00

it indicates that low-scoring examinees are more likely to answer the item correctly than high-scoring examinees. This situation calls for some action such as revision or elimination of the item.

Assume a teacher gave a test to 119 people and isolated the upper (U) and lower (L) 27% of the test papers with a total of 32 papers in each group. Data and item-discrimination indices for items 1 through 5 are presented in Table 7–1. Note that 20 testtakers in the U group answered item 1 correctly and 16 testtakers in the L group answered item 1 correctly. With an item-discrimination index equal to .13, item 1 is probably a reasonable item because more members of the U than of the L group answered it correctly. The higher the value of d, the more adequately the item discriminates the higher-scoring from the lower-scoring testtakers. For this reason, item 2 is a better item than item 1; its item-discrimination index is .63. The highest possible value of d is $+1.00$—all members of the U group answer the item correctly and all members of the L group answer the item incorrectly. If the same proportion of members of the U and L group pass the item, the item is not discriminating between testtakers at all, and d, appropriately enough, would be equal to 0. The lowest value that an index of item discrimination can take is -1. A d equal to -1 is a test developer's nightmare; it indicates a situation where all the members of the U group fail the item and all the members of the L group pass it. On the face of it, such an item is the worst possible type of item and is in dire need of revision or elimination. However, the test developer might learn or discover something new about the construct being measured through further investigation of this unanticipated finding.

Analysis of item alternatives   The quality of each alternative within a multiple-choice item can be readily assessed with reference to the comparative performance of upper and lower scorers. No formulas or statistics are really necessary here; by charting the number of testtakers in the U and L groups who chose each alternative, the test developer can get an idea of the effectiveness of a distractor by means of a simple eyeball test. To illustrate, let's analyze responses to five items on a hypothetical test, assuming that there were 32 scores in the upper level (U) of the distribution and 32 scores in the lower level (L) of the distribution. Let's begin by looking at the pattern of responses to item 1. In each case ★ denotes the correct alternative.

Alternatives

Item 1		★a	b	c	d	e
	U	24	3	2	0	3
	L	10	5	6	6	5

The response pattern to item 1 indicates that the item is a good one. More members of the U than of the L group answered the item correctly, and each of the distractors attracted some testtakers.

Item 2		a	b	c	d	★e
	U	2	13	3	2	12
	L	6	7	5	7	7

Item 2 signals a situation in which a relatively large number of members of the *U* group chose a particular distractor choice (in this case, "b"). This item could probably be improved upon revision, preferably one made after an interview with some or all of the *U* students who chose "b."

Item 3		a	b	★c	d	e
	U	0	0	32	0	0
	L	3	2	22	2	3

Item 3 indicates a most desirable pattern of testtaker response. All members of the *U* group answered the item correctly, and each distractor attracted one or more members of the *L* group.

Item 4		a	★b	c	d	e
	U	5	15	0	5	7
	L	4	5	4	4	15

Item 4 is more difficult than item 3—fewer examinees answered it correctly. Still, this item provides useful information about discrimination because it effectively discriminates higher-scoring from lower-scoring examinees. For some reason, one of the alternatives ("e") was particularly effective—perhaps too effective—as a distractor to students in the low-scoring group. The test developer may wish to further explore why this was the case.

Item 5		a	b	c	★d	e
	U	14	0	0	5	13
	L	7	0	0	16	9

Item 5 is a poor item because more members of the *L* than of the *U* group answered the item correctly. Furthermore, none of the examinees chose the "b" or "c" distractors.

Item-Characteristic Curves

A graphic representation of item difficulty and discrimination can be made in an **item-characteristic curve** (ICC). As shown in Figure 7–5, an ICC is a graph on which ability is plotted on the horizontal axis and probability of correct response is plotted on the vertical axis. Note that the extent to which an item discriminates high- from low-scoring examinees is apparent from the slope of the curve; the steeper the slope, the greater the item discrimination. Also note that if the slope is positive, more high scorers are getting the item correct than low scorers; if the slope is negative, the reverse is true. Now focus on the item-characteristic curve for item A; do you think this is a good item? The answer is that it is not; the probability of a testtaker's responding correctly is high for testtakers of low ability and low for testtakers of high ability. What about item B; is that a good item? Again, the answer is no. The curve tells us that testtakers of moderate ability have the highest probability of answering this item correctly; testtakers with the greatest amount of ability—as well as their counterparts at the other end of the ability spectrum—are unlikely to respond correctly to this item. Item B may be one of those items to which people who know too much or think too much are likely to respond incorrectly.

Item C is a good item; the probability of responding correctly to it increases with ability. What about item D? This item-characteristic curve profiles an item that discriminates at only one point on the continuum of ability; the probability is very high that all

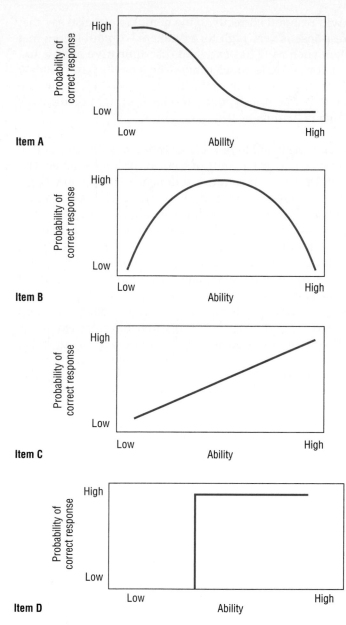

Figure 7–5
Some Sample Item-Characteristic Curves

(Source: Ghiselli et al., 1981)

In the interest of simplicity, we have omitted scale values for the axes. The vertical axis in such a graph lists probability of correct response in values ranging from 0 to 1. Values for the horizontal axis, which we have simply labeled "ability," are total scores on the test. In other sources you may find the vertical axis of an item-characteristic curve labeled something like "proportion of examinees who respond correctly to the item" and the horizontal axis labeled "total test score."

testtakers at or above this point will respond correctly to the item. We can also say that the probability of an incorrect response is very high for testtakers who fall below that particular point in ability. An item such as D has excellent discriminative ability and would be useful in a test designed, for example, to select applicants on the basis of some cutoff score. However, such an item might not be desirable in a test designed to provide detailed information on testtaker ability across all ability levels—as might be the case, for example, in a diagnostic reading or arithmetic test.

Latent-trait models A test is typically designed to provide an estimate of the amount of knowledge or ability (or strength of a particular trait) possessed by the testtaker. The variable on which performance on the test is presumed to depend—be it knowledge, ability, a personality trait, or something else—is never directly measurable itself; an estimate of the amount of the variable is obtained through the test. In this way, latent traits are like the factors in factor analysis, which are not directly measured but are reflected in the test items. According to the **latent-trait model** of measurement, this underlying, unobservable variable—this latent trait—is unidimensional. Presumably, all the items on a test are measuring this trait. An application of the latent-trait model can be found in the Illness Causality Scale, a measure of children's understanding of illness (Sayer et al., 1993). Researching the validity of the test, the authors expected that three latent traits would be found: an understanding of illness, level of cognitive development of the child, and verbal intelligence. They demonstrated the likely presence of these latent traits by correlating the Illness Causality Scale with other scales, each of which was designed to reflect one of the latent traits. For example, the authors found that the Illness Causality Scale was moderately correlated with a scale measuring verbal intelligence, presumably because the two scales share the latent trait of verbal intelligence.

Latent-trait models differ in some important ways from classical "true score" test theory. For example, in contrast to classical true score test theory, in which no assumptions are made about the frequency distribution of test scores, inherent in latent-trait models are assumptions regarding the probability of the occurrence of a particular observed score in testtakers with a particular true score. As Allen and Yen (1979, p. 240) put it, "Latent-trait theories propose models that describe how the latent trait influences performance on each test item. Unlike test scores or true scores, latent traits theoretically can take on values from $-\infty$ to $+\infty$ [minus to plus infinity]."

The applicability of latent-trait models to psychological tests has been questioned by some theoreticians. It has been argued, for example, that the assumption of test unidimensionality is violated when many psychological tests are considered. It has been further argued that even the same item on a psychological test may be tapping different abilities from the same testtaker, depending on the life experiences of the testtaker. Despite lingering theoretical questions, latent-trait models appear to be playing an increasingly dominant role in the design and development of new tests and testing programs.[5]

Other Considerations in Item Analysis

Guessing In achievement testing, the problem of how to handle testtaker guessing is one that has eluded any universally acceptable solution. It is true that a number of different procedures purporting to be corrections for guessing have been published, but none has

---

5. More detailed discussion of the various types of latent-trait models (also referred to as "item-response theory" in some of the literature) can be found in various sources (such as Hambleton, 1979, 1988; Hambleton & Cook, 1977; Lord, 1980; Lord & Novick, 1968; Weiss & Davison, 1981; Wright & Stone, 1979). One effort to bring the various latent-trait models together under a single theory culminated in the development of generalized linear item-response theory (Mellenbergh, 1994).

proven to be entirely satisfactory. The reason is that the problem of guessing is more complex than it first appears. To understand why, consider the following three criteria that any correction for guessing must meet as well as the interacting problems that must be addressed:

1. A correction for guessing must recognize that when a respondent guesses at an answer on an achievement test, the guess is not typically made on a totally random basis. It is more reasonable to assume that the testtaker's guess is based on some knowledge of the subject matter and the ability to rule out one or more of the distractor alternatives. However, the individual testtaker's amount of knowledge of the subject matter will vary from one item to the next.

2. A correction for guessing must also deal with the problem of omitted items. Sometimes, instead of guessing, the testtaker will simply omit a response to an item. Should the omitted item be scored "wrong"? Should the omitted item be excluded from the item analysis? Should the omitted item be scored as if the testtaker had made a random guess? Exactly how should the omitted item be handled?

3. Just as some people may be luckier than others in front of a Las Vegas slot machine, so some testtakers may be luckier than others in guessing the choices that are keyed correct. Any correction for guessing may seriously underestimate or overestimate the effects of guessing for lucky and unlucky testtakers.

A number of different solutions to the problem of guessing have been proposed. In addition to proposed interventions at the level of test scoring through the use of corrections for guessing (referred to as "formula scores"), intervention has also been proposed at the level of test instructions. Testtakers may be instructed to provide an answer only when they are certain (no guessing) or to complete all items and guess when in doubt. Individual differences in testtakers' willingness to take risks result in problems for this approach to guessing (Slakter et al., 1975). Some people who don't mind taking risks may guess even when instructed not to do so. Others, who tend to be reluctant to take risks, refuse to guess under any circumstances. This creates a situation in which one's predisposition to take risks can affect one's test score.

To date, no solution to the problem of guessing has been deemed to be entirely satisfactory. The responsible test developer addresses the problem of guessing by including in the test manual (1) explicit instructions regarding this point for the examiner to convey to the examinees, and (2) specific instructions for scoring and interpreting omitted items.

Guessing on responses to personality and related psychological tests is not thought of as a great problem; although it may sometimes be difficult to choose the most appropriate alternative on a selected-response format personality test (particularly one with forced-choice items), the presumption is that the testtaker does indeed make the best choice.

Item fairness Item-characteristic curves provide one tool for identifying which items are to be considered fair and which may be biased. Specific items are identified as biased in a statistical sense if they exhibit differential item functioning. Differential item functioning is exemplified by different shapes of item-characteristic curves for different groups (say, men and women) even though the two groups do not differ in total test score (Mellenbergh, 1994). Conversely, if an item is to be considered fair to different groups of testtakers, the item-characteristic curves for the different groups should not be significantly different:

> The essential rationale of this ICC criterion of item bias is that any persons showing the same ability as measured by the whole test should have the same probability of passing any given item that measures that ability, regardless of the person's race, social class, sex,

or any other background characteristics. In other words, the same proportion of persons from each group should pass any given item of the test, provided that the persons all earned the same total score on the test. (Jensen, 1980, p. 444)

A determination of the presence of differential item functioning requires a statistical test of the null hypothesis of no difference between the item-characteristic curves of the two groups. Advantages and problems of different statistical tests for detecting differential item functioning continue to be debated (for example, Raju et al., 1993). Items that show significant difference in item-characteristic curves should either be revised or be eliminated from the test. If a relatively large number of items biased in favor of one group coexist with approximately the same number of items biased in favor of another group, it cannot be claimed that the test measures the same abilities in the two groups— this although overall test scores between the individuals in the two groups may not be significantly different (Jensen, 1980).

Analysis of item-characteristic curves represents only one way of detecting item bias. Ironson and Subkoviak (1979) evaluated different methods for detecting item bias across different groups, including differences in item difficulty, item discrimination, item-characteristic curves, and the distribution of incorrect responses. These investigators concluded that the choice of item-analysis method does indeed affect determinations of item bias. Camilli and Shepard (1985) reported on the development of a computer program to aid in the detection of biased items on ability tests; a "biased item" was defined in the program as an item that favors one particular group of examinees in relation to another when differences in group ability are controlled.

Speed tests   Item analyses of tests taken under speed conditions yield misleading or uninterpretable results; the more toward the end of the test an item is, the more difficult it may appear to be—this simply because a testtaker may not have reached it. Similarly, measures of item discrimination may be artificially high for late-appearing items because examinees who know the material better may work faster and would be more likely to answer the later items. Thus, items appearing late in a speed test are more likely to show positive item-total correlations because of the select group of examinees reaching those items. One obvious solution to the problem is to restrict the item analysis of items on a speed test only to the items completed by the testtaker. However, this solution is *not* recommended for at least three reasons: (1) Item analyses of the later items would be based on a progressively smaller number of testtakers, yielding progressively more unreliable results; (2) if the more knowledgeable examinees reach the later items, part of the analysis is based on all testtakers and part of the analysis is based on a selected sample; and (3) because the more knowledgeable testtakers are more likely to score correctly, their performance will make items occurring toward the end of the test appear easier than they might in reality be.

An example drawn from the research literature illustrates the effects of a speed test on item score–total score correlations. Wesman (1949) administered the same test to comparable groups of female nursing school applicants. One group took the test under speed conditions, and the other group took the same test with generous time limits (power condition). The results showed that for items appearing toward the beginning of the test, there were no real differences under speed and power conditions. For items appearing late in the test, the item-total correlations were lower under the speed condition.

If speed is not an important element of the ability being measured by the test and because speed produces misleading information about item performance, the test developer should ideally administer the test to be item-analyzed with generous time limits to complete the test. Once the item analysis is completed, norms should be established using the speed conditions intended when the test is used in actual practice.

Qualitative Item Analysis

Test users have had a long-standing interest in understanding test performance from the perspective of testtakers (Fiske, 1967; Mosier, 1947). The calculation of item-validity, item-reliability, and other such quantitative indices represents one approach to understanding testtakers. Another general class of research methods is referred to as qualitative in nature. In contrast to quantitative methods, **qualitative methods** are techniques of data generation and analysis that rely primarily on verbal rather than mathematical or statistical procedures. Encouraging testtakers on a group or individual basis to discuss aspects of their testtaking experience is, in essence, eliciting or generating "data" (words). These data may then be used by test developers, users, and publishers to improve various aspects of the test.

Qualitative item analysis is a general term used to describe various nonstatistical procedures designed to explore how individual test items work, both as compared to other items in the test and in the context of the whole test. In contrast to statistically based procedures, qualitative methods involve exploration of the issues through verbal means such as interviews and group discussions conducted with testtakers and other relevant parties. Some of the topics researchers may wish to explore qualitatively are summarized in Table 7–2.

On a cautionary note, it is true that in some instances, providing testtakers with the opportunity to describe a test parallels providing students with the opportunity to describe their instructors. In both cases, there can be abuse of the process, especially by respondents who have extra-test (or extra-instructor) axes to grind. Respondents may be disgruntled for any number of reasons, ranging from a failure to prepare adequately for the test to disappointment in their test performance. In such cases, the opportunity to evaluate the test is tantamount to an opportunity to lash out. The test, the test administrator, and the institution, agency, or corporation responsible for the test administration may all become objects of criticism. For this reason, testtaker questionnaires, much like other qualitative research tools, if they are to be interpreted properly, must be interpreted with a grain of salt. At the very least, the fact that the testtaker is asked for an evaluation bespeaks sincere concern for his or her testtaking experience.

The "think aloud" test administration   An innovative approach to cognitive assessment entails having respondents verbalize thoughts as they come to them. Although different researchers use different procedures (see, for example, Davison et al., 1997; Hurlburt, 1997; Klinger, 1978), this general approach has been employed in a variety of research contexts including studies of adjustment (Kendall et al., 1979; Sutton-Simon & Goldfried, 1979), problem solving (Duncker, 1945; Montague, 1993), educational remediation (Randall et al., 1986), and clinical intervention (Gann & Davison, 1997; Haaga et al., 1993; White et al., 1992). Cohen et al. (1988) proposed the use of a **"think aloud" test administration** as a qualitative research tool designed to shed light on the testtaker's thought processes during the administration of a test. On a one-to-one basis with an examiner, examinees are asked to take a test, thinking aloud as they respond to each item. If the test is designed to measure achievement, such verbalizations may be useful in assessing not only if certain students (such as low or high scorers on previous examinations) are misinterpreting a particular item, but also why and how they are misinterpreting the item. If the test is designed to measure personality or some aspect of it, the think aloud technique may also yield valuable insights regarding the way individuals perceive, interpret, and respond to the items.

Expert panels   In addition to interviewing testtakers individually or in groups, **expert panels** may also provide qualitative analyses of test items. A *sensitivity review* is a study

Table 7-2
Potential Areas of Exploration by Means of Qualitative Item Analysis

This table lists sample topics and questions of possible interest to test users. The questions could be raised either orally or in writing shortly after a test's administration. Additionally, depending upon the objectives of the test user, the questions could be placed into other formats, such as true-false or multiple choice. Depending upon the specific questions to be asked and the number of testtakers being sampled, the test user may wish to guarantee the anonymity of the respondents.

Topic	Sample Question
Cultural Sensitivity	Did you feel that any item or aspect of this test was discriminatory with respect to any group of people? If so, why?
Face Validity	Did the test appear to measure what you expected it would measure? If not, what about this test was contrary to your expectations?
Test Administrator	Did the behavior of the test administrator affect your performance on this test in any way? If so, how?
Test Environment	Did any conditions in the room affect your performance on this test in any way? If so, how?
Test Fairness	Do you think the test was a fair test of what it sought to measure? Why or why not?
Test Language	Were there any instructions or other written aspects of the test that you had difficulty understanding?
Test Length	How did you feel about the length of the test with respect to (a) the time it took to complete, and (b) the number of items?
Testtaker's Guessing	Did you guess on any of the test items? About what percentage of the items would you estimate you guessed on? Did you employ any particular strategy for guessing, or was it basically random guessing?
Testtaker's Integrity	Do you think that there was any cheating during this test? If so, please describe the methods you think may have been used.
Testtaker's Mental/Physical State Upon Entry	How would you describe your mental state going into this test? Do you think that your mental state in any way affected the test outcome? If so, how? How would you describe your physical state going into this test? Do you think that your physical state in any way affected the test outcome? If so, how?
Testtaker's Mental/Physical State During the Test	How would you describe your mental state as you took this test? Do you think that your mental state in any way affected the test outcome? If so, how? How would you describe your physical state as you took this test? Do you think that your physical state in any way affected the test outcome? If so, how?
Testtaker's Overall Impressions	How would you describe your overall impression of this test? What suggestions would you offer the test developer for improvement?
Testtaker's Preferences	Was there any part of the test that you found educational, entertaining, or otherwise rewarding? What specifically did you like or dislike about the test? Was there any part of the test that you found anxiety-provoking, condescending, or otherwise upsetting? Why?
Testtaker's Preparation	How did you prepare for this test? If you were going to advise others as to how to prepare for it, what would you tell them?

of test items, typically conducted during the test development process, in which items are examined for fairness to all prospective testtakers and for the presence of offensive language, stereotypes, or situations. Sensitivity reviews have become a standard part of contemporary test development (Reckase, 1996). For example, in an effort to root out any possible bias in the Stanford Achievement Test Series (eighth edition), the test publisher formed an advisory panel of 12 minority group members, each a prominent member of the educational community. Panel members met with the publisher to obtain an understanding of the history and philosophy of the test battery and to discuss and define the problem of bias (Stanford Special Report, 1992). Some of the possible forms of content bias that may find their way into any achievement test were identified as follows:

Status: Are the members of a particular group shown in situations that do not involve authority or leadership?

Stereotype: Are the members of a particular group portrayed as uniformly having certain: (1) aptitudes, (2) interests, (3) occupations, or (4) personality characteristics?

Familiarity: Is there greater opportunity on the part of one group to: (1) be acquainted with the vocabulary, or (2) experience the situation presented by an item?

Offensive Choice of Words: (1) Has a demeaning label been applied, or (2) has a male term been used where a neutral term could be substituted?

Other: Panel members were asked to be specific regarding any other indication of bias they detected. (Stanford Special Report, 1992, pp. 3–4)

On the basis of qualitative information from an expert panel or testtakers themselves, a test user or developer may elect to modify or revise the test. In this sense, revision typically entails rewording items, deleting items, or creating new items. Note that there is another meaning of the term "test revision" beyond that associated with a stage in the development of a new test. After a period of time, many existing tests are scheduled for republication in new versions or editions. The development process that the test undergoes as it is modified and revised is called, not surprisingly, "test revision." The time, effort, and expense entailed in this latter variety of test revision may be quite extensive. For example, the revision may involve an age extension of the population for which the test is designed for use—upward for older testtakers and/or downward for younger testtakers—and corresponding new validation studies.

Test Revision

We now consider aspects of test revision as a stage in the development of a new test. Next, we consider aspects of test revision in the context of modifying an existing test to create a new edition. Much of our discussion of test revision in the development of a brand-new test may also apply to the development of subsequent editions of existing tests, depending on just how revised the revision really is.

Test Revision as a Stage in New Test Development

Having conceptualized the new test, constructed it, tried it out, and item-analyzed it both quantitatively and qualitatively, what remains is to act judiciously on all of the information and mold the test into its final form. A tremendous amount of information is generated at the item-analysis stage, particularly given that a developing test may have hundreds of items. On the basis of that information, some items from the original item pool will be eliminated and others will be rewritten. How is information about the difficulty, validity, reliability, discrimination, and bias of test items, along with information from the item-characteristic curves, integrated and used to revise the test? There are probably as many ways of approaching test revision as there are test developers. One approach would be to characterize each item according to its strengths and weaknesses: Some items may be highly reliable but lack criterion validity, whereas other items may be purely unbiased but too easy. Some items will be found to have many weaknesses, making them prime candidates for deletion or revision. For example, very difficult items have a restricted range (all or almost all testtakers get them wrong), which lowers correlation coefficients, as you may remember from Chapter 4. Because many reliability and validity coefficients are based on correlations, very difficult items will tend to lack reliability and validity because of their restricted range. The same is true of very easy items. Furthermore, test developers may find they must balance various strengths and weaknesses across items. For example, if many otherwise good items tend to be somewhat easy, the test developer may purposefully include some more difficult items even if they have other problems; those more difficult items may be specifically targeted for rewriting. The purpose of the test also influences the way the revision is done. If the test will be used to influence major decisions concerning educational placement or employment, the test developer will want to be scrupulously concerned with issues of item bias. If there is a need to identify the most highly skilled individuals among those being tested, items demonstrating excellent item discrimination, leading to the best possible test discrimination, will be emphasized.

As the test is being revised, the advantage of writing a large item pool becomes obvious; poor items can be eliminated in favor of those that were shown on the test tryout to be good items. Even when working with a large item pool, the test developer engaged in test revision must be aware of the domain from which the test should sample. For some aspects of the domain, it may be particularly difficult to write good items, and blind deletion of all poorly functioning items could cause those aspects of the domain to remain untested.

Having balanced all these concerns, the test developer comes out of the revision stage with a test of improved quality. The next step is to administer the revised test under standardized conditions to a second appropriate sample of examinees. On the basis of an item analysis of data derived from this administration of the second draft of the test, the test developer may deem the test to be in its finished form—in which case the test's norms may be developed from the data, and the test will be said to have been "standardized" on this (second) sample.

Standardization can be viewed as "the process employed to introduce objectivity and uniformity into test administration, scoring and interpretation" (Robertson, 1990, p. 75). A standardization sample represents the group(s) of individuals with whom examinees' performance will be compared. For norm-referenced tests, it is important that this sample be representative of the population on those variables that might affect performance. Ability tests, for example, are developed so that the standardization group is representative of the population on such characteristics as age, gender, geographic region, type of community, ethnic group, and parent education. The latest census data are usually utilized to ensure that the standardization sample closely matches the population on these demographic characteristics.

In those instances in which the item analysis of the data for a test administration indicates that the test is not yet in finished form, the steps of revision, tryout, and item analysis are repeated until the test is satisfactory and standardization can occur. Once the items of the test have been finalized, professional test development procedures dictate that conclusions about the test's validity await a *cross-validation* of findings. Cross-validation will be discussed shortly. For now, let's briefly consider some of the issues surrounding the development of a new edition of an existing test.

Test Revision in the Life Cycle of an Existing Test

Time waits for no person. We all get old; and tests get old too. Just like people, some tests seem to age more gracefully than others. For example, as we will see when we study projective techniques in Chapter 12, the stimulus materials for the Rorschach Inkblot Test seem to have held up quite well over the years. By contrast, the stimulus materials for another projective technique, the Thematic Apperception Test (TAT), tend to be showing their age. There comes a time in the life of most tests when either publication of the test will be discontinued or the test will be revised in some way. When is that time?

No hard-and-fast rules exist for when a test must be revised. APA (1996, Standard 3.18) offered the general suggestion that an existing test be kept in its present form as long as it remains "useful," and that it be revised "when significant changes in the domain represented, or new conditions of test use and interpretation make the test inappropriate for its intended use."

Practically speaking, many tests are deemed to be due for revision when any of the following conditions exist:

1. The stimulus materials look dated and current testtakers simply cannot relate to them.

2. The verbal content of the test, including the administration instructions and the test items, contains dated vocabulary that is not readily understood by current testtakers.

3. As popular culture changes and words take on new meanings, certain words or expressions in the test items or directions may be perceived as inappropriate or even offensive to a particular group and must therefore be changed.

4. The test norms are no longer adequate as a result of group membership changes in the population of potential testtakers.

5. The test norms are no longer adequate as a result of age-related shifts in the abilities measured over time, and an age extension to the norms (upward, downward, or in both directions) is necessary.

6. The reliability or the validity of the test, as well as the effectiveness of individual test items, can be significantly improved by a revision.

7. The theory on which the test was originally based has been improved significantly, and the changes should be reflected in the design and content of the test.

The steps taken to revise an existing test parallel those taken to create a brand-new test. In the test conceptualization phase, the test developer must think through exactly what the objectives of the revision are, and how those objectives can best be met. In the test construction phase, the action involves instituting the proposed changes. Test tryout, item analysis, and test revision (in the sense of making final refinements) follow. While all of that may sound relatively easy and straightforward, the process of creating a revised edition of an existing test can be a most ambitious undertaking. For example, recalling the revision of a test called the Strong Vocational Interest Blank, Campbell

(1972) reflected that the process of conceiving the revision started about ten years prior to actual revision work, and the revision work itself ran for another ten years. Butcher (2000) echoed these thoughts in an article that provided a detailed "inside view" of the process of revising a widely used personality test called the MMPI. Others have also noted the sundry considerations that must be kept in mind when contemplating the revision of an existing instrument (Adams, 2000; Okazaki & Sue, 2000; Reise et al., 2000; Silverstein & Nelson, 2000).

Once a successor to an established test has been published there will inevitably be questions about how equivalent the two editions of the tests are. For example, does a measured full-scale IQ of 110 on the first edition of an intelligence test mean exactly the same thing as a full-scale IQ of 110 on the second edition of the test? A number of researchers have advised caution in making interpretations from an original and a revised edition of a test, despite similarities in appearance (Reitan & Wolfson, 1990; Strauss et al., 2000). Even if the content of individual items does not change, the context in which the items appear may change, thus opening up the possibility of significant differences in testtakers' interpretation of the meaning of the items. Simply developing a computerized version of a test may make a difference, at least in terms of test scores achieved by members of different populations (Ozonoff, 1995). Formal item-analysis methods must be employed to evaluate the stability of items between revisions of the same test (Knowles & Condon, 2000). Ultimately, scores between a test and its updated version may not be directly comparable. As Tulsky and Ledbetter (2000) summed it up in the context of original and revised versions of tests of cognitive ability, "Any improvement or decrement in performance between the two cannot automatically be viewed as a change in examinee performance" (p. 260).

A key step in the development of all tests—brand-new or revised editions—is cross-validation. Next we discuss that important process, as well a more recent trend in test publishing, co-validation.

Cross-validation and co-validation   The term **cross-validation** refers to a revalidation of a test on a sample of testtakers other than the ones on whom test performance was originally found to be a valid predictor of some criterion. We expect that items selected for the final version of the test (in part because of their high correlations with a criterion measure) will have smaller item validities when administered to a second sample of testtakers—this because of the operation of chance factors. The decrease in item validities that inevitably occurs after cross-validation of findings is referred to as **validity shrinkage.** Such shrinkage is expected and is viewed as integral to the test development process. Further, such shrinkage is infinitely preferable to a scenario wherein (spuriously) high item validities are published in a test manual as a result of the inappropriate use of the identical sample of testtakers for test standardization and cross-validation of findings; users will in all likelihood be let down by the lower-than-expected validity of such a test. The test manual accompanying commercially prepared tests should outline the test development procedures used. Reliability information, including test-retest reliability and internal consistency estimates, should be reported along with evidence of the test's validity. Articles discussing cross-validation of tests are often published in scholarly journals. For example, Bank et al. (2000) provided a detailed account of the cross-validation of an instrument used to screen for cognitive impairment in older adults.

Not to be confused with "cross-validation," **co-validation** may be defined as a test validation process conducted on two or more tests using the same sample of testtakers. When used in conjunction with the creation of norms or the revision of existing norms, this process may also be referred to as **co-norming.** A current trend among test publishers that publish more than one test designed for use with the same population is to co-validate and/or co-norm tests. Co-validation of new tests and revisions of existing tests can be beneficial in various ways to all of the parties in the assessment enterprise.

Co-validation is beneficial to test publishers because of the economy of cost that can be achieved. During the process of validating a test, many prospective testtakers must first be identified. In many instances, after being identified as a possible participant in the validation study, a person will be prescreened for suitability by means of an interview conducted in person or over the telephone. All of this requires financial resources that are charged to the cost of developing the test. Time and money are saved if the same participant is deemed suitable in the validation studies for multiple tests and can be scheduled to do so with a minimum of administrative preliminaries. Qualified examiners to administer the test and other personnel to assist in scoring, interpretation, and statistical analysis must also be identified, retained, and scheduled to participate in the project. The cost of retaining such professional personnel on a per test basis is kept down when the work is done with multiple tests simultaneously.

Beyond benefits to the publisher, co-validation can hold potentially important benefits to test users and testtakers. Many tests that tend to be used together are published by the same publisher. For example, the third edition of the Wechsler Adult Intelligence Scale (WAIS-III) and the third edition of the Wechsler Memory Scale (WMS-III) might be used together in the clinical evaluation of an adult. And let's suppose that after an evaluation using these two tests, differences in measured memory ability emerged as a function of the test used. Had these two tests been normed on different samples, then sampling error would be one possible reason for the observed differences in measured memory. However, because the two tests were normed on the same population, sampling error as a causative factor has been greatly minimized, if not eliminated completely. A clinician might look to factors such as differences in the way that the two tests measure memory. One test, for example, might measure short-term memory using the recall of number sequences. The other test might measure the same variable using recalled comprehension of short reading passages. How each test measures the variable under study may yield important diagnostic insights.

On the other hand, consider two co-normed tests that are almost identical in how they measure the variable under study. With sampling error minimized by the co-norming process, a test user can be that much more confident that the scores on the two tests are comparable. So, for example, suppose a student transfers to a new school district that requires scores on Test A in each student's file. The transferring student has previously taken Test B, a test that was co-normed with Test A and that measures the same thing in much the same ways. The school psychologist might argue that retesting with Test A is unnecessary given the similarity between the tests and the fact that they were co-normed. In this case, the student benefits by being spared retesting, and by all of the useful diagnostic information from Test B that will be put to good use. And should the school insist on testing with Test A, even more diagnostic information will be available based on any difference scores; any planned interventions can be that much more focused in terms of their objectives.

Consider now the development of a real-life personality test in this chapter's *Close-up*. As you read about the development of the Personality Research Form (PRF), think about the general procedures involved in test development described in this chapter. What recommendations do you have for making the PRF a better test? If the test developer were to update validation research on the PRF, what type of validation study would you recommend? Would you recommend co-validation with another test of personality? Thinking about such "nuts and bolts" issues with regard to test development and construction will be a useful exercise as you are introduced to a number of different types of tests in the chapters to come.

Anatomy of the Development of a Test: The Personality Research Form

Test author Douglas N. Jackson afforded readers an "inside look" at the way his test, the Personality Research Form (PRF), was created in his detailed account of the sequential system used. According to Jackson (1970), the PRF was developed in the hope that "by a careful application of modern conceptions of personality and of psychometric theory and computer technology more rigorous and more valid assessment of important personality characteristics would result" (p. 62). More specifically, Jackson viewed four interrelated principles as essential to the development of the PRF (as well as other tests of personality). He described them as follows:

1. The importance of psychological theory (see Cronbach & Meehl, 1955; Loevinger, 1957)

2. The necessity for suppressing response style (for example, suppressing the tendency to respond in socially desirable ways or the tendency to respond nonpurposively or randomly) (see Jackson & Messick, 1958)

3. The importance of scale homogeneity and scale generalizability

4. The importance of fostering convergent and discriminant validity

Jackson (1970) labeled four major stages in the development of the PRF as follows:

I. The substantive definition of personality scale content

II. A sequential strategy in scale construction

III. The appraisal of the structural component of validity

IV. Evaluation of the external component of validity

In abbreviated, simplified fashion, each stage is described here.

I: The Substantive Definition of Personality Scale Content

A. The Choice of Appropriate Constructs

Jackson (1970) advised that "the first step in constructing a personality test is to decide what to measure" (p. 66). If, for example, a test or a scale within a test is to measure "aggressiveness," a clear definition of this construct must be arrived at; do we mean physical aggression? verbal aggression? overt aggression? covert aggression? all of these? The answers to these and related questions will depend on variables such as the objectives of the test and the costs involved—the latter term referring to factors such as the length of the test and the time it will take to administer (see

Cronbach & Gleser, 1965). An additional consideration in selecting a construct for measurement concerns how much is already known about it: "It is easier to prepare large numbers of items for dimensions whose correlates are well established" (Jackson, 1970, p. 67). The PRF was based on personality variables conceptualized and defined by Henry Murray and his colleagues (1938). To help lay the foundation for items to be written that will be high in validity, mutually exclusive definitions of each personality variable had to be derived if they did not already exist (for example, "exhibitionism" had to be distinguished from "need for social recognition").

B. The Development of Substantively Defined Item Sets

Jackson (1970, p. 67) described this step as "the most difficult of all—the creation and editing of the item pool of some three thousand items, comprising the set from which PRF scales were finally developed." He went on to describe the evaluation and editing of each item with respect to the following criteria:

- their conformity to the definition of the scale for which they were written

- the adequacy of the negative instances of the trait

- their clarity and freedom from ambiguity

- their judged freedom from extreme levels of desirability bias

- their judged discriminating power and popularity levels when administered to appropriate populations

- their judged freedom from various forms of content bias and their representativeness as a set

- the degree to which they conformed to the definition of the scale for which they were written as well as their "fortuitous convergence with irrelevant constructs, particularly those which were to be included in the PRF" (p. 68).

C. A Multidimensional Scaling Evaluation of Substantive Item Selection

The empirical value of rational judgment methods used in item selection was demonstrated by means of a technique called "multidimensional successive intervals scaling" (see Torgerson, 1958). Through the use of judges' ratings of descriptions of hypothetical people, information was obtained with respect to (1) the number of dimensions along which items were perceived to differ and (2) the scale value of each stimulus on each of the dimensions.

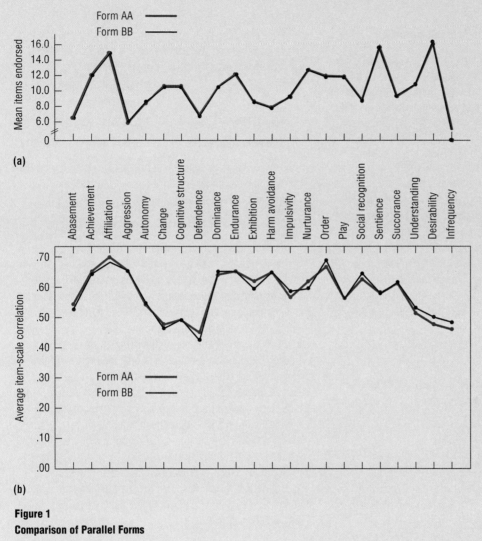

(a)

(b)

Figure 1
Comparison of Parallel Forms

(Source: Jackson, 1970)

D. Empirical Evaluation of Homogeneity
of Postulated Item Content
An empirical evaluation of the structured properties of the set of theoretically defined items was undertaken by means of the administration of provisional scales to an approximately equal number of male and female university students. Estimates of item reliability were obtained through the use of the KR-20 formula; the median reliability was found to be .925 with the highest reliability estimate being .94 for six of the scales: Aggression, Endurance, Exhibition, Harm Avoidance, Order, and Social Recognition. Interestingly, the lowest reliability estimate (.80) was obtained for the scale called "Defendence." Of this finding, Jackson (1970, pp. 71–72) wrote, "This is not at all surprising, since defensive people might be less willing to admit defensiveness consistently."

(continued)

Anatomy of the Development of a Test: The Personality Research Form
(continued)

II. A Sequential Strategy in Scale Construction

Responses to each of the items on the provisional PRF underwent a computerized item analysis to determine if the item would be retained or rejected. Some of the criteria employed at this stage of the test development process follow:

- Infrequently endorsed items—or items that almost everyone would endorse—were to be eliminated, because they reveal little about respondents. Stated more technically, they will fail to appreciably add to the reliability and validity of the test because of their small variances. Further, such items have been found to elicit stylistic tendencies to respond deviantly or nonpurposively. For these reasons, items with a *p* value of either below .05 or above .95 were eliminated. An obvious exception to this rule would be items deliberately selected for use in the Infrequency scale—a scale designed to detect nonpurposive or random responding and related response styles. A sample item on this scale might be one like "I have visited the Republic of Samoa during the past year."

- If an item correlated higher with any content-scale total score other than the one it was written for, the item was eliminated—a method of helping to ensure convergent and discriminant validity.

- An evaluation was made as to the degree to which the item elicited tendencies to respond desirably. This was accomplished, at least in part, by evaluating each item's correlation with a desirability scale.

- An evaluation was made of the item's saturation as indicated by the magnitude of its correlation with the total scale.

- An evaluation was made of the item's content saturation in relation to its desirability bias as indicated by a specially devised Differential Reliability Index.

- Items were assigned to parallel forms of the test on the basis of item and scale statistical properties. The rigor with which this process was executed can be seen graphically in Figure 1.

- Each item was subjected to a final substantive review designed to evaluate its generalizability and its representativeness with respect to scale content.

III. The Appraisal of the Structural Component of Validity

Steps were taken to ensure that optimal levels of homogeneity existed—homogeneity attributable to the test's content as opposed to response style or other variables.

IV. Evaluation of the External Component of Validity

Paid volunteers who lived in Stanford University housing and who were all "well acquainted with one another" served as the sample for the validity study. Jackson (1970, p. 88) informs us that each subject sat for a four-hour assessment battery including two forms of the PRF, a set of behavior ratings of 20 variables relevant to the 20 PRF content scales, and 600 adjectives measuring the same 20 traits relevant to each of the 20 scales. Subjects responded true or false to each of the 600 adjectives as self-descriptive, and later judged the desirability of each of them in other people. This latter task was included to appraise the hypothesis that a person's point of view about the desirability of a trait would tell us something valid about that person's own personality (Jackson, 1964; Stricker et al., 1968).

An examination of correlations between PRF scales and appropriate criterion measures revealed that there was substantial convergent and discriminant validity associated with PRF scales.

Self-Assessment

Test your understanding of elements of this chapter by seeing if you can explain each of the following terms, expressions, and abbreviations:

categorical scaling	comparative scaling
class scoring	constructed-response format

co-validation

cross-validation

cumulative scoring

expert panels

guessing

Guttman scale

item analysis

item-characteristic curve (ICC)

item-difficulty index

item-discrimination index

item-endorsement index

item fairness

item format

item pool

item-reliability index

item-validity index

latent-trait model

Likert scale

pilot work

qualitative item analysis

rating scale

scales

scaling

selected-response format

sensitivity review

summative scale

test conceptualization

test construction

test revision

test tryout

"think aloud" test administration

validity shrinkage

8

Intelligence and Its Measurement

Perhaps as long as there has been a discipline of psychology, there have been psychologists with their own definition of what intelligence is and how best to measure it.

In this chapter, we will look at the varied ways intelligence has been defined and survey the ways it has been measured. The chapter concludes with discussion of some of the many issues that have been raised about the practice of measuring intelligence, including an extended discussion of some complex issues with respect to culture and intelligence. Then, in Chapter 9, we look more closely at the "nuts and bolts" of intelligence tests and focus in detail on some representative tests. The measurement of intelligence and other ability- and achievement-related constructs in preschool and educational settings is the subject of Chapter 10. We begin, however, by raising a question that must logically precede any consideration of measurement issues related to intelligence.

What Is Intelligence?

We may define **intelligence** as a multifaceted capacity that manifests itself in different ways across the lifespan, but in general includes the abilities and capacities to acquire and apply knowledge, to reason logically, to plan effectively, to infer perceptively, to exhibit sound judgment and problem-solving ability, to grasp and visualize concepts, to be mentally alert and intuitive, to be able to find the right words and thoughts with facility, and to be able to cope, adjust, and make the most of new situations—but please do not interpret these words as the last word on what intelligence is. Rather, think of this definition as a point of departure for reflecting on the meaning of a most intriguing term; one that, as we will see, is paradoxically both simple and complex.

Intelligence is something that most people believe they can recognize when it is expressed in observable behavior. Yet a widely accepted definition has remained elusive. The concept just does not seem to lend itself to definition (Neisser, 1979). Still, it really should be defined (Neisser et al., 1996), especially if we are going to use the construct, design tests to measure it, and take action on the basis of the test results. Beyond attempts to create a definition that incorporates "all the right words," the search for an adequate and widely accepted definition has inspired cerebral glucose metabolism studies (Haier, 1993) and other such research on brain physiology (Vernon, 1993). Still, devising a widely acceptable definition of intelligence remains a challenge.

How do laypeople define intelligence? And how do lay definitions of intelligence contrast with those of scholars who have studied intelligence? Let's consider these questions now.

Intelligence Defined: Views of the Lay Public

Research conducted by Sternberg and his associates (Sternberg, 1981, 1982; Sternberg & Detterman, 1986; Sternberg et al., 1981) sought to shed light on this question. In one study, a total of 476 people (students, commuters, supermarket shoppers, people who answered newspaper ads, and people randomly selected from phone books) were asked to list behaviors they associated with "intelligence," "academic intelligence," "everyday intelligence," and "unintelligence." After a list of various behaviors characterizing intelligence was generated, 28 nonpsychologists in the New Haven area were asked to rate on a scale of 1 (low) to 9 (high) how characteristic each of the behaviors was for the ideal "intelligent" person, the ideal "academically intelligent" person, and the ideal "everyday intelligent" person. The views of 140 doctoral-level research psychologists who were experts in the area of intelligence were also solicited. These experts were themselves involved in research on intelligence in major universities and research centers around the United States.

All people polled in Sternberg's study had definite ideas about what intelligence, or the lack of it, was. For the nonpsychologists, the behaviors most commonly associated with intelligence were "reasons logically and well," "reads widely," "displays common sense," "keeps an open mind," and "reads with high comprehension." Leading the list of most frequently mentioned behaviors associated with "unintelligence" were "does not tolerate diversity of views," "does not display curiosity," and "behaves with insufficient consideration of others."

Sternberg and his colleagues grouped the list of 250 behaviors characterizing intelligence and unintelligence into subsets that were most strongly related to each other. The analysis indicated that the nonpsychologists and the experts conceived of intelligence in general as practical problem-solving ability (such as "listens to all sides of an argument"), verbal ability ("displays a good vocabulary"), and social competence ("is on time for appointments"). Each specific type of intelligence was characterized by various descriptors. "Academic intelligence" included verbal ability, problem-solving ability, and social competence, as well as specific behaviors associated with acquiring academic skills (such as "studying hard"). "Everyday intelligence" included practical problem-solving ability, social competence, character, and interest in learning and culture. In general, the researchers found a surprising degree of similarity between the experts' and laypeople's conceptions of intelligence. With respect to academic intelligence, however, the experts tended to stress motivation ("is persistent," "highly dedicated and motivated in chosen pursuits"), whereas laypeople stressed the interpersonal and social aspects of intelligence ("sensitivity to other people's needs and desires," "is frank and honest with self and others").

In another study (Siegler & Richards, 1980), students enrolled in college developmental psychology classes were asked to list behaviors associated with intelligence in infancy, childhood, and adulthood. Perhaps not surprisingly, different conceptions of intelligence as a function of developmental stage were noted. In infancy, intelligence was associated with physical coordination, awareness of people, verbal output, and attachment. In childhood, verbal facility, understanding, and characteristics of learning were most often listed. Verbal facility, use of logic, and problem solving were most frequently associated with adult intelligence.

A study conducted with first-, third-, and sixth-graders (Yussen & Kane, 1980) suggested that children as young as first grade also have notions about intelligence. Younger children's conceptions tended to emphasize interpersonal skills (acting nice, being helpful, being polite), whereas older children emphasized academic skills (being good at reading).

Intelligence Defined: Views of Scholars and Test Professionals

In a symposium published in the *Journal of Educational Psychology* in 1921, seventeen of the country's leading psychologists addressed the following questions: (1) What is intelligence? (2) How can it best be measured in group tests? and (3) What should the next steps in the research be? No two psychologists agreed (Thorndike et al., 1921). Six years later, Spearman (1927, p. 14) would reflect, "In truth, intelligence has become . . . a word with so many meanings that finally it has none." And decades after the symposium was first held, Wesman (1968, p. 267) concluded that there appeared to be "no more general agreement as to the nature of intelligence or the most valid means of measuring intelligence today than was the case 50 years ago."

As Neisser (1979) observed, although the *Journal* felt that the symposium would generate vigorous discussion, it generated more heat than light and led to a general increase in exasperation with discussion on the subject. Symptomatic of that exasperation was an unfortunate statement by a historian of psychology and—nonpsychometrician—experimental psychologist, Edwin G. Boring. Boring (1923, p. 5) attempted to quell the argument by pronouncing that "intelligence is what the tests test." Although such a view is not entirely devoid of merit (see Neisser, 1979, p. 225), it is an unsatisfactory, incomplete, and circular definition. The thoughts of some other behavioral scientists throughout history, as well as more contemporary views, follow.

Francis Galton   Among other accomplishments, Sir Francis Galton is remembered as the first person to publish on the heritability of intelligence, thus framing the contemporary nature/nurture debate (McGue, 1997). With regard to his own definition of intelligence, Galton (1883) believed that the most intelligent persons were those equipped with the best sensory abilities. This position was intuitively appealing because, as Galton observed, "The only information that reaches us concerning outward events appears to pass through the avenues of our senses; and the more perceptive the senses are of difference, the larger is the field upon which our judgment and intelligence can act" (p. 27). Following this logic, tests of visual acuity or hearing ability are in a sense, tests of intelligence. Galton attempted to measure this sort of intelligence in many of the sensorimotor and other perception-related tests he devised. In this respect, he anticipated more contemporary physiological research that examines, for example, the relationship between intelligence and speed of neural conductivity (Reed & Jensen, 1992, 1993).

Alfred Binet   Although his test at the turn of the century had the effect of launching the testing—intelligence and otherwise—movement, Alfred Binet did not leave us an explicit definition of intelligence. He did write that the components of intelligence included reasoning, judgment, memory, and abstraction (Varon, 1936). In papers critical of Galton's approach to intellectual assessment, Binet and a colleague called for more complex measurements of intellectual ability (Binet & Henri, 1895a, 1895b, 1895c). Unlike Galton, Binet was motivated by the very demanding and challenging task of developing a procedure for identifying intellectually limited Parisian schoolchildren who could not benefit from a regular instructional program and required special educational experiences. Galton viewed intelligence as a number of distinct processes or abilities that could be assessed only by separate tests. By contrast, Binet argued that when one solves a particular problem, the distinct abilities used cannot be separated but, rather, interact to produce the solution. For example, memory and concentration interact when a subject is asked to repeat digits presented orally. When analyzing a subject's response to such a task, it is difficult to determine the relative contribution of memory and concentration to the successful solution. This difficulty is the reason that Binet called for more complex measurements of intellectual ability.

David Wechsler David Wechsler's conceptualization of intelligence can perhaps best be summed up in his own words:

> Intelligence, operationally defined, is the aggregate or global capacity of the individual to act purposefully, to think rationally and to deal effectively with his environment. It is aggregate or global because it is composed of elements or abilities which, though not entirely independent, are qualitatively differentiable. By measurement of these abilities, we ultimately evaluate intelligence. But intelligence is not identical with the mere sum of these abilities, however inclusive. . . . The only way we can evaluate it quantitatively is by the measurement of the various aspects of these abilities. (1958, p. 7)

Elsewhere, Wechsler added that there are nonintellective factors that must be taken into account when assessing intelligence (Kaufman, 1990). Included among those factors are "capabilities more of the nature of conative, affective, or personality traits (which) include such traits as drive, persistence, and goal awareness (as well as) an individual's potential to perceive and respond to social, moral and aesthetic values" (Wechsler, 1975, p. 136). Binet also had observed that a comprehensive study of intelligence involved the study of personality as well.

Jean Piaget Since the early 1960s, the theoretical research of the Swiss developmental psychologist Jean Piaget (1954, 1971) has received increasing attention. Piaget's research focused on the development of cognition in children: how children think, how they understand themselves and the world around them, and how they reason and solve problems. For Piaget, intelligence may be conceived of as a kind of evolving biological adaptation to the outside world; as cognitive skills are gained, adaptation (at a symbolic level) increases and mental trial and error replaces actual physical trial and error. Yet, according to Piaget, the process of cognitive development is thought to occur neither solely through maturation nor solely through learning. He believed that as a consequence of interaction with the environment, psychological structures become reorganized. Piaget carefully described four stages of cognitive development through which, he theorized, all of us pass during our lifetimes. Although individuals can move through these stages at different rates and ages, he believed that their order was unchangeable. Piaget viewed the unfolding of these stages of cognitive development as the result of the interaction of biological factors and learning.

According to this theory, biological aspects of mental development are governed by inherent maturational mechanisms. As individual stages are reached and passed through, the child is also having experiences within the environment. Each new experience, according to Piaget, requires some form of cognitive organization or reorganization in a mental structure called a "schema." More specifically, Piaget used the term **schema** to refer to an organized action or mental structure that, when applied to the world, leads to knowing or understanding. Infants are born with several simple **schemata** (the plural of schema), including sucking and grasping. Learning initially by grasping and by putting almost anything in their mouths, infants use these schemata to understand and appreciate their world. As the infant grows older, schemata become more complicated and are tied less to overt action than to mental transformations. For example, when you add a series of numbers, you are transforming numbers mentally to

Table 8–1
Piaget's Stages of Cognitive Development

Stage	Age Span	Characteristics of Thought
Sensorimotor Period	Birth–2 years of age	Child develops ability to exhibit goal-directed, intentional behavior; develops the capacity to coordinate and integrate input from the five senses; acquires the capacity to recognize the world and its objects as permanent entities (that is, the infant develops "object permanence").
Preoperational Period	2–6 years of age	Child's understanding of concepts is based largely on what is seen; the child's comprehension of a situation, an event, or an object is typically based on a single, usually the most obvious, perceptual aspect of the stimulus; thought is irreversible (child focuses on static states of reality and cannot understand relations between states; for example, child believes the quantities of a set of beads change if the beads are pushed together or spread apart); animistic thinking (attributing human qualities to nonhuman objects and events).
Concrete Operations Period	7–12 years of age	Reversibility of thought now appears; conservation of thought (certain attributes of the world remain stable despite some modification in appearance); part-whole problems and serial ordering tasks can now be solved (able to put ideas in rank order); can deal only with relationships and things with which he or she has direct experience; able to look at more than one aspect of a problem and able to clearly differentiate between present and historical time.
Formal Operations Period	12 years of age and older	Increased ability to abstract and to deal with ideas independent of his or her own experience; greater capacity to generate hypotheses and test them in a systematic fashion ("if-then" statements, more alternatives); able to think about several variables acting together and their combined effects; can evaluate own thought; applies learning to new problems in a deductive way.

reach your answer. Infants, children, and adults continue to apply schemata to objects and events to achieve understanding, and these schemata are constantly being adjusted.

Piaget hypothesized that the individual learns through the two basic mental operations of **assimilation** (actively organizing new information so that it fits in with what already is perceived and thought) and **accommodation** (changing what is already perceived or thought to fit in with new information). For example, a child who sees a butterfly and calls it a "bird" has assimilated the idea of butterfly into an already existing mental structure, bird. However, when the new concept of "butterfly," separate from "bird," has additionally been formed, the mental operation of *accommodation* has been employed. Piaget also stressed the importance of physical activities and social peer interaction in promoting a disequilibrium that represents the process by which mental structures change. Disequilibrium causes the individual to discover new information, perceptions, and communication skills.

The four periods of cognitive development, each representing a more complex form of cognitive organization, are outlined in Table 8–1. The stages range from the sensorimotor period, wherein infants' thoughts are dominated by their perceptions, to the formal operations period, wherein an individual has the ability to construct theories and make logical deductions without the need for direct experience.

A major thread running through the theories of Binet, Wechsler, and Piaget is a focus on **interactionism.** Interactionism refers to the complex concept by which heredity

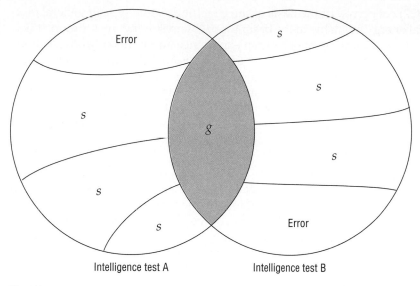

Figure 8–1
Spearman's Two-Factor Theory of Intelligence

Here, g *stands for a general intelligence factor and* s *stands for a specific factor of intelligence (specific to a single intellectual activity only).*

and environment are presumed to interact to influence the development of one's intelligence. As we will see in what follows, other theorists have focused on other aspects of intelligence. In factor-analytic theories, the focus is squarely on identifying the ability or groups of abilities deemed to constitute intelligence. In information-processing theories, the focus is on identifying the specific mental processes that constitute intelligence.

Factor-Analytic Theories of Intelligence

Factor analysis refers to a group of statistical techniques designed to determine if underlying relationships between sets of variables, including test scores, exist. In search of a definition of intelligence, theorists have used factor analysis to study correlations between tests measuring varied abilities presumed to reflect the underlying attribute of intelligence. As early as 1904, the British psychologist Charles Spearman pioneered new techniques to measure intercorrelations between tests. He found that measures of intelligence tended to correlate to various degrees with each other. Spearman (1927) formalized these observations into an influential theory of general intelligence that postulated the existence of a general intellectual ability factor (referred to with an italicized, lowercase *g*), which is partially tapped by all other mental abilities. This theory is sometimes referred to as a **two-factor theory of intelligence,** with *g* representing the portion of the variance that all intelligence tests have in common, and the remaining portions of the variance being accounted for either by specific components (**s**), or by error components (*e*) of this general factor (Figure 8–1). Tests that exhibited high, positive correlations with other intelligence tests were thought to be highly saturated with *g,* while tests with low or moderate correlations with other intelligence tests were thought of as possible measures of specific factors (such as visual or motor ability). The greater the magnitude of *g* in a test of intelligence, the better the test was thought to predict overall intelligence.

Spearman (1927) conceived of the basis of the g factor as some type of general electrochemical mental energy available to the brain for problem solving. In addition, it was associated with facility in thinking of one's own experience and in making observations and extracting principles. It was g rather than s that was assumed to afford the best prediction of overall intelligence. Abstract-reasoning problems were thought to be the best measures of g in formal tests. As Spearman and his students continued their research, they acknowledged the existence of an intermediate class of factors common to a group of activities but not to all. This class of factors, called **group factors,** is neither so general as g nor so specific as s. Examples of these broad group factors include linguistic, mechanical, and arithmetical abilities.

Other theorists attempted to "dig deeper" and be even more specific about identifying and describing factors other than g in intelligence. The number of factors listed to define intelligence in a factor-analytic theory of intelligence may depend, in part, on just how specific the theory is in terms of defining discrete cognitive abilities. These abilities may be conceived of in may ways, ranging from very broad to highly specific fashions. As an example, consider that one researcher has identified an ability "to repeat a chain of verbally presented numbers" that he labels "Factor R." Another researcher analyzes "Factor R" into three "facilitating abilities" or subfactors which she labels "ability to process sound" ("R1"), "ability to retain verbally presented stimuli" ("R2"), and "speed of processing verbally presented stimuli" ("R3"). Both researchers present factor-analytic evidence to support their respective positions.[1] Which of these two models will prevail? All other things being equal, it will probably be the model that is perceived as having the greater real-world application, the greater intuitive appeal in terms of how intelligence should be defined, and the greater amount of empirical support.

Many multiple-factor models of intelligence have been proposed. Some of these models, such as that developed by Guilford (1967), have sought to explain mental activities by deemphasizing, if not eliminating, any reference to g. Thurstone (1938) initially conceived of intelligence as being composed of seven "primary abilities." However, after designing tests to measure these abilities and noting a moderate correlation between the tests, Thurstone became convinced it was difficult if not impossible to develop an intelligence test that did not tap g. Gardner (1983, 1994) developed a theory of multiple (seven, actually) intelligences that included the following abilities: logical-mathematical, bodily-kinesthetic, linguistic, musical, spatial, interpersonal, and intrapersonal. Gardner (1983) described the latter two intelligences as follows:

> Interpersonal intelligence is the ability to understand other people: what motivates them, how they work, how to work cooperatively with them. Successful sales people, politicians, teachers, clinicians, and religious leaders are all likely to be individuals with high degrees of interpersonal intelligence. Intrapersonal intelligence, a seventh kind of intelligence, is a correlative ability, turned inward. It is a capacity to form an accurate, veridical model of oneself and to be able to use that model to operate effectively in life. (p. 9)

Aspects of Gardner's writings, particularly his descriptions of **interpersonal intelligence** and **intrapersonal intelligence,** have found expression in popular books written by others on the subject of so-called **emotional intelligence.** But whether or not constructs related to empathy and self-understanding qualify more for the study of emotion

---

1. Recall that factor analysis may take many forms. In exploratory factor analysis, the researcher is essentially exploring what relationships exist. In confirmatory factor analysis, the researcher is typically testing the viability of a proposed model or theory. Some factor-analytic studies are conducted on the subtests of a single test (such as a Wechsler test), while other studies are conducted on subtests from two (or more) tests (such as the current versions of a Wechsler test and the Binet test). The type of factor analysis employed by a theorist may well be the tool that will present that theorist's conclusions in the best possible light.

and personality than the study of intelligence has been a subject of debate (Davies et al., 1998).

In recent years, a theory of intelligence first proposed by Raymond B. Cattell (1941, 1971) and subsequently modified by Horn (Cattell & Horn, 1978; Horn & Cattell, 1966, 1967) has received increasing attention by test developers and test users. As originally conceived by Cattell, the theory postulated the existence of two major types of cognitive abilities: crystallized intelligence and fluid intelligence. The abilities that make up **crystallized intelligence** (symbolized Gc) include acquired skills and knowledge that are dependent on exposure to a particular culture as well as formal and informal education (vocabulary, for example). Retrieval of information and application of general knowledge are conceived of as elements of crystallized intelligence. The abilities that make up **fluid intelligence** (symbolized Gf) are nonverbal, relatively culture-free, and independent of specific instruction (such as memory for digits). Through the years, Horn (1968, 1985, 1988, 1991, 1994) proposed the addition of several additional factors: visual processing (Gv), auditory processing (Ga), quantitative processing (Gq), speed of processing (Gs), facility with reading and writing (Grw), short-term memory (Gsm), and long-term storage and retrieval (Glr). According to Horn (1989; Horn & Hofer, 1992), some of the abilities (such as Gv) are **vulnerable abilities** in that they decline with age and tend not to return to preinjury levels following brain damage. Others of these abilities (such as Gq) are **maintained abilities;** they tend not to decline with age and may return to preinjury levels following brain damage.

Another influential multiple intelligences model based on factor-analytic studies is the **three-stratum theory of cognitive abilities** (Carroll, 1997). In geology, a stratum is a layer of rock formation having the same composition throughout. Strata (the plural form of stratum) are illustrated in Figure 8–2, along with a representation of each of the three strata in Carroll's theory. The top stratum or level in Carroll's model is g or general intelligence. The second stratum is composed of eight abilities and processes: fluid intelligence (**Gf**), crystallized intelligence (**Gc**), general memory and learning (Y), broad visual perception (V), broad auditory perception (U), broad retrieval capacity (R), broad cognitive speediness (S), and processing/decision speed (T). Below each of the abilities in the second stratum are many "level factors" and/or "speed factors," each different depending on the second-level stratum to which they are linked. For example, three level factors linked to Gf are general reasoning, quantitative reasoning, and Piagetian reasoning. A speed factor linked to Gf is speed of reasoning. Four level factors linked to Gc are language development, comprehension, spelling ability, and communication ability. Two speed factors linked to Gc are oral fluency and writing ability. The three-stratum theory is a **hierarchical model,** meaning that all of the abilities listed in a stratum are subsumed or incorporated by the stratum or strata above it.

Moving from the concept of stratum and geology-based analogies, consider for a moment the periodic table of the elements that you became acquainted with in chemistry. There, in just one table, is a listing of all the known elements. Few scientists argue about which elements should or should not be listed in the table; rather, scientists tend to be in agreement about the list. For quite some time now, many psychologists have wondered whether it will ever be possible to develop a comparable, generally agreed upon listing of human abilities. If such a listing could be developed, it would have far-reaching implications for the way that cognitive abilities are understood, assessed, remediated, and enhanced.

In recent years, the desire for a comprehensive, consensually agreed upon conceptualization of human cognitive abilities has led some researchers to try to extract elements of existing models with the objective of creating a new, more complete model. Using factor analysis as well as other statistical tools, these researchers have attempted to

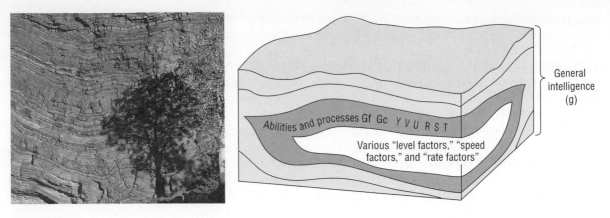

Figure 8–2
Strata in Geology and Carroll's Three-Stratum Theory

Erosion can bare multiple levels of strata on a cliff. In psychology, theory can bare the strata of hypothesized mental structure and function. In Carroll's three-stratum theory of cognitive ability, the first level is g, followed by a stratum made up of eight abilities and processes, followed by a stratum containing what Carroll refers to as varying "level factors" and "speed factors."

modify and reconfigure existing models to better fit empirical evidence. One such modification that has gained increasing attention blends the Cattell-Horn theory with Carroll's three-stratum theory. Although this blending was initiated by neither Cattell, nor Horn, nor Carroll, it is nonetheless referred to as the Cattell-Horn-Carroll (CHC) model of cognitive abilities.

The CHC model   The Cattell-Horn and Carroll models are similar in several respects, key among them the designation of broad abilities (second-stratum level in Carroll's theory), which subsume several narrow abilities (first-stratum level in Carroll's theory). Still, any prospective integration of the Cattell-Horn and Carroll models must somehow account for the differences between these two models. One difference has to do with the existence of a general intellectual (g) factor. For Carroll, g is the third-stratum factor, subsuming Gf, Gc, and the remaining six other broad, second-stratum abilities. By contrast, g has no place in the Cattell-Horn model. Another difference between the two models has to do with whether or not abilities labeled "quantitative knowledge" and "reading/writing ability" should each be considered a distinct, broad ability as they are in the Cattell-Horn model. For Carroll, all of these abilities are first-stratum, narrow abilities. Other differences between the two models have to do with the notation employed, the specific definitions of abilities, and the grouping of narrow factors related to memory.

An integration of the Cattell-Horn and Carroll models was proposed by Kevin S. McGrew (1997). On the basis of additional factor-analytic work, McGrew and Flanagan (1998) subsequently modified McGrew's initial CHC model. In its current form, the McGrew-Flanagan CHC model features ten "broad stratum" abilities and over seventy "narrow stratum" abilities, with each broad stratum ability subsuming two or more narrow stratum abilities. The ten broad stratum abilities, with their "code names" in parentheses, are labeled as follows: Fluid Intelligence (Gf), Crystallized Intelligence (Gc), Quantitative Knowledge (Gq), Reading/Writing Ability (Grw), Short-Term Memory (Gsm), Visual Processing (Gv), Auditory Processing (Ga), Long-Term Storage and Retrieval (Glr), Processing Speed (Gs), and Decision/Reaction Time or Speed (Gt).

In this model, there is no provision for the general intellectual ability factor (*g*). To understand the reason for this omission, it is important to understand why the authors undertook to create the model in the first place. The model was the product of efforts designed to improve the practice of psychological assessment in education (sometimes referred to as **psychoeducational assessment**) by identifying tests from different batteries that could be used to provide a comprehensive assessment of a student's abilities. Having identified key abilities, the authors made recommendations for **cross-battery assessment** of students, or assessment that employs tests from different test batteries and entails interpretation of data from specified subtests to provide a comprehensive assessment. According to these authors, *g* was not employed in their CHC model because it lacked utility in psychoeducational evaluations. They explained:

> The exclusion of *g* does not mean that the integrated model does not subscribe to a separate general human ability or that *g* does not exist. Rather, it was omitted by McGrew (1997) (and is similarly omitted in the current integrated model) since it has little practical relevance to cross-battery assessment and interpretation. (McGrew & Flanagan, 1998, p. 14)

Other differences between the Cattell-Horn and Carroll models were resolved more on the basis of factor-analytic studies than judgments regarding practical relevance to cross-battery assessment. The abilities labeled "quantitative knowledge" and "reading/writing" were conceived of as distinct broad abilities, much as they were by Horn and Cattell. McGrew and Flanagan drew heavily on Carroll's (1993) writings for definitions of many of the broad and narrow abilities listed, as well as the codes for these abilities.

At the very least, CHC theory as formulated by McGrew and Flanagan has great value from a heuristic standpoint. It compels practitioners and researchers alike to think about exactly how many human abilities really need to be measured, and how narrow or broad an approach is optimal in terms of being clinically useful. Further, it stimulates researchers to revisit other existing theories, which may also be ripe for reexamination by means of statistical methods such as factor analysis. The best features of such theories might then be combined with the goal of developing a clinically useful and actionable model of human abilities.

The Information-Processing View

Another approach to conceptualizing intelligence derives from the work of the Russian neuropsychologist Aleksandr Luria (1966a, 1966b, 1970, 1973, 1980). This approach focuses on the mechanisms by which information is processed—*how* information is processed, rather than *what* is processed. Two basic types of information-processing styles, simultaneous and successive, have been distinguished (Das et al., 1975; Luria, 1966a, 1966b). In **simultaneous** (or *parallel*) **processing,** information is integrated all at one time. In **successive** (or *sequential*) **processing,** each bit of information is individually processed in sequential fashion. As its name implies, sequential processing is logical and analytic in nature; piece by piece and one piece after the other, information is arranged and rearranged so that it makes sense. When you try to anticipate who the murderer is while watching a mystery movie, your thinking could be characterized as sequential in nature; you are constantly integrating bits of information that will lead you to a solution of the problem of "Whodunnit?" Memorizing a telephone number or learning the spelling of a new word is typical of the types of tasks that involve acquisition of information through successive processing.

By contrast, simultaneous processing may be described as synthesized in nature; information is integrated and synthesized at once and as a whole. As you stand before and appreciate a painting in an art museum, the information conveyed by the painting is processed in a manner that, at least for most of us, could reasonably be described as simultaneous—art critics and connoisseurs may be exceptions to this general rule. Tasks that involve the simultaneous mental representations of images or information, as is typical in map reading and in thinking about relationships between things, involve simultaneous processing.

Some tests, such as the Kaufman Assessment Battery for Children (Kaufman & Kaufman, 1983), which will be discussed in Chapter 10, rely heavily on this concept of a distinction between successive and simultaneous information processing. The strong influence of an information-processing perspective is also evident in the work of others (Das, 1972; Das et al., 1975; Naglieri, 1989, 1990; Naglieri & Das, 1988) who have developed a **PASS** model of intellectual functioning—PASS being an acronym for Planning, Attention, Simultaneous, and Successive. Within this model, "planning" refers to strategy development for problem solving, "attention" (also referred to as "arousal") refers to receptivity to information, and "simultaneous" and "successive" refer to the type of information processing employed. Proponents of the PASS model have argued that existing tests of intelligence do not adequately assess planning. Naglieri and Das (1997) developed the Cognitive Assessment System (CAS), a cognitive ability test expressly designed to tap PASS factors. Although these test authors presented evidence to support the construct validity of the CAS, other researchers have questioned whether the test is actually measuring what it purports to measure (Keith et al., in press; Keith & Kranzler, 1999; Kranzler & Keith, 1999; Kranzler et al., in press).

Robert Sternberg proposed another information-processing approach to intelligence, arguing that "the essence of intelligence is that it provides a means to govern ourselves so that our thoughts and actions are organized, coherent, and responsive to both our internally driven needs and to the needs of the environment" (Sternberg, 1986, p. 141). He proposed a triarchic theory of intelligence with three principal elements: metacomponents, performance components, and knowledge-acquisition components. Metacomponents are involved in planning what one is going to do, monitoring what one is doing, and evaluating what one has done upon completion. Performance components administer the instructions of metacomponents. Knowledge-acquisition components are involved in "learning how to do something in the first place" (Sternberg, 1994, p. 221).

Measuring Intelligence

The measurement of intelligence entails sampling an examinee's performance on different types of tests and tasks as a function of developmental level. At all developmental levels, the intellectual assessment process also provides a standardized situation from which the examinee's approach to the various tasks can be closely observed: an opportunity for assessment in itself, and one that can have great clinical utility. In the following two chapters, we will examine the components of some widely used cognitive ability tests. Here, we briefly view some of the types of tasks used in such tests, and reflect on the role of theory in the development of tests.

Types of Tasks Used in Intelligence Tests

In infancy (the period from birth through 18 months), intellectual assessment consists primarily of measurement of sensorimotor development. This includes, for example, the measurement of nonverbal, motor responses such as turning over, lifting the head, sit-

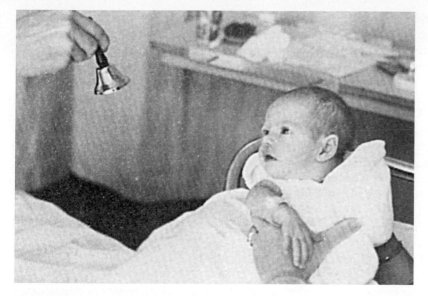

Figure 8–3
Testing the Alerting Response

One assessment technique common to infant development tests is a test of the alerting response. An **alerting response** *indicates an infant's capacity for responsiveness. It is deemed to be present when the infant's eyes brighten and widen—in contrast to the* **orienting response,** *which defines the response of turning in the direction of a stimulus. Here the child is exhibiting an alerting response to the sound of the bell.*

ting up, following a moving object with the eyes, imitating gestures, and reaching for a group of objects (Figure 8–3). The examiner who attempts to assess the intellectual and related abilities of infants must be skillful in establishing and maintaining rapport with examinees who do not yet know the meaning of words like *cooperation* and *patience.* Typically, measures of infant intelligence rely to a great degree on information obtained from a structured interview with the examinee's parents, guardians, or other caretakers.

The focus of evaluation in the older child shifts to verbal and performance abilities. More specifically, the child may be called on to perform tasks designed to yield a measure of general fund of information, vocabulary, social judgment, language, reasoning, numerical concepts, auditory and visual memory, attention, concentration, and spatial visualization. The administration of many of the items may be preceded, as prescribed by the test manual, with teaching items designed to provide the examinee with practice in what is required by a particular test item.

In a bygone era, many intelligence tests were scored and interpreted with reference to the concept of mental age. **Mental age** is an index that refers to the chronological age equivalent of one's performance on a test or a subtest. This index was typically derived by reference to norms that indicate the age at which most testtakers are able to pass or otherwise meet some criterion performance. More detailed discussion of this concept is presented in Cohen (2002), the companion student study guide for this textbook.

Especially when individually administered by a trained professional, tests administered to children, much like tests individually administered to adults, afford the examiner a unique opportunity to observe an examinee's reactions to success, failure, and frustration. The examiner can see, up close, the examinee's general approach to problem-solving and the test situation with its varied demands. Keen observation of such verbal and non-verbal behavior can yield a wealth of insights that in may cases will help to bring to light hitherto unidentified assets and deficits, and help to clarify ambiguities that arise in the test data. For schoolchildren, such observation may be useful with regard to a variety of objectives ranging from the individual tailoring of teaching agendas to class placement decisions.

According to Wechsler (1958), adult intelligence scales should tap such abilities as retention of general information, quantitative reasoning, expressive language and memory, and social judgment. The types of tasks used to reach these measurement objectives on the Wechsler scale for adults are the same as many of the tasks used on the Wechsler scales for children, although the content of specific items may vary. The fact that similar stimulus materials are used with children and adults has caused some to question whether children tend to be more motivated when presented with such materials (Marquette, 1976; Schaie, 1978), and whether the tasks fail to capture an adequate sampling of skills acquired by adults (Wesman, 1968). Publishers of intelligence tests have made available series of tests that can be used through a period that not quite, but almost, spans cradle to grave.

Tests of intelligence are seldom administered to adults for purposes of educational placement. Rather, they may be given to obtain clinically relevant information or some measure of learning potential and skill acquisition.

More basic than age as a factor to consider when developing a test of intelligence is the foundation or theory on which the test will sit. Let's consider the role of theory in the development of intelligence tests and the interpretation of data from intelligence tests.

Theory in Intelligence Test Development and Interpretation

How one measures intelligence has to do in large part with what one conceives intelligence to be. A chapter in Galton's (1869) *Hereditary Genius,* entitled "Classification of Men According to Their Natural Gifts," discussed sensory and other differences between people, which he believed were inherited. Perhaps not surprisingly, many Galtonian measures of cognitive ability were perceptual or sensorimotor in nature. Alfred Binet wrote extensively on what intelligence is, although the formal theory that the original Binet test is perhaps best associated with is that of Carl Spearman's (1904) "universal unity of the intellective function" with g as its centerpiece.

David Wechsler also wrote extensively on what intelligence is, and usually made a point of emphasizing that intelligence is multifaceted, consisting not only of cognitive abilities, but personality-related factors as well. Still, because his original test, the Wechsler-Bellevue (W-B) Scale (as well as all subsequent Wechsler tests), provided for the calculation of a Verbal IQ and a Performance IQ, some have misinterpreted his position as representing a two-factor theory of intelligence: verbal abilities and performance abilities. Commenting on the development of the W-B and on the Verbal subtests (numbered 1 through 6) and the Performance subtests (numbered 7 through 11), Matarazzo explained:

> The grouping of the subtests into Verbal (1 to 6) and Performance (7 to 11), while intending to emphasize a dichotomy as regards possible types of ability called for by the individual tests, does *not* imply that these are the only abilities involved in the tests. Nor does it presume that there are different kinds of intelligence, e.g., verbal, manipulative, etc. It merely implies that these are different ways in which intelligence may manifest itself. The subtests are different measures of intelligence, not measures of different kinds of intelligence, and the dichotomy into Verbal and Performance areas is only one of several ways in which the tests could be grouped. (Matarazzo, 1972, p. 196, emphasis in the original)

In a footnote accompanying the extracted text, Matarazzo pointed out that the verbal and performance areas presumably coincided with the so-called primary factors of mental ability (postulated by Thurstone, 1938). Regardless, decades of factor-analytic research on the Wechsler tests have pointed to the existence of more than two factors—although exactly how many factors are tapped by the various Wechsler tests and what they should be called have been matters of heated debate. And that brings us to an important point about theory and intelligence tests: Different theorists with different ideas about what factors are key in a theory of intelligence can look for (and probably find) their preferred factors in most widely used tests of intelligence. A Wechsler intelligence test, or any other such major test, could be factor-analyzed with an eye toward identifying subtests that tap the cognitive abilities deemed to be dominant in a particular theory. As a consequence, practitioners and researchers who find the Cattell-Horn model of intelligence most appealing may make interpretations from Wechsler test data (or other intelligence test data) with reference to that model. Practitioners and researchers who find Carroll's three-stratum theory most appealing may make interpretations with reference to that model. Practitioners and researchers who find an integration of the Cattell-Horn and Carroll models to be most appealing may make interpretations with reference to a Cattell-Horn-Carrol (CHC) model, such as that proposed by McGrew & Flanagan (1998).

Beyond putting new interpretation-related templates over existing tests, new tests designed to measure the abilities and related factors described in a theory may be developed. Imagine what it might be like to develop a test of intelligence from a theory of intelligence. In fact, don't imagine it; try your hand at it! As an exercise in converting a theory of intelligence into a test of intelligence, consider the multifactor theory of intelligence developed by a pioneer in psychometrics, E. L. Thorndike. According to Thorndike (Thorndike et al., 1909; Thorndike et al., 1921), intelligence can be conceived in terms of three clusters of ability: social intelligence (dealing with people), concrete intelligence (dealing with objects), and abstract intelligence (dealing with verbal and mathematical symbols). Thorndike also incorporated a general mental ability factor (g) into the theory, defining g as the total number of modifiable neural connections or "bonds" available in the brain. For Thorndike, one's ability to learn is determined by the number and speed of the bonds that can be marshaled. No major test of intelligence was ever developed based on Thorndike's multifactor theory. *This is your moment!* Jot down some notes outlining what you think a hypothetical "Thorndike Test of Intelligence" would look like. How might test items be grouped? What types of items would be found in each grouping? What types of summary scores might be reported for each testtaker? What types of interpretations would be made from the test data? What types of questions or comments would you anticipate from other professionals? From the general public? Come to your next class prepared to discuss your ideas.

Even in the course of completing this brief exercise, many issues surrounding the conversion of theory to practice may arise. In the real world, far more issues and questions will arise as soon as any attempt to define and measure "intelligence" is made. Let's look at some of those issues now.

Intelligence: Some Issues

Do you believe that intellectual ability is innate and that it simply unfolds from birth onward? How stable are intelligence test scores over time? What factors influence

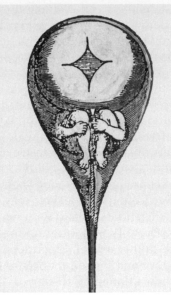

Figure 8–4
A Human Sperm Cell According to a Preformationist

This is how one scientist drew a human sperm cell as he saw it through a microscope—dramatic testimony to the way in which one's beliefs can affect perception (from Hartsoeker, 1694, cited in Needham, 1959, p. 20).

measured intelligence? These are some of the many questions and issues that have been raised with respect to intelligence and its measurement. Before reading on, make a note of your own answers to these questions—and then see if (and if so, how) your answers have changed when you reach the end of the chapter.

Nature Versus Nurture

Although most behavioral scientists today believe that measured intellectual ability represents an interaction between (1) innate ability and (2) environmental influences, such a belief was not always popular. As early as the seventeenth century, preformationism began to gain a foothold, as scientists of the day made discoveries that seemed to support this doctrine. **Preformationism** holds that all living organisms are preformed at birth. All of an organism's structures, including intelligence, are preformed at birth, and therefore unable to be improved upon. In 1672, one scientist reported that butterflies were preformed inside their cocoons and that their maturation was a result of an unfolding. In that same year, another scientist, this one studying chick embryos, generalized from his studies to draw a similar conclusion about humans (Malphigi, *De Formatione Pulli in Ovo*, 1672; cited in Needham, 1959, p. 167).

The invention of the compound microscope in the late seventeenth century provided a new tool with which preformationists could attempt to gather supportive evidence. Scientists confirmed their expectations by observing semen under the microscope. Various investigators "claimed to have seen a microscopic horse in the semen of a horse, an animalcule with very large ears in the semen of a donkey, and minute roosters in the semen of a rooster" (Hunt, 1961, p. 38; Figure 8–4).

The influence of preformationist theory waned slowly as evidence inconsistent with it was brought forth. For example, the theory could not explain the regeneration of limbs by crayfish and other organisms. With the progression of work in the area of genetics, preformationism as the dominant theory of development was slowly replaced by predeterminism. **Predeterminism** is the doctrine that holds that one's abilities are predetermined by genetic inheritance and that no amount of learning or other intervention can enhance what has been genetically encoded to unfold in time. Experimental work with animals was often cited in support of the predeterminist position. For example, a study by Carmichael (1927) showed that newly born salamanders and frogs, which had been anesthetized and deprived of an opportunity to swim, swam at about the same time as unanesthetized controls. Carmichael's work did not take into consideration the influence of the environment in the swimming behavior of salamanders and frogs. In parallel studies with humans, Dennis and Dennis (1940) observed the development of walking behavior in Hopi Indian children. Comparisons were made between children who spent much of their first year of life bound to a cradle board and children who had spent no such time constricted. Their conclusion was that there was no significant difference between the two groups of children at time of onset of walking and that walking was not a skill that could be enhanced by practice. Walking had been "proved" to be a human activity that unfolded with maturation.

Another proponent of the predeterminist view was Arnold Gesell. Generalizing from early twin studies that showed that practice had little effect on tasks such as climbing stairs, cutting with scissors, building with cubes, and buttoning buttons, Gesell (with Helen Thompson, 1929) concluded that "training does not transcend maturation." For Gesell, it was primarily the maturation of neural mechanisms and not learning or experience that was most important in the development of what might be referred to as intelligence. Gesell described mental development as a "progressive morphogenesis of patterns of behavior" (Gesell et al., 1940, p. 7) and argued that behavior patterns are determined by "innate processes of growth" that he viewed as synonymous with maturation (Gesell, 1945). Gesell (1954, p. 335) described infancy as "the period in which the individual realizes his racial inheritance" and has argued that this inheritance "is the end product of evolutionary processes that trace back to an extremely remote antiquity."

Is intelligence genetically encoded and something that unfolds with maturation? Or does the learning environment account for our intelligence? Nature/nurture questions like these have been raised for as long as there have been concepts of intelligence and tests to measure those concepts—sometimes amid great publicity and controversy. Galton firmly believed that genius was hereditary, a belief that was expressed in works such as *Hereditary Genius* (1869) and *English Men of Science* (1874). Richard Dugdale, another predeterminist, argued that degeneracy, like genius, was also inherited. Dugdale (1877) traced the immoral, lecherous lineage of the infamous Jukes family and hypothesized that the observed trail of poverty, harlotry, and laziness was a matter of heredity. Complementing the work of Dugdale was Henry Goddard's book, *The Kallikak Family* (1912). Goddard traced the family lineage resulting from the legitimate and illegitimate unions of a man given the pseudonym "Martin Kallikak" (the last name was a combination of the Greek words for "good" and "bad"). Kallikak had fathered children with a mentally defective waitress and with the reportedly normal woman he married. Goddard documented how Kallikak's illegitimate descendants were far less socially desirable than the legitimate ones.

Based on his testing of a sample of Mexican and Native American children, the father of the American version of Binet's test, Lewis M. Terman, concluded that people from these cultures were genetically inferior. The noted English statistician Karl Pearson wrote that as compared with the native British, immigrating Jews were "somewhat inferior physiologically and mentally" (Pearson & Moul, 1925, p. 126). Such observations seem flawed, even prejudiced—if not racist—by current standards, yet they tended to reflect the prevailing truisms of the day.

Although a scholarly consideration of the role of environmental and cultural factors (not to mention language barriers) is not evident in the writings of many behavioral scientists of the early twentieth century, a research literature that shed light on the environment side of the hereditary/environment issue subsequently began to mount. It was found, for example, that when identical twins are reared apart, they still show remarkably similar intelligence test scores, though not so similar as if they had been reared together (Johnson, 1963; Newman et al., 1937). Children born to poverty-stricken parents, but adopted at an early age by better-educated, middle-class families, tend to have higher intelligence test scores than do their counterparts who are not adopted by families of higher socioeconomic status—though the natural mothers with the higher IQs tend to have the children with the higher IQs irrespective of the family in which the adopted child is raised (Leahy, 1932, 1935).

In general, proponents of the "nurture" side of the nature/nurture controversy emphasize the crucial importance of factors such as prenatal and postnatal environment, socioeconomic status, educational opportunities, and parental modeling with respect to intellectual development. Proponents of this view characteristically suspect that opposing arguments that champion the role of nature in the controversy are based more on factors such as political leanings than on sound and impartial scientific inquiry and analysis.

Somewhere between the rhetoric arguing that heredity plays *no* part in intelligence (Kamin, 1974) and assertions such as "Nature has color coded groups of individuals so that statistically reliable predictions of their adaptability to intellectually rewarding and effective lives can easily be made and profitably be used by the pragmatic man-in-the-street" (Shockley, 1971, p. 375) lies the middle ground of the interactionist position: that intelligence, as measured by intelligence tests, is the result of the interaction between heredity and environment.

Inheritance and interactionism People differ in intelligence levels just as they differ in blood pressure levels, cerebrospinal fluid levels, sensitivity to pain (Sheffield et al., 2000), and many other ways. Once that is understood, it is natural to wonder *why* people differ in intellectual abilities, to wonder what accounts for the variability. According to the interactionist view, people inherit a certain intellectual potential. Exactly how much of that genetic potential is realized depends partially on the nature of the environment in which it is nurtured. No one to date has inherited the ability to fly or to have X-ray vision. You might spend your entire life in libraries or on mountaintops visiting gurus, but all your studies cannot result in your acquiring the ability to fly or to see through things, because those abilities have not been encoded in your genetic makeup. As a psychologist, you may one day administer an intelligence test to a mentally deficient adult who does not have the ability required to reiterate five digits or to tell you how a ball and an apple are similar. You may wonder to yourself, as you administer that test, whether the deficiency was inherited, whether it was the result of some environmental insult (anything from improper prenatal nutrition on the part of the mother to inferior educational opportunities), or whether it was the result of a combination of the two. Remember that the intelligence test data you obtain will indicate predefined strengths or weaknesses in various subject areas, but the data will not necessarily tell you why that deficiency exists.

The interactionist perspective on intellectual development tends to be a very optimistic one; according to it, we are free to become all that we can be. The notion that we can use the environment to push our genetic potential to the limit can be illustrated most graphically by reference to dedicated athletes. (See Figure 8–5.)

The Stability of Intelligence

Although research on the stability of measured intelligence in young children has yielded mixed findings (Dougherty & Haith, 1997; Lamp & Krohn, 1990: Smith, Bolin, &

Figure 8–5
What Does It Take to Win?

During the 1998 Winter Olympics in Nagano, Japan, the world looked on as Tara Lipinski became the youngest figure skater in Olympic history to win the gold. What does it take to do that? To what extent is such an accomplishment a matter of genes, training, motivation, and other factors?

Stovall, 1988; Wesman, 1968), intelligence does seem to be stable for much of one's adult life (Birren & Schaie, 1985; Shock et al., 1984; Youngjohn & Crook, 1993). Using archival intelligence test data from World War II, Gold et al. (1995) administered the same intelligence test to a sample of 326 veterans some 40 years later. In general, the data pointed to stability in measured intelligence over time. Increases in vocabulary were noted, as were decreases in arithmetic, verbal analogies, and other nonverbal skills. The researchers concluded that young adult intelligence was the most important determinant of cognitive performance as an older adult.

Longitudinal research on adult intelligence, especially with older subjects, can be complicated by many factors such as the extent to which one remains mentally active (Kaufman, 1990), the condition of one's physical health (Birren, 1968; Palmore, 1970), and myriad other potentially confounding factors (ranging from medication to personality). It is also important to distinguish between *group* similarities and differences in cognitive abilities over time and *intraindividual* similarities and differences. Addressing this latter point, Ivnik and colleagues (Ivnik et al., 1995; Malec et al., 1993) acknowledged that group means and standard deviations in studies where normal aging is controlled lend themselves to the conclusion that cognitive abilities are remarkably stable over the course of one's adult life. However, these researchers suggested that in a sample of normal adults, a focus on aging-related, within-individual variability in cognitive abilities may lead to different conclusions. Ivnik et al. (1995) found verbal intellectual skills to be highly stable over time, with delayed free recall of newly learned information being the least stable of the cognitive abilities they surveyed. The researchers concluded, "These data challenge the assumption that normal persons' cognitive abilities are stable over long periods of time. In actuality, none of the general cognitive abilities measured in this study is absolutely stable, although some are more stable than others" (p. 160).

A mounting body of research points to a decline in cognitive abilities in later adulthood, especially after age 75 (Nettelbeck & Rabbit, 1992; Ryan et al., 1990; Storandt, 1994). One study compared the performance of medical doctors over the age of 75 to the performance of younger colleagues on measures of cognitive ability. The resulting data indicated the performance of the elder physicians was about 26% lower than that of the younger group (Powell, 1994).

A popular stereotype that once existed about very bright children was "early ripe, early rot." A longitudinal study initiated by Terman at Stanford University in 1921 would subsequently expose this belief as myth. Terman and his colleagues identified 1,528 children (with an average age of 11) whose measured intelligence placed them within the top 1% in the country in intellectual functioning.[2] Terman followed these children for the remainder of his own life, taking measures of achievement, physical and social development, books read, character traits, and recreational interests. He conducted interviews with parents, teachers, and the subjects themselves. Some of the findings were published four years after the study had begun (Terman et al., 1925), although other researchers continued to collect and analyze data (Oden, 1968; Sears, 1977; Holahan & Sears, 1995). In general, the Terman studies suggested that gifted children tended to maintain their superior intellectual ability. However, more recent work suggests that there may come a point at which gifted children cease to pursue or exploit their gift. Winner (2000) writes that child prodigies may become "frozen into expertise"; their work has won them public acclaim and it becomes increasingly difficult to break away from their acknowledged expertise to become creative. Also, after having been pushed so hard by family or others to achieve at an early age, gifted children may lose motivation as adults (Winner, 1996).

From the Terman studies, we also know that the gifted tend to have lower mortality rates and be in better physical and mental health than their nongifted counterparts. They tend to hold moderate political and social views, and tend to be successful in educational and vocational pursuits. They commit less crime than the nongifted. This all sounds fine. But there is another side to being gifted—see *Everyday Psychometrics*.

Other Issues

Measured intelligence may vary as a result of factors related to the measurement process. A test author's definition of intelligence, the diligence of the examiner, as well as how much feedback the examiner gives the examinee (Vygotsky, 1978), the amount of previous practice or coaching the examinee has had, and the competence of the person interpreting the test data are just a few of the many factors that may affect measured intelligence.

A factor in measured intelligence that has received quite a bit of attention in recent years is the **Flynn effect.** James R. Flynn, of the department of political studies at the University of Otago in Dunedin, New Zealand, published findings that caused those who study and use intelligence tests in the United States to take notice. In his article entitled "The Mean IQ of Americans: Massive Gains 1932 to 1978," Flynn (1984) presented compelling evidence of what might be termed "intelligence inflation." He found that

---

2. The children followed in the Terman study were humorously referred to as "**Termites.**" One Termite, Lee Cronbach, would himself later earn his place as a luminary in the field of psychometrics. However, as Hirsch (1997) reported, Cronbach believed that serious errors were made in the scoring of the Termites' intelligence test protocols. Cronbach (cited in Hirsch, 1997, p. 214) reflected that "Terman was looking for high IQs and his assistants provided them. . . . Sears [a Stanford colleague of Terman] has found and recalculated my own IQ and it turns out that I have lived my life with an IQ that was 10 points too high."

Being Gifted

Who Is Gifted?

An informal answer to this question might be "one whose performance is consistently remarkable in any positively valued area" (Witty, 1940, p. 516). Criteria for **giftedness** cited in legislation such as PL 95-561 include intellectual ability ("consistently superior"), creative thinking, leadership ability, ability in performing arts, and mechanical or other psychomotor aptitudes. To that list, others have added many other variables ranging from diversity of interests to love of metaphors, abstract ideas, and novelty. The origin of giftedness is a matter of debate but factors such as heredity, atypical brain organization (O'Boyle et al., 1994; Hassler & Gupta, 1993), and environmental influences, including family environment (Gottfried et al., 1994), are frequently cited.

Identifying the Gifted

Tests of intelligence may aid in the identification of members of special populations at all points in the possible range of human abilities—including that group of exceptional people collectively referred to as "the gifted." As you may suspect, exactly who is identified as gifted may sometimes vary as a function of the measuring instrument. Wechsler tests of intelligence are commonly used. They contain subtests that are labeled "Verbal" in nature and subtests that are labeled "Performance." A composite or Full Scale score thought to reflect general intelligence is g, which in some cases has been used to identify the gifted. The practice of identification on the basis of a Wechsler Full Scale score has been questioned because the score obscures superior performance on individual subtests if the record as a whole is not superior. The Full Scale score further obscures a significant discrepancy, if one exists, between the Verbal and Performance scores. Additionally, each of the subtests does not contribute equally to g. In one study that employed gifted students as subjects, Malone et al. (1991) cautioned that their findings might be affected by a **ceiling effect.** That is, some of the test items were not sufficiently challenging—had too low a "ceiling"—to accurately gauge the gifted students' ability; a greater range of items at the high end of the difficulty continuum would have been preferable. Malone et al. (1991, p. 26) cautioned that "the use of the overall IQ score to classify students as gifted, or as a criterion for acceptance into special advanced programs, may contribute to the lack of recognition of the ability of some students."

Identification of the gifted should ideally be made not simply on the basis of an intelligence test but also on the basis of the goals of the program for which the test is being

Anyone who has ever watched the E! *television program,* Mysteries and Scandals, *knows that fame isn't always all that it seems to be. In each episode of that series, host A. J. Benza takes viewers on a journey through what he refers to as the "flip side of Hollywood's walk of fame." The inevitable moral of each story is that a gift can come with a price. Here, after some background about what giftedness is and how it is identified, we consider its price.*

conducted. Thus, for example, if an assessment program is undertaken to identify gifted writers, common sense indicates that a component of the assessment program should be a writing sample taken from the examinee and evaluated by an authority. It is true, however, that the most effective—and most frequently used—instrument for identifying gifted children is an intelligence test. School systems screening for candidates for gifted programs might employ a group test for the sake of economy. A group test frequently employed for this purpose is the Otis-Lennon School Ability Test. To screen for social abilities or aptitudes, tests such as the Differential Aptitude Test or Guilford et al.'s (1974) Structure of Intellect (SOI) test may be administered. Creativity might

(continued)

Being Gifted *(continued)*

be assessed through the use of the SOI, through personality and biographical inventories (Davis, 1989), or through other measures of creative thinking.

Other tools of assessment to identify the gifted include case studies, behavior rating scales, and nominating techniques. A **nominating technique** is a method of peer appraisal in which members of a class, team, work unit, or other type of group are asked to select (or "nominate") people in response to a question or statement. Class members, parents, or teachers might be asked, for example, to answer questions such as "Who has the most leadership ability?" "Who has the most original ideas?" and "Who would you most like to help you with this project?" Although teacher nomination is a widely used method of identifying gifted children, it is not necessarily the most reliable one (French, 1964; Gallagher, 1966; Jacobs, 1970; Tuttle & Becker, 1980). The gifted child may be a misbehaving child in the classroom, and this misbehavior may be due to boredom with the low level of the material being presented. The gifted child may ask questions of or make comments to the teacher that the teacher either doesn't understand or misconstrues as smart aleck in nature. Clark (1988) outlined specific behaviors that gifted children may display in the classroom.

The Pros and Cons of Giftedness

Most people can readily appreciate and list many benefits of being gifted. Depending on the nature of their gifts, gifted children may, for example, read at an age when their nongifted peers are learning the alphabet, do algebra at an age when their nongifted peers are learning addition, or play a musical instrument with expert proficiency at an age when their nongifted peers are struggling with introductory lessons. The gifted child can earn admiration and respect, and

the gifted adult may add to that a certain level of financial freedom.

The downside of being gifted is not as readily apparent. As Plucker and Levy (2001) remind us,

> . . . many talented people are not happy, regardless of whether they become experts in their fields. The literature contains a growing number of studies of underachievers who fail to develop their talents and achieve personal fulfillment. Furthermore, even the happiest, most talented individuals must face considerable personal and professional roadblocks emanating from their talent. The process of achieving professional success and personal happiness and adjustment involves overcoming many common, interrelated challenges. (p. 75)

Plucker and Levy (2001) cited the widely held assumption that the gifted will do just fine as a challenge to be overcome. Other challenges that must frequently be overcome by gifted individuals include depression and feelings of isolation (Jacobsen, 1999), sometimes to the point of suicidal ideation, gestures, or action (Weisse, 1990). Such negative feeling states may arise, at least in part, as a result of cultural pressure to be average or "normal," and even from stigma associated with talent and giftedness (Cross et al., 1991, 1993). Plucker and Levy add that there are self-imposed pressures, which often lead to long hours of study or practice—not without consequence:

> Being talented, or exceptional in almost any other way, entails a number of personal sacrifices. These sacrifices are not easy, especially when the issue is maintaining relationships, having a family, or maintaining a desirable quality of life. We would all like to believe that a person can work hard and develop his or her talent with few ramifications, but this is simply not realistic. (Plucker & Levy, 2001, p. 75)

measured intelligence seems to rise on average, year by year, starting with the year that the test is normed. The rise in measured IQ is not accompanied by any academic dividend, and so it is not thought to be due to any actual rise in "true intelligence." The phenomenon has since been well documented not only in the United States but other countries as well (Flynn, 1988). The exact amount of the rise in IQ will vary as a function of a number of factors, such as how culture-specific items are and whether the measure used is one of fluid or crystallized intelligence (Flynn, 2000).

The existence of a Flynn effect is of more than academic interest. It has real-world implications and consequences. According to Flynn (2000)—who was being sarcastic—

the state of affairs empowers psychologists and educators who examine children for placement in special classes. Flynn advised examiners who want the children they test to be eligible for special services to use the most recently normed version of an intelligence test they can find. Examiners who want the children they test to escape the stigma of any labeling were advised to use "the oldest test they can get away with," which should, according to Flynn, allow at least 10 points leeway in measured intelligence. A discussion of the ethics of Flynn's recommendations could make for a lively class session.

Let's briefly consider some other factors that to a greater or lesser degree may play a role in measured intelligence: personality, gender, family environment, and culture.

Personality   Sensitive to the manifestations of intelligence in *all* human behavior, Alfred Binet had conceived of the study of intelligence as being synonymous with the study of personality. David Wechsler (1958) also believed that all tests of intelligence measure traits of temperament and personality, such as drive, energy level, impulsiveness, persistence, and goal awareness. More contemporary researchers have expressed similar opinions regarding the great overlap between intelligence and personality (Ackerman & Heggestad, 1997).

Longitudinal and cross-sectional studies of children have explored the relationship between various personality characteristics and measured intelligence. Aggressiveness with peers, initiative, high need for achievement, competitive striving, curiosity, self-confidence, and emotional stability are some personality factors that are associated with gains in measured intelligence over time. Passivity, dependence, and maladjustment are some of the factors present in children whose measured intellectual ability has not increased over time.

In discussions of the role of personality in the measured intelligence of infants, the term *temperament* (rather than *personality*) is typically employed. In this context, **temperament** may be defined as the distinguishing manner of the child's observable actions and reactions. There is evidence to suggest that infants differ quite markedly in temperament with respect to a number of dimensions, including vigor of responding, general activity rate, restlessness during sleep, irritability, and "cuddliness" (Chess & Thomas, 1973). An infant's temperament can affect his or her measured intellectual ability in that irritable, restless children who do not enjoy being held have a negative reciprocal influence on their parents—and perhaps on test administrators as well. Parents are less likely to want to pick such children up and spend more time with them engaging in activities that are known to stimulate intellectual development, such as talking to them (White, 1971). One longitudinal study that began with assessment of temperament at age 3 and followed subjects through a personality assessment at age 21 concluded that differences in temperament were associated with differences in health-risk-related behaviors such as dangerous driving habits, alcohol dependence, unsafe sex, and violent crime (Caspi et al., 1997).

Gender   A great deal of research has been conducted on the cognitive differences between males and females. Although some differences have been found consistently (Table 8–2), exactly how significant these differences are has been a matter of controversy. Halpern (1997) attempted to place the issue in perspective: "It is about as meaningful to ask 'Which is the smarter sex?' or 'Which has the better brain?' as it is to ask 'Which has the better genitals?'" (p. 1092). Reasons advanced to account for observed gender differences have been psychosocial (Eccles, 1987) as well as physiological in nature (Hines, 1990; Hines et al., 1992; Shaywitz et al., 1995).

Family environment   To what extent does family environment contribute to measured intelligence? The answer to this relatively straightforward question is complicated, in part

Table 8–2
Cognitive Tests and Tasks That Usually Show Sex Differences

Type of Test/Task	Example
Tasks and tests on which women obtain higher average scores	
Tasks that require rapid access to and use of phonological, semantic, and other information in long-term memory	Verbal fluency—phonological retrieval (Hines, 1990) Synonym generation—meaning retrieval (Halpern & Wright, 1996) Associative memory (Birenbaum, Kelly, & Levi-Keren, 1994) Memory battery—multiple tests (Stumpf & Jackson, 1994) Spelling and anagrams (Stanley, Benbow, Brody, Dauber, & Lupkowski, 1992) Mathematical calculations (Hyde, Fennema, & Lamon, 1990) Memory for spatial location (Eals & Silverman, 1994) Memory for odors (Lehrner, 1993)
Knowledge areas	Literature (Stanley, 1993) Foreign languages (Stanley, 1992)
Production and comprehension of complex prose	Reading comprehension (Hedges & Nowell, 1995; Mullis et al., 1993) Writing (U.S. Department of Education, 1997)
Fine motor tasks	Mirror tracing—novel, complex figures (O'Boyle & Hoff, 1987) Pegboard tasks (Hall & Kimura, 1995) Matching and coding tasks (Gouchie & Kimura, 1991)
Perceptual speed	Multiple speeded tasks (Born, Bleichrodt, & van der Flier, 1987) "Finding As"—an embedded-letters test (Kimura & Hampson, 1994)
Decoding nonverbal communication	(Hall, 1985)
Perceptual thresholds (large, varied literature with multiple modalities)	Touch—lower thresholds (Ippolitov, 1973; Wolff, 1969) Taste—lower thresholds (Nisbett & Gurwitz, 1970) Hearing—males have greater hearing loss with age (Schaie, 1987) Odor—lower thresholds (Koelega & Koster, 1974)
Higher grades in school (all or most subjects)	(Striker, Rock, & Burton, 1993)
Speech articulation	Tongue twisters (Kimura & Hampson, 1994)
Tasks and tests on which men obtain higher average scores	
Tasks that require transformations in visual working memory	Mental rotation (Halpern & Wright, 1996; Voyer, Voyer, & Bryden, 1995) Piaget Water Level Test (Robert & Ohlmann, 1994; Vasta, Knott, & Gaze, 1996)
Tasks that involve moving objects	Dynamic spatiotemporal tasks (Law, Pelligrino, & Hunt, 1993)
Motor tasks that involve aiming	Accuracy in throwing balls or darts (Hall & Kimura, 1995)
Knowledge areas	General knowledge (Feingold, 1993; Wechsler Adult Intelligence Scale [Wechsler, 1991] Geography knowledge (Beller & Gafni, 1996) Math and science knowledge (Stanley, 1993; U.S. Department of Education, 1996)
Tests of fluid reasoning (especially in math and science domains)	Proportional reasoning tasks (Meehan, 1984) Scholastic Assessment Test—Mathematics Graduate Record Examination—Quantitative (Willingham & Cole, 1997) Mechanical Reasoning (Stanley et al., 1992) Verbal analogies (Lim, 1994) Scientific reasoning (Hedges & Nowell, 1995)

Males are also overrepresented at the low-ability end of many distributions, including the following examples: mental retardation (some types; Vandenberg, 1987), majority of attention deficit disorders (American Psychiatric Association, 1994), delayed speech (Hier, Atkins, & Perlo, 1980), dyslexia (even allowing for possible referral bias; DeFries & Gillis, 1993), stuttering (Yairi & Ambrose, 1992), and learning disabilities and emotional disturbances (Henning-Stout & Close-Conoley, 1992). In addition, males are generally more variable (Hedges & Nowell, 1995). References provided are examples of relevant research. The literature is too large to attempt a complete reference list here.

Source: Halpern (1997)

because of the intrusion of nature/nurture, or family environment versus genetic inheritance kinds of issues (Baumrind, 1993; Jackson, 1993; Scarr, 1992, 1993). Yet a new wrinkle in the controversy comes with the assertion that "family environment" begins in the womb and that a "maternal effects model" may more satisfactorily integrate data than a family effects model (Devlin et al., 1997). In this regard, it has been reported that "twins, and especially monozygotic twins, can experience radically different intrauterine environments even though they share the womb at the same time" (B. Price, cited in McGue, 1997, p. 417).

At a minimum, we can begin by stating what we hope is the obvious: Children thrive in a loving home where their safety and welfare are of the utmost concern, and they are given ample opportunity for learning and growth. Beyond that, other environmental factors may affect measured intelligence, such as the presence of resources (Gottfried, 1984), parental use of language (Hart & Risley, 1992), parental expression of concern over achievement (Honzik, 1967), and parental explanation for discipline policies in a warm, democratic home environment (Baldwin et al., 1945; Kent & Davis, 1957; Sontag et al., 1958).

The relationship of maternal age to measured IQ has also been studied. Generally, children of older mothers have higher mean IQ scores (Davis et al., 1972; Record et al., 1969). The effect of maternal age on measured intelligence is often attributed to social class, because younger mothers often tend to be of lower socioeconomic status. However, this positive relationship between maternal age and measured intelligence has also been reported after social class, birth order, and family size were controlled (Davis et al., 1972; Zybert et al., 1978).

Culture Much of our discussion of the relationship between culture and psychological assessment in general applies to any consideration of the role of culture in measured intelligence. A culture provides specific models for ways of thinking, acting, and feeling; it enables people to survive both physically and socially and to master and control the world around them (Chinoy, 1967). Because values may differ radically between cultural and subcultural groups, people from different cultural groups can have radically different views about what constitutes intelligence (Super, 1983; Wober, 1974). Moreover, because different cultural groups value and promote different types of abilities and pursuits, testtakers from different cultural groups can be expected to bring to a test situation differential levels of ability, achievement, and motivation. These differential levels may even find expression in measured perception and perceptual-motor skills, as observed by Serpell (1979) in his study of intelligence of members of a rural community in eastern Zambia. Serpell (1979) tested Zambian and English children on a task involving the reconstruction of models using pencil and paper, clay, or wire. The English children did best on the paper-and-pencil reconstructions, because those were the materials with which they were most familiar. By contrast, the Zambian children did best using wire, because that was the medium with which they were most familiar. Both groups of children did about equally well using clay.

Items on tests of intelligence tend to reflect the culture of the society where such tests are employed. To the extent that a score on such a test reflects the degree to which testtakers have been integrated into the society and the culture, it would be expected that members of subcultures (as well as others who for whatever reason choose not to perceive themselves as identified with the mainstream society) would score lower. In fact, Blacks (Baughman & Dahlstrom, 1968; Dreger & Miller, 1960; Lesser et al., 1965; Shuey, 1966), Hispanics (Gerry, 1973; Holland, 1960; Lesser et al., 1965; Mercer, 1976; Simpson, 1970), and Native Americans (Cundick, 1976) tend to score lower on intelligence tests than Whites or Asians (Flynn, 1991). These findings are controversial on many counts—ranging from the great diversity of the people who are grouped under each of these categories to sampling differences (Zuckerman, 1990). The meaningfulness of such findings can be questioned further when claims of genetic difference are made, because of the complexity of separating out the effects of genes versus the environment. For an authoritative and readable account of the complex issues involved when attempting to make such separations, see Neisser et al. (1996).

Ever since there have been tests of intelligence, developers of such tests have desired an instrument capable of measuring native intelligence. A reading of the work of Alfred Binet suggests that he too sought to develop a measure of intelligence that was as untainted as possible by factors such as prior education and economic advantages. The Binet-Simon test was designed to separate "natural intelligence from instruction" by "disregarding, in so far as possible, the degree of instruction which the subject possesses" (translated by Kite in Binet & Simon, 1908, p. 93). This desire to create what might be termed a **culture-free** intelligence test has resurfaced with various degrees of fervor throughout the history of intelligence testing. The assumption here is that if cultural factors can be controlled, differences between cultural groups will be lessened. A related assumption is that the effect of culture could be controlled through the elimination of verbal items and the exclusive reliance on nonverbal, performance items. Researchers thought that the nonverbal items represented the best available means for determining the cognitive ability of minority group children and adults. On the face of it, such an assumption seems reasonable. However, presuming that the use of nonverbal test items would eliminate the differences between minority and majority groups in measured intelligence has not been found to be true for native-born, English-speaking minority groups. For example, on the average, Blacks tended to score as low on performance as on verbal tests (Cole & Hunter, 1971; McGurk, 1975).

Superior performance on these nonlanguage tests as compared with more conventional IQ tests administered in English has been observed with non-English-speaking or bilingual groups such as Mexican Americans, Puerto Ricans, Chinese, Japanese, and Native American Indians (Jensen, 1980). This difference in performance on the two types of tests (verbal and performance) is attributed more to language effects than to intellectual abilities. It may be speculated that Blacks tend to score low on nonverbal tests for the same reasons that account for lower performance on verbal tests (for example, educational disadvantage). Another problem with exclusive reliance on nonverbal or nonlanguage tests was that they did not have the same high level of predictive validity as did the more verbally loaded tests, primarily because these items do not sample the same psychological processes as do the more verbally loaded, conventional tests of intelligence. Further, most academic courses and business and industrial jobs require at least some verbal facility. It should therefore come as no surprise to find that the nonverbal (performance) items have a low relation to success in the setting the tests were intended to predict for. The idea of developing a truly culture-free test has had great intuitive appeal but has proven to be a practical impossibility. All tests of intelligence, to a greater or lesser degree, reflect the culture in which they were devised and will be used.

The concept of culture loading is used in discussions regarding the magnitude with which cultural influence is reflected in the measured intelligence. **Culture loading** may be defined as the extent to which a test incorporates the vocabulary, concepts, traditions, knowledge, and feelings associated with a particular culture. A test item such as "Name three words for snow" is a highly culture-loaded item—one that draws heavily from the Eskimo culture where many words exist for snow. By contrast, people from Brooklyn would be hard put to come up with more than one word for snow (well, maybe two, if you count *slush*). Soon after it became evident that no test could legitimately be called "culture-free," a number of tests referred to as "culture-fair" began to be published. We

Table 8–3
Ways of Reducing the Culture Loading of Tests

Culture Loaded	Culture Loading Reduced
Paper-and-pencil tasks	Performance tests
Printed instructions	Oral instructions
Oral instructions	Pantomime instructions
No preliminary practice	Preliminary practice items
Reading required	Purely pictorial
Pictorial (objects)	Abstract figural
Written response	Oral response
Separate answer sheet	Answers written on test itself
Language	Nonlanguage
Speed tests	Power tests
Verbal content	Nonverbal content
Specific factual knowledge	Abstract reasoning
Scholastic skills	Nonscholastic skills
Recall of past-learned information	Solving novel problems
Content graded from familiar to rote	All item content highly familiar
Difficulty based on rarity of content	Difficulty based on complexity of relation education

Source: Jensen (1980)

may define **culture-fair** as a test or assessment process that has been designed to minimize the influence of culture with regard to various aspects of the evaluation procedures, such as administration instructions, item content, responses required of testtakers, and interpretations made from the resulting data. Table 8–3 lists techniques that have been used to reduce the culture loading of tests. Note that in contrast to the factor-analytic concept of "factor loading," which can be quantified, the culture loading of a test tends to be more of a subjective, qualitative, non-numerical judgment.

In general, the rationale behind culture-fair test items was to include only those tasks that seemed to reflect experiences, knowledge, and skills common to all different cultures. In addition, all the tasks were designed to be motivating to all groups (Samuda, 1982). An attempt was made to minimize the importance of factors such as verbal skills thought to be responsible for the lower mean scores of various minority groups. Therefore, the culture-fair tests tended to be nonverbal in nature, with directions that were simple, clear, and administered orally by the examiner. The nonverbal tasks typically consisted of assembling, classifying, selecting, or manipulating objects, and drawing or identifying geometric designs. Some sample items from the Cattell Culture Fair Test are illustrated in this chapter's *Close-up.* In general, although the culture loading of culture-fair intelligence tests has been reduced, so has their value as tests of intelligence. Culture-fair tests were found to lack what has been the hallmark of traditional tests of intelligence: predictive validity. And still, minority group members tended to score lower on these tests than did majority group members. Various subcultural characteristics have been presumed to penalize unfairly some minority group members who take intelligence tests that are culturally loaded with American White, middle-class values. Some have argued, for example, that Americans living in urban ghettos share common beliefs and values that are quite different from those of mainstream America. Included among these common beliefs and values, for example, are an inability to delay gratification, a "live for today" orientation, and a reliance on slang in verbal communication. Native Americans also share a common subculture with core values that may negatively influence their measured intelligence. Central to these values is the belief that individuals

Culture-Fair/Culture-Loaded

What types of test items are thought to be "culture-fair"—or at least more culture-fair than other, more culture-loaded items? The items reprinted below from the Culture Fair Test of Intelligence (Cattell, 1940) provide a sample. As you look at them, think about how culture-fair they really are.

Mazes

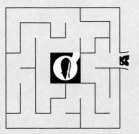

Classification
Pick out the two odd items in each row of figures.

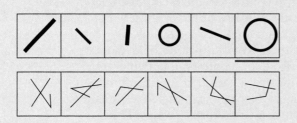

Figure Matrices
Choose from among the six alternatives the one that most logically completes the matrix pattern above it.

Series
Choose one figure from the six on the right that logically continues the series of three figures at the left.

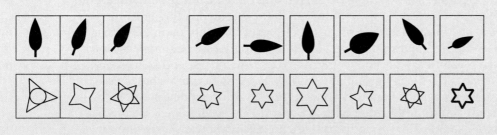

Items from the Culture Fair Test of Intelligence (Cattell, 1940)

In contrast to items designed to be culture-fair, consider the items on the Cultural/Regional Uppercrust Savvy Test (CRUST; Herlihy, 1977). This tongue-in-cheek test of intelligence was intentionally designed for illustrative purposes to be culture-loaded. Members of society's upper crust should have no problem at all achieving a perfect score.

1. When you are "posted" at the country club, (a) you ride horses with skill, (b) you are elected to the governance board, (c) you are publicly announced as not having paid your dues, (d) a table is reserved for you in the dining room, whether you use it or not.

2. An arabesque in ballet is (a) an intricate leap, (b) a posture in which the dancer stands on one leg, the other extended backward, (c) a series of steps performed by a male and a female dancer, (d) a bow similar to a curtsy.

3. The Blue Book is (a) the income tax guidelines, (b) a guide to pricing used cars, (c) a booklet used for writing essay exams, (d) a social register listing 400 prominent families.

4. Brookline is located (a) in suburban Boston, (b) on Cape Cod, (c) between Miami Beach and Fort Lauderdale, (d) on the north shore of Chicago.

5. Beef Wellington is (a) the king's cut of roast beef, (b) tenderloin in a pastry crust lined with pâté, (c) a hors d'oeuvre flavored with sherry, (d) roast beef with béarnaise sauce.

6. Choate is (a) a gelded colt used in fox hunts, (b) a prep school, (c) an imported brandy, (d) the curator of the Metropolitan Museum of Art.

7. The most formal dress for men is (a) white tie, (b) black tie, (c) tuxedo, (d) décolletage.

8. *The Stranger* is (a) the . . . family who moved into the neighborhood, (b) Howard Hughes, (c) a book by Camus, (d) an elegant restaurant in San Francisco.

9. Waterford is (a) a health spa for the hep set, (b) a "fat farm," (c) hand-cut crystal from Ireland, (d) the Rockefeller family estate in upper New York.

10. Dining "alfresco" means (a) by candlelight, (b) a buffet supper, (c) at a sidewalk cafe, (d) outdoors.

According to Herlihy (1977), the answers keyed correct are 1(c), 2(b), 3(d), 4(a), 5(b), 6(b), 7(a), 8(c), 9(c), 10(d).

should be judged with respect to their relative contribution to the group rather than individual accomplishments. Native Americans also value their relatively unhurried and present-time-oriented lifestyle (Foerster & Little Soldier, 1974).

Frustrated by their seeming inability to develop culture-fair equivalents of traditional intelligence tests, some test developers attempted to develop equivalents of traditional intelligence tests that were culture-specific. Expressly developed for members of a particular cultural group or subculture, such tests were thought to be able to yield a more valid measure of mental development. One culture-specific intelligence test developed expressly for use with Blacks was the Black Intelligence Test of Cultural Homogeneity (Williams, 1975), a 100-item multiple-choice test containing items such as the following:[3]

1. *Mother's Day* means
    a. Black independence day.
    b. a day when mothers are honored.
    c. a day the welfare checks come in.
    d. every first Sunday in church.

2. *Blood* means
    a. a vampire.
    b. a dependent individual.
    c. an injured person.
    d. a brother of color.

3. The following are popular brand names. Which one does not belong?
    a. Murray's
    b. Dixie Peach
    c. Royal Crown
    d. Preparation H

As you read the items above, you may be asking yourself, "Is this really an intelligence test? Should I be taking this seriously?" If you were thinking such questions, you are in good company; many psychologists probably asked themselves the same questions. In fact, a kind of parody of the BITCH (the acronym for the test) was published in the May 1974 issue of *Psychology Today* (p. 101), and it was called the "S.O.B. (Son of the Original BITCH) Test." However, the Williams (1975) test was purported to be a genuine culture-specific test of intelligence, one that was standardized on 100 Black high school students in the St. Louis area. Williams was awarded $153,000 by the National Institute of Mental Health to develop the BITCH.

In what was probably one of the few published studies designed to explore the test's validity, the Wechsler Adult Intelligence Scale (WAIS) and the BITCH were both administered to Black ($n = 17$) and White ($n = 116$) applicants for a job with the Portland, Oregon, police department. The Black subjects performed much better on the test than did the White subjects with a mean score that exceeded the White mean score by 2.83 standard deviations. The White mean IQ as measured by the WAIS exceeded the Black mean IQ by about 1.5 standard deviations. None of the correlations between the BITCH score and any of the following variables for either the Black or the White testtakers dif-

---

3. The answers keyed correct are as follows: 1(c), 2(d), and 3(d).

fered significantly from zero: WAIS Verbal IQ, WAIS Performance IQ, WAIS Full Scale IQ, and years of education. It was also noteworthy that even though the Black sample in this study had an average of more than 2½ years of college education, and even though their overall mean on the WAIS was about 20 points higher than Blacks in general, their scores on the BITCH fell below the average of the standardization sample (high school pupils ranging in age from 16 to 18). What, then, is the BITCH measuring? The study authors, Matarazzo and Wiens (1977), concluded that the test was measuring "street wiseness," though Jensen (1980, p. 681) questioned whether it is even a psychometrically good test of Black slang and "street wiseness."

Although many of the culture-specific tests did yield higher mean scores for the minority group they were specifically designed for use with, they lacked predictive validity and provided little useful and practical information.[4] The knowledge that is required to score high on all of the culture-specific and culture-reduced tests has not been seen as relevant for educational purposes within our pluralistic society. Such tests have low predictive validity for the criterion of success in academic as well as vocational settings.

At various phases in the life history of an intelligence test—including its development, administration, and interpretation—a number of approaches to reduce cultural bias may be employed. Panels of experts may evaluate the potential bias inherent in a newly developed test, and those items judged to be biased may be eliminated. The test may be devised so that relatively few verbal instructions are needed to administer it or provide for demonstrations of how to respond to what is required—all in an effort to minimize any possible language bias. A tryout or pilot testing with ethnically mixed samples of testtakers may be undertaken. If differences in scores emerge solely as a function of ethnic group membership, the individual items may be studied further for possible bias.

Major tests of intelligence have undergone a great deal of scrutiny for bias in many investigations—ranging from study of individual items to study of the validity of the predictions that can be made from their administration—and it has generally been concluded that these tests are relatively free of any systematic bias. However, even if an individual test is free of bias, it is important to remember that there are other potential sources of bias ranging from the criterion for referral for assessment, to the conduct of the assessment, to the scoring of items (particularly those items that are somewhat subjective), and, finally, to the interpretation of the findings.

A Perspective

So many decades after the publication of the 1921 Symposium, professionals still debate the nature of intelligence and how it should be measured (Sternberg & Detterman, 1986). In the wake of the controversial book, *The Bell Curve*,[5] the American Psychological Association commissioned a panel to write a report on intelligence that would carry

---

4. Perhaps the most psychometrically sound of the instruments designed especially for use with Black subjects was the Listening Comprehension Test (Carver, 1968–1969, 1969; Orr & Graham, 1968). On this test, however, Blacks tended to score lower than Whites even when the groups were matched with respect to socioeconomic status.

5. See Cohen (2002) for a discussion of *The Bell Curve*.

psychology's official imprimatur. The panel's report reflected wide disagreement with regard to the definition of intelligence but noted that "Such disagreements are not cause for dismay. Scientific research rarely begins with fully agreed definitions, though it may eventually lead to them" (Neisser et al., 1996, p. 77). The panel apparently ignored the fact that, in terms of the relative youth of psychology as a discipline (in contrast to, for example, geology, archaeology, or physics), research on intelligence may have only just begun. The panel also overlooked a number of newer approaches to intelligence, as well as some controversial evidence and viewpoints regarding differences between groups in measured intelligence (Frumkin, 1997; Lynn, 1997; Reed, 1997; Velden, 1997).

There has been no shortage of controversy when it comes to the subject of intelligence, beginning with how that word is defined. A trend in recent years has been to be much more liberal when defining and allowing for behavior presumed to be indicative of intelligence in the real world (Detterman, 1986). So, for example, we read discussions of "managerial intelligence" by no less an authority than Robert Sternberg (1997). Such work also reflects a trend toward context orientation in terms of defining intelligence; there seems to be more interest in specific types of intelligence as opposed to g. Still, disagreement over "the issue of the one versus the many" (Sternberg & Berg, 1986, p. 157) shows no sign of abatement.

Another issue that is not going to go away has to do with group differences in measured intelligence. Although human beings do certainly differ in size, shape, and color—and it is therefore reasonable to consider that there is also a physical base for differences in intellectual ability—discerning where and how nature can be differentiated from nurture is a laudable academic pursuit. Still, such differentiation remains a very complex business—one that is potentially fraught with social, political, and even legal consequences, some intended, some not. Claims about group differences can and have been used as political and social tools to oppress religious, ethnic, or other minority group members. This is most unfortunate, because as Jensen (1980) observed, variance attributable to group differences is far less than variance attributable to individual differences. As Neisser et al. (1996) said, it is essential in a democratic society that each individual be evaluated as an individual: "What matters for the next person you meet (to the extent that test scores matter at all) is that person's own particular score, not the mean of some reference group to which he or she happens to belong" (p. 90).

The relationship between intelligence and a wide range of social outcomes has been well documented. Scores on intelligence tests, especially when used with other indicators, have value in predicting outcomes such as school performance, years of education, even social status and income. Measured intelligence is negatively correlated with socially undesirable outcomes such as juvenile crime (Moffitt et al., 1981). For these and related reasons, we would do well to concentrate research attention on the environmental end of the heredity versus environment spectrum. We need to find ways to effectively boost measured intelligence through environmental interventions, the better to engender hope and optimism. In the latter context, consider that, "If social status is influenced by IQ, which is in turn substantially inherited, then social standing will, in part, be a function of one's genetic endowment. Hard work may be no guarantee of success, unless one has received a lucky draw in the genetic lottery" (McGue, 1997, p. 417).

Unfairly maligned by some and unduly worshiped by others, intelligence has endured, and will continue to endure, as a key construct in psychology and psychological assessment. For this reason, professionals who administer intelligence tests have a great responsibility, one in which thorough preparation is a necessity. That being said, and with this entire chapter as background, let's take a closer look at some widely used tests of intelligence.

Self-Assessment

Test your understanding of elements of this chapter by seeing if you can explain each of the following terms, expressions, and abbreviations:

accommodation

alerting response

assimilation

ceiling effect

CHC theory

cross-battery assessment

crystallized intelligence

culture-fair

culture-free

culture loading

emotional intelligence

factor-analytic theories of intelligence

fluid intelligence

Flynn effect

g

Gf-Gc

giftedness

hierarchical model

information-processing theories of intelligence

intelligence

interactionism

interpersonal intelligence

intrapersonal intelligence

maintained abilities

mental age

nominating technique

orienting response

parallel processing

PASS

predeterminism

preformationism

psychoeducational assessment

s

schema

schemata

sequential processing

simultaneous processing

structure of intellect model

successive processing

temperament

"Termites"

three-stratum theory of cognitive abilities

two-factor theory of intelligence

vulnerable abilities

9

Tests of Intelligence

Atest developer's conception of intelligence is, in a sense, the starting point and ending point in the development of a test of intelligence. If, for example, the test developer conceives of intelligence in terms of mental structures, the test will be designed to shed light on those structures. If the test developer conceives of intelligence in terms of processes, the test will be designed to shed light on those processes. Beginning with initial considerations regarding item content and item format, continuing with considerations related to scoring and interpretation, and later with plans for revising the test, the conception of intelligence at the test's foundation remains a guiding force—one that is reflected in decisions regarding almost every aspect of the test, not only its final form, but the uses to which the test will be put. The test manual may contain recommendations regarding the types of intervention, remediation, or other action deemed appropriate on the basis of an interpretation of the findings.

Many different intelligence tests exist. From the standpoint of a test user, the appeal of a particular test of intelligence derives from several variables. The theory of intelligence on which the test is based and the ease with which the test can be administered, scored, and interpreted for a particular purpose may be important considerations. Other "psychometric facts of life" may figure prominently in a test selection decision. For example, the adequacy and appropriateness of the norms are important, as is the acceptability of the published reliability and validity indices.

Some tests of intelligence were constructed on the basis of a theory. For example, Louis L. Thurstone conceived of intelligence as being composed of "primary mental abilities" or PMAs. Thurstone (1938) developed and published the Primary Mental Abilities test, which consisted of separate tests, each designed to measure one PMA: verbal meaning, perceptual speed, reasoning, number facility, rote memory, word fluency, and spatial relations. Although the test was not widely used, this early model of multiple abilities inspired other theorists and test developers to explore various components of intelligence, as well as ways to measure them.

An intelligence test may be developed on the basis of one theory, but then be reconceptualized in terms of another theory. For example, much has been written about a theory of intelligence that contains features of the Cattell-Horn model and the Carroll three-stratum model; it is becoming known as the Cattell-Horn-Carroll (CHC) theory. As receptivity to the Cattell-Horn-Carroll model has grown, books and manuals illustrating how this model can be used to supplement findings from Binet, Wechsler, and other intelligence tests have been published. Moreover, the tests that need to be administered from various test batteries in order to tap CHC abilities are specified.

Figure 9–1
Who Wants to Name the Cognitive Abilities Being Tapped?

If you have ever watched Who Wants to Be a Millionaire? *you probably sense that success on the show depends on a number of factors. But what are those factors?*

In this chapter, we will look at a sampling of individual and group tests of intelligence.[1] Before doing so, as a kind of warm-up exercise, consider the cognitive abilities tapped by a television game show that, at least in the eyes of many members of the general public, may well be a vehicle for identifying (and rewarding) highly intelligent people. Prospective contestants for *Who Wants to Be a Millionaire?* (Figure 9–1) are pre-screened by means of a telephone quiz in which general knowledge and speed are key factors. From the pool of people who are successful in the telephone screening, ten are selected (by lottery) for appearance on stage. These contestants are posed a time-limited, "fastest finger question" in which they must put four alternative responses in the correct order by means of keypad entry. The contestant who successfully does this the fastest advances to the "hot seat," where he or she is asked a series of multiple-choice questions deemed to be successively more difficult in nature. There is no time limit to respond to these questions. However, one wrong answer and it's curtains for the contestant in the hot seat. The contestant has three "lifelines" or aids to help answer the questions, each of which may be used only once. The "50/50" lifeline reduces the alternative responses from four to two. The "Ask the Audience" lifeline polls the studio audience for their opinion as to the correct answer. And the "Phone a Friend" lifeline allows the contestant to speak to one friend for 30 seconds (from a list of ten friends given to the show staff in advance of the taping).

---

1. As attested to by volumes such as *Tests in Print,* thousands of published tests exist. In a book such as this, we can provide only a brief description of a very small sample of tests in various categories for illustrative purposes. Readers are advised not to draw any conclusions about the value of any particular test from either its inclusion or omission in this textbook.

From the description above, as well as your own knowledge, if any, of this television program, how would you describe the way its creators might envision "intelligence"? In your answer, make sure to consider all of the myriad abilities related to the screening task, the fastest-finger task, and each of the lifelines. If you were asked to develop a test of intelligence based on this vision, what do you think that test would be like? What use would you foresee as appropriate—or inappropriate—for the findings from such a test?

In the pre-television days of the early twentieth century, Alfred Binet was charged with a very serious responsibility—developing a test to screen for developmentally disabled children in the Paris schools. Binet collaborated with Theodosius Simon to create the world's first formal test of intelligence in 1905. Adaptations and translations of Binet's work soon appeared in many countries throughout the world. The original Binet-Simon Scale was in use in the United States as early as 1908 (Goddard, 1908, 1910). By 1912 a modified version that extended the age range of the test downward to 3 months had been published (Kuhlmann, 1912). However, it was the work of Lewis Madison Terman at Stanford University that culminated in the ancestor of what we know now as the Stanford-Binet Intelligence Scale.

The Stanford-Binet Intelligence Scale

Although the first edition of the Stanford-Binet was certainly not without major flaws (such as the lack of representativeness of the standardization sample), it also contained some important innovations. It was the first published intelligence test to provide organized and detailed administration and scoring instructions. Another milestone was that it was the first American test to employ the concept of IQ. And it was also the first test to introduce the concept of an alternate item: an item to be used only under certain conditions, for instance, if the regular item had not been administered properly by the examiner.

In 1926, Terman began a collaboration with a Stanford colleague, Maude Merrill, in a project to revise the test—a project that would take 11 years to complete. Innovations in the 1937 scale included the development of two equivalent forms, labeled "L" and, "M," and new types of tasks for use with preschool-level and adult-level testtakers.[2] In addition, the manual for this test contained many scoring examples to aid the examiner. Although the test authors went to then-unprecedented lengths in attempting to achieve an adequate standardization sample (Flanagan, 1938) and the test was praised for its technical achievement in the areas of validity and especially reliability, a serious criticism of the test was, again, the lack of representativeness of the sample.

Another revision of the Stanford-Binet was well under way at the time of Terman's death at age 79 in 1956. The third edition of the Stanford-Binet, published in 1960, consisted of only a single form (labeled "L-M") composed of the items considered to be the best from the two forms of the 1937 test with no new items added to the test. A major innovation, however, in the 1960 test manual was the use of the deviation IQ tables in place of the ratio IQ tables. Earlier versions of the Stanford-Binet had employed the ratio IQ. The ratio IQ uses the concept of the mental age, which is the age level at which an individual appears to be functioning intellectually. The **ratio IQ** is the ratio of the testtaker's

---

2. Why the letters "L" and "M" for the two forms of the Stanford-Binet? What do these letters stand for? They are the first letters in the first names of the test's authors, Lewis and Maude. L. M. Terman left no clue as to what initials would have been used if his coauthor's name had not begun with the letter "M".

mental age divided by his or her chronological age, multiplied by 100 to eliminate decimals:

$$\text{ratio IQ} = \frac{\text{mental age}}{\text{chronological age}} \times 100$$

If the child's mental age was equal to his or her chronological age, the IQ would equal 100. In place of the ratio IQ, the deviation IQ was used beginning with the third edition of the Stanford-Binet. The deviation IQ reflects a comparison of the performance of the individual with the performance of others of the same age in the standardization sample. Essentially, test performance is converted into a standard score with a mean of 100 and a standard deviation of 16. If an individual performs at the same level as the average person of the same age, the deviation IQ is 100. If performance is a standard deviation above the mean for the examinee's age group, the deviation IQ is 116.

The Stanford-Binet was revised again in 1972, and, as with previous revisions, the quality of the standardization sample was criticized. Specifically, the manual was vague about the number of minority individuals in the standardization sample, stating only that a "substantial portion" of Black and Spanish-surnamed individuals was included. The 1972 norms may also have overrepresented the West and large, urban communities (Waddell, 1980).

The Stanford-Binet: Fourth Edition

The fourth edition of the Stanford-Binet Intelligence Scale (SB:FE; Thorndike et al., 1986) represented a significant departure from previous versions of the Stanford-Binet in theoretical organization, test organization, test administration, test scoring, and test interpretation. Previously, different items were grouped by age and the test was referred to as an **age scale.** The SB:FE is a point scale. In contrast to an age scale, a **point scale** is a test organized into subtests by category of item, not by age at which most testtakers are presumed capable of responding in the way keyed correct. The SB:FE contains 15 separate subtests yielding scores in the following four areas of cognitive ability: Verbal Reasoning, Abstract/Visual Reasoning, Quantitative Reasoning, and Short-Term Memory (Table 9–1). The rationale for the change was that clinically useful diagnostic information could more easily be obtained from such a format. Nine of the subtests were based on the types of items that appeared in previous versions of the test, and six of the subtests are new. In addition to scores in the four general areas listed, a test composite—formerly described as a deviation IQ score—may also be obtained. In general, a **test composite** may be defined as a test score or index derived from the combination of, and/or mathematical transformation of, one or more test scores. In the case of the SB:FE, the test composite is an index of general mental ability.

Unlike prior editions of the Binet test, the SB:FE contained an explicit exposition by the test's authors of the theoretical model of intelligence that guided the revision. Briefly, the model is a hierarchical one with general intelligence, or g, at the top of the hierarchy. The term "general mental ability" is wide-ranging but encompasses, among other things, (1) information-processing abilities, (2) planning and organizing abilities, and (3) reasoning and adaptation skills. Included in the second level of the theoretical hierarchy are (1) crystallized abilities (also referred to as "scholastic" or "academic abilities"), (2) fluid-analytic abilities (that is, nonlanguage abilities that relate to variables such as spatial skills and originality in problem solving), and (3) short-term memory. At the third level are the following areas: verbal reasoning, abstract/visual reasoning, and quantitative reasoning. These three areas, along with short-term memory at the second level of the hierarchy, make up what are called the "area scores" of the test. This theoretical model is based on the Cattell-Horn (1966) model of intelligence.

Table 9–1

The Subtests of the Stanford-Binet Intelligence Scale: Fourth Edition (SB:FE)

Subtest	Description
Verbal Reasoning	
Vocabulary	Consists of 14 picture vocabulary items (in which the subject's task is to identify the pictured object) and 32 items that are words the subject defines—words that may be presented visually as well as orally.
Comprehension	Items range in difficulty from identifying parts of the body to questions regarding social judgment, reasoning, and evaluation (such as "Why should people be quiet in a hospital?"). Again, items may be both read to the examinee and presented visually.
Absurdities	The examinee's task on these items is to identify what is wrong or silly about a picture. This type of item taps the subject's visual-analysis skills.
Verbal Relations	Each of these items presents the examinee with four words, and it is the examinee's task to state what it is that is similar about the first three things but different about the fourth. An example: "Newspaper. Magazine. Book. But not television." A correct response here would indicate that newspapers, magazines, and books are all read but television is not.
Abstract/Visual Reasoning	
Pattern Analysis	Exactly which items will be administered from this subtest will vary with the entry level of the examinee; the timed tasks range from placing cutout forms into a form-board to reproducing complex designs with blocks.
Copying	The examinee's task here is to copy a design. At the earliest level, the design is made from blocks. Subsequently, the designs are copied directly into a record booklet.
Matrices	Here the examinee's task is to solve increasingly difficult matrices that use geometric symbols, letters, and common objects as stimuli. Items on this nonverbal test are presented in a multiple-choice format, and the items are deemed to be especially useful in gauging the general mental ability of non-English-speaking people.
Paper Folding and Cutting	These multiple-choice items present the examinee with the task of identifying how a folded and cut piece of paper will look when unfolded.
Quantitative Reasoning	
Quantitative Subtest	Items on this subtest range from simple counting to knowledge of various arithmetic concepts and operations.
Number Series	The examinee's task is to complete a number sentence with the next logical number in the sequence. For example, consider the following sequence of numbers and determine which two numbers should come next: 1 2 4 _____. The answer is 8 and 16 and the reasoning is that each number in the sequence has been added to itself to yield the next number ($1 + 1 = 2$; $2 + 2 = 4$; $4 + 4 = 8$; $8 + 8 = 16$; and so on).
Equation Building	The examinee's task here is to rearrange a scrambled arithmetic equation so that it makes sense. As an example, rearrange the numbers and/or signs in the following equation to make a true number sentence: $5 + 12 = 7$. An acceptable rearrangement would be: $5 + 7 = 12$.
Short-Term Memory	
Bead Memory	Examinees study a picture of a bead sequence for five seconds and then must replicate the sequence using actual beads. The beads come in three different colors and four different shapes.
Memory for Sentences	The examiner orally presents a sentence and the examinee's task is to repeat it. The length of the sentence may vary from 2 to 22 words depending on the level of the examinee.
Memory for Digits	The examiner orally presents sequences of digits, forward and backward, and it is the examinee's task to repeat the digits presented in the same order.
Memory for Objects	Familiar objects are presented at one-second intervals and the examinee's task is to recall the presentation in the correct order.

Items from the previous edition of the test that were deemed to be outdated or biased or weakly correlated with a particular area of ability the item was supposed to tap were dropped. Items were balanced for gender, ethnic, racial, and disabled representation. Pictures of children representing various ethnic appearances, a child in a wheelchair, and related modifications were made in the test materials. The test's authors were assisted in the editorial process by a panel of minority-member psychologists who reviewed the materials and oversaw revisions where necessary. The word *brunette,* for example, was eliminated from the vocabulary test because of its lack of saliency to Black children.

The standardization sample   The standardization sample consisted of 5,013 subjects ranging in age from 2 years through 23 years, 11 months. The sample was stratified with respect to the following variables based on the 1980 U.S. census data: geographical region, community size, race/ethnic group, gender, parental occupation, and parental education. In approximating the population of the United States in the sample, Blacks were somewhat overrepresented and Whites were somewhat underrepresented. There was also an overrepresentation of families from higher-socioeconomic-status homes (43.1% of the sample versus 19.0% of the United States population). As a correction, the norms were weighted. This meant, for example, that a subject from a more advantaged background was counted as a fraction of a case in the construction of the norms but a subject from a less advantaged background was counted as more than one case. An assumption inherent in such a weighting process is that the examinees in the sample are indeed representative of the entire population (Glutting, 1989).

Treating the 18- to 23-year age range as a single group, rather than developing separate norms for different ages within this range, is another norm-related concern (Kaufman, 1990). Test performance may change enough between 18 and 23 years of age to warrant different norms for different ages within this range (Wechsler, 1981).

Psychometric properties   Thorndike, Hagen, and Sattler (1986b) reported Kuder-Richardson (KR-20) internal consistency measures of reliability, and test-retest measures of stability. The median reliabilities for all the tests with the exception of the Memory for Objects subtests were in the .80s to .90s range. The test composite has an internal consistency reliability of .95 to .99. No inter-scorer reliability estimates were reported.

A number of studies have examined the criterion validity of the SB:FE when used with normal subjects (Thorndike & Scott, 1986), and the validity coefficients have generally been acceptable. Criterion validity for the test when used with exceptional test-takers has also been established (Thorndike et al., 1986b). One independent study of developmentally delayed children found that SB:FE scores correlated well with measures of adaptive behavior (.67) and nonverbal intelligence (.78) that are frequently used with exceptional children (Atkinson et al., 1992). Reviewing the literature on the SB:FE's criterion-related validity, Laurent, Swerdlik, and Ryburn (1992) reported a median validity coefficient of .70, with a range from .21 to .91, depending on the range of abilities represented in the specific study and the criterion instrument used for comparison. The correlation of .21 was from a gifted sample, which would have a restricted range of intelligence test scores, thus lowering the correlation.

The construct validity of the SB:FE has been explored by means of factor analysis (Keith et al., 1988; Kline, 1989; Sattler, 1988; Thorndike et al., 1986b). Construct validity is supported by the identification of factors reflecting the hierarchical model of intelligence the test was designed to reflect. Consistent with the theoretical model, factor analyses of data for all age groups indicate that a general cognitive ability factor, or *g*, underlies test scores. A verbal factor, variously labeled "verbal comprehension," "verbal reasoning," or simply "verbal," has been identified by all researchers at all age levels. Factor structures that most clearly support the hierarchical model of intelligence were those obtained for the older age groups by Thorndike et al. (1986b) and Keith et al. (1988). With some exceptions, then, the research seems to support the SB:FE's four-factor model of intelligence, though not for testtakers under 6 years of age.

Test administration   Developers of intelligence tests, and particularly developers of intelligence tests designed for use with children, have traditionally been sensitive to the need for adaptive testing. **Adaptive testing** is testing that is individually tailored to the testtaker. Other terms used to refer to adaptive testing include **tailored testing, sequential testing, branched testing,** and **response-contingent testing.** As employed in intelligence tests, adaptive testing might pose a question in the middle range of difficulty. If the testtaker responds correctly to the item, an item of greater difficulty is posed next. If the testtaker responds incorrectly to the item, an item of lesser difficulty is posed. Adaptive testing is in essence designed "to mimic automatically what a wise examiner would do" (Wainer, 1990, p. 10). Adaptive testing helps ensure that the early test or subtest items will not be so difficult as to frustrate the testtaker, and not be so easy as to lull the testtaker into a false sense of security or a state of mind in which the task will not be taken seriously enough. Three other advantages of beginning an intelligence test or subtest at an optimal level of difficulty are these: (1) It allows the test user to collect the maximum amount of information in the minimum amount of time, (2) it facilitates rapport, and (3) it minimizes the potential for examinee fatigue as a result of being administered an overabundance of items.

After the examiner has established a rapport with the testtaker, the examination formally begins with an item from the Vocabulary subtest. The level of the item employed at the outset is determined by the examinee's chronological age, though the level of subsequent items will be based on the testtaker's performance; the highest level of the Vocabulary subtest wherein the examinee passes two consecutive items is the level at which further testing will begin. In this context, the Vocabulary subtest is termed the **routing test,** because it is used to direct or route the examinee to a particular level of questions. A purpose of the routing test, then, is to route the child to test items that have a high probability of being at an optimal level of difficulty. Vocabulary was selected as the routing test primarily because general word knowledge is highly correlated with overall intellectual ability.

Once the examinee has passed four items at two consecutive levels, a **basal** (base) **level** is said to have been established. After the examinee has failed three out of four or four out of four items at two consecutive levels, a **ceiling level** is said to have been reached and testing is discontinued. *The Examiner's Handbook: An Expanded Guide for Fourth Edition Users* (Delaney & Hopkins, 1987) elaborates on the administration and scoring procedures for each subtest and provides suggestions for administering the subtests to special populations.

Scoring and interpretation   A *Guide for Administering and Scoring the Fourth Edition* (Thorndike et al., 1986a) contains explicit directions for administering, scoring, and interpreting the test, as well as numerous examples of correct and incorrect responses useful in the scoring of individual items. Each item is scored either correct (1 point) or incorrect (0 points). Scores on the individual items of the various subtests are tallied to yield raw scores on each of the various subtests. The scorer then employs tables found in the manual to convert each of the subtest scores into a standard score. From these standard scores, a composite score as well as scores in each of the four general areas tested may be derived.

In addition to formal scoring, the occasion of an individually administered test affords the examiner an opportunity for behavioral observation; the way the examinee copes with frustration, how the examinee reacts to items considered very easy, the amount of support the examinee seems to require, the general approach to the task, how anxious, fatigued, cooperative, distractable, or compulsive the examinee appears to be—these are the types of behavioral observations that will supplement formal scores.

Information on test interpretation can be found in the test manual as well as in supplementary sources such as Delaney and Hopkins (1987), Sattler (1988), and Swerdlik and Dornback (1988). Delaney and Hopkins (1987) focus on the abilities presumed to underlie test performance. They point out, for example, that verbal expression underlies performance on the Vocabulary, Comprehension, Absurdities, and Verbal Relations subtests. Swerdlik and Dornback (1988) provide specific strategies for using SB:FE data in the classroom. On the basis of his own factor-analytic research, Sattler (1988) offered an alternative method of combining subtest data to yield composite test scores.

An evaluation   The SB:FE is a reliable and valid measure of overall general ability, including general reasoning and social judgment skills (Laurent et al., 1992). Strengths of the test include the large size of its standardization sample and the efforts of the publisher to eliminate problems of bias and discrimination in test items. The adaptive testing format is another plus, because it tends to minimize the number of test items that must be administered.

Although undeniably a strength of the test because of its sheer size, the sample used for standardization purposes may also be criticized. Children from the upper social class were overrepresented, as were children with college-educated parents. Norms were weighted in an effort to correct for the overrepresentations, but the full effect of the imbalance on scoring and interpreting data is open to question. Factor-analytic studies have not supported the hypothesized hierarchical factor structure of the test across all age levels. No inter-scorer reliability estimates are provided in the manual. KR-20 estimates of inter-item consistency are provided, but those estimates may be inflated. The estimates are based on the assumption that all items more difficult than a series of items failed by the testtaker would also be failed.[3] Another problem has to do with the test kit, which now contains only pictures of certain objects (such as a spoon or a thimble) instead of, as in previous editions, the actual objects. This economy may diminish the utility of the test for examinees who lack satisfactory visual representation skills and examinees of limited intellectual ability.

The Stanford-Binet has been a mainstay of assessors for decades, with traditionally good prediction rates of academic success at early age levels (Kaufman, 1973b) and psychometrically sound estimates of adult reasoning and judgment (Janzen, 1981). Yet recent years have witnessed a decline in the test's usage. One possible reason may be that it is difficult to learn to administer as compared to Wechsler tests. Whatever the reason, the publisher of this test is, at this writing in 2001, hard at work developing the fifth edition (SB5). Should the SB5 be published before the next edition of this text is published, it will be a useful exercise to locate and read published reviews of the test. For now, let's move on to a consideration of what is sure to remain a strong competitor in the marketplace of intelligence tests—the Wechsler tests.

---

3. Experienced clinicians who have had occasion to test the limits of an examinee will tell you that this assumption is not always correct. **Testing the limits** is a procedure that entails the administration of test items beyond the level at which the test manual dictates discontinuance. The procedure may be employed when an examiner has reason to believe that an examinee can respond correctly to items at the higher level. On a standardized ability test such as the SB:FE, the discontinue guidelines must be respected, at least in terms of scoring. Testtakers do not earn formal credit for passing the more difficult items. Rather, the examiner would simply note on the protocol that testing of the limits was conducted with regard to a particular subtest, and then record the findings.

The Wechsler Tests

David Wechsler designed a series of individually administered intelligence tests to assess the intellectual abilities of people from preschool through adulthood. In their current revisions, the three Wechsler intelligence tests are the Wechsler Adult Intelligence Scale-Third Edition (WAIS-III) for ages 16 through 89, the Wechsler Intelligence Scale for Children-Third Edition (WISC-III) for ages 6 through 16 years, and the Wechsler Preschool and Primary Scale of Intelligence-Revised (WPPSI-R), for ages 3 years to 7 years, 3 months. The tests are all similar in structure, with each containing a verbal and performance scale (Tables 9–2 and 9–3).

Although Wechsler tests are relatively easy to administer, administration errors can and do occur (Slate et al., 1993). Many of the items, especially for the younger testtakers, call for the examiner to demonstrate what is required. For such demonstrations, as well as for judgment in scoring responses and other facets of the test administration, thorough, supervised training in test administration is a must. For each test, the manual contains clear and explicit directions for administering the subtests, as well as a number of standard prompts for dealing with a variety of questions, comments, or other contingencies. The administration of Verbal and Performance subtests are alternated; first a Verbal subtest might be given, followed by a Performance subtest, followed by a Verbal subtest, and so forth. Each subtest has its own beginning point. For young children and adolescents, the testtaker's age is typically used to determine the starting point. The stopping point in a subtest occurs when the testtaker has either passed the last item in the subtest or has failed a certain prescribed number of items consecutively. Because there is so much overlap in subtests across the different tests, the examiner trained to administer one Wechsler test will typically have little difficulty in mastering another.

Table 9–2
The Wechsler Tests at a Glance

	WPPSI-R	WISC-III	WAIS-III
Verbal Scales			
Information	X	X	X
Comprehension	X	X	X
Similarities	X	X	X
Arithmetic	X	X	X
Vocabulary	X	X	X
Digit Span*	—	X[†]	X
Sentences	X	—	—
Letter-Number Sequencing	—	—	X[‡]
Performance Scales			
Picture Completion	X	X	X
Picture Arrangement	—	X	X
Block Design	X	X	X
Object Assembly	X	X	X[‡]
Coding[§]	—	X	—
Animal Pegs	X	—	—
Mazes	X	X[†]	—
Geometric Design	X	—	—
Symbol Search	—	X[†]	X[‡]
Matrix Reasoning	—	—	X
Digit Symbol	—	—	X

*The WPPSI-R equivalent of Digit Span is Sentences.
†Optional supplementary subtest that is not included to determine IQ score
‡Letter-Number Sequencing and Symbol Search (both supplementary WAIS-III subtests), as well as Object Assembly (an optional WAIS-III subtest) may be used in place of other subtests under certain conditions.
§The equivalent of this subtest on the WPPSI-R is Animal Pegs.

Table 9-3
Description of the Wechsler Subtests

Subtest	Description
Information	"In what continent is Brazil?" This is the type of question asked on the Wechsler Information subtests. In general, the questions tap general knowledge and in part assess learning and memory. Interests, education, cultural background, and reading skills are some influencing factors in the Information subtest score.
Comprehension	In general, these questions tap social comprehension, the ability to organize and apply knowledge, and what is colloquially referred to as "common sense." An illustrative question is "Why should children be cautious in speaking to strangers?"
Similarities	"How are a pen and a pencil alike?" This is illustrative of the general type of question that appears in this subtest; pairs of words are presented to the examinee and the task is to determine how they are alike. The ability to analyze relationships and engage in logical, abstract thinking are two of the intellectual functions tapped by this type of test.
Arithmetic	Arithmetic problems, presented and solved entirely verbally for older testtakers, are presented (at the lowest levels, this subtest may involve simple counting). Learning of arithmetic, alertness and concentration, and short-term auditory memory are some of the intellectual functions tapped by this test.
Vocabulary	The testtaker is called on to define words in this subtest that is generally viewed as the best measure of general intelligence, although education and cultural opportunity greatly influence scores on vocabulary tests as well.
Digit Span/Sentences	Digit Span, a subtest on the WISC-III, entails the examiner's verbally presenting a series of numbers, with the examinee's task being to then repeat the numbers in the same sequence. In the WPPSI-R equivalent of this task, Sentences, the examiner verbally presents sentences composed of vocabulary within preschoolers' range (such as "Jane goes to school"), and the child's task is to repeat the sentence verbatim. Both subtests tap attention, concentration, and short-term auditory memory, although Sentences appears to be more dependent on verbal skills.
Letter-Number Sequencing	Letters and numbers are orally presented in a mixed-up order. The task is to repeat the list with numbers in ascending order and letters in alphabetical order. Like Digit Span and Sentences, this test taps working memory.
Picture Completion	The subject's task here is to identify what important part is missing from a picture. For example, the testtaker might be shown a picture of a chair with one leg missing. This subtest draws on visual perception abilities, alertness, memory, concentration, attention to detail, and ability to differentiate essential from nonessential detail. Because respondents may point to the missing part, this test provides a good nonverbal estimate of intelligence. However, successful performance on a test such as this still tends to be highly influenced by cultural factors.
Picture Arrangement	In the genre of a comic strip panel, this subtest requires the testtaker to re-sort a scrambled set of cards with pictures on them into a story that makes sense. Because the testtaker must understand the whole story before a successful re-sorting will occur, this subtest is thought to tap the ability to comprehend or size up a whole situation. Additionally, attention, concentration, and ability to see temporal and cause-and-effect relationships are tapped.
Block Design	A design with colored blocks is illustrated either with blocks themselves or with a picture of the finished design, and the examinee's task is to reproduce the design. This test draws on perceptual-motor skills, psychomotor speed, and the ability to analyze and synthesize. Factors that may influence performance on this test include the examinee's color vision, frustration tolerance, and flexibility or rigidity in problem solving.
Object Assembly	The task here is to assemble, as quickly as possible, a cut-up picture of a familiar object. Some of the abilities called on here include pattern recognition, assembly skills, and psychomotor speed. Useful qualitative information pertinent to the examinee's work habits may also be obtained here by careful observation of the approach to the task (for example, does the examinee give up easily or persist in the face of difficulty?).
Coding	On the Coding subtest on the WISC-III, and the Animal Pegs subtest on the WPPSI-R, the examinee's task is to follow a code. If you were given the dot and dash equivalents of several letters in Morse code and then had to write out letters in Morse code as quickly as you could, you would be completing a coding task. The codes for the WISC-III are copied from a printed key. On the WPPSI-R, the task is to place pegs of different colors into an appropriate space based on a color code. This subtest taps learning ability, rote recall ability, psychomotor speed, concentration, and attention.
Mazes	This subtest does not appear on the WAIS-III and is a supplementary test (not included for purposes of calculating IQ) on the WISC-III. On the WPPSI-R, this subtest is composed of paper-and-pencil mazes, some of which are identical to those that appear on the WISC-III. Perceptual-motor skills, psychomotor speed, and visual planning abilities are tapped by this subtest.
Geometric Design	In no other Wechsler test but the WPPSI-R, this subtest consists of geometric designs that the child is required to copy with a pencil. In general, this subtest provides an index of the child's perceptual-motor skills.
Symbol Search	This is an optional performance subtest found on the WISC-III and the WAIS-III. The task is to visually scan two groups of symbols, one search group and one target group, and determine whether the target symbol appears in the search group. The test is presumed to tap cognitive processing speed.
Matrix Reasoning	A nonverbal analogy-like task designed to tap perceptual organizing abilities and reasoning.

Manuals for the Wechsler tests are clear about the scoring of responses, a fact that accounts for the usually high estimates of inter-rater reliability obtained in research studies. On some items, extra points may be earned depending on the quality of the response. On some Performance subtest items, extra points may be earned as a function of the speed with which the task is completed. Scores on the individual items are tallied to yield raw scores on each of the subtests. Using tables in the manual, the raw scores for each subtest are converted into scaled scores, and all the scaled scores on each subtest have a mean of 10 and a standard deviation of 3. From these scaled scores, a Verbal Scale IQ, a Performance Scale IQ, and a Full Scale IQ (composite) can be derived. On any one of the Wechsler tests, a Full Scale IQ calculated to be 100 will be considered average. And because the Wechsler tests are all point scales that yield deviation IQs with a mean of 100 (interpreted as average) and a standard deviation of 15, any Full Scale IQ in the range of 85 to 115 will also be considered average. On each of the Wechsler tests, a testtaker's performance is compared with scores earned by individuals in his or her own age group.

In general, the Wechsler tests have been evaluated favorably from a psychometric standpoint. Although the coefficients of reliability vary as a function of the specific type of reliability assessed, it is fair to say that the Wechsler tests are generally satisfactory with respect to internal consistency and test-retest reliability. Evidence for the criterion-related validity of each Wechsler test can be found in the individual test manuals along with a detailed presentation of the rationale for inclusion of the specific subtests. Factor-analytic studies by a number of independent investigators tend to support the construct validity of the Wechsler tests, as do studies of (1) correlations between a Wechsler test and other tests purporting to measure intelligence and (2) the intercorrelations of the individual subtests.

The manuals for the Wechsler tests tend to contain bare-bones guidelines for the interpretation of the test data. More detailed interpretive information can be obtained from any of a number of publications devoted to the subject. Kaufman (1994) described what he called a "successive levels" approach to Wechsler test interpretation, which entails successive evaluation of scale scores for the Verbal Scale, the Performance Scale, and the Full Scale, followed by an analysis and comparison of other data, such as clusters of selected subtests. In practice, a great deal of the data obtained during the testing, including and beyond scores and score clusters (such as the examiner's notes regarding the testtaker's extra-test behavior), may hold great interpretive significance for the capable examiner. Ultimately, test interpretation skills for a Wechsler test—like many other tests—are honed through a combination of activities, such as administering the test and observing firsthand a variety of testtakers as they take it; reading about test interpretation in various sources; and scoring and interpreting a number of test protocols under the tutelage of a skilled, experienced, and knowledgeable supervisor.

The WAIS-III

The WAIS-III is the latest in a series of instruments designed to measure the intelligence of adults. Its predecessors were the WAIS-R, the WAIS, the W-B II (Wechsler-Bellevue II), and the W-B I (Wechsler-Bellevue I). In the early 1930s, Wechsler's employer, Bellevue Hospital in Manhattan, needed an instrument suitable for evaluating the intellectual capacity of multilingual, multinational, and multicultural clients being referred there. Wechsler was dissatisfied with existing intelligence tests when used with such a population, and he began to experiment with various tests to find one more appropriate for measuring adult intelligence. The eventual result was the W-B I, published in 1939. This new test borrowed in format, though not in content, from existing tests.

Unlike the most popular individually administered intelligence test of the time, the Stanford-Binet, the W-B I was a point scale rather than an age scale; the items were classified by subtests rather than by age. The test was organized into six verbal subtests and five performance subtests, and all the items in each test were arranged in order of increasing difficulty. Another form of the test designed to be an equivalent alternate, the W-B II, was published in 1942, though it was never thoroughly standardized (Rapaport et al., 1968). Unless a specific reference is made to the W-B II, reference here (and in the literature in general) to "the Wechsler-Bellevue" is to the W-B I.

Although research had suggested that the W-B was indeed measuring something comparable to what other intelligence tests were measuring, the test had the following problems: (1) the standardization sample was rather restricted, (2) some subtests lacked sufficient inter-item reliability, (3) some of the subtests were made up of items that were too easy, (4) the scoring criteria for certain items were too ambiguous. Sixteen years after the publication of form I of the W-B, a revision with a new name, the Wechsler Adult Intelligence Scale (WAIS; Wechsler, 1955), was published.

Like its predecessor, the WAIS was organized into scales labeled "Verbal" and "Performance." Scoring yielded a Verbal IQ, a Performance IQ, and a Full Scale IQ. The test was carefully constructed and standardized and quickly became "the standard against which other adult tests can be compared" (Lyman, 1972, p. 429). The need for a more contemporary norm group soon became evident, and a revision of the test called the WAIS-R was published in 1981, shortly after Wechsler's death. In addition to new norms and updated materials, a change was made in the administration instructions mandating an alternation between verbal and performance tests.

The WAIS-III, with authorship credited to David Wechsler (1997), contains updated and colorized materials, along with norms expanded to include the age range of 74 to 89 (due to greater life expectancy). In some cases items were made physically larger to facilitate viewing by older adults. Some items were added to each of the subtests to extend the test's "floor" (more than 3 standard deviations below average) and to make the test more useful for evaluating people with extreme intellectual deficits. Analyses were undertaken to detect and replace any WAIS-R items found to be biased. The test was co-normed with another new edition of the Wechsler test, the Wechsler Memory Scale—Third Edition (WMS-III). The technical manual, which contains data for both the WAIS-III and the WMS-III (Tulsky et al., 1997), facilitates comparisons of memory with other indices of intellectual functioning when both the WAIS-III and the WMS-III are administered.

The materials of the WAIS-III will look quite familiar to examiners acquainted with other Wechsler signature tests. However, three subtests are new to the WAIS-III. As was the case when new subtests were added to the WISC-III (to be discussed shortly), the new subtests seemed designed to address concerns about the limited domains of cognitive functioning tapped in many intelligence tests (Lezak, 1988, 1995; Malec et al., 1992). Sample items from two of these new subtests, Symbol Search and Letter-Number Sequencing, are illustrated and explained in Figure 9–2. Symbol Search is a performance subtest designed to measure processing speed. Letter-Number Sequencing is a verbal subtest designed to measure attention and working memory. The third new subtest is Matrix Reasoning, a nonverbal, analogy-like task designed to tap perceptual organizing abilities and reasoning. Because it is an untimed performance test, it reduces the contribution of perceptual speed to performance test scores. A comprehensive guide to administration is presented in the *WAIS-III Administration and Scoring Manual*. Additionally, the test is packaged with a video that overviews changes in the test, reviews new features, and illustrates various aspects of test administration, scoring, and interpretation.

Standardization and norms   The WAIS-III standardization sample consisted of 2,450 adults aged 16 to 89 years, divided into 13 age bands from 16 to 17 years at one end of the spectrum, to 85 to 89 years at the other. The sample was stratified on the basis of 1995 U.S. census data with regard to variables such as age, sex, race/ethnicity, educational

Symbol Search

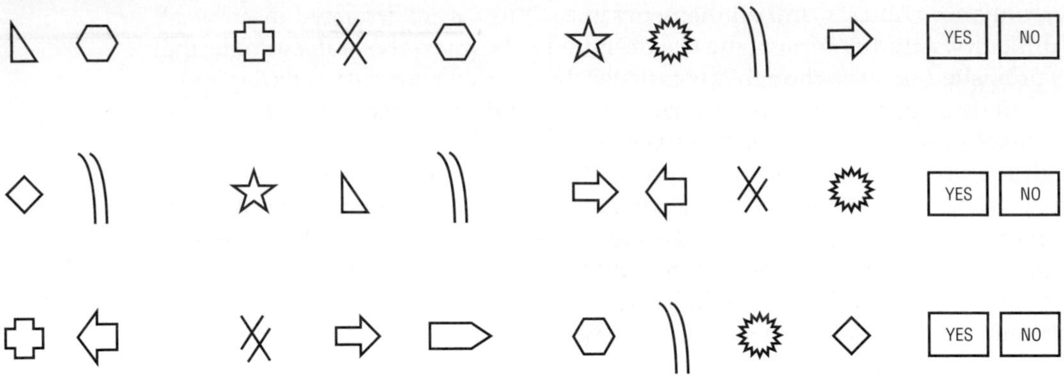

Letter-Number Sequencing

Item	Response
Q-3	3-Q
T-9-1	1-9-T
M-3-P-6	3-6-M-P
F-7-K-2-8	2-7-8-F-K
5-J-4-A-1-S	1-4-5-A-J-S
C-6-4-W-O-7-D	4-6-7-C-D-O-W

Figure 9–2
Sample Items From the WAIS-III

In the Symbol Search subtest, testtakers are presented with paired groups of stimuli, a target group (two symbols), and a search group. The testtaker marks a box to indicate whether either of the two target symbols appears in the search group. In the Letter-Number Sequencing subtest, the examiner verbalizes a list of letters and numbers. The testtaker's task is to repeat the list in reordered fashion—numbers in ascending order first, followed by letters in alphabetical order.

level, and geographic region. Consistent with census data, there were more females than males in the older age bands.

Following a Wechsler tradition, most subtest raw scores for each age group were converted to percentiles and then to a scale with a mean of 10 and a standard deviation of 3. There was, however, a break with tradition in terms of the derivation of the scaled scores. On the WAIS-R, scaled scores for each subtest had been based on the performance of a nonimpaired reference group of testtakers who were 20 to 34 years old. This was done because Wechsler believed that "optimal performance tended to occur at these ages" (Tulsky et al., 1997, p. 40). However, this belief has been challenged (Kaufman et al., 1989), and the use of the reference group for calculation of scaled scores contributed to a number of problems in WAIS-R interpretation, especially with older testtakers (Ivnik et al., 1992; Ryan et al., 1990; Tulsky et al., 1997). On the WAIS-III, scores obtained by the testtaker's same-age normative group serve as the basis for the testtaker's scaled score.

Psychometric issues The *WAIS-III Technical Manual* presents data from a number of studies attesting to the reliability, validity, and overall psychometric soundness of the test. What we found a bit surprising, however, is the relatively small sample sizes that were employed in the conduct of some of the studies. So, for example, to help document the criterion-related validity of the WAIS-III, correlations between scores on that test and the SB:FE were analyzed in a study that employed 26 adults. Those same 26 adults served as the sample for a similar criterion-related validity study that compared WAIS-III scores with scores on Raven's (1976) Standard Progressive Matrices. Use of the same, relatively small group of subjects in test validation research raises questions about the effect of practice on test performance. Larger samples were employed in similar, criterion-related validity studies for the WISC-III ($n = 184$ 16-year-olds) and the WAIS-R ($n = 192$ adults aged 16 to 74).

The evaluation of the construct validity of a test proceeds on the assumption that one knows in advance exactly what the test is supposed to measure. For intelligence tests, it is essential to know in advance how the test developer defined intelligence. If in a specific test intelligence was defined as Spearman's g, for example, then we would expect a factor analysis of such a test to yield a large, single common factor. The large, single common factor would indicate that the different questions or tasks on the test largely reflected the same underlying characteristic (intelligence or g). By contrast, if intelligence was defined by a test developer in accordance with Guilford's theory, no one factor would be expected to dominate. Instead, one would anticipate many different factors reflecting a diverse set of abilities. Recall that from Guilford's perspective, there is no single underlying intelligence for the different test items to reflect. Therefore, there would be no basis for a large common factor.

In a sense, a compromise between Spearman and Guilford is Thorndike. Thorndike's theory of intelligence leads us to look for one central factor, reflecting g, along with three additional factors representing social, concrete, and abstract intelligences. In this case, analysis would have to suggest that testtakers' responses to specific items reflected a general intelligence in part, but also different types of intelligence: social, concrete, and abstract.

Wechsler defined intelligence as being general in nature ("the global capacity of the individual") but having origins in distinct components ("composed of . . . abilities which . . . are quantitatively differentiable"). Recall that Wechsler (1974) said that there were two such components, verbal and performance. Historically, users of Wechsler tests have made interpretations from test data with reference to individual subtest scores, as well as the Verbal, Performance, and Full Scale scores, with the IQ calculated on the basis of these indices. Clinicians were trained to look for diagnostically significant discrepancies within and between these many indices—yet all within the Verbal/Performance framework. However, as early as the 1950s, alternative, multifactor models of what the Wechsler-Bellevue (Cohen, 1952a, 1952b) and the WAIS (Cohen, 1957a, 1957b) seemed to be measuring were in evidence.

In the years that followed, test users and theorists would begin wondering whether data derived from Wechsler tests might fit better conceptually with alternative, factorially derived models of cognitive ability (Hishinuma & Yamakawa, 1993; Kamphaus et al., 1994; Kaufman, 1990, 1994; Sattler, 1992; Shaw et al., 1993; Smith et al., 1992). The question, "How many factors are there *really* on the Wechsler tests?" seemed to have transformed from one of passing academic interest to pressing user obsession. The publishers of the Wechsler tests entered the fray in their revision of the children's test (discussed shortly). The issue was also addressed in the WAIS-III development, as evidenced by extensive exploratory and confirmatory factor-analytic investigations described in the test's technical manual. A result of these investigations, along with the addition of new subtests, was that in addition to the traditional Verbal/Performance dichotomy, WAIS-III users would be able to group test data by four factors: Verbal Comprehension, Working Memory, Perceptual Organization, and Processing Speed. Based on these four

Table 9–4
WAIS-III Subtests Grouped According to Indices

Verbal Comprehension	Working Memory	Perceptual Organization	Processing Speed
Vocabulary	Arithmetic	Picture Completion	Digit Symbol
Similarities	Digit Span	Block Design	Symbol Search
Information	Letter-Number Sequencing	Matrix Reasoning	

Source: The Psychological Corporation

factors, four "index scores," each with a mean set at 100 and a standard deviation set at 15, may be derived from the test data. A listing of the subtests used to derive each of these index scores is presented in Table 9–4. More on this four-factor alternative to the traditional Verbal/Performance dichotomy is presented in our discussion of the WISC-III.

The WISC-III

The Wechsler Intelligence Scale for Children (WISC) was first published in 1949. It represented a downward extension of the W-B I and actually incorporated many items contemplated for use in the (never-published) W-B II. "A well standardized, stable instrument correlating well with other tests of intelligence" (Burstein, 1972, p. 844), the WISC was not, however, without its flaws. The standardization sample contained only White children, and some of the test items were viewed as perpetuating gender and cultural stereotypes. Further, parts of the test manual were so unclear as to lead to ambiguities in the administration and scoring of the test. A revision of the WISC, called the Wechsler Intelligence Scale for Children-Revised (WISC-R), was published in 1974. The WISC-R included non-Whites in the standardization sample. Test material pictures were also made more culturally balanced. The test's language was modernized and "child-ized." The word *cigars,* in an arithmetic item, for example, was replaced with *candy bars.* There were also innovations in the administration and scoring of the test. For example, Verbal and Performance tests were administered in alternating fashion, a practice now common with respect to Wechsler and other tests.

The revision of the WISC-R yielded the Wechsler Intelligence Scale for Children-III, published in 1991. According to Sattler (1992), the primary reason for this latest revision was to update the normative data, though over a quarter of the WISC-III's items represent significant alterations from its predecessor. The artwork in the Picture Arrangement, Picture Completion, and Object Assembly subtests was modernized and rendered in color. The Mazes subtest was enlarged, as was the Coding subtest. The Coding key was set at the top of the sheet in the Coding subtest so that it would not be blocked by left-handed testtakers as they write. Other changes were designed to increase the range of possible scores on the subtests. For example, the Coding subtest was lengthened so that fewer testtakers would finish within the allotted time. Easier items were added to the Arithmetic scale to assess counting ability. At the other end of the Arithmetic scale, relatively difficult, multistep word problems were added.

A new Symbol Search subtest (similar to that described in our discussion of the WAIS-III) was introduced in the WISC-III. The test was added as the result of research on controlled attention, and it was thought to tap "freedom from distractibility." However, Sandoval (1995) perceived the addition of this subtest as significantly changing the factor structure of the test. Moreover, he objected to the retention of the label "freedom from distractibility" as "not a very good description of what the subtests Arithmetic and

Digit Span measure. . . . In the past the subtest Coding was included in this factor; because it has been moved, this would have been a good time to change the factor label" (p. 412). We will return to the issue of the nature (and number) of WISC-III factors shortly.

The development of the revision   The procedures used to revise the WISC-R and create the WISC-III illustrate many sound principles of test construction and revision. The publisher began the process with an in-house review of the test, including suggestions received from WISC-R users, recommendations solicited by experts, and ongoing correspondence with test users before and during the revision. New items and subtests were piloted, and a tryout version of the new test was administered to 500 children nationally. On the basis of the resulting data and in consultation with experts and high-volume users of the WISC-R, the WISC-III was then constructed. As has become standard practice in the development of new tests designed for wide commercial distribution, great pains were taken by the test developer to minimize any potential source of bias in any of the test's items. Using data from the WISC-R normative sample, each item was statistically analyzed with regard to performance as a function of gender, ethnicity, and age. Proposed replacement items underwent the same statistical review for item bias. WISC-R items and draft WISC-III items were reviewed by a panel of experts in an effort to balance references to ethnicity and gender. Items deemed to be outdated were deleted. Color vision experts were consulted to ensure that color-blind testtakers would not be adversely affected by the new color artwork in the test materials.

An attempt was made to make the WISC-III more user friendly to both examiners and examinees than prior versions of this test. In addition to changes in the test itself, improvements were made in the test materials. For example, the cardboard shield used by the examiner in administering the Object Assembly subtest was constructed so that it could stand on its own. Previously, this shield had to be held with one hand while the examiner awkwardly tried to arrange pieces of the object to be assembled with the other hand. A computer-based interpretive program called "WISC-III Writer" was designed to generate numerous interpretive options and statistical indices applicable to a variety of evaluation settings and purposes.

The standardization sample for the WISC-III consisted of 2,200 children between the ages of 6 and 16. There were 200 children in each of 11 age groups, divided equally by gender. Variables in the stratification were closely matched to 1988 U.S. census data for race/ethnicity, region of the country, and parental education level. Parental education level instead of parental occupation was used because prior research had indicated that parental education level accounts for more variance in test scores than parental occupation. Additional testing was conducted with Black and Hispanic children to ensure accuracy of item bias statistics. Additional testing was also conducted to compare same-subject performance on the WPPSI-R and the WISC-III (the subjects were 200 6-year-olds), the WAIS-R and the WISC-III (the subjects were 200 16-year-olds), and the WISC-R and the WISC-III (the subjects were 200 children across the age range). About 300 children who had taken the WISC-III were retested for research purposes within 4 to 8 weeks between test administrations. In all, upward of 4,500 test administrations at various sites around the country were conducted.

Who administered all these tests and how was quality control ensured? Most test publishers do not maintain an in-house staff of trained examiners who can arrange for the administration of, and actually administer, 4,500 tests throughout the country within a reasonable amount of time. Rather, the publisher contracts with experienced examiners who may be screened by means of a background questionnaire that solicits information on educational and background experience. This was the case with respect to the standardization of the WISC-III. Additionally, graduate students under the supervision of a qualified professional were employed. The test publisher used several tools of examiner quality control throughout the standardization, including

1. The completion and submission of practice protocols before testing
2. Information about the accuracy of administration and scoring of the practice protocol, provided to the examiner by telephone and letter
3. Frequent communication with examiners during the standardization process such as through a standardization newsletter
4. Rigorous checking procedures to evaluate each protocol for completeness and accuracy of administration and scoring

The reliability of persons responsible for checking the accuracy of the other examiners' scoring of test protocols was ensured by means such as the use of **anchor protocols**— that is, protocols generated by the test publisher and given to an examiner to check the accuracy of the examiner's scoring.

One question of psychometric intrigue looms: "What is the WISC-III really measuring?" Although most researchers agree it is clearly measuring more than one factor, the exact number of factors it is measuring, and what they should be called, are controversial. Not coincidentally, this is the subject of this chapter's *Close-up*. As you are probably aware by now, several different criteria may be used to determine how many factors exist (Gorsuch, 1983). In the case of the WISC-III, the criteria do not all point to the same number of factors (Wechsler, 1991). As different researchers depend to a greater or lesser extent on particular criteria, they will reach different conclusions concerning the number of factors they are willing to acknowledge. For example, some ways of doing the analysis point to a two-factor solution, with the subtests lining up neatly into "verbal" and "performance" camps. Sattler's (1992) analysis points to a three-factor solution, with factors he labeled "verbal comprehension," "perceptual organization," and "processing speed." The verbal comprehension factor includes the same subtests as Wechsler's original verbal factor, but Wechsler's original performance factor is split between perceptual organization and processing speed. This dichotomy reflects two different nonverbal abilities underlying performance on the test. The factor solution endorsed as best in the WISC-III manual and elsewhere (Kamphaus et al., 1994; Wechsler, 1991) involves four factors, including two major factors (verbal comprehension and perceptual organization) and two minor factors (freedom from distractibility and processing speed). Kamphaus et al. (1994) conceded that none of the factor solutions provided a very good fit with the data. Still, as you have probably noticed yourself, there are commonalities in the names of the factors; different investigators are probably not far apart conceptually.

In a general way, we can conclude that factor analysis supports the construct validity of the WISC-III relative to David Wechsler's definition of intelligence. After all, the WISC-III measures a general intelligence factor in addition to some more specific factors. Granted that with regard to these specific factors, there may be more than the two (verbal and performance) that Wechsler (1974) named. We are prepared, however, to cut some slack in this regard, because the test has undergone such substantial revision in the decades since Wechsler defined intelligence. We cannot ignore the addition, for example, of a new subtest, Symbol Search, designed to measure cognitive processing speed. Had David Wechsler been around when the decision was made to add this test, cognitive processing speed might well have been added to his list of specific factors in intelligence.

Hard-liners might hold the publisher of the WISC-III more strictly to the definition of intelligence put forth by Wechsler before deeming the test to be construct-valid. Yet in light of the ongoing debate among professionals about how intelligence shall be defined, Wechsler's pronouncements not only seem to hold up quite well but also continue to be measured by revisions of his test. Responsive to the changing interests and needs of the

Confirmatory Factor Analysis to Test the Structure of the WISC-III*

Confirmatory factor analysis (CFA) is an excellent method for determining whether a test really measures the abilities or constructs its authors believe it measures. It is, in other words, an excellent method for evaluating the *construct validity* of a test. Here, we describe how we used CFA to determine whether the Wechsler Intelligence Scale for Children-III (WISC-III) measures the constructs it is supposed to measure: Verbal Comprehension, Perceptual Organization, Freedom from Distractibility, and Processing Speed.

CFA often starts with a picture—a model—that describes the researcher's theory of what a test measures; this picture is often based on the researcher's reading of what the test is designed to measure. There is some judgment involved in converting a test's theory into a model, because test authors often do not describe their theory in enough detail to display it as a picture. A model of the constructs measured by the WISC-III is shown in Figure 1. The rectangles display its 13 subtests. These subtests supposedly measure four primary constructs: Verbal Comprehension, Perceptual Organization, Freedom from Distractibility, and Processing Speed. At the same time, the test supposedly measures general intelligence, or *g,* as implemented via the Full Scale IQ in the WISC-III. The constructs supposedly measured by the WISC-III are shown in ellipses. We have displayed this structure as a hierarchical model with the most general constructs leading to the most specific.

At first glance, the direction of the arrows in the model may seem counterintuitive. After all, psychologists estimate the scores for the constructs (such as Verbal Comprehension) by adding together the subtest scores. But the arrows make explicit the process psychologists believe occurs: that a person's level of Verbal Comprehension ability is one of the *primary* influences on his or her score on the Information or Similarities subtests, and so forth. Likewise, children's levels of general intelligence are an important influence on their Verbal Comprehension abilities.

The next step in CFA is to test the model against some data to determine whether the model does an adequate job of explaining the test. In this case, we tested the model with the WISC-III standardization data. This second step often involves examining "fit statistics," numerical descriptors of the extent to which the model, as drawn, describes the actual test data. The fit statistics suggested that the model shown

in the first figure does a fairly good job of explaining the abilities measured by the WISC-III.

Given a good fit of the model to the data, the next step in CFA is to interpret the findings of the analysis. The most salient findings for the WISC-III are shown in Figure 2. The numbers associated with the arrows from the factors to the subtests are called "factor loadings," and they describe the extent to which the subtests measure the same underlying ability, an ability that presumably is described by the name given to the factor. Stated differently, these numbers describe the relative validities of each of the subtests as measures of the corresponding underlying construct. For Verbal Comprehension, for example, all of these factor loadings are quite high, suggesting that each of the subtests (Information through Comprehension) provides a valid measure of Verbal Comprehension abilities. In contrast, the path from Perceptual Organization to Mazes was fairly low (.38) compared to the other factor loadings, suggesting that Mazes is not a particularly good measure of Perceptual Organization abilities. It may be that Mazes primarily measures some other ability besides Perceptual Organization or that Mazes measures some unique ability not shared by the other Perceptual tests, or that Mazes is simply not a very reliable measure to begin with.

The factor loadings from *g* to the first set of factors are also of interest, because they describe the extent to which each of these "first-order factors" measures general intelligence. Thus Verbal Comprehension, Perceptual Organization, and Freedom from Distractibility are largely a function of general intelligence, whereas Processing Speed is less affected by *g* and, presumably, more affected by other abilities, such as children's motor speed and facility.

The numbers associated with the various paths also provide feedback as to the constructs that supposedly underlie the test. The names given to the factors are to some extent arbitrary. For this research we chose the names used by the test developers who argue that the WISC-III measures the abilities named in the ellipses. The CFA provides evidence of the correctness of these names. This process of evaluating the factor names draws on other evidence—what we know about intelligence and its measurement—and requires thinking and judgment by the researchers. An examination of the paths from *g* to the first-order factors will illustrate this. We know from a great deal of other evidence that *g* is most closely connected with cognitive complexity, the ability to reason in novel situations, the ability to infer underlying

(continued)

*Our thanks to Timothy Z. Keith and E. Lea Witta for contributing this *Close-up*.

Confirmatory Factor Analysis
to Test the Structure of the WISC-III
(continued)

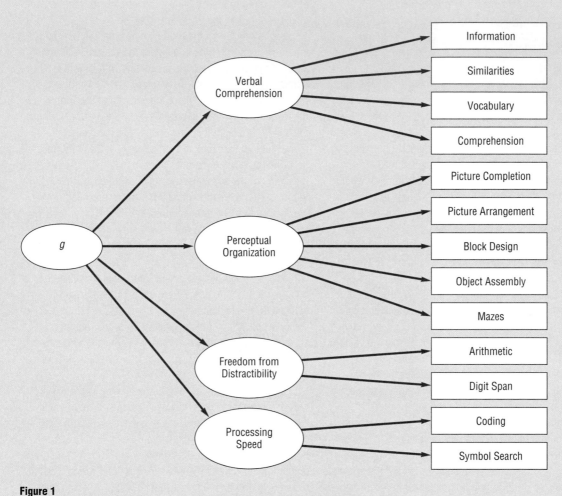

Figure 1
A Pictorial Representation of the Abilities Supposedly Measured by the WISC-III

According to the WISC-III manual, the test measures four narrow abilities—Verbal Comprehension, Perceptual Organization, Freedom from Distractibility, and Processing Speed—and one general ability—general intelligence, or g.

relations, and abstract reasoning; abilities widely associated with overall intelligence. If these abilities describe intelligence, and *g,* then it is reasonable that Verbal Comprehension and Perceptual Organization have high loadings on *g;* these constructs essentially describe aspects of verbal and nonverbal intelligence. In contrast, the even higher loading of Freedom from Distractibility on *g* (.90) makes little sense. Freedom from Distractibility has to do with the ability to tune out distractions in order to solve a problem; few theories of intelligence closely link such ability to general intelligence.

The fact that this factor is so closely related to *g* suggests that some other ability—not Freedom from Distractibility— is really being measured by the two subtests that make up this scale. Freedom from Distractibility may therefore be a misnomer for what is being measured.

What, then, would be a better name for this factor? We think that *Quantitative Reasoning* is a better name for several reasons. First, we looked at the subtests that make up the factor (Arithmetic and Digit Span). What might they both measure other than the ability to tune out distractions? One

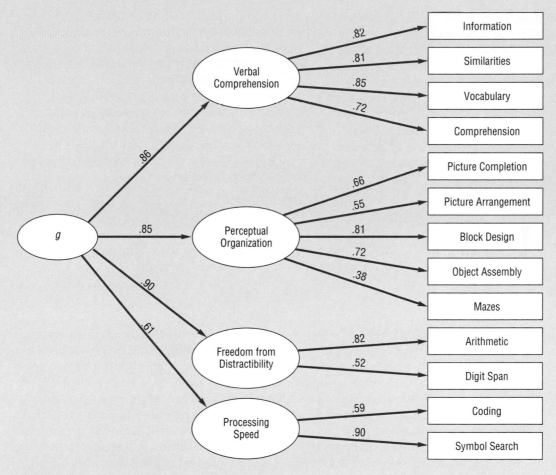

Figure 2
Model of the Structure of the WISC-III

The numbers associated with the paths are indices of the relative validities of the subtests and scales as measures of the corresponding constructs.

possibility is memory skill: Digit Span is primarily a memory task, and Arithmetic (in which children solve math problems read to them) is aided by remembering the different aspects of the problems. Another possibility is quantitative skill: Arithmetic requires the solving of math problems, whereas Digit Span requires children to remember series of numbers. The loadings of the subtest on the first-order factor—with Arithmetic having a considerably larger loading than Digit Span—argue for this factor-tapping numerical facility, however. In addition, our knowledge of the nature of *g* also suggests that *g* is not as closely related to the simple memory of numbers as it is to the mental manipulation of numbers, a much more cognitively demanding task. The second-order factor loadings also suggest the superiority of the name Quantitative Reasoning over the names Memory or Freedom from Distractibility. This conclusion, then, suggests that the Arithmetic and Digit Span subtests are not valid measures of Freedom from Distractibility (FFD), and that the FFD scale is not a valid measure of this construct. This conclusion, in turn, has implications for the interpretation of scores on the

(continued)

Confirmatory Factor Analysis
to Test the Structure of the WISC-III
(continued)

WISC-III. Most specifically, a child's score on the Freedom from Distractibility scale probably should not be interpreted as a measure of his or her ability to tune out distractions, but rather as a measure of his or her facility with mathematical concepts and reasoning with numbers.

CFA can also be used to compare competing models of the structure of a test. So, for example, if a test author thought his or her test measured one set of abilities, but others argued that the test measured another set of abilities, we could use CFA to test which model did a better job in explaining the data. Indeed, this would be a good approach for testing

our conclusions about the Quantitative Reasoning (FFD) factor. We could test this conclusion further by including other known measures of the three likely constructs—FFD, Memory, and Quantitative Reasoning—in another factor analysis to see which of several competing structures was best.

If you are interested in learning more about our CFA of the WISC-III (we did, in fact, compare several competing models of the WISC-III), please read Keith and Witta (1997). For more information about CFA, see Keith (1997), which also discusses CFAs of several other common intelligence tests that are discussed in your textbook.

community of test users, the publishers of the WISC-III recently published the WISC-III as a Process Instrument (WISC-III-PI).

The WISC-III-PI

The WISC-III-PI (Kaplan et al., 1999) was designed as an individually administered supplement to the WISC-III for the purpose of assessing the component processes involved in many WISC-III tasks. The test is appropriate for use with children from ages 6 through 16 years, 11 months. Using familiar WISC-III tasks, as well as some tasks developed especially for this test, data relevant to the child's test-taking strategies and cognitive functioning can be gleaned. In turn, these data may be used to profile the child's strengths and weaknesses in terms of cognitive processing, and to design appropriate interventions. In addition to normative data, a desirable feature of the test manual is the reporting of qualitative observations of the subject's test-taking behavior.

The WPPSI-R

Project Head Start as well as other 1960s programs for preschool children who were culturally different or exceptional (defined in this context as atypical in ability—gifted or retarded) fostered interest in the development of new tests (Zimmerman & Woo-Sam, 1978). The Stanford-Binet had traditionally been the test of choice for use with preschoolers, though test users were open to experimenting with alternative methods. Although some advocated a restandardization of the WISC for children under 6, Wechsler (1967) had decided that a new scale should be developed and standardized especially for children under age 6. The new test was the WPPSI (the Wechsler Preschool and Primary Scale of Intelligence), usually pronounced like "whipsy," and with its publication in 1967 the Wechsler series of intelligence tests was extended downward in age range to age 4. The WPPSI was the first major intelligence test that "adequately sampled the total population of the United States, including racial minorities" (Zimmerman & Woo-Sam, 1978,

p. 10)—a fact that contributed to the success of the WPPSI, especially in an era when standardized tests were under attack for not having adequate minority representation in the standardization sample.

The WPPSI-R was published in 1989 and is designed to assess the intelligence of children from ages 3 years through 7 years, 3 months. Major changes from the WPPSI included extension of the age range, addition of the Object Assembly subtest, and the renaming of the Animal Pegs subtest (formerly Animal House). Approximately 48% of the WPPSI items (excluding Animal Pegs) were retained intact or with only slight modifications from the WPPSI. New items were developed for the younger age range and for the older age range. There is a one-year overlap with the WISC-R at ages 6 years, 0 months (6–0) through 7 years, 3 months (7–3).

The WPPSI-R was standardized on 1,700 children, including 100 boys and 100 girls in each of eight age groups, ranging in half-year intervals from age 3 years to 7 years, and one age group of 50 boys and 50 girls in the 7 years to 7 years, 3 months interval. The sample closely reflects 1986 census estimates on stratification variables such as geographic region, ethnicity, parental education and occupation, and urban-rural residence.

Psychometric issues Reliability and validity coefficients presented in the WPPSI-R manual are acceptably high. Factor analyses of the data from the standardization sample yielded findings consistent with two previous studies of the WPPSI; a verbal factor and a performance factor were the two primary factors tapped by the test (Gyurke et al., 1990). Several validity studies, all of which support the validity of the test, are reported in the WPPSI-R manual. A number of other studies also support the test's validity (Bracken, 1992; Faust & Hollingsworth, 1991; Karr et al., 1993). Kaplan (1993) provided evidence for the test's predictive validity in a study that entailed its administration to 50 children before they entered kindergarten. Achievement test scores were evaluated with reference to test scores at the end of the first grade, two years later. Although Performance IQ before kindergarten was not found to predict academic achievement at the end of first grade, Verbal IQ and Full Scale IQ were found to be predictive of academic achievement. Achievement in the four areas covered by the achievement test—Listening, Math, Reading, and Word Analysis—was significantly correlated with Full Scale IQ (correlations ranged from .38 to .65) and with Verbal IQ (correlations ranged from .44 to .71). Given the phenomenon of IQ inflation discussed earlier, look for a revision of the WPPSI-R in the near future. And given the trends with regard to the WISC-III and the WAIS-III, we would not be surprised if the third edition of the WPPSI contained factor-analytically based index scores, much like its sister tests.

The Wechsler Tests in Perspective

Read the manual for a recently developed Wechsler intelligence test and the chances are good that you will find illustrations of exemplary practices in test development. Qualified examiners can learn to administer the tests relatively quickly, and examinees tend to find the test materials engaging. A number of computer-assisted scoring and interpretive aids are available for each of the tests, as are a number of manuals and guides. Moreover, the test developers are evidently making efforts to keep the scoring and interpretation of the tests fresh, as they extend the traditional Verbal/Performance model into one conducive to analysis by means of the more contemporary, multiple-factor conceptualization of intelligence.

An issue related to Wechsler tests, but certainly not exclusive to them, has to do with the development and use of short forms. The term **short form** refers to a test that has been abbreviated in length, typically to reduce the time needed for test administration, scoring, and interpretation. Sometimes, particularly when the testtaker is believed to have an atypically short attention span or other problems that would make an administration of the complete test impossible, a sampling of representative subtests is administered. Arguments for such use of Wechsler scales have been made with reference to testtakers from the general population (Kaufman et al., 1991), as well as elderly testtakers (Paolo & Ryan, 1991) and testtakers from psychiatric populations (Benedict et al., 1992; Boone, 1991; Grossman et al., 1993; Randolph et al., 1993; Sweet et al., 1990). More recently, arguments advanced in favor of shortened tests refer to the general reluctance of health care insurers to pay for psychological assessment services, and to many school psychologists' crowded calendar for assessment appointments. In addition, an overburdened criminal justice system is increasingly relying on psychological evaluations to assess intellectual capacity (Hayes, 1999). In response to these and other circumstances, it will come as no surprise that the validity of abbreviated forms of intelligence tests has been explored in recent years not only by independent researchers (Axelrod & Paolo, 1998; Campbell, 1998; Donders, 1997; Iverson et al., 1996), but by test developers and publishers as well (Kaufman & Kaufman, 1990; Prifitera et al., 1998).

Short forms of intelligence tests are nothing new. In fact, they have been around almost as long as the long forms. Soon after the Binet-Simon reached the United States, a short form of it was proposed (Doll, 1917). In 1958, Wechsler himself described the use of short forms as appropriate provided they were used only for screening purposes. But years later, perhaps in response to possible abuses of short forms, Wechsler (1967) advised that "reduction in the number of [subtests] as a time-saving device is unjustifiable and not to be encouraged" (p. 37). He further advised those who might claim that they do not have enough time to administer an intelligence test in its entirety to "find the time" (p. 37). Subsequent reviews of the literature on short forms tended to support Wechsler's later advice. Watkins (1986) concluded that short forms may be used for screening purposes only, and that they should not be used to make placement or educational decisions. Silverstein (1990) provided an incisive review of the history of short forms, focusing on four issues: (1) how to abbreviate the original test; (2) how to select subjects; (3) how to estimate scores on the original test; and (4) the criteria to apply when comparing the short form with the original. From a historical perspective, Smith et al. (2000) characterized views regarding the transfer of validity from the parent form to the short form as "overly optimistic." In contrast to some critics who have called for the abolishment of short forms altogether, Smith et al. (2000) argued that the standards for the validity of a short form must be high. They suggested a series of procedures to be used in the development of valid short forms.

From a psychometric standpoint, the validity of a test is affected by, and is somewhat dependent on, the test's reliability. Changes in a test that lessen its reliability may also lessen its validity. Reducing the number of items in a test typically reduces the test's reliability and, hence, its validity as well. For that reason, decisions made on the basis of data derived from administrations of a short form of a test must be made with caution (Nagle & Bell, 1993). In fact, when data from the administration of a short form of a test clearly suggest the need for intervention or placement, the "best practice" may be to take the time to administer the full form of the test for confirmation purposes.

Before leaving the subject of the Wechsler tests we pass along word "from the grapevine" that these tests too, like the Binet, are currently under revision. We expect to see a fourth edition of the WISC and a third edition of the WPPSI in the near future. And with new theories of human abilities being developed, not to mention recombinations of existing theories, it will not come as a surprise if any of these tests are based on a revised model of intelligence. Should any of these new editions be published before a new edition of this textbook is published, we strongly encourage students to locate and read reviews of the new tests.

Other Measures of Intelligence

Other Tests Designed for Individual Administration

In recent years, a growing number of tests purporting to measure intelligence have become available to test users. Some of these tests were developed by Alan and Nadeen Kaufman. This husband-wife team developed the Kaufman Adolescent and Adult Intelligence Test (KAIT; Kaufman & Kaufman, 1993) and the Kaufman Brief Intelligence Test (K-BIT; Kaufman & Kaufman, 1990). Their first flagship test was the Kaufman Assessment for Battery (K-ABC; Kaufman & Kaufman, 1983a, 1983b). The K-ABC departed conceptually from previously published intelligence tests with its focus on information processing and more specifically the distinction between sequential and simultaneous processing. The Kaufmans drew on the theoretical writings of A. R. Luria (1966a) in the design of the K-ABC, as did J. P. Das and Jack Naglieri in the development of their test called Cognitive Assessment System. Another test battery that deviated in many ways from prior measures of cognitive ability is the Differential Ability Scales. These and other tests widely used in educational settings will be discussed in the following chapter.

An estimate of intelligence can be derived from an assessee's paper-and-pencil rendering of a human figure and other drawings, according to some researchers and clinicians (Bardos, 1993; Buck, 1948; Holtzman, 1993; Naglieri, 1993). Many methods have been proposed for obtaining such estimates, the best-known of these being the Goodenough-Harris scoring system (Harris, 1963). A long-standing controversy, however, is whether the Goodenough system is indeed good enough. Although there is evidence that the system is reliable (Kamphaus & Pleiss, 1993; Scott, 1981), questions remain about its validity (Aikman et al., 1992; Motta et al., 1993; Sattler, 1992). Figure drawings hold out the promise of less time spent in evaluation, especially when the same drawings may be used for personality assessment. However, their use to assess intelligence—even as a screening device—remains controversial.

Tests Designed for Group Administration

Tests designed for administration to groups tend to differ in many ways from tests designed for individual administration. In contrast to the individual situation, the group situation affords little opportunity for examiner-examinee interaction. For this reason, examinees must be able to readily understand what is expected of them and then respond to test items independently. Typically, there is little, if any, provision for examinees to question instructions or explain their responses once a group testing has begun. Test items are usually in multiple-choice format. Examinee responses may be entered in various ways such as circling a particular choice or blackening a grid. If the group test is computer-administered, the response options increase. Responses may be entered through use of a keyboard, a mouse, a joystick, or some other data entry medium. If the computer is equipped with voice recognition capabilities, respondents may speak into a microphone.

Perhaps the most obvious advantage of group tests over individual tests is that they can be administered to large numbers of people at the same time and so are more efficient. Most group tests can be reliably machine- or computer-scored. They are also more economical than individual tests because, in most cases, only a one-page computer answer sheet is used, thus avoiding the necessity for expensive, nonreusable test booklets. Inherent in this efficiency is a lowered turnaround time in scoring. A larger and, in some instances, more representative sample of respondents can be tested. The test administrator need not be highly trained, thus further bringing down the cost and ease of administration. One advantage of limiting the role of the test administrator to reading instructions and keeping time is that the test administrator may have less effect on the examinee's score than a test administrator in a one-on-one situation. Because of the general ease of administering and scoring group tests, they often are normed on larger and more representative standardization samples than are many individual tests.

A primary use of group tests of intelligence is screening. Test results can suggest which subjects, students, or clients require more extensive assessment with individually administered tests. In the schools, group intelligence tests may also be helpful in identifying children who require extensive preparation or enrichment experience before beginning first grade. In research settings, group intelligence tests may be used, for example, to provide valuable information to an agency or institution (such as a school or the military) for program-planning purposes.

Lest we paint too rosy a picture of group tests, let us point out that these tests also carry distinct disadvantages. Two assumptions inherent in the use of group tests are that people taking the test understand what is expected of them and that they are motivated to perform on the test. If these assumptions are violated, the results obtained will be invalid. During an individually administered test, the examiner is able to observe the subject's individual learning style, such as a tendency to solve problems by trial and error or in an impulsive rather than a reflective manner. The examiner is also able to observe confusion, anxiety, lack of interest, or other factors that would hinder the examinee's performance; during the group test, the examiner has no such opportunity, and not only is the opportunity for observing extra-test behavior lost, but so might be important information bearing on the test score. Group tests are, as their name implies, designed for the masses, and they therefore place the atypical person (for example, the individual with some disability not identified before testing or the individual who walks to the beat of a different drummer) at a greater risk of obtaining a score on the test that does not accurately approximate that individual's hypothetical true score.

All examinees taking a group test, regardless of ability, typically start on the same item and frequently end on the last item as well. This state of affairs stands in marked contrast to the more custom-designed individually administered test situation in which all examinees need not start with or end on the same item and need not be exposed to all the items on the test. Most individually administered intelligence tests contain specific rules for beginning the test (such as "begin at the level of the examinee's chronological age provided he or she answers the first two consecutive items correctly; if not, work backward until the first two consecutive items of a level are answered correctly") and for discontinuing the test ("discontinue after four consecutive failures"). Such procedures prevent boredom or failure to take the test seriously (because of the administration of too many easy items) and feelings of discouragement resulting from a sequence of too-difficult items.

Most group intelligence tests require the testtaker to be able to read. And although the reading level required may be simpler than the cognitive demands of the item, the fact that the item does require reading may confound the value of the score achieved on the test by certain testtakers. In a study conducted with prisoners, a group test of intelligence identified 4% of the subjects as mentally retarded, in contrast to only 1% of the subjects when an individually administered intelligence test was used (Spruill & May, 1988). This pattern of lower scores on group intelligence tests could be the result of reading problems that are common in incarcerated populations. In another study, scores on a group-administered intelligence test predicted the reading achievement of high school students who were learning disabled better than scores on an individually administered intelligence test, presumably because of the greater need for reading skills when taking a group test of intelligence (Bracy-Nipper et al., 1987). By the way, the group test was also as good as the individual test in predicting success in other areas of academic achievement.

In addition to reading ability, another skill expected of the testtaker is the ability to manipulate a pencil and to mark an answer sheet—a task with which some normal first- and second-graders may have difficulty even if given prior practice sessions (Ramseyer & Cashen, 1971). Children who have difficulties with eye-hand coordination or concentration will be especially vulnerable to difficulties with a test administered in such a format.

Although the standardization samples for group intelligence tests are often large, they are rarely as representative as they may appear. Group intelligence tests designed for use in the schools, for example, tend to be standardized on school districts rather than on individuals. A particular district may be viewed as representative of a state, but the particular individuals who make up that district and who participate in the testing are not necessarily representative of the population of individuals the test publisher would like to sample from. This is so because (1) the particular district may have volunteered to take part in the standardization process, and (2) testtakers within the district may be required to obtain parental permission to participate. The latter situation will almost certainly bias the composition of the sample, since there is a tendency on the part of better-educated, higher socioeconomic-status parents to consent to testing, as opposed to parents of lower socioeconomic status with little education. That such subtle biasing factors exist may not be noted in a description of the sample in the test's manual.

The data from group intelligence tests—like the data from any test administration—can be misused. In the schools, for example, such data may be used to track students into various types of special educational programs—a misuse of the test, because such tracking should ideally be done only on the basis of a comprehensive evaluation that includes an individually administered intelligence test. Data from the administration of a group intelligence test—administered in a school, employment, military, or any other setting—may also be misused when they become the basis for unrealistic academic expectations.

Despite our list of limitations and caveats, it cannot be denied that group intelligence tests can be of great value when used as screening instruments. We now briefly discuss the application of such tests in various settings.

Group tests in the schools At one time, perhaps no more than a decade or two ago, approximately two-thirds of all school districts in the United States used group intelligence tests on a routine basis to screen 90% of their students; the other 10% were administered individual intelligence tests (Macmillan & Myers, 1980). Litigation and legislation surrounding the routine use of group intelligence tests have altered this picture somewhat (see Chapter 2), though the group intelligence test, now also referred to as a "school ability test," is by no means extinct. In many states, legal mandates prohibit the use of group intelligence data alone for tracking purposes. However, group intelligence test data, combined with other data, can be extremely useful in developing a profile of a child's intellectual assets.

Group intelligence test results provide school personnel with valuable information for instruction-related activities and increased understanding of the individual pupil. One primary function of data from a group intelligence test is to alert educators to students who require more extensive assessment with individually administered IQ tests— and possible placement in a special class or program. Group intelligence test data can also help a school district plan educational goals for all children.

Group intelligence tests in the schools are used in special forms as early as the kindergarten level. The tests are administered to groups of 10–15 children, each of whom receives a test booklet that includes printed pictures and diagrams. For the most part, simple motor responses are required to answer items; oversized alternatives in the form of pictures in a multiple-choice test might appear on the pages, and it is the child's job to circle or to place an "X" on the picture that represents the correct answer to the item presented orally by the examiner. In some tests, machine-scorable booklets are used as early as first grade, though reading or writing is not required. During such testing in small groups, the testtakers will be carefully monitored to make certain they are following the directions.

The California Test of Mental Maturity, the Kuhlmann-Anderson Intelligence Tests, the Henmon-Nelson Tests of Mental Ability, and the Cognitive Abilities Test are some of the many group intelligence tests available for use in school settings. The first group intelligence test to be used in U.S. schools was the Otis-Lennon School Ability Test, formerly the Otis Mental Ability Test. In its current (seventh) edition, the test is designed to measure abstract thinking and reasoning ability and to assist in school evaluation and placement decision-making. This nationally standardized test yields Verbal and Nonverbal score indexes, as well as an overall School Ability Index (SAI).

Group tests in the military   Group tests to measure various abilities such as the Army Alpha (primarily verbal in nature) and the Army Beta (primarily nonverbal in nature) were first developed in response to personnel problems of the military during World War I. At that time, there was the need to select potential officer candidates and to eliminate draftees who were mentally unfit for military service.

Today, group tests are still administered to prospective recruits, not only for routine screening purposes, but also as an aid in assigning soldiers to training programs and jobs. Data from group testing have indicated that there is a downward trend in the mean intelligence level of recruits since the ending of the draft and the inception of an all-volunteer army. In response to such findings, the military has developed new weapons training programs incorporating, for example, lower-level vocabulary in programmed instruction, a strategy designed to provide a better match between the learning ability of the trainee and the material to be learned.

Included among many group tests used by the armed forces are the Officer Qualifying Test (a 115-item multiple-choice test used by the Navy as an admissions test to Officer Candidate School), the Airman Qualifying Exam (a 200-item multiple-choice test given to all Air Force volunteers), and the Armed Services Vocational Aptitude Battery (ASVAB). The ASVAB is administered to prospective new recruits in all the armed services. It is also made available to high school students and other young adults who seek guidance and counseling about their future education and career plans (Wall, 1994). Annually, hundreds of thousands of people take the ASVAB, making it "the most widely used multiple aptitude test in the United States" (ASVAB, 1995, p. 1). Almost every day, the test is administered by school counselors as well as at various walk-in centers at no cost to the testtakers. In the context of a career exploration program, the ASVAB is designed to help testtakers learn about their interests, abilities, and personal preferences in relation to career opportunities in military and civilian settings. Illustrative items from each of the ten subtests are presented in this chapter's *Everyday Psychometrics*. The test is periodically revised, and in its current (1992) revision, it has norms based on a "nationally representative sample of American youth ages 16–23" (ASVAB, 1995, p. 1).

Through the years, various forms of the ASVAB have been produced, some for exclusive use in schools and some for exclusive use in the military. A set of 100 selected items included in the subtests of Arithmetic Reasoning, Numerical Operations, Word Knowledge, and Paragraph Comprehension make up a measure within the ASVAB called the Armed Forces Qualification Test (AFQT). The AFQT is a measure of general ability used in the selection of recruits into the military. The different armed services employ different cutoff scores in making accept/reject determinations for service based on considerations such as their preset quotas for people from a particular demographic group. In addition to the AFQT score, ten aptitude areas are also tapped on the ASVAB, including general technical, general mechanics, electrical, motor-mechanics, science,

The Armed Services Vocational Aptitude Battery (ASVAB): A Test You Can Take

If you would like firsthand experience in taking an ability test that can be useful in vocational guidance, do what about 900,000 other people do each year and take the Armed Services Vocational Aptitude Battery (ASVAB). Uncle Sam makes this test available to you free of charge—along with other elements of a career guidance package, including a workbook and other printed materials and test scoring and interpretation. Of course, although an objective is to get testtakers "into boots" (that is, into the military), taking the test entails no obligation of military service. For more information about how you can take the ASVAB, contact your school's counseling office or a military recruiter. Meanwhile, you may wish to warm up with the following ten sample items representing each of the ten ASVAB subtests.

I. General Science
Included here are general science questions, including questions from the areas of biology and physics.

1. An eclipse of the sun throws the shadow of the
   a. moon on the sun.
   b. moon on the earth.
   c. earth on the sun.
   d. earth on the moon.

II. Arithmetic Reasoning
The task here is to solve arithmetic problems. Testtakers are permitted to use (government-supplied) scratch paper.

2. It costs $0.50 per square yard to waterproof canvas. What will it cost to waterproof a canvas truck that is $15' \times 24'$?
   a. $ 6.67
   b. $18.00
   c. $ 20.00
   d. $180.00

III. Word Knowledge
Which of four possible definitions best defines the underlined word?

3. <u>Rudiments</u> most nearly means
   a. politics.
   b. minute details.
   c. promotion opportunities.
   d. basic methods and procedures.

IV. Paragraph Comprehension
A test of reading comprehension and reasoning.

4. Twenty-five percent of all household burglaries can be attributed to unlocked windows or doors. Crime is the result of opportunity plus desire. To prevent crime, it is each individual's responsibility to
   a. provide the desire.
   b. provide the opportunity.
   c. prevent the desire.
   d. prevent the opportunity.

V. Numerical Operations
This speeded test contains simple arithmetic problems that the testtaker must do quickly; it is one of two speeded tests on the ASVAB.

5. $6 - 5 =$
   a. 1
   b. 4
   c. 2
   d. 3

VI. Coding Speed
This subtest contains coding items that measure perceptual/motor speed among other factors.

KEY

| green . . . 2715 | man . . . 3451 | salt . . . 4586 |
| hat . . . 1413 | room . . . 2864 | tree . . . 5927 |

	a.	b.	c.	d.	e.
6. room	1413	2715	2864	3451	4586

(continued)

The Armed Services Vocational Aptitude Battery (ASVAB): A Test You Can Take
(continued)

VII. Auto and Shop Information
This test assesses knowledge of automobile shop practice and the use of tools.

7. What tool is shown above?
   a. hole saw
   b. keyhole saw
   c. counter saw
   d. grinding saw

VIII. Mathematics Knowledge
This is a test of ability to solve problems using high school–level mathematics. Use of scratch paper is permitted.

8. If $3X = -5$, then $X =$
   a. -2
   b. $-\frac{5}{3}$
   c. $-\frac{3}{5}$
   d. $\frac{3}{5}$

IX. Mechanical Comprehension
Knowledge and understanding of general mechanical and physical principles are probed by this test.

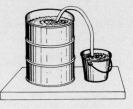

9. Liquid is being transferred from the barrel to the bucket by
   a. capillary action.
   b. gravitational forces.
   c. fluid pressure in the hose.
   d. water pressure in the barrel.

X. Electronics Information
Here, knowledge of electrical, radio, and electronics information is assessed.

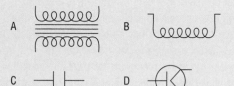

10. Which of the above is the symbol for a transformer?
    a. A
    b. B
    c. C
    d. D

Answer Key

1. b	6. c
2. c	7. a
3. d	8. b
4. d	9. b
5. Why are you looking this one up?	10. a

---

combat operations, and skill-technical. These are combined to assess aptitude in five separate career areas, including clerical, electronics, mechanics, skill-technical (medical, computers), and combat operations.

The test battery is continually reviewed and improved, based on data concerning how predictive scores are of actual performance in various occupations and military training programs. A large-scale study bearing on the validity of the test compared the performance of high- and low-scoring men who were all accepted into the Air Force. It was found that the lower-scoring men were less likely to complete basic training, had more unsuitable discharges, and were less likely to attain the required level of success (Grunzke et al., 1970). The ASVAB has been found to predict success in computer-programming and computer-operating roles (Besetsny et al., 1993) and grades in military technical schools across a variety of fields (Earles & Ree, 1992; Ree & Earles, 1990). A review of validity studies supports the construct, content, and criterion-related validity of the ASVAB as a device to guide training and selection decisions (Welsh et al., 1990). In general, the test has been deemed to be quite useful in making selection and placement decisions in the armed forces, and has held up well over time (Chan et al., 1999).

Measures of Specific Intellectual Abilities

There are certain intellectual abilities and talents that are not—or are only indirectly—assessed by the more widely used tests. One such ability is creativity. And although it is true that most tests of intelligence do not measure creativity, the reverse of that statement cannot be stated with equal certainty. To the extent that the components of creativity include numerous variables related to general intellectual ability (such as originality in problem solving, originality in perception, originality in abstraction, ideational fluency, and inductive reasoning abilities), measures of creativity may also be thought of as tools for assessing aspects of intellectual functioning.

A criticism frequently leveled at group standardized intelligence tests (as well as other ability and achievement tests) is that evaluation of test performance is too heavily focused on whether the answer is correct—as opposed to giving more weight to the examinee's thought process in arriving at the answer. On most achievement tests, for example, the skill that is required is called "convergent thinking"; after a consideration of the facts and after a logical series of logical judgments is made, a solution to a problem is arrived at. Convergent thinking is a deductive reasoning process that emphasizes one solution to a problem. In his structure of intellect model, Guilford (1967) drew a distinction between the intellectual processes of convergent and divergent types of thinking. Divergent thinking involves a reasoning process in which thought is permitted the freedom to move in many different directions, making several solutions possible. Divergent thinking requires flexibility of thought, originality, and imagination. There is much less emphasis on recall of facts than in convergent thinking. Guilford's model has served as a stimulus to focus research attention on not only the products of creative thought but the process as well.

A number of tests and test batteries designed to measure creativity in children and adults are available. Guilford (1954) described tasks such as Consequences ("Imagine what would happen if . . .") and Unusual Uses (for example, "Name as many uses as you can think of for a rubber band") as ways of assessing creativity. Included in Guilford et al.'s (1974) test battery, the Structure-of-Intellect Abilities, are Consequences and Unusual Uses subtests, four Christensen-Guilford Fluency tests (Word Fluency, Ideational Fluency, Expressional Fluency, and Associational Fluency), and other verbally oriented subtests (such as Simile Interpretation) as well as relatively nonverbal subtests (such as Sketches, Making Objects, and Decorations).

Based on the work of Mednick (1962), the Remote Associates Test (RAT) presents the testtaker with three words, and the task is to find a fourth word that is associated with the other three. The Torrance (1966, 1987a, 1987c) Tests of Creative Thinking consist of word-based, as well as picture-based and sound-based, test materials. In a subtest of different sounds administered with the aid of a phonograph record, for example, the examinee's task is to respond with the thoughts each sound conjures. Each subtest is designed to measure some or all of four characteristics deemed to be important in the process of creative thought: flexibility, originality, fluency, and elaboration—and responses are

Figure 9–3
Sample Item from the Meier Art Judgment Test

The Meier Art Tests (including the Meier Art Judgment Test and the Meier Aesthetic Perception Test) were based on the research of Norman Charles Meier in the area of aesthetic sensitivity. The task in the Aesthetic Perception Test is to rank four versions of the same work of art in order of perceived aesthetic merit. The Art Judgment Test consists of 100 pairs of paintings or drawings reproduced in black and white, one rendering of the original altered in some way. Examinees are informed of the difference between the two pictures (to control for potential problems in perception) and then asked which of the two versions of the artwork they like best. Here, the difference between the two pictures has to do with the positioning of the objects on the shelf.

scored in three or more of these four areas. Flexibility refers to the variety of ideas presented and the ability to shift from one approach to another. Fluency involves the number of ideas or total responses actually produced. Elaboration alludes to the richness of detail in a verbal explanation or pictorial display. Originality refers to the ability to produce nonobvious ideas or figures. Test-retest reliability on this battery has not been encouraging, though such findings may be similar with respect to other measures of creativity—an ability that may be highly susceptible to the effect of emotional or physical health, motivation, and related factors. And although a number of studies have explored aspects of the construct validity of this test (see, for example, Lieberman, 1965), many test reviewers (such as Wallach & Kogan, 1965) have remained skeptical, wondering aloud whether the test might more properly be thought of as one of intelligence. One large-scale factor-analytic study did not support the distinction of the fluency, flexibility, originality, and elaboration factors (Yamamoto & Frengel, 1966). A library of over 200 creativity tests exists at the University of Georgia and at the State University College at Buffalo (Haensly & Torrance, 1990).

A number of tests exist to measure specific intellectual abilities ranging from critical thinking (such as the Watson-Glaser Critical Thinking Appraisal) to music listening skills (such as the Seashore Measures of Musical Talents) to art judgment and aesthetic perception (Figure 9–3).

Creativity. Critical thinking. Music listening ability. Art judgment. As you read about each of these skills and how they all might be related to that intangible construct "intelligence," you may have said to yourself, "Why doesn't anyone create a test that measures all these diverse aspects of intelligence?" Although no one has undertaken that ambitious project, test packages have been developed, in recent years, to test not only intelligence but also related abilities in the context of an educational setting. These test packages, called psychoeducational batteries, are discussed in the following chapter, along with other tests used to measure academic abilities.

Self-Assessment

Test your understanding of elements of this chapter by seeing if you can explain each of the following terms, expressions, and abbreviations:

adaptive testing	ratio IQ
AFQT	routing test
anchor protocol	short form
Army Alpha	Stanford-Binet
Army Beta	Lewis Terman
ASVAB	test composite
basal level	testing the limits
Alfred Binet	WAIS-III
ceiling level	David Wechsler
deviation IQ	WISC-III
point scale	WISC-III-PI
RAT	WPPSI-R

10

Preschool and Educational Assessment

What are some of the things you associate with the word *school?* If the word *test* comes to mind, you probably have lots of company. This is so because many different tests are administered in public and private schools: intelligence tests, personality tests, tests of physical and sensory abilities—all kinds of tests. Educators are interested in answers to questions as diverse as "How good is your reading ability?" and "How far can you broad-jump?" In much of this chapter, we consider tests designed to facilitate the process of education: achievement and aptitude tests, as well as diagnostic tests. We begin, however, with a look at education-related tests that may be administered long before a child sets foot in a classroom.

Preschool Assessment

The first five years of life—the span of time referred to by the term *preschool period*—is a time of profound change. Basic reflexes develop and the child passes a number of sensorimotor milestones—crawling, sitting, standing, walking, running, grasping an object, and so forth. Usually between 18 and 24 months, the child becomes capable of symbolic thought and develops language skills. By age 2, the average child has a vocabulary of over two hundred words. Of course, all such observations about the development of children are of more than mere academic interest to professionals legally charged with the responsibility of assessment.

In the mid-1970s, Congress enacted Public Law (PL) 94-142, which mandated that children age 3 and up suspected of having physical or mental disabilities be evaluated professionally to determine what their special educational needs might be. The law also provided federal funds to help the states meet those educational needs. In 1986, a set of amendments to PL 94-142, known as PL 99-457, extended downward to birth the obligation of states toward children with disabilities. It further mandated that beginning with the school year 1990–1991, all disabled children from ages 3 to 5 be provided with a free, appropriate education. The law was expanded in scope in 1997 with the passage of PL 105-17. Among other things, PL 105-17 was intended to give greater attention to diversity issues, especially as they might be a factor in evaluation and the assignment of special services. The law also mandated that, effective July 1, 1998, infants and toddlers with disabilities must receive services in the home or in other natural settings, and such services are to continue in preschool programs. In 1999, attention deficit hyperactivity disorder (ADHD) was officially added to the list of disabling conditions that can qualify a child as eligible for special services. This, combined with other federal legislation and a growing movement toward "full-service schools" that dispense health and psychological services in addition to education (Reeder et al., 1997), all signal a growing societal reliance on infant and preschool assessment techniques.

Tools of Preschool Assessment

The tools of preschool assessment are, with age-appropriate variations built into them, the same types of tools used to assess school-age children and adults. These tools include, among others, checklists and rating scales, tests, and interviews.

Checklists and rating scales   Checklists and ratings scales are commonly used tools of assessment with preschoolers, although certainly not exclusive to this population. In general, a **checklist** is a questionnaire on which a person marks items to indicate the presence or absence of a specified behavior, thought, event, or circumstance. Checklists can cover broad areas and still be relatively economical and quick to administer—facts that greatly increase their appeal to busy clinicians (Kamphaus et al., 2000). Quite similar in definition, and sometimes even identical in form, is a rating scale. In general, a **rating scale** is a form completed by an evaluator (such as a rater, judge, examiner, and so forth) to make a judgment of relative standing with regard to a specified variable or variables. As with a checklist, the variables may reflect, for example, the frequency, magnitude, or presence/absence of an observable behavior or event, or a verbalized thought. Today, infants are likely to be greeted at birth by hospital delivery room staff equipped with a checklist or rating scale (see *Everyday Psychometrics*).

Two examples of commonly used checklists and rating scales are the Achenbach Child Behavior Checklist (CBCL) and the Connors Rating Scales-Revised (CRS-R). The CBCL comes in versions appropriate for use with children from ages 1½–5 (CBCL/1½–5), as well as a form for use with children through young adults, ages 4 through 18 (CBCL/4–18). Parents and others with a close relationship to the subject provide information for competence items covering the subject's activities, social relations, and school performance. The checklist also contains items that describe specific behavioral and emotional problems, as well as open-ended items for reporting additional problems. The protocols are hand-scored, machine-scored, or computer-scored, yielding scores on competence as well as clinical scales. The CRS-R is designed primarily to help assess attention deficit hyperactivity disorder and screen for other behavior problems. The instrument comes in various versions, each of which has a long form (15 to 20 minutes administration time) and a short form (5 to 10 minutes administration time). There is a parent version and a teacher version for use with children ages 3 to 17. An adolescent self-report version is for use by respondents ages 12 to 17. The instrument is hand-scored and has norms based on over eight thousand children ages 3 to 17.

Most checklists and rating scales serve the purpose of screening tools. Screening tools are used in all areas of psychology, usually to provide quick assessment of sundry populations (school-, work-, or military-related) ranging in age from children to older adults. In general, we may define a **screening tool** as an instrument or procedure used to identify a particular trait or constellation of traits at a gross or imprecise level—in contrast to more formal assessment by means of a more precise instrument such as a test or test battery, which would be used for more definitive diagnostic or evaluative purposes.

First Impressions

It's been said that every person in contemporary society is a number. We are represented by a Social Security number, a driver's license number, and myriad other numbers. Before any of those numbers, however, we are represented by what is called an Apgar number. The Apgar number is actually a score on a rating scale developed by physician Virginia Apgar (1909–1974), an obstetrical anesthesiologist who saw a need for a simple, rapid method of evaluating newborn infants and determining what immediate action, if any, is necessary.

As first presented in the early 1950s, the Apgar evaluation is conducted at one minute after birth to assess how well the infant tolerated the birthing process. The evaluation is conducted again at five minutes after birth to assess how well the infant is adapting to the environment. Each evaluation is made with respect to the same five variables, each variable can be scored on a range from 0 to 2, and each score (at 1 minute and 5 minutes) can range from 0 to 10. The five variables are heart rate, respiration, color, muscle tone, and reflex irritability, the latter measure being obtained by response to a stimulus such as a mild pinch. So, for example, with respect to the variable of reflex irritability, the infant will earn a score of 2 for a vigorous cry in response to the stimulus, a score of 1 for a grimace, and a score of 0 if it shows no reflex irritability. Few babies are "perfect 10's" on their 1-minute Apgar; many are 7's, 8's, and 9's. An Apgar score below 7 or 8 may indicate the need for assistance in being stabilized. A very low Apgar score, in the 0 to 3 range, may signal a more enduring problem such as neurological deficit. By the way, a useful acronym for remembering the five variables is the name "APGAR" itself: A stands for activity (or muscle tone), P for pulse (or heart rate), G for grimace (or reflex irritability), A for appearance (or color), and R for respiration.

Moving from the realm of the medical to the realm of the psychological, we focus on another evaluation of sorts that takes place shortly after birth—this one, far more informal

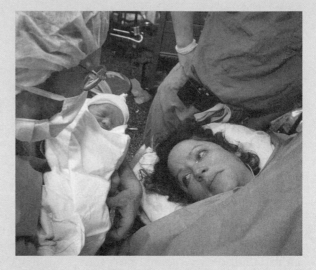

Welcome to the World of Evaluation
Only seconds after birth, a newborn infant is given its first formal evaluation by the hospital staff. The infant's next evaluation, conducted by the mother, may be no less momentous in its consequences.

in nature, by the child's mother. Judith Langlois and colleagues (1995) studied the relationship between infant attractiveness and maternal behavior and attitudes using a sample of 173 mothers and their firstborn infants (86 girls and 87 boys). Approximately one-third of the sample was identified as White, one-third was African American, and one-third was Mexican American. For the record, the mean first Apgar score for the infants in the study was 8.36, and the mean second Apgar score was 9.04.

To gauge attractiveness, the investigators used judges' ratings of photographs taken a standard distance from each infant's face while the child was either sleeping or otherwise had a neutral expression. Maternal behavior during feeding

In preschool assessment, screening tools may be used as a first step in identifying children who are said to be "at risk." This term came into vogue as an alternative to labeling a preschooler with a diagnostic label that might have a detrimental effect (Smith & Knudtson, 1990). Today, exactly what a child "at risk" is actually at risk for may vary in terms of not only the context of the discussion, but the state, even the jurisdiction. "At risk" has been used to refer to preschool children who may not be ready for first grade (Martin, 1986), and to children who, in some way, are not functioning within normal limits (Paget, 1985). In a most general sense, **at risk** refers to children who have documented and play was directly observed by trained raters in the hospital. A second set of observations was recorded around the time of the infant's three-month birthday. A measure developed by Parke and Sawin (1975) called The Parent Attitude Questionnaire was used to assess maternal attitudes both in the hospital and approximately three months later out of the hospital.

The researchers found that although all of the infants studied received adequate caregiving, the attractive infants received more positive treatment and attitudes from their mothers as compared with the unattractive infants. The mothers of the attractive infants were more affectionate and playful. The mothers of less attractive infants were more likely to be attentive to other people rather than to their infant. These mothers were also more likely to engage in routine caregiving than affectionate behavior. The attitudes of the mothers of less attractive infants, particularly during the first assessment, were also more negative than those of mothers of more attractive infants. At the time of the first assessment, the mothers of the less attractive infants were more likely than the mothers of more attractive infants to endorse the belief that their infant was interfering with their lives. Approximately three months later, the mothers of the less attractive infants, as compared with the mothers of more attractive infants, were more likely to endorse the belief that their infants needed more stimulation, although they no longer differed in beliefs regarding interference with their lives.

These findings are consistent with prior research suggesting that attractive children are treated less harshly by adults than unattractive children are (Berkowitz & Frodi, 1979; Dion, 1979; Elder et al., 1985), and that mothers of children with physical anomalies may behave in less desirable ways toward their children than mothers whose children had no such anomalies (Allen et al., 1990; Barden et al., 1989; Field & Vega-Lahr, 1984). Fathers, too, may behave differently as a function of the attractiveness of their offspring. Parke et al. (1977) found quality of paternal caregiving to 3-month-old infants to be significantly and positively correlated with infant attractiveness.

Langlois et al. (1995) cautioned that their correlational findings should not be interpreted as indicative of cause-and-effect; the results cannot be used to support statements indicating that attractiveness causes or affects maternal behavior and attitudes. It does seem the case, however, that for whatever reason, infant attractiveness tends to predict maternal behavior and attitudes. The researchers also wondered whether the results of their study would generalize to families of other income levels, or what effect the birth of additional children might have on the main findings. It may be that the mothers' relative inexperience with the range of infant behaviors led them to be more influenced by appearance than mothers who have had other children.

From moments after birth and onward, evaluation—in formal as well as informal ways—is very much a fact of life. We may define **informal evaluation** as a typically nonsystematic, relatively brief, and "off-the-record" assessment leading to the formation of an opinion or attitude conducted by any person, in any way, for any reason, in an unofficial context that is not subject to the ethics or other standards of an evaluation by a professional. The process of informal evaluation has not received a great deal of attention in the psychological assessment literature. Accordingly, the nature and extent of the influence of informal evaluations by people (such as parents, teachers, supervisors, personnel in the criminal justice system, and others) is largely unknown. On the one hand, considering the need for privacy, perhaps it is best that such private evaluations remain that way. On the other hand, research such as that conducted by Langlois and her colleagues brings to light the everyday implications of such informal evaluations—implications that may ultimately help to improve the quality of life for many people.

difficulties in one or more psychological, social, or academic areas and for whom intervention is or may be required. The need for intervention may be decided on the basis of a more complete evaluation, often involving psychological tests.

Psychological tests   One of the most widely used preschool tests is the WPPSI-R. discussed in the previous chapter. The Bayley Scales for Infant Development (Second Edition), the Battelle Developmental Inventory, the Early Screening Profile, the Developmental Indicators for the Assessment of Learning (Third Edition), the Mullen Scales of Early Learning, and the Miller Assessment for Preschoolers are some of many other tests used to gauge developmental strengths and weaknesses. These tests typically tap cognitive, motor, and social/behavioral content areas.

At the earliest levels, cognitive and social abilities are gauged by infant intelligence scales that, in essence, note the presence or absence of various developmental achievements through means such as observation and parental (or caretaker) interviews. By age 2, the child enters a challenging period for psychological assessors. Language and conceptual skills are beginning to emerge, yet the kinds of verbal and performance tests traditionally used with older children and adults are inappropriate. The attention span of the preschooler is short. Ideally, test materials are colorful, engaging, and attention-maintaining. Approximately one hour is a good rule-of-thumb limit for an entire test session with a preschooler, and less time is preferable; as testing time increases, so does the possibility of fatigue and distraction—with a resultant underestimation of the examinee's ability. Motivation of the young child may vary from one test session to the next, and this is something of which the examiner must be aware. Most welcomed by examiners who regularly work with preschoolers are tests that are relatively easy to administer, have simple start/discontinue rules, and allow the examiner ample opportunity to make behavioral observations of the child. Dual-easel test administration format (Figure 10–1), sample and teaching items for each subtest, and dichotomous scoring (for example, right/wrong) all facilitate test administration.

Data from infant intelligence tests, especially when combined with other information (such as birth history, emotional and social history, health history, data on the quality of the physical and emotional environment, and measures of adaptive behavior) have proved useful to health professionals when suspicions about developmental disability and related deficits have been raised. The tests have also proved useful in helping to define the abilities, as well as the extent of disability, in older, psychotic children. Furthermore, the tests have been in use for a number of years by many adoption agencies that will disclose and interpret such information to prospective adoptive parents. Infant tests also have wide application in the area of research and can play a part in selecting infants for specialized early educational experiences or measuring the outcome of educational, therapeutic, or prenatal care interventions.

What is the meaning of a score on an infant intelligence test? Whereas some of the developers infant tests (such as Cattell, 1940; Gesell et al., 1940) claimed that such tests could predict future intellectual ability because they measured the developmental precursors to such ability, others have insisted that performance on such tests at best reflects the infant's physical and neuropsychological intactness. The research literature supports a middle ground between these extreme positions. In general, the tests have not been found to predict performance on child or adult intelligence tests—tests that tap vastly different types of abilities and thought processes (Bayley, 1955, 1959, 1993; Bradway, 1945; Honzik et al., 1948; Welcher et al., 1971). The predictive efficacy of the tests does tend to increase with the extremes of the infant's performance; the test interpreter can say with authority more about the future performance of an infant whose performance was either profoundly below age expectancy or significantly precocious. Still, infancy is a developmental period of many spurts and lags, and infants who are slow or precocious at this age might catch up or fall back in later years. Perhaps the great value of preschool tests lies in their ability to help in the identification of children who are in a very low range of functioning and in need of intervention.

Other measures Many other instruments and assessment techniques are available for use with preschoolers including interviews, case history methods, portfolio evaluation, role-play methods—each modified in necessary ways to be age-appropriate for their in-

Figure 10–1
A Dual-Easel Format in Test Administration

An "easel format" in the context of test administration refers to test materials, usually some sort of book that contains test-stimulus materials and that can be folded and placed on a desk; the examiner turns the pages to reveal to the examinee, for example, objects to identify or designs to copy. When corresponding test-administration instructions or notes are printed on the reverse side of the test-stimulus pages for the examiner's convenience during test administration, the format is sometimes referred to as "dual easel."

tended use. Some instruments are designed to measure temperament (Fullard et al., 1984; McDevitt & Carey, 1978), language skills (Smith et al., 2000), and various aspects of parenting or caregiving (Arnold et al., 1993; Lovejoy et al., 1999) or the family environment in general (Moos & Moos, 1994). A proposed measure seeks to explore the preschooler's quality of life (Eiser et al., 2000). Some techniques, such as figure drawings to assess personality, will be covered in a subsequent chapter of this book. Some techniques are very specialized and would only be used under rather extraordinary conditions or in the context of research focused on a specific subject matter. An example of the latter is the Child Sexual Behavior Inventory (Friedrich et al., 2001), a 38-item behavior checklist that may be helpful in identifying sexually abused children as young as 2 years old. In sum, there is a growing number of instruments available for use with preschoolers to help evaluate, better understand, and address with appropriate intervention (if possible) a wide variety of areas related to personal, social, and academic development.

From here on in this chapter, we focus on school-age children and young adults, and various types of testing and assessment conducted with them in educational contexts.

We begin with achievement tests, a topic with which many students report that they are (all too) familiar.

Achievement Tests

Achievement tests are designed to measure accomplishment. An achievement test for a first-grader might have as its subject matter the English language alphabet, whereas an achievement test for someone such as yourself might contain questions relating to principles of psychological assessment. In short, achievement tests are designed to measure the degree of learning that has taken place as a result of exposure to a relatively defined learning experience. The "relatively defined learning experience" may be something as broad as a sampling of "what you learned from four years of college" or something as narrow as "administering first aid for snake bites." A test of achievement may be standardized nationally, regionally, or locally, or it may not be standardized at all; the pop quiz on the anatomy of a frog given by your high school biology teacher qualifies every bit as much for the title "achievement test" as does the statewide biology examination you may have been given at the completion of the school year. Like other tests, achievement tests vary widely with respect to their psychometric soundness. A sound achievement test is one that adequately samples the targeted subject matter and reliably gauges the extent to which all the examinees learned it.

Achievement tests assist school personnel in making decisions concerning a student's advancement to higher levels and the grouping of students for instructional purposes. Achievement tests are sometimes used to screen for difficulties, and in such instances they may precede the administration of diagnostic tests employed to identify areas where remediation will be necessary. Achievement test data can be used to gauge the quality of instruction in regard to one particular teacher, an entire school district, or a state, though such a use of test data presumes that students' abilities and related factors are relatively constant across situations—a tenuous assumption in some situations.

Achievement tests play an essential role in identifying children with learning disabilities. Although a definition in federal law was published over a quarter-century ago (see the Education for All Handicapped Children Act of 1975, Public Law 94-142, at Section 5b, 4), as have procedures for evaluation (Procedures for Evaluation, 1977), consensus among professionals regarding a definition of "learning disability" has been elusive, and a wide variety of assessment methods have been employed in an effort to comply with the law. For our purposes, we will define a **learning disability** as a disorder involving a discrepancy between ability and achievement, which may manifest itself in attentional, emotional, perceptual, and/or motor deficits, and/or in problems related to doing mathematical calculations, reading, writing, spelling, or using or understanding language, spoken or written. The term does not apply to persons who have academic problems that are cultural or economic in origin, nor to persons who have learning problems arising primarily from visual, hearing, or motor handicaps, or mental retardation.

Given a federal mandate to identify children with a "severe discrepancy between achievement and intellectual ability" (Procedures for Evaluating, 1977, p. 65083), it can readily be appreciated how achievement tests, as well as intelligence tests and other measures of cognitive ability and aptitude, could play a role in the diagnosis of a learning disability (or a "specific learning disability" as it is referred to in the legislation). A common approach to diagnosis is to administer tests of achievement and cognitive ability, and then determine by means of some formula whether a significant discrepancy exists. By law, a child will be diagnosed as learning disabled, and therefore be entitled to special school services, only if a significant discrepancy exists between the child's achievement and the child's expected level of achievement in one or more of the following areas: oral expression, listening comprehension, written expression, basic reading skills, reading comprehension, mathematics calculation, or mathematics reasoning. As we will see, in recent years test publishers have sought to provide "all-in-one" tests that provide means for determining whether a child should be diagnosed as learning disabled.

Measures of General Achievement

Measures of general achievement may survey learning in one or more academic areas. Tests that cover a number of academic areas are typically divided into several subtests and are referred to as "achievement batteries." Such batteries may be individually administered or group-administered. They may consist of a few subtests, as does the Wide Range Achievement Test-3 (Wilkinson, 1993) with its measures of reading, spelling, and arithmetic, or be as comprehensive as the STEP Series that includes subtests in reading, vocabulary, mathematics, writing skills, study skills, science, and social studies, a behavior inventory, an educational environment questionnaire, and an activities inventory. Some batteries, such as the SRA California Achievement Tests, span kindergarten through grade 12, whereas others are grade- or course-specific. Some batteries are constructed to provide both norm-referenced and criterion-referenced analyses. Others are concurrently normed with scholastic aptitude tests to enable a comparison between achievement and aptitude. Some batteries are constructed with practice tests that may be administered several days before actual testing to help students familiarize themselves with testtaking procedures. Other batteries contain **locator** or routing tests, pretests administered to determine the level of the actual test most appropriate for administration.

One popular instrument appropriate for use with persons age 4 through adult is the Wechsler Individual Achievement Test-Second Edition, otherwise known as the WIAT-II (Psychological Corporation, 2001). This instrument is used not only to gauge achievement, but to develop hypotheses about achievement versus ability. It features nine subtests that sample content in each of the seven areas required by the Individuals with Disabilities Education Act: oral expression, listening comprehension, written expression, basic reading skill, reading comprehension, mathematics calculation, and mathematics reasoning. The test was designed to facilitate understanding of the problem-solving processes and strategies that testtakers use in these areas. The manual provides age- and grade-based standard score information. Test scores allow for detailed skill analysis and specification of intervention targets for individualized education plans. Scoring is done either manually or by means of optional software capable of creating a basic report exportable to a word processor.

Of the many available achievement batteries, the test that is most appropriate for use is the one most consistent with the educational objectives of the individual teacher or school system. It may be that for a particular purpose, a battery that focuses on achievement in a few select areas is preferable to one that attempts to sample achievement in several areas. On the other hand, a test that samples many areas may be advantageous when an individual comparison of performance across subject areas is desirable. If a school or a local school district undertakes to follow the progress of a group of students as measured by a particular achievement battery, the battery of choice will be one that spans the targeted subject areas in all the grades to be tested. If ability to distinguish individual areas of difficulty is of primary concern, achievement tests with strong diagnostic features will be chosen. Although achievement batteries sampling a wide range of areas, across grades, and standardized on large, national samples of students have much to recommend them, they also have certain drawbacks. For example, such tests usually take years to develop; in the interim the items, especially in fields such as social studies and science, may become outdated. Further, any nationally standardized instrument is only as good as the extent to which it meets the (local) test user's objectives.

Measures of Achievement in Specific Subject Areas

Whereas achievement batteries tend to be standardized instruments, most measures of achievement in specific subject areas are teacher-made tests; every time a teacher gives a quiz, a test, or a final examination in a course, a test in a specific subject area has been created. Still, there are a number of standardized instruments designed to gauge achievement in specific areas.

At the elementary school level, the acquisition of basic skills such as reading, writing, and arithmetic is emphasized. The consumer of reading achievement tests has a great deal of choice with respect to variables such as individual or group administration, silent or oral reading, and type of subtest data provided. In general, the tests present the examinee with words, sentences, or paragraphs to be read silently or aloud, and reading ability is assessed by variables such as comprehension and vocabulary. When the material is read aloud, accuracy and speed will be measured. Tests of reading comprehension also vary with respect to the intellectual demands placed on the examinee over and above mere comprehension of the words read. Thus, some tests might require the examinee to simply recall facts from a passage, whereas others might require interpretation and drawing inferences.

At the secondary school level, one popular battery is the Cooperative Achievement Test. It consists of a series of separate achievement tests in areas as diverse as English, mathematics, literature, social studies, science, and foreign language. Each test was standardized on different populations appropriate to the grade level, and in general the tests tend to be technically sound instruments. For example, the American History component of the Social Studies series was standardized on seventh- and eighth-graders who represented 44 junior and 73 senior high schools. The sample was randomly selected and stratified according to public, parochial, and private schools. Alternate-form reliability for the test was found to be .87 for the junior high school sample and .79 for the senior high school sample. Kuder-Richardson reliability estimates of internal consistency at the junior high school level resulted in reliability coefficients of .88 and .90 for Forms A and B, respectively, and .90 for both forms at the high school level. Assessment of achievement in high school students may involve evaluation of minimum competencies, often as a requirement for a high school diploma (see this chapter's *Close-up*).

At the college level, there has been growing interest on the part of state legislatures to mandate end-of-major outcomes assessment in state colleges and universities. Apparently, taxpayers want some concrete affirmation that their education tax dollars are being well spent. Thus, for example, undergraduate psychology students attending a state-run institution could be required in their senior year to sit for a final—in the literal sense—examination encompassing a range of subject matter that could be described as "everything that an undergraduate psychology major should know." And if that sounds formidable to you, trust us when we advise you that the task of developing such examinations will be all the more formidable.

Another use for achievement tests at the college as well as the adult level is for the purpose of placement. The advanced placement program developed by the College Entrance Examination Board offers high school students the opportunity to achieve college credit for work completed while in high school. Successful completion of the advanced

Tests of Minimum Competency

Soon after the founding of the United States as an independent nation, one citizen commented in a book entitled *Letters from an American Farmer* that a "pleasing uniformity of decent competence appears throughout our habitations" (Crevecoeur, 1782, cited in Lerner, 1981). Over two hundred years later, widespread dissatisfaction with the *lack* of competence in this country has become evident. At about the time of the nation's bicentennial celebration, a grassroots movement aimed at eradicating illiteracy and anumeracy began taking shape. By 1980, 38 states had legislated regulations requiring that the schools administer a test to determine whether secondary school graduates had developed "minimum competence." Exactly what constituted minimum competence varied from one jurisdiction to the next, but it generally referred to some basic knowledge of reading, writing, and arithmetic. The movement has gained momentum with the realization that the illiterate and anumerate often wind up not only unemployed but unemployable as well. The unfortunate consequence is that too many of these individuals require public assistance or, alternatively, turn to crime—some finding their way to jail.

A minimum competency testing program is designed to ensure that the student given the high school diploma has at least acquired the minimal skills to become a productive member of society. Representative of such minimal skills necessary in everyday living are the ability to fill out an employment application and the ability to write checks, balance a checkbook, and interpret a bank statement.

As an example of one test for minimal competency, we focus attention on the Alabama High School Graduation Exam (AHSGE). A publication of the Alabama State Department of Education (Teague, 1983) sets forth very detailed specifications for items to be used in the AHSGE. The skills that are tested are based on ninth-grade minimal competencies in the areas of Reading, Language, and Mathematics. Some of the skills listed in the area of Language are:

- *Observe pronoun-antecedent agreement.*
  The student chooses the pronoun that agrees with its antecedent.
- *Use correct forms of nouns and verbs.*
  The student chooses the correct form of nouns (singular and/or plural) and of verbs (regular and/or irregular) and selects verbs that agree with the subjects.
- *Include in a message or request all necessary information (who, what, when, where, how, or why).*

The student demonstrates knowledge about what information is necessary in a message or request.

- *Determine what information is missing from a message, an announcement, or a process explanation; or what information is irrelevant.*
- *Identify the comma to separate works in a series.*
- *Identify question marks, periods, and exclamation points to punctuate sentences.*
- *Identify words frequently used in daily activities.*
  The student recognizes frequently used words that are spelled incorrectly.
- *Complete a common form, such as a driver's license application or change of address form.*
- *Identify the proper format of a friendly letter.*
- *Identify the proper format of a business letter.*
  The student demonstrates knowledge of the proper format of a business letter, which includes punctuation and capitalization. Test questions refer to business letters reproduced in the test booklet. An example appears at the end of this Close-up.

Although minimum competency may seem like a good idea, it has not gone unchallenged in the courts. Who should determine the skills necessary for minimum competence and the lack of minimum competence? What should the consequence be if an individual is not found to be minimally competent? Will a minimum competence requirement for a high school diploma act to motivate the academically unmotivated? In 1979, a federal judge in Florida held the scheduled application of that state's minimum competency law to be unconstitutional. Condemning the judge's decision, Lerner (1981) wrote that "disputes over empirical questions cannot be resolved by judicial fiat," and she went on to document that (1) substantial numbers of Americans are failing to master basic skills, such as reading, (2) the consequences of such deficits warrant action, and (3) the actions recommended by minimum competence advocates offer reasonable hope of bringing about the desired change (see also Lerner, 1980). Critics (such as Airasian et al., 1979; Haney & Madaus, 1978; Tyler, 1978) object primarily on grounds pertaining to the potential for abuse inherent in such programs, though some criticisms regarding the psychometric soundness of the instruments have also been voiced.

(continued)

Tests of Minimum Competency
(continued)

120 Drewry Road
Monroeville Alabama 36460

Miss Ann Andrews, Director
Parks and Recreation
Monroeville, Alabama 36460

Dear Miss Andrews:

Our class would like to use the Community House for our senior prom. The tentative date for the prom is April 30, 1982. Please let me know if the ballroom is available on this date and the charges for the use of this facility.

yours truly,

Jan Austin

1. What part of the letter is the salutation?

   a.   Jan Austin
   *b.   Dear Miss Andrews:
   c.   yours truly,
   d.   Miss Ann Andrews

2. Which part of the letter has an error in punctuation?

   a.   The salutation
   b.   The closing
   c.   The signature
   *d.   The heading

3. Which part of the letter has an error in capitalization?

   *a.   The closing
   b.   The body
   c.   The inside address
   d.   The heading

4. Which part of this business letter has been omitted?

   *a.   The date of the letter
   b.   The salutation
   c.   The closing
   d.   The inside address

Sample Items Designed to Evaluate the Testtaker's Knowledge of the Format for a Business Letter

placement test may result in advanced standing, advanced course credit, or both, depending on the college policy. Since its inception, the advanced placement program has resulted in advanced credit or standing for over one hundred thousand high school students in approximately two thousand colleges. Another type of test that has application for placement purposes, particularly in areas of the country where English may be spoken as a second language by a relatively large segment of the population (such as parts of California, Florida, and Texas) is a test of English proficiency. One way in which data from an English proficiency test are currently used is in the placement of applicants to college programs in an appropriate level of an English-as-a-second-language program. However, other uses of data from measures of English proficiency can be foreseen. In an era in which there appear to be growing numbers of native as well as immigrant Americans with limited English proficiency, and in a social climate that has legislators writing bills proclaiming English to be the official language of the state, one can foresee the increasing importance of issues related to the testing of English proficiency.

Achievement tests at the college or adult level may also assess whether college credit should be awarded for learning acquired outside a college classroom. Numerous programs are designed to systematically assess whether sufficient knowledge has been acquired to qualify for course credit. The College Level Examination Program (CLEP) is based on the premise that knowledge may be obtained through independent study and sources other than formal schooling. The program includes exams in subjects ranging from African American History to Tests and Measurement. Participants in programs such as CLEP tend to think very favorably of them (Losak, 1978). The Proficiency Examination Program (PEP) offered by the American College Testing Program is another service designed to assess achievement and skills learned outside the classroom.

The special needs of adults with a wide variety of educational backgrounds are addressed in tests such as the Adult Basic Learning Examination (ABLE), a test intended for use with examinees age 17 and older who did not complete eight years of formalized schooling. The test is designed to assess achievement in the areas of vocabulary, reading, spelling, and arithmetic; it was developed in consultation with experts in the field of adult education.

Achievement tests in nationwide use may test for information or concepts that are not taught within a specific school's curriculum. Some children will do well on such items anyway, having been exposed to the concepts or information independently. Performance on a school achievement test therefore does not depend entirely on school achievement. Concern about such issues has led to an interest in **curriculum-based assessment (CBA)**, assessment that clearly and faithfully reflects what is being taught in school. CBA tends to be viewed favorably but probably is not used consistently (Shapiro & Eckert, 1993) or with sufficient attention to the child's perspective (Frederickson, 1993). Curriculum-based measurement (CBM), a type of CBA, is characterized by the use of standardized measurement procedures to derive local norms to be used in the evaluation of student performance on curriculum-based tasks.

Before leaving the topic of achievement tests, we will briefly point out that there are at least two distinctly different types of achievement test items. One type demands only rote memory. An example of such an item on an examination designed to measure mastery of the material in this chapter might look like this:

1. One type of item that could be used in an achievement test is an item that requires

    a.   remote memory.

    b.   rote memory.

    c.   memory loss.

    d.   none of the above.

Alternatively, items in achievement tests could require the testtaker not only to know and understand the material but also to be able to apply it. In a test of English proficiency, for example, it might be important for the examinee to know more than vocabulary or rules of grammar; items that gauge the ability of the examinee to understand or speak conversational English might be of far greater importance.

Aptitude Tests

True or false: Achievement tests measure learned knowledge, whereas aptitude tests measure innate potential. The correct answer to this question is false. To understand why this is so, consider for a moment how we acquire knowledge. Each of us is born with a mental and a physical apparatus that does have certain limitations—not everyone is born with the same mental and physical gifts as everyone else. Working with the biological equipment we have in conjunction with psychological factors (such as motivation) and environmental factors (such as educational opportunities), we are constantly acquiring information through everyday life experiences and through formal learning experiences such as coursework in school. The primary difference between tests that are referred to as "achievement tests" and those that are referred to as "aptitude tests" is that **aptitude tests** tend to focus more on informal learning or life experiences as their subject matter, whereas achievement tests tend to focus on the learning that has occurred as a result of relatively structured input. Keeping this distinction in mind, consider the following two items, the first from a hypothetical achievement test and the second from a hypothetical aptitude test.

1. A correlation of .7 between variables X and Y in a predictive validity study accounts for what percentage of the variance?
   a. 7%
   b. 70%
   c. .7%
   d. 49%
   e. 25%

2. o is to O as x is to
   a. /
   b. %
   c. X
   d. Y

At least on the face of it, Item 1 appears to be more dependent on formal learning experiences than does Item 2. The successful completion of Item 1 hinges on familiarity with the concept of correlation and the knowledge that the variance accounted for by a correlation coefficient is equal to the square of the coefficient (in this case, $.7^2$, or .49—choice "d"). The successful completion of Item 2 requires experience with the concept of size, as well as the ability to grasp the concept of analogies, two abilities that tend to be gleaned from life experiences (witness how quickly you determined that the correct answer was choice "c"). It must also be kept in mind that the label "achievement" or "aptitude" for a test is very much dependent on the intended use of the test, not just on the type of items contained in it. It is possible for two tests to contain some of the same items and for one of the tests to be called an "aptitude" test, whereas the other is referred to as an "achievement" test. Item 2 in our example was presented as representing an item that might appear on some aptitude test, though it might well appear on an achievement test if the area of learning covered by the latter test encompassed the concept of size or analogous thinking. Similarly, Item 1, presented as an illustrative achievement test item, might well be used to assess aptitude (in statistics, or psychology, for example) were it to be included in a test that was not expressly designed to measure achievement in this area.

Aptitude tests, also referred to as **prognostic tests,** are tests typically used to make predictions. Some aptitude tests have been used to measure readiness for school, aptitude for college-level work or graduate school, and aptitude for work in a particular profession (such as medicine, law, art, or music). Achievement tests may also be used for predictive purposes. Thus, for example, an individual who performs well on a first-semester foreign-language achievement test might be considered a good candidate for the second term's work. The assumption is made that because the individual was able to master certain basic skills, he or she will be able to master more advanced skills—hence, the achievement test has been used as if it were a test of aptitude. Few situations exist where the reverse is true—where a test expressly designed to test for aptitude is used as an achievement test. Note that when achievement tests are used to make predictions, they tend to draw on narrower (more formal) learning experiences and are therefore typically used to make predictions with respect to some equally narrow variable (for example, success in Basic French predicts success in Advanced French). Aptitude tests draw on a broader fund of information and abilities and are typically used to predict to broader variables (just as "general fund of information" might be used to predict to success in higher education). Another hallmark of the aptitude test in contrast to the achievement test is the utilization of tasks that are not formally taught in the schools, such as figural analogies and number series. Such tasks are designed to reduce the likelihood that they had been specifically taught to the examinee.

To summarize the sometimes blurry distinction between achievement and aptitude tests: Although both types of tests measure learning to some degree, achievement tests are typically more limited in scope in the learning they assess. Achievement tests reflect learning that has occurred under controlled and definable conditions, usually where there has been specific training. Aptitude tests tap a combination of learning experiences and inborn potential that was obtained under uncontrolled and undefined conditions. Predictions about future learning and behavior can be made from both kinds of tests, though predictions made on the basis of achievement tests are usually limited to the subject matter of the test.

In the following sections, we survey some aptitude tests used in schools from entry level through graduate and professional institutions. Note that at the entry level an aptitude test is often referred to as a **readiness test,** because its primary purpose is to assess the child's readiness for learning. As the level of education climbs, however, the term *readiness* is dropped in favor of the term *aptitude,* although readiness is very much implied at all levels. The Scholastic Aptitude Test (SAT), given late in high school and widely used as a predictor of ability to do college-level work, might well have been called the "College Readiness Test." Similarly, the Graduate Record Examination (GRE), given in college and used as a predictor of ability to do graduate-level work, might have been christened the "Graduate School Readiness Examination." Both tests can be used effectively to predict aptitude for advanced-level work. For example, one *GRE Guide* indicated that correlations between the GRE and grades in the first year of graduate school ranged from .30 to .37, depending on the field of study. College grades are also predictive of first-year grades in graduate school, with correlations ranging between .35 and .39. Using college grades and GRE scores together results in even more accurate predictions of first-year graduate school grades. Correlations ranging from .44 to .48 indicate that between 19% and 23% of the variance in first-year graduate school grades can be accounted for by college grades and GRE scores together.

Aptitude tests such as the GRE and the SAT provide more than a mere indicator of readiness. Especially at the upper levels, educational standards vary not only from community to community but also from school to school—even from class to class.

Additionally, teacher prejudices as well as a host of other factors may enter into grading procedures. Aptitude tests represent a kind of equalizer, for they provide a sample of academic performance on a standardized test that can be compared with the performance of all other students taking the test. When used in conjunction with grades and various other criteria, aptitude test data can be a good predictor of future academic success.

The Elementary School Level

The age at which a child is mandated by law to enter school varies from state to state. Yet, individual children of the same chronological age may vary widely in how ready they are to separate from their parents and begin academic learning. Children entering the educational system come from a wide range of backgrounds and experiences, and their rates of physiological, psychological, and social development also vary widely. School readiness tests provide educators with a yardstick by which to assess pupils' abilities in areas as diverse as general information and sensory-motor skills. One of many instruments designed to assess children's readiness and aptitude for formal education is the Metropolitan Readiness Tests (MRT).

The Metropolitan Readiness Tests (MRT)   The MRT is a group-administered battery that assesses the development of reading and mathematics skills important in the early stages of formal, school learning. The test is divided into two levels: Level I, to be used with beginning and middle kindergarteners, and Level II, which spans the end of kindergarten through first grade (Table 10–1). There are two forms of the test at each level. The tests are orally administered in several sessions and are untimed, though they typically require about 90 minutes to administer. A practice test (especially useful with young children who have had minimal or no prior testtaking experience) may be ad-

Table 10–1
The Subtests of the Metropolitan Readiness Tests

Level I

Auditory Memory: Four pictures containing familiar objects are presented. The examiner reads aloud several words. The child must select the picture that corresponds to the same sequence of words that were presented orally.

Rhyming: The examiner supplies the names of each of the pictures presented and then gives a fifth word that rhymes with one of them. The child must select the picture that rhymes with the examiner's word.

Letter Recognition: The examiner names different letters and the child must identify each from the series presented in the test booklet.

Visual Matching: A sample is presented and the child must select the choice that matches the sample.

School Language and Listening: The examiner reads a sentence, and the child selects the picture that describes what was read. The task involves some inference-making and awareness of relevancy of detail.

Quantitative Language: The test assesses comprehension of quantitative terms and knowledge of ordinal numbers and simple mathematical operations.

Level II

Beginning Consonants: Four pictures representing familiar objects are presented in the test booklet and are named by the examiner. The examiner then supplies a fifth word (not presented), and the child must select the picture that begins with the same sound.

Sound-Letter Correspondence: A picture is presented followed by a series of letters. The examiner names the picture, and the child selects the choice that corresponds to the beginning sound of the pictured item.

Visual Matching: As in the corresponding subtest at Level I, a model is presented, and the child must select the choice that matches the model.

Finding Patterns: A stimulus consisting of several symbols is presented followed by a series of representative options. The child must select the option that contains the same sequence of symbols, even though presented in a larger grouping with more distractions.

School Language: As in the School Language and Listening Test at Level I, the child must select the picture that corresponds to an orally presented sentence.

Listening: Material is orally presented, and the child must select the picture that reflects comprehension of, and drawing conclusions from, that material.

Quantitative Concepts ⎫ Both are optional tests that, like the Quantitative Language of Level I, assess comprehension of basic mathematical concepts
Quantitative Operations ⎭ and operations.

ministered several days before the actual testing to help familiarize students with procedures and the format involved in taking such a test.

Normative data for the current edition of the MRT are based on a national sample of approximately thirty thousand children. The standardization sample was stratified according to geographic regions, socioeconomic factors, prior school experience, and ethnic background. Data were obtained from both public and parochial schools and from both large and small schools. Split-half reliability coefficients for both forms of both levels of the MRT as well as Kuder-Richardson measures of internal consistency were in the acceptably high range. Content validity was developed through an extensive review of the literature, analysis of the skills involved in the reading process, and the development of test items that reflected those skills. Items were reviewed by minority consultants in an attempt to reduce, if not eliminate, any potential ethnic bias. The predictive validity of MRT scores has been examined with reference to later school achievement indices, and the obtained validity coefficients have been acceptably high.

The Secondary School Level

Perhaps the most obvious example of an aptitude test widely used in the schools at the secondary level is the Scholastic Aptitude Test (SAT). The test has been of value not only in the college selection process but also as an aid to high school guidance and job placement counselors in advising students about what course of action might be best for them. In addition to the SAT, the American College Testing (ACT) programs provide another well-known aptitude test.

How much do colleges really rely on criteria such as SAT scores in making college entrance decisions? Probably less than most people believe. Institutions of higher learning in this country differ widely with respect to their admission criteria. Even among schools that require SAT or ACT test scores, varying weights are accorded to the scores with respect to admission decisions. Highly selective institutions may admit large numbers of students with lower test scores and reject large numbers of students with high test scores. It has been argued that higher education is available to any American citizen who wants it and that "in no major system of higher education in the world is access to higher education less dependent on the results of a single examination or set of examinations than in the United States" (Hargadon, 1981, p. 1112). That statement is even more reflective of the current state of affairs than it was when it was made over two decades ago. With that preface, we briefly describe the SAT.

The Scholastic Aptitude Test (SAT) The SAT was first introduced as an objective exam in 1926. Until 1995, the SAT was a three-hour test divided into two parts: Verbal and Mathematics. The Verbal part consisted of sections that included Analogies, Reading Comprehension, Antonyms, and Sentence Completion. The Reading Comprehension section consisted of reading passages containing subject material from a variety of academic areas, such as science, social studies, and the humanities. The Sentence Completion section consisted of single sentences or paragraphs in which one or two words had been omitted, and the examinee's task was to select the choice that best completed the written thought. Vocabulary knowledge was measured by performance on the Antonyms and Analogies items. In 1974, a Test of Standard Written English was introduced for the first time to assess the student's ability to comprehend the type of language utilized in most college textbooks. It consisted of 50 multiple-choice questions and required 30 minutes to complete. A Reading Comprehension score based on the Sentence Completion and Reading Comprehension sections was also computed. The Mathematics part of the SAT assessed the understanding and application of mathematical principles, as well as numerical reasoning ability. The subject matter of the test questions in this section assumed knowledge of the basic arithmetic operations such as addition, subtraction, multiplication, division, averages, percentages, odd-even integers, and geometric and algebraic concepts, including linear and quadratic equations, exponents, and factoring.

Test items for the SAT are constructed by experts in the field and pretested on national samples during the actual examination. The experimental items are placed in separately timed sections of the examination. Such a pretesting procedure on a sample of examinees who are representative of the group that will be taking future forms of the test provides the test constructors with useful information regarding the value of proposed new items. The responses of students are statistically analyzed to determine the percent answering each question correctly, the percent choosing each of the distractor items, and the percent who omit the item; and an index of the response to each item with the total score on the test (that is, a difficulty rating for each item) is computed. The test is under continual revision, and the total time to develop an item may be upward of 18 months.

The technical quality of the SAT is good. Reliability of recent forms of the test as measured by internal-consistency estimates have resulted in reliability coefficients in the .90s for both the Verbal and the Mathematics scales. Research concerning the validity of the SAT has focused mostly on correlations between SAT scores and college grades, or on a combination of SAT scores and high school grades with college grades. In general, high school grades have been found to correlate higher with college grades than do SAT scores. When SAT scores and high school grade-point average are combined, the correlation with college performance increases. For example, in one study, grades in the first year of college correlated .20 with SAT scores and .30 with high school class rank. Together, SAT scores and high school class rank correlated .34 with college grades, accounting for 11.3% of the variance in college grades (Baron & Norman, 1992). Correlations between the Verbal and Mathematics parts of the SAT have been in the high .60s, a finding that suggests that overlapping skills, probably verbal in nature, are tapped on both parts of the exam.

The SAT is administered several times a year under carefully controlled conditions in cities throughout the United States and in foreign countries. Foreign-language editions of the test have been made available, as have special editions for students with disabilities. A special form (the Preliminary Scholastic Aptitude Test, or PSAT) is available for administration as a practice exam and as a tool for counselors.

Major changes in the SAT's format and normative base were instituted in the early 1990s. The format changes were designed to make the test more "educationally relevant" with respect to its objective of predicting college performance (Moses, 1991). Essentially, the format change involved dichotomizing the SAT into two major components: Reasoning tests and Subject tests.

The first component is essentially a revised and expanded version of the preexisting SAT. It includes verbal and mathematical tests, and continues to measure ability or aptitude for college-level education. It also features increased emphasis on critical reading in the verbal sections. Some math questions require the student to produce a written answer. Students may use a calculator on math questions. The second SAT component consists of a set of achievement tests in the areas of writing, literature, history, foreign languages, mathematics, and sciences (College Board Review, 1990–1991; Q and A, 1994).

When the SAT was standardized in 1941, the average performance was reflected in a score of 500. In the years since 1941, SAT scores have declined, such that the average testtaker in 1993 received a verbal SAT score of 424 and a mathematics score of 478. Because the norms were anchored, the scores retained the same meaning in 1993 as they had in 1941; a score of 500 in 1993 meant that the testtaker performed at the average level of testtakers in 1941. This made possible the comparison of students taking the test during different years. A similar shift in GRE scores had taken place (see *Everyday Psychometrics* in Chapter 4). As of April 1995, the SAT norms were "recentered" so that a score of 500 indicates average performance among current testtakers. Test users, like college admissions offices, have been provided with tables to convert old SAT scores (based on the 1941 norms) to scores based on the 1995 norms for comparison purposes (Q and A, 1994). Unless recentering occurs in the meantime, an SAT score of 500 indicates an average level of performance relative to the immortalized performance of people who took the test in 1995.

The College Level and Beyond

If you are a college student planning to pursue further education after graduation, you are probably familiar with acronyms such as GRE, MAT, MCAT, and LSAT. Respectively, these acronyms stand for the Graduate Record Examination, the Miller Analogies Test, the Medical College Admissions Test, and the Law School Admission Test. The GRE is a test that may be used as one criterion for admission to many graduate school programs. The MAT is a 100-item multiple-choice analogy test that draws not only on the examinee's ability to perceive relationships but also on general intelligence, vocabulary, and academic learning. As an example, complete the following analogy:

Classical conditioning is to *Pavlov,* as *operant conditioning* is to

a. Freud.
b. Rogers.
c. Skinner.
d. Jung.
e. Westheimer.

Successful completion of this item demands not only the ability to understand the relationship between classical conditioning and Pavlov but also the knowledge that it was B. F. Skinner (choice "c") whose name—of the names listed—is best associated with operant conditioning.

Applicants for training in certain professions are required to take specialized examinations. Students applying to medical school are required to take the Medical College Admission Test (MCAT). Offered twice a year, the MCAT is a multiple-choice test divided into four separately timed sections. These include Verbal Ability (comprising 75 items to be completed in 20 minutes), Quantitative Ability (50 items to be completed in 45 minutes), General Information (75 items to be completed in 25 minutes), and Science (86 items to be completed in 60 minutes). Items in the Verbal Ability section consist of analogy items, synonyms, and antonyms. The Quantitative section assesses knowledge and application of algebraic, geometric, and arithmetic principles. The General Information section includes items pertaining to a variety of subject areas such as music and sports; and the Science section, probably the most closely related to the field of medicine, includes test items pertaining to biology, chemistry, and physics. Although the test continues to be used as one criterion in medical school admission, scores on it have not been found to be predictive of class rank in medical school.

Applicants to law school are required to take the Law School Admissions Test (LSAT). The test is presented in two testing sessions, one in the morning and one in the afternoon, and a separate score is obtained for each session. The morning session consists of five separately timed sections: Logical Reasoning, Practical Judgment, Data Interpretation, Quantitative Comparisons, and Principles and Cases. Based on the premise that the legal profession itself relies heavily on verbal skills (both in comprehension and in communication), the LSAT is purposely developed to primarily reflect verbal abilities. The test items are designed to assess comprehension, interpretation, critical analysis, evaluation, and application of information. To that end, each test item presents a body of information followed by multiple-choice items. The Logical Reasoning and Practical Judgment sections present information in the form of reading passages, and the Data Interpretation section employs graphs and tables. Subject matter representative of many different fields of study is included in the test. The only section that contains legally oriented subject material is the Principles and Cases section, which presents hypothetical situations involving legal principles. It is assumed, however, that the testtaker has had no previous legal training and that the answers may be obtained through general reasoning skills. The afternoon session is divided into three sections (Error Recognition, Sentence Correction, and Usage) that together form the Writing Ability Score. Taken together, these sections provide an indication of ability to express oneself in writing. Predictive validity studies examining the relationship between score obtained on the LSAT and grade-point average of first-year law students have yielded relatively low correlations.

Numerous other aptitude tests have been developed to assess specific kinds of academic and/or occupational aptitudes. For example, the Seashore Measures of Musical Talents (Seashore, 1938) is a musical aptitude test administered with the aid of a prerecorded record or tape. The six subtests measure specific aspects of musical talent (for example, comparing different notes and rhythms on variables such as loudness, pitch, time, and timbre). The Horn Art Aptitude Inventory is a measure of art aptitude that is divided into two sections. The Scribbles and Doodles section contains items thought to measure variables such as clarity of thought and originality. Items in the Imagery section contain key lines or "springboards" from art masterpieces to be incorporated in the examinee's artistic production. Scoring categories for the Imagery section include Design, Imagination, and Scope of Interests.

Diagnostic Tests

By the early twentieth century, it was recognized that tests of intelligence could be used to do more than simply measure cognitive ability. Binet and Simon (1908) wrote of their concept of "mental orthopedics" whereby intelligence test data could be used to improve learning. Today, a distinction is made between tests and test data that are used primarily for evaluative purposes, and tests and test data that are used primarily for diagnostic purposes. As implied in its name, the term **evaluative,** as used in phrases such as "evaluative purposes" or "evaluative information," is typically applied to tests or test data that are used to make judgments (such as pass/fail and admit/reject decisions). By contrast, the term **diagnostic,** as used in educational contexts and phrases such as "diagnostic purposes" or "diagnostic information," is typically applied to tests or test data that are used to pinpoint a student's difficulty for the purpose of remediating that difficulty.

A diagnostic reading test, for example, may contain a number of subtests, each designed to analyze a specific knowledge or skill required to read and to bring into full relief the specific problems, if any, that need to be addressed if the testtaker is to read at an appropriate grade level. By the way, diagnostic information can also be used for evaluative purposes. On the basis of a child's performance on a diagnostic reading test, for example, a teacher or administrator might make a class placement decision. Also, keep in mind that diagnostic tests do not necessarily provide information that will answer questions concerning *why* the learning difficulty exists; other educational, psychological, and perhaps medical examinations will have to answer the "why" question. In general, diagnostic tests are administered to students who have already demonstrated their problem with a particular subject area through their poor performance either in the classroom or on some achievement test. It is therefore understandable that diagnostic tests tend to contain simpler items than do achievement tests designed for use with members of the same grade.

Reading Tests

The ability to read is integral to virtually all classroom learning, and so it is not surprising that many diagnostic tests are available to help pinpoint difficulties in acquiring this skill (for example, the Stanford Diagnostic Reading Test, the Metropolitan Reading Instructional Tests, the Diagnostic Reading Scales, the Durrell Analysis of Reading Test). For illustrative purposes we briefly describe one such diagnostic battery, the Woodcock Reading Mastery Tests.

The Woodcock Reading Mastery Tests-Revised (WRMT-R) This test battery is suitable for children age 5 and older, and adults up to age 75—and beyond, according to the promotional literature. The subtests include:

- *Letter Identification.* Items that measure the ability to name letters presented in different forms. Both cursive/manuscript and uppercase/lowercase letters are presented.
- *Word Identification.* Words in isolation arranged in order of increasing difficulty. The student is asked to read each word aloud.
- *Word Attack.* Nonsense syllables that incorporate phonetic as well as structural analysis skills. The student is asked to pronounce each nonsense syllable.
- *Word Comprehension.* Items that assess word meaning by using a four-part analogy format.
- *Passage Comprehension.* Phrases, sentences, or short paragraphs read silently in which a word is missing. The student must supply the missing word.

The tests are individually administered and are designed to measure skills inherent in reading. The tests come in two forms labeled "G" and "H," and each form contains the five subtests listed above. Form G also contains a test labeled "Visual-Auditory Learning." A cassette tape is packaged with the tests and serves as a guide to the proper pronunciation of the Word Attack items and the Word Identification items. Test scores may be combined to form what are referred to as "clusters," such as a Readiness cluster (the Visual-Auditory Learning and Letter Identification tests), a Basic Skills cluster (the Word Identification and Word Attack tests), a Reading Comprehension cluster (the Word Comprehension and Passage Comprehension tests), a Total Reading-Full Scale cluster (the Word Identification, Word Attack, Word Comprehension, and Passage Comprehension tests), and a Total Reading-Short Scale (the Word Identification and Passage Comprehension tests). The last scale may be used for quick-screening (about 15 minutes) purposes, although each cluster of tests typically takes between 10 and 30 minutes to administer. An optional computer software program is also available for score conversion and storage of pre- and posttest scores.

Math Tests

The Stanford Diagnostic Mathematics Test, the Metropolitan Mathematics Instructional Tests, the Diagnostic Mathematics Inventory, and the KeyMath Revised: A Diagnostic Inventory of Essential Mathematics exemplify some of the many tests that have been developed to help diagnose difficulties with arithmetic and mathematical concepts. Items on such tests typically analyze the skills and knowledge necessary for segregating the parts of mathematical operations. The KeyMath Revised test, for example, contains 13 subtests designed to assess areas such as basic concepts (including knowledge of symbols, numbers, and fractions), operations (including skill in addition, subtraction, multiplication, division, and mental computation), and applications (numerical problems employing variables such as money and time). Diagnostic information is obtained from an evaluation of the examinee's performance in the various areas, subtests, and items. Total test scores are translated into grade equivalents, area performance may be translated into a general pattern of mathematical functioning, and subtest performance may be translated into a profile illustrating strengths and weaknesses. For each item on the test, the manual lists a description of the skill involved and a corresponding behavior objective—information useful in determining the skills to be included in a remedial program. A computerized scoring program converts raw scores into derived scores, summarizes the examinee's performance, and offers suggestions for remedial instruction.

Other Diagnostic Tests

In addition to individually administered diagnostic tests such as the KeyMath Revised, a number of diagnostic tests designed for group administration have been developed. Two examples of group diagnostic tests are the Stanford Diagnostic Reading Test (SDRT) and the Stanford Diagnostic Mathematics Test (SDMT). Although developed independently and standardized on separate populations, the two instruments share certain characteristics related to test design and format. Both instruments are available in two forms, and both are divided into four overlapping levels that assess performance from grade 1 through high school. The SDRT consists of ten subtests that reflect skills required in three major areas of reading: decoding, vocabulary, and comprehension. The SDMT consists of three subtests administered at all levels. Norm-referenced as well as criterion-referenced information is provided in the test manual for each of these tests. Normative data are presented as percentile ranks, stanines, grade equivalents, and scaled scores. Criterion-referenced information is provided for each skill through the use of a progress indicator, a cutoff score that shows if the student is sufficiently competent in that skill to progress to the next stage of the instructional program. The manuals for both instruments include an index of behavioral objectives useful in prescriptive teaching strategies. The most recent (fourth) edition of the SDRT also contains informal measures designed to probe students' attitudes toward reading, reading interests and habits, and ability to retell a read story. Although psychometric data is not provided for these measures, they may nonetheless have value in addressing the remedial needs of students (Swerdlik, 1998).

Psychoeducational Test Batteries

Psychoeducational test batteries are test kits that generally contain two types of tests: those that measure abilities related to academic success and those that measure educational achievement in areas such as reading and arithmetic. Data derived from these batteries allow for normative comparisons (how the student compares with other students within the same age group), as well as an evaluation of the testtaker's own strengths and weaknesses—all the better to plan educational interventions. Three such batteries are the Kaufman Assessment Battery for Children, the Differential Ability Scales, and the Woodcock-Johnson III.

Kaufman Assessment Battery for Children (K-ABC)

Alan and Nadeen Kaufman, a husband-wife team of psychologists, approached the task of test development with some experience; both had previously worked closely with Dorothea McCarthy in the development of the McCarthy Scales of Children's Abilities, and Alan Kaufman had worked with David Wechsler on the development of the WISC-R. Together, the Kaufmans developed the Kaufman Assessment Battery for Children (K-ABC). The K-ABC is an individually administered test battery that was designed for use with both normal and exceptional children from age 2½ through age 12½. The battery includes tests designed to measure both intelligence and achievement.

For the Kaufmans, intelligence is largely a matter of the problem-solving ability and the effectiveness of one's information-processing skills. The K-ABC intelligence subtests are divided into two groups, reflecting the two kinds of information-processing skills identified by Luria and his students (Das et al., 1975; Luria, 1966a, 1966b): simultaneous skills and sequential skills (see page 233). Table 10–2 presents the particular learning and teaching styles that reflect the two types of intelligence measured by the K-ABC. Scores on the simultaneous and sequential subtests are combined into a Mental Processing Composite, which is analogous to the IQ measure calculated on other tests.

The 16 subtests of the K-ABC are listed and summarized in Table 10–3. Three of the subtests assess the sequential processing type of intelligence, seven assess the simultaneous processing type of intelligence, and six assess achievement. Because some of the subtests are appropriate for limited age ranges, any one child will take no more than 13 of the subtests.

Standardization sample and psychometric properties   Two thousand children between the ages of 2½ and 12½ years served as subjects in the standardization sample. The sample was designed to be representative of the population of the United States based on 1980 census data. The sample was stratified at each age group by the variables of sex, race, socioeconomic status, geographic region, and community size. Exceptional children, including children with learning disabilities and children with behavior problems, were included in the standardization sample.

In general, satisfactory estimates of test-retest and split-half reliability for the test have been reported by the test's authors. Test-retest reliability coefficients ranged from .77 to .97 for 246 children who spanned the age range of the battery and were tested twice at intervals of two to four weeks.

The manual for the K-ABC presents the results of 43 validity studies conducted before publication of the test. Comparisons were made with other tests of ability and achievement using varied samples of subjects. In these studies, the correlation between the K-ABC Mental Processing Composite and the Full Scale IQ on the WISC-R and the WPPSI ranged from .55 to .77. The correlation between the K-ABC Mental Processing Composite and the Stanford-Binet (Form L-M) ranged from .36 to .74. In general, these and other data have been construed as supportive of the validity of the K-ABC (Bloom et al., 1988; Donders, 1992; Hayden et al., 1988; Klanderman et al., 1985; Krohn & Lamp, 1989; Krohn et al., 1988; Naglieri, 1985a, 1985b; Naglieri & Anderson, 1985; Smith & Lyon, 1987; Smith et al., 1989; Zucker, 1985; Zucker & Copeland, 1987). Noteworthy for its contrary conclusion, however, is research that examined the results of educational decisions based on the child's processing style as defined by the K-ABC. Good et al. (1993) found that using the K-ABC did not improve the quality of these decisions.

A number of studies have examined the factors measured by the K-ABC (Kamphaus et al., 1982; Kaufman, 1993; Kaufman & Kamphaus, 1984; Kaufman & McLean, 1987; Keith, 1985; Keith & Dunbar, 1984; Keith et al., 1985; Naglieri & Jensen, 1987; Willson et al., 1985). Many of the factor analyses suggested that the test was, indeed, tapping

Table 10–2

Characteristics and Teaching Guidelines for Sequential and Simultaneous Learners

Learner Characteristics

The Sequential Learner	The Simultaneous Learner
The sequential learner solves problems best by mentally arranging small amounts of information in consecutive, linear, step-by-step order. He/she is most at home with verbal instructions and cues, because the ability to interpret spoken language depends to a great extent on the sequence of words.	The simultaneous learner solves problems best by mentally integrating and synthesizing many parallel pieces of information at the same time. He/she is most at home with visual instructions and cues, because the ability to interpret the environment visually depends on perceiving and integrating many details at once.
Sequential processing is especially important in:	Simultaneous processing is especially important in:
• learning and retaining basic arithmetic facts • memorizing lists of spelling words • making associations between letters and their sounds • learning the rules of grammar, the chronology of historical events • remembering details • following a set of rules, directions, steps • solving problems by breaking them down into their components or steps	• recognizing the shape and physical appearance of letters and numbers • interpreting the overall effect or meaning of pictures and other visual stimuli, such as maps and charts • understanding the overall meaning of a story or poem • summarizing, comparing, evaluating • comprehending mathematical or scientific principles • solving problems by visualizing them in their entirety
Sequential learners who are weak in simultaneous processing may have difficulty with:	Simultaneous learners who are weak in sequential processing may have difficulty with:
• sight word recognition • reading comprehension • understanding mathematical or scientific principles • using concrete, hands-on materials • using diagrams, charts, maps • summarizing, comparing, evaluating	• word attack, decoding, phonics • breaking down science or arithmetic problems into parts • interpreting the parts and features of a design or drawing • understanding the rules of games • understanding and following oral instructions • remembering specific details and sequence of a story

Teaching Guidelines

For the Sequential Learner	For the Simultaneous Learner
1. Present material step by step, gradually approaching the overall concept or skill. Lead up to the big question with a series of smaller ones. Break the task into parts. 2. Get the child to verbalize what is to be learned. When you teach a new word, have the child say it, aloud or silently. Emphasize verbal cues, directions, and memory strategies. 3. Teach and rehearse the steps required to do a problem or complete a task. Continue to refer back to the details or steps already mentioned or mastered. Offer a logical structure or procedure by appealing to the child's verbal/temporal orientation.	1. Present the overall concept or question before asking the child to solve the problem. Continue to refer back to the task, question, or desired outcome. 2. Get the child to visualize what is to be learned. When you teach a new word, have the child write it and picture it mentally, see it on the page in the mind's eye. Emphasize visual cues, directions, and memory strategies. 3. Make tasks concrete wherever possible by providing manipulative materials, pictures, models, diagrams, graphs. Offer a sense of the whole by appealing to the child's visual/spatial orientation.
For example, the sequential learner may look at one or two details of a picture but miss the visual image as a whole. To help such a student toward an overall appreciation of the picture, start with the parts and work up to the whole. Rather than beginning with "What does the picture show?" or "How does the picture make you feel?" first ask about details:	The simultaneous learner may react to a picture as a whole but may miss details. To help such a student notice the parts that contribute to the total visual image, begin by establishing an overall interpretation or reaction:
"What is the little boy in the corner doing?" "Where is the dog?" "What expression do you see on the woman's face?" "What colors are used in the sky?"	"What does the picture show?" "How does the picture make you feel?"
Lead up to questions about the overall interpretation or appreciation:	Then consider the details:
"How do all these details give you clues about what is happening in this picture?" "How does this picture make you feel?"	"What is the expression on the woman's face?" "What is the little boy in the corner doing?" "What colors are used in the sky?"
The sequential learner prefers a step-by-step teaching approach, one that may emphasize the gradual accumulation of details.	Relate the details to the student's initial interpretation: "How do these details explain why the picture made you feel the way it did?" The simultaneous learner responds best to a holistic teaching approach that focuses on groups of details or images and stresses the overall meaning or configuration of the task.

Source: Kaufman et al. (1984)

Table 10–3
A Description of the K-ABC Subtests

Sequential Processing Scale

    Hand Movements (ages 2–6 through 12–5)—Performing a series of hand movements in the same sequence performed by the examiner.

    Number Recall (ages 2–6 through 12–5)—Repeating a series of digits in the same sequence spoken by the examiner.

    Word Order (ages 4–0 through 12–5)—Touching a series of silhouettes of common objects in the same sequence as these objects were named orally by the examiner.

Simultaneous Processing Scale

    Magic Window (ages 2–6 through 4–11)—Identifying a picture that the examiner exposes by slowly moving it behind a narrow window; hence, the picture is only partially visible at any one time.

    Face Recognition (ages 2–6 through 4–11)—Selecting from a group photograph the one or two faces that were exposed briefly.

    Gestalt Closure (ages 2–6 through 12–5)—Naming an object or a scene pictured in a partially completed inkblot drawing.

    Triangles (ages 4–0 through 12–5)—Assembling several identical triangles into an abstract pattern that matches a model.

    Matrix Analogies (ages 5–0 through 12–5)—Selecting the meaningful picture or abstract design that best completes a visual analogy.

    Spatial Memory (ages 5–0 through 12–5)—Recalling the placement of pictures on a page that was exposed briefly.

    Photo Series (ages 6–0 through 12–5)—Placing photographs of an event in chronological order.

Achievement Scale

    Expressive Vocabulary (ages 2–6 through 4–11)—Naming the object pictured in a photograph.

    Faces and Places (ages 2–6 through 12–5)—Naming the well-known person, fictional character, or place pictured in a photograph.

    Arithmetic (ages 3–0 through 12–5)—Demonstrating knowledge of numbers and mathematical concepts, counting and computational skills, and other school-related arithmetic abilities.

    Riddles (ages 3–0 through 12–5)—Inferring the name of a concrete or abstract concept when given a list of its characteristics.

    Reading/Decoding (ages 5–0 through 12–5)—Identifying letters and reading words.

    Reading/Understanding (ages 7–0 through 12–5)—Demonstrating reading comprehension by following commands given in sentences.

---

three factors—but which three? Although most factor analyses indicate the presence of simultaneous and sequential processing factors, there is some disagreement regarding the factor the K-ABC manual calls "achievement." Kaufman (1993) found evidence for the presence of an achievement factor, but others have different ideas about the third factor. Good and Lane (1988) identified it as verbal comprehension and reading achievement. Kaufman and McLean (1986) identified it as achievement and reading ability. Keith and Novak (1987) identified it as reading achievement and verbal reasoning. It is also true that although the Kaufmans have made a convincing case for the utility of the distinction between sequential and simultaneous learning, factor-analytic evidence suggests that these two types of learning are not entirely independent (Bracken, 1985; Keith, 1985).

Test administration, scoring, and interpretation   Starting and stopping points are based on the child's chronological age. The number of subtests administered varies from 7 at age 2½ years, to 13 at age 7 years and above. A dual-easel format is employed, with test items presented on an easel facing the child, and examiner instructions printed on the other side.

Oral instructions from the examiner and verbal responses from the examinee are minimal compared with other tests of intelligence, and the manual contains special instructions for test administration to bilingual and hearing-, speech-, or language-disabled testtakers. Some of the mental processing subtests require the examiner to teach or demonstrate what is required, although there are no sample or teaching items on the achievement portion of the test.

Subtest items are scored correct (1 point) or incorrect (0 points), and the manual provides explicit directions and criteria for administering and scoring the test. Scores on the individual items are tallied to yield raw scores on each of the subtests. Tables in the manual are then used to convert each of the subtest scores into a standard score. From these standard scores, Sequential Processing, Simultaneous Processing, Mental Processing Composite, and Achievement standard scores are derived. Sociocultural percentile ranks, based on the child's ethnic group and parents' educational level, can also be obtained.

One method of interpreting the K-ABC is the successive levels approach. As applied to the K-ABC, the test user evaluates processing style (simultaneous or sequential), as well as the relationship between ability and achievement as reflected respectively by the Mental Processing Composite and Achievement scores. A subtest-by-subtest evaluation of assets and deficits follows. An alternative to the interpretation of the Achievement score suggested in the manual has been proposed by Kamphaus and Reynolds (1987).

Recommendations for teaching based on Kaufman and Kaufman's (1983) idea of "processing strength" can be derived from the K-ABC test findings. It may be recommended, for example, that a student whose strength is processing sequentially should be taught using the teaching guidelines for sequential learners. Students who do not have any particular processing strength may be taught using a combination of methods. This model of test interpretation and consequential intervention has great intuitive appeal. However, research findings related to this approach have been mixed (Ayres & Cooley, 1986; Good et al., 1989; McCloskey, 1989; Salvia & Hritcko, 1984). Until this intervention model is employed in actual classrooms within the context of a regular curriculum over a reasonable period of time (one year or so), it will be impossible to be certain of its effectiveness.

An evaluation The K-ABC was introduced with extensive reliability and validity data supportive of its psychometric soundness. Factor-analytic studies were used to confirm that the test taps three primary factors, although, as noted earlier, controversy remains regarding the nature and naming of one of them. The well-defined theoretical basis of the test facilitates continuing research into the validity of the instrument from a theoretical perspective. The K-ABC was designed to be as culture-fair as possible, and researchers have found this to be the case (Bracken, 1985; Chattin & Bracken, 1989; Cummings & Merrell, 1993). The use of sample items, teaching items, and the minimal verbal emphasis on the mental processing subtests all contribute to making the test culture-fair.

The Differential Ability Scales

The Differential Ability Scales (DAS; Elliott, 1990a, 1990b) is actually an American adaptation of the BAS (British Ability Scales), which, in turn, was a descendant of a test called the BIT (British Intelligence Test). The BAS was first published in Great Britain in 1979, and a revision was published in 1983. Development of the American version of the DAS began in 1984, and the test was published about six years later (Elliott 1990a, 1990b). Appropriate for use with individuals from 2 years 6 months of age through 17 years 11 months, the DAS is not only a measure of ability (as one might expect from its name) but of achievement. As summarized in Table 10–4, the total battery consists of 17 cognitive subtests and 3 achievement subtests (tapping achievement in basic number skills, spelling, and word reading), though no more than 12 subtests are ever administered to any one testtaker. In the words of the test's developer, school psychologist Colin Elliott (1990b), the DAS was developed "to obtain and evaluate profiles of strengths and weaknesses. The achievement tests were co-normed with the cognitive battery to make direct ability-achievement discrepancy analyses possible" (p. 1).

The conception of intelligence (a term Elliott assiduously avoids) underlying the DAS is one that can best be described as a developmental, hierarchical model of cognitive abilities with three levels: general conceptual ability (GCA, also known as g) at the top of this hierarchy, followed by general verbal and nonverbal abilities (as measured by

Table 10-4
The Subtests of the DAS

Subtest	Description	Abilities Measured
Core Subtests		
Block Building (ages 2–6 through 3–5)	Copying a two- or three-dimensional design with blocks.	Perceptual-motor ability
Verbal Comprehension (ages 2–6 through 5–11)	Pointing to pictures and manipulating toys or objects in response to examiner instructions.	Receptive verbal knowledge
Picture Similarities (ages 2–6 through 5–11)	The child is shown a row of four pictures (such as geometric designs, or everyday objects) and is given a card with a fifth picture, which is to be placed under the picture sharing an element or concept.	Nonverbal reasoning
Naming Vocabulary (ages 2–6 through 5–11)	Naming objects and pictures.	Expressive verbal knowledge
Pattern Construction (ages 3–6 through 17–11)	Constructing a design with foam rubber squares or plastic blocks to match patterns depicted on cards.	Nonverbal, spatial reasoning
Early Number Concepts (ages 3–6 through 5–11)	Responding to questions about number, size, and other numerical concepts using colored chips or pictures.	Nonverbal and verbal knowledge
Copying (ages 3–6 through 5–11)	Copying drawings made by the examiner or displayed in a picture.	Perceptual-motor ability
Recall of Designs (ages 6–0 through 17–11)	Reproducing an abstract geometric design after being exposed to it.	Short-term visual spatial memory
Word Definitions (ages 6–0 through 17–11)	Defining words presented orally or visually.	Expressive verbal knowledge
Matrices (ages 6–0 through 17–11)	The testtaker is shown an incomplete matrix of abstract figures and selects the figure (from four or six choices) that completes the matrix.	Nonverbal reasoning
Similarities (ages 6–0 through 17–11)	Stating how things are similar or go together.	Verbal reasoning
Sequential and Quantitative Reasoning (ages 6–0 through 17–11)	The subtest is presented in two parts. The testtaker is first shown a series of abstract figures and must complete it. In the second part, the testtaker identifies a relationship within each pair of two pairs of numbers and then provides the missing number in an incomplete pair.	Detection of sequential patterns in figures or numbers
Diagnostic Subtests		
Recall of Objects—Immediate (ages 4–0 through 17–11)	Three immediate recall trials in which the testtaker views a card with pictures of 20 objects for 20 to 60 seconds and then tries to recall as many objects as possible.	Short-term verbal memory
Recall of Objects—Delayed (ages 4–0 through 17–11)	The testtaker recalls as many objects as possible from Recall of Ojects—Immediate subtest. Administration occurs 10 to 30 minutes after initial presentation of the objects.	Intermediate verbal memory
Matching Letterlike Forms (ages 4–6 through 5–11)	Choosing a figure (from six choices) that matches an abstract figure.	Visual perceptual matching
Recall of Digits (ages 3–0 through 17–11)	Repeating a sequence of digits presented orally at the rate of two digits per second.	Short-term auditory memory
Recognition of Pictures (ages 3–0 through 7–11)	After being shown black-and-white pictures of common objects for 5 or 10 seconds, a second picture with the same objects as well as distractors (objects not in the first picture) is shown, the task being to point to the object(s) that were in the first picture.	Short-term visual memory
Speed of Information Processing (ages 6–0 through 17–11)	The testtaker is presented with items consisting of rows of figures (circles containing small boxes or numbers). In each row the task is to mark the circle with the most boxes or highest number.	Quickness in performing mental operations
Achievement Subtests		
Basic Number Skills (ages 6–0 through 17–11)	Basic arithmetic skills, ranging from identifying numbers to problems requiring addition, subtracting, multiplication, or division. At upper age levels, word problems.	Numerical computation
Spelling (ages 6–0 through 17–11)	Writing words dictated by the examiner.	Spelling
Word Reading (ages 6–0 through 17–11)	Reading aloud words presented on a card.	Reading decoding skills

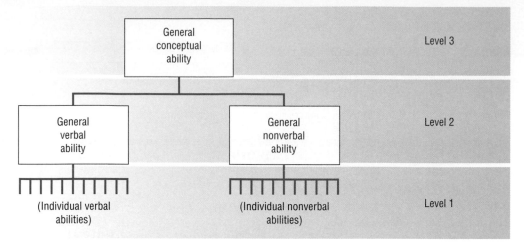

Figure 10–2
A Three-Level Hierarchical Model of Cognitive Abilities

The theory on which the DAS is based posits that individual abilities are at the first level and clusters of individual abilities are at the second level. At the third and highest level in this model is general conceptual ability (GCA)

cluster scores for clusters of subtests), followed by individual, specific verbal and nonverbal abilities as measured by individual subtests (Figure 10–2). GCA is a composite measure of intelligence, that is, a composite measure of conceptual and reasoning abilities derived from the scores on core subtests forming the foundation of the battery. Additionally, diagnostic subtests measure specific cognitive skills such as short-term auditory memory and visual discrimination. Developmentally, it is presumed that only certain abilities are present at certain ages, and the actual structure of the battery varies by age.

Standardization sample and psychometric properties   The standardization sample consisted of 3,475 subjects, with 175 subjects for each six-month age group from 2 years 6 months through 4 years 11 months and 200 subjects per age-group year in age-group years 5 through 17. The sample was stratified at each level on the basis of sex, race/ethnicity, parent education, geographic region, and preschool enrollment using 1988 census data as a criterion. Children enrolled in special education classes were included in the standardization sample. Children from smaller metropolitan and nonmetropolitan areas were underrepresented.

The DAS test developer reports generally satisfactory estimates of internal consistency and test-retest reliability. Test-retest reliability coefficients for the GCA range from .85 to .94. Test-retest reliability coefficients for the clusters range from .79 to .90 for 393 children randomly selected from three age levels and tested twice at intervals of two to seven weeks. Internal consistency was established through a procedure which, in the words of the test developer, "is based purely on the items expected to be taken by an individual and makes no assumptions about the person's performance on unadministered items" (Elliott, 1990b, p. 175). For subtests that entail subjective scoring (Copying, Recall of Designs, Similarities, and Word Definitions), mean inter-rater reliability estimates for each subtest were quite high, ranging from .90 to .96.

On the basis of factor-analytic research reported in the test's manual, the test taps one factor (GCA) at ages 2 years 6 months through 3 years 5 months; two factors (a verbal and a nonverbal factor) at ages 3 years 6 months through 5 years 11 months; and three factors (a verbal, a nonverbal reasoning, and a spatial ability factor) at ages 6 years 0 months through 17 years 11 months. Subsequent research with exceptional testtakers as well as testtakers from other populations will be necessary to further validate the factor structure of the DAS.

Several validity studies comparing the DAS to other measures of ability and achievement using nonhandicapped as well as exceptional children are reported in the test manual. Although the studies are limited in terms of sample size and region of the country, they tend to support the validity of the DAS as a measure of ability and achievement.

Test administration, scoring, and interpretation Administration instructions are clearly presented in the manual, with starting and stopping points based on the testtaker's chronological age and number of successes and failures. The core subtests are administered in a prescribed order, whereas the examiner has some discretion with regard to the sequence of administration of diagnostic and achievement subtests. Some subtests (1) make provision for sample items, teaching items, and examiner demonstration of items, (2) may be administered through gestures rather than verbal instructions to produce a Nonverbal Composite score, and/or (3) have an "out of level range" permitting their administration to high-ability or low-ability children—the net effect being an extension of the age and ability range of these subtests. Administration time for the complete battery ranges from about 35 minutes at age 2 years 6 months to about 90 minutes for the school-age testtaker.

Two record forms are provided, one for the preschool level and one for the school-age level. The record forms are user friendly, with clearly marked starting/stopping points and instructions for scoring. Most test items are scored correct (1 point) or incorrect (0 points), though some provide for 0, 1, or 2 scoring; bonus points are awarded for rapid, successful completion of timed items. Raw scores are tallied and converted to subtest scores, which, in turn, are converted into standard scores (having a mean of 50 and a standard deviation of 10 for the cognitive subtests, and a mean of 100 and a standard deviation of 15 for the achievement subtests). From these standard scores, the GCA and cluster scores, both of which have a mean of 100 and a standard deviation of 15, are derived.

Interpreting the DAS is similar in many ways to interpreting other ability-achievement batteries. Composite and cluster scores are compared and evaluated as are individual subtest scores—all in an effort to profile the testtaker's strengths and weaknesses. Additionally, extra-test behavior and other test-related findings may be included in the experienced examiner's interpretation of the testing.

An evaluation For preschool and school-age children alike, the DAS materials tend to be engaging; a variety of colorful, manipulable objects (as opposed to two-dimensional pictures) aid in maintaining interest and keeping testtakers task oriented. Because testing is tailored or adapted to the profile of responses—a style of testing known as adaptive testing—overall testing time is reduced. Because out-of-level norms were developed for the test, children within a broad ability range can be evaluated appropriately. The psychometric properties of the battery appear to be strong; reliability and validity data are in the acceptable range and the battery's factor structure has been confirmed in studies reported in the test manual. We would caution, however, that the samples with which the validity research was conducted tended to be relatively small and not geographically diverse. During the test's development, procedures were employed to reduce or eliminate

Table 10–5
WJ III Tests of Achievement

Curricular Area	Cluster	Standard Battery—Forms A & B	Extended Battery—Forms A & B
Reading	Basic Skills	Test 1 Letter-Word Identification	Test 13 Word Attack
	Fluency	Test 2 Reading Fluency	
	Comprehension	Test 9 Passage Comprehension	Test 17 Reading Vocabulary
	Broad	Tests 1, 2, 9	
Oral Language	Oral Expression	Test 3 Story Recall	Test 14 Picture Vocabulary
	Listening Comprehension	Test 4 Understanding Directions	Test 15 Oral Comprehension
Mathematics	Calculation Skills	Test 5 Calculation	
	Fluency	Test 6 Math Fluency	
	Reasoning	Test 10 Applied Problems	Test 18 Quantitative Concepts
	Broad	Tests 5, 6, 10	
Written Language	Basic Skills	Test 7 Spelling	Test 16 Editing
	Fluency	Test 8 Writing Fluency	
	Expression	Test 11 Writing Samples	
	Broad	Tests 7, 8, 11	
Knowledge			Test 19 Academic Knowledge
Supplemental		Test 12 Story Recall-Delayed	Test 20 Spelling of Sounds
		Handwriting Legibility Scale	Test 21 Sound Awareness
			Test 22 Punctuation & Capitalization

any possible race or gender bias, though the manual does not report any comparative data for White, Black, and Hispanic testtakers.

Woodcock-Johnson III (WJ III)

The WJ III (Woodcock et al., 2000) is a psychoeducational test package consisting of two co-normed batteries: Tests of Achievement and Tests of Cognitive Abilities, both of which are based on the Cattell-Horn-Carroll (CHC) theory of cognitive abilities. The WJ III was designed for use with persons as young as 2 and as old as "90+" according to the test manual. The WJ III yields a measure of general intellectual ability (g), as well as measures of specific cognitive abilities, achievement, scholastic aptitude, and oral language. It may be used to diagnose learning disabilities, determine discrepancies between ability and achievement, and plan educational programs and interventions.

The Tests of Achievement are packaged in parallel forms designated *A* and *B,* each of which are in turn divided into what is called a standard battery (12 subtests) and an extended battery (10 additional subtests). As illustrated in Table 10–5, interpretation of an achievement test is based on the testtaker's performance on clusters of tests in specific curricular areas.

The Tests of Cognitive Abilities may also be divided into a standard battery (10 subtests) and an extended battery (10 additional subtests). As illustrated in Table 10–6, the subtests tapping cognitive abilities are conceptualized in terms of broad cognitive factors, primary narrow abilities, and cognitive performance clusters.

When using either the achievement or cognitive abilities tests, the standard battery might be appropriate for screenings or brief reevaluations. The extended battery would likely be used to provide a more comprehensive and detailed assessment, complete with diagnostic information. In any case, cluster scores are used to help evaluate performance level, gauge educational progress, and identify individual strengths and weaknesses.

According to the test manual, the WJ III was normed on a sample of 8,818 subjects from ages 24 months to "90+" years who were representative of the population of the United States. Age-based norms are provided from ages 24 months to 19 years by month,

Table 10–6
WJ III Tests of Cognitive Abilities*

Broad Cognitive Factor	Test (Standard & Extended)	Primary Narrow Ability	Cognitive Performance
Comprehension-Knowledge *(Gc)*	Test 1 Verbal Comprehension	Lexical knowledge, language development	Verbal ability
	Test 11 General Information	General (verbal) information	
Long Term Retrieval *(Glr)*	Test 2 Visual-Auditory Learning	Associate memory	Thinking ability
	Test 12 Retrieval Fluency	Ideational fluency	
	Test 10 Visual-Auditory Learning-Delayed	*Associative memory*	
Visual-Spatial Thinking *(Gv)*	Test 3 Spatial Relations	Visualization, spatial relations	Thinking ability
	Test 13 Picture Recognition	Visual memory	
	Test 19 Planning (Gv/Gf)	*Spatial scanning, general sequential reasoning*	
Auditory Processing *(Ga)*	Test 4 Sound Blending	Phonetic coding, synthesis	Thinking ability
	Test 14 Auditory Attention	Speech-sound discrimination, resistance to auditory stimulus distortion	
	Test 8 Incomplete Words	*Phonetic coding, analysis*	
Fluid Reasoning *(Gf)*	Test 5 Concept Formation	Induction	Thinking ability
	Test 15 Analysis-Synthesis	General sequential reasoning	
	Test 19 Planning (Gv/Gf)	*Spatial scanning, general sequential reasoning*	
Processing Speed *(Gs)*	Test 6 Visual Matching	Perceptual speed	Cognitive efficiency
	Test 16 Decision Speed	Semantic processing speed	
	Test 18 Rapid Picture Naming	*Naming facility*	
	Test 20 Pair Cancellation	*Attention and concentration*	
Short-Term Memory *(Gsm)*	Test 7 Numbers Reversed	Working memory	Cognitive efficiency
	Test 17 Memory for Words	Memory span	
	Test 9 Auditory Working Memory	*Working memory*	

*Tests shown in italics are not part of the factor or cognitive performance cluster.

and by year after that. Grade-based norms are provided for kindergarten through grade 12, two-year college, and four-year college, including graduate school. Procedures for analysis of reliabilities for each subtest were appropriate depending upon the nature of the tests. For example, the reliability of tests that were not speeded and that did not have multiple-point scoring systems were analyzed by means of the split-half method, corrected for length using the Spearman-Brown correction formula. The test manual also presents concurrent validity data.

Scoring of the WJ III is accomplished with the aid of software provided in the test kit. Data from the raw scores are entered and the program produces a summary report (in English or Spanish) and a table of scores, including all derived scores for tests administered as well as clusters of tests. The program also provides age/grade profiles and standard score/percentile rank profiles. Optional interpretive software is also available (Riverside Publishing, 2001). This software features checklist protocols (a teacher checklist, a parent checklist, a self-report checklist, and a classroom observation form) in a form that integrates the checklist data into the report. The test publisher has also made available optional training materials, including CD-ROMs and videos, for assistance in administering and using the battery.

Other Tools of Assessment in Educational Settings

Beyond traditional achievement, aptitude, and diagnostic instruments lies a wide universe of other instruments and techniques of assessment that may be used in the service of students and society at large. Let's take a look at a sampling of these approaches, beginning with performance, portfolio, and authentic assessment.

Performance, Portfolio, and Authentic Assessment

For many years, the very broad label "performance assessment" has vaguely referred to any type of assessment that requires the examinee to do more than choose the correct response from a small group of alternatives. Thus, for example, essay questions and the development of an art project would be examples of performance tasks. By contrast, true-false questions and multiple-choice test items would not be considered performance tasks.

Among testing and assessment professionals, contemporary usage of performance-related terms focuses less on the type of item or task involved, and more on the knowledge, skills, and values that the examinee must marshal and exhibit. Additionally, there is a growing tendency to speak of performance tasks and performance assessment in the context of a particular domain of study, with experts in that particular domain of study typically being required to set the evaluation standards. For example, a performance task for an architecture student might be to construct a blueprint for a contemporary home. The overall quality of the student's work, as well as the knowledge, skill, and values inherent in that work, will be judged according to standards set by architects acknowledged by the community of architects to have expertise in the construction of contemporary homes. In keeping with contemporary trends, particularly in educational and work settings, we will define a **performance task** as a work sample designed to elicit representative knowledge, skills, and values from a particular domain of study. **Performance assessment** will be defined as an evaluation of performance tasks according to criteria developed by experts from the domain of study tapped by those tasks.

One of many possible types of performance assessment is portfolio assessment. *Portfolio* is a word with many meanings in different contexts. It may refer to a portable carrying case, most typically used to carry artwork, drawings, maps, and the like. Bankers and investors use it as a shorthand reference to one's financial holdings. In the language of psychological and educational assessment, **portfolio** is synonymous with "work sample." **Portfolio assessment** refers to the evaluation of one's work samples. In many educational settings, dissatisfaction with some more traditional methods of assessment has led to calls for more performance-based evaluations. "Authentic assessment" (discussed subsequently) is one name given to this trend toward more performance-based assessment. When used in the context of like-minded educational programs, portfolio assessment and authentic assessment are techniques designed to target academic teachings to real-world settings, external to the classroom.

As an example of portfolio assessment, consider how it might be implemented to gauge student progress in a high school algebra course. Students might be instructed to devise their own personal portfolios to illustrate all they have learned about algebra. An important aspect of portfolio assessment is the freedom of the person being evaluated to select the content of the portfolio. Some students might include narrative accounts of their understanding of various algebraic principles. Other students might reflect in writing on the ways algebra can be used in daily life. Still other students might attempt to make a convincing case that they can do some types of algebra problems that they could not do before taking the course. Throughout, the portfolio may be illustrated with items such as gas receipts (complete with algebraic formulas for calculating mileage), paychecks (complete with formulas used to calculate an hourly wage and taxes), and other items limited only by the student's imagination. The illustrations might go from simple to increasingly complex—providing compelling evidence regarding the student's grasp of the material.

The portfolio method has been used to assess giftedness (Hadaway & Marek-Schroer, 1992) and reading (Henk, 1993), among many other characteristics. Portfolios have also been applied at the college and graduate level as devices to assist students with career decisions (Bernhardt et al., 1993). Benefits of the portfolio approach include engaging students in the assessment process, giving them the opportunity to think generatively, and encouraging them to think about learning as an ongoing and integrated process. A key drawback, however, is the penalty such a technique may levy on the noncreative student. Exceptional portfolios are typically creative efforts; a person whose strengths do not lie in creativity may have learned the course material but be unable to adequately demonstrate that learning in such a medium. Another drawback, this one from the other side of the instructor's desk, concerns the evaluation of portfolios. Typically, a great deal of time and thoughtfulness must be devoted to their evaluation; in a lecture class of 300 people, for example, portfolio assessment would be impractical. Also, it is difficult to develop reliable criteria for portfolio assessment given the great diversity of work products. Hence, inter-rater reliability in portfolio assessment can become a problem.

A related form of assessment is **authentic assessment,** also known as **performance-based assessment** (Baker et al., 1993) and by other names. We may define authentic assessment in educational contexts as evaluation on relevant, meaningful tasks that may be conducted to examine learning of academic subject matter, but that demonstrate the student's transfer of that study to real-world activities. Authentic assessment of students' writing skills would therefore be based on writing samples rather than on responses to multiple-choice tests (Popham, 1993). Authentic assessment of students' reading would be based on tasks that have to do with reading—preferably authentic reading, such as an article in a local newspaper as opposed to a piece contrived especially for the purposes of assessment (Henk, 1993). Students in a college-level psychopathology course might be asked to identify patients' psychiatric diagnoses on the basis of videotaped interviews with the patients.

Authentic assessment is thought to increase student interest and the transfer of knowledge to settings outside the classroom. A drawback is that the assessment might assess prior knowledge and experience, not simply what was learned in the classroom (Henk, 1993). For example, students from homes where there has been a long-standing interest in legislative activities may well do better on an authentic assessment of reading skills using an article on legislative activity. Additionally, authentic skill may inadvertently entail the assessment of some skills that have little to do with classroom learning. For example, authentic assessment of learning a cooking school lesson on fileting fish may be confounded with an assessment of the would-be chef's perceptual-motor skills.

Peer Appraisal Techniques

One method of obtaining information about an individual is by asking that individual's peer group to make the evaluation. Techniques employed to obtain such information are termed **peer appraisal** methods. A teacher, a supervisor, or some other group leader may be interested in peer appraisals for a variety of reasons. Peer appraisals can help call needed attention to an individual who is experiencing academic, personal, social, or work-related difficulties—difficulties that for whatever reason have not come to the attention of the person in charge. Peer appraisals allow the individual in charge to view members of a group from a different perspective, the perspective of people who work, play, socialize, eat lunch, and walk home with the person being evaluated. In addition to providing information about behavior that is rarely observable, peer appraisals supply information about the group's dynamics: who takes which roles under what conditions. Knowledge of an individual's place within the group is an important aid in guiding the group to optimal efficiency.

Peer appraisal techniques may be used in university settings (Klockars, 1978) as well as in grade school, industrial, and military settings. Such techniques tend to be most useful in settings where the individuals doing the rating have functioned as a group long enough to be able to evaluate each other on specific variables. The nature of peer appraisals may change as a function of changes in the assessment situation and the membership of the group (Veldman & Sheffield, 1979); thus, for example, an individual who is rated as the "shyest" in the classroom can theoretically be quite gregarious—and perhaps even be rated the "rowdiest"—in a peer appraisal undertaken at an after-school center.

One method of peer appraisal that can be employed in elementary school (as well as other) settings is called the "Guess Who?" technique. Brief descriptive sentences (such as "This person is the most friendly") are read or handed out in the form of questionnaires to the class and the children are instructed to "Guess who?" Whether negative attributes should be included in the peer appraisal (for example, "This person is the least friendly") must be decided on an individual basis, considering the potential negative consequences such an appraisal could have on a member of the group.

The nominating technique is a method of peer appraisal in which individuals are asked to select or nominate other individuals for various types of activities. A child being interviewed in a psychiatric clinic may be asked, "Who would you most like to go to the moon with?" as a means of determining which parent or other individual is most important to the child. Members of a police department might be asked, "Who would you most like as your partner for your next tour of duty and why?" as a means of finding out which police officers are seen by their peers as being especially competent or incompetent.

The results of a peer appraisal can be graphically illustrated. One graphic method of organizing such data is called the **sociogram.** Figures such as circles or squares are drawn to represent different individuals, and lines and arrows are drawn to indicate various types of interaction. At a glance, the sociogram can provide information such as who is popular in the group, who tends to be rejected by the group, and who is relatively neutral in the opinion of the group. Nominating techniques have been the most widely researched of the peer appraisal techniques, and they have generally been found to be highly reliable and valid (Kane & Lawler, 1978, 1980). Still, the careful users of such techniques must be aware that an individual's perceptions within a group are constantly changing. As some members leave the group and others join it, the positions and roles the members hold within the group change; new alliances form, and members may be looked at in a new light. It is therefore important to periodically update and verify information.

Measuring Study Habits, Interests, and Attitudes

Academic performance is the result of a complex interplay of a number of factors. Ability and motivation are inseparable partners in the pursuit of academic success. A number of instruments designed to look beyond ability and toward factors such as study habits, interests, and attitudes have been published. For example, the Study Habits Checklist, designed for use with students in grades 9 through 14, consists of 37 items that assess study habits with respect to note taking, reading material, and general study practices. In the development of the test, potential items were presented for screening to 136 Phi Beta Kappa members at three colleges. This procedure was based on the premise that good students are the best judges of important and effective study techniques (Preston, 1961). The judges were asked to evaluate the items according to their usefulness to students having difficulty with college course material. Although the judges conceded that they did not always engage in these practices themselves, they identified the techniques they deemed to be the most useful in study activities. Standardization for the Checklist took place in 1966, and percentile norms were based on a sample of several thousand high school and college students residing in Pennsylvania. In one validity study, 302 college freshmen who had demonstrated learning difficulties and had been referred to a learning skills center were evaluated with the Checklist. As predicted, it was found that these students demonstrated poor study practices, particularly in the areas of note taking and proper use of study time (Bucofsky, 1971).

If a teacher knows a child's areas of interest, instructional activities engaging those interests can be employed. The What I Like to Do Interest Inventory (Meyers, 1975) consists of 150 forced-choice items that assess four areas of interests: academic interests, artistic interests, occupational interests, and interests in leisure time (play) activities. Included in the test materials are suggestions for designing instructional activities that are consonant with the designated areas of interest.

Attitude inventories used in educational settings assess student attitudes toward a variety of school-related factors. Interest in student attitudes is based on the premise that "positive reactions to school may increase the likelihood that students will stay in school, develop a lasting commitment to learning, and use the school setting to advantage" (Epstein & McPartland, 1978, p. 2). Some instruments assess attitudes in one specific subject area, such as reading (Engin et al., 1976; Heathington & Alexander, 1978; Wallbrown et al., 1978), as well as in several other areas (for example, the Survey of School Attitudes, the Quality of School Life Scales). Other instruments, such as the Survey of Study Habits and Attitudes (SSHA) and the Study Attitudes and Methods Survey, combine an attitude assessment with the assessment of study methods. The SSHA, intended for use in grades 7 through college, consists of 100 items tapping poor study skills and attitudes that could affect academic performance. Two forms, Form H for grades 7 to 12 and Form C for college, are available, each requiring 20 to 25 minutes to complete. Students respond to items on the following 5-point scale: "rarely," "sometimes," "frequently," "generally," or "almost always." Test items are divided into six areas, which include Delay Avoidance, Work Methods, Study Habits, Teacher Approval, Education Acceptance, and Study Attitudes. The test yields a study skills score, an attitude score, and a total orientation score.

While on the subject of study habits, skills, and attitudes, this seems an appropriate time to raise a question about how these variables are related to another, more global variable: personality. Are one's study habits, skills, and attitudes a part of one's personality? Why might it be useful to think about them as such? These are some questions to think about as we approach the following two chapters on personality and its assessment.

Self-Assessment

Test your understanding of elements of this chapter by seeing if you can explain each of the following terms, expressions, and abbreviations:

achievement test	checklist
Apgar	curriculum-based assessment
aptitude test	curriculum-based measurement
at risk	DAS
authentic assessment	diagnostic information

evaluative information

K-ABC

learning disability

locator test

peer appraisal

performance assessment

performance task

prognostic test

psychoeducational test battery

rating scale

readiness test

screening tool

sociogram

WJ III

11

Personality Assessment: An Overview

n a 1950s rock 'n' roll tune called "Personality," singer Lloyd Price described the subject of his song with the words *walk, talk, smile,* and *charm.* In so doing, Price used the term *personality* the way most people tend to use it. For laypeople, "personality" refers to components of an individual's makeup that can elicit positive or negative reactions from others. The individual who consistently tends to elicit positive reactions from others is thought to have a good personality. The individual who consistently tends to elicit not-so-good reactions from others is thought to have a bad personality or, perhaps worse yet, no personality. Descriptive epithets such as "aggressive personality," "cold personality," and "warm personality" also enjoy widespread usage. For behavioral scientists, the terms employed tend to be more rigorous than those describing simple social skills and are more precise than all-encompassing adjectives.

Personality and Personality Assessment Defined

Personality

Dozens of different definitions of personality exist in the psychology literature (Allport, 1937). Some definitions appear to be all-inclusive in nature. For example, McClelland (1951, p. 69) defined personality as "the most adequate conceptualization of a person's behavior in all its detail." Menninger (1953, p. 23) defined it as "the individual as a whole, his height and weight and love and hates and blood pressure and reflexes; his smiles and hopes and bowed legs and enlarged tonsils. It means all that anyone is and that he is trying to become." Some definitions rely heavily on a particular aspect of the person, such as the individual's phenomenal field (Goldstein, 1963) or the individual as a social being (Sullivan, 1953). At an extreme end of the spectrum of definitions are those proposed by theorists who have scrupulously avoided definition. For example, Byrne (1974, p. 26) characterized the entire area of personality psychology as "psychology's garbage bin in that any research which doesn't fit other existing categories can be labeled 'personality.'"

In their widely read and authoritative textbook *Theories of Personality*, Hall and Lindzey (1970, p. 9) wrote that "it is our conviction that *no substantive definition of personality can be applied with any generality*" and that "*personality is defined by the particular empirical concepts which are a part of the theory of personality employed by the observer*" [emphasis in the original]. They went on, "If this seems an unsatisfactory definition to the reader, let him take consolation in the thought that in the pages to follow he will encounter a number of specific definitions any one of which will become his if he chooses to adopt that particular theory" (p. 9). Hall and Lindzey (1970) noted that important theoretical differences underlie the various different types of definitions of personality that exist.

You may well ask, "If venerable authorities on personality such as Hall and Lindzey do not define personality, who are Cohen and Swerdlik to think that they can do it?" In response, we humbly offer our definition of **personality** as an individual's unique constellation of psychological traits and states. We view this definition as one that has the advantage of parsimony yet still is flexible enough to incorporate a wide variety of variables from the "whole person" types of definitions. Included in our definition, then, are variables on which individuals may differ, such as values, interests, attitudes, worldview, acculturation, personal identity, sense of humor, and cognitive and behavioral styles.

Personality Assessment

We define **personality assessment** as the measurement and evaluation of psychological traits, states, values, interests, attitudes, worldview, acculturation, personal identity, sense of humor, cognitive and behavioral styles, and/or related individual characteristics. In this chapter we will overview the process of personality assessment, including different approaches to the construction of personality tests. In the following chapter, we focus on various methods of personality assessment, including objective, projective, and behavioral methods. Before all of that, however, we need some background regarding the use of the terms trait, type, and state.

Traits, Types, and States

Personality traits Just as no universal consensus exists regarding the definition of personality, no consensus exists regarding the definition of *trait*. Theorists such as Gordon Allport (1937) have tended to view personality traits as real physical entities that are "bona fide mental structures in each personality" (p. 289). For Allport, a trait is a "generalized and focalized neuropsychic system (peculiar to the individual) with the capacity to render many stimuli functionally equivalent, and to initiate and guide consistent (equivalent) forms of adaptive and expressive behavior" (p. 295). Robert Holt (1971) noted that there "*are* real structures inside people that determine their behavior in lawful ways" (p. 6), and he went on to conceptualize these structures as changes in brain chemistry that might occur as a result of learning: "Learning causes submicroscopic structural changes in the brain, probably in the organization of its biochemical substance" (p. 7). Raymond Cattell (1950) also conceptualized traits as mental structures, but for him "structure" did not necessarily imply actual physical status.

Our own preference is to shy away from definitions that elevate *trait* to the status of physical existence. We view psychological traits as attributions made in an effort to identify threads of consistency in behavioral patterns. In this context, a definition of **trait** offered by Guilford (1959, p. 6) has great appeal: "Any distinguishable, relatively enduring way in which one individual varies from another."

Inherent in this relatively simple definition are commonalities with the writings of other personality theorists such as Allport (1937), Cattell (1950, 1965), and Eysenck (1961). The word *distinguishable* indicates that behaviors labeled with different trait terms are actually different from one another. For example, a behavior labeled "friendly" should be distinguishable from a behavior labeled "rude." The *context*, or the situation in which the behavior is displayed, is important in applying trait terms to behaviors. A behavior present in one context may be labeled with one trait term, but the same behavior exhibited in another context may be better described using another trait term. For example, if we observe someone involved in a lengthy, apparently interesting conversation, we would observe the context before drawing any conclusions about the person's traits. A person talking with a friend over lunch may be demonstrating friendliness, whereas a person talking during a wedding ceremony may be considered rude. Thus, the trait term selected by an observer is dependent both on the behavior itself and on the context in which that behavior appears. Behavior and its context may be observed using a wide variety of methods, from direct observation (watching the person with a variety of peers, hearing the person express attitudes about others, watching the person at work or at school) to an analysis of responses on a self-report questionnaire (on which the individual may describe relationships and interactions with others).

In his definition of trait, Guilford did not assert that traits represent enduring ways in which individuals vary from one another; rather, he used the term *relatively enduring way*. The modifier "relatively" emphasizes that exactly how a particular trait manifests itself is, at least to some extent, situation-dependent. For example, a "violent" parolee may generally be prone to behave in a rather subdued way with her parole officer and much more violently in the presence of her family and friends. John may be viewed as "dull" and "cheap" by his wife but as "charming" and "extravagant" by his secretary, business associates, and others he is keenly interested in impressing. Allport (1937) addressed the issue of cross-situational consistency of traits—or lack of it—as follows:

> Perfect consistency will never be found and must not be expected. . . . People may be ascendant and submissive, perhaps submissive only towards those individuals bearing traditional symbols of authority and prestige; and towards everyone else aggressive and domineering. . . . The ever changing environment raises now one trait and now another to a state of active tension. (p. 330)

For years, personality theorists and assessors have assumed that personality traits are relatively enduring over the course of one's life (West & Graziano, 1989). Roberts and DelVecchio (2000) explored just how enduring traits are by means of a meta-analysis of 152 longitudinal studies. These researchers concluded that trait consistency increases in a steplike pattern until one is 50 to 59 years old, at which time such consistency peaks. Their findings may be interpreted as compelling testimony to the relatively enduring nature of personality traits over the course of one's life. Do you think the physically aggressive high school students pictured in Figure 11–1 will still be physically aggressive when they approach retirement age?

Returning to our elaboration of Guilford's definition, note that *trait* is described as a way in which one individual varies from another. Here it is important to emphasize that the attribution of a trait term is always a *relative* phenomenon. For instance, some behavior described as patriotic may differ greatly from other behavior also described as patriotic. There are no absolute standards. In describing an individual as patriotic, we are, in essence, making an unstated comparison with the degree of patriotic behavior that could reasonably be expected to be emitted by the average person.

Research demonstrating a lack of cross-situational consistency in traits such as honesty (Hartshorne & May, 1928), punctuality (Dudycha, 1936), conformity (Hollander & Willis, 1967), attitude toward authority (Burwen & Campbell, 1957), and introversion/extraversion (Newcomb, 1929) are the types of studies typically cited by Mischel (1968, 1973, 1977, 1979) and others who have been critical of the predominant role of the concept of traits in personality theory. Such critics may also allude to the fact that some undetermined portion of behavior exhibited in public may be governed more by societal expectations and cultural role restrictions than by an individual's personality traits (see Barker, 1963; Goffman, 1963). Research designed to shed light on the primacy of

Figure 11–1
Trait Aggressiveness and Flare-Ups on the Ice

Bushman and Wells (1998) administered a self-report measure of trait aggressiveness (the Physical Aggression subscale of the Aggression Questionnaire) to 91 high school team hockey players before the start of the season. The players responded to items such as "Once in a while I cannot control my urge to strike another person" presented in Likert scale format ranging from 1 to 5 (where 1 corresponded to "extremely uncharacteristic of me" and 5 corresponded to "extremely characteristic of me"). At the end of the season, trait aggressiveness scores were examined with respect to minutes served in the penalty box for aggressive penalties such as fighting, slashing, and tripping. The preseason measure of trait aggressiveness predicted aggressive penalty minutes served. The study is particularly noteworthy because the test data were used to predict "real life" aggression, not a laboratory analogue of aggression such as the administration of electric shock. The authors recommended that the possible applications of the Aggression Questionnaire be explored in other settings where aggression is a problematic behavior. In what settings do you envision a possible use for the Aggression Questionnaire?

individual differences as opposed to situational factors in behavior is methodologically complex (see Golding, 1975), and a definitive verdict as to the primacy of the trait or the situation is simply not in.

Personality types   Having defined personality as a unique constellation of traits and states, we might define a personality **type** as a constellation of traits and states that is similar in pattern to one identified category of personality within a taxonomy of personalities. Whereas traits are frequently discussed as if they were characteristics possessed by an individual, types are more clearly descriptions of people. So, for example, describing an individual as "depressed" has a different meaning than describing that individual as a "depressed type." The latter term has more far-reaching implications regarding characteristic aspects of the individual, such as the person's worldview, activity level, capacity to enjoy life, and level of social interest.

At least since Hippocrates characterized people in terms such as the "melancholic type" and the "sanguine type," there has been no shortage of personality typologies through the ages. A typology devised by Carl Jung (1923) became the basis for the Myers-Briggs Type Indicator (MBTI; Myers & Briggs, 1943/1962). An assumption guiding the development of this test was that people exhibit definite preferences in the way that they perceive or become aware of, and judge or arrive at conclusions about, people, events, situations, and ideas. According to Myers (1962, p. 1), these differences in perception and judging result in "corresponding differences in their reactions, in their interests, values, needs, and motivations, in what they do best, and in what they like to do." For example, in one study designed to better understand the personality of chess players, the Myers-Briggs Type Indicator was administered to 2,165 chess players (including masters and senior masters). The chess players were found to be significantly more introverted, intuitive, and thinking (as opposed to feeling) than members of the general population. The investigator also found masters to be more judging than would be expected in the general population (Kelly, 1985).

John Holland (1973, 1985) argued that most people can be categorized as one of the following six personality types: Artistic, Enterprising, Investigative, Social, Realistic, or Conventional. His Self-Directed Search test (SDS; Holland et al., 1994) is a self-administered, self-scored, and self-interpreted aid used to type people according to this system and offer vocational guidance. Another personality typology, this one having only two categories, was devised by cardiologists Meyer Friedman and Ray Rosenman (1974; Rosenman et al., 1975). They conceived of a **Type A personality** as one characterized by competitiveness, haste, restlessness, impatience, feelings of being time-pressured, and strong needs for achievement and dominance. A **Type B personality** is one described by much the opposite of the Type A traits; in a word, "mellow" or "laid-back." A 52-item self-report inventory called the Jenkins Activity Survey (JAS; Jenkins et al., 1979), has been used to type respondents as Type A or Type B personalities.

The personality typology that has attracted the most attention by researchers and practitioners alike is that associated with scores on a test called the MMPI, and its successor, the MMPI-2 (both to be discussed shortly). Data from the administration of this test, as with other tests, are frequently discussed in terms of the patterns of scores that emerge on the subtests. The pattern is referred to as a profile. Defined in general terms, a **profile** is a narrative description, graph, table, or other representation of the extent to which a person has demonstrated certain targeted characteristics as a result of the administration or application of tools(s) of assessment.[1] As employed in the term **personality profile,** the targeted characteristics referred to in this definition are typically traits, states, or types. With specific reference to the MMPI, different profiles of scores are associated with different patterns of behavior. So, for example, a particular MMPI profile designated as "2-4-7" is associated with a type of individual who has a history of alcohol abuse alternating with sobriety and self-recrimination (Dahlstrom, 1995).

Beyond personality typologies associated with tests like the MMPI, the JAS, the SDS, and the MBTI, there was a trend away from the development of such typologies for several years. This was most likely due to a concerted effort to avoid any problems

---

1. The verb *to profile* refers to the creation of such a description. The term **profile analysis** refers to the interpretation of patterns of scores on a test or test battery. Profile analysis is frequently used to generate diagnostic hypotheses from intelligence test data. The noun **profiler** refers to an occupation best associated with the field of law enforcement: one who creates personality profiles of crime suspects to assist law enforcement personnel in capturing the profiled suspects.

associated with stereotyping. However, a resurgence of interest in personality types seems to be emerging (Dahlstrom, 1995), and typology-related research in diverse areas is burgeoning (see for example, Buck, 1999; Checcino, 1997; Kudryavstev & Ratinova, 1999; Millon & Davis, 1998; Minor, 2000; Robins et al., 1998; Rubenzer et al., 2000; Vansteelandt & Van Mechelen, 1998; Waltz et al., 2000).

Personality states   The word **state** has been used in at least two distinctly different ways in the personality assessment literature. In one usage, a personality state is an inferred psychodynamic disposition designed to convey the dynamic quality of id, ego, and superego in perpetual conflict. Assessment of these psychodynamic dispositions may be made through the use of various psychoanalytic techniques such as free association, word association, symbolic analysis of interview material, dream analysis, and analysis of slips of the tongue, accidents, jokes, and forgetting.

Presently, a more popular usage of the word *state*—and the one to which we refer in the discussion that follows—refers to the transitory exhibition of some personality trait. Put another way, the use of the word *trait* presupposes a relatively enduring behavioral predisposition, whereas the term *state* is indicative of a relatively temporary predisposition (Chaplin et al., 1988). Thus, for example, Sally may be described as being "in an anxious state" before her midterms, though no one who knows Sally well would describe her as "an anxious person."

Measuring personality states amounts, in essence, to a search for and an assessment of the strength of traits that are relatively transitory in nature or fairly situation-specific. Relatively few existing personality tests seek to distinguish traits from states. Seminal work in this area was done by Charles D. Spielberger and his associates. These researchers developed a number of personality inventories designed to distinguish various states from traits. In the manual for the State-Trait Anxiety Inventory (STAI), for example, we find that "state anxiety" refers to a transitory experience of tension because of a particular situation. By contrast, "trait anxiety" or "anxiety proneness" refers to a relatively stable or enduring personality characteristic. The STAI test items consist of short descriptive statements, and subjects are instructed to indicate either (1) how they feel right now or at this moment (and to indicate the intensity of the feeling), or (2) how they generally feel (and to record the frequency of the feeling). The test-retest reliability coefficients reported in the manual are consistent with the theoretical premise that trait anxiety is the more enduring characteristic, whereas state anxiety is transitory.

Personality Assessment: Some Basic Questions

- What type of employment is a person with this type of personality best suited for?
- Is this individual sufficiently well adjusted for military service?
- What emotional and other adjustment-related factors may be responsible for this student's level of academic achievement?
- What pattern of traits and states does this psychotherapy client evidence, and to what extent may this pattern be deemed to be pathological?
- How has this patient's personality been affected by neurological trauma?

These questions are a sampling of the kind that might lead to a referral for personality assessment. Collectively, these types of referral questions provide insight into the more general question, Why assess personality? We might add that personality assessment is also a staple of basic research in psychology, helping to validate or invalidate theories of behavior and to generate new hypotheses. Indeed, some of the measures used to assess personality are themselves theory-based, whereas others rely on more empirical underpinnings.

Beyond the "why" of personality assessment are several other questions that must be addressed in any overview of the enterprise. Approaches to personality assessment differ in terms of *who* is being assessed, *what* is being assessed, *where* the assessment is conducted, and *how* the assessment is conducted, as well as the ways in which the resulting data are scored and interpreted. Let's take a closer look at each of these basic issues.

Who?

Some methods of personality assessment rely on the assessee's own self-report. Assessees may respond to interview questions, answer questionnaires in writing, blacken squares on computer answer forms, or sort cards with various terms on them—all with the ultimate objective of providing the assessor with personality-related self-description. By contrast, other methods of personality assessment rely on informants other than the person being assessed to provide personality-related information. So, for example, parents or teachers may be asked to participate in the personality assessment of a child by providing ratings, judgments, opinions, and impressions relevant to the child's personality. These two different approaches to personality assessment vary in terms of the respondent's primary referent. In the self-report situation, the self is the primary referent.

The self as the primary referent   People undergo personality assessment so that they, as well as the assessor, can learn something about who they are. In many instances, the assessment or some aspect of it requires **self-report,** or a process wherein information about a person is supplied by that person. The information supplied by self-report may take many different forms: oral or written responses to questions or test items, keeping a diary, or reporting on self-monitored thoughts and/or behaviors. One variety of assessment-related information that is most typically obtained by means of self-report has to do with the assessee's self-concept. **Self-concept** may be defined as one's attitudes, beliefs, opinions, and related thoughts about oneself. Although inferences about an assessee's self-concept may be derived from other tools of assessment, the tool of choice is typically a **self-concept measure,** an instrument designed to yield information relevant to how an individual sees himself or herself with regard to selected psychological variables. Data from such an instrument are usually interpreted in the context of how others may see themselves on the same or similar variables. On the Beck Self-Concept Test (BST; Beck & Stein, 1961), for example, respondents are asked to compare themselves to other people on variables such as looks, knowledge, ability to tell jokes, and so forth. An awareness of the importance of self-concept in childhood compelled test developers to develop self-concept measures for children, including the Tennessee Self-Concept Scale (Fitts, 1965) and the Piers-Harris Self-Concept Scale (Piers, 1969). The latter test contains 80 self-statements (such as "I don't have any friends") to which respondents from grades 3 to 12 respond with either "yes" or "no" as the statement applies to them. Factor analysis of the test indicated that the items covered six general areas of self-concept: behavior, intellectual and school status, physical appearance and attributes, anxiety, popularity, and happiness and satisfaction.

Some measures of self-concept are based on the notion that states and traits related to self-concept are to a large degree context-dependent—that is, ever-changing as a result of the particular situation (Callero, 1992; Donahue et al., 1993). The term **self-concept differentiation** is used to refer to the degree to which a person has different self-concepts in different roles (Donahue et al., 1993). People characterized as "highly differentiated" are likely to perceive themselves quite differently in various roles. For example, a highly differentiated businessman in his forties may perceive himself as motivated and hard-driving in his role at work, conforming and people-pleasing in his role as son, and emotional and passionate in his role as husband. By contrast, people whose concept of self is not very differentiated tend to perceive themselves similarly across their social roles. According to Donahue et al. (1993), people with low levels of self-concept differentiation tend to be healthier psychologically, perhaps because of their more unified and coherent sense of self.

Assuming assessees have reasonably accurate insight into their own thinking and behavior, and assuming that they are motivated to respond to test items honestly, self-report measures can be extremely valuable. An assessee's candid and accurate self-report can illustrate what that individual is thinking, feeling, and doing. Unfortunately, some assessees may intentionally or unintentionally paint distorted pictures of themselves in self-report measures.

Consider what would happen if employers were to rely on job applicants' representations concerning their personality and their suitability for a particular job. They might receive universally glowing references—and still not hire the most suitable personnel. This is so because many job applicants, as well as other people in a wide variety of other contexts—contexts as diverse as singles bars, custody hearings, and high school reunions—attempt to "fake good" in their presentation of themselves to other people. The other side of the "faking good" coin is, as you might expect, "faking bad." Litigants in civil actions who claim injury may seek high awards to compensate them for their alleged pain, suffering, and emotional distress—all of which may be exaggerated and dramatized for the benefit of a judge and jury. The accused in a criminal action may view time in a mental institution as preferable to time in prison (or capital punishment) and strategically choose an insanity defense—with accompanying behavior and claims to make such a defense as believable as possible. A homeless person who prefers the environs of a mental hospital to that of the street may attempt to "fake bad" on tests and in interviews if failure to do so will result in discharge. In the days when a military draft existed, it was not uncommon for draft resisters to attempt to be deferred from their service obligation on psychiatric grounds—and many such people went to great lengths to "fake bad" when assessed.

Some testtakers, because of prevailing medical or psychological conditions at the time of testing, simply do not have sufficient insight into their own thinking to answer self-report questions in a way that will be most beneficial to them. The other side of the coin is the testtaker who has a great deal of self-insight and conveys it quite expertly on the self-report measure. For such testtakers, on the basis of self-report measure alone, Burisch (1984) argued that "clinicians cannot tell patients anything they do not already know" (p. 225). Well, Burisch may be overstating the case. Clinicians may well be able to accomplish that feat by looking at various patterns or clusters of responses. The more compelling question for us is, How much can the clinician tell about the assessee on the basis of self-report alone? And in the context of attempts to disguise oneself, we might rephrase that question: How much can the clinician *really* tell about the assessee on the basis of self-report alone? We return to this question later in this chapter.

Another person as the referent In some situations, the best available method for the assessment of personality, behavior, or both entails reporting by a third party such as a parent, teacher, peer, supervisor, spouse, or trained observer. Consider, for example, the assessment of a child for emotional difficulties. The child may be unable or unwilling to complete any measure (self-report, performance, or whatever) that will be of value in making a valid determination as to that child's emotional status. Even case history data may be of minimal value, because the problems may be so subtle as to become evident only after careful and sustained observation. In such cases, the use of a test in which the testtaker is an informant and not the subject of study may be valuable.

The Personality Inventory for Children (PIC), as well as its revision, the PIC-2, are examples of a kind of standardized interview of a child's parent; though the child is the subject of the test, the respondent is the parent (usually the mother), guardian, or other adult qualified to respond with reference to the child's characteristic behavior.[2] The test consists of a series of true-false items designed to be free of racial and gender bias (Kline & Lachar, 1992; Kline et al., 1993). The items may be administered by computer or paper and pencil. Test results yield scores that shed light on the validity of the testtaker's response patterns, as well as clinical information. A number of studies attest to the validity of the PIC for its intended purpose (Kline et al., 1992, 1993; Lachar & Wirt, 1981; Lachar et al., 1985; Wirt et al., 1984). However, as with any test that relies on the observations and judgment of a rater, some concerns about this instrument have also been expressed (Achenbach, 1981; Cornell, 1985).

In general, there are many cautions to consider when one person undertakes to evaluate another. For example, some raters may tend to be favorably lenient and generous, harshly severe, or relatively neutral in their ratings. Generalized biases to rate in a particular direction are referred to in terms such as **leniency** or **generosity error** and **severity error.** A general tendency to rate everyone near the midpoint of a rating scale is termed an **error of central tendency.** In some situations, a particular set of circumstances may create a certain bias. So, for example, a teacher might be very favorably disposed to judging one pupil, because that pupil's older sister was teacher's pet in a prior class. This variety of favorable response bias is sometimes referred to as a **halo effect.** As illustrated by the cartoon in Figure 11–2, raters may also make biased judgments, consciously or unconsciously, because it is in their own self-interest to do so. Therapists who passionately believe in the efficacy of a particular therapeutic approach may be more disposed than others to see the benefits of that approach. Proponents of alternative approaches may be more disposed to see the negative aspects of that same treatment.

Numerous other factors may contribute to bias in a rater's ratings. The rater may feel competitive with, physically attracted to, or physically repulsed by the subject of the ratings. The rater may not have the proper background, experience, and trained eye needed for the particular task. The rater's judgments may be limited by his or her general level of conscientiousness and willingness to devote the time and effort required to do the job properly. The rater may harbor biases concerning various stereotypes. Subjectivity based on the rater's own subjective preferences and taste may also enter into judgments; features that rate a "perfect 10" in one person's opinion may represent more like a "mediocre 5" in the eyes of another person.

Another factor to consider with regard to ratings is the context of the evaluation. A parent may indicate on a rating scale that a child is hyperactive, whereas that same child's teacher may indicate on that same rating scale that the child's activity level is within normal limits. Can they both be right? And can the information from both

2. The PIC was originally published in 1958, although a formal test manual was not published until 1977. Five years later, a "revised format manual supplement" (Lachar, 1982) was published. Since that time, the test has continually been referred to as the "PIC." This footnote is intended to address the confusion created by erroneous references to the PIC as the "PIC-R" and "PIC-Revised" (Kline et al., 1985, 1993; Kline & Lachar, 1992; Lachar et al., 1985, 1986; LaCombe et al., 1991; Wirt et al., 1984) prior to the publication of the Personality Inventory for Children, Second Edition (PIC-2) in 2001. By the way, in the course of a phone call to the test's publisher we learned that the test is referred to around the office as the "PIC," pronounced like the word "pick."

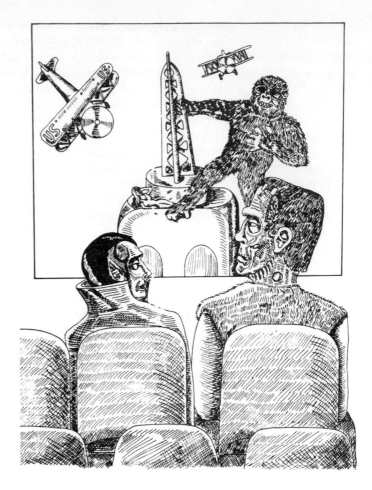

Figure 11–2
Ratings in One's Own
Self-Interest

"Monsters and screamers have always worked for me; I give it 'thumbs up,' Roger."

informants be integrated into a comprehensive and context-specific treatment plan? As Achenbach et al. (1987) reported on the basis of their meta-analysis of 119 articles in the scholarly literature, different informants may have different perspectives on the subjects of evaluation based on the different contexts in which they interact with the subjects. Interestingly, Achenbach et al. found that raters were more likely to agree about the difficulties of young children (ages 6 to 11) than about those of older children and adolescents. Raters also tended to show more agreement when the child was exhibiting problems of self-control (such as hyperactivity and mistreating other children) than when the child was exhibiting "overcontrol" problems (such as anxiety or depression). The researchers urged professionals to view the differences in evaluation that arise from different perspectives as something more than error in the evaluation process. In fact, Achenbach et al. (1987) advised professionals to employ these evaluative differences in planning treatment. Many of these ideas regarding context-dependent evaluation have been incorporated into Achenbach's (1993) Multiaxial Empirically Based Assessment system. The system is an approach to the assessment of children and adolescents that incorporates cognitive and physical assessments of the subject, self-report of the subject, and ratings by parents and teachers. Additionally, performance measures of the child alone, with the family, or in the classroom may be included.

The cultural background of assessees In recent years, test developers and users have shown increased sensitivity to issues of cultural diversity. A number of concerns have been raised regarding the use of personality tests and other tools of assessment with members of culturally and linguistically diverse populations (Anderson, 1995; Campos, 1989; Greene, 1987; Hinkle, 1994; Irvine & Berry, 1983; Lonner, 1985; Lopez & Hernandez, 1987; Sundberg & Gonzales, 1981). At the core of such concerns are questions related to how fair or generalizable the use of a particular instrument or measurement technique is or can be with a member of a particular cultural group. How a test was developed, how it is administered, and how scores on it are interpreted are all questions to be raised when considering the appropriateness of administering a particular personality test to members of culturally and linguistically diverse populations. These and related questions are further explored later in this chapter.

What?

What is being assessed when a personality assessment is conducted? For many personality tests, it is meaningful to answer this question with reference to the primary content area sampled by the test, as well as that portion of the test devoted to measuring aspects of the testtaker's general response style.

Primary content area sampled   Personality measures are tools used to gain insight into a wide array of thoughts, feelings, and behaviors associated with all aspects of the human experience. Some tests are designed to measure particular traits (such as introversion) or states (such as test anxiety), whereas others focus on descriptions of behavior, usually in particular contexts. For example, an observational checklist may concentrate on classroom behaviors associated with movement in order to assess a child's hyperactivity. Extended discussion of behavioral measures is presented in the following chapter.

One can begin to appreciate the broad range of variables in personality assessment by considering a sampling of the presentations made at a recent meeting of the Society for Personality Assessment (SPA).[3] In addition to presentations regarding research and clinical experience with widely used personality tests, measurement-related presentations were made on topics as diverse as optimism (Strassle et al., 1998), introversion (Colligan et al., 1998), shame (Harder & Greenwald, 1998; Thurston & Cradock, 1998), marital satisfaction (Snyder, 1998), narcissism (Lerner, 1998), chronic pain (Coolidge et al., 1998; Young & Wagner, 1998), creativity (Dudek, 1998; King & Pope, 1998), play and playfulness in children (Russ & Niec, 1998) and adults (Fowler, 1998; Handler, 1998), psychological aspects of Gulf War Syndrome (Horowitz, 1998; LaLone et al., 1998; Sloan et al., 1998), college student gambling (McCown et al., 1998), eating disorders (Franklin & Greene, 1998), human sexuality (Romei, 1998), sexual abuse (Boss, 1998; Ornduff, 1998; Silber et al., 1998), substance abuse (Craig, 1998; Baldrachi, et al., 1998), and vocational selection (Staal et al., 1998).

Many contemporary personality tests, especially tests that can be computer-scored and interpreted, are designed to measure not only some targeted trait or other personality variable, but some aspect of the testtaker's response style. For example, in addition to scales labeled "Introversion" and "Extraversion," a test of introversion/extraversion might contain other scales. These other scales could be designed to shed light on how

---

3. Founded by Bruno Klopfer and a group of his students, the Society for Personality Assessment (SPA) was incorporated in 1938 as the Rorschach Institute. The institute changed its name in 1971 to reflect its interest in the broad spectrum of activities in the area of personality assessment. Headquartered in Falls Church, Virginia, SPA sponsors conferences in partial fulfillment of the incorporator's objective "to provide an annual assembly of sharing research findings and clinical experiences." SPA members include measurement professionals and student affiliates. For more information, contact SPA at their e-mail address: *Klecksen@aol.com.*

Table 11–1
A Sampling of Test Response Styles

Response Style Name	Explanation: A Tendency To . . .
Socially desirable responding	Present oneself in a favorable (read "socially acceptable" or "socially desirable") light
Acquiescence	Agree with whatever is presented
Nonacquiescence	Disagree with whatever is presented
Deviance	Make unusual or uncommon responses
Extreme	Make extreme, as opposed to middle, ratings on a rating scale
Gambling/cautiousness	Guess — or not guess — when in doubt
Overly positive	Claim extreme virtue through self-presentation in a superlative manner (Butcher & Han, 1995)

honestly testtakers responded to the test, how consistently they answered the questions, and other matters related to the validity of the test findings. These measures of response pattern are also known as measures of response set or response style. Let's take a look at some different testtaker response styles, as well as the scales used to identify them.

Testtaker response styles   **Response style** refers to a tendency to respond to a test item or interview question in some characteristic manner regardless of the content of the item or question. For example, an individual may be more apt to respond with "yes" or "true" than "no" or "false" on a short-answer test. This particular pattern of responding is characterized as **acquiescent.** Table 11–1 shows a listing of other identified response styles.

Impression management is a term used to describe the behavior of attempting to manipulate others' impressions through "the selective exposure of some information (it may be false information) . . . coupled with suppression of [other] information" (Braginsky et al., 1969, p. 51). In the process of personality assessment, assessees might employ any number of impression management strategies for any number of reasons. Paulhaus (1984, 1986, 1990; Paulhus & Levitt, 1987) and his colleagues have explored impression management in testtaking as well as the related phenomena of enhancement (the claiming of positive attributes), denial (the repudiation of negative attributes), and self-deception ("the tendency to give favorably biased but honestly held self-descriptions" (Paulhus & Reid, 1991, p. 307). Testtakers who engage in impression management are exhibiting, in the broadest sense, a response style (Jackson & Messick, 1962).

Some personality tests contain items that are designed to detect different types of response styles. So, for example, a "true" response to an item like, "I Summer in Baghdad" would raise a number of questions, such as: Did the testtaker understand the instructions? take the test seriously? respond "true" to all items? respond randomly? endorse other infrequently endorsed items? Analysis of the entire protocol will help answer such questions.

Responding to a personality test in an inconsistent, contrarian, or random way, or attempting to fake good or bad, may have an effect on the validity of the interpretations made from the test data. Because a response style can affect the validity of the outcome, measures of response style are sometimes referred to as "validity scales." This label is a kind of shorthand reference to a measure of how honestly, diligently, and carefully a testtaker responded to test items. Some tests, such as the MMPI and its revision (to be discussed shortly), contain multiple validity scales. Although there are those who question the utility of formally assessing response styles (Costa & McCrae, 1997; Rorer, 1965) perhaps the more common view is that response styles are themselves important for what they reveal about testtakers. As Nunnally (1978, p. 660) observed, "To the extent that such stylistic variables can be measured independently of content relating to non-stylistic variables or to the extent that they can somehow be separated from the variance of other traits, they might prove useful as measures of personality traits."

Where?

Traditionally, personality assessment, as well as other varieties of assessment, have been conducted in places such as schools, clinics, hospitals, academic research laboratories, employment counseling and vocational selection centers, and the offices of psychologists and counselors. In addition to such traditional venues, contemporary assessors may be found observing behavior and making assessments in natural settings ranging from the assessee's own home (Marx, 1998; McElwain, 1998; Polizzi, 1998) to the incarcerated assessee's prison cell (Glassbrenner, 1998). As we will see in the discussion of behavioral assessment in the following chapter, behavioral observation may be undertaken just about anywhere.

How?

The "how" of personality assessment is a multidimensional subject. Some general facets of personality assessment, such as who the respondent is (self or someone else), exactly what is being assessed, and where the assessment is to occur, have already been addressed. Here, let's look at some other facets of the "how" question, including the scope of the assessment and its relationship to personality theory, the procedures and item formats employed, the frame of reference of the assessment, and variables related to scoring and interpretation.

Scope and theory   One dimension of the "how" of personality assessment concerns its scope. The scope of an evaluation may be very wide, seeking to take a kind of general inventory of personality, or relatively narrow, focusing on a selected aspect of it. The California Psychological Inventory (CPI; Gough & Bradley, 1996) is an example of an instrument with a relatively wide scope. This test contains 434 true-false items and is designed to yield information on many personality-related variables such as responsibility, self-acceptance, dominance, and locus of control (McAllister, 1996).

In contrast to instruments and procedures designed to take inventory of various aspects of personality are those designed to focus narrowly on as little as one particular aspect of personality. As an example, consider tests designed to measure a personality variable called "locus of control" (Rotter, 1966; Wallston et al., 1978). **Locus** (meaning "place" or "site") **of control** is the perception people have about the source of things that happen to them. In general, people who see themselves as largely responsible for what happens to them are said to have an internal locus of control. People who are prone to attribute what happens to them to external factors (such as fate or the action of others) are said to have an external locus. So, for example, a person who believes in the value of seatbelts, as opposed to a nonbuckling counterpart, would be expected to score closer to the internal as opposed to the external end of the continuum on a valid measure of locus of control. Research with different measures of locus of control (see Lefcourt, 1991) has yielded intriguing implications regarding the utility of this construct, especially with regard to health and lifestyle.

Instruments used in personality testing and assessment range from what we might label "theory-saturated" to relatively atheoretical—allowing the test users, should they so desire, to impose their own theoretical preferences on the interpretation of the findings. An example of a theory-saturated instrument is the Blacky Pictures Test (Blum, 1950). This test, now seldom if ever used, consists of pictures of Blacky, a dog, in various situations, each image designed to elicit fantasies associated with various psychoanalytic themes. For example, one card depicts Blacky with a knife hovering over his tail, a scene, according to the test's author, designed to elicit material related to the psychoanalytic concept of castration anxiety. The respondent's task is to make up stories in response to such cards, and the stories are then analyzed according to the guidelines set forth by Blum (1950). More contemporary psychoanalytically based assessment efforts can be found in other sources, such as the writings of Robert Plutchik, Hope Conte, and their associates (Conte & Plutchik, 1981; Conte et al., 1991; Plutchik & Conte, 1989).

Procedures and item formats   Personality may be assessed by many different methods such as face-to-face interviews, computer-administered tests, behavioral observation, paper-and-pencil tests, evaluation of case history data, evaluation of portfolio data, and recording of physiological responses. The equipment required for assessment varies greatly depending upon the method employed. In one technique, for example, all that may be required is a blank sheet of paper and a pencil; the assessee is asked to draw a person and the assessor makes inferences about the assessee's personality from the drawing. Other approaches to assessment, and in particular those conducted in academic research settings as opposed to homes or offices, may be far more elaborate in terms of the equipment they require (Figure 11–3).

Measures of personality vary in terms of the degree of structure built into them. For example, personality may be assessed by means of an interview, but it may also be assessed by a **structured interview.** In the latter method, the interviewer must typically follow an interview guide and has little leeway in terms of posing questions not in that guide. The variable of structure is also applicable to the tasks assessees are instructed to perform. In some approaches to personality assessment, the tasks are straightforward, highly structured, and unambiguous (as in, "Respond 'yes' or 'no' to the following questions"). In other approaches, what is required of the assessee is not so straightforward, not very structured, and intentionally ambiguous (as in being asked to respond to the presentation of inkblots with the question, "What might this be?").

The same personality trait or construct may be measured with different instruments in different ways. Consider the many possible ways of determining how aggressive a person is. Measurement of this trait could be made by the administration of a test, interviews with the assessee and others, reading official records and other case history data, a computerized test, behavioral observation at a hockey game, and a laboratory experiment using the administration of electric shock or other punishment as a dependent variable. Depending on how aggression is defined, it is even conceivable that psychophysiological variables, such as blood pressure, might be employed. Of course, criteria for what constitutes the trait being measured, in this case aggression, would have to be rigorously defined in advance. After all, psychological traits and constructs can and have been defined in many different ways, and virtually all such definitions tend to be context-dependent. For example, "aggressive" may be defined in ways ranging from hostile (as in assaultive) to bold or enterprising (as in aggressive salesperson). Whether or not the trait is socially desirable depends entirely on the context in which it is couched.

In personality assessment, as well as assessment in other areas, information may be gathered and questions may be answered in a variety of ways. So, for example, a researcher or practitioner interested in learning about the degree to which respondents are field dependent may construct a tilting chair/tilting room device like that pictured in Figure 11–3. In the interests of time and expense, an equivalent process administered by paper-and-pencil or computer may be more practical for everyday use. In this chapter's *Everyday Psychometrics,* we illustrate some of the more common types of item formats that have been employed in the study of personality and related psychological variables. These item formats, usually presented by means of a paper-and-pencil or

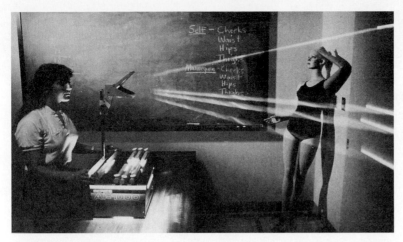

Body image distortion is a fairly common phenomenon in persons with eating disorders (Thompson & Smolak, 2001). The adjustable light beam apparatus has been used to measure just how distorted that image is. Assessees adjust four beams of light to reflect what they believe to be the width of their cheeks, waist, hips, and thighs.

During World War II, the assessment staff of the Office of Strategic Services (OSS) selected American secret agents using a variety of measures. One measure used to assess leadership ability and emotional stability in the field entailed a simulation that involved rebuilding a blown bridge. Candidates were deliberately supplied with insufficient materials for rebuilding the bridge. In some instances, "assistants" who were actually confederates of the experimenter further frustrated the efforts of the candidates.

Herman Witkin and his associates (Witkin & Berry, 1975; Witkin & Goodenough, 1981; Witkin et al., 1954, 1962) studied the cognitive style variable of field dependence/independence using this tilting room/tilting chair device, among other procedures. Here, the respondent's task was to determine which way was up without reliable visual cues. Findings were interpreted in terms of how field- or context-dependent an individual was, which in turn was interpreted in terms of social variables such as independence.

Figure 11–3
Some Laboratory and Field Procedures for Gaining Insights About Personality

There has been no shortage of innovation when it comes to ways of measuring aspects of personality. Pictured here are three of many such methods that require elaborate equipment or experimental setups to conduct. Although not typical of personality assessment as it is routinely conducted in consulting rooms, schools, and other settings, they illustrate the varied ways personality assessment has been approached in the laboratory and the field.

Some Common Item Formats

How may personality be assessed? Here are some of the more typical types of item formats.

ITEM 1

I enjoy being out and among other people.   TRUE   FALSE

This item illustrates the true-false format. Was your reaction something like "been there, done that" when you saw this item?

ITEM 2

Working with fellow community members
on organizing and staging a blood drive.   LIKE   DISLIKE

This two-choice item is designed to elicit information about the respondents' likes and dislikes. It is a common format in interest inventories, particularly those used in vocational counseling.

ITEM 3

How I feel when I am out and among other people

Warm	_:_:_:_:_:_:_	Cold
Tense	_:_:_:_:_:_:_	Relaxed
Weak	_:_:_:_:_:_:_	Strong
Brooks Brothers suit	_:_:_:_:_:_:_	Hawaiian shirt

This item format, called a **semantic differential** (Osgood et al., 1957), is characterized by bipolar adjectives separated by a 7-point rating scale on which respondents select one point to indicate their response. This type of item is useful for gauging the strength, degree, or magnitude of the direction of a particular response and has applications ranging from self-concept descriptions to opinion surveys.

ITEM 4

I enjoy being out and among other people.

or

I have an interest in learning about art.

ITEM 5

I am depressed too much of the time.

or

I am anxious too much of the time.

These are two examples of items written in a **forced-choice format,** where each of the two choices (there may be more than two choices) is ideally equal in social desirability. The Edwards Personal Preference Schedule (Edwards, 1953) is a classic forced-choice test. Edwards (1957a, 1957b, 1966) described in detail how he determined the items in this test to be equivalent in social desirability.

ITEM 6

naughty

needy

negativistic

new age

nerdy

nimble

nonproductive

numb

This illustrates an item written in an adjective checklist format. Respondents check the traits that apply to them.

computerized test, are far more common than apparatuses and procedures such as those illustrated in Figure 11–3.

Frame of reference   Frame of reference is another variable on which personality measures may differ. **Frame of reference** has to do with the temporal focus of the evaluation (the past, the present, or the future), as well as other contextual issues having to do with people, places, and events. Perhaps for most measures of personality, the frame of reference for the assessee may be described in phrases such as "what is" or "how I am right now." However, some techniques of measurement are easily adapted to tap alternative

ITEM 7

Complete this sentence.

I feel as if I _____.

Respondents are typically instructed to finish the sentence with their "real feelings" in what is called a sentence completion item. The Rotter Incomplete Sentence Blank (Rotter & Rafferty, 1950) is a standardized test that employs such items, and the manual features normative data (Rotter et al., 1992).

ITEM 8

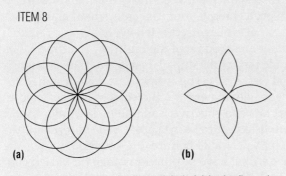

(a)   **(b)**

Can you distinguish the figure labeled *b* in the figure labeled *a?* This is the type of item found in embedded figures tests. Identifying hidden figures is a skill thought to tap the same field dependence/independence variable tapped by more elaborate apparatuses such as the tilting chair/tilting room illustrated in Figure 11–3.

ITEM 9

This is an item reminiscent of one of the Rorschach inkblot cards. We will have much more to say about the Rorschach in the following chapter.

ITEM 10

Much like the Rorschach test, which uses inkblots as an ambiguous stimulus, many other tests ask the respondent to "project" onto an ambiguous stimulus. This item is reminiscent of one such projective technique called the Hand Test. Respondents are asked to tell the examiner what they think the hands might be doing.

frames of reference such as "what could be ideally," "how I am in the office," "how others see me," "how I see others," and so forth. Obtaining self-reported information from different frames of reference is, in itself, a way of developing information related to states and traits. For example, in comparing self-perception in the present versus what is anticipated for the future, assessees who report that they will become better people may be presumed to be more optimistic than assessees who report a reverse trend.

Representative of methodologies that can be readily applied to varied frames of reference is the **Q-sort** technique. Originally developed by Stephenson (1953), the Q-sort is an assessment technique in which the task is to sort a group of statements, usually in perceived rank order ranging from "most descriptive" to "least descriptive." The statements, traditionally presented on index cards, may be sorted in ways designed to reflect various perceptions such as how respondents see themselves or how they would like to see themselves. Illustrative statements are, "I am confident," "I try hard to please others," and "I am uncomfortable in social situations." The technique is readily adaptable for use in sundry contexts with varying assessment objectives (Stephenson, 1980).

One of the best-known applications of Q-methodology in clinical and counseling settings was the use of the Q-sort as advocated by the personality theorist and psychotherapist Carl Rogers. Rogers (1959) used the Q-sort as a method of determining how much discrepancy there was between how clients saw themselves and how they would like to be; that is, the discrepancy between the actual and ideal self. At the beginning of psychotherapy, clients might be asked to sort cards twice, once according to how they perceived themselves to be and again according to how they would ultimately like to be. The larger the discrepancy between the sortings, the more work would be needed in therapy. Presumably the retesting of the client who successfully completed a course of psychotherapy would reveal much less discrepancy between the present and idealized selves. Beyond the application of the Q-sort technique in initial assessment and reevaluation of a therapy client, the technique has also been used extensively in basic research in the area of personality as well as in other areas. Some of the highly specialized kinds of Q-sorts that have been published include the Leadership Q-Test (Cassel, 1958) and the Tyler Vocational Classification System (Tyler, 1961). The former test was designed for use in military settings and contains cards with statements the subject is instructed to sort with respect to their perceived importance to effective leadership. The Tyler Q-sort contains cards on which occupations are listed. These cards are sorted in terms of the perceived desirability of each occupation. A desirable feature of Q-methodology is the ease with which it can be adapted for use with a wide population range for varied clinical and research purposes. DeMulder et al. (2000) described how Q-sort methodology was used with preschoolers to measure the variable of attachment security.

Two other item presentation formats that are readily adaptable to different frames of reference are the adjective checklist format and the sentence completion format (discussed in Chapter 12). Using an adjective checklist method, respondents simply check off from a list of adjectives those adjectives that apply to themselves (or to people they are rating). Using the same list of adjectives, the frame of reference can easily be changed by changing the instructions given to respondents. The Adjective Check List (Gough, 1960; Gough & Heilbrun, 1980) has been used in a wide range of research including studies focusing on managers' self-perceptions (Hills, 1985), parents' perceptions of their children (Brown, 1972), and clients' perceptions of their therapists (Reinehr, 1969). The Multiple Affect Adjective Check List-Revised (MAACL-R; Zuckerman & Lubin, 1985) consists of 132 adjectives arranged in alphabetical order. The test may be administered under two different types of instructions, both standardized. One set, the "Today" (or state) form, instructs testtakers to select those adjectives that describe how they feel at the time of testing.

Scoring and interpretation   Personality measures differ with respect to the way that conclusions are drawn from the data they provide. For some paper-and-pencil measures, a simple tally of responses to targeted items is presumed to provide a measure of the strength of a particular trait. For other measures, a computer programmed to apply highly technical manipulations of the data is required for purposes of scoring and interpretation.

Also with regard to scoring and interpretation, personality measures differ with respect to the nomothetic/idiographic variable. The **nomothetic approach** to assessment is characterized by efforts to learn how a limited number of personality traits can be applied to all people. By contrast, the **idiographic approach** is characterized by efforts to learn about each individual's unique constellation of personality traits, with no attempt to characterize each person according to any particular set of traits. A test such as the 16 PF (Cattell et al., 1993), which seeks to measure testtakers on 16 personality factors (which is what "PF" stands for), is representative of the nomothetic orientation to assessment. The idiographic orientation is evident in assessment procedures that are not only more flexible in terms of listing the observed traits, but in naming new trait terms.[4] The idiographic approach to personality assessment was described in detail by Allport (1937; Allport & Odbert, 1936).

Another dimension related to how meaning is attached to test scores has to do with whether interindividual or intraindividual comparisons are being made with respect to test scores. Most common in personality assessment is the normative approach, whereby a testtaker's responses and the presumed strength of a measured trait is interpreted relative to the strength of that trait in a sample of a larger population. In the **ipsative approach,** a testtaker's responses and the presumed strength of a measured trait is interpreted relative to the strength of measured traits for that same individual. On a test that employs ipsative scoring procedures, two people with the same score for a particular trait or personality characteristic may differ markedly with regard to the magnitude of that trait or characteristic relative to members of a larger population. The Edwards Personal Preference Schedule is a commonly cited example of one of the relatively few personality measures that employs ipsative scoring.

Issues in personality test development and use   Many of the issues inherent in the development process mirror the basic questions just discussed about personality assessment in general. Who will this test be designed for use with? Will the test entail self-report? Or will it require the use of raters or judges? If raters or judges are needed, what special training or other qualifications must they have? What content area will be sampled by the test? How will issues related to testtaker response sets be dealt with? What item format should be employed, and what is the optimal frame of reference? How will the test be scored and interpreted?

As we have previously noted, personality assessment that relies exclusively on self-report is a two-edged sword. On the one hand, the information is from "the source"; respondents are in most instances presumed to know themselves better than anyone else and therefore able to supply accurate responses about themselves. On the other hand, the consumer of such information has no way of knowing with certainty which self-reported information is entirely true, partly true, not really true, or an outright lie. Consider a response to a single item on a personality inventory written in a true-false format. The item reads: "I tend to enjoy meeting new people." A respondent indicates that this is "true." In reality, we do not know whether the respondent (1) veritably does enjoy meeting new people; (2) honestly believes that he or she enjoys meeting new people but really does not (in which case, the response is more the product of a lack of

---

4. Consider in this context the expression "new age" used as a personality trait (referring to a belief in spirituality). A personality assessment conducted with an idiographic orientation would be flexible enough to characterize the assessee as " new age" should this trait be judged applicable. Nomothetic instruments developed prior to the usage of such a new trait term would subsume cognitive and behavioral characteristics of the new trait term under whatever existing trait or traits in the nomothetic system were judged appropriate. So, for example, a nomothethic system that included "spiritual" as one of its core traits might subsume "new age" under "spiritual." At some point, if trends and usage warrant it, an existing nomothetic instrument could be revised to include a new trait term.

insight than a report of reality); (3) does not enjoy meeting new people but would have people think that he or she does; or (4) did not even bother to read the item, is not taking the test seriously, and is randomly responding true or false to each item.

One way developers of personality inventories have attempted to deal with the problems of self-report is by building into their tests so-called validity scales. We may define a **validity scale** as a subscale of a test designed to assist in judgments regarding how honestly the testtaker responded, and whether observed responses were products of response sets, carelessness, deliberate efforts to deceive, or unintentional misunderstanding. In the following section, when we discuss in detail the development of the MMPI and the MMPI-2, we will have more to say about the mechanics of validity scales.

In recent years, there has been some debate about whether validity scales should be included in personality tests. Some assert that "detection of an attempt to provide misleading information is a vital and absolutely necessary component of the clinical interpretation of test results" and that using any instrument without validity scales "runs counter to the basic tenets of clinical assessment" (Ben-Porath & Waller, 1992, p. 24). By contrast, the authors of the widely used Revised NEO Personality Inventory (NEO PI-R), Paul T. Costa, Jr., and Robert R. McCrae, perceived no need to include any validity scales in their instrument and have been less enthusiastic about the use of such scales in other tests (McCrae & Costa, 1983; McCrae et al., 1989; Piedmont & McCrae, 1996; Piedmont et al., 2000). Referring to validity scales as SD (for "social desirability") scales, Costa and McCrae (1997) opined:

> SD scales typically consist of items that have a clearly desirable response. We know that people who are trying falsely to appear to have good qualities will endorse many such items, and the creators of SD scales wish to infer from this that people who endorse many SD items are trying to create a good impression. That argument is formally identical to asserting that presidential candidates shake hands, and therefore people who shake hands are probably running for president. In fact, there are many more common reasons for shaking hands, and there is also a more common reason than impression management for endorsing SD items—namely, because the items are reasonably accurate self-descriptions. (p. 89)

According to Costa and McCrae, assessors can affirm that self-reported information is reasonably accurate by consulting external sources such as peer raters. Of course, the use of raters necessitates certain other precautions to guard against rater error and bias.

Education regarding the nature of various types of rater error and bias has been a key weapon in the fight against intentional or unintentional inaccuracies in ratings. Training sessions may be designed to accomplish several objectives such as clarifying terminology to increase the reliability of ratings. A term such as "satisfactory," for example, may have different meanings to different raters. During training, new raters can observe and work with more experienced raters to become acquainted with aspects of the task that may not be described in the rater's manual, to compare ratings with more experienced raters, and to discuss the thinking that went into the ratings.

The language that an assessment should be conducted in seems, at first blush, to be a nonissue. Yet a number of factors must be considered when an assessee is fluent in one or more languages. Words tend to lose—or gain—something in translation, and some words and expressions are not readily translatable into other languages. Consider the following item from the NEO PI-R: "I am known for my prudence and common sense." If you are a bilingual student, translate that statement now as an exercise in test item translation.

A French translation of this item is quite close, adding only an extra first-person possessive pronoun ("par ma prudence et *mon* bon sens"; McCrae et al., 1998, p. 176). However, the Filipino translation of this item reads, "I can be relied on to decide carefully and well on matters" (McCrae et al., 1998, p. 176).

In addition to sometimes significant differences in the meaning of individual items, the traits being measured by personality tests sometimes have different meanings as well. Acknowledging this fact, McCrae et al. (1998, p. 183) cautioned that "Personality-trait relations reported in Western studies should be considered promising hypotheses to be tested in new cultures."

The broader issue relevant to the development and use of personality tests with members of a culture that differs from the culture in which the test was normed concerns the applicability of the norms. So, for example, a number of MMPI studies conducted with members of groups from diverse backgrounds yield findings in which minority group members tend to present with more psychopathology than majority group members (see, for example, Montgomery & Orozco, 1985; Whitworth & Unterbrink, 1994). Such differences have elicited questions regarding the appropriateness of the use of the test with members of different populations (Dana, 1995; Dana & Whatley, 1991; Malgady et al., 1987). However, as Lopez (1988, p. 1096) observed, "To argue that the MMPI is culturally biased, one needs to go beyond reporting that ethnic groups differ in their group profiles." Lopez noted that many of the studies showing differences between the groups did not control for psychopathology; accordingly, there may well have been veritable differences across the groups in psychopathology. The size of the sample used in the research, as well as the appropriateness of the statistical analysis, are other extracultural factors to consider when evaluating cross-cultural research. Of course, if culture and "learned meanings" (Rohner, 1984, pp. 119–120), as opposed to psychopathology, are found to account for differences in measured psychopathology with members of a particular cultural group, the continued use of the measures with members of that cultural group must be questioned.

Armed with some background information regarding the nature of personality and its assessment, let's take a closer look at the process of developing instruments designed to assess personality.

Developing Instruments to Assess Personality

Tools such as logic, theory, and data reduction methods (such as factor analysis) are frequently used in the process of developing personality tests. Another tool in the test development process may be a criterion group. As we will see, most personality tests employ two or more of these of these tools in the course of their development.

Logic and Reason

Notwithstanding the grumblings of skeptics, there is a place for logic and reason in psychology, at least when it comes to writing items for a personality test. Logic and reason may dictate what content is covered by the items; indeed, the use of logic and reason in the development of test items is sometimes referred to as the "content" or "content-oriented" approach to test development. As an example, suppose you wished to create the "Evaluation of Anorexic Tendencies Test" (EATT), the purpose of which is to identify people who are at high risk for developing anorexia nervosa. Logically, the content of the test items would relate to what is known about this eating disorder. In writing the items for the test, you might rely on what you know about anorexia nervosa from reading, personal experience, and accounts by others. The fruit of your efforts might result in questions that look something like this:

1. Is your current weight at least 85% of expected body weight for your age and height?

2. Do you fear gaining weight?

3. Do you perceive your body as abnormal in any way?

The items above are written in a yes-no format and are based on the American Psychiatric Association's *Diagnostic and Statistical Manual* criteria for a diagnosis of anorexia nervosa. The items written by other test developers might be in the same or other formats (such as true-false) and tap the same or other content areas.

Efforts to use such direct, face-valid items can be traced at least as far back to an instrument used to screen World War I recruits for personality and adjustment problems. The Personal Data Sheet (Woodworth, 1917), later known as the Woodworth Psychoneurotic Inventory, contained items designed to elicit self-report of fears, sleep disorders, and other problems deemed to be symptomatic of psychoneuroticism. The greater the number of problems reported, the more psychoneurotic the respondent was presumed to be.

A relative newcomer among content-constructed instruments is the Symptom Checklist-90-R (SCL-90-R; Derogatis, 1994). This instrument employs a 5-point scale on which respondents report information relating to the severity of symptoms. The test manual provides normative data for four groups: nonpatient adults, nonpatient adolescents, psychiatric outpatients, and psychiatric inpatients. The test requires a sixth-grade reading level, and is designed for use with adolescents and adults no younger than 13 years old. It may be administered online, by paper and pencil, or by means of an audiotaped presentation and only takes about 15 minutes to administer. The resulting test data is organized into nine scales designed to alert clinicians to possible problems in areas such as depression, anxiety, and paranoid ideation.

When testtakers respond to such self-report instruments with candor and insight, these data can be a boon to the user. A great deal of clinically actionable information can be collected in relatively little time. A highly trained professional is not required to administer the test, and a computerized report of the findings can be available in minutes. Moreover, such instruments are particularly well suited to clinical settings in managed care environments, where drastic cost cutting has led to reductions in orders for assessment (Murray et al., 1992) and insurers are reluctant to authorize assessments (Acklin, 1996). In such environments, the preferred use of psychological tests is to identify conditions of "medical necessity" (Glazer et al., 1991), and the quicker and less expensive a test is, the better the insurer likes it. On the other hand, insurers also like quick and inexpensive-to-administer self-report measures, especially when the testtaker does not report any problems of "medical necessity." Absent a "medical necessity," a heavy burden of proof is placed on the test user to document the need for any treatment. Usually, only compelling proof that testtakers may be harmful to themselves or others will overrule the self-report of the testtaker.

Typical companions to logic, reason, and intuition in item development are research, clinical experience, or both. Another possible aid in the test development process is correspondence with experts on the subject matter of the test. And yet another possible tool—sometimes even the guiding force—is psychological theory.

Theory

As we noted earlier, personality measures differ in the extent to which they rely on a particular theory of personality in their development, as well as their interpretation. So, for example, if instead of logic and reason, psychoanalytic theory was the guiding force behind the development of the hypothetical "EATT," the items might be quite different. For example, based on the psychoanalytic notion that people with anorexia nervosa are unconsciously attempting to fade away into obscurity, EATT items might attempt to evaluate this possibility. Given that dreams are thought to reveal unconscious motivation, a question such as the following might be found on a psychoanalytically derived EATT: "Have you ever dreamed that you were fading away?"

A theory of "vocational personality" (Holland, 1992) lies at the core of a self-administered, self-scored, and self-interpreted measure called the Self-Directed Search (SDS; Holland et al., 1994). Holland (1959, 1966) views occupational choice as having a great deal to do with one's personality and self-perception. The SDS is a measure of one's interests, as well as of one's self-perceived abilities. Testtakers use their test scores to identify themselves in terms of occupational themes and then follow instructions to learn about various occupations that are consistent with their expressed pattern of interests and abilities.

Data Reduction Methods

Data reduction methods represent another class of widely used tool in contemporary test development. Data reduction methods include several types of statistical techniques collectively known as factor analysis or cluster analysis. One use of data reduction methods in the design of personality measures is to aid in the identification of the minimum number of variables or factors that account for the intercorrelations in observed phenomena. To illustrate, let's suppose that you want to paint your apartment but have no idea what color would go best with your "early undergraduate" decor. You go to the local paint stores in your area and obtain free card samples of every shade of paint known to humanity—thousands of color samples. Next you undertake a factor analysis of these thousands of color samples—that is, you attempt to identify the minimum number of variables or factors that account for the intercorrelations among all of these colors. You would discover that, accounting for the intercorrelations, there existed three factors (which might be labeled "primary" factors) and four more factors (which might be labeled "secondary" or "second-order" factors), the latter set of factors being combinations of the first set of factors. Because all colors can be reduced to three primary colors and their combinations, the three primary factors would correspond to the three primary colors, red, yellow, and blue (which you might christen factor R, factor Y, and factor B), and the four secondary or second-order factors would correspond to all the possible combinations that could be made from the primary factors (factors RY, RB, YB, and RYB).

The paint-sample illustration might be helpful to keep in mind as we review how factor analysis is used in test construction and personality assessment. In a way analogous to the factoring of all those shades of paint into three primary colors, think of all personality traits being factored into what one psychologist referred to as "the most important individual differences in human transactions" (Goldberg, 1993, p. 26). After all the factoring is over and the dust has settled, how many personality-related terms do you think would remain?

As the result of a pioneering research program in the 1940s, Raymond Bernard Cattell's answer to the question posed above was "16." Cattell (1946, 1947, 1948a, 1948b) reviewed previous research by Allport and Odbert (1936), which suggested that there were more than 18,000 personality trait names and terms in the English language. Of these, however, only about a quarter were "real traits of personality" or words and terms that designated "generalized and personalized determining tendencies—consistent and stable modes of an individual's adjustment to his environment . . . not . . . merely temporary and specific behavior" (Allport, 1937, p. 306). Cattell added to this list some trait names and terms employed in the professional psychology and psychiatric literature and then had judges rate "just distinguishable" differences between all the words (Cattell, 1957).

The result was a reduction in the size of the list to 171 trait names and terms. College students were asked to rate their friends with respect to these trait names and terms, and the factor-analyzed results of that rating further reduced the number of names and terms to 36, which Cattell referred to as "surface traits." Still more research indicated that 16 basic dimensions or "source traits" could be distilled. In 1949, Cattell's research culminated in the publication of a test called the Sixteen Personality Factor (16 PF) Questionnaire. Revisions of the test were published in 1956, 1962, 1968, and 1993.

Over the years, many questions have been raised regarding (1) whether the 16 factors identified by Cattell do indeed merit the description as the "source" traits of personality, and (2) whether, in fact, the 16 PF measures 16 distinct factors. Although some research supports Cattell's claims, give or take a factor or two depending on the sample (Cattell, 1986; Cattell & Krug, 1986; Lichtenstein et al., 1986), serious reservations regarding these assertions have also been expressed (Eysenck, 1985, 1991; Goldberg, 1993). Some have argued that the 16 PF may be measuring somewhat fewer than 16 factors, because several of the factors are substantially intercorrelated (Bloxom, 1978). Eysenck (1947, 1991) argued that as few as three factors are sufficient to describe personality. Other theorists have variously argued that three, four, five, or six factors can best describe personality (Church & Burke, 1994). At least four different five-factor models exist (Johnson & Ostendorf, 1993; Costa & McCrae, 1992a), and Waller and Zavala (1993) argued for a seven-factor model. In general, the trend among personality theorists has been toward what one might call "an economy of factors" when describing the factors that purportedly describe personality.

How and why can such extensive disagreement about the number of factors in personality exist? The variables entered into the factor analysis, and the range of personality attributes tapped by a test's items, will, of course, affect the factors that are identified; what comes out of the factor analysis is very much a consequence of what went into it in the first place. According to Cattell (1986), the 16 PF carefully sampled from a very broad range of personality traits whereas many other researchers incorporated a more limited range of personality features in their measures. Because fewer aspects of personality were reflected in test items, fewer factors are needed to represent them (Cattell & Krug, 1986).

It is also true, however, that even when working with the same variables, such as all the items on the 16 PF, factor analysts other than Cattell have reached different conclusions as to the number of common factors. These disagreements may be based upon differences in the criteria used to decide upon the number of factors (Cattell & Krug, 1986). Disagreements about the number of common factors may also reflect differences in the type of factor analysis used (H. E. P. Cattell, 1993; Eysenck, 1991; Russell & Karol, 1994). Some researchers, such as Cattell (1986), emphasize first-order or "primary" factors as having the greatest utility in explaining behavior; these are the factors derived from a factor analysis of the scale items themselves (Cattell & Krug, 1986). The scales derived from factor analysis may be somewhat intercorrelated, as they are on the 16 PF, and a factor analysis of those scales results in second-order factors (Comrey, 1992). By contrast, other researchers emphasize these second-order factors (Guastello, 1993). Second-order factor analyses of the 16 PF by Cattell and others reveal approximately five second-order factors (Cattell & Krug, 1986; Guastello, 1993; Russell & Karol, 1994; see also Terpylak & Schuerger, 1994). Still, Cattell has argued that the second-order factors are not the true "source" factors in personality and that they lack the predictive value of the first-order factors scored on the 16 PF (Cattell & Krug, 1986).

Although the 16PF has served as a kind of workhorse in the field of personality assessment for many years, the Revised NEO Personality Inventory (NEO PI-R; Costa & McCrae, 1992) is increasingly being used in research and clinical applications involving personality assessment and research. Based on a five-dimension (or factor) model of personality (referred to in shorthand fashion as the "Big 5"), the NEO PI-R is a measure of five major dimensions (or "domains") of personality and a total of 30 elements or "facets" that define each domain. The original version of the test was called the NEO Personality Inventory (NEO-PI; Costa & McCrae, 1985), where NEO was an acronym for the first three domains measured: Neuroticism, Extraversion, and Openness. The NEO PI-R provides for the measurement of two additional domains: Agreeableness and Conscientiousness. Stated briefly, the Neuroticism domain taps aspects of adjustment and emotional stability. The Extraversion domain taps aspects of sociability and assertiveness. Openness refers to openness to experience as well as active imagination, aesthetic sensitivity, attentiveness to inner feelings, preference for variety, intellectual curiosity, and independence of judgment. Agreeableness is primarily a dimension of interpersonal tendencies that include altruism, sympathy toward others, and the belief that others are similarly inclined. Conscientiousness is a dimension of personality that has to do with the active processes of planning, organizing, and following through. Each of these major dimensions or domains of personality may be subdivided into individual traits or facets measured by the NEO PI-R.

The NEO PI-R is designed for use with persons 17 years of age and older and is essentially self-administered. Computerized scoring and interpretation is available. Validity and reliability data are presented in the manual. A more detailed description of this test—one guest-authored by Costa and McCrae themselves—is presented in Cohen (2002).

We began our discussion of the tools of test development with a note that many personality tests have used two or more of the tools we mentioned in the process of their development. At this point you may begin to appreciate how, as well as why, two or more such tools might be used. A pool of items for an objective personality measure could be created, for example, on the basis of logic or theory, or both logic and theory. The items might then be arranged into scales on the basis of factor analysis. The draft version of the test could be administered to a criterion group and to a control group, in order to see if responses to the items differ as a function of group membership. But here we are getting just a bit ahead of ourselves; we need to define, discuss, and illustrate what is meant by "criterion group" in the context of personality test development.

Criterion Groups

A **criterion** may be defined as a standard on which a judgment or decision can be made. With regard to scale development, a **criterion group** is a reference group of testtakers who share specific characteristics and whose responses to test items serve as a standard by which items will be included or discarded from the final version of a scale. The process of using criterion groups to develop test items is referred to as **empirical criterion keying** because the scoring or keying of items has been demonstrated empirically to differentiate among groups of testtakers. The shared characteristic of the criterion group to be researched—a psychiatric diagnosis, a unique skill or ability, a genetic aberration, or whatever—will vary as a function of the nature and scope of the test. Development of a test by means of empirical criterion keying may be summed up as follows:

1. Create a large, preliminary pool of test items from which the test items for the final form of the test will be selected.
2. Administer the preliminary pool of items to at least two groups of people:

    Group 1: A criterion group composed of people known to possess the trait being measured

    Group 2: A randomly selected group of people (who may or may not possess the trait being measured)

3. Conduct an item analysis to select items indicative of membership in the criterion group. Items in the preliminary pool that discriminate between membership in the two groups in a statistically significant fashion will be retained and incorporated in the final form of the test.

4. Obtain data on test performance from a standardization sample of testtakers who are representative of the population from which future testtakers will come. The test performance data for Group 2 members on items incorporated into the final form of the test may be used for this purpose if deemed appropriate. The performance of Group 2 members on the test would then become the standard against which future testtakers will be evaluated. After the mean performance of Group 2 members on the individual items (or scales) of the test has been identified, future testtakers will be evaluated in terms of the extent to which their scores deviate, in either direction, from the Group 2 mean.

At this point you may ask, "But what about that initial pool of items? How is it created?" The answer is that the test developer may have found inspiration for each of the items from reviews of journals and books, interviews with patients, or consultations with colleagues. The test developer may have relied on logic or reason alone to write the items, or on other tests. Alternatively, the test developer may have relied on none of these and simply let imagination loose and committed to paper whatever emerged. An interesting aspect of test development by means of empirical criterion keying is that the content of the test items does not have to relate in a logical, rational, direct, or face-valid way to the measurement objective. Burisch (1984, p. 218) captured the essence of empirical criterion keying when he stated flatly, "If shoe size as a predictor improves your ability to predict performance as an airplane pilot, use it."[5] Burisch went on to offer this tongue-in-cheek description of how criterion groups could be used to develop an "M-F" test to differentiate males from females:

> Allegedly not knowing where the differences were, he or she would never dream of using an item such as "I can grow a beard if I want to" or "In a restaurant I tend to prefer the ladies' room to the men's room." Rather, a heterogeneous pool of items would be assembled and administered to a sample of men and women. Next, samples would be compared item by item. Any item discriminating sufficiently well would qualify for inclusion in the M-F test. (p. 214)

Now imagine that it is the 1930s. A team of researchers is keenly interested in devising a paper-and-pencil test that will improve reliability in psychiatric diagnosis. Their idea is to use empirical criterion keying to create the instrument. A preliminary version of the test will be administered to (1) several criterion groups of adult inpatients, each group homogeneous with respect to psychiatric diagnosis, and (2) a group of randomly selected normal adults. Using item analysis, items useful in differentiating members of the various clinical groups from members of the normal group will be retained to make up the final form of the test. The researchers envision that future users of the published test will be able to derive diagnostic insights by comparing a testtaker's response pattern to that of testtakers in the normal group.

And there you have the beginnings of a relatively simple idea that would, in time, win widespread approval from clinicians around the world. It is an idea for a test that stimulated the publication of thousands of research studies, an idea that led to the development of a test that would serve as a model for countless other instruments devised

---

5. It should come as no suprise, however, that any scale that is the product of such wildly empirical procedures would be expected to be extremely high in heterogeneity of item content and profoundly low in internal consistency measures.

through the use of criterion group research. The test, originally referred to as the "Medical and Psychiatric Inventory" (Dahlstrom & Dahlstrom, 1980), is the MMPI. Years after its tentative beginnings, the test's senior author recalled that "it was difficult to persuade a publisher to accept the MMPI" (Hathaway, cited in Dahlstrom & Welsh, 1960, p. vii). However, the University of Minnesota Press was obviously persuaded, because in 1943 it published the test, now under a new name, the Minnesota Multiphasic Personality Inventory (MMPI). The rest, as they say, is history.

In the next few pages, we describe the development of the original MMPI, as well as its more contemporary progeny, the MMPI-2 and the MMPI-A. Let's note at the outset that this test occupies a prominent place in psychometrics, having served as a model for so many other tests and having earned the distinction of being the most widely used psychological test in the world. As you read about the development and use of the MMPI in its original and revised forms, think about all that you have learned about test development and the assessment of personality. What questions would you like to ask the developers of this test if you were given the opportunity to chat with them?

The MMPI   The MMPI was the product of a collaboration between psychologist Starke R. Hathaway and psychiatrist/neurologist John Charnley McKinley (Hathaway & McKinley, 1940, 1942, 1943, 1951; McKinley & Hathaway, 1940, 1944). It was designed for administration to adolescents and adults, 14 years of age and older. Research preceding the selection of test items included review of textbooks, psychiatric reports, and previously published personality-test items. In this sense, the beginnings of the MMPI can be traced to an approach based on logic and reason with an emphasis on item content; the test authors hoped to be able to use the test for diagnostic purposes, and it was essential that the items covered a wide breadth of diagnostic territory. However, empirically keyed "clinical scales" were also planned. A listing of the ten clinical scales of the MMPI, including related information, is presented in Table 11–2. As you read about these scales, keep in mind that these same scales formed the core of not only the original MMPI but its 1989 revision, the MMPI-2. The clinical scales did undergo some modification for the MMPI-2, such as editing and reordering, and nine items were eliminated. Still, the MMPI-2 retains the ten original clinical scales—incorporating, of course, the decades-old data derived from relatively small (criterion) groups of psychiatric inpatients that formed the basis of these scales (Helmes & Reddon, 1993). It was the data from the standardization sample of normal subjects in the original MMPI that were renormed for the MMPI-2.

Before proceeding to describe the standardization sample—referred to as the normal "control group"—for the MMPI, it may be useful to clarify what is meant by a control group in this context. Indeed, given how the term control group has traditionally been used in the context of experimental research, its use in the context of test development by means of empirical criterion keying can create some confusion. In experimental research, an experimenter manipulates the situation so that the experimental group is exposed to something (the independent variable) and the control group is not. In the development of the MMPI, members of the criterion groups were drawn from a population of people diagnosed with a particular diagnostic label. Analogizing an experiment to this test development situation, it is as if the experimental treatment for the criterion group members were the diagnosed disorder itself. By contrast, members of the **control group** were normal (nondiagnosed) people who ostensibly received no such experimental treatment.

The standardization sample for the original MMPI consisted of approximately fifteen hundred subjects. Included in this were 724 people who happen to be visiting friends or relatives at University of Minnesota hospitals, 265 high school graduates seeking precollege guidance at the University of Minnesota Testing Bureau, 265 skilled workers participating in a local Works Progress Administration program, and 243 medical (nonpsychiatric) patients. The data from the 724 hospital visitors were used to derive T scores

Table 11-2

The Clinical Criterion Groups for MMPI Scales

Scale	Criterion Group
1. Hypochondriasis (Hs)	Patients who showed exaggerated concerns about their physical health
2. Depression (D)	Clinically depressed patients; unhappy and pessimistic about their future
3. Hysteria (Hy)	Patients with conversion reactions
4. Psychopathic deviate (Pd)	Patients who had had histories of delinquency and other antisocial behavior
5. Masculinity-femininity (Mf)	Minnesota draftees, airline stewardesses, and male homosexual college students from the University of Minnesota campus community
6. Paranoia (Pa)	Patients who exhibited paranoid symptomatology such as ideas of reference, suspiciousness, delusions of persecution, and delusions of grandeur
7. Psychasthenia (Pt)	Anxious, obsessive-compulsive, guilt-ridden, and self-doubting patients
8. Schizophrenia (Sc)	Patients who were diagnosed as schizophrenic (various subtypes)
9. Hypomania (Ma)	Patients, most diagnosed as manic-depressive, who exhibited manic symptomatology such as elevated mood, excessive activity, and easy distractibility
0. Social introversion (Si)	College students who had scored at the extremes on a test of introversion/extraversion

Note that the ten scales are numerically designated as "1" through "0." All of the scale names were popular diagnostic categories in the 1930s when the test was first conceived, although some names (such as "Psychopathic Deviate") are now relics of a bygone era. For this and other reasons, it is contemporary custom to refer to the scales by number rather than name.

MMPI clinical scale items were derived empirically by administration to clinical criterion groups and normal control groups; items that successfully differentiated between the two groups were retained in the final version of the test (Welsh & Dahlstrom, 1956). The clinical criterion group for the MMPI was for the most part made up of psychiatric inpatients at the University of Minnesota Hospital; we say "for the most part" because Scale 5 and Scale 0 were not derived in this way. The number of people included in each diagnostic category was relatively low by contemporary standards. For example, the criterion group for Scale 7 contained only 20 people, all diagnosed as psychasthenic; the test responses of these few people served as the criterion for inclusion or exclusion of test items in Scale 7 of the MMPI. Two of the "clinical" scales did not even use members of a clinical population in the criterion group. Scale 5 was originally designed to differentiate heterosexual from homosexual males. However, due to a dearth of items that effectively differentiated people on this variable, the test developers broadened the definition of Scale 5 and added items that discriminated between normal males (soldiers) and females (airline personnel). Some of the added items were obtained from the Attitude Interest Scale (Terman & Miles, 1936). Hathaway and McKinley also attempted to develop a scale to differentiate lesbians from female heterosexuals but were unable to do so. The other clinical scale derived from a nonclinical criterion group was the tenth scale, Scale 0. A latecomer to incorporation into the MMPI as a clinical scale, Scale 0 had been developed by Drake (1946) based on the MMPI responses of college students who had exhibited extreme introversion or extraversion scores on the Social Introversion–Extraversion Scale of the Minnesota T-S-E Inventory.

on the standard MMPI profile sheet, whereas the remaining data were used in various other stages of the test's development. Recall from Chapter 3 that a T score has a mean of 50 and a standard deviation of 10. Today, a testtaker who obtains a T score of 50 on any MMPI scale has therefore obtained the average or mean score of the sample of 724 people who, decades ago, happened to be visiting friends or relatives at University of Minnesota hospitals. A score of 70 is 2 standard deviations above the average score of those hospital visitors, and a score of 30 is 2 standard deviations below their average score. As we will see, persistent questions have been raised about the adequacy of the MMPI standardization group. But let's return to the 1930s and 1940s for just another moment.

By the 1930s, research on the Personal Data Sheet (Woodworth, 1917) and other such face-valid, logic-derived instruments had brought to light problems inherent in self-report methods (Anastasi, 1937; Landis, 1936; Landis et al., 1935). Hathaway and McKinley (1943) evidenced a keen awareness of such problems. They built into the MMPI three so-called validity scales: the L scale (the "Lie" scale), the F scale (the "Frequency" or more accurately the "Infrequency" scale), and the K ("Correction") scale. Note that these scales were not designed to measure validity in the technical, psychometric sense. There is, after all, something inherently self-serving, if not suspect, about a test that purports to gauge its own validity! Rather, "validity" here is a reference to a built-in indicator of the operation of the testtaker's response sets, carelessness, deliberate efforts to deceive, or unintentional misunderstanding that could affect the test results. The MMPI L scale contains 15 items that are somewhat negative but that apply to most people, such as "I do not always tell the truth" or "I gossip a little at times" (Dahlstrom et al., 1972, p. 109).

The preparedness of the examinee to reveal *anything* negative about himself or herself will be called into question if the score on the L scale does not fall within certain limits. The 64 items on the F scale (1) are infrequently endorsed by members of nonpsychiatric populations (that is, normal people) and (2) do not fit into any known pattern of deviance. A response of "true" to an item such as the following would be scored on the F scale: "It would be better if almost all laws were thrown away" (Dahlstrom et al., 1972, p. 115). An elevated F score may mean that the respondent did not take the test seriously and was just responding to items randomly. Alternatively, the individual with a high F score may be a very eccentric individual or someone who was attempting to "fake bad." Malingerers in the armed services, people intent on committing fraud with respect to health insurance, and criminals attempting to cop a psychiatric plea are some of the groups of people who might be expected to have elevated F scores on their profiles.

Like the L score and the F score, the K score is a reflection of the frankness of the test-taker's self-report. An elevated K score is associated with defensiveness and the desire to present a favorable impression. A low K score is associated with excessive self-criticism, desire to detail deviance, or desire to fake bad. A "true" response to the item "I certainly feel useless at times" and a "false" response to "At times I am all full of energy" (Dahlstrom et al., 1972, p. 125) would be scored on the K scale. The K scale is sometimes used to correct scores on five of the clinical scales; the scores are statistically corrected for an individual's overwillingness or unwillingness to admit deviancy.

Another scale that bears on the validity of a test administration is the "cannot say" scale, also referred to as the question mark ("?") scale. This scale is a simple frequency count of the number of items to which the examinee responded "cannot say" or failed to mark any response. Items may be omitted or marked "cannot say" for many reasons, including respondent indecisiveness, defensiveness, carelessness, and lack of experience relevant to the item (Graham, 1977). Traditionally, the validity of an answer sheet with a "cannot say" count of 30 or higher is called into question and is deemed uninterpretable (Dahlstrom et al., 1972). Even for tests with a "cannot say" score of 10, caution has been urged in test interpretation. High "cannot say" scores may be avoided by a proctor's emphasis in the initial instructions to answer all items and by the proctor's scanning of answer sheets for omitted items before the testtaker leaves the examination room.

The MMPI contains 550 true-false items, 16 of which are repeated on some forms of the test (for a total of 566 items administered). In addition to the clinical scales and the validity scales, there are MMPI content scales, supplementary scales, and Harris-Lingoes subscales. As its name implies, the content scales (sometimes referred to as the "Wiggins Content Scales" after Wiggins [1966]) are composed of groups of test items of similar content. Examples of content scales on the MMPI include the scales labeled "Depression" and "Family Problems."

"Supplementary scales" is a catch-all phrase for the hundreds of different MMPI scales that have been developed since the test's publication. These scales have been devised by different researchers using a variety of methods and statistical procedures, most notably factor analysis. There are supplementary scales that are fairly consistent with the original objectives of the MMPI, such as scales designed to shed light on matters such as alcoholism and ego strength. And then there are other supplementary scales, such as one labeled "Success in Baseball" and another labeled "Yeshiva College Subcultural Scale" (Graham, 1987).[6] The publisher of the MMPI makes available for

---

6. Here, astute reader, you may begin to obtain an appreciation for just how far from its original intended purpose the MMPI has strayed. In fact, the MMPI, and more recently the MMPI-2, has been used for an extraordinarily wide range of adventures that are related to psychiatric diagnosis in a tangential way, at best.

computerized scoring only a limited selection of the many hundreds of supplementary scales that have been developed and discussed in the professional literature. Clinicians are free to analyze the raw data in terms of whatever scales they choose, although they are advised that supplementary scales should be used along with, and not in place of, the clinical and validity scales. The Harris-Lingoes subscales (Harris & Lingoes, 1955, 1968), often referred to simply as the "Harris scales," are groupings of items into subscales (with labels such as "Brooding" and "Social Alienation") that were designed to be more internally consistent than the umbrella scale from which the subscale was derived.

Historically administered by means of paper-and-pencil, the MMPI is today administered by many methods: online, offline by means of disk, or through the use of items printed on index cards. An audio version for semiliterate testtakers is also available with instructions recorded on audiocassette. Testtakers respond to items by answering "true" or "false." Items left unanswered are construed as "cannot say." In the version of the test administered through the use of individual items printed on cards, testtakers are instructed to sort the cards into one of three piles labeled "true," "false," and "cannot say." At least a sixth-grade reading level is required to understand all of the items. There are no time limits, and the time required to administer 566 items is typically between 60 and 90 minutes.

It is possible to score MMPI answer sheets by hand, but the process is labor intensive. Today, with the exception of training exercises, scoring is almost always done by computer. Computer scoring of protocols is accomplished by means of software on personal computers, by computer transmission to a scoring service via modem, or by physically mailing the completed form to a computer-scoring service. Computer output may range from a simple numerical and graphic presentation of scores to a highly detailed narrative report complete with analysis of scores on selected supplementary scales.

Soon after the MMPI was published, it became evident that the test could not be used to neatly categorize testtakers into diagnostic categories. When testtakers had elevations in the pathological range of two or more scales, diagnostic dilemmas arose. Hathaway and McKinley (1943) had urged users of their test to opt for configural interpretation of scores—that is, interpretation based not on scores of single scales, but on the pattern or profile of scores. However, their proposed method for profile interpretation was extremely complicated, as were many of the proposed adjunctive and alternative procedures (Gilberstadt & Duker, 1965; Marks & Seeman, 1963). Paul Meehl (1951) proposed using a code made up of the numbers of the clinical scales on which the testtaker achieved the highest (most pathological) scores. If a testtaker achieved the highest score on Scale 1 and the second highest score on Scale 2, that testtaker's "2-point code type" would be 12. The 2-point code type for a highest score on Scale 2 and a second highest score on Scale 1 would be 21. Because each digit in the code is interchangeable, a code of 12 would be interpreted in exactly the same way as a code of 21. Before long, a wealth of research mounted on the interpretive meanings of the 40 code types that could be derived using ten scales and two interchangeable digits.[7] A code of 12 (or 21) for ex-

---

7. An assumption here is that each score elevation exceeds $T = 70$ in the MMPI 2-point code type. If the scale score does not exceed 70, this may be so indicated by the use of a prime (') after the scale number. By the way, a number of other coding systems have also been used to derive MMPI profiles. One 2-point coding scheme called for the first digit in the code to reflect the number of the scale on which the highest score was obtained and the second digit to reflect the number of the scale on which the lowest score was obtained. Another proposed system employed a 3-point code in which the first number is the highest score, the second number is the second highest score, and the third number is the third highest score. Research on the utility of these various coding systems contributed in no small way to a mushrooming research literature on the MMPI.

ample, is indicative of an individual in physical pain, whereas a code of 18 (or 81) is indicative of an individual harboring feelings of hostility and aggression. This coding scheme, and others, had great intuitive appeal and stimulated a great deal of research regarding the meaning of various MMPI score profiles. Another popular approach to scoring and interpretation came in the form of **Welsh codes**—referred to as such because they were created by Welsh (1948, 1956) and not because they were written in Welsh (although to the uninitiated, they may be equally incomprehensible). Here is an example of a Welsh code:

$$6*\underline{78}''1\text{-}53/4\text{:}2\#\underline{90}\ F'L\text{-}/K.$$

To the seasoned Welsh code user, this expression provides information about a test-taker's scores on the MMPI clinical and validity scales.[8]

Students interested in learning more about the MMPI need not expend a great deal of effort in tracking down sources. Chances are your university library is teeming with books and journal articles written on or about this multiphasic (many faceted) instrument that, for reasons to be discussed subsequently, has managed to obtain something akin to mythic status in the world of psychological tests. Of course, you will also want to become acquainted with the test's more contemporary revisions, the MMPI-2 and the MMPI-A.

The MMPI-2 Much of what has already been said about the MMPI in terms of its general structure as well as its administration, scoring, and interpretation is applicable to the MMPI-2. The most significant difference between the two tests has to do with the more representative standardization sample (normal control group) used in the norming of the MMPI-2 (discussed below). Approximately 14% of the MMPI items were rewritten to correct for grammatical errors and to make the language more contemporary, nonsexist, and readable. Items thought to be objectionable to present-day testtakers were eliminated. Added were items addressing topics such as drug abuse, suicide potential, marital adjustment, attitudes toward work, and Type A behavior patterns.[9] In all, the MMPI-2 contains a total of 567 true-false items, including 394 items that are identical to the original MMPI items, 66 items that were modified or rewritten, and 107 new items (Archer, 1992). The suggested age range of testtakers for the MMPI-2 is 18 years old and older as compared to 14 years old and older for the MMPI. The reading level required (sixth grade) is the same as for the MMPI. The MMPI-2, like its predecessor, may be administered online, offline by paper and pencil, or by audiocassette, and takes about the same time to administer.

The ten clinical scales of the MMPI are identical to those on the MMPI-2, as is the policy of referring to them primarily by number. Content component scales were added to the MMPI-2 to provide more focused indices of content. For example, Family Problems content is now subdivided into Family Discord and Familial Alienation content. The three original validity scales of the MMPI are included in the MMPI-2, as are three additional validity scales: Back-Page Infrequency (Fb), True Response Inconsistency (TRIN), and Variable Response Inconsistency (VRIN). The Back-Page Infrequency scale contains items seldom endorsed by testtakers who are candid, deliberate, and diligent in their approach to the test. Of course, some testtakers' diligence wanes as the test wears

---

8. With the instructor's approval, the motivated student may translate this code for extra credit.

9. Recall from our discussion of psychological types in the previous chapter (page 327) what constitutes Type A and Type B behavior.

on, so that by the "back pages" of the test a random or an inconsistent pattern of responses is evident. The Fb scale is designed to detect such a pattern. The TRIN scale is designed to identify acquiescent and nonacquiescent response patterns. It contains 23 pairs of items worded in opposite forms; consistency in responding dictates that, for example, a "true" response to the first item in the pair is followed by a "false" response to the second item in the pair. The VRIN scale is designed to identify indiscriminate response patterns. It too is made up of item pairs, each item in the pair worded either in opposite or similar forms. The senior author of the MMPI-2, James Butcher, developed yet another validity scale after the publication of that test. The *S* scale is a validity scale designed to detect self-presentation in a superlative manner (Butcher & Han, 1995; Lanyon, 1993; Lim & Butcher, 1996).

A nagging criticism of the original MMPI concerned the lack of representation of the standardization sample of the U.S. population. This criticism was addressed in the standardization of the MMPI-2. The 2,600 individuals (1,462 females, 1,138 males) from seven states who made up the MMPI-2 standardization sample had been matched to 1980 United States census data on the variables of age, gender, minority status, social class, and education (Butcher, 1990). Whereas the original MMPI did not contain any non-Whites in the standardization sample, the MMPI-2 sample was 81% White and 19% non-White. Age of subjects in the sample ranged from 18 years to 85 years. Formal education ranged from 3 years to 20+ years, with more highly educated people and people working in the professions overrepresented in the sample (Archer, 1992; Graham, 1990). Median annual family income for females in the sample was $25,000 to $30,000. Median annual family income for males in the sample was $30,000 to $35,000.

As with the original MMPI, the standardization sample data provided the basis for transforming the raw scores obtained by respondents into *T* scores for the MMPI-2. However, a technical adjustment was deemed to be in order. Recall from Chapter 3 that a linear *T* score has a mean set at 50 and a standard deviation set at 10. The *T* scores used for standardizing the MMPI clinical scales and content scales were linear *T* scores. For the MMPI-2, linear *T* scores were also used for standardization of the validity scales, the supplementary scales, and Scales 5 and 0 of the clinical scales. However, a different *T* score was used to standardize the remaining eight clinical scales, as well as all of the content scales; these scales were standardized with uniform *T* scores (*UT* scores). The *UT* scores were used in an effort to make the *T* scores corresponding to percentile scores more comparable across the MMPI-2 scales (Graham, 1990a; Tellegen & Ben-Porath, 1992).

The MMPI-A   Although its developers had recommended the original MMPI for use with adolescents, test users have evidenced some skepticism about this recommendation through the years. Early on it was noticed that adolescents as a group tended to score somewhat higher on the clinical scales than adults, a finding that left adolescents as a group in the unenviable position of appearing to suffer from more psychopathology than adults. In part for this reason, separate MMPI norms for adolescents were developed (Colligan & Offord, 1989; Dahlstrom et al., 1972; Marks et al., 1974). In the 1980s, with the MMPI revision under way, the test developers had a choice of simply renorming the MMPI-2 for adolescents or creating a new instrument. They opted to develop a new test that was in many key respects, a downward extension of the MMPI-2.

The Minnesota Multiphasic Personality Inventory-Adolescent (MMPI-A; Butcher et al., 1992) is a 478 true-false item test designed for use in clinical, counseling, and school settings for the purpose of assessing psychopathology and identifying personal, social, and behavioral problems. The individual items of the MMPI-A, much like the clinical and validity scales, largely parallel the MMPI-2, although there are 88 less items in total.

Some of the MMPI-2 items were discarded, others were rewritten, and some completely new ones were added. In its written (as opposed to audiocassette) form, the test is designed for administration to testtakers in the 14- to 18-year-old age range who have at least a sixth-grade reading ability. As with the MMPI-2, versions of the test are available for administration by computer, by paper and pencil, and by audiocassette. The time required for an administration of all the items typically is between 45 and 60 minutes.

The MMPI-A contains 16 basic scales including ten Clinical Scales (identical in name and number to those of the MMPI-2) and six Validity Scales (a total of eight Validity Scales given that the F scale is subdivided into F, F_1, and F_2 scales): Variable Response Inconsistency (VRIN), True Response Inconsistency (TRIN), Infrequency (F), Infrequency 1 (F_1), Infrequency 2 (F_2), Lie (L), Defensiveness (K), and "cannot say" (?). The F scale was divided into two subscales: F_1 applicable to the Clinical Scales, and F_2 applicable to the Content and Supplementary Scales.

In addition to basic Clinical and Validity Scales, the MMPI-A contains six Supplementary Scales (dealing with areas such as alcohol and drug use, immaturity, anxiety, and repression), 15 Content Scales (including areas such as Conduct Problems and School Problems), 28 Harris-Lingoes scales, and 3 scales labeled "Social Introversion." As with the MMPI-2, uniform T (UT) scales were employed for use with all of the Content Scales, and eight of the Clinical Scales (Scales 5 and 0 excluded), this to make percentile scores comparable across scales.

The normative sample for the MMPI-A consisted of 805 adolescent males and 815 adolescent females, drawn from schools in communities in California, Minnesota, New York, North Carolina, Ohio, Pennsylvania, Virginia, and Washington. The objective was to obtain a sample that was nationally representative in terms of demographic variables such as ethnic background, geographic region of the United States, and urban/rural residence. Concurrent with the norming of the MMPI-A, a clinical sample of 713 adolescents was tested for the purpose of obtaining validity data. However, no effort was made to ensure representativeness of the clinical sample; subjects were all drawn from the Minneapolis area, most from drug and alcohol treatment centers.

The MMPI-A has, in general, earned high marks from test reviewers and may well have quickly become the most widely used measure of psychopathology in adolescents. Research related to the 15 content scales of the MMPI-A suggests that these scales are particularly promising with regard to their utility in clinical and counseling settings (Butcher & Williams, 1992; Williams et al., 1992).

The MMPI and its revisions in perspective   We might analogize the original MMPI to a classic car. At its core is an engine (the ten clinical scales) that although clearly outdated, remains familiar and serviceable enough to maintain wide appeal. Many of the engine's component parts were named using a vocabulary of a bygone era. For this reason, these parts are today referred to by number rather than name. But although its engine may be technologically anachronistic, the car is a long-respected, known quantity with a strong brand heritage. It has been the subject of thousands of research studies since its introduction in the early 1940s. Moreover, an abundance of appealing bells, whistles, and options have been added to the vehicle (in terms of additional scales and a new normative sample), which attracts buyers to the showroom.

The MMPI-2 and MMPI-A revision processes had two seemingly contrary objectives to meet. One objective was to keep the revision as similar as possible to the original—this for the purpose of retaining the applicability and relevance of the many research studies that employed the MMPI. The second objective was to change the original test in ways that were responsive to the many constructive criticisms that had been leveled at the original over the years. In most ways, the developers of the MMPI-2 and the MMPI-A achieved this delicate balancing act, although, as might be expected, not everyone is entirely happy about the means to the end.

The most glaring problem with the MMPI was its lack of representative norms, a criticism addressed in both the MMPI-2 and the MMPI-A. However, it was only in the MMPI-A, and not the MMPI-2, that a clinical sample was concurrently tested for comparative and validation purposes. Comparable MMPI-2 data on a contemporary, nationally representative clinical sample would have gone a long way toward breathing new life and meaning into the tired but recycled clinical scales. Also puzzling is the fact that a nationally unrepresentative clinical sample was employed in the study of the MMPI-A. Once the decision had been made to employ a clinical sample, why wasn't the effort made to make that sample nationally representative? All of the subjects in the clinical sample cited in the MMPI-A manual were from Minnesota. In this respect, the MMPI-A retained a feature of the original MMPI it would have done better to change. In the late 1930s and early 1940s, when Hathaway and McKinley were feeling their way to develop a new diagnostic instrument, the lack of representativeness of the clinical subjects could be overlooked. Admittedly, obtaining such a sample, testing all of the subjects, and thoroughly analyzing all of the resulting data is a herculean and expensive undertaking. On the other hand, given the contemporary status of the MMPI (a veritable institution among psychological tests), and the great frequency with which it is used worldwide, why would the current test developers want to do any less? It is our opinion that the presentation of data from a nationally representative clinical sample would have been a most valuable—and eminently manageable—addition to the manuals of the two MMPI revisions.

The MMPI clinical scales each exhibit relatively low inter-item consistencies—not surprising given the empirical nature of their development. At the same time, the intercorrelations between the clinical scales is high. This combination of facts naturally raises questions such as, What are the clinical scales really measuring? Questions regarding exactly how scores on the clinical scales should be interpreted persist even with regard to the MMPI-2 and the MMPI-A. In large part, these questions have been addressed with reference to the use of other scales (such as the validity, content, Harris, and supplementary scales) as interpretive aids. Of course, scales other than the clinical scales carry their own interpretation-related baggage. For example, although an elevated F scale may reflect on the validity of the protocol, it may also reflect severe psychopathology. Here again, one needs to evaluate other scales in order to reach conclusions about the meaning of a particular scale.

A number of studies with the MMPI-2 and MMPI-A speak to the psychometric soundness of these instruments (see, for example, Archer & Gordon, 1994; Archer & Krishnamurthy, 1994; Butcher & Williams, 1992; Graham, 1990; Phelps, 1994; Williams et al., 1992). One study examining the criterion validity of the MMPI-2 compared clinical scale scores for normal subjects with the results of a rating scale completed by the subject's spouse. The various clinical scales were related to the ratings in ways that would be expected given interpretations of the scales. For example, people scoring high on Scale 2 (Depression) were rated by their spouses as lacking energy and interest, worrying, feeling sad, and not being self-confident. People scoring high on Scale 7 (Psychasthenia) were rated by their spouses as having bad dreams and many fears, being indecisive, and not being self-confident. Similar results were obtained by comparing the MMPI-2 scores of psychiatric patients with ratings by treatment professionals (Graham, 1990).

A common type of criterion validity study with a test such as the MMPI-2 entails asking people without mental disorders to respond to the test as though they had mental disorders (Bagby et al., 1994; Sivec et al., 1995; Wetter et al., 1994). The goal of such studies is to determine whether the validity scales on the MMPI-2 are sensitive to attempts to "faking bad," or presenting oneself as psychologically disordered. This is an important practical question relative to the use of the test, because individuals may try to fake bad for many reasons, such as to qualify for or maintain current disability benefits. Lamb and colleagues (1994) asked some of the college students in their study to complete the MMPI-2 without any special instructions (the control subjects). Other students were asked to respond as though they were experiencing psychological symptoms as the result of a closed head injury. The researchers encouraged students to make their responses believable, and they even offered monetary incentives for the most convincing test results. The validity scales did their stuff in this experiment. The profiles for the students attempting to appear disordered were less valid than those completed by the control subjects. Specifically, the profiles for the students who were faking bad had higher scores on the F and Fb scales, and lower scores on the K scale, than did the control students. This was true even of students who were given information about the symptoms of closed head injury and about the MMPI-2 validity scales. The results suggest that the MMPI-2 validity scales may successfully identify people who have been coached about how to respond dishonestly on the MMPI-2. A meta-analysis (Rogers et al., 1994) of this literature also concluded that the MMPI-2 validity scales are effective in this way.

Relationships between the content scales and the clinical scales have been explored to provide information about the construct validity of the content scales. Understanding the ways the content scales relate to the clinical scales helps the MMPI-2 user, already familiar with the clinical scales, to better understand what the content scales are measuring. For example, the Health Concerns content scale is correlated .89 to .91 with Scale 1, and the Social Discomfort content scale is correlated .84 to .85 with Scale 0. These correlations demonstrate convergent validity for the two content scales, and indicate that the content scales can be interpreted like the clinical scales with similar labels. By contrast, the Depression content scale and Scale 2 correlate only .52 to .63 (Graham, 1990). This suggests that elevations on the Depression content scale should not be interpreted like Scale 2 elevations. The difference between Scale 2 and the Depression content scale is also reflected in their relationships with other measures of depression: Correlations with other scales ranged from .55 to .83 (median = .69) for the Depression content scale, but only .35 to .55 (median = .48) for Scale 2. Thus, the Depression content scale seems to be tapping the same construct that other depression scales reflect (Boone, 1994).

Nichols (1992) notes that evidence of discriminative validity is lacking for several of the supplementary scales, including the two posttraumatic stress disorder scales, and the College Maladjustment, Type A, and Negative Treatment Indicators scales. Many of the people who score high on either of the posttraumatic stress disorder scales may not actually meet the criteria for being diagnosed with posttraumatic stress disorder (Nichols, 1992).

The reliability of the MMPI-2 is acceptable for the majority of the scales. The evidence for the validity of the original MMPI is impressive, and to the extent that such evidence is generalizable to the MMPI-2, there is reason to believe that the MMPI-2 may well be as valid as its predecessor. Still, much remains to be done to demonstrate the specific merits of the MMPI-2 with regard to its criterion-related and construct validity.

Although research studies with the original MMPI explored the test's efficacy with regard to populations at both ends of the normal–abnormal continuum, the trend in MMPI-2 research, with some exceptions, seems more focused on the abnormal end of the spectrum. This trend may be due, at least in part, to the proliferation of many tests designed to assess the "normal personality" (Ozer & Reise, 1994).

The usefulness of the MMPI-2 for non-Caucasian populations has received much attention since the test's publication. The original MMPI was standardized on Caucasians, but the MMPI-2 used a broader normative sample. Research has supported the adequacy of the MMPI-2 and its new norms for African Americans (Timbrook & Graham, 1994) and Hispanic Americans (Whitworth & Unterbrink, 1994).

As we have emphasized throughout this book, assessment professionals must be sensitive to cultural differences when conducting evaluations. Tests may be profoundly influential in one cultural milieu but of questionable consequence in another. So, for example, although Holland's notion of a vocational personality and its associated theory of six occupational themes has been received enthusiastically in the United States, questions have been raised concerning its applicability across cultures (Fouad & Dancer, 1992; Hansen, 1987; Khan et al., 1990; Swanson, 1992). Juni (1996) characterized the five-factor model of the NEO PI-R as "intrinsically bound to the culture and language that spawned it," although McCrae et al. (1998) have challenged this assertion. Let's now take a closer look at some culture-related issues in personality assessment.

Personality Assessment and Culture

Every day, assessment professionals across the United States are routinely called on to evaluate personality and related variables of people from culturally and linguistically diverse populations. Yet personality assessment is anything but routine with children, adolescents, and adults from Native American, Hispanic, Asian, African American and other cultures that may have been underrepresented in the development, standardization, and interpretation protocols of the measures used. Especially with members of culturally and linguistically diverse populations, a routine and business as usual approach to psychological testing and assessment impresses us as inappropriate, if not irresponsible. What is required is a professionally trained assessor capable of conducting a meaningful assessment, with sensitivity to how culture relates to the behaviors and cognitions being measured (Lopez, 2000).

Before any tool of personality assessment—an interview, a test, a protocol for behavioral observation, a portfolio, or something else—can be employed, and before data derived from an attempt at measurement can be imbued with meaning, the assessor will ideally consider some important issues with regard to assessment of a particular assessee. Many of these issues relate to the level of acculturation, values, identity, worldview, and language of the assessee. Professional exploration of these areas is capable of yielding not only information necessary as a prerequisite for formal personality assessment, but a wealth of personality-related information in its own right. Let's take a closer look.

Acculturation and Related Considerations

Acculturation is an ongoing process by which an individual's thoughts, behaviors, values, worldview, and identity develop in relation to the general thinking, behavior, customs, and values of a particular cultural group. The process of acculturation begins at birth, a time at which the newborn infant's family or caretakers serve as agents of the culture.[10] In the years to come, other family members, teachers, peers, books, films, theater, newspapers, television and radio programs, and other media serve as agents of acculturation. Through the process of acculturation, one develops culturally accepted ways of thinking, feeling, and behaving. Intimately entwined with acculturation is the learning of values.

---

10. The process of acculturation may begin before birth. It seems reasonable to assume that nutritional and other aspects of the mother's prenatal care may have implications for the newborn infant's taste and other preferences.

Table 11–3
Some Published Measures of Acculturation

Source	Description
Acculturation questionnaire (Smither & Rodriguez-Giegling, 1982)	Designed for use with members of various refugee populations, this questionnaire taps the assessee's willingness to acculturate.
Acculturation Rating Scale for Mexican Americans (Cuellar et al., 1980)	A test designed for use with Mexican Americans as a measure of Mexican acculturation.
African American acculturation (Snowden & Hines, 1999)	Taps race-related cultural and media preferences, degree of comfort in interracial social interaction, and attitudes regarding reliance on relatives for help and desirability of interracial marriage.
African Self-Consciousness Scale (Baldwin & Bell, 1985)	A test designed for use in conjunction with an Africentric personal theory (Baldwin, 1984). Includes components designed to measure several variables, such as those related to opposition to oppression. The validity of both the theory it is derived from and the test itself remains to be documented.
Asian Indian Acculturation Measure (Sodowsky & Carey, 1988)	This questionnaire published in the context of a journal article may have exploratory value in terms of the insights it yields regarding Asian Indian acculturation.
Asian Values Scale (Kim et al., 1999)	Developed to assist in the provision of culturally relevant and sensitive psychological services by focusing on the assessment of values.
Assimilation Measure for Spokane Indians (Roy, 1962)	A measure designed to assess degree of assimilation among other factors.
Children's Acculturation Scale (Franco, 1983)	Designed for use as a tool for learning about Mexican American children, this is a ten-item questionnaire completed by the child's teacher.
Chinese Acculturation Measures (Yao, 1979)	Two tests, one of traditional Chinese culture and the other of Chinese American assimilation, both of which may have value for exploratory purposes with immigrants from China.
Cuban Behavioral Identity Questionnaire (Garcia & Lega, 1979)	A brief scale to measure acculturation of Cuban Americans.
Cultural Health Attributions Questionnaire (Murguia et al., 2000)	Developed in response to a need for a measure that captures the full range of health beliefs among Latinos, and the Latino worldview that includes complex beliefs about the etiology, symptom expression, and treatment of illnesses.
Cultural Life Style Inventory (Mendoza, 1989)	A test designed for use with Mexican American adolescents and adults, this test measures various aspects of acculturation.
Ethnic Identity Questionnaire (Masuda et al., 1970)	A questionnaire designed for use with Japanese Americans. Some limited validity data is available (Marmot & Syme, 1976; Matsumoto et al., 1970).
Hawaiian Culture Scale-Adolescent Version (Hishinuma et al., 2000)	Measures variables such as sources of learning about the Hawaiian way of life, how much Hawaiian beliefs and non-Hawaiian beliefs are valued.
Indian Assimilation Scale (Howe Chief, 1940)	Test developed for use with young females that taps attitudes toward assimilation, Native American lineage, and related factors.
Intercultural Contact and Western Identification Scales (Chance, 1965)	Designed for use with Eskimo populations.
Multicultural Acculturation Scale (Wong-Rieger & Quintana, 1987)	Designed for use with members of people of various cultural backgrounds.
Multicultural Experience Inventory (Ramirez, 1984)	A test designed for use with Mexican American adults, it taps various aspects of acculturation, biculturalism, and multicultural participation.
Self-Identity Inventory (Sevig et al., 2000)	Developed to assist in the understanding of how minority group members differ within and across groups in their perceptions of and reaction to oppression.
Suinn-Lew Asian Self-Identity Acculturation Scale (Suinn et al., 1987)	A test designed for use with people of various Asian heritages, with some validity data.

A number of tests and questionnaires have been developed in recent years to yield insights regarding assessees' level of acculturation to their native culture or the dominant culture. A sampling of these measures is presented in Table 11–3. As you survey this list, keep in mind that the amount of psychometric research done on these instruments varies. Some of these instruments may be little more than content-valid, if that; in such cases, let the buyer beware. Should you wish to use any of these measures, you may wish to look up more information about it in a resource such as the *Mental Measurements Yearbook*. Alternatively, you might try to contact the developer of the instrument for updated information as to its psychometric soundness.

Perhaps the most appropriate use of many of these tests would be to derive hypotheses for future hypothesis testing by means of other tools of assessment. Unless compelling evidence exists to attest to the use of a particular instrument with members of a specific population, data derived from any of these tests and questionnaires should not be used alone to make selection, treatment, placement, or other momentous decisions.

Value is synonymous with worth, and **values** refers to that which an individual prizes or ideals an individual believes in. An early systematic treatment of the subject of values came in a book entitled *Types of Men* (Spranger, 1928), which listed different types of people based on whether they valued things like truth, practicality, and power. The book served as an inspiration for a yet more systematic treatment of the subject (Allport et al., 1951). Before long, a number of different systems for listing and categorizing values had been published. Rokeach (1973) differentiated what he called "instrumental" from "terminal" values. **Instrumental values** are guiding principles to help someone attain some objective. Honesty, imagination, ambition, and cheerfulness are some examples of instrumental values. **Terminal values** represent guiding principles and a mode of behavior that is an end-point objective. "A comfortable life," "an exciting life," "a sense of accomplishment," and "self-respect" are some examples of terminal values. Other value-categorization systems focus on values in specific contexts, such as employment settings. Super (1970), for example, explored factors related to work preferences and the extent to which values such as financial reward, job security, or prestige entered into employment decisions and job satisfaction.

Writing from an anthropological/cultural perspective, Kluckhohn (1954, 1960; Kluckhohn & Strodtbeck, 1961) conceived of values as answers to key questions with which civilizations must grapple. So, for example, from questions about how the individual should relate to the group, values emerge about individual versus group priorities. In one culture, the answers to such questions might take the form of norms and sanctions that encourage strict conformity and little competition among group members. In another culture, norms and sanctions may encourage individuality and competition among group members. In this context, one can begin to appreciate how members of different cultural groups can grow up with vastly different values, ranging from views on various "isms" (such as individualism versus collectivism) to views on what is trivial and what is worth dying for. The different values people from various cultures bring to the assessment situation may translate into widely varying motivational and incentive systems. Understanding what an individual values is an integral part of understanding personality.

Also intimately tied to the concept of acculturation is the concept of personal identity. **Identity** in this context may be defined as a set of cognitive and behavioral characteristics by which individuals define themselves as members of a particular group. Stated simply, identity refers to one's sense of self. Levine and Padilla (1980) defined **identification** as a process by which an individual assumes a pattern of behavior characteristic of other people and referred to it as one of the "central issues that ethnic minority groups must deal with" (p. 13). Echoing this sentiment, Zuniga (1988) suggested that a question such as, "What do you call yourself when asked about your ethnicity?" might be used as an icebreaker when assessing identification. She went on:

> How a minority client handles their response offers evidence of their comfortableness with their identity. A Mexican-American client who responds by saying, "I am an American, and I am just like everyone else," displays a defensiveness that demands gentle probing. One client sheepishly declared that she always called herself Spanish. She used this self-designation since she felt the term "Mexican" was dirty. (p. 291)

Another key culture-related personality variable concerns how an assessee tends to view the world. As its name implies, **worldview** is the unique way people interpret and make sense of their perceptions as a consequence of their learning experiences, cultural background, and related variables.

Culturally Sensitive Assessment

From time to time in recent years, there have been demands for cultural competence in psychological assessment. Usually defined in vague terms at best, "cultural competence" refers to knowledge of a particular culture achieved through academic study, life experience, or both. Presumably, the culturally competent assessor is knowledgeable with regard to the culture from which each assessee hails and has the ability to appropriately tailor assessments and interpretations of data accordingly. As well intentioned as this notion of cultural competence might be, we wonder how realistic it is. Particularly where there is a confluence of people from widely varied backgrounds, assessors must assess people from various cultures without the time or the resources to conduct in-depth culture-related research pertinent to the background of each assessee. Further, there will inevitably be many questions related to the criterion validity of the "cultural competence" construct. For example, what criteria shall be employed in deciding who is culturally competent to assess whom? And who among us has sufficient knowledge about our very own culture to be culturally competent to assess other people from the same culture? Even experts disagree on key assessment-related issues. Consider, for example, the opinion of two experts regarding one widely used personality test, the MMPI-2. In an article entitled, "Culturally Competent MMPI Assessment of Hispanic Populations," Dana (1995, p. 309) advised that "the MMPI-2 is neither better nor worse than [its predecessor] the MMPI for Hispanics." By contrast, Velasquez et al. (1997, p. 111) wrote, *"Counselors should always apply the MMPI-2, and not the MMPI, to Chicano clients"* (emphasis in the original). On the basis of clinical experience, Velasquez et al. (1997) concluded that as compared to the MMPI, the MMPI-2 "lessens the chances of overpathologization of Chicanos" (p. 111).

We view calls for cultural competence in assessment as a legitimate, albeit unrealistic, reaction to the rote cookie-cutter-type of psychological testing that has been the rule and not the exception for many years. But a middle ground exists between routine and impersonal psychological testing and the somewhat nebulous ideal of a cultural competence criterion. This middle ground is one characterized by a culturally sensitive approach. Lest we be as vague as we have observed others to be, we will define **culturally sensitive psychological assessment** as an approach to evaluation that is keenly perceptive of and responsive to issues of acculturation, values, identity, worldview, language, and other culture-related variables as they may impact the evaluation process or the interpretation of resulting data. We offer this definition not as the last word on the subject but rather as a first step designed to promote constructive and scholarly dialogue about what culturally sensitive psychological assessment really is, and all that it can be.

When planning an assessment in which there is some question regarding the projected impact of culture, language, or some related variable on the validity of the assessment, the culturally sensitive assessor can do a number of things. One thing is to carefully read existing case history data, if any. Such data may provide answers to key questions regarding the assessee's level of acculturation and other factors useful to know in advance of any formal assessment. Family, friends, clergy, professionals, and others who know the assessee may be able to provide valuable information regarding culture-related variables prior to the assessment. One administrative note here: If such informants are to be used, it will be necessary to have executed permission forms allowing

Assessing Acculturation and Related Variables

A number of important questions regarding acculturation and related variables may be raised with regard to assessees from culturally diverse populations. Many general types of interview questions may yield rich insights regarding the overlapping areas of acculturation, values, worldview, and identity. A sampling of such questions follows below. In advance of actually posing these or other questions with assessees, some caveats are in order. Keep in mind the critical importance of rapport when conducting an interview. Be sensitive to cultural differences in readiness to engage in self-disclosure about family or other matters that may be perceived as too personal to discuss with a stranger. Be ready and able to change the wording of these questions should you need to facilitate the assessee's understanding of them, and to change the order of these questions should an assessee respond to more than one question in the same response. Listen carefully and do not hesitate to probe for more information if you perceive value in doing so. Finally, note that the relevance of each of the questions below will vary with the background and unique socialization experiences of each assessee.

- Describe yourself.
- Describe your family. Who lives at home?
- Describe roles in your family, such as the role of mother, the role of father, the role of grandmother, the role of child, and so forth.
- What traditions, rituals, or customs were passed down to you by family members?
- What traditions, rituals, or customs do you think it is important to pass to the next generation?
- With regard to your family situation, what obligations do you see yourself as having? What obligations does your family have to you?
- What role does your family play in everyday life?
- How does the role of males and females differ from your own cultural perspective?
- What kind of music do you like?
- What kinds of foods do you eat most routinely?
- What do you consider fun things to do? When do you do these things?
- Describe yourself in the way that you think most other people would describe you. How would you say your own self-description would differ from that description?
- How might you respond to the question, "Who are you?" with reference to your own sense of personal identity?
- With which cultural group or groups do you identify most? Why?
- What aspect of the history of the group with which you most identify is most significant to you? Why?
- Who are some of the people who have influenced you most?

the exchange of information related to the assessee. Prior to the formal assessment, the assessor may consider a screening interview with the assessee, in which various culture-related issues are discussed. This chapter's *Close-up* lists some of the questions that may be raised during such an interview. After the assessment, the culturally sensitive assessor might reevaluate the data and conclusions for any possible adverse impact of culture-related factors. So, for example, with the cautions of Velasquez et al. (1997) firmly in mind, an assessor who happened to have administered the MMPI and not the MMPI-2 to a Chicano client might revisit the protocol and its interpretation with an eye toward identifying any possible sources of "overpathologization."

Translators are frequently used in clinic emergency rooms, crisis intervention cases, and other such situations. Whenever a translator is used, the interviewer must be wary not only of the translation of the words of the interviewee, but their intensity as well (Draguns, 1984). Members of the assessee's family are frequently enlisted to serve as translators although such a practice may not be desirable under some circumstances. For example, in some cultures, a younger person translating the words of an older person, particularly with regard to certain topics (such as sexual matters), may be perceived as very awkward, if not disrespectful (Ho, 1987). Case study and behavioral observation

- What are some things that have happened to you in the past that have influenced you most?

- What sources of satisfaction are associated with being you?

- What sources of dissatisfaction or conflict are associated with being you?

- What do you call yourself when asked about your ethnicity?

- What are your feelings regarding your racial and ethnic identity?

- Describe your most pleasant memory as a child.

- Describe your least pleasant memory as a child.

- Describe the ways in which you typically learn new things. In what ways might cultural factors have influenced this learning style?

- Describe the ways you typically resolve conflicts with other people. What influence might cultural factors have in this way of resolving conflicts?

- How would you describe your general view of the world?

- How would you characterize human nature in general?

- How much control do you believe you have over the things that happen to you? Why?

- How much control do you believe you have over your health? your mental health?

- What are your thoughts regarding the role of work in daily life? Has your cultural identity influenced your views about work in any way? If so, how?

- How would you characterize the role of doctors in the world around you?

- How would you characterize the role of lawyers in the world around you?

- How would you characterize the role of politicians in the world around you?

- How would you characterize the role of spirituality in your daily life?

- What are your feelings about the use of illegal drugs?

- What is the role of play in daily life?

- How would you characterize the ideal relationship between human beings and nature?

- What defines a person who has power?

- What happens when one dies?

- Do you tend to live your life more in the past, the present, or the future? What influences on you do you think helped shape this way of living?

- How would you characterize your attitudes and feelings about the older people in your family? older people in society in general?

- Describe your thinking about the local police and the criminal justice system.

- How do you see yourself ten years from now?

data must be interpreted with sensitivity to the meaning of the historical or behavioral data in a cultural context (Longabaugh, 1980; Williams, 1986).

Ultimately, culturally sensitive assessment entails raising important questions regarding the generalizability and appropriateness of the evaluative measures employed. In this discussion of personality assessment in general, we have endeavored to raise awareness regarding such issues. In the following chapter, we focus on common methods of assessment.

Self-Assessment

Text your understanding of elements of this chapter by seeing if you can explain each of the following terms, expressions, and abbreviations:

acculturation

acquiescence

control group for the MMPI

criterion

criterion groups

culturally sensitive psychological
  assessment

empirical criterion keying

error of central tendency

forced-choice format

frame of reference

gambling

generosity error

halo effect

identification

identify

identity

idiographic

impression management

instrumental values

ipsative

locus of control

MMPI

MMPI-A

MMPI-2

NEO PI-R

nomothetic

personality

personality assessment

personality state

personality trait

personality type

profile

Q-sort

response style

self-concept

self-concept measures

self-report

semantic differential

severity error

socially desirable responding

structured interview

terminal values

trait

type

Type A

Type B

values

Welsh code

worldview

12

Personality Assessment Methods

Some people see the world as filled with love and goodness, where others see hate and evil. Some people equate "living" with behavioral excess, whereas others strive for moderation in all things. Some people have relatively realistic perceptions of themselves and other people. Others labor under grossly distorted self-images and inaccurate perceptions of family, friends, and acquaintances. For psychologists and others interested in exploring differences among people with regard to these and other dimensions, many different tools are available. In the previous chapter, we viewed some of the many ways the multifaceted construct of personality can be measured. In this chapter, we focus on the different types of methods employed in the service of personality assessment.

Objective Methods

Typically associated with paper-and-pencil and computer-administered personality tests, **objective methods of personality assessment** characteristically contain short-answer items where the assessee's task is to select one response from the two or more provided and all scoring is done according to set procedures involving little, if any, judgment on the part of the scorer. As with tests of ability, objective methods of personality assessment may include items written in a multiple-choice, true-false, or matching-type format.

Whereas a particular response on an objective ability test may be scored "correct" or "incorrect," a response on an objective personality test is scored with reference to either the personality characteristic(s) being measured or the validity of the respondent's pattern of responses. So, for example, a number of "true" responses to true-false items on a personality test, where a "true" response is deemed indicative of the presence of a particular trait, will be interpreted with reference to the presumed strength of that trait in the testtaker. However, if the same respondent has also responded "true" to items indicative of the absence of the trait, as well as items rarely endorsed as "true" by testtakers, the validity of the protocol will be questioned. Scrutiny of the protocol may suggest an irregularity of some sort. For example, the items may have been responded to inconsistently, in random fashion, or with a "true" or "false" response bias. As we saw in the previous chapter, some objective personality tests are constructed with validity scales or other devices (such as a forced-choice format), which are designed to detect or deter response patterns that would call into question the meaningfulness of the scores.

As with objective ability tests, objective personality tests have many advantages. The items can be answered quickly, so testtakers can be administered many items, covering varied aspects of the trait or traits the test is designed to assess. The items, if well written, require little explanation, making them suitable for group administration or for independent computerized administration. Objective items can be quickly and reliably scored by machine, by hand (usually with the aid of a template held over the test form), or by computer. Especially with the aid of computers, some objective personality test protocols can be analyzed immediately after the testtaker is finished, for either normative or ipsative interpretations. In a normative analysis, the strength of a personality variable as evidenced on the test may be compared to a particular population as a whole. In an ipsative analysis, the strength of a personality variable as measured on the test may be compared to the strength of the testtaker's other personality variables as measured by the same test. The ipsative frame of reference is particularly useful in employment contexts where different intraindividual differences of interests or attitudes may point the way to different careers or job assignments.

Although objective personality test items share many characteristics with objective measures of ability, we should also point out that the term *objective* is something of a misnomer as applied to personality testing and assessment. With reference to short-answer items on ability tests, "objective" gained favor because the items—ideally—contained only one response that was correct. In contrast to the scoring of, say, essay tests, the scoring of objective, multiple-choice tests of ability left little room for emotion, bias, or favoritism on the part of the test scorer; scoring was dispassionate and objective. However, in contrast to objective ability tests, objective personality tests typically contain no one correct answer. Rather, the selection of a particular choice from multiple-choice items provides information relevant to the presence, absence, or strength of a personality-related variable, the validity of the test scores, or both. True, the scoring of such tests can still be dispassionate and objective. However, the extent of the objectivity of the derived scores may be quite controversial. So, for example, an individual may obtain a score on an objective personality test designed to detect the existence of an unresolved oedipal conflict. Yet the extent to which these test results will be viewed as objective is inextricably linked to one's views about the validity of psychoanalytic theory, and more specifically, the construct of an "oedipal conflict."

The objectivity of scores and related outcomes on personality tests, particularly of the objective variety, can also be questioned because they are derived from self-report. Testtakers typically report what they like or dislike, do or do not do, think or do not think, and so forth. One's self-report can be far from objective for many reasons. Some respondents may lack the insight to respond in what could reasonably be described as an objective manner. Some respondents may supply nonobjective responses on objective tests for deliberate reasons. They can respond in a manner that they believe will place them in the best or worst possible light, depending upon what their goal is. They can, in other words, attempt to manage impressions by faking good or faking bad.

Ultimately, the term *objective* as applied to most personality tests may be best thought of as shorthand for a test employing a short-answer, typically multiple-choice, format—a format that provides little, if any, room for discretion in terms of scoring. Traditionally, the description of a personality test as objective has served more to distinguish it from projective and other measurement methods than it has to impart information about how real, tangible, or objective any scores derived from it actually are. However, as we will see in our discussion of projective methods, tests can be objective as well as projective.

Projective Methods

Suppose the lights in your classroom were dimmed and everyone was told to stare at the clean chalkboard for a minute or so. And suppose everyone was then asked to take out some paper and write down what he or she thought could be seen on the chalkboard—other than the chalkboard itself. If you examined what each of your fellow students wrote, you might find as many different things seen on that blank chalkboard as there were students responding. You could assume that the students saw on the chalkboard—or, more accurately, *projected* onto the chalkboard—something that was not really there, but rather, in (or on) their own minds. You might further assume that each student's response to the blank chalkboard reflected something very telling about the student's personality structure.

The **projective hypothesis** holds that an individual supplies structure to unstructured stimuli in a manner consistent with the individual's own unique pattern of conscious and unconscious needs, fears, desires, impulses, conflicts, and ways of perceiving and responding. In like manner, we may define a **projective method** as a technique of personality assessment in which some judgment of the assessee's personality is made on the basis of performance on a task that involves supplying some sort of structure to relatively unstructured or incomplete stimuli. Almost any relatively unstructured stimulus will do for this purpose. In a scene in Shakespeare's play *Hamlet,* Polonius and Hamlet discuss what can be seen in clouds. Indeed, clouds could be used as a projective stimulus.[1] But psychologists, slaves to practicality (and scientific methods) as they are, have developed projective measures of personality that are more reliable than clouds and more portable than chalkboards. Inkblots, pictures, words, drawings, and other things have been used as projective stimuli.

Unlike self-report methods, projective tests are *indirect* methods of personality assessment; the examinee's task is to talk about something or someone other than herself or himself, and inferences about the examinee's personality will be made from the response. On such a task, the ability—and presumably the inclination—of examinees to fake is greatly minimized. Also somewhat minimized is the testtaker's need for great proficiency in the English language; minimal language skills are required to respond to—or create—a drawing. For that reason, and because some projective methods may be less culture-linked than other measures of personality, proponents of projective testing believe that there is a promise of cross-cultural utility with these tests that has yet to be fulfilled. Proponents of projective measures also argue that a major advantage of such measures is that they tap unconscious as well as conscious material. And in the words of the man who coined the term projective methods, "the most important things about an individual are what he cannot or will not say" (Frank, 1939, p. 395).[2]

Projective tests were born in the spirit of rebellion against normative data and through attempts by personality researchers to break down the study of personality into the study of specific traits of varying strengths. This orientation is exemplified by Frank (1939), who reflected, "It is interesting to see how the students of personality have

---

1. In fact, clouds *have* been used as projective stimuli. Wilhelm Stern's Cloud Picture Test, in which subjects were asked to tell what they saw in pictures of clouds, was one of the earliest projective measures.

2. The first published use of the term *projective methods* that we are aware of was in an article entitled "Projective Methods in the Psychological Study of Children," by Ruth Horowitz and Lois Barclay Murphy (1938). However, these authors had read Lawrence K. Frank's (1939) as-yet-unpublished manuscript and had credited him for having "applied the term 'projective methods.'"

attempted to meet the problem of individuality with methods and procedures designed for study of uniformities and norms that ignore or subordinate individuality, treating it as a troublesome deviation which derogates from the real, the superior, and only important central tendency, mode, average, etc." (pp. 392–393). Thus, in contrast to methods of personality assessment that focused on the individual from a statistics-based, normative perspective, projective techniques were at one time viewed as the technique of choice for focusing on the individual from a purely clinical perspective—a perspective that examined the unique way an individual projects onto an ambiguous stimulus "his way of seeing life, his meanings, significances, patterns, and especially his feelings" (Frank, 1939, p. 403). As we will see, however, years of clinical experience with these tests and a growing volume of research data have led interpretation of responses to projective stimuli to become increasingly norm-referenced in nature.

Inkblots as Projective Stimuli

Spill some ink in the center of a blank, white sheet of paper and fold it over. Allow to dry. There you have the recipe for an inkblot—recognized by assessment professionals as a projective stimulus and associated in the public eye with psychology itelf.

The Rorschach Hermann Rorschach (Figure 12–1) developed what he called a "form interpretation test" using inkblots as the forms to be interpreted. In 1921, he published his monograph on the technique, *Psychodiagnostics.* In the last section of that monograph, Rorschach proposed applications of his test to personality assessment, and he provided 28 case studies as examples employing normals and people with various psychiatric diagnoses (including neurosis, psychosis, and manic-depressive illness). Rorschach died suddenly and unexpectedly at the age of 38, just a year after his book was published. A paper by Rorschach co-authored by Emil Oberholzer entitled "The Application of the Form Interpretation Test" was published posthumously in 1923.

Like Rorschach, we will refer to his test as just that—a test. However, students should be aware of controversy surrounding whether it is more properly a test, a method, a technique, or something else. For example, Goldfried et al. (1971) view the Rorschach as a structured interview, and Korchin and Schuldberg (1981) regard it as "less of a test" and more as "an open and flexible arena for studying interpersonal transactions" (p. 1151). There has also been debate about whether or not the Rorschach is properly considered a projective instrument (Acklin, 1995; Aronow et al., 1995; Moreland et al., 1995b; Ritzler, 1995). For example, Exner, an authority on all things Rorschach, argued that the inkblots are "not completely ambiguous," that the task does not necessarily "force projection," and that "unfortunately, the Rorschach has been erroneously mislabeled a projective test for far too long" (1989, pp. 526–527; see also Exner, 1997). Regardless, "Rorschach" remains virtually synonymous with "projective tool" among assessment professionals.

The Rorschach consists of ten bilaterally symmetrical—mirror-imaged if folded in half—inkblots that are printed on separate cards. Five inkblots are achromatic (meaning "without color," or black and white); two are black, white, and red; and three are multicolored. The test comes with the cards only: no test manual, nor any administration, scoring, or interpretation instructions, nor any rationale for why some of the inkblots are achromatic and others are chromatic (with color). Filling the need for a test manual and administration, scoring, and interpretation instructions have been a number of manuals and handbooks that set forth a variety of methods (such as Aronow & Reznikoff, 1976, 1983; Beck, 1944, 1945, 1952, 1960; Exner, 1974, 1978, 1986; Exner & Weiner, 1982; Klopfer & Davidson, 1962; Lerner, 1991, 1996a, 1996b; Piotrowski, 1957). Although there are dif-

Figure 12–1
Herman Rorschach (1884–1922)

Rorschach was a Swiss psychiatrist whose father had been an art teacher and whose interests included art as well as psycho-analysis—particularly the work of Carl Jung, who had written extensively on methods of bringing unconscious material to light. In 1913 Rorschach published papers on how analysis of a patient's artwork could provide insights into personality. Rorschach's inkblot test was published in 1921 and it was not an immediate success. Rorschach died the following year of peritonitis at the age of 38, unaware of the great legacy he would leave. For more on Hermann Rorschach, read his Test Developer Profile on our companion Internet site at www.mhhe.com/psychtesting.

ferences among the systems in administration, scoring, and interpretation instructions, what follows is a description of the process in very general terms. The system that is most widely used is the one devised by Exner, and we will discuss it shortly. First, some general information regarding an administration and scoring of the Rorschach.

Each inkblot, printed on cards (Figure 12–2), is initially presented to the testtaker one at a time in numbered order, from 1 to 10. The testtaker is instructed to tell what is on each of the cards with a question such as, "What might this be?" Testtakers have a great deal of freedom with the Rorschach. They may, for example, rotate the cards and vary the number and length of their responses to each card. The examiner records all relevant information including the testtaker's verbatim responses, nonverbal gestures, the length of time required before the first response to each card, the position of the card, and so forth. The examiner does not engage in any discussion concerning the testtaker's responses during the initial administration of the cards. Every effort is made to provide the testtaker with the opportunity to "project," free from any outside distractions.

After the entire set of cards has been administered once, a second administration, referred to as the **inquiry,** is conducted. During the inquiry, the examiner attempts to determine what features of the inkblot played a role in formulating the testtaker's perceptions. Questions such as "What made it look like _____?" and "How do you see _____?" are asked in an attempt to clarify what was seen and which aspects of the inkblot were most influential in forming these percepts. The inquiry provides information that is useful in scoring and interpreting the responses. The examiner also learns in the inquiry whether the testtaker remembers earlier responses, whether the original percept is still seen, and whether any new responses are now perceived.

A third component of the administration, referred to as **testing the limits,** may also be included. This procedure enables the examiner to restructure the situation by asking specific questions that provide additional information concerning personality functioning.

If, for example, the testtaker has utilized the entire inkblot when forming percepts throughout the test, the examiner might want to determine if details within the inkblot could be elaborated on. Under those conditions, the examiner might say, "Sometimes

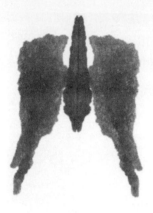

Figure 12–2
A Rorschach-Like Inkblot

people use a part of the blot to see something." Alternatively, the examiner might point to a specific area of the card and ask, "What does this look like?" A limit-testing procedure may also be undertaken, the objective being (1) to identify any confusion or misunderstanding concerning the task, (2) to aid the examiner in determining if the testtaker is able to refocus his or her percepts given a new frame of reference, and (3) to see if a testtaker made anxious by the ambiguous nature of the task is better able to perform given this added structure. At least one Rorschach researcher has advocated the technique of trying to elicit one last response from testtakers who think they have already given as many responses as they are going to give; the rationale is that endings have many meanings, and the one last response may provide a source of questions and inferences applicable to treatment considerations (Cerney, 1984).

Hypotheses concerning personality functioning will be formed on the basis of all the variables we have outlined (such as the content of the response, the location of the response, the length of time to respond) plus many additional ones. In general, Rorschach protocols are scored according to several categories, including location, determinants, content, popularity, and form. *Location* is the part of the inkblot that was utilized in forming the percept. Individuals may use the entire inkblot, a large section, a small section, a minute detail, or white spaces. *Determinants* are the qualities of the inkblot that determine what the individual perceives: the form, color, shading, or movement that the individual attributes to the inkblot. *Content* is the content category of the response; although different scoring systems vary in some of the categories scored, certain general content areas such as human figures, animal figures, anatomical parts, blood, clouds, X-rays, and sexual responses are usually included. *Popularity* is the frequency with which a certain response has been found to correspond with a particular inkblot or section of an inkblot. A popular response is one that has frequently been obtained from the general population. A rare response is one that has been perceived infrequently by the general population. The *form* of a response is how accurately the individual's perception matches or fits the corresponding part of the inkblot. Form level may be evaluated as being adequate or inadequate, or good or poor.

The scoring categories are considered to correspond to various aspects of personality functioning, and hypotheses concerning aspects of personality are based both on the number of responses that fall within each category and on the interrelationships among the categories. For example, the number of whole responses (using the entire inkblot) in a Rorschach record is thought to be associated with conceptual thought processes. Form level is associated with reality testing, human movement with imagination, and color responses with emotional reactivity. Patterns of response, recurrent themes, and the interrelationships among the different scoring categories are all considered in arriving at a final description of the individual from a Rorschach protocol. Data concerning the responses of various clinical and nonclinical groups of adults, adolescents, and children have been compiled and are available for comparisons (see Ames et al., 1971; Ames et al., 1974; Exner, 1978, 1986; Exner & Weiner, 1982; Goldfried et al., 1971).

Rorschach's "form interpretation test" was in its infancy at the time of its developer's death. The underdeveloped and orphaned test found a receptive home in the United States, where it was nurtured by several different schools, each with its own vision of how the test should be administered, scored, interpreted, and used. In this sense, the Rorschach is, as McDowell and Acklin (1996, p. 308) put it, "an anomaly in the field of psychological measurement when compared to objective and other projective techniques." Thus, although it is generally referred to as "the Rorschach," as if it were a standardized test, Rorschach practitioners and researchers have for many years employed a variety of Rorschach systems—on some occasions picking and choosing interpretive criteria from one or more systems. Consider in this context a study by Saunders (1991), which focused on Rorschach indicators of child abuse. Saunders (1991, p. 55) wrote, "Rorschach protocols were scored using Rapaport et al.'s (1945–46) system as the basic framework, but special scores of four different types were added. I borrowed two of these additional measures from other researchers . . . and developed the other two specifically for this study." Given the variation that existed in terminology and in administration and scoring practices, one readily appreciates how difficult it might be to muster consistent and credible evidence for the test's psychometric soundness.[3]

In a book that reviewed several Rorschach systems, Exner wrote of the advisability of approaching "the Rorschach problem through a research integration of the systems" (1969, p. 251). Exner would subsequently develop such an integration; a "comprehensive system" (Exner 1974, 1978, 1986, 1990, 1991, 1993; Exner & Weiner, 1982, 1995; see also Handler, 1996) for the administration, scoring, and interpretation of the Rorschach. Exner's system has been well received by clinicians and is, in all likelihood, the Rorschach system most used by them (Piotrowski, 1996a). Too, it is most often taught to graduate students (Hilsenroth & Handler, 1995).

Prior to the development of Exner's system and its widespread adoption by clinicians and researchers, evaluations of the Rorschach's psychometric soundness tended to be mixed at best (see, for example, Ames et al., 1952; Datel & Gengerelli, 1955; Guilford, 1948; Korner & Westwood, 1955; Lisansky, 1956; Remzy & Pickard, 1949; Rogers et al., 1951; Turner, 1966; Wittenborn & Holzberg, 1951). Exner's system brought a degree of uniformity to Rorschach use and thus facilitated "apples to apples" (or "bats to bats") comparison between research studies.

Yet regardless of the scoring system employed, there are a number of reasons why the evaluation of the psychometric soundness of the Rorschach is a tricky business. For example, because each inkblot is considered to have a unique stimulus quality, evaluation of reliability by a split-half method would be inappropriate. Of historical interest in this regard is the work of Behn, who, under Sigmund Freud's direction, attempted to develop a similar but not alternate form of the test called the "Behn-Rorschach" (Buckle & Holt, 1951; Eichler, 1951; Swift, 1944). Traditional test-retest reliability procedures also may not be appropriate for use with the Rorschach. This is so because of the effect of familiarity on response to the cards and because responses may reflect transient states as opposed to enduring traits. Commenting on this and related points, Exner (1983)

---

3. A test called the Holtzman Inkblot Technique (HIT; Holtzman et al., 1961) was designed to be more psychometrically sound than any existing inkblot test. A description of the HIT, as well as speculation as to why it never achieved the popularity and acceptance of the Rorschach, can be found in Cohen (2002).

concluded that "some Comprehensive System scores defy the axiom that something cannot be valid unless it is also reliable" (p. 411).

The widespread acceptance of Exner's system has advanced the cause of inter-scorer reliability. Indeed, a scholarly journal that regularly publishes Rorschach research now requires at least 80% inter-scorer agreement with regard to "variables central to the particular study" (Weiner, 1991, p. 1). Exner (1986, 1991, 1993), DeCato (1994), and others (for example, Parker et al., 1988) provided evidence that acceptable levels of inter-scorer reliability can be attained with the Rorschach. Using Exner's system, McDowell and Acklin (1996) reported an overall mean percentage agreement of 87% among Rorschach scorers. Still, as these researchers cautioned, "The complex types of data developed by the Rorschach introduce formidable obstacles to the application of standard procedures and canons of test development" (pp. 308–309). Far more pessimistic about such "formidable obstacles," and far less subtle in their conclusions, were Hunsley and Bailey (1999), who after reviewing the literature on the clinical utility of the Rorschach, wrote,

> Given the meager support from thousands of publications to date, the history of disagreements among proponents about the proper use of the Rorschach, and the uncertain acceptance by psychologists of a psychometrically and scientifically sound approach to Rorschach scoring and interpretation, we doubt that there will ever be sufficient evidence [sic] to suggest that the Rorschach or the Comprehensive System can contribute, in routine clinical practice, to scientifically informed psychological assessment. (p. 274)

Countering such pessimism are other reviews of the literature that are far more favorable to this test (Bornstein, 1998, 1999; Ganellen, 1996; Meyer & Handler, 1997; Viglione, 1999). In their meta-analysis designed to compare the validity of the Rorschach versus that of the MMPI, Hiller et al. (1999) concluded that "on average, both tests work about equally well when used for purposes deemed appropriate by experts" (p. 293). In a similar vein, Stricker and Gold (1999, p. 240) reflected that "A test is not valid or invalid; rather, there are as many validity coefficients as there are purposes for which the test is used. The Rorschach can demonstrate its utility for several purposes and can be found wanting for several others." They went on to argue for an approach to assessment that incorporated many different types of methods, and in so doing, sang the praises of the Rorschach test:

> Arguably, Walt Whitman's greatest poem was entitled "Song of Myself." We believe that everything that is done by the person being assessed is a song of the self. The Rorschach is one instrument available to the clinician, who has the task of hearing all of the music. (Stricker & Gold, 1999, p. 249)

Decades ago, Jensen (1965, p. 509) opined that "the rate of scientific progress in clinical psychology might well be measured by the speed and thoroughness with which it gets over the Rorschach." If this statement were true, then the rate of scientific progress in clinical psychology could be characterized as a crawl. The Rorschach remains one of the most frequently used (Camara et al., 1998; Watkins et al., 1995) and frequently taught (Watkins et al., 1990) psychological tests. It is widely used in forensic work (Piotrowski, 1996b, 1996c) and widely accepted by the courts (Meloy et al., 1997; Weiner et al., 1996). It is, as Weiner (1997) concluded in his evaluation of the status of the Rorschach at age 75: "Widely used and highly valued by clinicians and researchers in many countries of the world, it appears despite its fame not yet to have received the academic respect it deserves and, it can be hoped, will someday enjoy" (p. 17).

Pictures as Projective Stimuli

Look at Figure 12–3. Having looked at it, make up a story about it. Your story should have a beginning, a middle, and an end. Write it down, using as much paper as you

Figure 12–3
Ambiguous Picture for Use in Projective Story-Telling Task

need. Bring the story to class with you and compare it with some other student's story. What does the story reveal about your needs, fears, desires, impulse control, ways of viewing the world—your personality? What does the story written by your classmate reveal about her or him?

This exercise introduces you to the use of pictures as projective stimuli. Pictures used as projective stimuli may be photos of real persons, of animals, of objects, or of anything; they may be paintings, drawings, etchings, or any other variety of picture. One of the earliest uses of pictures as projective stimuli came at the beginning of the twentieth century. An article by Brittain (1907) in a journal called *The Pedagogical Seminary* reported sex differences in stories that children gave in response to nine pictures. The author reported that the girls were more interested in religious and moral themes than were the boys. The next year, another experimenter used pictures and a story-telling technique to investigate the imagination of children, and differences in themes as a function of age were observed (Libby, 1908). In 1932, a psychiatrist working at the Clinic for Juvenile Research in Detroit developed the Social Situation Picture Test (Schwartz, 1932), a projective instrument that contained pictures relevant to juvenile delinquents. Working at the Harvard Psychological Clinic in 1935, Christiana D. Morgan (Figure 12–4) and Henry Murray (Figure 12–5) published the Thematic Apperception Test (TAT)—pronounced by saying the letters and not by rhyming with "cat"—the instrument that has come to be the most widely used of all the picture/story-telling projective tests. We discuss the TAT as well as some related instruments.

The Thematic Apperception Test (TAT)   The TAT was originally designed as an aid to eliciting fantasy material from patients in psychoanalysis (Morgan & Murray, 1935). The stimulus materials consist of 31 cards, of which 1 is blank. The 30 picture cards, all black-and-white, contain a variety of scenes that were designed to present the testtaker with "certain classical human situations" (Murray, 1943). Some of the pictures contain a lone individual, some contain a group of people, and some contain no people. Some of the pictures appear to be as real as a photo, and others are surrealistic drawings. Examinees

Figure 12–4
Christiana D. Morgan (1897–1967)

On the box cover of the widely used TAT and in numerous other measurement-related books and articles, the authorship of the TAT is listed as "Henry A. Murray, Ph.D., and the Staff of the Harvard Psychological Clinic." However, the first articles describing the TAT were written by Christiana D. Morgan (Morgan, 1938), or Morgan and Murray with Morgan listed as senior author (Morgan & Murray, 1935, 1938). In a mimeographed manuscript in the Harvard University archives, an early version of the test was titled the "Morgan-Murray Thematic Apperception Test" (White et al., 1941). Wesley G. Morgan (1995) noted that because Christiana Morgan "had been senior author of the earlier publications a question is raised about why her name was omitted as an author of the 1943 version" (p. 238). W. G. Morgan (1995) took up that and related questions in a brief but fascinating account of the origin and history of the TAT images. More on the life of Christiana Morgan can be found in Translate This Darkness: The Life of Christiana Morgan *(Douglas, 1993). Her Test Developer Profile can be found on our Internet site at* www.mhhe.com/psychtesting.

are introduced to the examination with the cover story that it is a test of imagination in which it is their task to tell what events led up to the scene in the picture, what is happening at that moment, and what the outcome will be. Examinees are also asked to tell what the people depicted in the cards are thinking and feeling. In the TAT Manual, Murray (1943) also advised that the examiners attempt to find out what the source of the story was; in this context, it is noteworthy that the noun *apperception* is derived from the verb **apperceive,** which is defined as "to perceive in terms of past perceptions." The source of a story could be anything—a personal experience, a dream, an imagined event, a book, an episode of the *X-Files,* and so on. If the blank card is administered, examinees are instructed to imagine that there is a picture on the card and then proceed to tell a story about it.

In clinical practice, examiners tend to take liberties with various elements pertaining to the administration, scoring, and interpretation of the TAT. For example, although 20 cards is the recommended number for presentation, in practice an examiner might administer as few as 1 or 2 cards or as many as all 31. If a clinician is assessing a patient who has a penchant for telling stories that fill reams of the clinician's notepad, it's a good bet that fewer cards will be administered. If, on the other hand, a patient tells brief, one-

Figure 12–5
Henry A. Murray (1893–1988)

Henry Murray is perhaps best known for the influential theory of personality he developed, as well as his role as author of the Thematic Apperception Test. Biographies of Murray have been written by Anderson (1990) and Robinson (1992). Murray's Test Developer Profile can be found on the Internet at www.mhhe.com/psychtesting.

or two-sentence stories, more cards may be administered in an attempt to collect more raw data with which to work. Some of the cards are suggested for use with adult males, adult females, or both, and some are suggested for use with children. This is so because certain pictorial representations lend themselves more than others to identification and projection by members of these groups. In one study involving 75 males (25 each of 11-, 14-, and 17-year-olds), Cooper (1981) identified the ten most productive cards for use with adolescent males. In practice, however, any card—be it one recommended for use with males, with females, or with children—may be administered to any subject; the clinician administering selects the cards that he or she believes will elicit responses pertinent to the objective of the testing.

The raw material used in drawing conclusions about the individual examined with the TAT are (1) the stories as they were told by the examinee, (2) the clinician's notes about the way or the manner in which the examinee responded to the cards, and (3) the clinician's notes about extra-test behavior and verbalizations. The last two categories of raw data (test and extra-test behavior) are sources of clinical interpretations for almost any individually administered test. Analysis of the story content requires special training. One illustration of how a testtaker's behavior during testing may influence the examiner's interpretations of the findings was provided by Sugarman (1991, p. 140), who told of a "highly narcissistic patient [who] demonstrated contempt and devaluation of the examiner (and presumably others) by dictating TAT stories complete with spelling and punctuation as though the examiner was a stenographer."

A number of systems for interpreting TAT data exist, though all are based to a greater or lesser degree in Henry Murray's influential theory of personality, excellent summaries of which are available (in, for example, Hall & Lindzey, 1970; Murray, 1959; Murray & Kluckhohn, 1953). In particular, interpretive systems for the TAT tend to incorporate the Murrayan concepts of **need** (determinants of behavior arising from within the individual), **press** (determinants of behavior arising from within the environment), and **thema** (a unit of interaction between needs and press). In general, the guiding principle in interpreting TAT stories is that the testtaker is identifying with someone (the

Table 12–1
A Description of the Sample TAT-like Picture

Author's Description

A male and a female are seated in close proximity on a sofa. The female is talking on the phone. There is an end table with a magazine on it next to the sofa.

Manifest Stimulus Demand

Some explanation of the nature of the relationship between these two persons and some reason the woman is on the phone are required. Less frequently noted is the magazine on the table and its role in this scene.

Form Demand

Two large details, the woman and the man, must be integrated. Small details include the magazine and the telephone.

Latent Stimulus Demand

This picture is likely to elicit attitudes toward heterosexuality and, within that context, material relevant to the examinee's "place" on optimism-pessimism, security-insecurity, dependence-independence, passivity-assertiveness, and related continuums. Alternatively, attitudes toward family and friends may be elicited with the two primary figures being viewed as brother and sister, the female talking on the phone to a family member, and so on.

Frequent Plots

We haven't administered this card to enough people to make judgments about what constitutes "frequent plots." We have, however, provided a sampling of plots (Table 12–2).

Significant Variations

Just as we cannot provide information on frequent plots, we cannot report data on significant variations. We would guess, however, that most college students viewing this picture would perceive the two individuals in it as being involved in a heterosexual relationship. Were that to be the case, a significant variation would be a story in which the characters are not involved in a heterosexual relationship (for example, they are employer/employee). Close clinical attention will also be paid to the nature of the relationship of the characters to any "introduced figures" (persons not pictured in the card but introduced into the story by the examinee). The "pull" of this card is to introduce the figure to whom the woman is speaking. What is the phone call about? How will the story be resolved?

protagonist) in the story and that the needs, environmental demands, and conflicts of the protagonist in the story are in some way related to the concerns, hopes, fears, or desires of the examinee. In his discussion of the TAT from the perspective of a clinician, William Henry (1956) examined each of the cards in the test with regard to such variables as "manifest stimulus demand," "form demand," "latent stimulus demand," frequent plots, and significant variations. To get an idea of how some of these terms are used, look again at Figure 12–3—a picture that is *not* a TAT card—and then read Tables 12–1 and 12–2, which are descriptions of the card and some responses to the card from college-age respondents. Although a clinician may obtain bits of information from the stories told about every individual card, the clinician's final impressions will usually derive from a consideration of the overall patterns of themes that emerge.

TAT scoring and interpretation systems based on the work of personality theorists other than Murray may also be found. For example, an Affect Maturity Scale that has its basis in Anna Freud's notion of affect development and maturation has been described by Thompson (1986). Westen and his colleagues (Westen et al., 1985; Westen et al., 1988) have reported on the development of the Object Relations and Social Cognition Scale (ORSCS), a measure used in conjunction with the TAT and based in object relations theory as well as social-cognitive psychology.

As with the Rorschach and many other projective techniques, a debate between academics and practitioners regarding the psychometric soundness of the TAT has been

Table 12–2
Some Responses to the Sample Picture

Respondent	Story
1. (Male)	This guy has been involved with this girl for a few months. Things haven't been going all that well. He's suspected that she's been seeing a lot of guys. This is just one scene in a whole evening where the phone hasn't stopped ringing. Pretty soon he is just going to get up and leave.
2. (Female)	This couple is dating. They haven't made any plans for the evening and they are wondering what they should do. She is calling up another couple to ask if they want to get together. They will go out with the other couple and have a good time.
3. (Male)	This girl thinks she is pregnant and is calling the doctor for the results of her test. This guy is pretty worried because he has plans to finish college and go to graduate school. He is afraid she will want to get married, and he doesn't want to get trapped into anything. The doctor will tell her she isn't pregnant, and he'll be really relieved.
4. (Female)	This couple has been dating for about two years and they're very much in love. She's on the phone firming up plans for a down payment on a hall that's going to cater the wedding. That's a bridal magazine on the table over there. They look like they're really in love. I think things will work out for them even though the odds are against it—the divorce rates and all.
5. (Male)	These are two very close friends. The guy has a real problem and needs to talk to someone. He is feeling really depressed and that he is all alone in the world. Every time he starts to tell her how he feels, the phone rings. Pretty soon he will leave feeling like no one has time for him and even more alone. I don't know what will happen to him, but it doesn't look good.

unceasing through the years. Because of the general lack of standardization and uniformity with which administration, scoring, and interpretation procedures tend to be applied in everyday clinical practice, concern on psychometric grounds is clearly justified. However, in experimental tests where trained examiners are using the same procedures and scoring systems, inter-rater reliability coefficients can range from adequate to impressive (Leigh et al., 1992; Sivik & Hosterey, 1992; Stricker & Healy, 1990; Thomas & Dudek, 1985). Split-half, test-retest, and alternate-form reliability measures are inappropriate for use with the TAT (McClelland, 1980). Situational factors, including who the examiner is, how the test is administered, and the testtaker's experiences prior to and during the test's administration, may all affect test responses (Bellak, 1944; Bernstein, 1956; Feshback, 1961; Lindzey, 1950; Mussen & Scodel, 1955). Additionally, transient internal need states such as hunger, thirst, fatigue, and higher than ordinary levels of sexual tension can affect a testtaker's responses (Atkinson, 1958; McClelland & Atkinson, 1948; Sanford, 1936). Different TAT cards have different stimulus "pulls" (Goldfried & Zax, 1965; Murstein & Mathes, 1996). Some pictures are more likely than others to elicit stories with themes of despair, for example. Given that the pictures have different stimulus "pulls" or, more technically stated, different "latent stimulus demands," it becomes difficult if not impossible to determine the inter-item (inter-card) reliability of the test; card 1 might reliably elicit need achievement themes, whereas card 16, for example, might not usually elicit any such themes. The possibility of widely variable story lengths in response to the cards (Rubin, 1964; Webb & Hilden, 1953) presents yet another challenge to the documentation of inter-item reliability.

Conflicting opinions are presented in the scholarly literature concerning the validity of the TAT, including the validity of its assumptions and the validity of various applications (Barends et al., 1990; Cramer, 1996; Gluck, 1955; Hibbard et al., 1994; Kagan, 1956; Keiser & Prather, 1990; Mussen & Naylor, 1954; Ronan et al., 1995; Worchel & Dupree, 1990). Although the relationship between expression of fantasy stories and real-life behavior is tentative at best, and although the TAT is highly susceptible to faking (Hamsher & Farina, 1967; Holmes, 1974; Weisskopf & Dieppa, 1951), the test is widely used by practitioners. Yet in contrast to the test's apparently widespread use stand the findings of one survey of training directors of APA-approved programs in clinical psychology: The majority of these programs place very little emphasis on the test and typically rely on psychoanalytic writings in their teaching of it (Rossini & Moretti, 1997). The study authors provided a list of recommended books, chapters, and articles for in-depth study of the TAT.

Admittedly, the TAT and other tests like it do have great intuitive appeal; it does make sense that people would project their own motivation when asked to construct a story from an ambiguous stimulus. Another appeal for users of this test is that it is the clinician who tailors the test administration by selecting the cards and the nature of the inquiry—an undoubtedly welcome feature in the era of standardization, computer-adaptive testing, and computer-generated narrative summaries. But as with many projective tests, it seems the TAT must ultimately be judged by a different, more clinically than psychometrically oriented standard if its contribution to personality assessment is to be fully appreciated.

Other picture-story tests   Since the publication of the TAT, many modifications have been published employing pictures as a stimulus for projective story telling. In some of the earliest modifications, artwork designed to be more suitable for use with specific cultural groups was substituted for many of the original TAT cards. For example, the Thompson (1949) modification of the TAT was designed specifically for use with Black testtakers; its pictures contained both Black and White protagonists. Other modifications of the original TAT included tests designed for use with Native Americans, South Africans, and South Micronesians (Bellak, 1971). A TAT-like test called TEMAS was designed for use with urban Hispanic children (Costantino et al., 1988; Malgady et al., 1984).

A number of tests employing pictures as a stimulus for projective story telling were developed for use with respondents in a particular age group. For example, the Children's Apperception Test (CAT) developed by Leopold Bellak and first published in 1949 was designed for use with children ages 3 to 10. It featured animals instead of humans in the pictures. In response to research indicating that children might produce more clinically valuable responses with humans in the pictures (Murstein, 1963), an alternative version of the CAT called the "CAT-H" ("H" denoting the use of human figures in the pictures) was published (Bellak & Bellak, 1965). Whether to employ the CAT or the CAT-H was left to the clinician's judgment as a function of the maturity and personality of the individual testtaker (Bellak & Hurvich, 1966). Bellak subsequently developed a TAT-like test for testtakers at the other end of the age continuum, the Senior Apperception Technique (Bellak & Bellak, 1973).

The Picture Story Test (Symonds, 1949) was designed expressly for use with adolescents, and the 20 pictures contained in it were designed to elicit stories pertinent to those years (for example, coming home late, leaving home, and planning for the future). The Education Apperception Test (Thompson & Sones, 1973) and the School Apperception Method (Solomon & Starr, 1968) are two picture-story instruments designed to tap children's attitudes toward school and learning. The Michigan Picture Test was developed for use with children between the ages of 8 and 14, and it contains 16 pictures designed to elicit various responses, ranging from conflicts with authority figures to feelings of personal inadequacy (Andrew, 1953). The Roberts Apperception Test for Children (RATC; McArthur & Roberts, 1982) contains cards depicting a variety of situations, including family confrontation, parental conflict, parental affection, attitudes toward school, and peer action. It was developed to contain a standardized scoring system.

The Children's Apperceptive Story-Telling Test (CAST; Schneider, 1989; Schneider & Perney, 1990) has its basis in Adlerian theory. Another theoretically based projective instrument designed for use with children is the Blacky Pictures Test (Blum, 1950). This test features "Blacky" the dog, as well as family and friends, in scenes designed to elicit stories with psychoanalytic themes ranging from oedipal conflicts to castration anxiety. A highly ambiguous TAT-like test designed to assess object relations, developed by Phillipson (1955), has been described as "a cross between the TAT and the Rorschach" (Stricker & Healy, 1990, p. 226).

In one projective test, testtakers construct their own pictures and then tell a story. Designed for use with individuals 6 years of age or older, the Make A Picture Story Method (Shneidman, 1952) consists of 67 cut-out figures of people and animals that may be presented on any of 22 pictorial backgrounds. The figures (which vary in posture and position) represent males, females, children, nudes, minority groups (such as Blacks, Mexicans, and Asians), legendary characters, and well-known fictitious characters (such as Superman). A number of figures with blank faces are also included. The backgrounds represent diverse settings (for example, a living room, street, nursery, stage, school-room, bathroom, bridge, dream, camp, cave, raft, cemetery, cellar), and there is also one blank background, onto which the testtaker may assign any background. Examinees are instructed to arrange the figures on the backgrounds "as they might be in real life" (Shneidman, 1952, p. 7). The subject is then instructed to construct a story pertinent to their creation and indicate who the characters are, what they are doing, what they are thinking, how they are feeling, and what the outcome of the story will be.

Other tests using pictures as projective stimuli   A projective technique called the Hand Test (Wagner, 1983) consists of nine cards with pictures of hands on them and a tenth blank card. The testtaker is asked what the hands on each card might be doing. When presented with the blank card, the testtaker is instructed to imagine a pair of hands on the card and then describe what they might be doing. Testtakers may make several responses to each card, and all responses are recorded. Responses are interpreted according to 24 categories, such as affection, dependence, and aggression.

Another projective technique, the Rosenzweig Picture-Frustration Study (Rosenzweig, 1945, 1950, 1978; Rosenzweig et al., 1947, 1948), employs cartoons depicting frustrating situations (Figure 12–6). The testtaker's task is to fill in the response of the cartoon figure being frustrated. The test, which is based on the assumption that the testtaker

Figure 12–6
Sample Item From the Rosenzweig
Picture-Frustration Study

will identify with the person being frustrated, is available in forms for children, adolescents, and adults. Young children respond orally to the pictures, whereas older testtakers may respond either orally or in writing. An inquiry period is suggested after administration of all of the pictures in order to clarify the responses. Responses are scored in terms of the type of reaction elicited and the direction of the aggression expressed. The direction of the aggression may be "intropunitive" (aggression turned inward), "extrapunitive" (outwardly expressed), or "inpunitive" (aggression is evaded so as to avoid or gloss over the situation). Reactions are grouped into categories such as "obstacle dominance" (in which the response concentrates on the frustrating barrier), "ego defense" (in which attention is focused on protecting the frustrated person), and "need persistence" (in which attention is focused on solving the frustrating problem). For each scoring category, the percentage of responses is calculated and compared with normative data. A group conformity rating (GCR), representing the degree to which one's responses conform or are typical of those of the standardization group, is derived. The test has captured the imagination of researchers for decades (see Graybill, 1990, 1993; Wagner, 1985) although questions remain concerning how reactions to cartoons depicting frustrating situations are related to real-life situations.

One variation of the picture-story method may appeal to both "old school" clinicians and the more actuarily inclined. The Apperceptive Personality Test (APT; Karp et al., 1990) represented an attempt to address some long-standing criticisms of the TAT as a projective instrument while introducing objectivity into the scoring system. The test consists of eight stimulus cards "depicting recognizable people in everyday settings" (Holmstrom et al., 1990, p. 252), including males and females of different ages, as well as minority group members. This, by the way, is in contrast to the TAT stimulus cards, some of which depict fantastic or unreal types of scenes.[4] Another difference between the APT and the TAT is the emotional tone and draw of the stimulus cards. A long-standing criticism of the TAT cards has been their negative or gloomy tone, which might work to restrict the range of affect projected by a testtaker (Garfield & Eron, 1948; Ritzler et al., 1980). After telling a story about each of the pictures either orally or in writing, testtakers respond to a series of multiple-choice questions. In addition to supplying quantitative information, the questionnaire segment of the test was designed to fill in any information gaps from stories that would be too brief or cryptic to otherwise score. Responses are thus subjected to both clinical and actuarial interpretation and may, in fact, be scored and interpreted with computer software. If the norm base of the test is extended and made representative of census data, and if the test is found to be psychometrically sound on the basis of independent research with acceptably large samples of subjects, the APT is apt to become much more widely known in the years to come.

Words as Projective Stimuli

Although many projective techniques involve the use of verbalizations either in providing directions or in obtaining responses, some instruments use words as the projective stimulus material. Projective techniques that employ open-ended words, phrases, and sentences are referred to as semistructured techniques because, although they are open-ended and allow for a variety of responses, they still provide a framework within which the subject must operate. The two best-known examples of verbal projective techniques are word association and sentence completion tests.

---

4. Murray et al. (1938) believed that fantastic or unreal types of stimuli might be particularly effective in tapping unconscious processes.

Word association tests   The first attempt at investigating word association was made by Galton (1879). Galton's method consisted of presenting a series of unrelated stimulus words and instructing the subject to respond with the first word that came to mind. Continued interest in the phenomenon of word association resulted in additional studies being conducted. Precise methods for recording the responses given and the length of time elapsed before obtaining a response were developed (Cattell, 1887; Trautscholdt, 1883). Cattell and Bryant (1889) were the first to use cards with stimulus words printed on them, and Kraepelin's (1896) investigations studied the effect of physical states such as hunger and fatigue as well as the effect of practice on word association. Mounting experimental evidence led psychologists to believe that the associations individuals made to words were not chance happenings but, rather, the resultant interplay of the individual's life experiences, attitudes, and unique personality characteristics.

Jung (1910) maintained that by selecting certain key words that represented possible areas of conflict, word association techniques could be employed for psychodiagnostic purposes. Jung's experiments served as an inspiration to developers of such tests as the Word Association Test developed by Rapaport, Gill, and Schafer (1946) at the Menninger Clinic. This test consists of three parts. In the first part, each stimulus word is administered to the examinee, who has been instructed to respond quickly with the first word that comes to mind. The examiner records the length of time it takes the subject to respond to each item. In the second part of the test, each stimulus word is again presented to the examinee. Here the examinee is instructed to reproduce the original responses. Any deviation between the original and this second response is recorded, as is the length of time before reacting. The third part of the test is the inquiry. Here the examiner asks questions to try to clarify the relationship that exists between the stimulus word and the response (for example, "What were you thinking about?" or "What was going through your mind?"). In some cases, the relationship may be obvious, but in others the relationship between the two words may be idiosyncratic or even bizarre.

The test consists of 60 words, some considered neutral by the test authors (for example, *chair, book, water, dance, taxi*) and some labeled "traumatic." In the latter category are "words that are likely to touch upon sensitive personal material according to clinical experience, and also words that attract associative disturbances" (Rapaport et al., 1968, p. 257). Examples of words designated "traumatic" are *love, girlfriend, boyfriend, mother, father, suicide, fire, breast,* and *masturbation.*

Responses on the Word Association Test are evaluated with respect to variables such as popularity, reaction time, content, and test-retest responses. Normative data are provided on the percentage of occurrence of certain responses for college students and schizophrenic groups. For example, to the word *stomach,* 21% of the college group responded with "ache"; 13% with "ulcer." Ten percent of the schizophrenic group responded with "ulcer." To the word *mouth,* 20% of the college sample responded with "kiss"; 13% with "nose"; 11% with "tongue"; 11% with "lips"; and 11% with "eat." In the schizophrenic group, 19% responded with "teeth," and 10% responded with "eat."

The Kent-Rosanoff Free Association Test (1910) represents an attempt at standardizing the response of individuals to specific words.[5] The test consists of 100 stimulus words, all commonly used and believed to be neutral with respect to emotional impact.

---

5. The term **free association** refers to the technique of having subjects relate all their thoughts as they are occurring and is most frequently used in psychoanalysis; the only structure imposed is provided by the subjects themselves. The technique employed in the Kent-Rosanoff is that of *word association* (not free association), in which the examinee relates the first word that comes to mind in response to a stimulus word. The term *free association* in the test's title is, therefore, a misnomer.

The standardization sample consisted of 1,000 normal adults who varied in geographic location, educational level, occupation, age, and intellectual capacity. Frequency tables based on the responses of these 1,000 cases were developed. These tables were used to evaluate examinees' responses according to the clinical judgment of psychopathology. Psychiatric patients were found to have a lower frequency of popular responses than did the normals in the standardization group. However, as it became apparent that individuality of response may be influenced by many variables other than psychopathology (such as creativity, age, education, and socioeconomic factors), the popularity of the Kent-Rosanoff as a differential diagnostic instrument diminished. Damaging, too, is Ward et al.'s (1991) finding that scores on the Kent-Rosanoff were unrelated to other measures of psychotic thought. Still, the test endures as a standardized instrument of word association responses, and nearly ninety years after its publication, it continues to be used in experimental research and clinical practice.

Sentence completion tests   Other projective techniques that use verbal material as projective stimuli are sentence completion tests. How might *you* complete the following sentences?

I like to _____.

Someday, I will _____.

I will always remember the time _____.

I worry about _____.

I am most frightened when _____.

My feelings are hurt _____.

My mother _____.

I wish my parents _____.

Sentence completion tests may contain items that, like the items listed, tend to be quite general in nature and appropriate for administration in a wide variety of settings. Alternatively, sentence completion *stems* (the first part of the item) may be developed for use in specific types of settings (such as school or business) or for specific purposes. Sentence completion tests may be relatively atheoretical in nature or linked very closely to some theory. As an example of the latter, the Washington University Sentence Completion Test (Loevinger et al., 1970) was based on the writings of Loevinger and her colleagues in the area of ego development. Loevinger (1966; Loevinger & Ossorio, 1958) has argued that with maturity, knowledge, and awareness comes a transformation from a self-image that is essentially stereotypic and socially acceptable to one that is more personalized and realistic. The Washington University Sentence Completion Test was constructed in an attempt to assess self-concept according to Loevinger's theory. Inter-rater reliability for this test has been estimated to range from .74 to .88, internal consistency is in the high .80s, and test-retest reliability ranges from .67 to .76 or from .88 to .92, depending upon how the test is scored (Weiss et al., 1989). Some evidence for the validity of this test comes from its ability to predict social attitudes in a manner consistent with Loevinger's theory (Browning, 1987).

A number of standardized sentence completion tests are available to the clinician. One such test, the Rotter (pronounced like "rote," not "rot," with an "r" added) Incomplete Sentences Blank (Rotter & Rafferty, 1950) is the most popular of all (Lah, 1989a). Consisting of 40 incomplete sentences, the test was developed for use with populations from grade 9 through adulthood and is available in three levels: high school (grades 9 through 12), college (grades 13 through 16), and adult. Testtakers are instructed to respond to each item in a way that expresses their "real feelings." The manual suggests that responses on the test be interpreted according to several categories: family attitudes, social and sexual attitudes, general attitudes, and character traits. Each response is evaluated on a 7-point scale that ranges from "need for therapy" to "extremely good adjustment." The responses of several subjects on the Rotter, as well as some background information about the subjects, are presented in the test manual to provide illustrations of the different categories. The manual also contains normative data for a sample of 85 female and 214 male college freshmen but no norms for high school and adult populations. Reliability estimates for male and female college students were found to be .84 and .83, respectively. Estimates of inter-scorer reliability with respect to scoring categories were in the .90s. The majority of the validity studies with the Rotter were conducted in the 1950s and 1960s, and they employed "expert judge" and/or "known group" experimental designs. More recently, sociometric techniques have been used to demonstrate the validity of the Rotter as a measure of adjustment (Lah, 1989b).

In general, a sentence completion test may be a useful method for obtaining diverse information relating to an individual's interests, educational aspirations, future goals, fears, conflicts, needs, and so forth. The tests have a high degree of face validity; a child having difficulty in school, for example, would consider it appropriate to answer a list of questions or statements concerning feelings toward school. However, with this high degree of face validity comes a certain degree of transparency with respect to the objective of this type of test; for that reason, sentence completion tests are perhaps the most vulnerable of all the projective methods to faking on the part of the examinee intent on making a good—or a bad—impression.

Production of Figure Drawings

One relatively quick and easy-to-administer projective technique is the analysis of drawings. Drawings can provide the psychodiagnostician with a wealth of clinical hypotheses to be confirmed or discarded as the result of other findings (Figure 12–7). The use of drawings in clinical and research settings has extended beyond the area of personality assessment. Attempts have been made to use artistic productions as a source of information about intelligence, neurological intactness, visual-motor coordination, cognitive development, and even learning disabilities (Neale & Rosal, 1993; Oakland & Dowling, 1983). Figure drawings are an appealing source of diagnostic data, because the instructions for them can be administered individually or in a group by nonclinicians such as teachers and no materials other than a pencil and paper are required.

Figure-drawing tests The classic work on the use of figure drawings as a projective stimulus is a book entitled *Personality Projection in the Drawing of the Human Figure: A Method of Personality Investigation,* by Karen Machover (1949). Machover wrote that "the human figure drawn by an individual who is directed to 'draw a person' related intimately to the impulses, anxieties, conflicts, and compensations characteristic of that individual. In some sense, the figure drawn is the person, and the paper corresponds to the environment" (p. 35).

The instructions for administering the Draw A Person (DAP) test are quite simple; the examinee is given a pencil and an 8½-by-11-inch blank sheet of white paper and is told to "Draw a person." Inquiries on the part of the examinee concerning how the picture is to be drawn are met with statements such as "Make it the way you think it should be" or "Do the best you can." Immediately after the first drawing is completed, the

Drawing by a 25-year-old schoolteacher after becoming engaged. Previously, she had entered psychotherapy because of problems relating to men and a block against getting married. The positioning of the hands is indicative of a fear of sexual intercourse that remains.

Drawing by a male with a "Don Juan" complex—a man who pursued one affair after another. The collar pulled up to guard the neck and the excessive shading of the buttocks is suggestive of a fear of being attacked from the rear. It is possible that this man's Don Juanism is an outward defense against the lack of masculinity—even feelings of effeminacy—he may be struggling with within.

Drawing by an authoritarian and sadistic male who had been head disciplinarian of a reformatory for boys before he was suspended for child abuse. His description of this picture was that it "looked like a Prussian or a Nazi General."

The manacled hands, tied feet, exposed buttocks, and large foot drawn to the side of the drawing taken together are reflective, according to Hammer, of masochistic, homosexual, and exhibitionistic needs.

This drawing by an acutely paranoid, psychotic man was described by Hammer (1981, p. 170) as follows: "The savage mouth expresses the rage-filled projections loose within him. The emphasized eyes and ears with the eyes almost emanating magical rays reflect the visual and auditory hallucinations the patient actually experiences. The snake in the stomach points up his delusion of a reptile within, eating away and generating venom and evil."

Figure 12–7
Some Sample Interpretations Made From Figure Drawings

Source: Hammer, 1981

examinee is handed a second sheet of paper and instructed to draw a picture of a person of the opposite sex from the person just drawn.[6] Subsequently, many clinicians will ask questions concerning the drawings such as "Tell me a story about that figure," "Tell me about that boy/girl, man/lady," "What is the person doing?" "How is the person feeling?" "What is nice or not nice about the person?" Responses to these questions are used in forming various hypotheses and interpretations concerning personality functioning.

Traditionally, the drawings generated on the DAP have been formally evaluated through analysis of various characteristics of the drawing. Attention has been given to such factors as the length of time required to complete the picture, placement of the figures, the size of the figure, pencil pressure used, symmetry, line quality, shading, the presence of erasures, facial expressions, posture, clothing, and overall appearance. Various hypotheses have been generated based on these factors (Knoff, 1990a). For example, the placement of the figure on the paper is seen as representing how the individual functions within the environment; the person who draws a tiny figure at the bottom of the paper might have a poor self-concept or be insecure or depressed. The individual who draws a picture that cannot be contained on one sheet of paper and goes off the page is considered to be impulsive. Unusually light pressure suggests character disturbance (Exner, 1962). Placement of drawing on the right of the page suggests orientation to the future; to the left, orientation to the past; upper right suggests desire to suppress an unpleasant past plus excessive optimism about the future; lower left suggests depression with desire to flee into the past (Buck, 1948, 1950). Large eyes or large ears suggest suspiciousness, ideas of reference, or other paranoid characteristics (Machover, 1949; Shneidman, 1958). Unusually large breasts drawn by a male suggest unresolved oedipal problems with maternal dependence (Jolles, 1952). Long and conspicuous ties suggest sexual aggressiveness, perhaps overcompensating for fear of impotence (Machover, 1949). Button emphasis suggests dependent, infantile, inadequate personality (Halpern, 1958).

Another projective test employing figure drawings is the House-Tree-Person test (HTP) developed and popularized by Buck (1948). In this procedure, as its name implies, the subject is instructed to draw a picture of a house, a tree, and a person. In much the same way that different aspects of the human figure are presumed to be reflective of psychological functioning, the way in which an individual represents a house and a tree is considered to have symbolic significance. In this context, one might find, for example, an account of how the House-Tree-Person test has been used to identify physically abused children (Blain et al., 1981). A Draw An Animal procedure was developed based on the assumption that more projective material may be obtained through representations of animals as opposed to human figures (see Campo & Vilar, 1977, for an example of a study comparing the clinical utility of animal and human figure drawings).

Another projective drawing technique, this one thought to be of particular value in learning about the examinee in relation to her or his family, is the Kinetic Family Drawing (KFD). Derived from Hulse's (1951, 1952) Family Drawing Test, an administration of the KFD (Burns & Kaufman, 1970, 1972) begins with the examinee being given an 8½-by-11-inch piece of paper (which can be positioned any way) and a pencil with an eraser. The examinee, usually though not necessarily a child, is instructed as follows:

> Draw a picture of everyone in your family, including you, DOING something. Try to draw whole people, not cartoons or stick people. Remember, make everyone DOING something—some kind of actions. (Burns & Kaufman, 1972, p. 5)

---

6. Most people will draw a person of the same sex when instructed to simply "draw a person." It is deemed to be clinically significant if the person draws a person of the opposite sex when given these instructions. Rierdan and Koff (1981) found that in some cases, children are uncertain as to the sex of the figure drawn. They hypothesized that in such cases "the child has an indefinite or ill-defined notion of sexual identity" (p. 257).

In addition to yielding graphic representations of each family member for analysis, this procedure may yield a wealth of information in the form of examinee verbalizations while the drawing is being executed. After the examinee has completed the drawing, a rather detailed inquiry follows. The examinee is asked to identify each of the figures, talk about their relationship, and detail what they are doing in the picture and why (see Knoff & Prout, 1985). A number of formal scoring systems for the KFD are available (such as McPhee & Wegner, 1976; Meyers, 1978; Mostkoff & Lazarus, 1983). Related techniques include a school adaptation called the Kinetic School Drawing (KSD; Prout & Phillips, 1974), a test that combines aspects of the KFD and the KSD called the Kinetic Drawing System (KDS; Knoff & Prout, 1985), and the Collaborative Drawing Technique (Smith, 1985), a test that provides an occasion for family members to collaborate on the creation of a drawing—the better to "draw together."

The Draw A Person: Screening Procedure for Emotional Disturbance (DAP:SPED; Naglieri et al., 1991) features a standardized test administration and quantitative scoring system designed to screen testtakers (ages 6 through 17) for emotional problems. Based on the assumption that the rendering of unusual features in figure drawings signals emotional problems, 1 point is scored for each such feature. With age and normative information taken into account, high scores signal the need for more detailed evaluation. Validity data are presented in the test manual, but both an independent evaluation of the test (Motta et al. , 1993a, 1993b), as well as a study by two of the test's authors (McNeish & Naglieri, 1993), raised concerns about the number of misidentifications (both false positives and false negatives) that might result from the test's use as a screening tool.

Like other projective techniques, figure-drawing tests, although thought to be clinically useful, have had a rather embattled history in relation to their psychometric soundness (Cummings, 1981; Harris, 1978; Joiner & Schmidt, 1997; Joiner et al., 1996; Neale & Rosal, 1993). In general, the techniques are vulnerable with regard to the assumptions that drawings are essentially self-representations (Covetkovic, 1979; Kotkov & Goodman, 1953; Prater, 1957; Tharinger & Stark, 1990) and represent something far more than drawing ability (Sherman, 1958; Swensen, 1968; Whitmyre, 1953). Although a number of systems have been devised for scoring figure drawings (for example, Baugh & Carpenter, 1962; Hozier, 1959; Reznikoff & Tomblen, 1956), solid support for the validity of such approaches has been elusive (Watson et al., 1967). Experience and expertise do not necessarily correlate with greater clinical accuracy in drawing interpretation (Wanderer, 1967; Watson, 1967). Karen Machover (cited in Watson, 1967) herself reportedly had "grave misgivings" (p. 145) about the misuse of her test for diagnostic purposes.

To be sure, the clinical use of figure drawings has its academic defenders (Riethmiller & Handler, 1997a, 1997b). Waehler (1997), for example, cautioned that tests are not foolproof and that a person who comes across as rife with pathology in an interview might well seem benign on a psychological test. He went on to advise that figure drawings "can be considered more than 'tests'; they involve tasks that can also serve as stepping-off points for clients and examiners to discuss and clarify the picture" (p. 486).

Projective Methods in Perspective

In general critics have attacked projective methods on grounds related to the assumptions inherent in their use, the situational variables that attend their use, and the paucity of sound psychometric data to support their reliability and validity.

Assumptions Murstein (1961) examined ten assumptions of projective techniques and argued that none of them was scientifically compelling. Several assumptions concern the stimulus material. For example, it is assumed that the more ambiguous the stimuli, the more subjects reveal about their personality. However, Murstein describes the stimulus material as only one aspect of the "total stimulus situation." Environmental variables, response sets, reactions to the examiner, and related factors all contribute to response patterns. In addition, in situations where the stimulus properties of the projective material were designed to be unclear, or hazy, or are presented with uncompleted lines—thereby increasing ambiguity—projection on the part of the subject was not found to increase. Another assumption concerns the supposedly idiosyncratic nature of the responses evoked by projective stimuli. In fact, similarities in the response themes of different subjects to the same stimulus cards suggest that the stimulus material may not be as ambiguous and as amenable to projection as had been previously assumed. Some consideration of the stimulus properties and the ways in which they affect the subject's responses is therefore indicated. The assumption that projection is greater to stimulus material that is similar to the subject (in physical appearance, gender, occupation, and so on) has also been found to be questionable.

Other assumptions questioned by Murstein concern how responses on projective tests are interpreted. These include the assumption that every response provides meaning for personality analysis; that a relationship exists between the strength of a need and its manifestation on projective instruments; that subjects are unaware of what they are disclosing about themselves; that a projective protocol reflects sufficient data concerning personality functioning to formulate judgments; and, finally, that there is a parallel between behavior obtained on a projective instrument and behavior displayed in social situations. It is Murstein's contention that these "cherished beliefs have been accepted by some clinical psychologists without the support of sufficient research validation" (p. 343).

Another assumption basic to projective testing is that there is such a thing as an "unconscious." Though the term *unconscious* is used by many psychologists and laypeople as well, some academicians have questioned whether in fact the unconscious exists in the same way that the liver exists. The scientific studies typically cited to support the existence of the unconscious (or perhaps more accurately, the efficacy of the construct "unconscious") have used a very wide array of methodologies—see, for example, Diven (1937), Erdelyi (1974; Erdelyi & Goldberg, 1979; Erdelyi & Kleinbard, 1978), Greenspoon (1955), McGinnies (1949), and Razran (1961). The conclusions from each of these types of studies are subject to alternative explanations. Additionally, conclusions about the existence of the unconscious based on experimental testing of predictions derived from hypnotic phenomena, from signal detection theory, and from specific personality theories have been, at least, inconclusive (Brody, 1972).

Situational variables Proponents of projective techniques have claimed that such tests are capable of illuminating the recesses of the mind in a manner similar to the way that X-rays illuminate the body. Frank (1939) conceptualized projective tests as tapping personality patterns without disturbing the pattern being tapped. If that were true, then variables related to the test situation should have no effect on the data obtained. However, as we have seen, the variable of the examiner's being present or absent can significantly affect the responses of experimental subjects. TAT stories written in private are likely to be less guarded, less optimistic, and more affectively involved than those written in the presence of the examiner (Bernstein, 1956). The age of the examiner is likely to affect projective protocols (Mussen & Scodel, 1955), as are the specific instructions (Henry & Rotter, 1956) and the subtle reinforcement cues provided by the examiner (Wickes, 1956).

Masling (1960) reviewed the literature on the influence of situational and interpersonal variables in projective testing and concluded that there was strong evidence for the role of situational and interpersonal influences in projection. Moreover, Masling argued that it was not only the subjects who utilized every available cue in the testing situation (for example, the room or the actions and appearance of the examiner) but also the examiners, who capitalized on cues over and above their training and orientation. Examiners appeared to interpret projective data with regard to their own needs and expectations, their own subjective feelings about the person being tested, and their own constructions regarding the total test situation. In a later study, Masling (1965) experimentally demonstrated that Rorschach examiners are capable of unwittingly eliciting the responses they expect through postural, gestural, and facial cues.

Even in nonprojective situations such as taking a psychiatric history or taking an objective test, the effect of the clinician's training (Chapman & Chapman, 1967; Fitzgibbons & Shearn, 1972) and role perspective (Snyder et al., 1976), the patient's social class (Hollingshead & Redlich, 1958; Lee, 1968; Routh & King, 1972) and motivation to manage a desired impression (Edwards & Walsh, 1964; Wilcox & Krasnoff, 1967) may influence ratings of pathology (Langer & Abelson, 1974) as well as attribution of the locus of the problem (Batson, 1975). These and other variables are given wider latitude in the projective test situation in which the examiner may be at liberty to choose not only the test and extra-test data on which interpretation will be focused, but also the scoring system that will be used to arrive at that interpretation; as we have noted, for many of the projective methods, a number of different alternative scoring systems are available.

Psychometric considerations   The psychometric soundness of many widely used projective instruments has yet to be demonstrated. Kinslinger (1966) has cited the failure of researchers to cross-validate findings as a source of spurious validity estimates for projective techniques. Others (such as Cronbach, 1949; Vernon, 1964; Zubin et al., 1965) have called attention to variables such as uncontrolled variations in protocol length, inappropriate subject samples, inadequate control groups, and poor external criteria as factors contributing to spuriously increased ratings of validity. Recall that there are very real methodological difficulties in demonstrating the psychometric soundness of *any* instrument, let alone projective instruments where test-retest or split-half methods may be inappropriate. We must also mention the difficulty of designing reliability and validity studies that effectively rule out, limit, or statistically take into account the unique situational variables (such as extra-test cues) that attend the administration of such tests.

The debate between academicians who argue that projective tests are not technically sound instruments and clinicians who find such tests useful has been raging ever since projectives came into widespread use. Frank (1939) responded to those who would reject projective methods because of their lack of technical rigor:

> These leads to the study of personality have been rejected by many psychologists because they do not meet psychometric requirements for validity and reliability, but they are being employed in association with clinical and other studies of personality where they are finding increasing validation in the consistency of results for the same subject when independently assayed by each of these procedures. . . .
>
> If we face the problem of personality, in its full complexity, as an active dynamic process to be studied as a *process* rather than as entity or aggregate of traits, factors, or as static organization, then these projective methods offer many advantages for obtaining data on the process of organizing experience which is peculiar to each personality and has a life career. (Frank, 1939, p. 408) [emphasis in the original]

Behavioral Assessment Methods

Traits, states, motives, needs, drives, defenses, and related psychological constructs have no tangible existence; they are constructs whose existence must be inferred from behavior. In the traditional approach to clinical assessment, tests as well as other tools are employed to gather data; from these data, diagnoses and inferences are made concerning the existence and strength of psychological constructs. The traditional approach to assessment might therefore be labeled a "sign" approach, because test responses are deemed to be signs or clues to underlying personality or ability. In contrast to this traditional approach is an alternative philosophy of assessment that may be termed the "sample" approach. This approach focuses on the behavior itself; emitted behavior is not viewed as a sign of something but, rather, as a sample to be interpreted in its own right. The emphasis in **behavioral assessment** is on "what a person *does* in situations rather than on inferences about what attributes he *has* more globally" (Mischel, 1968, p. 10). Predicting what a person will do is thought to entail an understanding of the assessee with respect to both antecedent conditions (Smith & Iwata, 1997) and consequences for a particular situation. Upon close scrutiny, however, the trait concept is still present in many behavioral measures, though more narrowly defined and more closely linked to specific situations (Zuckerman, 1979).

To illustrate behavioral observation as an assessment strategy, consider the plight of the single female client who presents herself at the university counseling center complaining that even though all her friends tell her how attractive she is, she is experiencing great difficulty in meeting men—so much so that she doesn't even want to try anymore. A counselor confronted with such a client might, among other things, (1) interview the client with respect to this problem, (2) administer an appropriate test to the client, (3) ask the client to keep detailed diaries of her thoughts and behaviors with respect to her efforts to meet men, and/or (4) accompany the client to a singles bar and observe her behavior. The latter two strategies come under the heading of behavioral observation; in one situation, the counselor is doing the actual observing and, in another, it is the client herself.

The administration of a psychological test or test battery to a client such as this single woman might yield signs that then could be inferred to relate to the problem. For example, if a number of the client's TAT stories involved themes of demeaning, hostile, or otherwise unsatisfactory heterosexual encounters as a result of venturing out into the street, the counselor might make an interpretation at a deeper or second level of inference: The client's expressed fear of going outdoors (and ultimately her fear of meeting men) might in some way be related to an unconscious fear of promiscuity—a fear of becoming a streetwalker.

In contrast to the sign approach, the clinician employing the sample or behavioral approach to assessment might examine the behavioral diary that the client kept with respect to her problem and design an appropriate therapy program on the basis of those records. Thus, for example, the antecedent conditions under which the client would feel most distraught and unmotivated to do anything about the problem might be delineated and worked on in counseling sessions.

An advantage of the sign as opposed to the sample approach is that in the hands of a skillful, perceptive clinician, the client might be put in touch with feelings that even she was not really aware of before the assessment. The client may have been consciously (or unconsciously) avoiding certain thoughts and images (those attendant on the expression of her sexuality, for example), and this inability to deal with those thoughts and images may indeed have been a factor contributing to her ambivalence with respect to meeting men.

Behavioral assessors seldom make such deeper level inferences; and if sexuality is not raised as an area of difficulty by the client (in an interview, on a checklist, or by some other behavioral assessment technique), this problem area may well be ignored or given short shrift. The behavioral assessor does, however, tend to be more comprehensive and systematic in his or her approach to assessing the breadth and magnitude of the client's problem. Instead of searching for signs in Rorschach or other test protocols, the behaviorally oriented counselor or clinician might simply ask such a client a question like "What are some of the reasons you think you are unable to meet men?" and then take it from there. By obtaining a complete self-report either verbally or through a checklist and by obtaining behavioral observation data, the behaviorally oriented assessor will discover specific areas that need to be focused on in therapy. You can see that the behavioral approach does not require as much clinical creativity as the sign approach; perhaps for that reason, it is generally considered to be less of an art and more of a science.

Unlike traditional psychological assessors, behaviorally oriented clinicians have characteristically found little use for traditional psychological tests and procedures in their work. This division in the field of clinical psychology was noted as early as 1967 by Greenspoon and Gersten, who observed that "psychologists in the practicum agencies contend that tests are the 'bread and butter' of the clinical psychologist and the university personnel contend that if such is the case the clinical psychologist is on an ersatz diet" (p. 849). In their article entitled "A New Look at Psychological Testing: Psychological Testing from the Standpoint of a Behaviorist," they argued that "psychological tests should be able to provide the behavior therapist with information that should be of value in doing behavior therapy. This contention is based on the assumption that the behavior on any psychological test should be lawful" (Greenspoon & Gersten, 1967, p. 849). Accordingly, psychological tests could be useful, for example, in helping the behavior therapist to identify the kinds of contingent stimuli that would be most effective with a given patient. For example, patients with high percentages of color or color/form responses on the Rorschach and with IQs in excess of 90 might be most responsive to positive verbal contingencies (such as "good," "excellent"), whereas patients with high percentages of movement or vista (three-dimensional) responses and IQs in excess of 90 might be most responsive to negative verbal contingencies ("no," "wrong"). Although the ideas expressed by Greenspoon and Gersten seem not to have been greeted with a rush of experimental enthusiasm—perhaps because there exist more direct ways to assess responsiveness to various contingencies—their article did represent an innovative attempt to narrow a widening schism in the field of clinical assessment.

Differences between traditional and behavioral approaches to assessment have to do with varying assumptions about the nature of personality and the causes of behavior. The data from traditional assessment are used primarily to describe, classify, or diagnose, whereas the data from a behavioral assessment are typically more directly related to the formulation of a specific treatment program. Some of the other differences between the two approaches are summarized in Table 12–3.

The Who, What, When, Where, and How of It

The name says it all; *behavior* is the focus of assessment in behavioral assessment—not traits, states, or other constructs presumed to be present in various strengths, just behavior. This will become clear as we survey the who, what, when, where, and how of behavioral assessment.

Who is assessed? Most typically, only one person at a time. Regardless of whether the assessment is for research, clinical, or other purposes, the hallmark of behavioral assessment is intensive study of individuals—this is in contrast to mass testing of groups of people to obtain normative data with respect to some hypothesized trait or state. *Who* is the assessor? Depending on the particular assessment, the assessor may be a highly qualified professional, or a technician/assistant trained to conduct a particular assessment (such as recording the number of times young Johnny leaves his seat during writing class).

Table 12–3
Differences Between Behavioral and Traditional Approaches to Psychological Assessment

	Behavioral	Traditional
Assumptions		
Conception of personality	Personality constructs mainly employed to summarize specific behavior patterns, if at all	Personality as a reflection of enduring, underlying states or traits
Causes of behavior	Maintaining conditions sought in current environment	Intrapsychic or within the individual
Implications		
Role of behavior	Important as a sample of person's repertoire in specific situation	Behavior assumes importance only insofar as it indexes underlying causes
Role of history	Relatively unimportant, except, for example, to provide a retrospective baseline	Crucial in that present conditions seen as a product of the past
Consistency of behavior	Behavior thought to be specific to the situation	Behavior expected to be consistent across time and settings
Uses of data	To describe target behaviors and maintaining conditions	To describe personality functioning and etiology
	To select the appropriate treatment	To diagnose or classify
	To evaluate and revise treatment	To make prognosis; to predict
Other characteristics		
Level of inferences	Low	Medium to high
Comparisons	More emphasis on intraindividual or idiographic	More emphasis on interindividual or nomothetic
Methods of assessment	More emphasis on direct methods (e.g., observations of behavior in natural environment)	More emphasis on indirect methods (e.g., interviews and self-report)
Timing of assessment	More ongoing; prior, during, and after treatment	Pre- and perhaps posttreatment, or strictly to diagnose
Scope of assessment	Specific measures and of more variables (e.g., of target behaviors in various situations, of side effects, context, strengths as well as deficiencies)	More global measures (e.g., of cure, or improvement) but only of the individual

Source: Hartmann, Roper, and Bradford (1979)

What is measured in behavioral assessment? Not surprisingly, the behavior or behaviors targeted for assessment will vary as a function of the objectives of the assessment. Whatever behavior or behaviors are being measured, a careful definition of what constitutes a targeted behavior must be drawn. And for the purposes of assessment, the targeted behavior must be measurable—quantifiable in some way. Examples of such measurable behaviors can range from the number of seconds Johnny spends out of his seat during writing class to the number of degrees Celsius body temperature is altered—the latter being an observable event that may be considered behavior in its broadest sense. Note that descriptions of targeted behaviors in behavioral assessment typically begin with the phrase "the number of. . . ."

When is an assessment of behavior made? Beyond fairly general answers to this question (such as "during the school day except at lunch"), behavioral assessors may employ any of various schedules or formats of assessment. For example, one schedule of assessment is referred to as "frequency," or "event recording." Each time the targeted behavior occurs, it is recorded. Another schedule of assessment is referred to as "interval recording." Assessment according to this schedule occurs only during predefined intervals of time (for example, every other minute, every 48 hours, every third week). Beyond merely tallying the number of times a particular behavior is emitted, the assessor may also maintain a record of the intensity of the behavior as gauged by observable and quantifiable events such as the *duration* of the behavior, stated in number of seconds, minutes, hours, days, weeks, months, or years, or some ratio or percentage of time that the behavior occurs during a specified interval of time.

Where does the assessment take place? Unlike the administration of psychological tests, which are most likely to be administered in a psychologist's office or in some institutional setting such as a hospital or a school, behavioral assessment may take place virtually anywhere—preferably in the environment where the targeted behavior is most likely to occur naturally. For example, a behavioral assessor studying the obsessive-compulsive habits of a patient might wish to visit the patient at home to see firsthand the variety and intensity of the compulsive behavior the patient exhibits (for example, whether the patient checks the oven for having left the gas on and, if so, how many times per hour).

How is behavioral assessment conducted? The answer to this question will vary, of course, according to the purpose of the assessment. In some situations, the only special equipment required will be a trained observer with pad and pencil. In other types of situations, highly sophisticated recording equipment may be necessary. As an example of the latter situation, imagine that you are a NASA psychologist studying the psychological and behavioral effects of space travel on astronauts. What types of behavioral measures might you employ, and what special equipment would you need—or design—to obtain those measures?

Another "how" question relates to how data from behavioral assessment should be analyzed, and here there are essentially two camps. One camp may be characterized as accepting traditional psychometric assumptions with regard to behavioral assessment, including those assumptions related to the measurement of reliability (Russo et al., 1980) and validity (Haynes et al., 1979, 1981). Representative of this position are statements, such as that made by Bellack and Hersen (1988), that "the reliability, validity, and utility of any procedure should be paramount, regardless of its behavioral or nonbehavioral development" (p. 614).

Cone (1977) championed the traditionalist approach to behavioral assessment in an article entitled "The Relevance of Reliability and Validity for Behavioral Assessment." However, as the years passed, Cone (1986, 1987) became a leading proponent of an alternative position, one in which traditional psychometric standards are rejected as inappropriate yardsticks for behavioral assessment. Cone (1981) wrote, for example, that "a truly behavioral view of assessment is based on an approach to the study of behavior so radically different from the customary individual differences model that a correspondingly different approach must be taken in evaluating the adequacy of behavioral assessment procedures" (p. 51). Earlier, Nelson et al. (1977) had questioned the utility of traditional approaches to test reliability in behavioral assessment by noting that "the assessment tool may be precise, but the behavior being measured may have changed" (p. 428). Based on the conceptualization of each behavioral assessment as an experiment unto itself, Dickson (1975) wrote, "If one assumes that each target for assessment represents a single experiment, then what is needed is the scientific method of experimentation and research, rather than a formalized schedule for assessment. . . . Within this framework, each situation is seen as unique, and the reliability of the approach is not a function of standardization techniques . . . but rather is a function of following the experimental method in evaluation" (pp. 376–377).

The extent to which traditional psychometric standards are deemed applicable to behavioral assessment remains controversial, although the antitraditionalists would seem to be in the minority. As you learn more about various approaches to behavioral assessment, think about these types of issues and cultivate your own opinion regarding which of the two positions you personally find to be most appealing.

Approaches to Behavioral Assessment

Behavioral assessment may be accomplished through various means including behavioral observation and behavior rating scales, analogue studies, self-monitoring, and situational performance methods. Let's briefly take a closer look at each of these, as well as related methods.

Behavioral observation and rating scales A child psychologist observes a client in a playroom through a one-way mirror; a family therapist views a videotape of a troubled family attempting to resolve a conflict; a psychologist's assistant accompanies a patient lacking in interpersonal skills to a disco for the purpose of observing her; a school psychologist observes a child interacting with peers in the school cafeteria. These are all examples of the use of an assessment technique termed **behavioral observation.** As its name implies, this technique entails watching the activities of targeted clients or research subjects and, typically, maintaining some kind of record of those activities. Researchers, clinicians, or counselors may themselves serve as observers, or they may designate trained assistants or other people (such as parents, siblings, teachers, and supervisors) to be the observers. Even the observed person herself or himself can be the behavior observer, as in the case of the dieter maintaining a diary of food intake and emotional feelings—although in that instance, the term *self-observation* would be more appropriate than behavioral observation. In some instances, behavioral observation entails mechanical means, such as a videorecording of an event; this relieves the clinician, the researcher, or any other observer of the necessity to be physically present at the time the behavior occurs and allows him or her to view its occurrence when it is convenient to do so. Regardless of who actually does the observing, and whether the observation is accomplished through a live or a recorded viewing, factors noted in behavioral observation will typically include a notation of the presence or absence of specific, targeted behaviors, behavioral excesses, behavioral deficits, behavioral assets, and the situational antecedents and consequences of the emitted behaviors. Of course, because the people doing the observing and rating are human themselves, behavioral observation isn't always as cut-and-dried as it may appear at first blush (see *Everyday Psychometrics*).

Behavioral observation may take many forms. The observer may, in the tradition of the naturalist, record a running narrative of events, using tools such as pencil and paper, a video, film, or still camera, or a cassette recorder. Another form of behavioral observation employs what is called a "behavior rating scale"—a preprinted sheet on which the observer notes the presence or intensity of targeted behaviors, usually by checking boxes or by filling in coded terms. For example, if the focus of interest was whether an institutionalized patient took out the garbage on a daily basis, an Emptying Garbage behavioral scale or checklist (like the one reprinted in Cohen, 2002) might be employed. Sometimes the user of a behavior rating form writes in coded descriptions of various behaviors; the code is preferable to a running narrative, because it takes far less time to enter the data and frees the observer familiar with the code to enter data relating to any of hundreds of possible behaviors, not just the ones printed on the sheets. For example, a number of coding systems for observing the behavior of couples and families are available. Two such systems are the Marital Interaction Coding System (Weiss & Summers, 1983) and the Couples Interaction Scoring System (Notarius & Markman, 1981). In an attempt to facilitate the work of the observer, Filsinger (1983) describes the use of a handheld data-entry device for the observer to use while entering coded observations made from a combination of the Marital Interaction Coding System, the Couples Interaction Scoring System, and two other systems.

Behavior rating scales and systems, as approaches to behavioral assessment in general, may be categorized in different ways. A categorization of "direct" to "indirect" has to do with the setting in which the observed behavior occurs, and how closely that setting approximates the setting in which the behavior naturally occurs. The more natural the setting, the more direct the measure; the more removed from the natural setting, the

Confessions of a Behavior Rater

So often in discussions of behavioral assessment, the focus is placed squarely on the individual being evaluated. Only infrequently, if ever, is reference made to the thoughts and feelings of the person who has responsibility for evaluating the behavior of another person. What follows are the hypothetical thoughts of one behavior rater. We say hypothetical because these ideas are not really based on the thinking of one person but on a compilation of thoughts from many people responsible for conducting behavioral evaluations.

The behavior raters interviewed for this feature were all on the staff at a community-based, inpatient/outpatient facility in Brewster, New York. An objective of this facility is to prepare its adolescent and adult members for a constructive, independent life. Members live in residences with varying degrees of supervision, and their behavior is monitored on a 24-hour basis. Each day, members are issued an eight-page behavior rating sheet referred to as a "CDR" (clinical data recorder), which is circulated to supervising staff for rating through the course of the day. The staff records behavioral information for variables such as activities, social skills, support needed, and dysfunctional behavior.

On the basis of behavioral data, certain medical or other types of interventions may be recommended. Because behavioral monitoring is daily and consistent, changes in patient behavior as a function of medication, activities, or other variables are quickly noted and intervention strategies are adjusted. In short, the behavioral data may significantly affect the course of a patient's institutional stay—everything from amount of daily supervision, to privileges, to date of

discharge will be influenced by the behavioral data. Both patients and staff are aware of this fact of institutional life. Therefore, both patients and staff take the completion of the CDR very seriously. With that as background, here are some private thoughts of a behavior rater:

I record behavioral data in the presence of patients, and the patients are usually keenly aware of what I am doing. After I am through coding patients' CDRs for the time they are with me, other staff members will code them with respect to the time they spend with the patient. And so it goes. It is as if each patient is keeping a detailed diary of their life; only, it is we, the staff, who are keeping that diary for them.

Sometimes, especially for new staff, it feels odd to be rating the behavior of fellow human beings. One morning, perhaps out of empathy for a patient, I tossed a blank CDR to a patient and jokingly offered to let him rate my behavior. By dinner, long after I had forgotten that incident in the morning, I realized the patient was coding me for poor table manners. Outwardly, I laughed. Inwardly, I was really a bit offended. Subsequently, I told a joke to the assembled company that in retrospect probably was not in the best of taste. The patient coded me for being socially offensive. Now, I was genuinely becoming self-conscious. Later that evening, we drove to a local video store to return a tape we had rented, and the patient coded me for reckless driving. My discomfort level rose to the point that I thought it was time to end the joke. In retrospect, I had experienced firsthand the self-consciousness and discomfort some of our patients had experienced as they

---

less direct the measure (Shapiro & Skinner, 1990). According to this categorization, assessing a client's reactions in a real disco would provide a direct measure, whereas assessment of behavior in a simulated or videotaped evening at a dance would provide an indirect behavioral measure. Shapiro and Skinner (1990) also draw a distinction between "broad-band" instruments that seek to measure a wide variety of behaviors, and "narrow-band" instruments that may focus on behaviors related to single, specific constructs such as hyperactivity, shyness, or depression.

Analogue studies The behavioral approach to clinical assessment and treatment has been likened to the researcher's approach to experimentation; the behavioral assessor proceeds in many ways like a researcher, with the client's problem being the dependent variable and the factor(s) responsible for causing or maintaining the problem behavior being the independent variable(s). Behavioral assessors typically use the phrase **functional analysis** of behavior to convey the process of identifying the dependent and in-had their every move monitored on a daily basis by staff members.

Even though patients are not always comfortable having their behavior rated—and indeed many patients have outbursts with staff members that are in one way or another related to the rating system—it is also true that the system seems to work. Sometimes, self-consciousness is what is needed for people to get better. Here, I think of Sandy, a bright young man who gradually became fascinated by the CDR, and soon spent much of the day asking staff members various questions about it. Before long, Sandy asked if he could be allowed to code his own CDR. No one had ever asked to do that before, and a staff meeting was held to mull over the consequences of such an action. As an experiment, it was decided that this patient would be allowed to code his own CDR. The experiment paid off. Sandy's self-coding kept him relatively "on track" with regard to his behavioral goals, and he found himself trying even harder to get better as he showed signs of improvement. Upon discharge, Sandy said he would miss tracking his progress with the CDR.

Instruments such as the CDR can and probably have been used as weapons or rewards by staff. Staff may threaten patients with a poor behavioral evaluation. Overly negative evaluations in response to dysfunctional behavior that is particularly upsetting to the staff is also an ever-present possibility. Yet all the time you are keenly aware that the system works best when staff codes patients' behavior consistently and fairly.

A member receives training in kitchen skills for independent living as a staff member monitors behavior on the CDR.

dependent variables with respect to the presenting problem. However, just as it is true that experimenters must frequently employ independent and dependent variables that imitate how those variables occur in the real world, so behavioral assessors must, too. This type of study, where a variable or two are similar or analogous to the real variable the investigator wishes to examine, is termed an **analogue study.** The term "analogue study" is very broad in nature. It can be used, for example, to describe research conducted with white rats, when the experimenter really wishes to learn about humans. It can be used to describe research conducted with introductory psychology students, when the experimenter really wishes to learn about business people. It can be used to describe research on aggression with aggression defined as the laboratory administration of electric shock, when the experimenter really wishes to learn about real-world aggression outside the laboratory.

More specific than the term analogue study is **analogue behavioral observation,** which, after Haynes (2001a), may be defined as the observation of a person or persons in an environment that is designed to increase the chance that the assessor can observe targeted behaviors and interactions. The person or persons in this definition may be clients (including individual children and adults, families, or couples), or research subjects (including students, co-workers, or any other research sample). The targeted behavior, of course, depends on the objective of the research. For a client who avoids hiking because of a fear of snakes, the behavior targeted for assessment (and change) is the fear reaction to snakes, most typically elicited while hiking. This behavior may be assessed (and treated) in analogue fashion within the confines of a clinician's office using photos of snakes, videos of snakes, live snakes that are caged, and live snakes that are uncaged. A variety of environments designed to increase the chances that the assessor can observe the targeted behavior have been employed (see for example, Heyman, 2001; Mori & Armendariz, 2001; Norton & Hope, 2001; and Roberts, 2001). Situational performance measures and role-play measures, both discussed in more detail below, may also be thought of as analogue approaches to assessment.

Haynes (2001b) reviewed several principles of psychometric evaluation as applied to analogue behavioral observation and cautioned that researchers who develop analogue behavioral observation instruments, and clinicians who use them, must be cognizant of the judgments to be based on measures from such instruments, and of related issues having to do with the validity of the data derived.

Self-monitoring Self-monitoring may be defined as the act of systematically observing and recording aspects of one's own behavior and/or events related to that behavior. Self-monitoring is different from self-report. As noted by Cone (1999, p. 411), self-monitoring "relies on observations of *the* behavior of clinical interest . . . at the *time* . . . and *place* . . . of its actual occurrence. In contrast, self-report uses stand-ins or surrogates (verbal descriptions, reports) of the behavior of interest that are obtained at a time and place different from the time and place of the behavior's actual occurrence" (emphasis in the original). Self-monitoring may be used to record specific thoughts, feelings, or behaviors. The utility of self-monitoring depends in large part on the competence, diligence, and motivation of the assessee, although a number of ingenious methods have been devised to help assist in the process or assure compliance (Barton et al., 1999; Bornstein et al., 1986; Wilson & Vitousek, 1999). For example, palmtop computers have been programmed to beep as a cue to observe and record behavior (Shiffman et al., 1997).

Self-monitoring is both a tool of assessment and a tool of intervention. In some instances, the very act of engaging in self-monitoring (as in the self-monitoring of smoking, eating, anxiety, and panic) may be therapeutic.

Practical issues that must be considered in self-monitoring include the methodology employed, the targeting of specific thoughts, feelings, or behaviors, the sampling procedures put in place, the actual self-monitoring devices and procedures, and the training and preparation (Foster et al., 1999). There are also psychometric issues to be considered, including those related to the reliability and validity of the data obtained (Jackson, 1999). One potential problem with self-monitoring as well as other methods of behavioral assessment is the problem of reactivity. **Reactivity** refers to the possible changes in an assessee's behavior, thinking, or performance that may arise in response to being observed, assessed, or evaluated. So, for example, if you are on a weight-loss program and self-monitoring your food intake, you may be more inclined to forgo the cheesecake than to consume it. Education, training, and adequate preparation are some of the tools used to counter the effects of reactivity in self-monitoring. In addition, post-self-monitoring interviews on the effects of reactivity can provide additional insights with regard to the emission of the targeted thoughts or behaviors.

Situational performance measures   If you have ever applied for a part-time secretarial job and been required to take a typing test, you have had firsthand experience with what we are calling "situational performance measures." Broadly stated, a **situational performance measure** is a procedure that allows for observation and evaluation of an individual under a standard set of circumstances. A situational performance measure typically involves performance of some specific task under actual or simulated conditions. The road test you took to obtain your driver's license was a situational performance measure that entailed an evaluation of your driving skills in a real car, on a real road, in real traffic. On the other hand, situational performance measures used to assess the skills of prospective astronauts are done in rocket simulators in scientific laboratories that are firmly planted on Mother Earth.

The range of variables that may be focused on in situational performance measures is virtually limitless. In addition to evaluating skills such as typing and driving, situational performance measures have been used to assess a wide variety of variables related to personality. For example, the responses of prospective astronauts placed in simulated space conditions are closely observed with respect to such variables as tolerance for weightlessness; irritability; ability to eat, sleep, and exercise routine duties; and ability to get along with others under such conditions for a prolonged time. What all the situational performance measures have in common is that the construct they measure is thought to be more accurately assessed by examining behavior directly than by asking subjects to describe their behavior. In some cases, subjects may be motivated to misrepresent themselves, as when asked about moral behavior. In other situations, subjects may simply not know how they will respond under particular circumstances, as in a stress test.

The leaderless group is a situational assessment procedure in which the subjects being evaluated are usually aware that their behavior is being observed or recorded. The procedure involves organizing several people into a group for the purpose of carrying out a specific task. Although the group knows the objectives of the exercises, no one is placed in the position of leadership or authority. In addition, purposely vague instructions are provided for the group. The group determines how it will accomplish the task and who will be responsible for what duties. An observer monitors the group's progress and evaluates both the group's functioning as a whole and the way in which each individual member functions within the group. The leaderless-group situation provides an opportunity to observe the degree of cooperation exhibited by each individual group member and the extent to which each individual is able to function as part of a team.

The leaderless-group technique has been employed in military and industrial settings. Its use in the military developed out of attempts by the U.S. Office of Strategic Services (OSS, 1948) to assess such characteristics as cooperation, leadership, and initiative. The procedure was designed to aid in the establishment of cohesive military units—cockpit crews, tank crews, and so forth—in which members would work together well and each could make a significant contribution. Assessees might, for example, be assigned the task of transporting equipment over some obstacle-ridden terrain. The way in which the group as a group proceeded through the assignment, as well as how each individual member of the group contributed—or failed to contribute—to the group's progress would be carefully noted. From such a sample of behavior, information about an individual's leadership ability, initiative, organization and planning abilities, communication skills, social skills, and related skills and abilities could be obtained.

The use of the leaderless-group procedure in industrial settings has similarly been useful in identifying leaders—persons with managerial or executive potential. Less commonly, the technique has also been employed to identify those combinations of personnel that would have a high probability of functioning well together. Manz and Sims (1984) have called attention to a puzzling paradox that exists in an era when more and more organizations are adopting the self-managed work-group approach: How does one lead those who are supposed to lead themselves? On the basis of their research with 320 employees in a production plant that used a self-managed work system, Manz and Sims identified a unique type of leader required in such a work system—"the unleader." These authors described the effective unleader as primarily a facilitator who is able to balance both a hands-off and a directive management style in a variety of situations.

Situational stress tests are measures designed to assess how an individual will react to a specific type of anxiety, frustration, or stress. Most situational stress tests present a task that must be completed, an activity that must be carried out, or a problem that must be solved. Frustrating obstacles, such as a helper who hinders more than helps, are typically an essential part of the exercise. The way in which the examinee responds to this situation provides some indication of the way the examinee tends to respond to frustration in stressful situations.

Situational stress tests were frequently employed by the U.S. Office of Strategic Services (OSS, 1948) during the Second World War in efforts to select candidates for military intelligence and other positions. This technique is still widely used by military organizations for selection as well as research purposes. Tziner and Eden (1985) described the use of such techniques by the Israeli military to determine the ideal composition of a crew.

Role play   The technique of **role play,** or acting an improvised or partially improvised part in a simulated situation, can be used in teaching and in therapy. Police departments, for example, routinely prepare rookies for emergencies by having them play roles—such as that of an officer confronted by a criminal holding a hostage at gunpoint. A therapist might use role play to help a feuding couple avoid harmful shouting matches and learn more effective methods of conflict resolution. Role play may also be used as an assessment technique. For example, part of the prospective police officer's final exam may be successful performance of role-playing tasks. And a couple's successful resolution of role-played issues may be one of a therapist's criteria for terminating therapy.

A large and growing literature exists on role play as a method of assessment (see, for example, Becker & Heimberg, 1988; Bellack, 1983; Bellack et al., 1979; Helzel & Rice, 1985; Higgins et al., 1979; Wessberg et al., 1979). In general, role play can provide a relatively inexpensive and highly adaptable means for assessing various behavior potentials; we say "potentials" because of the uncertainty that role-played behavior will be elicited in a naturalistic situation (Kern et al., 1983; Kolotkin & Wielkiewicz, 1984). Bellack et al. (1990) employed role play for both evaluative and instructional purposes with psychiatric inpatients who were being prepared for independent living. While discussing the benefits of role play in assessing patients' readiness to return to the community, these authors acknowledged that "the ultimate validity criterion for any laboratory- or clinic-based assessment is unobtrusive observation of the target behavior in the community" (p. 253).

Psychophysiological methods   The search for clues to understanding and predicting human behavior has led researchers to the study of physiological indices (such as heart rate, blood pressure, and voice waves) known to be influenced by psychological factors—hence the term **psychophysiological** to describe these variables as well as the methods used to study them. Although these methods are arguably "behavioral" in nature, they do tend to be associated with behaviorally oriented clinicians and researchers (Haynes et al., 1989); consequently, we will cover them here.

One psychophysiological assessment method is based on assessees' monitoring of their own biological processes by means of instrumentation. Such instrumentation is generically referred to as "biofeedback" equipment, as is the physiological data obtained from such measurements. Measurements of variables such as heart rate, respiration rate, blood pressure, electrical resistance of the skin, brain waves, and voice waves may be "fed back" to the assessee via visual displays, such as lights and scales, or auditory stimuli, such as bells and buzzers (Schwitzgebel & Rugh, 1975). The use of biofeedback in humans was inspired by reports that animals given rewards (and hence feedback) for the emission of certain involuntary responses (such as heart rate) could successfully modify those responses (Miller, 1969). Early experimentation with humans demonstrated a capacity to produce certain types of brain waves on command (Kamiya, 1962, 1968). Since that time, biofeedback has been used in a wide range of therapeutic and assessment-related applications (Blanchard & Young, 1974; French et al., 1997; Hazlett et al., 1997; Hermann et al., 1997; Omizo & Williams, 1981; Sarnoff, 1982; Satinsky & Frerotte, 1981; Zhang et al., 1997).

The **plethysmograph** is an instrument that records changes in the volume of a part of the body arising from variations in blood supply. Investigators have been interested in determining any changes that occur in flow of blood as a result of personality factors. Kelly (1966) found significant differences in the blood supply of normal, anxiety-ridden, and psychoneurotic groups (the anxiety group having the highest mean) by using a plethysmograph to measure blood supply in the forearm. In another investigation, changes in finger volume by use of a plethysmograph were compared with results on the "emotional-stability" factor of the Bell Adjustment Inventory (Theron, 1948; Van der Merwe & Theron, 1947); those identified as emotionally labile were found to exhibit greater rates of change in finger volume.

A **penile plethysmograph** is designed to measure changes in penis volume as a function of sexual arousal. Freund (1963) developed one such instrument for use in his research concerning differences in penile volume of homosexual and heterosexual males when shown slides of male nudes. On the basis of summed reactions, Freund was able to correctly identify 48 of the 58 homosexuals who participated in the study, and all of the 65 heterosexual subjects. This type of device in variously modified forms, and the subsequent collection of what is referred to as "phallometric" data, have unique value in the assessment and treatment of male sexual offenders (Abel et al., 1981; Barbaree & Marshall, 1989; Blader & Marshall, 1984; Earls & Marshall, 1983; Earls et al., 1987; Farrall & Card, 1988; Freund & Blanchard, 1989; Freund et al., 1965; Hall et al., 1988; Laws & Osborne, 1983; Marshall et al., 1988; Quinsey et al., 1975). In one such type of application, the offender—a rapist, a child molester, an exhibitionist, or some other sexual offender— is exposed to visual and/or auditory stimuli depicting scenes of normal and deviant behavior while penile tumescence is simultaneously gauged (see, for example, Malcolm et al., 1985). In one study with rapists, the subjects demonstrated more sexual arousal to descriptions of rape and less arousal to consenting-sex stories than did control subjects (Quinsey et al., 1984). Offenders who continue to deny deviant sexual object choices may be confronted with the findings from such studies as a means of compelling them to speak more openly about their thoughts and behavior (Abel et al., 1986).

Researchers in this area have cautioned that it may be misleading to rely exclusively on phallometric data for the purposes of understanding sexual preferences; such data must ideally be complemented by other data, such as interviews (Haywood et al., 1990). Legal and ethical issues that attend the use of plethysmography have been discussed by Travin et al. (1988).

Another involuntary physiological response from which some researchers have sought to make inferences about psychological functioning is the response of the eye's pupil (the part of the eyeball through which light enters). Referred to as **pupillometrics,** the research conducted pertains to changes that occur in the pupil in response to a variety of personality aspects (Goldwater, 1972; Hess, 1972; Janisse, 1973). Among the dimensions found to affect the functioning of the pupil are interests, attitudes, and preferences (Hess, 1965; Hess & Polt, 1960, 1964, 1966). Some investigators have attempted to identify differences in the pupillary responses of different diagnostic groups (Rubin, 1974). Other investigators have applied pupillometrics to psychotherapeutic research. For example, in his work with alcoholics, Kennedy (1971) found that those patients nearing completion of treatment whose pupils dilated in response to their favored alcoholic beverage had a higher rate of recidivism than did those patients who exhibited decreased pupil dilation. Pupillometrics has also been employed to assess consumer preferences—with dubious results.

Perhaps best known of all psychophysiological measurement tools is what is commonly referred to as a "lie detector" or **polygraph** (more than one graph). Although not commonly associated with psychological assessment, the lie detection industry is, given the frequency with which such tests are administered and the potential consequences of the tests, "one of the most important branches of applied psychology" (Lykken, 1981, p. 4). Based on the assumption that detectable physical changes occur when an individual lies, the polygraph provides a continuous written record (known as a tracing, a graph, a chart, or a polygram) of several physiological indices (typically respiration, galvanic skin response, and blood volume/pulse rate) as an interviewer and instrument operator (polygrapher or polygraphist) asks the assessee a series of yes-no questions. Judgments as to the truthfulness of the responses are made either informally by surveying the charts or more formally by means of a scoring system. The reliability of such judgments is a matter of controversy (Iacono & Lykken, 1997). Different methods of conducting polygraphic examinations exist (Lykken, 1981), and polygraphic equipment is not standardized (Abrams, 1977; Skolnick, 1961). A problem with the method is a high false-positive rate for lying; the procedure "may label more than 50% of the innocent subjects as guilty" (Kleinmuntz & Szucko, 1984, p. 774). In light of the judgments polygraphers are called upon to make, education, training, and background requirements seem minimal; after as little as six weeks of training one may qualify as a polygrapher. From the available psychometric and related data, it seems reasonable to conclude that the promise of a machine purporting to have the capability of detecting dishonesty remains to be fulfilled (Alpher & Blanton, 1985).

Unobtrusive measures   A type of measure quite different from any we have discussed so far is one of the **unobtrusive** (Webb et al., 1966) or nonreactive variety. In many instances, an unobtrusive measure is a telling physical trace or record. In one study, it was garbage—literally (Cote et al., 1985). Due to their nature, unobtrusive measures do not necessarily require the presence or cooperation of respondents when measurements are being conducted. In a now classic book that was almost entitled *The Bullfighter's Beard,*[7] Webb et al. (1966) listed numerous examples of unobtrusive measures, including the following:

---

7. Webb et al. (1966) explained that the provocative, if uncommunicative, title *The Bullfighter's Beard* was a "title drawn from the observation that toreadors' beards are longer on the day of the fight than on any other day. No one seems to know if the toreador's beard really grows faster that day because of anxiety or if he simply stands further away from the blade, shaking razor in hand. Either way, there were not enough American aficionados to get the point" (p. v). The title they finally settled on was *Unobtrusive Measures: Nonreactive Research in the Social Sciences.*

- Popularity of a museum exhibit can be measured by examination of the erosion of the floor around it relative to the erosion around other exhibits.

- Amount of whiskey consumption in a town can be measured by counting the number of empty bottles in trashcans.

- The effect of the introduction of television into a community can, among other ways, be assessed by examining library book withdrawal records.

- The degree of fear induced by a ghost-story-telling session can be measured by noting the shrinking diameter of a circle of seated children.

In general, Webb et al. argued that unobtrusive measures were underutilized measurement techniques that could usefully complement other research techniques, such as interviews and questionnaires. More recently, in innovative research conducted by Harker and Keltner (2001), the telling record or unobtrusive measure employed was a college yearbook photo. As discussed in this chapter's *Close-up*, the study authors used such photos in combination with other existing data to study the relation between positive emotional expression and personality as well as other variables related to life outcome.

Issues in Behavioral Assessment

One issue—certainly not unique to behavioral assessment but an issue all the same—concerns the definition of what is being assessed. It is often difficult, if not impossible, to define a construct in a way that elicits consensus among all the people who would measure that construct. Clearly this has been the case with complex constructs such as "intelligence." However, it has also been the case with seemingly less abstract and more observable constructs such as "sexual orientation" (Sell, 1997).

Beyond definitional obstacles, tools of behavioral assessment must be of demonstrated value. However, as we have noted earlier, the best way to evaluate that value remains an open question. You may recall from Chapter 5 that classical test theory and generalizability theory conceptualize test score variation in somewhat different ways. In generalizability theory, rather than trying to estimate a single true score, consideration is given to how test scores would be expected to shift across situations as a result of changes in the characteristic being measured. It is for this and related reasons that generalizability theory seems particularly applicable in behavioral assessment as opposed to the measurement of personality traits (Cronbach, 1984). Behavior changes across situations, necessitating an approach to reliability that can account for those changes. By contrast, personality traits are presumed by many to be relatively stable across situations; hence, personality traits are presumed to be more appropriately measured by instruments with assumptions consistent with the true score model.

Regardless of whether behavioral measures are evaluated in accordance with classical test theory, generalizability theory, or something else (such as a Skinnerian experimental analysis), there are some things, it would seem, on which everyone can agree. One is that there must be an acceptable level of inter-rater reliability among behavior observers or raters. A potential source of error in behavioral ratings may arise in the situation where a dissimilarity in two or more of the observed behaviors or other things being rated leads to a more favorable or unfavorable rating than would have been made had the dissimilarity not existed. This source of error is referred to as a **contrast effect** (Bernardin & Buckley, 1981; Latham et al., 1975, Maurer & Alexander, 1991; Pulakos, 1986). Sometimes, for example, a rating may be excessively positive (or negative) because a prior rating was excessively negative (or positive). Figure skating judges exemplify the contrast effect when skaters who turn in performances worthy of very high marks are not given those marks only because a prior skater so excelled by contrast.

Personality, Life Outcomes, and College Yearbook Photos

It will come as a shock to few people to learn that individual differences in emotion are associated with differences in personality. Yet it will probably surprise many to learn that interpersonal differences in emotion may well have a pervasive effect on the course of one's life. In one study, it was observed that a tendency to express uncontrolled anger in early childhood was associated with ill-temper across the lifespan and with several negative life outcomes, such as lower educational attainment, lower status jobs, erratic work patterns, lower military rank, and divorce (Caspi et al., 1987). Suggestive findings such as these have prompted other investigators to wonder about the possible effects of positive emotions on personality and life outcomes.

Positive emotions have many beneficial effects, ranging from the broadening of thoughts and action repertoires (Cunningham, 1988; Frederickson, 1998; Isen, 1987) to the facilitation of the approach of other people (Berry & Hansen, 1996; Frijda & Mesquita, 1994; Ruch, 1993). A smile may send the message that one is friendly and nonthreatening (Henley & LaFrance, 1984; Keating et al., 1981), and may lead to positive attributions about one's sociability, friendliness, likeability, and stability (Borkenau & Liebler, 1992; Frank et al., 1993; Matsumoto & Kudoh, 1993). On the basis of such findings and related research, Harker and Keltner (2001) hypothesized that positive emotional expression would predict higher levels of well-being across adulthood. They tested the hypothesis by examining the relationship of individual differences in positive emotional expression to personality and other variables. A measure of positive emotional expression was obtained by coding judges' ratings of college yearbook photographs of women who participated in a longitudinal research project (Helson, 1967; Helson et al., 1984). These coded judgments were analyzed with respect to personality data on file (such as the subjects' responses to the Adjective Check List at ages 21, 27, 43, and 52) and life outcome data (including well-being as measured by the California Psychological Inventory, marital status, and the Marital Tensions Checklist).

Consistent with the researchers' hypothesis, positive emotional expression as evidenced in the college yearbook photos was found to correlate positively with life outcomes such as marital satisfaction and sense of personal well-being. This was the case even when the possible confounding influences of physical attractiveness or social desirability in responding were controlled for in the analysis of the data. The researchers cautioned, however, that the measure of emotional expression used in the study (the yearbook photo)

Is there a relationship between emotion expressed in college yearbook photos and personality and life outcomes? According to one study, the answer is "yes." Researchers found that positive emotional expression in women's college photos predicted favorable outcomes in marriage and personal well-being up to 30 years later.

consisted of a single instance of very limited behavior. They urged future researchers to consider the use of different measures of emotional expression obtained in different contexts. The researchers also cautioned that their findings are limited to research with women. Smiling may have different implications for the lives of men (Stoppard & Gruchy, 1993). In fact, smiling was negatively correlated with positive outcomes for a sample of male cadets at West Point (Mueller & Mazur, 1996).

This thought-provoking study was "one of the first to document that individual differences in expression relate to personality and may be stable aspects of personality" (Harker & Keltner, 2001, p. 121). The study authors reflected, "People photograph each other with casual ease and remarkable frequency, usually unaware that each snapshot may capture as much about the future as it does the passing emotions of the moment" (Harker & Keltner, 2001, p. 122).

Ratings are typically more favorable when the preceding performance being rated was very poor, and less favorable when the preceding performance being rated was very good. Contrast effects have been observed in interviews (Kopelman, 1975; Schuh, 1978), in behavioral diaries and checklists (Maurer et al., 1993), in laboratory-based performance evaluations (Murphy et al., 1985; Smither et al., 1988), and in field performance evaluations (Grey & Kipnis, 1976; Ivancevich, 1983). In a study by Wexley et al. (1972), as much as 80% of the total variance was thought to be due to contrast effects. Training raters to avoid contrast and other types of rating error may be costly in terms of time and labor. Teaching professionals how to use the behavior observation and coding system of the Marital Interaction Coding System "takes two to three months of weekly instruction and practice to learn how to use its 32 codes" (Fredman & Sherman, 1987, p. 28). Another approach to inter-rater reliability among behavioral raters is to employ a "composite judge" who, in essence, averages multiple judgments (Tsujimoto et al., 1990).

Some types of observer bias cannot practically or readily be remedied. For example, in behavioral observation involving the use of videotape equipment, it would on many occasions be advantageous if multiple cameras and recorders could be used to cover various angles of the ongoing action, to get close-ups, and so forth. The economic practicality of the situation (let alone other factors, such as the limited engineering skills on the part of the clinician using such equipment) is that more than one camera in a fixed position recording the action is seldom feasible. The camera in a sense is biased in that one fixed position, because in many instances it is recording information that may be quite different from the information that would have been obtained had it been placed in another position—or if multiple recordings were being made. The practicality of most such situations, however, mandates the use of one recording of the action.

As we have already noted in the context of self-monitoring, reactivity is another possible issue with regard to behavioral assessment. This term refers to the fact that people react differently in experimental as opposed to natural situations; microphones, cameras, and one-way mirrors may themselves alter the observed behavior. Some patients may attempt, for example, to minimize the amount of psychopathology they are willing to record for posterity, whereas others may exaggerate it. Illustrations of reactivity are probably quite familiar to you; even the most unruly child in the classroom can manage to appear angelic when the school principal is seated in the back with a pad and pencil. One possible solution to the problem of reactivity is the use of hidden observers or clandestine recording techniques, though such methods raise serious ethical issues. Many a time, all that is required to solve the problem is an adaptation period in which the people being observed are given some time to adjust to the idea of observation. They soon pay little attention to the observer or the recording device. Most clinicians are aware from personal experience that a tape recorder in the therapy room might put off some patients at first but in only a matter of minutes, the chances are good that it will be ignored. One form of reactivity that has received relatively little attention in the behavioral literature has to do with the relationship between the behavior rater and the person being rated; that, of course, was addressed in this chapter's *Everyday Psychometrics*.

A Perspective

More than a half-century ago, Theodor Reik's influential book, *Listening with the Third Ear*, intrigued clinicians with the possibilities of evaluation and intervention by means of skilled interviewing, active listening, and artful, depth-oriented interpretation. In one vignette, a female therapy patient recounted a visit to the dentist that entailed an injection and a tooth extraction. While speaking, she remarked on a book in Reik's bookcase that was "standing on its head"—to which Reik responded, "But why did you not tell me that you had had an abortion?" (Reik, 1948, p. 263). Reflecting on this bedazzling exhibition of clinical intuition, Masling (1997) wrote, "We would all have liked to have had Reik's magic touch, the ability to discern what is hidden and secret, to serve as oracle" (p. 259).

Historically, society has called upon mental health professionals to make diagnostic judgments and intervention recommendations, often on the basis of relatively little information. Early on, a promise of psychological tests, particularly in the area of personality assessment, was to empower clinicians—mere mortals—with a wondrous tool allowing them to play the oracle role that society imposed and expected. Soon, two very different philosophies of test design and use emerged. The clinical approach relied heavily on the clinician's judgment and intuition and was characterized by a lack of any preset and uniformly applied rules for drawing clinical conclusions and making predictions. By contrast, the statistical or actuarial approach relied heavily on standardization, norms, and preset, uniformly applied rules and procedures. Duels between various members of these two camps were common for many years and have been reviewed in detail elsewhere (Gough, 1962; Holt, 1978; Marchese, 1992; Meehl, 1954, 1959, 1965; Sawyer, 1966).

It seems fair to say that in those situations where there are insufficient data to formulate rules for decision making and prediction, the clinical approach wins out over the actuarial. For the most part, however, it is the actuarial approach that has been most enthusiastically embraced. This is so for a number of reasons ranging from a widespread desire to make assessment more a science than an art and from the fact that most of us are simply not clinically brilliant enough to spontaneously and consistently see through to what Reik (1952) characterized as the "secret self." Moreover, as Masling (1997) noted, the actuarial approach has the advantage of permitting hypotheses and predictions that have been found useful to be retained, whereas untenable hypotheses and predictions may be quickly discovered and discarded. Of course, in many instances, skill in clinical assessment can be conceptualized as an internalized, less formal, and more creative version of the actuarial approach. Holt (1978) made a similar point when he wrote, "There is no magic in clinical intuition that enables a clinician to predict a criterion about which he knows little, from data the relation of which to the criterion he has not studied, and to do so better than an actuarial formula based on just such prior study of predictor-criterion relations. In retrospect, it seems absurd to have expected that it could have been done" (p. 120).

The actuarial approach to personality assessment is increasingly common. Even projective instruments, once the bastion of the clinical approach, are increasingly published with norms and subsequently researched using rigorous statistical methods. Yet as Masling (1997) observed, "In academic psychology the climate of opinion about projective tests continues as though nothing has changed and clinicians were still reading tea leaves" (p. 263).

If the oracle-like, clinical orientation is characterized as the "third ear" approach, we might characterize the contemporary orientation as a "van Gogh" approach; in a sense, an ear has been dispatched. The day of the all-knowing oracle has passed. Today, it is incumbent upon the responsible clinician to rely on norms, inferential statistics, and related essentials of the actuarial approach. Sound clinical judgment is still desirable if not mandatory. However, it is required less for the purpose of making off-the-cuff interpretations and predictions and more for the purpose of organizing and interpreting information from different tools of assessment.

Self-Assessment

Test your understanding of elements of this chapter by seeing if you can explain each of the following terms, expressions, and abbreviations:

analogue studies

apperceive

behavioral assessment

contrast effect

Exner's Comprehensive System

figure drawing

free association test

functional analysis

HIT

inquiry

Murrayan concepts of need, press, and thema

objective methods of personality assessment

plethysmograph

penile plethysmograph

polygraph

projective hypothesis

projective techniques

reactivity

role play

Rorschach inquiry

Rorschach scoring system

Rorschach test

self-monitoring

sentence completion test

situational performance measure

TAT

testing the limits (on the Rorschach)

unconscious

unobtrusive measure

word association test

Clinical and Counseling Assessment

Clinical psychology is that branch of psychology that has as its primary focus the prevention, diagnosis, and treatment of abnormal behavior. Clinical psychologists receive training in psychological assessment and in psychotherapy and are employed in hospitals, public and private mental health centers, independent practice, and academia. Like clinical psychology, counseling psychology is a branch of psychology that is concerned with the prevention, diagnosis, and treatment of abnormal behavior; but its province tends to be the less severe behavior disorders and the everyday problems in living (such as marital and family communication problems, career decisions, and difficulties with school study habits). Although counseling psychologists work in a variety of settings, most are employed by schools, colleges, and universities, where they teach or work in the school counseling center. In general, the similarities between the two specialties outweigh the differences in terms of work setting, and service, research, and teaching activities (Brems & Johnson, 1997). Clinical psychologists are more apt to focus their research and treatment efforts on the more severe forms of behavior pathology while members of the two fields have in common the objective of fostering personal growth. Toward that end, clinical and counseling psychologists may use many of the same tools in the process of assessment—the interview, psychological tests, the case history, and behavioral measures. Counseling psychologists are most apt to employ psychological tests when the presenting problem involves a career-choice decision (Fee et al., 1982; Watkins & Campbell, 1989; Watkins et al., 1988).

Virtually any of the tests we have covered in this book to this point—tests of intelligence, general measures of personality, measures of self-concept, measures of cognitive style—would be appropriate for coverage in this chapter, for all have potential application in clinical and counseling contexts. Further, other specialized instruments might be covered here as well (such as tests and assessment procedures designed to measure various personal and social problems related to school, family, and employment). In an introductory text such as this, however, choices must be made as to coverage and organization.

In the previous chapter, a variety of behavioral measures were introduced, along with discussion of a sampling of applications in clinical and counseling contexts. In this chapter, we will look at the interview, the case history, and psychological tests in the context of clinical and counseling applications. The chapter concludes with a look at the end product of an assessment undertaken for clinical or counseling purposes—the psychological report.

An Overview

Clinical assessment may be undertaken for various reasons. For the clinical psychologist in a hospital, an independent practice, or some other clinical setting, tools of assessment are frequently used to clarify the nature of the psychological problem, make a diagnosis, and/or design a treatment plan. Let's review some specific types of assessment questions such a clinician might raise.

"Does this patient have a mental disorder? If so, what is the diagnosis?" In many cases, tools of assessment, including an interview, a test, and case history data can provide an answer. Before or after interviewing a patient, a clinician may administer tests such as the WAIS-III or the MMPI-2 to obtain estimates of the patient's intellectual functioning and level of psychopathology. The data from this testing may provide the clinician with initial hypotheses about the nature of the individual's difficulties, which will then guide the interview. Alternatively, the data from this testing can confirm or refute hypotheses made on the basis of the clinical interview. Interview and test data will be supplemented with case history data, especially when the patient will not or cannot cooperate. The clinician may interview people who know the patient, such as family members, co-workers, and friends, and obtain records relevant to the case.

"What is this person's current level of functioning? How does it compare with that of other people of the same age?" Consider the example of an individual who is suspected to have dementia resulting from Alzheimer's disease. The patient has experienced a steady and progressive loss of cognitive skills over a period of months. A diagnosis of dementia may involve tracking the individual's performance with repeated administrations of tests of cognitive ability, including memory. Periodic testing with various instruments may also provide information about the kinds of activities the patient should be advised to pursue, as well as the kinds of activities the patient should be encouraged to curtail or give up entirely.

"What type of treatment shall this patient be offered?" Tools of assessment can help guide decisions relating to treatment. Patients found to be high in intelligence, for example, tend to make good candidates for insight-oriented methods that require high levels of abstract ability. A person who complains of being depressed may be asked periodically to complete a measure of depression. If such a person is an inpatient, trends in the depth of depression as measured by the instrument may contribute to critical decisions regarding level of supervision within the institution, strength of medication administered, and date of discharge.

"How can this person's personality best be described?" Gaining an understanding of the individual need not focus on psychopathology. People who do not have any mental disorder sometimes seek psychotherapy for personal growth or for support in coping with a difficult set of life circumstances. In such instances, interviews and personality tests geared more to the normal testtaker might be employed.

Researchers may raise a wide variety of assessment-related questions, including "Which treatment approach is most effective?" or "What kind of client tends to benefit most from a particular kind of treatment?" A researcher may believe, for example, that people with a field-dependent cognitive style would be most likely to benefit from a cognitive-behavioral approach to treatment, and people with a field-independent cognitive style would be most likely to benefit from a humanistic approach to treatment. The researcher would use a variety of assessment tools to combine subjects into treatment groups and then to measure outcome in psychotherapy.

Counseling psychologists who do employment counseling may use a wide variety of assessment tools to help determine not only what kinds of occupations a person might enjoy doing but also which occupations would be sufficiently challenging without being overwhelming. School psychologists and counseling psychologists working in a school setting may assist students with a wide variety of problems, including those related to studying. Here, behavioral measures, including self-monitoring, might be employed to better understand exactly how, when, and where the student engages in study behavior. The answer to related questions such as "Why am I not doing well in school?" may in part be found in diagnostic educational tests, such as those designed to identify problem areas in reading and reading comprehension. Another part of the answer may be obtained through other tools of assessment, including the interview, which may focus on aspects of the student's motivation and other life circumstances.

Clinical Assessment and Managed Care

Any overview of contemporary clinical assessment would be incomplete without reference to managed care and its profound effect on clinical assessment. In general, **managed care** may be defined as a health care system wherein the products and services provided to patients by a network of participating health care providers are mediated by an administrative agency of the insurer that works to keep costs down by fixing schedules of reimbursement to the providers. Managed care companies have shown an unwillingness to allocate scarce health care dollars for psychological assessment services. The result has been a severe curtailment of the number of psychological tests ordered and administered (Backlar, 1996; Cushman & Guilford, 2000; Eisman et al., 2000; Miller, 1996). Approximately 75% of the clinicians in a recent survey indicated that managed care had affected their practice by reducing the number of psychological tests administered (Piotrowski et al., 1998). In general, reasons cited for the reduction in tests involved difficulty in obtaining approvals for such work and lower rates of reimbursement for testing. For the minority of psychologists who said that their work was unaffected by managed care, reasons given included (1) they had done relatively little testing previously, (2) they worked for institutions and had no personal contact with managed care agencies, and (3) their previous test use was primarily with tests (such as the MMPI-2) that tended to be authorized by managed care agencies. A few respondents reported that they simply absorbed the losses they incurred in work with managed care patients or that they avoided agreeing to assess such patients. The data also suggested that some of the tests most valued by many clinicians (such as the Rorschach) were the same tests judged most likely to be abandoned as the result of managed care policy.

As Piotrowski and his colleagues observed, "Economic reality will dictate, to a large extent, changes in psychological assessment practices, particularly the amount of time that psychologists may responsibly devote to assessment activities." These researchers went on to speculate that in the future, clinicians may spend more time focusing on specific symptoms targeted for change (such as anxiety, depression, or hostility) and less time on matters related to personality dynamics and intrapsychic processes. Alternatively, they may dispense with testing and assessment altogether, referring out assessment of managed care clients to "testing only" practices (Acklin, 1996). Such wholesale abandonment of assessment would be most unfortunate, given the compelling evidence to support the use of psychological tests in health care settings (Kubiszn et al., 2000). Few things about the future are certain, but it does seem that the nature of clinical assessment will be quite different—more abbreviated, more time limited, and less in-depth. Clinicians need to become more aware of their options (Kiesler, 2000; Levant et al., 2001; Stout et al., 2001) and more savvy about the needs of the marketplace (Reed et al., 2001). Of course, one of the key functions of clinical assessment—in or out of a managed care environment—is the diagnosis of mental disorders. Our overview continues with discussion of this aspect of clinical assessment.

The Diagnosis of Mental Disorders

Frequently, an objective of clinical assessment is to diagnose mental disorders. The reference source used for making such diagnoses is the current version of the American Psychiatric Association's *Diagnostic and Statistical Manual* (DSM), which presently is the **DSM-IV-TR** (where "IV" stands for "fourth edition" and "TR" stands for "text revision"). DSM-IV was published in 1994; its modified, "TR" version was published in 2000; and an electronic, searchable disk version of it was published in 2001.

DSM-IV-TR names and describes all known mental disorders and even includes a category called "conditions not attributable to a mental disorder that are a focus of attention or treatment." A DSM-IV-TR diagnosis immediately conveys a great deal of descriptive information about the nature of the behavioral deviance, deficits, or excesses in the diagnosed person.

Some clinical psychologists, most vocally the behaviorally oriented clinicians, have expressed dissatisfaction with DSM-IV-TR on many grounds, including the fact that it is firmly rooted in the medical model; patterns of behavior are described in DSM-IV-TR in a way akin to diseases as opposed to a scientific description of behavior. This diagnostic system has also been criticized for being relatively unreliable; different clinicians interviewing the same patient may well come up with different diagnoses. Even if the right diagnosis is made, this system of assessment provides no guidance as to what method of treatment will be optimally effective. Additional criticism has been made on cultural grounds, including proposed text revisions in sections of the guide that deal with dissociative disorders (Lewis-Fernandez, 1998).

Proponents of DSM-IV-TR argue that this diagnostic system is useful because of the wealth of information that is conveyed by a psychiatric diagnosis. They argue that perfect inter-diagnostician reliability cannot be achieved because of the nature of the subject matter. In response to the medical model criticism, DSM-IV-TR supporters maintain that the diagnostic system is useful whether any particular diagnostic category is or is not actually a disease; each of the disorders listed is associated with pain, suffering, or disability. The classification system, it is argued, provides useful subject headings under which practitioners can search for (or add to) the research literature with respect to the different diagnostic categories.

In DSM-IV-TR, diagnoses are coded according to five dimensions or axes. The types of disorders subsumed under each axis are as follows:

Axis I: Disorders of infancy, childhood, and adolescence; dementias such as those caused by Alzheimer's disease; disorders arising out of drug use; mood and anxiety disorders; and schizophrenia. Also included here are conditions that may be the focus of treatment (such as academic or social problems) but not attributable to mental disorder.

Axis II: Mental retardation and personality disorders.

Axis III: Physical conditions that may affect mental functioning—from migraine headaches to allergies—are included here.

Axis IV: Different problems or sources of stress may occur in an individual's life at any given time. Financial, legal, marital, occupational, or other problems may precipitate behavior ranging from starting to smoke after having quit to attempting suicide. The presence of such problems is noted on this axis.

Axis V: This axis calls for a global rating of overall functioning. At the high end of this scale are ratings indicative of no symptoms and everyday kinds of concerns. At the low end of this scale are ratings indicative of people who are a clear and present danger to themselves or others and must therefore be confined in a secure facility.

DSM-IV-TR diagnoses are descriptive and atheoretical; this is appropriate for an authoritative reference work designed to provide common language for clinicians and researchers with varied theoretical orientations toward the etiology and treatment of mental disorders (Widiger & Clark, 2000). The first two axes contain all the diagnostic categories for mental disorders, and the remaining three axes provide additional information regarding an individual's level of functioning and current life situation. Multiple diagnoses are possible; an individual may be diagnosed, for example, as exhibiting behavior indicative of the disorders listed on both Axis I and Axis II.

The fifth edition of the DSM is scheduled for publication in 2005 or 2006. One question that its authors may be grappling with seems most basic: What is a disorder? As it turns out, this seemingly simple question has generated a heated debate (Clark, 1999; Spitzer, 1999). The third edition of the DSM was the first edition of that manual to contain a definition of mental disorder. The published definition was criticized by Jerome C. Wakefield (1992a), who proposed as an alternative a "harmful dysfunction" (HD) definition. According to Wakefield, a disorder is conceived as a harmful failure of internal mechanisms to perform their naturally selected functions. Wakefield's position is termed **evolutionary** because he views the internal mechanisms that break down or fail as having been acquired through the Darwinian process of natural selection. For Wakefield, the attribution of disorder entails two things: (1) a scientific judgment that such an evolutionary failure exists, and (2) a value judgment that this failure is harmful to the individual (Wakefield, 1992b).

In contrast to Wakefield's evolutionary view of disorder are myriad other views, chief among them that the concept of disorder is so broad that it need not have any defining properties (Lilienfeld & Marino, 1995, 1999). Klein (1999) argued that proper evolutionary function cannot be determined, and that behavior labeled disordered may be the product of many involuntary or voluntary (as in role-playing) causes. Others have weighed in on this controversial issue by illuminating the role of culture (Kirmayer & Young, 1999), and by championing alternative vantage points such as the level of the neuron (Richters & Hinshaw, 1999).

Disputes about various aspects of the DSM, including the process by which it is developed, what should and should not be considered pathological, and how individual diagnostic categories should be derived, seem inevitable (Widiger & Clark, 2000). Even basic questions about what constitutes a disorder seem destined for long-term debate. Such debate is critically important, however, because much more than a semantic quibble is at stake. As Wakefield (1999) reflected, answers to questions about the nature of disorder shape the thoughts that result in research, diagnoses, treatment, and public policy.

Regardless of how disorder is defined, a key tool for identifying it will be the interview. If Jonathan Shedler has his way, it will be identified by patients themselves using a handheld computer. Shedler (2000) developed a diagnostic tool designed for self-administration by patients of primary care physicians. The patients are posed questions on the built-in display, and then respond yes or no on the keyboard. The physician may obtain a computer-generated report of the findings including specific DSM diagnoses. Of course, interviews with patients can still be conducted "the old-fashioned way," and it is to that variety of dialogue that we now turn our attention.

The Interview

An interview is a technique for gathering information by means of discussion. Except for rare circumstances (such as an individual known to be totally noncommunicative or an assessment conducted on someone who cannot be present), an interview will be part of every clinician's or counselor's typical individual assessment. In a clinical situation, for example, an interview may be conducted to arrive at a diagnosis, to pinpoint areas that must be addressed in psychotherapy, or to determine whether an individual will be harmful to himself or others. In a typical counseling application, an interview is conducted to assist the interviewee in learning more about himself or herself—the better to make a career or other life choice. Usually face-to-face in clinical and counseling applications, interviewers learn about interviewees not only from what the interviewees say but also from how they say it and how, in general, they present themselves during the interview.

Often, the interview guides decisions about what else needs to be done to assess the individual. If symptoms or complaints are described by the interviewee in a vague or inconsistent manner, the administration of a test designed to screen in a general way for psychopathology may be indicated. If the interviewee is unable to describe the frequency with which a particular problem occurs, a period of self-monitoring may be requested. If no clear presenting problem emerges during the interview, the interview may be used as a forum to solidify what is sometimes referred to as the therapeutic contract, a clarification and verbalization by both patient and therapist of goals, expectations, and obligations regarding the therapeutic process.

The training of most clinicians and counselors has sensitized them to issues concerning the role of the interviewer in an interview situation. Having been interviewed yourself on any number of occasions, you are probably aware that not only does the content of the interview vary from one situation to the next, but the tone of the interview as set by the interviewer may vary widely as well. Some interviewers, by virtue of their manner and their verbal and nonverbal responses to you and what you say, may make you feel relaxed and responsive, whereas others do not. Some interviewers may convey that they are "with you" and understand you, whereas others prompt you to feel that they have no comprehension of you or "where you're at." Some interviewers are warm and accepting; others are cold and aloof. Some interviewers prefer to ask open-ended questions (such as "Could you tell me something about yourself?"), and others prefer to pose closed questions—some posed so sharply as to be reminiscent of the Inquisition (such as "Are you now, or have you ever been, a member of the Communist party?").

Seasoned interviewers endeavor to create a positive, accepting climate in which to conduct the interview. They may use open-ended questions initially and then closed questions to obtain specific information. The effective interviewer conveys understanding to the interviewee by verbal or nonverbal means; a statement summarizing what the interviewee is trying to convey and an attentive posture and understanding facial expression are some of the ways by which understanding can be conveyed. Responses conveying that the interviewer is indeed listening attentively include head nodding and vocalizations such as "um-hmm." However, here the interviewer must exercise caution: Such vocalizations and head nodding have been observed to act as reinforcers that increase the emission of certain interviewee verbalizations (Greenspoon, 1955). For example, if a therapist vocalized an "um-hmm" every time an interviewee brought up material related to the subject of "mother," then—other things being equal—it is conceivable that the interviewee would spend more time talking about the subject of mother than would others not reinforced for bringing up that topic. An interview conducted to determine whether a student has the social skills and maturity to function effectively in a particular classroom setting will vary greatly in content from an interview designed to determine if an accused sex offender is competent to stand trial. Clearly, many types of interviews exist.

Types of Interviews

Interviews may be typed with respect to a number of different variables. One such variable is content. The content of some interviews, like personality inventories, is wide ranging. By contrast, other interviews focus narrowly on a particular subject matter. Another variable on which interviews differ is structure. A highly structured interview is one in which all the questions that will be asked are prepared in advance. In an interview with little structure, few or no questions are prepared in advance, leaving interviewers the freedom to delve into subject areas as their judgment dictates. An advantage of a structured interview is that it provides a uniform method of exploration. So, a structured interview, much like a test, may be employed as a pre/post measure of outcome for the purpose of gauging, for example, the therapeutic effects of psychotherapy, a new psychiatric drug, or some other intervention.

Many structured interviews are available for use by assessment professionals. For example, the Structured Clinical Interview for Dissociative Disorders (SCID-D) is designed to assist in the diagnosis of dissociative disorders (Steinberg et al., 1993). The Schedule for Affective Disorders and Schizophrenia (SADS; Endicott & Spitzer, 1978) is a standardized interview designed to detect schizophrenia and disorders of affect. A study with one form of the SADS suggested that this interview may be of particular value in detecting schizophrenia in mentally retarded adults (Meadows et al., 1991). A number of different approaches have been employed to detect psychologically related malingering: the feigning or deliberate exaggeration of symptoms related to mental disorder (Davidson, 1949; Greene, 1988; Lachar & Wrobel, 1979; Resnick, 1988; Ritson & Forest, 1970; Wachspress et al., 1953). One such approach employs the structured interview as the tool of choice. The Structured Interview of Reported Symptoms (SIRS; Rogers, 1986; Rogers et al., 1992) was conceived as a useful adjunct to standardized tests such as the MMPI, or even a substitute measure if the suspected malingerer refuses to take such tests.

Another variable on which interviews may differ is the extent to which the interviewer intentionally attempts to evoke stress in the interviewee. A **stress interview** is the general name applied to any interview where one objective is to place the interviewee in a pressured state for some particular reason. The stress may be induced to test for some aspect of personality (such as aggressiveness or hostility) that might be elicited only under such conditions. Screening for work in the security or intelligence fields might entail stress interviews if one of the criteria for the job is the ability to remain cool under pressure. Exactly what the source of the stress will be varies as a function of the specific purpose of the evaluation, though disapproving facial expressions, critical remarks, condescending reassurances, and relentless probing are among the interviewer behaviors that have been employed. To induce a stressed condition in a neurological examination, the examiner might say something like "You have only 5 seconds in which to complete this task." Then, the interviewer emphasizes the stressful condition by counting the numbers 1 through 5 while the examinee attempts to respond.

Another type of specialized interview is the **hypnotic interview,** conducted after a hypnotic state has been induced in the interviewee. Hypnotic interviews may be conducted as part of a therapeutic assessment or intervention, in situations where the interviewee has been an eyewitness to a crime or related situations. In all such cases, the prevailing belief is that the hypnotic state will focus the interviewee's concentration and enhance recall (McConkey & Sheehan, 1996; Reiser, 1980, 1990; Vingoe, 1995).

Critics of hypnotic interviewing suggest that any gains in recall may be offset by losses in accuracy and other possible negative outcomes (Kebbell & Wagstaff, 1998). Hypnotic interview procedures may inadvertently make interviewees more confident about their memories, regardless of the correctness of those memories (Dywan & Bowers, 1983; Sheehan et al., 1984). As compared to nonhypnotized interviewees, hypnotized interviewees may be more suggestible with regard to leading questions and thus more vulnerable to distortion of memories (Putnam, 1979; Zelig & Beidleman, 1981). Some researchers believe that hypnosis of witnesses may inadvertently produce memory distortion that is irreversible (Diamond, 1980; Orne, 1979). As a result, witnesses who have been hypnotized to enhance memory may be banned from testifying (Laurence & Perry, 1988; Perry & Laurence, 1990).

An interview procedure designed to retain the best features of a hypnotic interview—less the hypnotic induction—has been developed by Fisher and colleagues (Fisher & Geiselman, 1992; Fisher et al., 1989; Fisher et al., 1987; Mello & Fisher, 1996). In the **cognitive interview,** the procedure entails establishing rapport and encouraging the interviewee to use imagery and focused retrieval to recall information. If the interviewee is an eyewitness to a crime, he or she may be asked to shift perspective and describe events from the viewpoint of the perpetrator. Much like what typically occurs in hypnosis, a great deal of control of the interview shifts to the interviewee. And unlike many police interviews, there is an emphasis on open-ended as opposed to close-ended questions, and interviewees are allowed to speak without interruption. Although there has been little research designed to explore the comparative efficacy of hypnotic and cognitive interviews, the cognitive interview technique appears to hold promise (Kebbell & Wagstaff, 1998).

Regardless of the specific type of interview being conducted, questions with regard to the following areas are typically raised, and these are followed by additional queries as clinical judgment dictates:

- *Demographic data.* Name, age, sex, religion, number of persons in family, race, occupation, marital status, socioeconomic status, address, telephone numbers.

- *Reason for referral.* Why is this individual requesting or being sent for psychological assessment? Who is the referral source?

- *Past medical history.* What significant events are there in this individual's medical history?

- *Present medical condition.* What current medical complaints does this individual have? What medications are currently being used?

- *Familial medical history.* What chronic or familial types of disease are present in the family history?

- *Past psychological history.* What traumatic events has this individual suffered? What psychological problems (such as disorders of mood or disorders of thought content) have troubled this individual?

- *Current psychological conditions.* What psychological problems are currently troubling this person? How long have these problems persisted? What is causing these problems? What are the psychological strengths of this individual?

Throughout the interview, the interviewer may be jotting down subjective impressions about the interviewee's general appearance (appropriate?), personality (sociable? suspicious? shy?), mood (elated? depressed?), emotional reactivity (appropriate? blunted?), thought content (hallucinations? delusions? obsessions?), speech (normal conversational? slow and rambling? rhyming? singing? shouting?), and judgment (regarding such matters as prior behavior and plans for the future). During the interview, any chance actions by the patient that may be relevant to the purpose of the assessment are noted.[1]

---

1. Tangentially we note the experience of the senior author (RJC) while conducting a clinical interview in the Bellevue Hospital Emergency Psychiatric Service. Throughout the intake interview, the patient sporadically blinked his left eye. At one point in the interview, the interviewer said, "I notice that you keep blinking your left eye"—in response to which the interviewee said, "Oh, this . . ." as he proceeded to remove his (glass) eye. Once he regained his breath, the interviewer noted this vignette on the intake sheet.

One variety of clinical interview used frequently, especially in medical settings, is the mental status examination.

The mental status examination   A parallel to the general physical examination conducted by a physician is a **mental status examination** conducted by a clinician. This examination, used to screen for intellectual, emotional, and neurological deficits, typically includes provision for questioning or observation with respect to each area discussed in the following list.

- *Appearance.* Are the patient's dress and general appearance appropriate?
- *Behavior.* Is anything remarkably strange about the patient's speech or general behavior during the interview? Does the patient exhibit facial tics, involuntary movements, difficulties in coordination or gait?
- *Orientation.* Is the patient oriented to person; that is, does he know who he is? Is the patient oriented to place; that is, does she know where she is? Is the patient oriented to time; does he or she know the year, the month, and the day?
- *Memory.* How is the patient's memory for recent and long-past events?
- *Sensorium.* Are there any problems related to the five senses?
- *Psychomotor activity.* Does there appear to be any abnormal retardation or quickening of motor activity?
- *State of consciousness.* Does consciousness appear to be clear, or is the patient bewildered, confused, or stuporous?
- *Affect.* Is the patient's emotional expression appropriate? For example, does the patient (inappropriately) laugh while discussing the death of an immediate family member?
- *Mood.* Throughout the interview, has the patient generally been angry? depressed? anxious? apprehensive? what?
- *Personality.* In what terms can the patient best be described? sensitive? stubborn? apprehensive? what?
- *Thought content.* Is the patient hallucinating—seeing, hearing, or otherwise experiencing things that aren't really there? Is the patient delusional—expressing untrue, unfounded beliefs (such as the delusion that someone follows him or her everywhere)? Does the patient appear to be obsessive—does the patient appear to think the same thoughts over and over again?
- *Thought processes.* Is there under- or overproductivity of ideas? Do ideas seem to come to the patient abnormally slowly or quickly? Is there evidence of loosening of associations? Are the patient's verbal productions rambling or disconnected?
- *Intellectual resources.* What is the estimated intelligence of the interviewee?
- *Insight.* Does the patient realistically appreciate his or her situation and the necessity for professional assistance if such assistance is necessary?
- *Judgment.* How appropriate has the patient's decision making been with regard to past events and future plans?

A mental status examination begins at the first moment the interviewee enters the room. The examiner takes note of the examinee's appearance, gait, and so forth. **Orientation** is assessed by straightforward questions such as "What is your name?" "Where are you now?" and "What is today's date?" If the patient is indeed oriented to person, place, and time, the assessor may note in the record of the assessment "Oriented × 3" (read "oriented times 3"). Different kinds of questions based on the individual examiner's own preferences will be employed to assess the other areas in the examination. For example, to assess intellectual resources, a variety of questions may be asked, ranging from those of general information (such as "What is the capital of this state?"), to arithmetic calculations (such as "What is 81 divided by 9?"), to proverb interpretations (such as "What does this saying mean: People who live in glass houses shouldn't throw stones?"). Insight may be assessed, for example, simply by asking the interviewee why he or she is being interviewed; having little or no appreciation of the reason for the interview will indicate little insight (if not malingering). As a result of a mental status examination, a clinician might be better able to diagnose the interviewee, if in fact the purpose of the interview is diagnostic. The outcome of such an examination might be, for example, a decision to hospitalize, a decision not to hospitalize, or a request for a more in-depth psychological or neurological examination.

Psychometric Aspects of the Interview

Principles applied to estimate the reliability and validity of tests can also be used to evaluate interviews. After an interview, an interviewer usually reaches some conclusions about the interviewee. Those conclusions, like test scores, can be evaluated for their level of reliability and validity.

If more than one interviewer conducts an interview with the same individual, inter-rater reliability for interview data could be represented by the agreement that exists between the different interviewers' conclusions. In a study that explored the diagnosis of schizophrenia through two different types of interviews, one structured and one unstructured, Lindstrom et al. (1994) found that more structured interviews produced more reliable information, even though the content of the two types of interviews was similar.

Consistent with the findings of Lindstrom et al. (1994), the inter-rater reliability of interview data may be increased when different interviewers consider specific issues systematically. Systematic and specific consideration of various interview issues can be fostered in various ways. One way involves having interviewers complete a scale designed to rate the interviewee on targeted variables at the conclusion of the interview. In one study, family members were interviewed by several psychologists for the purpose of diagnosing depression. The actual content of the interviews was left to the discretion of the interviewers, although all interviewers completed the same rating scale at the conclusion of the interview. Completion of the postinterview rating scale improved inter-rater reliability (Miller et al., 1994).

In general, when an interview is undertaken for diagnostic purposes, the reliability and validity of the diagnostic conclusions made on the basis of the interview data are likely to increase when the diagnostic criteria are clear and specific. Efforts to increase inter-rater reliability for diagnostic purposes are evident in the third revision of the *Diagnostic and Statistical Manual* (DSM-III), published in 1980. Although its predecessor, DSM-II (1968), had provided descriptive information about the disorders listed, the descriptions were inconsistent in specific detail and in some cases could be fairly vague. For example, this is the DSM-II description of paranoid personality:

> This behavioral pattern is characterized by hypersensitivity, rigidity, unwarranted suspicion, jealousy, envy, excessive self-importance, and a tendency to blame others and ascribe evil motives to them. These characteristics often interfere with the patient's ability to maintain satisfactory interpersonal relations. Of course, the presence of suspicion itself does not justify the diagnosis, since suspicion may be warranted in some cases. (American Psychiatric Association, 1968, p. 42)

A description such as this may be helpful in communicating the nature of the disorder, but because of its nonspecificity and openness to interpretation, it is of only minimal value for diagnostic purposes. In an effort to bolster the reliability and validity of psychiatric diagnoses, the DSM-III (American Psychiatric Association, 1980) provided specific diagnostic guidelines, including a specific number of symptoms that had to be present for the diagnosis to be made. The diagnostic criteria for paranoid personality disorder, for example, listed eight ways in which suspicion might be displayed, at least three of which must be present for the diagnosis to be made. It listed four ways in which hypersensitivity might be displayed, two of which had to be present for the diagnosis to be made. It listed four ways in which restricted affect might be displayed, two of which had to be present for the diagnosis to be made (American Psychiatric Association, 1980). This tradition of increased specificity in diagnostic descriptions was evident in an interim revision of DSM-III (published in 1987 and referred to as DSM-III-R) as well as in the more recent revisions, DSM-IV (American Psychiatric Association, 1994) and DSM-IV-TR.

Evaluating the consistency of conclusions drawn from two interviews separated by some period of time produces a coefficient of reliability that conceptually parallels a coefficient of test-retest reliability. As an example, consider a study of the reliability of a semistructured interview for the diagnosis of alcoholism, as well as commonly co-occurring disorders (such as substance dependence, substance abuse, depression, and antisocial personality disorder). The authors found that some disorders (substance dependence and depression) were diagnosed with greater test-retest reliability than were other disorders (substance abuse and antisocial personality disorder; Bucholz et al., 1994).

Criterion validity of conclusions made on the basis of interviews is of as much concern to psychometricians as the criterion validity of conclusions made on the basis of test data. The degree to which an interviewer's findings or conclusions concur with other test results or other behavioral evidence reflects on the criterion-related validity of the conclusions. Consider in this context a study that compared the accuracy of two different tools of assessment, an objective test and a structured interview, in predicting the behavior of probationers. Harris (1994) concluded that the structured interview was much more accurate in predicting the criterion (later behavior of probationers) than was the test. In another study, this one having as a criterion the accurate reporting of the subject's drug use, a paper-and-pencil test was also pitted against an interview. The written test was found to be more criterion-valid than the interview, perhaps because people may be more disposed to admit to illegal drug use in writing than in a face-to-face interview (McElrath, 1994).

We conclude our discussion of the psychometric aspects of the interview with the reminder that an interview is a dynamic interaction between two or more people; on occasion, it may seem to develop a life of its own. Ultimately, the nature and form of any interview is determined by many factors such as the interview referral question; the nature, quality, and quantity of background information; constraints of time or the interview environment; and the willingness or ability of the interviewee to respond. Cultural factors may also play a role in this dynamic interaction.

Cultural Aspects of the Interview

When an interview is conducted in preparation for counseling or psychotherapy, it may be useful to explore a number of culture-related issues. To what extent does the client feel different from other people, and how much of a problem is this? What conflicts, if any, are evident with regard to motivation to assimilate versus commitment to a particular culture? To what extent does the client feel different as an individual vis-à-vis the cultural group with which she or he identifies most? What role, if any, does racism or prejudice play as an obstacle to this client's adjustment? What role, if any, do the dominant culture's standards (such as physical attractiveness) play in this client's adjustment? In what ways have culture-related factors affected this client's feelings of self-worth? What potential exists for cultural loss or feelings of rootlessness and loss of native heritage as a function of efforts to assimilate? Questions regarding physical health may also be appropriate, especially if the client is from a cultural group that has a documented tendency to express emotional distress through physical symptoms (Cheung & Lau, 1982; Kleinman & Lin, 1980).

The misspelled "ADRESSING" is an easy-to-remember acronym that may help the assessor remember various sources of cultural influence when assessing clients. As proposed by Pamela Hays (Hays, 1996, 2001), the letters in ADRESSING stand for *age*, *disability*, *religion*, *ethnicity*, *social status* (including variables such as income, occupation, and education), *sexual orientation*, *indigenous heritage*, *national origin*, and *gender*. How, for example, might a particular disability affect one's worldview in a particular context? Why might a deeply religious person feel strongly about a particular issue? These are the types of questions that could be raised by considering the ADRESSING acronym in the assessment of clients.

Whether using an interview, a test, or some other tool of assessment with a culturally different assessee, the assessor needs to be aware of ostensibly psychopathological responses that may be fairly commonplace in a particular culture. For example, claims of spirit involvement are not uncommon among some groups of depressed Native Americans (Johnson & Johnson, 1965), as well as others (Matchett, 1972). Diagnostic conclusions and judgments should attempt to distinguish veritable psychological and behavioral problems from behavior that may be deviant by the standards of the dominant culture but be customary by the standards of the assessee's culture. To be of maximum value, reports of assessment should go well beyond diagnostic determinations. Reports should provide a richly detailed account of what the problem is as well as what specific types of interventions are recommended.

Case History Data

Biographical and related data about an assessee may be obtained by interviewing the assessee and/or significant others in that person's life. Additional sources of case history data include hospital records, school records, employment records, and related documents. All such data are combined in an effort to obtain an understanding of the assessee, including insights into observed behavior patterns.[2] Case history data may be invaluable in helping a therapist develop a meaningful context in which to interpret data from other sources, such as interview transcripts and reports of psychological testing.

Psychological Tests

Clinicians and counselors may have occasion to use many different tests in the course of their practice, and nearly all of the tests we have described could conceivably be

---

2. For an example of a case study from the psychology literature, the interested reader is referred to "Socially Reinforced Obsessing: Etiology of a Disorder in a Christian Scientist" (Cohen & Smith, 1976), wherein the authors suggest that a woman's exposure to Christian Science predisposed her to an obsessive disorder. The article stirred some controversy and elicited a number of comments (for example, Coyne, 1976; Halleck, 1976; London, 1976; McLemore & Court, 1977), including one from a representative of the Christian Science church (Stokes, 1977)—all rebutted by Cohen (1977, 1979, pp. 76–83).

employed in clinical or counseling assessment. Often, more than one test is administered to an assessee. The phrase used to describe the group of tests administered is "test battery."

The Psychological Test Battery

If you are a culinary aficionado, or if you are a fan of *Iron Chef* on the Food Network, then you will know that the word *batter* refers to a beaten liquid mixture that typically contains a number of ingredients. Somewhat similar in meaning to this definition of batter is one definition of the word battery: an array or grouping of like things to be used together. When psychological assessors speak of a **battery,** they are referring to a group of tests administered together for the purpose of gathering information about an individual from a variety of instruments.

A personality test battery refers to a group of personality tests. A projective test battery also refers to a group of personality tests, though this term is more specific because it additionally tells us that the battery is confined to projective techniques (such as the Rorschach, the TAT, figure drawings, sentence completion, and word association tests). In shoptalk among clinicians, if the specific type of battery referred to is left unspecified or if the clinician refers to a battery of tests as a **standard battery,** what is usually being referred to is a group of tests including one intelligence test, at least one personality test, and a test designed to screen for neurological deficit (discussed in the following chapter).

Each test in the standard battery provides the clinician with information that goes beyond the specific area that the test is designed to tap. Thus, for example, a test of intelligence may yield not only information about intelligence but also information about personality and neurological functioning. Conversely, information about intelligence and neurological functioning can be gleaned from personality test data (and here we refer specifically to projective tests rather than personality inventories). The insistence on using a battery of tests and not a single test in evaluating patients was one of the many contributions of psychologist David Rapaport. At a time when using a battery of tests might mean using more than one projective test, Rapaport (1946/1967) argued that assessment would be incomplete if there weren't "right or wrong answers" to at least one of the tests administered; here he referred to a test of intellectual ability. This orientation is reflected in Rapaport's now-classic work in the area of clinical assessment, *Diagnostic Psychological Testing* (Rapaport et al., 1945–1946). Ogdon (1982) provides a useful sourcebook of studies from the research literature that sample the various interpretations that can be made from some of the tests typically used in a standard battery.

Diagnostic Tests

Some tests are designed primarily to be of diagnostic assistance to clinicians and counselors. One such group of tests was developed by Theodore Millon.

The Millon tests   The Millon Clinical Multiaxial Inventory (MCMI; Millon, 1983) consists of 175 true-false items that yield scores related to enduring personality features as well as acute clinical symptoms. The MCMI has been revised twice, resulting in the MCMI-II (Millon, 1987) and the MCMI-III (Millon et al., 1994). The MCMI-III yields scores for 14 personality scales that correspond to the DSM-IV personality disorders. There are also ten clinical scales, including scales to measure anxiety and depression, and four validity indices. Such information may be useful in assisting clinicians to make diagnoses with respect to the "multiaxial" DSM-IV and to assess outcome in psychotherapy. Because the MCMI tests are designed specifically for use with clinical populations, norms were gathered only on people with mental disorders; the standardization sample included 1,000 male and female patients with many different mental disorders. In scoring, raw scores on the scales are transformed into Base Rate scores, which are standard scores corresponding to known diagnostic prevalence data. In prior versions of the test, the validity of some of the scales had been a matter of concern to independent investigators. For example, Millon (1983) reported that the MCMI Drug Abuse scale correctly classified 94% of the sample tested. Yet in independent research with known alcohol and drug abusers, less than half that percentage of testtakers were correctly classified, and rates of false-positive identifications were as high as 50% (Bryer et al., 1990; Marsh et al., 1988). Concerns about the discriminant validity of certain scales have been noted (McCann, 1990), especially when a testtaker exhibits symptoms of a number of psychiatric conditions.

Although the MCMI-III authors cautioned that the instrument should not be used for "any purpose other than diagnostic screening or clinical assessment" (Millon et al., 1994, p. 5), the test seems to have inspired some strategies of intervention (Retzlaff, 1995a). Although generally received favorably, the MCMI-III retains some features of the MCMI-II that reviewers found controversial. For example, the sampling procedure employed to identify subjects for the standardization sample, the overlap of scales, and other technical matters prompted Haladyna and Reynolds (1992) to characterize the former version of the test as "a conceptual gem and psychometrically somewhere between a nightmare and an enigma" (p. 534).

The Millon Adolescent Clinical Inventory (MACI; Millon et al., 1993) is a revision of the Millon Adolescent Personality Inventory and its predecessor, the Millon Adolescent Inventory. Designed for use with adolescent clinical populations, the test yields clinical as well as personality-related data, includes validity and response bias scales, and has value in terms of DSM-IV diagnostic decision making. Administration time is an advantage, as most adolescents will complete the test's 160 items in about 20 minutes or so. A problem with the test is that the same responses to the 160 items are used repeatedly to derive scores on the test's 30 scales, with most scales containing 30 or more items. On average, each item is used on about six of the test's scales. As one reviewer observed, "The test should have more items, fewer scales, and/or fewer items per scale . . . so few items cannot be stretched that far" (Retzlaff, 1995b, p. 621).

A relative newcomer to the Millon family of tests is the Millon Index of Personality Styles (MIPS; Millon, 1994). Positioned as an instrument for the assessment of normal-range adult personality, the MIPS yields an overall adjustment index as well as information on 16 Jungian types. This computerized test may yield data of particular value to personnel working in vocational guidance and employee development programs.

At the foundation of each of these tests is Millon's (1969, 1981, 1986a, 1986b, 1990; Millon et al., 1996) notion of two primary dimensions of personality. One dimension, behavioral in nature, has to do with ways of gaining satisfaction and avoiding stress. The other has to do with an overall coping pattern that may be described as active or passive. Scores on Millon tests may be interpreted with respect to these two dimensions of personality, which, in turn, may be interpreted according to DSM-IV categories.

Evaluation of Specific Variables

Thousands of tests designed to focus on specific traits, states, interests, attitudes, and related variables are available to counselors and clinicians. Here, for illustrative purposes, we focus on what may be the most widely used of these fine-focused instruments—tests designed to assess depression.

Table 13–1
Criteria for Diagnosis of Depression

A. Five (or more) of the following symptoms have been present during the same 2-week period and represent a change from previous functioning; at least one of the symptoms is either depressed mood or loss of interest or pleasure.
   Note: Do not include symptoms that are clearly due to a general medical condition; or mood-incongruent delusions or hallucinations.

   1. Depressed mood most of the day, nearly every day, as indicated by either subjective report (e.g., feels sad or empty) or observation made by others (e.g., appears tearful). *Note:* In children and adolescents, can be irritable mood.
   2. Markedly diminished interest or pleasure in all, or almost all, activities most of the day, nearly every day (as indicated by either subjective account or observation made by others)
   3. Significant weight loss when not dieting or weight gain (e.g., a change of more than 5% of body weight in a month), or decrease or increase in appetite nearly every day. *Note:* In children, consider failure to make expected weight gains.
   4. Insomnia or hypersomnia nearly every day
   5. Psychomotor agitation or retardation nearly every day (observable by others, not merely subjective feelings of restlessness or being slowed down)
   6. Fatigue or loss of energy nearly every day
   7. Feelings of worthlessness or excessive or inappropriate guilt (which may be delusional) nearly every day (not merely self-reproach or guilt about being sick)
   8. Diminished ability to think or concentrate, or indecisiveness, nearly every day (either by subjective account or as observed by others)
   9. Recurrent thoughts of death (not just fear of dying), recurrent suicidal ideation without a specific plan, or a suicide attempt or a specific plan for committing suicide
B. The symptoms do not meet criteria for a Mixed Episode.
C. The symptoms cause clinically significant distress or impairment in social, occupational, or other important areas of functioning.
D. The symptoms are not due to the direct physiological effects of a substance (e.g., a drug of abuse, a medication) or a general medical condition (e.g., hypothyroidism).
E. The symptoms are not better accounted for by Bereavement, i.e., after the loss of a loved one, the symptoms persist for longer than 2 months or are characterized by marked functional impairment, morbid preoccupation with worthlessness, suicidal ideation, psychotic symptoms, or psychomotor retardation.

Source: American Psychiatric Association (1994)

Measures of depression   Depression is the most common mental health problem and reason for psychiatric hospitalization (Dean, 1985). From 5 to 9% of adult women, from 2 to 3% of adult men (American Psychiatric Association, 1994), and from 18 to 35% of adolescents (Clarizio, 1989) may experience depression at any time. Clinical depression is a risk factor for suicide and may even be the most universal of all such factors (Silverman, 1968). The DSM-IV criteria for diagnosing depression are presented in Table 13-1.

Depression may be diagnosed through an interview alone or through the use of varied other clinical tools (Ponterotto et al., 1989). Perhaps the most widely used test to measure the severity of depression is the Beck Depression Inventory-II (BDI-Il; Beck et al., 1996).

The BDI-II is a self-report measure of depression designed for use with respondents age 13 and older. For each item, testtakers circle one of four statements that best describes their feelings over the past two weeks. The statements reflect different intensities of feeling and are weighted in their scoring accordingly. Like the older version of this test, the Beck Depression Inventory (BDI), the BDI-II contains 21 items, each tapping a specific symptom or attitude associated with depression. However, the BDI-II differs from its predecessor in several key ways. The time frame of the older test was one week, whereas the time frame for the BDI-II is two weeks—this in keeping with DSM-IV diagnostic criteria for depression. Four BDI items (Weight Loss, Body Image Change, Somatic Preoccupation, and Work Difficulty) were retired and replaced by four new items on the BDI-II (Agitation, Worthlessness, Concentration Difficulty, and Loss of Energy). Beck et al. (1996) present data to document their assertion that on average, patients with mood disorders obtain higher scores on the BDI-II than patients with anxiety, adjustment, or other disorders. Additionally, they present data to support their claim that on average, patients with more serious depressive disorders score higher on the BDI-II than patients with less serious forms of depression. Because the items are so transparent and the test outcome so easily manipulated by the testtaker, the BDI-II should be used only with patients who have no known motivation to fake good or fake bad. Further, because the BDI-II contains no validity scales, it is probably advisable to administer it along with other tests that do have validity scales, such as the MMPI-2.

Although Beck's test is probably the most widely used measure of depression for adolescents and adults (Archer et al., 1991; Piotrowski & Keller, 1992), let's briefly take note of another instrument appropriate for use with younger respondents. The Children's Depression Inventory (CDI; Kovacs, 1977) is a 27-item, self-report questionnaire. Each item consists of three statements from which one is selected as reflective of how the respondent has felt over the course of the past two weeks. Appropriate for use with children and adolescents, the CDI has been studied extensively (see, for example, Carey et al., 1987; Kavan, 1990; Knoff, 1990b; Mattison et al., 1990; Saylor et al., 1984; Semrud-Clikeman, 1990; Siegel, 1986; Smucker et al., 1986). In general, the test has been shown to be reliable, valid, and capable of distinguishing depressed children and adolescents from normal controls. The CDI is less robust in its ability to distinguish children and adolescents diagnosed as depressed from children and adolescents with other psychiatric diagnoses. The factor structure of the test appears to vary as a function of the age of the children and adolescents tested. The CDI appears particularly useful in identifying children and adolescents as depressed when used as part of a multi-instrument battery (Kazdin et al., 1986).

One ten-year literature review of the validity and clinical utility of depression screening yielded a number of noteworthy findings. Schade et al. (1998) concluded that as a group, instruments used to screen for depression do detect clinically significant depression. Some evidence even suggested that screening instruments performed better than clinical impressions. An exception here is when severe dementia coexists with the depression. The researchers also found that screening instruments for depression lacked specificity and tended to measure more than depression. Another key finding was that "less is more" in depression screening with general populations. "Because short instruments with well-selected questions appear to perform as well as more elaborate ones (for case finding), brevity may be a key feature" (Schade et al., 1998, p. 60).

Short, long, and in-between length instruments are used in a number of specialty areas of clinical practice. Some of these instruments may be unique to a particular type of evaluation, whereas some types of evaluation require the use of traditional instruments in nontraditional ways. We now turn our attention to clinical assessment in special contexts.

Special Applications of Clinical Measures

Forensic Psychological Assessment

The word *forensic* means pertaining to or employed in legal proceedings, and the term **forensic psychological assessment** can be defined broadly as the theory and application of psychological evaluation and measurement in a legal context. Psychologists, psychiatrists, and other health professionals may be called on by courts, corrections and parole personnel, attorneys, and others involved in the criminal justice system to offer expert opinion on some matter. With respect to criminal proceedings, the opinion may, for example, concern an individual's competency to stand trial or his or her criminal responsibility (that is, sanity) at the time a crime is committed. With respect to a civil proceeding, the opinion may have to do with issues as diverse as the extent of emotional distress suffered in a personal injury suit, the suitability of one or the other parent in a custody proceeding, or the testamentary capacity (capacity to make a last will and testament) of a person before death.

Before discussing some of the assessment-related aspects in a sampling of the many areas of forensic psychology, it is important to note that there are important differences between forensic and general clinical practice. As noted by Rappeport (1982), the biggest difference is that in the forensic situation, the clinician is not serving the patient but a third party, such as a court or an attorney, and that fact (as well as its implications with respect to issues such as confidentiality) must be made clear to the assessee. Another difference is that the patient is consulting the professional not for therapy but for help in dealing with the third party. There is therefore "a great likelihood that the patient will not be as truthful as he or she would be in other circumstances" (Rappeport, 1982, p. 333). Consequently, it is imperative that the assessor rely not only on the assessee's representations but on all available documentation, such as police reports and interviews with persons who may have pertinent knowledge. The mental health professional who performs forensic work would do well to be educated in the language of the law. As Rappeport put it:

> To go into court and render the opinion that a person is not responsible for a crime because he is psychotic is to say nothing of value to the judge or jury. However, to go into the same court and state that a man is not responsible because as a result of a mental disorder, namely, paranoid schizophrenia, "he lacked substantial capacity to conform his behavior to the requirements of the law"—because he was hearing voices that told him he must commit the crime to protect his family from future harm—would be of great value to the judge or jury. It is not because the man had a psychosis that he is not responsible; it is how his illness affected his behavior and his ability to form the necessary criminal intent or to have the *mens rea*, or guilty mind, that is important. (p. 333)

Forensic assessors are sometimes placed in the role of psychohistorians, especially in cases involving questions of testamentary capacity. In such cases, assessors may be called on to offer opinions about people they have never personally interviewed or observed— a situation that seldom if ever arises in nonforensic assessments. Forensic assessment frequently entails rendering opinions about momentous matters such as whether a person is competent to stand trial, criminally responsible, or ready for parole. Some have challenged the role of mental health professionals in these and related matters, citing the unreliability of psychiatric diagnosis and the invalidity of various assessment tools for use with such objectives (Faust & Ziskin, 1988a, 1988b; see also Matarazzo, 1990, for a response). Still, judges, juries, district attorneys, the police, and other members of the criminal justice system rely on mental health professionals to provide them with their best judgments concerning such critical questions. One such question that is raised every day around the world—frequently with life or death hanging in the balance— concerns the prediction of dangerousness.

Dangerousness to oneself or others   An official determination that a person is dangerous to self or others is legal cause to deprive that individual of liberty. The individual so judged will, on a voluntary or involuntary basis, undergo psychotherapeutic intervention, typically in a secure treatment facility, until such time that he or she is no longer judged to be dangerous. This is so because the state has a clear and compelling interest in protecting its citizens from danger and in protecting suicidal people—presumed to be suffering from mental disorder—from their own self-destructive impulses. Mental health professionals—traditionally psychiatrists and increasingly psychologists—play a key role in decisions about who is and is not considered dangerous.

The determination of dangerousness is ideally made on the basis of multiple data sources, including interview data, case history data, and formal testing. When dealing with potentially homicidal or suicidal assessees, the professional assessor must have knowledge of the risk factors associated with such violent acts (such as previous attempts to commit the act, drug/alcohol abuse, and unemployment). If given an opportunity to interview the potentially dangerous individual, the assessor will typically explore the assessee's ideation and imagery associated with the violent act, as well as the availability and lethality of the method and means by which the violent act would be perpetrated. The assessor will assess how specific and detailed the plan, if any, is and the availability of helping resources such as family, friends, or roommates. If the assessor determines that a homicide is imminent, the assessor has a legal **duty to warn** the endangered third party—a duty that overrides the privileged communication between psychologist and client. As stated in the landmark 1974 case *Tarasoff v. the Regents of the University of California,* "Protective privilege ends where the public peril begins" (see Cohen, 1979, for elaboration of this and related principles).

Dangerousness manifests itself in sundry ways in varied settings ranging from the school playground to the post office lobby. Working together, members of the legal and mental health communities strive to keep people reasonably safe from themselves and others while not unduly depriving any citizens of their right to liberty. Toward that end, a rather large literature dealing with the assessment of dangerousness, including suicide, has emerged (see, for example, Baumeister, 1990; Blumenthal & Kupfer, 1990; Catalano et al., 1997; Copas & Tarling, 1986; Gardner et al., 1996; Jobes et al., 1997; Lewinsohn et al., 1996; Lidz et al., 1993; Monahan, 1981; Olweus, 1979; Rice & Harris, 1995; Steadman, 1983; van Praag et al., 1990; Wagner, 1997; Webster et al., 1994), along with a number of tests (Beck et al., 1989; Eyman & Eyman, 1990; Linehan et al., 1983; Patterson et al., 1983; Reynolds, 1987; Rothberg & Geer-Williams, 1992; Williams et al., 1996) and clinical interview guidelines (Sommers-Flanagan & Sommers-Flanagan, 1995; Truant et al., 1991; Wollersheim, 1974). Still, the prediction of dangerousness must, at this point in time, be considered more of an art than a science; clinicians have historically not been very accurate in their predictions of dangerousness. On a brighter note, there are many people and organizations working to better the odds when it comes to predicting dangerousness. As pointed out in this chapter's *Close-up,* among the organizations committed to the application of behavioral science to issues of dangerousness is the U.S. Secret Service.

Competency to stand trial   "Competency" in the legal sense has many different meanings. One may speak, for example, of competence to make a will, enter into a contract, commit a crime, waive constitutional rights, consent to medical treatment . . . the list goes on. Before convicted murderer Gary Gilmore was executed in Utah, he underwent an examination designed to determine whether or not he was competent to be executed. That is so because the law mandates that a certain propriety exists with respect to state-ordered executions, and it would not be morally proper to execute insane persons. **Competence to stand trial** has to do largely with a defendant's ability to understand the charges against him or her and assist in his or her own defense. As stated in the Supreme Court's ruling in *Dusky v. United States,* a defendant must have "sufficient present ability to consult with his lawyer with a reasonable degree of rational . . . (and) factual understanding of the proceedings against him." This "understand and assist" requirement, as it has come to be called, is in effect an extension of the constitutional prohibition against trials *in absentia;* a defendant must be not only physically present during the trial but mentally present as well.

The competency requirement protects an individual's right to choose and assist counsel, the right to act as a witness on one's own behalf, and the right to confront opposing

Assessment of Dangerousness
and the Secret Service

The Secret Service is charged by federal law with a number of responsibilities. The Service investigates crimes of counterfeiting, forgery, and fraud involving telecommunications, computers, and financial institutions. Perhaps best known, however, are its protective functions. The Secret Service is charged with protecting the following people and their families: the president of the United States, the vice president, former presidents and vice presidents, major candidates for or successors to these offices, and visiting foreign heads of state.

Like other law enforcement agencies, the Secret Service has a long tradition of experience in the area of criminal investigation. And again, much like other law enforcement agencies, the Secret Service cannot boast of special expertise in psychology or related areas of behavioral science that would be of value in its protective mission . . . or can it?

Law enforcement agencies, including the Secret Service, have evidenced a great deal of interest in terms of how behavioral science, and more specifically knowledge of dangerousness, can be applied in everyday functioning. In Los Angeles, where the stalking of celebrities has been a well-publicized problem, the police department established a threat management unit (Lane, 1992). When members of Congress or their staffs receive threats, the matter may be referred to a similar police unit established by the U.S. Capitol Police (Coggins, et al., 1998). Additionally, "the United States Marshals Service has initiated systematic efforts to formulate a protective investigative function to analyze inappropriate communications to, and to evaluate and manage potential threats against federal judicial officials" (Coggins et al., p. 53).

The Secret Service has been exemplary in its efforts to integrate behavioral research and clinical expertise into its policies and practices, including its risk assessment and protective activities. In the course of attempting to prevent a highly specific crime from taking place, some of the things the Service must do are (1) identify and investigate people who may pose a risk to a protectee; (2) make a determination as to level of risk the identified people pose; and (3) implement a case management program for those identified as possibly posing a genuine risk. To meet these and related objectives with maximum effectiveness, the Service established a behavioral research program. The head of that program is Margaret Coggins, Ph.D., and much of what we say here about that program is derived from a publication by Coggins and her colleagues (1998).

Charged with duties that entail conducting very specialized assessments of dangerousness on a regular basis, the Secret Service has a history of receiving input from clinical and forensic professionals. In 1980, the agency contracted with the Institute of Medicine to sponsor a conference of clinicians and behavioral scientists addressed to issues such as the prediction of dangerousness, case management of dangerous persons, and agent training needs (Takeuchi et al., 1981). Another conference in 1982 extended the agenda to issues such as the development of an internal research program on the assessment of people who threatened protectees and training for agents in the assessment and management of mentally ill threateners (Institute of Medicine, 1984). The Secret Service's behavioral research program evolved out of these conferences and today studies diverse matters such as risk assessment issues, factors in agent decision making, and attitudes of mental health professionals toward the Secret Service vis-à-vis their effect on the reporting of threats to the Service's protectees. A collaboration between researchers and practitioners was forged in order to achieve the program objectives:

Special agents and researchers, both internal Secret Service staff and external consultants, work together to identify practical study questions, prioritize areas of inquiry, design study methodologies, collect and analyze data, and disseminate research findings. Agents play a key role in ensuring that relevant investigative, risk assessment, and case management concerns are brought forward for study, and their participation in research design and data collection lends internal credibility to the importance of incorporating study findings into practice. Similarly, research staff and scholars from the academic and scientific communities ensure that principles of scientific integrity guide the research process and are instrumental in protecting the external validity of the data and

The Secret Service relies on research on the assessment of dangerousness in fulfilling its protective mission.

findings according to rigorous standards of peer review. (Coggins et al., 1998, p. 61)

The case study is a potentially useful tool of assessment and research, particularly in efforts to identify factors related to an individual's potential for violence against a Secret Service protectee. The Secret Service's Exceptional Case Study Project (ECSP) was designed to study persons who have either attacked or approached with lethal means an individual targeted on the basis of public status. Variables selected for study include behavior, thinking, planning, mental status, motivation, and communication patterns. One noteworthy finding from such research could be paraphrased in terms of the aphorism that actions speak louder than words; prior behavior takes precedence over threatening statements as a factor related to potential for violence (Vossekuil & Fein,

1997). This finding is consistent with the findings of psychiatrist Park Dietz in his research on individuals who stalk Hollywood celebrities. Dietz et al. (1991) concluded that there was little relation between writing a threatening letter to the celebrity and attempting to physically approach the celebrity; those who wrote such letters were no more or less likely to attempt to approach the celebrity than people who did not make threats.

Although the Secret Service has been exemplary in its organizational efforts to employ and generate behavioral research, it is also the case, as Coggins et al. (1998) put it, that "the operational mission always takes precedence over academic or scientific interest" (p. 68). Still, behavioral science, and in particular assessment-related research, has much to offer the Secret Service and other organizations involved in law enforcement and crime prevention.

Table 13–2
Georgetown Criteria for
Competency to Stand Trial

Factual Items

Defendant's ability to:

1. understand his [or her] current legal situation
2. understand the charges made against him [or her]
3. understand the legal issues and procedures in the case
4. understand the possible dispositions, pleas, and penalties
5. understand the facts relevant to the case
6. identify and locate witnesses

Inferential Items

Defendant's ability to communicate with counsel and to:

7. comprehend instructions and advice
8. make decisions after advice
9. follow testimony for contradictions or errors
10. maintain a collaborative relationship with his [or her] attorney
11. testify if necessary and be cross-examined
12. tolerate stress at the trial or while awaiting trial
13. refrain from irrational behavior during the trial

Source: Bukatman et al. (1971)

witnesses. The requirement also increases the probability that the truth of the case will be developed, since the competent defendant is able to monitor continuously the testimony of witnesses and help bring discrepancies in testimony to the attention of the court. In general, persons who are mentally retarded, psychotic, or suffering from a debilitating neurological disorder are persons held to be incompetent to stand trial. However, it cannot be overemphasized that any one of these three diagnoses is not sufficient in itself for a person to be found incompetent. Stated another way: It is possible for a person to be mentally retarded, psychotic, or suffering from a debilitating neurological disorder—or all three—and still be found competent to stand trial. The person will be found to be incompetent if and only if he or she is unable to understand the charges against him or her and is unable to assist in his or her own defense.

A number of instruments have been developed as aids in evaluating whether a defendant meets the "understand and assist" requirement. For example, researchers at Georgetown University Law School (Bukatman et al., 1971) enumerated 13 criteria of competency to stand trial (Table 13–2). Sample questions used in conjunction with these criteria include the following: What is your lawyer's job? What is the purpose of the judge? What does the jury do? What will the prosecutor do? What alibi or defense do you think you have now? What does incompetent to stand trial mean to you? Do you think there is any reason why you should be found incompetent? According to Bukatman et al., a thorough competency evaluation would entail answers to such questions "with sufficient information on each point to indicate whether there is, or might be in the future, a problem in that area" (p. 1226).

An alternative measure of competency, the Competency Screening Test (Lipsitt et al., 1971) employs a sentence completion format (Table 13–3) with each of 22 items relating to a legal criterion of competency to stand trial. The test is scored on a 3-point scale ranging from 0 to 2, with appropriate responses being scored 2, marginally appropriate responses being scored 1, and clearly inappropriate responses being scored 0. For example, a 2-point response to the item "When I go to court, the lawyer will _____" would be "defend me." Such a response indicates that the assessee has a clear understanding of the lawyer's role. By contrast, a 0-point response might be "have me guillotined," which would be indicative of an inappropriate perception of the lawyer's role. Lipsitt et al. re-

Table 13–3
Competency Screening Test

1. The lawyer told Bill that _____.
2. When I go to court, the lawyer will _____.
3. Jack felt that the judge _____.
4. When Phil was accused of the crime, he _____.
5. When I prepare to go to court with my lawyer _____.
6. If the jury finds me guilty, I _____.
7. The way a court trial is decided _____.
8. When the evidence in George's case was presented to the jury _____.
9. When the lawyer questioned his client in court, the client said _____.
10. If Jack had to try his own case, he _____.
11. Each time the D.A. asked me a question, I _____.
12. While listening to the witnesses testify against me, I _____.
13. When the witness testifying against Harry gave incorrect evidence, he _____.
14. When Bob disagreed with his lawyer on his defense, he _____.
15. When I was formally accused of the crime, I thought to myself _____.
16. If Ed's lawyer suggests that he plead guilty, he _____.
17. What concerns Fred most about his lawyer _____.
18. When they say a man is innocent until proven guilty _____.
19. When I think of being sent to prison, I _____.
20. When Phil thinks of what he is accused of, he _____.
21. When the [members of the jury hear] my case, they will _____.
22. If I had a chance to speak to the judge, I _____.

Source: Lipsitt et al. (1971)

ported the inter-rater reliability among trained scorers of this test to be $r = .93$. They also reported that their test was successful in discriminating seriously disturbed, state-hospitalized men from control groups consisting of students, community adults, club members, and civilly committed hospitalized patients. Subsequent research by independent investigators (Nottingham & Mattson, 1981) further supports the clinical utility of the Competency Screening Test.

Criminal responsibility "Not guilty by reason of insanity" is a plea to a criminal charge that we have all heard. But stop and think about the meaning of the legal term **insanity** to mental health professionals and the evaluation procedures by which psychological assessors could identify the insane. The insanity defense has its roots in the idea that only blameworthy persons (that is, those with a criminal mind) should be punished. Possibly exempt from blame, therefore, are children, mental incompetents, and others who may be irresponsible, lack control of their actions, or have no conception that what they are doing may be criminal. As early as the sixteenth century, it was argued in an English court that an offending act should not be considered a felony if the offender had no conception of good and evil. By the eighteenth century, the focus had shifted from good and evil as a criterion for evaluating criminal responsibility to the issue of whether the defendant "doth not know what he is doing no more than . . . a wild beast." Judicial history was made in nineteenth-century England when in 1843 Daniel M'Naghten was found not guilty by reason of insanity after attempting to assassinate the British prime minister (and mistakenly shooting and killing the prime minister's secretary). In the words of the court that acquitted M'Naghten, exculpation would be made if "at the time of the committing of the act, the party accused was laboring under such a defect of reason from disease of the mind as not to know the nature and quality of the act he was doing, or if he did know it, that he did not know he was doing what was wrong."

The decision in the **M'Naghten** case has come to be referred to as the "right or wrong test." To the present day, this test of sanity is used in England as well as in a number of jurisdictions in the United States. However, a deficiency in the "right or wrong test" is that it does not allow for the exculpation of persons who might know right from wrong but are unable to control impulses to commit criminal acts. In 1954, an opinion written by the United States Court of Appeal for the District of Columbia in the case of **Durham** v. United States held a defendant not to be culpable for criminal action "if his unlawful act was the product of a mental disease or defect." Still another standard of legal insanity was set forth by the American Law Institute (**ALI**) in 1956, and this standard has become one of the most widely used throughout the United States (Weiner, 1980). With slight alterations from one jurisdiction to another, this legal test of sanity provides as follows:

> A person is not responsible for criminal conduct i.e., insane if, at the time of such conduct, as a result of a mental disease or defect, he lacks substantial capacity either to appreciate the criminality (wrongfulness) of his conduct, or to conform his conduct to the requirements of the law.
>
> As used in this article, the terms "mental disease or defect" do not include an abnormality manifested only by repeated criminal or otherwise antisocial conduct.

In clinical practice, defendants who are mentally retarded, psychotic, or neurologically impaired are likely to be the ones found to be not guilty by reason of insanity. However, as was the case with considerations of competency to stand trial, the mere fact that a person is judged to be mentally retarded, psychotic, or neurologically impaired is in itself no guarantee that the individual will be found not guilty; other criteria, such as the ALI standards cited, must be met. To help psychological assessors determine if those standards are met, a number of instruments such as the Rogers Criminal Responsibility Assessment Scale (RCRAS) have been developed. Psychologist Richard Rogers and his colleagues (Rogers & Cavanaugh, 1980, 1981; Rogers et al., 1981) designed the RCRAS to be a systematic and empirical approach to insanity evaluations. This instrument consists of 25 items tapping both psychological and situational variables. The items are scored with respect to five scales: reliability (including malingering), organic factors, psychopathology, cognitive control, and behavioral control. After scoring, the examiner employs a hierarchical decision model for the purpose of arriving at a decision concerning the assessee's sanity. Validity studies done with this scale (for example, Rogers et al., 1983; Rogers et al., 1984) have shown it to be useful in discriminating between sane and insane patients/defendants.

Debate about the reasonableness of insanity as a defense has been a fact of life perhaps as long as there has been an insanity defense (Fingarette & Hasse, 1979; Finkel et al., 1985; Goldstein, 1967; Keilitz, 1987; Lanyon, 1986; Morse, 1985; Reynolds, 1984; Simon, 1967; Simon & Aaronson, 1988; Slobogin, 1985). In recent years, the disagreement has become even more heated, however, as attempts have been made at the federal and state levels to modify or even abolish existing statutes affecting a defense of insanity. Different insanity defense standards will have differential effects on court findings. Empirical research on how changed standards might affect court findings is currently in an exploratory stage (see, for example, Wettstein et al., 1991).

Readiness for parole or probation Some people convicted of a crime will pay their dues to society and go on to lead fulfilling, productive lives after their incarceration. At the other extreme are career criminals who will violate laws at the first opportunity upon their release—or escape—from prison. Predicting who is ready for parole or probation and what the outcome of such a release might be has proved no easy task, yet this has not deterred psychologists from trying to develop effective measures.

A classic work by Cleckley (1976) provided a detailed profile of *psychopaths*—people with few inhibitions who may pursue pleasure or money with callous disregard for the welfare of others. Based on a factor-analytic study of Cleckley's description, Robert D. Hare (1980) developed a 22-item Psychopathy Checklist (PCL) that reflects personality characteristics as rated by the assessor (such as callousness, impulsiveness, and empathy), as well as prior history as gleaned from the assessee's records (such as "criminal versatility"). In the revised version of the test, the Revised Psychopathy Checklist (PCL-R; Hare, 1985), two items from the original PCL were omitted because of their relatively low correlation with the rest of the scale, and the scoring criteria for some of the remaining items were modified. Hare et al. (1990) report that the two forms are equivalent.

Harris, Rice, and Cormier (1989) reported that in a maximum-security psychiatric sample, the PCL correctly identified 80% of the violent recidivists. A study by Hart, Kropp, and Hare (1988) indicates that psychopaths are four times more likely than nonpsychopaths to fail on release. A version of the PCL specially modified for use with young male offenders produced scores that correlated significantly with variables such as number of conduct disorder symptoms, previous violent offenses, violent recidivism, and violent behavior within the maximum security institution in which the study was conducted (Forth et al., 1990). In another study, psychopathy ratings were found to predict outcome for both temporary absence and parole release; psychopaths were recommitted four times more frequently than nonpsychopaths (Serin et al., 1990).

Another line of research in this area has been undertaken by Glenn Walters (1991) at the federal penitentiary in Leavenworth, Kansas. Walters and White (1989) have characterized the criminal lifestyle as one marked by self-indulgence, interpersonal intrusiveness, social rule breaking, and irresponsibility. The 14-item Lifestyle Criminality Screening Form (LCSF; Walters et al., 1991) yields scores on such characteristics based on information from an offender's presentence investigation report. In a study in which the subjects' probation officers served as the raters, offenders obtaining high scores on the LCSF exhibited a higher rate of parole and probation failure than offenders obtaining lower scores (Walters et al., 1990). Walters et al. (1990) caution, however, that additional research is required to explore the generalizability and implications of their findings.

Diagnosis and evaluation of emotional injury   **Emotional injury,** or psychological harm or damage, is a term that has sometimes been used synonymously with mental suffering, pain and suffering, and emotional harm. In cases involving myriad charges—among them discrimination, divorce, harassment, malpractice, personal injury, stalking, and unlawful termination of employment—psychological assessors may be responsible for evaluating alleged emotional injury. Such an evaluation will be designed to shed light on an individual's functioning prior to and then subsequent to the alleged injury (Melton et al., 1997). The court will evaluate the findings in light of all of the evidence, and make a determination regarding whether the alleged injury exists, and if so, the magnitude of the damage.

Many tools of assessment, including the interview, the case study, and psychological tests may be used in the process of evaluating and diagnosing claims of emotional injury. Interviews may be conducted with the person claiming the injury, as well as others who have knowledge relevant to the claim. Case study materials include documents such as physician or therapist records, school records, military records, employment records, and police records. The specific psychological tests used in an emotional injury evaluation will vary with the preferences of the assessor. In one study in which 140 forensic psychologists returned a survey dealing with assessment practices, it was found that no two practitioners routinely used the exact same combination of tests to assess emotional injury (Boccaccini & Brodsky, 1999). In order of frequency of usage, the top three tests preferred by the survey respondents were the MMPI (in its original form or the

MMPI-2), the WAIS-R or WAIS-III, and the MCMI (MCMI-II or MCMI-III). The reasons given for the use of specific tests and test batteries most frequently had to do with established norms, personal clinical experience, the widespread acceptance of the instrument, the research support, and content. Although such nonuniform use of tests to explore a specific variable has been criticized by some (see Ziskin, 1995), it has been defended on the grounds that claims of emotional injury arise from a wide range of causes, and the nature of the emotional injury claimed in each case may also be quite varied. Nonetheless, as Boccaccini and Brodsky (1999) recommend, greater consistency in test selection would be desirable. Such consistency could be achieved by studying the incremental validity each test adds to the task of assessing different types of emotional injury in specific contexts.

Custody Evaluations

As the number of divorces in this country continues to climb, so does the number of custody proceedings. Before the 1920s, it was fairly commonplace for the father to be granted custody of the children (Lamb, 1981). The pendulum swung, however, with the widespread adoption of what was referred to as the "tender years" doctrine, and the belief that the child's interest would be best served if the mother was granted custody. In recent years, and with the coming of age of the dual-career household, the courts have begun to be more egalitarian in their custody decisions; it is recognized that the best interest of the child may be served by father custody, mother custody, or joint custody (McClure-Butterfield, 1990). Psychological assessors can assist the court in making awards of custody with reports that detail the parental capacity of the parents or the parental preferences of the children (Weithorn, 1987). Ideally, one impartial expert in the mental health field should be responsible for assessing *all* family members and submitting a report to the court (Gardner, 1982). More often than not, however, the husband has his doctor, the wife has hers, and the battle is on.

Evaluation of the parent   The evaluation of the parental capacity typically entails a detailed interview that focuses primarily on various aspects of child rearing, though tests of intelligence, personality, and adjustment may be employed if questions remain after the interview. The assessor might begin with open-ended questions designed to let the parent ventilate some of his or her feelings and then proceed to more specific questions tapping a wide variety of areas, including

- the parent's own childhood: happy? abused?
- the parent's own relationship with parents, siblings, peers
- the circumstances that led up to the marriage and the degree of forethought that went into the decision to have (or adopt) children
- the adequacy of prenatal care and attitudes toward the pregnancy
- the parent's description of the child
- the parent's own evaluation of himself or herself as a parent, including strengths and weaknesses
- the parent's evaluation of his or her spouse regarding strengths and weaknesses as a parent
- the quantity and quality of time spent caring for and playing with children
- the parent's approach to discipline
- the parent's receptivity to the child's peer relationships

During the course of the interview, the assessor may find evidence that the interviewee really does not want custody of the children but is undertaking the custody battle for some other reason. For example, custody may be nothing more than another issue to bargain over with respect to the divorce settlement. Alternatively, a parent might, for example, be embarrassed to admit to himself or herself and to observers of the proceedings that he or she really doesn't want custody of the children. Sometimes a parent, emotionally scathed by all that has gone on before the divorce, may be employing the custody battle as a technique of vengeance—to threaten to take away that which is most prized and adored by the spouse. The clinician performing the evaluation must appreciate that such ill-motivated intentions do underlie some custody battles; and, in the best interest of the children, it is the obligation of the clinician to report such findings.

In certain cases an assessor may deem it desirable to assess any of many variables related to marriage and family life. A wide variety of such instruments are available including those designed to measure adjustment (Beier & Sternberg, 1977; Epstein et al., 1983; Locke & Wallace, 1959; McCubbin et al., 1985a, 1985b; Spanier, 1976; Spanier & Filsinger, 1983; Udry, 1981), assets (Olson et al., 1985), preferences (Price et al., 1982), intimacy (Waring & Reddon, 1983), jealousy (Bringle et al., 1979), communication (Bienvenu, 1978), feelings (Lowman, 1980), satisfaction (Roach et al., 1981; Snyder, 1981), stability (Booth & Edwards, 1983), trust (Larzelere & Huston, 1980), expectancies (Notarius & Vanzetti, 1983; Sabatelli, 1984), parenting ability (Bavolek, 1984), coping strategies (McCubbin et al., 1985a, 1985b; Straus, 1979), strength of family ties (Bardis, 1975), family interpersonal environment (Kinston et al., 1985; Moos & Moos, 1981; Robin et al., 1990), children's attitudes toward parents (Hudson, 1982), and overall quality of family life (Beavers, 1985; Olson & Barnes, 1985).

Evaluation of the child   The court will be interested in knowing if the child in a custody proceeding has a preference with respect to future living and visitation arrangements. Toward that end, the psychological assessor can be of assistance with a wide variety of tests and techniques. Most authorities agree that the preferences of children under the age of 5 are too unreliable and too influenced by recent experiences to be accorded much weight. However, if intelligence test data indicate that the child who is chronologically 5 is functioning at a higher level, then his or her preferences may be accorded greater weight. This is particularly true if the Comprehension subtest score on a Wechsler test (such as the Wechsler Preschool and Primary Scale of Intelligence-Revised) is elevated, for, you will recall, the Comprehension subtest requires the child to draw on the knowledge of social situations. Some methods that can be useful in assessing a child's parental preference include structured play exercises with dolls that represent the child and other family members, figure drawings of family members followed by story telling to the drawings, and the use of projective techniques such as the TAT and related tests (Figure 13–1). Sometimes impromptu innovation on the part of the examiner is required. In performing a custody evaluation on a 5-year-old child, the senior author of this text (RJC) noted that the child seemed to identify very strongly with the main character in a then-popular film, *E. T., the Extraterrestrial.* The child had seen the film three times, came into the test session carrying two *E. T.* bubble-gum cards, and identified as "E. T." the picture he drew when instructed to draw a person. To obtain a measure of parental preference, the examiner took four figures and represented them as "E. T.," "E. T.'s mother," "E. T.'s father," and "E. T.'s sister." An empty cardboard box was then labeled a "spaceship," and the child was told that E. T. (stranded on earth and longing to return to his home planet) had the opportunity to go home but that the spaceship had room for only two other passengers. The child boarded his mother and his sister in addition to "E. T." and told the examiner that E. T.'s father would "wave goodbye."

Figure 13–1
Projective Techniques Used in Custody Evaluation

The picture on the left is from the Children's Apperception Test-H (Bellak & Bellak, 1965), and the one on the right is from The Boys and Girls Book About Divorce *(Gardner, 1971). These, as well as TAT and other pictures used as projective stimuli, may be useful in evaluating children's parental preferences.*

Specially constructed sentence completion items can also be of value in the assessment of parental preferences. For example, the following items might be useful in examining children's differing perceptions of each parent:

Mothers _____.

If I do something wrong, my father _____.

It is best for children to live with _____.

Fathers _____.

Mommies are bad when _____.

I like to hug _____.

I don't like to hug _____.

Daddies are bad when _____.

The last time I cried _____.

My friends think that my mother _____.

My friends think that my father _____.

The data-gathering process for the evaluation begins at the moment the child and the parent(s) come into the office. The assessor takes careful note of the quality of the interaction between the parent(s) and the child. The child will then be interviewed alone and asked about the nature and quality of the relationship. If the child expresses a strong preference for one parent or the other, the assessor must evaluate how meaningful that preference is. For example, a child who sees his rancher father only every other weekend might have a good ol' time on the brief occasions that they are together and express a preference for living there—unaware that life in the country would soon become just as routine as life in the city with Mom. If children do not express a preference, insight into their feelings can be obtained by using the tests described earlier, combined with skillful interviewing. Included among the topics for discussion will be the child's physical description of his or her parents as well as his or her living quarters. Questions about the routine aspects of life (such as, "Who makes breakfast for you?") as well as questions about recreation, parental visitation, parental involvement with their education, their general well-being, and their siblings and friends will be asked.

Child Abuse and Neglect

A legal mandate exists in most states for many licensed professionals to report **child abuse** and **child neglect** when they have knowledge of it. The legal definitions of child abuse and child neglect vary from state to state. Typically, definitions of **abuse** refer to the creation of conditions that may give rise to abuse of a child (a person under the state-defined age of majority) by an adult responsible for the care of that person. The abuse may be in the form of (1) the infliction or allowing of infliction of physical injury or emotional impairment that is nonaccidental, (2) the creation or allowing the creation of substantial risk of physical injury or emotional impairment that is nonaccidental, or (3) the committing or allowing of a sexual offense to be committed against a child. Typical definitions of **neglect** refer to a failure on the part of an adult responsible for the care of a child to exercise a minimum degree of care in providing the child with food, clothing, shelter, education, medical care, and supervision.

A number of excellent general sources for the study of child abuse and child neglect are currently available (see, for example, Board of Professional Affairs, 1999; Cicchetti & Carlson, 1989; Ellerstein, 1981; Fischer, 1999; Fontana et al., 1963; Helfer & Kempe, 1988; Kelley, 1988; Reece & Groden, 1985). Resources are also available to assist professionals in recognizing specific forms of child abuse such as head injury (Billmire & Myers, 1985), eye injury (Gammon, 1981), mouth injury (Becker et al., 1978), emotional trauma (Brassard et al., 1986), burns (Alexander et al., 1987; Lung et al., 1977), bites (American Board of Forensic Odontology, 1986), fractures (Worlock et al., 1986), poisoning (Kresel & Lovejoy, 1981), sexual abuse (Adams-Tucker, 1982; Faller, 1988; Friedrich et al., 1986; Sanfilippo et al., 1986; Sebold, 1987), and shaken infant syndrome (Dykes, 1986). What follows are some brief, very general guidelines to the assessment of physical and emotional signs of child abuse.

Physical signs of abuse and neglect   Although psychologists and other mental health professionals without medical credentials do not typically have occasion to physically examine children, a knowledge of physical signs of abuse and neglect is important. Obvious physical injuries may be described by abused children or abusing adults as the result of an accident, and the knowledgeable professional needs a working familiarity with the various kinds of injuries that may signal more ominous causes. For example, in the case of injury to the face, in most veritable accidents, only one side of the face is injured. It may therefore be significant if a child evidences injury on both sides of the face—both eyes and both cheeks. Marks on the skin may be telling—grab marks made by an adult-size hand, marks that form a recognizable pattern, such as the tines of a fork, a belt buckle, a cord or rope, or human teeth. Burns from a cigarette or lighter may be in evidence as marks on the soles of the feet, the palms of the hands, the back, or the buttocks, and burns from scalding water may be in evidence as a glovelike redness on the hands or feet. Any bone fracture or dislocation should be investigated, as should head injuries, particularly when a patch of hair appears to be missing—as would be the case if the child's hair was pulled.

Physical signs that may or may not indicate neglect include dress that is inappropriate for the season, poor hygiene, and lagging physical development. Physical signs indicative of sexual abuse are not present in the majority of cases. In many instances, there is no penetration or only partial penetration by the abusing adult and no physical scars. In young children, physical signs that may or may not indicate sexual abuse include difficulty in sitting or walking; itching or reported pain or discomfort of genital areas; stained, bloody, or torn underclothing; and foreign bodies in orifices. In older children, the presence of sexually transmitted diseases or a pregnancy may or may not signal child sexual abuse.

Emotional and behavioral signs of abuse and neglect   Emotional and behavioral indicators may reflect something other than child abuse and neglect; child abuse or neglect is only one of several possible explanations underlying the appearance of such signs. Fear of going home or fear of adults in general and reluctance to remove outer garments may be signs of abuse. Other emotional and behavioral signs that may be abuse related include unusual reactions or apprehension in response to other children crying, low self-esteem, extreme or inappropriate moods, aggressiveness, social withdrawal, and nail biting, thumb sucking, or other habit disorders. Frequent lateness to or absence from school, chronic fatigue, chronic hunger, and age-inappropriate behavior (such as that of a child who has taken on the role of an adult because of the absence of a caregiver at home) may be signs of neglect.

In children under 8 years of age, problems such as fear of sleeping alone, eating disorders, enuresis, encopresis, sexual acting out, change in school behavior, tantrums, crying spells, sadness, and suicidal thoughts may or may not indicate sexual abuse. In older children, a professional might additionally observe memory problems, emotional numbness, violent fantasies, hyperalertness, self-mutilation, and sexual concerns or preoccupations, which may be accompanied by guilt or shame.

Interviews, behavioral observation, and psychological tests are all used in identifying child abuse. However, professionals disagree about the appropriate tools for such an assessment, particularly when the assessment involves sexual abuse. One technique involves observing children while they play with **anatomically detailed dolls (ADDs),** which are dolls having accurately represented genitalia. Sexually abused children may, on average, engage ADDs in more sexually oriented activities than other children, but differences between groups of abused and nonabused children are not large. Many nonabused children play in a sexually explicit way with ADDs, so such play is not necessarily diagnostic of sexual abuse (Elliott et al., 1993; Wolfner et al., 1993). Human-figure drawings are also used to assess sexual and physical abuse, though their accuracy in distinguishing abused from nonabused children is debated (Burgess et al., 1981; Chantler et al., 1993; Kelley, 1985). Questionnaires designed for administration to a child who may have been abused (Mannarino et al., 1994) or to adults such as teachers or parents who know that child well (Chantler et al., 1993) have been explored, though no well-developed and thoroughly validated instrument yet exists. In short, no widely accepted, reliable, and valid set of techniques for the assessment of sexual abuse is available (Hysjulien et al., 1994). That may be why Horner et al. (1993) found little consensus among professionals asked to make an evaluation of sexual abuse in a specific case. Lanyon (1993) encourages those doing sexual abuse assessment to integrate information from many assessment methods and sources and to avoid reliance on any single technique. However, selecting techniques to include in such an integrative evaluation is difficult, given the controversies surrounding specific assessment methods.

Issues in reporting child abuse and neglect   Child abuse, when it occurs, is a tragedy. A claim of child abuse when in fact there has been no such abuse is also a tragedy—one that can irrevocably scar an accused but innocent individual for life. It is incumbent on professionals who undertake the weighty obligation of assessing a child for potential abuse not to approach their task with any preconceived notions, because such notions can be conveyed to the child and be perceived as the right answer to questions (King & Yuille, 1987; White et al., 1988). Children from the ages of about 2 to 7 are highly suggestible and their memory is not as well developed as that of older children; for that reason, it is possible that events that occur after the alleged incident—including events only referred to in conversations—may be confused with the actual incident (Ceci et al., 1987; Goodman & Reed, 1986; Loftus & Davies, 1984). Other such considerations in the psychological examination of a child for abuse have been discussed in detail by Weissman (1991). Sensitivity to the rights of the accused in a child abuse proceeding are critical to making certain that justice is served (Ackerman, 1987; Besharov, 1985; Coleman, 1989; Corwin et al., 1987; Green, 1986; Jones & McGraw, 1987; Raskin & Yuille, 1987; Wong, 1987).

Risk assessment   In an effort to prevent child abuse, test developers have sought to create instruments useful in identifying parents and others who may be at risk for abusing children. The Child Abuse Potential Inventory (CAP; Milner et al., 1986; Milner, 1991) has demonstrated impressive validity in identifying abusers. Another test, the Parenting Stress Index (PSI; Loyd & Abidin, 1985), measures stress associated with the parental role. Parents are asked to reflect on their relationship with one child at a time. Some of the items focus on child characteristics that could engender stress, such as activity level and mood. Other PSI items reflect potentially stressful aspects of the parent's life, such as lack of social support and marital problems (Gresham, 1989). The test's authors report internal consistency reliability coefficients ranging from .89 to .95 for factors and total scores. Test-retest reliability coefficients range from .71 to .82 over three weeks, and .55 to .70 over a one-year interval (Loyd & Abidin, 1985). With respect to the test's validity, parents who physically abuse their children tend to score higher on the PSI than parents who do not (Wantz, 1989).

What are the appropriate uses of measures like the CAP and the PSI? Although positive relationships exist between child abuse and scores on the tests, the tests cannot be used to identify or prosecute child abusers in a legal context (Gresham, 1989). Because child abuse is a low base-rate phenomenon, even the use of highly reliable instruments will produce many false positives; that is, the test will erroneously identify the assessee as an abuser. For some parents, high levels of stress as measured by the PSI may indeed lead to physical abuse. However, for most parents, they will not. Some parent-child relationships, such as those involving children with disabilities, are inherently stressful (Innocenti et al., 1992; Orr et al., 1993). Still, most parents manage to weather the relationship without inflicting any harm. Some parents who experience high levels of stress as a result of their relationship with a child may themselves be harmed—even more stressed—to hear from a mental health official that they are at risk for child abuse. For that reason, great caution is called for in interpreting and acting on the results of a test designed to assess risk for child abuse.

On the other hand, high CAP or PSI scores may well point the way to an abusive situation, and they should alert concerned professionals to be watchful for signs of abuse. A second appropriate use of such scores concerns the allocation of resources designed to reduce parenting stress. Parents who score high on the CAP and the PSI could be given priority for placement in a parenting skills class, individualized parent training, child care assistance, and other such programs. If reducing the stress of the parent will reduce the risk of child abuse, everything that can possibly be done to reduce the parental stress should be attempted.

Assessment in Health Psychology

Clinical tools of assessment, as well as other tools of assessment, enjoy widespread use in the field of health psychology. **Health psychology** is a specialty area of psychology that focuses on understanding the role of psychological variables in the onset, course, treatment, and prevention of illness, disease, and disability (Cohen, 1994). Health psychologists are involved in teaching, research, or direct-service activities designed to promote good health.

Individual interviews, surveys, and paper-and-pencil tests are perhaps among the most frequently used tools of researchers in health psychology. Such instruments may be employed to help assess a current state of affairs with regard to some disease or condition, gauge treatment progress, and evaluate outcome of intervention (Brown, 1989). One general research approach entails reporting on the nature of the psychological adjustment of members of a targeted group. In this context, researchers have shown interest in a wide variety of populations. They have studied, for example, the postpartum adjustment of women shortly after childbirth (O'Hara et al., 1992), the postrelease adjustment of former defendants acquitted on an insanity plea (Wiederanders & Choate, 1994), and the health and happiness of the clinically obese (Bray, 1986). There has also been a steady stream of articles focusing on psychological adjustment to a variety of medical conditions, such as cancer (Heidrich et al., 1994; Schag et al., 1990), rheumatoid arthritis (Smith & Wallston, 1995), irritable bowel syndrome (Suls et al., 1994), and adult (Fleishman & Fogel, 1994) or pediatric (Boivin et al., 1995) HIV infection. Closely related variables such as quality of life (Goodwin et al., 1994; Walker & Rosser, 1988), satisfaction with life (Frisch et al., 1992; Huebner, 1994; Pavot & Diener, 1993), and reasons for living (Osman et al., 1993) have also received research attention. How people cope with physical setbacks (Barbarin & Chesler, 1986; Brown, 1984; Brown et al., 1989; Carver et al., 1991; Cohen & Lazarus, 1973; Derogatis et al., 1979; Dunkel-Schetter et al., 1992; Felton & Revenson, 1987; Hamburg & Adams, 1967; McCrae & Costa, 1986) or social disadvantage (Parron et al., 1982) is another topic of great interest, as is the assessment of coping behavior itself (Vitaliano et al., 1987).

Many studies in the health psychology literature focus on aspects of personality, behavior, or lifestyle and their relationship to physical health or longevity (Friedman, 1990). What personality traits or behavior patterns are predictive of what types of health or disease patterns? This question has taken many different forms in the health psychology literature (a sampling of which follow). What personality attributes are predictors of smoking initiation and cessation (Lipkus et al., 1994)? What factors are predictive of vigorous physical exercise in women and in men (Sallis et al., 1992)? What are the predictors of survival among hemodialysis patients (Christensen et al., 1994)? What are the predictors of cancer progression in young adult men and women (Epping-Jordan et al., 1994)? What psychological factors may influence one's immune function (Arnetz et al., 1987; Irwin et al., 1990; Keller et al., 1981; Kiecolt-Glaser & Glaser, 1988; McNaughton et al., 1990)? What effect do one's beliefs about health (Bond et al., 1992) and one's general outlook on life (Scheier & Carver, 1987) have on physical health? What are the psychological predictors of heart disease (Booth-Kewley & Friedman, 1987) and myocardial infarction (Connolly, 1976; Theorell et al., 1975)? What changes can be expected in alcoholics as they progress in treatment (DiClemente & Hughes, 1990)? What role might social support play in posthospitalization recovery (Wilcox et al., 1994), the rehabilitation of burn patients (Davidson et al., 1979), and the mortality rate in the population of an elderly community (Blazer, 1982)?

Another major area of inquiry concerns patients' compliance with doctors' instructions (Dunbar, 1990). What cognitive, behavioral, social, and related factors are critical in this context? Such questions have been studied with regard to conditions such as diabetes (Ary et al., 1986), rheumatoid arthritis (Corish et al., 1989), and alcoholism (Rees, 1985). Scales to measure degree of patient compliance have been developed (see, for example, DiMatteo et al., 1993; Haynes et al., 1979). In a somewhat related vein, researchers have examined causes of patient dissatisfaction with medical care (Marshall et al., 1993).

Other research questions raised by health psychologists probe areas such as the value of education efforts, skills training, or other such interventions in treatment or prevention (see, for example, Mazzuca, 1982). Gender-related (Cotton, 1992) and cultural (Bachman et al., 1991; Chan, 1994; Strassberg, 1992) factors, as well as relatively universal motivations for engaging in some health- or illness-related behavior (Allison et al.,

1992; Cooper, 1994; Nolan et al., 1994; Rakowski et al., 1992; Wright et al., 1992) have all been variables of interest.

In each of these and other areas, the need exists for reliable and valid tools to gauge change with regard to some psychological variable. When existing instruments are inappropriate, new ones have been created. Regardless, the assessment literature in health psychology reminds us that defining and measuring psychological variables is more complex than it may appear to the novice at first glance. For example, *stress* may be studied in the context of being an antecedent or a consequence of something—or both—and researchers have had to take that into account in defining and measuring it (Dohrenwend & Shrout, 1985; Kanner et al., 1981; Whitehead, 1994). The psychological concept of *social support* is ubiquitous in the health psychology literature, yet there is little agreement among researchers about exactly how it should be defined and measured (see, for example, Barrera, 1981; Brandt & Weinert, 1981; Cohen & Syme, 1985; Heitzmann & Kaplan, 1988; Norbeck et al., 1981; Procidano & Heller, 1983; Sallis et al., 1987; Sarason et al., 1983). In somewhat similar fashion, the measurement of variables related to obesity (Foreyt, 1987), alcoholism (Miller et al., 1991), pain (Melzack & Wall, 1982; Mikail et al., 1993; Turk & Rudy, 1986), and arthritis (Liang et al., 1988; Meenan & Pincus, 1987) has also proven a bit more complicated than one might expect.

Many tests useful in health psychology research may also be useful in clinical and counseling contexts. For example, the Condom Attitude Scale-Adolescent Version (Table 13–4) yields data that may be valuable not only in research applications but in

Table 13–4
Condom Attitude Scale-Adolescent Version

In an effort to learn more about the attitudes of adolescents toward condoms, Janet St. Lawrence and her colleagues (1994) modified an existing scale (Sacco et al., 1991) to create the following scale.

1. Using a condom takes the "wonder" out of sex. (R)
2. I am concerned about catching AIDS or some other sexually transmitted disease.
3. A condom is not necessary when you and your partner agree not to have sex with anyone else. (R)
4. Condoms are messy. (R)
5. A condom is not necessary if you know your partner. (R)
6. Using condoms shows my partner I care about him/her.
7. A condom is not necessary if you're pretty sure the other person doesn't have a sexually transmitted disease. (R)
8. If I'm not careful, I could catch a sexually transmitted disease.
9. I wouldn't use a condom if my partner refused. (R)
10. People who carry condoms would have sex with anyone. (R)
11. I wouldn't mind if my partner brought up the idea of using a condom.
12. Condoms create a sense of safety.
13. People who use condoms sleep around a lot. (R)
14. If I'm not careful, I could catch AIDS.
15. Condoms take away the pleasure of sex. (R)
16. If my partner suggested using a condom, I would respect him or her.
17. Other people should respect my desire to use a condom.
18. I worry that I could catch a sexually transmitted disease.
19. If my partner suggested using a condom, I would feel relieved.
20. People who carry condoms are just looking for sex. (R)
21. A condom is not necessary when you are with the same partner for a long time. (R)
22. If my partner suggested using a condom, I would think he/she was only being cautious.
23. Condoms protect against sexually transmitted diseases.

Note: Items marked with (R) are reverse scored.

individual and group counseling. Similarly, data from the Cocaine Expectancy Questionnaire (Jaffe & Kilbey, 1994) may assist counselors and therapists helping clients who might be at risk for using or are presently using cocaine. Below we focus in more detail on some aspects of psychological assessment as applied to problems of drug abuse.

Assessment of addiction and substance abuse   Assessment for drug addiction and for alcohol and substance abuse has become routine in a number of settings. Whether seeking outpatient psychotherapy services, being admitted for inpatient services, or even seeking employment, screening for drug use may be a prerequisite. Such screening can take varied forms ranging from straightforward physical tests involving the analysis of urine or blood samples, or much more imaginative laboratory procedures that involve the analysis of psychophysiological responses (Carter & Tiffany, 1999; Lang et al., 1993; Sayette et al., 2000). Exploration of personal history with drugs and alcohol may be accomplished by means of questionnaires or face-to-face interviews. However, such direct procedures are highly subject to impression management and all of the other potential drawbacks of a self-report instrument. Here, we will briefly discuss some psychological tests and other tools of assessment that have been used to screen for, or otherwise evaluate drug and alcohol abuse.

A number of tests and scales have been developed to assist in the assessment of abuse and addiction. The MMPI-2, for example, contains three scales useful in providing information about substance abuse potential. The oldest of these three scales is the MacAndrew Alcoholism Scale (MacAndrew, 1965), since revised and now referred to simply as the "MAC-R" (Butcher et al., 1989). This scale was originally constructed to aid in differentiating alcoholic from nonalcoholic psychiatric patients. The Addiction Potential Scale (APS, Weed et al., 1992) contains 39 items that substance abusers tended to endorse differently than either psychiatric patients or nonclinical samples. The Addiction Acknowledgment Scale (AAS; Weed et al., 1992) contains 13 items that make direct and obvious acknowledgments of substance abuse. The AAS is therefore a much more face-valid scale for substance abuse assessment than either the MAC-R or the APS. This is so because the endorsement of the transparent items of the AAS amounts to an outright admission of drug abuse. By contrast, the MAC-R and the APS "do not measure substance abuse directly but rather measure personality traits that often serve as pathways to substance abuse" (Rouse et al., 1999, p. 106).

The Addiction Severity Index (McDermott et al., 1996; McLellan et al., 1980) is one of the most widely used tests in the substance abuse field (Alterman et al., 2000), with applications in intake evaluations and follow-ups, as well as in the identification of patient subgroups in research. Raters assess severity of addiction in seven problem areas: medical condition, employment functioning, drug use, alcohol use, illegal activity, family/social relations, and psychiatric functioning. Items tap various problems experienced in each of these areas within the past 30 days, as well as lifetime problems. Estimates of the severity of the problems are derived from the scores.

Behavior associated with substance abuse or its potential has also been explored by analogue means such as role play. The Situational Competency Test (Chaney et al., 1978), the Alcohol Specific Role Play Test (Abrams et al., 1991), and the Cocaine Risk Response Test (Carroll, 1998; Carroll et al., 1999) are all measures that contain audiotaped role-play measures to which assessees respond. In the latter test, assessees are asked to orally respond with a description of what they would do under certain conditions—conditions known to prompt cocaine use in regular cocaine users. One scenario has to do with having had a difficult week, followed by cravings for cocaine to reward oneself. Another scenario takes place at a party where people are using cocaine in the next room. Assessees are asked to candidly detail their thinking and behavior in response to these and other situations. Of course, the value of the information elicited will vary as a function of many factors, among them the purpose of the assessment and the candor with which assessees respond. One might expect assessees to be straightforward in their responses if they were self-referred for addiction treatment. On the other hand, assessees might be less than straightforward if, for example, they were court-referred on suspicion of probation violation.

Efforts to reduce widespread substance abuse have led researchers to consider how culture may be a contributing factor to the problem, and how culturally informed intervention may be part of the solution. Using a wide variety of measures, researchers have explored substance abuse in the context of variables such as cultural identity and generational status (Ames & Stacy, 1998; Chappin & Brook, 2001; Duclos, 1999; Kail & DeLaRosa, 1998; Karlsen et al., 1998; Lessinger, 1998; O'Hare & Van Tran, 1998; Pilgrim et al., 1999), religious beliefs (Corwyn & Benda, 2000; Klonoff & Landrine, 1999), and sexual orientation (Kippax et al., 1998). Recovery from drug addiction has itself been conceptualized as a socially mediated process of reacculturation which can result in a new sense of identity (Hurst, 1997).

An important ethical concern when assessing substance abusers, especially in research contexts, has to do with obtaining fully informed consent to assessment. McCrady & Bux (1999) noted that substance abusers may be high or intoxicated at the time of consent and their ability to attend to and comprehend the requirements of the research might therefore be compromised. Further, because their habit may have thrust them into desperate financial straits, any payment offered to substance abusers for participation in a research study may have the appearance of being coercive. Procedures to maximize comprehension of consent and minimize the appearance of coercion are necessary elements of the consent process.

The Psychological Report

A critical component of any testing or assessment procedure is the reporting of the findings. The high reliability or validity of a test or assessment procedure may be cast to the wind if the assessment report is not written in an organized and readable fashion. Of course, what constitutes an organized and readable report will vary as a function of the goal of the assessment and the audience for whom the report is intended; a psychoanalyst's report exploring a patient's unresolved oedipal conflict designed for presentation to the New York Psychoanalytic Society will look and sound very different from a school psychologist's report to a teacher concerning a child's learning disability. Reports differ in the extent to which they rely on one or another assessment procedure. Of course, reports are written and used in widely different settings. Although we focus our attention on the writing of clinical reports in this chapter's *Everyday Psychometrics*, it should be clear that report writing is a skill necessary in educational, industrial/organizational, and other settings where psychological assessment takes place.

The Barnum Effect

The showman P. T. Barnum is credited with the quote "There's a sucker born every minute." Psychologists, among others, have taken P. T. Barnum's words about the widespread gullibility of people quite seriously. In fact, Barnum effect is a term that should be

Elements of a Typical Report
of Psychological Assessment

There is no one universally accepted style or form for a psychological report. Most assessors develop a style and form that they believe best suits the specific objectives of the assessment. Generally, however, most clinical reports contain the elements listed and briefly discussed below.

Demographic Data

Included here are all or some of the following: the patient's name, address, telephone number, education, occupation, religion, marital status, date of birth, place of birth, ethnic membership, citizenship, date of testing. The examiner's name must also be considered part of the identifying material in the report.

Reason for Referral

Why was this patient referred for psychological assessment? This section of the report may sometimes be as short as one sentence (for example, "Johnny was referred for evaluation to shed light on the question of whether his inattention in class is due to personality, neurological, or other difficulties"). Alternatively, this section of the report may be extended with all relevant background information (for example, "Johnny complained of hearing difficulties in his fourth-grade class according to a note in his records"). If all relevant background information is not covered in the "Reason for Referral" section of the report, it may be covered in a separate section labeled "Background" or in a section labeled "Findings."

Tests Administered

Here the examiner simply lists the names of the tests that were administered. Thus, for example, this section of the report may be as brief as the following:

- Wechsler Intelligence Scale for Children-III (1/8/02; 1/12/02)
- Bender Visual-Motor Gestalt Test (1/8/02)
- Rorschach Test (1/12/02)
- Thematic Apperception Test (1/12/02)
- Sentence Completion Test (1/8/02)
- Figure drawings (1/8/02)

Note that the date of the test administration has been inserted next to the name of each test administered. This is a good idea under any circumstances and particularly important if testing was executed over the course of a number of days, weeks, or longer. In the sample section above, note that the WISC-III was administered over the course of two testing sessions on two days (1/8/02 and 1/12/02); that the Bender, the Sentence Completion Test, and figure drawings were administered on 1/8/02; and that the Rorschach and the Thematic Apperception Test were administered on 1/12/02.

Also in this section, the examiner might place the names and the dates of tests known to have been previously administered to the examinee. If the examiner has a record of the findings (or better yet, the original test protocols) from this prior testing, this information may be integrated into the next section of the report, "Findings."

Findings

Here the examiner reports not only findings (for example, "On the WISC-III Johnny achieved a Verbal IQ of 100, a Performance IQ of 110, yielding a full-scale IQ of 106") but also

familiar to any psychologist called on to write a psychological report. Before reading on to find out exactly what the Barnum effect is, imagine that you have just completed a computerized personality test and that the printout describing the results reads as follows:

> You have a strong need for other people to like you and for them to admire you. You have a tendency to be critical of yourself. You have a great deal of unused capacity which you have not turned to your advantage. While you have some personality weaknesses, you are generally able to compensate for them. Your sexual adjustment has presented some problems for you. Disciplined and controlled on the outside, you tend to be worrisome and insecure inside. At times you have serious doubts as to whether you have made the

all extra-test considerations, such as observations concerning the examinee's motivation (for instance, "the examinee did/did not appear to be motivated to do well on the tests"), the examinee's level of fatigue, the nature of the relationship and rapport with the examiner, indices of anxiety, and method of approach to the task. The section labeled "Findings" may begin with a description of the examinee that is detailed enough for the reader of the report to almost visualize him or her. For example:

> John is a 20-year-old college student with brown, shoulder-length, stringy hair and a full beard. He came to the testing wearing a "psychedelic" shirt, cutoff and ragged shorts, and sandals. He sat slouched in his chair for most of the test session, tended to speak only when spoken to, and spoke in a slow, lethargic manner.

Also included in this section is mention of any extraneous variables that might in some way have affected the test results. Was testing in a school interrupted by any event such as a fire drill, an earth tremor, or some other disturbance? Did loud or atypical noise in or out of the test site affect the testtaker's concentration? Did the hospitalized patient receive any visitors just before an evaluation, and could such a visit have affected the findings? Answers to these types of questions may prove invaluable in interpreting assessment data.

The "Findings" section of the report is where all the background material, behavioral observations, and test data are integrated to provide an answer to the referral question. Whether or not the examiner makes reference to the actual test data is a matter of personal preference. Thus, for ex-

ample, one examiner might simply state, "There is evidence of neurological deficit in this record" and stop there. Another examiner would document exactly why this was being asserted: "There is evidence of neurological deficit as indicated by the rotation and perseveration errors in the Bender-Gestalt record. Further, on the TAT, this examinee failed to grasp the situation as a whole and simply enumerated single details. Additionally, this examinee had difficulty abstracting—still another index of neurological deficit—as evidenced by the unusually low score on the WISC-III Similarities subtest." The findings section should logically lead into the "Recommendations" section.

Recommendations

On the basis of the psychological assessment, with particular attention to factors such as the personal aspects and deficiencies of the examinee, recommendations addressed to ameliorating the presenting problem are given. The recommendation may be for psychotherapy, a consultation with a neurologist, placement in a special class, short-term family therapy addressed to a specific problem—whatever the examiner believes is required to ameliorate the situation is spelled out here.

Summary

The summary section includes in "short form" a statement concerning the reason for referral, the findings, and the recommendation. This section is usually only a paragraph or two, and it should provide a concise and succinct statement of who the examinee is, why the examinee was referred for testing, what was found, and what needs to be done.

right decision or done the right thing. You prefer a certain amount of change and variety and become dissatisfied when hemmed in by restrictions and limitations. You pride yourself on being an independent thinker and do not accept others' opinions without satisfactory proof. You have found it unwise to be too frank in revealing yourself to others. At times you are extraverted, affable, and sociable while at other times you are introverted, wary, and reserved. Some of your aspirations tend to be pretty unrealistic.

Still imagining that the preceding test results had been formulated specifically for you, please rate the accuracy of the description as it does or does not apply to you personally.

I feel that the interpretation was:

_____ excellent
_____ good
_____ average
_____ poor
_____ very poor

Now that you have completed the exercise we can say, "Welcome to the ranks of those who have been subject to the Barnum effect." This psychological profile is, as you no doubt have noticed, vague and general. The same paragraph (sometimes with slight modifications) has been used in a number of psychological studies (Forer, 1949; Jackson et al., 1982; Merrens & Richards, 1970; Sundberg, 1955; Ulrich et al., 1963), with similar findings: People tend to accept vague and general personality descriptions as uniquely applicable to themselves without realizing that the same description could be applied to just about anyone.

The finding that people tend to accept vague personality descriptions as accurate descriptions of themselves came to be known as the **Barnum effect** after psychologist Paul Meehl's (1956) condemnation of "personality description after the manner of P. T. Barnum."[3] Meehl suggested that the term Barnum effect be used "to stigmatize those pseudo-successful clinical procedures in which personality descriptions from tests are made to fit the patient largely or wholly by virtue of their triviality." Tallent (1958) made a related observation. Deploring the generality and vagueness that seemed to plague too many psychological reports, Tallent wrote:

> Quite similar to the Barnum phenomenon is what might be called the *Aunt Fanny description* in clinical reports. Superfluous statements, such as, "This client had difficulty in performing at optimal capacity when under stress," or "The client has unconscious hostile urges" might readily prompt the report reader to think "so has my Aunt Fanny!"

The "Barnum" or "Aunt Fanny" effect has been the subject of numerous research studies. In one study conducted by Ulrich, Stachnick, and Stainton (1963), 57 college students were given two personality tests by their psychology instructor, who promised to score the tests and have the results back to each individual student at a later date. One week later, all students were given the identical personality description—the one that appears earlier in this section—though the descriptions were arranged in different orders. The students were asked to rate the interpretations as "excellent," "good," "average," "poor," or "very poor" and to make any additional comments. The ratings were as follows:

excellent	27
good	26
average	3
poor	1
very poor	0

Some of the comments made by the students were:

> I feel that you have done a fine job with the material which you had to work with. I agree with almost all of your statements and think they answer the problems I may have.

> On the nose! Very good. I wish you had said more, all you did mention was all true without a doubt. I wish you could go further into this personality sometime.

---

3. Meehl credited D. G. Patterson with having first used the term *Barnum effect*.

The results have brought out several points which have worried me because I was not sure if I had imagined these to be personality traits of mine. Tests like this could be valuable to an individual in helping him to solve some of his own problems.

In a follow-up study executed by these same researchers, 79 other college students were shown how to administer two personality tests (the same tests that had been administered by the instructor in the first experiment). The students were then asked to play the role of test examiner and to use as an examinee any one available person, such as a roommate or a neighbor. At the completion of the test administration, the student examiner would tell the examinee that the test would be scored and returned with an interpretation. The "interpretation" was the same as in the prior study, and once again the ratings of its applicability were quite high:

excellent	29
good	30
average	15
poor	5
very poor	0

Some of the comments made by the examinees on the accuracy of the student examiners' "results" were as follows:

I believe this interpretation applied to me individually, as there are too many facets which fit me too well to be a generalization.

The interpretation is surprisingly accurate and specific in description. I shall take note of many of the things said.

I feel that the interpretation does apply to me individually. For the first time things I have been vaguely aware of have been put into concise and constructive statements which I would like to use as a plan for improving myself.

It appears to me that the results of this test are unbelievably close to the truth. For a short test of this type, I was expecting large generalizations for results, but this was not the case; and I give all the credit to the examiner whose conclusions were well calculated.

It can be seen that even in a situation in which nonexperienced student examiners were involved, 59 of the 79 examinees rated the generalized interpretation as excellent or good. In reviewing the surprising results of their experiments, Ulrich and his collaborators concluded that the persons given the phony test interpretations were not only taken in by the interpretations but also "very likely to praise highly the examiner on his conclusions."

Other research serves to underscore just how powerful the Barnum effect can be. In one study, students were unable to select their actual personal description when it was paired with a generalized description (Sundberg, 1955). In another, students preferred a generalized interpretation to an interpretation written on the basis of their actual psychological test scores (Merrens & Richards, 1970). The effect has since been explored with reference to situational variables (Hinrichsen & Bradley, 1974; Snyder & Shenkel, 1976; Snyder et al., 1977) such as the prestige of the diagnostician (Bradley & Bradley, 1977; Dmitruk et al., 1973; Halperin et al., 1976; Snyder & Larson, 1972), the sex of the diagnostician (Zeren & Bradley, 1982), the number of assessees (Snyder & Newburg, 1981), and the type of assessment instrument used (Snyder, 1974; Weinberger & Bradley, 1980). Cognizance of this effect and the factors that may heighten or diminish it is necessary if psychological assessors are to avoid making interpretations in the manner of P. T. Barnum.

Self-Assessment

Test your understanding of elements of this chapter by seeing if you can explain each of the following terms, expressions, and abbreviations:

abuse

ADRESSING acronym

ALI standard

Barnum effect

clinical psychology

cognitive interview

competence to stand trial

counseling psychology

custody evaluation

DSM

Durham standard

duty to warn

emotional and behavioral signs of abuse and neglect

emotional injury evaluation

evolutionary view of mental disorder

forensic psychological assessment

health psychology

hypnotic interview

interview

legal definitions of "insanity"

MAC-R

managed care

mental status examination

M'Naghten standard

neglect

orientation

"oriented times three"

physical signs of abuse and neglect

psychological report

standard battery

stress interview

Neuropsychological Assessment

Modern-day investigators exploring the link between the brain and the body use a number of varied tools and procedures in their work, including laboratory testing and field observation of head-trauma victims, experimentation involving the electrical or chemical stimulation of various human and animal brain sites, experimental lesioning of the brain of animal subjects, and autopsies of normal and abnormal human and animal subjects.

The branch of medicine that focuses on the nervous system and its disorders is **neurology.** The branch of psychology that focuses on the relationship between brain functioning and behavior is **neuropsychology.** Formerly a specialty area within clinical psychology, neuropsychology has evolved into a specialty in its own right in recent years. Psychologists doing routine clinical evaluations are trained to screen for signs and symptoms of neurological deficit. Such signs or symptoms may present themselves during history taking (for example, the examinee reports falling and losing consciousness for a few minutes), interviewing (the examinee complains of severe, long-lasting headaches), or testtaking (involuntary movements are observed); signs may also be evident in data derived from an intelligence test (such as a large discrepancy between measured verbal and performance IQ) or other tests. If, on the basis of such signs, neurological deficit is suspected, the examinee will be referred to a neurologist or a neuropsychologist for further evaluation. Succinctly put, the objective of the typical neuropsychological evaluation is "to draw inferences about the structural and functional characteristics of a person's brain by evaluating an individual's behavior in defined stimulus-response situations" (Benton, 1994, p. 1).

In this chapter, we survey some of the tools used by clinicians and neuropsychologists to screen for and diagnose neuropsychological and cognitive disorders. We begin with a brief introduction to neuroanatomy and brain–behavior relationships. This material is presented to help lay a foundation for appreciating how testtaking (as well as other) behavior can be evaluated to form hypotheses about the level of intactness or functioning in various parts of the brain.

The Nervous System and Behavior

The nervous system is composed of various kinds of *neurons* (nerve cells) and can be divided into the *central* nervous system (consisting of the brain and the spinal cord) and the *peripheral* nervous system (consisting of the neurons that convey messages to and

Table 14-1

Some Brain–Behavior Characteristics for Selected Nervous System Sites

Site	Characteristic
Temporal lobes	These lobes contain auditory reception areas as well as certain areas for the processing of visual information. Damage to the temporal lobe may affect sound discrimination, recognition, and comprehension; music appreciation; voice recognition; and auditory or visual memory storage.
Occipital lobes	These lobes contain visual reception areas. Damage to this area could result in blindness to all or part of the visual field or deficits in object recognition, visual scanning, visual integration of symbols into wholes, and recall of visual imagery.
Parietal lobes	These lobes contain reception areas for the sense of touch and for the sense of bodily position. Damage to this area may result in deficits in the sense of touch, disorganization, and distorted self-perception.
Frontal lobes	These lobes are integrally involved in ordering information and sorting out stimuli. Concentration and attention, abstract-thinking ability, concept-formation ability, foresight, problem-solving ability, speech, as well as gross and fine motor ability may be affected by damage to the frontal lobes.
Thalamus	The thalamus is a kind of communications relay station for all sensory information being transmitted to the cerebral cortex. Damage to the thalamus may result in altered states of arousal, memory defects, speech deficits, apathy, and disorientation.
Hypothalamus	The hypothalamus is involved in the regulation of bodily functions such as eating, drinking, body temperature, sexual behavior, and emotion. It is sensitive to changes in environment that call for a "fight or flight" response from the organism. Damage to it may elicit a variety of symptoms ranging from uncontrolled eating or drinking to mild alterations of mood states.
Cerebellum	Together with the pons (another brain site in the area of the brain referred to as the "hindbrain"), the cerebellum is involved in the regulation of balance, breathing, and posture, among other functions. Damage to the cerebellum may manifest as problems in fine motor control and coordination.
Reticular formation	In the core of the brain stem, the reticular formation contains fibers en route to and from the cortex. Because stimulation to this area can cause a sleeping organism to awaken and cause an awake organism to become even more alert, it is sometimes referred to as the "reticular activating system." Damage to this area can cause the organism to sleep for long periods of time.
Limbic system	Composed of the amygdala, the cingulate cortex, the hippocampus, and the septal areas of the brain, the limbic system is integral to the expression of emotions. Damage to this area may profoundly affect emotional behavior.
Spinal cord	Many reflexes necessary for survival (such as withdrawing from a hot surface) are carried out at the level of the spinal cord. In addition to its role in reflex activity, the spinal cord is integral to the coordination of motor movements. Spinal cord injuries may result in various degrees of paralysis or other motor difficulties.

from the rest of the body). Viewed from the top, the large, rounded portion of the brain called the cerebrum can be divided into two sections or hemispheres. This mass appears gray because mixtures of capillary blood vessels and cell bodies of neurons have a gray-brown color. Connecting the left and right hemispheres is a band of nerve fibers termed the *corpus callosum.* Much of the surface of the cerebral hemispheres constitutes the cerebral *cortex* (from the Latin meaning bark, shell, rind, or outer layer). The cortex appears wrinkled because of the many clefts or indentations in its surface. A cleft is technically termed a *fissure* or a *sulcus,* depending on its depth (fissures are deeper than sulci), and the ridge between the depression is a *gyrus* (the plural is *gyri*). Fissures divide each cerebral hemisphere into four areas termed *lobes:* the frontal, temporal, occipital, and parietal lobes. Just beneath the corpus callosum, at the approximate center of the brain, lies a group of nuclei called the *thalamus,* and below that lies another group of nuclei—the *hypothalamus* ("hypo" meaning "below"). The thalamus and the hypothalamus are actually part of the brain stem structure, which connects the brain to the spinal cord. Also part of the brain stem, just above the spinal cord, is a mass of nuclei and fibers—the *reticular formation.*

Some brain–behavior correlates are summarized in Table 14–1. Each of the two cerebral hemispheres receives sensory information from the opposite side of the body and also controls motor responses on the opposite side of the body—a phenomenon termed **contralateral control.** It is due to the brain's contralateral control of the body that an injury to the right side of the brain may result in sensory or motor defects on the left side of the body. The meeting ground of the two hemispheres is the corpus callosum, though one hemisphere, most frequently the left one, is dominant. It is because the left

Table 14–2
Technical Names for Various Kinds
of Sensory and Motor Deficits

Name	Description of Deficit
Acalculia	Inability to perform arithmetic calculations
Acopia	Inability to copy geometric designs
Agnosia	Deficit in recognizing sensory stimuli (for example, *auditory agnosia* is difficulty in recognizing auditory stimuli)
Agraphia	Deficit in writing ability
Akinesia	Deficit in motor movements
Alexia	Inability to read
Amnesia	Loss of memory
Amusia	Deficit in ability to produce or appreciate music
Anomia	Deficit associated with finding words to name things
Anopia	Deficit in sight
Anosmia	Deficit in sense of smell
Aphasia	Deficit in communication due to impaired speech or writing ability
Apraxia	Voluntary movement disorder in the absence of paralysis
Ataxia	Deficit in motor ability and muscular coordination

hemisphere is most frequently dominant that most people are right-handed. The dominant hemisphere dominates in activities such as reading, writing, arithmetic, and speech, and the nondominant hemisphere has as its forte tasks involving spatial and textural recognition as well as art and music appreciation. In the normal, neurologically intact individual, one hemisphere complements the other.

Neurological Damage and the Concept of Organicity

Neurological damage may take the form of a lesion in the brain or any other site within the central or peripheral nervous system. A **lesion** is a pathological alteration of tissue, such as that which could result from injury or infection. Neurological lesions may be physical or chemical in nature, and they may be focal (relatively circumscribed at one site) or diffuse (scattered at various sites). Because different sites of the brain control various functions, focal and diffuse lesions at different sites will manifest themselves in varying behavioral deficits. A partial listing of the technical names for the many varieties of sensory and motor deficits is presented in Table 14–2.

Note that a focal lesion may have diffuse ramifications with regard to behavioral deficits (that is, a circumscribed lesion in one area of the brain may affect many different kinds of behaviors). Conversely, it is possible that a diffuse lesion may affect one or more areas of functioning so severely that it masquerades as a focal lesion. In a sense, the neuropsychologist works backwards—examining behavior by means of a variety of tests and procedures and trying to determine from the pattern of findings where a neurological lesion, if any, exists. Neuropsychological assessment also plays a critical role in determining the extent of behavioral impairment that has occurred or can be expected to occur because of a neurological disorder. Such information is useful not only in designing remediation programs but also in assessing the consequences of drug treatments, physical training, and other therapy.

The terms "brain damage," "neurological damage," and "organicity" have, unfortunately, been used interchangeably in much of the psychological literature. The term *neurological damage* is most all-inclusive because it covers not only damage to the brain but also damage to the spinal cord and to all the components of the peripheral nervous system. Organicity, still a very popular term with clinicians, derives from the post–World

Figure 14-1
The Goldstein-Scheerer Tests
of Abstract and Concrete Thinking*

(a) The Stick Test is a measure of recent memory. The subject's task is to reproduce designs from memory using sticks. *(b)* The Cube Test challenges the subject to replicate with blocks a design printed in a booklet. This subtest was the predecessor of the Block Design task on Wechsler intelligence tests. It is used as a measure of non-verbal abstraction ability. *(c)* The Color-Form Sorting Test contains 12 objects, including 4 triangles, 4 circles, and 4 squares (each piece in one of four colors). The objects are presented in a random order, and the subject is instructed to sort according to which belong together. Once they are sorted, the subject is next asked to sort the objects a different way. The subject's flexibility in shifting from one sorting principle to another is noted. *(d)* The Object Sorting Test consists of 89 objects, which the subject is required to group. Concrete thinking and organic impairment may be inferred if the subject sorts, for example, by color instead of function. *(e)* The Color Sorting Test employs several woolen skeins of varying colors. The task here is to sort the skeins according to a sample sketch displayed by the examiner.

*The Goldstein-Scheerer Tests of Abstract and Concrete Thinking are now out of print.

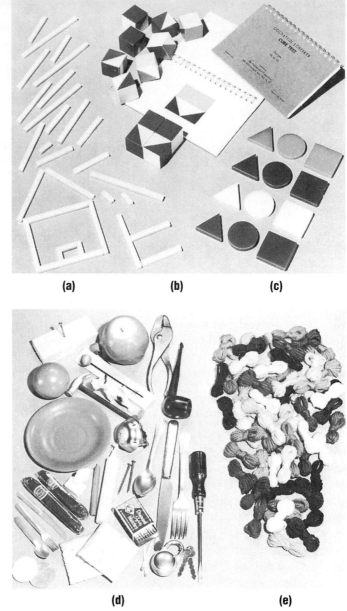

(a)   (b)   (c)

(d)   (e)

War I research of the German neurologist Kurt Goldstein. Studies of brain-injured soldiers led Goldstein to the conclusion that the factors differentiating organically impaired individuals ("organics" for short) from normals included the loss of abstraction ability, deficits in reasoning ability, and inflexibility in problem-solving tasks. Accordingly, Goldstein (1927, 1939, 1963a) and his colleagues developed psychological tests that tapped these factors and were designed to help in the diagnosis of organic brain syndrome, or **organicity** for short. Although these tests are now out of print, they remain representative of some of the types of tasks still used today to screen for neurological deficit (Figure 14-1).

In the tradition of Goldstein and his associates, two German psychologists, Heinz Werner and Alfred Strauss, examined brain–behavior correlates in brain-injured, mentally retarded children (Werner & Strauss, 1941; see also Strauss & Lehtinen, 1947). Like

Table 14–3
Evidence for the Nonunitary Nature of Organicity

Persons who have identical lesions in the brain may exhibit markedly different symptoms. Reed, Reitan, and Klove (1965) have observed that "behavior deficits associated with cerebral lesions in children may be quite different from the ability losses typically demonstrated by brain-damaged adults" (p. 250). In a similar vein, Pincus and Tucker (1974) noted that "large unilateral injuries in infants . . . tend to produce a more widespread deficit in intellectual abilities than similar injuries in adults" (pp. 123–124).

Many interacting factors such as the patient's premorbid functioning, the site and diffuseness of the lesion, the cause of the lesion and its rate of spread may make one "organic" appear quite dissimilar clinically from another (Goldfried et al., 1971; Reitan & Davison, 1974; Smith, 1962).

Considerable similarity may exist in the symptoms exhibited by persons who have entirely different types of lesions. Further, these different types of lesions may arise from a variety of causes, such as trauma with or without loss of consciousness, infection, nutritional deficiencies, tumor, stroke, neuronal degeneration, toxins, insufficient cardiac output, and a variety of metabolic disturbances. Many conditions that are not due to brain damage produce symptoms that mimic those produced by brain damage. For example, an individual who is psychotic, depressed, or simply fatigued may produce data on an examination for organic brain damage that is characteristically diagnostic of neuropsychological impairment.

Factors other than brain damage (such as psychosis, depression, fatigue) influence the responses of brain-damaged persons. Some types of responses are consequences (rather than correlates) of the brain damage. For example, if brain injured children as a group tend to be described as more aggressive than normals, this may reflect more on the way such children have been treated by parents, teachers, and peers than on the effect of any lesions per se. Conversely, persons who are in fact brain-damaged are sometimes able to compensate for their deficits to such an extent that some functions are actually taken over by other, more intact parts of the brain.

their predecessors who had worked with brain-injured adults, these investigators attempted to delineate characteristics common to *all* brain-injured people, including children. Although such work led to a better understanding of the behavioral consequences of brain injury in children, one unfortunate consequence was that a unitary picture of brain injury emerged; all "organic" children were presumed to share a similar pattern of cognitive, behavioral, sensory, and motor deficits—regardless of the specific nature or site of their impairment. The unitary concept of organicity prevailed through the 1950s. Toward the end of that time, researchers such as Birch and Diller (1959) began to complain about what they termed the "naivete of the concept of 'organicity'":

> It is abundantly clear that "brain damage" and "organicity" are terms which though overlapping are not identities and serve to designate interdependent events. "Brain-damage" refers to the fact of an anatomical destruction, whereas "organicity" represents one of the varieties of functional consequences which may attend such destruction. (p. 195)

Through the 1960s, a number of researchers echoed the view that "organicity" and "brain damage" should not be viewed as unitary in nature and that no one set of behavioral characteristics can be applied to all brain-injured persons. Thus, for example, Haynes and Sells (1963) observed that "both native practice and the overwhelming bulk of published research appear to accept the term brain damage as a unitary diagnostic entity, although the predominant evidence indicates that it represents a complex and multifaceted category" (p. 316). The conceptualization of organicity and brain damage as nonunitary in nature was supported by a number of observations, which are summarized in Table 14–3.

The Neuropsychological Examination

The tests and other procedures employed in a neuropsychological examination will vary as a function of several factors—such as the purpose of the examination, the neurological intactness of the examinee, and the thoroughness of the examination. In a sense, any routine administration of a battery of psychological tests in a clinical setting can also serve the purpose of neuropsychological screening. In the course of assessing intelligence, personality, or other variables the clinician may be alerted to suspicious findings signaling that a more in-depth neuropsychological examination should be conducted. Sometimes a patient is referred to a psychologist for screening for neurological problems. In such a case, a battery of tests will be administered—consisting, at a minimum, of an intelligence test, a personality test, and a perceptual-motor/memory test.[1] If neurological signs are discovered in the course of the evaluation, the examinee will be referred for further and more detailed evaluation.

Beyond general screening purposes, an individual might be referred for an in-depth neuropsychological evaluation because of the nature of the presenting problem (such as memory impairment). A neuropsychological examination might be ordered by a neurologist who seeks to find out more about the cognitive and behavioral consequences of a suspected or known lesion. A neurologist's referral note to a neuropsychologist in such an instance might read:

> My examination was negative but I feel I might be missing something. This patient did have a head injury about six months ago and he still complains of headaches and slight memory problems for recent events. I found no hard signs, some soft signs such as a right hand tremor (possibly due to anxiety), and a pattern of findings on laboratory tests ranging from negative to equivocal. Please evaluate this patient and let me know whether you find the headaches and other vague complaints to be organic or functional in origin.[2]

In addition to asking whether any observed deficits are organic (physically based) or functional (psychologically based), the referral note might also ask the neuropsychologist other kinds of questions, such as: Is this condition acute or chronic? Is this individual ready to go back to school or work? What skills require remediation? The neuropsychological examination will vary widely as a function of the nature of the referral question. Questions concerning the functional or organic origin of observed behavior will require more in-depth examination of personality and psychiatric history.

The content and nature of the examination will also vary as a function of the neurological intactness of the assessee. Neuropsychologists assess persons exhibiting a wide range of physical and psychological disabilities. Some, for example, have known visual or auditory deficits, concentration and attention problems, speech and language difficulties, and so forth. Allowance must be made for such deficits and a way must be found to administer the appropriate tests so that meaningful results can be obtained. Frequently, neuropsychologists will administer preliminary visual, auditory, and other such examinations to ascertain the gross intactness of sensory and motor functioning before proceeding with more specialized tests. An olfactory (sense of smell) deficit, for example, may be symptomatic of a great variety of neurological and nonneurological problems as diverse as Alzheimer's disease (Serby et al., 1991), Parkinson's disease (Serby et al., 1985), and AIDS (Brody et al., 1991). The discovery of such a deficit by means of a test such as

---

1. We have listed here what we believe to be the minimum amount of testing for an adequate neuropsychological screening. It is, however, not uncommon for some clinicians to administer only a perceptual-motor/memory test such as the Bender Visual Motor Gestalt test as a screening device. In the light of strong cautions against such practices (see, for example, Bigler & Ehrenfurth, 1981), some have stated flatly that the singular use of such a test "could certainly be considered negligent" (Kahn & Taft, 1983, p. 79).

2. In the jargon of neuropsychological assessment, a **hard sign** may be defined as an indicator of definite neurological deficit (for example, abnormal reflex performance). Hard signs may be contrasted with **soft signs,** which are suggestive of neurological deficit but not necessarily indicative of such deficit (for example, a 15-point discrepancy between the verbal and performance scales on a Wechsler intelligence test).

the University of Pennsylvania Smell Identification Test (Doty et al., 1984) would be a stimulus for continued diagnostic assessment.

Common to all thorough neuropsychological examinations is a history taking, a mental status examination, and the administration of tests and procedures designed to uncover any problems of neuropsychological functioning. Throughout the examination, the neuropsychologist's knowledge of neuroanatomy, neurochemistry, and neurophysiology will be essential for optimal interpretation of the data. In addition to guiding decisions concerning what to test for and how to test for it, such knowledge will also come into play with respect to the decisions concerning *when* to test. Thus, for example, it would be atypical for a neuropsychologist to psychologically test a stroke victim immediately after the stroke occurred. Because some recovery of function could be expected to spontaneously occur in the weeks and months following the stroke, testing the patient immediately after the stroke would therefore yield an erroneous picture of the extent of the damage.

The History

The typical neuropsychological examination begins with a careful history taking. Areas that will be of interest to the examiner include the following:

- The medical history of the patient.

- The medical history of the patient's immediate family and other relatives. A sample question here might be, Have you or any of your relatives experienced dizziness, fainting, blackouts, or spasms?

- The presence or absence of certain **developmental milestones;** a particularly critical part of the history-taking process when examining young children. A list of some of these milestones appears in Table 14–4.

- Psychosocial history, including level of academic achievement and estimated level of intelligence; an estimated level of adjustment at home and at work or school; observations regarding personality (for example, Is this individual hypochondriacal?), thought processes, and motivation (Is this person willing and able to respond accurately to these questions?).

- The character, severity, and progress of any history of complaints involving disturbances in sight, hearing, smell, touch, taste, or balance; disturbances in muscle tone, muscle strength, and muscle movement; disturbances in autonomic functions such as breathing, eliminating, and body temperature control; disturbances in speech; disturbances in thought and memory; pain (particularly headache and facial pain); and various types of thought disturbances.

A careful history is critical to the accuracy of the assessment. Consider, for example, a patient who exhibits flat affect, is listless, and doesn't seem to know what day it is or what time it is. Such an individual might be suffering from something neurological in origin (such as a dementia); however, a functional disorder (such as severe depression) might instead be causing the problem. A good history taking will shed light on whether the observed behavior is the result of a genuine dementia or a product of what is referred to as a pseudodementia. History-taking questions might include the following: How long has the patient been in this condition and what emotional or neurological trauma may have precipitated it? Does this patient have a personal or family history of depression or other psychiatric disturbance? What factors appear to be operating to maintain the patient in this state? Whether the disorder is organic or functional in origin, the history will also shed light on questions relative to its progressive or nonprogressive nature.

Table 14–4
Some Developmental Milestones

Age	Development
16 weeks	Gets excited, laughs aloud Spontaneous smile in response to people Anticipates eating at sight of food Sits propped for 10 to 15 minutes
28 weeks	Smiles and vocalizes to a mirror and pats at mirror image Many vowel sounds Sits unsupported for brief period and then leans on hands Takes solids well When lying on back, places feet to mouth Grasps objects and transfers objects from hand to hand When held standing, supports most of weight
12 months	Walks with only one hand held Says "mamma" and "dada" and perhaps two other words Gives a toy in response to a request or gesture When being dressed, will cooperate Plays "peek-a-boo" games
18 months	Has a vocabulary of some ten words Walks well, seldom falls, can run stiffly Looks at pictures in a book Feeds self, although spills Can pull a toy or hug a doll Can seat self in a small or adult chair Scribbles spontaneously with a crayon or pencil
24 months	Walks up and down stairs alone Runs well, no falling Can build a tower of six or seven blocks Uses personal pronouns ("I" and "you") and speaks a three-word sentence Identifies simple pictures by name and calls self by name Verbalizes needs fairly consistently May be dry at night Can pull on simple garment
36 months	Alternates feet when climbing stairs and jumps from bottom stair Rides a tricycle Can copy a circle and imitate a cross with a crayon or pencil Comprehends and answers questions Feeds self with little spilling May know and repeat a few simple rhymes
48 months	Can dry and wash hands, brushes teeth Laces shoes, dresses and undresses with supervision Can play cooperatively with other children Can draw figure of a person with at least two clear body parts
60 months	Knows and names colors, counts to 10 Skips on both feet Can print a few letters, can draw identifiable pictures

Source: Gesell and Amatruda (1947)

The Neuropsychological Mental Status Examination

An outline for a general mental status examination was presented in Chapter 13. The neuropsychological mental status examination overlaps the general examination with respect to questions concerning the assessee's consciousness, emotional state, thought content and clarity, memory, sensory perception, performance of action, language, speech, handwriting, and handedness. The mental status examination administered for the express purpose of evaluating neuropsychological functioning may delve more extensively into specific areas of interest. For example, during a routine mental status examination, the examiner might require the examinee to interpret the meaning of only one or two proverbs; on the neurological mental status examination, many proverbs may be presented to obtain a more comprehensive picture of the patient's capacity for abstract thought. Throughout the history taking and the mental status examination, the clinician will take note of gross and subtle observations pertinent to the evaluation. For example, the examiner will note the presence of involuntary movements (such as facial tics), locomotion difficulties, and other sensory and motor problems that may become apparent. The examiner may note, for example, that one corner of the mouth is slower to curl than the other when the patient smiles—a finding suggestive of damage to the seventh (facial) cranial nerve. As we will see in the upcoming section on interviews and rating scales, a number of prepackaged mental status examination "short forms" have been published.

The Physical Examination

Most neuropsychologists perform some kind of physical examination on patients, but the extent of this examination varies widely as a function of the expertise, competence, and confidence of the examiner. Some neuropsychologists have had extensive training in performing physical examinations under the tutelage of neurologists in teaching hospitals. Such psychologists feel confident in performing many of the same **noninvasive procedures** (procedures that do not involve any intrusion into the examinee's body) that neurologists perform as part of their neurological examination. In the course of the following discussion, we list some of these noninvasive procedures. We precede this discussion with the caveat that it is the physician and not the neuropsychologist who is always the final arbiter of medical questions.

In addition to making observations about the examinee's appearance, the examiner may also physically examine the scalp and skull for any unusual enlargements or depressions. Muscles may be inspected for their tone (soft? rigid?), strength (weak or tired?), and size relative to other muscles. With respect to the last point, the examiner might find, for example, that Ralph's right biceps are much larger than his left biceps. Such a finding could indicate muscular dystrophy in the left arm, but it also could reflect the fact that Ralph has been working as a shoemaker for the past 40 years—a job in which he is constantly hammering with and building up the muscle in his right arm. This patient's case underscores the importance of careful history taking when evaluating physical findings. In addition to physical examination of the skull and the musculature, simple reflexes may be tested. **Reflexes** are involuntary motor responses to stimuli. Many reflexes have survival value for infants but then disappear as the child grows older. One such reflex is the mastication (chewing) reflex. Stroking the tongue or lips will elicit chewing behavior in the normal infant; however, if chewing is elicited in the older child or adult, it indicates neurological deficit. In addition to testing for the presence or absence of various reflexes, the examiner might examine muscle coordination by using tests such as those listed in Table 14–5.

A complete examination is designed to assess not only the functioning of the brain but aspects of the functioning of the nerves, muscles, and other organs and systems as well. Some procedures used to shed light on the adequacy and functioning of some of the 12 cranial nerves are summarized in Table 14–6. Additional procedures of evaluation and measurement will be presented in the remainder of this chapter as we review several more specialized tools of neuropsychological assessment.

Table 14-5
Sample Tests Used to Evaluate Muscle Coordination

Walking-running-skipping

If the examiner has not had a chance to watch the patient walk for any distance, he or she may ask the patient to do so as part of the examination. We tend to take walking for granted; but, neurologically speaking, it is a highly complex activity that involves proper integration of many varied components of the nervous system. Sometimes abnormalities in gait may be due to nonneurological causes; if, for example, a severe case of bunions is suspected as the cause of the difficulty, the examiner may ask the patient to remove his or her shoes and socks so that the feet may be physically inspected. Highly trained examiners are additionally sensitive to subtle abnormalities in, for example, arm movements while the patient walks, runs, or skips.

Standing still (technically, the Romberg test)

The patient is asked to stand still with feet together, head erect, and eyes open. Whether patients have their arms extended straight out or at their sides and whether or not they are wearing shoes or other clothing will be a matter of the examiner's preference. Patients are next instructed to close their eyes. The critical variable is the amount of sway exhibited by the patient once the eyes are closed. Because normal persons may sway somewhat with their eyes closed, experience and training is required to determine when the amount of sway is indicative of pathology.

Nose-finger-nose

The patient's task is to touch her nose with the tip of her index finger, then touch the examiner's finger, and then touch her own nose again. The sequence is repeated many times with each hand. This test, as well as many similar ones (such as the toe-finger test, the finger-nose test, the heel-knee test), are designed to assess, among other things, cerebellar functioning.

Finger wiggle

The examiner models finger wiggling (that is, playing an imaginary piano or typing), and then the patient is asked to wiggle his own fingers. Typically, the non-dominant hand cannot be wiggled as quickly as the dominant hand, but it takes a trained eye to pick up a significant decrease in rate. The experienced examiner will also look for abnormalities in the precision of the movements and the rhythm of the movements, "mirror movements" (uncontrolled similar movements in the other hand when instructed to only wiggle one), and other abnormal involuntary movements. Like the nose-finger test, finger wiggling supplies information concerning the quality of involuntary movement and muscular coordination. A related task involves tongue wiggling.

Table 14-6
Sample Tests Used by Neurologists to Assess the Intactness of Some of the 12 Cranial Nerves

Cranial Nerve	Test
I (olfactory nerve)	Closing one nostril with a finger, the examiner places some odiferous substance under the nostril being tested and asks whether the smell is perceived. Subjects who perceive it are next asked to identify it. Failure to perceive an odor when one is presented may indicate lesions of the olfactory nerve, a brain tumor, or other medical conditions. Of course, failure may be due to other factors, such as oppositional tendencies on the part of the patient or intranasal disease, and such factors must be ruled out as causal.
II (optic nerve)	Assessment of the intactness of the second cranial nerve is a highly complicated procedure, for this is a sensory nerve with functions related to visual acuity and peripheral vision. A Snellen eye chart is one of the tools used by the physician in assessing optic nerve function. If the subject at a distance of 20 feet from the chart is able to read the small numbers or letters in the line labeled "20," then the subject is said to have 20/20 vision in the eye being tested. This is only a standard. Although many persons can read only the larger print at higher numbers on the chart (that is, a person who reads the letters on line "40" of the chart would be said to have a distance vision of 20/40), some persons have better than 20/20 vision. An individual who could read the line labeled "15" on the Snellen eye chart would be said to have 20/15 vision.
V (trigeminal nerve)	The trigeminal nerve supplies sensory information from the face, and it supplies motor information to and from the muscles involved in chewing. Information regarding the functioning of this nerve is examined by the use of tests for facial pain (pinpricks are made by the physician), facial sensitivity to different temperatures, and other sensations. Another part of the examination entails having the subject clamp his or her jaw shut. The physician will then feel and inspect the facial muscles for weakness and other abnormalities.
VIII (acoustic nerve)	The acoustic nerve has functions related to the sense of hearing and the sense of balance. Hearing is formally assessed with an audiometer. More frequently, the routine assessment of hearing involves the use of a "dollar watch." Provided the examination room is quiet, an individual with normal hearing should be able to hear a dollar watch ticking at a distance of about 40 inches from each ear (30 inches if the room is not very quiet). Other quick tests of hearing involve placing a vibrating tuning fork on various portions of the skull. Individuals who complain of dizziness, vertigo, disturbances in balance, and so forth may have their vestibular system examined by means of specific tests.

Tools of Neuropsychological Assessment

A number of tests and measurement procedures have been developed to assess all conceivable aspects of neuropsychological functioning. Here we present a sample of these specialized tools, beginning with interviews and rating scales.

Interviews and Rating Scales

A variety of structured interviews and rating forms are available as aids in the neuropsychological screening and evaluation process. Neuropsychological screening devices point the way to further areas of inquiry with more extensive evaluation methods. Such devices can be used economically with members of varied populations who may be at risk for neuropsychological impairment, such as psychiatric patients, the elderly, and alcoholics (Berg et al., 1987; Errico et al., 1990; Goldstein, 1986; Yozawitz, 1986). Some of these measures, such as the Short Portable Mental Status Questionnaire (Pfeiffer, 1975), are completed by an assessor, and others, such as the Neuropsychological Impairment Scale (NIS) (O'Donnell & Reynolds, 1983; O'Donnell, DeSoto, DeSoto, & Reynolds, 1993), are self-report instruments. The Mini-Mental State Exam (Folstein et al., 1975) has more than a quarter-century of history as a clinical and research tool used to screen for cognitive impairment. One study of its structure suggested it was measuring primarily concentration, language, orientation, memory, and attention (Jones & Gallo, 2000). Despite criticism of its internal structure for being amenable to obtaining acceptable levels of inter-rater reliability (Molloy et al., 1991; Anthony et al., 1982), it remains in wide use. Also in the category of brief, structured measures is the 7 Minute Screen, an instrument developed to help identify patients with symptoms characteristic of Alzheimer's disease (Solomon et al., 1998). Tasks on this test tap orientation, verbal fluency, and various aspects of memory. The respondent is also asked to draw a clock with all the numbers on it, and then asked to draw the hands pointing at 20 minutes before 4 o'clock. Lawrence et al. (2000) reported on a community-based pilot program for memory impairment screening that employed both the Mini-Mental State Examination and the 7 Minute Screen. They reported that the program identified a significant number of individuals with previously undetected cognitive impairment.

Case Histories and Case Studies

Case history files are valuable resources to all psychological assessors, but they are particularly valuable in neuropsychological assessment. In many instances, the referral question concerns the degree of damage that has been sustained relative to a patient's preexisting condition; the assessor must determine the level of the patient's functioning and neuropsychological intactness prior to any trauma, disease, or other disabling factors. In making such a determination about a premorbid level of functioning, the assessor may rely on a wide variety of case history data ranging from archival records to videotapes made with the family video camera.

In addition to historical records regarding the patient being assessed, published case studies on people who have suffered the same or similar type of neuropsychological deficit will be of great value to the assessor. Case study material can provide leads regarding areas of evaluation to explore in-depth, and can also suggest the course a particular disease or deficit will follow and how observed strengths or weaknesses may change over time. Additionally, case study material can be valuable in formulating plans for therapeutic intervention.

Tests

A wide variety of tests are used by neuropsychologists, clinical psychologists, school psychologists, educational evaluators, and others who are charged with finding answers to referral questions. Researchers may employ neuropsychological tests to gauge change in mental status or other variables as a result of the administration of medication or the onset of a disease or disorder. Forensic evaluators may employ tests to gain insight into how neuropsychological factors may have a bearing on issues such as criminal responsibility or competency to stand trial.

One symptom commonly associated with neuropsychological deficit, regardless of the site or exact cause of the problem, is inability or lessened ability to think abstractly. Tests that measure the ability to think abstractly are therefore frequently administered. One popular measure of verbal abstraction ability is the Wechsler Similarities subtest, isolated from the age-appropriate version of the Wechsler intelligence scale. The task is to identify how two objects (for instance, a ball and an orange) are alike. Proverb interpretation is another method used to assess ability to think abstractly. As an example, interpret the following proverb before reading on:

A stitch in time saves nine.

If your interpretation got across the idea that "haste makes waste," then you evidenced an ability to think abstractly. By contrast, some people with neurological deficits might have interpreted that proverb more concretely—with less abstraction. An interpretation such as "When sewing, take one stitch at a time—it'll save you from having to do it over nine times" might (or might not, depending on other factors) betray a deficit in abstraction ability. The Proverbs Test (Gorham, 1956) contains a number of proverbs along with standardized administration instructions and normative data. In one form of this test, the subject is instructed to write an explanation of the proverb. In another form of the test, this one multiple-choice, each proverb is followed by four choices, three of which may be either common misinterpretations or representative of a concrete-type response.

Nonverbal tests of abstraction include any of the various sorting tests—tests that require the respondent to sort objects in some logical way. Common to most of the sorting tests are instructions like "Group together all the ones that belong together," followed by questions such as "Why did you group those objects together?" Representative of such tests is the Object Sorting Test (refer back to Figure 14–1), which contains familiar objects the subject is asked to sort according to various categories (such as color or use). Alternatively, the examiner may group a few of the objects together and ask the subject to determine why those objects go together or to select the object that does not belong with the rest. Another such sorting test is the Color-Form Sorting Test (also known as Weigl's Test), wherein the subject's task is to sort objects of different shapes and colors according to the directions of the examiner. The Wisconsin Card Sorting Test-64 Card Version (WCST-64; Kongs et al., 2000) requires the testtaker to sort a pack of 64 cards that contain different geometric figures printed in different colors. The cards are to be sorted according to matching rules that must be inferred and that shift as the test progresses. Successful performance on this test requires several abilities associated with frontal lobe functioning including concentration, planning, organization, cognitive flexibility in shifting set, working memory, and inhibition of impulsive responding. The test may be useful in screening for neurological impairment, with or without suspected injury of the frontal lobe. Caution is suggested when using this or similar tests as some evidence suggests that the test may erroneously indicate that neurological impairment exists when in reality the testtaker has schizophrenia or a mood disorder (Heinrichs, 1990). It is there-

Figure 14–2
The Tower of Hanoi

This version of the Tower of Hanoi puzzle comes with 3 pegs and 8 rings. The puzzle begins with all of the rings on one of the pegs ordered from the bottom up in decreasing size. To solve the puzzle, all of the rings must be transferred to another peg following 3 rules: (1) Only one ring may be moved at a time; (2) the ring is moved from one peg to another; and (3) no ring may ever be placed on a smaller one.

fore important for clinicians to rule out alternative explanations for test performance indicative of neurological deficit.

Another tool useful in evaluating **executive functions** (organizing, planning, cognitive flexibility, and inhibition of impulses) associated with the frontal and prefrontal lobes of the brain is the Tower of Hanoi test (Figure 14–2). According to Rohl (1993), this puzzle made its first appearance in Paris in 1883. It is set up by stacking the rings on one of the pegs, beginning with the largest diameter ring, and with no succeeding ring resting on a smaller one. Probably because the appearance of these stacked rings looked reminiscent of a pagoda, the puzzle was christened *"La Tour de Hanoi."* The Tower of Hanoi, either in solid form for manipulation by hand or adapted for computerized administration, has been used to measure aspects of executive functioning in a number of different contexts (Aman et al., 1998; Arnett et al., 1997; Butters et al., 1985; Byrnes & Spitz, 1977; Glosser & Goodglass, 1990; Goel & Grafman, 1995; Goldberg et al., 1990; Grafman et al., 1992; Leon-Carrion et al., 1991; Mazzocco et al., 1992; Miller & Ozonoff, 2000; Minsky et al., 1985; Schmand et al., 1992; Spitz et al., 1985).

As early as the 1930s, psychologist Stanley D. Porteus became enamored with the potential for psychological assessment of the seemingly simple task of identifying the correct path in a maze and then tracing a line to the end-point of that maze. This type of task was originally introduced to yield a quantitative estimate of "prudence, forethought, mental alertness, and power of sustained attention" (Porteus, 1942). Porteus urged colleagues to use mazes for varied research purposes ranging from the exploration of cultural differences (Porteus, 1933), to the study of social inadequacy (Porteus, 1955), to the study of personality traits by means of qualitative analysis of a testtaker's performance (Porteus, 1942). Today, maze tasks like those in the Porteus Maze Test (Figure 14–3) are used primarily as measures of executive function (Daigneault et al., 1992; Krikorian & Bartok, 1998; Mack & Patterson, 1995). Although useful in measuring such functioning in adults, its utility for that purpose in children has been questioned. Shum et al. (2000) observed no adverse impact on Porteus maze performance of children with traumatic brain injury.

Representative items for four other types of tasks that may be used in neuropsychological assessment are illustrated in Figure 14–4. Part (a) illustrates a **trail making item.** The task is to connect the circles in a logical way. This type of task is thought to tap

Figure 14–3
"Where do we go from here, Charly?"

A Porteus-maze-like task is being illustrated by the woman in the white coat to actor Cliff Robertson as "Charly" in the now-classic film of the same name.

many abilities including visual-conceptual, visual-motor, planning, and other cognitive abilities, although exactly which abilities are tapped has been a matter of longstanding debate (Stanczak et al., 1998). The Trail Making Tests in the Halstead-Reitan Neuropsychological Battery (a fixed battery to be discussed shortly) are among the most widely used measures of brain damage (Salthouse et al., 2000; Thompson et al., 1999) and have been employed in a variety of studies (Bassett, 1999; Compton et al., 2000; King et al., 2000; Nathan et al., 2001; Ruffolo et al., 2000; Sherrill-Pattison et al., 2000; Wecker et al., 2000) with diverse subject populations ranging from Vietnam combat veterans (Beckham et al., 1998) to patients with silicone gel breast implants (Klein, 1998). Currently, a test that employs color trails is being explored to see if it represents a more culture-fair analogue of the trail making test (Lee & Chan, 2000; Lee et al., 2000).

Illustration (b) in Figure 14–4 is an example of a field of search item. Shown a sample item, the testtaker must scan this field of items to match the sample as quickly as possible. Field of search has traditionally been, and today remains, an important area in neuropsychological research and clinical neuropsychology. Field of search ability has strong adaptive value and can have life or death consequences for predator and prey. Field of search research has many applications, enhancing our understanding of everyday functions such as driving a car (Crundall et al., 1998; Duchek et al., 1998; Guerrier et al., 1999; Recarte & Nunes, 2000; Zwahlen et al., 1998) to more specialized activities such as piloting aircraft (Seagull & Gopher, 1997) and monitoring air traffic (Remington et al., 2000).

Illustration (c) is an example of a simple line drawing reminiscent of the type of item that appears in instruments such as the Boston Naming Test (Goodglass & Kaplan, 1983). The testtaker's task on the Boston (as it is often abbreviated) is **confrontation naming;**

**Figure 14–4
Sample Items Used
in Neuropsychological Assessment**

(a) The Trail Making Test
The testtaker's task is to connect the dots
in logical fashion.

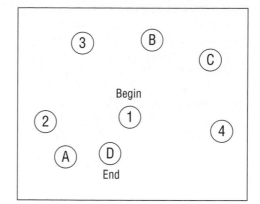

(b) The Field of Search
After being shown a sample stimulus, the testtaker's
task is to locate a match as quickly as possible.

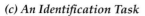

(c) An Identification Task
A task entailing what is referred to as confrontation
naming.

(d) A Picture Absurdity
The testtaker answers questions like, "What's wrong
or silly about this picture?"

that is, naming each stimulus presented. This seemingly simple task entails three component operations necessary for success: a perceptual component (perceiving the visual features of the stimulus), a semantic component (accessing the underlying conceptual representation or core meaning of whatever is pictured), and a lexical component (accessing and expressing the appropriate name). Difficulty with the naming task could therefore be due to deficits in any or all of these components. Persons who are neurologically compromised as a result of Alzheimer's disease or other dementia typically experience difficulty with naming tasks.

Illustration (d) in Figure 14–4 is what is called a picture absurdity item; the pictorial equivalent of a verbal absurdity item. The testtaker must identify what is wrong or silly about the picture. It is similar to the picture absurdity items on the Stanford-Binet intelligence test. As with Wechsler-type Comprehension items, this item can provide insight into the testtaker's social comprehension and reasoning abilities. Although once popular in cognitive ability testing, picture and verbal absurdity-type items have largely been replaced in many tests and batteries by other types of items. In one fairly atypical but nonetheless innovative application, absurdity items were used in the context of training autistic youth in appropriate affective behavior (Gena, 1995).

A number of other item types (such as recall of digits forward or backward) and tests (such as the MMPI-2) may be employed in a neuropsychological evaluation. Some of the most commonly used neuropsychological tests include tests of general intellectual ability, tests of verbal functioning, memory tests, and tests designed to evaluate general perceptual, motor, and perceptual-motor functioning.

Tests of general intellectual ability   Tests of intellectual ability, particularly Wechsler tests, occupy a prominent position among the diagnostic tools available to the neuropsychologist. In fact, a survey of members of the APA Division of Clinical Neuropsychology and members of the National Academy of Neuropsychologists indicated that of all psychological tests and test batteries, the Wechsler scales were the most frequently used in practice by neuropsychologists; although many neuropsychologists use a variety of different techniques in their daily practice, one test virtually all of them use is a Wechsler intelligence test (Seretny et al., 1986).

The varied nature of the tasks on the Wechsler scales and the wide variety of responses required make it a good bet that if a neuropsychological deficit exists, some clue to the existence of the deficit will be brought to light. Thus, for example, difficulties in attention, concentration, or conceptualization might be noted during the administration of the Arithmetic items—a possible clue to a neurological deficit as opposed to a lack of arithmetic ability. Because certain patterns of test response indicate particular deficits, the examiner will look beyond performance on individual tests to a study of the pattern of test scores, a process termed **pattern analysis.** Thus, for example, extremely poor performance on the Block Design and other performance subtests in a record that contains relatively high scores on all the verbal subtests might, in combination with other data, lead the examiner to suspect damage in the right hemisphere. A number of researchers intent on developing a definitive sign of brain damage have devised various ratios and quotients based on patterns of subtest scores. David Wechsler himself referred to one such pattern called a **deterioration quotient** or "DQ" (also referred to by some as a "deterioration index"). However, neither Wechsler's DQ nor any other WAIS-based index has performed satisfactorily enough to be deemed a stand-alone measure of neuropsychological impairment. Fuld (1984) proposed that patients with Alzheimer's disease would present with WAIS-R profiles featuring high scores on Information and Vocabulary, low scores on Digit Symbol and Block Design, and middle-range scores on the Digit Symbol, Block Design, and Object Assembly subtests. However, independent research has not supported the predictive validity of this profile (Logstdon et al., 1989).

We have already noted the need to administer standardized tests in a manner that rigidly conforms to the instructions in the test manual. Yet because of the limited ability of the testtaker, such "by the book" test administrations are not always possible or desirable when testing members of the neurologically impaired population. Because of various problems or potential problems (such as the shortened attention span of some neurologically impaired individuals), the experienced examiner may find it necessary to modify the test administration in ways that will accommodate the testtaker yet yield clinically useful information. The examiner administering a Wechsler scale may deviate from the prescribed order of test administration when administering the test to an individual who becomes fatigued quickly; in such cases, the more taxing subtests will be administered early in the exam. In the interest of shortening the total test administration time, the trained examiner might omit certain subtests that he or she suspects will not provide any information over and above that already obtained. Let us reiterate that such deviations in the administration of standardized tests such as the Wechsler scales can be made—and meaningfully interpreted—by trained and experienced neuropsychologists. For the rest of us, it's *by the book!*

Tests of verbal functioning   **Aphasia,** not to be confused with *aphagia,* refers to a loss of ability to express oneself or to understand spoken or written language because of some neurological deficit.[3] A number of batteries such as the Neurosensory Center Comprehensive Examination of Aphasia (NCCEA) have been designed to help identify the extent and nature of the communication deficit. The NCCEA (Spreen & Benton, 1969), for example, is composed of 24 subtests, 20 of which are designed to assess various aspects of auditory and visual comprehension and oral/written expression. The remaining four subtests address visual and tactile functioning, and these subtests are administered only when the examiner suspects a visual or tactile sensory deficit. Perhaps a more culturally relevant instrument, especially for testtakers of Hispanic descent, is the Multilingual Aphasia Examination. Rey et al. (1999) found the published norms to be comparable to their own data using a sample of Hispanic testtakers. They also discussed specific problems encountered in neuropsychological research with Hispanics and suggested guidelines and directions for future research.

Verbal fluency and fluency in writing are sometimes affected by injury to the brain, and there are tests to assess the extent of the deficit in such skills. In the Controlled Word Association Test (formerly the Verbal Associative Fluency Test), the examiner says a letter of the alphabet and it is the subject's task to say as many words as he or she can think of that begin with that letter. Each of three trials employing three different letters as a stimulus lasts one minute, and the testtaker's final score on the test reflects the total number of correct words produced weighted by factors such as the gender, age, and education of the testtaker. Controlled Word Association Test scores are related in the predicted direction to the ability of dementia patients to complete tasks of daily living, such as using the telephone or writing a check (Loewenstein et al., 1992). And although people with dementia tend to do poorly on the test as compared with controls, the differences observed have not been significant enough to justify using the test as an indicator of dementia (Nelson et al., 1993).

Aphasia is assessed more broadly with the Reitan-Indiana Aphasia Screening Test (AST); (Reitan, 1984a). Available in both a child and an adult form, this test contains a variety of items involving the use of language, including naming common objects, following verbal instructions, and writing familiar words. Factor analysis has suggested that these tasks load on two factors: language abilities and coordination involved in writing

---

3. **Aphagia** is a condition in which the ability to eat is lost or diminished.

words or drawing objects (Williams & Shane, 1986). Both forms of the test were designed to be screening devices that can be administered in 15 minutes or less. As with other neuropsychological screening tools, if any problems are observed, more extensive assessment would be in order. Used alone as a screening tool (Reitan, 1984a, 1984b; Reitan & Wolfson, 1992), or in combination with other tests (Tramontana & Boyd, 1986), the AST may be of value in distinguishing testtakers who have and do not have brain damage.

The Sequenced Inventory of Communication Development (SICD) is a test designed to assess the development of receptive and expressive communication in children aged 4 months to 4 years. The test contains a number of observation and test procedures designed to assess various aspects of the young child's awareness and understanding. In support of the test's construct validity, two studies showed that chronic middle ear infections (otitis media) in young children produce a delay in language development as measured by the SICD (Friel-Patti & Finitzo, 1990; Wallace et al., 1988).

Tests of memory   Memory is a complex, multifaceted cognitive function that has defied simple explanation. To appreciate just how complex it is, consider the following:

> Humans possess an estimated 1 trillion neurons, plus 70 trillion synaptic connections between them. . . . A single neuron may have as many as 10,000 synapses, but during the process of memory formation perhaps only 12 synapses will be strengthened while another 100 will be weakened. The sum of those changes, multiplied neuron by neuron, creates a weighted circuit that amounts to memory. (Hall, 1998, p. 30)

Different models of memory compete for recognition in the scientific community, and no one model has garnered universal acceptance. For our purposes, a sample model is presented in Figure 14–5—along with the caveat that this relatively simple model, which was pieced together from various sources, is incomplete at best and *not* universally accepted. Moreover, the model contains elements that are still very much a matter of debate among contemporary researchers.

According to our model, memory results from information processing by the nervous system of external (actual) sensory input such as sights, sounds, smells, tastes, and so forth. Your stored vision of a loved one's face, the song you will never forget, and the smell of freshly mowed grass are examples of memories formed on the basis of actual sensory input. Memory of a sort may also result from what one produces internally, in the absence of actual sensation. What one imagines, dreams, and misperceives are all examples of this latter sort of memory. Of course, dominance of imagined or fabricated sorts of memories can become a matter of clinical significance. The line between the sensory input channel and conscious awareness is broken to indicate that not all sensory input automatically makes it into conscious awareness. Attention, concentration, and related factors play a key role in determining which input actually make it into conscious awareness.

Contrary to the popular image of memory as a storehouse of sorts, memory is a very active process, presumed to entail both short-term and long-term processes (Atkinson & Shiffrin, 1968). Incoming information is processed in short-term memory, where it is temporarily stored for as little as seconds or as long as a minute or two. "Short-term memory" has also been characterized by some researchers as virtually synonymous with "working memory" (Daneman & Carpenter, 1980; Newell, 1973). The more traditional view of short-term memory is that it serves as a passive buffer in which information is either transferred to long-term memory or dissipated (that is, forgotten). Our model allows for both passive and active components of short-term memory, with encoding of long-term memory made from the active, "working" component of short-term memory. In our model, note that the path between short-term memory and conscious awareness is two way: Stimuli from conscious awareness can be fed into short-term memory, and short-term memory can feed stimuli back into conscious awareness. Note also that the

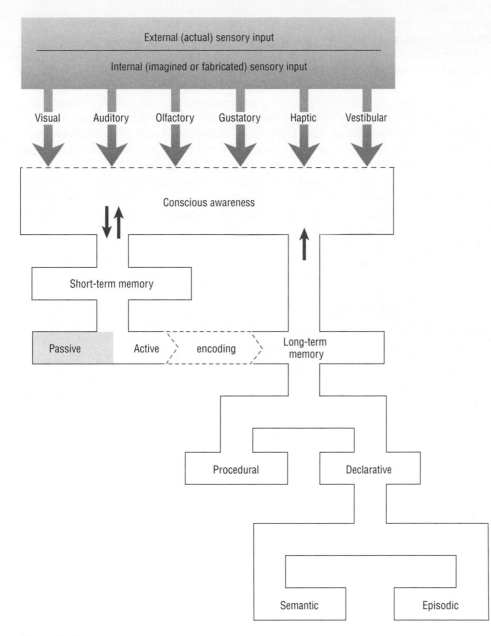

Figure 14–5
A Model of Memory

path to long-term memory is illustrated by a broken line—this to indicate that not all information in short-term memory is encoded in long-term memory.

With regard to long-term memory, researchers have distinguished between procedural and declarative memory. **Procedural memory** is memory for things like driving a car, making entries on a keyboard, or riding a bicycle; most of us can draw on procedural memory with little effort and concentration. **Declarative memory** refers to memory of factual material—such as the differences between procedural and declarative memory. We have compartmentalized the procedural and declarative components of long-term memory for illustrative purposes. We have also compartmentalized what are widely believed to be two components of declarative memory: semantic and episodic memory. Semantic memory is, strictly speaking, memory for facts. Episodic memory is memory for facts in a particular context or situation. An example of episodic or context-dependent memory might be the recollection of a classmate's name while in class, but not at a chance meeting at a social event. Being asked to repeat digits in the context of a memory test is another example of episodic memory because it is linked so intimately with the (testing) context. As indicated by the one-way pathway from long-term memory to consciousness, information stored in long-term memory is available for retrieval. Whether information so retrieved can be restored directly to long-term memory, or must instead be processed again through short-term memory, is a matter of debate.

Neuropsychological tests designed to evaluate memory tap different components of memory as outlined in our model. One of the most widely used tests of memory, the Wechsler Memory Scale-III (WMS-III), taps primarily declarative episodic memory. As stated in its technical manual, "The information that is presented is novel and contextually bound by the testing situation and requires the examinee to learn and retrieve information" (Tulsky et al., 1997, p. 3). Much like its predecessor (the WMS-R), the WMS-III is an individually administered memory test designed for use with older adolescents and adults. However, there are many significant differences between the WMS-R and the WMS-III in terms of the test's subtests and scales, norm development, index structure and index scoring, and related factors (see Tulsky et al., 1997). The WMS-III requires examinees to complete tasks such as retelling a story read aloud, sequencing letters and numbers (similar to the Letter-Number Sequencing task previously described for the WAIS-III), and learning word pairs that are seemingly unrelated. There are also subtests involving the recognition of pictures of faces. Examinees are first presented with an array of "target" faces. They must then identify which of these target faces are included among a second array of faces that includes both target and other faces. Optional tests include those involving tasks such as reproduction of designs presented on cards, and "multitasking" (that is, doing more than one thing at a time such as reciting the alphabet while counting backward from 30). Factor-analytic studies performed with the WMS-III supported different factor solutions as a function of age group but were interpreted by the test developers as generally supportive of their notion of the following dimensions underlying the test: immediate and delayed auditory memory, immediate and delayed visual memory, and working memory.

Two other approaches to memory testing are illustrated in Figure 14–6. In an approach devised by Milner (1971) "tactile nonsense figures" are employed to measure immediate tactile (or haptic) memory. Another tactile memory test involves an adaptation in the administration of the Seguin-Goddard Formboard. Initially designed to assess visuopractic ability, Halstead (1947a) suggested that the formboard could be used to assess tactile memory if examinees were blindfolded during the test and a recall trial was added. One effort to make memory tests more real world in nature is to integrate in them tasks that people must perform each day. A computerized test battery developed by Thomas Crook and described by Hostetler (1987) uses a number of real-world tasks (such as telephone dialing and name-face association). The battery has been employed as an outcome measure in studies of the efficacy of various drugs in the treatment of Alzheimer's disease.

Tests of perceptual, motor, and perceptual-motor functions   Neurologically impaired individuals may exhibit difficulty in making sense out of fragmented or jumbled stimuli, and tests such as Mooney's Closure Faces Test are designed to assess the existence and extent of this deficit. People with right hemisphere lesions may exhibit deficits in visual scanning ability, and a test such as the Field of Search can be of value in discovering such deficits. The Ishihara (1964) test screens for color blindness, though more specialized in-

(a) **(b)**

Figure 14–6
Two Tools Used in the Measurement of Tactile Memory

(a) *Four pieces of wire bent into what are in essence "tactile nonsense figures" can be used in a tactile test of immediate memory. Examinees may be instructed to feel one of the figures with their right or left hand (or both hands) and then locate a matching figure.* **(b)** *Shown here is one form of the Seguin-Goddard Formboard. Blindfolded examinees are instructed to fit each of the ten wooden blocks into the appropriate space in the formboard with each hand separately and then with both hands. Afterward, the examinee may be asked to draw the formboard from memory. All responses are timed and scored for accuracy.*

struments are available if rare forms of color perception deficit are suspected. Among the tests available for measuring deficit in auditory functioning is the Wepman Auditory Discrimination Test. This brief, easy-to-administer test requires that the examiner read a list of 40 pairs of monosyllabic meaningful words (such as *muss/much*) pronounced with lips covered. The examinee's task is simply to determine if the two words just presented are the same or different. It's quite a straightforward test—provided that the examiner (1) isn't suffering from a speech defect, (2) has no heavy foreign accent, and (3) doesn't mutter. The standardization sample for the test represented a broad range within the population, but there is little information available about the reliability and validity of the test. The test manual also fails to outline standardized administration conditions, which are particularly critical for the test, given the nature of the stimuli (Pannbacker & Middleton, 1992).

An example of a test designed to assess gross and fine motor skills is the Bruininks-Oseretsky Test of Motor Proficiency. Designed for use with children aged 4½ to 14½, this instrument includes subtests that assess running speed and agility, balance, strength, response speed, and dexterity. A sphere referred to by its manufacturer as a "Neuro Developmental Training Ball" (Figure 14–7) may be used to assess balance and the vestibular sense. Performance on specified tasks with this tool of assessment has been shown to improve in response to interventions designed to improve sensorimotor skills (Polatajko et al., 1991). Additional evidence for the validity of this measure comes from a correlational study that compared the performance of developmentally disabled individuals on

Figure 14–7
A Tool Used to Measure Vestibular Functioning

it with the Papcsy-DePaepe test (a test that entails walking on beams of varying heights and widths). The correlation between the two measures was .64 (DePaepe & Ciccaglione, 1993). A measure of manual dexterity that was originally developed in the late 1940s as an aid in employee selection is the Purdue Pegboard Test (Figure 14–8). The object here is to insert pegs into holes using one hand, then the other hand, and then both hands. Each of these 3 segments of the test has a time limit of 30 seconds, and the score is equal to the number of pegs correctly placed. Normative data are available, and it is noteworthy that in a non-brain-injured population, women generally perform slightly better on this task than men. With brain-injured subjects, this test may help answer questions regarding the lateralization of a lesion.

A number of tests are designed to assess visual-motor integration. In the Beery-Buktenica Development Test of Visual-Motor Integration, the examinee's task is to copy geometric forms arranged in increasing order of difficulty. In studies with subjects from a geriatric population, the test was found to correlate .64 to .70 with WAIS-R scores and .40 with ratings of adaptive functioning (Ferere et al., 1992). The Frostig Developmental Test of Visual Perception measures some aspects of visual perception and eye-hand coordination by means of subtests that entail drawing lines between boundaries, finding embedded figures, distinguishing target shapes from other shapes, locating a rotated figure, and copying simple forms and patterns by joining dots. The test as a whole demonstrates moderate internal consistency (.72), with individual subtests demonstrating relatively low internal consistency reliability (.31 to .58). Item analysis suggested that more than half of the items are either passed or failed by a very large majority of testtakers—that is, some items are passed by almost all testtakers, and other items are failed by almost all testtakers—indicating that the items are poor sources of information about differences between testtakers (Brand, 1989).

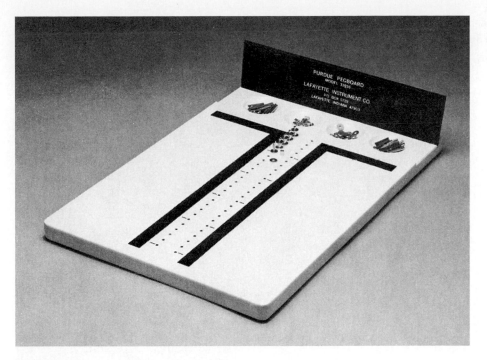

Figure 14–8
A Tool Used to Measure Manual Dexterity

One test widely used as a neuropsychological screening device is the **Bender-Gestalt test.** Interestingly, although the test enjoys widespread use by clinicians and school psychologists (Golden & Kupperman, 1980; Lubin et al., 1971), it is not particularly popular among neuropsychologists (Seretny et al., 1986), perhaps because they have more specialized instruments at their disposal.

Usually referred to as the "Bender-Gestalt" or simply "the Bender," the test consists of nine cards, on each of which is printed one design. The designs had been used by psychologist Max Wertheimer (1923) in his study of the perception of *gestalten* (German for "configurational wholes"). Lauretta Bender (Figure 14–9) believed they could be used to assess perceptual maturation and neurological impairment. Bender (1938) proposed that a testtaker be shown each of the cards in turn and instructed, "Copy it as best you can." There is no time limit for response, and usually all cards are copied in no more than five minutes. Unusually long or short administration times for this part of the test can be of diagnostic significance. After all nine designs have been copied, a fresh, blank piece of paper is placed before the testtaker with the instructions, "Now please draw all of the designs you can remember." Referred to as the "recall" phase of the test, this second phase was not an element of the original test. Gobetz (1953) proposed this procedure as a means of testing a hypothesis about differential performance on the Bender as a function of personality.[4] At the conclusion of the test, the testtaker may be asked to sign and

---

4. Gobetz (1953) had hypothesized that, owing to the pressure of the unexpected second test, subjects diagnosed as neurotic would be able to recall fewer figures on the recall portion of the test than would normal subjects. The recall procedure is routinely used with the Bender today not to provide personality data but rather to provide additional neuropsychological data.

Figure 14–9
Lauretta Bender (1896–1987)

Bender (1970) reflected that the objective in her visual-motor test was not to get a perfect reproduction of the test figures, but "a record of perceptual motor experience—a living experience unique and never twice the same, even with the same individual . . ." (p. 30).

date each sheet of paper. The examiner may draw an arrow on the back of the sheets to indicate the direction in which the paper was slanted. Related extra-test considerations, such as the handedness of the testtaker and distractions that may have occurred during administration, are also noted on the reverse side of the sheets.

Bender (1938, 1970) intended the test to be scored by means of clinical judgment. Still, a number of quantitative scoring systems for this appealingly simple test soon became available for adult (Hutt, 1985; Pascal & Suttell, 1951; Reichenberg & Raphael, 1992; Watkins, 1976) and child (Koppitz, 1963, 1975; Reichenberg & Raphael, 1992) protocols. A sampling of scoring terms common to many of these systems is presented in Figure 14–10. In addition, the test has inspired the creation of various alternative versions, including the so-called BIP Bender (a Bender that employs a background interference procedure; Canter, 1963, 1966), a multiple-choice Bender (designed to better distinguish perceptual from motor problems; Labrentz et al., 1976), and procedures instructing testtakers to verbalize associations to the designs (Hutt, 1977; Suczek & Klopfer, 1952). Like Halpern (1951) and others, Koppitz (1963, 1975) attributed symbolic significance to errors in producing specific Bender designs (Table 14–7).

Evidence in support of the use of the Bender-Gestalt as an instrument to assess personality is tenuous (Holmes et al., 1984). And although early reviews of the Bender's validity as a neuropsychological screening tool tended to be quite favorable (for example, Heaton et al., 1978; Spreen & Benton, 1965), the use of the test for neuropsychological screening purposes has also been questioned by research showing high rates of false negatives (Bigler & Ehrenfurth, 1980, 1981) as well as false positives (Margolis et al., 1989). The extent to which such findings are artifacts of the methodology or the scoring system employed is not known. Regardless, the Bender, after so many decades of service, is cur-

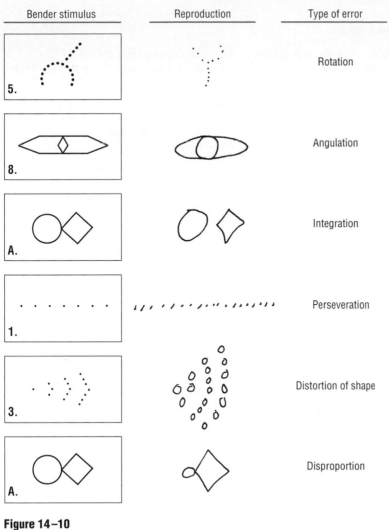

Bender stimulus	Reproduction	Type of error
5.		Rotation
8.		Angulation
A.		Integration
1.		Perseveration
3.		Distortion of shape
A.		Disproportion

Figure 14–10
Sample Errors on the Bender-Gestalt

These types of errors may suggest organic impairment. Not all the illustrated errors are signs of organic impairment at all ages.

rently under revision and is being co-normed with the Stanford-Binet. The revised Bender will contain new items as well as new administration procedures.

Other Tools of Neuropsychological Assessment

Space limitations prohibit extended discussion of the burgeoning array of tools available to clinicians, neuropsychologists, school psychologists, and others who conduct neuropsychological evaluations. As a result, only a few other tools will be mentioned here. Through the years, the Benton Visual Retention Test has been a widely used screening measure that has good predictive validity when used with other tests such as the Hooper Visual Organization Test and the Weigl Color-Form Sorting Test (Tamkin & Kunce, 1985). The latest (fifth) edition of the Benton provides for direct copy of designs and/or

Table 14–7
Emotional Indicators on the Bender

The following are the 12 Bender "emotional indicators" (EIs) enumerated by Koppitz (1963, 1975). Koppitz (1975, p. 92) cautioned that the "presence of three or more EIs on a Bender test protocol tends to reflect emotional difficulties that warrant further investigation."

1. *Confused order.* Associated with poor planning and inability to organize material.
2. *Wavy line on Figures 1 and 2.* Associated with poor motor coordination and/or emotional instability.
3. *Dashes substituted for circles on Figure 2.* Associated with impulsivity and lack of interest in young children.
4. *Increasing size on Figures 1, 2, or 3.* Associated with low frustration tolerance and explosiveness.
5. *Large size.* Associated with acting-out behavior in children.
6. *Small size.* Associated with anxiety, withdrawal, and timidity in children.
7. *Fine line.* Associated with timidity, shyness, and withdrawal in young children.
8. *Careless overwork or heavily reinforced lines.* Associated with impulsivity, aggressiveness, and acting-out behavior in children, although some researchers have found it to be related to high intelligence and good achievement.
9. *Second attempt.* Associated with impulsivity and anxiety.
10. *Expansion.* Associated with impulsivity and acting-out behavior in children.
11. *Box around design.* Associated with children who have weak inner control. They need and want limits and controls to function in school and at home.
12. *Spontaneous elaboration or additions to design.* Associated with children who are overwhelmed by fears and anxieties and are totally preoccupied with their own thoughts; they often have a tenuous hold on reality and may confuse fact and fantasy.

a memory format of administration. One authority in neuropsychology cited the Benton as an instrument of choice when perseveration or visual-spatial deficits are suspected (Lezak, 1995). A possible limitation, however, is that left-brain conceptualization can confound what were designed to be right-brain-type tasks.

Perhaps the greatest advances in the field of neuropsychological assessment have come in the form of high technology and the mutually beneficial relationship that has developed between psychologists and medical personnel. For example, recent advances in genetic research have led to exciting suggestive evidence regarding the origins of autism. Mutations in a gene essential to brain development may predict the onset of this debilitating developmental disorder (O'Connor, 2001). Beyond the level of the gene, more "everyday" miracles in diagnosis and treatment are brought about using imaging technology, and related technology discussed in this chapter's *Everyday Psychometrics.*

Neuropsychological Test Batteries

The Flexible Battery

The tests we've listed only begin to illustrate the diversity of the numerous techniques and methods available to the clinician doing neuropsychological assessment. On the basis of the mental status examination, the physical examination, and the case history data, the neuropsychologist will typically administer a **flexible battery** of neuropsychological tests; specific tests will be chosen for some purpose relevant to the unique aspects of the patient and the presenting problem. This so-called flexible battery of tests handpicked by the neuropsychologist stands in contrast to a fixed or prepackaged battery of neuropsychological tests, wherein all examinees are administered the same subtests in the context of a standardized procedure (see Williams, 2000).

The clinician who administers a flexible battery has not only the responsibility of selecting the tests to be used but also the burden of integrating all the findings from each

Medical Diagnostic Aids and Neuropsychological Assessment

Data from neuropsychological assessment combined with data derived from various medical procedures can in some cases yield a thorough understanding of a neurological problem. For example, certain behavioral indices evident in neuropsychological testing may lead the neuropsychologist to recommend that a particular site in the brain be further explored for the presence of lesions—a suspicion that may be confirmed by a diagnostic procedure that yields cross-sectional pictures of the site.

The trained neuropsychologist has a working familiarity with the array of nonpsychological—medical—tests that may be brought to bear on neuropsychological problems. In this discussion, we describe a sampling of such tests and measurement procedures. We begin with a brief description of the medical procedure and apparatus that is perhaps most familiar to us all—whether from experience in a dentist's chair or elsewhere—the X-ray.

To the radiologist, the X-ray photograph's varying shades convey information about the corresponding density of the tissue through which the X-rays have been passed. With front, side, back, and other X-ray views of the brain and the spinal column, the diagnosis of tumors, lesions, infections, and other abnormalities can frequently be made. There are many different types of neuroradiologic procedures. These range from the simple X-ray of the skull to more complicated procedures involving the injection of some tracer element into the bloodstream (as is required for a cerebral angiogram).

Perhaps you have also heard or read about another X-ray-type of procedure, the "CAT (computerized axial tomography) scan" or "CT" scan (Figure 1). The *CT scan* is superior to traditional X-rays because the structures in the brain may be represented in a systematic series of three-dimensional views, a feature that is extremely important in assessing conditions such as spinal anomalies. *PET* (positron emission tomography) scans are a tool of nuclear medicine particularly useful in diagnosing biochemical lesions in the brain. PET has also been used as a tool in evaluation research with schizophrenics and other psychiatric patients (Trimble, 1986). Conceptually related to the PET scan is *SPECT* (single photon emission computed tomography), a technology that records the course of a radioactive tracer fluid (iodine) producing exceptionally clear photographs of organs and tissues (Figure 2).

Figure 1

The CT scan is useful in pinpointing the location of tumors, cysts, degenerated tissue, or other abnormalities, and its use may eliminate the need for exploratory surgery or painful diagnostic procedures used in brain or spinal studies.

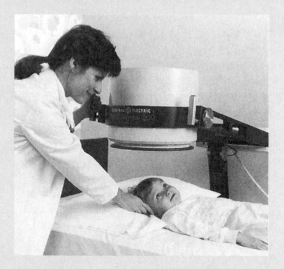

Figure 2

SPECT technology has been found to be of promising value in evaluating conditions such as cerebral vascular disease, Alzheimer's disease, and seizure disorders.

(continued)

Medical Diagnostic Aids and Neuropsychological Assessment *(continued)*

Also referred to as a "radioisotope scan," the *brain scan* procedure involves the introduction of radioactive materials into the brain through an injection. The cranial surface is then scanned with a special camera to track the flow of material. Alterations in blood supply to the brain are noted, including alterations that may be associated with disease such as tumors.

The *electroencephalograph* (EEG) is a machine that measures the electrical activity of the brain by means of electrodes pasted to the scalp. It is a relatively safe, painless procedure that can be of significant value in diagnosing and treating seizure and other disorders. The electroencephalographer is trained to distinguish normal from abnormal brainwave activity. EEG activity will vary as a function of age, level of arousal (awake, drowsy, asleep), and other variables in addition to brain abnormalities. EEG technology has been used to study a wide variety of neuropsychological phenomena such as electrical activity of the brain in Alzheimer's disease (see, for example, Martin-Loeches et al., 1991).

The *electromyograph* (EMG) is a machine that records electrical activity of muscles by means of an electrode that is inserted directly into the muscle. Abnormalities found in the EMG can be used with other clinical and historical data as an aid in making a final diagnosis. The *echoencephalograph* is a machine that transforms electric energy into sound (sonic) energy. The sonic energy ("echoes") transversing the tissue area under study is then converted back into electric energy and displayed as a printout. This printout is used as an adjunct to other procedures in helping the neurologist to determine the nature and location of certain types of lesions in the brain. Radio waves in combination with a magnetic field can also be used to create detailed anatomical images, as illustrated in Figure 3.

Information about nerve damage and related abnormalities may be obtained by direct electrical stimulation of nerves and notation of movement or lack of movement in corresponding muscle tissue. Examination of the cerebrospinal fluid for blood and other abnormalities is an important diagnostic aid to the neurologist. A sample of the

Figure 3

This magnetic resonance system utilizes a magnetic field and radio waves to create detailed images of the body. These and related imaging techniques may be employed not only in the study of neuropsychological functioning but in the study of abnormal behavior as well; see, for example, Kellner et al.'s (1991) study of obsessive-compulsive disorder.

fluid is obtained by means of a medical procedure termed a *lumbar puncture*—in everyday terminology, a spinal tap. This procedure entails inserting a special needle into the widest spinal interspace, after a local anesthetic has been applied. In addition to providing information concerning the chemical normality of the fluid, the test also lets the neurologist gauge the normality of the intracranial pressure.

Laboratory analysis of blood, urine, and other cells will provide the physician with a wealth of leads concerning possible bases for suspected neurological difficulties. For example, a presenting problem of decreased sensation may be due to a number of different causes, such as diabetes mellitus (which could be diagnosed by a glucose tolerance test).

of the individual tests—no simple task because each test may have been normed on different populations. Another problem inherent in the use of a flexible battery is that the tests administered frequently overlap with respect to some of the functions tested, and the result is some waste in testing and scoring time. Regardless of these and other drawbacks, the preference of most highly trained neuropsychologists has traditionally been to tailor a battery of tests to the specific demands of a particular testing situation. Of course, all of that may change as a result of judicial action (see this chapter's *Close-up*).

The Fixed Battery

A **fixed battery** is a prepackaged test battery containing a number of standardized tests to be administered in a prescribed fashion. Fixed neuropsychological test batteries are designed to comprehensively sample the patient's neuropsychological functioning. The fixed battery is appealing to clinicians, especially clinicians who are relatively new to neuropsychological assessment, because it tends to be less demanding in many ways. Whereas a great deal of expertise and skill is required to fashion a flexible battery that will adequately answer the referral question, a prepackaged battery represents a non-tailor-made but comprehensive alternative. Various tests sampling various areas are included in the battery, and each is supplied with clear scoring methods. One major drawback of the prepackaged tests, however, is that the specific disability of the patient may greatly—and adversely—influence performance on the test; thus, an individual with a visual impairment, for example, may perform poorly on many of the other subtests of a battery that require certain visual skills.

Keeping in mind that trained neuropsychologists may administer a fixed battery, may modify a fixed battery for the purposes of a particular case at hand, or administer their own hand-picked assortment of tests, we now look at some representative fixed batteries.

Halstead-Reitan Neuropsychological Battery   Ward C. Halstead (1908–1969) was an experimental psychologist whose interest in the study of brain–behavior correlates led him to establish a laboratory for that purpose at the University of Chicago in 1935—the first such laboratory of its kind in the world. During the course of 35 years of research, Halstead studied over 1,100 brain-damaged persons. From his observations, Halstead (1947a, 1947b) derived a series of 27 tests designed to assess the presence or absence of organic brain damage—the Halstead Neurological Test Battery. A student of Halstead's, Ralph M. Reitan, later elaborated on his mentor's findings. In 1955, Reitan published two papers that dealt with the differential intellectual effects of various brain lesion sites (Reitan, 1955a, 1955b). Fourteen years and much research later, Reitan (1969) privately published a book entitled *Manual for Administration of Neuropsychological Test Batteries for Adults and Children*—the forerunner of the Halstead-Reitan Neuropsychological Test Battery (H-R; see also Reitan & Wolfson, 1993).

Administration of the H-R requires a highly trained examiner conversant with the procedures necessary to administer the various subtests (Table 14–8 and Figure 14–11). Even with such an examiner, the test generally requires a full workday to complete. Subtest scores are interpreted not only with respect to what they mean by themselves but also by their relation to scores on other subtests. Appropriate interpretation of the findings requires the eye of a trained neuropsychologist, though H-R computer interpretation software—no substitute for clinical judgment but an aid to it—is available. Scoring yields a number referred to as the "Halstead Impairment Index," and an index of .5 or above, the cutoff point, is indicative of a neurologic problem. Data on over 10,000 patients in the standardization sample were used to establish that cutoff point. Normative information has also been published with respect to other populations, such as people

Fixed Versus Flexible Neuropsychological Test Batteries and the Law

Do courts have any preferences regarding the specific tests administered by assessors who function as expert witnesses in litigation? With reference to neuropsychological assessment, does it matter if the assessor administered a fixed or a flexible battery? The ruling of a federal court in *Chapple v. Ganger* is enlightening with regard to such questions. In the *Chapple* case, the court applied the *Daubert* standard with regard to the admission of scientific evidence.

The *Chapple* Case

The *Chapple* case originated in an automobile accident in which a 10-year-old boy sustained closed head injuries. The plaintiff claimed that these injuries impaired brain functioning and were permanent, whereas the defendant denied this claim. Three neuropsychological examinations of the boy by three different assessors at three different times were undertaken. The first was conducted by a clinical psychologist who administered a flexible battery of tests. The second, about a year later, also entailed the administration of a flexible battery, this time by a neuropsychologist.* The third neuropsychological examination, commissioned by the defendant and conducted by neuropsychologist Ralph Reitan, entailed an administration of most of the subtests of the Halstead-Reitan Neuropsychological Test Battery for Older Children. In the two earlier examinations, the findings referred to some degree of brain trauma as a result of the accident, which in turn left the child with some degree of permanent impairment. By contrast, Reitan concluded that the child scored in the normal range on most of the tests in his fixed battery and presented much like other children in the non-brain-damaged population. Reitan did allow, however, for the possibility of some mild impairment attributable to some minor brain dysfunction. Reitan's opinions were formed on the basis of the child's test performance and evaluation of other materials including school and other records, as well as the reports of the other two psychologists. The other two psychologists also reviewed the child's records and historical data in coming to their conclusions.

Invoking the *Daubert* standard, the court ruled in favor of the defendant, finding no evidence to support permanent organic brain damage. Although no explicit reference to the value of flexible versus fixed batteries was made, the court seemed to find the results of the fixed battery administration more compelling: "The focus is on the methodology of the experts, and not the conclusions which they generate. This does not mean, however, that a conclusion will be admissible merely because some part of the methodology is scientifically valid. The entire reasoning process must be valid. A credible link must be established between the reasoning and the conclusion." In *Chapple,* then, testimony regarding the administration of a fixed battery was accepted by the court as medical evidence, whereas testimony regarding the administration of flexible batteries was not accepted by the court.

The Implications of *Daubert* and *Chapple*

On its face, the implications of *Daubert* seem vague and open to multiple interpretations (Black et al., 1994; Faigman, 1995; Larvie, 1994). However, there may be a lesson to be learned from *Chapple,* at least with regard to the admissibility of evidence obtained as the result of fixed versus flexible neuropsychological batteries. Although administration of flexible batteries is generally accepted in the professional community, a court may look more favorably on conclusions reached as the result of a fixed, standardized battery. Echoing *Daubert,* the court in *Chapple* wrote, "General acceptance is a factor to be considered; however, it is not dispositive." The *Chapple* court's decision also suggested that it might accept as evidence results from individual standardized tests, as those test results were used to supplement the findings from a fixed neuropsychological test battery.

---

*A listing of some of the tests administered in both flexible batteries can be found in Chapter 14 of Cohen (2002).

Table 14–8
Subtests of the Halstead-Reitan Battery

Category

This is a measure of abstracting ability in which stimulus figures of varying size, shape, number, intensity, color, and location are flashed on an opaque screen. Subjects must determine what principle ties the stimulus figures together (such as color) and indicate their answer among four choices by pressing the appropriate key on a simple keyboard. If the response is correct, a bell rings; if incorrect, a buzzer sounds. The test primarily taps frontal lobe functioning of the brain.

Tactual performance

Blindfolded examinees complete the Seguin-Goddard Formboard (see Figure 14–6) with their dominant and nondominant hands and then with both hands. Time taken to complete each of the tasks is recorded. The formboard is then removed, the blindfold is taken off, and the examinee is given a pencil and paper and asked to draw the formboard from memory. Two scores are computed from the drawing: the *memory* score, which includes the number of shapes reproduced with a fair amount of accuracy, and the *localization* score, which is the total number of blocks drawn in the proper relationship to the other blocks and the board. Interpretation of the data includes consideration of the total time to complete this task, the number of figures drawn from memory, and the number of blocks drawn in the proper relationship to the other blocks.

Rhythm

First published as a subtest of the Seashore Test of Musical Talent and subsequently included as a subtest in Halstead's (1947a) original battery, the subject's task here is to discriminate between like and unlike pairs of musical beats. Difficulty with this task has been associated with right temporal brain damage (Milner, 1971).

Speech sounds perception

This test consists of 60 nonsense words administered by means of an audiotape adjusted to the examinee's preferred volume. The task is to discriminate a spoken syllable, selecting from four alternatives presented on a printed form. Performance on this subtest is related to left hemisphere functioning.

Finger-tapping

Originally called the "finger oscillation test," this test of manual dexterity measures the tapping speed of the index finger of each hand on a tapping key. The number of taps from each hand is counted by an automatic counter over 5 consecutive, 10-second trials with a brief rest period between trials. The total score on this subtest represents the average of the five trials for each hand. A typical, normal score is approximately 50 taps per 10-second period for the dominant hand and 45 taps for the nondominant hand (a 10% faster rate is expected for the dominant hand). Cortical lesions may differentially affect finger-tapping rate of the two hands.

Time sense

The examinee watches the hand of a clock sweep across the clock and then has the task of reproducing that movement from sight. This test taps visual motor skills as well as ability to estimate time span.

Other tests

Also included in the battery is the Trail Making Test (see Figure 14–4), in which the examinee's task is to correctly connect numbered and lettered circles. A strength-of-grip test is also included; strength of grip may be measured informally by a handshake grasp and more scientifically by a dynamometer (see Figure 14–11).

To determine which eye is the preferred or dominant eye, the Miles ABC Test of Ocular Dominance is administered. Also recommended is the administration of a Wechsler intelligence test, the MMPI (useful in this context for shedding light on questions concerning the possible functional origin of abnormal behavior), and an aphasia screening test adapted from the work of Halstead and Wepman (1959).

Various other sensorimotor tests may also be included. A test called the "critical flicker fusion test" was once part of this battery but has been discontinued by most examiners. If you have ever been in a disco and watched the action of the strobe light, you can appreciate what is meant by a light that flickers. In the flicker fusion test, an apparatus that emits a flickering light at varying speeds is turned on, and the examinee is instructed to adjust the rate of the flicker until the light appears to be steady or fused.

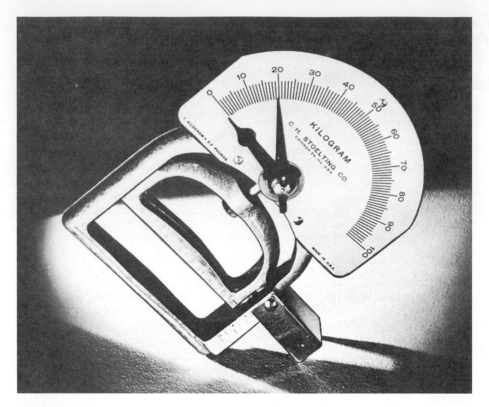

Figure 14–11
A Dynamometer

This instrument measures strength of hand grip. The examinee is instructed to squeeze the grips as hard as possible, two trials with each hand. The score is recorded in number of pounds of pressure exerted.

with epilepsy (Klove & Matthews, 1974), people who are mentally retarded (Matthews, 1974), and neurologically intact, nonpsychiatric adults (Fromm-Auch & Yeudall, 1983). Leckliter and Matarazzo (1989) cautioned that H-R performance may be affected by factors such as age, education, IQ, and gender, and that there is a "critical need to use clinical judgment in the selection of appropriate reference norms" (p. 509). Cultural factors must also be considered when administering this battery (Evans et al., 2000).

Conducting test-retest reliability studies on the H-R is a prohibitive endeavor in light of the amount of time it may take to complete one administration of the battery, as well as other factors (such as practice effects and effects of memory). Still, as Matarazzo et al. (1976) observed after their review of a number of reliability studies, "Despite the lack of comparability across the four samples on many dimensions, including age and test-retest intervals, the results again reveal a high degree of clinical as well as purely psychometric reliability for most of the tests in the neuropsychological battery" (pp. 348–349). A growing body of literature attests to the validity of the instrument in differentiating brain-damaged subjects from subjects without brain damage, and for assisting in making judgments relative to the severity of a deficit and its possible site (Reitan, 1994; Reitan & Wolfson, 2000). The battery has also been used to identify neuropsychological impairment associated with learning disabilities (Batchelor et al., 1990; Batchelor et al., 1991), as well as cognitive, perceptual, motor, and behavioral deficits associated with particular neurological lesions (Guilmette & Faust, 1991; Guilmette et al., 1990; Heaton et al., 2001; Whitworth, 1984).

Other fixed neuropsychological batteries The writings of the Russian neuropsychologist Aleksandr Luria served as the inspiration for a group of standardized tests (Christenson, 1975) that were subsequently revised (Golden et al., 1980, 1985) and became known as the Luria-Nebraska Neuropsychological Battery (LNNB). The LNNB in its various published forms contains clinical scales designed to assess cognitive processes and functions. Analysis of scores on these scales may lead to judgments as to whether neuropsychological impairment exists, and if so, the area of the brain that is affected. The LNNB takes about one-third the time it takes to administer the Halstead-Reitan battery. Still, evidence suggests that the Halstead-Reitan is the battery of choice for experienced neuropsychological assessors (Guilmette & Faust, 1991). This may be due to the fact that the LNNB may be overdependent on language skills (Franzen, 1985) or that it may yield a high rate of false-negative findings, especially with regard to aphasia (Crosson & Warren, 1982; Delis & Kaplan, 1982). A neuropsychological test battery for children, also derived in part on the basis of Luria's work, is the NEPSY (Korkman et al., 1997), the inspiration for which was detailed by its senior author (Korkman, 1999).

Among the other available neuropsychological batteries is the Montreal Neurological Institute Battery (Taylor, 1979), a test devised in large part as a result of intensive observation of neurosurgical patients. This battery contains many published tests, including the Wechsler intelligence tests, the Mooney Closure Faces Test, and the Wisconsin Card Sorting Test. The battery is particularly useful to trained neuropsychologists in locating specific kinds of lesions. The battery was administered preoperatively and postoperatively to hundreds of patients who underwent surgical excision of a defined area of brain tissue as the method of treatment for a brain tumor or epilepsy. Because the research on the battery was executed primarily with individuals who had surgically induced focal lesions, it is understandable that the battery has more utility in cases involving focal as opposed to diffuse lesions.

Many published and unpublished neuropsychological test batteries are designed to probe deeply into one area of neuropsychological functioning instead of surveying for possible behavioral deficit in a variety of areas. Thus, test batteries exist that focus on visual, sensory, memory, and communication problems; indeed, batteries can focus on virtually any specific area of brain–behavior functioning. One such specialized battery is the Southern California Sensory Integration Tests. Designed to assess sensory-integrative and motor functioning in children 4 to 9 years of age, this battery consists of 18 standardized subtests. The Southern California is helpful not only in identifying children who are having sensorimotor problems but also in identifying the nature of those problems.

A neuropsychological battery called the Severe Impairment Battery (SIB; Saxton et al., 1990) is designed for use with severely impaired assessees who might otherwise perform at or near the floor of existing tests. The battery is divided into six subscales: Attention, Orientation, Language, Memory, Visuoperception, and Construction. Another specialized battery is the Cognitive Behavioral Driver's Inventory, which was specifically designed to assist in determining whether individuals with brain damage are capable of driving a motor vehicle (Lambert & Engum, 1992).

A Perspective

As we saw in this chapter's *Everyday Psychometrics*, medical diagnostic tools in the areas of neurological and neuropsychological assessment are technologically sophisticated. With increasing precision, these tools may soon be able to pinpoint areas of the nervous system that have been damaged or compromised in some way. Given this state of affairs, will the role of the neuropsychologist and the enterprise of neuropsychological assessment become obsolete? Hardly. If anything, neuropsychological assessment is a growing and vital area. Beyond physically locating areas of damage or deficit, there is a great need to understand cognitive strengths and weaknesses and to put that understanding to work in prevention, treatment, and rehabilitation efforts. Increasingly, neuropsychologists have shown a willingness to reach out to the community and share their expertise (Schopp et al., 2000; Lawrence et al., 2000).

Self-Assessment

Test your understanding of elements of this chapter by seeing if you can explain each of the following terms, expressions, and abbreviations:

aphasia

Bender Visual-Motor Gestalt Test

brain–behavior relationships

brain damage

central nervous system

confrontation naming

contralateral control

declarative memory

deterioration quotient

executive functions

fixed battery

flexible battery

memory tests

motor tests

NEPSY

neurological damage

neurology

neuropsychological assessment

neuropsychological history

neuropsychological mental status examination

neuropsychological physical examination

neuropsychological tools of assessment

noninvasive procedures

organicity

pattern analysis

perceptual-motor tests

perceptual tests

peripheral nervous system

PET scan

physical examination

procedural memory

tools of neuropsychological assessment

Tower of Hanoi

trail-making item

15

The Assessment of People With Disabilities

After Hurricane Andrew hit south Florida, death, destruction, and a great deal of emotional distress was left in its wake. One who had been traumatized by this natural disaster was Neil Tugg. Tugg was a 40-year-old deaf man who received counseling from the Deaf Services Bureau (DSB) with a counselor proficient in American Sign Language (ASL). Tugg still required counseling after the State of Florida's consulting contract with the DSB had expired, so he was referred to a new provider. The new provider did not have a counselor proficient in ASL, so a translator was used. Citing the Americans with Disabilities Act (ADA), Tugg brought a lawsuit, claiming that "the presence of an interpreter in a therapeutic setting [deprived him of] an equal opportunity to achieve the same results as a hearing individual" (*Tugg v. Towey*, 1994, p. 1001). In the lawsuit, the plaintiffs argued that in addition to—or even in place of—conceptualizing deafness as a medical disability, deafness could be considered a cultural identity. They further intimated that this culturally distinct group, like other culturally distinct groups, could be unjustly stigmatized or discriminated against.

Tugg was adjudicated, and we will have more to say about it and the issues it raised later in this chapter. The case, which we may reasonably presume to be illustrative of many other such cases, is dramatic evidence of the aggressiveness with which claims of ADA violations are making their way to the courts. The case also serves as a useful point of departure for thinking about broader issues concerning the rights of people with disabilities, and more to the focus of this chapter, the rights of people with disabilities vis-à-vis psychological assessment.

An Overview

As many as one in seven Americans has a disability that interferes with activities of daily living (O'Keefe, 1993). In recent years, society has acknowledged more than ever before the special needs of citizens challenged by physical and/or mental disabilities. The effects of this ever-increasing acknowledgment are visibly evident in things like special access ramps alongside flights of stairs; specially equipped buses designed to accommodate passengers in wheelchairs; large-print newspapers, books, and magazines for the visually impaired; captioned television programming for the hearing-impaired;

and signing and pantomiming of important speeches for the hearing-impaired.[1] As medical technology continues to increase the chances that society's disabled citizenry will survive, so society has responded with environmental aids and legal protection for the exceptional individual.[2]

Disability and the Law

In 1973, Congress passed the Rehabilitation Act, a law that has been referred to as the "Bill of Rights for Handicapped Citizens" because it addressed many of the special needs of people with disabilities and outlawed job discrimination on the basis of disability by agencies of the federal government and by entities receiving federal funds. This protection was extended to disabled people involved with private companies through the Americans with Disabilities Act of 1990 (Public Law 101-336). Similar protections have been extended to children as well. In 1975, Congress passed Public Law 94-142, the Education for All Handicapped Children Act, mandating appropriate educational assessment and programs to meet the needs of handicapped children aged 3 to 18. This act was amended in 1986 (Public Law 99-457) to extend the age range covered by the law to birth. A 1990 amendment of the same act (Public Law 101-476) specified the broad range of conditions covered by the law: "mental retardation, hearing impairments including deafness, speech or language impairments, visual impairments including blindness, serious emotional disturbance, orthopedic impairments, autism, traumatic brain injury, other health impairments, or specific learning disabilities" (Section 101). Psychologists assessing individuals with such disabling conditions were obliged by law to "use tests and other assessment materials which have been validated for the purposes for which they are being used" (Department of Health, Education, and Welfare, 1977a, 1977b)—this in the face of a paucity of psychological tests that have been standardized on disabled populations.

The Education for All Handicapped Children Act of 1975 (PL 94-142) was amended some 27 years later by Public Law 105-17 (see this chapter's *Everyday Psychometrics*). Also referred to as the "Individuals with Disabilities Education Act Amendments of 1997" (IDEA), this act defined the terms "infant or toddler with a disability" and "child with a disability." An **infant or toddler with a disability** was defined as

> an individual under 3 years of age who needs early intervention services because the individual (i) is experiencing developmental delays, as measured by appropriate diagnostic instruments and procedures in one or more of the areas of cognitive development, physical development, communication development, social or emotional development, and adaptive development; or (ii) has a diagnosed physical or mental condition which has a high probability of resulting in developmental delay; and . . . may also include, at a State's discretion, at-risk infants and toddlers. (p. 108)

The term **at-risk infants and toddlers** was defined in the act as "an individual under 3 years of age who would be at risk of experiencing a substantial developmental delay if early intervention services were not provided to the individual" (p. 106). The IDEA

---

1. Like the noun *mime,* the verb *pantomime* has to do with communication by gesturing. As used in the context of psychological testing, pantomime is something that a test administrator might do with an examinee who is deaf or hearing impaired to help convey the meaning of some instruction, question, or response.

2. In accordance with general usage of the word in educational contexts, the word *exceptional* is used here in its broadest sense; an *exceptional* individual is someone who differs from most other people with respect to some physical and/or mental ability. People with disabling conditions—as well as the gifted—may in this context be referred to as "exceptional."

Public Law 105-17
and Everyday Practice

Public Law (PL) 105-17 is the Individuals with Disabilities Act Amendments of 1997. This act contains a number of provisions that are relevant to the everyday practice of measurement professionals who have occasion to evaluate school-age children. It affects not only the way that children are evaluated but the recommendations for intervention that are made as a result of the evaluation. The provisions of PL 105-17 include requirements concerning the following:

- *A "least restrictive environment" for learning*
  "To the maximum extent appropriate, children with disabilities, including children in public or private institutions or other care facilities, are educated with children who are not disabled, and special classes, separate schooling, or other removal of children with disabilities from the regular educational environment occurs only when the nature or severity of the disability of a child is such that education in regular classes with the use of supplementary aids and services cannot be achieved satisfactorily" (p. 61).

- *An individualized education program*
  "An individualized education program, or an individualized family service plan . . . is developed, reviewed, and revised for each child with a disability" (p. 61).

- *Evaluation materials that are culturally appropriate*
  "testing and evaluation materials and procedures utilized for the purposes of evaluation and placement of children with disabilities will be selected and administered so as not to be racially or culturally discriminatory. Such materials or procedures shall be provided and administered in the child's native language or mode of communication, unless it is clearly not feasible to do so, and no single procedure shall be the sole criterion for determining an appropriate educational program for a child" (p. 62).

- *Regular State and district-wide performance evaluations, including "alternate assessments" where necessary*
  "Children with disabilities are included in general State and district-wide assessment programs, with appropriate accommodations, where necessary. As appropriate, the State or local educational agency (i) develops guidelines for the participation of children with disabilities in alternate assessments for those children who cannot participate in State and district-wide assessment programs; and (ii) develops and, beginning not later than July 1, 2000, conducts those alternate assessments" (p. 67).

- *Parental involvement in the education of the child, including parental consent for evaluation*
  "The agency proposing to conduct an initial evaluation to determine if the child qualifies as a child with a disability . . . shall obtain an informed consent from the parent of such child before the evaluation is conducted. Parental consent shall not be construed as consent for placement for receipt of special education and related services. . . . If the parents of such child refuse consent for the evaluation, the agency may continue to pursue an evaluation by utilizing the mediation and due process procedures . . . except to the extent inconsistent with State law relating to parental consent" (p. 81).

- *Conduct of evaluations*
  "In conducting the evaluation, the local educational agency shall (A) use a variety of assessment tools and strategies to gather relevant functional and developmental information, including information provided by the parent, that may assist in determining whether the child is a child with a disability and the content of the child's individualized education program, including information related to enabling the child to be involved in and progress in the general curriculum or, for preschool children, to participate in appropriate activities; (B) not use any single procedure as the sole criterion for determining whether a child is a child with a disability or determining an appropriate educational program for the child; and (C) use technically sound instruments that may assess the relative contribution of cognitive and behavioral factors, in addition to physical or developmental factors. . . . Each local educational agency shall ensure that—(A) tests and other evaluation materials used to assess a child under this section—(i) are selected and administered so as not to be discriminatory on a racial or cultural basis; and (ii) are provided and administered in the child's native language or other mode of communication, unless it is clearly not feasible to do so; and (B) any standardized tests that are given to the child—(i) have been validated for the specific purpose for which they are used; (ii) are administered by trained and knowledgeable personnel; and (iii) are administered in accordance with any instructions provided by the producer of such tests; (C) the child is assessed in all areas of suspected disability; and (D) assessment tools and strategies that provide relevant information that directly assists persons in determining the educational needs of the child are provided" (pp. 81–82).

- *Review of existing data*
  "As part of an initial evaluation (if appropriate) and as part of any reevaluation . . . qualified professionals, as appropriate shall (A) review existing evaluation data on the child, including evaluations and information provided by the parents of the child, current classroom-based assessments and observations, and teacher and related services providers observation; and (B) on the basis of that review, and input from the child's parents, identify what

(continued)

Public Law 105-17
and Everyday Practice
(*continued*)

additional data, if any, are needed to determine—(i) whether the child has a particular category of disability, as described in section 602(3), or, in case of a re-evaluation of a child, whether the child continues to have such a disability; (ii) the present levels of performance and educational needs of the child; (iii) whether the child needs special education and related services, or in the case of a reevaluation of a child, whether the child continues to need special education and related services; and (iv) whether any additions or modifications to the special education and related services are needed to enable the child to meet the measurable annual goals set out in the individualized education program of the child and to participate, as appropriate, in the general curriculum" (pp. 82–83).

- *Determinations of eligibility*
  "The determination of whether the child is a child with a disability . . . shall be made by a team of qualified professionals and the parent of the child. . . . In making a determination of eligibility . . . a child shall not be determined to be a child with a disability if the determinant factor for such determination is lack of instruction in reading or math or limited English proficiency" (p. 82).

- *Assessment of infants and toddlers with disabilities and development of individualized family service plans*
  "A statewide system . . . shall provide, at a minimum, for each infant or toddler with a disability . . . (1) a multidisciplinary assessment of the unique strengths and needs of the infant or toddler and the identification of services appropriate to meet such needs; (2) a family-directed assessment of the resources, priorities, and concerns of the family and the identification of the supports and services necessary to enhance the family's capacity to meet the developmental needs of the infant or toddler; and (3) a written individualized family service plan developed by a multidisciplinary team, including the parents, as required by subsection (e). (b) Periodic Review.—The individualized family service plan shall be evaluated once a year and the family shall be pro-vided a review of the plan at 6-month intervals (or more often where appropriate based on infant or toddler and family needs). (c) Promptness After Assessment.—The individualized family service plan shall be developed within a reasonable time after the assessment required by subsection (a)(1) is completed. With the parents' consent, early intervention services may commence prior to the completion of the assessment. (d) Content of Plan.—The individualized family service plan shall be in writing and con-tain—(1) a statement of the infant's or toddler's present levels of physical development, cognitive development, communication development, social or emotional development, and adaptive development, based on objective criteria; (2) a statement of the family's resources, priorities, and concerns relating to enhancing the development of the family's infant or toddler with a disability; (3) a statement of the major outcomes expected to be achieved for the infant or toddler and the family, and the criteria, procedures, and timelines used to determine the degree to which progress toward achieving the outcomes is being made and whether modifications or revisions of the outcomes or services are necessary; (4) a statement of specific early intervention services necessary to meet the unique needs of the infant or toddler and the family, including the frequency, intensity, and method of delivering services; (5) a statement of the natural environments in which early intervention services shall appropriately be provided, including a justification of the extent, if any, to which the services will not be provided in a natural environment; (6) the projected dates for initiation of services and the anticipated duration of the services; (7) the identification of the service coordinator from the profession most immediately relevant to the infant's or toddler's or family's needs (or who is otherwise qualified to carry out all applicable responsibilities under this part) who will be responsible for the implementation of the plan and coordination with other agencies and persons; and (8) the steps to be taken to support the transition of the toddler with a disability to preschool or other appropriate services" (pp. 111–112).

defined *child with a disability* in two ways; one way with reference to a child "in general," and one way for children aged 3 through 9. "In general," a **child with a disability** refers to a child

with mental retardation, hearing impairments (including deafness), speech or language impairments, visual impairments (including blindness), serious emotional disturbance . . . orthopedic impairments, autism, traumatic brain injury, other health impairments, or specific learning disabilities. (p. 43)

For a child aged 3 through 9, the term *child with a disability* may, at the discretion of the state or local educational agency, include a child

> experiencing developmental delays, as defined by the State and as measured by appropriate diagnostic instruments and procedures, in one or more of the following areas: physical development, cognitive development, communication development, social or emotional development, or adaptive development. (p. 43)

Reading these definitions, as well as this chapter's *Everyday Psychometrics*, you may have concluded that what constitutes a disability is a fairly clear-cut matter. In practice, however, applying such definitions can be less than straightforward. "Disability" itself has been defined in many different ways (Walkup, 2000), and the federal legislation left considerable leeway to the states in terms of defining who is disabled and who shall be entitled to services. One source of that leeway is the term "developmental delay," which may be defined in different ways by different states. We will define **developmental delay** as slower than expected progress, usually on the basis of age norms, with regard to physical, cognitive, social, emotional, adaptive, or communication-related expression of one's ability or potential. However, exactly how it is defined by individual states will vary. Moreover, there is room for differences of opinion among knowledgeable professionals and school staff, as well as parents, when it comes to official determinations about who is in need of services or accommodation in the classroom. These issues are further discussed below, first as they apply to assessment in school settings, and then as they apply more generally in employment settings.

Who has a disability?   In everyday practice, the determination of whether an individual shall be considered disabled and therefore be entitled to special services is made by a multidisciplinary committee, often with the child's parent in attendance. In clear-cut cases of disability (as is the case with blindness, deafness, and so forth), all parties tend to agree on the evaluation, as well as plans for intervention. However, many borderline cases also come before committees. These cases often involve mild developmental lags—the significance of which is arguable. Sometimes professionals disagree among themselves about the extent of a disability and whether or not special services are required. For example, on the basis of the very same data about a child described by a teacher as "hyperactive" and "impulsive," some professionals may see "exuberance" (and thus no need for intervention), whereas other professionals might diagnose "attention deficit disorder" and see a need for intervention. Some parents want their children to be recognized as having a disability and therefore be entitled to special services—contrary to the recommendations of a committee of professionals. On the other hand, some parents, perhaps because of a fear that their child will be stigmatized, reject committees' recommendations for special services. Even when there is complete agreement as to the facts presented before the professionals, parents, and other members of such multidisciplinary committees, the individual committee members may privately accord different emphasis and weight to different facts, thus leaving the door open to conflicting opinions and conclusions.

Professional organizations, state and local agencies, individual professionals involved in assessment and intervention, and even members of a population with a particular disability may have their own ideas about definition, assessment, and intervention in relation to a particular disability. Indeed, whether what has traditionally been conceived of as a disability should remain a disability conceptually has in some instances become a matter of debate. For example, as we will see, many people who are deaf have begun to view deafness not as a disability but rather as a distinct culture within the majority culture; in this context, Deaf (with a capital "D") culture becomes a diversity issue and not an issue of disability. Mental retardation is another condition that has had a stormy history in terms of definition, assessment, and classification (Baumeister & Muma, 1975; Lowitzer et al., 1987; Roszkowski & Spreat, 1981; Taylor, 1980; Utley et al., 1987; Wilson & Spitzer, 1969). Even today, experts are divided regarding the extent to which the new AAMR (American Association on Mental Retardation) classification system draws on the values of science and professionalism versus advocacy and consumerism (MacMillan et al., 1995). You can begin to appreciate that although matters related to disability definition and assessment are relatively straightforward in theory, they are fraught with controversy and pitfalls in everyday practice.

Another definitional issue, one not touched on in PL 105-17, has to do with what is called a "functional disability." A **functional disability** may be defined as a condition in which one's ability to perform in some characteristic physical, social, or other way—that is, one's ability to function—has been disrupted. Measures of functional disability first began to appear in the 1930s, primarily for the purpose of assessing compensation for claims of accident and injury (McDowell & Newell, 1987). Since that time, the term functional disability, and a sister term, functional assessment, have been applied in an increasingly wide range of contexts (Bombadier & Tugwell, 1987; Feinstein et al., 1986; Granger & Gresham, 1984; Halpern & Fuherer, 1984; Slater et al., 1974; Spiegel et al., 1988). Although the term "functional disability" was once applied primarily to matters concerning one's ability to earn a living, it is now used in sundry contexts ranging from housework to recreation. One may speak, for example, of a functional social interaction disability or a communication disability. The term is even used with reference to children (Walker & Greene, 1991), in which case one might speak of functional disability at home, at school, or in the community.[3] Various tests and measurement procedures have been developed to assess functional disability in different contexts (see, for example, Brady & Halle, 1997; Desrochers et al., 1997; Neath et al., 1997).

To what extent are functional disabilities considered real disabilities? To what extent are schools required to supply services to people with functional disabilities? To what extent are guidelines for alternate assessment of children with functional disabilities required in school district–wide and statewide examinations? To what extent must accommodations in testing and in other services be made for people with functional disabilities? Such questions are matters of academic debate among assessment professionals. Conceivably, future laws will provide more specific guidelines for the assessment and intervention of functional disabilities.

Alternate assessment: Some issues   PL 105-17 contains a general mandate for the development and implementation of alternate assessment programs for children who, as a result of a disability, could not otherwise participate in state- and district-wide assessments. The law left open the definition of "alternate assessment," as well as many related questions of definition, procedure, and interpretation. It was left to the states and/or the local school districts to define who requires alternate assessment, how such assessments are conducted, and how meaningful inferences are drawn from the data derived from such assessments.

Alternate assessment is typically accomplished by means of some **accommodation** made to the assessee. The verb *to accommodate* may be defined as "to adapt, adjust, or make suitable." In the context of everyday life, we are all familiar with many varied examples of accommodation. Buses that lower for wheelchair passengers and elevator but-

---

3. Walker and Greene (1991) described the development of the Functional Disability Inventory, a scale to measure functional disability in child-relevant contexts including home, school, and community. The measure is available in both self-report and parent-report formats.

tons coded in Braille are two of many such examples. In the context of psychological testing and assessment, there are many different ways that people with disabilities can be accommodated. Accommodation may take the form of a modification in the way that a test is presented or in the way that the assessee responds to the test. Accommodation may mean that one test or measurement procedure is substituted for another. Accommodation may take the form of extended time limits or a change in the physical or interpersonal environment in which a test is administered. Let's take a closer look at these methods of accommodation, as well as some general considerations regarding the appropriateness of various methods for members of different populations.

Assessment and Accommodation

People with disabilities may be assessed for several reasons. They may be assessed for the purpose of evaluating the extent to which their disability affects their ability to carry out activities in some sphere of daily life. Perhaps in combination with such diagnostic evaluations, an assessment may be conducted for the purpose of determining the appropriateness of various interventions, ranging from treatment to special services. Additionally, people with disabilities are assessed for the exact same reasons that people with no disabilities are assessed: to obtain employment, to earn a professional credential, to be screened for psychopathology—the list goes on.

Depending on the nature of one's disability and other factors, modifications may have to be made in a test (or measurement procedure) in order for an evaluation to proceed. These accommodations may take many forms. One method of accommodation entails a modification of the way a test is presented to a testtaker. For example, a written test may be modified for presentation to a visually impaired testtaker by having it set in larger type. Another method of accommodation entails a modification in response format. For example, a speech-impaired individual may be accommodated by writing out responses in an examination that would otherwise be administered orally. Students with learning disabilities may be accommodated by being permitted to read test questions aloud (Fuchs et al., 2000). Extension of a time limit represents yet another type of accommodation. Time limits may be extended when a disability interferes with an individual's ability to concentrate, move, or otherwise respond within the test's prescribed limit.

The physical environment in which a test is conducted might have to be modified in order to accommodate an individual with a disability. For example, standardized tests usually administered at central locations in group administrations may, on occasion, be administered individually to a disabled person in his or her home. An extremely obese individual may require special furniture to be accommodated for a test. For an individual with a visual deficit, modified lighting may be required. Beyond the physical environment, the interpersonal environment may also require some modification. Routinely, individual testtakers come unaccompanied to test sites. However, depending on the nature of an individual's disability, a helper, translator, or even a guide dog may have to be present during the testing.

Some types of accommodation involve the modification of the test or measurement procedure itself. The test may have to be shortened or in some cases administered over the course of several sessions. Depending on the nature of the testtaker's disability, some tasks of a test composed of several subtests may have to be omitted. For example, consider a situation in which an individual who has a fine motor disability is being assessed with a test of cognitive ability. The test includes a subtest that requires the manipulation of blocks. The assessor might omit the block design subtest and/or substitute an optional test that does not rely on fine motor coordination. An estimate of cognitive ability would then be made from the data on the remaining tests.

The demands of a particular situation may require the substitution of one test for another. For example, a young preschooler or school-age child with severe cerebral palsy may not be able to be screened for cognitive deficit with any of the popular instruments used for this purpose. Alternatively, a test such as the Peabody Picture Vocabulary Test (PPVT-III; Dunn & Dunn, 1997) might be used for such screening because neither an oral nor a pointing response is required from the testtaker. The child would simply have to signal "yes" or "no," in whatever fashion is possible, to indicate to the examiner which of four pictures matches the word spoken by the examiner.

In some situations, an alternative test might be better suited for use with a particular individual owing to the availability of norms for people with the identical disability. In most cases, however, clinical judgment is the key to decisions about if, when, and how an accommodation will be made. A blind person who cannot complete a paper-and-pencil, multiple-choice examination will have to take the test in some type of alternate format. The alternate format might be a Braille administration, a paper-and-pencil administration modified by means of large type, an individually given oral administration, or a computer format with electronically administered (aural) instructions (with responses keyboarded in). Which of these alternate formats shall be employed? Ideally, this question will be answered not on the basis of convenience or the availability of one or another alternate forms, but rather on the basis of an informed consideration of what is known about the assessee, as well as other factors, which include the capabilities of the assessor, the purpose of the assessment, and the meaning attached to test scores.

The capabilities of the assessee   Which of several alternate means of assessment will be best tailored to the needs and capabilities of the assessee? Case history data, records of prior assessments, and interviews with friends, family, teachers, and others who know the assessee can all provide a wealth of useful information. In addition, the assessor might pre-interview the assessee to learn about the potential benefits and drawbacks of using any available alternate means of assessment. What an assessor should not do is simply presume that a particular alternate method of assessment is equivalent to the original method. In the case of blind assessees, for example, proficiencies in Braille and keyboarding may vary widely. Additionally, some people who are sight impaired are also hearing impaired, thus raising obstacles to the use of methods involving auditory input. No method of alternate assessment is the correct choice for everyone, and the unique needs and capabilities of the assessee must be considered on a case-by-case basis.

The capabilities of the assessor   Early in his career, the senior author (RJC), as part of his clinical psychology internship at Bellevue Hospital in New York City, did a rotation through the children's ward. At that time, the children's ward contained a female patient who was severely disabled as a result of her mother's use of the fertility drug thalidomide. This patient had failed to develop normal limbs, and instead had stumps for arms and legs. She delighted in getting a rise out of new visitors to the ward by repeatedly slapping all four of her malformed limbs against them. On one occasion, a visitor to the ward was a researcher, there to conduct an evaluation of this patient, among others. Perhaps not surprisingly, the researcher was somewhat taken aback by the appearance of the patient with the malformed limbs—and horrified to the point of being visibly shaken when she was greeted with the patient's most vigorous, though playful, attack. An outside observer could not help but wonder if the researcher could ever recover enough to develop a rapport with the assessee so that a meaningful evaluation could be conducted.

This vignette illustrates the fact that in assessments involving people with disabilities the state of mind and capabilities of the assessor can play a role. We probably would all like to think that we can deal professionally with any assessee we are assigned to evaluate. However, the comfort level of the assessor in a particular assessment situation can affect the results; in this context, it is important to acknowledge that some assessors may feel extremely uncomfortable in the presence of people with certain disabilities. Should an assessee perceive such discomfort on the part of the assessor, the working relationship between the two will be jeopardized, as will the validity of any data obtained. If assessors have concerns about their performance in assessing people with any sort of disability, these concerns should be discussed candidly with a supervisor or a colleague. A course of action that takes into account the needs of both the assessor and the assessee will have to be charted. It may be that prior to administering any tests to people with disabilities the assessor should receive additional training, including practice trials with members of certain populations. Alternatively, the assessor may refer such assessment assignments to another assessor with more training and experience in dealing with members of a particular population.

The purpose of the assessment Accommodation is appropriate under some circumstances and inappropriate under other circumstances. In general, one looks to the purpose of the assessment and the consequences of the accommodation in order to judge the appropriateness of modifying a test to accommodate a person with a disability. For example, modifying a written driving test—or a road test—so that a blind person could be tested for a driver's license is clearly inappropriate. For their own as well as the public's safety, the blind are prohibited from driving automobiles. On the other hand, changing the form of a written philosophy test so that a blind person could take the test is another matter entirely; blindness has no bearing on the purpose of the test, which presumably has to do with gauging the testtaker's knowledge of philosophy. Moreover, the consequences of any accommodation made so that a disabled person could take such a test are congruent with social policy that encourages equal opportunity and treatment for all citizens and fairness for people with disabilities.

Issues related to the purpose of an assessment and whether some form of accommodation should be made are seldom as straightforward as the two examples cited above. Whether a particular disability will significantly affect one's ability to perform in a particular employment setting, for example, is a question debated not only in academic journals but in corporate offices and the courts. One survey of accommodation policies by state found that states tend to offer more accommodations on criterion-referenced as opposed to norm-referenced tests (Thurlow et al., 2000). Even in cases where parties agree that some sort of accommodation is appropriate, one side may claim that a particular variety of accommodation goes too far, whereas the other argues that it does not go far enough. In mediating such disputes, the courts tend to evaluate how reasonable a particular accommodation is given the circumstances, including the nature of one's duties, the purpose of the assessment, and related variables.

Inferences made from test scores After administering a standardized test, the test user looks to the test manual for guidelines in interpreting the meaning of the test score. It is in the context of the normative data that scores on standardized tests are imbued with meaning. It is also in the context of normative data that test users can make reasonable inferences and predictions on the basis of scores on standardized tests. But what happens to the meaning of a score on a standardized test when that test has not been administered in the prescribed, standardized fashion? If there are published norms relevant to the modifications or abbreviations made, then a sound basis exists for interpretation of such scores. More often than not, however, when a standardized test is modified, the

A Modest Proposal for a Model Form

Accommodation in some form may be undertaken for a variety of reasons during the course of psychological testing and assessment. It is useful for test users and other consumers of assessment data to be aware of what ways, if any, a standardized test was modified for administration to people with disabilities. However, test users' need to know such information must be balanced against social policies and laws designed to safeguard people with disabilities from discrimination. Accordingly, in assessment situations involving employment, academic, and other matters where some accommodation has been made as a result of the assessee's disability, it would seem that a note limited to a description of the accommodation, rather than a description of the assessee's disability, is in order. Exceptions to this are assessment situations that are specifically focused on the assessee's disability, undertaken for diagnostic or evaluative purposes. Another exception would be the case where scores on a particular modification of a test are known to be equivalent to scores on the unmodified version of the test; in such a case, there would seem to be no need to report details of the modification. Of course, another exception is when such an addendum is prohibited by law or inadvisable according to the standards of a profession. Due to changes in laws and professional standards having to do with the assessment of people with disabilities, professionals who conduct such assessments need to keep abreast of the relevant literature.

In the absence of any laws, regulations, or professional standards to the contrary, we propose that an addendum be added to reports of psychological testing in which a standardized test or measurement procedure was in some way modified to accommodate the special needs of a particular assessee. The addendum should describe the nature of the change made, the rationale for the change, and any other information relevant to test users who may make inferences from the test scores. As illustrated, the proposed "Accommodation Addendum" would therefore contain three headings:

Accommodation Addendum

Nature of the Accommodation
Exactly how was the test or measurement procedure modified or adapted? A sample response might be as simple

meaning of the score on that test becomes questionable at best. Test users are left to their own devices with regard to making interpretations from such data.

Interpreting scores from standardized tests that have been modified is an unenviable task. Professional judgment, expertise, and, quite frankly, guesswork, can all enter into the process of drawing inferences from scores on modified tests; and still the inferences will most likely be vulnerable to legitimate challenges. Accordingly, the process of interpreting scores made from standardized tests that have been modified is not a task for the timid, the inexperienced, or the professional who lacks the background or training needed to make an educated guess when necessary.

A burgeoning scholarly literature has focused on various aspects of accommodation including issues related to general policies (Burns, 1998; Shriner, 2000; Simpson et al., 1999; Thurlow et al., 2000), method of test administration (Calhoon et al., 2000; Danford & Steinfeld, 1999), score comparability (Elliott et al., 2001; Johnson, 2000; Pomplun & Omar, 2000, 2001), and documentation (Schulte et al., 2000). Before a decision related to accommodation is made for any individual testtaker, due consideration must be given to issues regarding the meaning of scores derived from modified instruments and the validity of the inferences that one will be able to make from the data derived. After any such accommodation, some notation on the record regarding the nature of a modification to a standardized test may be in order. The issues relevant to such notations are the subject of this chapter's *Close-up*.

as follows: "Instead of being administered in a group administration in its usual written (paper-and-pencil) format, the test was administered individually and read to the assessee who orally responded." This section of the addendum provides a clear description of the accommodation that was made.

Rationale for the Accommodation

Not to be confused with an entry designed to describe the assessee's disability, "rationale" in this sense refers to the basis for the accommodation vis-à-vis the test manual, the scholarly literature, or other research and clinical experience. Here, test users can explain, preferably with reference to test manuals, published studies, or pilot research, the rationale for the modification of the test. For example, a test user may draw on a study cited in the test manual that has to do with the comparability of test scores when the test is administered in an unmodified way versus an administration with a particular modification. If such sources cannot be drawn on, test users must draw on their own psychometric expertise and judgment to provide the reader of the report with a rationale for the modifications. Let's also emphasize that the modification of any standardized test procedure should only be made by, or in consultation with, professionals with expertise in psychometrics.

Other Remarks

This space is for any other noteworthy aspect of the test administration that might affect inferences made from the test score. For many tests administered under accommodated conditions, this section will include a caution regarding interpretations made from the test score.

This proposal has been set in type, not in stone. We are interested in any comments you may have, including comments about what we left out, what we should have put in, or how this form might be improved. Please send your comments to us ℅ the publisher, McGraw-Hill Higher Education, 55 Francisco St., Suite 200, San Francisco, CA 94133-2217.

Disability, Assessment, and the Workplace

The Americans with Disabilities Act of 1990 (ADA) mandated that employers with 15 or more employees not discriminate against people with disabilities in hiring, in access to facilities, and in the terms, conditions, and benefits of employment. As defined in the ADA, a **disability** is a physical or mental impairment that substantially limits one or more of an individual's major life activities. Any psychological disorder, such as mental retardation, organic brain syndrome, mental illness, or specific learning disability, may qualify under the ADA guidelines as a disability. An individual need not even be diagnosed as having such a disability to be protected under the ADA. Rather, the mere perception that an individual is disabled may qualify him or her for protection (*Sutton v. United Airlines*, 1999). A claim of discrimination brought because a person is regarded as having an impairment and is discriminated against as a result of that perception is termed a **perceived disability case.**

Limitation of a "major life activity" is a key element of the ADA definition of disability, but exactly what constitutes such a limitation is not defined in the act. Goodman-Delahunty (2000) provides some assistance in this context by noting that a **major life activity** can be presumed to constitute functions such as caring for oneself, performing manual tasks, walking, seeing, hearing, speaking, breathing, learning, sitting, standing, lifting, reading, reaching, reproducing, and working. She pointed out that assessment of whether a substantial impairment exists requires consideration of three factors: (1) the nature and severity of the impairment, (2) the duration or expected duration of the impairment, and (3) the long-term impact of the impairment. If the claimed impairment is not deemed to be severe or long-term in nature, it may not qualify as a disability. So, for example, in *Pack v. Kmart* (1999), the plaintiff claimed impairment of the major life activity of sleeping, due to the fact that she was depressed. The court rejected the claim because the sleep problem was controlled by medication, and there was insufficient evidence to prove that the problem was severe, long-term, or permanent.

An employee who is deemed to be a "qualified individual with a disability" (QUID) is entitled to accommodation in the workplace. Such accommodation typically takes the form of modification of job functions or circumstances (National Council on Disability, 1996). A **QUID** is a disabled employee who meets the employer's standards for education, skill, and other job-related qualifications, and who can perform the essential functions of the job with or without accommodation in the workplace. The essential functions of a job are those fundamental duties that cannot be delegated to others and may require specific expertise, knowledge, or skill.

Since the passage of the ADA, upward of 20,000 claims have been filed with the federal agency charged with enforcing antidiscrimination laws in employment settings (Wylonis, 1999). Claims of discrimination on the basis of emotional, neurological, or other psychological impairment comprise about 30% of the cases, but that proportion may increase in the future (Moss et al., 1999). Courts have ruled that even prison inmates are entitled to protection from discrimination under the ADA (Clements, 1999). For example, a prison inmate denied access to a motivational boot camp because of a history of hypertension claimed successfully that his rights under the ADA had been violated (*Pennsylvania Department of Corrections v. Yeskey,* 1998).

Psychologists and others with expertise in psychological assessment have many possible roles to play with regard to ADA-related claims of discrimination (Blanck & Berven, 1999). Such experts may serve as advisers to companies putting hiring and other policies in place to prevent violations of law. Presently, relatively few companies have such policies with regard to hiring persons with mental impairments (Scheid, 1999). Psychologists and other assessment professionals may serve as advisers to parties in the claims, or to the courts, regarding the nature and course of claimed disabilities and the effects that therapy or other intervention may have on the claimed disability. On the basis of an evaluation of workplace demands and the individual claimant, a clinician may be able to offer useful suggestions regarding what constitutes a reasonable accommodation in the workplace. On the basis of an evaluation of a job description, an industrial/organizational psychologist may be able to render an educated, third-party opinion regarding what the essential functions of the job are. In cases where it is determined that discrimination has taken place, assessment professionals can provide useful input into the question of damages by providing testimony regarding the emotional or other injury suffered by the claimant (Goodman-Delahunty & Foote, 1995).

Assessment and Specific Disabilities

A number of special considerations must be taken into account when conducting individual evaluations of people with disabilities. In general, it is desirable for the assessor to achieve an understanding of the assessee not only with respect to the assessee's deficits and strengths in terms of a particular disability but with respect to deficits and strengths in other areas (for example, language development, socialization skills, and personality in general)—areas that may or may not be related to the primary disability. Such information will be essential in making appropriate accommodations (if any are deemed necessary), selecting appropriate test materials (if the assessor has this discretion), and interpreting interview, test, observational, and related data derived from the assessment. Sources for such information include case files, as well as teachers, parents, friends, family members, and others acquainted with the assessee. A good rule of thumb is to try to obtain data from as many different sources as possible, to better understand the assessee's functioning in different types of situations and under a wide variety of conditions. Exactly which variables to focus on in such preassessment activities will of course depend on the objectives of the assessment. What follows are some considerations applicable in many types of assessment situations with people who have sensory, motor, and cognitive disabilities. We begin with some general issues applicable to the assessment of people who are visually impaired.

Visual Disabilities

A three-category taxonomy of visual impairment useful in considerations related to testing and assessment was proposed by Bauman (1974). Included in the first category are people for whom vision is of no practical use in a testing or working assignment. The totally blind fall into this classification. Also included in this category are individuals who can differentiate between light and dark or even some who can distinguish shapes but can do so only when those shapes are held between the eyes and the source of light. The next category includes people for whom vision is of some assistance in handling large objects, locating test pieces in a work space, or following the hand movements of the examiner during a demonstration, but who cannot read even enlarged ink print effectively enough to be tested using such materials. Such individuals may be tested with materials that do not rely heavily on vision but, rather, require a combination of vision and touch. The third category includes people who read ink print efficiently, although they may need large type, may hold the page very close to their eyes, or may use a magnifier or some other special visual aid.

Accommodation of a testtaker who is visually impaired may take many different forms, depending of course, on the nature and extent of the impairment. In general, it may be necessary to modify the lighting in the room. Some testtakers may require more light; others may be disturbed by excessive light and glare. Some other types of modification that may be made are as follows:

- For the partially seeing examinee, writing instruments and written materials should be appropriate for the task. Thus, for example, a black felt-tip pen or crayon may be more appropriate than a fine-point ballpoint pen. Similarly, special wide-lined paper may be required.

- In general, persons with impaired vision require more time than do nonimpaired individuals. It may take longer to dictate materials than for the examinees to read the materials themselves. When the partially sighted person is asked to use residual vision, test fatigue may set in, shown by behavior such as eye rubbing or other extraneous movements. Adequate time must be allowed when testing the visually impaired, and speeded tests may be inappropriate (Nester, 1993).

- Multiple-choice questions, even in Braille, are frowned on by experts in this area, because this type of question places an extra burden of concentration on the visually impaired examinee.

- In the introduction to the test, the examinee with a severe visual impairment may need time to touch all the materials he or she will be working with. During testing, more verbal information about what is going on may be required than for a sighted individual.

- It is important under any testing conditions to have a quiet testing room that is free of distractions. However, this requirement takes on added importance in the testing of blind or visually impaired people, because these individuals may be more distracted by extraneous sounds than are the fully sighted.

- The work space should be relatively compact so that all equipment is within the examinee's grasp.

- If the test stimulus materials require some reading and the test is being administered to a partially seeing person, then it may be advisable to retype the materials in large type. An administration in Braille may be appropriate; however, relatively few blind individuals read Braille and relatively few of these people read it well.

If an objective of the test is assessment of intellectual ability, many tests and subtests, such as the Verbal Scale of a Wechsler test, have been used for purposes of estimation. Some research has called this fairly common practice into question. In one study, children who were blind or who had severe visual impairment tended to perform about 1 standard deviation below the mean of sighted children on the Comprehension subtest (Groenveld & Jan, 1992). Although these testtakers' scores were close to the average for sighted children on the Information, Similarities, Vocabulary, and Arithmetic subtests, the study calls attention to the need for norms specifically developed for blind and visually impaired testtakers.

In the area of personality assessment, most existing methods available for use with the sighted can be readily adapted for use with the visually impaired and the blind. Test materials that must be read can be reprinted in large type, read to the examinee, or prerecorded on tape. Even a test such as the Thematic Apperception Test can be administered to a blind person if the blind person hears a description of the card and then proceeds to tell a story about it. A specially developed TAT-like test for the blind is the Sound Test, which contains prerecorded sounds such as footsteps, running water, and music, combined in some instances with verbal interchanges; the examinee's task is to construct a story about such aural stimuli. Other specially devised personality tests include the Emotional Factors Inventory and the Adolescent Emotional Factors Inventory, two tests that include scales measuring the examinee's adjustment to blindness. The Maxfield-Bucholz Social Competency Scale for Blind Preschool Children is a measure of social competence and adaptive behavior designed for use with blind children from birth to age 6. The scale is administered to a third party such as the parent, guardian, or primary caregiver, and it is designed to explore areas such as the subject's physical development, ability with respect to self-care, and social competency.

Tests have also been developed to help the blind and the visually impaired with vocational guidance. Many of the available tests of finger and hand dexterity are used with this population. Available vocational interest inventories are administered to this population in large-print editions, Braille, or other adaptations. One such test, the PRG Interest Inventory, was based entirely on the content of the types of jobs held by and the types of hobbies indulged in by blind respondents. In the test's instructions, examinees are advised to respond as if they have the visual capabilities to handle the description of the various jobs. The instructions were worded this way so that the test would yield a veritable measure of interest as opposed to perceived capability.

Visual impairment may affect the outcome of neuropsychological tests (Kempen et al., 1994), thus prompting a neurologically oriented neuropsychologist to look to the brain for answers about the poor test performance. However, as Kempen et al. (1994) have advised, a simple vision test may be all that is necessary in some cases to answer key questions about poor test performance.

It bears repeating that extreme care must be taken when attempting to make inferences from test scores on standardized tests that were modified to accommodate the test-taker. Even when no test modification was made, the interpretation of test scores on testings conducted with people with disabilities contains many pitfalls. Based on experiences at the Texas School for the Blind and Visually Impaired, for example, Loftin (1997) cautioned that a number of diagnosed conditions may be directly related to vision deficit, and congenital blindness in particular. A partial listing of these conditions includes delayed motor milestones, echolalic speech, tangential or egocentric conversations, over-identification with adults, and a tendency to be passive in problem solving.

Sensitivity to the needs of a particular population can be developed by work with members of that population, either in a professional or volunteer capacity. The prospective assessment professional may also wish to read about the experience of other assessment professionals in working with members of various populations. Resources in the literature having to do with the assessment of the blind and the visually impaired include Bauman and Kropf (1979), Bradley-Johnson (1994), Bradley-Johnson and Harris (1990), Chase (1986), Drinkwater (1976), Evans (1978), Levack (1991), Loftin (1997), Swallow (1981), Tillman (1973), and Vander Kolk (1977).

Hearing Disabilities

People with hearing impairment differ with respect to variables such as magnitude of hearing loss, age at onset of loss, and consequential effects of the loss on language skills, social adjustment, and other abilities and personality characteristics. From a cultural perspective (to be discussed in greater detail later in this chapter), people with profound hearing loss prior to the age of 3 belong to a different culture than members of the relatively small segment of the deaf population who experienced a profound loss of hearing in later life (Raifman & Vernon, 1996). The latter group use speech and may perceive themselves as part of the majority culture. By contrast, people who are deaf from an early age use a language that is visual, tend to work with their hands rather than words, and due to their isolation from the majority culture, interact primarily with others who are deaf (Higgins, 1983; Lane, 1992; Padden & Humphries, 1988; Vernon & Andrews, 1990). When a hearing assessor has the task of assessing a nonhearing assessee, the problem, at least at first glance, is one of communication. Unfortunately, the problem may go well beyond communication; in fact, it may better be characterized as a "culture clash" (Phillips, 1996).

For assessees who are hearing impaired and/or did not lose their hearing at an early age, a number of test modification strategies may be employed to facilitate assessor-assessee communication. These strategies include (1) presenting written instructions at a reading level appropriate to the assessee (printed on paper or electronically by means of computer or a special teletype device), (2) amplification of the assessor's voice (through amplification equipment or the assessee's own hearing aid), and (3) using an interpreter proficient in a sign language in which the assessee is proficient.[4] For assessees with early onset deafness, it is highly recommended that only assessors who are fluent themselves in American Sign Language (ASL) and familiar with the culture be used (Leigh et al., 1996; Raifman & Vernon, 1996). This is essential for reasons related to rapport, communication, and accuracy in interpretation of test findings. To facilitate such examinations,

---

4. One source for information and a directory of certified interpreters is the Registry of Interpreters for the Deaf. Their Web address is *http://www.rid.org*.

special test materials may be employed. For example, Barbara Brauer, a psychologist who is deaf, developed a videotaped version of an MMPI administration in American Sign Language (Brauer, 1993).

Essential as one or more of the adaptations listed above may be, there are drawbacks associated with each (Orr et al., 1987). For example, using written communication instead of spoken communication introduces another variable (reading proficiency) into the task where no such variable had existed before. Pantomiming instructions and cues in the absence of explicit directions for doing so in the test manual results in a situation where different pantomimists (that is, different test administrators) may well have different ideas about how to get a point across by gestures; hence, the standardization of the instructions to the examinee will suffer. The introduction of an interpreter into the situation may have the effect of diminishing the rapport between the examiner and the examinee. Further, a certain amount of error in expressive and receptive translations can also be expected. The interpreter's signing skills must be compatible with the assessee's receptive skills. It would be inappropriate, for example, for the interpreter to sign in Coded Sign English (a method of communication more closely linked to the written/verbal expression of people with no hearing impairment) if the assessee is more fluent in ASL. Verbal information, especially idioms and proverbs, is not readily amenable to translation into sign, and the assessor must carefully examine test materials in advance with that fact in mind—and appropriately modify the administration materials if need be. Sign language is, in fact, a different language from English, and translations of tests into sign language should be treated with as much care as any foreign-language translation (Nester, 1993).

Performance subtests of Kaufman tests (Gibbins, 1988; Kennedy & Hiltonsmith, 1988; Phelps & Branyan, 1988) and Wechsler tests have been used to gauge the intellectual functioning of people who are deaf and hearing impaired. Jeffrey Braden (1985, 1990, 1992; Maller & Braden, 1993) and Patricia Sullivan (1982) and colleagues (Maller, 1997; Sullivan & Brookhouser, 1996; Sullivan & Burley, 1990; Sullivan & Montoya, 1997; Sullivan & Schulte, 1992) have written extensively on the use of the Wechsler and other tests with people who are deaf or hard-of-hearing. Sullivan recently urged a reevaluation of the historic taboo against the use of verbal intelligence tests with members of this population. Sullivan and Montoya (1997) argued that the majority of people who are deaf and hard-of-hearing are now competing with hearing persons in academic as well as employment environments. Face-to-face communication skills and English literacy are typically required for higher paying jobs (Allen, 1994; Schildroth et al., 1991).

In contrast to tests originally designed for use with the general population, some tests designed to measure cognitive ability were standardized on hearing as well as non-hearing respondents; the Hiskey-Nebraska Test of Learning Aptitude is one such test. Developed for use with children and adolescents ages 3 to 17 by Marshall S. Hiskey (1966), the Hiskey-Nebraska was developed with sensitivity to the needs of testtakers who are deaf or hard-of-hearing. The test includes pantomine practice exercises, as well as a manual replete with helpful guidelines for testing deaf and hard-of-hearing respondents. Although the norms are in need of updating, the test has endured as a useful measure of cognitive ability (Sullivan & Burley, 1990). It has international appeal as the test of choice in clinical and research applications with deaf and hard-of-hearing assessees (see, for example, Collins et al., 1987; Nagyne Rez & Zsoldos, 1991; Qu et al., 1992).

Measures of academic achievement using tests such as the Metropolitan Achievement Test and the Stanford Achievement Tests can be useful because both of these tests have been standardized with members of this population. In general, hearing-impaired and deaf children do not perform as well on such tests as do their hearing peers. This is due not only to their language impairment but also to the lack of curriculum methods developed specifically to meet the educational needs of the deaf. Only 5% of graduates from educational programs for the deaf attain a tenth-grade education; 41% achieve a seventh- or eighth-grade education, and 30% are functionally illiterate.

Tools used for personality assessment with the deaf and hard-of-hearing, as with other people, include the interview (appropriately modified such as with signing or amplification), case history evaluation, and tests. In some cases, personality tests that minimize requirements for verbal ability are preferred (Leigh et al., 1996). So, for example, tests involving drawing (such as the Draw A Person and the House-Tree-Person) are frequently used with assessees who are deaf. Personality assessment with children and adults using paper-and-pencil personality tests should be used only if the reading level of the test is known and the assessee is known to be reading at or above that level.

The Rorschach has been recommended for use with only those deaf people known to be above average in intelligence and able to sign fluently (Vernon & Brown, 1964), although clinicians experienced with this special population may be able to use it more routinely (Sachs, 1976). Other projective measures, such as those involving drawings (Johnson, 1989; Ouellette, 1988), the Bender Visual-Motor Gestalt Test used projectively (Gibbins, 1989), and the TAT (Vernon & Brown, 1964), may prove insightful. Cates and Lapham (1991) caution that although the TAT may be useful, deaf children and adolescents may concretely label the cards, then perseverate on themes in an effort to supply the "right" answer:

> A potential difficulty in administering apperception techniques to deaf children and adolescents is a tendency toward response perseveration. For example, if unfamiliar with the task, the deaf student may initially attempt to label the picture. If this response is corrected, the deaf student may then perceive the first story told as the correct response. If the first correct response is a story containing a violent theme, then the deaf client may assume that violence is desired or appropriate in the stories and perseverate on violent themes. The clinician must decide whether to allow the perseveration or restructure the response set of the child or adolescent. The authors generally noted the perseverative phenomenon, then restructured the response set, indicating that each picture may elicit differing themes. (p. 125)

Cates and Lapham (1991) also reported on concrete types of response that may be given on another projective measure, the Hand Test. They found that

> Deaf children and adolescents give a higher frequency of concrete responses to the Hand Test than do their hearing counterparts. For example, in response to the first card—a hand held up, palm outward—the deaf child may initially provide a description of the hand (e.g., "It's a hand, held up. Five fingers.") rather than describe the hand in some form of activity, as requested in the instructions. In the Hand Test scoring system, this type of descriptive response is considered indicative of severe disturbance. The clinician using the Hand Test, then, may wish to administer the test according to standardized procedure, followed by a testing-the-limits procedure, in which the deaf child is urged to provide more appropriate responses. Alternatively, following the first descriptive response, the clinician may wish to reemphasize the instructions, elicit a more appropriate response, and consider the initial response as training. The deaf subject may also benefit from an inclusion to the standard directions that the hands are not signing. (p. 122)

Behavior checklists and rating scales can prove to be valuable tools of assessment with the deaf (McCoy, 1972). The most extensively used checklist with deaf children and adolescents is the Meadow-Kendall Social-Emotional Assessment Inventory (Meadow et al., 1980), appropriate for use with individuals age 7 to 21 years old. Other such instruments, not necessarily designed especially for the deaf, include the Behavior Problem Checklist (Quay & Peterson, 1967, 1983), the Devereaux Adolescent Behavior Rating Scale (Spivack et al., 1967), the Devereaux Child Behavior Rating Scale (Spivack & Spotts,

1966), the Child Behavior Checklist (Achenbach, 1978), and the Walker Problem Behavior Identification Checklist (Walker, 1976).

As is frequently the case when testing people who are deaf or hard-of-hearing, appropriate norms for the test employed may be scant or nonexistent. In such circumstances, assessors must draw on their own training and experience—or, if necessary, that of a more experienced and highly trained colleague—in an effort to make reasonable inferences from the resulting data. Where appropriate, conclusions should be supported by multiple sources of data, including case history data, data from behavioral observation, as well as reports from parents, teachers, therapists, or other caregivers.

Before administering psychological and educational tests to hearing-impaired and deaf testtakers, most psychologists and other test users would profit from education, supervised experience, and training relevant to hearing loss and deafness (Cates & Lapham, 1991; Elliot et al., 1987; Elliott & Carroll, 1997; Pollard, 1993; Weaver & Bradley-Johnson, 1993; Zieziula, 1982). Such specialized preparation is critical if accurate interpretations are to be made from assessment data. Misiaszek et al. (1985) cautioned that mental health professionals who are unfamiliar with the effects of prelingual deafness on personality, communication, cognition, and socialization are prone to make diagnostic errors. People who suffer prelingual deafness may exhibit behavior that seems similar to the concrete and sometimes fragmented behavior patterns typical of people with schizophrenia. Other products of deaf enculturation, such as egocentric and rigid behaviors, may be mistaken for personality disorders. Consideration of such potential pitfalls leads to a general conclusion that cannot be overemphasized in any discussion of assessment with members of a population who have a particular disability: Specialized education, training, and supervised experience is highly desirable, if not mandatory.

Visual/Hearing Disabilities

Ten Regional Centers for Deaf-Blind Youth and Adults were created by Congress in 1967 in response to an increase in babies born with multiple handicaps as the result of a rubella epidemic that spread across the United States from 1963 to 1965. The centers were charged with the responsibility of identifying and assessing such children. The assessment of members of this population represents the "most difficult diagnosis task a psychologist can be asked to do" (Vernon et al., 1979, p. 291). The assessor must be particularly wary of diagnostic errors that might lead to the placement of such children into programs for the mentally or emotionally impaired when, in fact, such programs would be inappropriate for the particular child.

Few standardized tests are appropriate for use with the deaf-blind. Standardized tests developed for and standardized on individuals with other disabling conditions do not adequately take into account the multiplicity and the pervasiveness of impairments of the deaf-blind. Psychological assessment of the deaf-blind most typically involves assessment of adaptive behavior (to be discussed later in greater detail) as well as interviews with caregivers and analysis of case history material. One of the few tests designed for use with, and standardized on, this population is the Callier-Azusa Scale (CAS).

The CAS is a behavior checklist that enables the examiner to compare the subject's development in a number of areas (motor, perceptual, language, daily living skills, and socialization) with typical development for deaf-blind children, from birth to 9 years, who have received appropriate interventions. The test is useful both in educational program planning and as a posttest to assess behavior change after a specific intervention. Stillman (1974) recommends that more than one rater assess the child's behavior both at home and at school for at least two weeks. Information is usually provided by a parent, the teacher, or some other person having extensive contact with the child. Adequate reliability has been reported with respect to the test's 16 subscales. The test authors also reported that the scale's reliability was not significantly influenced by the child's educational setting or the number of people rating the child (Bennett et al., 1979). Related to validity evidence, Diebold, Curtis, and Dubose (1978) have demonstrated the strong relationship for a sample of 6- to 13-year-old deaf-blind children between systematic observation of daily behavior measures and performance on CAS developmental scales. The 16 subscales of the CAS yield an age-equivalent score rather than IQ, but the conversion table is psychometrically unsound and therefore few professionals use it. Credit for particular items is awarded only if the behavior is "present fully and regularly." Behaviors that are just emerging are not credited. If the deaf-blind child has additional disabilities, such as a motor deficit, specific CAS items can be omitted.

Another standardized test that can be used with the deaf-blind is the Assessment of Development Levels by Observation (ADLO; Wolf-Schein, 1993). As its name implies, the ADLO entails systematic observation of behavior and classification of it by developmental level. Behavior is assessed and classified on variables related to self-help skills, fine and gross motor skills, receptive (listening and understanding) and expressive language, and relationships with adults. Typically, the test is conducted in a setting familiar to the child; an observer evaluates the child playing alone, interacting with familiar and unfamiliar adults, and working with a language specialist. Norms are available for children from birth to 8 years of age. Measured inter-rater reliability for this test is good (in the range of .86 to .92). Work remains to be done to establish the test's validity (Wolf-Schein, 1993).

Motor Disabilities

Motor deficits come in many forms and from many varied causes, and may involve any muscle or muscle group in the body. Paralysis, tremors, involuntary movement, gait difficulties, and problems with volitional movement and speech are some of the many types of motor problems that may exist. The cause of the motor problem may be an inherited muscular or neurological difficulty or one acquired as a result of a trauma to the muscle, the brain, or the spinal cord. Other causal factors include the wide range of neuromuscular diseases. Cases of cerebral palsy, for example, are believed to occur at the rate of 1.6 to 5 per 1,000 in the under-21 population. The palsy may be caused by an endocrine imbalance, low blood sugar, anoxia, a high forceps delivery, or any of a variety of other factors before, during, or after birth.

Most of the tests used to assess intellectual functioning rely at least in part on the respondent's ability to manipulate some materials—cards, blocks, beads, or whatever; the test that does not contain such tasks would be criticized by experts as being too loaded on verbal as opposed to performance measures of intelligence. Examiners wishing to assess the intelligence of motor-handicapped people will attempt to select an existing test that does not need to be modified in any way for administration to the particular individual being assessed. If all available tests were to require modification, the test requiring the least modification would be selected. An example of a modification that might be employed when administering a block design task, for example, would require the examiner to physically turn the blocks until the examinee indicates that the rotation of the block is his or her response. The examinee might indicate this with a verbal response or, if there is a speech deficit, with some other response, such as a wink of the eye. On paper-and-pencil tasks that require fine motor coordination, such as tests that involve blackening tiny grids with number 2 pencils, the motor-handicapped individual might require a writer to enter the responses. The alternative (not to administer any motor tasks to the motor-handicapped examinee) is the approach taken by some examiners; the rationale here is that a verbal test such as the Vocabulary subtest of a Wechsler examination correlates highly with the rest of the examination and may therefore be used as a rough estimate of both verbal and nonverbal intelligence. However, such a procedure provides only a *rough estimate* and is never a good practice if used for placement decisions in the absence of other assessment data.

Psychologists and special educators who assess variables such as the severity of a motor deficit have a number of tests at their disposal for use. Four test batteries in current use are the Purdue Perceptual-Motor Survey, the Bruininks-Oseretsky Test of Motor Proficiency, the Frostig Movement Skills Test Battery, and the Southern California Sensory Integration Tests. The Purdue is a screening device that provides guidelines for assessing various gross and fine motor functions in children aged 6 to 10 years. The Bruininks-Oseretsky also tests gross and fine motor skills as well as general motor proficiency. It is a technically sound test but one that requires (1) a very well-trained examiner to administer and interpret, and (2) extensive space to administer (such as a playground or a specially equipped room). The Frostig is designed to assess sensorimotor development, gross and fine motor coordination, balance, strength, and flexibility in children aged 6 to 12 years. It is popular among many examiners because it is relatively simple to administer, contains a relatively wide range of motor skills sampled, and is easy to score. The Southern California is also a measure of sensory integrative functioning designed for use with children aged 4 to 9 years. However, this time-consuming test must be administered and interpreted by a highly trained examiner. Other motor skills tests have been developed for use with elderly individuals, including the Physical Disability Index (PDI; Gerety et al., 1993). Designed specifically for frail elderly populations, the PDI assesses strength, balance, mobility, and range of motion. The test authors report good levels of inter-rater (.81 to .99) and test-retest (.97) reliability, and criterion-related validity coefficients ranging from .27 to .56.

Cognitive Disabilities

The term **cognitive disability** covers a broad spectrum of disabling conditions including various neurological deficits, learning disabilities, autism, and mental retardation. Elsewhere in this book, we have discussed many issues relative to the assessment of some of these cognitive disabilities. Here we focus on assessment issues related to mental retardation.

Mental retardation and adaptive behavior   Definitions of mental retardation and associated classification systems vary by source. Most definitions make reference to significantly subaverage general intellectual functioning existing along with deficits in adaptive behavior, all manifested during the developmental period. Here, **adaptive behavior** refers to the personal and social effectiveness and appropriateness of one's actions. One's behavior is characterized as adaptive to the extent that one acts or modifies one's behavior in a way that is consistent with age-appropriate adjustment, social maturity, and personal and social competence (Cain et al., 1963; Doll, 1953; Fullan & Loubser, 1972). In 1905, Alfred Binet made indirect reference to the concept of adaptive behavior when he said "an individual is normal if he is able to conduct his affairs of life without having need of supervision of others, if he is able to work sufficiently . . . to supply his own personal needs" (Binet, quoted in Goddard, 1916).

Traditionally, mental retardation has been diagnosed primarily on the basis of intelligence tests, and then classified in terms of one of four categories: mild, moderate, severe, and profound. These categories designate progressively lower measured IQs and are associated with characteristic deficits in adaptive behavior with regard to specific contexts throughout the lifespan. In 1992, a manual published by the American Association on Mental Retardation (AAMR) replaced these four categories with four new ways of classifying people with mental retardation. AAMR (1992) defined mental retardation as a condition that develops before the age of 18 in which there is significant subaverage intellectual functioning (measured IQ of 75 or less) concurrent with limitations in at least two of ten adaptive skill areas. Adaptive skill areas ranged from leisure to academics to work, and included areas such as communication, self-care, and social skills. The new AAMR classification system emphasized the role of adaptive behavior in the definition of mental retardation by replacing the qualitative labels associated with deficit (mild, moderate, and so on) with a qualifier indicative of intensity of support required across various environments. Required intensity of support was categorized as "intermittent" (support required on an as-needed basis), "limited" (time-limited but consistent over time), "extensive" (daily in at least some environments), or "pervasive" (constant support required across environments; see AAMR, 1992).

Heavily criticized by many, the 1992 AAMR system has been characterized as a "dead manual walking" (Greenspan, 1997). The manual raises a host of new problems in terms of assessing and classifying intelligence, adaptive behavior, and intensities of needed supports (Gresham et al., 1995; Hodapp, 1995), especially with young children (Vig & Jedrysek, 1996). For some, the 1992 manual represents an abandonment of a pragmatic/ scientific perspective on mental retardation for one that is primarily political (Matson, 1995). The AAMR's Committee on Terminology and Classification responded to such criticisms by arguing, in part, that a system based on required intensity of supports has more utility than one based on IQ level (Luckasson et al., 1996). Still, years after the AAMR recommendations, many descriptions of research subjects in the scholarly literature employ the mild-to-profound classification system. Scanning the recent literature, one finds, for example, a case study of a 9-year-old boy diagnosed with moderate retardation (Richman et al., 1997), research on the application of Piagetian techniques with 25 profoundly mentally retarded 27- to 70-year-old men (Williams, 1996), and research on self-esteem and job satisfaction of 200 adults with mild mental retardation (Griffin et al., 1996).

The diagnosis of mental retardation is typically made on the basis of data from an appropriate measure of intelligence, as well as a measure of adaptive behavior. Especially for very young assessees, measures of sensory, motor, and sensorimotor ability will be included as part of an evaluation designed to distinguish deficit from developmental delay. If an evaluation of the assessee's understanding of basic concepts is desired, a test such as the Boehm Test of Basic Concepts or the Bracken Basic Concept Scale-Revised may be employed. If autism is suspected or needs to be ruled out, specialized diagnostic instruments, such as the Childhood Autism Rating Scale or the Diagnostic Assessment for the Severely Handicapped-II, may be administered (Matson et al., 1998). An invaluable contribution can be made by the assessee's family in such assessments (Parette & Brotherson, 1996). Ideally, the net result of the assessment will be an understanding of the assessee—not only in terms of scores on standardized tests and standing relative to peers but an understanding of the individual in terms of his or her unique behavioral deficits and excesses across environments (Desrochers et al., 1997; Harris et al., 1996).

Many standardized measures of adaptive behavior exist, and test users must be aware of the pros and cons of these varied instruments. For example, the AAMR Adaptive Behavior Scale-School:2 (ABS-S:2; Lambert et al., 1993) is something of an anomaly; it was designed to measure typical performance in coping with various environmental demands, but the domains assessed are mismatched with the AAMR's 1992 manual (Stinnett, 1997). Further, although the standardization sample for this measure was quite large, including people with mental retardation ($n = 2{,}074$) as well as a nonchallenged sample ($n = 1{,}254$), high-functioning people with mental retardation were underrepresented. The result is the potential for an error in interpretation, whereby the adaptive functioning of members of this population is overestimated (Stinnett, 1997).

The Adaptive Behavior Assessment System (ABAS; Harrison & Oakland, 2000) was designed to provide a comprehensive assessment of persons from ages 5 through 89 in areas of adaptive skills specified in the AAMR manual, such as communication, community, home living, work, and health and safety. The instrument, available in English and Spanish, comes in three different forms, one each for parents and teachers (available for ages 5 through 21), and an adult form which may be completed by assessees themselves or by a spouse, a relative, or other caretaker. Scores allow for both evaluation of functioning and pinpointing of strengths and weaknesses. According to the manual, it may also have application in specifying goals for persons with learning disabilities. The test was published relatively recently. A more "classic" approach to assessment of adaptive behavior is embodied in a test referred to simply as "the Vineland."

The Vineland Social Maturity Scale was developed by Edgar A. Doll (1953), then the director of research at the Vineland Training School in Vineland, New Jersey. Three decades later, the test was revised and published as the Vineland Adaptive Behavior Scales (VABS; Sparrow et al., 1984). The revised test, like its predecessor, is usually referred to simply as "the Vineland." In the tradition of its predecessor, it emphasizes social competence, which Doll (1953, p. 2) conceived of as "a functional composite of human traits which subserves social usefulness as reflected in self-sufficiency and service to others." The primary use of the Vineland is to assess the adaptive behavior of developmentally disabled individuals.

The revised Vineland is available in three forms: the Survey Form of the Interview Edition, the Expanded Form of the Interview Edition, and the Classroom Edition. The two Interview Edition forms (Sparrow et al., 1984a, 1984b) were designed for use with individuals from birth to age 18, as well as with low-functioning adults. They are both structured interviews undertaken with a parent or some other informant who is very familiar with the assessee. The Survey Form contains 297 items and requires 20 to 60 minutes to administer. The Expanded Form is a more detailed version of the interview that contains 577 items (including the 297 items in the briefer form). It takes between 60 and 90 minutes to administer. The third form of the Vineland, the Classroom Edition (Sparrow et al., 1985), is a 244-item form completed by a teacher that focuses primarily on behavior in an academic context. It is designed for use with assessees ranging in age from 3 to 13 years old.

All three forms of the test tap the areas, or domains, of daily living, socialization, motor function, and communication. In addition, the two Interview Edition forms contain items relevant to maladaptive behavior. In each domain, the informant is asked to provide information relative to actual behaviors. Skills are broken down into component behaviors so that the level of ability can be specified. For example, in the area of daily living skills, the informant is asked about the individual's ability to put on shoes, including the individual elements of this ability, such as lacing shoes and tying a bowknot. In the area of socialization skills, the informant may be asked about the assessee's table manners, and everything from using a napkin to requesting items on the table.

Normative data are available for all forms of the Vineland. For the Interview Edition, data were gathered on about 4,800 people without disabilities. For the Classroom Edition, approximately three thousand children and adolescents constituted the normative sample. All standardization data were gathered from normative groups that had been drawn nationally and were stratified according to the 1980 U.S. census for sex, geographical region, size of community, parents' education, and race and ethnicity. Raw scores on the test are converted into standard scores with a mean of 100 and a standard deviation of 15. Scores are calculated separately for each domain. A total score, called the Adaptive Behavior Composite, incorporates evaluative data from each of the domains. More on psychometric aspects of this test is presented in Cohen (2002).

As in the assessment of members of other populations, education, training, and experience with members of the population of people with mental retardation is essential for understanding and dealing with the special diagnostic questions unique to this pop-

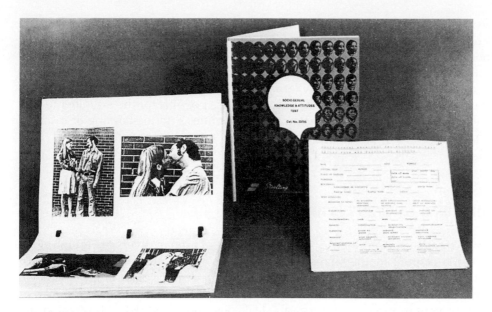

Figure 15–1
The Socio-Sexual Knowledge & Attitudes Test

ulation (Silka & Hauser, 1997). In pervasive developmental disorders, multidisciplinary collaboration in the assessment is particularly critical (Volkmar et al., 1996).

Quality of life   Along with interest in the assessment of adaptive behavior is increasing interest in the measurement of variables related to the quality of life of people with mental retardation (Hughes et al., 1995; Rosen et al., 1995) as well as other disabilities (Renwick et al., 1996; Storey, 1997). Researchers have examined sundry variables such as stress, loneliness, sources of satisfaction, and quality of friendships (Rosen et al., 1995; Siperstein et al., 1997). Researchers have sought to understand the needs and desires of parents of intellectually challenged children (Westling, 1996) and have explored how quality-of-life and related issues may vary by age (Mast & Lichtenberg, 2000), disability (Gallagher & MacLachlan, 2000), and culture (Keith et al., 1996). The definition of "quality of life" has varied in different studies. In some research, "quality of life" was a reference to an observer's judgment of a subject's lifestyle. In other research, this same term referred to a more subjective appraisal of the subject's own life. In the interest of uniformity, Felce (1997) proposed a definition of quality of life based in part on an assessment of one's personal values, life conditions, and personal satisfaction. Alternatively, Storey (1997) acknowledged that the assessment of quality-of-life issues must necessarily be quite broad because the relevant dependent measures change over time and with different populations.

Related to quality-of-life issues has been a great deal of research interest in social information processing (Gomez & Hazeldine, 1996), including matters related to sexual activity (Lumley & Miltenberger, 1997; Lumley et al., 1998) and consent to same (Parker & Abramson, 1995). One instrument specifically designed for use in assessing the sexual knowledge and attitudes of the developmentally disabled is the Socio-Sexual Knowledge & Attitudes Test (Wish et al., 1980). Topic areas covered by the instrument include anatomy terminology, menstruation, masturbation, dating, marriage, intimacy, intercourse, pregnancy, childbirth, alcohol and drugs, homosexuality, and venereal disease (Figure 15–1). Because expressive language required by the examinee is minimal—most responses are made by pointing or indicating "yes" or "no"—the test is suitable for administration to those with limited language skills or ability. Though the test manual includes normative data on developmentally disabled individuals aged 18 to 42, the intent of the test authors is that the test be used in a criterion-referenced as opposed to a norm-referenced fashion, as a measure of what the individual testtaker knows, believes, or doesn't know. Using a testing-the-limits procedure, it is possible for the examiner to employ some of the pictorial stimuli to explore the examinee's understanding of diseases such as AIDS and concepts such as sexual abuse and sexual harassment.

Disability as a Diversity Issue

It is uncontroversial to assert that "disabilities are part of human diversity" (Leigh et al., 1996, p. 364). It is quite another matter, however, to assert that the members of a group of people who all have the same disability constitute a distinct cultural group. As we noted at the beginning of this chapter, the plaintiffs in *Tugg v. Towey* alleged just that. In *Tugg,* the argument was that people who are deaf constitute a distinct cultural minority, one that may be discriminated against in many of the same ways as other cultural minorities. In what follows, we examine this assertion as it applies to the population singled out in the lawsuit—deaf individuals—keeping in mind that analogous arguments could be applied to most any population of people who have the same or a similar disability.

Disability, Diversity, and Culture

Most of the half-million or so people who cannot hear speech well enough to understand it were deaf before they were 3 years old (Schein & Delk, 1974). These people communicate with one another using American Sign Language and have as their primary social contacts other deaf people. As a group, members of this population have in common not only their language, but many of their beliefs, attitudes, values, nonverbal behavior, norms, and traditions. In short, they have in common many of the things used to define a distinct cultural group (Dolnick, 1993; Padden, 1980; Paul & Jackson, 1993; Phillips, 1996; Sacks, 1989; Tyler, 1993). In fact, members of this cultural group can assimilate with relative ease into any of the many deaf communities that exist throughout the country (Jankowski, 1991; Padden & Humphries, 1988). By contrast, members of this group assimilate into the hearing world only with great effort (Higgins, 1983).

Conceiving members of the deaf population as a distinct cultural minority rather than as people who have the same handicap is useful and therapeutic in the sense that it shifts the focus of attention from deficit to the richness of Deaf culture (Lane, 1992). Recall that "Deaf" in this context is spelled with a capital "D" to emphasize that the people so described really do share a common culture—as opposed to a medical condition (Padden, 1980; Padden & Humphries, 1988; Woodward, 1972). Members of the Deaf culture tend to be held in high esteem by others who also identify themselves as culturally Deaf (Phillips, 1996). Let's also point out that many members of the culture see themselves as multicultural in that they are members of more than one minority culture. The resulting multicultural issues to be considered in clinical assessment, as well as intervention, can be complex (Akamatsu, 1993–1994; Anderson & Grace, 1991; Christensen & Delgado, 1993; Cohen et al., 1990; Eldredge, 1993; Freeman, 1989; Rodriguez & Santiviago, 1991).

The Need for Sensitivity

Throughout this book we have made repeated reference to the need for sensitivity in the assessment of people from cultures with which an assessor may have little or no acquaintance. Much of what we have said in this context seems eminently applicable to the assessment of people with disabilities. People from different cultures may view or understand certain experiences in different ways and interpret them against backdrops of widely varying cultural wisdoms. These people may act in ways that seem odd, even pathological, from one's own cultural perspective. So, for example, in Deaf culture, it is critically important to gain eye contact before communication can proceed—this because communication is very much a visual, and not an aural, medium. Consequently, the rules in Deaf culture for attention getting and turn taking in conversation are quite different from the rules for the broader society (Phillips, 1996). Culturally accepted ways of gaining visual attention include firmly tapping the hand of the person with whom one wishes to communicate or, if out of reach, waving one's hand to attract attention. Such behavior may strike a nonaccustomed individual as odd but is very much "everyday" in Deaf culture.

As we have stated many times and in many different ways throughout this book, it is incumbent upon mental health professionals to avoid culture-related pitfalls in assessment and treatment. One such pitfall derives from reflexive adherence to one's own cultural truths while giving insufficient consideration to the world as seen through the eyes of people from diverse backgrounds, including people with disabling conditions.

Self-Assessment

Test your understanding of elements of this chapter by seeing if you can explain each of the following terms, expressions, and abbreviations:

AAMR

accommodation

accommodation by alternate assessment

ADA

adaptive behavior

Americans with Disabilities Act of 1990

at-risk infant or toddlers (according to IDEA)

child aged 3 through 9 with a disability (according to IDEA)

child with a disability (in general, according to IDEA)

cognitive disability

disability (ADA definition)

disability as a diversity issue

Education for All Handicapped Children Act

functional disability

IDEA

Individuals with Disabilities Education Act Amendments of 1997

intensity of support (in AAMR definition)

issues in alternate assessment

major life activity (as implied in ADA)

perceived disability case

Public Law 94-142

Public Law 99-457

Public Law 101-336

Public Law 101-476

Public Law 105-17

16

Assessment, Careers, and Business

Many people contemplating momentous career decisions believe that if they take a battery of tests, they will gain insight into the types of work for which they might be best suited. They are right. In fact, tests and other tools of assessment can be useful in directing people to personally fulfilling careers, while steering them away from jobs and work environments in which they might burn out prematurely or be very unhappy. From the perspective of employers, tools of assessment can provide welcome assistance in screening and selecting applicants, as well as in identifying specific job assignments for personnel.

In this chapter, we survey a wide variety of assessment tools and procedures used to accomplish various ends in business and other organizational contexts. We begin with a look at some commonly used instruments in career counseling.

Career Counseling

"What do you want to be when you grow up?" It seems as if it was just yesterday that we were asked that question. For some of us, it really was just yesterday. Professionals involved in career counseling have hundreds of tools at their disposal to help their clients identify what work they might succeed at. For example, there are tests specifically designed to measure interests, aptitudes, skills, special talents, attitudes toward work, assumptions about careers, perceptions regarding career barriers, dysfunctional career thoughts, confidence in one's skills, and readiness for making career and educational choices. There is an instrument designed to measure psychological resources of adults in career transition (Heppner, 1998) and one to identify students who are undecided about career objectives (Larson & Majors, 1998). Variables thought to be important in occupational choice range from whether one is a "people person" (Roe & Klos, 1969; Roe & Siegelman, 1964) to whether a work environment brings out the best in the worker (Moos, 1986).

One variable that has been historically considered closely related to occupational fulfillment and success is personal interests. It may be that by age 15, students' interests are sufficiently solidified so as to be useful in course and career planning (Care, 1996). Let's begin our survey of testing and assessment in the world of work with a brief look at how and why tests of interests are used in career counseling.

Figure 16–1
It's Not Just a Job, It's an Adventure!

Had Orin Scrivello, D.D.S. (Steve Martin) in the comedy Little Shop of Horrors *taken an interest survey, the results might have been quite bizarre. As a child, young Orin's interests leaned toward bashing the heads of pussycats, shooting puppies with a BB gun, and poisoning guppies. He was able to put what his mother described as his "natural tendencies" to use in gainful employment: He became a dentist.*

Measures of Interest

On the presumption that interest in one's work promotes better performance, greater productivity, and greater job satisfaction, both employers and prospective employees have much to gain from methods that can help individuals identify their interests and a job tailored to those interests. Using such methods, individuals can discover, for example, if their interests lie in being a starship captain and "seeking new worlds and exploring new civilizations" or in something more along the lines of dentistry (Figure 16–1). Employers can use information about their employees' interest patterns in formulating job descriptions and attracting new personnel. For example, a company could design an employment campaign emphasizing that the position offers security if security was found to be the chief interest of the successful workers currently holding the same job. Although many instruments designed to measure interests have been published (Table 16–1), our discussion will focus on the one with the longest history of continuous use, the Strong Interest Inventory (SII).

Strong Interest Inventory As early as 1907, psychologist G. Stanley Hall had developed a questionnaire to assess children's recreational interests. However, it was not until the early 1920s that Edward K. Strong, Jr., after attending a seminar on the measurement of

Table 16–1
Some Measures of Interest

Test	Description
Campbell Interest and Skill Survey	Developed by David Campbell, who revised the Strong Interest Inventory, this instrument focuses on occupations that require four or more years of postsecondary education. In addition to assessing interests, it is designed to provide an estimate of the individual's confidence in performing various occupational activities.
Career Interest Inventory	Designed for use with students in grades 7 through 12 as well as adults, this test introduces testtakers to the world of occupational and educational alternatives. In addition to career-related interests, the test taps interest in school subjects and school-related activities.
Guidance Information System (GIS 3.0)	Available only on disk or CD-ROM, this combination assessment instrument and information retrieval system contains a number of components ranging from information on colleges to information on the types of jobs college majors in different areas tend to get. The interest assessment component of the system is called the Career Decision-Making System. After probing the assessee's interests, interest scores are calculated, and the system provides lists of suggested careers and occupations to explore.
Jackson Vocational Interest Survey	A forced-choice measure of interests as they relate to 26 work roles (what one does at work) and 8 work styles (the type of work environment preferred, usually related to one's personal values). Designed for use with high school and college students, the test yields scores on ten Holland-like themes, as well as validity-related indices. The development of this test has been described in detail by Jackson (1977; Jackson & Williams, 1975).
Kuder Occupational Interest Survey (KOIS)	This classic interest measuring instrument is an outgrowth of the Kuder Preference Survey, which was originally published in 1939. Each item presents testtakers with three choices of activity, and their task is to select their most and least preferred of the choices. Scores are reported in terms of magnitude of interest in various occupational categories. The test has been criticized for its lack of predictive validity, an assertion that has been addressed by the test's author and his colleagues (Kuder et al. 1998; Zytowski, 1996).
Reading-Free Vocational Interest Inventory (R-FVII)	Designed for use with people 10 years of age and older with learning disabilities, mental retardation, or other special needs, this test measures vocational likes and dislikes using pictures of people at work in different occupations. For each item, respondents select one of three drawings depicting the preferred job task. The protocol yields scores on 11 occupational categories that represent types of occupations at which members of special populations might be employed.
Self-Directed Search-Form R	Developed by John L. Holland, this is a self-administered, self-scored, and self-interpreted interest inventory, appropriate for use by individuals 12 years of age and older. Form-R (1994) contains updated norms. Testtakers complete a booklet in which they are asked questions about various interest-related areas including activities, aspirations, and competencies.

interest, began a program of systematic investigation into the measurement of human interests. One product of this work was the 420-item Strong Vocational Interest Blank (SVIB) for men, published with a test manual by Stanford University Press in 1928 and revised in 1938. In 1935, a 410-item SVIB for women was published, along with a test manual. The women's SVIB was revised in 1946. Both the men's and the women's SVIB were again revised in the mid-1960s. Amid concern about sex-specific forms of the test in the late 1960s and early 1970s (McArthur, 1992), a merged form was published in 1974. Developed under the direction of David P. Campbell, the merged form was called the Strong-Campbell Interest Inventory (SCII). The test was revised in 1985 and again in 1994 and is now known as the Strong Interest Inventory (SII; Strong et al., 1985; Harmon et al., 1994).

Strong's approach to test construction was empirical and straightforward: (1) Select hundreds of items that might conceivably distinguish the interests of a person by that person's occupation, (2) administer this rough cut of the test to several hundred people selected so as to be representative of certain occupations or professions, (3) sort out which items seemed of interest to persons by occupational group and discard items with no discriminative ability, and (4) construct a final version of the test that would yield scores describing how an examinee's pattern of interest corresponded to that of people actually employed in various occupations and professions. With such a test, college students majoring in psychology could, for example, see how closely their pattern of interests paralleled that of working psychologists. Presumably, if your interests closely match those of psychologists (in contrast to the interests of, say, tow truck operators), you would probably enjoy the work of a psychologist.

Test items, all written in multiple-choice format, probe personal preferences for school subjects, occupations, amusement, activities, and other variables. Respondents are also asked to describe themselves with self-descriptive statements (such as, "win friends easily") by indicating "yes," "no," or "uncertain." Protocols are computer-scored and interpreted, yielding information on the testtaker's personal style, basic interests, and other data useful in determining how similar or dissimilar the respondent's interests are to those of people holding a variety of jobs.

The standardization sample for the 1994 revision included an occupational reference group consisting of adults employed in 50 different occupations, and a general reference group. To qualify for membership in the occupational reference group, respondents must have reported that they liked their work and were employed at it for a minimum of three years. The general reference group served as a kind of control group; its members were selected to represent men and women in general. Minorities were represented in both the occupational and general reference groups. Lattimore and Borgen (1999) studied the criterion-related validity of the SII across racial-ethnic groups and in general, their findings supported the use of the test with respondents from diverse cultural backgrounds, particularly college-educated respondents.

In addition to the SII, many other interest inventories (for example, Holland et al., 1994; Kuder, 1979) are now in widespread use by counseling psychologists. The Minnesota Vocational Interest Inventory is an empirically keyed instrument designed to compare the respondents' interest patterns with those of persons employed in a variety of nonprofessional occupations (such as stock clerks, painters, printers, truck drivers). An instrument called the "Career Decision Scale" has been used to examine cognitive processes associated with general career indecision (see Osipow & Reed, 1985) as well as specialty indecision among people who have decided on a career (Savickas et al., 1985). A number of interest tests designed for use with people who do not read well use drawings and other pictures in media such as slides and filmstrips (Elksnin & Elksnin, 1993).

How well do interest measures predict the kind of work in which individuals will be successful and happy? In considering this question, let's note the finding from one study that interest and aptitude measures correlated in the range of .40 to .72 (Lam et al., 1993). From this study, one might infer that people are interested in things that they do well or that they develop abilities in areas that interest them.

In one of the few studies examining the accuracy with which interest and aptitude tests predict future job performance and satisfaction, Bizot and Goldman (1993) identified people who had been tested in high school with measures of vocational interest and aptitude. Eight years later, these individuals reported on their satisfaction with their jobs. Further, they permitted the researchers to contact their employers for information about the quality of their work. The researchers found that when a good match existed between subjects' aptitudes in high school and the level of their current job, then their job performance was likely to be evaluated positively by the employer. When a poor match existed between the subjects' aptitude as measured in high school and the level of their current job, they would be more likely to be rated as poor in job performance by the employer. The extent to which employees were satisfied with their jobs was not related to aptitudes as measured in high school. As for the predictive validity of

Figure 16–2
The O'Connor Tweezer Dexterity Test

the interest tests administered in high school, the tests predicted neither job performance nor job satisfaction eight years later. The results of this study, as well as of related studies (for example, Jagger et al., 1992), sound a caution to counselors regarding overreliance on interest inventories. Still, this genre of test seems to have value in bringing a dimension to vocational counseling that is not typically found in many other tests.

Measures of Ability and Aptitude

As we saw in Chapter 10, achievement, ability, and aptitude tests measure prior learning to some degree, but they differ in the uses to which the test data will be put. Beyond that, aptitude tests may tap a greater amount of informal learning than do achievement tests. Achievement tests may be more limited and focused in scope than aptitude tests.

Ability and aptitude measures vary widely in topics covered, specificity of coverage, and other variables. The Wonderlic Personnel Test measures mental ability in a general sense. This brief (12-minute) test includes items that assess spatial skill, abstract thought, and mathematical skill. The Bennet Mechanical Comprehension Test is a widely used paper-and-pencil measure of a testtaker's ability to understand the relationship between physical forces and various tools (for example, pulleys and gears) as well as other common objects (carts, steps, and seesaws). Other mechanical tests, such as the Hand-Tool Dexterity Test, blur the lines among aptitude, achievement, and performance tests by requiring the testtaker to actually take apart, reassemble, or otherwise manipulate materials, usually in a prescribed sequence and within some prescribed time limit. If a job consists mainly of securing tiny transistors into the inner workings of an electronic appliance or game, then the employer's focus of interest might well be on prospective employees' perceptual-motor abilities, finger dexterity, and related variables. In such an instance, the O'Connor Tweezer Dexterity Test might be the instrument of choice (Figure 16–2). This test requires the examinee to insert brass pins into a metal plate using a pair of tweezers. Other tests designed to measure specific aptitudes exist for a wide variety of occupational fields. For the professions, a number of psychometrically sophisticated assessment programs are in place to screen or select applicants by means of aptitude tests. These programs include the Medical College Admissions Tests, the Law School Admission Test, the Dental Admission Testing Program, and the specialized tests that are part of the Graduate Record Examination, such as the specialty examination in psychology.

For a while, one of the most widely used of all aptitude tests was the General Aptitude Test Battery. A description of the test, as well as the controversy surrounding it, follows.

The General Aptitude Test Battery   The United States Employment Service (USES) developed the General Aptitude Test Battery (GATB) and first put it into use in 1947 after extensive research and development. The GATB (pronounced like "Gatsby" without the *s*) is available for use by state employment services as well as other agencies and organizations (such as certain school districts and nonprofit organizations that have obtained official permission from the government to administer the test). The GATB is a tool used to identify aptitudes for occupations, and it is a test just about anyone of working age can take. The test is administered regularly at local state offices (referred to by names such as the "Job Service," "Employment Security Commission," and "Labor Security Commission") to people who want the agency to help find them a job, to people who are unemployed and have been referred by a state office of unemployment, or to employees of a company that has requested such aptitude assessment. If you are curious about your own aptitude for work in fields as diverse as psychology, education, and plumbing, you may want to visit your local state employment office. Be prepared to sit for an examination that will take about three hours if you take the entire test; the GATB consists of twelve timed tests that measure nine aptitudes that in turn can be divided into three composite aptitudes. About one-half the time will be spent on psychomotor tasks, and the other half on paper-and-pencil tasks. In some instances, depending on factors such as the reason assessment is undertaken, only selected tests of the battery will be administered (referred to as a "Special Aptitude Test Battery" or SATB) to measure aptitude for a specific line of work. And even if you take the full GATB, various SATBs—aptitudes deemed necessary for specific occupations—can be isolated for study from the other test data.

In recent years, the GATB has evolved from a test with multiple cutoffs to one that employs regression and validity generalization for making recommendations based on test results. The rationale and process by which the GATB has made this evolution has been described by John E. Hunter (1980, 1986), Frank Schmidt, and their associates (Hunter & Schmidt, 1983; Hunter et al., 1982; Hunter & Hunter, 1984—the latter Hunter is more than an associate; she's John's wife), and validity generalization is the subject of our chapter *Close-up*. Briefly, recommendations with respect to aptitude for a particular job had in the past been made on the basis of GATB validity studies bearing on specific jobs; if, for example, there existed 500 job descriptions covering 500 jobs for which scores on the GATB were to be applied, there would be 500 individual validation studies with the GATB—one validation study for each individual job, typically with a relatively small sample size (many of these single studies containing an average of only 76 subjects). Further, there were no validation studies for the other 12,000-plus jobs in the American economy (according to the *Dictionary of Occupational Titles* published by the United States Department of Labor, 1977). Using meta-analysis to cumulate results across a number of validation studies and statistically correct for error such as sampling error, Hunter demonstrated that all the jobs could be categorized within five families of jobs, based on what are called "worker function codes" of the *Dictionary of Occupational Titles*. The five families of jobs are (1) Setting Up, (2) Feeding and Off-Bearing, (3) Synthesizing

Validity Generalization and the GATB

Can a test validated for use in personnel selection for one occupation also be valid for use in personnel selection for another occupation? Must the validation of a test used in personnel selection be situation-specific? Stated more generally, can validity evidence for a test be meaningfully applied to situations other than those in which the evidence was obtained? These are the types of questions that are raised when the topic of validity generalization is discussed.

As applied to employment-related decision making on the basis of test scores achieved on the General Aptitude Test Battery (GATB), *validity generalization* refers to the fact that the same test-score data may be predictive of aptitude for all jobs; the implication is that if a test is validated for a few jobs selected from a much larger cluster of jobs—each requiring similar skills at approximately the same level of complexity—the test is valid for all jobs in that cluster. For example, if a validation study conclusively indicated that GATB scores are predictive of aptitude for (and ultimately proficiency in) the occupation of assembler in an aircraft assembly plant, an entirely new validation study may not be needed to apply such data to the occupation of assembler in a shipbuilding plant; if the type and level of skill required in the two occupations can be shown to be sufficiently similar, it may be that the same or similar procedures used to select aircraft assemblers can profitably be used to select assemblers of ships.

Validity generalization (VG) as applied to personnel selection using the GATB makes unnecessary the burden of conducting a separate validation study with the test for every one of the over 12,000 jobs in the American economy. The application of VG to GATB scores also enables GATB users to supply employers with more precise information about testtakers. To understand why this is so, let's begin by consulting the pie chart in Figure 1.

Note that the inner circle of the chart lists the 12 tests in the General Aptitude Test Battery and that the next ring of the circle lists eight aptitudes derived from the 12 tests. Not illustrated here is a ninth aptitude, General Learning Ability, which is derived from scores on the Vocabulary, Arithmetic Reasoning, and Three-Dimensional Space tests. A brief description of each of the nine aptitudes measured by the GATB follows:

General Learning Ability (also referred to as *intelligence*) (G)—"Catching on" and understanding instructions and principles as well as reasoning and judgment are tapped here. G is measured by Tests 3, 4, and 6 in the diagram.

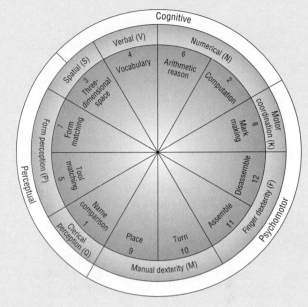

Figure 1
Aptitudes Measured by the General Aptitude Test Battery

Verbal Aptitude (V)—Understanding the meaning of words and relationships between them as well as using words effectively are some of the abilities tapped here. V is measured by Test 4.

Numerical Aptitude (N)—N is measured by tasks requiring the quick performance of arithmetic operations. It is measured by Tests 2 and 6.

Spatial Aptitude (S)—The ability to visualize and mentally manipulate geometric forms is tapped here. S is measured by Test 3.

Form Perception (P)—Attention to detail, including the ability to discriminate slight differences in shapes, shading, lengths, and widths, as well as ability to perceive pertinent detail is measured. P is measured by Tests 5 and 7.

Clerical Perception (Q)—Attention to detail in written or tabular material as well as the ability to proofread words and numbers and to avoid perceptual errors in arithmetic computation is tapped here. Q is measured by Test 1.

Motor Coordination (K)—This test taps the ability to quickly make precise movements that require eye-hand coordination. K is measured by Test 8.

(continued)

Validity Generalization and the GATB
(continued)

Finger Dexterity (F)—This test taps the ability to quickly manipulate small objects with the fingers. F is measured by Tests 11 and 12.

Manual Dexterity (M)—The ability to work with one's hands in placing and turning motions is measured here. M is measured by Tests 9 and 10.

Referring back to the diagram and more specifically to the outermost ring, note that the three composite aptitudes can be derived from the nine specific aptitudes: a Cognitive composite, a Perceptual composite, and a Psychomotor composite. The nine aptitudes that compose the three composite aptitudes may be summarized as follows:

The Nine GATB Aptitudes	The Three Composite Scores
G General Learning Ability (also referred to as *intelligence*)	
V Verbal Aptitude	Cognitive
N Numerical Aptitude	
S Spatial Aptitude	
P Form Perception	Perceptual
Q Clerical Perception	
K Motor Coordination	
F Finger Dexterity	Psychomotor
M Manual Dexterity	

Traditionally—before the advent of VG—testtakers who sat for the GATB might subsequently receive counseling as to how they did in each of the nine aptitude areas. Further they might have been informed (1) how their own pattern of GATB scores compared with patterns of aptitude (referred to as "Occupational Aptitude Patterns" or OAPs) deemed necessary for proficiency in various occupations, and/or (2) how they performed with respect to any of the 467 constellations of a Special Aptitude Test Battery (SATB) that could potentially be extracted from a GATB protocol. Using VG makes possible additional information useful in advising prospective employers and counseling prospective employees. Such information includes more precise data concerning a testtaker's performance with respect to OAPs, as well as scores (usually expressed in percentiles) with respect to

the five job families. Research (Hunter, 1982) has indicated that the three composite aptitudes can be used to validly predict job proficiency for all jobs in the United States economy. All jobs may be categorized according to five job families, and the aptitude required for each of these families can be described with respect to various contributions of the three composite GATB scores. For example, Job Family 1 (Set-up Jobs) is 59% Cognitive, 30% Perceptual, and 11% Psychomotor in nature. GATB scoring is done by computer as is weighting of scores to determine suitability for employment in jobs in each of the five job families.

Proponents of VG as applied to use with the GATB list the following advantages:

1. *The decreased emphasis on multiple cutoffs as a selection strategy has advantages for both prospective employers and prospective employees.* In a multiple cutoff selection model, a prospective employee would have to achieve certain minimum GATB scores in each of the aptitudes deemed critical for proficiency in a given occupation; failure to meet the minimal cutting score in these aptitudes would mean elimination from the candidate pool for that occupation. Using VG, a potential benefit for the prospective employee is that the requirement of a minimum cutting score on any specific aptitude is eliminated. For employers, VG encourages the use of a top-down hiring policy: one in which the best-qualified people (as measured by the GATB) are offered jobs first.

2. *Research has suggested that the relationship between aptitude test scores and job performance is linear (Waldman & Avolio, 1989), a relationship that is statistically better suited to VG than to the multiple cutoff selection model.* The nature of the relationship between scores on a valid test of aptitude and ratings of job performance is illustrated in Figure 2. Given that such a relationship exists, Hunter (1980, 1982) notes that from a technical standpoint, linear data are better suited to analysis using a VG model than using a model with multiple cutoffs.

3. *More precise information can be reported to employers regarding a testtaker's relative standing in the continuum of aptitude test scores.* Consider in this context Figure 3, and let's suppose that an established and validated cutoff score for selection in a particular occupation using this hypothetical test of aptitude is 155. Examinee *X* and Examinee *Y* both meet the cutoff requirement, but Examinee *Y* is probably better qualified for the job—we say "probably" because there may be exceptions to this general rule depending on variables such as the actual demands of the specific

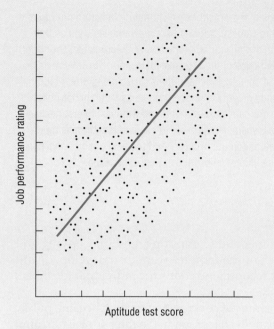

Figure 2
**The Linear Relationship Between Aptitude Test Scores
and Job Performance Ratings**

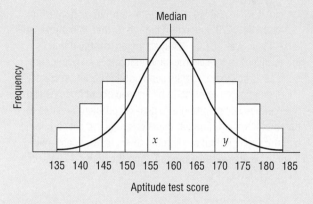

Figure 3
Results of a Hypothetical Aptitude Test

job. Although the score for Examinee *X* falls below the median score for all testtakers, the score for Examinee *Y* lies at the high end of the distribution of scores. All other factors being equal, which individual would you prefer to hire if you owned the company? Using a simple cutoff procedure, no distinction with respect to aptitude score would have been made between Examinee *X* and Examinee *Y* provided both scores met the cutoff criterion.

4. *VG better assists employers in their efforts to hire qualified employees.* Studies such as one conducted at the Philip Morris Company suggest that a significant increase in the rate of training success can be expected for employees hired using a selection procedure that uses VG as compared with employees hired by other means (Warmke, 1984).

Is VG "the answer" to all personnel selection problems? Not at all. VG is simply one rationale for justifiably avoiding the time and expense of conducting a separate validation study for every single test with every possible group of testtakers under every possible set of circumstances—too often

with too few subjects to achieve meaningful findings. Note, however, that with the convenience of VG come many concerns about the efficacy of the procedures employed. And although we have devoted a fair amount of time to acquainting you with this important concept in the personnel selection literature, it is equally important for you to be aware that a number of technical issues with respect to VG are currently being debated in the professional literature.

You will recall that in the development of VG as applied to personnel selection, Hunter and his colleagues used a process called meta-analysis to cumulate findings across a number of studies. One important aspect of this work involved statistically correcting for the small sample sizes that occurred in the studies analyzed. The types of procedures used in such a process and the types of interpretations that can legitimately be made as a result have been the subject of a number of critical analyses of VG. The amount of unexplained variance that remains even after statistical corrections for differences in sample size have been made (Cascio, 1987), the unknown influence of a potential restriction-of-range problem with respect to subject self-selection (Cronbach, 1984), objections with respect to using employer ratings as a criterion (Burke, 1984), and the fact that alternative models may explain variation in validity coefficients as well as the cross-situational consistency model (James et al., 1986) are some of the technical issues that have been raised with respect to the use of VG (see also Zedeck &

(continued)

Validity Generalization and the GATB
(continued)

Cascio, 1984). With specific reference to VG as applied to use with the GATB, one might inquire further: What problems arise when over 12,000 occupations are grouped into five job families? Is it really meaningful to place an occupation such as "truck driver" in the same job family as "secretary"?

Clearly, much remains to be learned about how VG can most effectively be brought to bear on problems related to personnel testing. Difficult questions—some psychometric in nature, others that relate more to societal values—will have to be addressed. Compounding the task is a litany of

variables that are neither psychometric in nature nor directly related to values; included here are variables such as the strength of the economy, the size of the available labor pool, the experience of the available labor pool, the general desirability of specific jobs, and the salaries being offered for various kinds of work. Whether one looks favorably or not at the government's experimentation with VG in personnel selection, it seems reasonable to assume that there is much to be learned in the process, and the field of personnel selection may ultimately profit from the experience.

and Coordinating, (4) Analyzing, Compiling, and Computing, and (5) Copying and Comparing. Regression equations for each of the families were then developed, and using these equations Hunter found that recommendations for individual testtakers could be generalized to various jobs.

In the late 1980s, the GATB became a center of controversy when it became public knowledge that the test had been race normed. Discussed in Chapter 4, race norming refers to the process of adjusting scores to show an individual testtaker's standing within his or her own racial group. With the race-normed GATB, high-scorers within racial groups were recommended for employment. For example, among people being considered for a skilled job, a GATB raw score of 300 was "translated into percentile scores of 79, 62, and 38, respectively, for Blacks, Hispanics, and others" (Gottfredson, 1994, p. 966). Only percentile scores and not raw scores were reported to employers.

In an attempt to address the ensuing controversy, the U.S. Department of Labor asked the National Academy of Sciences (NAS) to conduct a study. The NAS issued a report (Hartigan & Wigdor, 1989) that was generally supportive of race norming. The NAS noted that the GATB appeared to suffer from slope bias such that the test correlated more highly with criterion measures for White samples (.19) than for Black samples (.12). Intercept bias was also present, with the result that the performance of Blacks would be overpredicted relative to the performance of Whites if the same regression line were used for both groups. The practice of race norming amounted to using different regression lines, each with the accurate slope and intercept for the specific racial group. The NAS found race norming to be a reasonable method for correcting for the bias of the test.

The NAS report also addressed more general issues concerning the utility of the GATB as a predictor of job performance. Using a database of 755 studies, the NAS noted the GATB correlated approximately .22 with criteria such as supervisory ratings. Others have estimated the test's validity to be .20 (Vevea et al., 1993) and .21 (Waldman & Avolio, 1989). These relatively small coefficients were viewed by the NAS as modest but acceptable. To understand why they were considered acceptable, recall from Chapter 6 that criterion validity is limited by the reliability of the measures. Although the GATB has adequate test-retest reliability (around .81), the likely poor reliability of supervisory ratings may depress the GATB's validity coefficient. Such depression of a validity coefficient could be expected to occur for any test designed to predict job performance that is validated against supervisors' ratings (Hartigan & Wigdor, 1989). Of course, even predictors with modest criterion validity can improve personnel selection decisions. Thus, despite the low criterion validity coefficients, the GATB is widely viewed as a valid means for selecting employees.

The NAS recommendation to continue the practice of race norming the test may have done more to fan the flames of controversy than to quell them. In July of 1990, the Department of Labor proposed a two-year suspension in the use of the GATB, during which time the efficacy of the test and its scoring procedures would be further researched. The legality of the practice of race norming had also become a heated topic of debate by that time (Baydoun & Neuman, 1992; Delahunty, 1988). The question of whether race norming of the GATB should continue became moot after Congress passed the Civil Rights Act of 1991, a law that made the practice of race norming illegal.

Today, the GATB is still in use by the U.S. Employment Service. However, reports to employers are no longer race-normed. The raw scores of people from all racial groups are now converted to interpretable standard scores using the same norms. In addition to its potential applied value, the GATB remains a valuable resource for researchers in areas such as theory validation (see, for example, Farrell & McDaniel, 2001).

Measures of Personality

Although ample research may be cited to cast doubt on the application of personality tests in various career counseling contexts (Ghiselli, 1973; Ghiselli & Barthol, 1953; Guion & Gottier, 1965; Kinslinger, 1966; Schmitt et al., 1984), a trend seems to be toward a more charitable view of personality tests, especially when such tests are carefully selected for a particular study and used properly (Day & Silverman, 1989; Fontanna, 2000; Lord et al., 1986; Schneider, 1987; Weiss & Adler, 1984). In the past, methodological problems as well as theoretical inadequacies in research plagued many studies that employed personality measures (Hollenbeck & Whitener, 1988). Additionally, past studies deemphasized the specific role requirements of various jobs, and inappropriate personality tests may have been employed in the research. The role requirements of, say, an emergency medical technician are quite different from those of a computer programmer or a salesperson. Different personality traits are of greater or lesser importance in considering each of these occupations, and the same personality test might not be well suited for each of them. Cascio (1982) drew attention to the distinction between task-related and people-related aspects of an occupation and the differential role each of these variables might play in predicting overall success in an occupation or a particular job. Keeping this distinction in mind, as well as the caveat that personality measures must be job-relevant, it would appear that personality measures have an important place in career counseling (Day & Silverman, 1989; Hogan et al., 1985; Wright & Cropanzano, 2000).

A personality test such as the MMPI-2, widely used in clinical settings, may have limited application in the career counseling context. Other personality tests, such as the Guilford-Zimmerman Temperament Survey and the Edwards Personal Preference Schedule may be preferred, perhaps because the measurements they yield tend to be more related to the specific variables under study. One test that seems to be riding a wave of popularity for use in workplace-related measurements is the Myers-Briggs Type Indicator (MBTI). Isabel Briggs Myers and her mother, Katharine Cook Briggs, two women with no formal training in psychology or assessment, were inspired by the writings of Carl Jung (1923) and his ideas about different psychological types. That inspiration culminated in the creation of the MBTI (Myers & Briggs, 1943/1962), an instrument used to identify testtakers by psychological type and to shed light on "basic differences in the ways human beings take in information and make decisions" (McCaulley, 2000, p. 117). Despite many concerns about the test's validity and related matters (Girelli & Stake, 1993; Harvey & Murry, 1994; Lorr, 1991; Martin & Bartol, 1986; Pittenger, 1993; Zumbo & Taylor, 1993), the MBTI remains very popular, especially among counselors and organizational consultants, perhaps because of the strong intuitive appeal of a test that purports to classify people by psychological type. A more detailed description of this instrument can be found in the companion workbook to this textbook (Cohen, 2002), as well as in many published articles (see, for example, McCaulley, 2000).

Before leaving the subject of personality assessment in the world of work, let's mention an intriguing line of research that raised the question, "Does the emotional disposition of children have anything to do with how satisfied they are with their jobs as adults?" If you think the question itself is somewhat surprising, hold on to your hats when we tell you that the answer to the question (a resounding "yes") is even more surprising. Using data from three separate longitudinal studies, Staw et al. (1986) found that dispositional data obtained in infancy predicted job-related attitudes over a time span of some 50 years. Although the interpretation of the data does have its critics, it clearly has found a growing base of support among other researchers (Arvey et al., 1989; House et al., 1996; Judge et al., 2000; Motowidlo, 1996). It may be that one's temperament mediates emotionally significant events, including those at work, which in turn influence one's level of job satisfaction (Weiss & Cropanzano, 1996).

Tests of integrity   Integrity tests may serve to screen new employees as well as to keep honest those already hired. Screening instruments purporting to predict who will and will not be an honest employee—so-called **integrity tests**—have been around for many years. However, the use of such tests has increased dramatically with the passage of legislation prohibiting the use of polygraphs (lie detectors) in most employment settings. In fact, it has been estimated that integrity testing has mushroomed into a $30 million a year industry (Lawlor, 1990), with an estimated 15 million people taking such tests annually (Gavzer, 1990).

Sackett et al. (1989) dichotomized existing instruments into what they term "overt integrity tests" (which may straightforwardly ask the examinee questions like "Do you always tell the truth?"), and "personality-based measures," which resemble in many ways objective personality inventories such as the MMPI. Items on the latter type of test may be far more subtle than on the former. Also, responses to items on the personality-based measures are less likely to be interpreted on the basis of the face validity of the item and more likely to be interpreted with reference to the responses of groups of people known to have or lack integrity, as defined by the particular test.

Whether integrity tests measure what they purport to measure is debatable. Reviews of the validity of such measures have ranged from mixed (APA, 1991a; Sackett & Harris, 1984; Sackett et al., 1989) to positive (DePaulo, 1994; Honts, 1994; Sackett, 1994; Saxe, 1994). Perhaps the fairest conclusion from this literature is that when the test has been professionally developed, it stands an excellent chance of meeting acceptable standards of validity. *Model Guidelines for Preemployment Integrity Testing Programs* is a document developed by the Association of Personnel Test Publishers (APTP, 1990) that addresses many of the issues surrounding integrity tests, including issues relating to test development, administration, scoring, interpretation, confidentiality, public statements regarding the tests, and test-marketing practices. Specific guidelines in these areas are provided, and the responsibilities of test users and publishers are discussed (see Jones et al., 1990, for an overview).

Beyond issues regarding the validity of integrity tests lie broader questions that relate to various aspects of the use of such tests (Camara & Schneider, 1994). For example, is privacy being invaded when a prospective employee is asked to sit for such a test? Can such tests be used in support of discrimination practices? Should such tests be used alone or in combination with other measurement procedures as a basis for granting or denying employment? Interestingly, White (1984) suggests that pre-employment honesty testing may induce negative work-related attitudes. Having to undergo such a test may be interpreted by prospective employees as evidence of high levels of employee theft— with the (paradoxical) result being a new and higher norm of stealing by employees.

Other Measures

Numerous other tools of assessment may be used in career planning and pre-employment contexts, even if they were not specifically designed for that purpose. For example, the Checklist of Adaptive Living Skills (CALS; Morreau & Bruininks, 1991) surveys the life skills needed to make a successful transition from school to work. Organized into four broad domains (Personal Living Skills, Home Living Skills, Community Living Skills, and Employment Skills), this test is designed for evaluation of 794 life skills. The checklist is designed for use with assessees of any age. According to the manual, the individual completing the checklist must have had the opportunity to observe the assessee for at least three months in natural settings. Assessees are judged to be "independent" with regard to a specific skill if they perform the task with good quality, at least 75% of the time, when needed without reminder. This criterion-based instrument may be particularly useful in career and pre-employment counseling with members of special populations.

Researchers are interested in the role of culture in various aspects of assessment for employment (Blustein & Ellis, 2000; Hofstede, 1998; Leong & Hartung, 2000; Ponterotto et al., 2000; Rotundo & Sackett, 1999; Ryan et al., 2000; Sandoval et al., 1998; Subich, 1996). According to Meyers (1994), the fact that a new job can sometimes result in a kind of "culture shock" prompted the creation of an instrument called the Cross-Cultural Adaptability Inventory (CCAI; Kelley & Meyers, 1992). The CCAI is a self-administered and self-scored instrument designed to provide information on the testtaker's ability to adapt to other cultures. Testtakers respond to 50 items written in a 6-point, Likert format. The test yields information with regard to one's readiness to adapt to new situations, tolerate ambiguity, maintain one's personal identity in new surroundings, and interact with people from other cultures. The report is organized into information with regard to four factors thought to be relevant to cross-cultural adaptability: Emotional Resilience, Flexibility/Openness, Perceptual Acuity, and Personal Autonomy. The test may hold value in evaluating readiness to take a job or be relocated to a position involving overseas employment.

Tests and other tools of assessment may be valuable not only at the pre-employment end of the career planning spectrum, but at the other end of that spectrum, when retirement becomes a viable option. The decision to retire is momentous and multifaceted; such a decision should not be made on the basis of analyzing a single criterion such as global satisfaction or financial security (Parnes & Less, 1985). Counselors may offer assistance to persons considering retirement by means of probing interviews, as well as the administration of various measures such as tests that assess life satisfaction, goal-directedness, leisure satisfaction, and interpersonal support. More specifically, the Goal Instability Scale (Robbins & Patton, 1985), the Life Satisfaction Index A (Neugarten et al., 1961), the

Leisure Satisfaction Scale (Beard & Ragheb, 1980), and the Interpersonal Support Evaluations List (Cohen et al., 1985) are some of the instruments that may provide valuable data. Floyd et al. (1992) developed the Retirement Satisfaction Inventory to help assess adjustment in retirement.

Tests and other tools of assessment may be used by businesses and other organizations to assist in making staffing and other personnel-related decisions. Some of the issues in such decision making are discussed below.

Screening, Selection, Classification, and Placement

In the context of employment, **screening** refers to a relatively superficial process of evaluation based on certain minimal standards, criteria, or requirements. For example, a municipal fire department may screen for certain minimal requirements for height, weight, physical health, physical strength, and cognitive ability for admission to a training program for firefighters. The government may use a group-administered test of intelligence to screen out people unsuited for military service or to identify intellectually gifted recruits for special assignments. **Selection** refers to a process whereby each person evaluated for a position will either be accepted or rejected for that position. By contrast, **classification** does not imply acceptance or rejection but, rather, a rating, categorization, or "pigeonholing" with respect to two or more criteria. The military, for example, classifies personnel with respect to security clearance on the basis of variables such as rank, personal history of political activity, and known associations. As a result of such evaluations, one individual might have access to documents labeled "Secret" whereas another might have access to documents labeled "Top Secret." Like classification, **placement** need not carry any implication of acceptance or rejection; it is a disposition, transfer, or assignment to a group or category that may be made on the basis of one criterion. If, for example, you took a college-level course when still in high school, the score you earned on the advanced placement test in that subject area may have been the sole criterion used to place you in an appropriate section of that college course upon your acceptance to college.

Businesses, schools, the military, and other organizations regularly screen, select, classify, or place individuals. A wide array of tests can be used as aids to decision making. Measures of ability, aptitude, interest, and personality may all be of value, depending on the demands of the particular decision. In the high-profile world of professional sports, where selection errors can be extremely costly, psychological tests may be used to help assess whether a new draft choice player will live up to his or her potential (Gardner, 2001). Of course, for more everyday types of employment decision making, and especially at the pre-employment stage, some of the most common tools of assessment include the letter of application and the résumé, the job application form, the letter of recommendation, and the interview.

The Résumé and the Letter of Application

There is no one standard résumé; résumés can be "as unique as the individuals they represent" (Cohen, 1994, p. 394). Typically, information related to one's work objectives, qualifications, education, and experience is included on a résumé. A companion cover letter to a résumé, called a letter of application, lets a job applicant demonstrate motivation, businesslike writing skills, and his or her unique personality. Neither a résumé nor a letter of application is likely to be the sole vehicle through which employment is secured. At best, both of these documents are stepping-stones to personal interviews or

Table 16–2
Checklist for an Application Form Item

1. Is the item necessary for identifying the applicant?
2. Is it necessary for screening out those who are ineligible under the company's basic hiring policies?
3. Does it help to decide whether the candidate is qualified?
4. Is it based on analysis of the job or jobs for which applicants will be selected?
5. Has it been pretested on the company's employees and found to correlate with success?
6. Will the information be used? How?
7. Is the application form the proper place to ask for it?
8. To what extent will answers duplicate information to be obtained at another step in the selection procedure—for example, through interviews, tests, or medical examinations?
9. Is the information needed for selection at all, or should it be obtained at induction or even later?
10. Is it probable that the applicants' replies will be reliable?
11. Does the question violate any applicable federal or state legislation?

Source: Ahern (1949)

other evaluation situations. On the other hand, the employer, the personnel psychologist, or some other individual reading the applicant's résumé and cover letter may use these documents as a basis for rejecting an application. The cover letter and the résumé may be analyzed for details such as quality of written communication, perceived sincerity, and appropriateness of the applicant's objectives, education, motivation, and prior experience with regard to the available position. From the perspective of the evaluator, much the same is true of another common tool of assessment in employment settings, the application form.

The Application Form

Application forms may be thought of as biographical sketches that supply employers with information pertinent to the acceptability of job candidates. In addition to demographic information (such as name, address, and telephone number), pertinent details about other areas, such as educational background, military service, and previous work experience, may be requested. As noted in Table 16–2, each item in an application form should be relevant to consideration for employment. The application form is a highly useful tool for quick screening in numerous settings.

Letters of Recommendation

Another useful tool in the preliminary screening of applicants is the letter of recommendation (Arvey, 1979; Glueck, 1978). Such letters may be a unique source of detailed information about how the applicant has performed in the past, the quality of the applicant's relationships with peers, and so forth. Of course, such letters are not without their drawbacks. It is no secret that applicants solicit letters from those who they believe will say only positive things about them. Another possible drawback to letters of recommendation is the variance in the observational and writing skills of the letter writers. In research that employed application files for admission to graduate school in psychology, it was found that an applicant might variously be described as "analytically oriented, reserved, and highly motivated" or "free-spirited, imaginative, and outgoing" depending on the letter writer's perspective. As the authors of that study pointed out, "Although favorable recommendations may be intended in both cases, the details of and bases for such recommendations are varied" (Baxter et al., 1981, p. 300). Efforts to minimize the drawbacks inherent in the open-ended letter of recommendation have sometimes taken the form of "questionnaires of recommendation" wherein former employers, professors, and other letter writers respond to structured questions concerning the applicant's prior performance. Some questionnaires employ a forced-choice format designed to force respondents to make negative as well as positive statements about the applicant.

Although they were originally written to provide a prospective employer with an opinion about an applicant, some letters of reference now serve the function of an archival record—one that provides a glimpse of an unfortunate chapter of American history and the prevailing prejudices of an era. Winston (1996, 1998) documented how letters of reference written by prominent psychologists in the United States for Jewish psychology students and psychologists during the 1920s through the 1950s followed a common practice of identifying the job candidates as Jews. The letters went on to disclose whether or not, in the letter-writers' opinion, the candidate evidenced the "objectionable traits" thought to characterize Jews. These letters support a compelling argument that although anti-Semitism tends to be treated in American history as a problem from which European immigrants fled, negative stereotypes associated with being Jewish were very much a part of the cultural landscape in the United States.

Interviews

Interviews, be they individual or group in nature, provide an occasion for the face-to-face exchange of information. Like other interviews, the employment interview may fall anywhere on a continuum from highly structured, with uniform questions being asked to all, to highly unstructured, with the questions left largely to the interviewer's discretion. As with other interviews, too, the interviewer's biases and prejudices may creep into the evaluation and influence the outcome. Other factors, such as the order of interviewing, might also affect outcomes by reason of contrast effects. For example, an average applicant may appear better or less qualified depending on whether the preceding candidate was particularly poor or outstanding. Factors that may affect the outcome of an employment interview, according to Schmitt (1976), include the backgrounds, attitudes, motivations, perceptions, expectations, knowledge about the job, and interview behavior of both the interviewer and the interviewee. Situational factors, such as the nature of the job market, may also affect the outcome of the interview.

Portfolio Assessment

In the context of industrial/organizational assessment, portfolio assessment entails an evaluation of an individual's work sample for the purpose of making some screening, selection, classification, or placement decision. A video journalist applying for a position at a new television station may present a portfolio of video clips, including rehearsal footage and outtakes. An art director for a magazine may present a portfolio of art to a prospective employer, including material such as rough drafts and notes about how to solve a particular design-related problem. In portfolio assessment, the assessor may have the opportunity to (1) evaluate many work samples created by the assessee, (2) obtain some understanding of the assessee's work-related thought processes and habits through an analysis of the materials from rough draft to finished form, and (3) question the assessee further regarding various aspects of his or her work-related thinking and habits. The result may be a more complete picture of the prospective employee at work in the new setting than might otherwise be available.

Performance Tests

As its name implies, a performance test requires assessees to demonstrate certain skills or abilities under a specified set of circumstances. The typical objective of such an exercise is to obtain a job-related performance sample. If you have ever taken a word processing test as a prerequisite for employment, you have had firsthand experience with performance tests. Sometimes the line between performance tests and achievement and aptitude tests is blurred, as when the work sample required is to complete a standardized test of skill or ability. For example, the Seashore Bennett Stenographic Proficiency Test is a standardized measure of stenographic competence. The test materials include a recording in which a voice dictates a series of letters and manuscripts that the assessee must transcribe in shorthand and then type. The recorded directions provide a uniform clarity of voice and rate of dictation. Whether one views the test protocol as an achievement test, an aptitude test, or a performance sample is, in practice, up to the discretion of the test user.

One widely used instrument designed to measure clerical aptitude and skills is the Minnesota Clerical Test (MCT). The MCT comprises two subtests, Number Comparison and Name Comparison. Each subtest contains 200 items, with each item consisting of either a pair of names or a pair of numbers (depending upon the subtest) to be compared. For each item, the assessee's task is to check whether the two names (or numbers) in the pair are the same or different. A score is obtained by simply subtracting the number of incorrect responses from the number of correct ones. Because speed and accuracy in clerical work is important to so many employers, this deceptively simple test has been used for decades as an effective screening tool in the workplace (Dorcus & Jones, 1950; Ghiselli, 1973; Selover, 1949). Not only can it be administered and scored quickly and easily, but also the pattern of the testtakers' errors or omissions on this timed test may suggest whether the testtaker values speed over accuracy or vice versa.

More sophisticated varieties of performance assessment are regularly employed in the field of aviation in the training and evaluation of pilots (Kennedy et al., 1982), air traffic controllers (Ackerman & Kanfer, 1993), and others (Retzlaff & Gibertini, 1988). Kennedy et al. (1982) lauded commercially available video games for the extent to which they compare favorably with more conventional tests of psychomotor skills and cognition. Ackerman and Kanfer (1993) noted that computer simulations permit assessors to evaluate assessees' response to a standardized set of air traffic control tasks and to precisely monitor the time of response.

The kind of special equipment necessary for performance tests varies widely (Figure 16–3). For example, during World War II, the assessment staff of the Office of Strategic Services (OSS) selected American secret agents, saboteurs, propaganda experts, and other personnel for overseas assignments. In addition to interviews, personality tests, and other paper-and-pencil tests, OSS administered situational performance tests. Today, the Israelis, among other military powers, use similar methods. Tziner and Eden (1985) described experiments with three-person military crews performing military tasks in a military field setting. Individuals were assigned to the crews on the basis of levels of ability and motivation, and assignment by all possible combinations of these levels was varied in an effort to determine the optimal composition of a crew.

A commonly used performance test in the assessment of business leadership ability is a leaderless–group situation. Communication skills, problem-solving ability, the ability to cope with stress, and other skills can also be assessed economically by a group exercise in which the participants' task is to work together in the solution of some problem or the achievement of some goal. As group members interact, the assessors make judgments with respect to questions such as "Who is the leader?" and "What role do other members play in this group?" The answers to such questions will no doubt figure into

Figure 16–3
Games Psychologists Play

Psychologists have long recognized the value of gamelike situations in the process of evaluating prospective personnel. A task referred to as the "Manufacturing Problem" was used as part of the AT&T Management Progress Study conducted in 1957. The assessee's task here is to collaborate with others in buying parts and manufacturing a "product."

decisions concerning the individual assessee's future position in the organization. Another performance test frequently used to assess leadership or managerial ability is the "in-basket" technique. This technique simulates the way a manager or an executive deals with his or her in-basket filled with mail, memos, announcements, and various other notices and directives. Assessees are instructed that they have only a limited amount of time, usually two or three hours, to deal with all the items in the basket (more commonly, a manila envelope). Through posttest interviews and an examination of the way that the assessee handled the materials, assessors can make judgments concerning variables such as organizing and planning, problem solving, decision making, creativity, leadership, and written communication skills.

The assessment center A widely used tool in selection, classification, and placement is the **assessment center.** Although it sounds as if it might be a place, the term actually denotes an organizationally standardized procedure for evaluation involving multiple assessment techniques such as paper-and-pencil tests and situational performance tests. The assessment center concept had its origins in the writings of Henry Murray and his associates (1938). Assessment center activities were pioneered by military organizations both in the United States and abroad (Thornton & Byham, 1982). In 1956, the first application of the idea in an industrial setting occurred with the initiation of the Management Progress Study (MPS) at American Telephone and Telegraph (Bray, 1964). MPS was to be a longitudinal study that would follow the lives of over four hundred telephone company

Table 16–3
Original Management Progress Study Dimensions

Area	Dimension
Administrative skills	Organizing and planning—How effectively can this person organize work, and how well does he or she plan ahead?
	Decision making—How ready is this person to make decisions, and how good are the decisions made?
	Creativity—How likely is this person to solve a management problem in a novel way?
Interpersonal skills	Leadership skills—How effectively can this person lead a group to accomplish a task without arousing hostility?
	Oral communication skills—How well would this person present an oral report to a small conference group on a subject he or she knew well?
	Behavior flexibility—How readily can this person, when motivated, modify his or her behavior to reach a goal? How able is this person to change roles or style of behavior to accomplish objectives?
	Personal impact—How forceful and likable an early impression does this person make?
	Social objectivity—How free is this person from prejudices against racial, ethnic, socioeconomic, educational, and other social groups?
	Perceptions of threshold social cues—How readily does this person perceive minimal cues in the behavior of others?
Cognitive skills	General mental ability—How able is this person in the functions measured by tests of intelligence, scholastic aptitude, and learning ability?
	Range of interests—To what extent is this person interested in a variety of fields of activity such as science, politics, sports, music, art?
	Written communication skill—How well would this person compose a communicative and formally correct memorandum on a subject he or she knew well? How well written are memos and reports likely to be?
Stability of performance	Tolerance of uncertainty—To what extent will this person's work performance stand up under uncertain or unstructured conditions?
	Resistance to stress—To what extent will this person's work performance stand up in the face of personal stress?
Work motivation	Primacy of work—To what extent does this person find satisfactions from work more important than satisfactions from other areas of life?
	Inner work standards—To what extent will this person want to do a good job, even if a less good one is acceptable to the boss and others?
	Energy—How continuously can this person sustain a high level of work activity?
	Self-objectivity—How realistic a view does this person have of his or her own assets and liabilities, and how much insight into his or her own motives?
Career orientation	Need for advancement—To what extent does this person need to be promoted significantly earlier than his or her peers? To what extent are further promotions needed for career satisfaction?
	Need for security—How strongly does this person want a secure job?
	Ability to delay gratification—To what extent will this person be willing to wait patiently for advancement if confident advancement will come?
	Realism of expectations—To what extent do this person's expectations about his or her work life with the company conform to what is likely to be true?
	Bell System value orientation—To what extent has this person incorporated Bell System values such as service, friendliness, justice of company position on earnings, rates, wages?
Dependency	Need for superior approval—To what extent does this person need warmth and nurturant support from immediate supervisors?
	Need for peer approval—To what extent does this person need warmth and acceptance from peers and subordinates?
	Goal flexibility—To what extent is this person likely to reorient his or her life toward a different goal?

Source: Bray (1982)

management and nonmanagement personnel. Participants attended a 3½-day assessment center in which they were interviewed for two hours. They then took a number of paper-and-pencil tests designed to shed light on cognitive abilities and personality (for example, the School and College Ability Test and the Edwards Personal Preference Schedule), and participated in individual and group situational exercises (such as the in-basket test and a leaderless group). Additionally, projective tests such as the Thematic Apperception Test and the Sentence Completion Test were administered. All the data on each of the assessees were integrated at a meeting of the assessors, at which judgments on a number of dimensions were made. The dimensions, grouped by area, are listed in Table 16–3.

The use of the assessment center method has mushroomed, with an estimated two thousand or more business organizations relying on some form of it for selection, classification, placement, promotion, career training, and early identification of leadership potential (Gaugler et al., 1987). The method has been subject to numerous studies concerning its validity, and the consensus is that the method has much to recommend it (Cohen et al., 1977; Gaugler et al., 1987; Hunter & Hunter, 1984; McEvoy & Beatty, 1989; Schmitt et al., 1984). Perhaps the most critical question related to assessment centers is not *if* the assessment center method is valid but *why* it is valid (Klimoski & Brickner, 1987).

Physical Tests

A lifeguard who is visually impaired is seriously compromised in his or her ability to perform the job. A wine taster with damaged tastebuds is of little value to a vintner. An aircraft pilot who has lost the use of his arms . . . the point is clear: Physical requirements of a job must be taken into consideration when screening, selecting, classifying, and placing applicants. Depending on the specific requirements of the job, a number of physical subtests may be used. Thus, for example, for a job in which a number of components of vision are critical, a test of visual acuity might be administered along with tests of visual efficiency, stereopsis (distance/depth perception), and color blindness. General physical fitness is required in many jobs, such as in police work where successful candidates might one day have to chase a fleeing suspect on foot or defend themselves against a suspect resisting arrest. The tests used in assessing such fitness might include a complete physical examination, tests of physical strength, and a performance test that meets some determined criterion with respect to running speed and running agility. Tasks like vaulting some object, stepping through tires, and going through a window frame would be included to simulate running on difficult terrain.

In some instances, an employer's setting certain physical requirements for employment are so reasonable and so necessary that they would readily be upheld by any court if challenged. Other physical requirements for employment, however, may fall into a gray area. How reasonable is it, for example, for a municipal police or fire department to maintain height and weight standards or weight-lifting requirements? In general, the law favors physical standards that are both nondiscriminatory and job related. As we will see in the discussion of legal/ethical issues later in this chapter, exceptions do exist to this general rule.

Also included under the heading of physical tests are tests of sensory intactness/impairment, including tests to measure color blindness, visual acuity, visual depth perception, and auditory acuity. These types of tests are routinely employed in industrial settings in which the ability to perceive color or the possession of reasonably good eyesight or hearing is essential to the job. Additionally, physical techniques have been applied in the assessment of integrity and honesty, as is the case with the polygraph and drug testing.

Drug testing   Beyond concerns about traditional physical, emotional, and cognitive job requirements lies great concern about employee drug use. Personnel and human resource managers are increasingly seeking assurance that the people they hire, and the staff currently employed, do not and will not use illegal drugs. The dollar amounts vary by source, but estimates of corporate losses in the workplace that are due, directly or indirectly, to employee drug or alcohol use run into the tens of billions of dollars. Revenue may be lost because of injury to people or animals, damage to products and the environment, or employee absenteeism, tardiness, or sick leave. And no dollar amount can be attached to the tragic loss of life that may result from a drug- or alcohol-related mishap. For those reasons, testing for drug use is a growing practice in corporate America. It has been estimated that 40–50% of companies use drug testing in some form (West

& Ackerman, 1993), with large companies and industries more likely to test than small companies and service organizations. Companies that do drug testing most commonly test all applicants during the selection process and test actual employees only if drug use is suspected. Random drug testing is relatively unusual in private companies, although it is common in government agencies and in the military (Murphy & Thornton, 1992).

Methods of drug testing vary. One method, the Immunoassay Test, employs the subject's urine to determine the presence or absence of drugs in the body by identifying the metabolized by-products of the drug (metabolites). Although widely used in workplace settings, the test can be criticized for its inability to specify the precise amount of the drug that was taken, when it was taken, and which of several possible drugs in a particular category was taken. Further, there is no way to estimate the degree of impairment that occurred in response to the drug. The Gas Chromatography/Mass Spectrometry (GCMS) Test also examines metabolites in urine to determine the presence or absence of drugs, but it can more accurately specify which drug was used. GCMS technology cannot, however, pinpoint the time at which the drug was taken or the degree of impairment that occurred as a consequence.

Many employees object to drug testing as a condition of employment (Labig, 1992) and have argued that such testing violates their constitutional rights to privacy and freedom from unreasonable search and seizure. In the course of legal proceedings, a question that emerges frequently is the validity of drug testing. The consequences of **false positives** (an individual tests positively for drug use when in reality there has been no drug use) and **false negatives** (an individual tests negatively for drug use when in reality there has been drug use) in such cases can be momentous. A false positive may result in, among other things, the loss of one's livelihood. A false negative may result in an impaired person working in a position of responsibility and placing others at risk.

Modern laboratory techniques tend to be relatively accurate in detecting tell-tale metabolites. Error rates are generally well under 2% (West & Ackerman, 1993). However, laboratory techniques may not always be used correctly. By one estimate, fully 93% of laboratories that do drug testing fail to meet standards designed to reduce human error (Comer, 1993). Error may also occur in the interpretation of results. Metabolites may be identified accurately, but whether their origin was in the abuse of some illicit drug or in some over-the-counter medication cannot always be determined. To help prevent such confusion, administrators of the urine test typically ask the subject to compile a list of any medications currently being taken. However, not all subjects are willing or able to remember all medications they may have taken. Further, some employees are reluctant to report some prescription medications they may have taken to treat conditions to which any possible social stigma may be attached, such as depression or epilepsy. Additionally, some foods may also produce metabolites that mimic the metabolites of some illegal drugs. For example, metabolites of opiates will be detected following the subject's ingestion of (perfectly legal) poppy seeds (West & Ackerman, 1993).

Another question related to the validity of drug tests concerns the degree to which drugs identified through testing actually affect job performance. Some drugs leave the body very slowly. For example, a person may test positive for marijuana use up to a month after the last exposure to it. Thus, the residue of the drug remains long after any discernible impairment from having taken the drug. By contrast, cocaine leaves the body in only three days. It is possible for a habitual cocaine user to be off the drug for three days, be highly impaired as a result of cocaine withdrawal, yet still test negative for drug use. Thus, neither a positive nor a negative finding with regard to a drug test necessarily means that behavior has or has not been impaired by drug use (Comer, 1993).

An alternative to drug testing involves directly examining impairment using performance tests. For example, sophisticated video-game-style tests of coordination, judgment, and reaction time are available to compare current performance with baseline performance as established on earlier tests. The advantages of these performance tests over drug testing include a more direct assessment of impairment, fewer ethical concerns regarding invasion of privacy, and immediate information about impairment. The last advantage is particularly vital in preventing potentially impaired individuals from hurting themselves or others. Organizations using such electronic tests have reported benefits with regard to employee satisfaction and fewer accidents (Comer, 1993).

Productivity, Motivation, Attitude, and Culture

Beyond their use in pre-employment counseling and in the screening, selection, classification, and placement of personnel, tools of measurement are used to assess employee productivity, motivation, and job satisfaction, as well as sundry aspects of the work environment, including aspects of the organizational welfare.

Tests of Cognitive Ability

Selection decisions regarding personnel, as well as other types of selection decisions such as those regarding professional licensure or acceptance for academic training, are often based, at least in part, on performance on tests that tap acquired knowledge, as well as various cognitive skills and abilities. In general, cognitive-based tests are popular tools of selection because they have been shown to be valid predictors of future performance (Schmidt & Hunter, 1998). However, along with that impressive track record comes a dilemma with regard to diversity issues.

Personnel selection and diversity issues   The continued use of tests that tap primarily cognitive abilities and skills for screening, selection, classification, and placement has become controversial. This controversy stems from a well-documented body of evidence that points to consistent group differences on cognitive ability tests. For example, on average, Asians tend to score higher than Whites on mathematical and quantitative ability measures, while Whites score higher than Asians on measures of comprehension and verbal ability. On average, Whites also tend to score higher on cognitive ability tests than Blacks and Hispanics. Given that the test scores may differ on average by as much as one standard deviation (Sackett et al., 2001), such differences may carry a great impact in terms of who gets what job or who is admitted to an institution of higher learning; average differences between groups on tests of cognitive ability may contribute to limiting diversity in employment settings, in the professions, and in access to education and training.

It is in society's interest to promote diversity in employment settings, in the professions, and in access to education and training. Toward that end, diversity has, in the past, been encouraged by various means. One approach entailed the use of cut scores on tests defined on the basis of group membership. However, there has been a general trend away from efforts to promote diversity that entail preferential treatment to any group with regard to test scores. This trend is evident in legislation, court actions, and public referendums. For example, the Civil Rights Act of 1991 made it illegal for employers to adjust test scores as a function of group membership. In 1996, Proposition 209 was passed in California, prohibiting the use of group membership as a basis for any selection decision in that state. In that same year, a federal court ruled that race was not a relevant criterion in selecting university applicants (*Hopwood v. State of Texas*, 1996). In the state of Washington, voters approved legislation that banned the use of race as a criterion in college admissions, contracting, and hiring (Verhovek & Ayres, 1998).

How may diversity in the workplace and other settings be achieved while still using tests known to be good predictors of performance, and while not building in a preference for any group in the selection criteria? Although no one answer to this complex question is likely to be satisfactory to all concerned, there are jobs waiting to be filled and seats waiting to be occupied at educational and training institutions; some strategy for balancing the various interests must be found. Sackett et al. (2001) proposed that employers and other users of cognitive ability tests use video- and computer-based formats for administering such tests, as well as any other format that may minimize verbal content and the demand for testtakers' verbal skills and abilities. They also recommended other strategies such as greater reliance on relevant job or life experience as selection criteria. However, Sackett et al. (2001) also advised that "subgroup differences are not simply artifacts of paper-and-pencil technologies" (p. 316) and it is incumbent upon society at large to effectively address such extra-test issues.

Productivity

Productivity may be defined simply as output or value yielded relative to work effort made. The term is used here in its broadest sense, equally applicable to workers who produce products and workers who provide services. If a business endeavor is to succeed, monitoring output with the ultimate goal of maximizing output is essential. Measures of productivity help to define not only where a business is but also what it needs to do to get where it wants to be. A manufacturer of television sets, for example, might find that the people who are manufacturing the housing are working at optimal efficiency but that the people responsible for installing the picture tubes in the cabinets are working at one-half the expected efficiency. A productivity evaluation can help identify the factors responsible for the sagging performance of the picture-tube installers.

Using techniques such as supervisor ratings, interviews with employees, and planting undercover employees in the picture-tube workshop, management might determine what—or who in particular—is responsible for the unsatisfactory performance. Perhaps the most common method of evaluating worker productivity or performance is through the use of rating and ranking procedures by superiors in the organization. One type of ranking procedure used when large numbers of employees are being assessed is the **forced distribution technique.** This procedure involves distributing a predetermined number or percentage of assessees into various categories that describe performance (such as "unsatisfactory," "poor," "fair," "average," "good," "superior"). Another index of on-the-job performance is number of absences within a given period. It typically reflects more poorly on an employee if he or she is absent on, say, 20 separate occasions than on 20 consecutive dates as the result of illness. The **critical incidents technique** (Flanagan & Burns, 1955) involves the supervisor recording positive and negative employee behaviors. The supervisor catalogues the notations according to various categories (for example, "dependability; initiative") for ready reference when an evaluation needs to be made. There is some evidence to suggest that a honeymoon period of about three months or so occurs when a new worker starts a job and that supervisory ratings will more truly reflect the worker at the conclusion of that period (see Helmreich et al., 1986).

Peer ratings or evaluations made by other workers of the same level have proved to be a valuable method of identifying talent among employees. Although peers have a tendency to rate their counterparts higher than these people would be rated by superiors, the information obtained from the ratings and rankings of peers can be highly predictive of future performance. For example, one study involved 117 inexperienced life insurance agents who attended a three-week training class. At the conclusion of the course, the budding insurance agents were asked to list the three best people in their class with respect to each of 12 situations. From these data, a composite score for each of the 117

Table 16–4
Peer Ratings and Performance of Life Insurance Salespeople

	Job Tenure		Production	
	6 months	1 year	6 months	1 year
Peer rating	.18*	.29[†]	.29[†]	.30[†]
Age	.18*	.24[†]	.06	.09
Starting salary	.01	.03	.13	.26[†]
Final course grade	.02	.06	−.02	.02

Source: Mayfield (1972)

*$p = .05$ (one-tailed test)

[†]$p = .01$ (one-tailed test)

agents was obtained. After one year, these peer ratings and three other variables were correlated with job tenure (number of weeks on the job) and with production (number of dollars of insurance sold). As can be seen from Table 16–4, peer ratings had the highest validity in all of the categories. By contrast, a near zero correlation was obtained between final course grade and all categories.

In many organizations, people work in teams. In an organizational or workplace context, a **team** may be defined as two or more people who interact interdependently toward a common and valued goal, who have each been assigned specific roles or functions to perform. For a sales team, the division of labor may simply reflect division of sales territories. In the creation of complicated software, the division of labor may involve the assignment of tasks that are too complicated for any one individual. The operation of a cruise ship or military vessel requires a trained team due to the multitude of things that must be done if the ship is to sail. To achieve greater productivity, organizations ask questions such as "What does the team know?" and "How does the collective knowledge of the team differ qualitatively from the individual knowledge and expertise of each of the team members?" Addressing these and related questions, a literature exploring different ways of measuring team knowledge has begun to emerge (see, for example, Cannon-Bowers et al., 1998; Cooke et al., 2000; Salas et al., 1998).

Motivation

Why do some people skip lunch, work overtime, and take home work nightly, whereas others strive to do as little as possible and live a life of leisure at work? At a practical level, light may be shed on such questions using assessment instruments that tap the values of the assessee. Dealing with a population of unskilled personnel may require specially devised techniques. Champagne (1969) responded to the challenge of knowing little about what might appeal to rural, unskilled people in attempts to attract them to work, so he devised a motivational questionnaire. As illustrated by the three items in Figure 16–4, the questionnaire used a paired comparison (forced-choice) format that required the subject to make choices relative to 12 factors used by companies to entice employment applications: fair pay, steady job, vacations and holidays with pay, job extras such as pensions and sick benefits, a fair boss, interesting work, good working conditions, chance for promotion, a job close to home, working with friends and neighbors, nice people to work with, and praise for good work. The job-seeking factor found to be most important in Champagne's sample of 349 male and female, rural, unskilled subjects was "steady job." The least important factor was found to be "working with friends and neighbors." "Praise for good work" was a close runner-up for being least in importance. In interpreting the findings, Champagne cautioned that "the factors reported here relate to the job-seeking behavior of the unskilled and are not measures of how to retain and

Vacations and holidays with pay . . .   OR   

. . . Job extras such as pensions, sick benefits, etc. □

A job close to home . . .   OR   

. . . A fair boss □

Working with friends and neighbors . . .   OR   

. . . chance for a promotion □

Figure 16–4
Studying Values with the Unskilled

Champagne (1969) used test items such as those pictured in a recruitment study with a rural, unskilled population.

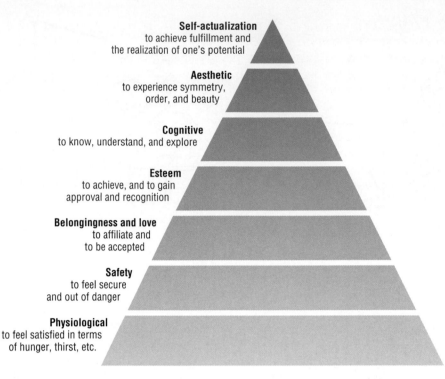

Figure 16–5
Maslow's Hierarchy of Needs (adapted from Maslow, 1970)

motivate the unskilled once employed. . . . What prompts a person to accept a job is not necessarily the same as what prompts a person to retain a job or do well in it" (p. 268).

On a theoretical level, an abundance of theories seek to delineate the specific needs, attitudes, social influences, and other factors that might account for differences in motivation. For example, Vroom (1964) proposed an expectancy theory of motivation, which essentially holds that employees expend energy in ways designed to achieve the outcome they want; the greater the expectancy that an action will achieve a certain outcome, the more energy that will be expended to achieve that outcome. Maslow (1943, 1970) constructed a theoretical hierarchy of human needs (Figure 16–5) and proposed that as one category of need is met, people move on to satisfy the next category of need. Employers who subscribe to Maslow's theory would seek to identify (1) the need level the job requires of the employee and (2) the need level the prospective employee is at. Alderfer (1972) proposed an alternative need theory of motivation, one that was not hierarchical in nature. Whereas Maslow saw the satisfaction of one need leading to the satisfaction of the next need in the hierarchy, Alderfer proposed that once a need was satisfied it was possible that the organism strove to satisfy it to an even greater degree. The Alderfer theory also provides that frustrating one need might lead to channeling energy into the achievement of a need at another level.

In a widely cited program that undertook to define the characteristics of achievement motivation, McClelland (1961) used as his measure of that motivation stories written under special instructions about TAT and TAT-like pictures. McClelland described the individual with a high need for achievement as one who prefers a task that is not too simple or extremely difficult, something with moderate as opposed to extreme risks. A situation with little or no risk will not lead to feelings of accomplishment if the individual succeeds. On the other hand, an extremely high-risk situation may not lead to feelings of accomplishment because of the high probability of failure. Persons with high need for achievement enjoy taking responsibility for their actions because they desire the credit and recognition for their accomplishments. Such individuals also desire information about their performance to constantly improve their output. Other researchers also used TAT-like pictures and their own specially devised scoring systems to study related areas of human motivation such as the fear of failure (Birney et al., 1969; Cohen & Houston, 1975; Cohen & Parker, 1974; Cohen & Teevan, 1974, 1975; Cohen et al., 1975) and the fear of success (Horner, 1973).

Motivation may be conceptualized as stemming from incentives that are either primarily internal or primarily external in origin. Another way of stating this is to speak of **intrinsic motivation** (where the primary force driving the individual stems from things such as the individual's involvement in work or satisfaction with work products) as opposed to **extrinsic motivation** (where the primary force driving the individual stems from rewards, such as salary and bonuses, or from constraints, such as job loss). A scale designed to assess aspects of intrinsic and extrinsic motivation is the Work Preference Inventory (WPI; Amabile et al., 1994). The WPI contains 30 items rated on a 4-point scale based on how much the testtaker believes the item to be self-descriptive. Factor analysis indicates that the test does appear to tap two distinct factors, intrinsic and extrinsic motivation. Each of these two factors may be divided into two subfactors. The intrinsic motivation factor may be divided into one subfactor that has to do with the challenge of the work tasks and another that has to do with the enjoyment of work. The extrinsic motivation factor may be divided into one subfactor that has to do with compensation for work and another that has to do with external influences (such as recognition by others of one's work). The WPI correlates in the predicted direction with behavioral and other questionnaire measures of motivation, as well as with measures of vocational interest, personality, and creativity. The test is internally consistent (the reliability coefficient was .70 for the extrinsic scale and .75 for the intrinsic scale) and evidences good test-retest reliability (.80 for the extrinsic scale, .89 for the intrinsic scale over a six-month interval).

In some instances, it seems as if the motivation to perform a particular job becomes markedly reduced as compared to previous levels. Such is the case with a phenomenon referred to as "burnout."

Burnout and its measurement   **Burnout** may be defined as "a psychological syndrome of emotional exhaustion, depersonalization, and reduced personal accomplishment that can occur among individuals who work with other people in some capacity" (Maslach et al., 1997, p. 192). In this definition, *emotional exhaustion* refers to an inability to give of oneself emotionally to others, and *depersonalization* refers to distancing other people, and even developing cynical attitudes toward them. The potential consequences of burnout range from a deterioration in service provided, to absenteeism and job turnover. The potential effects of burnout on a worker suffering from it range from insomnia to alcohol and drug use.

The most widely used measure of burnout is the Maslach Burnout Inventory, Third Edition (Maslach et al., 1996). Developed by Christina Maslach and her colleagues, this test contains 22 items divided into 3 subscales: Emotional Exhaustion (9 items), Depersonalization (5 items), and Personal Accomplishment (8 items). Testtakers respond to items like, "I don't really care what happens to some recipients" ("recipients" referring to people for whom the testtaker provides care) on a scale ranging from 0 ("never") to 6 ("every day"). The test form is labeled "MBI Human Services Survey" in order to minimize the reactive effect of the respondent's personal beliefs on the subject of burnout. To distinguish it from two other forms of the MBI subsequently developed, the original

MBI is cited as "Maslach Burnout Inventory—Human Services Survey" (MBI-HSS). One version of the MBI, referred to as the "MBI Educators Survey" (MBI-ES), is used to assess burnout in the teaching profession. This is basically the same as the MBI-HSS with the word *student* substituted for *recipient*. The other version, designed for use with people in occupations other than human services, is the MBI-General Survey (MBI-GS). Items from the original scale were modified so that they would have broad applicability. For example, an item from the Exhaustion scale, "Working with people all day is really a strain for me," was changed to "Working all day is really a strain for me." The MBI manual contains data relevant to the psychometric soundness of the tests. Included is a discussion of discriminant validity in which burnout is conceptually distinguished from similar concepts such as depression and job dissatisfaction.

Attitude

An **attitude** may be formally defined as a presumably learned disposition to react in some characteristic manner to a particular stimulus. The stimulus may be an object, a group, an institution—virtually anything. Later in this chapter, we will see how attitudes toward goods and services are measured. More immediately, however, we focus on workplace-related attitudes. Although attitudes do not necessarily predict behavior (Tittle & Hill, 1967; Wicker, 1969), there has been great interest in measuring the attitudes of employers and employees toward each other, as well as toward numerous variables in the workplace. Much research has been done, for example, on the subject of job satisfaction.

Job satisfaction Compared with dissatisfied workers, satisfied workers in the workplace are believed to be more productive (Petty et al., 1984), more consistent in work output (Locke, 1976), less likely to complain (Burke, 1970; Locke, 1976), and less likely to be absent from work or to be replaced (Herzberg et al., 1957; Vroom, 1964). Although these assumptions are somewhat controversial (Iaffaldano & Muchinsky, 1985) and should probably be considered on a case-by-case basis, employers, employees, researchers, and consultants have maintained a long-standing interest in the measurement of job satisfaction. Traditionally, **job satisfaction** has been defined as "a pleasurable or positive emotional state resulting from the appraisal of one's job or job experiences" (Locke, 1976, p. 300).

One diagnostic measure of job satisfaction (or in this case, *dis*satisfaction) entails video-recording an employee at work and then playing back the video for the employee via a computer-assisted setup (Johansson & Forsman, 2001). The employee clicks on virtual controls to indicate when an unsatisfactory situation arises, and a window of questions automatically opens. According to data from studies of manual workers, analysis of the responses can be useful in creating a more satisfactory work environment (Johansson & Forsman, 2001).

Of course, contemporary measures of job satisfaction may focus on other elements of the job including cognitive evaluations of the work (Organ & Near, 1985) and the work schedule (Baltes et al., 1999; Barnett & Gareis, 2000), perceived sources of stress (Brown & Peterson, 1993; Vagg & Spielberger, 1998), various aspects of well-being (Daniels, 2000), and mismatches between an employee's cultural background and the prevailing organizational culture (Aycan et al., 2000; Early et al., 1999; Parkes et al., 2001).

In addition to job satisfaction, other job-related constructs that have attracted the attention of theorists and assessment professionals include job involvement, work centrality, organizational socialization, and organizational commitment (Caught et al., 2000; Nystedt et al., 1999; Paullay et al., 1994; Taormina & Bauer, 2000). Before focusing on the

Table 16-5

Consequences of Organizational Commitment Level for Individual Employees and the Organization

| | Level of Organizational Commitment | | |
	Low	Moderate	High
The Individual Employee	Potentially positive consequences for opportunity for expression of originality and innovation, but an overall negative effect on career advancement opportunities	Enhanced feeling of belongingness and security, along with doubts about the opportunity for advancement	Greater opportunity for advancement and compensation for efforts, along with less opportunity for personal growth and potential for stress in family relationships
The Organization	Absenteeism, tardiness, workforce turnover, and poor quality of work	As compared with low commitment, less absenteeism, tardiness, turnover, and better quality of work, as well as increased level of job satisfaction	Potential for high productivity, but sometimes accompanied by lack of critical/ethical review of employee behavior and by reduced organizational flexibility

broader construct of organizational culture, let's briefly take a closer look at the concept of organizational commitment.

Organizational commitment Organizational commitment has been defined as "the strength of an individual's identification with and involvement in a particular organization" (Porter et al., 1974, p. 604). This "strength" has been conceptualized and measured in ways that emphasize both its attitudinal and behavioral components (Mathieu & Zajac, 1990). In general, it refers to a person's feelings of loyalty to, identification with, and involvement in an organization. Presumed correlates of high and low organizational commitment as observed by Randall (1987) are summarized in Table 16–5. The most widely used measure of this construct is the Organizational Commitment Questionnaire (OCQ; Porter et al., 1974), a 15-item Likert scale, wherein respondents express their commitment-related attitudes toward an organization. Despite its widespread use for over a quarter-century, however, there is relatively little evidence to support its construct validity (Bozeman & Perrewe, 2001). The viability of alternative measures, such as a multidimensional instrument developed Allen & Meyer (1990), has been explored in several investigations (Dunham et al., 1994).

Organizational Culture

Organizational culture, or corporate culture, as it is known when applied to a company or corporation, has been defined in many ways. For our purposes, we will define **organizational culture** after Cohen (2001) as the totality of socially transmitted behavior patterns characteristic of a particular organization or company, including the structure of the organization and the roles within it, the leadership style, the prevailing values, norms, sanctions, and support mechanisms, as well as the past traditions and folklore, methods of enculturation, and characteristic ways of interacting with people and institutions outside of the culture (such as customers, suppliers, the competition, government agencies, and the general public).

Much like different places at different times throughout history, organizations and corporations have developed distinctive cultures. They have distinctive ceremonies, rights, and privileges—formal as well as informal—tied to success and advancement, as well as various types of sanctions tied to failure (Trice & Beyer, 1984). Organizational cultures have observable artifacts, which may be in the form of an annual report or a

Assessment of Corporate and Organizational Culture

Corporations and other organizations have shown growing interest in self-examination and self-improvement. The Discussion of Organizational Culture (DOC; Cohen, 2001) was devised to assist in those efforts. This interview and discussion guide, designed for administration by a trained interviewer or focus-group moderator, is divided into 10 discussion topics. The questions under each discussion topic explore various aspects of organizational culture. Beginning with "First Impressions" and proceeding through other topics that tap content related to the physical space, prevailing values, and other areas, the objective is to develop a sense of what is unique about the culture at a particular company or organization. Diagnostic insights useful in determining where and how the corporate or organizational culture may be improved can be derived from such data. Space limitations preclude the publication of all ten parts of this comprehensive discussion guide. However, a sense of the types of questions raised for discussion can be gleaned from just the first few parts, reprinted below.

Discussion of Organizational Culture (DOC; Cohen, 2001)*

I. First Impressions

1. What does it mean to be an employee of this corporation? (*Note:* Substitute terminology as appropriate throughout. For example, this question might be rephrased as "What does it mean to be a volunteer at this organization?" or "What does it mean to be an 'IBMer'?"

2. a. How is working here the same as working anyplace else?

   b. How is working here different from working anyplace else?

   c. What makes working here special?

3. a. How does working here make you feel part of a team?

   b. How does working here let you shine as an individual?

4. a. What is obvious about this company to any visitor who has ever taken a tour of it?

   b. What is obvious about this company only to you?

5. In general, how would you describe the compatibility of the fit between personnel at this company and the jobs they are assigned to do?

   a. How much role ambiguity exists in job descriptions?

   b. If such role ambiguity exists, how do you and others deal with it?

II. The Physical Space

1. In general terms, describe the physical space of this company.

2. Comment specifically on the physical space with reference to:

   a. the grounds

   b. parking spaces

videotape of the office Christmas party. Organizational cultures also typically have a set of core values or beliefs that guide the actions taken by the organization, as well as the direction in which it moves.

Just as the term "culture" is traditionally applied to a group of people who share a particular way of life, the term "organizational culture" applies to a "way of work." An organizational culture provides a way of coping with internal and external challenges and demands. And just as conflicts between ways of thinking and doing things can cause conflicts between groups of people, so conflicts between organizational cultures may develop. Such conflicts are perhaps most evident when a company with one type of corporate culture acquires or merges with a company that has a very different corporate culture (Brannen & Salk, 2000; Veiga et al., 2000). Any effort to remedy such a clash in corporate cultures must be preceded by sober study and understanding of the cultures involved.

Perhaps because the concept of organizational culture is so multifaceted, obtaining a measure of it is no simple feat. To appreciate just how complex the task of describing an organizational culture is, consider how you would describe any other type of culture— American culture, NASCAR culture, or antiquing culture.

c. the general "feel" of the exteriors and interiors

d. the offices

e. the dining areas

f. the restrooms

g. the storage facilities

h. other aspects of the physical space

3. a. Overall, what works about the physical space?

b. What does not work about it, and how can it be improved?

4. What does the way that space is laid out here tell you about this company?

III. Corporate Structure and Roles

1. Describe the administrative structure of this company, including a brief description of who reports to whom.

   a. What works about this structure?

   b. What does not work about structure?

   c. What is unique about this structure?

   d. What does this structure tell you about this company?

2. Describe the roles associated with key job titles in the organizational structure.

   a. Is there ambiguity in roles, or do employees have a clear idea of their function in the company?

b. Are there any roles within the company that seem antiquated or not necessary?

c. Are there any roles within the company that need to be created? strengthened? better defined?

d. Describe your own role in the company and how you fit into the "grand scheme" of things.

e. How might your role be improved for your own personal benefit?

f. How might your role be improved for the benefit of the company?

3. What can one tell about this company by analyzing

   a. its annual reports

   b. its company records

   c. the type of information that it makes public

   d. the type of information it maintains as private

   e. the products or services it provides

   f. the way it provides those products or services

   g. the corporate vision as articulated by senior management

As a qualitative research consultant to many companies, the senior author of this textbook was presented with the challenge of assessing several organizational cultures. Because no satisfactory measure existed for conducting such an assessment, he created an instrument to do so; that instrument is the subject of this chapter's *Everyday Psychometrics*.

Other Applications of Assessment

Psychometric expertise is applied in a wide variety of industrial, organizational, and business-related settings. For example, experimental and engineering psychologists use a variety of assessment tools in their ergonomic (work-related) and human factors research, as they help develop the plans from everything from household items (Hsu & Peng, 1993) to components for automobiles (Chira-Chavala & Yoo, 1994) and aircraft (Begault, 1993). These researchers may use custom-designed measurement instruments, standardized tests, or both in their efforts to better understand human response to specific equipment or instrumentation in a particular work environment.

Another business-related area where tests and other tools of assessment are used extensively is consumer psychology.

Consumer Psychology

Consumer psychology is that branch of social psychology that deals primarily with the development, advertising, and marketing of products and services. As is true of almost all other specialty areas in psychology, some consumer psychologists work exclusively in academia, some work in applied settings, and many do both (Tybout & Artz, 1994). In both applied and research studies, consumer psychologists can be found working closely with professionals in fields such as marketing and advertising to help answer questions such as the following:

- Does a market exist for this new product?
- Does a market exist for this new use of an existing product?
- Exactly who, with respect to age, sex, race, social class, and other demographic variables, constitutes the market for this product?
- How can the targeted consumer population cost effectively be made aware of this product?
- How can the targeted consumer population most cost effectively be persuaded to purchase this product?
- What is the best way to package this product?[1]

One area of interest shared by the consumer psychologist and psychologists in other specialty areas is the measurement of attitudes; for the consumer psychologist, however, the attitude of interest might be one toward a particular product or concept.

The Measurement of Attitudes

Attitudes formed about products, services, or brand names are a frequent focus of interest in consumer attitude research. Attitude is typically measured by self-report, using tests and questionnaires. A limitation of this approach is that people differ in their ability to be introspective and in their level of self-awareness. People also differ in the extent to which they are willing to be candid about their attitudes. In some instances, the use of an attitude measure may, in essence, create an attitude where none existed before; in such studies, the attitude being measured may be viewed as an artifact of the measurement procedure (Sandelands & Larson, 1985).

Questionnaires and other self-report instruments designed to measure consumer attitudes are developed in ways similar to those previously described for psychological tests in general (see Chapter 7). A more detailed description of the preparation of measures of attitude can be found in the now-classic work *The Measurement of Attitude* (Thurstone & Chave, 1929). A monograph entitled "A Technique for the Measurement of Attitudes" (Likert, 1932) provided researchers with a simple procedure for constructing an instrument for measuring attitudes. Essentially, this procedure consists of listing statements (either favorable or unfavorable) that reflect a particular attitude. These statements are then administered to a group of respondents whose responses are analyzed to identify the most discriminating statements—items that best discriminate people at different points on the hypothetical continuum—which are then included in the final

---

1. Questions concerning packaging and how to make a product stand out on the shelf have been referred to as issues of "shelf-esteem" by consumer psychologists with a sense of humor.

scale. Each statement included in the final scale is accompanied by a 5-point continuum of alternative responses that may range, for example, from "strongly agree" to "strongly disagree." Scoring is accomplished by assigning numerical weights of 1 through 5 to each category such that 5 represents the strongest favorable response and 1 reflects the least favorable response.

Measures of attitude found in the psychological literature run the gamut from instruments devised solely for research and testing of academic, theoretical formulations, to scales with wide-ranging, real-world applications. In the latter context, we might find sophisticated industrial/organizational measures designed to gauge workers' attitudes toward their work, or scales designed to measure the general public's attitudes toward some politician or issue. The Self-Help Agency Satisfaction Scale, for example, designed to gauge self-help agency clients' satisfaction with aspects of the support they receive (Segal et al., 2000), is representative of measures designed to measure consumer satisfaction with a product or service. Attitude scales with applied utility may also be found in the educational psychology literature—consider, for example, measures such as the Study Attitudes and Methods Survey (a scale designed to assess study habits) and the Minnesota Teacher Attitude Survey (a scale designed to assess student-teacher relations).

To answer questions such as those posed at the beginning of this section, consumer psychologists rely on other methods, used individually or in combination with each other, such as surveys, motivation research, and behavioral observation.

Surveys   In consumer psychology, a **survey** is a fixed list of questions administered to a selected sample of persons for the purpose of learning about consumers' attitudes, beliefs, opinions, and/or behavior with regard to the targeted products, services, or advertising. There are many different ways to conduct a survey, and these various methods all have specific pros and cons in terms of study design and data interpretation (Johnson et al., 2000; Lavrakas, 1998; Massey, 2000; Schwartz et al., 1998; Visser et al., 2000). One specialized type of survey, called a **poll,** is much like an instrument to record votes, and usually contains questions that can be answered with a simple "yes-no" or "for-against" type of response. Politicians, news organizations, and special interest organizations may retain researchers who conduct polls (pollsters) for the purpose of gauging public opinion about controversial issues.

Surveys and polls may be conducted by means of face-to-face, online, and telephone interviews, as well as by mail. The personal interaction of the face-to-face interview helps ensure that questions are understood and adequate clarification of queries is provided. Another advantage of this survey method is the ability to present interviewees with stimuli (such as products) that they can hold in their hands and evaluate. However, the face-to-face approach may also introduce a source of bias into the study as some respondents act to manage favorable impressions or seek to provide responses they believe the interviewer would like to hear. The face-to-face approach may not be the best when the topic being discussed is particularly sensitive, or when responses may be embarrassing or otherwise place the respondent in a bad light (Midanik et al., 2001). The face-to-face approach is also labor-intensive and therefore can be quite costly when it comes to selecting, training, and employing interviewers.

Surveying by means of a face-to-face interview is a very common method of survey research, and it can be conducted almost anywhere—on a commuter bus or ferry, at a ball game, or near an election polling station. A common site for face-to-face survey research on consumer products is a shopping mall; "mall intercept studies" (as they are called) can be conducted by interviewers with clipboards who approach shoppers. The shopper may be asked to participate in a survey by answering some questions right then and there or may be led to a booth or room where a more extended interview takes place. Another face-to-face survey method, this one more popular with political pollsters, is the door-to-door approach; here an entire neighborhood may be polled by knocking on the door at individual households and soliciting responses to the questionnaire.

Online, telephone, and mail surveys do not necessarily require personal contact between the researcher and respondent and may, in many instances, reduce the biases associated with personal interaction. Further, survey methods conducted in the absence of face-to-face interaction tend to be more cost-effective due to automation of process components, the need for fewer personnel and less training, and the possibility of executing the entire study from a central location. The online survey holds great potential due to its easy access and feedback potential (Kaye & Johnson, 1999) and can be particularly useful for learning about various aspects of online behavior such as purchasing (Li et al., 1999) and teamwork (Levesque et al., 2001), as well as self-improvement (Mueller et al., 2000) and deviant online behavior (Greenfield, 1999; Houston et al., 2001; Young et al., 1999). However, unsolicited online surveys are viewed by many as unwanted e-mail or "spam," and such perceptions may result not only in low response rates, but in a sense that one's privacy has been violated (Cho & LaRose, 1999). Researchers may also feel a certain degree of doubt regarding whether or not respondents actually are who they say they are; in this regard, there is no substitute for a face-to-face interview complete with identity verification.

The telephone survey offers a number of advantages, but it does suffer from some limitations. Generally, the amount of information that can be obtained by telephone is less than that which can be obtained by personal interview or mail. It is not possible to show respondents visual stimuli over the phone. In addition, bias may be introduced if telephone directories are used for identifying respondents. As many as 40 percent of all telephones in some cities are not listed. A partial solution to this last problem is random-digit dialing, a procedure that randomly changes the last one or two digits of a telephone number taken from a directory. Use of this process generally yields contacts with households that have unlisted telephone numbers, as well as those with listed numbers. Of course, the reason many people obtain unlisted numbers in the first place is that they do not want to be bothered with phone solicitations. And this speaks to a key disadvantage of phone surveys: They are viewed by many as an unwelcome annoyance and invasion of privacy.

A mail survey may be the most appropriate survey method when the survey questionnaire is particularly long and will require some time to complete. In general, mail surveys tend to be relatively low in cost, since they do not require the services of a trained interviewer and can provide large amounts of information. They are also well suited for obtaining information about which respondents may be sensitive or shy in a face-to-face or even a telephone interview. They are ideal for posing questions that require the use of records or consultation with others (such as family members) for an answer. Note also that much of what we say about mail surveys also applies to electronic mail surveys or surveys conducted by means of fax machines.

The major disadvantages of mail questionnaires are (1) the possibility of no response at all from the intended recipient of the survey (for whatever reason—the survey was never delivered, or it was thrown out as junk mail as soon as it arrived); (2) the possibility of response from someone (perhaps a family member) who was not the intended recipient of the survey; and (3) the possibility of a late—and hence useless for tabulation purposes—response. If large numbers of people fail to respond to a mail questionnaire, it is impossible to determine whether those individuals who did respond are representative of those who did not. People may not respond to a mail questionnaire for many different reasons; and various techniques, ranging from incentives to follow-up mailings, have been suggested for dealing with various types of nonresponse (Furse & Stewart, 1984).

It is possible to combine the various survey methods to obtain the advantages of each. For example, the survey researcher might mail a lengthy questionnaire to potential respondents, then obtain responses by telephone. Alternatively, those individuals not returning their responses by mail might be contacted by telephone or in person.

Many commercial research firms maintain a list of a large number of people or families who have agreed to respond to questionnaires that are sent to them; the people who make up this list are referred to as a **consumer panel.** In return for their participation, panel members may receive incentives such as cash and free samples of all the products about which they are asked to respond in surveys. One special type of panel is called a **diary panel.** Respondents must keep detailed records of their behavior (for example, keeping a record of products they purchased, use of coupons, radio stations they listened to while driving to and from work, or what newspapers and magazines they read). Specialized panels monitor general product or advertising awareness, attitudes, and opinions on social issues, as well as a variety of other variables.

Survey research may employ a wide variety of item types. One approach to item-writing, particularly popular for surveys administered in writing, is referred to as the **semantic differential technique** (Osgood et al., 1957). Originally developed as a clinical tool for defining the meaning of concepts and relating concepts to one another in a "semantic space," the technique entails graphically placing a pair of bipolar adjectives (such as good/bad or strong/weak) on a 7-point scale such as this one:

GOOD _____ /_____ /_____ /_____ /_____ /_____ /_____ BAD

Respondents are instructed to place a mark on this continuum that corresponds to their judgment or rating. In research involving certain consumer applications, the bipolar adjectives may be replaced by descriptive expressions more consistent with the research objectives (such as "just another drink" at one end of the rating continuum and "a very special beverage" at the other).

As with any research, care must be exercised when interpreting the results of a survey. Both the quantity and the quality of the data may vary from survey to survey. Response rates may differ, questions may be asked in different forms, and data collection procedures may vary from one survey to another (Henry, 1984). Ultimately, the utility of any conclusions rests on the integrity of the data and the analytic procedures used. Some guidelines for designing survey research are presented in Cohen (2002).

Occasions arise when research questions cannot be answered through a survey or a poll; consumers may be unable or unwilling to cooperate. As an example of an inability to cooperate, consider the hypothetical case of "Ralph," who smokes a hypothetical brand of cigarettes we will call "Cowboy." When asked why he chooses to smoke "Cowboy" brand cigarettes, Ralph might reply "taste." It may be the case, however, that Ralph began smoking "Cowboy" because the advertising for this brand appealed to Ralph's image of himself as an independent, macho type. It matters not that Ralph is employed as a clerk for a dry cleaner. Consumers may also be unwilling or reluctant to respond to some survey or poll questions. Suppose, for example, that the manufacturers of Cowboy cigarettes wished to know where on the product's packaging the Surgeon General's warning could be placed so that it would be least likely to be read. How many consumers would be willing to entertain such a question? Indeed, what would even posing such a question do for the public image of the product? It can be seen that if this hypothetical company was interested in obtaining an answer to such a question, it would have to do so through other means, such as motivation research.

Motivation Research Methods

Motivation research is so named because it typically involves analyzing motives for consumer behavior and attitudes. **Motivation research methods** include individual interviews and focus groups, two qualitative research methods used to examine in depth the reactions of consumers representative of the group of people who use a particular product or service. Unlike quantitative research, which typically involves large numbers of subjects and elaborate statistical analyses, qualitative research typically involves few respondents and little or no statistical analyses; the emphasis in the latter type of research is not on quantity (of subjects or of data) but on the qualities of whatever is under study. Qualitative research often provides the data from which to develop hypotheses that may then be tested with larger numbers of consumers. Qualitative research also has diagnostic value. The best way to obtain highly detailed information about what a consumer likes and dislikes about a product, a store, or an advertisement is to use qualitative research.

A **focus group** is a group interview led by a trained, independent moderator who, ideally, has a knowledge of group-discussion facilitation techniques and group dynamics.[2] As their name implies, focus groups are designed to focus group discussion on something—such as a particular commercial, a concept for a new product, or packaging for a new product. Focus groups have examined everything from the choice to purchase organically grown rather than conventionally grown produce (Hammitt, 1990) to issues surrounding the purchase of condoms by college students (Mays et al., 1993).

Focus groups usually consist of 6 to 12 participants who may have been recruited off the floor of a shopping mall or may have been selected in advance to meet some preset qualifications for participation in the group; the usual objective here is to have the members of the group represent in some way the population of targeted consumers for the product or service. Thus, for example, only beer drinkers (defined, for example, as males who drink at least two six-packs per week and females who drink at least one six-pack per week) might be solicited for participation in a focus group designed to explore one or various attributes of a new brand of beer—including such variables as its taste, its packaging, its advertising, and its "bar call," this last phrase being an industry term that refers to the ease with which one could order the brew in a bar. Because of the high costs associated with introducing a new product and advertising a new or established product, professionally conducted focus groups, complete with a representative sampling of the targeted consumer population, are a valuable tool in market research.

Depending on the requirements of the moderator's client (an advertiser, a manufacturer, etc.), the group discussion can be relatively structured (with a number of points to be covered) or relatively unstructured (with few points to be covered exhaustively). After establishing a rapport with the group, the moderator may, for example, show some advertising or a product to the group and then pose a general question (such as "What did you think of the beer commercial?") to be followed up by more specific kinds of questions (such as "Were the people in that commercial the kind of people *you* would like to have a beer with?"). The responses of the group members may build on those of other group members, and the result of the free-flowing discussion may be new information, new perspectives, or some previously overlooked problems with the advertising or product.

Focus groups typically last from one to two hours and are usually conducted in rooms (either conference rooms or living rooms) equipped with one-way mirrors (from which the client's staff may observe the proceedings) and audio or video equipment so that a record of the group session will be preserved. Aside from being an active listener and an individual who is careful not to suggest answers to questions or draw conclu-

---

2. Focus-group moderators vary greatly in training and experience (McDonald, 1993). Ideally, a focus-group moderator should be independent so that he or she can dispassionately discuss the topics with some distance and perspective. However, some advertising agencies maintain an in-house focus-group moderator staff to test the advertising produced by the agency. Critics of this practice have likened the process to assigning wolves to guard the henhouse.

sions for the respondents, the moderator's duties include (1) following a discussion guide and keeping the discussion on the topic; (2) drawing out silent group members so that everyone is heard from; (3) limiting the response time of group members who might dominate the group discussion; and (4) writing a report that provides not only a summary of the group discussion but also offers psychological or marketing insights to the client. In recent years researchers have experimented with computer equipment in focus groups so that second-by-second reaction to stimulus materials such as commercials can be monitored. Cohen described the advantages (1985) and limitations (1987) of a technique whereby respondents watching television commercials pressed a calculatorlike keypad to indicate how positive or negative they were feeling on a moment-to-moment basis while watching television. The response could then be visually displayed as a graph and played back for the respondent, who could be asked about the reasons for the spontaneous response.

Focus groups are widely employed in consumer research for varied reasons, such as:

1. to generate hypotheses that can be further tested quantitatively
2. to generate information for designing or modifying consumer questionnaires
3. to provide general background information about a product category
4. to get impressions on new product concepts for which little information is available
5. to obtain new ideas about older products
6. to generate ideas for product development or names for existing products
7. to interpret the results of previously obtained quantitative results

In general, the focus group is a highly useful technique for exploratory research, a technique that can provide a valuable springboard to more comprehensive quantitative studies. Because so few respondents are typically involved in such groups, the findings from them cannot automatically be thought of as representative of the larger population. Still, many a client (including advertising agency creative staff) has received inspiration from the words spoken by ordinary consumers on the other side of a one-way mirror.

Although widely used in consumer research, the focus group is a qualitative research tool also used by researchers with varied objectives. Focus groups have been used to explore such topics as adolescent perceptions of smoking imagery in films (McCool et al., 2001), sources of stress in caregivers (Ducharme et al., 2001), ethical dilemmas among medical students (Hicks et al., 2001), influences on meat consumption (Lea & Worsley, 2001), behavior related to feminine hygiene (Lichtenstein & Nansel, 2000), positive by-products of struggles with chemical dependency (McMillen et al., 2001), and the needs of persons who are at risk of suicide (Pullen & Gow, 2000).

Focus groups provide a forum for open-ended probing of thoughts, which ideally stimulates dialogue and discussion among the participants. Although the open-ended nature of the experience is a strength, the lack of any systematic framework for exploring human motivation is not; no two focus group moderators charged with answering the same questions may approach their task in quite the same way. Addressing this issue, Cohen (1999) proposed a "dimensional" approach to qualitative research. This approach attempted to apply the overlapping psychological modalities or dimensions found so important by clinician Arnold Lazarus (1973, 1989) in his "multimodal" diagnostic and therapeutic efforts (Lazarus, 1973, 1989) to nonclinical objectives in qualitative research. Specifically, **dimensional qualitative research** is an approach to qualitative research that seeks to ensure that a study is comprehensive and systematic from a psychological perspective, by guiding the study design and proposed questions for discussion on the basis of "BASIC ID" dimensions. BASIC ID is an acronym for the key dimensions in Lazarus's approach to diagnosis and intervention; the letters stand for behavior, affect, sensation, imagery, cognition, interpersonal relations, and drugs. Cohen's adaptation of Lazarus's work adds an eighth dimension, a sociocultural one, thus adding an *s* to the acronym and changing it to its plural form (BASIC IDS). Reflecting on this approach, Cohen wrote,

> The dimensions of the BASIC IDS can provide a uniform yet systematic framework for exploration and intervention, yet be flexible enough to allow for the implementation of new techniques and innovation. Anchored in logic, it is an approach that is accessible by nonpsychologists who seek to become more knowledgeable in the ways that psychology can be applied in marketing contexts. . . . Regardless of the specific framework adopted by a researcher, it seems high time to acknowledge that we are all feeling, sensing, behaving, imagining, thinking, socially relating, and biochemical beings who are products of our culture. Once this acknowledgment is made, and once we strive to routinely and systematically account for such variables in marketing research, we can begin to appreciate the added value psychologists bring to qualitative research with consumers in a marketing context. (1999, p. 365)

Behavioral observation   In October 1982, the sales of pain relievers such as aspirin, Bufferin, Anacin, and Excedrin rose sharply. Was this rise in sales due to the effectiveness of the advertising campaigns for these products? No. The sales rose sharply in 1982 when it was learned that seven people had died from Tylenol capsules that had been laced with cyanide. As Tylenol, the pain reliever with the largest share of the market, was withdrawn from the shelves of stores nationwide, there was a corresponding rise in the sale of alternative preparations. A similar phenomenon occurred in 1986. The point here is that if market researchers were to base their judgments concerning the effectiveness of an ad campaign on sales figures alone, the interpretation of the data would, no doubt, be spurious. Thus, it is not unusual for market researchers to station behavioral observers in stores as a technique for monitoring what really prompts a consumer to buy this or that product at the point of choice. Such an observer at a store selling pain relievers in October of 1982 might have observed, for example, a conversation with the clerk about what the best alternative to Tylenol would be. Behavioral observers in a supermarket who studied the purchasing habits of people buying breakfast cereal concluded that children accompanying the purchaser requested or demanded a specific brand of cereal (Atkin, 1978). Hence, it would be wise for breakfast cereal manufacturers to gear their advertising to children and not the adult consumer.

Other methods   A number of other methods and tools may be brought to bear on marketing and advertising questions. Consumer psychologists sometimes employ projective tests—existing as well as custom-designed—as an aid in answering the questions raised by their clients. Special instrumentation, including tachistoscopes and electroencephalographs, have also been used in efforts to uncover consumer motivation. Special computer programs may be used to derive brand names for new products. Thus, for example, when Honda wished to position a new line of its cars as "advanced precision automobiles," a company specializing in the naming of new products conducted a computer search of over 6,900 English-language morphemes to locate word roots that mean or imply "advanced precision." The applicable morphemes were then computer-combined in ways the phonetic rules of English would allow. From the resulting list, the best word (that is, one that has visibility among other printed words, one that will be recognizable as a brand name, and so forth) was then selected; in this case, that word was *Acura* (Brewer, 1987).

Literature reviews are another method available to consumer psychologists. A literature review might suggest, for example, that certain sounds or imagery in a particular brand tend to be more popular with consumers than other sounds or imagery (Figure 16–6). Schloss (1981) observed that the sound of the letter *K* was represented better

Figure 16–6
What's in a Name?

"What's in a name? A rose by any other name would smell as sweet." Sentiments such as this may be touching to read and beautiful to behold when spoken by talented actors on Broadway. However, they wouldn't have taken William Shakespeare very far on Madison Avenue. The name given to a product is an important part of what is referred to as the "marketing mix": the way a product is positioned, marketed, and promoted in the marketplace. The ad shown, reproduced from a 1927 magazine, touts the benefits of a toothbrush with the name Pro-phy-lac-tic. The creator of this brand name no doubt wished to position this toothbrush as being particularly useful in preventing disease. However, the word prophylactic *(defined as "protective") became more identified in the public's mind with condoms, a fact that could not have helped the longevity of this brand of toothbrush in the marketplace. Today, researchers use a variety of methods, including word association, to create brand names.*

than six times more than would be expected by chance in the initial letters of 200 top brand-name products (such as Sanka, Quaker, Nabisco—and, we might add, Acura). Schloss went on to speculate about the ability of this as well as other sounds of words to elicit emotional as opposed to rational reactions. Coincidentally, the sound of the letter *k* is well represented in the final chapter of this textbook, a chapter dealing with the burgeoning use of computers in the assessment enterprise.

Self-Assessment

Test your understanding of elements of this chapter by seeing if you can explain each of the following terms, expressions, and abbreviations:

ability and aptitude measures

assessment in career counseling

assessment center

attitude

burnout

classification

consumer panel

consumer psychology

critical incidents technique

diary panel

dimensional qualitative research

drug test

extrinsic motivation

false negative

false positive

focus group

forced distribution technique

GATB

integrity test

interest measures

intrinsic motivation

job satisfaction

MBTI

organizational commitment

organizational culture

performance test

personality assessment and the workplace

physical test

placement

poll

portfolio assessment

pre-employment assessment

productivity

race norming

screening

selection

semantic differential technique

SII

survey

team

Computer-Assisted Psychological Assessment

Computers, whether in desktop, laptop, or palm-held form, are increasingly a part of the essential office of clinicians and consultants (Garb, 2000a, 2000b; Sturges, 1998). Professionals who specialize in psychological and educational assessment have long recognized the value of computers in administering, scoring, and interpreting tests. As early as 1930, electromechanical scoring for at least one psychological test, the Strong Vocational Interest Blank (SVIB), was available (Campbell, 1971). In 1946, thanks to the efforts of a Minneapolis engineer named Elmer Hankes, SVIB scoring and profiling had become mechanized. One year later, Hankes adopted the same technology to score and profile the MMPI (Dahlstrom et al., 1972). By the late 1950s, computers were being used not merely to score or develop profiles but also to interpret test data (Rome et al., 1965). And by 1965, the Roche Psychiatric Service Institute had initiated the first national, mail-in MMPI service; clinicians could administer the MMPI, mail in the protocol, and get back a computer-scored and computer-interpreted report. With the advent of the personal computer in the 1970s, office-based, computer-assisted psychological assessment (CAPA) would become increasingly accessible to great numbers of test users.

In this chapter, we survey the pros and cons of CAPA and discuss issues related to it, including controversies surrounding paper-and-pencil versus computer-administered tests, and questions that have been raised about computer-based test interpretation (CBTI). We conclude with a brief discussion of standards for CAPA products, and some thoughts regarding what lies on the horizon for the field of psychological testing and assessment.

An Overview

From the standpoint of test users, computer-assisted assessment refers to the convenience and economy of time in administering, scoring, and interpreting tests; thus, the "assistance" typically referred to in the phrase "computer assisted" is assistance to test users, not testtakers. CAPA allows testtakers to work independently, responding to items presented on a video screen and entering data onto a hard drive. The computer then scores the test, analyzes response patterns, and provides some sort of report. For test users, this computer-mediated process represents a great advance over the not too distant past when they had to personally administer a test and possibly even place the responses in some other form for analysis (manually using a scoring template or other device), before beginning the often laborious tasks of scoring and interpreting the resulting data.

The CAPA process typically entails computerized test administration. A testtaker sits at a computer setup and responds to visually and/or aurally presented items by means of some data entry process: keystroke, mouse, voice, touching the screen, or light pen. More inventive means of data entry have been devised for physically challenged testtakers, such as a dental plate activated by the tongue for testtakers who lack the capacity for speech or the use of their limbs (Wilson et al., 1982). One increasingly popular method of computer-assisted assessment is called **computerized adaptive testing (CAT).** CAT may be defined as an interactive, computer-administered testtaking process wherein items presented to the testtaker are based, in part, on the testtaker's performance on previous items. As in the more traditional process of test administration, the test might begin with some sample, practice items. However, the computer may not permit the testtaker to continue with the test until the practice items have been responded to in a satisfactory manner and the testtaker has provided evidence that he or she understands the test procedure. A test may be different for each testtaker, depending on individual performance on the items presented. Each item on an achievement test, for example, may have a known difficulty level and discrimination index. These data as well as other data (such as a statistical allowance for blind guessing) will be factored in when it comes time to derive a final score on the items administered—we do not say "final score on the test" because "the test" is ultimately different for different testtakers. The advantage of CAT is that only a sample of the total number of items in the item pool are administered to any one testtaker. On the basis of previous responses patterns, items that have a very high probability of being answered in a particular fashion (correctly, if an ability test) are not presented, thus providing economy in terms of testing time and total number of items presented (Embretson, 1996). Computer-adaptive testing has been found to reduce the number of test items that need to be administered by as much as 50% while simultaneously reducing measurement error by 50% (Weiss & Vale, 1987). The item statistics used in such tests must be very precise, so very large samples of respondents are needed to establish those statistics.

In this brief introduction to CAPA, we have already touched on some of the advantages of the process. Can you think of any additional advantages? What about disadvantages? Give these questions some thought before reading on.

The Advantages

In general, the potential advantages afforded by CAPA have to do with the objectivity, accuracy, and efficiency that computers and software can bring to various aspects of testing and assessment. More specifically, Jackson (1986, p. 5) listed the following advantages:

1. the economy of professional time
2. the possibility of employing trained assistants to monitor test administration when no psychologist is available
3. the negligible time lag between the administration of a test and its scoring and interpretation
4. the virtual elimination of scoring errors resulting from human lapses of attention or judgment

5. the capacity of a computer to combine data according to a rule more accurately than the capacities of humans

6. the standardization of interpretations by eliminating unreliability traceable to differing points of view in professional judgment

7. the potential for systematically gathering and accessing extensive normative databases that transcend the capacities of human test interpreters

8. the possibility of employing complex scoring and data combination strategies that are not otherwise practical

9. the application of computer-based assessment to special populations

Technology has been a boon to behavioral assessment by providing innovative ways to keep records of targeted behaviors and their antecedents and consequences (Farrell, 1986; Flowers, 1982; Paul, 1987). As compared with other varieties of assessment data, including clinical impressions, patient self-report, and psychological test reports, ongoing behavioral assessment (1) requires a lower level of inference regarding personality-related constructs; (2) need not be linked to any particular theory of personality; (3) helps identify environmental conditions that are acting to maintain certain behaviors; (4) provides behavioral baseline data with which other behavioral data, after intervention, may be compared; (5) provides a record of patients' behavioral strengths and weaknesses across a variety of situations; (6) helps target specific behavioral patterns for modification through interventions; (7) can be organized or graphically displayed in ways that may stimulate innovative or more effective treatment approaches; and (8) provides a ready means for standardizing evaluations in both the psychometric sense (for example, reporting inter-rater reliability on a behavioral observation measure) and the procedural sense (for example, the protocols used in the course of behavioral observation). Third-party payers for mental health services (such as insurance companies) increasingly demand uniformity and accountability in the reporting of assessment-related data. Behavior-based assessment systems are well suited to such an environment because client progress is gauged on the basis of documented behavioral events.

Computer programs designed to facilitate the construction of administration, scoring, and interpretation of assessor-made tests, such as teacher-made achievement tests, are proliferating in record numbers. These programs, some with names such as *Make-A-Test* (Figure 17–1), *Create-A-Test, The Grand Inquisitor,* and *The First National Item Bank and Criterion-Referenced Scoring System,* typically make use of two advantages of computerized testing: the ability to store items in an item bank and the ability to individualize testing through a technique called "item branching."

Item banking   An **item bank** is a relatively large, easily accessible collection of test questions. Instructors who regularly teach a particular course sometimes create their own item bank of questions they have found to be useful on examinations. One of the many potential advantages of an item bank is accessibility to a large number of test items conveniently classified by subject area, item statistics, or other variables. And just as funds may be added to or withdrawn from a more traditional bank, so items may be added to, withdrawn from, and even modified in an item bank (see this chapter's *Close-up*).

Item branching   One of the major advantages of computer-based test administration is the capability of **item branching**—the ability of the computer to tailor the content and order of presentation of test items on the basis of responses to previous items. A computer may have a bank, for example, of achievement test items of different difficulty levels. The computer may be programmed (1) not to present an item of the next difficulty

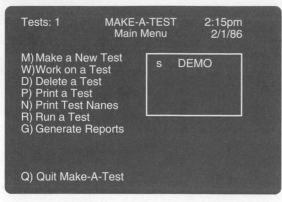

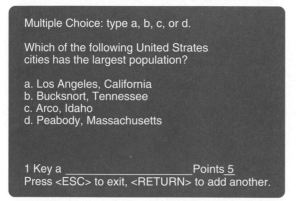

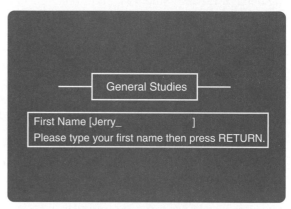

```
Tests: 1        MAKE-A-TEST        2:15pm
                Main Menu          2/1/86

M) Make a New Test       ┌─────────────┐
W) Work on a Test        │ s   DEMO    │
D) Delete a Test         │             │
P) Print a Test          │             │
N) Print Test Nanes      │             │
R) Run a Test            │             │
G) Generate Reports      └─────────────┘



Q) Quit Make-A-Test
```

Manager Main Menu Screen: All program options are accessed through simple menu structures. Submenus and prompts help users know available options.

```
Test: General Studies              11:25am
Items: 23    Edit Test Information  3/15/86

A) Long Test Name          :General Studies
B) Teacher's Name          :Jerry St. Vincent
C) Response Mode           :Forced Choice
D) Sequencing Mode         :Sequential
E) Test Time Limit         :2 minutes
F) Item Time Limit         :20 seconds
G) Show Item Number        :Yes
H) Show Points Possible    :Yes
I) Show Item Feedback      :Yes
J) Correct Feedback        :Good Job!
K) Incorrect Feedback      :Keep trying.
L) Show Student Score      :Yes
>
Press <ESC> to go back.
```

Edit Test Information Screen: Tests of up to 500 items may be given with one of several presentation options.

```
Multiple Choice: type a, b, c, or d.

Which of the following United Strates
cities has the largest population?

a. Los Angeles, California
b. Bucksnort, Tennessee
c. Arco, Idaho
d. Peabody, Massachusetts



1 Key a _____ Points 5
Press <ESC> to exit, <RETURN> to add another.
```

Test Item Creation Screen: Test items are created with a simple text editor. Editing is performed using the same word processing–style editor.

```
        ┌──────────────────┐
        │ General Studies  │
  ──────┘                  └──────────
  ┌───────────────────────────────────┐
  │ First Name [Jerry_            ]    │
  │ Please type your first name then press RETURN. │
  └───────────────────────────────────┘
```

Run a Test Screen: The Run a Test option allows instructor preview of the test in student mode with timing and scoring.

```
  ┌─────────────────────────────────────┐
  │         General Studies             │
  │                                     │
  │   Your Score: 43                    │
  │                                     │
  │   Number Right . . . . . . . .7/9   │
  │                                     │
  │   Average Time . . . . . . . 147 seconds │
  │   Time-Outs    . . . . . . . .0      │
  │                                     │
  │              Press <RETURN>         │
  └─────────────────────────────────────┘
```

Online Test Completion Screen: At the end of a computer-administered test, immediate scoring results can be displayed to the student.

```
Test     : General Studies         2:39pm
Selected: 6       Print a Report   6/28/86

A) Individual       ┌────────────────────────┐
B) Group            │ Report Options         │
C) Item Response    │                        │
D) Item Statistics  │ 1) # Per Page:Multiple │
E) Test Statistics  │ 2) Sort By    :Name    │
                    │ 3) Print Items :No     │
Individual Report   │ 4) Destination:Printer │
                    └────────────────────────┘
>_

Press <RETURN> to print a report
Press <ESC> to go back
```

Individual Report Screen: A wide range of report types and styles can be ordered by the user. Reports can also be viewed online before printing.

Figure 17–1
Sample Display Screens from the WICAT Make-A-Test Program

Designing an Item Bank

Developing a bank of items for an item bank is no easy chore; many questions and issues relating to the development of such a bank and to the maintenance of a satisfactory pool of items need to be resolved (Hiscox, 1983; Hiscox & Brzezinski, 1980). As an introduction to the potential problems inherent in developing an item bank, suppose that you are a consultant who has been asked by the "Association of Personal Physical Trainers Who Make House Calls" (APPTHC)—to develop an item bank of questions that any physical trainer who makes house calls should reasonably be able to answer. APPTHC officials inform you that their ultimate objective will be to use this item bank to develop an APPTHC certification examination. How would you go about developing such an item bank? What questions need to be raised in advance about the items, the test as a whole, and the administration, scoring, and interpretation of the test? Try tackling this question on your own before looking at the following outline; as an APPTHC member in good standing might say, "No pain, no gain!"

Questions to Be Answered in Designing an Item Bank

I. Items

   A. *Acquisition and development*

      1. Develop/use your own item collection or use collections of others?

         a. If develop your own item collection, what development procedures will be followed?

         b. If use collections of others, will the items be leased or purchased; is the classification scheme sufficiently documented and are the item format specifications sufficiently compatible for easy transfer and use?

      2. What types of items will be permitted?

         a. Will open-ended (constructed response) items, opinion questions, instructional objectives, or descriptions of performance tasks be included in the bank?

         b. Will all the items be made to fit a common format (for example, all multiple-choice with options "a," "b," "c," and "d")?

         c. Must the items be calibrated, be validated, or otherwise carry additional information?

      3. What will be the size of the item collection?

         a. How many items per objective/subtopic (collection depth)?

         b. How many different topics (collection breadth)?

      4. What review, tryout, and editing procedures will be used?

         a. Who will perform the review/editing?

         b. Will there be a field tryout, and if so, what statistics will be gathered, and what criteria will be used for inclusion in the bank?

   B. *Classification*

      1. How will the subject matter classifications be performed?

         a. Will the classification by subject matter use fixed categories, keywords, or some combination of the two?

         b. Who will be responsible for preparing, expanding, and refining the taxonomy?

         c. How detailed will the taxonomy be? Will it be hierarchically or nonhierarchically arranged?

         d. Who will assign classification indices to each item, and how will this assignment be verified?

      2. What other assigned information about the items will be stored in the item bank?

      3. What measured information about the items will be stored in the bank? How will the item measures be calculated?*

   C. *Management*

      1. Will provision be made for updating the classification scheme and items? If so:

         a. Who will be permitted to make additions, deletions, and revisions?

         b. What review procedures will be followed?

         c. How will the changes be disseminated?

         d. How will duplicate (or near-duplicate) items be detected and eliminated?

---

*This question is the subject of considerable controversy and discussion in the technical-measurement literature. For example, to obtain a latent-trait difficulty parameter, concern has been expressed about sample size, calibration procedure (Rasch, 3-parameter), linking models (major axis, least squares, maximum likelihood), and number of items common to the equating forms.

(continued)

Designing an Item Bank *(continued)*

e. When will a revision of an item be trivial enough that item statistics from a previous version can be aggregated with revisions from the current version?

f. Will item statistics be stored from each use, or from last use, or will they be aggregated across uses?

2. How will items that require pictures, graphs, special characters, or other types of enhanced printing be handled?

3. How will items that must accompany other items, such as a series of questions about the same reading passage, be handled?

II. Tests

A. *Assembly*

1. Must the test constructor specify the specific items to appear on the test, or will the items be selected by computer?

2. If the items are selected by computer:

a. How will one item out of several that matches the search specification be selected (randomly, time since last usage, frequency of previous use)?

b. What happens if no item meets the search specifications?

c. Will a test constructor have the option to reject a selected item, and if so, what will be the mechanism for doing so?

d. What precautions will be taken to ensure that examinees who are tested more than once do not receive the same items?

3. What item or test parameters can be specified for test assembly (item format restrictions, limits on difficulty levels, expected score distribution, expected test reliability, and so on)?

4. What assembly procedures will be available (options to multiple-choice items placed in random order, the test items placed in random order, different items on each test)?

5. Will the system print tests or just specify which items to use? If the former, how will the tests be printed or duplicated and where will the answers be displayed?

B. *Administration, scoring, and reporting*

1. Will the system be capable of online test administration? If so:

a. How will access be managed?

b. Will test administration be adaptive, and if so, using what procedures?

2. Will the system provide for test scoring? If so:

a. What scoring formula will be used (rights only, correction for guessing, partial credit for some answers, weighting by discrimination values)?

b. How will constructed responses be evaluated (offline by the instructor, online/offline by examiners comparing their answers to a key, online by computer with/without employing a spelling algorithm)?

3. Will the system provide for test reporting? If so:

a. What records will be kept (the tests themselves, individual student item responses, individual student test scores, school or other group scores) and for how long? Will new scores for individuals and groups supplement or replace old scores?

b. What reporting options (content/format) will be available?

c. To whom will the reports be sent?

C. *Evaluation*

1. Will reliability and validity data be collected? If so, what data will be collected by whom, and how will they be used?

2. Will norms be made available and, if so, based on what norm-referenced measures?

III. System

A. *Acquisition and development*

1. Who will be responsible for acquisition/development, given what resources, and operating under what constraints?

2. Will the system be made transportable to others? What levels and what degree of documentation will be available?

B. *Software/hardware features*

1. What aspects of the system will be computer-assisted?

a. Where will the items be stored (computer, paper, card file)?

b. Will requests be filled using a batch, online, or manual mode?

2. Will a microcomputer be used and, if so, what special limits does such a choice place on item text, item-bank size, and test development options?

3. Will items be stored as one large collection or will separate files be maintained for each user?

4. How will the item-banking system be constructed (from scratch; by piecing together word processing, database management, and other general-purpose programs; by adopting existing item-banking systems)?

5. What specific equipment will be needed (for storage, retrieval, interactions with the system, and so on)?

6. How user- and maintenance-friendly will the equipment and support programs be?

7. Who will be responsible for equipment maintenance?

C. *Monitoring and training*

1. What system features will be monitored (number of items per classification category, usage by user group, number of revisions until a user is satisfied, distribution of test lengths or other test characteristics, and so on)?

2. Who will monitor the system, train users, and give support (initially, ongoing)?

3. How will information about changes in system procedures be disseminated?

D. *Access and security*

1. Who will have access to the items and other information in the bank (authors/owners, teachers, students)? Who can request tests?

2. Will users have direct access to the system or must they go through an intermediary?

3. What procedures will be followed to secure the contents of the item bank (if they are to be secure)?

4. Where will the contents of the item bank be housed (centrally or will each user also have a copy)?

5. Who will have access to score reports?

IV. Use and Acceptance

A. *General*

1. Who decides to what uses the item bank will be put? And will these uses be the ones that the test users need and want?

2. Who will develop the tests and who will be allowed to use the system? Will those people be acceptable to the examinees and recipients of the test information?

3. Will the system be able to handle the expected demand for use?

4. Is the output of the system likely to be used and used as intended?

5. How will user acceptance and item-bank credibility be enhanced?

B. *Instructional improvement.* If this is an intended use:

1. Will the item bank be part of a larger instructional/decision-making system?

2. Which textbooks, curriculum guidelines, and other materials, if any, will be keyed to the bank's items? Who will make that decision and how will the assignments be validated?

3. Will items be available for drill and practice as well as for testing?

4. Will information be available to users that will assist in the diagnosis of educational needs?

C. *Adaptive testing.* If this is an option:

1. How will the scheduling of the test administrations take place?

2. How will the items be selected to ensure testing efficiency yet maintain content representation and avoid duplication between successive test administrations?

3. What criteria will be used to terminate testing?

4. What scoring procedures will be followed?

D. *Certification of competence.* If this is an intended use:

1. Will the item bank contain measures that cover all the important component skills of the competence being assessed?

2. How many attempts at passing the test will be allowed; when? How will these attempts be monitored?

(continued)

Designing an Item Bank *(continued)*

E. *Program/curriculum evaluation.* If this is an intended use:

1. Will it be possible to implement the system so as to provide reliable measures of student achievement in a large number of specific performance areas?

2. Will the item bank contain measures that cover all the important stated objectives of the curriculum? That go beyond the stated objectives of the curriculum?

3. Will the item bank yield commensurable data that permit valid comparisons over time?

F. *Testing and reporting requirements imposed by external agencies.* If meeting these requirements is an intended use:

1. Will the system be able to handle requirements for program evaluation, student selection for specially funded programs, assessing educational needs, and reporting?

2. Will the system be able to accommodate minor modifications in the testing and reporting requirements?

V. Costs

A. *Cost feasibility*

1. What are the (fixed, variable) costs (financial, time, space, equipment, and supplies) to create and support the system?

2. Are those costs affordable?

B. *Cost comparisons*

1. How do the item-banking system costs compare with the present or other testing systems that achieve the same goals?

2. Do any expanded capabilities justify the extra cost? Are any restricted capabilities balanced by cost savings?

Source: Millman and Arter (1984).

---

level until two consecutive items of the previous difficulty level are answered correctly and (2) to terminate the test when five consecutive items of a given level of difficulty have been answered incorrectly. Alternatively, the pattern of items to which the testtaker is exposed may be based not on the testtaker's response to preceding items but on a random drawing from the total pool of test items. Green (1984) commented on the advantage of such a procedure:

> Conventional tests can be compromised by theft of test forms, or by each of several applicants memorizing a few items for later mutual benefit. Future applicants can then be coached on specific item content, or even furnished with test answer keys. But when the computer selects items at random from its pool, each applicant gets a different test form, and such specific coaching is much less effective. In fact, if the item pool is sufficiently large and extensive, it can be published for all to see, on the grounds that anyone who can answer all these items knows the material being tested.

Green went on to cite the case of a computer-administered driver's license test—the written portion—as that might be particularly amenable to the administration of randomly drawn items. And given a large enough bank of items, it would even be possible to keep a record of the items administered to an applicant on a first administration of the test—an administration on which the applicant did not receive a passing score—and randomly draw from the remaining (unused) items in the bank for succeeding administrations to the same applicant.

Jackson (1986) mused about how item branching might be employed in a computer-administered personality test to get a more accurate picture of the testtaker:

> If a respondent has already responded to four items in such a way as to deny visual hallucinations, it would be reasonable to conclude that this [is] a less fruitful avenue of investigation than that of depression, where three or four items have been endorsed. By selecting

items to present to the respondent from the depression area, one might obtain a more complete and accurate picture of psychopathology in terms of such sub-dimensions as suicidal tendencies, despair over the future, fatigue and eating disorders. (p. 11)

Another potential application of item-branching technology in personality tests has to do with monitoring the purposefulness of examinees' responses. Should a profile of responses make it appear that the examinee is responding in a nonpurposive or inconsistent fashion or even faking, the computer may be programmed to respond in a prescribed way, such as by admonishing the respondent to be more careful or refusing to proceed until a purposive response is given. For example, on a computer-based true-false test, if the examinee responds "true" to an item such as "I spent Christmas in Beirut last year," there would be reason to suspect that the examinee is responding nonpurposively, randomly, or in some way other than genuinely.

You might conclude that automation has done for psychological assessment exactly what it has done in many other spheres of daily living—greatly enhanced the quality of life. Is that, in fact, the case? As our overview continues, you will become acquainted with some of the problems and issues that computer technology has left in its wake.

The Disadvantages

From the perspective of a testtaker, particularly one who is not computer savvy or experienced, a computer-administered test may be an intimidating experience. Testtakers may find themselves prevented from engaging in various testtaking strategies that have worked for them in the past, such as previewing or reviewing test materials and skipping around to answer only questions they are certain of first. Examinees whose practice is to skim through and survey all the items on a test at the outset may not be able to do so during a computerized test administration. Typically, an item must be answered before the computer's cursor proceeds to the next. Having completed the test or any portion of it, testtakers may be electronically prohibited from reviewing previously entered answers. During the test, because an answer may be required before the next item is presented for response, the examinee is deprived of the option of purposefully omitting items. And because every item must be answered (and in many instances verified with a prompt from the computer, such as "You answered TRUE; if that is correct press RETURN"), the computer administration of a test may actually take longer for some testtakers than the administration of the same test with paper and pencil. Note, however, that computer administrations of tests typically take less time than conventional administrations for the average examinee (White et al., 1985). Such a time savings has been found with the computerized Differential Aptitude Test (Dimock & Cormier, 1991) and the computerized MMPI (Watson et al., 1992).

A great paradox of the computer era is that although such technology is designed to be timesaving, many long hours must frequently be invested by the test user in reading tomes of documentation—perhaps even a number of ancillary books written as easy guides to the primary books—before the technology can be used. Once the obstacle of learning to use computer software or specially designed hardware is overcome and the inevitable bugs have been worked out, other problems may arise.

In contrast to psychological tests administered by clinicians themselves, automated testing is typically designed for administration by a nonprofessional member of the clinician's staff or for self-administration by the assessee. Thus, in contrast to the clinician-administered test, an automated testing situation may provide diminished, if any, opportunity for the assessor to (1) establish a rapport with the assessee, (2) observe the assessee's testtaking behavior, and (3) note any unusual extra-test conditions that may have affected responses.

The use of computers in the service of behavioral observation carries with it a unique set of problems, among them the fact that: (1) The system may not be feasible due to the great expense associated with it. Some computer-assisted behavioral assessment systems, such as that conceptualized by Paul (1987), require highly trained personnel who do little but observe patients' behavior. Thus, in addition to the initial cost of setting up and maintaining such a system, financial outlays are necessary to train and employ dedicated behavioral observers. It is clearly desirable to have highly trained professionals whose job description includes little more than behavioral observation and rating. However, there is a real question as to whether such an employment position is economically feasible. (2) An important consideration in evaluating the utility of behavioral data gathered by two or more assessors is the degree to which inter-rater reliability between the assessors has been established. Clearly, the institution of such a program requires a commitment to training staff members who will be performing the assessments. (3) Staff may be concerned that behavior-rating tasks will diminish their effectiveness in other spheres of their work. Clinicians conducting individual or group therapy, as well as other staff members performing other duties, may view the minute or two it takes to complete a behavioral observation form as a distraction from their other duties. In such cases, practicing with the system or entering data after the activity is completed will often allay such concerns. (4) Staff may be "computerphobic" or harbor otherwise negative attitudes toward the introduction of computers into their daily routine. Many legitimate concerns about the use of computers in mental health settings have been expressed by both clinicians (Elliott, 1988; Hartman, 1986a, 1986b; Reimers et al., 1987; Skinner & Pakula, 1986; Witt & Elliott, 1985) and their clients (Romanczyk, 1986). In addition, certain mental health professionals, presumably like members of other occupations, are reluctant to trade in more traditional ways of working for a lifestyle that relies on computer hardware and software. The challenge here is to effectively address all legitimate concerns, while eradicating irrational "computerphobia," by exposure to the benefits of the computerized approach.

The age of computers has brought with it new kinds of crime: computer theft and computer mischief, the latter exemplified by computer viruses capable of altering or erasing a computer's memory. Just as clinicians have for decades protected the security of tests and test data with tools such as locked steel filing cabinets, so clinicians who use CAPA technology have the obligation to protect these tests and test data. A significant obstacle modern clinicians face, however, is the time and expense entailed in keeping up with the latest and most effective means of electronic security.

Perhaps the most vexing concern of clinicians who use computerized assessment software, particularly software that provides automated interpretations of findings, are questions regarding the validity of computer-generated interpretations of findings. Related questions have to do with the equivalence of data obtained from a computerized version of a test with data derived from the more traditional paper-and-pencil administration.

Despite these questions and issues, CAPA is here to stay. So, in the interest of gaining a better understanding of it, let's examine some CAPA-related inputs and outputs—that is, what goes into and what comes out of the computer.

Data In, Data Out

Data In

For purposes of discussion, let's dichotomize computer input into two categories: (1) input of responses by a testtaker, and (2) input of test data by a test user.

Input by testtakers   Most tests that are currently available for computer administration were originally developed for conventional (that is, paper-and-pencil) administration. A primary concern of test users is how factors related to computerized test administration—factors that are irrelevant to the original design of the test—might influence testtaker performance. For example, in a computer-assisted administration of a test, testtakers typically must enter their responses through a keyboard. But what if the testtaker is woefully unfamiliar with it? In some tests, such as one in which the testtaker's task is to quickly list words (as in some tests of divergent thinking or creativity), testtakers unfamiliar with computer keyboards are penalized. Concerns have also been expressed regarding the applicability of published norms and of reliability and validity data; typically such data are obtained using conventional test administrations, and generalizing those data to a computer-assisted test administration is risky at best, and inappropriate at worst.

There is evidence that certain types of items may yield significantly different scores as a function of the mode of test administration. Significant differences in scores on speeded arithmetic tests as a function of whether the tests were conventionally administered or computer-administered have been found (Greaud & Green, 1986). By contrast, on tests involving mostly multiple-choice and true-false items, the two modes of test administration were deemed equivalent (Hoffman & Lundberg, 1976). A clear exception to the latter finding was matching-type items: the computer presentation of matching items resulted in significantly lower scores, different numbers of changed responses, and different patterns of changed responses, as compared with conventionally presented matching items.

On paper-and-pencil tests, a testtaker can, by design or omission, fail to respond to a particular item. But if the computer will not proceed unless an item is responded to in some way, the testtaker who wishes not to respond is compelled to enter this "nonresponse." This fact of life of computerized test administration has implications for the data obtained in many types of tests, including personality tests (Honaker, 1988). For example, when the Adjective Checklist is administered by computer, respondents must actively reject an adjective, rather than passively fail to endorse it—a fact that may lead to differences in scores (Allred & Harris, 1984).

Responses to items as a function of item content may also be affected by mode of administration. Writing decades ago, Smith (1963) mused that testtakers might prefer an impersonal computer to face-to-face contact when confession-type questions were being asked. This hypothesis has been explored in a number of studies, some of which have yielded conflicting findings (Lukin et al., 1985). Skinner and Allen (1983) found no differences in respondents' willingness to describe their alcohol and illegal drug use when using a paper-and-pencil questionnaire or a computer, though such differences have been observed by others (Evan & Miller, 1969; Hart & Goldstein, 1985; Koson et al., 1970). Koson et al. (1970) found that females tended to be more honest than males on computerized tests. More pathological MMPI scores were found as a function of computerized as opposed to conventional test administration (Bresolin, 1984). Rezmovic (1977) found mode-of-administration effects most pronounced at the extreme ends of a distribution of test scores; computer administration caused extreme scorers to become even more extreme.

Input by test users   Placing yourself in the shoes of a test user, consider some of your options with regard to having the tests you administer computer-scored and/or interpreted: central processing, teleprocessing, and local processing.

Central processing entails sending test protocols completed on paper or some other form at one location to some other central location for processing—that is, for scoring or interpretation. The results may then be returned to the test user in an oral report by telephone or in a written report by mail or fax. Because ownership of hardware or software is not required, the chief advantage of central processing is its low cost. Particularly when test results do not have to be turned around very quickly, and when there are large numbers of protocols to be processed, central processing offers the most economical test-scoring and interpretation alternative. Clinicians who test clients only on occasion may find central processing to be best suited to their needs. However, as the prices of technology such as computers and optical mark readers continue to go down, and as mailing, shipping, and related costs rise, the cost-efficiency edge of central processing will dwindle. In the interest of protecting the proprietary nature of the programs used to score and interpret a test, central processing may be the only variety of processing made available by the test publisher.

In contrast to central processing (physically shipping test protocols or other data to a central location), it is possible to transmit test data stored in a computer to a central computer over telephone lines using a modem as an interface. **Teleprocessing** refers to the computerized scoring, interpretation, or other conversion of raw test data that have been sent for processing over telephone lines by modem from one test site to a central facility. Unlike central processing, a teleprocessing arrangement requires that test users purchase, lease, or otherwise maintain computer hardware suitable for interfacing with the teleprocessor.

In an era of efficient but relatively inexpensive personal computers, local processing is the hands-down option of choice for most test users. **Local processing** may be defined simply as on-site computerized scoring, interpretation, or other conversion of raw test data. With the appropriate hardware and software, the test user may use the same computer to administer and then score a test. Two key advantages of local processing are control and flexibility. By having the system entirely in-house, the test user has total control over every facet of the processing of the tests, including factors such as hours of operation, when servicing of the system will take place, and quality control of the operation. And because the user of local processing typically has at least one powerful computer on the premises, the flexibility to use that computer for test-administration purposes—or some other non-assessment-related purpose—is another advantage.

Software for local test processing is plentiful; such software is not necessarily published by the test publisher and may be produced by any number of competing manufacturers. One variety of such software yields an interpretive report but seldom contains a program for administering the test or a scoring program. This is because of legal issues surrounding ownership of the items in the test and the system used to score the test. Test items and scoring information are owned by the test developer or publisher and cannot legally be copied into a computer without the owner's permission—permission that is seldom forthcoming. Central-processing and teleprocessing services that involve scoring are available legally only from the test publisher or licensees. By contrast, local processing involves the generation of interpretive findings (in various forms, such as a narrative report), based on scoring that was done either by hand or by owner-licensed computer software. Most test publishers offer only one "official" interpretive system for a given application of a particular test, though independent companies may offer a variety of test-interpretation software.

Local processing may also take the form of a test package containing software for the administration, scoring, and/or interpretation of a test. Such packages are only available from the test publisher or its licensees. In some cases, local processing is effected through an online link via a modem to a central computer. The test user connects to that central computer via a modem and feeds in the testtaker's responses. In a relatively brief amount of time, typically only minutes, the raw data has been converted into one or more types of interpretable scores, perhaps even complete with graphics. The scoring service may also provide for timely comparison of an individual's test scores with the scores of other testtakers—thus making what has been traditionally referred to as "local" scoring a bit more "global."

Data Out

Every day, computers around the world receive input in the form of test responses, demographic information, and other data, and generate psychological reports from this input. These reports can take many different forms. At one end of the spectrum, a computer-generated report may consist only of a number representing a test score. At the other end, a report may contain test scores along with a narrative interpretation of the scores that integrates all the findings, as well as any additional relevant information. We discuss different types of computer-generated reports in this chapter's *Everyday Psychometrics.*

Issues in CAPA

In general, many of the issues that exist with regard to CAPA can be categorized as relating to (1) computer-assisted test administration, (2) computer-assisted test interpretation, (3) clinical versus mechanical judgment, (4) standards for CAPA products, and (5) access to CAPA products.

Computer-Assisted Test Administration: Equivalence

A key issue regarding the computerized administration of tests that were originally developed for paper-and-pencil administration is that of equivalence. Beyond psychometric concerns, questions about the equivalence of paper-and-pencil versus computerized administration of tests have been raised with regard to the total testtaking experience, including perceptual and attitudinal components (Honaker & Fowler, 1990). Addressing the equivalence question over a decade ago, Honaker (1990) observed that research had left unanswered many of the essential questions (such as those listed in Table 17–1) about equivalence of test formats. For the most part, contemporary researchers are still raising many of these same concerns with regard to a variety of tests now available for both paper-and-pencil and computerized test administration. Butcher

Table 17–1
Questions to Raise When Considering the Use
of a Computer-Administered Version of a Conventional Test

1. Is the computer administration psychometrically equivalent to its traditional counterpart?
   a. Are there differences in the rank order of the scores? If so, data from the conventional version of the test cannot be used with the computerized version.
   b. Are there differences in the mean scores or in the shape of the distribution of scores? If so, data from the conventional version of the test can be used with the computerized version only if an equating formula has been used to adjust the computerized scores for these differences.
2. Has this particular program of a computerized version of the test been shown to be equivalent?
3. Will this computerized version be equivalent on my particular computer? Is my computer different, in some critical way, from the computers used to do the equivalency research?
4. For which of my clients will this computerized version be equivalent? Stated another way: For what types of clients has the program been demonstrated to be equivalent?
5. How will my clients react to the computerized test?

Source: Adapted from Hofer and Green (1985) and Honaker (1990)

Types of Computer-Generated Psychological Reports

Test scoring and interpretation software varies in many ways, including the complexity of the report provided. For example, some elements of a report that may or may not be included are tallies of scores, graphics of profiles, item analysis data, and interpretations of findings.

We may categorize types of computer-generated psychological reports in terms of whether they are scoring reports, interpretive reports, or integrative reports. Here we define each of these types of reports and describe the type of information that might be found in them.

Scoring Reports

In general, a **scoring report** may be defined as a formal or official computer-generated account of test performance, usually presented in numeric form. One type of scoring report, a **simple scoring report,** simply lists test scores. In tests with multiple scales, a simple scoring report might list, for example, number of points scored on each scale. Another type of scoring report is an **extended scoring report.** Beyond a simple listing of test scores, an extended scoring report may contain more detailed information, such as item analysis statistics. Extended scoring reports are particularly useful when it is important for the test user to know at a glance whether certain differences between subtest or scale scores are statistically significant.

Interpretive Reports

In general, an **interpretive report** is a formal or official computer-generated account of test performance, presented in numeric as well as narrative form, including an explanation of the findings. There are three varieties of interpretive report: a descriptive report, a screening report, and a consultative report.

A **descriptive report** is a type of interpretive report that features brief, scale-by-scale narrative summaries. In fact, the "description" in a descriptive report may be so brief as to amount to a one-sentence comment regarding where a particular score stands from a normative perspective. Descriptive reports are particularly helpful when a test contains scales reported in different types of scores, since they help the test user quickly identify which scores should be focused on.

A **screening report** provides more information than a descriptive report, but less than a consultative report; it provides narrative information on each of the scales on the test, as well as analysis or commentary regarding relation-

ships between the scores. As its name implies, a screening report is particularly useful for screening purposes. Programmed into the software are various criteria that must be met before the software causes a line of narrative text to be automatically printed on a screening report. As an example, consider the decision rules of an instrument once used to screen personnel based on an administration of the MMPI (University of Minnesota, 1984). For this screening instrument to report an interpretive comment such as "The client may keep problems to himself too much," the following conditions would have to be met:

- Lie and Correction scales are greater than the Infrequency scale, *and*
- the Infrequency scale is less than a T score of 55, *and*
- the Depression, Paranoia, Psychasthenia, and Schizophrenia scales are less than a T score of 65, *and*
- the Conversion Hysteria scale is greater than 69 T, *or*
- the Need for Affection subscale is greater than 63 T, *or*
- the Conversion Hysteria scale is greater than 64 T, and the Denial of Social Anxiety subscale or Inhibition of Aggression subscale is greater than 59 T, *or*
- the Repression scale is greater than 59 T, *or*
- the Brooding subscale is greater than 59 T

More than a bare-bones descriptive report and less tentative in its conclusions than a screening report is a consultative report. A **consultative report** is a type of interpretive report that provides a detailed analysis of test data in language appropriate for communication between assessment professionals. It provides the expert opinion of an individual or group of individuals, who may have devoted years of study to the interpretation of a particular instrument.

Integrative Reports

The newest breed of computer-generated report is an **integrated report:** one that not only provides a level of description and analysis found in interpretive reports, but integrates into the report data from other sources such as behavioral observations or medication records. From a report that integrates behavioral observation data with medication records, for example, a clinician might receive valuable assistance concerning optimal medications and dosages for a client.

et al. (2000) reviewed the literature on equivalence of paper-and-pencil versus computer administration of tests, as well as the literature on orally administered clinical interviews versus computer-administered interviews. Although these researchers concluded that paper-and-pencil and computer administration of tests were equivalent, they noted that this conclusion was limited to equivalence studies conducted using the MMPI or the MMPI-2. Meaningful equivalence studies on tests other than the MMPI and MMPI-2 are few and far between, when they exist at all (Butcher et al., 2000; Honaker & Fowler, 1990), and no definitive answers are evident. Studies have reported major differences as a function of mode of administration (French & Beaumont, 1991), as well as relatively moderate differences (Watson et al., 1992).

Butcher et al. (2000) observed that the mode of administration of clinical interviews yielded significantly different results. Somewhat paradoxically, as noted by Snyder (2000) and others (Kobak et al., 1993), the lack of equivalence between face-to-face and computer administration of clinical interviews may be due to respondents' greater willingness to divulge personal information to an impersonal computer.

If a test user has any doubts regarding the equivalence of a computer-administered version of a paper-and-pencil test, caution in interpreting the findings is indicated. Greater caution is required if computer-obtained scores are to be used with norms that were obtained as a result of paper-and-pencil administrations of the same test (Hofer & Green, 1985).

Computer-Assisted Test Interpretation: Validity

Perhaps the thorniest issue regarding computer-assisted test interpretation has to do with the validity of the growing number of such interpretation programs available (Butcher, 1994). Is this system valid for administration to the people I test? is the key question for users of CAPA products. For test users in many settings, especially settings that differ markedly from the setting where the CAPA instrument was developed, the answer to this question is probably no (Mitchell, 1986).

Studies regarding the validity of computer-based test interpretation programs have not been encouraging. Lanyon (1984) characterized the lack of demonstrated program validity as more the norm than the exception. Butcher (1987) wrote of "misstatements of staggering proportions" in some test interpretation programs. More recently, Butcher and his colleagues were more charitable regarding computer-generated reports of personality tests, concluding that the interpretive statements in such reports are generally "comparable to clinician-generated statements" (Butcher et al., 2000, p. 11). However, as observed by Garb (2000a), Butcher et al. (2000) found only four studies that had been conducted during the 1990s, two that reported negative findings and two that reported mixed findings. Garb (2000a) commented that implicit in Butcher et al.'s data was the finding that "as many as 40% of the computer-generated narrative statements were less than appropriate in 87% of the reports" (p. 4).

One approach to validating a computer-based test interpretation program is by a consumer satisfaction study. In this approach, testtakers review and comment on the computer-generated findings with regard to variables such as overall accuracy, omission of relevant information, and inclusion of trivial or misleading information. Due to a tendency to assign greater accuracy to narratives with a number of nonspecific statements (Butcher et al., 2000), it is important that such studies control for the Barnum effect (Eyde et al., 1990; Guastello & Rieke, 1990; Prince & Guastello, 1990).

Other strategies for evaluating the validity of computer-based test interpretations (CBTIs) are external criterion studies and expert opinion modeling. In an external criterion study, the validity of a CBTI is examined relative to other test data or the ratings of a clinician or other person who knows the testtaker well. In a validation study regarding expert opinion modeling, at issue is the question of how well a computer-generated narrative output captures what an expert consultant might opine given the same data (Vale & Keller, 1987; Vale et al., 1986). At its best, then, a CBTI interpretation is no better than that of the best experts available. Honaker and Fowler (1990, p. 538) questioned the wisdom of the expert simulation strategy, writing that it "essentially maintains the status quo and produces improvements in assessment accuracy only to the degree that the emulated expert (or experts) improves." An issue related to the one regarding expert simulation—and one that has been debated almost since the notion of expert simulation was conceived—is whether or not computer simulation of clinical judgment is actually superior to clinical judgment.

Clinical Versus Mechanical Prediction

Should clinicians review test results and related assessment data and then draw conclusions, make recommendations, and take actions that are based on their own education, training, and clinical experience? Alternatively, should clinicians review test results and related assessment data and then draw conclusions, make recommendations, and take actions on the basis of known statistical probabilities, much like an actuary or statistician whose occupation is to calculate risks? A debate regarding the respective merits of what has become known as "clinical versus actuarial prediction" and "clinical versus actuarial assessment" began to simmer over a half-century ago with the publication of a monograph on the subject by Paul Meehl (1954; see also Dawes et al., 1989; Garb, 1994; Holt, 1970; and Marchese, 1992).[1]

The increasing popularity of CBTIs has resurrected elements of the debate about clinical versus actuarial prediction approaches. The battleground has shifted to the frontier of new technology, the focus has shifted to CBTI software (and questions regarding how it compares to clinical judgment), and "actuarial prediction" has become subsumed under the somewhat broader label "mechanical prediction." Contemporary scholars and practitioners tend not to debate whether clinicians should be using actuary-like methods to make clinical judgments. It is more au courant to debate whether clinicians should be using software that uses actuary-like methods to make clinical judgments.

Some clarification and definition of terms may be helpful here. In the context of clinical decision-making, **actuarial assessment** and **actuarial prediction** have been used synonymously to refer to the application of empirically demonstrated statistical rules and probabilities as a determining factor in clinical judgment and actions. As asserted by Butcher et al. (2000), "actuarial assessment" is not synonymous with "computerized assessment." Citing Sines (1966), Butcher et al. (2000, p. 6) noted that, "A computer-based test interpretation (CBTI) system is actuarial only if its interpretive output is wholly determined by statistical rules that have been demonstrated empirically to exist between the output and the input data." It is possible for the interpretive output of a CBTI system to be determined by things other than statistical rules. The output may be based, for example, not on any statistical formulas or actuarial calculations, but rather on the clinical judgment, opinions, and expertise of the author of the software. "Computerized assessment" in such an instance would amount to a computerized application of clinical opinion; that is, the application of a clinician's (or group of clinicians') judg-

---

1. Although this debate has traditionally been couched in terms of *clinical assessment* (or prediction) as compared to statistical or actuarial assessment (or prediction), a parallel debate could pit other applied areas of assessment (including educational, personnel, or organizational assessment, for example) against statistically based methods. At the heart of the debate are questions concerning the utility of a rather subjective approach to assessment that is based on one's training and experience, as compared to a more objective and statistically sophisticated approach that is strictly based on preset rules for analyzing the data.

ments, opinions, and expertise to a particular set of data as processed by the computer software.

Clinical prediction refers to the application of a clinician's own training and clinical experience as a determining factor in clinical judgment and actions. Clinical prediction relies on clinical judgment, which Grove et al. (2000) characterized as

> the typical procedure long used by applied psychologists and physicians, in which the judge puts data together using informal, subjective methods. Clinicians differ in how they do this: The very nature of the process tends to preclude precise specification. (p. 19)

Grove et al. (2000) proceeded to compare clinical judgment with what they termed **mechanical prediction,** or the application of empirically demonstrated statistical rules and probabilities, as well as computer algorithms, to the computer generation of findings and recommendations. These authors reported the results of a meta-analysis of 136 studies that pitted the accuracy of clinical prediction against mechanical prediction. In some studies, the two approaches to assessment seemed to be about equal in accuracy. On average, however, Grove et al. concluded that the mechanical approach was about 10% more accurate than the clinical approach. The clinical approach fared least well when the predictors included clinical interview data. Perhaps this was because, as these investigators noted, unlike computer programs, human clinicians make errors in judgment, failing to take account, for example, of base rates or other statistical mediators of accurate assessment. The study authors also hinted that the cost of mechanical prediction probably was less than the cost of clinical prediction since the mechanical route obviated the necessity for highly paid professionals and team meetings; "a clerk, or a computer program can make the prediction for a pittance" (Grove et al., 2000, p. 26).

Based on Grove et al.'s (2000) findings, as well as other studies that have supported the use of statistical prediction over clinical prediction, one may wonder why many clinicians prefer to conduct their assessments "the old-fashioned way," without the benefit of computer software. One reason is that some of the methods used in the comparison research seem to tip the scales in favor of the statistical approach (Holt, 1970; Karon, 2000). For example, as Karon (2000) observed, "clinical data" in many of the studies is defined not in terms of qualitative information elicited by a clinician, but rather in terms of MMPI or MMPI-2 scores. Perhaps the more compelling reason, as Karon (1981) argued, is that the variables in the study of personality (as well as other areas of psychology) are infinite; exactly which variables need to be focused on can be a very individual matter, one decided on an individual basis. Combine these variables with other variables, such as English-speaking ability, cooperativeness, and ethnic and cultural differences, and the size of the computer database needed for accurate prediction becomes extraordinarily large.

Standards for CAPA Products

Professional groups like the American Psychological Association develop guidelines and standards for the use of CAPA products (Bartram et al., 1987; Moreland, 1987). Unfortunately, it is only APA members who can be held to adherence to such guidelines and standards. Many people who use tests do not belong to professional organizations and, indeed, may not even be members of a licensed profession.

Traditionally, quality control in test-related materials has been maintained by a combination of factors, including (1) efforts made by commercial publishers to publish only materials that pass muster with their professional reviewers, and (2) a professional marketplace sufficiently knowledgeable about such products to embrace or reject them. But the computer era in testing is, in at least some respects, changing all that. Mom-and-pop-type operations offering CAPA-related products are getting into the publishing game in record numbers. Just about anyone with a computer, something the person feels he or she has to offer professionals in the field, and an entrepreneurial bent can play. The phenomenon is due at least in part to the small amount of capital needed to start such a business, in comparison with the large investment that would be needed to found a more traditional publishing company. With a computer, many aspects of such a business—from accounting on spreadsheet programs to designing advertising on desktop publishing programs—can be done rather cheaply in-house. The major cash outlay for the would-be publisher may be not for the development of or research into the product but, rather, for its advertising and marketing. The CAPA-related product itself, usually a piece of software, may be available in the form of a floppy disk that the publisher purchases blank for small change. Once the publisher's program has been copied onto the disk, that same disk might be sold for hundreds of dollars. Of course, the validity of the test-interpretation (or other) program that the publisher has copied onto the disk is an entirely different matter; it may not be worth the small change spent on the blank floppy disk.

Currently, the government does not regulate CAPA-related publishing or traditional psychological test publishing. Opinion is divided as to whether such regulation should be introduced. Some have called for governmental regulation of psychological tests, in a manner akin to the way that the Food and Drug Administration oversees the pharmaceutical and cosmetics industries. Others believe that the hodgepodge of checks and balances currently in place for years with respect to traditional tests will also be sufficient for CAPA-related products; according to this view, the marketplace has sufficient sophistication to reject products lacking professional merit. It is probably reasonable to expect no governmental regulation of published psychological testing–related products until solid evidence of public harm comes as the result of the actions of some unscrupulous publisher.

Access to CAPA Products

The issue of access to CAPA-related products is perhaps the least controversial of the many issues facing test users; professionals tend to agree that only qualified professionals should have access to CAPA-related products. The problem, of course, is much the same as the one that has existed, and continues to exist, with regard to more traditional testing products; and that is the definition of a qualified professional. Licensing laws help solve that problem in some, but not all, states, and even where licensing laws exist, they often are sufficiently vague that they allow just about anyone access to the use of psychological assessment–related products.

Many testing professionals fear that the widespread availability of testing software increases the danger that test security will be breached. Further, as such software falls into the wrong hands, the stage will be set for abuse of such tests and public disenchantment with, if not rejection of, psychological tests altogether. To date, there is no research to confirm or disconfirm the gnawing suspicion of many testing professionals that CAPA products are being abused more than conventional paper-and-pencil test-related products.

A Perspective

Computers have a long history of distinction as workhorses when it comes to scoring test protocols and organizing test data. Their value when it comes to interpreting data and printing out reports is a bit more controversial. On the positive side, computers apply the decision rules they are programmed to apply reliably. Unlike inter-rater reliability, "inter-computer" reliability is perfect—barring any program glitches, power outages, or the like. Computers carry no biases regarding race, social class, gender, or sexual orientation. And unlike some clinicians, they don't fall back on a favored personality theory when in doubt about making a test-related decision. Rather, computers diligently play by the rules they are programmed with. It is only when those rules are flawed that their output is flawed. And here we come to the many questions that have been raised about the lack of validation or improper validation of many computer programs (Garb & Schramke, 1996; Moreland, 1985; Snyder et al., 1990).

We share with others (Garb, 2000a, 2000b; Marks, 1999) the view that computers will become increasingly important for psychological assessment. However, for this prophecy to become a reality beneficial to clients, thoughtful solutions to obstacles must continue to be developed (Drasgow & Olson-Buchanan, 1999), and users of assessment-related programs must become more discriminating consumers (Snyder, 2000). Hopefully, users will become better clinicians as well. The development, enhancement, and sharpening of clinical skills will ideally proceed along tracks parallel to the development of new technology. After all, it is in human hands that even the most eloquent computer narratives are placed. It is human judgment that processes and interprets these reports. Ultimately, there is no substitute for clinical judgment (Karon, 1981), and the optimal combination of actuarial methods and clinical judgment must be identified for all types of predictive enterprises (Holt, 1958).

On the Horizon

We foresee more research comparing varied aspects of computer-administered tests with tests administered in more traditional ways. We foresee more research focusing on the validity of computer-based test interpretation. In the area of interface between behavioral assessment and new technology, we foresee research focused on questions related to how a wide range of interventions in inpatient and outpatient settings (ranging from leisure activities to medication) affect behavior. As a consequence of such research, we hope, better prediction of outcomes as a result of intervention will result.

And moving from a consideration of computer-related assessment issues to the broader topic of assessment in general, we foresee a new generation of psychologists, diagnosticians, and educators: students very much like you who have acquired a firm grounding in principles of testing and assessment through reading and thinking about the issues discussed in books such as this one. Should you decide to pursue a career in which you have occasion to use psychological or educational tests, we hope this book will continue to serve as a useful reference and resource for some basic but nonetheless essential assessment-related information. Should you decide to pursue a career in which you have occasion to write about or research psychological or educational tests, perhaps it will be *your* contributions and insights we will be privileged to cite in some future edition of *Psychological Testing and Assessment: An Introduction to Tests and Measurement.*

Self-Assessment

Test your understanding of elements of this chapter by seeing if you can explain each of the following terms, expressions, and abbreviations:

access to CAPA products	**advantages of CAPA**
actuarial methods	**behavioral assessment and CAPA**

CAPA

CAT

CBTI

central processing

computerized adaptive testing

consultative report

descriptive report

disadvantages of CAPA

equivalence issue in CAPA

extended scoring report

integrative report

interpretive report

item bank

item branching

local processing

mechanical prediction

screening report

simple scoring report

standards for CAPA products

teleprocessing

validity issues in CAPA

References

Abel, G. G., Blanchard, E. B., Murphy, W. D., Becker, J. V., & Djenderedjian, A. (1981). Two methods of measuring penile response. *Behavior Therapy, 12,* 320–328.

Abel, G. G., Rouleau, J., & Cunningham-Rathner, J. (1986). Sexually aggressive behavior. In W. J. Curran, A. L. McGarry, & S. Shah (Eds.), *Forensic psychiatry and psychology: Perspectives and standards for interdisciplinary practice* (pp. 289–314). Philadelphia: Davis.

Abeles, N., & Barlev, A. (1999). End of life decisions and assisted suicide. *Professional Psychology: Research and Practice, 30,* 229–234.

Abidin, R. R. (1990). *Parenting stress index* (3rd ed.). Odessa, FL: Psychological Assessment Resources.

Abrams, D. B., Binkoff, J. A., Zwick, W. R., et al. (1991). Alcohol abusers' and social drinkers' responses to alcohol-relevant and general situations. *Journal of Studies on Alcohol, 52,* 409–414.

Abrams, S. (1977). *A polygraph handbook for attorneys.* Lexington, MA: Heath.

Achenbach, T. M. (1978). *Child Behavior Profile.* Bethesda, MD: Laboratory of Developmental Psychology, National Institutes of Mental Health.

Achenbach, T. M. (1981). A junior MMPI? *Journal of Personality Assessment, 45,* 332–333.

Achenbach, T. M. (1993). Implications of Multiaxial Empirically Based Assessment for behavior therapy with children. *Behavior Therapy, 24,* 91–116.

Achenbach, T. M., McConaughy, S. H., & Howell, C. T. (1987). Child/adolescent behavioral and emotional problems: Implications of cross-informant correlations for situational specificity. *Psychological Bulletin, 101,* 213–232.

Ackerman, M. (1987). Child sexual abuse: Bona fide or fabricated? *American Journal of Family Law, 2,* 181–185.

Ackerman, M. J. (1995). *Clinician's guide to child custody evaluations.* New York: Wiley-Interscience.

Ackerman, P. L., & Heggestad, E. D. (1997). Intelligence, personality, and interests: Evidence for overlapping traits. *Psychological Bulletin, 121,* 219–245.

Ackerman, P. L., & Kanfer, R. (1993). Integrating laboratory and field study for improving selection: Development of a battery for predicting air traffic controller success. *Journal of Applied Psychology, 78,* 413–432.

Acklin, M. W. (1995). Avoiding Rorschach dichotomies: Integrating Rorschach interpretation. *Journal of Personality Assessment, 64,* 235–238.

Acklin, M. W. (1996). Personality assessment and managed care. *Journal of Personality Assessment, 66,* 194–201.

Acklin, M. W. (1997). Swimming with sharks. *Journal of Personality Assessment, 69,* 448–451.

Adams, K. M. (1984). Luria left in the lurch: Unfulfilled promises are not valid tests. *Journal of Clinical Neuropsychology, 6,* 455–458.

Adams, K. M. (2000). Practical and ethical issues pertaining to test revisions. *Psychological Assessment, 12,* 281–286.

Adams-Tucker, C. (1982). Proximate effects of sexual abuse in childhood: A report on 28 children. *American Journal of Psychiatry, 139,* 1252–1256.

Addeo, R. R., Greene, A. F., & Geisser, M. E. (1994). Construct validity of the Robson Self-Esteem Questionnaire in a sample of college students. *Educational and Psychological Measurement, 54,* 439–446.

Adelman, S. A., Fletcher, K. E., Bahnassi, A., & Munetz, M. R. (1991). The Scale for Treatment Integration of the Dually Diagnosed (STIDD): An instrument for assessing intervention strategies in the pharmacotherapy of mentally ill substance abusers. *Drug and Alcohol Dependence, 27,* 35–42.

Adler, A. (1927/1965). *Understanding human nature.* Greenwich, CT: Fawcett.

Adler, A. (1933/1964). *Social interest: A challenge to mankind.* New York: Capricorn.

Adler, T. (1990). Does the "new" MMPI beat the "classic"? *APA Monitor, 20,* (4), 18–19.

Ahern, E. (1949). *Handbook of personnel forms and records.* New York: American Management Association.

Aikman, K. G., Belter, R. W., & Finch, A. J. (1992). Human figure drawings: Validity in assessing intellectual level and academic achievement. *Journal of Clinical Psychology, 48,* 114–120.

Airasian, P. W., Madaus, G. F., & Pedulla, J. J. (1979). *Minimal competency testing.* Englewood Cliffs, NJ: Educational Technology Publications.

Akamatsu, C. T. (1993–1994). The view from within and without: Conducting research on deaf Asian-Americans. *Journal of the American Deafness and Rehabilitation Association, 27,* 12–16.

Alderfer, C. (1972). *Existence, relatedness and growth: Human needs in organizational settings.* New York: Free Press.

Alderson, J. C., Krahnke, K. J., & Stansfield, C. W. (1987). *Reviews of English language proficiency tests.* Washington, DC: TESOL.

Alessandri, S. M., Bendersky, M., & Lewis, M. (1998). Cognitive functioning in 8- to 18-month-old drug-exposed infants. *Developmental Psychology, 34,* 565–573.

Alexander, R. C., Surrell, J. A., & Cohle, S. D. (1987). Microwave oven burns in children: An unusual manifestation of child abuse. *Pediatrics, 79,* 255–260.

Allen, M. J., & Yen, W. M. (1979). *Introduction to measurement theory.* Monterey: Brooks/Cole.

Allen, N. J., & Meyer, J. P. (1990). The measurement and antecedents of affective, continuance, and normative commitment to the organization. *Journal of Occupational Psychology, 63,* 1–18.

Allen, R., Wasserman, G. A., & Seidman, S. (1990). Children with congenital anomalies: The preschool period. *Journal of Pediatric Psychology, 15,* 327–345.

Allen, T. E. (1994). *Who are the deaf and hard-of-hearing students leaving high school and entering postsecondary education?* (pp. 1–16). U.S. Office of Special Education and Rehabilitative Services: Pelavin Research Institute.

Allison, D. B., Kalinsky, L. B., & Gorman, B. S. (1992). A comparison of the psychometric properties of three measures of dietary restraint. *Psychological Assessment, 4,* 391–398.

Allport, G. W. (1937). *Personality: A psychological interpretation.* New York: Holt.

Allport, G. W., & Odbert, H. S. (1936). Trait-names: A psycholexical study. *Psychological Monographs, 47* (Whole No. 211).

Allport, G. W., Vernon, P. E., & Lindzey, G. (1951). *Study of values* (rev. ed.). Boston: Houghton Mifflin.

Allred, L. J., & Harris, W. G. (1984). *The nonequivalence of computerized and conventional administrations of the Adjective Checklist.* Unpublished manuscript, Johns Hopkins University.

Alpher, V. S., & Blanton, R. L. (1985). The accuracy of lie detection: Why lie tests based on the polygraph should not be admitted into evidence today. *Law & Psychology Review, 9*, 67–75.

Alterman, A. I., McDermott, P. A., Cook, T. G., et al. (2000). Generalizability of the clinical dimensions of the Addiction Severity Index to nonopioid-dependent patients. *Psychology of Addictive Behaviors, 14*, 287–294.

Amabile, T. M., Hill, K. G., Hennessey, B. A., & Tighe, E. M. (1994). The Work Preference Inventory: Assessing intrinsic and extrinsic motivational orientations. *Journal of Personality and Social Psychology, 66*, 950–967.

Amada, G. (1996). You can't please all of the people all of the time: Normative institutional resistances to college psychological services. *Journal of College Student Psychotherapy, 10*, 45–63.

Aman, C. J., Roberts, R. J., & Pennington, B. F. (1998). A neuropsychological examination of the underlying deficit in attention deficit hyperactivity disorder: Frontal lobe versus right parietal lobe theories. *Developmental Psychology, 34*, 956–969.

Ambrosini, P. J., Metz, C., Bianchi, M. D., Rabinovich, H., & Undie, A. (1991). Concurrent validity and psychometric properties of the Beck Depression Inventory in outpatient adolescents. *Journal of the American Academy of Child and Adolescent Psychiatry, 30*, 51–57.

American Association on Mental Retardation. (1992). *Mental retardation: Definition, classification, and systems of supports* (9th ed.). Washington, DC: Author.

American Board of Forensic Odontology, Inc. (1986). Guidelines for analysis of bite marks in forensic investigation. *Journal of the American Dental Association, 12*, 383–386.

American Education Research Association, American Psychological Association, & National Council on Measurement in Education. (1998). *Standards for educational and psychological testing*. Manuscript in preparation.

American Educational Research Association, American Psychological Association, & National Council on Measurement in Education. (1999). *Standards for educational and psychological testing*. Washington, DC: Author.

American Law Institute. (1956). *Model penal code*. Tentative Draft Number 4.

American Psychiatric Association. (1968). *Diagnostic and statistical manual of mental disorders* (2nd ed.). Washington, DC: Author.

American Psychiatric Association. (1980). *Diagnostic and statistical manual of mental disorders* (3rd ed.). Washington, DC: Author.

American Psychiatric Association. (1987). *Diagnostic and statistical manual of mental disorders* (3rd ed., rev.). Washington, DC: Author.

American Psychiatric Association. (1994). *Diagnostic and statistical manual of mental disorders* (4th ed.). Washington, DC: Author.

American Psychiatric Association. (2000). *Diagnostic and statistical manual of mental disorders,* (4th ed.; text rev.). Washington, DC: Author.

American Psychiatric Association (2001). *Diagnostic and statistical manual of mental disorders,* (4th ed.; text rev.). [CD-ROM (Windows)]. Washington, DC: Author.

American Psychological Association. (1953). *Ethical standards of psychologists*. Washington, DC: Author.

American Psychological Association. (1954). *Technical recommendations for psychological tests and diagnostic techniques*. Washington, DC: Author.

American Psychological Association. (1967). *Casebook on ethical standards of psychologists*. Washington, DC: Author.

American Psychological Association. (1981). Ethical principles of psychologists. *American Psychologist, 36*, 633–638.

American Psychological Association. (1985). *Standards for educational and psychological testing*. Washington, DC: Author.

American Psychological Association. (1987). *Casebook on ethical principles of psychologists*. Washington, DC: Author.

American Psychological Association. (1991). *Questionnaires used in the prediction of trustworthiness in pre-employment selection decisions: An APA Task Force Report*. Washington, DC: Author.

American Psychological Association. (1992). Ethical principles of psychologists and code of conduct. *American Psychologist, 47*, 1597–1611.

American Psychological Association. (1993, January). Call for book proposals for test instruments. *APA Monitor, 24*, 12.

American Psychological Association, Committee on Professional Practice and Standards. (1994a). Guidelines for child custody evaluations in divorce proceedings. *American Psychologist, 49*, 677–680.

American Psychological Association. (1994b). C. H. Lawshe. *American Psychologist, 49*, 549–551.

American Psychological Association. (1995). *Finding information about psychological tests*. Washington, DC: Author.

American Psychological Association (1996). *Standards for psychological tests*. Washington, DC: Author.

Ames, L. B., Learned, J., Metraux, R. W., & Walker, R. N. (1952). *Child Rorschach responses*. New York: Paul B. Hoeber.

Ames, L. B., Metraux, R. W., Rodell, J. L., & Walker, R. N. (1974). *Child Rorschach responses: Developmental trends from two to ten years* (rev. ed.). New York: Brunner/Mazel.

Ames, L. B., Metraux, R. W., & Walker, R. N. (1971). *Adolescent Rorschach responses: Developmental trends from ten to sixteen years*. New York: Brunner/Mazel.

Ames, S. L., & Stacy, A. W. (1998). Implicit cognition in the prediction of substance use among drug offenders. *Psychology of Addictive Behaviors, 12*, 272–281.

Amrine, M. (Ed.). (1965). Special issue. *American Psychologist, 20*, 857–991.

Anastasi, A. (1937). *Differential psychology*. New York: Macmillan.

Anderson, G., & Grace, C. (1991). The Black deaf adolescent: A diverse and underserved population. *Volta Review, 93*, 73–86.

Anderson, J. W. (1990). The life of Henry A. Murray: 1893–1988. In A. I. Rabin, R. A. Zucker, R. A. Emmons, & S. Frank (Eds.), *Studying persons and lives* (pp. 304–333). New York: Springer.

Anderson, W. P. (1995). Ethnic and cross-cultural differences on the MMPI-2. In J. C. Duckworth & W. P. Anderson (Eds.), *MMPI and MMPI-2: Interpretation manual for counselors and clinicians* (4th ed.; pp. 439–460). Bristol, PA: Accelerated Development.

Andrew, G. (1953). The selection and appraisal of test pictures. In G. Andrew, S. W. Hartwell, M. L. Hutt, & R. E. Walton (Eds.), *The Michigan Picture Test* (No. 7-2144). Chicago: Science Research Associates.

Angoff, W. H. (1962). Scales with nonmeaningful origins and units of measurement. *Educational and Psychological Measurement, 22*, 27–34.

Angoff, W. H. (1964). Technical problems of obtaining equivalent scores on tests. *Educational and Psychological Measurement, 1*, 11–13.

Angoff, W. H. (1966). Can useful general-purpose equivalency tables be prepared for different college admissions tests? In A. Anastasi (Ed.), *Testing problems in perspective* (pp. 251–264). Washington, DC: American Council on Education.

Angoff, W. H. (1971). Scales, norms, and equivalent scores. In R. L. Thorndike (Ed.), *Educational measurement* (2nd ed.). Washington, DC: American Council on Education.

Anthony, L., LeResche, L., Niaz, U., et al. (1982). Limits of the "Mini-Mental State" as a screening test for dementia and delirium among hospital patients. *Psychological Medicine, 12,* 397–408.

Appelbaum, P., & Grisso, T. (1995a). The MacArthur Treatment Competence Study: I. Mental illness and competence to consent to treatment. *Law and Human Behavior, 19,* 105–126.

Appelbaum, P., & Grisso, T. (1995b). The MacArthur Treatment Competence Study: III. Abilities of patients to consent to psychiatric and medical treatments. *Law and Human Behavior, 19,* 149–174.

Archer, R. P. (1992). Review of the Minnesota Multiphasic Personality Inventory—2. In J. J. Kramer & J. C. Conoley (Eds.), *The eleventh mental measurements yearbook.* Lincoln: Buros Institute of Mental Measurements, University of Nebraska.

Archer, R. P., & Gordon, R. (1994). Psychometric stability of MMPI-A item modification. *Journal of Personality Assessment, 62,* 416–426.

Archer, R. P., & Krishnamurthy, R. (1994). A structural summary approach for the MMPI-A: Development and empirical correlates. *Journal of Personality Assessment, 63,* 554–573.

Archer, R. P., Maruish, M., Imhof, E. A., & Piotrowski, C. (1991). Psychological test usage with adolescent clients: 1990 survey findings. *Professional Psychology: Research and Practice, 22,* 247–252.

Arnett, P. A., Rao, S. M., Grafman, J., et al. (1997). Executive functions in multiple sclerosis: An analysis of temporal ordering, semantic encoding, and planning abilities. *Neuropsychology, 11,* 535–544.

Arnetz, B. B., Wasserman, J., Petrini, B., et al. (1987). Immune function in unemployed women. *Psychosomatic Medicine, 19,* 3–12.

Arnold, D. S., O'Leary, S. G., Wolff, L. S., & Acker, M. M. (1993). The Parenting Scale: A measure of dysfunctional parenting in discipline situations. *Psychological Assessment, 5,* 137–144.

Aronow, E., & Reznikoff, M. (1976). *Rorschach content interpretation.* Orlando: Grune & Stratton.

Aronow, E., & Reznikoff, M. (1983). *A Rorschach introduction: Content and perceptual approaches.* Orlando: Grune & Stratton.

Aronow, E., Reznikoff, M., & Moreland, K. L. (1995). The Rorschach: Projective technique or psychometric test? *Journal of Personality Assessment, 64,* 213–228.

Arvey, R. D. (1979). *Fairness in selecting employees.* Reading, MA: Addison-Wesley.

Arvey, R. D., Bouchard, T. J., Segal, N. L., & Abraham, L. M. (1989). Job satisfaction: Environmental and genetic components. *Journal of Applied Psychology, 74,* 187–192.

Ary, D. D., Toobert, D., Wilson, W., & Glasgow, R. E. (1986). Patient perspectives on factors contributing to non-adherence to diabetes regimen. *Diabetes Care, 9,* 168–172.

Asch, S. E. (1951). Effects of group pressure upon the modification and distortion of judgment. In H. Guetzkow (Ed.), *Groups, leadership, and men.* Pittsburgh: Carnegie.

Asch, S. E. (1955). Opinions and social pressure. *Scientific American, 193,* 33–35.

Asch, S. E. (1957a). Studies of independence and conformity. A minority of one against a unanimous majority. *Psychological Monographs, 70* (9, Whole No. 416).

Asch, S. E. (1957b). An experimental investigation of group influence. In Walter Reed Army Institute of Research (Ed.), *Symposium on preventive and social psychiatry.* Washington, DC: U.S. Government Printing Office.

Association of Personnel Test Publishers (APTP). (1990). Model guidelines for preemployment integrity testing programs. Washington, DC: APTP.

ASVAB 18/19 Counselor Manual: The ASVAB career exploration program. (1995). Washington, DC: U.S. Department of Defense.

Atkin, C. K. (1978). Observation of parent-child interaction in supermarket decision-making. *Journal of Marketing, 42,* 41–45.

Atkinson, J. W. (Ed.). (1958). *Motives in fantasy, action, and society.* Princeton, NJ: Van Nostrand.

Atkinson, J. W. (1981). Studying personality in the context of an advanced motivational psychology. *American Psychologist, 36,* 117–128.

Atkinson, L., Bevc, I., Dickens, S., & Blackwell, J. (1992). Concurrent validities of the Stanford-Binet (Fourth Edition), Leiter, and Vineland with developmentally delayed children. *Journal of School Psychology, 30,* 165–173.

Atkinson, R. C., & Shiffrin, R. M. (1968). A proposed system and its control processes. In K. W. Spence & J. T. Spence (Eds.), *The psychology of learning and motivation: Advances in research and theory* (Vol. 2; pp. 82–90). Oxford: Oxford University.

Axelrod, B. N., & Paolo, A. M. (1998). Utility of the WAIS-R seven subtest short form as applied to the standardization sample. *Psychological Assessment, 10,* 33–37.

Aycan, Z., Kanungo, R. N., Mendonca, M., et al. (2000). Impact of culture on human resource management practices: A 10-country comparison. *Applied Psychology: An International Review, 49,* 192–221.

Ayres, R. R., & Cooley, E. J. (1986). Sequential versus simultaneous processing on the K-ABC: Validity in predicting learning success. *Journal of Psychoeducational Assessment, 4,* 211–220.

Bachman, J. G., Wallace, J. M., O'Malley, P. M., et al. (1991). Racial/ethnic differences in smoking, drinking, and illicit drug use among American high school seniors, 1976–1989. *American Journal of Public Health, 812,* 372–377.

Back, R., & Dana, R. H. (1977). Examiner sex bias and Wechsler Intelligence Scale for Children scores. *Journal of Consulting and Clinical Psychology, 45,* 500.

Backlar, P. (1996). Managed mental health care: Conflict of interest in provider/client relationships. *Community Mental Health Journal, 32,* 101–110.

Bagby, R. M., Rogers, R., Buiis, T., & Kalemba, V. (1994). Malingered and defensive response styles on the MMPI-2: An examination of the validity scales. *Assessment, 1,* 31–38.

Baker, E. L., O'Neill, H. F., & Linn, R. L. (1993). Policy and validity prospects for performance-based assessment. *American Psychologist, 48,* 1210–1218.

Baldrachi, R., et al. (1998). MMPI-2 assessment of substance abuse in PTSD Vietnam combat veterans. In P. Sloan & J. H. Quillen (Chairs), *Assessment of cognitive, emotional and physical functioning in war veterans.* Symposium presented at the Society for Personality Assessment 1998 Midwinter Meeting, February 20.

Baldwin, A. L., Kalhorn, J., & Breese, F. H. (1945). Patterns of parent behavior. *Psychological Monographs, 58* (Whole No. 268).

Baldwin, J. A. (1984). African self-consciousness and the mental health of African-Americans. *Journal of Black Studies, 15,* 177–194.

Baldwin, J. A., & Bell, Y. R. (1985). The African Self-Consciousness Scale: An Africentric personality questionnaire. *Western Journal of Black Studies, 9*(2), 65–68.

Ball, J. D., Archer, R. P., Gordon, R. A., & French, J. (1991). Rorschach depression indices with children and adolescents: Concurrent validity findings. *Journal of Personality Assessment, 57,* 465–476.

Baltes, B. B., Briggs, T. E., Huff, J. W., et al. (1999). Flexible and compressed workweek schedules: A meta-analysis of their effects on work-related criteria. *Journal of Applied Psychology, 84*, 496–513.

Bank, A. L., MacNeill, S. E., & Lichtenberg, P. A. (2000). Cross validation of the MacNeill-Lichtenberg Decision Tree triaging mental health problems in geriatric rehabilitation patients. *Rehabilitation Psychology, 45*, 193–204.

Barbaree, H. E., & Marshall, W. L. (1989). Erectile responses among heterosexual child molesters, father-daughter incest offenders, and matched non-offenders: Five distinct age preference profiles. *Canadian Journal of Behavioral Science, 21*, 70–82.

Barbarin, O. A., & Chesler, M. (1986). The medical context of parental coping with childhood cancer. *American Journal of Community Psychology, 14*, 221–235.

Barden, R. C., Ford, M. E., Jensen, A. G., Rogers-Salyer, M., & Salyer, K. E. (1989). Effects of craniofacial deformity in infancy on the quality of mother-infant interactions. *Child Development, 60*, 819–824.

Bardis, P. D. (1975). The Borromean family. *Social Science, 50*, 144–158.

Bardos, A. N. (1993). Human figure drawings: Abusing the abused. *School Psychology Quarterly, 8*, 177–181.

Barends, A., Westen, D., Leigh, J., Silbert, D., & Byers, S. (1990). Assessing affect-tone of relationship paradigms from TAT and interview data. *Psychological Assessment, 2*, 329–332.

Barker, R. (1963). On the nature of the environment. *Journal of Social Issues, 19*, 17–38.

Barko, N. (1993, August). What's your child's emotional IQ? *Working Mother, 16*, 33–35.

Barnett, L. A., Far, J. M., Mauss, A. L., & Miller, J. A. (1996). Changing perceptions of peer norms as a drinking reduction program for college students. *Journal of Alcohol & Drug Education, 41*(2), 39–62.

Barnett, R. C., & Gareis, K. C. (2000). Reduced hours, job-role quality, and life satisfaction among married women physicians with children. *Psychology of Women Quarterly, 24*, 358–364.

Baron, J., & Norman, M. F. (1992). SATs, achievement tests, and high-school class rank as predictors of college performance. *Educational and Psychological Measurement, 52*, 1047–1055.

Barrera, M. (1981). Preliminary development of a scale of social support. *American Journal of Community Psychology, 9*, 435–447.

Bartholomew, D. (1996a). "Metaphor taken as math: Indeterminacy in the factor analysis model": Comment. *Multivariate Behavioral Research, 31*, 551–554.

Bartholomew, D. (1996b). Response to Dr. Maraun's first reply to discussion of his paper. *Multivariate Behavioral Research, 31*, 631–636.

Barton, K. A., Blanchard, E. B., & Veazy, C. (1999). Self-monitoring as an assessment strategy in behavioral medicine. *Psychological Assessment, 11*, 490–497.

Bartram, D., Beaumont, J. G., Cornford, T., & Dann, P. L. (1987). Recommendations for the design of software for computer based assessment: Summary statement. *Bulletin of the British Psychological Society, 40*, 86–87.

Bass, B. M. (1956). Development of a structured disguised personality test. *Journal of Applied Psychology, 40*, 393–397.

Bass, B. M. (1957). Validity studies of proverbs personality test. *Journal of Applied Psychology, 41*, 158–160.

Bass, B. M. (1958). Famous Sayings Test: General manual. *Psychological Reports, 4*, Monograph Number 6.

Bassett, S. S. (1999). Attention: Neuropsychological predictor of competency in Alzheimer's disease. *Journal of Geriatric Psychiatry and Neurology, 12*, 200–205.

Batchelor, E., Jr., Sowles, G., Dean, R. S., & Fischer, W. (1991). Construct validity of the Halstead-Reitan Neuropsychological Battery for children with learning disorders. *Journal of Psychoeducational Assessment, 9*, 16–31.

Batchelor, E. S., Gray, J. W., & Dean, R. S. (1990). Empirical testing of a cognitive model to account for neuropsychological functioning underlying arithmetic problem solving. *Journal of Learning Disabilities, 23*(1), 38–42.

Batson, D. C. (1975). Attribution as a mediator of bias in helping. *Journal of Personality and Social Psychology, 32*, 455–466.

Baugh, V. S., & Carpenter, B. L. (1962). Comparison of delinquents and non-delinquents. *Journal of Social Psychology, 56*, 73–78.

Baughman, E. E., & Dahlstrom, W. B. (1968). *Negro and white children: A psychological study in the rural South.* New York: Academic Press.

Bauman, M. K. (1974). Blind and partially sighted. In M. V. Wisland (Ed.), *Psychoeducational diagnosis of exceptional children* (pp. 159–189). Springfield, IL: Charles C Thomas.

Bauman, M. K., & Kropf, C. A. (1979). Psychological tests used with blind and visually handicapped persons. *School Psychology Digest, 8*, 257–270.

Baumeister, A. A., & Muma, J. R. (1975). On defining mental retardation. *Journal of Special Education, 9*, 293–306.

Baumeister, R. F. (1990). Suicide as escape from self. *Psychological Review, 97*, 90–113.

Baumrind, D. (1993). The average expectable environment is not good enough: A response to Scarr. *Child Development, 64*, 1299–1317.

Bavolek, S. J. (1984). *Handbook for the Adult-Adolescent Parenting Inventory.* Eau Claire, WI: Family Development Associates.

Baxter, J. C., Brock, B., Hill, P. C., & Rozelle, R. M. (1981). Letters of recommendation: A question of value. *Journal of Applied Psychology, 66*, 296–301.

Baydoun, R. B., & Neuman, G. A. (1992). The future of the General Aptitude Test Battery (GATB) for use in public and private testing. *Journal of Business and Psychology, 7*, 81–91.

Bayley, N. (1955). On the growth of intelligence. *American Psychologist, 10*, 805–818.

Bayley, N. (1959). Value and limitations of infant testing. *Children, 5*, 129–133.

Bayley, N. (1969). *Bayley Scales of Infant Development: Birth to Two Years.* New York: Psychological Corporation.

Bayley, N. (1993). *Bayley Scales of Infant Development (2nd Edition) Manual.* San Antonio: Psychological Corporation.

Beard, J. G., & Ragheb, M. G. (1980). Measuring leisure satisfaction. *Journal of Leisure Research, 12*, 20–33.

Beavers, R. (1985). *Manual of Beavers-Timberlawn Family Evaluation Scale and Family Style Evaluation.* Dallas: Southwest Family Institute.

Beck, A. T., Brown, G., & Steer, R. A. (1989). Prediction of eventual suicide in psychiatric inpatients by clinical ratings of hopelessness. *Journal of Consulting and Clinical Psychology, 57*, 309–310.

Beck, A. T., Rush, A. J., Shaw, B. F., & Emery, G. (1979). *Cognitive therapy for depression.* New York: Guilford.

Beck, A. T., & Steer, R. A. (1993). *Beck Depression Inventory manual.* San Antonio: Psychological Corporation.

Beck, A. T., Steer, R. A., & Brown, G. K. (1996). *Manual for the Beck Depression Inventory, 2nd ed.* San Antonio: Psychological Corporation.

Beck, A. T., & Stein, D. (1961). Development of a Self-Concept test. Unpublished manuscript, University of Pennsylvania School of Medicine, Center for Cognitive Therapy, Philadelphia.

Beck, A. T., Ward, C. H., Mendelson, M., Mock, J., & Erbaugh, J. (1961). An inventory for measuring depression. *Archives of General Psychiatry, 4*, 561–571.

Beck, S. J. (1944). *Rorschach's test: Vol. 1. Basic processes.* New York: Grune & Stratton.

Beck, S. J. (1945). *Rorschach's test: Vol. 2. A variety of personality pictures.* New York: Grune & Stratton.

Beck, S. J. (1952). *Rorschach's test: Vol. 3. Advances in interpretation.* New York: Grune & Stratton.

Beck, S. J. (1960). *The Rorschach experiment.* New York: Grune & Stratton.

Becker, H. A., Needleman, H. L., & Kotelchuck, M. (1978). Child abuse and dentistry: Orificial trauma and its recognition by dentists. *Journal of the American Dental Association, 97*(1), 24–28.

Becker, R. E., & Heimberg, R. G. (1988). Assessment of social skills. In A. S. Bellack & M. Hersen (Eds.), *Behavioral assessment: A practical handbook* (3rd ed.). New York: Pergamon.

Beckham, J. C., Crawford, A. L., & Feldman, M. E. (1998). Trail Making Test performance in Vietnam combat veterans with and without posttraumatic stress disorder. *Journal of Traumatic Stress, 11*, 811–819.

Beebe, S. A., Casey, R., & Pinto-Martin, J. (1993). Association of reported infant crying and maternal parenting stress. *Clinical Pediatrics, 32*, 15–19.

Begault, D. R. (1993). Head-up auditory displays for traffic collision avoidance advisories: A preliminary investigation. *Human Factors, 35*, 707–717.

Beier, E. G., & Sternberg, D. P. (1977). Marital communication. *Journal of Communication, 27*, 92–100.

Bellack, A. S. (1983). Recurrent problems in the behavioral assessment of social skill. *Behaviour Research and Therapy, 21*, 29–42.

Bellack, A. S., & Hersen, M. (Eds.). (1988). *Behavioral assessment: A practical guide* (3rd ed.). Elmsford, NY: Pergamon.

Bellack, A. S., Hersen, M., & Lamparski, D. (1979). Role-play tests for assessing social skills: Are they valid? Are they useful? *Journal of Consulting and Clinical Psychology, 47*, 335–342.

Bellack, A. S., Morrison, R. L., Mueser, K. T., Wade, J. H., & Sayers, S. L. (1990). Role play for assessing the social competence of psychiatric patients. *Psychological Assessment, 2*, 248–255.

Bellak, L. (1944). The concept of projection: An experimental investigation and study of the concept. *Psychiatry, 7*, 353–370.

Bellak, L. (1971). *The TAT and CAT in clinical use* (2nd ed.). New York: Grune & Stratton.

Bellak, L., & Bellak, S. (1965). *The CAT-H—A human modification.* Larchmont, NY: C.P.S.

Bellak, L., & Bellak, S. S. (1973). *Senior Apperception Technique.* New York: C.P.S.

Bellak, L., & Hurvich, M. (1966). A human modification of the Children's Apperception Test. *Journal of Projective Techniques, 30*, 228–242.

Benbow, C. P., & Stanley, J. C. (1996). Inequity in equity: How "equity" can lead to inequity for high-potential students. *Psychology, Public Policy, and Law, 2*, 249–292.

Bender, L. (1938). A visual-motor gestalt test and its clinical use. *American Orthopsychiatric Association Research Monographs*, No. 3.

Bender, L. (1970). The visual-motor gestalt test in the diagnosis of learning disabilities. *Journal of Special Education, 4*, 29–39.

Benedict, R. H., Schretlen, D., & Bobholz, J. H. (1992). Concurrent validity of three WAIS-R short forms in psychiatric inpatients. *Psychological Assessment, 4*, 322–328.

Bennett, F., Hughes, A., & Hughes, H. (1979). Assessment techniques for deaf-blind children. *Exceptional Children, 45*, 287–288.

Ben-Porath, Y. S. (1990). Cross-cultural assessment of personality: The case for replicatory factor analysis. In J. N. Butcher & C. D. Spielberger (Eds.), *Advances in personality assessment* (Vol. 8; pp. 1–26). Hillsdale, NJ: Erlbaum.

Ben-Porath, Y. S., & Waller, N. G. (1992). Five big issues in clinical personality assessment: A rejoinder to Costa and McCrae. *Psychological Assessment, 4*, 23–25.

Benton, A. L. (1994). Neuropsychological assessment. *Annual Review of Psychology, 45*, 1–25.

Berg, M. (1985). The feedback process in diagnostic psychological testing. *Bulletin of the Menninger Clinic, 49*, 52–68.

Berg, R., Franzen, M., & Wedding, D. (1987). *Screening for brain impairment: A manual for mental health practice.* New York: Springer.

Berk, R. A. (Ed.). (1982). *Handbook of methods for detecting test bias.* Baltimore: Johns Hopkins University.

Berkowitz, L., & Frodi, A. (1979). Reactions to a child's mistakes as affected by her/his looks and speech. *Social Psychology Quarterly, 42*, 420–425.

Bernardin, H. J. (1978). Effects of rater training on leniency and halo errors in student ratings of instructors. *Journal of Applied Psychology, 63*, 301–308.

Bernardin, H. J., & Buckley, M. R. (1981). Strategies in rater training. *Academy of Management Review, 6*, 205–212.

Bernhardt, G. R., Cole, D. J., & Ryan, C. W. (1993). Improving career decision making with adults: Use of portfolios. *Journal of Employment Counseling, 30*, 67–72.

Bernstein, L. (1956). The examiner as an inhibiting factor in clinical testing. *Journal of Consulting Psychology, 20*, 287–290.

Berry, D. S., & Hansen, J. S. (1996). Positive affect, negative affect, and social interaction. *Journal of Personality and Social Psychology, 71*, 796–809.

Besetsny, L. K., Ree, M. J., & Earles, J. A. (1993). Special test for computer programmers? Not needed: The predictive efficiency of the Electronic Data Processing Test for a sample of Air Force recruits. *Educational and Psychological Measurement, 53*, 507–511.

Besharov, D. J. (1985). "Doing something" about child abuse: The need to narrow the grounds for state intervention. *Harvard Journal of Law and Public Policy, 8*, 539–589.

Bienvenu, M. J., Sr. (1978). *A counselor's guide to accompany a Marital Communication Inventory.* Saluda, NC: Family Life.

Bigler, E. D., & Ehrenfurth, J. W. (1980). Critical limitations of the Bender-Gestalt test in clinical neuropsychology: Response to Lacks. *Clinical Neuropsychology, 2*, 88–90.

Bigler, E. D., & Ehrenfurth, J. W. (1981). The continued inappropriate singular use of the Bender Visual Motor Gestalt Test. *Professional Psychology, 12*, 562–569.

Billmire, M. G., & Myers, P. A. (1985). Serious head injury in infants: Accident or abuse? *Pediatrics, 75*, 341–342.

Binet, A., & Henri, V. (1895a). La psychologie individuelle. *L'Année Psychologique, 2*, 411–465.

Binet, A., & Henri, V. (1895b). La mémoire des mots. *L'Année Psychologique, 1*, 1–23.

Binet, A., & Henri, V. (1895c). La mémoire des phrases. *L'Année Psychologique, 1*, 24–59.

Binet, A., & Simon, T. (1905). Méthodes nouvelles pour le diagnostic du niveau intellectuel des anormaux. *L'Année Psychologique, 11*, 191–244.

Binet, A., & Simon, T. (1908). La developpement de l'intelligence chez les enfants [The development of intelligence in children] (E. S. Kite, Trans.). In J. J. Jenkins & D. G. Paterson (reprint Eds.), *Studies in individual differences: The search for intelligence* (pp. 90–96). New York: Appleton-Century-Crofts. (Reprinted in 1961).

Bingham, W. V. (1937). *Aptitudes and aptitude testing.* New York: Harper.

Birch, H. G., & Diller, L. (1959). Rorschach signs of "organic-ity": A physiological basis for perceptual disturbances. *Journal of Projective Techniques, 23,* 184–197.

Birney, R. C., Burdick, H., & Teevan, R. C. (1969). *Fear of failure.* New York: Van Nostrand Reinhold.

Birren, J. E. (1968). Increments and decrements in the intellectual status of the aged. *Psychiatric Research Reports, 23,* 207–214.

Birren, J. E., & Schaie, K. W. (1985). *Handbook of psychology of aging* (2nd ed.). New York: Van Nostrand Reinhold.

Bizot, E. B., & Goldman, S. H. (1993). Prediction of satisfactoriness and satisfaction: An 8-year follow up. Special issue: The theory of work adjustment. *Journal of Vocational Behavior, 43,* 19–29.

Black, B., Ayala, F., & Saffran-Brinks, C. (1994). Science and the law in the wake of Daubert: A new search for scientific knowledge. *Texas Law Review, 72,* 715–802.

Black, H. (1963). *They shall not pass.* New York: Morrow.

Black, H. C. (1979). *Black's law dictionary* (rev. ed.). St. Paul: West.

Black, M., Schuler, M., & Nair, P. (1993). Prenatal drug exposure: Neurodevelopment outcome and parenting environment. *Journal of Pediatric Psychology, 18,* 605–620.

Blader, J. C., & Marshall, W. L. (1984). The relationship between cognitive and erectile measures of sexual arousal in non-rapist males as a function of depicted aggression. *Behaviour Research and Therapy, 22,* 623–630.

Blain, G. H., Bergner, R. M., Lewis, M. L., & Goldstein, M. A. (1981). The use of objectively scorable House-Tree-Person indicators to establish child abuse. *Journal of Clinical Psychology, 37,* 667–673.

Blanchard, E. B., & Young, L. D. (1974). Clinical applications of biofeedback training: A review of evidence. *Archives of General Psychiatry, 30,* 573–589.

Blanck, P. D., & Berven, H. M. (1999). Evidence of disability after *Daubert. Psychology, Public Policy, and Law, 5,* 16–40.

Blazer, D. (1982). Social support and mortality in an elderly community population. *American Journal of Epidemiology, 115,* 684–694.

Bloom, A. S., Allard, A. M., Zelko, F. A. J., Brill, W. J., Topinka, C. W., & Pfohl, W. (1988). Differential validity of the K-ABC for lower functioning preschool children versus those of higher ability. *American Journal of Mental Retardation, 93*(3), 273–277.

Bloxom, B. M. (1978). Review of the 16 PF. In O. K. Buros (Ed.), *The eighth mental measurements yearbook.* Lincoln: Buros Institute of Mental Measurements, University of Nebraska.

Blum, G. S. (1950). *The Blacky pictures: A technique for the exploration of personality dynamics.* New York: Psychological Corporation.

Blum, M. L., & Naylor, J. C. (1968). *Industrial psychology: Its theoretical and social foundations* (rev. ed.). New York: Harper & Row.

Blumenthal, J. A. (1998). The reasonable woman standard: A meta-analytic review of gender differences in perceptions of sexual harassment. *Law & Human Behavior, 22,* 33–57.

Blumenthal, S. J., & Kupfer, D. J. (Eds.). (1990). *Suicide over the life cycle: Risk factors, assessment, and treatment of suicidal patients.* Washington, DC: American Psychiatric Press.

Blustein, D. L., & Ellis, M. V. (2000). The cultural context of career assessment. *Journal of Career Assessment, 8,* 379–390.

Board of Professional Affairs, Committee on Professional Practice & Standards, Practice Directorate, American Psychological Association. (1999). Guidelines for psychological evaluations in child protection matters. *American Psychologist, 54,* 586–593.

Boccaccini, M. T., & Brodsky, S. L. (1999). Diagnostic test usage by forensic psychologists in emotional injury cases. *Professional Psychology: Research and Practice, 30,* 253–259.

Boivin, M. J., Green, S. D. R., Davies, A. G., et al. (1995). A preliminary evaluation of the cognitive and motor effects of pediatric HIV infection in Zairian children. *Health Psychology, 14,* 13–21.

Bombadier, C., & Tugwell, P. (1987). Methodological considerations in functional assessment. *Journal of Rheumatology, 14,* 6–10.

Bond, G. G., Aiken, L. S., & Somerville, S. C. (1992). The health belief model and adolescents with insulin-dependent diabetes mellitus. *Health Psychology, 11,* 190–198.

Bond, M. H., & Forgas, J. P. (1984). Linking person perception to behavior intention across cultures: The role of cultural collectivism. *Journal of Cross-Cultural Psychology, 1,* 185–216.

Bond, R., & Smith, P. B. (1996). Culture and conformity. A meta-analysis of studies using Asch's line judgment task. *Psychological Bulletin, 119,* 111–137.

Boone, D. E. (1991). Item-reduction vs. subtest-reduction short forms on the WAIS-R with psychiatric inpatients. *Journal of Clinical Psychology, 47,* 271–276.

Boone, D. E. (1994). Validity of the MMPI-2 Depression content scale with psychiatric inpatients. *Psychological Reports, 74,* 159–162.

Booth, A., & Edwards, J. (1983). Measuring marital instability. *Journal of Marriage and the Family, 45,* 387–393.

Booth-Kewley, S., & Friedman, H. S. (1987). Psychological predictors of heart disease: A quantitative review. *Psychological Bulletin, 101,* 343–362.

Boring, E. G. (1923, June 6). Intelligence as the tests test it. *New Republic,* pp. 35–37.

Boring, E. G. (1950). *A history of experimental psychology* (rev. ed.). New York: Appleton-Century-Crofts.

Borkenau, P., & Liebler, A. (1992). Trait inferences: Sources of validity at zero acquaintance. *Journal of Personality and Social Psychology, 62,* 645–657.

Bornstein, P. H., Hamilton, S. B., & Bornstein, M. T. (1986). Self-monitoring procedures. In A. R. Ciminero, C. S. Calhoun, & H. E. Adams (Eds.), *Handbook of behavioral assessment* (pp. 176–222). New York: Wiley.

Bornstein, R. F. (1998). Interpersonal dependency and physical illness: A meta-analytic review of retrospective and prospective studies. *Journal of Research in Personality, 32,* 480–497.

Bornstein, R. F. (1999). Criterion validity of objective and projective dependency tests: A meta-analytic assessment of behavioral prediction. *Psychological Assessment, 11,* 48–57.

Bornstein, R. F., Rossner, S. C., Hill, E. L., & Stepanian, M. L. (1994). Face validity and fakability of objective and projective measures of dependency. *Journal of Personality Assessment, 63,* 363–386.

Boss, A. L. (1998). The man who tried to merge with his victim: A case of attempted sexual homicide. In B. Ritzler (Chair), *Individual case studies.* Paper session presentation at the Society for Personality Assessment 1998 Midwinter Meeting, February 20.

Box, G. E. P., & Cox, D. R. (1964). An analysis of transformations. *Journal of the Royal Statistical Society, 59,* 211–243.

Boyle, J. P. (1987). Intelligence, reasoning, and language proficiency. *Modern Language Journal, 71,* 277–288.

Bozeman, D. P., & Perrewe, P. L. (2001). The effect of item content overlap on Organizational Commitment Questionnaire–turnover cognitions relationships. *Journal of Applied Psychology, 86,* 161–173.

Bracken, B. A. (1985). A critical review of the Kaufman Assessment Battery for Children (K-ABC). *School Psychology Review, 14,* 21–36.

Bracken, B. A. (1992). Review of the Wechsler Preschool and Primary Scale of Intelligence—Revised. In J. J. Kramer & J. C. Conoley (Eds.), *The eleventh mental measurements year-*

book. Lincoln: Buros Institute of Mental Measurements, University of Nebraska.

Bracken, B. A., & Barona, A. (1991). State of the art procedures for translating, validating, and using psychoeducational tests in cross-cultural assessment. *School Psychology International, 12,* 119–132.

Bracy-Nipper, D., Karmos, J. S., & Mouw, J. (1987). WISC-R vs. DCAT for predicting academic performance in a high school learning disabled population. *Journal of Instructional Psychology, 14,* 41–47.

Braden, J. P. (1985). *Deafness, deprivation, and IQ.* New York: Plenum.

Braden, J. P. (1990). Do deaf persons have a characteristic psychometric profile on the Wechsler Performance Scales? *Journal of Psychoeducational Assessment, 8,* 518–526.

Braden, J. P. (1992). Intellectual assessment of deaf and hard-of-hearing people: A quantitative and qualitative research synthesis. *School Psychology Review, 21,* 82–84.

Bradley, G. W., & Bradley, L. A. (1977). Experimenter prestige and feedback related to acceptance of genuine personality interpretations and self-attitude. *Journal of Personality Assessment, 41,* 178–185.

Bradley-Johnson, S. (1994). *Psychoeducational assessment of students who are visually impaired or blind: Infancy through high school.* Austin: PRO-ED.

Bradley-Johnson, S., & Harris, S. (1990). Best practices in working with students with a visual loss. In A. Thomas & J. Grimes (Eds.), *Best practices in school psychology II* (pp. 871–885). Washington, DC: National Association of School Psychologists.

Bradway, K. P. (1945). Predictive values of Stanford-Binet preschool items. *Journal of Educational Psychology, 36,* 1–16.

Brady, N. C., & Halle, J. W. (1997). Functional analysis of communicative behaviors. *Focus on Autism and Other Developmental Disabilities, 12*(2), 95–104.

Braginsky, B. M., Braginsky, D. D., & Ring, K. (1969). *Methods of madness.* New York: Holt, Rinehart & Winston.

Brand, H. J. (1989). Reliability of the Frostig Test of Visual Perception in a South African sample. *Perceptual and Motor Skills, 69,* 273–274.

Brandt, P. A., & Weinert, C. (1981). The PRQ—A social support measure. *Nursing Research, 30,* 277–280.

Brannen, M. Y., & Salk, J. E. (2000). Partnering across borders: Negotiating organizational culture in a German-Japanese joint venture. *Human Relations, 53,* 451–487.

Brassard, M., et al. (Eds.). (1986). *The psychological maltreatment of children and youth.* Elmsford, NY: Pergamon.

Brauer, B. (1993). Adequacy of a translation of the MMPI into American Sign Language for use with deaf individuals: Linguistic equivalency issues. *Rehabilitation Psychology, 38,* 247–259.

Bray, D. W. (1964). The management progress study. *American Psychologist, 19,* 419–429.

Bray, D. W. (1982). The assessment center and the study of lives. *American Psychologist, 37,* 180–189.

Bray, G. A. (1986). Effects of obesity on health and happiness. In K. D. Brownell & J. P. Foreyt (Eds.), *Handbook of eating disorders* (pp. 3–44). New York: Basic.

Brems, C., & Johnson, M. E. (1997). Comparison of recent graduates of clinical versus counseling psychology programs. *Journal of Psychology, 13,* 91–99.

Bresolin, M. J., Jr. (1984). A comparative study of computer administration of the Minnesota Multiphasic Personality Inventory in an inpatient psychiatric setting. *Dissertation Abstracts International, 46,* 295B. (University Microfilms No. 85-06, 377).

Brewer, S. (1987, January 11). A perfect package, yes, but how 'bout the name? *Journal-News* (Rockland County, NY), pp. H-1, H-18.

Bricklin, B. (1984). *The Bricklin Perceptual Scales: Child-Perception-of-Parents-Series.* Furlong, PA: Village.

Bringle, R., Roach, S., Andler, C., & Evenbeck, S. (1979). Measuring the intensity of jealous reactions. *Catalogue of Selected Documents in Psychology, 9,* 23–24.

Brittain, H. L. (1907). A study in imagination. *Pedagogical Seminary, 14,* 137–207.

Brody, D., Serby, M., Etienne, N., & Kalkstein, D. S. (1991). Olfactory identification deficits in HIV infection. *American Journal of Psychiatry, 148,* 248–250.

Brody, M. L., Walsh, B. T., & Devlin, M. J. (1994). Binge eating disorder: Reliability and validity of a new diagnostic category. *Journal of Consulting and Clinical Psychology, 62,* 381–386.

Brody, N. (1972). *Personality: Research and theory.* New York: Academic Press.

Brodzinsky, D. M. (1993). On the use and misuse of psychological testing in child custody evaluations. *Professional Psychology: Research and Practice, 24,* 213–219.

Brogden, H. E. (1946). On the interpretation of the correlation coefficient as a measure of predictive efficiency. *Journal of Educational Psychology, 37,* 65–76.

Brogden, H. E. (1949). When tests pay off. *Personnel Psychology, 2,* 171–183.

Brotemarkle, R. A. (1947). Clinical psychology, 1896–1946. *Journal of Consulting and Clinical Psychology, 11,* 1–4.

Brown, D. C. (1994). Subgroup norming: Legitimate testing practice or reverse discrimination. *American Psychologist, 49,* 927–928.

Brown, G., Nicassio, P. W., & Wallston, K. A. (1989). Pain coping strategies and depression in rheumatoid arthritis. *Journal of Consulting and Clinical Psychology, 57,* 652–657.

Brown, G. W. (1989). Life events and measurement. In G. W. Brown & T. Harris (Eds.), *Life events and illness.* New York: Guilford.

Brown, J. M. (1984). Imagery coping strategies in the treatment of migraine. *Pain, 18,* 157–167.

Brown, R. D. (1972). The relationship of parental perceptions of university life and their characterizations of their college sons and daughters. *Educational and Psychological Measurement, 32,* 365–375.

Brown, R. T., Reynolds, C. R., & Whitaker, J. S. (1999). Bias in mental testing since *Bias in Mental Testing. School Psychology Quarterly, 14,* 208–238.

Brown, S. P., & Peterson, R. A. (1993). Antecedents and consequences of salesperson job satisfaction: Meta-analysis and assessment of causal effects. *Journal of Marketing Research, 30,* 63–77.

Browning, D. L. (1987). Ego development, authoritarianism, and social status: An investigation of the incremental validity of Loevinger's Sentence Completion Test (Short Form). *Journal of Personality and Social Psychology, 53,* 113–118.

Bryer, J. B., Martines, K. A., & Dignan, M. A. (1990). Millon Clinical Multiaxial Inventory Alcohol Abuse and Drug Abuse scales and the identification of substance-abuse patients. *Psychological Assessment, 2,* 438–441.

Bucholz, K. K., Cadoret, R., Cloninger, C. R., & Dinwiddie, S. H. (1994). A new, semi-structured psychiatric interview for use in genetic linkage studies: A report on the reliability of the SSAGA. *Journal of Studies on Alcohol, 55,* 149–158.

Buck, J. N. (1948). The H-T-P technique: A qualitative and quantitative scoring manual. *Journal of Clinical Psychology, 4,* 317–396.

Buck, J. N. (1950). *Administration and interpretation of the H-T-P test: Proceedings of the H-T-P workshop at Veterans Administration Hospital, Richmond, Virginia.* Beverly Hills: Western Psychological Services.

Buck, R. (1999). The biological affects: A typology. *Psychological Review, 106,* 301–336.

Buckle, M. B., & Holt, N. F. (1951). Comparison of Rorschach and Behn Inkblots. *Journal of Projective Techniques, 15,* 486–493.

Buckner, F., & Firestone, M. (2000). "Where the public peril begins": 25 years after *Tarasoff. Journal of Legal Medicine, 21,* 187–222.

Bucofsky, D. (1971). Any learning skills taught in the high school? *Journal of Reading, 15*(3), 195–198.

Bukatman, B. A., Foy, J. L., & De Grazia, E. (1971). What is competency to stand trial? *American Journal of Psychiatry, 127,* 1225–1229.

Burger, J. M., Horita, M., Kinoshita, L., et al. (1997). Effects of time on the norm of reciprocity. *Basic and Applied Social Psychology, 19,* 91–100.

Burgess, A. W., McCausland, M. P., & Wolbert, W. A. (1981, February). Children's drawings as indicators of sexual trauma. *Perspectives in Psychiatric Care, 19,* 50–58.

Burisch, M. (1984). Approaches to personality inventory construction: A comparison of merits. *American Psychologist, 39,* 214–227.

Burke, M. J. (1984). Validity generalization: A review and critique of the correlation model. *Personnel Psychology, 37,* 93–115.

Burke, R. J. (1970). Occupational and life strains, satisfactions, and mental health. *Journal of Business Administration, 1,* 35–41.

Burns, A., Jacoby, R., & Levy, R. (1991). Progression of cognitive impairment in Alzheimer's disease. *Journal of the American Geriatrics Society, 39,* 39–45.

Burns, E. (1998). *Test accommodations for students with disabilities.* Springfield, IL: Charles C Thomas.

Burns, R. C., & Kaufman, S. H. (1970). *Kinetic Family Drawings (K-F-D): An introduction to understanding through kinetic drawings.* New York: Brunner/Mazel.

Burns, R. C., & Kaufman, S. H. (1972). *Actions, styles, and symbols in Kinetic Family Drawings (K-F-D).* New York: Brunner/Mazel.

Buros, O. K. (1938). *The 1938 mental measurements yearbook.* New Brunswick, NJ: Rutgers University Press.

Buros, O. K. (1968). The story behind the mental measurements yearbooks. *Measurement and Evaluation in Guidance, 1*(2), 86–95.

Burstein, A. G. (1972). Review of the Wechsler Adult Intelligence Scale. In O. K. Buros (Ed.), *The seventh mental measurements yearbook* (pp. 786–788). Highland Park, NJ: Gryphon.

Burwen, L. S., & Campbell, D. T. (1957). The generality of attitudes toward authority and nonauthority figures. *Journal of Abnormal and Social Psychology, 54,* 24–31.

Bushard, P., & Howard, D. A. (Eds.). (1994). *Resource guide for custody evaluators: A handbook for parenting evaluations.* Madison, WI: Association for Family and Conciliation Courts.

Bushman, B. J., & Wells, G. L. (1998). Trait aggressiveness and hockey penalties: Predicting hot tempers on the ice. *Journal of Applied Psychology, 83,* 969–974.

Butcher, J. N. (1987). The use of computers in psychological assessment: An overview of practices and issues. In J. N. Butcher (Ed.), *Computerized psychological assessment: A practitioner's guide* (pp. 3–14). New York: Basic.

Butcher, J. N. (1990). *MMPI-2 in psychological treatment.* New York: Oxford University.

Butcher, J. N. (1994). Psychological assessment by computer: Potential gains and problems to avoid. *Psychiatric Annals, 24,* 20–24.

Butcher, J. N. (2000). Revising psychological tests: Lessons learned from the revision of the MMPI. *Psychological Assessment, 12,* 263–271.

Butcher, J. N., Dahlstrom, W. G., Graham, J. R., Tellegen, A., & Kaemmer, B. (1989). *Minnesota Multiphasic Personality Inventory—2 (MMPI-2): Manual for administration and scoring.* Minneapolis: University of Minnesota.

Butcher, J. N., & Han, K. (1995). Development of an MMPI-2 scale to assess the presentation of self in a superlative manner: The *S* Scale. In J. N. Butcher & C. D. Spielberger (Eds.), *Advances in personality assessment* (Vol. 10; pp. 25–50). Hillsdale, NJ: Erlbaum.

Butcher, J. N., Perry, J. N., & Atlis, M. M. (2000). Validity and utility of computer-based test interpretation. *Psychological Assessment, 12,* 6–18.

Butcher, J. N., & Williams, C. L. (1992). *Essentials of MMPI-2 and MMPI-A interpretation.* Minneapolis: University of Minnesota.

Butcher, J. N., Williams, C. L., Graham, J. R., et al. (1992). *Minnesota Multiphasic Personality Inventory-Adolescent (MMPI-A): Manual for administration, scoring, and interpretation.* Minneapolis: University of Minnesota Press.

Butters, N., Wolfe, J., Martone, M., et al. (1985). Memory disorders associated with Huntington's disease: Verbal recall, verbal recognition and procedural memory. *Neuropsychologia, 23,* 729–743.

Byrne, D. (1974). *An introduction to personality* (2nd ed.). Englewood Cliffs, NJ: Prentice-Hall.

Byrnes, M. M., & Spitz, H. H. (1977). Performance of retarded adolescents and non-retarded children on the Tower of Hanoi problem. *American Journal of Mental Deficiency, 81,* 561–569.

Cain, L. F., Levine, S., & Elsey, F. F. (1963). *Cain-Levine Social Competency Scale.* Palo Alto, CA: Consulting Psychologists Press.

Calhoon, M. B., Fuchs, L. S., & Hamlett, C. L. (2000). Effects of computer-based test accommodations on mathematics performance assessments for secondary students with learning disabilities. *Learning Disability Quarterly, 23,* 271–282.

Callahan, J. (1994). The ethics of assisted suicide. *Health and Social Work, 19,* 237–244.

Callero, P. L. (1992). The meaning of self-in-role: A modified measure of role-identity. *Social Forces, 71,* 485–501.

Camara, W. J., Nathan, J. S., & Puente, A. E. (1998). *Psychological test usage in professional psychology: Report to the APA Practice and Science Directorates.* Washington, DC: American Psychological Association.

Camara, W. J., Nathan, J. S., & Puente, A. E. (2000). Psychological test usage: Implications in professional psychology. *Professional Psychology: Research and Practice, 31,* 141–154.

Camara, W. J., & Schneider, D. L. (1994). Integrity tests: Facts and unresolved issues. *American Psychologist, 49,* 112–119.

Camilli, G., & Shepard, L. A. (1985). A computer program to aid the detection of biased test items. *Educational & Psychological Measurement, 45,* 595–600.

Campbell, D. P. (1971). *Handbook for the Strong Vocational Interest Blank.* Palo Alto, CA: Stanford University Press.

Campbell, D. P. (1972). The practical problems of revising an established psychological test. In J. N. Butcher (Ed.), *Objective personality assessment: Changing perspectives* (pp. 117–130). New York: Academic Press.

Campbell, D. T., & Fiske, D. W. (1959). Convergent and discriminant validation by the multitrait-multimethod matrix. *Psychological Bulletin, 56,* 81–105.

Campbell, J. M. (1998). Internal and external validity of seven Wechsler Intelligence Scale for Children-Third Edition short forms in a sample of psychiatric inpatients. *Psychological Assessment, 10,* 431–434.

Campo, V., & Vilar, N. P. (1977). Clinical usefulness of the Draw-An-Animal Test. *British Journal of Projective Psychology and Personality Study, 22*(1), 1–7.

Campos, L. P. (1989). Adverse impact, unfairness, and bias in the psychological screening of Hispanic peace officers. *Hispanic Journal of Behavioral Sciences, 11*, 122–135.

Cannon-Bowers, J. A., Salas, E., Blickensderfer, E., & Bowers, C. A. (1998). The impact of cross-training and workload on team functioning: A replication and extension of initial findings. *Human Factors, 40*, 92–101.

Canter, A. (1963). A background interference procedure for grapho-motor tests in the study of deficit. *Perceptual and Motor Skills, 16*, 914.

Canter, A. (1966). A background interference procedure to increase the sensitivity of the Bender Gestalt Test to organic brain disorders. *Journal of Consulting Psychology, 30*, 91–97.

Care, E. (1996). The structure of interests related to college course destinations. *Journal of Career Assessment, 4*, 77–89.

Carey, M. P., Faulstich, M. E., Gresham, F. M., Ruggerio, L., & Enyart, P. (1987). Children's Depression Inventory: Construct and discriminant validity across clinical and non-referred (control) populations. *Journal of Consulting and Clinical Psychology, 55*, 755–761.

Carey, N. B. (1994). Computer predictors of mechanical job performance: Marine Corps findings. *Military Psychology, 6*, 1–30.

Carmichael, L. (1927). A further study of the development of behavior in vertebrates experimentally removed from the influence of external stimulation. *Psychological Review, 34*, 34–47.

Carroll, J. B. (1985, May). Domains of cognitive ability. Symposium: Current theories and findings on cognitive abilities. Los Angeles: AAAS.

Carroll, J. B. (1993). *Human cognitive abilities: A survey of factor-analytic studies.* Cambridge, England: Cambridge University Press.

Carroll, J. B. (1997). The three-stratum theory of cognitive abilities. In D. P. Flanagan et al. (Eds.), *Contemporary intellectual assessment: Theories, tests, and issues* (pp. 122–130). New York: Guilford.

Carroll, K. M. (1998). *A cognitive-behavioral approach: Treating cocaine addiction.* NIH Publication No. 98-4308. Rockville, MD: National Institute on Drug Abuse.

Carroll, K. M., Nich, C., Frankforter, T. L., & Bisighini, R. M. (1999). Do patients change in the ways we intend? Assessing acquisition of coping skills among cocaine-dependent patients. *Psychological Assessment, 11*, 77–85.

Carter, B. L., & Tiffany, S. T. (1999). Meta-analysis of cue reactivity in addiction research. *Addiction, 94*, 327–340.

Carver, C. S., Scheier, M. F., & Pozo, C. (1991). Conceptualizing the process of coping with health problems. In H. Friedman (Ed.), *Hostility, coping, and health* (pp. 167–187). Washington, DC: American Psychological Association.

Carver, R. P. (1968/1969). Designing an aural aptitude test for Negroes: An experiment that failed. *College Board Review, 70*, 10–14.

Carver, R. P. (1969). Use of a recently developed listening comprehension test to investigate the effect of disadvantagement upon verbal proficiency. *American Educational Research Journal, 6*, 263–270.

Cascio, W. F. (1982). *Applied psychology in personnel management* (2nd ed.). Reston, VA: Reston Publishing Company.

Cascio, W. F. (1987). *Applied psychology in personnel management* (3rd ed.). Englewood Cliffs, NJ: Prentice-Hall.

Cascio, W. F., Outtz, J., Zedeck, S., & Goldstein, I. L. (1991). Statistical implications of six methods of test score use in personnel selection. *Personnel Psychology, 4*, 233–264.

Caspi, A., Begg, D., Dickson, N., et al. (1997). Personality differences predict health-risk behaviors in young adulthood: Evidence from a longitudinal study. *Journal of Personality and Social Psychology, 73*, 1052–1063.

Caspi, A., Elder, G., & Bem, D. J. (1987). Moving against the world: Life-course patterns of explosive children. *Developmental Psychology, 23*, 308–313.

Cassel, R. N. (1958). *The leadership q-sort test: A test of leadership values.* Murfreesboro, TN: Psychometric Affiliates.

Catalano, R., Novaco, R., & McConnell, W. (1997). A model of the net effect of job loss on violence. *Journal of Personality and Social Psychology, 72*, 1440–1447.

Cates, J. A., & Lapham, R. F. (1991). Personality assessment of the prelingual, profoundly deaf child or adolescent. *Journal of Personality Assessment, 56*, 118–129.

Cattell, H. E. P. (1993). Comment on Goldberg. *American Psychologist, 48*, 1302–1303.

Cattell, J. M. (1887). Experiments on the association of ideas. *Mind, 12*, 68–74.

Cattell, J. M., & Bryant, S. (1889). Mental association investigated by experiment. *Mind, 14*, 230–250.

Cattell, P. (1940). *Cattell Infant Intelligence Scale.* New York: Psychological Corporation.

Cattell, R. B. (1940). A culture free intelligence test, Part I. *Journal of Educational Psychology, 31*, 161–179.

Cattell, R. B. (1941). Some theoretical issues in adult intelligence testing. *Psychological Bulletin, 38*, 592.

Cattell, R. B. (1946). *The description and measurement of personality.* New York: Harcourt, Brace & World.

Cattell, R. B. (1947). Confirmation and clarification of the primary personality factors. *Psychometrika, 12*, 197–220.

Cattell, R. B. (1948a). The primary personality factors in the realm of objective tests. *Journal of Personality, 16*, 459–487.

Cattell, R. B. (1948b). The primary personality factors in women compared with those in men. *British Journal of Psychology, Statistical Section, 1*, 114–130.

Cattell, R. B. (1950). *Personality: A systematic theoretical and factual study.* New York: McGraw-Hill.

Cattell, R. B. (1957). *Personality and motivation, structure and measurement.* Yonkers, NY: World Book.

Cattell, R. B. (1965). *The scientific analysis of personality.* Baltimore: Penguin.

Cattell, R. B. (1971). *Abilities: Their structure, growth, and action.* Boston: Houghton Mifflin.

Cattell, R. B. (1986). The 16 PF personality structure and Dr. Eysenck. *Journal of Social Behavior and Personality, 1*, 153–160.

Cattell, R. B., Cattell, A. K. S., & Cattell, H. E. P. (1993). *16 PF, Fifth Edition.* Champaign, IL: Institute for Personality and Ability Testing.

Cattell, R. B., & Horn, J. L. (1978). A check on the theory of fluid and crystallized intelligence with description of new subtest design. *Journal of Educational Measurement, 15*, 139–164.

Cattell, R. B., & Krug, S. E. (1986). The number of factors in the 16 PF: A review of the evidence with special emphasis on methodological problems. *Educational and Psychological Measurement, 46*, 509–522.

Caught, K., Shadur, M. A., & Rodwell, J. J. (2000). The measurement artifact in the Organizational Commitment Questionnaire. *Psychological Reports, 87*, 777–788.

Ceci, S. J., Ross, D. F., & Toglia, M. P. (1987). Suggestibility of children's memory: Psycholegal implications. *Journal of Experimental Psychology, 116*, 38–49.

Celis, W., III. (1994, December 16). Computer admissions test found to be ripe for abuse. *New York Times*, pp. A1, A32.

Cerney, M. S. (1984). One last response to the Rorschach test: A second chance to reveal oneself. *Journal of Personality Assessment, 48*, 338–344.

Champagne, J. E. (1969). Job recruitment of the unskilled. *Personnel Journal, 48,* 259–268.

Chan, D. W. (1994). The Chinese Ways of Coping Questionnaire: Assessing coping in secondary school teachers and students in Hong Kong. *Psychological Assessment, 6,* 108–116.

Chan, K.-Y., Drasgow, F., & Sawin, L. L. (1999). What is the shelf life of a test? The effect of time on the psychometrics of a cognitive ability test battery. *Journal of Applied Psychology, 84,* 610–619.

Chance, N. A. (1965). Acculturation, self-identification, and personality adjustment. *American Anthropologist, 67,* 372–393.

Chaney, E. F., O'Leary, M. R., & Marlatt, G. A. (1978). Skill training with problem drinkers. *Journal of Consulting and Clinical Psychology, 46,* 1092–1104.

Chantler, L., Pelco, L., & Mertin, P. (1993). The psychological evaluation of child sexual abuse using the Louisville Behavior Checklist and human figure drawing. *Child Abuse and Neglect, 17,* 271–279.

Chaplin, W. F., John, O. P., & Goldberg, L. R. (1988). Conceptions of state and traits: Dimensional attributes with ideals as prototypes. *Journal of Personality and Social Psychology, 54,* 541–557.

Chapman, J. C. (1921). *Trade tests.* New York: Holt.

Chapman, L., & Chapman, J. (1967). Genesis of popular but erroneous psychodiagnostic observations. *Journal of Abnormal Psychology, 72,* 193–204.

Chappin, S. R., & Brook, J. S. (2001). The influence of generational status and psychosocial variables on marijuana use among Black and Puerto Rican adolescents. *Hispanic Journal of Behavioral Sciences, 23,* 22–36.

Charlton, B. G. (1996). The uses and abuses of meta-analysis. *Family Practice, 13,* 397–401.

Chase, J. (1986). Application of assessment techniques to the totally blind. In P. Lazarus & S. Storchart (Eds.), *Psychoeducational evaluation of children and adolescents with low incidence handicaps.* New York: Grune & Stratton.

Chase, S., & Schlink, F. J. (1927). *Your money's worth: A study in the waste of the consumer's dollar.* New York: Macmillan.

Chattin, S. H., & Bracken, B. A. (1989). School psychologists' evaluation of the K-ABC, McCarthy Scales, Stanford-Binet IV, and WISC-R. *Journal of Psychoeducational Assessment, 7*(2), 112–130.

Checcino, D. J. (1997). Relationships among personality type, self-concept, grade point average, and gender of seventh graders. *Dissertation Abstracts International, Section A: Humanities and Social Sciences, 57*(8-A), 3401.

Chess, S., & Thomas, A. (1973). Temperament in the normal infant. In J. C. Westman (Ed.), *Individual differences in children.* New York: Wiley.

Cheung, F. M., & Lau, B. (1982). Situational variations of helpseeking behavior among Chinese patients. *Comprehensive Psychiatry, 23,* 252–262.

Chinoy, E. (1967). *Society: An introduction to sociology.* New York: Random House.

Chira-Chavala, T., & Yoo, S. M. (1994). Potential safety benefits on intelligence cruise control systems. *Accident Analysis & Prevention, 26,* 135–146.

Cho, H., & LaRose, R. (1999). Privacy issues in Internet surveys. *Social Science Computer Review, 17,* 421–434.

Christiansen, A. J., Weibe, J. S., Smith, T. W., & Turner, C. W. (1994). Predictors of survival among hemodialysis patients: Effects of perceived family support. *Health Psychology, 13,* 521–525.

Christensen, A. L. (1975). *Luria's neuropsychological investigation.* New York: Spectrum.

Christensen, K. M., & Delgado, G. L. (1993). *Multicultural issues in deafness.* White Plains, NY: Longman.

Church, A. T., & Burke, P. J. (1994). Exploratory and confirmatory tests of the Big Five and Tellegen's three- and four-dimensional models. *Journal of Personality and Social Psychology, 66,* 93–114.

Cicchetti, D., & Carlson, V. (Eds.). (1989). *Child maltreatment: Theory and research on the causes and consequences of child abuse and neglect.* New York: Cambridge University.

Cieutat, V. J. (1965). Examiner differences with the Stanford-Binet IQ. *Perceptual and Motor Skills, 20,* 317–318.

Clarizio, H. F. (1989). *Assessment and treatment of depression in children and adolescents.* Brandon, VT: Clinical Psychological Publishing.

Clark, B. (1979). *Growing up gifted.* Columbus, OH: Merrill.

Clark, B. (1988). *Growing up gifted* (3rd ed.). Columbus, OH: Merrill.

Clark, L. A. (1999). Introduction to the special section on the concept of disorder. *Journal of Abnormal Psychology, 108,* 371–373.

Clawson, T. W. (1997). Control of psychological testing: The threat and a response. *Journal of Counseling Development, 76,* 90–93.

Cleckley, H. (1976). *The mask of sanity* (5th ed.). St. Louis, MO: Mosby.

Clements, C. B. (1999). Psychology, attitude shifts, and prison growth. *American Psychologist, 54,* 785–786.

Cliff, N. (1984). An improved internal consistency reliability estimate. *Journal of Educational Statistics, 9,* 151–161.

Cloninger, C. R., Przybeck, T. R., & Svrakis, D. M. (1991). The Tridimensional Personality Questionnaire: U.S. normative data. *Psychological Reports, 69,* 1047–1057.

Code of Fair Testing Practices in Education. (1988). Washington, DC: Joint Committee on Testing Practices.

Coggins, M. H., Pynchon, M. R., & Dvoskin, J. A. (1998). Integrating research and practice in federal law enforcement: Secret Service applications of behavioral science expertise to protect the president. *Behavioral Sciences and the Law, 16,* 51–70.

Cohen, B. M., Moses, J. L., & Byham, W. C. (1977). *The validity of assessment centers: A literature review* (rev. ed.; monograph no. 2). Pittsburgh: Development Dimensions.

Cohen, E. (1965). Examiner differences with individual intelligence tests. *Perceptual and Motor Skills, 20,* 1324.

Cohen, F., & Lazarus, R. S. (1973). Active coping processes, coping dispositions, and recovery from surgery. *Psychosomatic Medicine, 35,* 375–389.

Cohen, J. (1952a). A factor-analytically based rationale for the Wechsler-Bellevue. *Journal of Consulting Psychology, 16,* 272–277.

Cohen, J. (1952b). Factors underlying Wechsler-Bellevue performance of three neuropsychiatric groups. *Journal of Abnormal and School Psychology, 47,* 359–364.

Cohen, J. (1957a). The factorial structure of the WAIS between early adulthood and old age. *Journal of Consulting Psychology, 21,* 283–290.

Cohen, J. (1957b). A factor-analytically based rationale for the Wechsler Adult Intelligence Scale. *Journal of Consulting Psychology, 21,* 451–457.

Cohen, J. (1960). A coefficient of agreement for nominal scales. *Educational and Psychological Measurement, 20,* 37–46.

Cohen, O., Fischgrund, J., & Redding, R. (1990). Deaf children from ethnic, linguistic, and racial minority backgrounds: An overview. *American Annals of the Deaf, 135,* 67–73.

Cohen, R. J. (1977). Socially reinforced obsessing: A reply. *Journal of Consulting and Clinical Psychology, 45,* 1166–1171.

Cohen, R. J. (1979). *Malpractice: A guide for mental health professionals.* New York: Free Press.

Cohen, R. J. (1985). Computer-enhanced qualitative research. *Journal of Advertising Research, 25*(3), 48–52.

Cohen, R. J. (1987). Overview of emerging evaluative and diagnostic methods technologies. In *Proceedings of the fourth annual Advertising Research Foundation workshop: Broadening the horizons of copy research.* New York: Advertising Research Foundation.

Cohen, R. J. (1994). *Psychology & adjustment: Values, culture, and change.* Boston: Allyn & Bacon.

Cohen, R. J. (1999). *Exercises in psychological testing and assessment.* Mountain View, CA: Mayfield.

Cohen, R. J. (1999). What qualitative research can be. *Psychology & Marketing, 16,* 351–368.

Cohen, R. J. (2001). *Discussion of Organizational Culture* (DOC). Jamaica, NY: Author.

Cohen, R. J. (2002). *Exercises in psychological testing and assessment* (5th ed.). New York: McGraw-Hill.

Cohen, R. J., Becker, R. E., & Teevan, R. C. (1975). Perceived somatic reaction to stress and hostile press. *Psychological Reports, 37,* 676–678.

Cohen, R. J., & Houston, D. R. (1975). Fear of failure and rigidity in problem solving. *Perceptual and Motor Skills, 40,* 930.

Cohen, R. J., & Mariano, W. E. (1982). *Legal guidebook in mental health.* New York: Free Press.

Cohen, R. J., Montague, P., Nathonson, L. S., & Swerdlik, M. E. (1988). *Psychological testing: An introduction to tests and measurement.* Mountain View, CA: Mayfield.

Cohen, R. J., & Parker, C. (1974). Fear of failure and death. *Psychological Reports, 34,* 54.

Cohen, R. J., & Smith, F. J. (1976). Socially reinforced obsessing: Etiology of a disorder in a Christian Scientist. *Journal of Consulting and Clinical Psychology, 44,* 142–144.

Cohen, R. J., & Teevan, R. C. (1974). Fear of failure and impression management: An exploratory study. *Psychological Reports, 35,* 1332.

Cohen, R. J., & Teevan, R. C. (1975). Philosophies of human nature and hostile press. *Psychological Reports, 37,* 460–462.

Cohen, S., Nermelstein, R., Karmack, T., & Hoberman, H. (1985). Measuring the functional components of social support. In I. G. Sarason & B. Sarason (Eds.), *Social support: Theory, research, and practice* (pp. 73–94). Dordrecht, Netherlands: Martinus Nijhoff.

Cohen, S., & Syme, S. L. (1985). *Social support and health.* San Francisco: Academic Press.

Cole, S. T., & Hunter, M. (1971). Pattern analysis of WISC scores achieved by culturally disadvantaged children. *Psychological Reports, 20,* 191–194.

Coleman, L. (1989). Medical examination for sexual abuse: Are we being told the truth? *Family Law News, 12*(2).

College Board Review, The (1990–1991, Winter). Roundtable: The new SAT: Debating its implications. *College Board Review, 158,* 22–27.

Colligan, R. C., & Offord, K. P. (1989). The aging MMPI: Contemporary norms for contemporary teenagers. *Mayo Clinic Proceedings, 64,* 3–27.

Colligan, R. C., Osborne, D., & Offord, K. P. (1980). Linear transformation and the interpretation of MMPI *T* scores. *Journal of Clinical Psychology, 36,* 162–165.

Colligan, R. C., Osborne, D., & Offord, K. P. (1984a). Normalized transformation and the interpretation of MMPI *T* scores: A reply to Hsu. *Journal of Consulting and Clinical Psychology, 52,* 824–826.

Colligan, R. C., Osborne, D., Swenson, W. M., & Offord, K. P. (1983). *The MMPI: A contemporary normative study of adults* (2nd ed.). Odessa, FL: Psychological Assessment Resources.

Colligan, R. C., Osborne, D., Swenson, W. M., & Offord, K. P. (1984b). The aging MMPI: Development of contemporary norms. *Mayo Clinic Proceedings, 59,* 377–390.

Colligan, R. C., et al. (1998). Introversion-extroversion, optimism-pessimism, and the risk for Alzheimer's disease. In R. J. Craig (Chair), *Assessment, decision-making, and classification.* Paper session presentation at the Society for Personality Assessment 1998 Midwinter Meeting, February 21.

Colligan, R. C., Osborne, D., Swenson, W. M., & Offord, K. P. (1984c). *Contemporary norms for the MMPI: Summarizing one year of clinical experience.* Paper presented at the 93rd annual meeting of the American Psychological Association, Toronto, Ontario, Canada.

Collins, J. K., Jupp, J. J., Maberly, G. F., et al. (1987). An exploratory study of the intellectual functioning of neurological and myxoedematous cretins in China. *Australia & New Zealand Journal of Developmental Disabilities, 13,* 13–20.

Collins, L. M. (1996). Is reliability obsolete? A commentary on "Are simple gain scores obsolete?" *Applied Psychological Measurement, 20,* 289–292.

Comer, D. R. (1993). Workplace drug testing reconsidered. *Journal of Managerial Issues, 5,* 517–531.

Commons, M. (1985, April). How novelty produces continuity in cognitive development within a domain and accounts for unequal development across domains. Toronto: SRCD, Ontario, Canada.

Compton, D. M., Bachman, L. D., Brand, D., & Avet, T. L. (2000). Age-associated changes in cognitive function in highly educated adults: Emerging myths and realities. *International Journal of Geriatric Psychiatry, 15,* 75–85.

Comrey, A. L. (1992). *A first course in factor analysis.* Hillsdale, NJ: Erlbaum.

Cone, J. D. (1977). The relevance of reliability and validity for behavioral assessment. *Behavior Therapy, 8,* 411–426.

Cone, J. D. (1981). Psychometric considerations. In M. Hersen & A. S. Bellack (Eds.), *Behavioral assessment: A practical handbook* (2nd ed.). New York: Pergamon.

Cone, J. D. (1986). Idiographic, nomothetic, and related perspectives in behavioral assessment. In R. O. Nelson & S. C. Hayes (Eds.), *Conceptual foundations of behavioral assessment.* New York: Guilford.

Cone, J. D. (1987). Behavioral assessment: Some things old, some things new, some things borrowed? *Behavioral Assessment, 9,* 1–4.

Cone, J. D. (1999). Introduction to the special section on self-monitoring: A major assessment method in clinical psychology. *Psychological Assessment, 11,* 411–414.

Conger, A. J. (1985). Kappa reliabilities for continuing behaviors and events. *Educational and Psychological Measurement, 45,* 861–868.

Connolly, J. (1976). Life events before myocardial infarction. *Journal of Human Stress, 3,* 3–17.

Conte, H. R., & Plutchik, R. (1981). A circumplex model for interpersonal personality traits. *Journal of Personality and Social Psychology, 40,* 701–711.

Conte, H. R., Plutchik, R., Buck, L., Picard, S., & Karasu, T. B. (1991). Interrelations between ego functions and personality traits: Their relation to psychotherapy outcome. *American Journal of Psychotherapy, 45,* 69–77.

Cook, T. D., Cooper, H., Cordray, D. S., et al. (1992). *Meta-analysis for explanation: A casebook.* New York: Russell Sage Foundation.

Cooke, N. J., Salas, E., Cannon-Bowers, J. A., & Stout, R. J. (2000). Measuring team knowledge. *Human Factors, 42,* 151–173.

Coolidge, F. L., et al. (1998). Personality disorders in chronic pain patients. In F. Coolidge (Chair), *Validity studies.* Paper session presentation at the Society for Personality Assessment 1998 Midwinter Meeting, February 20.

Cooper, A. (1981). A basic TAT set for adolescent males. *Journal of Clinical Psychology, 37*(2), 411–414.

Cooper, M. L. (1994). Motivations for alcohol use among adolescents: Development and validation of a four-factor model. *Psychological Assessment, 6,* 117–128.

Copas, J. B., & Tarling, R. (1986). Some methodological issues in making predictions. In A. Blumstein et al. (Eds.), *Criminal careers and "career criminals"* (pp. 291–313). Washington, DC: National Academy.

Corish, C. D., Richard, B., & Brown, S. (1989). Missed medication doses in rheumatoid arthritis patients: Intentional and unintentional reasons. *Arthritis Care and Research, 2*, 3–9.

Cornell, D. G. (1985). External validation of the Personality Inventory for Children—Comment on Lachar, Gdowski, and Snyder. *Journal of Consulting and Clinical Psychology, 53*, 273–274.

Corwin, D., Berlinger, L., Goodman, G., Goodwin, J., & White, S. (1987). Child sexual abuse and custody disputes: No easy answers. *Journal of Interpersonal Violence, 2*, 91–105.

Corwyn, R. F., & Benda, B. B. (2000). Religiosity and church attendance: The effects on use of "hard drugs" controlling for sociodemographic and theoretical factors. *International Journal for the Psychology of Religion, 10*, 241–258.

Costa, P. T., Jr., & McCrae, R. R. (1985). *The NEO Personality Inventory manual.* Odessa, FL: Psychological Assessment Resources.

Costa, P. T., Jr., & McCrae, R. R. (1986). Major contributions to personality psychology. In S. Modgil & C. Modgil (Eds.), *Hans Eysenck: Consensus and controversy* (pp. 63–72, 86, 87). Barcombe Lewes Sussex, England: Falmer.

Costa, P. T., Jr., & McCrae, R. R. (1987). On the need for longitudinal evidence and multiple measures in behavior-genetics studies of adult personality. *Behavioral and Brain Sciences, 10*, 22–23.

Costa, P. T., Jr., & McCrae, R. R. (1992a). Four ways five factors are basic. *Personality and Individual Differences, 13*, 653–665.

Costa, P. T., Jr., & McCrae, R. R. (1992b). Reply to Eysenck. *Personality and Individual Differences, 13*, 861–865.

Costa, P. T., Jr., & McCrae, R. R. (1992c). *Revised NEO Personality Inventory (NEO-PI-R) and NEO Five-Factor Inventory (NEO-FFI) professional manual.* Odessa, FL: Psychological Assessment Resources.

Costa, P. T., Jr., & McCrae, R. R. (1997). Stability and change in personality assessment: The Revised NEO Personality Inventory in the year 2000. *Journal of Personality Assessment, 68*, 86–94.

Costantino, G., Malgady, R., & Rogler, L. H. (1988). *Tell-Me-A-Story—TEMAS—manual.* Los Angeles: Western Psychological Services.

Cote, J. A., McCullough, J., & Reilly, M. (1985). Effects of unexpected situations on behavior-intention differences: A garbology analysis. *Journal of Consumer Research, 12*, 188–194.

Cotton, P. (1992). Women's health initiative leads way as research begins to fill gender gaps. *Journal of the American Medical Association, 267*(4), 469–470, 473.

Covetkovic, R. (1979). Conception and representation of space in human figure drawings by schizophrenic and normal subjects. *Journal of Personality Assessment, 43*(3), 247–256.

Coyne, J. C. (1976). The place of informed consent in ethical dilemmas. *Journal of Consulting and Clinical Psychology, 44*, 1015–1017.

Craig, R. J. (1998). MCMI-III typological analysis of cocaine and heroine addicts. In R. J. Craig (Chair), *Assessment, decision-making, and classification.* Paper session presentation at the Society for Personality Assessment 1998 Midwinter Meeting, February 21.

Cramer, P. (1996). *Storytelling, narrative, and the Thematic Apperception Test.* New York: Guilford.

Crawford, A. M. (1996). Stigma associated with AIDS: A meta-analysis. *Journal of Applied Social Psychology, 26*, 398–416.

Crevecoeur, M. G. St. J. de (1951). What is an American letter? In H. S. Commager (Ed.), *Living ideas in America.* New York: Harper. (Originally published in *Letters from an American farmer*, 1762)

Crick, N. R. (1997). Engagement in gender normative versus nonnormative forms of aggression: Links to social-psychological adjustment. *Developmental Psychology, 33*, 610–617.

Crick, N. R., Bigbee, M. A., & Howes, C. (1996). Gender differences in children's normative beliefs about aggression: How do I hurt thee? Let me count the ways. *Child Development, 67*, 1003–1014.

Crocker, L., Llabre, M., & Miller, M. D. (1988). The generalizability of content validity ratings. *Journal of Educational Measurement, 25*, 287–299.

Cronbach, L. J. (1949). Statistical methods applied to Rorschach scores: A review. *Psychological Bulletin, 46*, 393–429.

Cronbach, L. J. (1951). Coefficient alpha and the internal structure of tests. *Psychometrika, 16*, 297–334.

Cronbach, L. J. (1970). *Essentials of psychological testing* (3rd ed.). New York: Harper & Row.

Cronbach, L. J. (1975). Five decades of public controversy over mental testing. *American Psychologist, 30*, 1–13.

Cronbach, L. J. (1984). *Essentials of psychological testing* (4th ed.). New York: Harper & Row.

Cronbach, L. J., & Gleser, G. C. (1965). *Psychological tests and personnel decisions* (2nd ed.). Urbana: University of Illinois.

Cronbach, L. J., Gleser, G. C., Nanda, H., & Rajaratnam, N. (1972). *The dependability of behavioral measurement: Theory of generalizability for scores and profiles.* New York: Wiley.

Cronbach, L. J., & Meehl, P. E. (1955). Construct validity in psychological tests. *Psychological Bulletin, 52*, 281–302.

Cross, T. L., Coleman, L. J., & Stewart, R. A. (1993). The social cognition of gifted adolescents: An exploration of the stigma of the giftedness paradigm. *Roeper Review, 16*, 37–40.

Cross, T. L., Coleman, L. J., & Terhaar-Yonkers, M. (1991). The social cognition of gifted adolescents in schools: Managing the stigma of giftedness. *Journal for the Education of the Gifted, 15*, 44–55.

Crosson, B., & Warren, R. L. (1982). Use of the Luria-Nebraska Neuropsychological Battery in aphasia: A conceptual critique. *Journal of Consulting and Clinical Psychology, 50*, 22–31.

Crowne, D. P., & Marlowe, D. (1964). *The approval motive: Studies in evaluative dependence.* New York: Wiley.

Crundall, D. E., Underwood, G., & Chapman, P. R. (1998). How much do drivers see? The effects of demand on visual search strategies in novice and experienced drivers. In G. Underwood (Ed.), *Eye guidance in reading and scene perception* (pp. 395–417). Oxford, England: Elsevier.

Cuellar, I., Harris, I. C., & Jasso, R. (1980). An acculturation scale for Mexican American normal and clinical populations. *Hispanic Journal of Behavioral Science, 2*, 199–217.

Cummings, J. A. (1981). An evaluation of Kinetic Family Drawings. Paper presented at the annual meeting of the American Psychological Association, Los Angeles.

Cummings, M. A., & Merrell, K. W. (1993). K-ABC score patterns of Sioux children: Mental processing styles, effects of school attendance, and relationship between raw scores and age. *Journal of Psychoeducational Assessment, 11*, 38–45.

Cundick, B. P. (1976). Measures of intelligence on Southwest Indian students. *Journal of Social Psychology, 81*, 151–156.

Cunningham, M. R. (1988). What do you do when you're happy or blue? Mood, expectancies, and behavioral interests. *Motivation and Emotion, 12*, 309–331.

Cureton, E. E. (1957). The upper and lower twenty-seven per cent rule. *Psychometrika, 22*, 293–296.

Cushman, P., & Guilford, P. (2000). Will managed care change our way of being? *American Psychologist, 55*, 985–996.

Dahlstrom, W. G. (1995). Pigeons, people, and pigeon holes. *Journal of Personality Assessment, 64*, 2–20.

Dahlstrom, W. G., & Dahlstrom, L. E. (Eds.). (1980). *Basic readings on the MMPI: A new selection on personality measurement*. Minneapolis: University of Minnesota.

Dahlstrom, W. G., & Welsh, G. S. (1960). *An MMPI handbook: A guide to use in clinical practice and research*. Minneapolis: University of Minnesota.

Dahlstrom, W. G., Welsh, G. S., & Dahlstrom, L. E. (1972). *An MMPI handbook: Vol. 1. Clinical interpretation*. Minneapolis: University of Minnesota.

Daigneault, S., Braun, C. M. J., & Whitaker, H. A. (1992). Early effects of normal aging on perseverative and non-perseverative prefrontal measures. *Developmental Neuropsychology, 8*, 99–114.

Dana, R. H. (1995). Culturally competent MMPI assessment of Hispanic populations. *Hispanic Journal of Behavioral Sciences, 17*, 305–319.

Dana, R. H., & Whatley, P. R. (1991). When does a difference make a difference? MMPI scores and African-Americans. *Journal of Clinical Psychology, 47*, 400–406.

Daneman, M., & Carpenter, P. A. (1980). Individual differences in working memory and reading. *Journal of Verbal Learning and Verbal Behavior, 19*, 450–466.

Danford, G. S., & Steinfeld, E. (1999). Measuring the influences of physical environments on the behaviors of people with impairments. In E. Steinfeld & G. S. Danford (Eds.), *Enabling environments: Measuring the impact of environment on disability and rehabilitation* (pp. 111–137). New York: Kluwer Academic/Plenum.

Daniels, K. (2000). Measures of five aspects of affective well-being at work. *Human Relations, 53*, 275–294.

Darwin, C. (1859). *On the origin of species by means of natural selection*. London: Murray.

Das, J. P. (1972). Patterns of cognitive ability in nonretarded and retarded children. *American Journal of Mental Deficiency, 77*, 6–12.

Das, J. P., Kirby, J., & Jarman, R. F. (1975). Simultaneous and successive synthesis: An alternative model for cognitive abilities. *Psychological Bulletin, 82*, 87–103.

Datel, W. E., & Gengerelli, J. A. (1955). Reliability of Rorschach interpretations. *Journal of Projective Techniques, 19*, 322–338.

Daubert v. Merrell Dow Pharmaceuticals (1993). 113 S.Ct. 2786.

Davidson, H. A. (1949). Malingered psychosis. *Bulletin of the Menninger Clinic, 13*, 157–163.

Davidson, T. N., Bowden, L., & Tholen, D. (1979). Social support as a moderator of burn rehabilitation. *Archives of Physical Medicine and Rehabilitation, 60*, 556.

Davies, M., Stankov, L., & Roberts, R. D. (1998). Emotional intelligence: In search of an elusive construct. *Journal of Personality and Social Psychology, 75*, 989–1015.

Davies, P. L., & Gavin, W. J. (1994). Comparison of individual and group/consultation treatment methods for preschool children with developmental delays. *American Journal of Occupational Therapy, 48*, 155–161.

Davis, G. A. (1989). Testing for creative potential. *Contemporary Educational Psychology, 14*, 257–274.

Davis, R., Butler, N., & Goldstein, H. (1972). *From birth to seven: A report of the National Child Development Study*. London: Longman.

Davison, G. C., Vogel, R. S., & Coffman, S. G. (1997). Think-aloud approaches to cognitive assessment and the articulated thoughts in simulated situations paradigm. *Journal of Consulting and Clinical Psychology, 65*, 950–958.

Dawes, R. M., Faust, D., & Meehl, P. E. (1989, March 31). Clinical versus actuarial judgment. *Science, 243*, 1668–1674.

Day, D. V., & Silverman, S. B. (1989). Personality and job performance: Evidence of incremental validity. *Personnel Psychology, 42*, 25–36.

Dean, A. (Ed.). (1985). *Depression in multidisciplinary perspective*. New York: Brunner/Mazel.

DeCato, C. M. (1994). Toward a training model for Rorschach scoring revisited: A follow-up study on a training system for interscorer agreement. *Perceptual and Motor Skills, 78*, 3–10.

Delahunty, R. J. (1988). Perspectives on within-group scoring. *Journal of Vocational Behavior, 33*, 463–477.

Delaney, E. A., & Hopkins, T. F. (1987). *Examiner's handbook: An expanded guide for Fourth Edition users*. Chicago: Riverside.

Delis, D. C., & Kaplan, E. (1982). The assessment of aphasia with the Luria Nebraska Neuropsychological Battery: A case critique. *Journal of Consulting and Clinical Psychology, 50*, 32–39.

Deloria, D. J. (1985). Review of the Miller Assessment for Preschoolers. In J. V. Mitchell, Jr. (Ed.), *The ninth mental measurements yearbook*. Lincoln: Buros Institute of Mental Measurements, University of Nebraska.

DeMulder, E. K., Denham, S., Schmidt, M., & Mitchell, J. (2000). Q-sort assessment of attachment security during the preschool years: Links from home to school. *Developmental Psychology, 36*, 274–282.

Dennis, W., & Dennis, M. G. (1940). The effect of cradling practice upon the onset of walking in Hopi children. *Journal of Genetic Psychology, 56*, 77–86.

DePaepe, J. L., & Ciccaglione, S. (1993). A dynamic balance measure for persons with severe and profound mental retardation. *Perceptual and Motor Skills, 76*, 619–627.

Department of Health, Education, and Welfare. (1977a). Nondiscrimination on basis of handicap: Implementation of Section 504 of the Rehabilitation Act of 1973. *Federal Register, 42*(86), 22676–22702.

Department of Health, Education, and Welfare. (1977b). Education of Handicapped Children: Implementation of Part B of the Education of the Handicapped Act. *Federal Register, 42*(163), 42474–42518.

DePaulo, B. M. (1994). Spotting lies: Can humans learn to do better? *Current Directions in Psychological Science, 3*, 83–86.

Derogatis, L. R. (1994). *SCL-90-R: Symptom Checklist-90-R: Administration, scoring and procedures manual* (3rd ed.). Minneapolis: NCS.

Derogatis, L. R., Abeloff, M. D., & Melisaratos, N. (1979). Psychological coping mechanisms and survival time in metastatic breast cancer. *Journal of the American Medical Association, 242*, 1504–1508.

Desrochers, M. N., Hile, M. G., & Williams-Mosely, T. L. (1997). Survey of functional assessment procedures used with individuals who display mental retardation and severe problem behaviors. *American Journal on Mental Retardation, 101*, 535–546.

Detterman, D. K. (1986). Qualitative integration: The last word? In R. J. Sternberg & D. K. Detterman (Eds.), *What is intelligence?* (pp. 163–166). Norwood, NJ: Ablex.

Devlin, B., Daniels, M., & Roeder, K. (1997). The heritability of IQ. *Nature, 388*, 468–471.

Diamond, B. L. (1980). Inherent problems in the use of pretrial hypnosis on a prospective witness. *California Law Review, 68*, 313–349.

Dickson, C. R. (1975). Role of assessment in behavior therapy. In P. McReynolds (Ed.), *Advances in psychological assessment* (Vol. 3). San Francisco: Jossey-Bass.

DiClemente, C. C., & Hughes, S. O. (1990). Stages of change profiles in outpatient alcoholism treatment. *Journal of Substance Abuse, 2*, 217–235.

Diebold, M. H., Curtis, W. S., & DuBose, R. F. (1978). Developmental scales versus observational measures for deaf-blind children. *Exceptional Children, 44*, 275–278.

Dietz, P. E., Matthews, D. B., Van Duyne, C., et al. (1991). Threatening and otherwise inappropriate letters to Hollywood celebrities. *Journal of Forensic Sciences, 36*, 185–209.

DiMatteo, M. R., Hays, R. D., Grita, E. R., et al. (1993). Patient adherence to cancer control regimens: Scale development and initial validation. *Psychological Assessment, 5,* 102–112.

Dimock, P. H., & Cormier, P. (1991). The effects of format differences and computer experience on performance and anxiety on a computer-administered test. *Measurement and Evaluation in Counseling and Development, 24,* 119–126.

Dion, K. K. (1979). Physical attractiveness and evaluation of children's transgressions. *Journal of Personality and Social Psychology, 24,* 207–213.

Diven, K. (1937). Certain determinants in the conditioning of anxiety reactions. *Journal of Psychology, 3,* 291–308.

Dmitruk, V. M., Collins, R. W., & Clinger, D. I. (1973). The Barnum effect and acceptance of negative personal evaluation. *Journal of Consulting and Clinical Psychology, 41,* 192–194.

Dohrenwend, B. P., & Shrout, P. E. (1985). Hassles in the conceptualization and measurement of life stresses variables. *American Psychologist, 40,* 780–785.

Doll, E. A. (1917). A brief Binet-Simon scale. *Psychological Clinic, 11,* 197–211, 254–261.

Doll, E. A. (1953). *Measurement of social competence: A manual for the Vineland Social Maturity Scale.* Circle Pines, MN: American Guidance Service.

Dolnick, E. (1993). Deafness as culture. *Atlantic, 272*(3), 37–53.

Donahue, E. M., Robins, R. W., Roberts, B. W., & John, O. P. (1993). The divided self: Concurrent and longitudinal effects of psychological adjustment and social roles on self-concept differentiation. *Journal of Personality and Social Psychology, 64,* 834–846.

Donders, J. (1992). Validity of the Kaufman Assessment Battery for Children when employed with children with traumatic brain injury. *Journal of Clinical Psychology, 48,* 225–230.

Donders, J. (1997). A short form of the WISC-III for clinical use. *Psychological Assessment, 9,* 15–20.

Dorcus, R. M., & Jones, M. H. (1950). *Handbook of employee selection.* New York: McGraw-Hill.

Doty, R. L., Shaman, P., & Dann, M. (1984). Development of the University of Pennsylvania Smell Identification Test: A standard microencapsulated test of olfactory dysfunction. *Physiological Behavior, 32,* 489–502.

Dougherty, T. M., & Haith, M. M. (1997). Infant expectations and reaction time as predictors of childhood speed of processing and IQ. *Developmental Psychology, 33,* 146–155.

Douglas, C. (1993). *Translate this darkness: The life of Christiana Morgan.* New York: Simon & Schuster.

Draguns, J. G. (1984). Assessing mental health and disorder across cultures. In P. Pedersen, N. Sartorius, & A. J. Marsella (Eds.), *Mental health services: The cross-cultural context* (pp. 31–57). Beverly Hills: Sage.

Drake, L. E. (1946). A social I.E. scale for the MMPI. *Journal of Applied Psychology, 30,* 51–54.

Drasgow, F., & Olson-Buchanan, J. B. (Eds.). (1999). *Innovations in computerized assessment.* Mahwah, NJ: Erlbaum.

Dreger, R. M., & Miller, K. S. (1960). Comparative studies of Negroes and Whites in the U.S. *Psychological Bulletin, 51,* 361–402.

Drinkwater, M. J. (1976). Psychological evaluation of visually handicapped children. *Massachusetts School Psychologists Association Newsletter, 6.*

Drotar, D., Olness, K., & Wiznitzer, M., et al. (1999). Neurodevelopmental outcomes of Ugandan infants with HIV infection: An application of growth curve analysis. *Health Psychology, 18,* 114–121.

DuBois, P. H. (1966). A test-dominated society: China 1115 B.C.—1905 A.D. In A. Anastasi (Ed.), *Testing problems in perspective* (pp. 29–36). Washington, DC: American Council on Education.

DuBois, P. H. (1970). *A history of psychological testing.* Boston: Allyn & Bacon.

Ducharme, F., Levesque, L., Gendron, M., & Legault, A. (2001). Development process and qualitative evaluation of a program to promote the mental health of family caregivers. *Clinical Nursing Research, 10,* 182–201.

Duchek, J. M., Hunt, L., Ball, K., et al. (1998). Attention and driving performance in Alzheimer's disease. *Journal of Gerontology: Series B: Psychological Science & Social Sciences, 53B*(2), 130–141.

Duclos, C. W. (1999). Factors associated with alcohol, drug, and mental health service utilization among a sample of American Indian adolescent detainees. *Dissertation Abstracts International, Section B: The Sciences & Engineering, 40*(4-B), 1524.

Dudek, S. Z. (1998). Depression in creative painters. In M. A. Blais et al. (Chairs), *Assessment of emotional distress and depression.* Paper session presented at the Society for Personality Assessment 1998 Midwinter Meeting, February 21.

Dudycha, G. J. (1936). An objective study of punctuality in relation to personality and achievement. *Archives of Psychology, 204,* 1–319.

Dugdale, R. (1877). *The Jukes: A study in crime, pauperism, disease, and heredity.* New York: Putnam.

Dunbar, J. (1990). Predictors of patient adherence: Patient characteristics. In S. A. Shumaker, E. B. Schron, & J. D. Ockene (Eds.), *The handbook of health behavior change* (pp. 348–360). New York: Springer.

Duncker, K. (1945). On problem solving. *Psychological Monographs, 5,* 1–13.

Dunham, R. B., Grube, J. A., & Castaneda, M. B. (1994). Organizational commitment: The utility of an integrative definition. *Journal of Applied Psychology, 79,* 370–380.

Dunkel-Schetter, C., Feinstein, L. G., Taylor, S. E., & Falke, R. L. (1992). Patterns of coping with cancer. *Health Psychology, 11,* 79–87.

Dunn, L. M., & Dunn, L. M. (1997). *Examiner's manual for the PPVT-III, Peabody Picture Vocabulary Test, Third Edition.* Circle Pines, MN: American Guidance Service.

Dwyer, C. A. (1996). Cut scores and testing: Statistics, judgment, truth, and error. *Psychological Assessment, 8,* 360–362.

Dykes, L. (1986). The whiplash shaken infant syndrome: What has been learned? *Child Abuse and Neglect, 10,* 211.

Dywan, J., & Bowers, K. (1983). The use of hypnosis to enhance recall. *Science, 22,* 184–185.

Earles, J. A., & Ree, M. J. (1992). The predictive validity of the ASVAB for training grades. *Educational and Psychological Measurement, 52,* 721–725.

Earls, C. M., & Marshall, W. L. (1983). The current state of technology in the laboratory assessment of sexual arousal patterns. In J. G. Greer & I. R. Stuart (Eds.), *The sexual aggressor: Current perspectives on treatment* (pp. 336–362). New York: Van Nostrand Reinhold.

Earls, C. M., Quinsey, V. L., & Castonguay, L. G. (1987). A comparison of three methods of scoring penile circumference changes. *Archives of Sexual Behavior, 6,* 493–500.

Early, P. C., Gibson, C. B., & Chen, C. C. (1999). "How did I do?" versus "How did we do?": Cultural contrasts of performance feedback use and self-efficacy. *Journal of Cross-Cultural Psychology, 30,* 594–619.

Eccles, J. S. (1987). Gender roles and women's achievement-related decisions. *Psychology of Women Quarterly, 11,* 135–171.

Edwards, A. L. (1953). *Edwards Personal Preference Schedule.* New York: Psychological Corporation.

Edwards, A. L. (1957a). *Techniques of attitude scale construction.* New York: Appleton-Century-Crofts.

Edwards, A. L. (1957b). *The social desirability variable in personality assessment and research.* New York: Dryden.

Edwards, A. L. (1966). Relationship between probability of endorsement and social desirability scale value for a set of 2,824 personality statements. *Journal of Applied Psychology, 50,* 238–239.

Edwards, A. L., & Walsh, J. A. (1964). Response sets in standard and experimental personality scales. *American Education Research Journal, 1,* 52–60.

Eichler, R. M. (1951). A comparison of the Rorschach and Behn-Rorschach inkblot tests. *Journal of Consulting Psychology, 15,* 185–189.

Eiser, C., Mohay, H., & Morse, R. (2000). The measurement of quality of life in young children. *Child: Care, Health & Development, 26,* 401–413.

Eisman, E. J., Dies, R. R., Finn, S. E., et al. (1998). *Problems and limitations in the use of psychological assessment in contemporary healthcare delivery: Report of the Board of Professional Affairs Psychological Assessment Work Group, Part II.* Washington, DC: American Psychological Association.

Eisman, E. J., Dies, R. R., Finn, S. E., et al. (2000). Problems and limitations in using psychological assessment in the contemporary health care delivery system. *Professional Psychology: Research and Practice, 31,* 131–140.

Elder, G. H., Van Nguyen, T., & Caspi, A. (1985). Linking family hardship to children's lives. *Child Development, 56,* 361–375.

Eldredge, N. (1993). Culturally affirmative counseling with American Indians who are deaf. *Journal of the American Deafness and Rehabilitation Association, 26,* 1–18.

Elksnin, L. K., & Elksnin, N. (1993). A review of picture interest inventories: Implications for vocational assessment of students with disabilities. *Journal of Psychoeducational Assessment, 11,* 323–336.

Ellerstein, N. S. (Ed.). (1981). *Child abuse and neglect: A medical reference.* New York: Wiley.

Elliot, H., Glass, L., & Evans, J. (Eds.). (1987). *Mental health assessment of deaf clients: A practical manual.* Boston: Little, Brown.

Elliott, A. N., O'Donohue, W. T., & Nickerson, M. A. (1993). The use of sexually anatomically detailed dolls in the assessment of sexual abuse. *Clinical Psychology Review, 13,* 207–221.

Elliott, C. D. (1990a). *The Differential Ability Scales.* San Antonio: Psychological Corporation.

Elliott, C. D. (1990b). *Technical Handbook: The Differential Ability Scales.* San Antonio: Psychological Corporation.

Elliott, S. N. (1988). Acceptability of behavioral treatments in educational settings. In J. C. Witt, S. N. Elliott, & F. M. Greshma (Eds.), *The handbook of behavior therapy education* (pp. 121–150). New York: Plenum.

Elliott, S. N., Katochwill, T. R., & McKevitt, B. C. (2001). Experimental analysis of the effects of testing accommodations on the scores of students with and without disabilities. *Journal of School Psychology, 39,* 3–24.

Elliott, T. R., & Carroll, M. N. (1997). Issues in psychological assessment for rehabilitation services. Paper presented at the annual convention of the American Psychological Association, August, Chicago.

Embretson, S. E. (1996). The new rules of measurement. *Psychological Assessment, 8,* 341–349.

Endicott, J., & Spitzer, R. L. (1978). A diagnostic interview: The Schedule for Affective Disorders and Schizophrenia. *Archives of General Psychiatry, 35,* 837–844.

Engin, A., Wallbrown, F., & Brown, D. (1976). The dimensions of reading attitude for children in the intermediate grades. *Psychology in the Schools, 13*(3), 309–316.

Epping-Jordan, J. E., Compas, B. E., & Howell, D. C. (1994). Predictors of cancer progression in young adult men and women: Avoidance, intrusive thoughts, and psychological symptoms. *Health Psychology, 13,* 539–547.

Epstein, J. L., & McPartland, J. M. (1978). *The Quality of School Life Scale administration and technical manual.* Boston: Houghton Mifflin.

Epstein, N., Baldwin, L., & Bishop, S. (1983). The McMaster Family Assessment Device. *Journal of Marital and Family Therapy, 9,* 171–180.

Erdelyi, M. H. (1974). A new look at the new look: Perceptual defense and vigilance. *Psychological Review, 81,* 1–25.

Erdelyi, M. H., & Goldberg, B. (1979). Let's not sweep repression under the rug: Toward a cognitive psychology of repression. In J. F. Kihlstrom & F. J. Evans (Ed.), *Functional disorders of memory.* Hillsdale, NJ: Erlbaum.

Erdelyi, M. H., & Kleinbard, J. (1978). Has Ebbinghaus decayed with time? The growth of recall (hypermnesia) over days. *Journal of Experimental Psychology: Human Learning and Memory, 4,* 275–289.

Errico, A. L., Nixon, S. J., Parsons, O. A., & Tassey, J. (1990). Screening for neuropsychological impairment in alcoholics. *Psychological Assessment, 2,* 45–50.

Evan, W. M., & Miller, J. R. (1969). Differential effects of response bias of computer vs. conventional administration of a social science questionnaire. *Behavioral Science, 14,* 216–227.

Evans, J. D., et al. (2000). Cross-cultural applications of the Halstead-Reitan batteries. In E. Fletcher-Janzen et al. (Eds.), *Handbook of cross-cultural neuropsychology* (pp. 287–303). New York: Kluwer Academic/Plenum.

Evans, M. (1978). Unbiased assessment of locally low incidence handicapped children. *IRRC practitioners talk to practitioners.* Springfield, IL: Illinois Regional Resource Center.

Exner, J. E. (1962). A comparison of human figure drawings of psychoneurotics, character disturbances, normals, and subjects experiencing experimentally induced fears. *Journal of Projective Techniques, 26,* 292–317.

Exner, J. E. (1966). Variations in WISC performance as influenced by difference in pretest rapport. *Journal of General Psychology, 74,* 299–306.

Exner, J. E. (1969). *The Rorschach systems.* New York: Grune & Stratton.

Exner, J. E. (1974). *The Rorschach: A comprehensive system.* New York: Wiley.

Exner, J. E. (1978). *The Rorschach: A comprehensive system: Vol. 2. Current research and advanced interpretations.* New York: Wiley-Interscience.

Exner, J. E. (1983). Rorschach assessment. In I. B. Weiner (Ed.), *Methods in clinical psychology* (2nd ed.). New York: Wiley.

Exner, J. E. (1986). *The Rorschach: A comprehensive system: Vol. 1. Basic foundations* (2nd ed.). New York: Wiley.

Exner, J. E. (1989). Searching for projection in the Rorschach. *Journal of Personality Assessment, 53,* 520–536.

Exner, J. E. (1990). *Workbook for the comprehensive system* (3rd ed.). Asheville, NC: Rorschach Workshops.

Exner, J. E. (1993). *The Rorschach: A comprehensive system: Vol. 2. Interpretations.* New York: Wiley.

Exner, J. E., Jr. (1991). *The Rorschach: A comprehensive system: Vol. 2. Interpretation* (2nd ed.). New York: Wiley.

Exner, J. E., Jr. (1993). *The Rorschach: A comprehensive system: Vol. 1. Basic foundations* (3rd ed.). New York: Wiley.

Exner, J. E., Jr. (1997). Critical bits and the Rorschach response process. *Journal of Personality Assessment, 67,* 464–477.

Exner, J. E., & Weiner, I. B. (1982). *The Rorschach: A comprehensive system: Vol. 3. Assessment of children and adolescents.* New York: Wiley.

Exner, J. E., & Weiner, I. B. (1995). *The Rorschach: A comprehensive system: Vol. 3. Assessment of children and adolescents,* (2nd ed.). New York: Wiley.

Eyde, L. D., Kowal, D. M., & Fishburne, F. J., Jr. (1990). The validity of computer-based test interpretations of the MMPI. In S. Wise & T. B. Gutkin (Eds.), *The computer as adjunct to the decision-making process.* Lincoln: Buros Institute of Mental Measurements, University of Nebraska.

Eyde, L. D., Moreland, K. L., Robertson, G. J., Primoff, E. S., & Most, R. B. (1988). Test user qualifications: A data-based approach to promoting good test use. *Issues in Scientific Psychology: Report of the Test User Qualifications Working Group of the Joint Committee on Testing Practices.* Washington, DC: American Psychological Association.

Eyman, J. R., & Eyman, S. K. (1990). Suicide risk and assessment instruments. In P. Cimbolic & D. A. Jobes (Eds.), *Youth suicide: Issues, assessment, and intervention* (pp. 9–32). Springfield, IL: Charles C Thomas.

Eysenck, H. J. (1947). *Dimensions of personality.* New York: Praeger.

Eysenck, H. J. (1961). The effects of psychotherapy. In H. J. Eysenck (Ed.), *Handbook of abnormal psychology: An experimental approach* (pp. 697–725). New York: Basic.

Eysenck, H. J. (1967). Intelligence assessment: A theoretical and experimental approach. *British Journal of Educational Psychology, 37,* 81–98.

Eysenck, H. J. (1985). Can personality study ever be scientific? *Journal of Social Behavior and Personality, 1,* 3–19.

Eysenck, H. J. (1991). Dimensions of personality: 16, 5, or 3?—Criteria for a taxonomic paradigm. *Personality and Individual Differences, 12,* 773–790.

Faigman, D. L. (1995). The evidentiary status of social science under Daubert: Is it "scientific," "technical," or "other" knowledge? *Psychology, Public Policy, and Law, 1,* 960–979.

Faller, K. C. (1988). *Child sexual abuse.* New York: Columbia University.

Farrall, F. R., & Card, R. D. (1988). Advancements in physiological evaluation of assessment and treatment of the sexual transgressor. In R. A. Prentky & V. L. Quinsey (Eds.), *Human sexual aggression: Current perspectives* (pp. 261–273). New York: Annals of the New York Academy of Sciences.

Farrell, A. D. (1986). The microcomputer as a tool for behavioral assessment. *Behavior Therapist, 1,* 16–17.

Farrell, J. N., & McDaniel, M. A. (2001). The stability of validity coefficients over time: Ackerman's (1988) model and the General Aptitude Test Battery. *Journal of Applied Psychology, 86,* 60–79.

Farrenkopf, T., & Bryan, J. (1999). Psychological consultation under Oregon's 1994 Death With Dignity Act: Ethics and procedures. *Professional Psychology: Research and Practice, 30,* 245–249.

Faust, D. S., & Hollingsworth, J. O. (1991). Concurrent validation of the Wechsler Preschool and Primary Scale of Intelligence—Revised (WPPSI-R) with two criteria of cognitive abilities. Special issue: Wechsler Preschool and Primary Scale of Intelligence (WPPSI-R). *Journal of Psychoeducational Assessment, 9,* 224–229.

Faust, D. S., & Ziskin, J. (1988a). The expert witness in psychology and psychiatry. *Science, 241,* 31–35.

Faust, D. S., & Ziskin, J. (1988b). Response to Fowler and Matarrazo. *Science, 242,* 1143–1144.

Federal Rules of Evidence. (1975). Eagan, MN: West Group Publishing.

Fee, A. F., Elkins, G. R., & Boyd, L. (1982). Testing and counseling psychologists: Current practices and implications for training. *Journal of Personality Assessment, 46,* 116–118.

Feinstein, A. R., Josephy, B. R., & Wells, C. K. (1986). Scientific and clinical problems in indexes of functional disability. *Annals of Internal Medicine, 105,* 413–520.

Felce, D. (1997). Defining and applying the concept of quality of life. *Journal of Intellectual and Research, 41,* 126–135.

Felton, B. J., & Revenson, T. A. (1987). Age differences in coping with chronic illness. *Psychology and Aging, 2,* 164–170.

Fenn, D. S., & Ganzini, L. (1999). Attitudes of Oregon psychologists toward physician-assisted suicide and the Oregon Death With Dignity Act. *Professional Psychology: Research and Practice, 30,* 235–244.

Ferere, H., Burns, W. J., & Roth, L. (1992). Use of the Revised Developmental Test of Visual-Motor Integration with chronic mentally ill adult population. *Perceptual and Motor Skills, 74,* 287–290.

Ferguson, R. L., & Novick, M. R. (1973). Implementation of a Bayesian system for decision analysis in a program of individually prescribed instruction. *ACT Research Report, Number 60.*

Feshback, S. (1961). The influence of drive arousal and conflict. In J. Kagan & G. Lesser (Eds.), *Contemporary issues in thematic apperception methods.* Springfield, IL: Charles C Thomas.

Field, T. M., & Vega-Lahr, N. (1984). Early interactions between infants with cranio-facial anomalies and their mothers. *Infant Behavior and Development, 7,* 527–530.

Filsinger, E. (1983). A machine-aided marital observation technique: The Dyadic Interaction Scoring Code. *Journal of Marriage and the Family, 2,* 623–632.

Finding Information About Psychological Tests. (1995). Washington, DC: American Psychological Association, Science Directorate.

Fingarette, H., & Hasse, A. F. (1979). *Mental disabilities and criminal responsibility.* Berkeley: University of California.

Finkel, N. J., Shaw, R., Bercaw, S., et al. (1985). Insanity defenses: From the jurors' perspective. *Law and Psychology Review, 9,* 77–92.

Finkelhor, D., & Dziuba-Leatherman, J. (1994). Victimization of children. *American Psychologist, 49,* 173–183.

Fischer, H. (1999). Exemptions from child abuse reporting. *American Psychologist, 54,* 145.

Fisher, R. P., & Geiselman, R. E. (1992). *Memory-enhancing techniques for investigative interviewing.* Springfield, IL: Charles C Thomas.

Fisher, R. P., Geiselman, R. E., & Amador, M. (1989). Field test of the cognitive interview: Enhancing the recollection of actual victims and witnesses of crime. *Journal of Applied Psychology, 74,* 722–727.

Fisher, R. P., Geiselman, R. E., Raymond, D. S., et al. (1987). Enhancing enhanced eyewitness memory: Refining the cognitive interview. *Journal of Police Science & Administration, 15,* 291–297.

Fiske, D. W. (1967). The subjects react to tests. *American Psychologist, 22,* 287–296.

Fitts, W. H. (1965). *Manual for the Tennessee Self-Concept Scale.* Nashville: Counselor Recordings and Tests.

Fitzgibbons, D. J., & Shearn, C. R. (1972). Concepts of schizophrenia among mental health professionals: A factor-analytic study. *Journal of Consulting and Clinical Psychology, 38,* 288–295.

Flanagan, D. P., & McGrew, K. S. (1997). A cross-battery approach to assessing and interpreting cognitive abilities: Narrowing the gap between practice and cognitive science. In D. P. Flanagan, J. L. Genshaft, & P. L. Harrison (Eds.), *Contemporary intellectual assessment: Theories, tests, and issues* (pp. 314–325). New York: Guilford.

Flanagan, J. C. (1938). Review of Measuring Intelligence by Terman and Merrill. *Harvard Educational Review, 8,* 130–133.

Flanagan, J. C., & Burns, R. K. (1955). The employee business record: A new appraisal and development tool. *Harvard Business Review, 33*(5), 99–102.

Fleishman, J. A., & Fogel, B. (1994). Coping and depressive symptoms among people with AIDS. *Health Psychology, 13,* 156–169.

Fliess, J. L. (1971). Measuring nominal scale agreement among many raters. *Psychological Bulletin, 76,* 378–382.

Flowers, J. H. (1982). Some simple Apple II software for the collection and analysis of observational data. *Behavior Research Methods and Instrumentation, 14,* 241–249.

Floyd, F. J., Haynes, S. N., Doll, E. R., et al. (1992). Assessing retirement satisfaction and perceptions of retirement experiences. *Psychology and Aging, 7,* 609–621.

Floyd, F. J., & Widaman, K. F. (1995). Factor analysis in the development and refinement of clinical assessment instruments. *Psychological Assessment, 7,* 286–299.

Flynn, J. R. (1984). The mean IQ of Americans: Massive gains 1932 to 1978. *Psychological Bulletin, 95,* 29–51.

Flynn, J. R. (1988). Massive IQ gains in 14 nations: What IQ tests really measure. *Psychological Bulletin, 101,* 171–191.

Flynn, J. R. (1991). *Asian-Americans: Achievement beyond IQ.* Hillsdale, NJ: Erlbaum.

Flynn, J. R. (2000). The hidden history of IQ and special education: Can the problems be solved? *Psychology, Public Policy, and Law, 6,* 191–198.

Foerster, L. M., & Little Soldier, D. (1974). Open education and native American values. *Educational Leadership, 32,* 41–45.

Folstein, M. F., Folstein, S. E., & McHugh, P. R. (1975). "Mini-Mental State": A practical method for grading the cognitive state of patients for the clinician. *Journal of Psychiatric Research, 12,* 189–198.

Fontana, V. J., Donovan, D., & Wong, R. J. (1963, December 8). The maltreatment syndrome in children. *New England Journal of Medicine, 269,* 1389–1394.

Fontanna, D. (2000). *Personality in the workplace.* Lewiston, NY: Macmillan Press.

Forer, B. R. (1949). The fallacy of personal validation: A classroom demonstration of gullibility. *Journal of Abnormal and Social Psychology, 44,* 118–123.

Foreyt, J. P. (1987). Issues in the assessment and treatment of obesity. *Journal of Consulting and Clinical Psychology, 55,* 677–684.

Forrest, D. W. (1974). *Francis Galton: The life and works of a Victorian genius.* New York: Taplinger.

Forth, A. E., Hart, S. D., & Hare, R. D. (1990). Assessment of psychopathy in male young offenders. *Psychological Assessment, 2,* 342–344.

Foster, S. L., Laverty-Finch, C., Gizzo, D. P., & Osantowski, J. (1999). Practical issues in self-observation. *Psychological Assessment, 11,* 426–438.

Fouad, N. A., & Dancer, L. S. (1992). Cross-cultural structure of interests: Mexico and the United States. *Journal of Vocational Behavior, 40,* 129–143.

Fowler, D. R., Finkelstein, A., & Penk, W. (1986). *Measuring treatment responses by computer interview.* Paper presented at the 94th annual meeting of the American Psychological Association, Washington, DC.

Fowler, J. C. (1998). Transitional relating and healthy play in treatment. In H. M. Potash (Chair), *The assessment of psychological health.* Symposium presented at the Society for Personality Assessment 1998 Midwinter Meeting, February 21.

Franco, J. N. (1983). An acculturation scale for Mexican-American children. *Journal of General Psychology, 108,* 175–181.

Frank, L. K. (1939). Projective methods for the study of personality. *Journal of Psychology, 8,* 389–413.

Frank, M. G., Ekman, P., & Friesen, W. V. (1993). Behavioral markers and recognizability of the smile of enjoyment. *Journal of Personality and Social Psychology, 64,* 83–93.

Franklin, C. L., & Greene, R. L. (1998). The use of the MMPI-2 in eating-disordered patients. In R. Greene (Chair), *MMPI-MMPI-2 Empirical Studies II.* Symposium presented at the Society for Personality Assessment 1998 Midwinter Meeting, February 21.

Frantz, D., & Nordheimer, J. (1997, September 28). Giant of exam business keeps quiet on cheating. *New York Times,* pp. A1, A32.

Franzen, M. D. (1985). Review of Luria-Nebraska Neuropsychological Battery. In D. J. Keyser & R. C. Sweetland (Eds.), *Test critiques* (Vol. 3; pp. 402–414). Kansas City, MO: Test Corporation of America.

Frederickson, B. L. (1998). What good are positive emotions? *Review of General Psychology, 2,* 300–319.

Fredman, N., & Sherman, R. (1987). *Handbook of measurements for marriage & family therapy.* New York: Brunner/Mazel.

Fredrickson, N. (1993). CRA: Has it had its day? *Educational and Child Psychology, 10,* 14–26.

Freeman, S. T. (1989). Cultural and linguistic bias in mental health evaluations of deaf people. *Rehabilitation Psychology, 34,* 51–63.

French, C. C., & Beaumont, J. G. (1991). The Differential Aptitude Test (Language Usage and Spelling): A clinical study of a computerized form. *Current Psychology: Research and Reviews, 10,* 31–48.

French, D. J., Gauthier, J. G., Roberge, C., et al. (1997). Self-efficacy in the thermal biofeedback treatment of migraine sufferers. *Behavior Therapy, 28,* 109–125.

French, J. L. (Ed.). (1964). *Educating the gifted.* New York: Holt, Rinehart & Winston.

Freud, S. (1913/1959). Further recommendations in the technique of psychoanalysis. In E. Jones (Ed.) and J. Riviere (Trans.), *Collected papers* (Vol. 2). New York: Basic.

Freund, K. (1963). A laboratory method for diagnosing predominance of homosexual and heterosexual erotic interest in the male. *Behavior Research and Therapy, 1,* 85–93.

Freund, K., & Blanchard, R. (1989). Phallometric diagnosis of pedophilia. *Journal of Consulting and Clinical Psychology, 57,* 100–105.

Freund, K., Sedlacek, E., & Knob, K. (1965). A simple transducer for mechanical plethysmography of the male genital. *Journal of Experimental Analysis of Behavior, 8,* 169–170.

Friedman, H. S. (Ed.). (1990). *Personality and disease.* New York: Wiley.

Friedman, M., & Rosenman, R. H. (1974). *Type A behavior and your heart.* New York: Knopf.

Friedrich, W. M., Urquiza, A. J., & Beike, R. (1986). Behavioral problems in sexually abused young children. *Journal of Pediatric Psychiatry, 11,* 47–57.

Friedrich, W. N., Fisher, J. L., Dittner, C. A., et al. (2001). Child Sexual Behavior Inventory: Normative, psychiatric, and sexual abuse comparisons. *Child Maltreatment: Journal of the American Professional Society on the Abuse of Children, 6,* 37–49.

Friel-Patti, S., & Finitzo, T. (1990). Language learning in a prospective study of otitis media with effusion in the first two years of life. *Journal of Speech and Hearing Research, 33,* 188–194.

Frijda, N. H., & Mesquita, B. (1994). The social roles and functions of emotions. In S. Kitayama & H. R. Markus (Eds.), *Emotion and Culture: Empirical studies of mutual influence* (pp. 51–87). Washington, DC: American Psychological Association.

Frisch, M. B., Cornell, J., Villanueva, M., & Retzlaff, P. J. (1992). Clinical validation of the Quality of Life Inventory: A measure of life satisfaction for use in treatment planning and outcome assessment. *Psychological Assessment, 4,* 92–101.

Frolik, L. A. (1999). Science, common sense, and the determination of mental capacity. *Psychology, Public Policy, and Law, 5,* 41–58.

Fromm-Auch, D., & Yeudall, L. T. (1983). Normative data for the Halstead-Reitan Neuropsychological Tests. *Journal of Clinical Neuropsychology, 5,* 221–238.

Frumkin, R. M. (1997). Significant neglected sociocultural and physical factors affecting intelligence. *American Psychologist, 52,* 76–77.

Frye v. United States, 293 Fed. 1013 (D.C. cir. 1923).

Fuchs, L. S., Fuchs, D., Eaton, S. B., et al. (2000). Using objective data sources to enhance teacher judgments about test accommodations. *Exceptional Children, 67,* 67–81.

Fuld, P. A. (1984). Test profile of cholinergic dysfunction and of Alzheimer-type dementia. *Journal of Clinical Neuropsychology, 6,* 380–392.

Fullan, M., & Loubser, J. (1972). Education and adaptive capacity. *Sociology of Education, 45,* 271–287.

Fullard, W., McDevitt, S. C., & Carey, W. B. (1984). Assessing temperament in one- to three-year-old children. *Journal of Pediatric Psychology, 9,* 205–217.

Furse, D. H., & Stewart, D. W. (1984). Manipulating dissonance to improve mail survey response. *Psychology & Marketing, 1,* 71–84.

Gallagher, J. J. (1966). *Research summary on gifted child education.* Springfield, IL: State Department of Public Instruction.

Gallagher, P., & MacLachlan, M. (2000). Development and psychometric evaluation of the Trinity Amputation and Prosthesis Experience Scales. *Rehabilitation Psychology, 45,* 130–154.

Galton, F. (1869). *Hereditary genius.* London: Macmillan. (Republished in 1892.)

Galton, F. (1874). *English men of science.* New York: Appleton.

Galton, F. (1879). Psychometric experiments. *Brain, 2,* 149–162.

Galton, F. (1883). *Inquiries into human faculty and its development.* London: Macmillan.

Gammon, J. A. (1981). Ophthalmic manifestations of child abuse. In N. S. Ellerstein (Ed.), *Child abuse and neglect: A medical reference* (pp. 121–139). New York: Wiley.

Ganellen, R. J. (1996). Comparing the diagnostic efficiency of the MMPI, MCMI-II, and Rorschach: A review. *Journal of Personality Assessment, 67,* 219–243.

Gann, M. K., & Davison, G. C. (1997). *Cognitive assessment of reactance using the articulated thoughts in simulated situations paradigm.* Unpublished manuscript, University of Southern California.

Garb, H. N. (1994). Toward a second generation of statistical prediction rules in psychodiagnosis and personality assessment. *Computers in Human Behavior, 11,* 313–324.

Garb, H. N. (2000a). Introduction to the special section on the use of computers for making judgments and decisions. *Psychological Assessment, 12,* 3–5.

Garb, H. N. (2000b). Computers will become increasingly important for psychological assessment: Not that there's anything wrong with that! *Psychological Assessment, 12,* 31–39.

Garb, H. N., & Schramke, C. J. (1996). Judgment research and neuropsychological assessment: A narrative review and meta-analyses. *Psychological Bulletin, 120,* 140–153.

Garcia, M., & Lega, L. I. (1979). Development of a Cuban Ethnic Identity Questionnaire. *Hispanic Journal of Behavioral Sciences, 1,* 247–261.

Gardner, F. L. (2001). Applied sport psychology in professional sports: The team psychologist. *Professional Psychology: Research and Practice, 32,* 34–39.

Gardner, H. (1983). *Frames of mind: The theory of multiple intelligences.* New York: Basic.

Gardner, H. (1994). Multiple intelligences theory. In R. J. Stern-berg, (Ed.), *Encyclopedia of human intelligence* (pp. 740–742). New York: Macmillan.

Gardner, R. A. (1971). *The boys and girls book about divorce.* New York: Bantam.

Gardner, R. A. (1982). *Family evaluation in child custody litigation.* Cresskill, NJ: Creative Therapeutics.

Gardner, W., Lidz, C. W., Mulvey, E. P., & Shaw, E. C. (1996). Clinical versus actuarial prediction of violence in patients with mental illnesses. *Journal of Consulting and Clinical Psychology, 64,* 602–609.

Garfield, S. L., & Eron, L. D. (1948). Interpreting mood and activity in TAT stories. *Journal of Abnormal and Social Psychology, 43,* 338–345.

Garrett, H. E., & Schneck, M. R. (1933). *Psychological tests, methods and results.* New York: Harper.

Gaugler, B. B., Rosenthal, D. B., Thornton, G. C., III, & Bentson, C. (1987). Meta-analysis of assessment center validity. *Journal of Applied Psychology, 72,* 493–511.

Gavzer, B. (1990, May 27). Should you tell all? *Parade Magazine,* pp. 4–7.

Gena, A. (1995). Training and generalization of affective behavior displayed by youth with autism. *Dissertation Abstracts International, Section B: The Sciences & Engineering, 55*(11-B), 5103.

General Electric Co. v. Joiner, 118 S. Ct. 512 (1997).

Gerety, M. B., Mulrow, C. D., Tuley, M. R., Hazuda, H. P., Lichtenstein, M. J., Bohannon, R., Kanten, D. N., O'Neil, M. B., & Gorton, A. (1993). Development and validation of a physical performance instrument for the functionally impaired elderly: The Physical Disability Index (PDI). *Journal of Gerontology, 48,* M33–M38.

Gerry, M. H. (1973). Cultural myopia: The need for a corrective lens. *Journal of School Psychology, 11,* 307–315.

Gesell, A. (1945). *The embryology of behavior. The beginnings of the human mind.* New York: Harper.

Gesell, A. (1954).The ontogenesis of infant behavior. In L. Carmichael (Ed.), *Manual of child psychology.* New York: Wiley.

Gesell, A., & Amatruda, C. S. (1947). *Development diagnosis: Normal and abnormal child development* (2nd ed.). New York: Harper & Row.

Gesell, A., & Thompson, H. (1929). Learning and growth in identical twin infants. *Genetic Psychology Monographs, 6,* 1–124.

Gesell, A., et al. (1940). *The first five years of life.* New York: Harper.

Ghiselli, E. E. (1973). The variety of aptitude tests in personnel selection. *Personnel Psychology, 26,* 461–477.

Ghiselli, E. E., & Barthol, R. P. (1953). The validity of personality inventories in the selection of employees. *Journal of Applied Psychology, 38,* 18–20.

Ghiselli, E. E., Campbell, J. P., & Zedeck, S. (1981). *Measurement theory for the behavioral sciences.* San Francisco: Freeman.

Gibbins, S. (1988, April). *Use of the K-ABC and WISC-R with deaf children.* Paper presented at the Annual Meeting of the National Association of School Psychologists, Chicago.

Gibbins, S. (1989). The provision of school psychological assessment services for the hearing impaired: A national survey. *Volta Review, 91,* 95–103.

Gilberstadt, H., & Duker, J. (1965). *A handbook for clinical and actuarial MMPI interpretations.* Philadelphia: Saunders.

Gillingham, W. H. (1970). An investigation of examiner influence on Wechsler Intelligence Scale for Children scores (Doctoral dissertation, Michigan State University). *Dissertation Abstracts International, 31,* 2178A. (University Microfilms No. Order 70-20, 458)

Girelli, S. A., & Stake, J. E. (1993). Bipolarity in Jungian type theory and the Myers-Briggs Type Indicator. *Journal of Personality Assessment, 60,* 290–301.

Glaser, R., & Nitko, A. J. (1971). Measurement in learning and instruction. In R. L. Thorndike (Ed.), *Educational measurement* (2nd ed.). Washington, DC: American Council on Education.

Glassbrenner, J. (1998). Continuity across contexts: Prison, women's counseling center, and home. In L. Handler (Chair), *Conducting assessments in clients' homes: Contexts, surprises, dilemmas, opportunities.* Symposium presented at the Society for Personality Assessment 1998 Midwinter Meeting, February 20.

Glazer, W. M., Kramer, R., Montgomery, J. S., & Myers, L. (1991). Use of medical necessity scales in concurrent review of psychiatric inpatient care. *Hospital and Community Psychiatry, 42,* 1199–1200.

Glosser, G., & Goodglass, H. (1990). Disorders in executive control functions among aphasic and other brain-damaged patients. *Journal of Clinical and Experimental Neuropsychology, 12,* 485–501.

Gluck, M. R. (1955). The relationship between hostility in the TAT and behavioral hostility. *Journal of Projective Techniques, 19,* 21–26.

Glueck, W. F. (1978). *Personnel: A diagnostic approach.* Dallas: Business Publications.

Glutting, J. J. (1989). Introduction to the structure and application of the Stanford-Binet Intelligence Scale—Fourth Edition. *Journal of School Psychology, 27,* 69–80.

Gobetz, W. A. (1953). Quantification, standardization, and validation of the Bender-Gestalt test on normal and neurotic adults. *Psychological Monographs, 67,* No. 6.

Goddard, H. H. (1908). The Binet and Simon tests of intellectual capacity. *Training School, 5,* 3–9.

Goddard, H. H. (1910). A measuring scale of intelligence. *Training School, 6,* 146–155.

Goddard, H. H. (1912). *The Kallikak family.* New York: Macmillan.

Goddard, H. H. (1913). The Binet tests in relation to immigration. *Journal of Psycho-Asthenics, 18,* 105–107.

Goddard, H. H. (1916). *Feeblemindedness.* New York: Macmillan.

Goddard, H. H. (1917). Mental tests and the immigrant. *Journal of Delinquency, 2,* 243–277.

Goel, V., & Grafman, J. (1995). Are the frontal lobes implicated in "planning" functions? Interpreting data from the Tower of Hanoi. *Neuropsychologia, 33,* 623–642.

Goffman, E. (1963). *Behavior in public places.* Glencoe, IL: Free Press.

Gokhale, D. V., & Kullback, S. (1978). *The information in contingency tables.* New York: Marcel Dekker.

Gold, D. P., Andres, D., Etezadi, J., et al. (1995). Structural equation model of intellectual change and continuity and predictors of intelligence in older men. *Psychology & Aging, 10,* 294–303.

Goldberg, L. R. (1993). The structure of phenotypic personality traits. *American Psychologist, 48,* 26–34.

Goldberg, T. E., Gold, J. M. Greenberg, R., Griffin, S., Schulz, S. C., Pickar, D., Kleinman, J. E., & Weinberger, D. R. (1993). Contrasts between patients with affective disorders and patients with schizophrenia on a neuropsychological test battery. *American Journal of Psychiatry, 150,* 1355–1362.

Goldberg, T. E., Saint-Cyr, J. A., & Weinberger, D. R. (1990). Assessment of procedural learning and problem solving in schizophrenic patients by Tower of Hanoi type tasks. *Journal of Neuropsychiatry, 2,* 165–173.

Golden, C. J., Hammeke, T. A., & Purisch, A. D. (1980). *The Luria-Nebraska Neuropsychological Battery: Manual.* Los Angeles: Western Psychological Services.

Golden, C. J., & Kupperman, S. K. (1980). Graduate training in clinical neuropsychology. *Professional Psychology, 11,* 55–63.

Golden, C. J., Purisch, A. D., & Hammeke, T. A. (1985). *Luria-Nebraska Neuropsychological Battery: Forms I and II, manual.* Los Angeles: Western Psychological Services.

Goldfried, M., & Zax, M. (1965). The stimulus value of the TAT. *Journal of Projective Techniques, 29,* 46–57.

Goldfried, M. R., & Davison, G. C. (1976). *Clinical behavior therapy.* New York: Holt, Rinehart & Winston.

Goldfried, M. R., Stricker, G., & Weiner, I. B. (1971). *Rorschach handbook of clinical and research applications.* Englewood Cliffs, NJ: Prentice-Hall.

Golding, S. L. (1975). Flies in the ointment: Methodological problems in the analysis of the percentage of variance due to persons and situations. *Psychological Bulletin, 82,* 278–288.

Goldman, B. A., & Mitchell, D. F. (1995). *Directory of unpublished experimental measures* (Vol. 6). Washington, DC: American Psychological Association.

Goldstein, A. S. (1967). *The insanity defense.* New Haven, CT: Yale University.

Goldstein, G. (1986). The neuropsychology of schizophrenia. In I. Grant & K. M. Adams (Eds.), *Neuropsychological assessment of neuropsychiatric disorders* (pp. 146–171). New York: Oxford University.

Goldstein, K. (1927). Die lokalisation in her grosshim rinde. *Handb. norm. pathol. psychologie.* Berlin: J. Springer.

Goldstein, K. (1939). *The organism.* New York: American Book.

Goldstein, K. (1963a). *The organism.* Boston: Beacon.

Goldstein, K. (1963b). The modifications of behavior consequent to cerebral lesions. *Psychiatric Quarterly, 10,* 586–610.

Goldwater, B. C. (1972). Psychological significance of pupillary movements. *Psychological Bulletin, 77,* 340–355.

Gomez, R., & Hazeldine, P. (1996). Social information processing in mild mentally retarded children. *Research in Developmental Disabilities, 17,* 217–227.

Good, R. H., Chowdhri, S., Katz, L., Vollman, M., & Creek, R. (1989, March). *Effect of matching instruction and simultaneous/sequential processing strength.* Paper presented at the Annual Meeting of the National Association of School Psychologists, Boston.

Good, R. H., & Lane, S. (1988). *Confirmatory factor analysis of the K-ABC and WISC-R: Hierarchical models.* Paper presented at the Annual Meeting of the American Psychological Association, Atlanta.

Good, R. H., Vollmer, M., Creek, R. J., & Katz, L. (1993). Treatment utility of the Kaufman Assessment Battery for Children: Effects of matching instruction and student processing strength. *School Psychology Review, 22,* 8–26.

Goodglass, H., & Kaplan, E. (1983). *Boston Naming Test.* Philadelphia: Lea & Febiger.

Goodman, G. S., & Reed, R. S. (1986). Age differences in eyewitness testimony. *Law and Human Behavior, 10,* 317–332.

Goodman-Delahunty, J. (2000). Psychological impairment under the American with Disabilities Act: Legal guidelines. *Professional Psychology: Research and Practice, 31,* 197–205.

Goodman-Delahunty, J., & Foote, W. E. (1995). Compensation for pain, suffering and other psychological injuries: The impact of *Daubert* on employment discrimination claims. *Behavioral Sciences and the Law, 13,* 183–206.

Goodwin, D. A. J., Boggs, S. R., & Grahm-Pole, J. (1994). Development and validation of the Pediatric Oncology Quality of Life Scale. *Psychological Assessment, 6,* 321–328.

Gorham, D. R. (1956). A Proverbs Test for clinical and experimental use. *Psychological Reports, Monograph Supplement, 2,* No. 1, 2–12.

Gorsuch, R. L. (1983). *Factor analysis* (2nd ed.). Hillsdale, NJ: Erlbaum.

Gorsuch, R. L. (1997). Exploratory factor analysis: Its role in item analysis. *Journal of Personality Assessment, 68,* 532–560.

Gottfredson, L. G. (2000). Skills gaps, not tests, make racial proportionality impossible. *Psychology, Public Policy, and Law, 6,* 129–143.

Gottfredson, L. S. (1988). Reconsidering fairness: A matter of social and ethical priorities. *Journal of Vocational Behavior, 33,* 293–319.

Gottfredson, L. S. (1994). The science and politics of race-norming. *American Psychologist, 49,* 955–963.

Gottfried, A. W. (Ed.). (1984). *Home environment and early cognitive development: Longitudinal research.* New York: Academic Press.

Gottfried, A. W., Gottfried, A. E., Bathurst, K., & Guerin, D. W. (1994). *Gifted IQ: Early developmental aspects.* New York: Plenum.

Gough, H. G. (1960). The Adjective Check List as a personality assessment research technique. *Psychological Reports, 6,* 107–122.

Gough, H. G. (1962). Clinical versus statistical prediction in psychology. In L. Postman (Ed.), *Psychology in the making: Histories of selected research problems* (pp. 526–584). New York: Knopf.

Gough, H. G., & Bradley, P. (1996). *CPI manual* (3rd ed.). Palo Alto, CA: Consulting Psychologists Press.

Gough, H. G., & Heilbrun, A. B., Jr. (1980). *The Adjective Checklist manual (Revised).* Palo Alto, CA: Consulting Psychologists Press.

Grafman, J., Litvan, I., Massaquoi, S., & Stewart, M. (1992). Cognitive planning deficit in patients with cerebellar atrophy. *Neurology, 42,* 1493–1496.

Graham, J. R. (1977). *The MMPI: A practical guide.* New York: Oxford University.

Graham, J. R. (1987). *The MMPI: A practical guide* (2nd ed.). New York: Oxford University.

Graham, J. R. (1990). *MMPI-2: Assessing personality and psychopathology.* New York: Oxford University.

Granger, C. V., & Gresham, G. E. (Eds.). (1984). *Functional assessment in rehabilitation medicine.* Baltimore: Williams & Wilkins.

Grant, C. D., & Nash, M. R. (1995). The Computer-Assisted Hypnosis Scale: Standardization of a computer-administered measure of hypnotic ability. *Psychological Assessment, 7,* 49–58.

Graybill, D. (1990). Developmental changes in the response types versus aggression categories on the Rosenzweig Picture Frustration Study, Children's Form. *Journal of Personality Assessment, 55,* 603–609.

Graybill, D. (1993). A longitudinal study of changes in children's thought content in response to frustration on the Children's Picture-Frustration Study. *Journal of Personality Assessment, 61,* 531–535.

Greaud, V. A., & Green, B. F. (1986). Equivalence of conventional and computer presentation of speed tests. *Applied Psychological Measurement, 10,* 23–34.

Green, A. (1986). True and false allegations of sexual abuse in child custody disputes. *Journal of the American Academy of Child Psychology, 25,* 449–456.

Green, B. F. (1984). *Computer-based ability testing.* Paper delivered at the 91st annual meeting of the American Psychological Association, Toronto, Ontario, Canada.

Green, C. W. (1998). Normative influence on the acceptance of information technology: Measurement and effects. *Small Group Research, 29,* 85–123.

Greene, R. L. (1987). Ethnicity and MMPI performance: A review. *Journal of Consulting and Clinical Psychology, 55,* 497–512.

Greene, R. L. (1988). Assessment of malingering and defensiveness by objective personality measures. In R. Rogers (Ed.), *Clinical assessment of malingering and deception* (pp. 123–158). New York: Guilford.

Greenfield, D. N. (1999). Psychological characteristics of compulsive Internet use: A preliminary analysis. *Cyber-Psychology & Behavior, 2,* 403–412.

Greenlaw, P. S., & Jensen, S. S. (1996). Race-norming and the Civil Rights Act of 1991. *Public Personnel Management, 25,* 13–24.

Greenspan, S. (1997). Dead manual walking? Why the AAMR definition needs redoing. *Education & Training in Mental Retardation & Developmental Disabilities, 32,* 179–190.

Greenspoon, J. (1955). The reinforcing effect of two spoken sounds on the frequency of two responses. *American Journal of Psychology, 68,* 409–416.

Greenspoon, J., & Gersten, C. D. (1967). A new look at psychological testing: Psychological testing from the standpoint of a behaviorist. *American Psychologist, 22,* 848–853.

Gregoire, J. (1999). Emerging standards for test applications in the French-speaking countries of Europe. *European Journal of Psychological Assessment, 15,* 158–164.

Gresham, F. M. (1989). Review of the Parenting Stress Index. In J. C. Conoley & J. J. Kramer (Eds.), *The tenth mental measurements yearbook.* Lincoln: Buros Institute of Mental Measurements, University of Nebraska.

Gresham, F. M., MacMillan, D. L., & Siperstein, G. N. (1995). Critical analysis of the 1992 AAMR definition: Implications for school psychology. *School Psychology Quarterly, 10*(1), 1–19.

Grey, R. J., & Kipnis, D. (1976). Untangling the performance appraisal dilemma: The influence of perceived organizational context on evaluative processes. *Journal of Applied Psychology, 61,* 329–335.

Griffin, D. K., Rosenberg, H., Cheyney, W., & Greenberg, B. (1996). A comparison of self-esteem and job satisfaction of adults with mild mental retardation in sheltered workshops and supported employment. *Education and Training in Mental Retardation and Developmental Disabilities, 31*(2) 142–150.

Griffith, L. (1997). Surviving no-frills mental health care: The future of psychological assessment. *Journal of Practical Psychiatry and Behavioral Health, 3,* 255–258.

Grisso, T. (1986). *Evaluating competencies: Forensic assessments and instruments.* New York: Plenum.

Groeger, J. A., & Chapman, P. R. (1997). Normative influences on decisions to offend. *Applied Psychology: An International Review, 46,* 265–285.

Groenveld, M., & Jan, J. E. (1992). Intelligence profiles of low vision and blind children. *Journal of Visual Impairment and Blindness, 86,* 68–71.

Gross, M. L. (1962). *The brain watchers.* New York: Random House.

Grossman, I., Mednitsky, S., Dennis, B., & Scharff, L. (1993). Validation of an "amazingly" short form of the WAIS-R for a clinically depressed sample. *Journal of Psychoeducational Assessment, 11,* 173–181.

Grove, W. M., & Barden, R. C. (1999). Protecting the integrity of the legal system: The admissibility of testimony from mental health experts under *Dauberg/Kumho* analyses. *Psychology, Public Policy, and Law, 5,* 224–242.

Grove, W. M., Zald, D. H., Lebow, B. S., et al. (2000). Clinical versus mechanical prediction: A meta-analysis. *Psychological Assessment, 12,* 19–30.

Grunzke, N., Gunn, N., & Staufer, G. (1970). *Comparative performance of low-ability airmen* (Technical Report 70-4). Lackland AFB, TX: Air Force Human Resources Laboratory.

Guastello, S. J. (1993). A two-(and-a-half)-tiered trait taxonomy. *American Psychologist, 48,* 1298–1299.

Guastello, S. J., & Rieke, M. L. (1990). The Barnum Effect and the validity of computer-based test interpretations: The Human Resource Development Report. *Psychological Assessment, 2,* 186–190.

Guerrier, J. H., Manivannan, P., & Nair, S. N. (1999). The role of working memory, field dependence, visual search, and reaction time in the left turn performance of older female drivers. *Applied Ergonomics, 30,* 109–119.

Guilford, J. P. (1948). Some lessons from aviation psychology. *American Journal of Psychology, 3,* 3–11.

Guilford, J. P. (1954). A factor analytic study across the domains of reasoning, creativity, and evaluation. I. Hypothesis and description of tests. *Reports from the psychology laboratory.* Los Angeles: University of Southern California.

Guilford, J. P. (1959). *Personality.* New York: McGraw-Hill.

Guilford, J. P. (1967). *The nature of human intelligence.* New York: McGraw-Hill.

Guilford, J. P., et al. (1974). *Structure-of-Intellect Abilities.* Orange, CA: Sheridan Psychological Services.

Guilmette, T. J., & Faust, D. (1991). Characteristics of neuropsychologists who prefer the Halstead-Reitan Battery or the Luria-Nebraska Neuropsychological Battery. *Professional Psychology: Research and Practice, 22*(1), 80–83.

Guilmette, T. J., Faust, D., Hart, K. & Arkes, H. R. (1990). A national survey of psychologists who offer neuropsychological services. *Archives of Clinical Neuropsychology, 5*, 373–392.

Guion, R. M. (1980). On trinitarian doctrines of validity. *Professional Psychology, 11*, 385–398.

Guion, R. M., & Gottier, R. F. (1965). Validity of personality measures in personnel selection. *Personnel Psychology, 18*, 81–91.

Gulliksen, H., & Messick, S. (Eds.). (1960). *Psychological scaling: Theory and applications.* New York: Wiley, 1960.

Guttman, L. (1947). The Cornell technique for scale and intensity analysis. *Educational and Psychological Measurement, 7*, 247–280.

Guttman, L. A. (1944a). A basis for scaling qualitative data. *American Sociological Review, 9*, 139–150.

Guttman, L. A. (1944b). A basis for scaling qualitative data. *American Sociological Review, 9*, 179–190.

Gyurke, J. S., Stone, B., & Beyer, M. (1990). A confirmatory factor analysis of the WPPSI-R. *Journal of Psychoeducational Assessment, 8*(1), 15–21.

Haaga, D. A., Davison, G. C., McDermut, W., Hillis, S. L., & Twomey, H. B. (1993). "State of mind" analysis of the articulated thoughts of ex-smokers. *Cognitive Therapy and Research, 17*, 427–439.

Hadaway, N., & Marek-Schroer, M. F. (1992). Multidimensional assessment of the gifted minority student. *Roeper Review, 15*, 73–77.

Haensly, P. A., & Torrance, E. P. (1990). Assessment of creativity in children and adolescents. In C. R. Reynolds & R. W. Kamphaus (Eds.), *Handbook of psychological and educational assessment of children: Intelligence & achievement* (pp. 697–722). New York: Guilford.

Hafemeister, T. L. (2001, February). Ninth Circuit rejects immunity from liability for mental health evaluations. *Monitor on Psychology, 32.*

Haier, R. J. (1993). Cerebral glucose metabolism and intelligence. In P. A. Vernon (Ed.), *Biological approaches to the study of human intelligence* (pp. 317–332). Norwood, NJ: Ablex.

Haines, M., & Spear, S. F. (1996). Changing the perception of the norm: A strategy to decrease binge drinking among college students. *Journal of American College Health, 45*(3), 134–140.

Haladyna, T. M., & Reynolds, C. R. (1992). Review of Millon Clinical Multiaxial Inventory II. In J. J. Kramer & J. C. Conoley (Eds.), *The eleventh mental measurements yearbook* (pp. 530–535). Lincoln: Buros Institute of Mental Measurements, University of Nebraska.

Haley, K., & Lee, M. (Eds.). (1998). *The Oregon Death With Dignity Act: A guidebook for health care providers.* Portland, OR: Oregon Health Sciences University, Center for Ethics in Health Care.

Hall, C. S., & Lindzey, G. (1970). *Theories of personality.* New York: Wiley.

Hall, G. C. N., Proctor, W. C., & Nelson, G. M. (1988). Validity of physiological measures of pedophilic sexual arousal in a sexual offender population. *Journal of Consulting and Clinical Psychology, 56*, 118–122.

Hall, J. A., & Rosenthal, R. (1995). Interpreting and evaluating meta-analysis. *Evaluation and the Health Professions, 18*, 393–407.

Hall, S. S. (1998, February 15). Our memories, our selves. *New York Times Magazine,* pp. 26–33, 49, 56–57.

Halleck, S. L. (1976). Discussion of "Socially Reinforced Obsessing." *Journal of Consulting and Clinical Psychology, 44*, 146–147.

Halperin, K., Snyder, C. R., Shenkel, R. J., & Houston, B. K. (1976). Effects of source status and message favorability on acceptance of personality feedback. *Journal of Applied Psychology, 61*, 85–88.

Halpern, A. S., & Fuherer, M. J. (Eds.). (1984). *Functional assessment in rehabilitation.* Baltimore: Paul H. Brookes.

Halpern, D. F. (1997). Sex differences in intelligence: Implications for education. *American Psychologist, 52*, 1091–1102.

Halpern, D. F. (2000). Validity, fairness, and group differences: Tough questions for selection testing. *Psychology, Public Policy, & Law, 6*, 56–62.

Halpern, F. (1951). The Bender Visual Motor Test. In H. H. Anderson & G. Anderson (Eds.), *An introduction to projective techniques* (pp. 324–341). Englewood Cliffs, NJ: Prentice-Hall.

Halpern, F. (1958). Child case study. In E. F. Hammer (Ed.), *The clinical application of projective drawings* (pp. 113–129). Springfield, IL: Charles C Thomas.

Halstead, W. C. (1947a). *Brain and intelligence.* Chicago: University of Chicago.

Halstead, W. C. (1947b). *Brain and intelligence: A quantitative study of the frontal lobes.* Chicago: University of Chicago.

Halstead, W. C., & Wepman, J. M. (1959). The Halstead-Wepman Aphasia Screening Test. *Journal of Speech and Hearing Disorders, 14*, 9–15.

Hambleton, R. K. (1979). Latent trait models and their application. *New Directions in Testing and Measurement, 4*, 13–32.

Hambleton, R. K. (1988). Principles and applications of item response theory. In R. L. Linn (Ed.), *Educational measurement* (3rd ed.). New York: American Council on Education/Macmillan.

Hambleton, R. K. (1994). Guidelines for adapting educational and psychological tests: A progress report. *European Journal of Psychological Assessment, 10*, 229–244.

Hambleton, R. K., & Cook, L. L. (1977). Latent trait models and their use in the analysis of educational test data. *Journal of Educational Measurement, 14*, 75–96.

Hambleton, R. K., & Jurgensen, C. (1990). Criterion-referenced assessment of school achievement. In C. R. Reynolds & R. W. Kamphaus (Eds.), *Handbook of psychological and educational assessment of children: Intelligence & achievement* (pp. 456–476). New York: Guilford.

Hamburg, D., & Adams, J. E. (1967). A perspective on coping behavior: Seeking and utilizing information in major transitions. *Archives of General Psychiatry, 17*, 277–284.

Hamera, E., & Brown, C. E. (2000). Developing a context-based performance measure for persons with schizophrenia: The test of grocery shopping skills. *American Journal of Occupational Therapy, 54*, 20–25.

Hammer, E. F. (1958). *The clinical application of projective drawings.* Springfield, IL: Charles C Thomas.

Hammer, E. F. (1981). Projective drawings. In A. I. Rabin (Ed.), *Assessment with projective techniques: A concise introduction* (pp. 151–185). New York: Springer.

Hammitt, J. K. (1990). Risk perceptions and food choice: An exploratory analysis of organic—versus conventional—produce buyers. *Risk Analysis, 10*, 367–374.

Hamsher, J. H., & Farina, A. (1967). "Openness" as a dimension of projective test responses. *Journal of Consulting Psychology, 31,* 525–528.

Handler, L. (1996). John Exner and the book that started it all: A review of *The Rorschach Systems. Journal of Personality Assessment, 66,* 441–471.

Handler, L. (1998). The importance of assessing playfulness. In H. M. Potash (Chair), *The assessment of psychological health.* Symposium presented at the Society for Personality Assessment 1998 Midwinter Meeting, February 21.

Haney, W. (1981). Validity, vaudeville, and values: A short history of social concerns over standardized testing. *American Psychologist, 36,* 1021–1034.

Haney, W., & Madaus, G. F. (1978). Making sense of the competency testing movement. *Harvard Educational Review, 48,* 462–484.

Hansen, J. C. (1987). Cross-cultural research on vocational interests. *Measurement and Evaluation in Counseling and Development, 19,* 163–176.

Harder, D. W., & Greenwald, D. (1998). Further validation of the Harder PFQ2 Shame and Guilt Scales. In J. Butcher (Chair), *New measures and instruments in assessment.* Paper session presentation at the Society for Personality Assessment 1998 Midwinter Meeting, February 19.

Hare, R. D. (1980). A research scale for the assessment of psychopathy in criminal populations. *Personality and Individual Differences, 1,* 111–119.

Hare, R. D. (1985). *The Psychopathy Checklist.* Unpublished manuscript. University of British Columbia, Vancouver, Canada.

Hare, R. D., Harpur, A. R., Hakstian, A. R., Forth, A. E., Hart, S. D., & Newman, J. P. (1990). The Revised Psychopathy Checklist: Reliability and Factor Structure. *Psychological Assessment, 2,* 338–341.

Hargadon, F. (1981). Tests and college admissions. *American Psychologist, 36,* 1112–1119.

Harker, L., & Keltner, D. (2001). Expressions of positive emotion in women's college yearbook pictures and their relationship to personality and life outcomes across adulthood. *Journal of Personality and Social Psychology, 80,* 112–124.

Harmon, L. W., Hansen, J. C., Borgen, F. H., & Hammer, A. L. (1994). *Strong Interest Inventory: Applications and technical guide.* Palo Alto, CA: Consulting Psychologists Press.

Harris, D. (1963). *Children's drawings as measures of intellectual maturity.* New York: Harcourt Brace Jovanovich.

Harris, D. B. (1978). A review of Kinetic Family Drawings. In O. K. Buros (Ed.), *The eighth mental measurements yearbook* (Vol. 1; pp. 884–885). Highland Park, NJ: Gryphon.

Harris, G. T., Rice, M. E., & Cormier, C. A. (1989). Violent recidivism among psychopaths and non-psychopaths treated in a therapeutic community. *Penetanguishene Mental Health Centre Research Report VI* (No. 181). Penetanguishene, Ontario, Canada: Penetanguishene Mental Health Centre.

Harris, P. M. (1994). Client management classification and prediction of probation outcome. *Crime and Delinquency, 40,* 154–174.

Harris, R., & Lingoes, J. (1955). *Subscales for the Minnesota Multiphasic Personality Inventory* [mimeograph]. San Francisco: The Langley Porter Clinic.

Harris, R., & Lingoes, J. (1968). *Subscales for the Minnesota Multiphasic Personality Inventory* [mimeograph]. San Francisco: The Langley Porter Clinic.

Harris, S. L., Delmolino, L., & Glasberg, B. A. (1996). Psychological and behavioral assessment in mental retardation. *Child & Adolescent Psychiatric Clinics of North America, 5,* 797–808.

Harrison, P., & Oakland, T. (2000). *Adaptive Behavior Assessment System.* San Antonio: Psychological Corporation.

Harrison, P. L. (1990). *AGS Early Screening Profiles.* Circle Pines, MN: American Guidance Service.

Hart, B., & Risley, T. R. (1992). American parenting of language-learning children: Persisting differences in family-child interactions observed in natural home environments. *Developmental Psychology, 28,* 1096–1105.

Hart, R. R., & Goldstein, M. A. (1985). Computer-assisted psychological assessment. *Computers in Human Services, 1,* 69–75.

Hart, S. D., Kropp, P. R., & Hare, R. D. (1988). Performance of male psychopaths following conditional release from prison. *Journal of Consulting and Clinical Psychology, 56,* 227–232.

Hart, V. (1992). Review of the Infant Mullen Scales of Early Development. In J. J. Kramer & J. C. Conoley (Eds.), *The eleventh mental measurements yearbook.* Lincoln: Buros Institute of Mental Measurements, University of Nebraska.

Hartigan, J. A., & Wigdor, A. K. (1989). *Fairness in employment testing: Validity generalization, minority issues, and the General Aptitude Test Battery.* Washington, DC: National Academy.

Hartman, D. E. (1986a). On the use of clinical psychology software: Practical, legal, and ethical concerns. *Professional Psychology: Research and Practice, 17,* 462–465.

Hartman, D. E. (1986b). Artificial intelligence or artificial psychologist? Conceptual issues in clinical microcomputer use. *Professional Psychology: Research and Practice, 17,* 528–534.

Hartmann, D. P., Roper, B. L., & Bradford, D. C. (1979). Some relationships between behavioral and traditional assessment. *Journal of Behavioral Assessment, 1,* 3–21.

Hartshorne, H., & May, M. A. (1928). *Studies in the nature of character. Vol. 1: Studies in deceit.* New York: Macmillan.

Harvey, R. J., & Murry, W. D. (1994). Scoring the Myers-Briggs Type Indicator: Empirical comparison of preference score versus latent-trait methods. *Journal of Personality Assessment, 62,* 116–129.

Hasselblad, V., & Hedges, L. V. (1995). Meta-analysis of screening and diagnostic tests. *Psychological Bulletin, 117,* 167–178.

Hassler, M., & Gupta, D. (1993). Functional brain organization, handedness, and immune vulnerability in musicians and nonmusicians. *Neuropsychologia, 31,* 655–660.

Hathaway, S. R., & McKinley, J. C. (1940). A multiphasic personality schedule (Minnesota): 1. Construction of the schedule. *Journal of Psychology, 10,* 249–254.

Hathaway, S. R., & McKinley, J. C. (1942). A multiphasic personality schedule (Minnesota): III. The measurement of symptomatic depression. *Journal of Psychology, 14,* 73–84.

Hathaway, S. R., & McKinley, J. C. (1943). *The Minnesota Multiphasic Personality Inventory* (rev. ed.). Minneapolis: University of Minnesota.

Hathaway, S. R., & McKinley, J. C. (1951). *The MMPI manual.* New York: Psychological Corporation.

Hayden, D. C., Frulong, M. J., & Linnemeyer, S. (1988). A comparison of the Kaufman Assessment Battery for Children and the Stanford-Binet IV for the assessment of gifted children. *Psychology in the Schools, 25,* 239–243.

Hayes, S. C. (1999). Comparison of the Kaufman Brief Intelligence Test and the Matrix Analogies Test-Short Form in an adolescent forensic population. *Psychological Assessment, 11,* 108–110.

Haynes, J. R., & Sells, S. G. (1963). Assessment of organic brain damage by psychological tests. *Psychological Bulletin, 60,* 316–325.

Haynes, R. B., Taylor, D. W., & Sackett, D. L. (Eds.). (1979). *Compliance in health care.* Baltimore: Johns Hopkins University.

Haynes, S. N. (2001a). Introduction to the special section on clinical applications of analogue behavioral observation. *Psychological Assessment, 13,* 3–4.

Haynes, S. N. (2001b). Clinical applications of analogue behavioral observation: Dimensions of psychometric evaluation. *Psychological Assessment, 13,* 73–85.

Haynes, S. N., Falkin, S., & Sexton-Radek, K. (1989). Psychophysiological measurement in behavior therapy. In G. Turpin (Ed.), *Handbook of clinical psychophysiology* (pp. 175–214). London: Wiley.

Haynes, S. N., Follingstad, D. R., & Sullivan, J. (1979). Assessment of marital satisfaction and interaction. *Journal of Consulting and Clinical Psychology, 47,* 789–791.

Haynes, S. N., Jensen, B. J., Wise, E., & Sherman, D. (1981). The marital intake interview: A multimethod criterion validity assessment. *Journal of Consulting and Clinical Psychology, 49,* 379–387.

Hays, P. A. (1996). Culturally responsive assessment with diverse older clients. *Professional Psychology: Research and Practice, 27,* 188–193.

Hays, P. A., & LeVine, P. (2001). *Addressing cultural complexities in practice: A framework for clinicians and counselors.* Washington, D. C.: American Psychological Association.

Haywood, T. W., Grossman, L. S., & Cavanaugh, J. L. (1990). Subjective versus objective measurements of deviant sexual arousal in clinical evaluations of alleged child molesters. *Psychological Assessment, 2,* 269–275.

Hazlett, R. L., Falkin, S., Lawhorn, W., Friedman, E., & Haynes, S. N. (1997). Cardiovascular reactivity to a naturally occurring stressor: Development and psychometric evaluation of psychophysiological assessment procedure. *Journal of Behavioral Medicine, 20,* 551–571.

Heathington, B. S., & Alexander, J. E. (1978). A child-based observation checklist to assess attitudes toward reading. *Reading Teacher, 31,* 769–771.

Heaton, R. K., Baade, L. E., & John, K. L. (1978). Neuropsychological test results associated with psychiatric disorders in adults. *Psychological Bulletin, 85,* 141–162.

Heaton, R. K., Temkin, N., Dikmen, S., et al. (2001). Detecting change: A comparison of three neuropsychological methods, using normal and clinical samples. *Archives of Clinical Neuropsychology, 16,* 75–91.

Hedges, C. (1997, November 25). In Bosnia's schools, 3 ways never to learn from history. *New York Times,* pp. A1, A4.

Heidrich, S. M., Forsthoff, C. A., & Ward, S. E. (1994). Psychological adjustment in adults with cancer: The self as mediator. *Health Psychology, 13,* 346–353.

Heinrichs, R. W. (1990). Variables associated with Wisconsin Card Sorting Test performance in neuropsychiatric patients referred for assessment. *Neuropsychiatry, Neuropsychology, and Behavioral Neurology, 3,* 107–112.

Heinze, M. C., & Grisso, T. (1996). Review of instruments assessing parenting competencies used in child custody evaluations. *Behavioral Sciences and the Law, 14,* 293–313.

Heitzmann, C., & Kaplan, R. M. (1988). Assessment of methods for measuring social support. *Health Psychology, 7,* 75–109.

Helfer, R. E., & Kempe, R. S. (Eds.). (1988). *The battered child* (4th ed.). Chicago: University of Chicago Press.

Helmes, E., & Reddon, J. R. (1993). A perspective on developments in assessment psychopathology: A critical review of the MMPI and MMPI-2. *Psychological Bulletin, 113,* 453–471.

Helmreich, R. L., Sawin, L. L., & Carsrud, A. L. (1986). The honeymoon effect in job performance: Temporal increases in the predictive power of achievement motivation. *Journal of Applied Psychology, 71,* 185–188.

Helson, R. (1967). Personality characteristics and developmental history of creative college women. *Genetic Psychology Monographs, 76,* 205–256.

Helson, R., Mitchell, V., & Moane, G. (1984). Personality and patterns of adherence and nonadherence to the so-cial clock. *Journal of Personality and Social Psychology, 46,* 1079–1096.

Helzel, M. F., & Rice, M. E. (1985). On the validity of social skills assessments: An analysis of role-playing and ward staff ratings of social behavior in a maximum security setting. *Canadian Journal of Behavioral Science, 17,* 400–411.

Henk, W. A. (1993). New directions in reading assessment. *Reading and Writing Quarterly: Overcoming Learning Difficulties, 9,* 103–120.

Henley, N. M., & LaFrance, M. (1984). Gender as culture: Difference in dominance in nonverbal behavior. In. A. Wolfgang (Ed.), *Nonverbal behavior: Perspectives, applications, intercultural insights* (pp. 351–371). Lewiston, NY: Hogrefe & Huber.

Henry, E. M., & Rotter, J. B. (1956). Situational influences on Rorschach responses. *Journal of Consulting Psychology, 20,* 457–462.

Henry, J. D. (1984). Syndicated public opinion polls: Some thoughts for consideration. *Journal of Advertising Research, 24,* I-5–I-8.

Henry, W. E. (1956). *The analysis of fantasy.* New York: Wiley.

Heppner, M. J. (1998). The Career Transitions Inventory: Measuring internal resources in adulthood. *Journal of Career Assessment, 6,* 135–145.

Herlihy, B. (1977). Watch out, IQ myth: Here comes another debunker. *Phi Delta Kappan, 59,* 298.

Hermann, C., Blanchard, E. B., & Flor, H. (1997). Biofeedback treatment for pediatric migraine: Prediction of treatment outcome. *Journal of Consulting and Clinical Psychology, 65,* 611–616.

Herrnstein, R., & Murray, C. (1994). *The bell curve.* New York: Free Press.

Herzberg, F., Mausner, B., Peterson, R. O., & Capwell, D. F. (1957). Job attitudes: Review of research and opinion. *Journal of Applied Psychology, 63,* 596–601.

Hess, E. H. (1965). Attitude and pupil size. *Scientific American, 212,* 46–54.

Hess, E. H. (1972). Pupillometrics: A method of studying mental, emotional and sensory processes. In N. S. Greenfield & R. A. Sternbach (Eds.), *Handbook of psychophysiology* (pp. 491–531). New York: Holt, Rinehart & Winston.

Hess, E. H., & Polt, J. M. (1960). Pupil size as related to interest value of visual stimuli. *Science, 132,* 349–350.

Hess, E. H., & Polt, J. M. (1964). Pupil size in relation to mental activity during simple problem solving. *Science, 143,* 1190–1192.

Hess, E. H., & Polt, J. M. (1966). Changes in pupil size as a measure of taste difference. *Perceptual and Motor Skills, 23,* 451–455.

Hetherington, E. M., & Parke, R. D. (1993). *Child psychology: A contemporary viewpoint* (4th ed.). New York: McGraw-Hill.

Heyman, R. E. (2001). Observation of couple conflicts: Clinical assessment applications, stubborn truths, and shaky foundations. *Psychological Assessment, 13,* 5–35.

Hibbard, S., Farmer, L., Wells, C., et al., (1994). Validation of Cramer's defense mechanism manual for the TAT. *Journal of Personality Assessment, 63,* 197–210.

Hicks, L. K., Lin, Y., Robertson, D. W., et al. (2001). Understanding the clinical dilemmas that shape medical students' ethical development: Questionnaire survey and focus group study. *British Medical Journal, 322,* 709–710.

Higgins, P. C. (1983). *Outsiders in a hearing world.* Beverly Hills: Sage.

Higgins, R. L., Alonso, R. R., & Pendleton, M. G. (1979). The validity of role-play assessments of assertiveness. *Behavior Therapy, 10,* 655–662.

Hiller, J. B., Rosenthal, R., Bornstein, R. F., & Brunell-Neuleib, S. (1999). A comparative meta-analysis of Rorschach and MMPI validity. *Psychological Assessment, 11,* 278–296.

Hills, D. A. (1985). Prediction of effectiveness in leaderless group discussions with the Adjective Check List. *Journal of Applied Psychology, 15,* 443–447.

Hilsenroth, M. J., & Handler, L. (1995). A survey of graduate students' experiences, interests, and attitudes about learning the Rorschach. *Journal of Personality Assessment, 64,* 243–257.

Hines, M. (1990). Gonadal hormones and human cognition development. In J. Balthazart (Ed.), *Hormones, brains, and behaviors in vertebrates: I. Sexual differentiation, neuroanatomical aspects, neurotransmitters, and neuropeptides* (pp. 51–63). Basel, Switzerland: Karger.

Hines, M., Chiu, L., McAdams, L. A., Bentler, M. P., & Lipcamon, J. (1992). Cognition and the corpus callosum: Verbal fluency, visuospatial ability, language lateralization related to midsagittal surface areas of the corpus callosum. *Behavioral Neuroscience, 106,* 3–14.

Hinkle, J. S. (1994). Counselors and cross-cultural assessment: A practical guide to information and training. *Measurement and Evaluation in Counseling and Development, 27,* 103–115.

Hinrichsen, J. J., & Bradley, L. A. (1974). Situational determinants of personal validation of general personality interpretations: A re-examination. *Journal of Personality Assessment, 38,* 530–534.

Hirsch, J. (1997). Some history of heredity-vs-environment, genetic inferiority at Harvard(?), and *The* (incredible) *bell curve. Genetics, 99,* 207–224.

Hiscox, M. D. (1983). *A balance sheet for educational item banking.* Paper presented at the annual meeting of the National Council for Measurement in Education, Montreal, Canada.

Hiscox, M. D., & Brzezinski, E. (1980). *A guide to item banking in education.* Portland, OR: Northwest Regional Educational Laboratory, Assessment and Education Division.

Hishinuma, E. S., Andrade, N. N., Johnson, R. C., et al. (2000). Psychometric properties of the Hawaiian Culture Scale-Adolescent Version. *Psychological Assessment, 12,* 140–157.

Hishinuma, E. S., & Yamakawa, R. (1993). Construct and criterion-related validity of the WISC-III for exceptional students and those who are "at risk." In B. A. Bracken (Ed.), *Monograph series, Advances in psychoeducational assessment: Wechsler Intelligence Scale for Children, Third Edition; Journal of Psychoeducational Assessment* (pp. 94–104). Brandon, VT: Clinical Psychology Publishing.

Hiskey, M. S. (1966). *Hiskey-Nebraska Test of Learning Aptitude.* Lincoln: Union College.

Ho, M. K. (1987). *Family therapy with ethnic minorities.* Newbury Park, CA: Sage.

Hodapp, R. M. (1995). Definitions in mental retardation: Effects on research, practice, and perceptions. *School Psychology Quarterly, 10*(1), 24–28.

Hofer, P. J., & Green, B. F. (1985). The challenge of competence and creativity in computerized psychological testing. *Journal of Consulting and Clinical Psychology, 53,* 826–838.

Hoffman, B. (1962). *The tyranny of testing.* New York: Crowell-Collier.

Hoffman, K. I., & Lundberg, G. D. (1976). A comparison of computer monitored group tests and paper-and-pencil tests. *Educational and Psychological Measurement, 36,* 791–809.

Hofstede, G. (1998). Attitudes, values, and organizational culture: Disentangling the concepts. *Organization Studies, 19,* 477–493.

Hogan, R., Carpenter, B., Briggs, S., & Hanson, R. (1985). Personality assessment and personnel selection. In H. J. Bernardin & D. A. Bownes (Eds.), *Personality assessment in organizations.* New York: Praeger.

Holahan, C., & Sears, R. (1995). *The gifted group in later maturity.* Stanford, CA: Stanford University Press.

Holden, G. W., & Edwards, L. A. (1989). Parental attitudes toward child rearing: Instruments, issues, and implications. *Psychological Bulletin, 106,* 29–58.

Holland, A. (1980). *Communicative abilities in daily living: A test of functional communication for aphasic adults.* Baltimore: University Park.

Holland, J. L. (1959). A theory of vocational choice. *Journal of Counseling Psychology, 59,* 35–45.

Holland, J. L. (1966). *The psychology of vocational choice.* Waltham, MA: Blaisdell.

Holland, J. L. (1973). *Making vocational choices.* Englewood Cliffs, NJ: Prentice-Hall.

Holland, J. L. (1985). *Manual for the vocational preference inventory.* Odessa, FL: Psychological Assessment Resources.

Holland, J. L. (1992). *Making vocational choices: A theory of vocational personalities and work environments* (2nd ed.). Odessa, FL: Psychological Assessment Resources.

Holland, J. L., Powell, A. B., & Fritzsche, B. A. (1994). *The Self-Directed Search (SDS) Professional user's guide—1994 edition.* Odessa, FL: Psychological Assessment Resources.

Holland, W. R. (1960). Language barrier as an educational problem of Spanish speaking children. *Exceptional Children, 27,* 42–47.

Hollander, E. P., & Willis, R. H. (1967). Some current issues in the psychology of conformity and nonconformity. *Psychological Bulletin, 68,* 62–76.

Hollenbeck, J. R., & Whitener, E. M. (1988). Reclaiming personality traits for personal selection: Self-esteem as an illustrative case. *Journal of Management, 14,* 81–91.

Hollingshead, A. B., & Redlich, F. C. (1958). *Social class and mental illness: A community study.* New York: Wiley.

Holmes, C. B., Dungan, D. S., & Medlin, W. J. (1984). Reassessment of inferring personality traits from Bender-Gestalt drawing styles. *Journal of Clinical Psychology, 40,* 1241–1243.

Holmes, D. S. (1974). The conscious control of thematic projection. *Journal of Consulting and Clinical Psychology, 42,* 323–329.

Holmstrom, R. W., Silber, D. E., & Karp, S. A. (1990). Development of the Apperceptive Personality Test. *Journal of Personality Assessment, 54,* 252–264.

Holt, R. R. (1958). Clinical and statistical prediction: A reformulation and some new data. *Journal of Abnormal and Social Psychology, 56,* 1–12.

Holt, R. R. (1970). Yet another look at clinical and statistical prediction: Or, is clinical psychology worthwhile? *American Psychologist, 25,* 337–349.

Holt, R. R. (1971). *Assessing personality.* New York: Harcourt Brace Jovanovich.

Holt, R. R. (1978). *Methods in clinical psychology: Vol. 2. Prediction and research.* New York: Plenum.

Holtzman, W. H. (1993). An unjustified, sweeping indictment by Motta et al. of human figure drawings for assessing psychological functioning. *School Psychology Quarterly, 8,* 189–190.

Holtzman, W. H., Thorpe, J. S., Swartz, J. D., & Herron, E. W. (1961). *Inkblot perception and personality: Holtzman Inkblot Technique.* Austin: University of Texas Press.

Honaker, L. M. (1988). The equivalency of computerized and conventional MMPI administration: A review. *Clinical Psychology Review, 8,* 561–577.

Honaker, L. M. (1990, August). Recommended guidelines for computer equivalency research (or everything you should know about computer administration but will be disappointed if you ask). In W. J. Camara (Chair), *The state of computer-based testing and interpretation: Consensus or chaos?* Symposium conducted at the Annual Convention of the American Psychological Association, Boston.

Honaker, L. M., & Fowler, R. D. (1990). Computer-assisted psychological assessment. In G. Goldstein & M. Hersen (Eds.), *Handbook of psychological assessment* (2nd ed. pp. 521–546). New York: Pergamon.

Honts, C. R. (1994). Psychophysiological detection of deception. *Current Directions in Psychological Science, 3,* 77–82.

Honzik, M. P. (1967). Environmental correlates of mental growth: Prediction from the family setting at 21 months. *Child Development, 38,* 337–364.

Honzik, M. P., McFarlane, J. W., & Allen, L. (1948). The stability of mental test performance between 2 and 18 years. *Journal of Experimental Education, 17,* 309–324.

Hopkins, K. D., & Glass, G. V. (1978). *Basic statistics for the behavioral sciences.* Englewood Cliffs, NJ: Prentice-Hall.

Hopwood v. State of Texas, 78 F. 3d 932, 948 (5th Cir., 1996).

Horn, J. (1988). Thinking about human abilities. In J. R. Nesselroade & R. B. Cattell (Eds.), *Handbook of multivariate psychology.* New York: Plenum.

Horn, J. L. (1968). Organization of abilities and the development of intelligence. *Psychological Review, 75,* 242–259.

Horn, J. L. (1985). Remodeling old theories of intelligence: GF-Gc theory. In B. B. Wolman (Ed.), *Handbook of intelligence* (pp. 267–300). New York: Wiley.

Horn, J. L. (1988). Thinking about human abilities. In J. R. Nesselroade & R. B. Cattell (Eds.), *Handbook of multivariate psychology* (rev. ed.); (pp. 645–685). New York: Academic Press.

Horn, J. L. (1989). Cognitive diversity: A framework for learning. In P. L. Ackerman et al. (Eds.), *Learning and individual differences* (pp. 61–116). New York: W. H. Freeman.

Horn, J. L. (1991). Measurement of intellectual capabilities: A review of theory. In K. S. McGrew et al. (Eds.), *Woodcock-Johnson technical manual* (pp. 197–232). Chicago: Riverside.

Horn, J. L. (1994). Theory of fluid and crystallized intelligence. In R. J. Sternberg (Ed.), *Encyclopedia of human intelligence* (pp. 443–451).

Horn, J. L., & Cattell, R. B. (1966). Refinement and test of the theory of fluid and crystallized intelligence. *Journal of Educational Psychology, 57,* 253–270.

Horn, J. L., & Cattell, R. B. (1967). Age differences in fluid and crystallized intelligence. *Acta Psychologica, 26,* 107–129.

Horn, J. L., & Hofer, S. M. (1992). Major abilities and development in the adult period. In R. J. Sternberg & C. A. Berg (Eds.), *Intellectual development* (pp. 44–99). Boston, MA: Cambridge University Press.

Horner, M. S. (1973). A psychological barrier to achievement in women: The motive to avoid success. In D. C. McClelland & R. S. Steele (Eds.), *Human motivation* (pp. 222–230). Morristown, NJ: General Learning.

Horner, T. M., Guyer, M. J., & Kalter, N. M. (1993). Clinical expertise and the assessment of child sexual abuse. *Journal of the American Academy of Child and Adolescent Psychiatry, 32,* 925–931.

Horowitz, R., & Murphy, L. B. (1938). Projective methods in the psychological study of children. *Journal of Experimental Education, 7,* 133–140.

Horowitz, T. (1998). Gulf War symptomatology: Neuropsychological consequences without post-traumatic stress disorder. In P. Sloan & J. H. Quillen (Chairs), *Assessment of cognitive, emotional and physical functioning in war veterans.* Symposium presented at the Society for Personality Assessment 1998 Midwinter Meeting, February 20.

Horst, P. (1953). Correcting the Kuder-Richardson reliability for dispersion of item difficulties. *Psychological Bulletin, 50,* 371–374.

Hostetler, A. J. (1987). Try to remember. *APA Monitor 18*(5), 18.

House, R. J., Shane, S. A., & Herold, D. M. (1996). Rumors of the death of dispositional research are vastly exaggerated. *Academy of Management Review, 20,* 203–224.

Houston, T. K., Cooper, L. A., Vu, H., et al. (2001). Screening the public for depression through the Internet. *Psychiatric Services, 52,* 362–367.

Howard, M. N. (1991). The neutral expert: A plausible threat to justice. *Criminal Law Review.*

Howe Chief, E. (1940). An assimilation study of Indian girls. *Journal of Social Psychology, 11,* 19–30.

Hozier, A. (1959). On the breakdown of the sense of reality: A study of spatial perception in schizophrenia. *Journal of Consulting Psychology, 23,* 185–194.

Hsu, S-H, & Peng, Y. (1993). Control/display relationship of the four-burner stove: A re-examination. *Human Factors, 35,* 745–749.

Hudson, W. W. (1982). *The clinical measurement package: A field manual.* Chicago: Dorsey.

Huebner, E. S. (1994). Preliminary development and validation of a multidimensional life satisfaction scale for children. *Psychological Assessment, 6,* 149–158.

Huesmann, L. R., & Guerra, N. G. (1997). Children's normative beliefs about aggression and aggressive behavior. *Journal of Personality and Social Psychology, 72,* 408–419.

Hughes, C., Hwang, B., Kim, J.-H., et al. (1995). Quality of life in applied research: A review and analysis of empirical measures. *American Journal on Mental Retardation, 99,* 623–641.

Hull, C. L. (1922). *Aptitude testing.* Yonkers, NY: World Book.

Hulse, W. G. (1951). The emotionally disturbed child draws his family. *Quarterly Journal of Child Behavior, 3,* 151–174.

Hulse, W. G. (1952). Childhood conflict expressed through family drawings. *Quarterly Journal of Child Behavior, 16,* 152–174.

Humphreys, L. G. (1996). Linear dependence of gain scores on their components imposes constraints on their use and interpretation: Comment on "Are simple gain scores obsolete?" *Applied Psychological Measurement, 20,* 293–294.

Hunsley, J., & Bailey, J. M. (1999). The clinical utility of the Rorschach: Unfulfilled promises and an uncertain future. *Psychological Assessment, 11,* 266–277.

Hunt, J. McV. (1961). *Intelligence and experience.* New York: Ronald.

Hunter, J. E. (1980). *Validity generalization for 12,000 jobs: An application of synthetic validity and validity generalization to the General Aptitude Test Battery (GATB).* Washington, DC: U.S. Employment Service, Department of Labor.

Hunter, J. E. (1982). *The dimensionality of the General Aptitude Test Battery and the dominance of general factors over specific factors in the prediction of job performance.* Washington, DC: U.S. Employment Service, Department of Labor.

Hunter, J. E. (1986). Cognitive ability, cognitive aptitudes, job knowledge, and job performance. *Journal of Vocational Behavior, 29,* 340–362.

Hunter, J. E., & Hunter, R. (1984). Validity and utility of alternate predictors of job performance. *Psychological Bulletin, 96,* 72–98.

Hunter, J. E., & Schmidt, F. L. (1976). A critical analysis of the statistical and ethical implications of various definitions of "test bias." *Psychological Bulletin, 83,* 1053–1071.

Hunter, J. E., & Schmidt, F. L. (1981). Fitting people into jobs: The impact of personal selection on normal productivity. In M. D. Dunnette & E. A. Fleishman (Eds.), *Human performance and productivity: Vol. 1. Human capability assessment.* Hillsdale, NJ: Erlbaum.

Hunter, J. E., & Schmidt, F. L. (1983). Quantifying the effects of psychological interventions on employee job performance and work-force productivity. *American Psychologist, 38,* 473–478.

Hunter, J. E., & Schmidt, F. L. (1990). *Methods of meta-analysis.* Newbury Park, CA: Sage.

Hunter, J. E., Schmidt, F. L., & Jackson, G. B. (1982). *Meta-analysis: Cumulating research findings across studies.* Beverly Hills: Sage.

Hunter, M. S. (1992). The Women's Health Questionnaire: A measure of mid-aged women's perceptions of their emotional and physical health. *Psychology and Health, 7,* 45–54.

Hurlburt, R. T. (1997). Randomly sampling thinking in the natural environment. *Journal of Consulting and Clinical Psychology, 65,* 941–949.

Hurst, N. H. (1997). A narrative analysis of identity change in treated substance abusers. *Dissertation Abstracts International, Section B: The Sciences & Engineering, 58*(4-B), 2124.

Hutt, M. L. (1977). *The Hutt adaptation of the Bender-Gestalt* (3rd ed.). New York: Grune & Stratton.

Hutt, M. L. (1985). *The Hutt adaptation of the Bender-Gestalt Test* (4th ed.). Orlando: Grune & Stratton.

Hutton, J. B., Dubes, R., & Moir, S. (1992). Assessment practices of school psychologists: Ten years later. *School Psychology Review, 21,* 271–284.

Hysjulien, C., Wood, B., Benjamin, G., Andrew, H. (1994). Child custody evaluations: A review of methods used in litigation and alternative dispute resolution. *Family and Conciliation Courts Review, 32,* 466–489.

Iacono, W. G., & Lykken, D. T. (1997). The validity of the lie detector: Two surveys of scientific opinion. *Journal of Applied Psychology, 82,* 425–433.

Iaffaldano, M. T., & Muchinsky, P. M. (1985). Job satisfaction and job performance: A meta-analysis. *Psychological Bulletin, 97,* 251–273.

Ilyin, D. (1976). *The Ilyin oral interview.* Rowley, MA: Newbury House.

Impara, J. C., & Plake, B. S. (Eds.). (1998). *The thirteenth mental measurements yearbook.* Lincoln: Buros Institute of Mental Measurements, University of Nebraska.

Innocenti, M. S., Huh, K., & Boyce, G. C. (1992). Families of children with disabilities: Normative data and other considerations on parenting stress. *Topics in Early Childhood Special Education, 12,* 403–427.

Institute for Juvenile Research. (1937). *Child guidance procedures, methods and techniques employed at the Institute for Juvenile Research.* New York: Appleton-Century.

Institute of Medicine. (1984). *Research and training for the Secret Service: Behavioral science and mental health perspectives: A report of the Institute of Medicine* (IOM Publication No. IOM-84-01). Washington, DC: National Academy Press.

International Test Commission. (1993). *Technical standards for translating tests and establishing test score equivalence.* Amherst, MA: Author. (Available from Dr. Ronald Hambleton, School of Education, University of Massachusetts, Amherst, MA 01003).

Ioannidis, J. P. A., Cappelleri, J. C., & Lau, J. (1998). Issues in comparisons between meta-analysis and large trials. *Journal of the American Medical Association, 279,* 1089–1093.

Ironson, G. H., & Subkoviak, M. J. (1979). A comparison of several methods of assessing item bias. *Journal of Educational Measurement, 16,* 209–225.

Irvine, S. H., & Berry, J. W. (Eds.). (1983). *Human assessment and cultural factors.* New York: Plenum.

Irwin, M. R., Patterson, T. L., Smith, T. L., et al. (1990). Reduction of immune function in life stress and depression. *Biological Psychiatry, 27,* 22–30.

Isen, A. M. (1987). Positive affect, cognitive processes, and social behavior. *Advances in Experimental Social Psychology, 20,* 203–253.

Ishihara, S. (1964). *Tests for color blindness* (11th ed.). Tokyo: Kanehara Shuppan.

Ivancevich, J. M. (1983). Contrast effects in performance evaluation and reward practices. *Academy of Management Journal, 26,* 465–476.

Iverson, G. L., Myers, B., Bengston, M. L., & Adams, R. L. (1996). Concurrent validity of a WAIS-R seven subtest short form in patients with brain impairment. *Psychological Assessment, 8,* 319–332.

Ivnik, R. J., Malec, J. F., Smith, G. E., Tangalos, E. G., Petersen, R. C., Kokmen, E., & Kurland, L. T. (1992). Mayo's older American normative studies: WAIS-R norms for ages 56–97. *Clinical Neuropsychologist, 6*(Suppl.), 1–30.

Ivnik, R. J., Smith, G. E., Malec, J. F., Petersen, R. C., & Tangalos, E. G. (1995). Long-term stability and intercorrelations of cognitive abilities in older persons. *Psychological Assessment, 7,* 155–161.

Jackson, D. E., O'Dell, J. W., & Olson, D. (1982). Acceptance of bogus personality interpretations: Face validity reconsidered. *Journal of Clinical Psychology, 38,* 588–592.

Jackson, D. N. (1964). Desirability judgments as a method of personality assessment. *Educational and Psychological Measurement, 24,* 223–238.

Jackson, D. N. (1970). A sequential system for personality scale development. In C. D. Spielberger (Ed.), *Current topics in clinical and community psychology.* New York: Academic Press.

Jackson, D. N. (1977). *Jackson Vocational Interest Survey manual.* Port Huron, MI: Research Psychologists.

Jackson, D. N. (1986). *Computer-based personality testing.* Washington, DC: Scientific Affairs Office, American Psychological Association.

Jackson, D. N., & Messick, S. (1958). Content and style in personality assessment. *Psychological Bulletin, 55,* 243–252.

Jackson, D. N., & Messick, S. (1962). Response styles and the assessment of psychopathology. In S. Messick & J. Ross (Eds.), *Measurement in personality and cognition.* New York: Wiley.

Jackson, D. N., & Williams, D. R. (1975). Occupational classification in terms of interest patterns. *Journal of Vocational Behavior, 6,* 269–280.

Jackson, J. F. (1993). Human behavioral genetics, Scarr's theory, and her views on interventions: A critical review and commentary on their implications for African American children. *Child Development, 64,* 1318–1332.

Jackson, J. L. (1999). Psychometric considerations in self-monitoring assessment. *Psychological Assessment, 11,* 439–447.

Jacobs, J. (1970). Are we being misled by fifty years of research on our gifted children? *Gifted Child Quarterly, 14,* 120–123.

Jacobsen, M. E. (1999). Arousing the sleeping giant: Giftedness in adult psychotherapy. *Roeper Review, 22,* 36–41.

Jacob-Timm, S., & Hartshorne, T. (1998). *Ethics and law for school psychologists* (3rd ed.). New York: John Wiley & Sons.

Jaffe, A. J., & Kilbey, M. M. (1994). The Cocaine Expectancy Questionnaire (CEQ): Construction and predictive utility. *Psychological Assessment, 6,* 18–26.

Jagger, L., Neukrug, E., & McAuliffe, G. (1992). Congruence between personality traits and chosen occupation as a predictor of job satisfaction for people with disabilities. *Rehabilitation Counseling Bulletin, 36,* 53–60.

Jagim, R. D., Wittman, W. D., & Noll, J. O. (1978). Mental health professionals' attitudes towards confidentiality, privilege, and third-party disclosure. *Professional Psychology, 9,* 458–466.

James, L. R., Demaree, R. G., & Mulaik, S. A. (1986). A note on validity generalization procedures. *Journal of Applied Psychology, 71,* 440–450.

James, L. R., Demaree, R. G., & Wolf, G. (1984). Estimating within-group interrater reliability with and without response bias. *Journal of Applied Psychology, 69,* 85–98.

Janisse, M. P. (1973). Pupil size and affect: A critical review of the literature since 1960. *Canadian Psychologist, 14,* 311–329.

Jankowski, K. (1991). On communicating with deaf people. In L. A. Samovar & R. E. Belmont (Eds.), *Intercultural communication: A reader.* (6th ed.); (pp. 142–150). Belmont, CA: Wadsworth.

Janzen, H. L. (1981). Why use the Binet? *Alberta School Psychologist, 2,* 25–38.

Jastak, J. F., & Jastak, S. (1984). *Wide Range Achievement Test—Revised.* Wilmington, DE: Jastak Associates.

Jenkins, C. D., Zyzanski, S. J., & Rosenman, R. H. (1979). *Jenkins Activity Survey: Manual.* San Antonio: Psychological Corporation.

Jennings, B. (1991). Active euthanasia and forgoing life-sustaining treatment: Can we hold the line? *Journal of Pain, 6,* 312–316.

Jensen, A. R. (1965). A review of the Rorschach. In O. K. Buros (Ed.), *The sixth mental measurements yearbook* (pp. 501–509). Lincoln: Buros Institute of Mental Measurement, University of Nebraska.

Jensen, A. R. (1969). How much can we boost IQ and scholastic achievement? *Harvard Educational Review, 39,* 1–123.

Jensen, A. R. (1980). *Bias in mental testing.* New York: Free Press.

Jensen, A. R. (2000). Testing: The dilemma of group differences. *Psychology, Public Policy, and Law, 6,* 121–127.

Jobes, D. A., Jacoby, A. M., Cimbolic, P., & Hustead, L. A. T. (1997). Assessment and treatment of suicidal clients in a university. *Journal of Consulting Psychology, 44,* 368–377.

Johansson, H. J., & Forsman, M. (2001). Identification and analysis of unsatisfactory psychosocial work situations: A participatory approach employing video-computer interaction. *Applied Ergonomics, 32,* 23–29.

Johnson, D. L., & Johnson, C. A. (1965). Totally discouraged: A depressive syndrome of the Dakota Sioux. *Psychiatric Research Review, 2,* 141–143.

Johnson, E. S. (2000). The effects of accommodation on performance assessments. *Remedial and Special Education, 21,* 261–267.

Johnson, G. S. (1989). Emotional indicators in the human figure drawings of hearing-impaired children: A small sample validation study. *American Annals of the Deaf, 134,* 205–208.

Johnson, J. A., & Ostendorf, F. (1993). Clarification of the five-factor model with the abridged big five dimensional circumplex. *Journal of Personality and Social Psychology, 65,* 563–576.

Johnson, L. C., Beaton, R., Murphy, S., & Pike, K. (2000). Sampling bias and other methodological threats to the validity of health survey research. *International Journal of Stress Management, 7,* 247–267.

Johnson, L. J., Cook, M. J., & Kullman, A. J. (1992). An examination of the concurrent validity of the Battelle Developmental Inventory as compared with the Vineland Adaptive Scales and the Bayley Scales of Infant Development. *Journal of Early Intervention, 16,* 353–359.

Johnson, R. C. (1963). Similarity in IQ of separated identical twins as related to length of time spent in same environment. *Child Development, 34,* 745–749.

Joiner, T. E., Jr., & Schmidt, K. L. (1997). Drawing conclusions—or not—from drawings. *Journal of Personality Assessment, 69,* 476–481.

Joiner, T. E., Jr., Schmidt, K. L., & Barnett, J. (1996). Size, detail, and line heaviness in children's drawings as correlates of emotional distress: (More) negative evidence. *Journal of Personality Assessment, 67,* 127–141.

Jolles, J. (1952). *A catalogue for the qualitative interpretation of the H-T-P.* Los Angeles: Western Psychological Services.

Jones, D. P., & McGraw, J. M. (1987). Reliable and fictitious accounts of sexual abuse to children. *Journal of Interpersonal Violence, 2,* 27–45.

Jones, J. W., Arnold, D., & Harris, W. G. (1990). Introduction to the Model Guidelines for Preemployment Integrity Testing. *Journal of Business and Psychology, 4,* 525–532.

Jones, P., & Rodgers, B. (1993). Estimating premorbid IQ in schizophrenia. *British Journal of Psychiatry, 162,* 273–274.

Jones, R. N., & Gallo, J. J. (2000). Dimensions of the Mini-Mental State Examination among community dwelling older adults. *Psychological Medicine, 30,* 605–618.

Jones, S. E. (2001, February). Ethics Code Draft published for comment. *APA Monitor, 32.*

Judge, T. A., Bono, J. E., & Locke, E. A. (2000). Personality and job satisfaction: The mediating role of job characteristics. *Journal of Applied Psychology, 85,* 237–249.

Jung, C. G. (1910). The association method. *American Journal of Psychology, 21,* 219–269.

Jung, C. G. (1923). *Psychological types.* London: Rutledge & Kegan Paul.

Juni, S. (1996). Review of the revised NEO Personality Inventory. In J. C. Conoley & J. C. Impara (Eds.), *The twelfth mental measurements yearbook* (pp. 863–868). Lincoln: Buros Institute of Mental Measurements, University of Nebraska.

Kagan, J. (1956). The measurement of overt aggression from fantasy. *Journal of Abnormal and Social Psychology, 52,* 390–393.

Kahn, M., & Taft, G. (1983). The application of the standard of care doctrine to psychological testing. *Behavioral Sciences and the Law, 1,* 71–84.

Kail, B. L., & DeLaRosa, M. (1998). Challenges to treating the elderly Latino substance abuser: A not so hidden research agenda. *Journal of Gerontological Social Work, 30,* 128–141.

Kaiser, H. F. (1958). A modified stanine scale. *Journal of Experimental Education, 26,* 261.

Kaiser, H. F., & Michael, W. B. (1975). Domain validity and generalizability. *Educational and Psychological Measurement, 35,* 31–35.

Kalat, J. W., & Matlin, M. W. (2000). The GRE Psychology Test: A useful but poorly understood test. *Teaching of Psychology, 27,* 24–27.

Kamin, L. J. (1974). *The science and politics of IQ.* New York: Wiley.

Kamiya, J. (1962). *Conditional discrimination of the EEG alpha rhythm in humans.* Paper presented at the annual meeting of the Western Psychological Association, April.

Kamiya, J. (1968). Conscious control of brain waves. *Psychology Today, 1*(11), 56–60.

Kamphaus, R. W., Benson, J., Hutchinson, S., & Platt, L. O. (1994). Identification of factor models for the WISC-III. *Educational and Psychological Measurement, 54,* 174–186.

Kamphaus, R. W., Kaufman, A. S., & Kaufman, N. L. (1982). *A cross-validation study of sequential-simultaneous processing at ages 2½–12½ using the Kaufman Assessment Battery for Children (K-ABC).* Paper presented at the Annual Meeting of the American Psychological Association, Washington, DC.

Kamphaus, R. W., Petoskey, M. D., & Rowe, E. W. (2000). Current trends in psychological testing of children. *Professional Psychology: Research and Practice, 31,* 155–164.

Kamphaus, R. W., & Pleiss, K. L. (1993). Comment on "The use and abuse of human figure drawings." *School Psychology Quarterly, 8,* 187–188.

Kamphaus, R. W., & Reynolds, C. R. (1987). *Clinical and research applications of the K-ABC.* Circle Pines, MN: American Guidance Service.

Kane, J. S., & Lawler, E. E., III. (1978). Methods of peer assessment. *Psychological Bulletin, 85,* 555–586.

Kane, J. S., & Lawler, E. E., III. (1980). In defense of peer assessment: A rebuttal to Brief's critique. *Psychological Bulletin, 85,* 555–586.

Kanner, A. D., Coyne, J. C., Schaefer, C., & Lazarus, R. S. (1981). Comparison of two modes of stress measurement:

Daily hassles and uplifts versus major life events. *Journal of Behavioral Medicine, 4,* 1–39.

Kaplan, C. (1993). Predicting first-grade achievement from pre-kindergarten WPPSI-R scores. *Journal of Psychoeducational Assessment, 11,* 133–138.

Kaplan, E., Fein, D., Kramer, J., Delis, D., & Morris, R. (1999). *WISC-III as a Process Instrument (WISC-III PI).* San Antonio: Psychological Corporation.

Karlsen, S., Rogers, A., & McCarthy, M. (1998). Social environment and substance misuse: A study of ethnic variations among inner London adolescents. *Ethnicity & Health, 3,* 265–273.

Karon, B. P. (1981). The Thematic Apperception Test (TAT). In A. I. Rabin (Ed.), *Assessment with projective techniques: A concise introduction* (pp. 85–120). New York: Springer.

Karon, B. P. (2000). The clinical interpretation of the Thematic Apperception Test, Rorschach, and other clinical data: A reexamination of statistical versus clinical prediction. *Professional Psychology: Research and Practice, 31,* 230–233.

Karp, S. A., Holmstrom, R. W., & Silber, D. E. (1990). *Apperceptive Personality Test Manual* (Version 2.0). Orland Park, IL: International Diagnostic Systems, Inc.

Karr, S. K., Carvajal, H. H., Elser, D., & Bays, K. (1993). Concurrent validity of the WPPSI-R and the McCarthy Scales of Children's Abilities. *Psychological Reports, 72,* 940–942.

Katz, R. C., Santman, J., & Lonero, P. (1994). Findings on the Revised Morally Debatable Behaviors Scale. *Journal of Psychology, 128,* 15–21.

Katz, W. F., Curtiss, S., & Tallal, P. (1992). Rapid automatized naming and gesture by normal and language-impaired children. *Brain and Language, 43,* 623–641.

Kaufman, A. S. (1973b). Comparison of the WPPSI, Stanford-Binet, McCarthy Scales as predictors of first-grade achievement. *Perceptual and Motor Skills, 36,* 67–73.

Kaufman, A. S. (1994). *Intelligence testing with the WISC-R.* New York: Wiley.

Kaufman, A. S. (1990). *Assessing adolescent and adult intelligence.* Needham Heights, MA: Allyn & Bacon.

Kaufman, A. S. (1993). Joint exploratory factor analysis of the Kaufman Battery for Children and the Kaufman Adolescent and Adult Intelligence Test for 11- and 12-year olds. *Journal of Clinical Child Psychology, 22,* 355–364.

Kaufman, A. S. (1994). *Intelligent testing with the WISC-III.* New York: Wiley.

Kaufman, A. S., Ishkuma, T., & Kaufman-Packer, J. L. (1991). Amazingly short forms of the WAIS-R. *Journal of Psychoeducational Assessment, 9,* 4–15.

Kaufman, A. S., & Kamphaus, R. W. (1984). Factor analysis of the Kaufman Assessment Battery for Children (K-ABC) for ages 2½ through 12½ years. *Journal of Educational Psychology, 76*(4), 623–637.

Kaufman, A. S., & Kaufman, N. L. (1983a). *Kaufman Assessment Battery for Children (K-ABC): Administration and scoring manual.* Circle Pines, MN: American Guidance Service.

Kaufman, A. S., & Kaufman, N. L. (1983b). *Kaufman Assessment Battery for Children (K-ABC) interpretative manual.* Circle Pines, MN: American Guidance Service.

Kaufman, A. S., & Kaufman, N. L. (1990). *Kaufman Brief Intelligence Test (K-BIT): Manual.* Circle Pines, MN: American Guidance Service.

Kaufman, A. S., & Kaufman, N. L. (1993). *Kaufman Adolescent and Adult Intelligence Test (KAIT) manual.* Circle Pines, MN: American Guidance Service.

Kaufman, A. S., Kaufman, N. L., & Goldsmith, B. (1984). *Kaufman Sequential or Simultaneous (K-SOS).* Circle Pines, MN: American Guidance Service.

Kaufman, A. S., & McLean, J. E. (1986). K-ABC/WISC-R factor analysis for a learning disabled population. *Journal of Learning Disabilities, 19,* 145–153.

Kaufman, A. S., & McLean, J. E. (1987). Joint factor analysis of the K-ABC and WISC-R with normal children. *Journal of School Psychiatry, 25,* 105–118.

Kaufman, A. S., Reynolds, C. R., & McLean, J. E. (1989). Age and WAIS-R intelligence in a national sample of adults in the 20- to 74-year age range: A cross-sectional analysis with educational level controlled. *Intelligence, 13,* 235–253.

Kavale, K. A. (1995). Meta-analysis at 20: Retrospect and prospect. *Evaluation and the Health Professionals, 18,* 349–369.

Kavan, M. G. (1990). Review of *Children's Depression Inventory.* In J. J. Kramer & J. C. Conoley (Eds.), *The supplement to the tenth mental measurements yearbook* (pp. 46–48). Lincoln: Buros Institute of Mental Measurements, University of Nebraska.

Kaye, B. K., & Johnson, T. J. (1999). Taming the cyber frontier: Techniques for improving online surveys. *Social Science Computer Review, 17,* 323–337.

Kazdin, A. E., Colbus, D., & Rodgers, A. (1986). Assessment of depression and diagnosis of depressive disorder among psychiatrically disturbed children. *Journal of Abnormal Child Psychology, 14,* 499–515.

Keating, C. F., Mazur, A., Segall, M. H., et al. (1981). Culture and the perception of social dominance from facial expression. *Journal of Personality and Social Psychology, 40,* 615–626.

Kebbell, M. R., & Wagstaff, G. F. (1998). Hypnotic interviewing: The best way to interview eyewitnesses? *Behavioral Sciences & the Law, 16,* 115–129.

Kehoe, J. F., & Tenopyr, M. L. (1994). Adjustment in assessment scores and their usage: A taxonomy and evaluation of methods. *Psychological Assessment, 6,* 291–303.

Keilitz, I. (1987). Researching and reforming the insanity defense. *Rutgers Law Review, 39,* 289–322.

Keiser, R. E., & Prather, E. N. (1990). What is the TAT? A review of ten years of research. *Journal of Personality Assessment, 55,* 800–803.

Keith, K. D., Heal, L. W., & Schalock, R. L. (1996). Crosscultural measurement of critical quality of life concepts. *Journal of Intellectual and Disability Research, 21,* 273–293.

Keith, T. Z. (1985). Questioning the K-ABC: What does it measure? *School Psychology Review, 1,* 21–36.

Keith, T. Z. (1997). Using confirmatory factor analysis to aid in understanding the constructs measured by intelligence tests. In D. P. Flanagan, J. L. Genshaft, & P. L. Harrison (Eds.), *Contemporary intellectual assessment: Theories, tests, and issues* (pp. 373–402). New York: Guilford.

Keith, T. Z., Cool, V. A., Novak, C. G., White, L. J., & Pottebaum, S. M. (1988). Confirmatory factor analysis of the Stanford-Binet Fourth Edition: Testing the theory-test match. *Journal of School Psychology, 26*(3), 253–274.

Keith, T. Z., & Dunbar, S. B. (1984). Hierarchical factor analysis of the K-ABC: Testing alternate models. *Journal of Special Education, 18,* 367–375.

Keith, T. Z., Hood, C., Eberhart, S., & Pottebaum, S. M. (1985). *Factor structure of the K-ABC for referred school children.* Paper presented at the Annual Meeting of the National Association of School Psychologists, Las Vegas.

Keith, T. Z., & Kranzler, J. H. (1999). The absence of structural fidelity precludes construct validity: Rejoinder to Naglieri on what the Cognitive Assessment System does and does not measure. *School Psychology Review, 28,* 117–144.

Keith, T. Z., Kranzler, J. H., & Flanagan, D. F. (in press). What does the Cognitive Assessment System measure? *School Psychology Review.*

Keith, T. Z., & Novak, C. G. (1987). Joint factor structure of the WISC-R and K-ABC for referred school children. *Journal of Psychoeducational Assessment, 5*(4), 370–386.

Keith, T. Z., & Witta, L. (1997). Hierarchical and cross-age confirmatory factor analysis of the WISC-III: What does it measure? *School Psychology Quarterly, 12,* 80–107.

Keller, S. W., Weiss, J. M., Schleifer, S. J., Miller, N. E., & Stein, M. (1981). Suppression of immunity by stress: Effect of graded series of stressors on lymphocyte proliferation. *Science, 213,* 1397–1400.

Kelley, C., & Meyers, J. (1992). *Cross-Cultural Adaptability Inventory.* Minneapolis: NCS Assessments.

Kelley, S. J. (1985). Drawings: Critical communications for the sexually abused child. *Pediatric Nursing, 11,* 421–426.

Kelley, S. J. (1988). Physical abuse of children: Recognition and reporting. *Journal of Emergency Nursing, 14*(2), 82–90.

Kelley, T. L. (1927). *Interpretation of educational measurements.* Yonkers, NY: World Book.

Kelley, T. L. (1939). The selection of upper and lower groups for the validation of test items. *Journal of Educational Psychology, 30,* 17–24.

Kellner, C. H., Jolley, R. R., Holgate, R. C., Austin, L., Lydiard, R. B., Laraia, M., & Ballenger, J. C. (1991). Brain MRI in obsessive-compulsive disorder. *Psychiatry Research, 36,* 45–49.

Kelly, D. H. (1966). Measurement of anxiety by forearm blood flow. *British Journal of Psychiatry, 112,* 789–798.

Kempen, J. H., Kritchevsky, M., & Feldman, S. T. (1994). Effect of visual impairment on neuropsychological test performance. *Journal of Clinical and Experimental Neuropsychology, 16,* 223–231.

Kendall, M. G. (1948). *Rank correlation methods.* London: Griffin.

Kendall, P. C., Williams, L., Pechacek, T. F., Graham, L. E., Shisslak, C., & Herzof, N. (1979). Cognitive-behavioral and patient education interventions in cardiac catherization procedures: The Palo Alto Medical Psychology Project. *Journal of Consulting and Clinical Psychology, 47,* 48–59.

Kennedy, M. H., & Hiltonsmith, R. W. (1988). Relationships among the K-ABC Nonverbal Scale, the Pictorial Test of Intelligence and the Hiskey-Nebraska Test of Learning Aptitude for speech- and language-disabled preschool children. *Journal of Psychoeducational Assessment, 6*(1), 49–54.

Kennedy, O. A. (1971). Pupillometrics as an aid in the assessment of motivation, impact of treatment, and prognosis of chronic alcoholics. *Dissertation Abstracts International, 32,* 1214B–1215B.

Kennedy, R. S., Bittner, A. C., Harbeson, M., & Jones, M. B. (1982). Television computer games: A "new look" in performance testing. *Aviation, Space and Environmental Medicine, 53,* 49–53.

Kent, G. H., & Rosanoff, A. J. (1910). A study of association in insanity. *American Journal of Insanity, 67,* 37–96, 317–390.

Kent, N., & Davis, D. R. (1957). Discipline in the home and intellectual development. *British Journal of Medical Psychology, 30,* 27–33.

Kerlinger, F. N. (1973). *Foundations of behavioral research* (2nd ed.). New York: Holt.

Kern, J. M., Miller, C., & Eggers, J. (1983). Enhancing the validity of role-play tests: A comparison of three role-play methodologies. *Behavior Therapy, 14,* 482–492.

Khan, S. B., Alvi, S. A., Shaukat, N., & Hussain, M. A. (1990). A study of the validity of Holland's theory in a non-Western culture. *Journal of Vocational Behavior, 36,* 132–146.

Kiecolt-Glaser, J. K., & Glaser, R. (1988). Psychological influences on immunity: Implications for AIDS. *American Psychologist, 43,* 892–898.

Kiesler, C. A. (2000). The next wave of change for psychology and mental health services in the health care revolution. *American Psychologist, 55,* 481–487.

Kim, B. S. K., Atkinson, D. R., & Yang, P. H. (1999). The Asian Values Scale: Development, factor analysis, validation, and reliability. *Journal of Counseling Psychology, 46,* 342–352.

King, B. J., & Pope, B. W. (1998). The measurement and appraisal of creativity in the assessment battery. In H. M. Potash (Chair), *The assessment of psychological health.* Symposium presented at the Society for Personality Assessment 1998 Midwinter Meeting, February 21.

King, D. A., Conwell, Y., Cox, C., et al. (2000). A neuropsychological comparison of depressed suicide attempters and nonattempters. *Journal of Neuropsychiatry and Clinical Neurosciences, 12,* 64–70.

King, M. A., & Yuille, J. C. (1987). Suggestibility and the child witness. In S. J. Ceci, M. P. Toglia, & D. F. Ross (Eds.), *Children's eyewitness testimony.* New York: Springer-Verlag.

Kinslinger, H. J. (1966). Application of projective techniques in personnel psychology since 1940. *Psychological Bulletin, 66,* 134–149.

Kinston, W., Loader, P., & Miller, L. (1985). *Clinical assessment of family health.* London: Hospital for Sick Children, Family Studies Group.

Kippax, S., Campbell, D., Van de Ven, P., et al. (1998). Cultures of sexual adventurism as markers of HIV seroconversion: A case control study in a cohort of Sydney gay men. *AIDS Care, 10,* 677–688.

Kirchner, W. K. (1966). A note on the effect of privacy in taking typing tests. *Journal of Applied Psychology, 50,* 373–374.

Kirmayer, L. J., & Young, A. (1999). Culture and context in the evolutionary concept of mental disorder. *Journal of Abnormal Psychology, 108,* 446–452.

Klanderman, J. W., Perney, J., & Kroeschell, Z. B. (1985). Comparison of the K-ABC and WISC-R for LD children. *Journal of Learning Disabilities, 18,* 524–527.

Klein, D. F. (1999). Harmful dysfunction, disorder, disease, illness, and evolution. *Journal of Abnormal Psychology, 108,* 421–429.

Klein, S. H. (1998). Cognitive dysfunction in patients with silicone gel breast implants. *Clinical Neuropsychologist, 12,* 500–502.

Kleinman, A. M., & Lin, T. Y. (1980). Introduction. In A. M. Kleinman & T. Y. Lin (Eds.), *Normal and abnormal behavior in Chinese cultures* (pp. 1–6). Dordrecht, Netherlands: Reidel.

Kleinmuntz, B., & Szucko, J. J. (1984). Lie detection in ancient and modern times: A call for contemporary scientific study. *American Psychologist, 39,* 766–776.

Klimoski, R., & Brickner, M. (1987). Why do assessment centers work? The puzzle of assessment center validity. *Personnel Psychology, 40,* 243–259.

Kline, R. B. (1989). Is the Fourth Edition Stanford-Binet a four factor test? Confirmatory factor analyses of alternative models for ages 2 through 23. *Journal of Psychoeducational Assessment, 7,* 4–13.

Kline, R. B., & Lachar, D. (1992). Evaluation of age, sex, and race bias in the Personality Inventory for Children (PIC). *Psychological Assessment, 4,* 333–339.

Kline, R. B., Lachar, D., & Boersma, D. C. (1993). Identification of special education needs with the Personality Inventory for Children (PIC): A hierarchical classification model. *Psychological Assessment, 5,* 307–316.

Kline, R. B., Lachar, D., & Gdowski, C. L. (1992). Clinical validity of a Personality Inventory for Children (PIC) profile typology. *Psychological Assessment, 58,* 591–605.

Kline, R. B., Lachar, D., & Sprague, D. J. (1985). The Personality Inventory for Children (PIC): An unbiased predictor of cognitive and academic status. *Journal of Pediatric Psychology, 10,* 461–477.

Kline, R. B., Snyder, J., Guilmette, S., & Castellanos, M. (1993). External validity of the Profile Variability Index for the K-ABC, Stanford-Binet, and WISC- R: Another cul-de-sac. *Journal of Learning Disabilities, 26,* 557–567.

Klinger, E. (1978). Modes of normal conscious flow. In K. S. Pope & J. L. Singer (Eds.), *The stream of consciousness: Scientific investigations into the flow of human experience* (pp. 225–258). New York: Plenum.

Klockars, A. J. (1978). Personality variables related to peer selection. *Educational and Psychological Measurement, 32,* 513–517.

Klonoff, E. A., & Landrine, H. (1999). Acculturation and alcohol use among Blacks: The benefits of remaining culturally traditional. *Western Journal of Black Studies, 23,* 211–216.

Klopfer, B., Ainsworth, M., Klopfer, W., & Holt, R. R. (1954). *Developments in the Rorschach technique: Vol. 1. Technique and theory.* Yonkers-on-Hudson, NY: World.

Klopfer, B., & Davidson, H. (1962). *The Rorschach technique: An introductory manual.* New York: Harcourt.

Klove, H., & Matthews, C. G. (1974). Neuropsychological studies of patients with epilepsy. In R. M. Reitan & L. A. Davidson (Eds.), *Clinical neuropsychology: Current status and applications* (pp. 237–365). New York: Winston.

Kluckhohn, F. R. (1954). Dominant and variant value orientations. In C. Kluckhohn & H. A. Murray (Eds.), *Personality in nature, society, and culture* (pp. 342–358). New York: Knopf.

Kluckhohn, F. R. (1960). A method for eliciting value orientations. *Anthropological Linguistics, 2*(2), 1–23.

Kluckhohn, F. R., & Strodtbeck, F. L. (1961). *Variations in value orientations.* Homewood, IL: Dorsey.

Knapp, R. R. (1960). The effects of time limits on the intelligence test performance of Mexican and American subjects. *Journal of Educational Psychology, 51,* 14–20.

Knoff, H. M. (1990a). Evaluation of projective drawings. In C. R. Reynolds and T. B. Gutkin (Eds.), *Handbook of school psychology* (2nd ed.; pp. 898–946). New York: Wiley.

Knoff, H. M. (1990b). Review of Children's Depression Inventory. In J. J. Kramer & J. C. Conoley (Eds.), *The supplement to the tenth mental measurements yearbook* (pp. 48–50). Lincoln: Buros Institute of Mental Measurements, University of Nebraska.

Knoff, H. M., & Prout, H. T. (1985). *The Kinetic Drawing System: Family and School.* Los Angeles: Western Psychological Services.

Knowles, E. S., & Condon, C. A. (2000). Does the rose still smell as sweet? Item variability across test forms and revisions. *Psychological Assessment, 12,* 245–252.

Kobak, K. A., Reynolds, W. M., & Greist, J. H. (1993). Development and validation of a computer administered version of the Hamilton Anxiety Scale. *Psychological Assessment, 5,* 487–492.

Kolotkin, R. A., & Wielkiewicz, R. M. (1984). Effects of situational demand in the role-play assessment of assertive behavior. *Journal of Behavioral Assessment, 6,* 59–70.

Kongs, S. K., Thompson, L. L., Iverson, G. L., & Heaton, R. K. (2000). *Wisconsin Card Sorting Test-64 Card Version* (WCST-64). Odessa, FL: Psychological Assessment Resources.

Kopelman, M. D. (1975). The contrast effect in the selection interview. *British Journal of Educational Psychology, 45,* 333–336.

Koppitz, E. M. (1963). *The Bender-Gestalt Test for young children.* New York: Grune & Stratton.

Koppitz, E. M. (1975). *The Bender-Gestalt Test for young children* (Vol. 2). New York: Grune & Stratton.

Korchin, S. J., & Schuldberg, D. (1981). The future of clinical assessment. *American Psychologist, 36,* 1147–1158.

Korkman, M. (1999). Applying Luria's diagnostic principles in the neuropsychological assessment of children. *Neuropsychology Review, 9,* 89–105.

Korkman, M., Kirk, U., & Kemp, S. (1997). NEPSY. San Antonio: Psychological Corporation.

Korman, A. K. (1988). *The outsiders: Jews and corporate America.* Lexington, MA: Lexington.

Korner, I. N., & Westwood, D. (1955). Inter-rater agreement in judging student adjustment from projective tests. *Journal of Clinical Psychology, 11,* 167–170.

Koson, D., Kitchen, C., Kochen, M., & Stodolsky, D. (1970). Psychological testing by computer: Effect on response bias. *Educational and Psychological Measurement, 30,* 803–810.

Kotkov, B., & Goodman, M. (1953). The Draw-A-Person tests of obese women. *Journal of Clinical Psychology, 9,* 362–364.

Kovacs, M. (1977). *Children's Depression Inventory.* Pittsburgh: Western Psychiatric Institute and Clinic.

Kraepelin, E. (1892). *Uber die Beeinflussung einfacher psychischer Vorgange durch einige Arzneimittel.* Jena: Fischer.

Kraepelin, E. (1895). Der psychologische versuch in der psychiatrie. *Psychologische Arbeiten, 1,* 1–91.

Kraepelin, E. (1896). Der psychologische versuch in der psychiatrie. *Psychologische Arbeiten, 1,* 1–91.

Kranzler, J. H., & Keith, T. Z. (1999). Independent confirmatory factor analysis of the Cognitive Assessment System (CAS): What does the CAS measure? *School Psychology Review, 28,* 117–144.

Kranzler, J. H., Keith, T. Z., & Flanagan, D. P. (in press). Independent examination of the factor structure of the Cognitive Assessment System (CAS): Further evidence disputing the construct validity of the CAS. *Journal of Psychoeducational Assessment.*

Krauss, D. A., & Sales, B. D. (1999). The problem of "helpfulness" in applying *Daubert* to expert testimony: Child custody determinations in family law as an exemplar. *Psychology, Public Policy, and Law, 5,* 78–99.

Krauss, M. W. (1993). Child-related and parenting stress: Similarities and differences between mothers and fathers of children with disabilities. *American Journal on Mental Retardation, 97,* 393–404.

Kresel, J. J., & Lovejoy, F. H. (1981). Poisonings and child abuse. In N. S. Ellerstein (Ed.), *Child abuse and neglect: A medical reference* (pp. 307–313). New York: Wiley.

Krikorian, R., & Bartok, J. A. (1998). Developmental data for the Porteus Maze Test. *Clinical Neuropsychologist, 12,* 305–310.

Krohn, E. J., & Lamp, R. E. (1989). Concurrent validity of the K-ABC and Stanford-Binet—Fourth Edition for Head Start Children. *Journal of School Psychology, 27*(1), 59–67.

Krohn, E. J., Lamp, R. E., & Phelps, C. G. (1988). Validity of the K-ABC for a black preschool population. *Psychology in the Schools, 25,* 15–21.

Kronholz, J. (1998, February 12). As states end racial preferences, pressure rises to drop SAT to maintain minority enrollment. *Wall Street Journal,* p. A24.

Kubiszyn, T. W., Meyer, G. J., Finn, S. E., et al. (2000). Empirical support for psychological assessment in clinical health care settings. *Professional Psychology: Research and Practice, 31,* 119–130.

Kuder, F., Diamond, E. E., & Zytowski, D. G. (1998). Differentiation as fundamental validity for criterion-group and scaled interest inventories. *Educational and Psychological Measurement, 58,* 38–41.

Kuder, G. F. (1979). *Kuder Occupational Interest Survey, Revised: General manual.* Chicago: Science Research Associates.

Kuder, G. F., & Richardson, M. W. (1937). The theory of the estimation of reliability. *Psychometrika, 2,* 151–160.

Kudryavstev, J. A., & Ratinova, N. (1999). The psychological typology of criminal homicidal aggression. *International Journal of Offender Therapy & Comparative Criminology, 43,* 459–472.

Kuhlmann, F. (1912). A revision of the Binet-Simon system for measuring the intelligence of children. *Journal of Psycho-Asthenics Monograph Supplement, 1*(1), 1–41.

Kumho Tire Co. Ltd. v. Carmichael, 119 S. Ct. 1167 (1999).

Kuncel, N. R., Hezlett, S. A., & Ones, D. S. (2001). A comprehensive meta-analysis of the predictive validity of the Graduate Record Examinations: Implications for graduate student selection and performance. *Psychological Bulletin, 127,* 162–181.

Labig, C. E., Jr. (1992). Supervisor and nonsupervisory employee attitudes about drug testing. *Employee Responsibilities and Rights Journal, 5,* 131–141.

Labrentz, E., Linkenhoker, F., & Aaron, P. G. (1976). Recognition and reproduction of Bender-Gestalt figures: A developmental study of the lag between perception and performance. *Psychology in the Schools, 13,* 128–133.

Lachar, D. (1982). *Personality Inventory for Children (PIC): Revised format manual supplement.* Los Angeles: Western Psychological Services.

Lachar, D., Gdowski, C. L., & Snyder, D. K. (1985). Consistency of maternal report and the Personality Inventory for Children: Always useful and sometimes sufficient—Reply to Cornell. *Journal of Consulting and Clinical Psychology, 53,* 275–276.

Lachar, D., & Gruber, C. P. (2001). *The Personality Inventory for Children, Second Edition (PIC-2).* Los Angeles: Western Psychological Services.

Lachar, D., Kline, R. B., & Boersma, D. C. (1986). The Personality Inventory for Children: Approaches to actuarial interpretation in clinic and school settings. In H. M. Knoff (Ed.), *The psychological assessment of child and adolescent personality* (pp. 273–308). New York: Guilford.

Lachar, D., & Wirt, R. D. (1981). A data-based analysis of the psychometric performance of the Personality Inventory for Children (PIC): An alternative to the Achenbach review. *Journal of Personality Assessment, 45,* 614–616.

Lachar, D., & Wrobel, T. A. (1979). Validating clinicians' hunches: Construction of a new MMPI critical item set. *Journal of Consulting and Clinical Psychology, 47,* 277–284.

LaCombe, J. A., Kline, R. B., Lachar, D., Butkus, M., & Hillman, S. B. (1991). Case history correlates of a Personality Inventory for Children (PIC) profile typology. *Psychological Assessment, 3,* 678–687.

Lah, M. I. (1989a). Sentence completion tests. In C. S. Newmark (Ed.), *Major psychological assessment instruments* (Vol. 2; pp. 133–163). Needham Heights, MA: Allyn & Bacon.

Lah, M. I. (1989b). New validity, normative, and scoring data for the Rotter Incomplete Sentences Blank. *Journal of Personality Assessment, 53,* 607–620.

Laidlaw, T. M. (1999). Designer testing: Using subjects' personal vocabulary to produce individualised tests. *Personality and Individual Differences, 27,* 1197–1207.

LaLone, L. V., et al. (1998). Psychological aspects of the Gulf War Syndrome hypothesis: Examination of the MMPI-2 profiles generated by Gulf War veterans. In R. D. Merritt (Chair), *MMPI/MMPI-2 Empirical studies I.* Paper session presented at the Society for Personality Assessment 1998 Midwinter Meeting, February 20.

Lam, C. S., Chan, F., Hilburger, J., Heimburger, M., Hill, V., & Kaplan, S. (1993). Canonical relationships between vocational interests and aptitudes. *Vocational Evaluation and Work Adjustment Bulletin, 26,* 155–160.

Lamb, D. G., Berry, D. T. R., Wetter, M. W., & Baer, R. A. (1994). Effects of two types of information on malingering of closed head injury on the MMPI-2: An analog investigation. *Psychological Assessment, 6,* 8–13.

Lamb, M. E. (Ed.). (1981). *The role of the father in child development* (2nd ed.). New York: Wiley.

Lambert, E. W., & Engum, E. S. (1992). Construct validity of the Cognitive Behavioral Driver's Inventory: Age, diagnosis, and driving ability. *Journal of Cognitive Rehabilitation, 10,* 32–45.

Lambert, N., Nihira, K., & Leland, H. (1993). *AAMR Adaptive Behavior Scale-School-Second Edition: Examiner's manual.* Austin: PRO-ED.

Lamp, R. E., & Krohn, E. J. (1990). Stability of the Stanford-Binet Fourth Edition and K-ABC for young black and white children from low income families. *Journal of Psychoeducational Assessment, 8,* 139–149.

Landers, S. (1986, December). Judge reiterates I.Q. test ban. *APA Monitor 17,* 18.

Landis, C. (1936). Questionnaires and the study of personality. *Journal of Nervous and Mental Disease, 83,* 125–134.

Landis, C., Zubin, J., & Katz, S. E. (1935). Empirical evaluation of three personality adjustment inventories. *Journal of Educational Psychology, 26,* 321–330.

Landrum, M. S., & Ward, S. B. (1993). Behavioral assessment of gifted learners. *Journal of Behavioral Education, 3,* 211–215.

Landy, F. J. (1986). Stamp collecting versus science. *American Psychologist, 41,* 1183–1192.

Landy, F. J., & Farr, J. H. (1980). Performance rating. *Psychological Bulletin, 87,* 72–107.

Lane, H. (1992). *The mask of benevolence: Disabling the deaf community.* New York: Vintage.

Lane, J. C. (1992, August). Threat management fills void in police services. *Police Chief,* pp. 27–29, 31.

Lang, P. J., Greenwald, M. K., Bradley, M. M., & Hamm, A. O. (1993). Looking at pictures: Affective, facial, visceral, and behavioral reactions. *Psychophysiology, 30,* 261–273.

Langer, E. J., & Abelson, R. P. (1974). A patient by any other name: Clinician group difference in labeling bias. *Journal of Consulting and Clinical Psychology, 42,* 4–9.

Langlois, J. H., Ritter, J. M., Casey, R. J., & Sawin, D. B. (1995). Infant attractiveness predicts maternal behaviors and attitudes. *Developmental Psychology, 31,* 464–472.

Lanyon, R. I. (1984). Personality assessment. *Annual Review of Psychology, 35,* 667–701.

Lanyon, R. I. (1986). Psychological assessment procedures in court-related settings. *Professional Psychology: Research and Practice, 17,* 260–268.

Lanyon, R. I. (1993a). Assessment of truthfulness in accusations of child molestation. *American Journal of Forensic Psychology, 11,* 29–44.

Lanyon, R. I. (1993b). Development of scales to assess specific deception strategies on the Psychological Screening Inventory. *Psychological Assessment, 5,* 324–329.

Larson, L. M., & Majors, M. S. (1998). Applications of the Coping with Career Indecision instrument with adolescents. *Journal of Career Assessment, 6,* 163–179.

La Rue, A., & Watson, J. (1998). Psychological assessment of older adults. *Professional Psychology: Research and Practice, 29,* 5–14.

Larvie, V. (1994). Evidence—Admissability of scientific evidence in federal courts—The Supreme Court decides Frye is dead and the Federal Rules of Evidence provide the standard, but is there a skeleton in the closet? Daubert v. Pharmaceuticals, 113 S. Ct. 2786. *Land & Water Review, 29,* 275–309.

Larzelere, R., & Huston, T. (1980). The Dyadic Trust Scale: Toward understanding interpersonal trust in close relationships. *Journal of Marriage and the Family, 43,* 595–604.

Latham, G. P., Wexley, K. N., & Pursell, E. D. (1975). Training managers to minimize rating errors in the observation of behavior. *Journal of Applied Psychology, 60,* 550–555.

Latimer, E. J. (1991). Ethical decision-making in the care of the dying and its applications to clinical practice. *Journal of Pain and Symptom Management, 6,* 329–336.

Lattimore, R. R., & Borgen, F. H. (1999). Validity of the 1994 Strong Interest Inventory with racial and ethnic groups in the United States. *Journal of Counseling Psychology, 46,* 185–195.

Laurence, J. R., & Perry, C. W. (1988). *Hypnosis, will, and memory.* New York: Guilford.

Laurent, J., Swerdlik, M., & Ryburn, M. (1992). Review of validity research on the Stanford-Binet Intelligence Scale: Fourth Edition. *Psychological Assessment, 4,* 102–112.

Lavin, M. (1992). The Hopkins Competency Assessment Test: A brief method for evaluating patients' capacity to give informed consent. *Hospital and Community Psychiatry, 646,* 132–136.

Lavrakas, P. J. (1998). Methods for sampling and interviewing in telephone surveys. In L. Bickman & D. J. Rog (Eds.), *Handbook of applied social research methods* (pp. 429–472). Thousand Oaks, CA: Sage.

Lawlor, J. (1990, September 27). Loopholes found in truth tests. *USA Today,* p. D-1.

Lawrence, B. S. (1996). Organizational age norms: Why is it so hard to know one when you see one? *Gerontologist, 36,* 209–220.

Lawrence, J., Davidoff, D. A., Katt-Lloyd, D., et al. (2000). A pilot program of community-based screening for memory impairment. *Journal of the American Geriatrics Society, 48,* 854–855.

Laws, D. R., & Osborne, C. A. (1983). How to build and operate a behavioral laboratory to evaluate and treat sexual deviance. In J. G. Greer & I. R. Stuart (Eds.), *The sexual aggressor: Current perspectives on treatment* (pp. 293–335). New York: Van Nostrand Reinhold.

Lawshe, C. H. (1975). A quantitative approach to content validity. *Personnel Psychology, 28,* 563–575.

Lazarus, A. A. (1973). Multimodal behavior therapy: Treating the BASIC ID. *Journal of Nervous and Mental Disease, 156,* 404–411.

Lazarus, A. A. (1989). *The practice of multimodal therapy.* Baltimore: Johns Hopkins University Press.

Lea, E., & Worsley, A. (2001). Influences on meat consumption in Australia. *Appetite, 36,* 127–136.

Leahy, A. (1932). A study of certain selective factors influencing prediction of the mental status of adopted children or adopted children in nature-nurture research. *Journal of Genetic Psychology, 41,* 294–329.

Leahy, A. M. (1935). Nature-nurture and intelligence. *Genetic Psychology Monographs, 17,* 241–306.

Leckliter, I. N., & Matarazzo, J. D. (1989). The influence of age, education, IQ, gender, and alcohol abuse on Halstead-Reitan Neuropsychological Test Battery performance. *Journal of Clinical Psychology, 45,* 484–512.

Lee, S. D. (1968). *Social class bias in the diagnosis of mental illness.* Unpublished doctoral dissertation, University of Oklahoma.

Lee, S.-J., & Tedeschi, J. T. (1996). Effects of norms and norm-violations on inhibition and instigation of aggression. *Aggressive Behavior, 22,* 17–25.

Lee, T. M. C., & Chan, C. C. H. (2000). Are Trail Making and Color Trails Tests of equivalent constructs? *Journal of Clinical and Experimental Neuropsychology, 22,* 529–534.

Lee, T. M. C., Cheung, C. C. Y., Chan, J. K. P., et al. (2000). Trail making across languages. *Journal of Clinical and Experimental Neuropsychology, 22,* 772–778.

Lees-Haley, P. R., Smith, H. H., Williams, C. W., & Dunn, J. T. (1996). Forensic neuropsychological test usage: An empirical survey. *Archives of Clinical Neuropsychology, 11,* 45–51.

Lefcourt, H. M. (1991). Locus of control. In J. P. Robinson, P. R. Shaver, & L. S. Wrightsman (Eds.), *Measures of personality social psychological attitudes* (pp. 413–499). San Diego: Academic Press.

Leigh, I. W., Corbett, C. A., Gutman, V., & Moore, D. A. (1996). Providing psychological services to deaf individuals: A response to new perceptions of diversity. *Professional Psychology: Research and Practice, 27,* 364–371.

Leigh, J., Westen, D., Barends, A., Mendel, M. J., & Byers, S. (1992). The assessment of complexity of representations of people using TAT and interview data. *Journal of Personality, 60,* 809–837.

Leon-Carrion, J., et al. (1991). The computerized Tower of Hanoi: A new form of administration and suggestions for interpretation. *Perceptual and Motor Skills, 73,* 63–66.

Leong, F. T., & Hartung, P. J. (2000). Cross-cultural career assessment: Review and prospects for the new millennium. *Journal of Career Assessment, 8,* 391–401.

Lepper, M. R. (1995). Theory by the numbers? Some concerns about meta-analysis as a theoretical tool. *Applied Cognitive Psychology, 9,* 411–422.

Lerner, B. (1980). *Minimum competence, maximum choice: Second chance legislation.* New York: Irvington.

Lerner, B. (1981). The minimum competence testing movement: Social, scientific, and legal implications. *American Psychologist, 36,* 1056–1066.

Lerner, P. (1998). Narcissism: The relationship among method, theory, and research. In A. Schwartz (Chair), *Exploring along the narcissistic continuum.* Symposium presented at the Society for Personality Assessment 1998 Midwinter Meeting, February 21.

Lerner, P. M. (1991). *Psychoanalytic theory and the Rorschach.* New York: Analytic.

Lerner, P. M. (1996a). Current perspectives on psychoanalytic Rorschach assessment. *Journal of Personality Assessment, 67,* 450–461.

Lerner, P. M. (1996b). The interpretive process in Rorschach testing. *Journal of Personality Assessment, 67,* 494–500.

Lesser, G. S., Fifer, G., & Clark, D. H. (1965). Mental abilities of children from different social-class and cultural groups. *Monographs of the Society for Research in Child Development, 30* (Serial No. 102).

Lessinger, L. H. (1998). The relationship between cultural identity and MMPI-2 scores of Mexican-American substance abuse patients. *Dissertation Abstracts International, Section B: The Sciences & Engineering, 59*(2-B), 877.

Levack, N. (1991). *Low vision: A resource guide with adaptations for students with visual impairments.* Austin: Texas School for the Blind and Visually Impaired.

Levant, R. F., Reed, G. M., & Ragusea, S. A. (2001). Envisioning and accessing new roles for professional psychology. *Professional Psychology: Research and Practice, 32,* 79–87.

Levesque, L. L., Wilson, J. M., & Wholey, D. R. (2001). Cognitive divergence and shared mental models in software development project teams. *Journal of Organizational Behavior, 22,* 135–144.

Levine, E., & Padilla, A. (1980). *Crossing cultures in therapy.* Monterey: Brooks/Cole.

Levy-Shiff, R., Dimitrovsky, L., Shulman, S., & Har-Even, D. (1998). Cognitive appraisals, coping strategies, and support resources as correlates of parenting and infant development. *Developmental Psychology, 34,* 1417–1427.

Lewinsohn, P. M., Rohde, P., & Seeley, J. R. (1996). Adolescent suicidal ideation and attempts: Prevalence, risk factors and clinical implications. *Clinical Psychology: Science and Practice, 3,* 25–46.

Lewis-Fernandez, R. (1998). A cultural critique of the DSM-IV dissociative disorders section. *Transcultural Psychiatry, 35,* 387–400.

Lezak, M. D. (1988). IQ: R.I.P. *Journal of Clinical and Experimental Neuropsychology, 10,* 351–361.

Lezak, M. D. (1995). *Neuropsychological assessment* (3rd ed.). New York: Oxford University.

Li, H., Kuo, C., & Russel, M. G. (1999). The impact of perceived channel utilities, shopping orientations, and demographics on the consumer's online buying behavior. *Journal of Computer-Mediated Communication, 5*(2).

Liang, M. H., Larson, M. G., Cullen, K. E., & Schwartz, J. A. (1988). Comparative measurement efficiency and sensitivity of five health status instruments in arthritis research. *Arthritis and Rheumatism, 28,* 542–547.

Libby, W. (1908). The imagination of adolescents. *American Journal of Psychology, 19,* 249–252.

Lichtenstein, B., & Nansel, T. R. (2000). Women's douching practices and related attitudes: Findings from four focus groups. *Women and Health, 31,* 117–131.

Lichtenstein, D., Dreger, R. M., & Cattell, R. B. (1986). Factor structure and standardization of the Preschool Personality Questionnaire. *Journal of Social Behavior and Personality, 1,* 165–181.

Lidz, C. W., Mulvey, E. P., & Gardner, W. (1993). The accuracy of predictions of violence to others. *Journal of the American Medical Association, 269,* 1007–1011.

Lieberman, J. N. (1965). Playfulness and divergent thinking: An investigation of their relationship at the kindergarten level. *Journal of Genetic Psychology, 107,* 219–224.

Likert, R. (1932). A technique for the measurement of attitudes. *Archives of Psychology,* Number 140.

Lilienfeld, S. O., & Marino, L. (1995). Mental disorder as a Roschian concept: A critique of Wakefield's "harmful dysfunction" analysis. *Journal of Abnormal Psychology, 104,* 411–420.

Lilienfeld, S. O., & Marino, L. (1999). Essentialism revisited: Evolutionary theory and the concept of mental disorder. *Journal of Abnormal Psychology, 108,* 400–411.

Lim, J., & Butcher, J. N. (1996). Detection of faking on the MMPI-2: Differentiation among faking-bad, denial, and claiming extreme virtue. *Journal of Personality Assessment, 67,* 1–25.

Lindell, M. K., Brandt, C. J., & Whitney, D. J. (1999). A revised index of interrater agreement for multi-item ratings of a single target. *Applied Psychological Measurement, 23,* 127–135.

Lindgren, B. (1983, August). N or N–1? [Letter to the editor]. *American Statistician,* p. 52.

Lindstrom, E., Wieselgren, I. M., & von Knorring, L. (1994). Interrater reliability of the Structured Clinical Interview for the Positive and Negative Syndrome Scale for schizophrenia. *Acta Psychiatrica Scandinavica, 89,* 192–195.

Lindzey, G. (1950). An experimental examination of the scapegoat theory of prejudice. *Journal of Abnormal and Social Psychology, 45,* 296–309.

Linehan, M. M., Goodstein, J. L., Nielsen, S. L., & Chiles, J. A. (1983). Reasons for staying alive when you are thinking of killing yourself: The Reasons for Living Inventory. *Journal of Consulting and Clinical Psychology, 51,* 276–286.

Lipkus, I. M., Barefoot, J. C., Williams, R. B., & Siegler, I. C. (1994). Personality measures as predictors of smoking initiation and cessation in the UNC Alumni Heart Study. *Health Psychology, 13,* 149–155.

Lippmann, W. (1922, October). The mental age of Americans. *New Republic.*

Lipsitt, P. D., Lelos, D., & McGarry, A. L. (1971). Competency for trial: A screening instrument. *American Journal of Psychiatry, 128,* 105–109.

Lipton, J. P. (1999). The use and acceptance of social science evidence in business litigation after *Daubert. Psychology, Public Policy, and Law, 5,* 59–77.

Lisansky, E. S. (1956). The inter-examiner reliability of the Rorschach test. *Journal of Projective Techniques, 20,* 310–317.

Locke, E. A. (1976). The nature and causes of job satisfaction. In M. D. Dunnette (Ed.), *Handbook of industrial and organizational psychology.* Chicago: Rand McNally.

Locke, H. J., & Wallace, K. M. (1959). Short marital adjustment and prediction tests: Their reliability and validity. *Marriage and Family Living, 21,* 251–255.

Loevinger, J. (1957). Objective tests as instruments of psychological theory. *Psychological Reports, 3,* 635–694.

Loevinger, J. (1966). The meaning and measurement of ego development. *American Psychologist, 21,* 195–206.

Loevinger, J., & Ossorio, A. G. (1958). Evaluation of therapy by self-report: A paradox. *American Psychologist, 13,* 366.

Loevinger, J., Wessler, R., & Redmore, C. (1970). *Measuring ego development: Vol. 1. Construction and use of a sentence completion test. Vol. 2. Scoring manual for women and girls.* San Francisco: Jossey-Bass.

Loewenstein, D. A., Rubert, M. P., Berkowitz-Zimmer, N., Guterman, A., Morgan, R., & Hayden, S. (1992). Neuropsychological test performance and prediction of functional capacities in dementia. *Behavior, Health, and Aging, 2,* 149–158.

Loftin, M. (1997). Critical factors in assessment of students with visual impairments. *RE:view, 28,* 149–159.

Loftus, E. F., & Davies, G. M. (1984). Distortions in the memory of children. *Journal of Social Issues, 40,* 51–67.

Logstdon, R. G., Teri, L., Williams, D. E., Vitiello, M. V., & Prinz, P. N. (1989). The WAIS-R profile: A diagnostic tool for Alzheimer's Disease? *Journal of Clinical and Experimental Neuropsychology, 11,* 892–898.

Lohman, D. F. (1989). Human intelligence: An introduction to advances in theory and research. *Review of Educational Research, 59,* 333–373.

London, P. (1976). Psychotherapy for religious neuroses? Comments on Cohen and Smith. *Journal of Consulting and Clinical Psychology, 44,* 145–147.

Longabaugh, R. (1980). The systematic observation of behavior in naturalistic settings. In H. C. Triandis & J. W. Berry (Eds.), *Handbook of cross-cultural psychology: Vol. 2. Methodology* (pp. 57–126). Boston: Allyn & Bacon.

Lonner, W. J. (1985). Issues in testing and assessment in cross-cultural counseling. *Counseling Psychologist, 13,* 599–614.

Lopez, S. (1988). The empirical basis of ethnocultural and linguistic bias in mental health evaluations of Hispanics. *American Psychologist, 42,* 228–234.

Lopez, S., & Hernandez, P. (1987). When culture is considered in the evaluation and treatment of Hispanic patients. *Psychotherapy, 24,* 120–127.

Lopez, S. R. (2000). Teaching culturally informed psychological assessment. In R. H. Dana (Ed.), *Handbook of cross-cultural and multicultural personality assessment* (pp. 669–687). Mahwah, NJ: Erlbaum.

Lord, F. M. (1980). *Applications of item response theory to practical testing problems.* Hillsdale, NJ: Erlbaum.

Lord, F. M., & Novick, M. R. (1968). *Statistical theories of mental test scores.* Menlo Park, CA: Addison-Wesley.

Lord, R. G., De Vader, C. L., & Alliger, G. M. (1986). A meta-analysis of the relation between personality traits and leadership perceptions: An application of validity generalization procedures. *Journal of Applied Psychology, 71,* 402–410.

Lorr, M. (1991). An empirical evaluation of the MBTI typology. *Personality and Individual Differences, 12,* 1141–1145.

Losak, J. (1978). What do the students say? *College Board Review, 108,* 25–27.

Lovejoy, M. C., Weis, R., O'Hare, E., & Rubin, E. (1999). Development and initial validation of the Parent Behavior Inventory. *Psychological Assessment, 11,* 534–545.

Lowitzer, A. C., Utley, C. A., & Baumeister, A. A. (1987). AAMD's 1983 Classification in Mental Retardation as utilized by state mental retardation/developmental disabilities agencies. *Mental Retardation, 25,* 287–291.

Lowman, J. C. (1980). Measurement of family affective structure. *Journal of Personality Assessment, 44,* 130–141.

Loyd, B. H., & Abidin, R. R. (1985). Revision of the Parenting Stress Index. *Journal of Pediatric Psychology, 10,* 169–177.

Lubin, B., Larsen, R. M., Matarazzo, J. D., & Seever, M. F. (1985). Psychological test usage patterns in five professional settings. *American Psychologist, 40,* 857–861.

Lubin, B., Wallis, R. R., & Paine, C. (1971). Patterns of psychological test usage in the United States: 1935–1969. *Professional Psychology, 2,* 70–74.

Luckasson, R., Schalock, R. L., Snell, M. E., & Spitalnik, D. M. (1996). The 1992 AAMR definition and preschool children: Response from the Committee on Terminology and Classification. *Mental Retardation, 34,* 247–253.

Lukin, M. E., Dowd, E. T., Plake, B. S., & Kraft, R. G. (1985). Comparing computerized versus traditional psychological assessment. *Computers in Human Behavior, 1,* 49–58.

Lumley, V. A., & Miltenberger, R. G. (1997). Sexual abuse prevention for persons with mental retardation. *American Journal on Mental Retardation, 101,* 459–472.

Lumley, V. A., Miltenberger, R. G., Long, E. S., Rapp, J. T., & Roberts, J. A. (1998). Evaluation of a sexual abuse prevention program for adults with mental retardation. *Journal of Applied Behavior Analysis, 31,* 91–101.

Lung, R. J., Miller, S. H., Davis, T. S., & Graham, W. P. (1977). Recognizing burn injuries as abuse. *American Family Physician, 15,* 134–135.

Luria, A. R. (1966a). *Human brain and psychological processes.* New York: Harper & Row.

Luria, A. R. (1966b). *Higher cortical functions in man.* New York: Basic.

Luria, A. R. (1970, March). The functional organization of the brain. *Scientific American, 222,* 66–78.

Luria, A. R. (1973). *The working brain: An introduction to neuropsychology.* New York: Basic.

Luria, A. R. (1980). *Higher cortical functions in man* (2nd ed.). New York: Basic.

Lutey, C., & Copeland, E. P. (1982). Cognitive assessment of the school-age child. In C. R. Reynolds & T. B. Gutkin (Eds.), *The handbook of school psychology.* New York: Wiley.

Lykken, D. T. (1981). *A tremor in the blood: Uses and abuses of the lie detector.* New York: McGraw-Hill.

Lyman, H. B. (1972). Review of the Wechsler Adult Intelligence Scale. In O. K. Buros (Ed.), *The seventh mental measurements yearbook* (pp. 788–790). Highland Park, NJ: Gryphon.

Lynn, R. (1997). Direct evidence for a genetic basis for black-white differences in IQ. *American Psychologist, 5,* 73–74.

Lyons, J. A., & Scotti, J. R. (1994). Comparability of two administration formats of the Keane Posttraumatic Stress Disorder Scale. *Psychological Assessment, 6,* 209–211.

MacAndrew, C. (1965). The differentiation of male alcoholic outpatients from nonalcoholic psychiatric outpatients by means of the MMPI. *Quarterly Journal of Studies on Alcohol, 26,* 238–246.

Machover, K. (1949). *Personality projection in the drawing of the human figure: A method of personality investigation.* Springfield, IL: Charles C Thomas.

Mack, J. L., & Patterson, M. B. (1995). Executive dysfunction and Alzheimer's disease: Performance on a test of planning ability—the Porteus Maze Test. *Neuropsychology, 9,* 556–564.

Macmillan, D. L., Gresham, F. M., & Siperstein, G. N. (1995). Heightened concerns over the 1992 AAMR definition: Advocacy versus precision. *American Journal on Mental Retardation, 100,* 87–95.

Macmillan, D. L., & Meyers, C. E. (1980). Larry P.: An education interpretation. *School Psychology Review, 9,* 136–148.

Mael, F. A. (1991). Career constraints of observant Jews. *Career Development Quarterly, 39,* 341–349.

Magnello, M. E., & Spies, C. J. (1984). Francis Galton: Historical antecedents of the correlation calculus. In B. Laver (Chair), *History of mental measurement: Correlation, quantification, and institutionalization.* Paper session presented at the 92nd annual convention of the American Psychological Association, Toronto, Ontario, Canada.

Maher, L. (1996). Hidden in the light: Occupational norms among crack-using street-level sex workers. *Journal of Drug Issues, 26,* 143–173.

Malcolm, P. B., Davidson, P. R., & Marshall, W. L. (1985). Control of penile tumescence: The effects of arousal level and stimulus content. *Behaviour Research & Therapy, 23,* 273–280.

Malec, J. F., Ivnik, R. J., & Smith, G. E. (1993). *Neuropsychology and normal aging.* In R. W. Parks, R. F. Zec, & R. S. Wilson (Eds.), *Neuropsychology of Alzheimer's disease and other dementias* (pp. 81–111). New York: Oxford University.

Malec, J. F., Ivnik, R. J., Smith, G. E., et al. (1992). Mayo's older adult normative studies: Utility of corrections for age and education for the WAIS-R. *Clinical Neuropsychologist, 6*(Suppl.), 31–47.

Malgady, R. G., Costantino, G., & Rogler, L. H. (1984). Development of a Thematic Apperception Test (TEMAS) for urban Hispanic children. *Journal of Consulting and Clinical Psychology, 52,* 986–996.

Malgady, R. G., Rogler, L. H., & Constantino, G. (1987). Ethnocultural and linguistic bias in mental health evaluations of Hispanics. *American Psychologist, 42,* 228–234.

Maller, S. J. (1997). Deafness and WISC-III item difficulty: Invariance and fit. *Journal of School Psychology, 35,* 299–314.

Maller, S. J., & Braden, J. P. (1993). The construct and criterion-related validity of the WISC-III with deaf adolescents. *Journal of Psychoeducational Assessment, WISC-III Monograph,* 105–113.

Malone, P. S., Brounstein, P J., van Brock, A., & Shaywitz, S. S. (1991). Components of IQ scores across levels of measured ability. *Journal of Applied Social Psychology, 21,* 15–28.

Maloney, M. P., & Ward, M. P. (1976). *Psychological assessment.* New York: Oxford University.

Mannarino, A. P., Cohen, J. A., & Berman, S. R. (1994). The Children's Attributions and Perceptions Scale: A new measure of sexual-abuse related factors. *Journal of Clinical Child Psychology, 23,* 204–211.

Manz, C. C., & Sims, H. P. (1984). Searching for the "unleader": Organizational member views on leading self-managed groups. *Human Relations, 37,* 409–424.

Maranell, G. M. (1974). *Scaling: A sourcebook for behavioral scientists.* Chicago: Aldine.

Maraun, M. D. (1996a). Metaphor taken as math: Indeterminacy in the factor analysis model. *Multivariate Behavioral Research, 31,* 517–538.

Maraun, M. D. (1996b). Meaning and mythology in the factor analysis model. *Multivariate Behavioral Research, 31,* 603–616.

Maraun, M. D. (1996c). The claims of factor analysis. *Multivariate Behavioral Research, 31,* 673–689.

Marchese, M. C. (1992). Clinical versus actuarial prediction: A review of the literature. *Perceptual and Motor Skills, 75,* 583–594.

Mardell-Czudnowski, C. D., & Goldenberg, D. S. (1983, 1990). *Developmental Indicators for the Assessment of Learning—Revised.* Circle Pines, MN: American Guidance Service.

Mardell-Czudnowski, C., & Goldenberg, D. S. (1998). *Developmental Indicators for the Assessment of Learning—3* (DIAL-3). Circle Pines, MN: American Guidance Service.

Margolis, R. B., Williger, N. R., Greenlief, C. L., Dunn, E. J., & Gfeller, J. D. (1989). The sensitivity of the Bender-Gestalt Test as a screening instrument for neuropsychological impairment in older adults. *Journal of Psychology, 123,* 179–186.

Mark, M. M. (1999). Social science evidence in the courtroom: *Daubert* and beyond? *Psychology, Public Policy, and Law, 5,* 175–193.

Marks, I. (1999). Computer aids to mental health care. *Canadian Journal of Psychiatry, 44*, 548–555.

Marks, P. A., Seeman, W., & Haller, D. L. (1974). *The actuarial use of the MMPI with adolescents and adults.* Baltimore: Williams & Wilkins.

Marks, P. E., & Seeman, W. (1963). *The actuarial description of personality: An atlas for use with the MMPI.* Baltimore: Williams & Wilkins.

Marmot, M. G., & Syme, S. L. (1976). Acculturation and coronary heart disease in Japanese-Americans. *American Journal of Epidemiology, 104*, 225–247.

Marquette, B. W. (1976). *Limitations on the generalizability of adult competency across all situations.* Paper presented at the annual meeting of the Western Psychological Association, Los Angeles.

Marsh, D. T., Stile, S. A., Stoughton, N. L., & Trout-Landen, B. L. (1988). Psychopathology of opiate addiction: Comparative data from the MMPI and MCMI. *American Journal of Drug and Alcohol Abuse, 14*, 17–21.

Marshall, G. N., Hays, R. D., Sherbourne, C. D., & Wells, K. B. (1993). The structure of patient satisfaction with outpatient medical care. *Psychological Assessment, 5*, 477–483.

Marshall, W. L., Barbaree, H. E., & Butt, J. (1988). Sexual offenders against male children: Sexual preferences. *Behavior Research and Therapy, 26*, 383–391.

Martin, D. C., & Bartol, K. M. (1986). Holland's Vocational Preference Inventory and the Myers-Briggs Type Indicator as predictors of vocational choice among Master's of Business Administration. *Journal of Vocational Behavior, 29*, 51–65.

Martin, R. P. (1986). Assessment of the social and emotional functioning of preschool children. *School Psychology Review, 15*, 216–232.

Martin-Loeches, M., Gil, P., Jimenez, F., Exposito, F. J., Miguel, F., Cacabelos, R., & Rubia, F. J. (1991). Topographic maps of brain electrical activity in primary degenerative dementia of the Alzheimer type and multiinfarct dementia. *Biological Psychiatry, 29*, 211–223.

Marx, E. (1998). Sibling antagonism transformed during assessment in the home. In L. Handler (Chair), *Conducting assessments in clients' homes: Contexts, surprises, dilemmas, opportunities.* Symposium presented at the Society for Personality Assessment 1998 Midwinter Meeting, February 20.

Maslach, C., Jackson, S. E., & Leiter, M. P. (1996). *The Maslach Burnout Inventory* (3rd ed.). Palo Alto, CA: Consulting Psychologists Press.

Maslach, C., Jackson, S. E., & Leiter, M. P. (1997). The Maslach Burnout Inventory. In C. P. Zalaquett & R. J. Wood (Eds.), *Evaluating stress: A book of resources* (3rd ed.; pp. 191–218). Lanham, MD: Scarecrow.

Masling, J. (1959). The effects of warm and cold interaction on the administration and scoring of an intelligence test. *Journal of Consulting Psychology, 23*, 336–341.

Masling, J. (1960). The influence of situational and interpersonal variables in projective testing. *Psychological Bulletin, 57*, 65–85.

Masling, J. (1965). Differential indoctrination of examiners and Rorschach responses. *Journal of Consulting Psychology, 29*, 198–201.

Masling, J. M. (1997). On the nature and utility of projective tests and objective tests. *Journal of Personality Assessment, 69*, 257–270.

Maslow, A. H. (1943). A theory of motivation. *Psychological Review, 50*, 370–396.

Maslow, A. H. (1970). *Motivation and personality* (2nd ed.). New York: Harper & Row.

Massey, D. S. (2000). When surveys fail: An alternative for data collection. In A. A. Stone et al. (Eds.), *The science of self-report: Implications for research and practice* (pp. 145–160). Mahwah, NJ: Erlbaum.

Massil, H. (1995). Postpartum sexual function: What is the norm? *Sexual and Marital Therapy, 10*, 263–276.

Mast, B. T., & Lichtenberg, P. A. (2000). Assessment of functional abilities among geriatric patients: A MIMIC model of the functional independence measure. *Rehabilitation Psychology, 45*, 49–64.

Masuda, M., Matsumoto, G. H., & Meredith, G. M. (1970). Ethnic identity in three generations of Japanese Americans. *Journal of Social Psychology, 81*, 199–207.

Matarazzo, J. D. (1972). *Wechsler's measurement and appraisal of adult intelligence* (5th ed.) Baltimore: Williams & Wilkins.

Matarazzo, J. D. (1990). Psychological assessment versus psychological testing: Validation from Binet to the school, clinic, and courtroom. *American Psychologist, 45*, 999–1017.

Matarazzo, J. D., Matarazzo, R. G., Wiens, A. N., Gallo, A. E., & Klonoff, H. (1976). Retest reliability of the Halstead Impairment Index in a normal, a schizophrenic and two samples of organic patients. *Journal of Clinical Psychology, 32*, 338–349.

Matarazzo, J. D., & Wiens, A. N. (1977). Black Intelligence Test of Cultural Homogeneity and Wechsler Adult Intelligence Scale scores of black and white police applicants. *Journal of Applied Psychology, 62*, 57–63.

Matchett, W. F. (1972). Repeated hallucinatory experiences as part of the mourning process. *Psychiatry, 35*, 185–194.

Mathieu, J. E., & Zajac, D. M. (1990). A review and meta-analysis of the antecedents, correlates, and consequences of organizational commitment. *Psychological Bulletin, 108*, 171–194.

Matson, J. L. (1995). Comments on Gresham, MacMillan, and Siperstein's paper "Critical analysis of the 1992 AAMR definition: Implications for school psychology." *School Psychology Quarterly, 10*(1), 20–23.

Matson, J. L., Smiroldo, B. B., & Hastings, T. L. (1998). Validity of the Autism/Pervasive Developmental Disorder subscale of the Diagnostic Assessment for the Severely Handicapped-II. *Journal of Autism & Developmental Disorders, 28*, 77–81.

Matsumoto, D., & Kudoh, T. (1993). American-Japanese cultural differences in attributions of personality based on smiles. *Journal of Nonverbal Behavior, 17*, 231–243.

Matsumoto, G. M., Meredith, G. M., & Masuda, M. (1970). Ethnic identification: Honolulu and Seattle Japanese-Americans. *Journal of Cross-Cultural Psychology, 1*, 63–76.

Matthews, C. G. (1974). Applications of neuropsychological test methods in mentally retarded subjects. In R. M. Reitan & L. A. Davison (Eds.), *Clinical neuropsychology: Current status and applications* (pp. 267–287). New York: Winston.

Mattison, R. E., Handford, A., Kales, H. C., Goodman, A. L., & McLaughlin, R. E. (1990). Four-year predictive value of the Children's Depression Inventory. *Psychological Assessment, 2*, 169–174.

Maurer, T. J., & Alexander, R. A. (1991). Contrast effects in behavioral measurement: An investigation of alternative process explanations. *Journal of Applied Psychology, 76*, 3–10.

Maurer, T. J., Palmer, J. K., & Ashe, D. K. (1993). Diaries, checklists, evaluations, and contrast effects in measurement of behavior. *Journal of Applied Psychology, 78*, 226–231.

Mayfield, E. C. (1972). Value of peer nominations in predicting life insurance sales performance. *Journal of Applied Psychology, 56*, 319–323.

Mays, V. M., Cochran, S. D., Hamilton, E., & Miller, N. (1993). Just cover up: Barriers to heterosexual and gay young adults' use of condoms. *Health Values: The Journal of Health Behavior, Education, and Promotion, 17*, 41–47.

Mazzocco, M. M. M., Hagerman, R. J., & Pennington, B. F. (1992). Problem solving limitations among cytogenetically expressing Fragile X women. *American Journal of Medical Genetics, 43*, 78–86.

Mazzuca, S. A. (1982). Does patient education in chronic disease have therapeutic value? *Journal of Chronic Diseases, 35*, 521–529.

McAllister, L. W. (1996). *A practical guide to CPI interpretation* (3rd ed.). Palo Alto, CA: Consulting Psychologists Press.

McArthur, C. (1992). Rumblings of a distant drum. *Journal of Counseling and Development, 70*, 517–519.

McArthur, D. S., & Roberts, G. E. (1982). *Roberts Apperception Test for Children manual.* Los Angeles: Western Psychological Services.

McBride, B. A. (1989). Stress and fathers' parental competence: Implications for family life and parent educators. *Family Relations, 38*, 385–389.

McCall, W. A. (1922). *How to measure in education.* New York: Macmillan.

McCall, W. A. (1939). *Measurement.* New York: Macmillan.

McCann, J. T. (1990). A multitrait-multimethod analysis of the MCMI-II clinical syndrome scales. *Journal of Personality Assessment, 55*, 465–476.

McCaulley, M. H. (2000). Myers-Briggs Type Indicator: A bridge between counseling and consulting. *Consulting Psychology Journal: Practice and Research, 52*, 117–132.

McClelland, D. C. (1951). *Personality.* New York: Holt-Dryden.

McClelland, D. C. (1961). *The achieving society.* Princeton, NJ: Van Nostrand.

McClelland, D. C. (1980). Motive dispositions: The merits of operant and respondent measures. In L. Wheeler (Ed.), *Review of personality and social psychology* (Vol. 1; pp. 10–41). Beverly Hills: Sage.

McClelland, D. C., & Atkinson, J. W. (1948). The projective expression of needs: I. The effect of different intensities of the hunger drive on perception. *Journal of Psychology, 25*, 205–222.

McCloskey, G. W. (1989, March). *The K-ABC sequential simultaneous information processing model and classroom intervention: A report—the Dade County Classroom research study.* Paper presented at the Annual Meeting of the National Association of School Psychologists, Boston.

McClure-Butterfield, P. (1990). Issues in child custody evaluation and testimony. In C. R. Reynolds & R. W. Kamphaus (Eds.), *Handbook of psychological and educational assessment of children: Personality, behavior and context* (pp. 576–588). New York: Guilford.

McConkey, K. M., & Sheehan, P. W. (1996). *Hypnosis, memory, and behavior in criminal investigation.* New York: Guilford.

McCool, J. P., Cameron, L. D., & Petrie, K. J. (2001). Adolescent perceptions of smoking imagery in film. *Social Science & Medicine, 52*, 1577–1587.

McCown, W. (1998). An inventory to predict severity of impact of college student gambling. In J. Butcher (Chair), *New measures and instruments in assessment.* Paper session presentation at the Society for Personality Assessment 1998 Midwinter Meeting, February 19.

McCoy, G. F. (1972). *Diagnostic evaluation and educational programming for hearing impaired children.* Springfield, IL: Office of the Illinois Superintendent of Public Instruction.

McCrady, B. S., & Bux, D. A. (1999). Ethical issues of informed consent with substance abusers. *Journal of Consulting and Clinical Psychology, 67*, 186–193.

McCrae, R. R., & Costa, P. T., Jr. (1983). Social desirability and scales: More substance than style. *Journal of Consulting and Clinical Psychology, 51*, 882–888.

McCrae, R. R., & Costa, P. T., Jr. (1986). Personality, coping, and coping effectiveness in an adult sample. *Journal of Personality, 54*, 385–405.

McCrae, R. R., Costa, P. T., Jr., Dahlstrom, W. G., Barefoot, J. C., Siegler, I. C., & Williams, R. B., Jr. (1989). A caution on the use of the MMPI K-correction in research on psychosomatic medicine. *Psychosomatic Medicine, 51*, 58–65.

McCrae, R. R., Costa, P. T., Jr., Del Pilar, G. H., Rolland, J.-P., & Parker, W. D. (1998). Cross-cultural assessment of the five-factor model: The Revised NEO Personality Inventory. *Journal of Cross-Cultural Psychology, 29*, 171–188.

McCubbin, H., Larsen, A., & Olson, D. (1985a). F-COPES: Family Crisis Oriented Personal Evaluation Scales. In D. H. Olson, H. I. McCubbin, H. L. Barnes, A. S. Larsen, M. Muxen, & M. Wilson (Eds.), *Family inventories* (rev. ed.). St. Paul: Family Social Science, University of Minnesota.

McCubbin, H. I., Patterson, J. M., & Wilson, L. R. (1985b). FILE: Family Inventory of Life Events and Changes. In D. H. Olson, H. I. McCubbin, H. L. Barnes, A. S. Larsen, M. Muxen, & M. Wilson (Eds.), *Family inventories* (rev. ed.). St. Paul: Family Social Science, University of Minnesota.

McCubbin, J. A., Wilson, J. F., Bruehl, S., Brady, M., Clark, K., & Kort, E. (1991). Gender effects on blood pressures obtained during an on-campus screening. *Psychosomatic Medicine, 53*, 90–100.

McCusker, P. J. (1994). Validation of Kaufman, Ishikuma, Kaufman-Packer's Weschsler Adult Intelligence Scale—Revised short forms on a clinical sample. *Psychological Assessment, 6*, 246–248.

McDermott, P. A., Alterman, A. I., Brown, L., et al. (1996). Construct refinement and confirmation for the Addiction Severity Index. *Psychological Assessment, 8*, 182–189.

McDevitt, S. C., & Carey, W. B. (1978). The measurement of temperament in 3–7 year old children. *Journal of Child Psychology & Psychiatry & Allied Disciplines, 19*, 245–253.

McDonald, R. P. (1996a). Latent traits and the possibility of motion. *Multivariate Behavioral Research, 31*, 593–601.

McDonald, R. P. (1996b). Consensus emerges: A matter of interpretation. *Multivariate Behavioral Research, 31*, 663–672.

McDonald, W. J. (1993). Focus group research dynamics and reporting: An examination of research objectives and moderator influences. *Journal of the Academy of Marketing Science, 21*, 161–168.

McDowell, C., & Acklin, M. W. (1996). Standardizing procedures for calculating Rorschach interrater reliability: Conceptual and empirical foundations. *Journal of Personality Assessment, 66*, 308–320.

McDowell, I., & Newell, C. (1987). *Measuring health: A guide to rating scales and questionnaires.* New York: Oxford University.

McElrath, K. (1994). A comparison of two methods for examining inmates' self-reported drug use. *International Journal of the Addictions, 29*, 517–524.

McElwain, B. A. (1998). On seeing Beth at home and in a different light. In L. Handler (Chair), *Conducting assessments in clients' homes: Contexts, surprises, dilemmas, opportunities.* Symposium presented at the Society for Personality Assessment 1998 Midwinter Meeting, February 20.

McEvoy, G. M., & Beatty, R. W. (1989). Assessment centers and subordinate appraisals of managers: A seven-year examination of predictive validity. *Personnel Psychology, 42*, 37–52.

McGinnies, E. (1949). Emotionality and perceptual defense. *Psychological Review, 56*, 244–251.

McGrew, K. S. (1997). Analysis of the major intelligence batteries according to a proposed comprehensive *Gf-Gc* framework. In D. P. Flanagan, J. L. Genshaft, & P. L. Harrison (Eds.), *Contemporary intellectual assessment: Theories, tests, and issues* (pp. 151–180). New York: Guilford.

McGrew, K. S., & Flanagan, D. P. (1998). *The intelligence test desk reference: Gf-Gc cross-battery assessment.* Boston: Allyn & Bacon.

McGue, M. (1997). The democracy of the genes. *Nature, 388*, 417–418.

McGurk, F. J. (1975). Race differences—twenty years later. *Homo, 26,* 219–239.

McKinley, J. C., & Hathaway, S. R. (1940). A multiphasic schedule (Minnesota): II. A differential study of hypochondriases. *Journal of Psychology, 10,* 255–268.

McKinley, J. C., & Hathaway, S. R. (1944). The MMPI: V. Hysteria, hypomania, and psychopathic deviate. *Journal of Applied Psychology, 28,* 153–174.

McLellan, A. T., Luborsky, L., Woody, G. E., & O'Brien, C. P. (1980). An improved diagnostic evaluation instrument for substance abuse patients. *Journal of Nervous and Mental Disease, 168,* 26–33.

McLemore, C. W., & Court, J. H. (1977). Religion and psychotherapy—ethics, civil liberties, and clinical savvy: A critique. *Journal of Consulting and Clinical Psychology, 45,* 1172–1175.

McMillen, C., Howard, M. O., Nower, L., & Chung, S. (2001). Positive by-products of the struggle with chemical dependency. *Journal of Substance Abuse Treatment, 20,* 69–79.

McNaughton, M. E., Smith, L. W., Patterson, T. L., & Grant, I. (1990). Stress, social support, coping resources, and immune status in the elderly. *Journal of Nervous and Mental Disease, 178,* 460–461.

McNeish, T. J., & Naglieri, J. A. (1993). Identification of individuals with serious emotional disturbance using the Draw A Person: Screening Procedure for Emotional Disturbance. *Journal of Special Education, 27,* 115–121.

McNemar, Q. (1964). Lost: Our intelligence. Why? *American Psychologist, 19,* 871–882.

McNemar, Q. (1975). On so-called test bias. *American Psychologist, 30,* 848–851.

McPhee, J. P., & Wegner, K. W. (1976). Kinetic-Family-Drawing styles and emotionally disturbed childhood behavior. *Journal of Personality Assessment, 40,* 487–491.

McReynolds, P. (1987). Lightner Witmer: Little-known founder of clinical psychology. *American Psychologist, 42,* 849–858.

McReynolds, P., & Ludwig, K. (1984). Christian Thomasius and the origin of psychological rating scales. *ISIS, 75,* 546–553.

Meadow, K. P., Karchmer, M. A., Petersen, L. M., & Rudner, L. (1980). *Meadow-Kendall Social-Emotional Assessment Inventory.* Washington, DC: Gallaudet University.

Meadows, G., Turner, T., Campbell, L., Lewis, S. W., Reveley, M. A., & Murray, R. M. (1991). Assessing schizophrenia in adults with mental retardation: A comparative study. *British Journal of Psychiatry, 158,* 103–105.

Mednick, S. A. (1962). The associative basis of the creative process. *Psychological Review, 69,* 220–232.

Mednick, S. A., Higgins, J., & Kirschenbaum, J. (1975). *Psychology.* New York: Wiley.

Medvec, V. H., Madey, S. F., & Gilovich, T. (1995). When less is more: Counterfactual thinking and satisfaction among Olympic medalists. *Journal of Personality and Social Psychology, 69,* 603–610.

Medvec, V. H., & Savitsky, K. (1997). When doing better means feeling worse: The efforts of categorical cutoff points on counterfactual thinking and satisfaction. *Journal of Personality and Social Psychology, 72,* 1284–1296.

Meehl, P. E. (1951). *Research results for counselors.* St. Paul, MN: State Department of Education.

Meehl, P. E. (1954). *Clinical versus statistical prediction: A theoretical analysis and a review of the evidence.* Minneapolis: University of Minnesota.

Meehl, P. E. (1956). Wanted: A good cookbook. *American Psychologist, 11,* 263–272.

Meehl, P. E. (1959). A comparison of clinicians with five statistical methods of identifying psychotic MMPI profiles. *Journal of Clinical Psychology, 6,* 102–109.

Meehl, P. E. (1965). Seer over sign: The first good example. *Journal of Experimental Research in Personality, 1,* 27–32.

Meenan, R. F., & Pincus, T. (1987). The status of patient status measures. *Journal of Rheumatology, 14,* 411–414.

Meier, S. T. (1984). The construct validity of burnout. *Journal of Occupational Psychology, 57,* 211–219.

Meier, S. T. (1991). Tests of the construct validity of occupational stress measures with college students: Failure to support discriminant validity. *Journal of Counseling Psychology, 38,* 91–97.

Melchert, T. P., & Patterson, M. M. (1999). Duty to warn and interventions with HIV-positive clients. *Professional Psychology: Research and Practice, 30,* 180–186.

Mellenbergh, G. J. (1994). Generalized linear item response theory. *Psychological Bulletin, 115,* 300–307.

Mello, E. W., & Fisher, R. P. (1996). Enhancing older adult eyewitness memory with the cognitive interview. *Applied Cognitive Psychology, 10,* 403–418.

Meloy, J. R., Hansen, T. L., & Weiner, I. B. (1997). Authority of the Rorschach: Legal citations during the past 50 years. *Journal of Personality Assessment, 69,* 53–62.

Melton, G. (1988). Ethical and legal issues in AIDS-related practice. *American Psychologist, 43,* 941–947.

Melton, G., Petrila, J., Poythress, N. G., & Slobogin, C. (1997). *Psychological evaluations for the courts: A handbook for mental health professionals and lawyers* (2nd ed.). New York: Guilford.

Melton, G. B. (1989). Review of the Child Abuse Protection Inventory, Form VI. In J. C. Conoley & J. J. Kramer (Eds.), *The tenth mental measurements yearbook.* Lincoln: Buros Institute of Mental Measurements, University of Nebraska.

Melton, G. B., & Limber, S. (1989). Psychologists' involvement in cases of child maltreatment. *American Psychologist, 44,* 1225–1233.

Melzack, R., & Wall, P. D. (1982). *The challenge of pain.* New York: Basic.

Mendoza, R. H. (1989). An empirical scale to measure type and degree of acculturation in Mexican-American adolescents and adults. *Journal of Cross-Cultural Psychology, 20,* 372–385.

Menninger, K. A. (1953). *The human mind* (3rd ed.). New York: Knopf.

Mercer, J. R. (1976). A system of multicultural pluralistic assessment (SOMPA). In *Proceedings: With bias toward none.* Lexington: Coordinating Office for Regional Resource Centers, University of Kentucky.

Merrens, M. R., & Richards, W. S. (1970). Acceptance of generalized versus "bona fide" personality interpretation. *Psychological Reports, 27,* 691–694.

Mershon, B., & Gorsuch, R. L. (1988). Number of factors in the personality sphere: Does increase in factors increase predictability of real-life criteria? *Journal of Personality and Social Psychology, 55,* 675–680.

Messick, S. (1995). Validity of psychological assessment. *American Psychologist, 50,* 741–749.

Meyer, G. J., & Handler, L. (1997). The ability of the Rorschach to predict subsequent outcome: Meta-analysis of the Rorschach Prognostic Rating Scale. *Journal of Personality Assessment, 69,* 1–38.

Meyers, C. E. (1975). *What I Like To Do—An inventory of students' interests.* Chicago: Science Research Associates.

Meyers, D. V. (1978). Toward an objective procedure evaluation of the Kinetic Family Drawings (KFD). *Journal of Personality Assessment, 42,* 358–365.

Meyers, J. (1994, January/February). Assessing cross-cultural adaptability with the CCAI. *San Diego Psychological Association Newsletter, 3*(1 & 2).

Micceri, T. (1989). The unicorn, the normal curve and other improbable creatures. *Psychological Bulletin, 105,* 156–166.

Midanik, L. T., Greenfield, T. K., & Rogers, J. D. (2001). Reports of alcohol-related harm: Telephone versus face-to-face interviews. *Journal of Studies on Alcohol, 62,* 74–78.

Mikail, S. F., DuBreuil S., & D'Eon, J. L. (1993). A comparative analysis of measures used in the assessment of chronic pain patients. *Psychological Assessment, 5,* 117–120.

Miller, I. J. (1996). Managed care is harmful to outpatient mental health services: A call for accountability. *Professional Psychology: Research and Practice, 27,* 349–363.

Miller, I. W., Kabacoff, R. I., Epstein, N. B., & Bishop, D. S. (1994). The development of a clinical rating scale for the McMaster Model of Family Functioning. *Family Process, 33,* 53–69.

Miller, J. N., & Ozonoff, S. (2000). The external validity of Asperger disorder: Lack of evidence from the domain of neuropsychology. *Journal of Abnormal Psychology, 109,* 227–238.

Miller, N. E. (1969). Learning of visceral and glandular responses. *Science, 163,* 434–445.

Miller, W. R., Heather, N., & Hall, W. (1991). Calculating standard drink units: International comparisons. *British Journal of Addiction, 86,* 43–47.

Millman, J., & Arter, J. A. (1984). Issues in item banking. *Journal of Educational Measurement, 21,* 315–330.

Millon, T. (1969). *Modern psychopathology.* Philadelphia: Saunders.

Millon, T. (1981). *Disorders of personality: DSM-III, Axis II.* New York: Wiley.

Millon, T. (1983). *Millon Clinical Multiaxial Inventory manual.* Minneapolis: National Computer Systems.

Millon, T. (1986a). Personality prototypes and their diagnostic criteria. In T. Millon & G. L. Klerman (Eds.), *Contemporary directions in psychopathology: Toward the DSM-IV.* New York: Guilford.

Millon, T. (1986b). A theoretical derivation of pathological personalities. In T. Millon & G. L. Klerman (Eds.), *Contemporary directions in psychopathology: Toward the DSM-IV.* New York: Guilford.

Millon, T. (1987). *Millon Clinical Multiaxial Inventory II manual.* Minneapolis: National Computer Systems.

Millon, T. (1990). *Toward a new personology: An evolutionary model.* New York: Wiley.

Millon, T. (1994). *Millon Index of Personality Styles manual.* San Antonio: Psychological Corporation.

Millon, T., & Davis, R. D. (1998). Ten subtypes of psychopathy. In T. Millon et al. (Eds.), *Psychopathy: Antisocial, criminal, and violent behavior* (pp. 161–170). New York: Guilford.

Millon, T., Millon, C., & Davis, R. (1993). *Millon Adolescent Clinical Inventory.* Minneapolis: National Computer Systems.

Millon, T., Millon, C., & Davis, R. (1994). *MCMI-III manual: Millon Clinical Multiaxial Inventory-III.* Minneapolis: National Computer Systems.

Millon, T., et al. (1996). *Disorders of personality: DSM-IV and beyond* (2nd ed.). New York: Wiley.

Milner, B. (1971). Interhemispheric differences in the localization of psychological processes in man. *British Medical Bulletin, 27,* 272–277.

Milner, J. (1989). Additional cross-validation of the Child Abuse Potential Inventory. *Psychological Assessment, 1,* 219–223.

Milner, J. S. (1986). *The Child Abuse Potential Inventory: Manual* (2nd ed.). Webster, NC: Psytec Corporation.

Milner, J. S. (1989). Applications of the Child Abuse Potential Inventory. *Journal of Clinical Psychology, 45,* 450–454.

Milner, J. S. (1991). Additional issues in child abuse assessment. *American Psychologist, 46,* 82–84.

Milner, J. S., Gold, R. G., & Wimberley, R. C. (1986). Prediction and explanation of child abuse: Cross-validation of the Child Abuse Protection Inventory. *Journal of Consulting and Clinical Psychology, 54,* 865–866.

Miner, J. B. (2000). Testing a psychological typology of entrepreneurship using business founders. *Journal of Applied Behavioral Science, 36,* 43–69.

Minsky, S. K., Spitz, H. H., & Bessellieu, C. L. (1985). Maintenance and transfer of training by mentally retarded young adults on the Tower of Hanoi problem. *American Journal of Mental Deficiency, 90,* 190–197.

Mirka, G. A., Kelaher, D. P., Nay, T., & Lawrence, B. M. (2000). Continuous assessment of back stress (CABS): A new method to quantify low-back stress in jobs with variable biomechanical demands. *Human Factors, 42,* 209–225.

Mischel, W. (1968). *Personality and assessment.* New York: Wiley.

Mischel, W. (1973). Toward a cognitive social learning reconceptualization of personality. *Psychological Review, 80,* 252–283.

Mischel, W. (1977). On the future of personality measurement. *American Psychologist, 32,* 246–254.

Mischel, W. (1979). On the interface of cognition and personality: Beyond the person-situation debate. *American Psychologist, 34,* 740–754.

Misiaszek, J., Dooling, J., Gieseke, M., Melman, H., Misiaszek, J. G., & Jorgensen, K. (1985). Diagnostic considerations in deaf patients. *Comprehensive Psychiatry, 26,* 513–521.

Mitchell, J. V., Jr. (Ed.). (1985). *The ninth mental measurements yearbook.* Lincoln: Buros Institute of Mental Measurements, University of Nebraska.

Mitchell, J. V., Jr. (1986). Measurement in the larger context: Critical current issues. *Professional Psychology: Research and Practice, 17,* 544–550.

Moffitt, T. E., Caspi, A., Krueger, R. F., et al. (1997). Do partners agree about abuse in their relationship? A psychometric evaluation of interpartner agreement. *Psychological Assessment, 9,* 47–56.

Moffitt, T. E., Gabrielli, W. F., Mednick, S. A., & Schulsinger, F. (1981). Socioeconomic status, IQ, and delinquency. *Journal of Abnormal Psychology, 90,* 152–156.

Molloy, D. W., Alemayehu, E., & Roberts, R. (1991). Reliability of a standardized Mini-Mental State Examination compared with the traditional Mini-Mental State Examination. *American Journal of Psychiatry, 148,* 102–105.

Monahan, J. (1981). *The clinical prediction of violent behavior.* Washington, DC: U.S. Government Printing Office.

Montague, M. (1993). Middle school students' mathematical problem solving: An analysis of think-aloud protocols. *Learning Disability Quarterly, 16,* 19–32.

Montana Health and Safety Code. (1997). *8 Mont. Code Ann.,* §50-16-1003.

Montgomery, G. T., & Orozco, S. (1985). Mexican Americans' performance on the MMPI as a function of level of acculturation. *Journal of Clinical Psychology, 41,* 203–212.

Moore, M. S., & McLaughlin, L. (1992). Assessment of the preschool child with visual impairment. In E. Vasquez Nutall, I. Romero & J. Kalesnik (Eds.), *Assessing and screening preschoolers: Psychological and educational dimensions* (pp. 345–368). Boston: Allyn & Bacon.

Moos, R. H. (1986). *Work Environment Scale* (2nd ed.). Palo Alto, CA: Consulting Psychologists Press.

Moos, R. H., & Moos, B. S. (1981). *Family Environment Scale manual.* Palo Alto, CA: Consulting Psychologists Press.

Moos, R. H., & Moos, B. S. (1994). *Family environment manual: Development, applications, research.* Palo Alto, CA: Consulting Psychologists Press.

Moreland, K. L. (1985). Validation of computer-based test interpretations: Problems and prospects. *Journal of Consulting and Clinical Psychology, 53,* 816–825.

Moreland, K. L. (1986). An introduction to the problem of test user qualifications. In R. B. Most (Chair), *Test purchaser qualifications: Present practice, professional needs, and a proposed system*. Symposium presented at the 94th annual convention of the American Psychological Association, Washington, DC.

Moreland, K. L. (1987). Computerized psychological assessment: What's available. In J. N. Butcher (Ed.), *Computerized psychological assessment: A practitioner's guide* (pp. 26–49). New York: Basic.

Moreland, K. L., Eyde, L. D., Robertson, G. J., Primoff, E. S., & Most, R. B. (1995a). Assessment of test user qualifications: A research-based measurement procedure. *American Psychologist, 50,* 14–23.

Moreland, K. L., Reznikoff, M., & Aronow, E. (1995b). Integrating Rorschach interpretation by *carefully* placing *more* of your eggs in the content basket. *Journal of Personality Assessment, 64,* 239–242.

Morgan, C. D. (1938). Thematic apperception test. In H. A. Murray (Ed.), *Explorations in personality: A clinical and experimental study of fifty men of college age* (pp. 673–680). New York: Oxford University.

Morgan, C. D., & Murray, H. A. (1935). A method for investigating fantasies: The Thematic Apperception Test. *Archives of Neurology and Psychiatry, 34,* 289–306.

Morgan, D. D., & Murray, H. W. (1938). Thematic Apperception Test. In H. A. Murray (Ed.), *Explorations in personality: A clinical and experimental study of fifty men of college age* (pp. 530–545). New York: Oxford University.

Morgan, W. G. (1995). Origin and history of Thematic Apperception Test images. *Journal of Personality Assessment, 65,* 237–254.

Mori, L. T., & Armendariz, G. M. (2001). Analogue assessment of child behavior problems. *Psychological Assessment, 13,* 36–45.

Morreau, L. E., & Bruininks, R. H. (1991). *Checklist of Adaptive Living Skills.* Itasca, IL: Riverside.

Morse, S. J. (1985). Excusing the crazy: The insanity defense reconsidered. *Southern California Law Review, 58,* 777–836.

Moses, S. (1991). Major revision of SAT goes into effect in 1994. *APA Monitor, 22*(1), 35.

Mosier, C. I. (1947). A critical examination of the concepts of face validity. *Educational and Psychological Measurement, 7,* 191–206.

Moss, K., Ullman, M., Johnsen, M. C., et al. (1999). Different paths to justice: The ADA, employment, and administrative enforcement by the EEOC and FEPAs. *Behavioral Sciences and the Law, 17,* 29–46.

Mostkoff, D. L., & Lazarus, P. J. (1983). The Kinetic Family Drawing: The reliability of an objective scoring system. *Psychology in the Schools, 20,* 16–20.

Motowidlo, S. J. (1996). Orientation toward the job and organization. In K. R. Murphy (Ed.), *Individual differences and behavior in organizations* (pp. 20–175). San Francisco: Jossey-Bass.

Motta, R. W., Little, S. G., & Tobin, M. I. (1993a). The use and abuse of human figure drawings. *School Psychology Quarterly, 8,* 162–169.

Motta, R. W., Little, S. G., & Tobin, M. I. (1993b). A picture is worth less than a thousand words: Response to reviewers. *School Psychology Quarterly, 8,* 197–199.

Mueller, C. G. (1949). Numerical transformations in the analysis of experimental data. *Psychological Bulletin, 46,* 198–223.

Mueller, J. H., Jacobsen, D. M., & Schwarzer, R. (2000). What are computers good for? A case study in online research. In M. H. Birnbaum (Ed.), *Psychological experiments on the Internet* (pp. 195–216). San Diego, CA: Academic Press.

Mueller, U., & Mazur, A. (1996). Facial dominance in *homo sapiens* as honest signaling of male quality. *Behavioral Ecology, 8,* 569–579.

Mulaik, S. A. (1996a). On Maraun's deconstructing of factor indeterminacy with constructed factors. *Multivariate Behavioral Research, 31,* 579–592.

Mulaik, S. A. (1996b). Factor analysis is not just a model in pure mathematics. *Multivariate Behavioral Research, 31,* 655–661.

Mulvey, E. P., & Lidz, C. W. (1984). Clinical considerations in the prediction of dangerousness in mental patients. *Clinical Psychology Review, 4,* 379–401.

Murguia, A., Zea, M. C., Reisen, C. A., & Peterson, R. A. (2000). The development of the Cultural Health Attributions Questionnaire (CHAQ). *Cultural Diversity and Ethnic Minority Psychology, 6,* 268–283.

Murphy, G. E. (1984). The prediction of suicide: Why is it so difficult? *American Journal of Psychotherapy, 38,* 341–349.

Murphy, K. R., Balzer, W. K., Lockhart, M. C., & Eisenman, E. J. (1985). Effects of previous performance on evaluations of present performance. *Journal of Applied Psychology, 70,* 72–84.

Murphy, K. R., & Thornton, G. C., III. (1992). Characteristics of employee drug testing policies. *Journal of Business and Psychology, 6,* 295–309.

Murphy, L. L., Conoley, J. C., & Impara, J. C. (1994). *Tests in print IV: An index to tests, test reviews, and the literature on specific tests.* Lincoln: Buros Institute of Mental Measurements, University of Nebraska.

Murphy-Berman, V. (1994). A conceptual framework for thinking about risk assessment and case management in child protective service. *Child Abuse and Neglect, 18,* 193–201.

Murray, H. A. (1943). *Thematic Apperception Test manual.* Cambridge, MA: Harvard University.

Murray, H. A. (1959). Preparations for the scaffold of a comprehensive system. In S. Koch (Ed.), *Psychology: A study of science* (Vol. 3). New York: McGraw-Hill.

Murray, H. A., et al. (1938). *Explorations in personality.* Cambridge, MA: Harvard University.

Murray, H. A., & Kluckhohn, C. (1953). Outline of a conception of personality. In C. Kluckholn, H. A. Murray, & D. Schneider (Eds.), *Personality in nature, society, and culture* (2nd ed.; pp. 3–52). New York: Knopf.

Murray, H. A., & MacKinnon, D. W. (1946). Assessment of OSS personnel. *Journal of Consulting Psychology, 10,* 76–80.

Murray, J. P., Greenfield, S., Kaplan, S. H., & Yano, E. M. (1992). Ambulatory testing for capitation and fee for service patients in the same practice setting. Relationship to outcome. *Medical Care, 30,* 252–261.

Murstein, B. I., & Mathes, S. (1996). Projection on projective techniques = pathology: The problem that is not being addressed. *Journal of Personality Assessment, 66,* 337–349.

Murstein, B. J. (1961). Assumptions, adaptation level, and projective techniques. *Perceptual and Motor Skills, 12,* 107–125.

Murstein, B. J. (1963). *Theory and research in projective techniques.* New York: Wiley.

Mussen, P. H., & Naylor, H. K. (1954). The relationship between overt and fantasy aggression. *Journal of Abnormal and Social Psychology, 49,* 235–240.

Mussen, P. H., & Scodel, A. (1955). The effects of sexual stimulation under varying conditions on TAT sexual responsiveness. *Journal of Consulting and Clinical Psychology, 19,* 90.

Myers, I. B. (1962). *The Myers-Briggs Type Indicator: Manual.* Palo Alto, CA: Consulting Psychologists Press.

Myers, I. B., & Briggs, K. C. (1943/1962). *The Myers-Briggs Type Indicator.* Palo Alto, CA: Consulting Psychologists Press.

Nagle, R. J., & Bell, N. L. (1993). Validation of Stanford-Binet Intelligence Scale: Fourth Edition Abbreviated Batteries with college students. *Psychology in the Schools, 30,* 227–231.

Naglieri, J. A. (1985a). Use of the WISC-R and K-ABC with learning disabled, borderline mentally retarded, and normal children. *Psychology in the Schools, 22,* 133–141.

Naglieri, J. A. (1985b). Normal children's performance on the McCarthy Scales, Kaufman Assessment Battery and Peabody Individual Achievement Test. *Journal of Psychoeducational Assessment, 3,* 123–129.

Naglieri, J. A. (1989). A cognitive processing theory for the measurement of intelligence. *Educational Psychologist, 24,* 185–206.

Naglieri, J. A. (1990). *Das-Naglieri Cognitive Assessment System.* Paper presented at the conference "Intelligence: Theories and Practice," Memphis.

Naglieri, J. A. (1993). Human figure drawings in perspective. *School Psychology Quarterly, 8,* 170–176.

Naglieri, J. A. (1997). IQ: Knowns and unknowns, hits and misses. *American Psychologist, 52,* 75–76.

Naglieri, J. A., & Anderson, D. F. (1985). Comparison of the WISC-R and K-ABC with gifted students. *Journal of Psychoeducational Assessment, 3,* 175–179.

Naglieri, J. A., & Das, J. P. (1988). Planning-arousal-simultaneous-successive (PASS): A model for assessment. *Journal of School Psychology, 26,* 35–48.

Naglieri, J. A., & Das, J. P. (1997). *Das-Naglieri Cognitive Assessment System: Interpretive handbook.* Itasca, IL: Riverside.

Naglieri, J. A., & Jensen, A. R. (1987). Comparison of black-white differences on the WISC-R and the K-ABC: Spearman's hypothesis. *Intelligence, 11,* 21–43.

Naglieri, J. A., McNeish, T. J., & Bardos, A. N. (1991). *Draw A Person: Screening Procedure for Emotional Disturbance—Examiner's manual.* Austin: PRO-ED.

Nagyne Rez, I., & Zsoldos, M. (1991). Issues of diagnosis of learning problems in patients with impaired hearing on the basis of observations gained during the application of the Hiskey-Nebraska Test of Learning Aptitude. *Magyar Pszichologiai Szemle, 47,* 393–402.

Narens, L., & Luce, R. D. (1986). Measurement: The theory of numerical assignments. *Psychological Bulletin, 99,* 166–180.

Nathan, J., Wilkinson, D., Stammers, S., & Low, L. (2001). The role of tests of frontal executive function in the detection of mild dementia. *International Journal of Geriatric Psychiatry, 16,* 18–26.

National Association of School Psychologists. (2000). *Professional conduct manual* (4th ed.). Washington, DC: Author.

National Council on Disability. (1996). *Cognitive impairments and the application of Title I of the Americans with Disabilities Act.* Washington, DC: Author.

National Joint Committee on Learning Disabilities. (1985). *Learning disabilities and the preschool child: A position paper of the National Joint Committee on Learning Disabilities.* Baltimore: Author.

Naylor, J. C., & Shine, L. C. (1965). A table for determining the increase in mean criterion score obtained by using a selection device. *Journal of Industrial Psychology, 3,* 33–42.

Neagoe, A. D. (2000). Abducted by aliens: A case study. *Psychiatry, 63,* 202–207.

Neale, E. L., & Rosal, M. L. (1993). What can art therapists learn from projective drawing techniques for children? A review of the literature. *Arts in Psychotherapy, 20,* 37–49.

Neath, J., Bellini, J., & Bolton, B. (1997). Dimensions of the Functional Assessment Inventory for five disability groups. *Rehabilitation Psychology, 42,* 183–207.

Needham, J. (1959). *A history of embryology.* New York: Abelard-Schuman.

Neisser, U. (1979). The concept of intelligence. *Intelligence, 3,* 217–227.

Neisser, U., Boodoo, G., Bouchard, T. J., Jr., et al. (1996). Intelligence: Knowns and unknowns. *American Psychologist, 51,* 77–101.

Nellis, L. & Gridley, B. E. (1994). Review of the Bayley Scales of Infant Development—Second Edition. *Journal of School Psychology, 32,* 201–209.

Nelson, C. A., Wewerka, S., Thomas, K. M., et al. (2000). Neurocognitive sequelae of infants of diabetic mothers. *Behavioral Neuroscience, 114,* 950–956.

Nelson, D. V., Harper, R. G., Kotik-Harper, D., & Kirby, H. B. (1993). Brief neuropsychologic differentiation of demented versus depressed elderly inpatients. *General Hospital Psychiatry, 15,* 409–416.

Nelson, L. D. (1994). Introduction to the special section on normative assessment. *Psychological Assessment, 4,* 283.

Nelson, R. O., Hay, L. R., & Hay, W. M. (1977). Comment on Cone's "The relevance of reliability and validity for behavior assessment." *Behavior Therapy, 8,* 427–430.

Nester, M. A. (1993). Psychometric testing and reasonable accommodation for persons with disabilities. *Rehabilitation Psychology, 38,* 75–85.

Nettelbeck, T., & Rabbit, P. M. A. (1992). Aging, cognitive performance, and mental speed. *Intelligence, 16,* 189–205.

Neugarten, B., Havighurst, R. J., & Tobin, S. (1961). The measurement of life satisfaction. *Journal of Gerontology, 16,* 134–143.

Newborg, J., Stock, J. R., Wnek, L., et al. (1984). *Battelle Developmental Inventory.* Allen, TX: DLM Teaching Resources.

Newcomb, T. M. (1929). *Consistency of certain extrovert-introvert behavior patterns in 51 problem boys.* New York: Columbia University Bureau of Publications.

Newell, A. (1973). Production systems: Models of control structures. In W. G. Chase (Ed.), *Visual information processing* (pp. 463–526). New York: Academic Press.

Newman, H. H., Freeman, F. N., & Holzinger, K. J. (1937). *Twins.* Chicago: University of Chicago.

Nichols, D. S. (1992). Review of the Minnesota Multiphasic Personality Inventory—2. In J. J. Kramer & J. C. Conoley (Eds.), *The eleventh mental measurements yearbook.* Lincoln: Buros Institute of Mental Measurements, University of Nebraska.

Nolan, Y., Johnson, J. A., & Pincus, A. L. (1994). Personality and drunk driving: Identification of DUI types using the Hogan Personality Inventory. *Psychological Assessment, 6,* 33–40.

Norbeck, J. S., Lindsey, A. M., & Carrieri, V. L. (1981). The development of an instrument to measure social support. *Nursing Research, 30,* 264–269.

Norton, P. J., & Hope, D. A. (2001). Analogue observational methods in the assessment of social functioning in adults. *Psychological Assessment, 13,* 59–72.

Notarius, C., & Markman, H. (1981). Couples Interaction Scoring System. In E. Filsinger & R. Lewis, (Eds.), *Assessing marriage: New behavioral approaches.* Beverly Hills: Sage.

Notarius, C. I., & Vanzetti, N. A. (1983). The Marital Agendas Protocol. In E. Filsinger (Ed.), *Marriage and family assessment: A sourcebook for family therapy.* Beverly Hills: Sage.

Nottingham, E. J., IV, & Mattson, R. E. (1981). A validation study of the Competency Screening Test. *Law and Human Behavior, 5,* 329–335.

Novick, M. R., & Lewis, C. (1967). Coefficient alpha and the reliability of composite measurements. *Psychometrika, 32,* 1–13.

Nunnally, J. C. (1978). *Psychometric theory* (2nd ed.). New York: McGraw-Hill.

Nyborg, H., & Jensen, A. R. (2000). Black-white differences on various psychometric tests: Spearman's hypothesis tested on American armed services veterans. *Personality and Individual Differences, 28,* 593–599.

Nystedt, L., Sjoeberg, A., & Haegglund, G. (1999). Discriminant validation of measures of organizational commitment, job involvement, and job satisfaction among Swedish army officers. *Scandinavian Journal of Psychology, 40,* 49–55.

Oakland, T., & Dowling, L. (1983). The Draw-A-Person Test: Validity properties for nonbiased assessment. *Learning Disability Quarterly, 6,* 526–534.

O'Boyle, M. W., Gill, H. S., Benbow, C. P., & Alexander, J. E. (1994). Concurrent finger-tapping in mathematically gifted males: Evidence for enhanced right hemispheric involvement during linguistic processing. *Cortex, 30,* 519–526.

O'Connor, E. (2001, February). Researchers pinpoint potential cause of autism. *Monitor on Psychology, 32*(2), p. 13.

Oden, M. H. (1968). The fulfillment of promise: 40-year-follow-up of the Terman gifted group. *Genetic Psychology Monographs, 77,* 3–93.

O'Donnell, W. E., DeSoto, C. B., & DeSoto, J. L. (1993). Validity and reliability of the Revised Neuropsychological Impairment Scales (NIS). *Journal of Clinical Psychology, 49,* 372–382.

O'Donnell, W. E., DeSoto, C. B., DeSoto, J. L., & Reynolds, D. M. (1993). *The Neuropsychological Impairment Scale (NIS) manual.* Los Angeles: Western Psychological Services.

O'Donnell, W. E., & Reynolds, D. McQ. (1983). *Neuropsychological Impairment Scale (NIS) manual.* Annapolis, MD: Annapolis Neuropsychological Services.

Ogdon, D. P. (1982). *Psychodiagnosis and personality assessment: A handbook.* Los Angeles: Western Psychological Services.

O'Hara, M. W., Hoffman, J. G., Phillips, L. H. C., & Wright, E. J. (1992). Adjustment in childbearing women: The Postpartum Adjustment Questionnaire. *Psychological Assessment, 4,* 160–169.

O'Hare, T., & Van Tran, T. (1998). Substance abuse among Southeast Asians in the U.S.: Implications for practice and research. *Social Work in Health Care, 26,* 69–80.

Okazaki, S., & Sue, S. (2000). Implications of test revisions for assessment with Asian Americans. *Psychological Assessment, 12,* 272–280.

O'Keeffe, J. (1993). Disability, discrimination, and the Americans with Disabilities Act. *Consulting Psychology Journal, 45*(2), 3–9.

O'Leary, K. D., & Arias, I. (1988). Assessing agreement of reports of spouse abuse. In G. T. Hotaling, D. Finkelhor, J. T. Kirkpatrick, & M. A. Straus (Eds.), *Family abuse and its consequences* (pp. 218–227). Newbury Park, CA: Sage.

Olson, D. H., & Barnes, H. L. (1985). Quality of Life. In D. H. Olson, H. I. McCubbin, H. L. Barnes, A. S. Larsen, M. Muxen, & M. Wilson (Eds.), *Family inventories* (rev. ed.). St. Paul: Family Social Science, University of Minnesota.

Olson, D. H., Larsen, A. S., & McCubbin, H. I. (1985). Family Strengths. In D. H. Olson, H. I. McCubbin, H. L. Barnes, A. S. Larsen, M. Muxen, & M. Wilson (Eds.), *Family inventories* (rev. ed.). St. Paul: Family Social Science, University of Minnesota.

Olweus, D. (1979). Stability of aggressive reaction patterns in males: A review. *Psychological Bulletin, 86,* 852–875.

Omizo, M. M., & Williams, R. E. (1981). Biofeedback training can calm the hyperactive child. *Academic Therapy, 17,* 43–46.

Oregon Death With Dignity Act, 2 Ore. Rev. Stat. §§ 127.800-127.897 (1997).

Organ, D. W., & Near, J. P. (1985). Cognition versus affect in measures of job satisfaction. *International Journal of Psychology, 20,* 241–253.

Ornduff, S. (1998). Rorschach variables and other data in the assessment of sexually abused girls. In B. Ritzler (Chair), *Cross-validation in projective assessment.* Symposium presented at the Society for Personality Assessment 1998 Midwinter Meeting, February 21.

Orne, M. T. (1979). The use and misuse of hypnosis in court. *International Journal of Clinical and Experimental Hypnosis, 27,* 311–341.

Orr, D. B., & Graham, W. R. (1968). Development of a listening comprehension test to identify educational potential among disadvantaged junior high school students. *American Educational Researcher Journal, 5,* 167–180.

Orr, F. C., DeMatteo, A., Heller, B., Lee, M., & Nguyen, M. (1987). Psychological assessment. In H. Elliott, L. Glass, & J. W. Evans (Eds.), *Mental health assessment of deaf clients* (pp. 93–106). Boston: Little, Brown.

Orr, R. R., Cameron, S. J., Dobson, L. A., & Day, D. M. (1993). Age-related changes in stress experienced by families with a child who has developmental delays. *Mental Retardation, 31,* 171–176.

Osgood, C. E., Suci, G. J., & Tannenbaum, P. H. (1957). *The measurement of meaning.* Urbana: University of Illinois.

Osipow, S. H., & Reed, R. (1985). Decision making style and career indecision in college students. *Journal of Vocational Behavior, 27,* 368–373.

Osman, A., Gifford, J., Jones, T., et al. (1993). Psychometric evaluation of the Reasons for Living Inventory. *Psychological Assessment, 5,* 154–158.

OSS Assessment Staff. (1948). *Assessment of men: Selection of personnel for the Office of Strategic Service.* New York: Rinehart.

Ouellette, S. E. (1988). The use of projective drawing techniques in the personality assessment of prelingually deafened young adults: A pilot study. *American Annals of the Deaf, 133,* 212–217.

Outtz, J. (1994, June). Cited In T. DeAngelis, New tests allow takers to tackle real-life problems. *APA Monitor, 25,* 14.

Ozer, D. J. (1985). Correlation and the coefficient of determination. *Psychological Bulletin, 97,* 307–315.

Ozer, D. J., & Reise, S. P. (1994). Personality assessment. *Annual Review of Psychology, 45,* 357–388.

Ozonoff, S. (1995). Reliability and validity of the Wisconsin Card Sorting Test in studies of autism. *Neuropsychology, 9,* 491–500.

Pack v. K-Mart. (1999). 166 F. 3d, 1300 (10th Cir.).

Padden, C. (1980). The deaf community and the culture of deaf people. In C. Baker & R. Battison (Eds.), *Sign language and the deaf community* (pp. 89–103). Washington, DC: National Association of the Deaf.

Padden, C., & Humphries, T. (1988). *Deaf in America: Voices from a culture.* Cambridge, MA: Harvard University.

Paget, K. D. (1985). Assessment in early childhood education. *Diagnostique, 10,* 76–87.

Palmore, E. (Ed.). (1970). *Normal aging.* Durham, NC: Duke University.

Panell, R. C., & Laabs, G. J. (1979). Construction of a criterion-referenced, diagnostic test for an individualized instruction program. *Journal of Applied Psychology, 64,* 255–261.

Pannbacker, M., & Middleton, G. (1992). Review of Wepman's Auditory Discrimination Test, Second Edition. In J. J. Kramer & J. C. Conoley (Eds.), *The eleventh mental measurements yearbook.* Lincoln: Buros Institute of Mental Measurements, University of Nebraska.

Panter, A. T., Swygert, K. A., Dahlstrom, W. G., & Tanaka, J. S. (1997). Factor analytic approaches to personality item-level data. *Journal of Personality Assessment, 68,* 561–589.

Paolo, A. M., & Ryan, J. J. (1991). Application of WAIS-R short forms to persons 75 years of age and older. *Journal of Psychoeducational Assessment, 9,* 345–352.

Parette, H. P., & Brotherson, M. J. (1996). Family participation in assistive technology assessment for young children with mental retardation and developmental disabilities. *Education & Training in Mental Retardation & Developmental Disabilities, 31,* 29–43.

Parke, R. D., Hymel, S., Power, T., & Tinsley, B. (1977, November). Fathers and risk: A hospital based model of intervention. In D. B. Sawin (Chair), *Symposium on psychosocial risks during infancy.* Austin: University of Texas at Austin.

Parke, R. D., & Sawin, D. B. (1975, April). *Infant characteristics and behavior as elicitors of maternal and paternal responsivity in the newborn period.* Paper presented at themeetings of the Society for Research in Child Development, Denver, CO.

Parker, K. C. H., Hanson, R. K., & Hunsley, J. (1988). MMPI, Rorschach, and WAIS: A meta-analytic comparison of reliability, stability, and validity. *Psychological Bulletin, 103,* 367–373.

Parker, T., & Abramson, P. R. (1995). The law hath not been dead: Protecting adults with mental retardation from sexual abuse and violation of their sexual freedom. *Mental Retardation, 33,* 257–263.

Parkes, L. P., Bochner, S., & Schneider, S. K. (2001). Person-organisation fit across cultures: An empirical investigation of individualism and collectivism. *Applied Psychology: An International Review, 50,* 81–108.

Parnes, H. S., & Less, L. J. (1985). Introduction and overview. In H. S. Parnes, J. E. Crowley, R. J. Haurin, et al. (Eds.), *Retirement among American men.* Lexington, MA: Lexington Books.

Parron, D. C., Solomon, F., & Jenkins, C. D. (Eds.). (1982). *Behavior, health risks, and social disadvantage.* Washington, DC: National Academy.

Pascal, G. R., & Suttell, B. J. (1951). *The Bender-Gestalt Test: Quantification and validity for adults.* New York: Grune & Stratton.

Patterson, W. M., Dohn, H. H., Bird, J., & Patterson, G. A. (1983). Evaluation of suicidal patients: The SAD PERSONS scale. *Psychosomatics, 24,* 343–349.

Paul, G. L. (1987). *The time-sample behavioral checklist: Observational assessment instrumentation for service and research.* Champaign, IL: Research.

Paul, V., & Jackson, D. W. (1993). *Toward a psychology of deafness.* Boston: Allyn & Bacon.

Paulhus, D. L. (1984). Two-component models of socially desirable responding. *Journal of Personality and Social Psychology, 46,* 598–609.

Paulhus, D. L. (1986). Self-deception and impression management in test responses. In A. Angleitner & J. S. Wiggins (Eds.), *Personality assessment via questionnaire* (pp. 142–165). New York: Springer.

Paulhus, D. L. (1990). Measurement and control of response bias. In J. P. Robinson, P. R. Shaver, & L. Wrightsman (Eds.), *Measures of personality and social-psychological attitudes* (pp. 17–59). San Diego, CA: Academic Press.

Paulhus, D. L., & Levitt, K. (1987). Desirable response triggered by affect: Automatic egotism? *Journal of Personality and Social Psychology, 52,* 245–259.

Paulhus, D. L., & Reid, D. B. (1991). Enhancement and denial in socially desirable responding. *Journal of Personality and Social Psychology, 60,* 307–317.

Paullay, I. M., Alliger, G. M., & Stone-Romero, E. F. (1994). Construct validation of two instruments designed to measure job involvement and work centrality. *Journal of Applied Psychology, 79,* 224–228.

Pavot, W., & Diener, E. (1993). Review of the Satisfaction with Life Scale. *Psychological Assessment, 5,* 164–172.

Pearson, K., & Moul, M. (1925). The problem of alien immigration of Great Britain illustrated by an examination of Russian and Polish Jewish children. *Annals of Eugenics, 1,* 5–127.

Pedersen, D. M., Shinedling, M. M., & Johnson, D. L. (1968). Effects of sex of examiner and subject on children's quan-titative test performance. *Journal of Personality and Social Psychology, 10,* 251–254.

Pennsylvania Department of Corrections v. Yeskey (1998). 118 F. 3d, 168.

Perez, J. A., Dasi, F., & Lucas, A. (1997). Length overestimation bias as a product of normative pressure arising from anthropocentric vs. geocentric representations of length. *Swiss Journal of Psychology, 56,* 243–255.

Perry, C., & Laurence, J. R. (1990). Hypnosis with a criminal defendant and a crime witness: Two recent related cases. *International Journal of Clinical and Experimental Hypnosis, 38,* 266–282.

Perry, S. (1989). Warning third parties at risk for AIDS: Policy is barrier to treatment. *Hospital and Community Psychiatry, 40,* 158–161.

Peterson, C. A. (1997). *The twelfth mental measurements yearbook:* Testing the tests. *Journal of Personality Assessment, 68,* 717–719.

Peterson, N. S., & Novick, M. R. (1976). An evaluation of some models for culture-fair selection. *Journal of Educational Measurement, 13,* 3–29.

Petrie, K., & Chamberlain, K. (1985). The predictive validity of the Zung Index of Potential Suicide. *Journal of Personality Assessment, 49,* 100–102.

Petty, M. M., McGhee, G. W., & Cavender, J. W. (1984). A meta-analysis of the relationships between individual job satisfaction and individual performance. *Academy of Management Review, 9,* 712–721.

Pfeiffer, E. (1975). A Short Portable Mental Status Questionnaire for the assessment of organic brain deficit in elderly patients. *Journal of the American Geriatric Society, 23,* 433–441.

Phelps, L. (1994). MMPI-2 and MMPI-A computerized interpretation: An adjunct to quality mental health service. *Measurement and Evaluation in Counseling and Development, 27,* 186–189.

Phelps, L., & Branyon, B. (1988). Correlations among the Hiskey, K-ABC Nonverbal Scale, Leiter, and WISC-R Performance Scale with public school deaf children. *Journal of Psychoeducational Assessment, 6,* 354–358.

Phillips, B. A. (1996). Bringing culture to the forefront: Formulating diagnostic impressions of deaf and hard-of-hearing people at times of medical crisis. *Professional Psychology: Research and Practice, 27,* 137–144.

Phillipson, H. (1955). *The object relations technique.* Glencoe, IL: Free Press.

Piaget, J. (1954). *The construction of reality on the child.* New York: Basic.

Piaget, J. (1971). *Biology and knowledge.* Chicago: University of Chicago.

Piedmont, R. L., & McCrae, R. R. (1996). *Are validity scales valid in volunteer samples? Evidence from self-reports and observer ratings.* Unpublished manuscript, Loyola College, Maryland.

Piedmont, R. L., McCrae, R. R., Riemann, R., & Angleitner, A. (2000). On the invalidity of validity scales: Evidence from self-reports and observer ratings in volunteer samples. *Journal of Personality and Social Psychology, 78,* 582–593.

Piers, E. V. (1969). *Manual for the Piers-Harris Children's Self-Concept Scale.* Nashville: Counselor Recordings and Tests.

Pilgrim, C., Luo, Q., Urberg, K. A., & Fang, X. (1999). Influence of peers, parents, and individual characteristics on adolescent drug use in two cultures. *Merrill-Palmer Quarterly, 45,* 85–107.

Pincus, J. H., & Tucker, G. J. (1974). *Behavioral neurology.* New York: Oxford University.

Pintner, R. (1931). *Intelligence testing.* New York: Holt.

Piotrowski, C. (1996a). The status of Exner's Comprehensive System in contemporary research. *Perceptual and Motor Skills, 82,* 1341–1342.

Piotrowski, C. (1996b). The Rorschach in contemporary forensic psychology. *Psychological Reports, 78,* 458.

Piotrowski, C. (1996c). Use of the Rorschach in forensic practice. *Perceptual and Motor Skills, 82,* 254.

Piotrowski, C., Belter, R. W., & Keller, J. W. (1998). The impact of "managed care" on the practice of psychological testing: Preliminary findings. *Journal of Personality Assessment, 70,* 441–446.

Piotrowski, C., & Keller, J. W. (1989). Psychological testing in outpatient mental health facilities: A national study. *Professional Psychology: Research and Practice, 20*(4), 423–425.

Piotrowski, C., & Keller, J. W. (1992). Psychological testing in applied settings: A literature review from 1982–1992. *Journal of Training and Practice in Professional Psychology, 6,* 74–82.

Piotrowski, C., & Lubin, B. (1990). Assessment practices of health psychologists: Survey of APA Division 38 clinicians. *Professional Psychology: Research and Practice, 21,* 99–106.

Piotrowski, Z. (1957). *Perceptanalysis.* New York: Macmillan.

Pitasky, V. M. (1998). IDEA: The year in review. *Today's School Psychologist, 6*(1), 1, 7–12.

Pittenger, D. J. (1993). The utility of the Myers-Briggs Type Indicator. *Review of Educational Research, 63,* 467–488.

Plucker, J. A., & Levy, J. J. (2001). The downside of being talented. *American Psychologist, 56,* 75–76.

Plutchik, R., & Conte, H. R. (1989). Measuring emotions and the derivatives of emotions: Personality traits, ego defenses, and coping styles. In S. Wetzler & M. M. Katz (Eds.), *Contemporary approaches to psychological assessment.* New York: Brunner/Mazel.

Polatajko, H. J., Law, M., Miller, J., Schaffer, R., & Macnab, J. (1991). The effect of a sensory integration program on academic achievement, motor performance, and self-esteem in children identified as learning disabled. *Occupational Therapy Journal of Research, 11,* 155–176.

Polizzi, D. (1998). Contested space: Assessment in the home and the combative marriage. In L. Handler (Chair), *Conducting assessments in clients' homes: Contexts, surprises, dilemmas, opportunities.* Symposium presented at the Society for Personality Assessment 1998 Midwinter Meeting, February 20.

Pollard, R. Q. (1993). 100 years in psychology and deafness: A centennial retrospective. *Journal of the American Deafness & Rehabilitation Association, 26,* 32–46.

Pomplun, M., & Omar, M. H. (2000). Score comparability of a state mathematics assessment across students with and without reading accommodations. *Journal of Applied Psychology, 85,* 21–29.

Pomplun, M., & Omar, M. H. (2001). Score comparability of a state reading assessment across selected groups of students with disabilities. *Structural Equation Modeling, 8,* 257–274.

Ponterotto, J. G., Pace, T. M., & Kaven, M. G. (1989). A counselor's guide to the assessment of depression. *Journal of Counseling and Development, 67,* 301–309.

Ponterotto, J. G., Rivera, L., & Sueyoshi, L. A. (2000). The Career-in-Culture interview: A semi-structured protocol for the cross-cultural intake interview. *Career Development Quarterly, 49,* 85–96.

Popham, W. J. (1993). Educational testing in America: What's right, what's wrong? *Educational Measurement: Issues and Practice, 12,* 11–14.

Porter, L., Steers, R. T., Mowday, R. T., & Boulian, P. V. (1974). Organizational commitment, job satisfaction and individual performance. *Journal of Applied Psychology, 59,* 603–609.

Porter, L. W., Steers, R. W., Mowday, R. T., & Boulian, P. V. (1974). Organizational commitment, job satisfaction, and

turnover among psychiatric technicians. *Journal of Applied Psychology, 59,* 603–609.

Porteus, S. D. (1933). *The Maze Test and mental differences.* Vineland, NJ: Smith Printing & Publishing.

Porteus, S. D. (1942). *Qualitative performance in the Maze Test.* San Antonio: Psychological Corporation.

Porteus, S. D. (1955). *The Maze Test: Recent advances.* Palo Alto, CA: Pacific Books.

Powell, D. H. (1994). *Profiles in cognitive aging.* Cambridge, MA: Harvard University Press.

Prater, G. F. (1957). Cited in Swenson, C. H., Jr. Empirical evaluations of human figure drawings. *Psychological Bulletin, 54,* 431–466.

Preston, R. (1961). Improving the item validity of study habits inventories. *Educational and Psychological Measurement, 21,* 129–131.

Price, G., Dunn, R., & Dunn, K. (1982). *Productivity Environmental Survey manual.* Lawrence, KS: Price Systems.

Prifitera, A., Weiss, L. G., & Saklofske, D. (1998). The WISC-III in context. In A. Prifitera & D. Saklofske (Eds.), *WISC-III clinical use and interpretation: A scientist-practitioner perspective* (pp. 1–39). San Diego, CA: Academic Press.

Prince, R. J., & Guastello, S. J. (1990). The Barnum Effect in a computerized Rorschach interpretation system. *Journal of Psychology: Interdisciplinary and Applied, 124,* 217–222.

Procedures for evaluating specific learning disabilities. (1977). *Federal Register,* December 29, Part III.

Procidano, M. E., & Heller, K. (1983). Measures of perceived social support from friends and from family: Three validation studies. *American Journal of Community Psychology, 11,* 1–24.

Prout, H. T., & Phillips, P. D. (1974). A clinical note: The kinetic school drawing. *Psychology in the Schools, 11,* 303–396.

Psychological Corporation, The. (1992a). *Wechsler Individual Achievement Test.* San Antonio: Author.

Psychological Corporation, The. (1992b). *Wechsler Individual Achievement Test manual.* San Antonio: Author.

Psychological Corporation, The. (2001). *Wechsler Individual Achievement Test-Second Edition.* San Antonio: Author.

Pulakos, E. D. (1986). The development of training programs to increase accuracy with different rating tasks. *Organizational Behavior and Human Decision Processes, 38,* 76–91.

Pullen, L., & Gow, K. (2000). University students elaborate on what young persons "at risk of suicide" need from listeners. *Journal of Applied Health Behaviour, 2,* 32–39.

Putnam, W. H. (1979). Hypnosis and distortions in eyewitness memory. *The International Journal of Clinical and Experimental Hypnosis, 27,* 437–448.

Q and A on balancing the SAT scores. (1994). New York: College Board.

Qu, C., Zhang, P., Zheng, R., et al. (1992). An examination of the IQs of 319 hearing-impaired students in 5 cities in China. *Chinese Mental Health Journal, 6,* 219–221.

Quay, H. C., & Peterson, C. (1983). *Manual for the Revised Behavior Problem Checklist.* Coral Gables, FL: Authors.

Quay, H. C., & Peterson, D. R. (1967). *Behavior Problem Checklist.* Champaign: University of Illinois Press.

Quill, T. E., Cassel, C. K., & Meier, D. E. (1992). Care of the hopelessly ill: Proposed clinical criteria for physician-assisted suicide. *New England Journal of Medicine, 327,* 1380–1384.

Quinsey, V. L., Chaplin, T. C., & Upfold, D. (1984). Sexual arousal to nonsexual violence and sadomasochistic themes among rapists and nonsex-offenders. *Journal of Consulting and Clinical Psychology, 52,* 651–657.

Quinsey, V. L., Steinman, C. M., Bergersen, S. G., & Holmes, T. F. (1975). Penile circumference, skin conductance, and ranking responses of child molesters and "normals" to sexual and non-sexual visual stimuli. *Behavior Therapy, 6*, 213–219.

Raifman, L. J., & Vernon, M. (1996). Important implications for psychologists of the Americans with Disabilities Act: Case in point, the patient who is deaf. *Professional Psychology: Research and Practice, 27*, 372–377.

Raju, N. S., Drasgow, F., & Slinde, J. A. (1993). An empirical comparison of the area methods, Lord's chi-square test, and the Mantel-Haenszel technique for assessing differential item functioning. *Educational and Psychological Measurement, 53*, 301–314.

Rakowski, W., Dube, C. E., Marcus, B. H., et al. (1992). Assessing elements of women's decisions about mammography. *Health Psychology, 11*, 111–118.

Ramirez, M., III. (1984). Assessing and understanding biculturalism-multiculturalism in Mexican-American adults. In J. L. Martinez, Jr., & R. H. Mendoza (Eds.), *Chicano psychology* (pp. 77–94). Orlando: Academic Press.

Ramseyer, G. C., & Cashen, V. M. (1971). The effect of practice sessions on the use of separate answer sheets by first and second graders. *Journal of Educational Measurement, 8*, 177–181.

Randall, A., Fairbanks, M. M., & Kennedy, M. L. (1986). Using think-aloud protocols diagnostically with college readers. *Reading Research & Instruction, 25*, 240–253.

Randall, D. M. (1987). Commitment and the organization: The organization man revisited. *Academy of Management Review, 12*, 460–471.

Randolph, C., Mohr, E., & Chase, T. N. (1993). Assessment of intellectual function in dementing disorders: Validity of WAIS-R short forms for patients with Alzheimer's, Huntington's, and Parkinson's disease. *Journal of Clinical and Experimental Neuropsychology, 15*, 743–753.

Ranseen, J. D., & Humphries, L. L. (1992). The intellectual functioning of eating disorder patients. *Journal of the American Academy of Child and Adolescent Psychiatry, 31*, 844–846.

Rapaport, D. (1946–1967). Principles underlying nonprojective tests of personality. In M. M. Gill (Ed.), *David Rapaport: Collected papers*. New York: Basic.

Rapaport, D., Gill, M. M., & Schafer, R. (1945–1946). *Diagnostic psychological testing* (2 vols.). Chicago: Year Book.

Rapaport, D., Gill, M. M., & Schafer, R. (1968). R. R. Holt (Ed.), *Diagnostic psychological testing*. (rev. ed.). New York: International Universities.

Rappeport, J. R. (1982). Differences between forensic and general psychiatry. *American Journal of Psychiatry, 139*, 331–334.

Raskin, D. C., & Yuille, J. C. (1987). Problems of evaluating interviews of children in sexual abuse cases. In S. J. Ceci, M. P. Toglia, & D. F. Ross (Eds.), *New perspectives on the child witness*. New York: Springer-Verlag.

Raven, J. C. (1976). *Standard Progressive Matrices*. Oxford: Oxford Psychologists.

Raz, S., Glogowski-Kawamoto, B., Yu, A. W., et al. (1998). The effects of perinatal hypoxic risk on developmental outcome in early and middle childhood: A twin study. *Neuropsychology, 12*, 459–467.

Razran, G. (1961). The observable unconscious and the inferable conscious in current Soviet psychophysiology: Introceptive conditioning, semantic conditioning, and the orienting reflex. *Psychological Review, 68*, 81–147.

Recarte, M. A., & Nunes, L. M. (2000). Effects of verbal and spatial-imagery tasks on eye fixations while driving. *Journal of Experimental Psychology: Applied, 6*, 31–43.

Reckase, M. D. (1996). Test construction in the 1990s: Recent approaches every psychologist should know. *Psychological Assessment, 8*, 354–359.

Record, R. G., McKeown, T., & Edwards, J. H. (1969). The relationship of measured intelligence to birth order and maternal age. *Annals of Human Genetics, 33*, 61–69.

Ree, M. J., & Earles, J. A. (1990). *Differential validity of a differential aptitude test* (Rpt 89–59). Texas: Brooks Air Force Base.

Reece, R. N., & Groden, M. A. (1985). Recognition of non-accidental injury. *Pediatric Clinics of North America, 32*, 41–60.

Reed, G. M., Levant, R. F., Stout, C. E., et al. (2001). Psychology in the current mental health marketplace. *Professional Psychology: Research and Practice, 32*, 65–70.

Reed, H. B. C., Jr., Reitan, R. M., & Klove, H. (1965). Influence of cerebral lesions on psychological test performances of older children. *Journal of Consulting Psychology, 19*, 247–251.

Reed, T. E. (1997). "The genetic hypothesis": It was not tested but it could have been. *American Psychologist, 52*, 77–78.

Reed, T. E., & Jensen, A. R. (1992). Conduction velocity in a brain nerve pathway of normal adults correlates with intelligence level. *Intelligence, 16*, 259–272.

Reed, T. E., & Jensen, A. R. (1993). Choice reaction time and visual pathway conduction velocity both correlate with intelligence but appear not to correlate with each other: Implications for information processing. *Intelligence, 17*, 191–203.

Reeder, G. D., Maccow, G. C., Shaw, S. R., Swerdlik, M. E., Horton, C. B., & Foster, P. (1997). School psychologists and full-service schools: Partnerships with medical, mental health, and social services. *School Psychology Review, 26*, 603–621.

Rees, D. W. (1985). Health beliefs and compliance with alcohol treatment. *Journal of Studies of Alcohol, 46*, 517–524.

Reichenberg, N., & Raphael, A. J. (1992). *Advanced psychodiagnostic interpretation of the Bender Gestalt Test: Adults and children*. Westport, CT: Praeger.

Reik, T. (1948). *Listening with the third ear*. New York: Farrar, Strauss.

Reik, T. (1952). *The secret self*. New York: Grove.

Reimers, T. M., Wacker, D. P., & Koeppel, G. (1987). Acceptability of behavioral treatments: A review of the literature. *School Psychology Review, 16*, 212–227.

Reinehr, R. C. (1969). Therapist and patient perceptions of hospitalized alcoholics. *Journal of Clinical Psychology, 25*, 443–445.

Reise, S. P., Waller, N. G., & Comrey, A. L. (2000). Factor analysis and scale revision. *Psychological Assessment, 12*, 287–297.

Reiser, M. (1980). *Handbook of investigative hypnosis*. Los Angeles: Lehi.

Reiser, M. (1990). Investigative hypnosis. In D. C. Raskin (Ed.), *Psychological methods in criminal investigation evidence* (pp. 151–190). New York: Springer.

Reitan, R. (1994, July). *Child neuropsychology and learning disabilities*. Advanced Workshop, Los Angeles.

Reitan, R. M. (1955a). An investigation of the validity of Halstead's measures of biological intelligence. *Archives of Neurology and Psychiatry, 73*, 28–35.

Reitan, R. M. (1955b). Certain differential effects of left and right cerebral lesions in human adults. *Journal of Comparative and Physiological Psychology, 48*, 474–477.

Reitan, R. M. (1969). *Manual for administration of neuropsychological test batteries for adults and children*. Indianapolis: Author.

Reitan, R. M. (1984a). *Aphasia and sensory-perceptual disorders in adults*. South Tucson, AZ: Neuropsychology Press.

Reitan, R. M. (1984b). *Aphasia and sensory-perceptual disorders in children*. South Tucson, AZ: Neuropsychology Press.

Reitan, R. M. (1994). Ward Halstead's contributions to neuropsychology and the Halstead-Reitan Neuropsychological Test Battery. *Journal of Clinical Psychology, 50*, 47–70.

Reitan, R. M., & Davison, L. A. (1974). *Clinical neuropsychology: Current status and applications*. New York: Winston/Wiley.

Reitan, R. M., & Wolfson, D. (1990). A consideration of the comparability of the WAIS and WAIS-R. *Clinical Neuropsychologist, 4,* 80–85.

Reitan, R. M., & Wolfson, D. (1992). A short screening examination for impaired brain functions in early school-age children. *Clinical Neuropsychologist, 6,* 287–294.

Reitan, R. M., & Wolfson, D. (1993). *The Halstead-Reitan Neuropsychological Test Battery: Theory and clinical interpretation* (2nd ed.). Tucson: Neuropsychology Press.

Reitan, R. M., & Wolfson, D. (2000). The neuropsychological similarities of mild and more severe head injury. *Archives of Clinical Neuropsychology, 15,* 433–442.

Remington, R. W., Johnston, J. C., Ruthruff, E., et al. (2000). Visual search in complex displays: Factors affecting conflict detection by air traffic controllers. *Visual Cognition, 7,* 769–784.

Remzy, I., & Pickard, P. M. (1949). A study in the reliability of scoring the Rorschach inkblot test. *Journal of General Psychology, 40,* 3–10.

Renwick, R., et al. (Eds.). (1996). *Quality of life in health promotion and rehabilitation: Conceptual approaches, issues, and applications.* Thousand Oaks, CA: Sage.

Resnick, P. J. (1988). Malingered psychosis. In R. Rogers (Ed.), *Clinical assessment of malingering and deception* (pp. 34–53). New York: Guilford.

Retzlaff, P. (1995a). *Tactical psychotherapy of the personality disorders: An MCMI-III-based approach.* Boston: Allyn & Bacon.

Retzlaff, P. (1995b). Review of the Millon Adolescent Clinical Inventory. In J. C. Conoley & J. C. Impara (Eds.), *The twelfth mental measurements yearbook* (pp. 620–622). Lincoln: Buros Institute of Mental Measurements, University of Nebraska.

Retzlaff, P. D., & Gibertini, M. (1988). Objective psychological testing of U.S. Air Force officers in pilot training. *Aviation, Space, and Environmental Medicine, 59,* 661–663.

Rey, G. J., Feldman, E., Rivas-Vazquez, R., et al. (1999). Neuropsychological test development and normative data on Hispanics. *Archives of Clinical Neuropsychology, 14,* 593–601.

Reynolds, C. E., & Brown, R. T. (Eds.). (1984). *Perspectives on bias in mental testing.* New York: Plenum.

Reynolds, C. R., Sanchez, S., & Wilson, V. L. (1996). Normative tables for calculating the WISC-III Performance and Full Scale IQs when Symbol Search is substituted for Coding. *Psychological Assessment, 8,* 378–382.

Reynolds, S. E. (1984). Battle of the experts revisited: 1983 Oregon legislation on the insanity defense. *Willamette Law Review, 20,* 303–317.

Reynolds, W. M. (1987). *Suicidal Ideation Questionnaire.* Odessa, FL: Psychological Assessment Resources.

Rezmovic, V. (1977). The effects of computerized experimentation on response variance. *Behavior Research Methods and Instrumentation, 9,* 144–147.

Reznikoff, M., & Tomblen, D. (1956). The use of human figure drawings in the diagnosis of organic pathology. *Journal of Consulting Psychology, 20,* 467–470.

Rice, M. E., & Harris, G. T. (1995). Violent recidivism: Assessing predictive validity. *Journal of Consulting and Clinical Psychology, 63,* 737–748.

Richardson, M. W., & Kuder, G. F. (1939). The calculation of test reliability based upon the method of rational equivalence. *Journal of Educational Psychology, 30,* 681–687.

Richman, D. M., Berg, W. K., Wacker, D. P., Stephens, T., Rankin, B., & Kilroy, J. (1997). Using pretreatment and posttreatment assessments to enhance and evaluate existing treatment packages. *Journal of Applied Behavior Analysis, 30,* 709–712.

Richman, J. (1988). The case against rational suicide. *Suicide & Life-Threatening Behavior, 18,* 285–289.

Richters, J. E., & Hinshaw, S. (1999). The abduction of disorder in psychiatry. *Journal of Abnormal Psychology, 108,* 438–445.

Rierdan, J., & Koff, E. (1981). Sexual ambiguity in children's human figure drawings. *Journal of Personality Assessment, 45,* 256–257.

Riethmiller, R. J., & Handler, L. (1997a). Problematic methods and unwarranted conclusions in DAP research: Suggestions for improved research procedures. *Journal of Personality Assessment, 69,* 459–475.

Riethmiller, R. J., & Handler, L. (1997b). The great figure drawing controversy: The integration of research and clinical practice. *Journal of Personality Assessment, 69,* 488–496.

Riggs, D. S., Murphy, C. M., & O'Leary, K. D. (1989). Intentional falsification in reports of interpartner aggression. *Journal of Interpersonal Violence, 4,* 220–232.

Ritson, B., & Forest, A. (1970). The simulation of psychosis: A contemporary presentation. *British Journal of Medical Psychology, 43,* 31–37.

Ritzler, B. (1995). Putting your eggs in the content analysis basket: A response to Aronow, Reznikoff and Moreland. *Journal of Personality Assessment, 64,* 229–234.

Ritzler, B. A., Sharkey, K. J., & Chudy, J. F. (1980). A comprehensive projective alternative to the TAT. *Journal of Personality Assessment, 44,* 358–362.

Riverside Publishing. (2001). *Report Writer for the WJ III.* Itasca, IL: Author.

Roach, R. J., Frazier, L. P., & Bowden, S. R. (1981). The Marital Satisfaction Scale: Development of a measure for intervention research. *Journal of Marriage and the Family, 21,* 251–255.

Roback, A. A. (1961). *History of psychology and psychiatry.* New York: Philosophical Library.

Robbins, S. B., & Patton, M. J. (1985). Self-psychology and career development: Construction of the Superiority and Goal Instability Scales. *Journal of Counseling Psychology, 32,* 221–231.

Roberts, B. W., & DelVecchio, W. F. (2000). The rank-order consistency of personality traits from childhood to old age: A quantitative review of longitudinal studies. *Psychological Bulletin, 126,* 3–25.

Roberts, M. W. (2001). Clinic observations of structured parent-child interaction designed to evaluate externalizing disorders. *Psychological Assessment, 13,* 46–58.

Roberts, R. N., & Magrab, P. R. (1991). Psychologists' role in a family-centered approach to practice, training, and research with young children. *American Psychologist, 46,* 144–148.

Robertson, G. J. (1990). A practical model for test development. In C. R. Reynolds & R. W. Kamphaus (Eds.), *Handbook of psychological and educational assessment of children: Intelligence & achievement* (pp. 62–85). New York: Guilford.

Robin, A. L., Koepke, T., & Moye, A. (1990). Multidimensional assessment of parent-adolescent relations. *Psychological Assessment, 2,* 451–459.

Robins, R. W., John, O. P., & Caspi, A. (1998). The typological approach to studying personality. In R. B. Cairns et al. (Eds.), *Methods and models for studying the individual* (pp. 135–160). Thousand Oaks, CA: Sage.

Robinson, F. G. (1992). *Love's story untold: The life of Henry A. Murray.* Cambridge, MA: Harvard University.

Robinson, N. M., Zigler, E., & Gallagher, J. J. (2000). Two tails of the normal curve: Similarities and differences in the study of mental retardation and giftedness. *American Psychologist, 55,* 1413–1424.

Rodriguez, O., & Santiviago, M. (1991). Hispanic deaf adolescents: A multicultural minority. *Volta Review, 93,* 89–97.

Roe, A., & Klos, D. (1969). Occupational classification. *Counseling Psychologist, 1,* 84–92.

Roe, A., & Siegelman, M. (1964). *The origin of interests.* Washington, DC: American Personnel and Guidance Association.

Rogers, C. R. (1959). A theory of therapy, personality, and interpersonal relationships, as developed in the client-centered framework In S. Koch (Ed.), *Psychology: A study of a science* (Vol. 3; pp. 184–256). New York: McGraw-Hill.

Rogers, L. S., Knauss, J., & Hammond, K. R. (1951). Predicting continuation in therapy by means of the Rorschach Test. *Journal of Consulting Psychology, 15*, 368–371.

Rogers, R. (1986). *Structured interview of reported symptoms (SIRS).* Unpublished scale. Toronto: Clarke Institute of Psychiatry.

Rogers, R., Bagby, R. M., & Dickens, S. E. (1992). *Structured Interview of Reported Symptoms (SIRS) and professional manual.* Odessa, FL: Psychological Assessment Resources.

Rogers, R., & Cavanaugh, J. L. (1980). Differences in psychological variables between criminally responsible and insane patients: A preliminary study. *American Journal of Forensic Psychiatry, 1*, 29–37.

Rogers, R., & Cavanaugh, J. L. (1981). Rogers Criminal Responsibility Assessment Scales. *Illinois Medical Journal, 160*, 164–169.

Rogers, R., Dolmetsch, R., & Cavanaugh, J. L. (1981). An empirical approach to insanity evaluations. *Journal of Clinical Psychology, 37*, 683–687.

Rogers, R., Seman, W., & Wasyliw, D. E. (1983). The RCRAS and legal insanity: A cross validation study. *Journal of Clinical Psychology, 39*, 554–559.

Rogers, R., Sewell, K. W., & Salekin, R. T. (1994). A meta-analysis of malingering on the MMPI-2. *Assessment, 1*, 227–237.

Rogers, R., Wasyliw, D. E., & Cavanaugh, J. L. (1984). Evaluating insanity: A study of construct validity. *Law & Human Behavior, 8*, 293–303.

Rohl, J. S. (1993). The Tower of Hanoi. Supplementary information supplied with *Jarrah Wooden Tower of Hanoi.* Mt. Lawley, Australia: Built-Rite Sales.

Rohner, R. P. (1984). Toward a conception of culture for cross-cultural psychology. *Journal of Cross-Cultural Psychology, 15*, 111–138.

Rokeach, M. (1973). *The nature of human values.* New York: Free Press.

Romanczyk, R. G. (1986). *Clinical utilization of microcomputer technology.* New York: Pergamon.

Romano, J. (1994, November 7). Do drunken drivers get railroaded? *New York Times,* pp. NNJ1, NNJ19.

Rome, H. P., Mataya, P., Pearson, J. S., Swenson, W., & Brannick, T. L. (1965). Automatic personality assessment. In R. W. Stacey & B. Waxman (Eds.), *Computers in biomedical research* (Vol. 1; pp. 505–524). New York: Academic Press.

Romei, J. (1998). Evaluating sexuality and separation-individuation on the SCT and TAT. In H. Potash (Chair), *TAT and SCT: New scorings, interpretations and intercorrelations.* Symposium presented at the Society for Personality Assessment 1998 Midwinter Meeting, February 21.

Ronan, G. G., Date, A. L., & Weisbrod, M. (1995). Personal problem-solving scoring of the TAT: Sensitivity to training. *Journal of Personality Assessment, 64*, 119–131.

Rorer, L. G. (1965). The great response-style myth. *Psychological Bulletin, 63*, 129–156.

Rorschach, H. (1921/1942). *Psycho-diagnostics: A diagnostic test based on perception* (P. Lemkau & B. Kronenburg, Trans.). Berne: Huber. (First German edition: 1921. Distributed in the United States by Grune & Stratton.)

Rorschach, H., & Oberholzer, E. (1923). The application of the interpretation of form to psychoanalysis. *Journal of Nervous and Mental Diseases, 60*, 225–248, 359–379.

Rosen, J. (1998, February 23/March 2). Damage control. *New Yorker, 74*, 64–68.

Rosen, M., Simon, E. W., & McKinsey, L. (1995). Subjective measure of quality of life. *Mental Retardation, 33*, 31–34.

Rosenman, R. H., Brand, R. J., Jenkins, C. D., Friedman, M., Straus, R., & Wurm, M. (1975). Coronary heart disease in the Western Collaborative Group Study: Final followup experience of 8½ years. *Journal of the American Medical Association, 233*, 872–877.

Rosenthal, R. (1991). *Meta-analytic procedures for social research* (rev. ed.). Newbury Park, CA: Sage.

Rosenzweig, S. (1945). The picture-association method and its application in a study of reactions to frustration. *Journal of Personality, 14*, 3–23.

Rosenzweig, S. (1950). *Revised scoring manual for the Rosenzweig Picture-Frustration Study, Form for Adults.* St. Louis, MO: Author.

Rosenzweig, S. (1978). *The Rosenzweig Picture Frustration (P-F) Study: Basic Manual.* St. Louis, MO: Rana House.

Rosenzweig, S., Fleming, E. E., & Clarke, H. J. (1947). Revised scoring manual for the Rosenzweig Picture-Frustration Study. *Journal of Psychology, 26*, 141–191.

Rosenzweig, S., Fleming, E. E., & Rosenzweig, L. (1948). The children's form of the Rosenzweig Picture-Frustration Study. *Journal of Psychology, 24*, 165–208.

Rossini, E. D., & Moretti, R. J. (1997). Thematic Apperception Test (TAT) interpretation: Practice recommendations from a survey of clinical psychology doctoral programs accredited by the American Psychological Association. *Professional Psychology, 28*, 393–398.

Roszkowski, M. J., & Spreat, S. (1981). A comparison of the psychometric and clinical methods of determining level of mental retardation. *Applied Research in Mental Retardation, 2*, 359–366.

Rothberg, J. M., & Geer-Williams, C. (1992). A comparison and review of suicide prediction scales. In R. W. Maris et al. (Eds.), *Assessment and prediction of suicide* (pp. 202–217). New York: Guilford.

Rotter, J. B. (1966). Generalized expectancies for internal versus external control of reinforcement. *Psychological Monographs, 80* (Whole Number 609).

Rotter, J. B., Lah, M. I., & Rafferty, J. E. (1992). *Rotter Incomplete Sentences Blank manual.* San Antonio: Psychological Corporation.

Rotter, J. B., & Rafferty, J. E. (1950). *The manual for the Rotter Incomplete Sentences Blank.* New York: Psychological Corporation.

Rotton, J., & Kelly, I. W. (1985). Much ado about the full moon: A meta-analysis of lunar-lunacy research. *Psychological Bulletin, 97*, 286–306.

Rotundo, M., & Sackett, P. R. (1999). Effect of rater race on conclusions regarding differential prediction in cognitive ability tests. *Journal of Applied Psychology, 84*, 815–822.

Rouse, S. V., Butcher, J. N., & Miller, K. B. (1999). Assessment of substance abuse in psychotherapy clients: The effectiveness of MMPI-2 substance abuse scales. *Psychological Assessment, 11*, 101–107.

Routh, D. K., & King, K. W. (1972). Social class bias in clinical judgment. *Journal of Consulting and Clinical Psychology, 38*, 202–207.

Roy, P. (1962). The measurement of assimilation: The Spokane Indians. *American Journal of Sociology, 67*, 541–551.

Rozeboom, W. W. (1996a). What might common factors be? *Multivariate Behavioral Research, 31*, 555–570.

Rozeboom, W. W. (1996b). Factor-indeterminacy issues are not linguistic confusions. *Multivariate Behavioral Research, 31*, 637–650.

Rubenzer, S. J., Faschingbauer, T. R., & Ones, D. S. (2000). Assessing the U.S. presidents using the revised NEO Personality Inventory. *Assessment, 7*, 403–420.

Rubin, L. S. (1974). The utilization of pupillometry in the differential diagnosis and treatment of psychotic and behavioral disorders. In M. P. Janisse (Ed.), *Pupillary dynamics and behavior* (pp. 75–134). New York: Plenum.

Rubin, S. (1964). A comparison of the Thematic Apperception Test stories of two IQ groups. *Journal of Projective Techniques, 28,* 81–85.

Ruch, G. M. (1925). Minimum essentials in reporting data on standard tests. *Journal of Educational Research, 12,* 349–358.

Ruch, G. M. (1933). Recent developments in statistical procedures. *Review of Educational Research, 3,* 33–40.

Ruch, W. (1993). Exhilaration and humor. In M. Lewis & J. M. Haviland (Eds.), *Handbook of emotions* (pp. 605–616). New York: Guilford.

Ruffolo, L. F., Guilmette, T. J., & Grant, W. W. (2000). Comparison of time and error rates on the Trail Making Test among patients with head injuries, experimental malingerers, patients with suspect effort on testing, and normal controls. *Clinical Neuropsychologist, 14,* 223–230.

Rulon, P. J. (1939). A simplified procedure for determining the reliability of a test by split-halves. *Harvard Educational Review, 9,* 99–103.

Rupert, P. A., Kozlowski, N. F., Hoffman, L. A., et al. (1999). Practical and ethical issues in teaching psychological testing. *Professional Psychology: Research and Practice, 30,* 209–214.

Russ, S. W., & Niec, L. (1998). *Assessment of children's play and treatment planning.* Workshop presented at the Society for Personality Assessment 1998 Midwinter Meeting, February 18.

Russell, J. S. (1984). A review of fair employment cases in the field of training. *Personnel Psychology, 37,* 261–276.

Russell, M., & Karol, D. (1994). *The 16PF fifth edition administrator's manual.* Champaign, IL: Institute for Personality and Ability Testing.

Russo, D. C., Bird, B. L., & Masek, B. J. (1980). Assessment issues in behavioral medicine. *Behavioral Assessment, 2,* 1–18.

Ryan, A. M., Sacco, J. M., McFarland, L. A., & Kriska, S. D. (2000). Applicant self-selection: Correlates of withdrawal from a multiple hurdle process. *Journal of Applied Psychology, 85,* 163–169.

Ryan, J. J., Paolo, A. M., & Brungardt, T. M. (1990). Standardization of the Wechsler Adult Intelligence Scale—Revised for persons 75 years and older. *Psychological Assessment, 2,* 404–411.

Sabatelli, R. M. (1984). The Marital Comparison Level Index: A measure for assessing outcomes relative to expectations. *Journal of Marriage and the Family, 46,* 651–662.

Sacco, W. P., Levine, B., Reed, D. L., & Thompson, K. (1991). Attitudes about condom use as an AIDS-relevant behavior: Their factor structure and relation to condom use. *Psychological Assessment, 3,* 311–326.

Sachs, B. B. (1976). Some views of a deaf Rorschacher on the personality of deaf individuals. *Hearing Rehabilitation Quarterly, 2,* 13–14.

Sackett, P. R. (1994). Integrity testing for personnel selection. *Current Directions in Psychological Science, 3,* 73–76.

Sackett, P. R., Burris, L. R., & Callahan, C. (1989). Integrity testing for personnel selection: An update. *Personnel Psychology, 42,* 491–529.

Sackett, P. R., & Harris, M. M. (1984). Honesty testing for personnel selection: A review and critique. *Personnel Psychology, 37,* 221–245.

Sackett, P. R., Schmitt, N., Ellingson, J. E., & Kabin, M. B. (2001). High-stakes testing in employment, credentialing, and higher education: Prospects in a post-affirmative action world. *American Psychologist, 56,* 302–318.

Sackett, P. R., & Wilk, S. L. (1994). Within group norming and other forms of score adjustment in preemployment testing. *American Psychologist, 49,* 929–954.

Sacks, E. (1952). Intelligence scores as a function of experimentally established social relationships between child and examiner. *Journal of Abnormal and Social Psychology, 47,* 354–358.

Sacks, O. (1989). *Seeing voices: A journey into the world of the deaf.* Berkeley: University of California.

Salas, E., Cannon-Bowers, J. A., Church-Payne, S., & Smith-Jentsch, K. A. (1998). Teams and teamwork in the military. In C. Cronin (Ed.), *Military psychology: An introduction* (pp. 71–87). Needham Heights, MA: Simon & Schuster.

Sallis, J. F., Grossman, R. M., Pinsky, R. B., et al. (1987). The development of scales to measure social support for diet and exercise behaviors. *Preventive Medicine, 16,* 825–836.

Sallis, J. F., Hovell, M. F., & Hofstetter, C. R. (1992). Predictors of adaptation and maintenance of vigorous physical activity in men and women. *Preventive Medicine, 21,* 237–251.

Salthouse, T. A., Toth, J., Daniels, K., et al. (2000). Effects of aging on efficiency of task switching in a variant of the Trail Making Test. *Neuropsychology, 14,* 102–111.

Salvia, J., & Hritcko, T. (1984). The K-ABC and ability training. *Journal of Special Education, 18,* 345–356.

Samuda, R. J. (1982). *Psychological testing of American minorities: Issues and consequences.* New York: Harper & Row.

Samuel, W. (1977). Observed IQ as a function of test atmosphere, tester expectation, and race of tester: A replication for female subjects. *Journal of Educational Psychology, 69,* 593–604.

Sandelands, L. E., & Larson, J. R. (1985). When measurement causes task attitudes: A note from the laboratory. *Journal of Applied Psychology, 70,* 116–121.

Sandoval, J. (1995). Review of the Wechsler Intelligence Scale for Children, Third Edition. In J. C. Conoley & J. C. Impara (Eds.), *The twelfth mental measurements yearbook.* Lincoln: Buros Institute of Measurements, University of Nebraska.

Sandoval, J., et al. (Eds.) (1998). *Test interpretation and diversity: Achieving equity in assessment.* Washington, DC: American Psychological Association.

Sanfilippo, J., et al. (1986). Identifying the sexually molested preadolescent girl. *Pediatric Annals, 15,* 621–624.

Sanford, R. N. (1936). The effects of abstinence from food upon imaginal processes: A preliminary experiment. *Journal of Psychology, 2,* 129–136.

Sarason, I. G., Levine, H. M., Basham, R. B., & Sarason, B. R. (1983). Assessing social support: The Social Support Questionnaire. *Journal of Personality and Social Psychology, 44,* 127–139.

Sarnoff, D. (1982). Biofeedback: New uses in counseling. *Personnel and Guidance Journal, 60,* 357–360.

Satinsky, D., & Frerotte, A. (1981). Biofeedback treatment for headache: A two-year follow-up study. *American Journal of Clinical Biofeedback, 4,* 62–65.

Sattler, J. M. (1988). *Assessment of children* (3rd ed.). San Diego: Author.

Sattler, J. M. (1991). How good are federal judges in detecting differences in item difficulty on intelligence tests for ethnic groups? *Psychological Assessment, 3,* 125–129.

Sattler, J. M. (1992). Assessment of children: WISC-III and WPPSI-R supplement. San Diego: Author.

Sattler, J. M., & Gwynne, J. (1982). White examiners generally do not impede the intelligence test performance of black children: To debunk a myth. *Journal of Consulting and Clinical Psychology, 50,* 196–208.

Saunders, E. A. (1991). Rorschach indicators of chronic childhood sexual abuse in female borderline inpatients. *Bulletin of the Menninger Clinic, 55,* 48–65.

Savickas, M. L., Alexander, D. E., Osipow, S. H., & Wolf, F. M. (1985). Measuring specialty indecision among career-decided students. *Journal of Vocational Behavior, 27*, 356–357.

Sawyer, J. (1966). Measurement and prediction, clinical and statistical. *Psychological Bulletin, 66*, 178–200.

Saxe, L. (1994). Detection of deception: Polygraph and integrity tests. *Current Directions in Psychological Science, 3*, 69–73.

Saxe, L., & Ben-Shakhar, G. (1999). Admissibility of polygraph tests: The application of scientific standards post-*Daubert. Psychology, Public Policy, and Law, 5*, 203–223.

Saxton, J., McGonigle-Gibson, K. L., Swihart, A. A., Miller, V. J., & Boller, F. (1990). Assessment of the severely impaired patient: Description and validation of a new neuropsychological test battery. *Psychological Assessment, 2*, 298–303.

Sayer, A. G., Willett, J. B., & Perrin, E. C. (1993). Measuring understanding of illness causality in healthy children and in children with chronic illness: A construct validation. *Journal of Applied Developmental Psychology, 14*, 11–36.

Sayette, M. A., Shiffman, S., Tiffany, S. T., et al. (2000). The measurement of drug craving. *Addiction, 93*(Suppl. 2), S189–S210.

Saylor, C. F., Finch, A. J., Spirito, A., & Bennett, B. (1984). The Children's Depression Inventory: A systematic evaluation of psychometric properties. *Journal of Consulting and Clinical Psychology, 52*, 955–967.

Scarr, S. (1992). Developmental theories for the 1990s: Development and individual differences. *Child Development, 63*, 1–19.

Scarr, S. (1993). Biological and cultural diversity: The legacy of Darwin for development. *Child Development, 64*, 1333–1353.

Schade, C. P., Jones, E. R., Jr., & Wittlin, B. J. (1998, January). A ten-year review of the validity and clinical utility of depression screening. *Psychiatric Services, 49*, 55–61.

Schag, C. A., Heinrich, R. L., Aadland, R. L., & Ganz, P. A. (1990). Assessing problems of cancer patients: Psychometric properties of the cancer inventory of problem situations. *Health Psychology, 9*, 83–102.

Schaie, K. W. (1978). External validity in the assessment of intellectual development in adulthood. *Journal of Gerontology, 33*, 695–701.

Scheid, T. L. (1999). Employment of individuals with mental disabilities: Business response to the ADA's challenge. *Behavioral Sciences and the Law, 17*, 73–91.

Scheier, M., & Carver, C. (1987). Dispositional optimism and physical well-being: The influence of generalized outcome expectancies on health. *Journal of Personality, 55*, 169–210.

Schein, J. D., & Delk, M. T., Jr. (1974). *The deaf population in the United States.* Silver Springs, MD: National Association for the Deaf.

Schildroth, A., Rawlings, B., & Allen, T. (1991). Deaf students in transition: Education and employment issues for deaf adolescents. In O. Cohen & G. Long (Eds.), Selected issues in adolescence and deafness [Special issue]. *Volta Review, 93*(5), 41–53.

Schloss, I. (1981). Chicken and pickles. *Journal of Advertising Research, 21*, 47–49.

Schmand, B., Brand, N., & Kuipers, T. (1992). Procedural learning of cognitive and motor skills in psychotic patients. *Schizophrenia Research, 8*, 157–170.

Schmidt, F. L. (1988). The problem of group differences in ability scores in employment selection. *Journal of Vocational Behavior, 33*, 272–292.

Schmidt, F. L., & Hunter, J. E. (1974). Racial and ethnic bias in psychological tests: Divergent implications of two definitions of test bias. *American Psychologist, 29*, 1–8.

Schmidt, F. L., & Hunter, J. E. (1992). Development of a causal model of processes determining job performance. *Current Directions in Psychological Science, 1*, 89–92.

Schmidt, F. L., & Hunter, J. E. (1998). The validity and utility of selection methods in personnel psychology: Practical and theoretical implications of 85 years of research findings. *Psychological Bulletin, 124*, 262–274.

Schmidt, F. L., P. L., Hunter, J. E., McKenzie, R. C., & Muldrow, T. W. (1979). Impact of valid selection procedures on work force productivity. *Journal of Applied Psychology, 64*, 609–626.

Schmidt, F. L., Hunter, J. E., Outerbridge, A. N., & Trattner, M. H. (1986). The economic impact of job selection methods on size, productivity, and payroll costs of the federal work force: An empirically based demonstration. *Personnel Psychology, 32*, 1–29.

Schmitt, N. (1976). Social and situational determinants of interview decisions: Implications for the employment interview. *Personnel Psychology, 29*, 79–101.

Schmitt, N., Gooding, R., Noe, R., & Kirsch, M. (1984). Meta-analysis of validity studies published between 1964 and 1982 and the investigation of study characteristics. *Personnel Psychology, 37*, 407–422.

Schneider, B. (1987). The people make the place. *Personnel Psychology, 40*, 437–453.

Schneider, M. F. (1989). Children's Apperceptive Story-telling Test. Austin: PRO-ED.

Schneider, M. F., & Perney, J. (1990). Development of the Children's Apperceptive Story-Telling Test. *Psychological Assessment, 2*, 179–185.

Schönemann, P. H. (1966). A generalized solution of the orthogonal Procrustes problem. *Psychometrika, 31*, 1–10.

Schönemann, P. H. (1996a). The psychopathology of factor indeterminacy. *Multivariate Behavioral Research, 31*, 571–577.

Schönemann, P. H. (1996b). Syllogisms of factor indeterminacy. *Multivariate Behavioral Research, 31*, 651–654.

Schopp, L., Johnstone, B., & Merrell, D. (2000). Telehealth and neuropsychological assessment: New opportunities for psychologists. *Professional Psychology: Research and Practice, 31*, 179–183.

Schouten, P. G. W., & Kirkpatrick, L. A. (1993). Questions and concerns about the Miller Assessment for Preschoolers. *Occupational Therapy Journal of Research, 13*, 7–28.

Schuh, A. J. (1978). Contrast effect in the interview. *Bulletin of the Psychonomic Society, 11*, 195–196.

Schulte, A. A., Gilbertson, L., & Kratochwil, T. R. (2000). Educators' perceptions and documentation of testing accommodations for students with disabilities. *Special Services in the Schools, 16*, 35–56.

Schultz, B. M., Dixon, E. B., Lindenberger, J. C., & Ruther, N. J. (1989). *Solomon's sword: A practical guide to conducting child custody evaluations.* San Francisco: Jossey-Bass.

Schwartz, L. A. (1932). Social situation pictures in the psychiatric interview. *American Journal of Orthopsychiatry, 2*, 124–132.

Schwartz, N., Groves, R. M., & Schuman, H. (1998). Survey methods. In D. T. Gilbert et al. (Eds.), *The handbook of social psychology* (4th ed.; Vol. 1; pp. 143–179). New York: McGraw-Hill.

Schwitzgebel, R. L., & Rugh, J. D. (1975). Of bread, circuses and alpha machines. *American Psychologist, 30*, 363–370.

Scott, L. H. (1981). Measuring intelligence with the Goodenough-Harris Drawing Test. *Psychological Bulletin, 89*, 483–505.

Seagull, F. J., & Gopher, D. (1997). Training head movement in visual scanning: An embedded approach to the development of piloting skills with helmet-mounted displays. *Journal of Experimental Psychology: Applied, 3*, 163–180.

Sears, R. R. (1977). Sources of life satisfaction of the Terman gifted men. *American Psychologist, 32,* 119–281.

Seashore, C. E. (1938). *Psychology of music.* New York: McGraw-Hill.

Sebold, J. (1987). Indicators of child sexual abuse in males. *Social Casework, 68,* 75–80.

Segal, S. P., Redman, D., & Silverman, C. (2000). Measuring clients' satisfaction with self-help agencies. *Psychiatric Services, 51,* 1148–1152.

Sell, R. L. (1997). Defining and measuring sexual orientation: A review. *Archives of Sexual Behavior, 26,* 643–658.

Selover, R. B. (1949). Review of the Minnesota Clerical Test. In O. K. Buros (Ed.), *The third mental measurements yearbook* (pp. 635–636). New Brunswick, NJ: Rutgers University.

Semrud-Clikeman, M. (1990). Assessment of childhood depression. In C. R. Reynolds & R. W. Kamphaus (Eds.), *Handbook of psychological and educational assessment of children: Personality, behavior & context* (pp. 279–297). New York: Guilford.

Serby, M., Corwin, J., Conrad, P., et al. (1985). Olfactory dysfunction in Alzheimer's disease and Parkinson's disease. *American Journal of Psychiatry, 142,* 781–782.

Serby, M., Larson, P., & Kalkstein, D. (1991). The nature and course of olfactory deficits in Alzheimer's disease. *American Journal of Psychiatry, 148,* 357–360.

Seretny, M. L., Dean, R. S., Gray, J. W., & Hartlage, L. C. (1986). The practice of clinical neuropsychology in the United States. *Archives of Clinical Neuropsychology, 1,* 5–12.

Serin, R. C., Peters, R. DeV., & Barbaree, H. E. (1990). Predictors of psychopathy and release outcome in a criminal population. *Psychological Assessment, 2,* 419–422.

Serpell, R. (1979). How specific are perceptual skills? A cross-cultural study of pattern reproduction. *British Journal of Psychology, 70,* 365–380.

Sevig, T. D., Highlen, P. S., & Adams, E. M. (2000). Development and validation of the Self-Identity Inventory (SII): A multicultural identity development instrument. *Cultural Diversity and Ethnic Minority Psychology, 6,* 168–182.

Shadish, W. R. (1996). Meta-analysis and the exploration of causal mediating processes: A primer of examples, methods, and issues. *Psychological Methods, 1,* 47–65.

Shah, S. A. (1969). Privileged communications, confidentiality, and privacy: Privileged communications. *Professional Psychology, 1,* 56–59.

Shapiro, E. S., & Eckert, T. L. (1993). Curriculum-based assessment among school psychologists: Knowledge, use, and attitudes. *Journal of School Psychology, 31,* 375–383.

Shapiro, E. S., & Skinner, C. H. (1990). Principles of behavior assessment. In C. R. Reynolds & R. W. Kamphaus (Eds.), *Handbook of psychological and educational assessment of children: Personality, behavior & context* (pp. 343–363). New York: Guilford.

Sharpe, D. (1997). Of apples and oranges, file drawers and garbage: Why validity issues in meta-analysis will not go away. *Clinical Psychology Review, 17,* 881–901.

Shavelson, R. J., Webb, N. M., & Rowley, G. L. (1989). Generalizability theory. *American Psychologist, 44,* 922–932.

Shaw, S. R., Swerdlik, M. E., & Laurent, J. (1993). Review of the WISC-III. In B. A. Bracken (Ed.), *Monograph series, Advances in psychoeducational assessment: Wechsler Intelligence Scale for Children, Third Edition: Journal of Psychoeducational Assessment* (pp. 151–159). Brandon, VT: Clinical Psychology Publishing.

Shaywitz, B. A., Shaywitz, S. E., Pugh, K. R., et al. (1995). Sex differences in the functional organization of the brain for language. *Nature, 373,* 607–609.

Shedler, J. (2000). The Shedler QPD Panel (Quick PsychDiagnostics Panel): A psychiatric "lab test" for primary care. In M. E. Maruish (Ed.), *Handbook of psychological assessment in primary care settings* (pp. 277–296). Mahwah, NJ: Erlbaum.

Sheehan, P. W., Grigg, L., & McCann, T. (1984). Memory distortion following exposure to false information in hypnosis. *Journal of Abnormal Psychology, 93,* 259–296.

Sheffield, D., Biles, P. L., Orom, H., Maixner, W., & Sheps, D. S. (2000). Race and sex differences in cutaneous pain perception. *Psychosomatic Medicine, 62,* 517–523.

Shell, R. W. (1980). Psychiatric testimony: Science or fortune telling? *Barrister, 7,* 6–12.

Shepard, L. A. (1983). The role of measurement in educational policy: Lessons from the identification of learning disabilities. *Journal of Special Education, 14,* 79–91.

Sherman, L. J. (1958). The influence of artistic quality on judgments of patient and non-patient status from human figure drawings. *Journal of Projective Techniques, 22,* 338–340.

Sherrill-Pattison, S., Donders, J., & Thompson, E. (2000). Influence of demographic variables on neuropsychological test performance after traumatic brain injury. *Clinical Neuropsychologist, 14,* 496–503.

Shiffman, S., Hufford, M., Hickcox, M., et al. (1997). Remember that? A comparison of real-time versus retrospective recall of smoking lapses. *Journal of Consulting and Clinical Psychology, 65,* 292–300.

Shneidman, E. S. (1952). Manual for the Make a Picture Story Method. *Projective Techniques Monographs, 2.*

Shneidman, E. S. (1958). Some relationships between thematic and drawing materials. In E. F. Hammer (Ed.), *The clinical applications of projective drawings* (pp. 296–307). Springfield, IL: Charles C Thomas.

Shock, N. W., Greulich, R. C., Andres, R., et al. (1984). *Normal human aging: The Baltimore longitudinal study of aging* (NIH Publication No. 84-2450). Washington, DC: U.S. Government Printing Office.

Shockley, W. (1971). Models, mathematics, and the moral obligation to diagnose the origin of Negro IQ deficits. *Review of Educational Research, 41,* 369–377.

Shriner, J. G. (2000). Legal perspectives on school outcomes assessment for students with disabilities. *Journal of Special Education, 33,* 232–239.

Shuey, A. M. (1966). *The testing of Negro intelligence* (2nd ed.). New York: Social Science.

Shum, D., Short, L., Tunstall, J., et al. (2000). Performance of children with traumatic brain injury on a 4-disk version of the Tower of London and the Porteus Maze. *Brain & Cognition, 44,* 59–62.

Shuman, D. W., & Sales, B. D. (1999). The impact of *Daubert* and its progeny on the admissibility of behavioral and social science evidence. *Psychology, Public Policy, and Law, 5,* 3–15.

Siegel, L. J. (1986). Review of the Children's Depression Inventory. In D. J. Keyser & R. C. Sweetland (Eds.), *Test critiques* (Vol. 5). Kansas City, MO: Test Corporation of America.

Siegler, R. S., & Richards, D. (1980). The development of intelligence. In R. S. Sternberg (Chair), *People's conception of the nature of intelligence.* Symposium presented at the 88th annual convention of the American Psychological Association, Montreal, Canada.

Silber, D. E., et al. (1998). *Personality of sexual assault survivors.* Poster session presentation at the Society for Personality Assessment 1998 Midwinter Meeting, February 21.

Silka, V. R., & Hauser, M. J. (1997). Psychiatric assessment of the person with mental retardation. *Psychiatric Annals, 27*(3), 162–169.

Silverman, C. (1968). The epidemiology of depression: A review. *American Journal of Psychiatry, 124,* 883–891.

Silverstein, A. B. (1990). Short forms of individual intelligence tests. *Psychological Assessment, 2,* 3–11.

Silverstein, M. L., & Nelson, L. D. (2000). Clinical and research implications of revising psychological tests. *Psychological Assessment, 12,* 298–303.

Simon, R. J. (1967). *The jury and the defense of insanity.* Boston: Little, Brown.

Simon, R. J., & Aaronson, D. E. (1988). *The insanity defense.* New York: Praeger.

Simpson, R. (1970). Study of the comparability of the WISC and WAIS. *Journal of Consulting and Clinical Psychology, 2,* 156–158.

Simpson, R. L., Griswold, D. E., & Myles, B. S. (1999). Educators' assessment accommodation preferences for students with autism. *Focus on Autism and Other Developmental Disabilities, 14*(4), 212–219, 230.

Sines, J. O. (1966). Actuarial methods in personality assessment. In B. A. Maher (Ed.), *Progress in experimental personality research* (Vol. 3; pp. 133–193). New York: Academic Press.

Siperstein, G. N., Leffert, J. S., & Wenz-Gross, M. (1997). The quality of friendships between children with and without learning problems. *American Journal on Mental Retardation, 102,* 111–125.

Sivec, H. J., Hilsenroth, M. J., & Lynn, S. J. (1995). Impact of simulating borderline personality on the MMPI-2: A costs-benefits model employing base rates. *Journal of Personality Assessment, 64,* 295–311.

Sivec, H. J., Lynn, S. J., & Garske, J. P. (1994). The effect of somatoform disorders and paranoid psychotic role-related dissimulations as a response set on the MMPI-2. *Assessment, 1,* 69–81.

Sivik, T. M., & Hoesterey, U. (1992). The Thematic Apperception Test as an aid in understanding the psychodynamics of development of chronic idiopathic pain syndrome. *Psychotherapy and Psychosomatics, 57,* 57–60.

Skafte, D. (1985). *Child custody evaluations: A practical guide.* Beverly Hills: Sage.

Skinner, H. A., & Allen, B. A. (1983). Does the computer make a difference? Computerized versus face-to-face versus self-report assessment of alcohol, drug, and tobacco use. *Journal of Consulting and Clinical Psychology, 51,* 267–275.

Skinner, H. A., & Pakula, A. (1986). Challenge of computers in psychological assessment. *Professional Psychology: Research and Practice, 17,* 44–50.

Skolnick, J. H. (1961). Scientific theory and scientific evidence: An analysis of lie detection. *Yale Law Journal, 70,* 694–728.

Slakter, M. J., Crehan, K. D., & Koehler, R. A. (1975). Longitudinal studies of risk taking on objective examinations. *Educational and Psychological Measurement, 35,* 97–105.

Slate, J. R., Jones, C. H., Murray, R. A., & Coulter, C. (1993). Evidence that practitioners err in administering and scoring the WAIS-R. *Measurement and Evaluation in Counseling and Development, 25,* 156–161.

Slater, S. B., Vukmanovic, C., Macukanovic, P., Prvulovic, T., & Cutler, J. L. (1974). The definition and measurement of disability. *Social Science and Medicine, 8,* 305–308.

Slay, D. K. (1984). A portable Halstead-Reitan Category Test. *Journal of Clinical Psychology, 40,* 1023–1027.

Sloan, P., et al. (1998). MMPI-2 prediction of physical symptoms in Gulf War veterans. In P. Sloan & J. H. Quillen (Chairs), *Assessment of cognitive, emotional and physical functioning in war veterans.* Symposium presented at the Society for Personality Assessment 1998 Midwinter Meeting, February 20.

Slobogin, C. (1985). The guilty but mentally ill verdict: An idea whose time should not have come. *George Washington Law Review, 53,* 494–527.

Slobogin, C. (1999). The admissibility of behavioral science information in criminal trials: From primitivism to *Daubert* to Voice. *Psychology, Public Policy, and Law, 5,* 100–119.

Smith, A. (1962). Ambiguities in concepts and studies of "brain damage" and "organicity." *Journal of Nervous and Mental Disease, 135,* 311–326.

Smith, C. A., & Wallston, K. A. (1995). On babies and bathwater: Disease impact and negative affectivity in the self-reports of persons with rheumatoid arthritis. *Health Psychology, 14,* 64–73.

Smith, D. E. (1986). Training programs for performance appraisal: A review. *Academy of Management Review, 11,* 22–40.

Smith, D. K. (1985). *Test use and perceived competency: A survey of school psychologists.* Unpublished manuscript, University of Wisconsin–River Falls, School Psychology Program.

Smith, D. K., Bolin, J. A., & Stovall, D. R. (1988). K-ABC stability in a preschool sample: A longitudinal study. *Journal of Psychoeducational Assessment, 6,* 396–403.

Smith, D. K., & Knudtson, L. S. (1990). *K-ABC and S-B:FE relationships in an at-risk preschool sample.* Paper presented at the Annual Meeting of the American Psychological Association, Boston.

Smith, D. K., Lasee, M. J., & McCloskey, G. M. (1990). *Test-retest reliability of the AGS Early Screening Profiles.* Paper presented at the Annual Meeting of the National Association of School Psychologists, San Francisco.

Smith, D. K., & Lyon, M. A. (1987). *Children with learning difficulties: Differences in ability patterns as a function of placement.* Paper presented at the Annual Meeting of the American Educational Research Association, Washington, DC. (ERIC Document Reproduction Service No. ED 285 317)

Smith, D. K., St. Martin, M. E., & Lyon, M. A. (1989). A validity study of the Stanford-Binet Fourth Edition with students with learning disabilities. *Journal of Learning Disabilities, 22,* 260–261.

Smith, G. E., Ivnik, R. J., Malec, J. F., Kokmen, E., Tangalos, E. G., & Kurland, L. T. (1992). Mayo's older Americans normative studies (MOANS): Factor structure of a core battery. *Psychological Assessment, 4,* 382–390.

Smith, G. T., McCarthy, D. M., & Anderson, K. G. (2000). On the sins of short form development. *Psychological Assessment, 12,* 102–111.

Smith, M. (1948). Cautions concerning the use of the Taylor-Russell tables in employee selection. *Journal of Applied Psychology, 32,* 595–600.

Smith, M. H., May, W. T., & Lebovitz, L. (1966). Testing experience and Stanford-Binet scores. *Journal of Educational Measurement, 3,* 229–233.

Smith, R. E. (1963). Examination by computer. *Behavioral Science, 8,* 76–79.

Smith, R. G., & Iwata, B. A. (1997). Antecedent influences on behavior disorders. *Journal of Applied Behavior Analysis, 30,* 343–375.

Smith, T. T., Myers-Jennings, C., & Coleman, T. (2000). Assessment of language skills in rural preschool children. *Communication Disorders Quarterly, 21,* 98–113.

Smither, J. W., Reilly, R. R., & Buda, R. (1988). Effect of prior performance information on ratings of present performance: Contrast versus assimilation revisited. *Journal of Applied Psychology, 73,* 487–496.

Smither, R., & Rodriguez-Giegling, M. (1982). Personality, demographics, and acculturation of Vietnamese and Nicaraguan refugees to the United States. *International Journal of Psychology, 17,* 19–25.

Smucker, M. R., Craighead, W. E., Craighead, L. W., & Green, B. J. (1986). Normative and reliability data for the Children's Depression Inventory. *Journal of Abnormal Child Psychology, 14,* 25–39.

Snowden, L. R., & Hines, A. M. (1999). A scale to assess African American acculturation. *Journal of Black Psychology, 25,* 36–47.

Snyder, C. R. (1974). Acceptance of personality interpretations as a function of assessment procedures. *Journal of Consulting and Clinical Psychology, 42,* 150.

Snyder, C. R., & Larson, G. R. (1972). A further look at student acceptance of general personality interpretations. *Journal of Consulting and Clinical Psychology, 38,* 384–388.

Snyder, C. R., & Newburg, C. L. (1981). The Barnum effect in a group setting. *Journal of Personality Assessment, 45,* 622–629.

Snyder, C. R., & Shenkel, R. J. (1976). Effects of "favorability," modality, and relevance on acceptance of general personality interpretations prior to and after receiving diagnostician feedback. *Journal of Consulting and Clinical Psychology, 44,* 34–41.

Snyder, C. R., Shenkel, R. J., & Lowery, C. R. (1977). Acceptance of personality interpretations: The "Barnum effect" and beyond. *Journal of Consulting and Clinical Psychology, 45,* 104–114.

Snyder, C. R., Shenkel, R. J., & Schmidt, A. (1976). Effect of role perspective and client psychiatric history on locus of problem. *Journal of Consulting and Clinical Psychology, 44,* 467–472.

Snyder, D. (1998). *Assessing couples using the Marital Satisfaction Inventory, Revised (MIS-R).* Workshop presented at the Society for Personality Assessment 1998 Midwinter Meeting, February 22.

Snyder, D. K. (1981). *Marital Satisfaction Inventory (MSI) manual.* Los Angeles: Western Psychological Services.

Snyder, D. K. (2000). Computer-assisted judgment: Defining strengths and liabilities. *Psychological Assessment, 12,* 52–60.

Snyder, D. K., Widiger, T. A., & Hoover, D. W. (1990). Methodological considerations in validating computer-based test interpretations: Controlling for response bias. *Psychological Assessment, 2,* 470–477.

Snyder, P., Lawson, S., Thompson, B., Stricklin, S., & Sexton, D. (1993). Evaluating the psychometric integrity of instruments used in early intervention research: The Battelle Developmental Inventory. *Topics in Early Childhood Special Education, 32,* 273–280.

Sodowsky, G. R., & Carey, J. C. (1988). Relationships between acculturation-related demographics and cultural attitudes of an Asian-Indian immigrant group. *Journal of Multicultural Counseling and Development, 16*(July), 117–136.

Sokal, M. M. (1991). Psyche Cattell (1893–1989). *American Psychologist, 46,* 72.

Solomon, I. L., & Starr, B. D. (1968). *The School Apperception Method.* New York: Springer.

Solomon, P. R., Hirschoff, A., Kelly, B., et al. (1998). A 7-minute neurocognitive screening battery highly sensitive to Alzheimer's disease. *Archives of Neurology, 55,* 349–355.

Sommers-Flanagan, J., & Sommers-Flanagan, R. (1995). Intake interviewing with suicidal patients: A systematic approach. *Professional Psychology: Research and Practice, 26,* 41–47.

Sontag, L. W., Baker, C. T., & Nelson, V. L. (1958). Personality as a determinant of performance. *American Journal of Orthopsychiatry, 25,* 555–562.

Spanier, G. (1976). Measuring dyadic adjustment: New scales for assessing the quality of marriage and similar dyads. *Journal of Marriage and the Family, 38,* 15–28.

Spanier, G. B., & Filsinger, E. (1983). The Dyadic Adjustment Scale. In E. Filsinger (Ed.), *Marriage and family assessment.* Beverly Hills: Sage.

Sparks, K., Cooper, C., Ried, Y., & Shirom, A. (1997). The effects of hours of work on health: A meta-analytic review. *Journal of Occupational and Organizational Psychology, 70,* 391–408.

Sparrow, S. S., Balla, D. A., & Cicchetti, D. V. (1984a). *Vineland Adaptive Behavior Scales, Interview Edition: Expanded form manual.* Circle Pines, MN: American Guidance Service.

Sparrow, S. S., Balla, D. A., & Cicchetti, D. V. (1984b). *Vineland Adaptive Behavior Scales, Interview Edition: Survey form manual.* Circle Pines, MN: American Guidance Service.

Sparrow, S. S., Balla, D. A., & Cicchetti, D. V. (1985). *Vineland Adaptive Behavior Scales, Classroom Edition manual.* Circle Pines, MN: American Guidance Service.

Spearman, C. (1927). *The abilities of man: Their nature and measurement.* New York: Macmillan.

Spearman, C. E. (1904). "General intelligence" objectively determined and measured. *American Journal of Psychiatry, 15,* 201–293.

Spearman, C. S. (1930–1936). Autobiography. In C. Murchison (Ed.), *A history of psychology in autobiography* (3 vols.). Worcester, MA: Clark University Press.

Speth, E. B. (1992). *Test-retest reliabilities of Bricklin Perceptual Scales.* Unpublished doctoral dissertation, Hahneman University Graduate School, Philadelphia.

Spiegel, J. S., Leake, B., Spiegel, T. M., et al. (1988). What are we measuring? An examination of self-reported functional status measures. *Arthritis and Rheumatism, 31,* 721–728.

Spielberger, C. D., et al. (1980). *Test Anxiety Inventory: Preliminary professional manual.* Palo Alto, CA: Consulting Psychologists Press.

Spitz, H. H., Minsky, S. K., & Bessellieu, C. L. (1985). Influence of planning time and first-move strategy on Tower of Hanoi problem-solving performance of mentally retarded young adults and non-retarded children. *American Journal of Mental Deficiency, 90,* 46–56.

Spitzer, R. L. (1999). Harmful dysfunction and the *DSM* definition of mental disorder. *Journal of Abnormal Psychology, 108,* 430–432.

Spitznagel, E. L., & Helzer, J. E. (1985). A proposed solution to the base rate problem in the kappa statistic. *Archives of General Psychiatry, 42,* 725–728.

Spivack, G., & Spotts, J. (1966). *Devereux Child Behavior Rating Scale manual.* Devon, PA: Devereux Foundation.

Spivack, G., Spotts, J., & Haimes, P. E. (1967). *Devereux Adolescent Behavior Rating Scale.* Devon, PA: Devereux Foundation.

Spranger, E. (1928). *Types of men* (P. J. W. Pigors, Trans.). Halle: Niemeyer.

Spreen, O., & Benton, A. L. (1965). Comparative studies of some psychological tests for cerebral damage. *Journal of Nervous and Mental Disease, 140,* 323–333.

Spreen, O., & Benton, A. L. (1969). *Neurosensory Center Comprehensive Examination for Aphasia.* Victoria, Canada: University of Victoria.

Spruill, J., & May, J. (1988). The mentally retarded offender: Prevalence rates based on individual versus group intelligence tests. *Criminal Justice and Behavior, 15,* 484–491.

Spruill, J. A. (1993). Secondary assessment: Structuring the transition process. *Learning Disabilities Research & Practice, 8,* 127–132.

Staal, M. A., et al. (1998). Selection decisions in Air Force basic trainees seen for a mental health evaluation. In R. J. Craig (Chair), *Assessment, decision-making, and classification.*

Paper session presentation at the Society for Personality Assessment 1998 Midwinter Meeting, February 21.

Stahl, P. M. (1995). *Conducting child custody evaluations.* Thousand Oaks, CA: Sage.

St. Lawrence, J. S., Reitman, D., Jefferson, K. W., et al. (1994). Factor structure and validation of an adolescent version of the Condom Attitude Scale: An instrument for measuring adolescents' attitudes toward condoms. *Psychological Assessment, 6,* 352–359.

Stanczak, D. E., Lynch, M. D., McNeil, C. K., & Brown, B. (1998). The Expanded Trail Making Test: Rationale, development, and psychometric properties. *Archives of Clinical Neuropsychology, 13,* 473–487.

Stanford Special Report, Number 9. (1992). Bias control. San Antonio: Psychological Corporation/Harcourt Brace Jovanovich.

Stanley, J. C. (1971). Reliability. In R. L. Thorndike (Ed.), *Educational measurement* (2nd ed.). Washington, DC: American Council on Education.

Starch, D., & Elliot, E. C. (1912). Reliability of grading of high school work in English. *School Review, 20,* 442–457.

Staw, B. M., Bell, N. E., & Clausen, J. A. (1986). The dispositional approach to job attitudes: A lifetime longitudinal test. *Administrative Science Quarterly, 31,* 56–77.

Steadman, H. J. (1983). Predicting dangerousness among the mentally ill: Art, magic, and science. *International Journal of Law and Psychiatry, 6,* 381–390.

Stedman, J. M., Hatch, J. P., & Schoenfeld, L. S. (2000). Pre-internship preparation in psychological testing and psychotherapy: What internship directors say they expect. *Professional Psychology: Research and Practice, 31,* 321–326.

Steiger, J. H. (1996a). Dispelling some myths about factor indeterminacy. *Multivariate Behavioral Research, 31,* 539–550.

Steiger, J. H. (1996b). Coming full circle in the history of factor indeterminacy. *Multivariate Behavioral Research, 31,* 617–630.

Steinberg, M., Cicchetti, D., Buchanan, J., & Hall, P. (1993). Clinical assessment of dissociative symptoms and disorders: The Structured Clinical Interview for DSM-IV Dissociative Disorders (SCID-D). *Dissociation: Progress in Dissociative Disorders, 6,* 3–15.

Stephens, J. J. (1992). Assessing ethnic minorities. *SPA Exchange, 2*(1), 4–6.

Stephenson, W. (1953). *The study of behavior: Q-technique and its methodology.* Chicago: University of Chicago.

Stephenson, W. (1980). Newton's fifth rule and Q-methodology: Application to educational psychology. *American Psychologist, 35,* 882–889.

Sternberg, R. J. (1981). The nature of intelligence. *New York Education Quarterly, 12*(3), 10–17.

Sternberg, R. J. (1982, April). Who's intelligent? *Psychology Today,* pp. 30–33, 35–36, 38–39.

Sternberg, R. J. (1985). *Beyond IQ: A triarchic theory of human intelligence.* Cambridge: Cambridge University Press.

Sternberg, R. J. (1986). Intelligence is mental self-government. In R. J. Sternberg & D. K. Detterman (Eds.), *What is intelligence?* (pp. 141–148). Norwood, NJ: Ablex.

Sternberg, R. J. (1994). PRSVL: An integrative framework for understanding mind in context. In R. J. Sternberg & R. K. Wagner (Eds.), *Mind in context* (pp. 218–232). Cambridge: Cambridge University Press.

Sternberg, R. J. (1997). Managerial intelligence. *Journal of Management, 23,* 475–493.

Sternberg, R. J., & Berg, C. A. (1986). Quantitative integration: Definitions of intelligence: A comparison of the 1921 and 1986 symposia. In R. J. Sternberg & D. K. Detterman (Eds.), *What is intelligence?* (pp. 155–162). Norwood, NJ: Ablex.

Sternberg, R. J., Conway, B. E., Ketron, J. L., & Bernstein, M. (1981). People's conceptions of intelligence. *Journal of Personality and Social Psychology, 41,* 37–55.

Sternberg, R. J., & Detterman, D. K. (Eds.). (1986). *What is intelligence?* Norwood, NJ: Ablex.

Stillman, R. (1974). *Assessment of deaf-blind children: The Callier-Azusa Scale.* Paper presented at the Intercom '74, Hyannis, MA.

Stinnett, T. A. (1997). "AAMR Adaptive Behavior Scale-School: 2" Test review. *Journal of Psychoeducational Assessment, 15,* 361–372.

Stokes, J. B. (1977). Comment on "Socially reinforced obsessing: Etiology of a disorder in a Christian Scientist." *Journal of Consulting and Clinical Psychology, 45,* 1164–1165.

Stone, A. A. (1986). Vermont adopts *Tarasoff:* A real barnburner. *American Journal of Psychiatry, 143,* 352–355.

Stone, B. J. (1992). Prediction of achievement by Asian-American and White children. *Journal of School Psychology, 30,* 91–99.

Stoppard, J. M., & Gruchy, C. D. G. (1993). Gender, context, and expression of positive emotion. *Personality and Social Psychology Bulletin, 19,* 143–150.

Storandt, M. (1994). General principles of assessment of older adults. In M. Storandt & G. R. VandenBos (Eds.), *Neuropsychological assessment of dementia and depression in older adults: A clinician's guide* (pp. 7–32). Washington, DC: American Psychological Association.

Storey, K. (1997). Quality of life issues in social skills assessment of persons with disabilities. *Education and Training in Mental Retardation and Developmental Disabilities, 32,* 197–200.

Storzbach, D., Campbell, K. A., Binder, L. M., et al. (2000). Psychological differences between veterans with and without Gulf War unexplained symptoms. *Psychosomatic Medicine, 62,* 726–735.

Stout, C. E., Levant, R. F., Reed, G. M., & Murphy, M. J. (2001). Contracts: A primer for psychologists. *Professional Psychology: Research and Practice, 32,* 89–91.

Strassberg, D. S., Tilley, D., Bristone, S., & Oei, T. P. S. (1992). The MMPI and chronic pain: A cross-cultural view. *Psychological Assessment, 4,* 493–497.

Strassle, C. G., et al. (1998). Optimism: An important neglected variable in personality assessment. In H. M. Potash (Chair), *The assessment of psychological health.* Symposium presented at the Society for Personality Assessment 1998 Midwinter Meeting, February 21.

Straus, M. A. (1979). Measuring intrafamily conflict and violence: The Conflict Tactics (CT) Scales. *Journal of Marriage and the Family, 41,* 75–85.

Strauss, A. A., & Lehtinen, L. E. (1947). *Psychopathology and education of the brain injured child.* New York: Grune & Stratton.

Strauss, E., Ottfried, S., & Hunter, M. (2000). Implications of test revisions for research. *Psychological Assessment, 12,* 237–244.

Stricker, G., & Gold, J. R. (1999). The Rorschach: Toward a nomothetically based, idiographically applicable configurational model. *Psychological Assessment, 11,* 240–250.

Stricker, G., & Healey, B. J. (1990). Projective assessment of object relations: A review of the empirical literature. *Psychological Assessment, 2,* 219–230.

Stricker, L. J., Messick, S., & Jackson, D. N. (1968). Desirability judgments and self-reports as predictors of social behavior. *Journal of Experimental Research in Personality, 3,* 151–167.

Strong, E. K., Jr., Hansen, J. C., & Campbell, D. C. (1985). *Strong Vocational Interest Blank. Revised edition of Form T325,*

Strong-Campbell Interest Inventory. Stanford, CA: Stanford University. (Distributed by Consulting Psychologists Press)

Sturges, J. W. (1998). Practical use of technology in professional practice. *Professional Psychology: Research and Practice, 29,* 183–188.

Subich, L. M. (1996). Addressing diversity in the process of career assessment. In M. L. Savickas & W. B. Walsh (Eds.), *Handbook of career counseling: Theory and practice* (pp. 277–289). Palo Alto, CA: Davies-Black.

Suczek, R. F., & Klopfer, W. G. (1952). Interpretation of the Bender-Gestalt Test: The associative value of the figures. *American Journal of Orthopsychiatry, 22,* 62–75.

Sugarman, A. (1991). Where's the beef? Putting personality back into personality assessment. *Journal of Personality Assessment, 56,* 130–144.

Suinn, R. M., Rickard-Figueroa, K., Lew, S., & Vigil, S. (1987). The Suinn-Lew Asian Self-Identity Acculturation Scale: An initial report. *Educational and Psychological Measurement, 47,* 401–407.

Sullivan, G., Burnam, A., Koegel, P., & Hollenberg, J. (2000). Quality of life of homeless persons with mental illness: Results from the Course-of-Homelessness study. *Psychiatric Services, 51,* 1135–1141.

Sullivan, H. S. (1953). *The interpersonal theory of psychiatry.* New York: Norton.

Sullivan, P. M. (1982). Administration modifications on the WISC-R Performance Scale with different categories of deaf children. *American Annals of the Deaf, 127,* 780–788.

Sullivan, P. M., & Brookhouser, P. E. (Eds.). (1996). *Proceedings of the Fourth Annual Conference on the Habilitation and Rehabilitation of Hearing Impaired Adolescents.* Boys Town, NE: Boys Town.

Sullivan, P. M., & Burley, S. K. (1990). Mental testing of the deaf child. In C. Reynolds & R. Kamphaus (Eds.), *Handbook of psychological and educational assessment of children* (pp. 761–788). New York: Guilford.

Sullivan, P. M., & Montoya, L. A. (1997). Factor analysis of the WISC-III with deaf and hard-of-hearing children. *Psychological Assessment, 9,* 317–321.

Sullivan, P. M., & Schulte, L. E. (1992). Factor analysis of WISC-R with deaf and hard-of-hearing children. *Psychological Assessment, 4,* 537–540.

Suls, J., Wan, C. K., & Blanchard, E. B. (1994). A multilevel data-analytic approach for evaluation of relationships between daily life stressors and symptomatology: Patients with irritable bowel syndrome. *Health Psychology, 13,* 103–113.

Sundberg, N. D. (1955). The acceptability of "fake" versus "bona fide" personality test interpretations. *Journal of Abnormal and Social Psychology, 50,* 145–147.

Sundberg, N. D., & Gonzales, L. R. (1981). Cross-cultural and cross-ethnic assessment: Overview and issues. In P. McReynolds (Ed.), *Advances in psychological assessment* (Vol. 5; pp. 460–541). San Francisco: Jossey-Bass.

Sundberg, N. D., & Tyler, L. E. (1962). *Clinical psychology.* New York: Appleton-Century-Crofts.

Super, C. M. (1983). Cultural variation in the meaning and uses of children's "intelligence." In J. B. Deregowski, S. Dziurawiec, & R. C. Annis (Eds.), *Explorations in cross-cultural psychology.* Lisse, Netherlands: Swets & Zeitlinger.

Super, D. E. (1970). *Work Values Inventory.* Boston: Houghton Mifflin.

Sutton v. United Airlines. (1999). 527 US 471, 119 S. Ct. 213.

Sutton-Simon, K., & Goldfried, M. R. (1979). Faulty thinking patterns in two types of anxiety. *Cognitive Therapy and Research, 3,* 193–203.

Swallow, R. (1981). Fifty assessment instruments commonly used with blind and partially seeing individuals. *Journal of Visual Impairment and Blindness, 75,* 65–72.

Swanson, J. L. (1992). The structure of vocational interests for African-American college students. *Journal of Vocational Behavior, 40,* 144–157.

Sweeney, J. A., Clarkin, J. F., & Fitzgibbon, M. L. (1987). Current practice of psychological assessment. *Professional Psychology: Research and Practice, 18,* 377–380.

Sweet, J. J., Moberg, P. J., & Tovian, S. M. (1990). Evaluation of Wechsler Adult Intelligence Scale—Revised premorbid IQ formulas in clinical populations. *Psychological Assessment, 2,* 41–44.

Swensen, C. H. (1968). Empirical evaluations of human figure drawings: 1957–1966. *Psychological Bulletin, 70,* 20–44.

Swerdlik, M. E. (1985). Review of Brigance Diagnostic Comprehensive Inventory of Basic Skills. In J. V. Mitchell, Jr. (Ed.), *The ninth mental measurements yearbook* (pp. 214–215). Lincoln: Buros Institute of Mental Measurements, University of Nebraska.

Swerdlik, M. E. (1992). Review of the Otis-Lennon School Ability Test. In J. J. Kramer & J. C. Conoley (Eds.), *The eleventh mental measurements yearbook.* Lincoln: Buros Institute of Mental Measurements, University of Nebraska.

Swerdlik, M. E. (1998). Review of Stanford Diagnostic Reading Test, Fourth Edition. In J. C. Impara & B. S. Plake (Eds.), *The thirteenth mental measurements yearbook.* Lincoln: Buros Institute of Mental Measurements, University of Nebraska.

Swerdlik, M. E., & Dornback, F. (1988, April). *An interpretation guide to the fourth edition of the Stanford-Binet Intelligence Scale.* Paper presented at the annual meeting of the National Association of School Psychologists, Chicago.

Swift, J. W. (1944). Reliability of Rorschach scoring categories with pre-school children. *Child Development, 15,* 207–216.

Swoboda, J. S., Elwork, A., Sales, B. D., & Levine, D. (1978). Knowledge of and compliance with privileged communication and child-abuse-reporting laws. *Professional Psychology, 9,* 448–457.

Sylvester, R. H. (1913). Clinical psychology adversely criticized. *Psychological Clinic, 7,* 182–188.

Symonds, P. M. (1949). *Adolescent fantasy: An investigation of the picture-story method of personality study.* New York: Columbia University.

Takeuchi, J., Solomon, F., & Menninger, W. W. (Eds.). (1981). *Behavioral science and the Secret Service: Toward the prevention of assassination.* Washington, DC: National Academy.

Tallent, N. (1958). On individualizing the psychologist's clinical evaluation. *Journal of Clinical Psychology, 114,* 243–244.

Tamkin, A. S., & Kunce, J. T. (1985). A comparison of three neuropsychological tests: The Weigl, Hooper and Benton. *Journal of Clinical Psychology, 41,* 660–664.

Tan, U. (1993). Normal distribution of hand preference and its bimodality. *International Journal of Neuroscience, 68,* 61–65.

Taormina, R. J., & Bauer, T. N. (2000). Organizational socialization in two cultures: Results from the United States and Hong Kong. *International Journal of Organizational Analysis, 8,* 262–289.

Taylor, H. C., & Russell, J. T. (1939). The relationship of validity coefficients to the practical effectiveness of tests in selection. *Journal of Applied Psychology, 23,* 565–578.

Taylor, L. B. (1979). Psychological assessment of neurosurgical patients. In T. Rasmussen & R. Marino (Eds.), *Functional neurosurgery.* New York: Raven.

Taylor, R. L. (1980). Use of the AAMD classification system: A review of recent research. *American Journal of Mental Deficiency, 85,* 116–119.

Teague, W. (State Superintendent of Education). (1983). *Basic competency education: Reading, language, mathematics specifications for the Alabama High School Graduation Examination* (Bulletin No. 4). Montgomery: Alabama State Department of Education.

Tein, J.-Y., Sandler, I. N., & Zautra, A. J. (2000). Stressful life events, psychological distress, coping, and parenting of divorced mothers: A longitudinal study. *Journal of Family Psychology, 14,* 27–41.

Tellegen, A., & Ben-Porath, Y. S. (1992). The new uniform *T* scores for the MMPI-2: Rationale, derivation, and appraisal. *Psychological Assessment, 4,* 145–155.

Tenopyr, M. L. (1999). A scientist-practitioner's viewpoint on the admissibility of behavioral and social scientific information. *Psychology, Public Policy, and Law, 5,* 194–202.

Teplin, S. W., et al. (1991). Neurodevelopmental health, and growth status at age 6 years of children with birth weights less than 1001 grams. *Journal of Pediatrics, 118,* 768–777.

Terman, L. M., et al. (1925). *The mental and physical traits of a thousand gifted children: Vol. 1. Genetic studies of genius.* Stanford, CA: Stanford University.

Terman, L. M., & Miles, C. C. (1936). *Sex and personality: Studies in masculinity and femininity.* New York: McGraw-Hill.

Terpylak, O., & Schuerger, J. M. (1994). Broad factor scales of the 16 PF fifth edition and Millon personality disorder scales: A replication. *Psychological Reports, 74,* 124–126.

Tharinger, D. J., & Stark, K. (1990). A qualitative versus quantitative approach to evaluating the Draw-A-Person and Kinetic Family Drawing: A study of mood- and anxiety-disorder children. *Psychological Assessment, 2,* 365–375.

Theorell, T., Lind, E., & Folderus, B. (1975). The relationship of disturbing life changes and emotions to the early development of myocardial infarction and some other serious illnesses. *International Journal of Epidemiology, 4,* 281–293.

Theron, P. A. (1948). Peripheral vasomotor reactions as indices of basic emotional tension and lability. *Psychosomatic Medicine, 10,* 335–346.

Thomas, A. D., & Dudek, S. Z. (1985). Interpersonal affect in Thematic Apperception Test responses: A scoring system. *Journal of Personality Assessment, 49,* 30–36.

Thompson, A. E. (1986). An object relational theory of affect maturity: Applications to the Thematic Apperception Test. In M. Kissen (Ed.), *Assessing object relations phenomena* (pp. 207–224). Madison, CT: International Universities.

Thompson, C. (1949). The Thompson modification of the Thematic Apperception Test. *Journal of Projective Techniques, 13,* 469–478.

Thompson, J. K., & Smolak, L. (Eds.). (2001). *Body image, eating disorders, and obesity in youth: Assessment, prevention, and treatment.* Washington, DC: APA Books.

Thompson, J. K. & Thompson, C. M. (1986). Body size distortion and self-esteem in asymptomatic, normal weight males and females. *International Journal of Eating Disorders, 5,* 1061–1068.

Thompson, J. M. & Sones, R. (1973). *The Education Apperception Test.* Los Angeles: Western Psychological Services.

Thompson, M. D., Scott, J. G., Dickson, S. W. (1999). Clinical utility of the Trail Making Test practice time. *Clinical Neuropsychologist, 13,* 450–455.

Thompson, R. J., Gustafson, K. E., Meghdadpour, S., & Harrell, E. S. (1992). The role of biomedical and psychosocial processes in the intellectual and academic functioning of children and adolescents with cystic fibrosis. *Journal of Clinical Psychology, 48,* 3–10.

Thorndike, E. L., et al. (1921). Intelligence and its measurement: A symposium. *Journal of Educational Psychology, 12,* 123–147, 195–216.

Thorndike, E. L., Bregman, E. O., Cobb, M. V., Woodward, E., & the staff of the Division of Psychology of the Institute of Educational Research of Teachers College, Columbia University. (1927). *The measurement of intelligence.* New York: Bureau of Publications, Teachers College, Columbia University.

Thorndike, E. L., Lay, W., & Dean, P. R. (1909). The relation of accuracy in sensory discrimination to general intelligence. *American Journal of Psychology, 20,* 364–369.

Thorndike, R. (1985). Reliability. *Journal of Counseling & Development, 63,* 528–530.

Thorndike, R. L. (1971). Concepts of cultural fairness. *Journal of Educational Measurement, 8,* 63–70.

Thorndike, R. L., Hagen, E. P., & Sattler, J. P. (1986a). *Guide for administering and scoring the fourth edition of the Stanford-Binet Intelligence Scale.* Chicago: Riverside.

Thorndike, R. L., Hagen, E. P., & Sattler, J. P. (1986b). *Technical manual for the Stanford-Binet Intelligence Scale, Fourth Edition.* Chicago: Riverside.

Thorndike, R. L., & Scott, J. (1986). Assessing the pattern and level of cognitive abilities with the fourth edition of the Stanford-Binet. In G. J. Robertson (Chair), *Perspectives on intelligence assessments: 1986.* Symposium presented at the 94th annual convention of the American Psychological Association, Washington, DC.

Thornton, G. C., & Byham, W. C. (1982). *Assessment centers and managerial performance.* New York: Academic Press.

Thurlow, M. L., House, A. L., Scott, D. L., & Ysseldyke, J. E. (2000). Students with disabilities in large-scale assessments: State participation and accommodation policies. *Journal of Special Education, 34,* 154–163.

Thurston, N. S., & Cradock, J. A. (1998). Projective assessment of shame with the Thurston-Cradock Test (TCT). In J. Butcher (Chair), *New measures and instruments in assessment.* Paper session presentation at the Society for Personality Assessment 1998 Midwinter Meeting, February 19.

Thurstone, L. L. (1925). A method of scaling psychological and educational tests. *Journal of Educational Psychology, 16,* 433–451.

Thurstone, L. L. (1927). A law of comparative judgment. *Psychological Review, 34,* 273–286.

Thurstone, L. L. (1929). Theory of attitude measurement. *Psychological Bulletin, 36,* 222–241.

Thurstone, L. L. (1938). Primary mental abilities. *Psychometric Monographs,* No. 1. Chicago: University of Chicago Press.

Thurstone, L. L. (1947). *Multiple factor analysis.* Chicago: University of Chicago.

Thurstone, L. L. (1959). *The measurement of values.* Chicago: University of Chicago.

Thurstone, L. L. & Chave, E. J. (1929). *The measurement of attitude.* Chicago: University of Chicago.

Tillman, M. H. (1973). Intelligence scale for the blind: A review with implications for research. *Journal of School Psychology, 11,* 80–87.

Timbrook, R. E., & Graham, J. R. (1994). Ethnic differences on the MMPI-2? *Psychological Assessment, 6,* 212–217.

Tinsley, H. E. A., & Weiss, D. J. (1975). Interrater reliability and agreement of subjective judgments. *Journal of Counseling Psychology, 22,* 358–376.

Tittle, C. R., & Hill, R. J. (1967). Attitude measurement and prediction of behavior: An evaluation of conditions and measurement techniques. *Sociometry, 30,* 199–213.

Tobler, N. S., & Stratton, H. H. (1997). Effectiveness of school-based drug prevention programs: A meta-analysis of the research. *Journal of Primary Prevention, 18,* 71–128.

Torgerson, W. S. (1958). *Theory and methods of scaling.* New York: Wiley.

Torrance, E. P. (1966). *Torrance Tests of Creative Thinking.* Bensenville, IL: Scholastic Testing Service.

Torrance, E. P. (1987a). *Guidelines for administration and scoring/ Comments on using the Torrance Tests of Creative Thinking.* Bensenville, IL: Scholastic Testing Service.

Torrance, E. P. (1987c). *Survey of the uses of the Torrance Tests of Creative Thinking.* Bensenville, IL: Scholastic Testing Service.

Touliatos, J., Perlmutter, B. F., & Strauss, M. A. (1991). *Handbook of family measurements.* Newbury Park, CA: Sage.

Tramontana, M. G., & Boyd, T. A. (1986). Psychometric screening of neuropsychological abnormality in older children. *International Journal of Clinical Neuropsychology, 8,* 53–59.

Trappey, C. (1996). A meta-analysis of consumer choice and subliminal advertising. *Psychology & Marketing, 13,* 517–530.

Trautscholdt, M. (1883). Experimentelle unterschungen uber die association der vorstellungen. *Philosophesche Studien, 1,* 213–250.

Travin, S., Cullen, K., & Melella, J. T. (1988). The use and abuse of erection measurements: A forensic perspective. *Bulletin of the American Academy of Psychiatry and Law, 16,* 235–250.

Trice, H. M., & Beyer, J. M. (1984). Studying organizational cultures through rites and ceremonies. *Academy of Management Review, 9,* 653–669.

Trimble, M. R. (Ed.). (1986). *New brain imaging techniques and psychopharmacology.* Oxford: Oxford University.

Truant, G. S., O'Reilly, R., & Donaldson, L. (1991). How psychiatrists weigh risk factors when assessing suicide risk. *Suicide and Life-Threatening Behavior, 21,* 106–114.

Tryon, R. C. (1957). Reliability and behavior domain validity: Reformulation and historical critique. *Psychological Bulletin, 54,* 229–249.

Tsudzuki, A., Hata, Y., & Kuze, T. (1957). A study of rapport between examiner and subject. *Japanese Journal of Psychology, 27,* 22–28.

Tsujimoto, R. N., Hamilton, M., & Berger, D. E. (1990). Averaging multiple judges to improve validity: Aid to planning cost-effective research. *Psychological Assessment, 2,* 432–437.

Tugg v. Towey (1994, July 19). *National Disability Law Reporter, 5,* 999–1005.

Tulchin, S. H. (1939). The clinical training of psychologists and allied specialists. *Journal of Consulting Psychology, 3,* 105–112.

Tulsky, D., Zhu, J., & Ledbetter, M. F. (Project directors). (1997). *WAIS-III, WMS-III Technical manual.* San Antonio: Psychological Corporation.

Tulsky, D. S., & Ledbetter, M. F. (2000). Updating to the WAIS-III and WMS-III: Considerations for research and clinical practice. *Psychological Assessment, 12,* 253–262.

Turk, D. C., & Rudy, T. E. (1986). Assessment of cognitive factors in pain: A worthwhile enterprise? *Journal of Consulting and Clinical Psychology, 54,* 760–768.

Turner, D. R. (1966). Predictive efficiency as a function of amount of information and level of professional experience. *Journal of Projective Techniques and Personality Assessment, 30,* 4–11.

Tuttle, F. B., & Becker, A. (1980). *Characteristics and identification of gifted and talented students.* Washington, DC: National Education Association.

Tybout, A. M., & Artz, N. (1994). Consumer psychology. *Annual Review of Psychology, 45,* 131–169.

Tyler, L. E. (1961). Research explorations in the realm of choice. *Journal of Counseling Psychology, 8,* 195–202.

Tyler, L. E. (1965). *The psychology of human differences* (3rd ed.). New York: Appleton-Century-Crofts.

Tyler, R. S. (1993). Cochlear implants and the deaf culture. *American Journal of Audiology, 2,* 26–32.

Tyler, R. W. (1978). *The Florida accountability program: An evaluation of its educational soundness and implementation.* Washington, DC: National Education Association.

Tziner, A., & Eden, D. (1985). Effects of crew composition on crew performance: Does the whole equal the sum of its parts? *Journal of Applied Psychology, 70,* 85–93.

Udry, J. R. (1981). Marital alternatives and marital disruption. *Journal of Marriage and the Family, 13,* 889–897.

Ulrich, R. E., Stachnik, T. J., & Stainton, N. R. (1963). Student acceptance of generalized personality interpretations. *Psychological Reports, 13,* 831–834.

University of Minnesota. (1984). *User's guide for the Minnesota Report: Personal Selection System.* Minneapolis: National Computer Systems.

Ussher, J. M., & Wilding, J. M. (1991). Performance and state changes during the menstrual cycle, conceptualised within a broadband testing framework. *Social Science and Medicine, 32,* 525–534.

Utley, C. A., Lowitzer, A. C., & Baumeister, A. A. (1987). A comparison of the AAMD's definition, eligibility criteria, and classification schemes with state departments of education guidelines. *Education and Training in Mental Retardation, 22*(1), 35–43.

Vagg, P. R., & Spielberger, C. D. (1998). Occupational stress: Measuring job pressure and organizational support in the workplace. *Journal of Occupational Health Psychology, 3,* 294–305.

Vale, C. D., & Keller, L. S. (1987). Developing expert computer systems to interpret psychological tests. In J. N. Butcher (Ed.), *Computerized psychological assessment: A practitioner's guide* (pp. 64–83). New York: Basic.

Vale, C. D., Keller, L. S., & Bentz, V. J. (1986). Development and validation of a computerized interpretation system for personnel tests. *Personnel Psychology, 39,* 525–542.

Vander Kolk, C. J. (1977). Intelligence testing for visually impaired persons. *Journal of Visual Impairment & Blindness, 71,* 158–163.

Van der Merwe, A. B., & Theron, P. A. (1947). A new method of measuring emotional stability. *Journal of General Psychology, 37,* 109–124.

Van de Vijver, F., & Hambleton, R. K. (1996). Translating tests: Some practical guidelines. *European Psychologist, 1,* 89–99.

van Praag, H. M., Plutchik, R., & Apter, A. (Eds.). (1990). *Violence and suicidality: Perspectives in clinical and psychobiological research* (pp. 37–65). New York: Brunner/Mazel.

Vansteelandt, K., & Van Mechelen, I. (1998). Individual differences in situation-behavior profiles: A triple typology model. *Journal of Personality and Social Psychology, 75,* 751–765.

Varon, E. J. (1936). Alfred Binet's concept of intelligence. *Psychological Review, 43,* 32–49.

Veiga, J., Lubatkin, M., Calori, R., & Very, P. (2000). Measuring organizational culture clashes: A two-nation post-hoc analysis of a cultural compatibility index. *Human Relations, 53,* 539–557.

Velasquez, R. J., Gonzales, M., Butcher, J. N., et al. (1997). Use of the MMPI-2 with Chicanos: Strategies for counselors. *Journal of Multicultural Counseling and Development, 25,* 107–120.

Veldman, D. J., & Sheffield, J. R. (1979). The scaling of sociometric nominations. *Educational and Psychological Measurement, 39,* 99–106.

Veldon, M. (1997). The heritability of intelligence: Neither known nor unknown. *American Psychologist, 52*, 72–73.

Verhovek, S. H., & Ayres, B. D., Jr. (1998, November 4). The 1998 elections: The nation—referendums. *New York Times*, p. B2.

Vernon, M., & Andrews, J. E., Jr. (1990). *Psychology of deafness: Understanding deaf and hard of hearing people.* New York: Longman.

Vernon, M., Blair, R., & Lotz, S. (1979). Psychological evaluation and testing of children who are deaf-blind. *School Psychology Digest, 8*, 291–295.

Vernon, M., & Brown, D. W. (1964). A guide to psychological tests and testing procedures in the evaluation of deaf and hard-of-hearing children. *Journal of Speech and Hearing Disorders, 29*, 414–423.

Vernon, P. A. (1993). *Biological approaches to the study of human intelligence.* Norwood, NJ: Ablex.

Vernon, P. E. (1950). *The structure of human abilities.* New York: Wiley.

Vernon, P. E. (1964). *Personality assessment: A critical survey.* New York: Wiley.

Vevea, J. L., Clements, N. C., & Hedges, L. V. (1993). Assess the effects of selection bias on validity data for the General Aptitude Test Battery. *Journal of Applied Psychology, 78*, 981–987.

Vig, S., & Jedrysek, E. (1996). Application of the 1992 AAMR definition: Issues for preschool children. *Mental Retardation, 34*, 244–246.

Viglione, D. J. (1999). A review of recent research addressing the utility of the Rorschach. *Psychological Assessment, 11*, 251–265.

Vingoe, F. J. (1995). Beliefs of British law and medical students compared to expert criterion group on forensic hypnosis. *Contemporary Hypnosis, 12*, 173–187.

Visser, P. S., Krosnick, J. A., & Lavrakas, P. J. (2000). Survey research. In H. T. Reis & C. M. Judd (Eds.), *Handbook of research methods in social and personality psychology* (pp. 223–252). New York: Cambridge University Press.

Vitaliano, M. A., Maiuro, R. D., Russo, J., & Becker, J. (1987). Raw versus relative scores in the assessment of coping strategies. *Journal of Behavioral Medicine, 10*, 1–19.

Volkmar, F. R., Klin, A., Marans, W., & Cohen, D. J. (1996). The pervasive developmental disorders: Diagnosis and assessment. *Child & Adolescent Psychiatric Clinics of North America, 5*, 963–977.

von Knorring, L., & Lindstrom, E. (1992). The Swedish version of the Positive and Negative Syndrome Scale (PANSS) for schizophrenia: Construct validity and interrater reliability. *Acta Psychiatrica Scandinavica, 86*, 463–468.

von Wolff, C. (1732). *Psychologia empirica.*

von Wolff, C. (1734). *Psychologia rationalis.*

Vossekuil, B., & Fein, R. A. (1997). *Final report: Secret Service Exceptional Case Study Project.* Washington, DC: U.S. Secret Service, Intelligence Division.

Vroom, V. H. (1964). *Work and motivation.* New York: Wiley.

Vygotsky, L. S. (1978). *Mind in society: The development of higher psychological processes.* Cambridge, MA: Harvard University.

Wachspress, M., Berenberg, A. N., & Jacobson, A. (1953). Simulation of psychosis: A report of three cases. *Psychiatric Quarterly, 27*, 463–473.

Waddell, D. D. (1980). The Stanford-Binet: An evaluation of the technical data available since the 1972 restandardization. *Journal of School Psychology, 18*, 203–209.

Waehler, C. A. (1997). Drawing bridges between science and practice. *Journal of Personality Assessment, 69*, 482–487.

Wagner, B. M. (1997). Family risk factors for child and adolescent suicidal behavior. *Psychological Bulletin, 121*, 246–298.

Wagner, E. E. (1983). *The Hand Test.* Los Angeles: Western Psychological Services.

Wagner, E. E. (1985). Review of the Rosenzweig Picture-Frustration Study. *The ninth mental measurements yearbook*, (Vol. 2; pp. 1297–1298). Lincoln: Buros Institute of Mental Measurements, University of Nebraska.

Wainer, H. (1990). *Computerized adaptive testing: A primer.* Hillsdale, NJ: Erlbaum.

Wakefield, J. C. (1992a). Disorder as harmful dysfunction: A conceptual critique of DSM-III-R's definition of mental disorder. *Psychological Review, 99*, 232–247.

Wakefield, J. C. (1992b). The concept of mental disorder: On the boundary between biological facts and social values. *American Psychologist,47*, 373–388.

Wakefield, J. C. (1999). Evolutionary versus prototype analyses of the concept of disorder. *Journal of Abnormal Psychology, 108*, 374–399.

Wald, A. (1947). *Sequential analysis.* New York: Wiley.

Wald, A. (1950). *Statistical decision function.* New York: Wiley.

Waldman, D. A., & Avolio, B. J. (1989). Homogeneity of test validity. *Journal of Applied Psychology, 74*, 371–374.

Walker, H. M. (1976). *Walker Problem Behavior Identification Checklist.* Los Angeles: Western Psychological Services.

Walker, L. S., & Greene, J. W. (1991). The Functional Disability Inventory: Measuring a neglected dimension of child health status. *Journal of Pediatric Psychology, 16*, 39–58.

Walker, S., & Rosser, R. (Eds.). (1988). *Quality of life: Assessment and application.* London: MTP Press.

Walkup, J. (2000). Disability, health care, and public policy. *Rehabilitation Psychology, 45*, 409–422.

Wall, J. E. (1994). An example of assessment's role in career exploration. *Journal of Counseling Development, 72*, 608–613.

Wallace, I. F., Gravel, J. S., McCarton, C. M., & Ruben, R. J. (1988). Otitis media and language development at 1 year of age. *Journal of Speech and Hearing Disorders, 53*, 245–251.

Wallach, M. A., & Kogan, N. (1965). *Modes of thinking in young children.* New York: Holt, Rinehart & Winston.

Wallbrown, F., Brown, D., & Engin, A. (1978). A factor analysis of reading attitudes along with measures of reading achievement and scholastic aptitude. *Psychology in the Schools, 15*, 160–165.

Waller, N. G., & Zavala, J. D. (1993). Evaluating the big five. *Psychological Inquiry, 4*, 131–135.

Wallston, K. A., Wallston, B. S., & DeVellis, R. (1978). Development of the Multidimensional Health Locus of Control (MHLC) Scales. *Health Education Monographs, 6*, 160–170.

Walters, G. D. (1991). Predicting the disciplinary adjustment of maximum and minimum security prison inmates using the Lifestyle Criminality Screening Form. *International Journal of Offender Therapy and Comparative Criminology, 1*, 2–9.

Walters, G. D., Revella, L., & Baltrusaitis, W. J., II. (1990). Predicting parole/probation outcome with the aid of the Lifestyle Criminality Screening form. *Psychological Assessment, 2*, 313–316.

Walters, G. D., & White, T. W. (1989). The thinking criminal: A cognitive model of lifestyle criminality. *Criminal Justice Research Bulletin, 4*(4), 1–10.

Walters, G. D., White, T. W., & Denney, D. (1991). The Lifestyle Criminality Screening Form: Preliminary data. *Criminal Justice and Behavior, 18*, 406–418.

Waltz, J., Babcock, J. C., Jacobson, N. S., & Gottman, J. M. (2000). Testing a typology of batterers. *Journal of Consulting and Clinical Psychology, 68*, 658–669.

Wanderer, Z. W. (1967). *The validity of diagnostic judgments based on "blind" Machover figure drawings.* Unpublished doctoral dissertation, Columbia University, New York.

Wantz, R. A. (1989). Review of the Parenting Stress Index. In J. C. Conoley & J. J. Kramer (Eds.), *The tenth mental measurements yearbook*. Lincoln: Buros Institute of Mental Measurements, University of Nebraska.

Ward, P. B., McConaghy, N., & Catts, S. V. (1991). Word association and measures of psychosis proneness in university students. *Personality and Individual Differences, 12*, 473–480.

Waring, E. M., & Reddon, J. (1983). The measurement of intimacy in marriage: The Waring Questionnaire. *Journal of Clinical Psychology, 39*, 53–57.

Warmke, D. L. (1984). *Successful implementation of the "new" GATB in entry-level selection*. Presentation at the American Society for Personnel Administrators Region 4 Conference, October 15, Norfolk, VA.

Watkins, C. E., Jr. (1986). Validity and usefulness of WAIS-R, WISC-R, and WPPSI short forms. *Professional Psychology: Research and Practice, 17*, 36–43.

Watkins, C. E., Jr., & Campbell, V. L. (1989). Personality assessment and counseling psychology. *Journal of Personality Assessment, 53*, 296–307.

Watkins, C. E., Campbell, V. L., & Manus, M. (1990). Personality assessment training in counseling psychology programs. *Journal of Personality Assessment, 55*, 380–383.

Watkins, C. E., Jr., Campbell, V. L., & McGregor, P. (1988). Counseling psychologists' uses of and opinions about psychological tests: A contemporary perspective. *Counseling Psychologist, 16*, 476–486.

Watkins, C. E., Jr., Campbell, V. L., Nieberding, R., & Hallmark, R. (1995). Contemporary practice of psychological assessment by clinical psychologists. *Professional Psychology: Research and Practice, 26*, 54–60.

Watkins, E. O. (1976). *Watkins Bender-Gestalt Scoring System*. Novato, CA: Academic Therapy.

Watson, C. G. (1967). Relationship of distortion to DAP diagnostic accuracy among psychologists at three levels of sophistication. *Journal of Consulting Psychology, 31*, 142–146.

Watson, C. G., Felling, J., & Maceacherr, D. G. (1967). Objective draw-a-person scales: An attempted cross-validation. *Journal of Clinical Psychology, 23*, 382–386.

Watson, C. G., Thomas, D., & Anderson, P. E. D. (1992). Do computer-administered Minnesota Multiphasic Personality Inventories underestimate booklet-based scores? *Journal of Clinical Psychology, 48*, 744–748.

Weaver, C. B., & Bradley-Johnson, S. (1993). A national survey of school psychological services for deaf and hard of hearing students. *American Annals of the Deaf, 138*, 267–274.

Webb, E. J., Campbell, D. T., Schwartz, R. D., & Sechrest, L. (1966). *Unobtrusive measures: Nonreactive research in the social sciences*. Chicago: Rand McNally.

Webb, W. B., & Hilden, A. H. (1953). Verbal and intellectual ability as factors in projective test results. *Journal of Projective Techniques, 17*, 102–103.

Webster, C. D., Harris, G. T., Rice, M. E., Cormier, C., & Quinsey, V. L. (1994). *The violence prediction scheme*. Ontario, Canada: University of Toronto Centre of Criminology.

Wechsler, D. (1939). *The measurement of adult intelligence*. Baltimore: Williams & Wilkins.

Wechsler, D. (1944). *The measurement of adult intelligence* (3rd ed.). Baltimore: Williams & Wilkins.

Wechsler, D. (1955). *Manual for the Wechsler Adult Intelligence Scale*. New York: Psychological Corporation.

Wechsler, D. (1958). *The measurement and appraisal of adult intelligence* (4th ed.). Baltimore: Williams & Wilkins.

Wechsler, D. (1967). *Manual for the Wechsler Preschool and Primary Scale of Intelligence*. New York: Psychological Corporation.

Wechsler, D. (1974). *Manual for the Wechsler Intelligence Scale for Children—Revised*. New York: Psychological Corporation.

Wechsler, D. (1975). Intelligence defined and undefined: A relativistic appraisal. *American Psychologist, 30*, 135–139.

Wechsler, D. (1981). *Manual for the Wechsler Adult Intelligence Scale—Revised*. New York: Psychological Corporation.

Wechsler, D. (1991). *Manual for the Wechsler Intelligence Scale for Children—Third Edition*. San Antonio: Psychological Corporation.

Wechsler, D. (1997). *Wechsler Adult Intelligence Scale—Third Edition*. San Antonio: Psychological Corporation.

Wecker, N. S., Kramer, J. H., Wisniewski, A., et al. (2000). Age effects on executive ability. *Neuropsychology, 14*, 409–414.

Weed, N. C., Butcher, J. N., McKenna, T., & Ben-Porath, Y. S. (1992). New measures for assessing alcohol and drug abuse with the MMPI-2: The APS and AAS. *Journal of Personality Assessment, 58*, 389–404.

Weinberger, L. J., & Bradley, L. A. (1980). Effects of "favorability" and type of assessment device upon acceptance of general personality interpretations. *Journal of Personality Assessment, 44*, 44–47.

Weiner, B. A. (1980). Not guilty by reason of insanity: A sane approach. *Chicago Kent Law Review, 56*, 1057–1085.

Weiner, I. B. (1966). *Psychodiagnosis in schizophrenia*. New York: Wiley.

Weiner, I. B. (1991). Editor's note: Interscorer agreement in Rorschach research. *Journal of Personality Assessment, 56*, 1.

Weiner, I. B. (1997). Current status of the Rorschach Inkblot Method. *Journal of Personality Assessment, 68*, 5–19.

Weiner, I. B., Exner, J. E., Jr., & Sciara, A. (1996). Is the Rorschach welcome in the courtroom? *Journal of Personality Assessment, 67*, 422–424.

Weir, R. F. (1992). The morality of physician-assisted suicide. *Law, Medicine and Health Care, 20*, 116–126.

Weiss, D. J. (1985). Adaptive testing by computer. *Journal of Consulting and Clinical Psychology, 53*, 774–789.

Weiss, D. J., & Davison, M. L. (1981). Test theory and methods. *Annual Review of Psychology, 32*, 629–658.

Weiss, D. J., & Vale, C. D. (1987). Computerized adaptive testing for measuring abilities and other psychological variables. In J. N. Butcher (Ed.), *Computerized psychological assessment: A practitioner's guide* (pp. 325–343). New York: Basic.

Weiss, D. S., Zilberg, N. J., & Genevro, J. L. (1989). Psychometric properties of Loevinger's Sentence Completion Test in an adult psychiatric outpatient sample. *Journal of Personality Assessment, 53*, 478–486.

Weiss, H. M., & Adler, S. (1984). Personality and organizational behavior. In B. M. Straw & L. L. Cummings (Eds.), *Research in organizational behavior* (Vol. 6; pp. 1–50). Greenwich, CT: JAI.

Weiss, H. M., & Cropanzano, R. (1996). Affective events theory: A theoretical discussion of the structure, causes, and consequences of affective experiences at work. *Research in Organizational Behavior, 18*, 1–74.

Weiss, R., & Summers, K. (1983). Marital Interaction Coding System III. In E. Filsinger (Ed.), *Marriage and family assessment: A sourcebook of family therapy*. Beverly Hills: Sage.

Weisse, D. E. (1990). Gifted adolescents and suicide. *School Counselor, 37*, 351–358.

Weisskopf, E. A., & Dieppa, J. J. (1951). Experimentally induced faking of TAT responses. *Journal of Consulting Psychology, 15*, 469–474.

Weissman, H. N. (1991). Forensic psychological examination of the child witness in cases of alleged sexual abuse. *American Journal of Orthopsychiatry, 6*, 48–58.

Weithorn, L. A. (Ed.). (1987). *Psychology and child custody determinations*. Lincoln: University of Nebraska.

Welcher, D., Mellitis, E. D., & Hardy, J. B. (1971). A multivariate analysis of factors affecting psychological performance. *Johns Hopkins Medical Journal, 129,* 19–35.

Welsh, G. S. (1948). An extension of Hathaway's MMPI profile coding system. *Journal of Consulting Psychology, 12,* 343–344.

Welsh, G. S. (1956). Factor dimensions A and R. In G. S. Welsh & W. G. Dahlstrom (Eds.), *Basic readings on the MMPI in psychology and medicine* (pp. 264–281). Minneapolis: University of Minnesota.

Welsh, G. S., & Dahlstrom, W. G. (Eds.). (1956). *Basic readings on the MMPI in psychology and medicine.* Minneapolis: University of Minnesota.

Welsh, J. R., Kucinkas, S. K., & Curran, L. T. (1990). *Armed Services Vocational Aptitude Battery (ASVAB): Integrative review of validity studies* (Rpt 90-22). San Antonio: Operational Technologies Corp.

Werner, H., & Strauss, A. A. (1941). Pathology of figure-background relation in the child. *Journal of Abnormal and Social Psychology, 36,* 236–248.

Wertheimer, M. (1923). Untersuchungen zur Lehre von der Gestalt. *Psychologische Forschung* [Studies in the theory of Gestalt Psychology. *Psychology for Schools*], *4,* 301–303. Translated by Don Cantor in R. J. Herrnstein & E. G. Boring (1965), *A sourcebook in the history of psychology.* Cambridge, MA: Harvard University.

Wesman, A. G. (1949). Effect of speed on item-test correlation coefficients. *Educational and Psychological Measurement, 9,* 51–57.

Wesman, A. G. (1968). Intelligent testing. *American Psychologist, 23,* 267–274.

Wessberg, H. W., Mariotto, M. J., Conger, A. J., & Farrell, A. D. (1979). The ecological validity of role plays for assessing heterosocial anxiety and skill of male college students. *Journal of Consulting and Clinical Psychology, 47,* 525–535.

West, L. J., & Ackerman, D. L. (1993). The drug-testing controversy. *Journal of Drug Issues, 23,* 579–595.

West, S. G., & Graziano, W. G. (1989). Long-term stability and change in personality: An introduction. *Journal of Personality, 57,* 175–193.

Westen, D., Barends, A., Leigh, J., Mendel, M., & Silbert, D. (1988). *Manual for coding dimensions of object relations and social cognition from interview data.* Unpublished manuscript, University of Michigan, Ann Arbor.

Westen, D., Silk, K. R., Lohr, N., & Kerber, K. (1985). *Object relations and social cognition: TAT scoring manual.* Unpublished manuscript, University of Michigan, Ann Arbor.

Westling, D. L. (1996). What do parents of children with moderate and severe mental disabilities want? *Education and Training in Mental Retardation and Developmental Disabilities, 31,* 86–114.

Wetter, M. W., Baer, R. A., Berry, D. T. R., & Reynolds, S. K. (1994). The effect of symptom information on faking on the MMPI-2. *Assessment, 1,* 199–207.

Wettstein, R. M., Mulvey, E. P., & Rogers, R. (1991). A prospective comparison of four insanity defense standards. *American Journal of Psychiatry, 148,* 21–27.

Wexley, K. N., Yukl, G. A., Kovacs, S. Z., & Sanders, R. E. (1972). Importance of contrast effects in employment interviews. *Journal of Applied Psychology, 56,* 45–48.

White, B. L. (1971). *Human infants: Experience and psychological development.* Englewood Cliffs, NJ: Prentice-Hall.

White, D. M., Clements, C. B., & Fowler, R. D. (1985). A comparison of computer administration with standard administration of the MMPI. *Computers in Human Behavior, 1,* 153–162.

White, J. A., Davison, G. C., Haaga, D. A. F., & White, K. L. (1992). Cognitive bias in the articulated thoughts of depressed and nondepressed psychiatric patients. *Journal of Nervous and Mental Disease, 180,* 77–81.

White, L. T. (1984). Attitudinal consequences of the preemployment polygraph examination. *Journal of Applied Social Psychology, 14,* 364–374.

White, R. W., Sanford, R. N., Murray, H. A., & Bellak, L. (1941, September). *Morgan-Murray Thematic Apperception Test: Manual of directions* [mimeograph]. Cambridge, MA: Harvard Psychological Clinic.

White, S., Santilli, G., & Quinn, K. (1988). Child evaluator's roles in child sexual abuse assessments. In E. B. Nicholson & J. Bulkley (Eds.), *Sexual abuse allegations in custody and visitation cases: A resource book for judges and court personnel* (pp. 94–105). Washington, DC: American Bar Association.

Whitehead, W. E. (1994). Assessing the effects of stress on physical symptoms. *Health Psychology, 13,* 99–102.

Whitmyre, J. W. (1953). The significance of artistic excellence in the judgment of adjustment inferred from human figure drawings. *Journal of Consulting Psychology, 17,* 421–424.

Whitworth, R. H. (1984). Review of Halstead-Reitan Neuropsychological Battery and allied procedures. In D. J. Keyser & R. C. Sweetland (Eds.), *Test critiques* (Vol. 1; pp. 305–314). Kansas City, MO: Test Corporation of America.

Whitworth, R. H., & Unterbrink, C. (1994). Comparison of MMPI-2 clinical and content scales administered to Hispanic and Anglo-Americans. *Hispanic Journal of Behavioral Sciences, 16,* 255–264.

Wicker, A. W. (1969). Attitudes versus actions: The relationship of verbal and overt behavioral responses to attitude objects. *Journal of Social Issues, 25,* 41–78.

Wickes, T. A., Jr. (1956). Examiner influences in a testing situation. *Journal of Consulting Psychology, 20,* 23–26.

Widiger, T. A., & Clark, L. A. (2000). Toward DSM-V and the classification of psychopathology. *Psychological Bulletin, 126,* 946–963.

Wiederanders, M. R., & Choate, P. A. (1994). Beyond recidivism: Community adjustments of conditionally released insanity acquittees. *Psychological Assessment, 6,* 61–66.

Wigdor, A. K., & Garner, W. R. (1982). *Ability testing: Uses, consequences, and controversies.* Washington, DC: National Academy.

Wiggins, N. (1966). Individual viewpoints of social desirability. *Psychological Bulletin, 66,* 68–77.

Wilcox, R., & Krasnoff, A. (1967). Influence of test-taking attitudes on personality inventory scores. *Journal of Consulting Psychology, 31,* 185–194.

Wilcox, V. L., Kasal, S. V., & Berkman, L. F (1994). Social support and physical disability in older people after hospitalization: A prospective study. *Health Psychology, 13,* 170–179.

Wilkenson, G. S. (1993). *Wide Range Achievement Test-3.* Wilmington, DE: Wide Range, Inc.

Williams, A. D. (2000). Fixed versus flexible batteries. In R. J. McCaffrey et al. (Eds.), *The practice of forensic neuropsychology: Meeting challenges in the courtroom* (pp. 57–70). New York: Plenum.

Williams, C. L. (1986). Mental health assessment of refugees. In C. L. Williams & J. Westermeyer (Eds.), *Refugee mental health in resettlement countries* (pp. 175–188). New York: Hemisphere.

Williams, C. L., Butcher, J. N., Ben-Porath, Y. S., & Graham, J. R. (1992). *MMPI-A content scales: Assessing psychopathology in adolescents.* Minneapolis: University of Minnesota.

Williams, J. M., & Shane, B. (1986). The Reitan-Indiana Aphasia Screening Test: Scoring and factor analysis. *Journal of Clinical Psychology, 42,* 156–160.

Williams, K. C. (1996). Piagetian principles: Simple and effective application. *Journal of Intellectual Disability Research, 40*(2), 110–119.

Williams, R. (1975). The BITCH-100: A culture-specific test. *Journal of Afro-American Issues, 3,* 103–116.

Williams, R. H., & Zimmerman, D. W. (1996a). Are simple gains obsolete? *Applied Psychological Measurement, 20,* 59–69.

Williams, R. H., & Zimmerman, D. W. (1996b). Are simple gain scores obsolete: Commentary on the commentaries of Collins and Humphreys. *Applied Psychological Measurement, 20,* 295–297.

Williams, S. K., Jr. (1978). The Vocational Card Sort: A tool for vocational exploration. *Vocational Guidance Quarterly, 26,* 237–243.

Williams, T. Y., Boyd, J. C., Cascardi, M. A., & Poythress, N. (1996). Factor structure and convergent validity of the Aggression Questionnaire in an offender population. *Psychological Assessment, 8,* 398–403.

Willson, V. L., Reynolds, C. R., Chatman, S. P., & Kaufman, A. S. (1985). Confirmatory analysis of simultaneous, sequential and achievement factors on the K-ABC at 11 age levels ranging from 2½ to 12½ years. *Journal of School Psychology, 23,* 261–269.

Wilson, G. G., & Vitousek, K. M. (1999). Self-monitoring in the assessment of eating disorders. *Psychological Assessment, 11,* 480–489.

Wilson, P. T., & Spitzer, R. L. (1969). A comparison of three current classification systems for mental retardation. *American Journal of Mental Deficiency, 74,* 428–435.

Wilson, S. L., Thompson, J. A., & Wylie, G. (1982). Automated psychological testing for the severely physically handicapped. *International Journal of Man-Machine Studies, 17,* 291–296.

Winner, E. (1996). *Gifted children: Myths and realities.* New York: Basic.

Winner, E. (2000). The origins and ends of giftedness. *American Psychologist, 55,* 159–169.

Winston, A. S. (1996). "As his name indicates": R. S. Woodworth's letters of reference and employment for Jewish psychologists in the 1930s. *Journal of the History of the Behavioral Sciences, 32,* 30–43.

Winston, A. S. (1998). "The defects of his race": E. G. Boring and antisemitism in American psychology, 1923–1953. *History of Psychology, 1,* 27–51.

Wirt, R. D., Lachar, D., Klinedinst, J. K., & Seat, P. D. (1984). *Multidimensional description of child personality: A manual for the Personality Inventory for Children.* (1984 revision by David Lachar). Los Angeles: Western Psychological Services.

Wish, J., McCombs, K. F., & Edmonson, B. (1980). *Socio-Sexual Knowledge & Attitudes Test.* Chicago: Stoelting.

Witkin, H. A., & Berry, J. W. (1975). Psychological differentiation in cross-cultural perspective. *Journal of Cross-Cultural Psychology, 6,* 4–87.

Witkin, H. A., Dyk, R. B., Faterson, H. F., Goodenough, D. R., & Karp, S. A. (1962). *Psychological differentiation.* New York: Wiley.

Witkin, H. A., & Goodenough, D. R. (1977). Field dependence and interpersonal behavior. *Psychological Bulletin, 84,* 661–689.

Witkin, H. A., & Goodenough, D. R. (1981). *Cognitive styles: Essence and origins* (Psychological Issues Monograph 51). New York: International Universities.

Witkin, H. A., Lewis, H. B., Hertzman, M., Machover, K., Meissner, P. B., & Wapner, S. (1954). *Personality through perception: An experimental and clinical study.* New York: Harper.

Witmer, L. (1907). Clinical psychology. *Psychological Clinic, 1,* 1–9.

Witt, J. C., & Elliott, S. N. (1985). Acceptability of classroom management strategies. In T. R. Kratochwill (Ed.), *Advances in school psychology, Vol. 4* (pp. 251–288). Hillsdale, NJ: Erlbaum.

Wittenborn, J. R., & Holzberg, J. D. (1951). The Rorschach and descriptive diagnosis. *Journal of Consulting Psychology, 15,* 460–463.

Witty, P. (1940). Some considerations in the education of gifted children. *Educational Administration and Supervision, 26,* 512–521.

Wober, M. (1974). Towards an understanding of the Kiganda concept of intelligence. In J. W. Berry & P. R. Dasen (Eds.), *Culture and cognition: Readings in cross-cultural psychology* (pp. 261–280). London: Methuen.

Wolfner, G., Fause, D., & Dawes, R. M. (1993). The use of anatomically detailed dolls in sexual abuse evaluations: The state of the science. *Applied and Preventive Psychology, 2,* 1–11.

Wolfram, W. A. (1971). Social dialects from a linguistic perspective: Assumptions, current research, and future directions. In R. Shuy (Ed.), *Social dialects and interdisciplinary perspectives.* Washington, DC: Center for Applied Linguistics.

Wolf-Schein, E. G. (1993). Assessing the "untestable" client: ADLO. *Developmental Disabilities Bulletin, 21,* 52–70.

Wollersheim, J. P. (1974). The assessment of suicide potential via interview methods. *Psychotherapy, 11,* 222–225.

Wong, D. L. (1987). False allegations of child abuse: The other side of the tragedy. *Pediatric Nursing, 13,* 329–333.

Wong-Rieger, D., & Quintana, D. (1987). Comparative acculturation of Southeast Asians and Hispanic immigrants and sojourners. *Journal of Cross-Cultural Psychology, 18,* 145–162.

Woodcock, R. W. (1990). Theoretical foundations of the WJ-R measures of cognitive ability. *Journal of Psychoeducational Assessment, 8,* 231–258.

Woodcock, R. W. (1997). The Woodcock-Johnson Tests of Cognitive Ability—Revised. In D. P. Flanagan, J. L. Genshaft, & P. L. Harrison (Eds.), *Contemporary intellectual assessment: Theories, tests, and issues* (pp. 230–246). New York: Guilford.

Woodcock, R. W., & Mather, N. (1989). *WJ-R Tests of Cognitive Ability—Standard and Supplemental Batteries: Examiners manual.* In R. W. Woodcock & M. B. Johnson, *Woodcock-Johnson Psychoeducational Battery—Revised.* Allen, TX: DLM Teaching Resources.

Woodcock, R. W., & Mather, N. (1989, 1990). *WJ-R Tests of Achievement: Examiner's manual.* In R. W. Woodcock & M. B. Johnson, *Woodcock-Johnson Psychoeducational Battery—Revised.* Allen, TX: DLM Teaching Resources.

Woodcock, R. W., McGrew, K. S., & Mather, N. (2000). *Woodcock-Johnson III.* Itasca, IL: Riverside Publishing.

Woodward, J. (1972). Implications for sociolinguistics research among the deaf. *Sign Language Studies, 1,* 1–7.

Woodworth, R. S. (1917). *Personal Data Sheet.* Chicago: Stoelting.

Worchel, F. F., & Dupree, J. L. (1990). Projective story-telling techniques. In C. R. Reynolds & R. W. Kamphaus (Eds.), *Handbook of psychological and educational assessment of children: Personality, behavior, & context* (pp. 70–88). New York: Guilford.

Worlock, P., et al. (1986). Patterns of fractures in accidental and non-accidental injury in children. *British Medical Journal, 293,* 100–103.

Wright, B. D., & Stone, M. H. (1979). *Best test design: Rasch measurement.* Chicago: Mesa.

Wright, L., McCurdy, S., & Rogoll, G. (1992). The TUPA Scale: A self-report measure for the Type A subcomponent of time urgency and perpetual activation. *Psychological Assessment, 4,* 352–356.

Wright, T. A., & Cropanzano, R. (2000). Psychological well-being and job satisfaction as predictors of job performance. *Journal of Occupational Health Psychology, 5,* 84–94.

Wylonis, L. (1999). Psychiatric disability, employment, and the Americans with Disabilities Act. *Psychiatric Clinics of North America, 22,* 147–158.

Yamamoto, K., & Frengel, B. A. (1966). An exploratory component analysis of the Minnesota tests of creative thinking. *California Journal of Educational Research, 17,* 220–229.

Yan, L. (1999). Ancient Chinese mental tests and the features and values. *Psychological Science (China), 22,* 132–135.

Yao, E. L. (1979). The assimilation of contemporary Chinese immigrants. *Journal of Psychology, 101,* 107–113.

Yarnitsky, D., Sprecher, E., Zaslansky, R., & Hemli, J. A. (1995). Heat pain thresholds: Normative data and repeatability. *Pain, 60,* 329–332.

Young, G., & Wagner, E. E. (1998). Hand test characteristics of pain clinic patients. In P. Panek (Chair), *Research applications of the Hand Test.* Symposium presented at the Society for Personality Assessment 1998 Midwinter Meeting, February 21.

Young, K. S., Pistner, M., O'Mara, J., & Buchanan, J. (1999). Cyber disorders: The mental health concern for the new millennium. *CyberPsychology & Behavior, 2,* 475–479.

Younger, J. B. (1991). A model of parenting stress. *Research on Nursing and Health, 14,* 197–204.

Youngjohn, J. R., & Crook, T. H., III. (1993). Stability of everyday memory in age-associated memory impairment: A longitudinal study. *Neuropsychology, 7,* 406–416.

Yozawitz, A. (1986). Applied neuropsychology in a psychiatric center. In I. Grant & K. M. Adams (Eds.), *Neuropsychological assessment of neuropsychiatric disorders* (pp. 121–146). New York: Oxford University.

Yussen, S. R., & Kane, P. T. (1980). *Children's conception of intelligence.* Madison report for the project on studies of instructional programming for the individual student, University of Wisconsin, Technical Report #546.

Zedeck, S., & Cascio, W. F. (1984). Psychological issues in personnel decisions. *Annual Review of Psychology, 35,* 461–518.

Zelig, M., & Beidleman, W. B. (1981). Investigative hypnosis: A word of caution. *International Journal of Clinical and Experimental Hypnosis, 29,* 401–412.

Zeren, A. S., & Bradley, L. A. (1982). Effects of diagnostician prestige and sex upon subjects: Acceptance of genuine personality feedback. *Journal of Personality Assessment, 46,* 169–174.

Zhang, L.-M., Yu, L.-S., Wang, K.-N., et al. (1997). The psychophysiological assessment method for pilot's professional reliability. *Aviation, Space, & Environmental Medicine, 68,* 368–372.

Zieziula, F. R. (Ed.). (1982). *Assessment of hearing-impaired people.* Washington, DC: Gallaudet College.

Zimmerman, I. L., & Woo-Sam, J. M. (1978). Intelligence testing today: Relevance to the school age child. In L. Oettinger (Ed.), *Psychologists and the school age child with MBD/LD.* New York: Grune & Stratton.

Ziskin, J. (1995). *Coping with psychiatric and psychological testimony* (5th ed.; Vols. 1–3). Marina del Rey, CA: Law and Psychology Press.

Zubin, J., Eron, L. D., & Schumer, F. (1965). *An experimental approach to projective techniques.* New York: Wiley.

Zucker, S. (1985). *MSCA/K-ABC with high risk pre-schoolers.* Paper presented at the Annual Meeting of the National Association of School Psychologists, Las Vegas.

Zucker, S., & Copeland, E. P. (1987). *K-ABC/McCarthy Scale performance among three groups of "at-risk" pre-schoolers.* Paper presented at the Annual Meeting of the National Association of School Psychologists, Las Vegas.

Zuckerman, M. (1979). Traits, states, situations, and uncertainty. *Journal of Behavioral Assessment, 1,* 43–54.

Zuckerman, M. (1990). Some dubious premises in research and theory on racial differences. *American Psychologist, 45,* 1297–1303.

Zuckerman, M., & Lubin, B. (1985). *Manual for the Multiple Affect Adjective Check List—Revised.* San Diego: Educational and Industrial Testing Service.

Zumbo, B. D., & Taylor, S. V. (1993). The construct validity of the Extraversion subscales of the Myers-Briggs Type Indicator. *Canadian Journal of Behavioural Science, 25,* 590–604.

Zuniga, M. E. (1988). Assessment issues with Chicanas: Practice implications. *Psychotherapy, 25,* 288–293.

Zwahlen, H. T., Schnell, T., Liu, A., et al. (1998). Driver's visual search behaviour. In A. G. Gale et al. (Eds.), *Vision in vehicles-VI* (pp. 3–40). Oxford, England: Elsevier.

Zweigenhaft, R. L. (1984). *Who gets to the top? Executive suite discrimination in the eighties.* New York: American Jewish Committee Institute of Human Relations.

Zybert, P., Stein, Z., & Belmont, L. (1978). Maternal age and children's ability. *Perceptual and Motor Skills, 47,* 815–818.

Zytowski, D. G. (1996). Three decades of interest inventory results: A case study. *Career Development Quarterly, 45,* 141–148.

Illustration Credits

Chapter 1—p. 7, © 2001 Ronald J. Cohen. All rights reserved; p. 9, © AP/Wide World Photos; p. 11, Courtesy Gary A. Mirka, Department of Industrial Engineering, North Carolina State University; p. 15, © AP/Wide World Photos; p. 23, Courtesy National Archives; p. 34, Photo courtesy of Buros Center for Testing

Chapter 2—p. 39, © Maynard Owen Williams/National Geographic Society Image Collection; p. 41L, Photo of James McKeen Cattell from the *Journal of Consulting Psychology*, Vol. 1, Number 1 (1937); p. 41R, Photo of Psyche Cattell courtesy of Hudson Cattell; p. 45, © Brown Brothers; p. 65, © Bettmann/Corbis

Chapter 4—p. 102, © Jason Childs/STL/NewSport; p. 114, Courtesy University College, London; p. 117, Courtesy University College, London

Chapter 5—p. 143, Photo courtesy of Nancy Bayley; p. 146, © Amy Ramey/PhotoEdit

Chapter 6—p. 159L, © Bettmann/Corbis; p. 159R, © Bettmann/Corbis

Chapter 8—p. 232, © Bill Bachman/Photo Researchers, Inc.; p. 235, Reproduced with permission of the authors from Well, *Assessment and Management of Developmental Changes and Problems in Children*, 2/e, C.V. Mosby, 1981; p. 238, © The Granger Collection, New York; p. 241, © Wally McNamee/Corbis; p. 243, Courtesy E! Entertainment Television; p. 251, © 2001 Ronald J. Cohen. All rights reserved

Chapter 9—p. 257, Maria Melin/© 2001 ABC, Inc./ABC Photography Archives; p. 286, © 1940 Meier Art Judgment Test. The University of Iowa, Iowa City, IA

Chapter 10—p. 290, © Annie Griffiths Belt/Corbis; p. 293, Courtesy of Mark E. Swerdlik

Chapter 11—p. 326, Photo courtesy VarsityOnline; p. 337T, © 2001 Ronald J. Cohen. All rights reserved; p. 337M, Photo of "blown bridge," JET videogame. © 1985 Sublogic

Corporation; p. 337B, Tilting chair/tilting room photo by David Linton, from *Scientific American*, February 1959; p. 339, "Item 9" courtesy of Century Diagnostics Computer Interpreted Rorschach Report, Tempe, AZ

Chapter 12—p. 369, © Hans Huber Publishers, Bern; p. 370, Courtesy of Century Diagnostics Computer Interpreted Rorschach Report, Tempe, AZ; p. 374, Courtesy of the Harvard Archives; p. 375, Courtesy Henry A. Murray; p. 395, Courtesy of Supervised Lifestyles, Inc.; p. 402, © 2001 by Shirley Eberson. All rights reserved. May not be reproduced without permission.

Chapter 13—p. 425, © Rick Wilking/Reuters/Timepix; p. 432, Left: CAT-H card reproduced with permission of the publisher, CPS, Inc., Larchmont, NY, Right: reproduced by permission of Jason Aronson, Inc.

Chapter 14—p. 448, Goldstein-Scheerer Tests of Abstract and Concrete Thinking. © 1945, renewed 1972 by Psychological Corporation. Reproduced by permission. All rights reserved; p. 457, © 2001 S. Cohen. All rights reserved. May not be reproduced without permission. Jarrah wooden Tower of Hanoi courtesy of Built-Rite Sales, 6 Hillview Road, Mt. Lawley, W.A. Australia 6050; p. 458. © Archive Photos; p. 465, Sequin formboard courtesy of the C.H. Stoelting Company, Chicago, IL; p. 466, Photo of Neuro Lafayette Instrument Company, a Bissell Healthcare Company; p. 467, Photo of the Purdue Pegboard used by permission of the Lafayette Instrument Company, a Bissell Healthcare Company; p. 468, Photo courtesy Dr. Peter Schilder; p. 471, Photos courtesy General Electric Medical Systems; p. 472, Photos courtesy General Electric Medical Systems; p. 476, Courtesy of the C.H. Stoelting Company, Chicago, IL

Chapter 15—p. 501, Reproduced by permission of Stoelting Co., Wood Dale, IL 60191

Chapter 16—p. 509, Photo of the O'Connor Tweezer Dexterity Test by permission of the Lafayette Instrument Company, Lafayette, IN; p. 522, Photo of "manufacturing problem" courtesy of Dr. Douglas Bray

Name Index

Rosanoff, A. J., 381
Rosen, J., 57
Rosen, M., 501
Rosenman, R. H., 327, 353n
Rosenthal, R., 124
Rosenzweig, S., 379
Rosser, R., 436
Rossini, E. D., 378
Roszkowski, M. J., 484
Rothberg, J. M., 423
Rotter, J. B., 335, 339, 382, 387
Rotundo, M., 517
Rouse, S. V., 438
Routh, D. K., 388
Roy, P., 359
Rozeboom, W. W., 178
Rubenzer, S. J., 328
Rubin, L. S., 400
Rubin, S., 377
Ruch, G. M., 53
Ruch, W., 402
Rudy, T. E., 437
Ruffolo, L. F., 458
Rugh, J. D., 399
Rulon, P. J., 137
Rupert, P. A., 67
Russ, S. W., 333
Russell, J. S., 182n
Russell, J. T., 165, 168
Russell, M., 346
Russo, D. C., 392
Ryan, J. J., 242, 268, 278, 517
Ryburn, M., 261

Sabatelli, R. M., 431
Sacco, W. P., 437
Sachs, B. B., 495
Sackett, P. R., 184, 185, 516, 517, 526, 527
Sacks, E., 23
Sacks, O., 502
Salas, E., 528
Sales, B. D., 61
Salk, J. E., 534
Sallis, J. F., 436, 437
Salthouse, T. A., 458
Salvia, J., 312
Samuda, R. J., 249
Samuel, W., 23
Sandelands, L. E., 536
Sandoval, J., 270, 517
Sanfilippo, J., 433
Sanford, R. N., 377
Santiviago, M., 502
Sarason, I. G., 437
Sarnoff, D., 399
Satinsky, D., 399
Sattler, J. M., 24, 179, 261, 263, 269, 270, 272, 279
Saunders, E. A., 371
Savickas, M. L., 508

Savitsky, K., 102
Sawin, D. B., 291
Sawyer, J., 404
Saxe, L., 61, 516
Saxton, J., 477
Sayer, A. G., 210
Sayette, M. A., 438
Saylor, C. F., 421
Scarr, S., 247
Schade, C. P., 421
Schafer, R., 381
Schag, C. A., 436
Schaie, K. W., 236, 241, 246
Scheid, T. L., 490
Scheier, M., 436
Schein, J. D., 502
Schildroth, A., 494
Schloss, I., 542
Schmand, B., 457
Schmidt, F. L., 51, 124, 172, 173, 184, 510, 526
Schmidt, K. L., 386
Schmitt, N., 515, 520, 524
Schneck, M. R., 42
Schneider, B., 515
Schneider, D. L., 517
Schneider, M. F., 378
Schonemann, P. H., 178
Schopp, L., 478
Schramke, C. J., 563
Schuerger, J. M., 346
Schuh, A. J., 403
Schuldberg, D., 368
Schulte, A. A., 488
Schulte, L. E., 494
Schultz, B. M., 32
Schwartz, L. A., 373
Schwartz, N., 537
Schwitzgebel, R. L., 399
Scodel, A., 377, 387
Scott, J., 261
Scott, L. H., 279
Scotti, J. R., 126n
Seagull, F. J., 458
Sears, R. R., 242
Seashore, C. E., 306
Sebold, J., 433
Seeman, W., 352
Segal, S. P., 537
Sell, R. L., 401
Sells, S. G., 449
Selover, R. B., 521
Semrud-Clikeman, M., 421
Serby, M., 450
Seretny, M. L., 460, 467
Serin, R. C., 429
Serpell, R., 247
Sevig, T. D., 359
Shadish, W. R., 124
Shah, S. A., 68
Shane, B., 462

Shapiro, E. S., 299, 394
Sharpe, D., 124
Shavelson, R. J., 145
Shaw, S. R., 269
Shaywitz, B. A., 245
Shearn, C. R., 388
Shedler, J., 410
Sheehan, P. W., 412
Sheffield, J. R., 240, 320
Shell, R. W., 59
Shenkel, R. J., 443
Shepard, L. A., 212
Sherman, L. J., 386
Sherman, R., 403
Sherrill-Pattison, S., 458
Shiffman, S., 396
Shiffrin, R. M., 462
Shine, L. C., 168
Shinedling, M. M., 23
Shneidman, E. S., 379
Shock, N. W., 241
Shockley, W., 240
Shriner, J. G., 488
Shrout, P. E., 437
Shuey, A. M., 247
Shuman, D. W., 61
Siegel, L. J., 421
Siegelman, M., 505
Siegler, R. S., 225
Silber, D. E., 333
Silka, V. R., 501
Silverman, C., 420
Silverman, I., 246
Silverman, S. B., 515
Silverstein, M. L., 218
Simon, R. J., 428
Simon, T., 42, 248, 258, 306
Simpson, R., 247
Simpson, R. L., 488
Sims, H. P., 398
Sines, J. O., 560
Siperstein, G. N., 501
Sivec, H. J., 356
Sivik, T. M., 377
Skinner, C. H., 394
Skinner, H. A., 555
Skolnick, J. H., 400
Slakter, M. J., 211
Slate, J. R., 264
Slater, S. B., 484
Sloan, P., 333
Slobogin, C., 61, 428
Smith, A., 449
Smith, C. A., 436
Smith, D. E., 139
Smith, D. K., 240, 290, 309, 386
Smith, F. J., 417n
Smith, G. E., 269
Smith, G. T., 278
Smith, M., 169

Smith, M. H., 23
Smith, P. B., 125
Smith, R. E., 555
Smith, R. G., 389
Smith, T. T., 293
Smither, J. W., 403
Smither, R., 359
Smolak, L., 337
Smucker, M. R., 421
Snowden, L. R., 359
Snyder, C. R., 388, 443
Snyder, D. K., 333, 431, 559, 563
Sodowsky, G. R., 359
Sokal, M. M., 41
Solomon, I. L., 378
Solomon, P. R., 455
Sommers-Flanagan, J., 423
Sommers-Flanagan, R., 423
Sones, R., 378
Sontag, L. W., 247
Spanier, G. B., 431
Sparks, K., 124
Sparrow, S. S., 500
Spearman, C. S., 2, 41, 117, 226, 229–230, 236
Speth, E. B., 32
Spiegel, J. S., 484
Spielberger, C. D., 328, 532
Spies, C. J., 40, 115
Spitz, H. H., 457
Spitzer, R. L., 410, 412, 484
Spitznagel, E. L., 139
Spivack, G., 495
Spotts, J., 495
Spranger, E., 360
Spreat, S., 484
Spreen, O., 461, 468
Staal, M. A., 333
Stachnik, T. J., 442
Stacy, A. W., 439
Stahl, P. M., 32
Stainton, N. R., 442
Stake, J. E., 516
Stanczak, D. E., 458
Stanley, J. C., 51, 131, 246
Starch, D., 138
Stark, K., 386
Starr, B. D., 378
Staw, B. M., 516
Steadman, H. J., 423
Steer, R. A., 162
Steiger, J. H., 178
Stein, D., 329
Steinberg, M., 412
Steinfeld, E., 488
Stephens, J. J., 48
Stephenson, W., 339, 340
Stern, H., 9
Stern, W., 367n
Sternberg, D. P., 431

Glossary/Index

Alternate forms: Different versions of the same test or measure; contrast with *parallel forms*, 132

Alternate-forms reliability: An estimate of the extent to which item sampling and other error have affected scores on two versions of the same test; contrast with *parallel forms reliability*, 132–133. *See also* Internal consistency reliability, Inter-scorer reliability, Split-half reliability, Test-retest reliability, Reliability, and Coefficient of equivalence

American Association on Mental Retardation (AAMR), 484, 498–499

American Board of Assessment Psychology (ABAP), 28, 64

American Board of Professional Psychology (ABPP), 28

American College Testing (ACT) programs, 303

American Educational Research Association, 21

American Law Institute (ALI), 428

American Psychiatric Association (APA), 74, 409, 416, 420

American Psychological Association (APA), 21
  CAPA product guidelines and standards, 561
  Committee on Professional Practices and Standards, 31
  death-with-dignity legislation, 65, 66
  legal and ethical concerns, 60–67
  online databases, 35
  report on intelligence, 253–254

American Sign Language (ASL), 479, 493–494

Americans with Disabilities Act (ADA), 54, 479, 480, 489–490

Analogue behavioral observation: The observation of a person or persons in an environment designed to increase the assessor's chance of observing targeted behaviors and interactions, 395–396

Analogue study: Research or behavioral intervention that replicates a variable or variables in ways that are similar to or analogous to the real variables the experimenter wishes to study; for example, a laboratory study designed to research a phobia of snakes in the wild, 395

Analyzing test items. *See* Item analysis

Anatomically detailed doll (ADD): A human figure in doll form with accurately represented genitalia, typically used to assist in the evaluation of sexually abused children, 434

Anchoring, 108

Anchor protocol: A test answer sheet developed by a test publisher to check the accuracy of examiners' scoring, 272

APA: American Psychological Association. In other sources, particularly medical texts, this may refer to the American Psychiatric Association. *See* American Psychiatric Association; American Psychological Association

Apgar number, 290

Aphagia: A condition in which the ability to eat is lost or diminished, 461n

Aphasia: A loss of ability to express oneself or to understand spoken or written language due to a neurological deficit, 461

Aphasia Screening Test (AST), 461–462

Apperceive: To perceive in terms of past perceptions (from this verb, the noun apperception is derived), 374

Apperceptive Personality Test (APT), 380

Application form, 519

Aptitude test: A test that usually focuses more on informal as opposed to formal learning experiences and is designed to measure both learning and inborn potential for the purpose of making predictions about the test-taker's future performance; also referred to as a *prognostic test* and, especially with young children, a *readiness test*, 300–306, 509–515
  achievement tests vs., 300–301
  career counseling and, 509–515
  college level, 305–306
  elementary school level, 302–303
  secondary school level, 303–305

Arithmetic mean: Also referred to simply as the *mean*, a measure of central tendency derived by calculating an average of all scores in a distribution, 81, 83

Armed Forces Qualification Test (AFQT), 282

Armed Services Vocational Aptitude Battery (ASVAB), 282, 283–284, 285

Army Alpha and Beta tests, 282

ASL. *See* American Sign Language

Assessee capabilities, 486

Assessment. *See* Psychological assessment

Assessment center: An organizationally standardized procedure for evaluation involving multiple assessment techniques, 522–524

Assessment of Developmental Levels by Observation (ADLO), 497

Assessment of Men (OSS), 2

Assessor capabilities, 486–487

Assimilation: In Piagetian theory, one of two basic mental operations through which humans learn, this one involving the active organization of new information into what is already perceived, known, and thought; contrast with *accommodation*, 228

Association of Personnel Test Publishers (APTP), 516

Association of Test Publishers, 63

Asymptotic curve, 91

At risk: Defined in different ways by different school districts, but in general, a reference to functioning that is deficient and possibly in need of intervention, 290–291, 480

At-risk infant or toddler: According to IDEA, a child under 3 years of age who would be in danger of experiencing a substantial developmental delay if early intervention services were not provided, 480

Attention Deficit Hyperactivity Disorder (ADHD), 289

Attitude: A presumably learned disposition to react in some characteristic manner to a particular stimulus, 532
  job satisfaction and, 532–533
  measurement of, 321, 536–539
  organizational commitment and, 533

Attractiveness, and maternal behavior, 290–291

Aunt Fanny effect. *See* Barnum effect

Authentic assessment: Also known as performance-based assessment, evaluation on relevant, meaningful tasks that may be conducted to examine learning of academic subject matter but that demonstrates the student's transfer of that study to real-world activities, 319

Autism, 499

Average deviation: A measure of variability derived by summing the absolute value of all the scores in a distribution and dividing by the total number of scores, 87

Banding, 185

Bar graph: A graphic illustration of data wherein numbers indicative of frequency are set on the vertical axis, categories are set on the horizontal axis, and the rectangle bars that describe the data are typically noncontiguous, 80

Barnum effect: The consequence of one's belief that a vague personality description truly describes oneself, when in reality that description may apply to almost anyone; sometimes referred to as the "Aunt Fanny effect," because the same personality might be applied to anyone's Aunt Fanny, 439–443

Basal level: A stage in a test achieved by a testtaker by meeting some preset criterion to continue to be tested, for example, responding correctly to two consecutive items on an ability test that contains increasingly difficult items may establish a "base" from which to continue testing; contrast with *ceiling level*, 262

Base rate: An index, usually expressed as a proportion, of the extent to which a particular trait, behavior, characteristic, or attribute exists in a population, 169
predictive validity and, 170–171
BASIC ID dimensions, 541–542
Battelle Development Inventory, 291
Battery. *See* test battery.
Bayley Scales of Infant Development (BSID-II), 142–143, 291
Beck Depression Inventory (BDI), 162, 420–421
Beck Self-Concept Test (BST), 329
Beery-Buktenica Development Test of Visual-Motor Integration, 466
Behavior
adaptive, 498–501
brain anatomy and, 446
domain of, 145
nonverbal, 48–49
sampling, 20
test-related, 19–20
Behavioral assessment: An approach to evaluation based on the analysis of samples of behavior, including the antecedents and consequences of the behavior, 388–403
analogue studies and, 394–396
approaches to, 392–401
characteristics of, 390–392
computer-assisted, 554
issues in, 401, 403
overview of, 388–390
personal account of, 394–395
psychophysiological methods of, 398–400
rating scales and, 393–394
role play and, 398

self-monitoring in, 396
situational performance measures and, 397–398
traditional assessment compared to, 391
unobtrusive measures used in, 400–401, 402
Behavioral observation: Monitoring the actions of others or oneself by visual or electronic means while recording quantitative and/or qualitative information regarding the actions, typically for diagnostic or related purposes and either to design intervention or to measure the outcome of an intervention, 10, 393, 542
Behavior Problem Checklist, 495
Behn-Rorschach test, 371
Bell Adjustment Inventory, 399
Bell Curve, The (Herrnstein & Murray), 54, 253
Bender-Gestalt test: A widely used screening tool for neuropsychological deficit that entails copying designs; also referred to simply as "the Bender;" developed by Lauretta Bender, M.D., 450n, 467–469, 470, 495
Bennet Mechanical Comprehension Test, 509
Benton Visual Retention Test, 469–470
Bias: As applied to tests, a factor inherent within a test that systematically prevents accurate, impartial measurement, 179
intercept, 180
slope, 180–181
translation, 47
See also Intercept bias, Slope bias, and Test bias
Bimodal distribution: A distribution in which the central tendency consists of two scores occurring an equal number of times, both the most frequently occurring scores in the distribution, 85. *See also* Mode
Biofeedback equipment, 12, 399
Black Intelligence Test of Cultural Homogeneity (BITCH), 252–253
Blacky Pictures Test, 335, 378–379
Blindness
accommodation for, 491–492
assessment of, 491–493
deafness with, 496–497
Blueprinting, 157
Body image distortion, 337
Boehm Test of Basic Concepts, 499
Boston Naming Test, 458
Boys and Girls Book About Divorce, The (Gardner), 432

Bracken Basic Concepts Scale-Revised, 499
Brain
anatomical overview of, 445–447
behavioral correlates to, 446
medical diagnostic aids and, 471–472
neurological damage to, 447–449
Brain scan, 472
Branched testing. *See* Adaptive testing
Brand names, 543
Breathalyzer test, 146
Bricklin Perception of Relationships Test, 31
Bricklin Perceptual Scales (BPS), 31, 32
British Ability Scales (BAS), 312
Bruininks-Oseretsky Test of Motor Proficiency, 465, 498
Burnout: A psychological syndrome of emotional exhaustion, depersonalization, and reduced personal accomplishment, 531–532
Buros Institute of Mental Measurements, 34
Business-related assessment, 27, 535–544
attitude measures in, 536–539
behavioral observation in, 542
consumer psychology and, 536
motivation research methods in, 539–544
qualitative research in, 539–540, 541
See also Employment issues

California Test of Mental Maturity, 282
Callier-Azusa Scale (CAS), 496–497
Campbell Interest and Skill Survey, 507
CAPA. *See* Computer-assisted psychological assessment
Career counseling, 505–518
ability and aptitude measures for, 509–515
interest measures for, 506–509
personality measures for, 515–517
See also Employment issues
Career Interest Inventory, 507
Case history data: Records, transcripts, and other accounts in written, pictorial, or other form, in any media, that preserve archival information, official and informal accounts, and other data and items relevant to an assessee, 9–10, 417, 455
Case studies, 455
CAT. *See* Computerized adaptive testing
Catalogues of tests, 33–34
Categorical scaling: A system of scaling in which stimuli are placed into one of two or more alternative categories that differ quantitatively with respect to some continuum, 196

for by the correlation coefficient, 116–117

Coefficient of equivalence: An estimate of parallel-forms reliability or alternate-forms reliability, 132. *See also* Parallel-forms reliability; Alternate-forms reliability

Coefficient of generalizability: In generalizability theory, an index of the influence that particular facets have on a test score, 147

Coefficient of reliability. *See* Reliability coefficient

Coefficient of stability: An estimate of test-retest reliability obtained during time intervals of six months or longer, 132. *See also* Test-retest reliability; Reliability

Coefficient of validity. *See* Validity coefficient

Cognitive Abilities Test, 282

Cognitive Assessment System, 279

Cognitive disability: A general reference to a broad spectrum of disabling conditions, including various neurological deficits, learning disabilities, autism, and mental retardation, 498–502

Cognitive interview: A type of hypnotic interview without the hypnotic induction; the interviewee is encouraged to use imagery and focused retrieval to recall information, 413

Collaborative Drawing Technique, 386

College Entrance Examination Board, 296

College level aptitude tests, 305–306

College Level Examination Program (CLEP), 299

College yearbook photos, 402

Color-Form Sorting Test, 448, 456, 469

Color Sorting Test, 448

Committee on Emotional Fitness, 43

Communication
   nonverbal, 48–49
   verbal, 46–48

Comparative scaling: In test development, a method of developing ordinal scales through the use of a sorting task that entails judging a stimulus in comparison with every other stimulus used on the test, 196

Competence to stand trial: Understanding the charges against one and being able to assist in one's own defense, 423, 426–427

Competency Screening Test, 426–427

Computer-Assisted Hypnosis Scale, 101

Computer-assisted psychological assessment (CAPA), 11–12, 545–564

access to CAPA-related products, 562
actuarial prediction and, 560–561
advantages of, 546–553
central processing of, 555–556
clinical prediction and, 561
disadvantages of, 553–554
equivalence issues, 557, 559
ethical issues related to, 64, 66
evaluation of, 562–563
future of, 563
item banking and, 547, 549–552
item branching and, 547, 552–553
local processing of, 556–557
mechanical prediction and, 561
overview of, 545–554
programs designed for, 547
reports generated from, 557, 558
standards for CAPA products, 561–562
teleprocessing of, 556
testtaker input issues, 554
validity issues, 559–560

Computer-based test interpretation (CBTI), 545, 559–560

Computerized adaptive testing (CAT): An interactive, computer-administered testtaking process wherein items presented to the testtaker are based in part on the testtaker's performance on previous items, 546

Computers
   availability of psychological tests on, 64, 66
   using in assessment, 11–12

Conceptualization of tests, 188–191
   item development issues, 190–191
   pilot work, 191
   preliminary questions, 189–190

Concurrent validity: A form of criterion-related validity that is an index of the degree to which a test score is related to some criterion measure obtained at the same time (concurrently), 160, 161–162. *See also* Construct validity; Content validity; Criterion-related validity; Face validity; Predictive validity; Validity

Condom Attitude Scale-Adolescent Version, 437–438

Confidence interval: A range or band of test scores that is likely to contain the "true score," 149–150

Confidential information: Communication between a professional and a client, along with other data obtained by the professional in the course of a professional relationship that the professional has an ethical obligation not to disclose; contrast with *privileged information*, 68

Confidentiality: The ethical obligation of professionals to keep confidential all communications made or entrusted to them in confidence. Professionals may be compelled to disclose such confidential communications under court order or other extraordinary conditions, such as when such communications refer to a third party in imminent danger; contrast with privacy right.
   ethical issues related to, 68–69
   test results and, 70

Confirmatory factor analysis (CFA): A class of mathematical procedures employed when a factor structure that has been explicitly hypothesized is tested for its fit with the observed relationships between the variables, 178, 273–276. *See also* Factor analysis

Conformity, 125

Confrontation naming: Identifying a pictured stimulus in a neuropsychological context, such as in response to administration of items in the Boston Naming Test, 458, 459, 460

Connors Rating Scales-Revised (CRS-R), 289

Co-norming: The test norming process conducted on two or more tests using the same sample of testtakers; when used to validate all of the tests being normed, this process may also be referred to as co-validation, 107n, 218–219

Consensus translation, 47

Consistency, 29

Construct: An informed, scientific idea developed or generated to describe or explain behavior; some examples of constructs include "intelligence," "personality," "anxiety," and "job satisfaction," 14, 173

Construct bias, 47

Constructed-response format: A form of test item requiring the testtaker to construct or create a response, as opposed to simply selecting a response. Items on essay examinations, fill-in-the-blank, and short-answer tests are examples of items in a constructed-response format; contrast with *selected-response format*, 199, 201

Construction of tests, 192–202
   scaling process, 193–198
   scoring items, 201–202
   writing items, 198–201

Developmental Indicators for the Assessment of Learning, 291

Developmental milestone: Important event during the course of one's life that may be marked by the acquisition, presence, or growth of certain abilities or skills, or the failure, impairment, or cessation of such abilities or skills, 451, 452

Devereaux Adolescent Behavior Rating Scale, 495

Devereaux Child Behavior Rating Scale, 495

Deviates, 115

Deviation IQ: A variety of standard score used to report "intelligence quotients" (IQs) with a mean set at 100 and a standard deviation set at 15. On the Stanford-Binet, it is also referred to as a test composite, and it represents an index of intelligence derived from a comparison between the performance of an individual testtaker and the performance of other testtakers of the same age in the test's standardization sample, 97, 259

Diagnosis: A description or conclusion reached on the basis of evidence and opinion through a process of distinguishing the nature of something and ruling out alternative conclusions, 17–18, 409–410

Diagnostic and Statistical Manual of Mental Disorders (DSM), 74, 344, 409–410
criteria for diagnosing depression, 420
DSM-IV-TR edition, 409–410
nominal scales, 74
revisions to diagnostic descriptions, 415–416

Diagnostic Assessment for the Severely Handicapped-II, 499

Diagnostic information: In educational contexts, test or other data used to pinpoint a student's difficulties for the purpose of remediating them, 306

Diagnostic Psychological Testing (Rapaport), 418

Diagnostic test: A tool used to make a diagnosis, usually to identify areas of deficit to be targeted for intervention, 17–18, 306–308
math tests, 307–308
Millon tests, 418–419
reading tests, 307

Diana v. State Board of Education (1970), 57

Diary panel: A variety of consumer panel in which respondents have

agreed to keep diaries of their thoughts and/or behaviors, 539. *See also* Consumer panel

Dictionary of Occupational Titles, 510

Differential Abilities Scale (DAS), 180, 279, 312–316
administration of, 315
evaluation of, 315–316
psychometric properties of, 314–315
scoring and interpretation of, 315
standardization sample for, 314
subtests of, 313

Differential Aptitude Test (DAT), 165, 243

Differential cutoffs, 185

Differential scoring, 185

Dimensional qualitative research: An adaptation of Lazarus's multimodal clinical approach for use in qualitative research applications, designed to ensure that the research is comprehensive and systematic from a psychological perspective and guided by discussion questions based on the seven modalities (or dimensions) named in Lazarus's model, which are summarized by the acronym BASIC ID (behavior, affect, sensation, imagery, cognition, interpersonal relations, and drugs). Cohen's adaptation of Lazarus's work adds an eighth dimension, sociocultural, changing the acronym to BASIC IDS, 541–542

Directory of Unpublished Experimental Measures, 35

Disability: As defined in the Americans with Disabilities Act of 1990, a physical or mental impairment that substantially limits one or more of the major life activities of an individual, 479–504
accommodation and, 484–488
alternate assessment and, 4–6, 484–485
children with, 482–483
cognitive, 498–502
culture of, 502–503
deaf-blindness, 496–497
employment issues and, 489–490
ethics of testing individuals with, 64
functional, 484
hearing, 493–497
infants or toddlers with, 480
legal issues and, 480–485
motor, 497–498
need for sensitivity toward, 503
overview of, 479–480
professional determination of, 483–484

visual, 491–493, 496–497
See also Major life activity

Discriminant evidence: With reference to construct validity, data from a test or other measurement instrument showing little relationship between test scores or other variables with which the scores on the test being construct-validated should not theoretically be correlated; contrast with *convergent evidence,* 177

Discriminant validity, 177

Discrimination
group differences and, 50–51
item-discrimination index, 206–208

Discussion of Organizational Culture (DOC), 534–535

Distribution: In a psychometric context, a set of test scores arrayed for recording or study, 78
bimodal, 85
frequency, 78–81
kurtosis of, 90
measures of central tendency, 81–85
measures of variability, 85–89
skewness of, 89–90

Divergent thinking, 285

Domain-referenced tests, 109. *See* Criterion-referenced testing and assessment

Domain sampling: (1) A sample of behaviors from all possible behaviors that could be indicative of a particular construct; (2) a sample of test items from all possible items that could be used to measure a particular construct, 15n, 145

Draw An Animal procedure, 385

Draw A Person (DAP) test, 383, 385, 495
Screening Procedure for Emotional Disturbance (DAP:SPED), 386

Drug testing, 524–526

DSM. *See Diagnostic and Statistical Manual of Mental Disorders*

DSM-IV-TR: Abbreviation for *Diagnostic and Statistical Manual of Mental Disorders, Fourth Edition, Text Revision,* published in May 2000, a slightly modified version of DSM-IV, which was published in 1994, 409. *See also Diagnostic and Statistical Manual of Mental Disorders*

Dual-easel test administration format, 292, 293

Durham standard: A standard of legal insanity in *Durham v. United States* wherein the defendant was not found culpable for criminal action if his unlawful act was the product of a mental disease or defect; contrast with *ALI standard* and *M'Naghten standard,* 428

Durham v. United States (1954), 428

Dusky v. United States, 423

Duty to warn: A legally mandated obligation to advise an endangered third party of their peril that may override patient privilege. Therapists and assessors may have a legal duty to warn when a client expresses intent to hurt a third party in any way, ranging from physical violence to disease transmission, 69, 423

Dynamic characteristics, 141

Early Screening Profile, 291

Eating disorders, 337

Echoencephalograph, 472

Educable mentally retarded (EMR), 57

Educational assessment, 25–26, 288–322
   achievement tests, 294–299
   aptitude tests, 300–306
   attitude inventories, 321
   authentic assessment, 319
   diagnostic tests, 306–308
   interest inventories, 321
   peer appraisal techniques, 319–320
   performance assessment, 318
   portfolio assessment, 318–319
   preschool assessment, 288–294
   psychoeducational test batteries, 308–317
   study habits assessment, 320–321
   See also Schools

Educational Testing Service (ETS), 35, 110–111

Education Apperception Test, 378

Education for All Handicapped Children Act, 55, 294, 480

Edwards Personal Preference Schedule (EPPS), 202, 515

Electroencephalograph (EEG), 472

Electromyograph (EMG), 472

Elementary school aptitude tests, 302–303

Ellis Island, 45

Emotional exhaustion, 531

Emotional injury: A term sometimes used synonymously with *mental suffering, emotional harm,* and *pain and suffering,* to convey psychological damage, 429–430

Emotional intelligence: A popularization of aspects of Gardner's theory of multiple intelligences, with emphasis on the notions of interpersonal and intrapersonal intelligence, 230–231

Emotional issues
   behavioral assessment of, 402
   child abuse indicated through, 434

Empirical criterion keying: The process of using criterion groups to develop test items, wherein the scoring or keying of items has been demonstrated empirically to differentiate among groups of testtakers, 347–348. *See also* Criterion group

Empirical keying by group, 185

Employment issues, 505–535
   application form, 519
   aptitude tests, 509–515
   assessment centers, 522–524
   attitude, 532–533
   burnout, 531–532
   career counseling, 505–518
   classification, 518–526
   cognitive ability tests, 526–527
   cultural diversity, 526–527
   disabilities, 489–490
   drug testing, 524–526
   integrity tests, 516–517
   interest inventories, 506–509
   interviews, 520
   job satisfaction, 532–533
   letters of recommendation, 519–520
   motivation, 528–532
   organizational commitment, 533
   organizational culture, 533–535
   performance tests, 521–524
   personality assessment, 515–517
   physical tests, 524
   placement, 518–526
   portfolio assessment, 520
   productivity, 527–528
   résumés, 518–519
   screening and selection, 518–526

English Men of Science (Galton), 239

English proficiency tests, 298–299

Environment, Intelligence, and Scholastic Achievement, 54

Episodic memory, 464

Equal Employment Opportunity Commission (EEOC), 56

Equal Opportunity Employment Act (1991), 55

Equipercentile method: A procedure for comparing scores on two or more tests, as in the creation of national anchor norms, which entails the calculating of percentile norms for each test and identifying the score on each test that corresponds to the percentile, 107

Equivalence issues, 557, 559

Erg: A unit of work, 27n

Ergonomics: The study of work, 27n

Error: Collectively, all of the factors other than what a test purports to measure that contribute to scores on the test; error is a variable in all testing and assessment, 18
   leniency, 181–182
   rating, 181–182
   severity, 182
   sources of, 129–131
   standard, of measurement, 19

Error of central tendency: Less than accurate rating or evaluation by a rater or judge due to that rater's general tendency to make ratings at or near the midpoint of the scale; contrast with *generosity error* and *severity error,* 182, 331

Error variance: In the true score model, the component of variance attributable to random sources irrelevant to the trait or ability the test purports to measure in an observed score or distribution of scores. Common sources of error variance include those related to test construction (including item or content sampling), test administration, and test scoring and interpretation, 18, 129
   administration of tests and, 129–130
   construction of tests and, 129
   interpretation of tests and, 130–131
   scoring of tests and, 130–131

E.T., the Extraterrestrial (film), 431

Eta squared, 120n

Ethical issues, 52–70
   death-with-dignity legislation and, 65–66
   privacy and disclosure principles and, 68–69
   professional concerns and, 60–64
   public concerns and, 53–58

Ethical Standards for the Distribution of Psychological Tests and Diagnostic Aids (APA), 62

Ethical Standards of Psychologists (APA), 62, 68–69

Ethics: A body of principles of right, proper, or good conduct; contrast with *laws,* 53

Evaluation
   cultural standards of, 49
   informal, 291
   of test quality, 28–36

Evaluative information: Test or other data used to make judgments such as class placement, pass/fail, and admit/reject decisions; contrast with *diagnostic information,* 306

Evolutionary view of mental disorder: The view that an attribution of mental disorder requires both a scientific judgment (from an

Evolutionary view of mental disorder: *(continued)* evolutionary perspective) that there exists a failure of function, and a value judgment (from the perspective of social values) that the failure is harmful to the individual, 410

Examiner's Handbook: An Expanded Guide for Fourth Edition Users, The (Delaney & Hopkins), 262

Exceptional Case Study Project (ECSP), 425

Exceptional individuals, 480n

Executive functions: In neuropsychology, organizing, planning, cognitive flexibility, inhibition of impulses, and other activities associated with the frontal and prefrontal lobes of the brain, 457

Exercises in Psychological Testing and Assessment (Cohen), 37

Exner's Comprehensive System, 371, 372

Expectancy chart: Graphic representation of an expectancy table, 165, 167

Expectancy data: Information, usually in the form of an expectancy table, illustrating the likelihood that an individual testtaker will score within some interval of scores on a criterion measure, 165–169

Expectancy table: Information presented in tabular form illustrating the likelihood that an individual testtaker will score within some interval of scores on a criterion measure, 165–169
  creating, 166
  Naylor-Shine tables, 168
  Taylor-Russell tables, 165, 167–168

Expert panel: In the test development process, a group of people knowledgeable about the subject matter being tested and/or the population for whom the test was designed who can provide input to improve the test's content, fairness, and other related ways, 213, 215

Expert testimony, 59–61

Exploratory factor analysis: A class of mathematical procedures employed to estimate factors, extract factors, or decide how many factors to retain, 178. *See also* Factor analysis

Extended scoring report: A type of scoring report that provides not only a listing of scores but statistical data as well, 558. *See also* Scoring report

Extrinsic motivation: A state in which the primary force driving an individual comes from external sources (such as a salary or bonus) and external constraints (such as job loss), 531

Facet: In generalizability theory, variables of interest in the universe including, for example, the number of items in the test, the amount of training the test scorers have had, and the purpose of the test administration, 145

Face-to-face surveys, 537–538

Face validity: A judgment regarding how well a test or other tool of measurement measures what it purports to measure, based solely on "appearances" such as the content of the test's items, 155–156. *See also* Validity

Factor analysis: A class of mathematical procedures, frequently employed as data reduction methods, designed to identify variables on which people may differ (or factors). In measurement, two types of factor analysis are common, exploratory factor analysis and confirmatory factor analysis.
  confirmatory, 178
  construct validity and, 177–178
  exploratory, 178
  intelligence theories based on, 229–233
  inter-item consistency and, 205–206

Factor loading: In factor analysis, a metaphor suggesting that test (or an individual test item) carries a certain amount of one or more abilities which, in turn, has a determining influence on the test score (or on the response to the individual test item). Unlike other metaphors, however, a factor loading can be quantified, 178, 273

Fair Access Coalition on Testing (FACT), 63

Fairness: As applied to tests, the extent to which a test is used in an impartial, just, and equitable way, 182–186
  affirmative action and, 185
  item analysis and, 211–212
  test score adjustments and, 184–185

False negative: (1) In the general context of the miss rate of a test, an inaccurate prediction of classification indicating that a testtaker did not possess a trait or other attribute being measured when in reality the testtaker did; (2) in drug testing, an individual tests negative for drug use when in reality there has been drug use, 169, 525

False positive: (1) In the general context of the miss rate of a test, an inaccurate prediction or classification indicating that a testtaker did possess a trait or other attribute being measured when in reality the testtaker did not; (2) in drug testing, an individual tests positive for drug use when in reality there has been no drug use, 169, 525

Family Education Rights and Privacy Act (1974), 55

Family environment, 245, 247

Federal Rules of Evidence, 60

Field of Search test, 458, 459, 464

Figure-drawing tests, 383–386

Finding Information About Psychological Tests (APA), 35

First National Item Bank and Criterion-Referenced Scoring System program, 547

Fissure, 446

Fit statistics, 273

Five-dimension model of personality, 346–347

Fixed battery: A prepackaged test battery containing a number of standardized tests to be administered in a prescribed fashion, such as the Halstead-Reitan Neuropsychological Battery; contrast with *flexible battery,* 473, 474, 475–476

Fixed reference group scoring system: A system of scoring wherein the distribution of scores obtained on the test from one group of testtakers (the fixed reference group) is used as the basis for the calculation of test scores for future administrations; the SAT and the GRE are scored this way, 108–109

Flexible battery: Best associated with neuropsychological assessment, a group of tests hand-picked by the assessor to provide an answer to the referral question; contrast with *fixed battery,* 470, 473, 474

Flip-coin test (FCT), 179

Fluid intelligence: In Cattell's two-factor theory of intelligence, nonverbal abilities, less dependent on culture and formal instruction than crystallized intelligence; contrast with *crystallized intelligence,* 231

Flynn effect: "Intelligence inflation"; the fact that intelligence measured using a normed instrument rises each year after the test was

meta-analysis and, 124–125
statistical tools and, 123–124
Inflation of range: Also referred to as *inflation of variance,* a reference to a phenomenon associated with reliability estimates wherein the variance of either variable in a correlational analysis is inflated by the sampling procedure used and the resulting correlation coefficient tends to be higher as a consequence; contrast with *restriction of range,* 141
Inflation of variance. *See* Inflation of range
Informal evaluation: A typically nonsystematic, relatively brief, and "off-the-record" assessment leading to the formation of an opinion or attitude, conducted by any person in any way for any reason, in an unofficial context and not subject to the same ethics or standards as evaluation by a professional; contrast with *formal evaluation,* 291
Information-processing theories of intelligence, 233–234
Informed consent: Permission to proceed with a (typically) diagnostic, evaluative, or therapeutic service on the basis of knowledge about the service and its risks and potential benefits, 67
Inkblot techniques, 368–372
Inquiry: A typical element of Rorschach test administration; following the initial presentation of all ten cards, the assessor asks specific questions designed, among other things, to determine what about each card led to the assessee's perceptions, 369
Insanity: A legal term denoting an inability to tell right from wrong, a lack of control, or a state of other mental incompetence or disorder sufficient to prevent that person from standing trial, being judged guilty, or entering into a contract or other legal relationship, 427–428
Institute for Juvenile Research, 42
Instrumental values: Guiding principles in the attainment of some objective; for example, honesty and ambition, 360
Integrative report: A form of interpretive report of psychological assessment, usually computer-generated, in which data from behavioral, medical, administrative, and/or other sources are inte-

grated; contrast with *scoring report* and *interpretive report,* 558
Integrity test: A screening instrument designed to predict who will and will not be an honest employee, 516–517
Intelligence: A simple yet controversial term that has been defined in many ways, such as: a multifaceted capacity that manifests itself in different ways across the lifespan but in general includes the abilities and capacities to acquire and apply knowledge, to reason effectively and logically, to exhibit sound judgment, to be perceptive, intuitive, mentally alert, and able to find the right words and thoughts with facility, and to be able to cope with and adjust to new situations and new types of problems, 224–255
Binet's view of, 226–227
CHC model of, 232–233, 237
common views of, 225–226
controversy on nature of, 253–254
culture and, 247–253
factor-analytic theories of, 229–233
family environment and, 245, 247
Galton's view of, 226
gender and, 245, 246
giftedness and, 242, 243–244
information-processing theories of, 233–234
interactionist perspective on, 228–229, 240
measurement of, 234–237
multi-factor models of, 230–231
nature vs. nurture controversy about, 238–240
personality characteristics and, 245
Piaget's view of, 227–229
stability of, 240–242
triarchic theory of, 234
two-factor theory of, 229–230
Wechsler's view of, 227
Intelligence tests, 256–287
controversy about, 254
cultural issues related to, 44–46, 247–253
developing and interpreting, 236–237
Flynn effect and, 242, 244–245
group administration of, 42, 279–285
historical overview of, 42
identifying giftedness with, 243–244
measuring specific abilities with, 285–287
minority groups and, 44–46, 57–58, 247–248
neuropsychological assessment and, 460–461

short forms of, 277–278
standard scoring of, 97
Stanford-Binet Intelligence Scale, 258–263
types of tasks used in, 234–236
Wechsler tests, 264–278
Interactionism: The belief that heredity and environment interact to influence the development of one's mental capacity and abilities, 228–229, 240
Intercept: In the equation for a regression line, $Y = a + bX$, the letter a, which stands for a constant indicating where the line crosses the vertical or Y-axis, 122
Intercept bias: Refers to the point at which a regression line intercepts the Y-axis; refers to a test or measurement procedure systematically underpredicting or overpredicting the performance of members of a group; contrast with *slope bias,* 180
Interest inventories, 321, 506–509
Inter-item consistency. *See* Internal consistency
Internal consistency: Also referred to as *inter-item consistency,* an estimate of how consistently the items of a test measure a single construct obtained from a single administration of a single form of the test and the measurement of the degree of correlation among all of the test items, 135, 205–206
Interpersonal intelligence: In Gardner's theory of multiple intelligences, the ability to understand other people, what motivates them, how they work, and how to work cooperatively with them; contrast with *intrapersonal intelligence,* 230
Interpersonal Support Evaluation List, 518
Interpretation
computer-based, 545, 559–560
culture and, 125–126
error variance and, 130–131
intelligence test, 262–263, 311–312, 315
personality assessment, 340–341
Interpretive report: A formal or official computer-generated account of test performance, presented in both numeric and narrative form and including an explanation of the findings; the three varieties of interpretive report are descriptive, screening, and consultative; contrast with *scoring report* and *integrative report,* 558

Maintained abilities *(continued)* pre-injury levels after brain damage; contrast with *vulnerable abilities,* 231

Major life activity: Although not expressly defined by the Americans with Disabilities Act of 1990, presumed to constitute functions such as caring for oneself, performing manual tasks, walking, seeing, hearing, speaking, breathing, learning, sitting, standing, lifting, reading, reaching, reproducing, and working, 489. *See also* Disability

Make A Picture Story Method, 379

Make-A-Test program, 547, 548

Mall intercept studies, 537

Managed care: A health care system wherein the products and services provided to patients by a participating network of health care providers are mediated by an administrative agency of the insurer that works to keep costs down by fixing schedules of reimbursement to providers, 408

Management Progress Study (MPS), 523–524

Manual for Administration of Neuropsychological Test Batteries for Adults and Children (Reitan), 473

Manuals for tests, 33

Marital Interaction Coding System, 393, 403

Marital Satisfaction Scale (MSS), 174, 177

Marlowe-Crowne Social Desirability Scale, 177

Maslach Burnout Inventory (MBI), 531–532

Maslow's hierarchy of needs, 530

Math tests, 307–308

Maxfield-Bucholz Social Competency Scale for Blind Preschool Children, 492

Maze tests, 457

MBTI. *See* Myers-Briggs Type Indicator

Meadow-Kendall Social-Emotional Assessment Inventory, 495

Mean: Also called the *arithmetic mean,* a measure of central tendency derived by calculating an average of all scores in a distribution, 81, 83

Measurement: Assigning numbers or symbols to characteristics of people or objects according to rules, 15–16, 73
inference from, 123–126
scales of, 73–76
standard error of, 19

Measurement of Attitude, The (Thurstone & Chave), 536

Measurement of Intelligence in Infants and Young Children, The (P. Cattell), 41

Measure of central tendency: A statistic indicating the average or middlemost score between the extreme scores in a distribution. The *mean* is a measure of central tendency and a statistic at the ratio level of measurement; the *median* is a measure of central tendency that takes into account the order of scores and is ordinal in nature; the *mode* is a measure of central tendency that is nominal in nature, 81–85.
arithmetic mean, 81, 83
median, 83–84
mode, 84–85

Measure of variability: A statistic indicating how scores in a distribution are scattered or dispersed; range, standard deviation, and variance are common measures of variability, 85–89

Mechanical prediction: In clinical practice and other fields, the application of statistical rules and probabilities, as well as computer algorithms, in the computer generation of findings and recommendations; contrast with *clinical prediction* and *actuarial prediction,* 561

Median: A measure of central tendency derived by identifying the middlemost score in a distribution, 83–84

Medical College Admissions Test (MCAT), 305

Medical diagnostic aids, 471–472

Meier Art Tests, 286

Memory
models of, 462–464
neuropsychological tests of, 464

Mental age: An index, now seldom used, that refers to the chronological age equivalent of one's performance on a test or subtest; derived by reference to norms indicating the age at which most testtakers can pass or meet some performance criterion with respect to individual or groups of items, 235

Mental disorders
diagnosis of, 409–410
new views of, 410

Mental Measurements Yearbook (MMY), 34, 360

Mental orthopedics, 306

Mental retardation
adaptive behavior and, 498–501
classification of, 483–484, 498–499
diagnosis of, 499

Mental status examination: A specialized interview and observation used to screen for intellectual, emotional, and neurological deficits by touching on areas such as the interviewee's appearance, behavior, memory, affect, mood, judgment, personality, thought content, thought processes, and state of consciousness, 414–415
neuropsychological, 452–453

Mesokurtic: A description of the kurtosis of a distribution where the distribution is not extremely peaked or flat in its center, 90. *See also* Kurtosis

Meta-analysis: A research tool and the result of combining statistical information across various studies, 124–125

Method bias, 47

Method of contrasted groups: A procedure for gathering construct validity evidence that entails demonstrating that scores on the test vary in a predictable way as a function of membership in a particular group, 176

Metropolitan Readiness Tests (MRT), 302–303

Michigan Picture Test, 378

Milestone. *See* Developmental milestone

Military, group tests in, 282–285

Miller Analogies Test (MAT), 305

Miller Assessment for Preschoolers, 292

Millon Adolescent Clinical Inventory (MACI), 419

Millon Clinical Multiaxial Inventory (MCMI), 418–419

Millon Index of Personality Styles (MIPS), 419

Mini-Mental State Examination, 455

Minimum competency testing program: Formal evaluation program in basic skills such as reading, writing, and arithmetic, designed for use in various aspects of educational decision making ranging from remediation to grade promotions to graduation, 55, 297–298

Minnesota Clerical Test (MCT), 521

Minnesota Multiphasic Personality Inventory (MMPI), 95, 349–358
adolescent version of (MMPI-A), 354–355
clinical scales for, 349, 350, 353–354, 355
content scales for, 351
equivalence studies on, 559

Projective hypothesis: The thesis that an individual supplies structure to unstructured stimuli in a manner consistent with the individual's own unique pattern of conscious and unconscious needs, fears, desires, impulses, conflicts, and ways of perceiving and responding, 367

Projective method: A technique of personality assessment in which some judgment of the assessee's personality is made on the basis of his or her performance on a task that involves supplying structure to relatively unstructured or incomplete stimuli, 367

Projective personality tests, 367–388
  assumptions inherent in, 386–387
  custody evaluations and, 431, 432
  deaf people and, 495
  figure-drawing tests, 383–386
  inkblot tests, 368–372
  picture-based tests, 372–380
  psychometric soundness of, 388
  situational variables for, 387–388
  word-based tests, 380–383

Projective tests, 43

Protocol: (1) The form or sheet on which testtaker's responses are entered; (2) a method or procedure for evaluation or scoring, 22n

Proverbs Test, 456

PsycARTICLES database, 35

Psychoanalytic theory, 344–345

Psychodiagnostics (Rorschach), 368

Psychoeducational assessment: Psychological evaluation in a school or other setting, usually conducted to diagnose, remedy, or measure academic or social progress or to otherwise enrich a student's education, 233

Psychoeducational test battery: A packaged kit containing tests that measure educational achievement and abilities related to academic success, 308–317
  Differential Ability Scale, 312–316
  Kaufman Assessment Battery for Children, 309–312
  Woodcock-Johnson III, 316–317

Psychological Assessment (Maloney & Ward), 3

Psychological assessment: The gathering and integrating of psychological data for psychological evaluation, through the use of tests, interviews, case studies, behavioral observation, and specially designed apparatuses and mea-

surement procedures; contrast with *psychological testing*, 4
  accommodation and, 484–488
  alternate assessment and, 4–6, 484–485
  assumptions in, 13–21
  cultural issues in, 44–52, 361–363
  future of, 563
  group membership and, 50–52
  historical overview of, 38–43
  legal and ethical issues in, 52–70
  parties in process of, 21–25
  public policy and, 52
  rights of individuals in, 67–70
  settings for, 25–28
  testing distinguished from, 2–4
  tools of, 6–12

Psychological autopsy: A reconstruction of a dead person's psychological profile on the basis of archival records, artifacts, and interviews with the assessee while living or with people who knew him or her, 24

Psychological Bulletin, 177

Psychological Clinic (journal), 42

Psychological Corporation, 41

Psychological reports, 439–443
  Barnum effect and, 442–443
  elements of, 440–441

Psychological test: A measuring device or procedure designed to measure psychology-related variables, 6

Psychological testing: The measuring of psychology-related variables by means of devices or procedures designed to obtain samples of behavior, 4
  adaptive testing and, 262
  assessment distinguished from, 2–4
  assumptions in, 13–21
  contemporary roots of, 1–2
  cultural issues in, 44–52
  group membership and, 50–52
  historical overview of, 38–43
  legal and ethical issues in, 52–70
  normal curve and, 92–93
  parties in process of, 21–25
  public policy and, 52
  settings for, 25–28
  testtaker rights and, 67–70

Psychological Tests and Personnel Decisions (Cronbach & Gleser), 169

Psychological trait: 14. *See* Trait

Psychology Today, 252

Psychometrician: A professional in testing and assessment who typically holds a doctoral degree in psychology or education and specializes in areas such as indi-

vidual differences, quantitative psychology, or theory of assessment; contrast with *psychometrist*, 29n

Psychometrics: The science of psychological measurement (synonymous with the antiquated term *psychometry*), 29
  application of, 31–32
  classroom tests and, 192–193
  intelligence tests and, 261–262, 268–270, 309, 311, 314–315
  interviews and, 415–416
  projective personality tests and, 376–377, 388

Psychometrist: A professional in testing and assessment who typically holds a master's degree in psychology or education and is qualified to administer specific tests; contrast with *psychometrician*, 29n

Psychopathy Checklist (PCL), 429

Psychophysiological assessment methods: Techniques for monitoring physiological changes known to be influenced by psychological factors, such as heart rate and blood pressure, 398–400

PsycINFO: An online electronic database maintained by the American Psychological Association and leased to institutional users, designed to help individuals locate relevant documents from psychology, education, nursing, social work, law, medicine, and other disciplines, 35

PsycLAW database, 35

PsycSCAN database, 35

Public Law 94-142, 25, 55, 288, 294, 480

Public Law 95-561, 243

Public Law 99-457, 25, 288, 480

Public Law 101-336, 480

Public Law 101-476, 480

Public Law 105-17, 4, 55, 288, 480, 481–482

Public policy, 52

Pupillometrics: The study and measurement of the involuntary physiological response of the eye's pupil to various stimuli, 400

Purdue Pegboard Test, 466

Purdue Perceptual-Motor Survey, 498

Purposive sampling: The arbitrary selection of people to be part of a sample because they are thought to be representative of the population being studied, 103. *See also* Sample, Sampling, Stratified sampling, Stratified random sampling, and Incidental sampling

Q-sort technique: An assessment technique in which the task is to sort a group of statements, usually in perceived rank order ranging from "most descriptive" to "least descriptive"; the statements, traditionally presented on index cards, may be sorted in ways that reflect various perceptions, such as how respondents see themselves or would like to see themselves, 339–340

Qualitative item analysis: A general term for various nonstatistical procedures designed to explore how individual test items work, both compared to other items in the test and in the context of the whole test; in contrast to statistically based procedures, qualitative methods involve exploration of the issues by verbal means such as interviews and group discussions conducted with testtakers and other relevant parties, 213–215

expert panels and, 213, 215

potential areas of exploration for, 214

"think aloud" test administration and, 213

Quality-of-life issues, 501–502

Quantitative methods: Techniques of data generation and analysis that rely primarily on mathematical or statistical rather than verbal procedures, 213, 539–540, 541

Quartile: One of three dividing points between the four quarters of a distribution, each typically labeled Q_1, Q_2, or Q_3, 86

QUID: Acronym for "qualified individual with a disability," especially with respect to the Americans with Disabilities Act of 1990; a disabled employee who meets the employer's standards for education, skill, and other job-related qualifications and who can perform the essential functions of the job with or without accommodation in the workplace, 490

Race norming: The controversial practice of norming on the basis of race or ethnic background, 101, 185, 514. *See also* Norms

Radioisotope scans, 472

Raising Children with Love and Limits (P. Cattell), 41

Range: A descriptive statistic of variability derived by calculating the difference between the highest and lowest scores in a distribution, 86

restriction or inflation of, 141

scatterplots of, 121

See also Interquartile range and Semi-interquartile range

Rank-difference/rank-order correlation coefficient. *See* Spearman's rho

Ranking: The ordinal ordering of persons, scores, or variables into relative positions or degrees of value, 182

Rapport: A working relationship between examiner and examinee in testing or assessment, 22–23

Rating: A numerical or verbal judgment that places a person or attribute along a continuum identified by a scale of numerical or word descriptors called a *rating scale*, 181

Rating error: A judgment that results from the intentional or unintentional misuse of a rating scale; two types of rating error are *leniency error* (or *generosity error*) and *severity error*, 181–182

Rating scale: A system of ordered numerical or verbal descriptors on which judgments about the presence/absence or magnitude of a particular trait, attitude, emotion, or other variable are indicated by raters, judges, or examiners or, when the rating scale reflects self-report, the assessee, 181, 194–196

behavioral observation and, 393–394

neuropsychological assessment and, 455

preschool assessment and, 289

Ratio IQ: An index of intelligence derived from the ratio of the testtaker's mental age as calculated from a test, divided by his or her chronological age and multiplied by 100 to eliminate decimals, 258–259

Ratio scale: A system of measurement in which all things measured can be rank-ordered, the rank ordering does imply something about exactly how much greater one ranking is than another, equal intervals exist between each number on the scale, and all mathematical operations can be performed meaningfully because a true or absolute zero point exists; few scales in psychology or education are ratio scales, 76

Raw score: A straightforward, unmodified accounting of performance, usually numerical and typically used for evaluation or diagnosis, 101

Reactivity: Changes in an assessee's behavior, thinking, or performance that arise in response to being observed, assessed, or evaluated, 396

Readiness test: A tool of assessment designed to evaluate whether an individual has the requisites to begin a program or perform a task; sometimes synonymous with *aptitude test*, 301

Reading-Free Vocational Interest Inventory (R-FVII), 507

Reading tests, 307

Reason and logic, 343–344

Reference volumes, 34

Reflex: Involuntary motor response to a stimulus, 453

Regression: The analysis of relationships among variables to understand how one variable may predict another, 121–123. *See also* Simple regression and Multiple regression

multiple, 123

simple, 121

Regression coefficient: In the formula $Y = a + bX$, the letter a symbolizing the ordinate intercept is a regression coefficient, as is the letter b, which is equal to the slope of the line; in practice, the actual values of a and b are determined by simple algebraic calculation, 121–122

Regression line: The result of simple regression analysis, the graphic "line of best fit" that comes closest to the greatest number of points on the scatterplot of the two variables, 115, 121. *See* Simple regression and Scatterplot

Rehabilitation Act (1973), 480

Reitan-Indiana Aphasia Screening Test (AST), 461–462

Reliability: The extent to which measurements are consistent or repeatable; also, the extent to which measurements differ from occasion to occasion as a function of measurement error, 29, 32, 128–153

alternate-forms, 132–133

breathalyzer test, 146

BSID-II, 142–143

classroom tests and, 193

clinical interviews and, 415–416

processing whereby information is integrated and synthesized all at once and as a whole; contrast with *successive processing*, 233–234, 310, 311

Situational Competency Test, 438

Situational performance measure: A procedure that typically involves the performance of a task by the assessee under actual or simulated conditions while allowing for observation and evaluation by an assessor, 397–398

Situational stress tests, 398

Sixteen Personality Factor (16PF) Questionnaire, 346

Skewness: An indication of the nature and extent to which symmetry is absent in a distribution; a distribution is said to be skewed positively when relatively few scores fall at the positive end and skewed negatively when relatively few scores fall at the negative end, 89–90

Sliding band, 185

Slope bias: A reference to the slope of a regression line being different between groups, this term refers to a test or measurement procedure systematically yielding different validity coefficients for members of different groups; contrast with *intercept bias*, 180

Smell Identification Test, 451

Social information processing, 501

Socially desirable responding, 334

Social Situation Picture Test, 373

Social support, 437

Society
  assessment process and, 24–25
  legal and ethical concerns of, 53–58

Society for Personality Assessment (SPA), 333

Sociogram: A graphic representation of peer appraisal data or other interpersonal information, 320

Socio-Sexual Knowledge & Attitudes Test, 501–502

Soft sign: In neuropsychological assessment, an indication that neurological deficit may be present; for example, a significant discrepancy between Verbal and Performance subtests on a Wechsler test, 450n

Sorting tests, 456

Southern California Sensory Integration Tests, 477, 498

Spearman-Brown formula: An equation used to estimate internal consistency reliability from a correlation of two halves of a test that has been lengthened or shortened; inappropriate for use with heterogeneous tests or speed tests, 134–135

Spearman's rho: Also referred to as the *rank-order correlation coefficient* and the *rank-difference correlation coefficient*, this index of correlation may be the statistic of choice when the sample size is small and both sets of measurements are ordinal, 117

Specific intelligence (*s*) factor, 229

SPECT technology, 471

Speed test: A test, usually of achievement or ability, with a time limit; speed tests usually contain items of uniform difficulty level, 142
  item analysis and, 212
  reliability coefficient and, 142–144

Split-half reliability: An estimate of the internal consistency of a test obtained by correlating two pairs of scores obtained from equivalent halves of a single test administered once, 133–135. *See also* Alternate forms reliability, Internal consistency reliability, Inter-scorer reliability, Parallel forms reliability, Test-retest reliability, Reliability, and Odd-even reliability.

Standard battery: Usually, the administration of a group of at least three different types of tests for the purpose of evaluating different spheres of functioning: an intelligence test, a personality test, and a neuropsychological test, 418

Standard deviation: A measure of variability equal to the square root of the averaged squared deviations about the mean; a measure of variability equal to the square root of the variance, 87–89. *See also* Variance

Standard error of measurement: In true score theory, a statistic designed to estimate the extent to which an observed score deviates from a true score; also called the *standard error of a score*, 19, 148
  reliability coefficient and, 148–150

Standard error of the difference: A statistic designed to aid in determining how large a difference between two scores should be before it is considered statistically significant, 150–152

Standard error of the estimate: In regression, an estimate of the magnitude of error; the lower the degree of correlation, the higher the standard error of the estimate, 123

Standardization: A process of test development wherein the test is administered to a representative sample of testtakers under clearly specified conditions and the data are scored and interpreted, to establish a context for future test administrations with other testtakers, 102–104

Standardization sample, 100
  for Differential Abilities Scale, 314
  for Kaufman Assessment Battery for Children, 309
  for Minnesota Multiphasic Personality Inventory, 349–350, 353, 354
  for Stanford-Binet Intelligence Scale, 261
  for Wechsler Adult Intelligence Scale-III, 267–268
  for Wechsler Intelligence Scale for Children-III, 271

Standardized test: A test or measure that has undergone standardization, 102. *See* Standardization

Standard score: A raw score that has been converted from one scale into another, the latter scale (1) having some arbitrarily set mean and standard deviation and (2) being more widely used and readily interpretable; examples of standard scores are z scores and T scores, 94–98
  deviation IQ, 97
  normalized, 98
  stanine, 96–97
  transformation of, 97
  T scores, 95–96
  z scores, 94–95

Standards for Educational and Psychological Testing, 21

Stanford Achievement Test Series, 215

Stanford-Binet Intelligence Scale, 44, 258–263
  administration of, 262
  development of, 258–259
  evaluation of, 263
  fourth edition of, 259–263
  psychometric properties of, 261–262
  scoring and interpretation of, 262–263
  standardization sample of, 261
  subtests of, 260

Stanford Diagnostic Mathematics Test (SDMT), 308

Stanford Diagnostic Reading Test (SDRT), 308

Stanine: A standard score derived from a scale with a mean of 5 and a standard deviation of approximately 2, 96–97

State: As in *personality state,* (1) the transitory exhibition of a trait, indicative of a relatively temporary predisposition to behave in a particular way; (2) in psychoanalytic theory, an inferred psychodynamic disposition designed to convey the dynamic quality of id, ego, and superego in perpetual conflict, 13, 14–16, 328

Static characteristics, 141

Statistics
  central tendency measures and, 81–85
  correlation and, 112–121
  frequency distributions and, 78–81
  kurtosis and, 90
  normal curve and, 90–94
  regression and, 121–123
  scales of measurement and, 72–76
  skewness and, 89–90
  standard scores and, 94–98
  variability measures and, 85–89

Stick Test, 448

Stigmatizing labels, 69–70

Stratified-random sampling: The process of developing a sample based on specific subgroups of a population in which every member has the same chance of being included in the sample, 103. *See also* Sample, Sampling, Stratified sampling, Purposive sampling, and Incidental sampling

Stratified sampling: The process of developing a sample based on specific subgroups of a population, 103. *See also* Sample, Sampling, Stratified-random sampling, Purposive sampling, and Incidental sampling

Stress interview: An interview purposely designed to pressure or stress the interviewee in order to gauge reaction to that stress, 412

Strong Interest Inventory (SII), 507

Strong Vocational Interest Blank (SVIB), 507, 545

Structured Clinical Interview for Dissociative Disorders (SCID-D), 412

Structured interview: Questions posed from a guide with little if any leeway to deviate from the guide, 336, 412

Structured Interview of Reported Symptoms (SIRS), 412

Structure of Intellect (SOI) test, 243–244, 285

Study Attitudes and Methods Survey, 537

Study Habits Checklist, 320–321

Subgroup norms: Norms for any defined group within a larger group, 107–108. *See also* Norms.

Substance-abuse assessment, 438–439

Successive processing: Also referred to as *sequential processing*; based on Luria's writings, a type of information processing whereby information is processed in a sequential, bit-by-bit fashion and arranged and rearranged until it is logical; contrast with *simultaneous processing,* 233–234

Sulcus, 446

Summative scale: An index derived from the summing of selected scores on a test or subtest, 195

Supplementary scales, 351–352

Survey: In consumer psychology, a fixed list of questions administered to a selected sample of persons, typically to learn about consumers' attitudes, beliefs, opinions, and/or behavior regarding targeted products, services, or advertising, 537–539

Survey of Study Habits and Attitudes (SSHA), 321

Sutton v. United Airlines (1999), 489

Symptom Checklist-90-R (SCL-90-R), 344

Tactile memory test, 464

Tail: The area on the normal curve between 2 and 3 standard deviations above the mean, and the area on the normal curve between −2 and −3 standard deviations below the mean; a normal curve has two tails, 93–94

Tailored testing. *See* Adaptive testing

Tarasoff v. Regents of University of California (1974), 69, 423

TAT. *See* Thematic Apperception Test

Taylor-Russell tables, 165, 167–168

Team: Two or more people acting interdependently toward a common goal, who have each been assigned specific roles or functions, 528

Technical Recommendations for Achievement Tests (NCME), 61

Technical Recommendations for Psychological Tests and Diagnostic Tests (APA), 61

Telephone surveys, 538

Teleprocessing: Computerized scoring, interpretation, or other conversion of raw test data sent over telephone lines by modem from a test site to a central location for computer processing; contrast with *central processing* and *local processing,* 556

TEMAS test, 378

Temperament: With reference to personality assessments of infants, the distinguishing manner of the child's observable actions and reactions, 245

Tennessee Self-Concept Scale, 329

Terminal values: Guiding principles and a mode of behavior that are an end-point objective; for example, "a comfortable life" and "an exciting life"; contrast with *instrumental values,* 360

"Termites": Humorous reference to gifted children who participated in Lewis M. Terman's study of intelligence initiated in 1916, 242n

Test: A measuring device or procedure, 6–8
  reliability, 29, 32, 128–153
  translation, 47, 362
  validity, 29–30, 32–33

Test administration
  error variance and, 129–130
  group intelligence tests and, 279–280
  qualifications for, 62–64
  "think aloud" technique for, 213

Test battery: A selection of tests and assessment procedures typically composed of tests designed to measure different variables but having a common objective; for example, an intelligence test, a personality test, and a neuropsychological test might be used to obtain a general psychological profile of an individual, 136n. *See also* Psychoeducational test battery

Test bias, 20, 179–182
  intercept bias and, 180
  rating error and, 181–182
  slope bias and, 180–181
  translations and, 47
  validity and, 179–182

Test catalogues, 33–34

Test composite: A test score or index derived from the combination and/or mathematical transformation of one or more test scores, 259

Test conceptualization, 188–191

Test construction, 192–202

Test Developer Profiles, 21, 375

Test developers, 21

Test development, 21, 188–223
  conceptualization stage in, 188–191
  construction stage in, 192–202
  criterion groups used in, 347–348
  data reduction methods in, 345–347
  example of, 220–222